The
Paperback
PRICE GUIDE™
No. 2

By
Kevin B. Hancer

With the Assistance of

R. Reginald

Special Research Advisor to this Edition

Rahn Kollander

Harmony Books/New York

This second edition is dedicated to the family and friends whose support made it possible, and also to Lt. Col. Ray Trautman, whose love of books served his country well in a time of need.

The Paperback Price GuideTM **No. 2** is copyrighted 1982 by Kevin B. Hancer, Editor, 5813 York Ave. S., Edina, MN 55410. All rights are reserved. Send all pricing and corrective data to above address. Printed in U.S.A.

Published and distributed to the collectors market by Overstreet Publications, Inc., 780 Hunt Cliff Dr. N.W., Cleveland, TN 37311.

Distributed to the book trade by Harmony Books, a division of Crown Publishers, Inc., One Park Ave., New York, NY 10016.

ISBN: 0-517-544539
ISSN: 0730-2932

Second Edition

Library of Congress Cataloging in Publication Data

Hancer, Kevin.
  The paperback price guide #2.

  Rev. ed. of: The paperback price guide. 1st ed. c1980.
    1. Paperbacks—Bibliography—Prices—United States.   2. Out-of-print books—Prices—United States.   3. Paperbacks—Collectors and collecting—United States.
I. Title. II. Title: Paperback price guide number two.
Z1033.P3H35   1982   018'.4   82-11790
ISBN O-517-54453-9 (pbk.)

The following people have also contributed much-needed data for this edition:

Lawrence Abbott
Vince Amero
Red Anderson
Tanya Anderson
Paul Aronoff
Newton Baird
Gary A. Barrenger
Larry Barrett
Jack Beck
Victor A. Berch
Luther Blalock
B. Bruce-Briggs
Ron Burgess
Gordon Chalmers
Austin Chamberlain
LaNelle Chapman
Tom Claggett
William F. Coffey
John Coltrane
Ina Cooke
R. Crandall
Mrs. Charles Crosby
Kevin S. Dacey
Don Davidson
Michael DeLong
Liz Downey
Winona M. Eads
Dennis Earle
H. E. Ericson
Jim Estes
Dave Farah
Doug Finn
Russ Francetich
Sharon Frisbie
George Gagliardi
Ric Gelman
Gerald Glenn
Daniel Gobbett
Mark Goodman
James Goolsby
David M. Gorski
Mike Grinley
David Grothe
Philip Gunderson
Joe Hagen

Robert C. Hahn
S. J. Haitaian
William Hartz
Claude Held
Bob Hencey
Patrick M. Hickey
Melville C. Hill
Michael F. Hopkins
Jim Hossen
Paul Hunt
Richard Hurt
Norral Johnson
Wayne Kadik
Norman Kagan
Kathy Kauppi
Greg Ketter
Mike Krizman
Mike L. Laird
Robert Lambert
James Laurie
Henry Lexau
Denny Lien
Daniel J. Lobel
Glen H. Loveland
Bob Lurie
Bill Lyles
Jack Maier
Dale Manesis
Pete Manesis
Bev Mason
Wilf Mattenley
James May
Dave McClintock
Ken McDaniel
John Meyer
Dave Miller
Gene Miller
Terry Moore
George R. Morgan
Harry Nudel
Lynn Oliver
Charles Orr
Don Osier
Robert Overstreet
Jeff Patton

Curtis Paul
Scott Pell
Richard A. Pender
Dennis Petilli
Don Petterson
Paul Petterson
Frank Puncer
Russ Reed
Warren Rohrer
Paul Rollinson
Bob Sampon
Stephen Sayles
R. J. Schneider
Piet Schreuders
Herb Scott
Denver Sherry
Maxine Shupe
John Songas
Tom Strong
Jon M. Suter
Mary Flanders Sykes
Richard L. Sykes
Jay Taylor-Henderson
J. Grant Thiessen
Joel Thingvall
Ned Thomas
Andy Thurnauer
Mike Tickal
Jan Tonnesen
J. Barry Traylor
David Wallace
Don Wallace
Sidney R. Wallace
Jon Warren
Howard Waterhouse
G. Weinberger
Doug Welch
Mel White
Tom Williams
Robert Wilson
Steve Wilson
Thure Wilson
Odelene B. Worden
Peter Young
Lesley Zartens

ABOUT THE AUTHOR

Kevin Hancer was born in 1950 in Minneapolis, Minnesota. At the age of ten he began to deal books as a means of earning money to buy books that he wanted, and he has been a fixture in the book business ever since as a dealer, collector, publisher, and fan. He has organized fan clubs, most notably the Minneapolis chapter of The Burroughs Bibliophiles, and has worked with many colleges and schools on both courses or special collections in the area of fantastic literature. He has more than 75 publications to his credit, with **The Fantasy Journal**, **The Burroughs Newsbeat** and **Paperback Market** being most notable. Edgar Rice Burroughs, creator of Tarzan, has long been a special interest, and Kevin has written numerous articles about Burroughs for books, magazines, newspapers, and fanzines. He has long been working on a definitive pictorial history of the ape-man.

Currently Kevin resides in Edina, Minnesota, and works as a freelance writer and lecturer, as well as a specialist book dealer. He spends a lot of time traveling, in search of either a good story or a good book. He has two young children, Aileen and Colin, who have already displayed some of the same love for books as has their father.

TABLE OF CONTENTS

Acknowledgements A-3

About the Author A-4

Introduction A-6

Format of This Book A-6

Why People Collect Paperbacks A-8

How to Start Collecting A-9

Selling Paperbacks A-10

The Care of a Paperback Collection A-12

The Grading of Paperback Books A-12

A Word About Reprints A-13

A Special Plea A-13

Further Reading A-13

Market Report for 1982 . . . . .A-14

Article "Over There! Over There! The Yanks Are Coming!" A-16

Main Listing begins 1

Author Cross-Index 380

INTRODUCTION

In the mid-eleventh century A.D., a Chinaman named Pi Sheng introduced movable type to the world. As the wonders of the far East became known to the rest of civilization through the explorations of Marco Polo and others, Eastern technology was gradually adapted for use in Europe. Four hundred years after Pi Sheng, Johann Gutenberg introduced the use of movable type to Europeans. This revolutionary development made books available to people who previously could not afford to buy laboriously handwritten copies.

Books became even more accessible to the general public when cheap paperback editions were introduced, but paperback publication was generally not a commercial success until the mid-20th century. Much as mechanically printed books were not initially accepted, neither was the paperback book. It was not until the growth of leisure time for the modern working classes, coupled with the development of proper sales and marketing techniques, that publishing became a widespread, profitable venture.

The modern era of the paperback book, which is the subject of this volume, began in 1939 with the issuance of ten titles by Pocket Books, each in a limited test printing of no more than 10,000 copies each, and only distributed within New York City. Once the floodgates were opened, nothing could close them again.

The paperback book has grown to become a multi-million dollar business today. As inflation drives the price of hardcover books higher and higher, industry insiders predict that the future of the book industry may largely belong to that once scorned and unsuccessful item—the paperback book.

FORMAT OF THIS BOOK

The Paperback Price Guide is an attempt to list all mass market paperback books published in the United States between 1939 and 1959. Selected Canadian and post-1959 books are included also, based on collector interest, and more will be added to future editions of this book.

Book listings are arranged according to the imprint name, which is the identifiable series title, and then listed in numerical order. Where there is no identifiable series title, entries are listed under the publisher's name. The resultant groupings are then organized in alphabetical order. Rather than organizing by title or author, this method was chosen to assist those collectors interested in collecting individual series. A selected cross-index of important authors in all fields will be found after the regular listings.

Where available, data has been included to identify books that are either first or original editions. A first edition is the first appearance of a novel or collection of short stories in book form. An original edition is the first appearance of a novel or collection of short stories in any form. An original edition is always a first edition.

Publication dates are included for each identified first or original edition. Dates are also noted periodically for other entries, as a means of helping provide a time reference for all entries. It is worth correcting a major mistake committed by many people. The copyright date of a book is **not** the same as the publication date, because books usually do not require a new copyright each time they are published.

Because cover art is of so much interest to so many, selected cover artists have their work identified where such knowledge is available. The artists so identified are selected based on interest in them within the collector's market. This informational area will increase as more and more collectors increase their sense of awareness about cover art and artists. The abbreviation 'c-' indicates identification of a cover artist. The identified artists include:

Robert Abbett	Roy Krenkel
Rudolph Belarski	Robert Maguire
Earle Bergey	Richard Powers
L. B. Cole	Mac Raboy
Frank Frazetta	Norman Saunders
R. C. M. Heade	Alex Schomburg
Everett Raymond Kinstler	Wally Wood

Additional notes are included where called for. These include identification of movie and TV tie-in editions.

Pricing is provided for each book in each of three different conditions. These are Good, Fine, and Near Mint. These grades were chosen because, although the majority of books within the market may be found to be only in fair, good, or very good condition, books in the higher grades receive the largest interest. So, it is a mistake to think that the middle price, the Fine price, reflects the value of an average copy because it most certainly does not. These prices are given as a guiding reference. A very good copy would value out somewhere between the Good and Fine prices, closer to one price or the other depending on how close the book's condition is to Good or Fine. The same would apply to books falling between Fine and Near Mint in condition. Prices given are an educated opinion of the average current retail value within the collector's marketplace, they are not quotations of the prices at which private parties can sell their books. Prices are for first printings only, with just one exception being that of paperbacks in dust jackets, as dust jacketed books were virtually always reprints or later issues.

Many entries also include a letter code at the far right margin. This is a genre classification, used to identify books that belong to a particular area of interest within the book world. The genre codes used are:

A—Adventure
B—Biography
C—Combat
E—Esoteric(a)/Exotic(a)/Exploitation. All these terms have been used by publishers and collectors alike, but no matter how you say it, it adds up to a book in which a sexual emphasis has been exploited. This is not to be confused with pornographic novels including explicit sexual material.
H—Humor
HO—Horror
JD—Juvenile Delinquency
M—Mystery
NF—Non-Fiction
R—Romance
S—Sports
SF—Science-Fiction
W—Western

This book also includes over 1100 photographs, both black-and-white and color, designed to illustrate both key books and a general sampling of the listed entries in different time periods. The number of black-and-white and color photographs has grown due to popular demand. With so many new collectors on the scene, a lot of desire has been expressed for more photographs because a lot of collectors have never seen most of the books listed. The color section of this book has been specially selected to present a quality selection of interesting and/or important covers by a wide variety of artists as published by different publishers.

The following abbreviations are used with the cover reproductions throughout the book for copyright credit purposes. The companies they represent are listed here:

(Abra) Abrams, Harry N., Inc.
(Ace) Ace Books, Inc.
(Anson) Anson Bond Publ., Inc.
(Archer) The Archer Press, Ltd.
(Argyle) Argyle Press
(Arrow) Arrow Publ.
(Astro) Astro Dist. Corp.
(Atomic) Atomic Books, Inc.
(Avon) Avon Publ., Inc.
(Banner) Banner Mystery
(Bantam) Bantam Books
(Bard) Bard Publ. Corp.
(Bart) Bartholomew House, Inc.
(BB) Ballantine Books
(Belmt) Belmont Books
(Berk) Berkley Publ. Corp.
(Bowker) R. R. Bowker Co.
(CBS) Columbia Broadcasting System
(Cen) Century Publications
(Check) Checkerbooks, Inc.
(Close) Close-up, Inc.
(Col) Columbia Publ. Inc.
(Cor) Corinth Publ., Inc.
(CP) Colonial Press, Inc.
(Crest) Crestwood Publ., Inc.
(Cross) Crossword Pleasure, Inc.
(Croy) Croyden Publ. Co.
(Daggar) Daggar House, Inc.
(DD) Doubleday & Co., Inc.
(Death) Death Library, Inc.
(Dell) Dell Publ. Co., Inc.
(Delta) Delta Library, Inc.
(Design) Design Publ. Corp.
(Det) Detective House, Inc.
(Div) Diversey Publ. Corp.
(Duch) Duchess Printing & Publ. Co., Ltd.
(Edell) Edell Co.
(Eerie) Eerie Publ. Co.
(ERB) Edgar Rice Burroughs
(Eton) Eton Books, Inc.
(Export) Export Publ. Ent., Ltd.
(Falcon) Falcon Books, Inc.
(Faw) Fawcett Publ., Inc.
(Fed) Federal Publ. Co.
(Fem) Femack Co., The
(Glxy) Galaxy Publ. Corp.
(Great) Great American Publ., Inc.
(Green) Green Publ. Co.
(GW) Golden Willow Press, Inc.
(Handi) Handi-book Publ.
(Hanro) Hanro Corp.
(Hart) Horace Hart, Inc.
(HB) Harlequin Books
(HH) Hangman's House
(Hill) Hillman Periodicals, Inc.
(Holl) Holloway House Publ. Co.
(How) Howard Publ.
(Ideal) Ideal Dist. Co.
(Infan) Infantry Journal, Inc.

(Jon) Jonathan Press, Inc.
(Knic) Knickerbocker Publ., Inc.
(KW) Keep-Worthy Books, Inc.
(Larch) Larch Publ.
(Leisure) Leisure Library, Inc.
(Lion) Lion Books, Inc.
(Mag) Magazine Village, Inc.
(MCG) Marvel Comics Group (Atlas)
(Merc) Mercury Publs.
(Metro) Metro Publ.
(MH) Mohawk Publ. Corp.
(Mid) Midwood Ent., Inc.
(Mil) Military Service Publ. Co.
(MP) Magazine Productions, Inc.
(NA) New American Library
(New) New International Library, Inc.
(NH) National Home Library Foundation
(Novel) Novel Library
(NS) Novel Selections, Inc.
(Oceana) Oceana Publ.
(Orig) Original Novels, Inc.
(Padell) Padell Book & Magazine Co.
(Par) Parsee Publ.
(Pen) Penguin Books
(Perma) Perma Books
(Phan) Phantom Mystery Publ.
(Phoen) Phoenix Books
(PI) Parents' Institute
(Pitman) Pitman Publ. Corp.
(Pkb) Pocket Books
(Poplib) Popular Library, Inc.
(Pub) Publishers Productions, Inc.
(Put) Putnam's Sons, G. P.
(Pyb) Pyramid Books
(QB) Quarter Books
(Quinn) Quinn Publ. Co.
(RC) Readers Choice Library
(Red) Red Arrow Books
(Retail) Retail Distributors, Inc.
(Rio) Rio Publ. Corp.
(RL) Reader's League of America
(RN) Romantic Novels
(Royce) Royce Publ.
(S&S) Street & Smith
(SB) Scholastic Book Services
(SG) Star Guidance, Inc.
(SH) Stamford House
(Sigb) Signet Books
(Simon) Simon & Schuster
(Sol) Solomon & Gelman, Inc.
(Spot) Spotlight Publ.
(Star) Star Publ., Inc.
(Stj) St. John Publ. Co.
(Tech) Tech Books, Inc.
(Toby) Toby Press, Inc.
(Univ) Universal Publ. Co., Inc.
(Value) Value Books, Inc.
(Vulcan) Vulcan Publ., Inc.
(ZD) Ziff-Davis

WHY PEOPLE COLLECT PAPERBACKS

Anything that exists or was produced on this planet is undoubtedly collected by someone, somewhere. Collecting is a peculiar passion that affects many people in varying degrees and in many different ways.

Book collecting has been a popular hobby for many years, and paperback book collecting often follows traditional patterns.

Since books are, of course, meant to be read, many collectors collect those books that they enjoy reading, although collectors generally treasure their higher grade copies and do not decrease their condition by reading them, which often creates, for many collectors, the necessity of obtaining a "reading" copy in lesser condition. A reader might collect all the books by a favorite author or group of authors, or might collect all books within a particular genre, or even books with a similar theme. Different collectors limit their reading by different degrees, so this could mean anything from a small number of books to many hundreds or even thousands.

Cover art has become a larger collecting factor in recent years, and is the aspect of this hobby that seems to intrigue the media most. There are many different artists and artistic styles, but some of the more lurid cover art has been the most popular in the United States while fine art has been more popular in Europe. As collectors learn more about artists, it seems that this area gains importance in the field.

Some people collect original or first editions, often within a particular genre.

Some people collect paperbacks as examples of our popular culture because they are reflective of the time in which they were produced. While a book might have been written centuries or just years earlier, the design, packaging, and cover art will reflect contemporary marketing appeal. For example, the 1932 Jacket Library edition of Rostand's **Cyrano de Bergerac** was packaged with a classic, stylish look, but when reprinted years later the book was retitled as **The Art of Love** by "a Parisian Casanova" and the cover depicts a young couple in a heated embrace! The trend to lurid appeal perhaps reached a high (or low) point when Royal Books packaged a reprint of Mark Twain's **Pudd'nhead Wilson** as **The Unnatural Son** in order to increase its mass market appeal. America's fascination with things sexual has long been an easy mark for exploitation, and paperback publishers of the '40s and '50s were well aware of it. This was particularly exploited in the '40s, becoming more subdued in the '50s as paperbacks began to come under attack by various moral-minded groups, much in the same way as comic books.

Some people collect paperbacks because of the totally outrageous nature and bizarre aspect of the design and packaging of certain books. A book like **Naked on Roller Skates** or **Ten Toes Up** may be utterly wretched reading, but the titles and cover art are so outrageous that they have appeal for certain collectors. There are all kinds of collectors in this area. Some are especially interested in books like **Nigger Heaven** or **Hot Chocolate** that deal with black people, for example. This type of collector is unlikely to be taking the books seriously, but is instead attracted by the very outrageousness of them.

HOW TO START COLLECTING

A good place to begin collecting is your neighborhood. Local swap shops, trading posts, second-hand stores, and retail stores operated by charitable groups (such as the Salvation Army) contain many bargains for the collector. Local used bookstores can also contain a lot of reasonably priced items.

There are a lot of mail-order dealers that specialize in vintage paperbacks and issue catalogues periodically. There is often a charge for these catalogues, but at the current time this is the way that collectors can get the widest selection of books. Collectors should compare catalogues, the more the better, in order to see where the best value can be obtained. There can be a great difference in price between one catalogue and another. This can often happen where one dealer may be part-time, only selling those items he obtains in his local area, while another dealer may be full-time, traveling and buying through the mails. The former has a lower overhead and can offer a smaller selection at cheaper prices. The latter will generally charge more but has a wider variety of items. This can become even more extreme in the case of a specialist in a particular field. The specialist will charge a lot more for the items in his field, but has invested time and effort in order to offer a wide selection. Each collector must judge for himself the benefits of buying the item from a specialist, therefore paying more (usually) but getting the book wanted, as opposed to waiting for a more attractive price.

Many dealers work from want lists. These should be submitted in a clean, orderly fashion and a SASE (self-addressed, stamped envelope) should be included.

Collectors have to take the responsibility of keeping themselves informed. **The Paperback Price Guide** has been designed and created to be a valuable reference tool, and each new yearly edition will further expand and clarify information. Examining this book, revised editions, and other references such as dealer lists will keep a buyer reasonably informed. Collectors should be aware of the fact that some dealers incorrectly state facts about their books, or inaccurately represent values. This often can merely be a case of ignorance. Collectors must remember that dealers exist with varying degrees of expertise. As in any consumer market, defensive buying makes good sense. Caveat emptor.

Another way to start collecting is at your local bookstore or newsstand. Each and every month, new books appear that will be collector's items in the future. These can include first or original editions, movie and TV tie-ins, and books with cover art by popular artists, such as Michael Whelan and Rowena Morrill (there are many others as well).

SELLING PAPERBACKS

If you have paperbacks that you wish to sell, there are several methods to consider.

The easiest method is to sell your books to a dealer who sells collectible paperbacks. Often, this will mean selling all items as one group. This method is known as wholesaling, which means selling books to a dealer who will try to resell them for his own profit. In order to understand what this means to the dealer, a few background facts are worth discussing.

A serious book dealer is very likely to be a highly individualistic businessman. Known to other book people as a "bookman," the dealer is often a person who has begun to deal out of a love for books rather than as a means to high income. The big profits in the book business are far more likely to be with the new book field rather than the used book market, and many used book dealers will work a 50-60 hour week. Many of the businesses are either one person operations or they center on one person. Because of this, most operations reflect the personality of the owner and different operations can be radically different from one another. These operations have one thing in common, however. The people who run them are free-style businessmen trying to turn a profit in an area where many businesses routinely go out of business after only a few months or years. The dealer tries to buy material at a price where he can resell at a reasonable profit. Novices need to understand that this often means the absorbing of overhead, which is the cost of operating a business, such as rent, utilities, postage, advertising, taxes, etc.

When a dealer considers the purchase of a group of books, he will likely consider carefully the desirability of the material—how many books does he have an immediate call for, how many books are top quality items, what is the overall condition of the group, etc. Collectible books are not like coins, which can be cashed in for their bullion value. In order to profit, and thereby survive in business, the dealer must resell the books he buys. This is the most difficult part of the business, as any veteran book dealer knows that finding material to buy is not a problem. Any dealer, if he stays in business long enough, will find himself offered far more books than he could ever buy. It is unrealistic for the layman to think that he can sell all of his or her books to a dealer for what he/she considers a fair percentage of their value. Mediocre books exist in such profusion that no dealer has to pay a high price to get them. They are extremely common and obtainable for relatively pennies. A dealer will be looking for the items that are uncommon, and this is the material that he will make a special effort to buy. The dealer will consider his wholesale offer based on **his** retail (which can vary a lot from one dealer to another) and his offer will be a percentage of that. This can mean as high as 70 percent for the extraordinarily high quality items down to 10 percent for low interest items. This often will mean an overall percentage of 25 percent, although that certainly is not an "official" figure and can vary in either direction. When trying to get the best price on material, especially the better books in top condition, a person trying to wholesale should try to find out which dealers may be specifically interested in the type of material they have. A dealer who specializes in military books, for example, would probably pay more for good books in that field than a dealer who specializes in science fiction, and so on. The dealer who specializes in certain areas is likely to have a ready list of interested buyers within his specialty, and the power of a good mailing list cannot be overemphasized, for when the dealer's ability to sell is enhanced by a healthy clientele, that dealer can and will buy more material.

Wholesaling to a dealer means the preparation of a listing giving him the information he needs to make a meaningful bid. This will mean the title, author, publisher, book number, condition, and indication of first printing (where possible). Books must be individually graded. Many novice wholesalers make the mistake of including only the most general statement of condition. Example: "all books grade from good to mint." This kind of statement is totally worthless, because a difference in condition on key books can mean a great difference in the wholesale price, even to determining whether the dealer wants to buy at any price. This book gives some detailed information on book grading that should help a lot in this area.

Some people have turned wholesaling into a profitable second income, searching at rummage sales, estate sales, farm auctions, etc., locating books that they believe are suitable for dealers with whom they are acquainted. In the trade, these people are usually referred to as "scouts." Because they don't have the contacts to sell directly to an interested public, they are content with a smaller, faster profit on their material.

If wholesaling does not appeal to a person with books they want to sell, there is only one alternative and that is trying to sell directly to the public. This also means the preparation of a detailed listing, with books individually graded and priced. Lists can be fairly inexpensively printed at any of the many instant printing establishments throughout the country.

This method has several drawbacks. Not having an established mailing list, the seller must try to find names of interested parties wherever he can. Collector publications like this one can be helpful in this, but are still limited, and other dealers will not be willing to share the names of their customers. Selling also involves the creation of overhead costs, because the seller is, in effect, becoming a dealer. Also, if the list does not reach interested buyers, or enough of them, a lot of books could be left over. If successful, however, a higher percentage of value could be realized.

No matter which method is chosen, it should be pointed out that a lot of trial and error is likely to occur. Experience is not only helpful in the book business, it is essential, and there are no short cuts, but the learning can often be pleasurable in itself for the book lover.

THE CARE OF A PAPERBACK COLLECTION

The physical condition of a paperback book is subject to all the ills that affect other paper collectibles, and rare or collectible books should be protected from damage that would reduce their value.

Books should be stored in a cool, dry, and dark place. The paper on which most paperbacks were printed will get brown and brittle with age. Heat, humidity, and light will hasten the deterioration of books.

Many collectors use specially designed bags to protect their paperbacks. Because of non-inert elements in plastic bags that might damage books over the years, some collectors prefer not to use them. Protective coverings made of polyester film is far preferable, although more costly.

Some collectors have used protective sprays such as Krylon Crystal Clear to coat the covers of their books. This method is destructive and should not be used under any circumstances.

THE GRADING OF PAPERBACK BOOKS

The condition of a book is the most important factor affecting its value as a collectible item. The following guidelines are suggested, and collectors and dealers should be careful not to let "wishful thinking" affect their use of these definitions.

MINT (M): As issued. The book is absolutely brand-new and perfect in every way, and just as clean and bright as the day it was printed. This condition grade is seldom, if ever, found.

NEAR MINT (NM): Almost perfect. The cover will still be bright, crisp, and unfaded, with only the most minor signs of wear. Plastic lamination (if any) might be very slightly chipped. The spine will be very tight, square and clean, with only the most minor wear spots. Pages will still be virtually white. Any defects will be very, very minor in nature.

VERY FINE (VF): Slight wear is beginning to show. There may be some slight fading of the cover or spine, and possibly a very slight crease along the edge of the spine to indicate that the book was carefully read once. All aspects of the book will be clean and fresh with no major signs of wear anywhere.

FINE (FN): This copy may have been read carefully several times, but the spine will still be very clean although perhaps slightly bent. The stress lines on the spine will be noticeable but still minor in nature. No creases or bends in the covers themselves. Pages will still be largely white or slightly browning. Cover lamination (if any) may be slightly peeling at corners or other spots. Edge staining could be slightly faded. Light wear, minor color flaking, or minor rubbing noticeable on the extremities. An assortment of minor indications of wear are present, but this still is a very nice copy.

VERY GOOD (VG): An obviously read copy, but still fairly tight. Cover lustre and gloss is largely gone. Plastic lamination (if any) is noticeably peeling in spots. Slight bends or creases in the cover. Pages fairly fresh but browning. Spine is bent from several readings but not broken or torn. Wear spots, chipping, and rubbing is noticeable but not major. No tears in the spine and no tape repairs. Possibly very minor spine splits are noticeable at top and bottom.

GOOD (G): The average used copy but still complete with no pages missing. Cover has bends, creases, and is faded. Spine is loose and possibly splitting on either end but still intact. Spine could be rolled. Minor tears could be present on some pages. No pieces of the cover will be missing. While this copy has been read numerous times, it will still be holding together although showing signs of wear.

FAIR (f): Very heavily read and possibly soiled, but still complete and readable. Torn cover or pages is likely, as is a rolled spine. Possible stains or damage from the elements. This is a reading copy only.

POOR (p): Damaged, heavily worn and soiled. Pages or parts of the cover are missing. Unreadable and unsuitable for collecting.

IMPORTANT: Books that are misbound, miscut, or have covers misprinted are not worth as much as they would be without these defects. The use of tape or colored inks used to hide rubbing spots also detracts from the attractiveness of a book. Condition grades are not on a sliding scale according to age. The ofttimes quoted statement "it's very good for its age" is totally ridiculous and without any validity whatsoever to the collector.

A WORD ABOUT REPRINTS

Reprint editions of most paperback books will not be worth the same as first printings. Fortunately, in these cases the reprints are usually easy to detect.

Some publishers, like Pocket Books, made this quite easy. If collectors check the indicia or copyright page of the book (almost always on the reverse side of the title page), reprintings will generally be noted. On the subject of Pocket Books, it is useful to mention that the accuracy of their reprint information on some books has been questioned, but I have yet to hear the validity of the first printing identification made suspect.

For many publishers, it was easier to reissue a book under a new number rather than reprint it under the old number. Still others, like Dell and Popular Library, would sometimes add 1000 to the original number. For example, the reprint of Popular Library No. 392 became No. 1392.

Reprints are often worth 25 to 50 percent less than the original printings with a number of exceptions. Perhaps the most striking example of this exists with the first ten Pocket Book titles. Because the first printings were limited to no more than 10,000 copies each and distributed within the New York City area only, reprints will be worth significantly less—at least 90 percent less.

A SPECIAL PLEA

Inasmuch as future editions of **The Paperback Price Guide** will be forthcoming, the editor requests that notification of omissions or corrections be sent to me at the following address for possible inclusion in future editions: 5813 York Avenue South, Edina, Minnesota 55410.

I welcome comments from dealers or collectors about this book, for it is a fact that thoughtful feedback is helpful in increasing the accuracy and usefulness of this book within the hobby.

FURTHER READING

For those who wish to increase their knowledge of paperback books, the following publications are suggested.

Hardboiled America by Geoffrey O'Brien, Van Nostrand Reinhold, 1981, $16.95. A study of hardboiled mysteries.

Paperback Market, 5813 York Avenue South, Edina, MN 55410. $10/four issues. An adzine with informational articles.

Paperback Quarterly, 1710 Vincent Street, Brownwood, TX 76801. $10/four issues. A high quality, scholarly journal on the history of paperbacks.

Paperbacks, USA, A Graphic History, 1939-1959, Blue Dolphin, 1981, $10.95. An absolute must for those interested in cover art. Exceptionally informative.

GOOD LUCK AND HAPPY COLLECTING!

MARKET REPORT FOR 1982

The newly emerging paperback market has been the subject of a great deal of activity since the first edition of this book.

As expected, large quantities of books were uncovered as publicity about the possible value of books was made known to the general public. The greatest majority of this material was not of high grade quality, creating an obvious surplus of books in the lower grades.

There were exceptions, however. The warehouse caches of Ace, Archer, and Pyramid appeared in the market. The Ace backstock, along with a lot of original cover paintings, was of high grade condition but not great quantity on early and valuable titles. In the case of the American warehouse of Archer, it was learned that much of the warehouse stock was destroyed by fire and so many of the surfacing copies showed signs of smoke and water damage. The books from the Pyramid backstock was unceremoniously wholesaled through discount stores in parts of the country, and much did not reach the collector market, although small quantities of several Ellison and Woolrich titles were located by dealers.

Publicity on the paperback collectible field appeared in many sources, from the front page of *The Wall Street Journal* to feature articles in *The National Enquirer* and elsewhere. There was also a reasonable amount of radio and TV mentions. As expected, however, the media concentrated on only the most valuable books, which are a relative handful in the field. This led to a lot of disappointments, as many people seemed to feel that any old paperback, in any condition, was worth good money. This was not surprising, all in all, for the approach was the same as the media takes with all collectibles.

The paperback field was subject to the same ills as the rest of the national economy. Tight money caused the market on many books to drop, especially in the lower grades. This was also partly due to the many small accumulations that were dropped into the market.

The greatest interest and activity was in the top line books in the high condition grades. Some of this is certainly no surprise, for the top material always gets the highest degree of attention, but there was another strong factor present. It became very obvious that a lot of people began collecting for the first time. A lot of these people were former comic book collectors with some degree of expertise and a lot of them did what they felt was the best economic move for a new collector—trying to buy the best books in the highest grades. This caused a lot of demand for key books and there were many record prices reached on key books in top condition. This trend is likely to continue as more new collectors enter the market, for experience in other collectible fields has shown them that the best books do go up in value at a faster rate than any others. Some feel that if they are ever to own some of these books, they should buy them as soon as they can.

The top line books were most often first or original editions by important authors. In this regard, Harlan Ellison was probably the most consistent top seller, while Hillman's **The Dying Earth** by Jack Vance was probably the most sought-after single book. Oddities and short series publishers were very popular, as were digest size novels. Drug books maintained their desirability in some areas, and there was a lot of activity in some of the most outrageously lurid cover art titles in top condition.

My best opinion is that the top line material will be strong in the future as well. Lesser material will regain ground as the economy improves and as surplus stocks are absorbed. Dealers will likely have to be flexible in the lower grades, but this has long been a standard in all collectible fields.

OVER THERE! OVER THERE! THE YANKS ARE COMING!
The Story of Armed Services Editions

Books can be used as a weapon, both in peace and wartime. In World War II, the United States government sponsored a publishing effort in which books became a very important weapon for democracy. The books were known as Armed Services Editions, and millions of lives were influenced by them.

This incredible publishing venture was initiated through The Council on Books in Wartime, which was an organization of publishers, editors, librarians, and booksellers. In February of 1943, publisher and Council member W. W. Norton made an ambitious proposal to the organization. "It has long been felt," he wrote, "that a major contribution of the industry could properly lie along a new and completely different line, that of making freely available to our armed forces...the entertainment, the information, the morale, and even the inspiration, which is in books." The proposal was enthusiastically endorsed and was quickly moved from mere words to positive action.

Philip Van Doren Stern was chosen to manage the operation of Armed Services Editions. He and a small staff of eight were responsible for preparing the volumes, handling all accounts, and attending to all aspects of production—truly a Herculean effort.

The books to be published were carefully selected. Publishers were asked to submit the titles of books that they believed would be suitable. A special committee of six people (later ten) used the publishers' lists to prepare a list of recommendations. Final selection, however, was in the hands of Lt. Col. Ray L. Trautman, of the Special Services Division of the Army, and Isabel DuBois, librarian of the United States Navy. "We tried to select a quality variety of titles from those available," recalled Trautman, "and it was no easy task." That Trautman and DuBois succeeded is obvious from checking the complete listing of Armed Services Editions in this book. Armed Services Editions published more classic titles, in all fields, than any other paperback publisher.

Armed Services Editions contracted with authors in a very simple arrangement. Titles were assigned for a period extending to twelve months after repeal of the Selective Service Act. It was agreed that the books would be kept out of the private sector, so as to not compete with regular editions of the books. Although the books were to be free to servicemen and servicewomen, a royalty of 1¢-per-copy would be paid to the publisher. This last condition was sometimes set aside. In early 1944, John Steinbeck suggested to his publisher, Viking Press, that they waive future royalties on the edition of his **Cup of Gold**. Viking Press generously agreed. Other publishers and authors, being assured that lower costs would result in the distribution of more books, agreed to waive all or part of their royalty payments.

The United States Government financed the publication of the books, which cost between four and seven cents apiece. The government's War Production Board allocated metal for printing plates, and special exemptions were secured to allow for the acquisition of paper. The project managed to work its way through wartime red tape rather quickly, as the Army and Navy were asking for a staggering 50,000 copies each of 50 different titles each month!

The first Armed Services Editions appeared in September of 1943. 30 titles a month were initially produced, and that amount went up to 40 titles a month one year later.

The books were produced in the most economical format possible, a saddle-stitched, oblong edition. The cover dimensions were either 5½" x 3-7/8" or 6½" x 4½" depending on the length of the book. Text was printed in two columns per page. Eventually, some of the very last titles appeared in a traditional paperback format.

Concerned primarily with content, Stern's staff spent little time in the area of cover art. They were overworked to begin with, and with saleability not a factor there was no need to produce the kind of colorful covers that commercial paperback publishers were using. Covers of Armed Services Editions would either reproduce a small picture of the original hardcover dust jacket illustration or a specially designed, simple mock-up.

Once published, the books were shipped to each and every corner of the globe in which American armed forces were stationed, as well as to military hospitals in the States. In this respect, the G. I. of World War II was far better off than his allied counterparts. One disgruntled British officer reported his dismay after a landing operation in the Pacific Theater. "There was still a lot of fierce fighting all over that island, but the Americans were already unloading beer, cigarettes, and paperback books for their soldiers."

The books were definitely a great morale booster. Any G. I. could shut out the all-too-real horrors of war by opening the pages of an Armed Services Edition. The books were highly prized and often read until they literally fell apart. Lt. Col. Trautman toured the European Theater, and recalled that some soldiers in France were willing to pay $10 just to be able to read one. "Mind you, these boys were only being paid $55 a month!" he remembered. An incident in Italy was typical of how many G. I.s felt about their reading material. One G. I. had his nose broken by another, because the offending soul had torn a page out for use as a cigarette paper!

Popular author Edgar Rice Burroughs served as a war correspondent in the Pacific Theater, and received many requests for copies of his books. This was hardly unique, with many other authors receiving requests, and then thanks for the books published in Armed Services Editions. "I still get letters," says E. B. White.

Armed Services Editions were an exceptional effort—"one of the great altruistic movements in American publishing, which introduced millions of servicemen and servicewomen to a habit some of them never broke." When the project ended in 1947, 126 million books had been published and distributed, lifting the hearts and spirits of American troops everywhere, and the benefits didn't stop there. As troops returned home, many copies were abandoned. It was through this that many American authors received exposure to new readers in other lands, spreading the cream of American literature to other parts of the world.

The people involved in the Armed Services Editions project performed a great service, and can be proud of their efforts. Their good work deserves the praise of booklovers everywhere.

Note: The author gratefully acknowledges the following reference sources:
A History of the Council on Books in Wartime, Robert Ballou, 1946.
"Of Armed Services Editions I Sing" by Max Wilk, **Publisher's Weekly**, January 2, 1981.
Personal conversations and correspondence with the late Lt. Col. Ray L. Trautman.

Ace D1, © Ace

Ace D11, © Ace

Ace D21, © Ace

ACE

Ace Books, Inc./A. A. Wynn, Inc.

		Good	Fine	N/Mint	
D 1	The Grinning Gismo—Samuel W. Taylor; c-Saunders				M
	Too Hot for Hell—Keith Vining; c-Saunders	20.00	60.00	100.00	M
D 2	Bad Man's Return—W. Colt MacDonald				W
	Bloody Hoofs—J. Edward Leithead; c-Saunders	3.00	9.00	15.00	M
D 3	Twist the Knife Slowly—Kate Clugston; aka A Murderer in the House				W
	The Big Fix—Mel Colton; orig., 1952	4.00	12.00	20.00	M
D 4	Rimrock Rider—Walter A. Tompkins; c-Saunders				M
	Massacre at White River—L. B. Patten; orig., 1952	3.00	9.00	15.00	W
D 5	Drawn to Evil—Harry Whittington; orig., 1952, c-Saunders				M
	The Scarlet Spade—Eaton K. Goldthwaite; aka Cut for Partners, c-Saunders	4.00	12.00	20.00	M
D 6	The Branded Lawman—William E. Vance				W
	Plundor Valley—Nelson Nye	3.00	9.00	15.00	W
D 7	So Dead My Love—Harry Whittington				M
	I, the Executioner—Stephen Ransome; 1953	3.00	9.00	15.00	M
D 8	Terror Rides the Range—Alan K. Echols; orig., 1953				W
	Gunsmoke Gold—Tom West	3.00	9.00	15.00	W
D 9	Decoy—Michael Morgan; orig., 1953				M
	If I Die Before I Wake—Sherwood King	4.00	12.00	20.00	M
D10	The Brazos Firebrand—Leslie Scott; orig., 1953, c-Saunders				W
	Hell on Hoofs—Gordon Young; aka Quarter Horse, c-Ralph Smith	3.00	9.00	15.00	W
D11	Mrs. Homicide—Day Keene; orig., 1953				M
	Dead Ahead—William L. Stuart; aka The Dead Lie Still	3.00	9.00	15.00	M
D12	The Man From Boot Hill—Dean Owen; orig., 1953				W
	Wild Horse Range—Dan J. Stevens	3.00	9.00	15.00	W
D13	The Judas Goat—Leslie Edgley				M
	Cry Plague!—Theodore S. Drachman	12.50	37.50	60.00	SF
D14	Maverick With a Star—George Kilrain				W
	Vultures on Horseback—Paul Evan Lehman	3.00	9.00	15.00	W
D15	Junkie—William Lee (William Burroughs); orig., 1953				E
	Narcotic Agent—Maurice Helbrant	25.00	75.00	125.00	E
D16	Germinie—Jules de Goncourt & Edmond de Goncourt; c-Saunders				
	Crime d'Amour—Paul Bourget	3.00	9.00 *	15.00	
D17	Shakedown—Roney Scott				
	The Darkness Within—Walter Ericson	3.00	9.00	15.00	M
D18	The Lead Slingers—J. Edward Leithead; c-Saunders				M
	The Hanging Hills—Brad Ward	3.00	9.00	15.00	W
D19	Fear No More—Leslie Edgley				W
	Never Kill a Cop—Mel Colton	3.00	9.00	15.00	M
D20	The Desperate Code—Roy Manning; aka Six-Gun Sheriff				M
	Double-Cross Brand—Alan K. Echols; orig., 1953	3.00	9.00	15.00	W
D21	Nightshade—John N. Makris; orig., 1953, c-Saunders				M
	High Stakes—Lester Dent; aka Dead at the Take-off	4.00	12.00	20.00	M
D22	Badlands Masquerader—Leslie Scott				W
	Mavericks of the Plains—Bliss Lomax	3.00	9.00	15.00	W
D23	Bring Back Her Body—Stuart Brock; orig., 1953				M
	Passing Strange—Richard Sale	3.00	9.00	15.00	M
D24	Vulture Valley—Tom West				W
	The Sidewinders—John Callahan	3.00	9.00	15.00	W
D25	The Code of the Wooster—P. G. Wodehouse; c-Saunders				H
	Quick Service—P. G. Wodehouse; c-Saunders	4.00	12.00	20.00	H
D26	The Impotent General—Charles Pettit; c-Saunders				E
	Love in a Junk & Other Exotic Tales—Harold Acton & Lee Yi-Hsieh; aka Four Cautionary Tales, c-Saunders	6.00	18.00	30.00	E
D27	The Fingered Man—Bruno Fischer; c-Saunders				M
	Double Take—Mel Colton	3.00	9.00	15.00	M
D28	Gunsmoke Kingdom—Paul Evan				W
	Avenger From Nowhere—William E. Vance; orig., 1953	3.00	9.00	15.00	W

1

(ACE, continued)

	Good	Fine	N/Mint	
				M
D29 Dead Man Friday—J. F. Hutton; aka Too Good to Be True				M
The Fast Buck—Ross Laurence; orig., 1953	3.00	9.00	15.00	W
D30 Johnny Sundance—Brad Ward; c-Saunders				W
South to Santa Fe—George Kilrain; orig., 1953	3.00	9.00	15.00	SF
D31 Universe Maker—A. E. Van Vogt; orig., 1953				SF
The World of Null-A—A. E. Van Vogt	3.00	9.00	15.00	NF
D32 Cookbook for Beginners—Dorothy Malone; aka Cookbook for Brides	2.00	6.00	10.00	M
D33 Murder by the Pack—Carl G. Hodges; orig., 1953, c-Saunders				M
About Face—Frank Kane	3.00	9.00	15.00	W
D34 Hellion's Hole—Ken Murray; orig., 1953				W
Feud in Piney Flats—Ken Murray; orig., 1953, c-Saunders	3.00	9.00	15.00	E
D35 Open All Night—Jack Houston; orig., 1953				E
The Marina Street Girls—Rae Loomis	3.00	9.00	15.00	SF
D36 Conan the Conqueror—Robert E. Howard; aka Hour of the Dragon, c-Saunders				SF
The Sword of Rhiannon—Leigh Brackett; orig., 1953......................	9.00	27.00	45.00	M
D37 The Drowning Wire—Marvin Claire				M
Departure Delayed—Will Oursler	3.00	9.00	15.00	W
D38 Showdown at Yellow Butte—Jim Mayo; orig., 1953				W
Outlaw River—Bliss Lomax; c-Saunders	3.00	9.00	15.00	W
D39 Quantrill's Raiders—Frank Gruber; orig., 1954, c-Saunders				W
Rebel Road—Frank Gruber; 1954, aka Outlaw	3.00	9.00	15.00	M
D40 Waltz Into Darkness—William Irish				M
Scylla—Malden Grange Bishop; orig., 1954	4.00	12.00	20.00	M
D41 Mourning After—Thomas B. Dewey				M
Death House Doll—Day Keene; orig., 1954	3.00	9.00	15.00	W
D42 One Against a Bullet Horde—Walker A. Tompkins				W
Law for Tombstone—Charles M. (Chuck) Martin	3.00	9.00	15.00	SF
D43 Salome, My First 2,000 Years of Love—George Sylvester Viereck & Paul Eldridge ...	4.00	12.00	20.00	SF
D44 Sentinels of Space—Eric Frank Russell				SF
The Ultimate Invader—Don Wollheim; orig., 1954	3.00	9.00	15.00	M
D45 Death Hitches a Ride—Martin L. Weiss				M
Tracked Down—Leslie Edgley; aka The Angry Heat	3.00	9.00	15.00	W
D46 Vengeance Valley—Roy Manning				W
Law From Back Beyond—Chuck Martin; orig., 1954, c-Saunders	3.00	9.00	15.00	M
D47 Kiss and Kill—Joe Barry; orig., 1954				M
On the Hook—Richard Powell; aka Shark River	3.00	9.00	15.00	W
D48 Utah Blaine—Jim Mayo; orig., 1954				W
Desert Showdown—Brad Ward; aka The Spell of the Desert, c-Saunders	3.00	9.00	15.00	E
D49 The Golden Temptress—Charles Grayson; aka The Broken Gate				M
Tongking!—Dan Cushman; orig., 1954	4.00	12.00	20.00	E
D50 The Mating Call—Wilene Shaw				M
Ban 'un—Ozro Grant	3.00	9.00	15.00	E
D51 Over the Edge—Lawrence Treat				M
Switcheroo—Emmett McDowell; orig., 1954	3.00	9.00	15.00	M
D52 Crossfire Trail—Louis L'amour; orig., 1954				W
Boomtown Buccaneers—William Colt MacDonald	3.00	9.00	15.00	SF
D53 Gateway to Elsewhere—Murray Leinster; orig., 1954				SF
The Weapon Shops of Isher—A. E. Van Vogt	2.00	6.00	10.00	E
S54 The Naked Fear—Carl Offord; orig., 1954	2.00	6.00	10.00	M
D55 Kill-box—Michael Stark; aka Run for Your Life				M
The Tobacco Auction Murders—Robert Turner; orig., 1954	3.00	9.00	15.00	W
D56 Ambush at Coffin Canyon—Bliss Lomax				W
Hellbent for a Hangrope—Clement Hardin	3.00	9.00	15.00	A
D57 Treachery in Trieste—Charles L. Leonard				A
Counterspy Express—A. S. Fleischman; orig., 1954	3.00	9.00	15.00	E
S58 Vice, Inc.—Joachim Joesten	2.00	6.00	10.00	M
D59 Spiderweb—Robert Bloch; orig., 1954				M
The Corpse in My Bed—David Alexander; aka Most Men Don't Kill..........	5.00	15.00	25.00	M

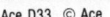

Ace D33, © Ace

Ace D40, © Ace

Ace D48, © Ace

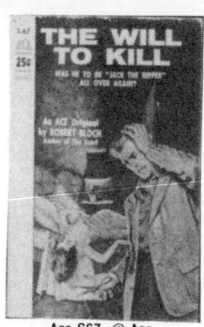

Ace S67, © Ace

Ace S75, © Ace

Ace S90, © Ace

(ACE, continued)

#	Title	Good	Fine	N/Mint	
S60	The Marshal of Medicine Bend—Brad Ward	2.00	6.00	10.00	W
D61	Cosmic Manhunt—L. Sprague de Camp; 1st ed., 1954				SF
	Ring Around the Sun—Clifford D. Simak				SF
D62	Ken Murray's Giant Joke Book—Ken Murray	3.00	9.00	15.00	SF
D63	You'll Die Next—Harry Whittington; orig., 1954	3.00	9.00	15.00	H
	Drag the Dark—Frederick C. Davis				M
D64	Bullets Don't Bluff—Paul Evan Lehman; orig., 1954	3.00	9.00	15.00	M
	Under the Mesa Rim—Chandler Whipple				W
D65	Tornado—Juanita Osborne; orig., 1954	3.00	9.00	15.00	W
	Night Fire—Edward Kimbrough				E
S66	Return to Tomorrow—L. Ron Hubbard	3.00	9.00	15.00	E
S67	The Will to Kill—Robert Bloch	4.00	12.00	20.00	SF
D68	Deadwood—Walker A. Tompkins	4.00	12.00	20.00	M
	Bullet Brand Empire—William Hopson				W
D69	Daybreak-2250 A.D.—Andre Norton; aka Star Man's Son	3.00	9.00	15.00	W
	Beyond Earth's Gates—C. W. Moore & Lewis Padgett				SF
S70	Luisita—Rae Loomis	2.00	6.00	10.00	
D71	Drop Dead—Gordon Ashe	2.00	6.00	10.00	E
	The Case of the Hated Senator—Margaret Scherf; aka Dead: Senate Office Building				M
D72	Nightrider Deputy—Ralph R. Perry	3.00	9.00	15.00	M
	The Devil's Saddle—Norman A. Fox				W
D73	Adventures in the Far Future—D. A. Wollheim	2.00	6.00	10.00	W
	Tales of Outer Space—Donald A. Wollheim				SF
S74	Heat Lightning—Wilene Shaw	2.00	6.00	10.00	SF
S75	Cartoon Annual—Ralph Shikes	1.60	4.80	8.00	E
S76	Shame—Emile Zola	3.00	9.00	15.00	H
D77	Catch the Brass Ring—Stephen Marlowe	1.60	4.80	8.00	E
	Stranger at Home—George Sanders				M
D78	Lobo Legacy—Tom West	2.00	6.00	10.00	M
	The One-Shot Kid—Nelson Nye				W
D79	The Brain Stealers—Murray Leinster	2.00	6.00	10.00	W
	Atta—Francis Rufus Bellamy				SF
S80	The Fear and the Guilt—Wilene Shaw	2.00	6.00	10.00	SF
D81	Too Many Sinners—Sheldon Stark	1.60	4.80	8.00	E
	Liability Limited—John A. Saxon				M
S82	Kilkenny—Louis L'Amour	2.00	6.00	10.00	M
S83	The Steel Noose—Arnold Drake	2.00	6.00	10.00	W
D84	An Earth Gone Mad—Roger Dee	1.60	4.80	8.00	E
	The Rebellious Stars—Isaac Asimov; aka The Stars, Like Dust				SF
S85	The Bachelor's Widow—Maurice Dekobra	1.60	4.80	8.00	SF
D86	Tangled Trail—Roy Manning	1.60	4.80	8.00	E
	Sentinel Peak—Richard Brister				W
S87	Why Am I So Beat—Nolan Miler; 1955	1.60	4.80	8.00	W
D88	The 7-Day System for Gaining Self-Confidence, Popularity and Financial Success—Dexter Davis	1.20	3.60	6.00	E
D89	Death Watch—Ruth Wilson & Alexander Wilson; aka The Town Is Full of Rumors	1.20	3.60	6.00	NF
	Turn Left for Murder—Stephen Marlowe				M
S90	The Chaos Fighters—Robert Moore Williams	1.60	4.80	8.00	W
S91	End of the Line—Stanley Baron	1.60	4.80	8.00	SF
D92	The Drifter—Burt Arthur	1.60	4.80	8.00	E
	The Longhorn Trail—Richard Wormser & Dan Gordon				W
S93	Modern Casanovas Handbook—Horace T. Elmo	1.60	4.80	8.00	W
D94	One Against Eternity—A. E. Van Vogt; aka The Weapon Makers	2.00	6.00	10.00	H
	The Other Side of Here—Murray Leinster				SF
S95	The Naked Jungle—Harry Whittington; orig., 1955	1.60	4.80	8.00	SF
D96	The Last Planet—Andre Norton; aka Star Rangers	1.60	4.80	8.00	M
	A Man Obsessed—Alan E. Nourse				SF
D96	The Last Planet—Andre Norton; special edition	1.60	4.80	8.00	SF

	Good	Fine	N/Mint	
S97 Death Has 2 Faces—Norman Herries	1.20	3.60	6.00	M
D98 The Lobo Horseman—Sam Peoples				W
The Texas Tornado—Nelson Nye; aka Rustler's Roost	1.60	4.80	8.00	W
				SF
D99 The Galactic Breed—Leigh Brackett; aka The Starmen	1.60	4.80	8.00	SF
Conquest of the Space Sea—Robert Moore Williams	1.20	3.60	6.00	E
S100 The Caves—Henry Lewis Nixon				M
D101 Knock 'em Dead—Jack Karney	1.60	4.80	8.00	
Point of No Escape—Mel Colton	1.60	4.80	8.00	A
S102 Oath of Seven—George Albert Glay				SF
D103 Solar Lottery—Phillip K. Dick	1.60	4.80	8.00	SF
The Big Jump—Leigh Brackett	1.20	3.60	6.00	E
S104 Left Bank of Desire—R. V. Cassill & Eric Protter	1.20	3.60	6.00	JD
S105 The Fires of Youth—Edward DeRoo; orig., 1955				W
D106 Lawman Without a Badge—Dorothy L. Bonar	1.20	3.60	6.00	W
Four Texans North—Lee Floren	1.20	3.60	6.00	E
S107 The Gilded Hideaway—Peter Twist	1.20	3.60	6.00	E
S108 Lie Like a Lady—C. S. Cody				M
D109 I See Red—Sterling Noel	1.60	4.80	8.00	M
Mambo to Murder—Dale Clark				SF
D110 No World of Their Own—Poul Anderson	1.60	4.80	8.00	SF
The 1000 Year Plan—Isaac Asimov; aka Foundation	1.60	4.80	8.00	SF
D110 The 1000 Year Plan—Isaac Asimov; special edition	1.20	3.60	6.00	E
S111 The Smoldering Fire—Harry Harrison Kroll				W
D112 Trigger Gospel—Henry Sinclair Drago	1.60	4.80	8.00	W
Border Buccaneers—Frank Castle				SF
D113 The Transposed Man—Dwight V. Swain; 1st ed., 1955	1.60	4.80	8.00	
One in 300—J. T. McIntosh	1.20	3.60	6.00	E
S114 Living It Up—Edward Adler				M
D115 Shady Lady—Cleve F. Adams	1.60	4.80	8.00	M
One Got Away—Harry Whittington	1.60	4.80	8.00	H
S116 Words Fail Me!—Brant House	1.20	3.60	6.00	E
S117 Dark Rapture—Kim Darien				SF
D118 Dome Around America—Jack Williamson	1.60	4.80	8.00	SF
The Paradox Men—Charles L. Harness	1.20	3.60	6.00	E
S119 The Driven Flesh—Lawrence Easton				W
D120 Bounty Man—John McGreevey	1.60	4.80	8.00	W
Call of the Gun—Samuel A. Peeples				SF
D121 3 Faces of Time—Sam Merwin, Jr.	1.60	4.80	8.00	SF
The Stars Are Ours!—Andre Norton	1.60	4.80	8.00	SF
D121 The Stars Are Ours!—Andre Norton; special edition	1.20	3.60	6.00	E
D122 The Preying Streets—Ledru Baker, Jr.				M
D123 Love Me to Death—Frank Diamond	1.20	3.60	6.00	M
The Squeeze—Gil Brewer	1.20	3.60	6.00	E
S124 House of Deceit—Rae Loomis	1.60	4.80	8.00	SF
D125 The Man Who Upset the Universe—Isaac Asimov; aka Foundation and Empire	1.20	3.60	6.00	E
S126 Washington Bachelor—A. H. Berzen	1.60	4.80	8.00	A
D127 Alexander and the Camp Follower—Robert Payne; aka Alexander the God				W
D128 Way Station West—William E. Vance	1.20	3.60	6.00	W
High Saddle—William Hopson				M
D129 Silenced Witnesses—Norman C. Rosenthal	1.60	4.80	8.00	M
The Dangling Carrot—Day Keene; orig., 1955	1.20	3.60	6.00	
S130 Backlash—Sidney Weissman	1.20	3.60	6.00	E
D131 The Ripening—Eugene Wyble	1.60	4.80	8.00	H
S132 Cartoon Annual No. 2—Brant House	1.60	4.80	8.00	SF
S133 Adventures on Other Planets—Donald A. Wollheim				W
D134 Tornado on Horseback—Nelson Nye; aka Fiddle-Back Ranch	1.20	3.60	6.00	W
The Outsiders—Gene Olson				M
D135 Dead Ringer—James Hadley Chase	1.60	4.80	8.00	M
Maid for Murder—Milton K. Ozaki				

Ace D109, © Ace

Ace D127, © Ace

Ace D135, © Ace

Ace S140, © Ace   Ace D178, © Ace   Ace D181, © Ace

(ACE, continued)

		Good	Fine	N/Mint	
S136	A Taste of Sin—R. V. Cassill	1.20	3.60	6.00	E
S137	Violent Night—Ralph Jackson	1.20	3.60	6.00	E
D138	Haven of the Hunted—T. V. Olsen				W
	Gunsmoke Over Sabado—Paul Evan; 1956	1.20	3.60	6.00	W
D139	The Atom Curtain—Nick Bodie Williams				SF
	Alien From Arcturus—Gordon R. Dickson	1.20	3.60	6.00	SF
S140	Honeymoon Humor—Horace T. Elmo	1.60	4.80	8.00	H
S141	Blood on the Branches—Oliver Crawford	1.20	3.60	6.00	
S142	Masquerade in Blue—Glenn M. Barns	1.20	3.60	6.00	E
S143	A Woman on the Place—Harry Whittington	1.20	3.60	6.00	E
D144	The Man From Stony Lonesome—Jay Albert				W
	A Killer Comes Riding—Rod Patterson	1.20	3.60	6.00	W
S145	The Little Monsters—Brant House	1.60	4.80	8.00	H
D146	The Forgotten Planet—Murray Leinster				SF
	Contraband Rocket—Lee Correy	1.60	4.80	8.00	SF
D146	The Forgotten Planet—Murray Leinster; special edition	1.60	4.80	8.00	SF
D147	Prowl Cop—Gregory Jones				M
	My Private Hangman—Norman Herries	1.60	4.80	8.00	M
S148	The Man From Andersonville—Brad Ward	1.20	3.60	6.00	W
D149	A Run for the Money—Dale Clark				M
	The Thin Edge of Mania—Mark Macklin	1.20	3.60	6.00	M
D150	Agent of the Unknown—Margaret St. Clair				SF
	The World Jones Made—Philip K. Dick	1.60	4.80	8.00	SF
S151	Climb a Broken Ladder—Robert Novak	1.00	3.00	5.00	E
S152	Medic Mirth—Henry G. Felsen	1.60	4.80	8.00	H
S153	The Wild Seed—Hallam Whitney & Harry Whittington	1.20	3.60	6.00	E
D154	Voyage to Somewhere—Sloan Wilson	1.20	3.60	6.00	C
D155	Journey to the Center of the Earth—Jules Verne	1.00	3.00	5.00	SF
D156	Thruway West—Lee Floren; c-Leone				W
	The Naked Range—Stephen C. Lawrence	1.20	3.60	6.00	W
D157	Stab in the Dark—Louis Trimble				M
	Never Say No to a Killer—Jonathan Gant	1.20	3.60	6.00	M
S158	Golden Girl—Kim Darien	1.20	3.60	6.00	E
S159	She Shark—John Farr	1.20	3.60	6.00	
D160	Decision at Sundown—Michael Carder				W
	Action Along the Humboldt—Karl Kramer	1.20	3.60	6.00	W
S161	Gag Writer's Private Joke Book—Eddie Davis	1.20	3.60	6.00	H
D162	The Mars Monopoly—Jerry Sohl				SF
	The Man Who Lived Forever—R. DeWitt Miller & Anna Hunger	1.60	4.80	8.00	SF
D163	Woman's Doctor—Russell Boltar	1.20	3.60	6.00	E
D164	Mankind on the Run—Gordon R. Dickson				SF
	The Crossroads of Time—Andre Norton	1.60	4.80	8.00	SF
S165	Love and Hisses—Brant House	1.60	4.80	8.00	H
D166	Whispering Canyon—Stuart Breck				W
	Terror of Tres Alamos—Samuel A. Peeples	1.20	3.60	6.00	W
D167	Destroying Angel—John Creighton				M
	Never Say Die—Milton K. Ozaki	1.20	3.60	6.00	M
S168	Riverboat Girl—P. A. Hoover	1.20	3.60	6.00	E
D169	Star Bridge—Jack Williamson & James E. Gunn	1.20	3.60	6.00	SF
D170	Black Fire—Lawrence Goldman				
	Flight by Night—Day Keene; orig., 1956	1.20	3.60	6.00	
S171	Campus Joke Book—Eddie Davis	1.60	4.80	8.00	H
D172	Johnny No-Name—Ben Smith				W
	Stages South—Robert Steelman	1.20	3.60	6.00	W
D173	Overlords From Space—Joseph E. Kelleam				SF
	The Man Who Mastered Time—Ray Cummings	1.20	3.60	6.00	SF
S174	B-Girl—Robert Novak	1.20	3.60	6.00	E
D175	Best TV Humor of the Year—Irving Settel ed.	1.20	3.60	6.00	H

	Good	Fine	N/Mint	
D176 3 Thousand Years—Thomas Calvert McClary				SF
The Green Queen—Margaret St. Clair	1.20	3.60	6.00	SF
D177 The Girl in the Cop's Pocket—Robert Turner				M
Violence Is Golden—C. H. Thames	1.20	3.60	6.00	M
D178 The Savage City—Jean Paradise	2.00	6.00	10.00	A
S179 Squelches—Brant House	1.60	4.80	8.00	H
D180 The No-Gun Fighter—Nelson Nye				W
One Step Ahead of the Posse—Walt Coburn	1.20	3.60	6.00	W
D181 The Exploits of Sherlock Holmes—John Dickson Carr & Adrian Conan Doyle	1.60	4.80	8.00	M
D182 Shame—Emile Zola				E
Therese Raquin—Emile Zola	1.20	3.60	6.00	
S183 The End of the World—Don Wollheim; orig., 1956	1.60	4.80	8.00	SF
D184 The Big Ivy—James McCague	1.00	3.00	5.00	
D185 The Humming Box—Harry Whittington				M
Build My Gallows High—Geoffrey Homes	1.20	3.60	6.00	M
D186 Ex-Marshal—Ray Hogan				W
Steel Horizon—Edward Churchill	1.20	3.60	6.00	W
D187 The Pawns of Null-A—A. E. Van Vogt; 1st ed., 1956	3.00	9.00	15.00	SF
S188 They Goofed—Brant House	1.60	4.80	8.00	H
D189 Dead on Arrival—Stephen Marlowe				M
Weep for a Wanton—Lawrence Treat	1.20	3.60	6.00	M
S190 The Golden Couch—Henry Lewis Nixon	1.00	3.00	5.00	
D191 Apalachee Gold—Frank G. Slaughter	1.00	3.00	5.00	
D192 Beware of This Tenderfoot—Roy Manning				W
Bad Blood at Black Range—John Callahan	1.20	3.60	6.00	W
D193 The Man Who Japed—Philip K. Dick				SF
The Space Born—E. C. Tubb	2.00	6.00	10.00	SF
D194 Moscow—Theodor Plievier	1.00	3.00	5.00	C
D195 The Deep End—Owen Dudley				M
The Quaking Widow—Robert Colby	1.20	3.60	6.00	M
196 The Night Branders—Walt Coburn				W
The Highwayman—Frank Gruber	1.20	3.60	6.00	W
D197 Counterfeit Corpse—Ferguson Findley				M
TNT for Two—James Byron	1.20	3.60	6.00	M
S198 Tokyo Intrigue—William Bender, Jr	1.20	3.60	6.00	
D199 Planet of No Return—Poul Anderson				SF
Star Guard—Andre Norton; 1957	1.60	4.80	8.00	SF
D200 Report on Unidentified Flying Objects—Edward J. Ruppett	.80	2.40	4.00	UFO
D201 Saturday Mountain—Nathaniel Jones				E
Across That River—Harry Whittington	1.20	3.60	6.00	E
D202 The Color of Green—Leonard Kaufman	.80	2.40	4.00	
D203 Uneasy Lies the Head—William L. Rohde				M
Cain's Girl Friend—William Grote	1.20	3.60	6.00	M
D204 The Desperate Donigans—Gordon Donalds				
John Law, Keep Out!—Paul Durst	1.00	3.00	5.00	
D205 Who Speaks of Conquest?—Lan Wright				SF
The Earth in Peril—Don A. Wollheim	1.20	3.60	6.00	SF
D206 Great Day in the Morning—Robert Hardy Andrews	1.00	3.00	5.00	W
D207 Hollywood Doctor—Charles Grayson	1.00	3.00	5.00	E
D208 Blind Man's Bullets—Glenn Balch				W
The Prodigal Gun—Barry Cord	1.00	3.00	5.00	W
D209 Three Times a Victim—F. L. Wallace				M
A Night for Treason—John Jakes	1.20	3.60	6.00	
D210 The Lion at Morning—Stephen Longstreet	.80	2.40	4.00	E
D211 Eye in the Sky—Philip K. Dick	1.00	3.00	5.00	SF
S212 Hollywood Humor—Horace T. Elmo	1.60	4.80	8.00	H
D213 How to Stop Killing Yourself—Peter J. Steincrohn	1.20	3.60	6.00	NF
D214 Hate Alley—Martin Weiss	1.20	3.60	6.00	

Ace D187, © Ace

Ace D209, © Ace

Ace S212, © Ace

Ace D238, © Ace

Ace D270, © Ace

Ace D274, © Ace

(ACE, continued)

		Good	Fine	N/Mint	
D215	Three to Conquer—Eric Frank Russell				SF
	Doomsday Eve—Robert Moore Williams	1.60	4.80	8.00	SF
D216	Ridin' Through—William Colt MacDonald				W
	Savage Valley—Barry Cord; aka Dry Range	1.00	3.00	5.00	W
D217	Downwind—Bob McKnight				M
	A Rage to Kill—B. E. Lovell	1.00	3.00	5.00	M
D218	Tigrero!—Sasha Siemel	.80	2.40	4.00	A
S219	Backwater Woman—P. A. Hoover	1.00	3.00	5.00	E
D220	Wear a Fast Gun—John Jakes				W
	The Friendless One—Ray Hogan	1.20	3.60	6.00	W
D221	The Terror Package—Robert Chavis				M
	You've Bet Your Life—Gordon Ashe	1.00	3.00	5.00	M
D222	First on the Rope—R. Frison-Roche	.80	2.40	4.00	A
D223	This Fortress World—James E. Gunn				SF
	The 13th Immortal—Robert Silverberg	1.20	3.60	6.00	SF
D224	Desire in the Ozarks—Shelby Steger	1.00	3.00	5.00	E
D225	A Lonely Walk—M. E. Chaber				M
	Loser by a Head—Harry Giddings	1.20	3.60	6.00	M
D226	Doc Colt—Samuel A. Peeples				M
	Showdown at Warbird—Edwin Booth	1.00	3.00	5.00	W
D227	Crisis in 2140—H. Beam Piper & John J. McGuire				SF
	Gunner Cade—Cyril Judd	1.20	3.60	6.00	SF
D228	We Die Alone—David Howarth	.80	2.40	4.00	NF
D229	Take It Out in Trade—Walter Whitney	1.00	3.00	5.00	E
D230	Boss of Barbed Wire—Barry Cord				W
	Burn 'Em Out—Lee Floren	1.00	3.00	5.00	W
D231	Point of Peril—Edward Ronns				M
	Murder for Charity—Owen Dudley	1.00	3.00	5.00	M
D232	The Fixers—Willard Manus	.80	2.40	4.00	E
D233	First on Mars—Rex Gordon	.80	2.40	4.00	SF
D234	Look of the Eagle—Robert L. Scott, Jr.	.80	2.40	4.00	
D235	The Lady and the Snake—John Farr				M
	Nothing to Lose but My Life—Louis Trimble	1.00	3.00	5.00	M
D236	Jinx Rider—Edwin Booth				W
	Walk a Lonely Trail—Ray Hogan	1.00	3.00	5.00	W
D237	The Secret Visitors—James White				SF
	Master of Life and Death—Robert Silverberg	1.20	3.60	6.00	SF
D238	Go—Clellon Holmes	3.00	9.00	15.00	JD
D239	Earth Satellites and the Race for Space Superiority—G. Harry Stine	.80	2.40	4.00	NF
D240	Broken Wheel Ranch—Wayne C. Lee				W
	Torture Trail—Tom West	1.00	3.00	5.00	W
D241	The Hired Target—Wilson Tucker				M
	One Deadly Dawn—Harry Whittington	1.20	3.60	6.00	M
D242	Empire of the Atom—A. E. Van Vogt				SF
	Space Station No. 1—Frank B. Long	1.00	3.00	5.00	SF
D243	The Roving Eye—Michael Wells	.80	2.40	4.00	E
D244	Night Raider of the Atlantic—Terrence Robertson	.80	2.40	4.00	C
D245	Off on a Comet—Jules Verne	.80	2.40	4.00	SF
D246	The Magnate—John Harriman	.80	2.40	4.00	
D247	Look Out Behind You—Ken Lewis				M
	Not So Evil as Eve—John Creighton	1.00	3.00	5.00	M
D248	Longhorn Law—Ray Hogan				W
	Cross Me in Gunsmoke—Clement Hardin	1.00	3.00	5.00	W
D249	The Cosmic Puppets—Philip K. Dick				SF
	Sargasso of Space—Andrew North	1.00	3.00	5.00	SF
D250	The Terrible Swift Sword—Arthur Steuer	.80	2.40	4.00	M
D251	Windward Passage—Hamilton Cochran	.80	2.40	4.00	A
D252	The Rawhide Breed—John Callahan				W

		Good	Fine	N/Mint	
(ACE, continued)					
	Prairie Terror—Rod Patterson	1.00	3.00	5.00	W
D253	The Buried Motive—Bruce Cassiday				M
	Marked Down for Murder—Spencer Dean	1.00	3.00	5.00	M
D254	The Lash of Desire—Marcos Spinelli	1.20	3.60	6.00	E
D255	Star Ways—Poul Anderson; c-Emsh				SF
	City Under the Sea—Kenneth Bulmer	1.20	3.60	6.00	
S256	The General—Karl Ludwig Opitz	.80	2.40	4.00	C
D257	Tiger in the Streets—Louis Malley	1.20	3.60	6.00	JD
D258	The Long Walk—Slavomir Rawicz	.80	2.40	4.00	NF
D259	The Case of the Violent Virgin—Michael Avallone				M
	The Case of the Bouncing Betty—Michael Avallone	1.00	3.00	5.00	M
D260	Land of the Stranger—Ray Hogan				W
	The Saddle Wolves—Lee Floren	1.00	3.00	5.00	W
D261	The Variable Man and Other Stories—Philip K. Dick; c-Emsh	1.00	3.00	5.00	SF
S262	Attack!—Leland Jamieson; c-Emsh	1.00	3.00	5.00	C
S263	See How They Run—Wilene Shaw	.80	2.40	4.00	E
D264	Cain Basin—Barry Cord				W
	Brother Outlaw—Lee E. Wells	1.00	3.00	5.00	W
D265	Terror in the Night and Other Stories—Robert Bloch				M
	Shooting Star—Robert Bloch	3.00	9.00	15.00	M
D266	Twice Upon a Time—Charles L. Fontenay; c-Emsh				SF
	The Mechanical Monarch—E. C. Tubb	1.60	4.80	8.00	SF
D267	Speed Demon—Jim Bosworth	1.00	3.00	5.00	E
D268	Lincoln's Wit—Brant House, ed.	1.00	3.00	5.00	H
D269	Death in the South Atlantic—Michael Powell	.80	2.40	4.00	NF
D270	D for Delinquent—Bud Clifton	1.60	4.80	8.00	JD
D271	Lovers and Libertines—Cliff Howe	1.20	3.60	6.00	NF
D272	Riders in the Night—Lee Floren				W
	Backlash at Cajon Pass—William Hopson	1.00	3.00	5.00	W
D273	The Midnight Eye—Mike Roscoe				M
	Shakedown Hotel—Ernest Jason Fredericks	1.00	3.00	5.00	M
D274	World Without Men—Charles Eric Maine; c-Emsh	6.00	18.00	30.00	SF
S275	Cartoon Annual No. 3—Brant House	1.60	4.80	8.00	H
D276	The Gunsmoke Trail—Barry Cord				W
	Lead in His Fists—Tom West	1.00	3.00	5.00	W
D277	City on the Moon—Murray Leinster; c-Emsh				SF
	Men on the Moon—Donald A. Wollheim	1.20	3.60	6.00	SF
D278	This Bright Sword—Donald Barr Chidsey	.80	2.40	4.00	
D279	Bye-Bye, Baby!—J. Harvey Bond				M
	Murder Mutual—Bob McKnight	1.20	3.60	6.00	M
D280	The Story of Wake Island—James P. S. Devereux	.80	2.40	4.00	NF
D281	Guideposts—Norman Vincent Peale	.80	2.40	4.00	NF
D282	Scoundrels, Fiends & Human Monsters—Cliff Howe	1.20	3.60	6.00	NF
D283	City—Clifford D. Simak	1.00	3.00	5.00	SF
D284	The Man Who Killed Tex—Edwin Booth				W
	The Guns of Hammer—Barry Cord	1.00	3.00	5.00	W
D285	The Brass Shroud—Bruce Cassiday				M
	Odd Woman Out—Joseph Linklater	1.00	3.00	5.00	M
D286	Invaders From Earth—Robert Silverberg; c-Emsh				SF
	Across Time—David Grinnell	1.00	3.00	5.00	SF
D287	Coral and Brass—Gen. Holland M. Smith & Percy Finch	.80	2.40	4.00	NF
D288	The Trail to Tomahawk—Edwin Booth				W
	Law Beyond the Law—John Callahan	1.00	3.00	5.00	W
D289	This'll Slay You—Alan Payne				M
	Violent City—John & Ward Hawkins; 1958	1.00	3.00	5.00	M
D290	A Woman Called Trouble—P. A. Hoover	1.00	3.00	5.00	E
D291	Lest We Forget Thee, Earth—Calvin M. Knox				SF
	People Minus X—Raymond Z. Gallun; c-Emsh	1.60	4.80	8.00	SF
D292	The Insiders—Booth Mooney	1.00	3.00	5.00	E
D293	The Unknown Soldier—Vaino Linna	1.00	3.00	5.00	C
D294	Beyond the Wild Missouri—Walt Coburn				W
	Bad Bunch of the Brasada—John H. Latham	1.00	3.00	5.00	W
D295	Big Planet—Jack Vance				SF
	Slaves of the Klau—Jack Vance	3.00	9.00	15.00	SF
D296	Run the River Gauntlet—John Clagett	1.00	3.00	5.00	A
D297	The Cut of the Whip—Peter Rabe				M
	Kill One, Kill Two—Robert H. Kelston	1.00	3.00	5.00	M
D298	Thunder Creek Range—Paul Evan				W
	Outlaw's Welcome—William E. Vance	1.00	3.00	5.00	W
D299	A Planet for Texans—John J. McGuire				SF
	Star Born—Andre Norton	1.20	3.60	6.00	SF
D300	The Dance Merchants—J. Walter Small	1.00	3.00	5.00	E
D301	The Deadly Combo—John Farr				M
	Murder Isn't Funny—J. Harvey Bond	1.20	3.60	6.00	M
D302	The Iron King—Maurice Druon	1.00	3.00	5.00	A
D303	War of the Wing-Men—Poul Anderson				SF
	The Snows of Ganymede—Poul Anderson	1.20	3.60	6.00	SF

8

Ace D312, © Ace

Ace D315, © Ace

Ace D343, © Ace

(ACE, continued)

		Good	Fine	N/Mint	
D304	River to the Sunset—Archie Joscelyn				W
	Trouble at Breakdam—Ben Smith	1.00	3.00	5.00	W
D305	Free-Lance Murder—Vic Rodell				M
	Cornered—Louis King	1.00	3.00	5.00	M
D306	All Shook Up—Peyson Antholz	1.60	4.80	8.00	JD
D307	From Eve On—Brant House	1.60	4.80	8.00	H
D308	Gunman's Gamble—Jack M. Bickham				W
	Draw and Die!—Roy Manning	1.00	3.00	5.00	W
D309	The Island of Dr. Moreau—H. G. Wells	1.20	3.60	6.00	SF
D310	Mocambu—Marcos Spinell	1.20	3.60	6.00	E
D311	Stepsons of Terra—Robert Silverberg				SF
	A Man Called Destiny—Lan Wright	1.20	3.60	6.00	SF
D312	The Deadly Streets—Harlan Ellison; 1st ed., 1958	12.50	37.50	60.00	JD
D313	The Deadly Boodle—J. M. Flynn				M
	Design for Dying—Samuel A. Krasney	1.00	3.00	5.00	M
D314	Deeds of Darkness—Blair Ashton	1.00	3.00	5.00	
D315	Six Worlds Yonder—Eric Frank Russell				SF
	The Space Willies—Eric Frank Russell	2.00	6.00	10.00	SF
D316	Mesquite Johnny—Barry Cord				W
	A Time for Guns—Rod Patterson	1.00	3.00	5.00	W
D317	The Wayward Blonde—John Creighton				M
	The Big Bite—Gerry Travis	1.20	3.60	6.00	M
D318	Captain Crossbones—Donald Barr Chidsey	1.20	3.60	6.00	A
D319	The Man With Three Faces—Hans-Otto Meissner	.50	1.50	2.50	NF
D320	The Last Shoot Out—William Hopson				W
	The Rangemaster—Robert McCaig	1.00	3.00	5.00	W
D321	The Smell of Trouble—Louis Trimble				M
	Trial by Perjury—John Creighton	1.00	3.00	5.00	M
D322	The Void Beyond and Other Stories—Robert Moore Williams				SF
	The Blue Atom—Robert Moore Williams	1.20	3.60	6.00	SF
D323	The Violent Ones—Brant House, ed.	1.60	4.80	8.00	JD
D324	Brigands of the Moon—Ray Cummings; c-Emsh	1.20	3.60	6.00	SF
D325	July, 1863—Irving Werstein	1.00	3.00	5.00	NF
D326	Battling the Bombers—Wilhelm Johnen	1.00	3.00	5.00	C
D327	First on the Moon—Jeff Satton; c-Emsh	.80	2.40	4.00	SF
D328	The Fourth Gunman—Merle Constiner				W
	Slick on the Draw—Tom West	.80	2.40	4.00	W
D329	Stamped for Death—Emmett McDowell				M
	Three for the Gallows—Emmett McDowell	1.20	3.60	6.00	M
D330	Muscle Boy—Bud Clifton	1.20	3.60	6.00	E
D331	The Secret of Zi—Kenneth Bultner; c-Emsh				SF
	Beyond the Vanishing Point—Ray Cummings	1.20	3.60	6.00	SF
D332	Stranger in Sundown—Ben Smith				W
	Blood on Boot Hill—Kermit Welles; 1959	1.00	3.00	5.00	W
D333	Scream Street—Mike Brett				M
	Stranglehold—John Creighton	1.20	3.60	6.00	M
D334	Queen of the Flat-tops—Stanley Johnston	.80	2.40	4.00	NF
D335	War of Two Worlds—Poul Anderson				SF
	Threshold of Eternity—John Brunner	1.20	3.60	6.00	SF
D336	Morals Squad—Samuel A. Krasney	1.20	3.60	6.00	E
D337	Play It Cool—Jack Gerstine	1.60	4.80	8.00	JD
D338	The Fires of Youth—Edward DeRoo	1.60	4.80	8.00	JD
D339	Ring Around the Sun—Clifford D. Simak	1.20	3.60	6.00	SF
D340	Solar Lottery—Philip K. Dick	1.20	3.60	6.00	SF
D341	The Marina Street Girls—Rae Loomis	1.60	4.80	8.00	E
D342	Queen's Blade—Nicholas Gorham	1.00	3.00	5.00	A
D343	The Young Wolves—Edward DeRoo	1.60	4.80	8.00	JD
D344	Desert Fury—Gordon Landsborough; aka Battery From Hellfire	1.00	3.00	5.00	C

(ACE, continued)

		Good	Fine	N/Mint	
D345	Plague Ship—Andrew North				SF
	Voodoo Planet—Andrew North	1.00	3.00	5.00	SF
					W
D346	Sheriff of Big Hat—Barry Cord				W
	Wanted! Alive!—Ray Hogan	1.00	3.00	5.00	W
					M
D347	The Corpse Without a Country—Louis Trimble				M
	Play for Keeps—Harry Whittington	1.20	3.60	6.00	M
					W
D348	The Man From Nowhere—T. V. Olsen				W
	The Avenging Gun—John L. Shelley	1.00	3.00	5.00	W
					M
D349	The Guilty Bystander—Mike Brett				M
	Kill Me With Kindness—J. Harvey Bond	1.00	3.00	5.00	M
D350	Red Alert—Peter Bryant	.80	2.40	4.00	SF
					SF
D351	The Sun Smasher—Edmond Hamilton				SF
	Star Haven—Ivar Jorgenson	1.20	3.60	6.00	SF
G352	Fire and Morning—Francis Leary	1.00	3.00	5.00	A
D353	The Macabre Reader—Donald A. Wollheim, ed.	1.60	4.80	8.00	HO
D354	The Hidden Planet—Donald A. Wollheim	1.20	3.60	6.00	SF
D355	The Beachhead Spies—Bill Strutton & Michael Pearson; aka The Secret Invaders	1.00	3.00	5.00	C
					W
D356	Kansan Guns—Paul Durst				W
	The Cactus Kid—Tom West	1.00	3.00	5.00	W
					M
D357	Lady in Peril—Lester Dent				M
	Wired for Scandal—F. L. Wallace	3.00	9.00	15.00	M
					SF
D358	The Plot Against Earth—Calvin M. Knox				SF
	Recruit for Andromeda—Milton Lesser	1.00	3.00	5.00	SF
D359	The Haunted Strangler—John C. Cooper; aka The Grip of the Strangler, movie tie-in	3.00	9.00	15.00	HO
					W
D360	War in Peaceful Valley—Barry Cord				W
	Johnny Sixgun—John H. Latham	1.00	3.00	5.00	W
					M
D361	Murder Mistress—Robert Colby				M
	Dangerous to Know—James P. Duff	1.20	3.60	6.00	M
					SF
D362	The 100th Millenium—John Brunner				SF
	Edge of Time—David Grinnell	1.20	3.60	6.00	SF
D363	The Rapist—Samuel A. Krasney	1.20	3.60	6.00	E
D364	The Pipes Are Calling—Donald Barr Chidsey; 1st ed., 1959	1.00	3.00	5.00	A
D365	Mig Alley—Robert Eunson; 1st ed., 1959.	.80	2.40	4.00	C
D366	The Invaders Are Coming—Alan E. Nourse & J. A. Meyer; c-Emsh	1.00	3.00	5.00	SF
					M
D367	Negative of a Nude—Charles E. Fritch; 1st ed., 1959				M
	Till Death Do Us Part—Louis Trimble	1.00	3.00	5.00	M
					W
D368	A Score to Settle—Joseph Gage				W
	Hangman's Valley—Ray Hogan; 1st ed., 1959	1.00	3.00	5.00	W
					SF
D369	Vanguard From Alpha—Brian Aldiss				SF
	The Changeling Worlds—Kenneth Bulmer	1.00	3.00	5.00	SF
D370	Cry Flood!—Ernest Jason Fredericks	.80	2.40	4.00	E
G371	Berlin—Theodor Plievier	.80	2.40	4.00	C
					W
D372	Grass Greed—Glenn Balch				W
	Cimarron Territory—Dan Kirby	1.00	3.00	5.00	W
					M
D373	Scarlet Starlet—Doug Warren				M
	The Knave of Diamonds—Jack Karney; 1st ed., 1959	1.00	3.00	5.00	M
D374	The Thoroughbred and the Tramp—Burgess Leonard; 1st ed., 1959	1.00	3.00	5.00	E
					SF
D375	Masters of Evolution—Damon Knight; c-Emsh				SF
	Fire in the Heavens—George O. Smith	1.00	3.00	5.00	SF
G376	The Big Company Look—J. Harvey Howells	.80	2.40	4.00	
D377	Bombs in Orbit—Jeff Sutton; 1st ed., 1959	.80	2.40	4.00	SF
D378	Out for Kicks—Wilene Shaw	1.00	3.00	5.00	
					M
D379	Drink With the Dead—J. M. Flynn				M
	Mistress of Horror House—William Woody	1.00	3.00	5.00	M
					W
D380	Concho Valley—Barry Cord				W
	My Brother the Gunman—William Heuman	1.00	3.00	5.00	W
					SF
D381	Secret of the Lost Race—Andre Norton; 1st ed., 1959				SF
	One Against Herculum—Jerry Sohl	1.00	3.00	5.00	SF
G382	The Willing Maid—C. T. Ritchie	1.00	3.00	5.00	A

Ace D359, © Ace

Ace D378, © Ace

Ace G386, © Ace

Ace D417, © Ace

Ace D420, © Ace

Ace D435, © Ace

(ACE, continued)

		Good	Fine	N/Mint	
D383	The Murder Specialist—Bud Clifton; 1st ed., 1959	1.00	3.00	5.00	M
D384	Feud Fury—Jack M. Bickham; 1st ed., 1959				W
	Mountain Ambush—Louis Trimble	1.00	3.00	5.00	W
D385	Echo in the Skull—John Brunner				SF
	Rocket to Limbo—Alan E. Nourse; c-Emsh	1.00	3.00	5.00	SF
G386	The Sulu Sword—Richard O'Connor	1.00	3.00	5.00	A
D387	Fare Prey—Laine Fisher				M
	The Bikini Bombshell—Bob McKnight	1.00	3.00	5.00	M
D388	When the Sleeper Wakes—H. G. Wells; c-Emsh	.80	2.40	4.00	SF
D389	No Entry—Manning Coles	.80	2.40	4.00	
G390	Long Pig—Russell Foreman	1.00	3.00	5.00	
D391	The World Swappers—John Brunner; 1st ed., 1959				SF
	Seige of the Unseen—A. E. Van Vogt	1.00	3.00	5.00	SF
D392	Twisted Trail—Tom West				W
	The Man From Salt Creek—Archie Joscelyn	.80	2.40	4.00	W
D393	Dictators Die Hard—Robert A. Levey				M
	Evil Is the Night—John Creighton; 1st ed., 1959	1.00	3.00	5.00	M
D394	The Flaming Island—Donald Barr Chidsey	1.00	3.00	5.00	A
D395	Thunder at Harper's Ferry—Allan Keller	.80	2.40	4.00	NF
D396	Luisita—Rae Loomis	.80	2.40	4.00	E
D397	Journey to the Center of the Earth—Jules Verne	.50	1.50	2.50	SF
D398	Why I Am So Beat—Nolan Miller	.80	2.40	4.00	E
D399	Living It Up—Edward Adler	.80	2.40	4.00	
D400	Last Chance at Devil's Canyon—Barry Cord				W
	Shadow of a Gunman—Gordon D. Shirreffs	1.00	3.00	5.00	W
D401	Obit Deferred—Louis Trimble; 1st ed., 1959				M
	I Want Out—Tedd Thomey	1.00	3.00	5.00	M
G402	Kiboko—Daniel P. Mannix	1.20	3.60	6.00	A
D403	The Pirates of Zan—Murray Leinster; 1st ed., 1959, c-Emsh				SF
	The Mutant Weapon—Murray Leinster	1.20	3.60	6.00	SF
D404	The Hollow Hero—Clifford Anderson; 1st ed., 1959	.80	2.40	4.00	
D405	First to the Stars—Rex Gordon; 1st ed., 1959	.80	2.40	4.00	SF
D406	Go, Man, Go!—Edward De Roo; 1st ed., 1959	1.60	4.80	8.00	JD
D407	The Planet Killers—Robert Silverberg				SF
	We Claim These Stars!—Poul Anderson	1.00	3.00	5.00	SF
D408	Wyoming Welcome—Edwin Booth				W
	Law of the Trigger—Giles A. Lutz	1.00	3.00	5.00	W
D409	Terror Tournament—J. M. Flynn				M
	Cargo for the Styx—Louis Trimble; 1st ed., 1959	1.00	3.00	5.00	M
D410	Buccaneer's Blade—Donald Barr Chidsey; 1st ed., 1959	1.00	3.00	5.00	A
D411	Swamp Sanctuary—Bob McKnight; 1st ed., 1959	1.20	3.60	6.00	E
D412	Apache Butte—Gordon R. Shirreffs				W
	Ride the Long Night—E. A. Alman; 1st ed., 1960	1.00	3.00	5.00	W
D413	A Touch of Infinity—Harlan Ellison				SF
	The Man With Nine Lives—Harlan Ellison	4.00	12.00	20.00	SF
G414	The Companions of Jehu—Alexandre Dumas	1.00	3.00	5.00	A
D415	Dead Certain—Stewart Sterling; 1st ed., 1960				M
	Fire on Fear Street—Stewart Sterling	1.00	3.00	5.00	M
D416	The Big Question—John Kenneth; 1st ed., 1960	.80	2.40	4.00	E
D417	Rumble at the Housing Project—Edward DeRoo	1.60	4.80	8.00	
D418	Nothing but My Gun—Tom West				W
	The Quiet Ones—C. S. Park	1.00	3.00	5.00	W
D419	A Slice of Death—Bob McKnight; 1st ed., 1960				M
	Open Season—Bernard Thielen	1.00	3.00	5.00	M
D420	The Angry Ones—John A. Williams; 1st ed., 1960	1.00	3.00	5.00	E
D421	Dr. Futurity—Philip K. Dick; 1st ed., 1960				SF
	Slavers of Space—John Brunner	1.00	3.00	5.00	SF
D422	The Best From Fantasy and Science Fiction, 3rd Series—ed. Anthony Boucher &				

		Good	Fine	N/Mint	
	J. Francis McComas	1.00	3.00	5.00	SF
D423	Tidal Wave—Browning Norton; 1st ed., 1960.	1.00	3.00	5.00	
D424	Wild Justice—Robert McCaig				W
	Shoot-out at the Way Station—Lee Richards	1.00	3.00	5.00	W
D425	Dig Her a Grave—Paul Kruger				M
	A Half Interest in Murder—John Creighton; 1st ed., 1960	1.00	3.00	5.00	M
D426	Penal Colony—Robert S. Close; aka Eliza Callaghan	1.60	4.80	8.00	E
D427	World of the Masterminds—Robert Moore Williams				SF
	To the End of Time and Other Stories—Robert Moore Williams; 1st ed., 1960	1.00	3.00	5.00	SF
D428	Scowtown Woman—P. A. Hoover	1.00	3.00	5.00	E
D429	The Anatomy of Violence—Charles Runyon; 1st ed., 1960	1.00	3.00	5.00	E
D430	Born Savage—William Hopson; c-Basil Gogos				W
	The Hasty Hangman—Ray Hogan; 1st ed., 1960	1.00	3.00	5.00	W
D431	Lost in Space—George O. Smith				SF
	Earth's Last Fortress—A. E. Van Vogt; 1st ed., 1960	1.00	3.00	5.00	SF
D432	Convention Queen—Donn Broward; 1st ed., 1960	1.00	3.00	5.00	E
D433	If Hate Could Kill—Jack Bradley; 1st ed., 1960				M
	The Smasher—Talmage Powell.	1.00	3.00	5.00	M
D434	The Purchase of the North Pole—Jules Verne	.80	2.40	4.00	SF
D435	Lady in Bondage—C. T. Ritchie; aka Black Angels	1.20	3.60	6.00	A
D436	The Challenger—Giles A. Lutz				W
	The Phantom Pistoleer—Tom West	1.00	3.00	5.00	W
D437	And Then the Town Took Off—Richard Wilson				SF
	The Sioux Spaceman—Andre Norton; 1st ed., 1960.	1.00	3.00	5.00	SF
D438	The Panic Button—Charles Fogg; 1st ed., 1960	.80	2.40	4.00	C
D439	Run If You Can—Owen Dudley; 1st ed., 1960				M
	The Devil's Punchbowl—Duane Decker	1.00	3.00	5.00	M
G440	Letter of Marque—Andrew Hepburn	1.00	3.00	5.00	A
D441	Skip Bomber—Lloyd E. Olson	.80	2.40	4.00	C
D442	Rider of the Rincon—Rod Patterson				W
	Killer's Paradise—Jack M. Bickham	1.00	3.00	5.00	W
D443	Bow Down to Nul—Brian W. Aldiss; 1st ed., 1960				SF
	The Dark Destroyers—Manly Wade Wellman	1.00	3.00	5.00	SF
D444	Desire Island—Shepard Rifkin; 1st ed., 1960	1.20	3.60	6.00	E
D445	Bloodline to Murder—Emmett McDowell; 1st ed., 1960				M
	In at the Kill—Emmett McDowell	1.00	3.00	5.00	M
D446	Flight 685 Is Overdue—Edward Moore; 1st ed., 1960	.80	2.40	4.00	M
D447	The Hot Chariot—J. M. Flynn				M
	Kiss the Babe Goodbye—Bob McKnight; 1st ed., 1960	1.00	3.00	5.00	M
D448	Pistol-Whipper—Lee Floren				W
	Winter Range—Al Cody	1.00	3.00	5.00	W
D449	The Genetic General—Gordon R. Dickson; 1st ed., 1960				SF
	Time to Teleport—Gordon R. Dickson	2.00	6.00	10.00	SF
D450	Side Me With Sixes—Tom West				W
	The Ridgerunner—Ray Hogan	1.00	3.00	5.00	W
D451	Odds Against Linda—Steve Ward; 1st ed., 1960				M
	A Key to the Morgue—Robert Martin	1.00	3.00	5.00	M
D452	The Color of Hate—Joe L. Hensley	1.00	3.00	5.00	M
D453	The Games of Neith—Margaret St. Clair; 1st ed., 1960				SF
	The Earth Gods Are Coming—Kenneth Bulmer	1.00	3.00	5.00	SF
G454	Ride East! Ride West!—Anne Powers; aka Rogue's Honor	1.00	3.00	5.00	A
D455	The Best From Fantasy and Science Fiction - Fourth Series—Anthony Boucher, ed. . .	1.00	3.00	5.00	SF
D456	The Desperate Dude—Edwin Booth				W
	Danger Trail—Edwin Booth	1.00	3.00	5.00	W
D457	Vulcan's Hammer—Philip K. Dick; 1st ed., 1960				SF
	The Skynappers—John Brunner.	1.00	3.00	5.00	SF
D458	Womanhunt—Mark Derby	1.00	3.00	5.00	A
D459	The Hot Diary—Howard J. Olmsted; 1st ed., 1960				M
	Ring Around a Rogue—J. M. Flynn	1.00	3.00	5.00	M
D460	When the Ship Sank—James MacGregor	.80	2.40	4.00	C
D461	The Time Traders—Andre Norton	.80	2.40	4.00	SF
D462	The Useless Gun—Jack M. Bickham				W
	The Long Fuse—John H. Latham; 1st ed., 1960	1.00	3.00	5.00	W
D463	Dying Room Only—Stewart Sterling				M
	The Body in the Bed—Stewart Sterling	1.00	3.00	5.00	M
D464	Tame the Wild Flesh—Wilene Shaw; 1st ed., 1960	1.00	3.00	5.00	E
D465	The Martian Missile—David Grinnell				SF
	The Atlantic Abomination—John Brunner; 1st ed., 1960	1.00	3.00	5.00	SF
D466	Wild Bill Hickok—Richard O'Connor	.80	2.40	4.00	W
D467	Five, Four, Three, Two, One - Pfftt—William C. Anderson; 1st ed., 1960.	1.60	4.80	8.00	SF-H
D468	Sentinels of Space—Eric Frank Russell; c-Schulz	1.00	3.00	5.00	SF
D469	Running Scared—Bob McKnight; 1st ed., 1960				M
	Man-Killer—Talmage Powell	1.00	3.00	5.00	M
D470	The Maverick—Ben Smith				W
	The Man Who Was Morgan—Gene Olson	.80	2.40	4.00	W
D471	Sanctuary in the Sky—John Brunner				SF
	The Secret Martians—Jack Sharkey; 1st ed., 1960	1.00	3.00	5.00	SF

Ace D472, © Ace

Ace D493, © Ace

Ace D513, © Ace

		Good	Fine	N/Mint	
(ACE, continued)					
D472	A Night for Screaming—Harry Whittington	1.20	3.60	6.00	M
D473	The Greatest Adventure—John Taine	1.60	4.80	8.00	SF
G474	Lost Mines and Hidden Treasure—Leland Lovelace	.80	2.40	4.00	NF
475					
D476	Double-Cross Dinero—Tom West				W
	Lost Valley—Edwin Booth	1.00	3.00	5.00	W
D477	The Duchess of Skid Row—Louis Trimble				M
	Love Me and Die—Louis Trimble	1.00	3.00	5.00	M
D478	Spacehive—Jeff Sutton; 1st ed. 1960	.80	2.40	4.00	SF
D479	To the Tombaugh Station—Wilson Tucker; 1st ed., 1960				SF
	Earthman Go Home!—Poul Anderson	1.20	3.60	6.00	SF
G480	The Strong Men—John Brick	1.00	3.00	5.00	A
D481	The Biggest Holdup—Joseph F. Dinneen; aka The Alternate Case	1.00	3.00	5.00	NF
D482	The Weapon Shops of Isher—A. E. Van Vogt	1.00	3.00	5.00	SF
D483	The Corpse in the Picture Window—Bruce Cassidy				M
	If Wishes Were Hearses—J. Harvey Bond; 1st ed., 1961	1.00	3.00	5.00	M
D484	Dead Man's Spurs—Al Cody; 1st ed., 1961				W
	Ambush at Riflestock—Ray Hogan	1.00	3.00	5.00	W
D485	The Puzzle Planet—Robert A. W. Lowndes; 1st ed., 1961				SF
	The Angry Espers—Lloyd Biggle, Jr.	1.00	3.00	5.00	SF
D486	The Little Caesars—Edward DeRoo	1.20	3.60	6.00	JD
D487	Four-Year Hitch—Leonard Sanders; 1st ed., 1961	.80	2.40	4.00	C
D488	Third Time Down—Dan Brennan; 1st ed., 1961	1.00	3.00	5.00	C
D489	Somebody's Walking Over My Grave—Robert Arthur; 1st ed. 1961				M
	Dally With a Deadly Doll—John Miles	1.00	3.00	5.00	M
D490	Adventures on Other Planets—Donald A. Wollheim	.80	2.40	4.00	SF
D491	The Big Time—Fritz Leiber; 1st ed., 1961				SF
	The Mind Spider and Other Stories—Fritz Leiber	2.00	6.00	10.00	SF
D492	Winter Drive—William Hopson				W
	The Wild Quarry—Giles A. Lutz	1.00	3.00	5.00	W
D493	The Queen's Awards/Fifth Series—ed. Ellery Queen; c-Maguire	1.20	3.60	6.00	M
D494	Log Jam—Leslie Turner White	1.00	3.00	5.00	A
D495	A Mania for Blondes—Samuel A. Krasney; 1st ed., 1961	1.00	3.00	5.00	M
D496	With Blood in Their Eyes—Steven Lawrence				W
	Killer's Canyon—Tom West	.80	2.40	4.00	W
D497	Wandl the Invader—Ray Cummings; 1st ed., 1961				SF
	I Speak for Earth—Keith Woodcott	1.20	3.60	6.00	SF
D498	Galactic Derelict—Andre Norton	1.00	3.00	5.00	SF
D499	Night Drop—Frederick C. Davis				M
	High Heel Homicide—Frederick C. Davis	1.00	3.00	5.00	M
G500	The Bad Man of the West—George D. Hendricks	1.00	3.00	5.00	NF
D501	Let Him Go Hang—Bud Clifton	1.00	3.00	5.00	M
D502	Long Night at Lodgepole—Al Cody; 1st ed., 1961				W
	Troubled Range—Paul Evan Lehman	1.00	3.00	5.00	W
D503	The Girl in the Death Seat—Fan Nichols	1.00	3.00	5.00	M
D504	Master of the World—Jules Verne; movie tie-in	.80	2.40	4.00	SF
D505	The Surfside Caper—Louis Trimble				M
	In a Vanishing Room—Robert Colby; 1st ed., 1961	1.00	3.00	5.00	M
D506	The Brazen Dream—Harry Harrison Kroll; 1st ed., 1961	1.00	3.00	5.00	E
D507	Meeting at Infinity—John Brunner; 1st ed., 1961				SF
	Beyond the Silver Sky—Kenneth Bulmer	1.00	3.00	5.00	SF
D508	More Macabre—Donald A. Wollheim	1.60	4.80	8.00	HO
D509	Star Hunter—Andre Norton; 1st ed., 1961				SF
	The Beast Master—Andre Norton	1.20	3.60	6.00	SF
D510	The Searching Rider—Harry Whittington				W
	Hangman's Territory—Jack M. Bickham	1.20	3.60	6.00	W
D511	Drop Dead, Please—Bob McKnight; 1st ed. 1961				M
	One for the Death House—J. M. Flynn	1.00	3.00	5.00	M

(ACE, continued)

		Good	Fine	N/Mint	
D512	Marooned—Donald Barr Chidsey; 1st ed., 1961	1.00	3.00	5.00	A
D513	The Juvies—Harlan Ellison	12.50	37.50	60.00	JD
D514	Ride a Lone Trail—Gordon D. Shirreffs				W
	Hangin' Pards—Gordon D. Shirreffs	1.00	3.00	5.00	W
D515	Kill Me a Fortune—Robert Colby; 1st ed., 1961				M
	Five Alarm Funeral—Stewart Sterling	1.00	3.00	5.00	M
D516	The Swordsman of Mars—Otis Adelbert Kline	1.20	3.60	6.00	SF
D517	The Trouble With Tycho—Clifford D. Simak				SF
	Bring Back Yesterday—A. Bertram Chandler; 1st ed., 1961	1.20	3.60	6.00	SF
D518	Nightmare Cruise—Wade Miller	1.20	3.60	6.00	M
D519	Air Rescue—Carroll V. Glines, Jr. & Wendell F. Moseley	1.00	3.00	5.00	NF
D520	One Foot in Hell—Wilene Shaw; 1st ed., 1961	1.00	3.00	5.00	E
D521	The Girl in the White Cap—Margaret Howe	.80	2.40	4.00	R
D522	A Nest of Fear—Hal Ellson	1.00	3.00	5.00	JD
D523	Strike the Black Flag—Jay Scotland (John Jakes); 1st ed., 1961	1.20	3.60	6.00	A
D524	Overseas Nurse—Jennifer Ames	.80	2.40	4.00	R
D525	This World Is Taboo—Murray Leimster; 1st ed., 1961	1.20	3.60	6.00	SF
D526	Obsession—Kim Darien	1.00	3.00	5.00	E
D527	Star Guard—Andre Norton	1.00	3.00	5.00	SF
D528	Forgotten Planet—Murray Leinster	1.00	3.00	5.00	SF
D529	The Pirate and the Lady—Leslie Turner White; 1st ed., 1961	1.00	3.00	5.00	A
D530	The Day They H-Bombed Los Angeles—Robert Moore Williams; 1st ed., 1961	2.00	6.00	10.00	SF
D531	The Outlaws of Mars—Otis Adelbert Kline	1.20	3.60	6.00	SF
D532	Nurse Craig—Isabel Cabot	.80	2.40	4.00	R
D533	Mad Ave—H. T. Elmo	1.60	4.80	8.00	H
D534	Daybreak - 2250 A.D.—Andre Norton; 1962, aka Star Man's Son	.80	2.40	4.00	SF
D535	The Shadow Girl—Ray Cummings	1.00	3.00	5.00	SF
D536	The Nurse and the Pirate—Peggy Gaddis	.80	2.40	4.00	R
D537	The Island of Dr. Moreau—H. G. Wells	.80	2.40	4.00	SF
D538	The 1,000 Year Plan—Isaac Asimov; aka Foundation	1.00	3.00	5.00	SF
D539	Psychiatric Nurse—Mary Mann Fletcher; 1st ed., 1962	.80	2.40	4.00	R
D540	School Nurse—Arlene Hale	.80	2.40	4.00	R
D541	Scavengers in Space—Alan E. Nourse	.80	2.40	4.00	SF
D542	The Last Planet—Andre Norton; aka Star Rangers	1.00	3.00	5.00	SF
D543	Small Town Nurse—Harriet Kathryn Myers; 1st ed., 1962	.80	2.40	4.00	R
D544	Space Station No. 1—Frank Belknap Long	1.20	3.60	6.00	SF
D545	Emergency Nurse—Suzanne Roberts; 1st ed., 1962	.80	2.40	4.00	R
D546	The Crossroads of Time—Andre Norton	1.00	3.00	5.00	SF
D547	The Super Barbarians—John Brunner	1.00	3.00	5.00	SF
D548	End of the World—Dean Owen; movie tie-in	1.60	4.80	8.00	SF
D549	Spotlight on Nurse Thorne—Tracy Adams; 1st ed., 1962	.80	2.40	4.00	R
D550	No World of Their Own—Poul Anderson	1.00	3.00	5.00	SF
D551	Red Alert—Peter Bryant	.50	1.50	2.50	SF
D552	Hollywood Nurse—Patricia Libby	.80	2.40	4.00	R
D553	The House on the Borderland—William Hope Hodgson	1.00	3.00	5.00	SF
D554	Runaway Nurse—Ethel Hamill	.80	2.40	4.00	R
D555	The Trial of Terra—Jack Williamson; 1st ed., 1962	1.00	3.00	5.00	SF
D556	A Nurse for Dr. Sterling—Ruth MacLeod	.50	1.50	2.50	R
D557	Hope Wears White—Florence Stuart	.50	1.50	2.50	R
D558	Campus Nurse—Suzanne Roberts	.50	1.50	2.50	R
D559	Ski Resort Nurse—Jane L. Sears	.50	1.50	2.50	R
D560	Medic in Love—Rowena Boylan	.50	1.50	2.50	R
D561	Nell Shannon, R.N.—Ann Rush; 1963	.50	1.50	2.50	R
D562	Cover Girl Nurse—Patricia Libby	.50	1.50	2.50	R
D563	Leave It to Nurse Kathy—Arlene Hale	.50	1.50	2.50	R
D564	Prodigal Nurse—Harriet Kathryn Myers	.50	1.50	2.50	R
D565	The Heart of Dr. Hilary—Ray Dorien	.50	1.50	2.50	R
D566	Julie Jones, Cape Canaveral Nurse—Suzanne Roberts; 1st ed., 1963	.50	1.50	2.50	R

Ace D518, © Ace

Ace D530, © Ace

Ace D548, © Ace

Ace D599, © Ace	Ace F101, © Ace	Ace F156, © Ace		

(ACE, continued)		Good	Fine	N/Mint	
D567	A Challenge for Nurse Melanie—Isabel Moore; 1st ed. 1963	.50	1.50	2.50	R
D568	Star Ways—Poul Anderson	.80	2.40	4.00	SF
D569	Dude Ranch Nurse—Arlene Hale; 1st ed., 1963	.50	1.50	2.50	R
D570	Spanish Grant—L. L. Foreman	.80	2.40	4.00	W
D571	Princess of White Starch—Katherine McComb; 1st ed., 1963	.50	1.50	2.50	R
D572	Arizona Rider—Frank Wynne	.80	2.40	4.00	W
D573	Whispering Canyon—Stuart Brock	.80	2.40	4.00	W
D574	Kilkenny—Louis L'Amour	1.20	3.60	6.00	W
D575	A Nurse Called Hope—Peggy Dern	.50	1.50	2.50	R
D576	Border Nurse—Dorothy Dowdell	.50	1.50	2.50	R
D577	Legacy of Love—Frances Sarah Moore; c-Schinella	.50	1.50	2.50	R
D578	The Lawbringers—Brian Wynne Garfield	.80	2.40	4.00	W
D579	Hootenanny Nurse—Suzanne Roberts; 1st ed., 1964	.50	1.50	2.50	R
D580	Symptoms of Love—Arlene Hale	.50	1.50	2.50	R
D581	Co-ed in White—Suzanne Roberts; 1st ed., 1964	.50	1.50	2.50	R
D582	My Love an Altar—Joan Sargent; c-Schinella	.50	1.50	2.50	R
D583	Hotel Nurse—Tracy Adams; 1st ed., 1964	.50	1.50	2.50	R
D584	Airport Nurse—Monica Edwards	.50	1.50	2.50	R
D585	Nurse Marcie's Island—Arlene Hale; 1st ed., 1964	.50	1.50	2.50	R
D586	San Francisco Nurse—Barbara Grabendike; 1st ed., 1964	.50	1.50	2.50	R
D587	Nurse Connor Comes Home—Arlene Hale; 1st ed., 1964	.50	1.50	2.50	R
D588	Short-trigger Man—Merle Constiner; 1st ed., 1964	.80	2.40	4.00	W
D589	The Nurse With the Silver Skates—Virginia B. McDonnell	.50	1.50	2.50	R
D590	Stampede at Hourglass—Lin Searles; 1st ed., 1964	.80	2.40	4.00	W
D591	Northwest Nurse—Arlene Fitzgerald; 1st ed., 1964	.50	1.50	2.50	R
D592	Gunslick Mountain—Nelson Nye	.80	2.40	4.00	W
D593	Sisters in White—Suzanne Roberts; 1st ed., 1965	.50	1.50	2.50	R
D594	The Desperate Deputy of Cougar Hill—Louis Trimble; 1st ed., 1965	.80	2.40	4.00	W
D595	Nurse Ann in Surgery—Ruth MacLeod; 1st ed., 1965	.50	1.50	2.50	R
D596	Nurse on the Run—Arlene Hale; 1st ed., 1965	.50	1.50	2.50	R
D597	The Hardest Man in the Sierras—L. P. Holmes; 1st ed., 1965	.80	2.40	4.00	W
D598	Disaster Area Nurse—Arlene Hale; 1st ed., 1965	.50	1.50	2.50	R
D599	Winged Victory for Nurse Kerry—Patricia Libby	.50	1.50	2.50	R

ACE F-SERIES
Ace Books, Inc./A. A. Wynn, Inc.

F101	Cruise Nurse—Joan Sargent; 1961				R
	Calling Dr. Merryman—Margaret Howe	.50	1.50	2.50	R
F102	Never Forget, Never Forgive—Clayton Fox				M
	The Flying Eye—Bob McKnight	.50	1.50	2.50	M
F103	A Trap for Sam Dodge—Harry Whittington				W
	High Thunder—Lee Floren	.80	2.40	4.00	W
F104	Mayday Orbit—Poul Anderson; 1961				SF
	No Man's World—Kenneth Bulmer	.80	2.40	4.00	SF
F105	The Best From Fantasy and Science Fiction, 5th Series—ed. Anthony Boucher	.80	2.40	4.00	SF
F106	The Gun From Nowhere—Tom West				W
	Justice at Spanish Flat—Brian Wynne	.50	1.50	2.50	W
F107	Scratch a Thief—John Trinian				M
	My Pal, the Killer—Chester Warwick	.50	1.50	2.50	M
F108	The Sun Saboteurs—Damon Knight				SF
	The Light of Lilith—G. McDonald Wallis	.80	2.40	4.00	SF
F109	Storm Over Warlock—Andre Norton; 1961	.80	2.40	4.00	SF
F110	Track the Man Down—Ray Hogan				W
	Savage Range—Lee E. Wells	.50	1.50	2.50	W
F111	To Have and to Kill—Robert Martin				M
	The Girl From Las Vegas—J. M. Flynn	.50	1.50	2.50	M
F112	Barbara Ames, Private Secretary—Jeanne Judson				R

Dell 183, 1947 © Dell

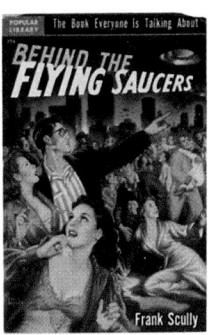

Popular Library 326, 1951
© Poplib; c-Earle Bergey

Avon 307, 1951 © Avon

Pocket Book 133, 1941 © PkB
c-Sol Immerman & H. Lawrence Hoffman

Dell Unnumbered, 1947 © Dell
c-Chic Young (?)

Avon 362, 1951 © Avon

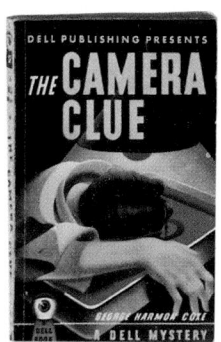

Dell 27, 1943 © Dell

Dell 320, 1949 © Dell
c-Jean des Vignes

Popular Library 131, 1948 © Poplib
c-Fiedler

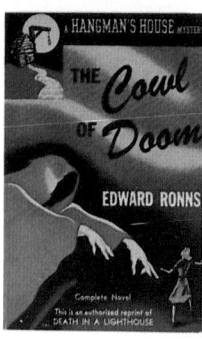

Hangman's House 13, 1946 © HH

Archer Books 5, 1951 © Archer
c-C.M. Heade

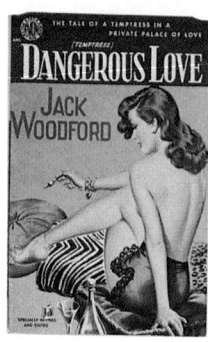

Avon 280, 1950 © Avon

Ace D-41, 1954 © Ace

Signet 1351, 1956 © Sigb
c-Robert Maguire

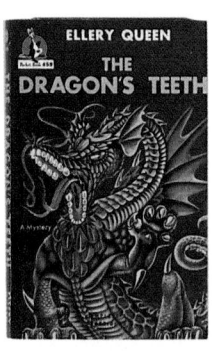

Pocket Book 459, 1947 © Pkb

Pocket Book 123, 1941 © Pkb

Popular Library 219, 1950 © Poplib
c-Rudolph Belarski

Avon 127, 1947 © Avon
c-George Mayers

Pocket Book 212, 1943 © Pkb
c-H. Lawrence Hoffman

Bantam A883, 1951 © Bantam
c-Earl Mayan

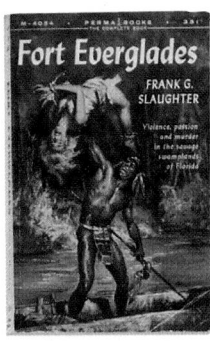

Perma Books M-4054, 1958 © Perma
c-James Meese

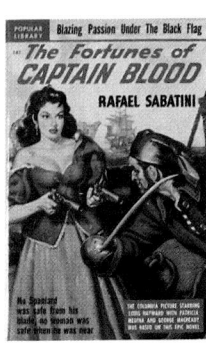

Popular Library 241, 1950 © Poplib
c-Rudolph Belarski

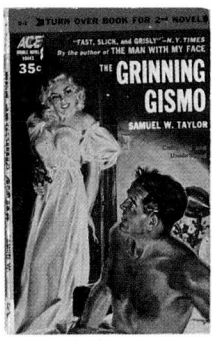

Ace D-1, 1952 © Ace
c-Norman Saunders

Avon 652, 1955 © Avon
c-Jimmy Hatlo

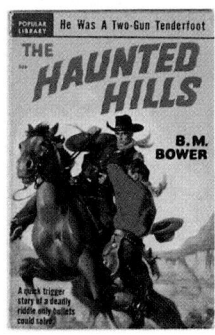

Popular Library 306, 1951 © Poplib
c-George Rozen

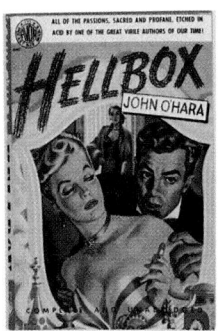

Avon 293, 1951 © Avon

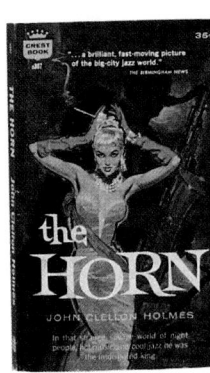

Crest Books s307, 1959 © Crest
c-Mitch Hooks

Dell 21, 1943 © Dell

Bronze Books 2, 1952 © Bronze

Signet 754, 1949 © Sigb
c-James Avati

Mentor Books M39, 1949 © Mentor
c-Robert Jonas

Signet 1287, 1956 © Sigb
c-Robert Schulz

Quarter Books 37, 1949 © QB
c-George Gross

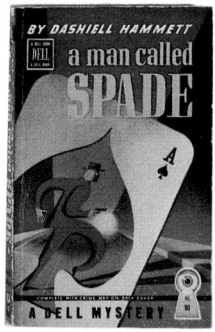

Avon 187, 1949 © Avon

Avon 276, 1951 © Avon

Dell 90, 1945 © Dell

Avon 315, 1951 © Avon

**Pocket Book 903, 1952 © Pkb
c-Frederick Banberry**

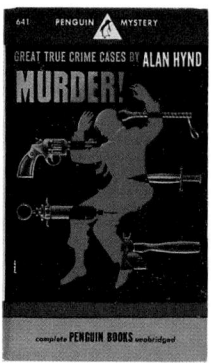

**Penguin 641, 1947 © Pen
c-Robert Jonas**

**Dell 10 Cent 32, 1951 © Dell
c-Rafael de Soto**

Avon 308, 1951 © Avon

**Gold Medal 158, 1951 © Faw
c-Barye Phillips**

**Fighting Forces Series nn, 1945
© Felix Keesing**

Avon 314, 1951 © Avon

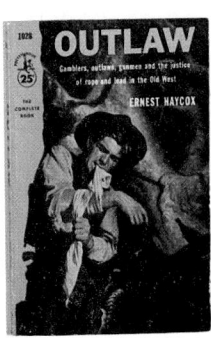

**Pocket Book 1028, 1954 © Pkb
c-Tom Ryan**

Pocket Book 253, 1944 © Pkb
c-Lee Manso

Dell 307, 1949 © Dell

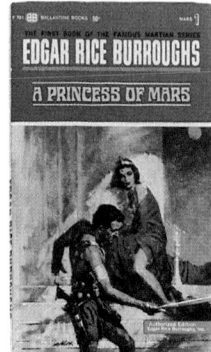

Ballantine F701, 1963 © ERB
c-Robert Abbett

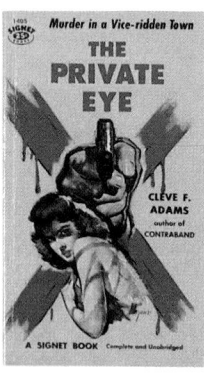

Signet 1405, 1957 © Sigb
c-Robert Maguire

Popular Library 234, 1950 © Poplib
c-A. Leslie Ross

Dell F-Series F85, 1959 © Dell
c-Warren Baumgartner

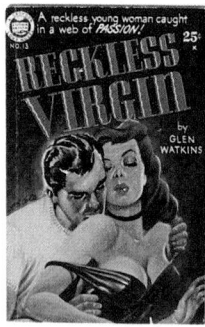

Croydon 13, 1949 © Croy
c-L.B. Cole

Hillman 19, 1949 © Hill

Dell 330, 1949 © Dell

Pocket Book 426, 1948 © Pkb
c-Robert Ripley

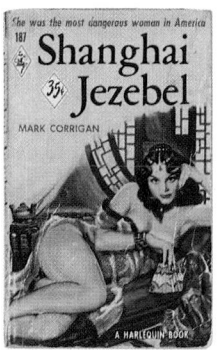

Harlequin 187, 1952 © HB

Pocket Book 621, 1949 © Pkb
c-Al Capp

Ballantine 55, 1953 © BB
c-Richard Powers

Pyramid 39, 1951 © Pyb

Ballantine U2106, 1964 © Wm. Gaines
c-Frank Frazetta

Dell 20, 1943 © Dell

Ace F-Series F-189, 1963 © ERB
c-Frank Frazetta

Dell 426, 1950 © Dell
c-Robert Stanley

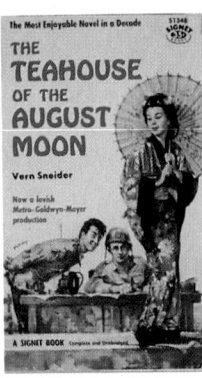

Signet s1348, 1956 © Sigb
c-Stanley Zuckerberg

Pyramid 20, 1950 © Pyb

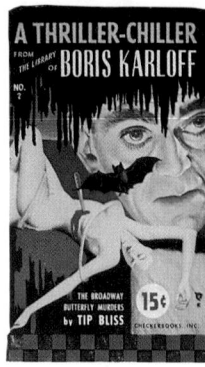

Checker Books 2, 1949 © Check

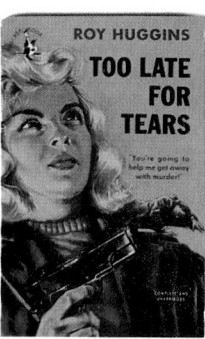

Pocket Book 602, 1949 © Pkb
c-Bernard Safran

Pocket Book 25, 1939 © Pkb

Leisure Library 8, 1952 © Leisure
c-R.C.M. Heade

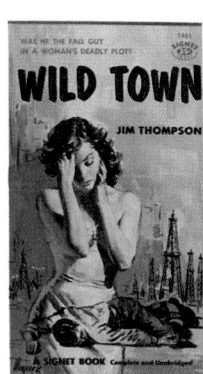

Signet 1461, 1957 © Sigb
c-Robert Maguire

Century 124, 1950 © Cen
c-Malcolm Smith

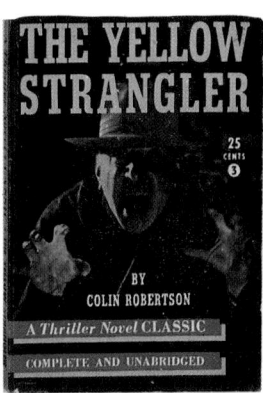

Thriller Novel Classic 3
© Novel Selections

	Good	Fine	N/Mint	
Fashions for Carol—Nell Marr Dean	.40	1.20	2.00	R
F113 Rebels of the Red Planet—Charles L. Fontenay				SF
200 Years to Christmas—J. T. McIntosh	1.00	3.00	5.00	SF
F114 The Bird of Time—Wallace West	.40	1.20	2.00	SF
F115 The Blonde Cried Murder—John Creighton; 1961				M
Killing Cousins—Fletcher Flora	.50	1.50	2.50	M
F116 Deadman Canyon—Louis Trimble; 1961				W
The Lurking Gun—Clement Hardin	.50	1.50	2.50	W
F117 The Door Through Space—Marion Zimmer Bradley				SF
Rendezvous on a Lost World—A. Bertram Chandler; 1961	1.00	3.00	5.00	SF
F118 Making Profits in the Stock Market—Jacob O. Kamm, Ph.D.	.50	1.50	2.50	NF
F119 Delusion World—Gordon R. Dickson				SF
Spacial Delivery—Gordon R. Dickson	1.60	4.80	8.00	SF
F120 Gunmen Can't Hide—Jack M. Bickham				W
Come in Shooting—John Callahan	.50	1.50	2.50	W
F121 Sing Me a Murder—Helen Nielsen				M
Woman Missing and Other Stories—Helen Nielsen	.50	1.50	2.50	M
F122 Dr. Kilbourne Comes Home—Dorothy Worley				R
Calling Nurse Linda—Patti Stone	.40	1.20	2.00	R
F123 The Nemesis From Terra—Leigh Brackett				SF
Collision Course—Robert Silverberg	.80	2.40	4.00	SF
F124 Slattery—Steven G. Lawrence				W
Bullet Welcome for Slattery—Steven G. Lawrence	.50	1.50	2.50	W
F125 The Widow Maker—Frank Diamond				M
Deep Six—J. M. Flynn	.50	1.50	2.50	M
F126 The Troublemaker—Edwin Booth				W
A Marshal for Lawless—Ray Hogan	.50	1.50	2.50	W
F127 Seven From the Stars—Marion Zimmer Bradley				SF
Worlds of the Imperium—Keith Laumer	1.00	3.00	5.00	SF
F128 The Buzzard's Nest—Tom West				W
Siege at High Meadow—Louis Trimble	.50	1.50	2.50	W
F129 The Automated Goliath—William F. Temple				SF
The Three Suns of Amara—William F. Temple	.40	1.20	2.00	SF
F130 The Bullet-Proof Martyr—James A. Howard				M
The Screaming Cargo—J. M. Flynn	.50	1.50	2.50	M
F131 The Best From Fantasy and Science Fiction, 6th Series—ed. Anthony Boucher	.80	2.40	4.00	SF
F132				
F133 Secret Agent of Terra—John Brunner				SF
The Rim of Space—A. Bertram Chandler	1.20	3.60	6.00	SF
F134 Tumbleweed Trigger—Gordon D. Shirreffs				W
A Shooting at Sundust—Rod Patterson	.50	1.50	2.50	W
F135 The Long Tomorrow—Leigh Brackett	.80	2.40	4.00	SF
F136 Childbirth: True Accounts of Unusual Experiences—ed. Dr. Myron Harkary	.50	1.50	2.50	NF
F137 Impossible—Yet It Happened!—R. Dewitt Miller; aka Forgotton Mysteries	.50	1.50	2.50	NF
F138 A Noose for Slattery—Steven G. Lawrence				W
Walk a Narrow Trail—Steven G. Lawrence	.50	1.50	2.50	W
F139 The Makeshift Rocket—Poul Anderson				SF
Un-man—Poul Anderson	1.00	3.00	5.00	SF
F140 Love With a Harvard Accent—Leonie St. John; 1962	.50	1.50	2.50	
F141 The Darkness Before Tomorrow—Robert Moore Williams				SF
The Ladder in the Sky—Keith Woodcott	.40	1.20	2.00	SF
F142 Smoky Pass—L. P. Holmes; 1962				W
Wolf Brand—L. P. Holmes	.50	1.50	2.50	W
F143 End of a Big Wheel—Clayton Fox				M
A Stone Around Her Neck—Bob McKnight	.50	1.50	2.50	M
F144 The Badge Shooters—Clement Hardin				W
Massacre Basin—Frank Wynne	.50	1.50	2.50	W
F145 Next Stop the Stars—Robert Silverberg				SF
The Seed of Earth—Robert Silverberg	1.20	3.60	6.00	SF
F146 Sir Scoundrel—Jay Scotland (John Jakes)	.80	2.40	4.00	A
F147 Eye of the Monster—Andre Norton; 1962				SF
Sea Siege—Andre Norton	.80	2.40	4.00	SF
F148 Wild Sky—Harry Whittington				W
Dead Man's Double Cross—Tom West	.80	2.40	4.00	W
F149 Cosmic Checkmate—Katherine MacLean & Charles V. deVet				SF
King of the Fourth Planet—Robert Moore Williams	.40	1.20	2.00	SF
F150 Rafe—Nelson Nye				W
Hideout Mountain—Nelson Nye	.50	1.50	2.50	W
F151				
F152 Rio Desperado—Gordon D. Shirreffs				W
Voice of the Gun—Gordon D. Shirreffs	.50	1.50	2.50	W
F153 The Planet Savers—Marion Zimmer Bradley				SF
The Sword of Aldones—Marion Zimmer Bradley	.80	2.40	4.00	SF
F154 The Wizard of Linn—A. E. Van Vogt	.80	2.40	4.00	SF
F155 The Time of Terror—Lionel White				M
A Death at Sea—Lionel White	.80	2.40	4.00	M

Ace F166, © Ace Ace F170, © Ace Ace F189, © Ace

(ACE F-SERIES, continued)

		Good	Fine	N/Mint	
F156	At the Earth's Core—Edgar Rice Burroughs; c-Krenkel	.80	2.40	4.00	SF
F157	The Moon Maid—Edgar Rice Burroughs; c-Krenkel	.80	2.40	4.00	SF
F158	Pellucidar—Edgar Rice Burroughs; c-Krenkel	.80	2.40	4.00	SF
F159	The Moon Men—Edgar Rice Burroughs; c-Emsh	.80	2.40	4.00	SF
F160	The Shotgunner—Ray Hogan				W
	New Gun for Kingdom City—Ray Hogan	.50	1.50	2.50	W
F161	Times Without Number—John Brunner				SF
	Destiny's Orbit—David Grinnell	.40	1.20	2.00	SF
F162	The Best From Fantasy and Science Fiction, 7th Series—ed. Anthony Boucher	.80	2.40	4.00	SF
F163	Doctor Ellen—Adele De Leeuw	.40	1.20	2.00	
F164					
F165	Cache From Outer Space—Philip Jose Farmer				SF
	The Celestial Blueprint—Philip Jose Farmer	2.00	6.00	10.00	SF
F166	Maigret and the Reluctant Witness—Georges Simenon				M
	Maigret Has Scruples—Georges Simenon	.80	2.40	4.00	M
F167	Catseye—Andre Norton; 1962	.80	2.40	4.00	SF
F168	Thuvia, Maid of Mars—Edgar Rice Burroughs; c-Krenkel	1.20	3.60	6.00	SF
F169	Tarzan and the Lost Empire—Edgar Rice Burroughs; c-Frazetta	1.20	3.60	6.00	SF
F170	The Chessmen of Mars—Edgar Rice Burroughs; c-Krenkel	1.20	3.60	6.00	SF
F171	Tanar of Pellucidar—Edgar Rice Burroughs; c-Krenkel	.80	2.40	4.00	SF
F172	Gun Rich—Giles A. Lutz				W
	Battling Buckeroos—Tom West	.50	1.50	2.50	W
F173	The Jewels of Aptor—Samuel R. Delany				SF
	Second Ending—James White	1.00	3.00	5.00	SF
F174	First Through Time—Rex Gordon	.80	2.40	4.00	SF
F175	Lament for Four Brides—Evelyn Berckman	.50	1.50	2.50	R
F176	The Outside Gun—Ray Hogan				W
	Gun Trap at Bright Water—Dan J. Stevens	.50	1.50	2.50	W
F177	Warlord of Kor—Terry Carr				SF
	The Star Wasps—Robert Moore Williams	.80	2.40	4.00	SF
F178	More Adventures on Other Planets—ed. Donald A. Wollheim	.50	1.50	2.50	SF
F179	Pirates of Venus—Edgar Rice Burroughs; c-Krenkel	.80	2.40	4.00	SF
F180	Tarzan at the Earth's Core—Edgar Rice Burroughs; c-Frazetta	1.00	3.00	5.00	SF
F181	The Mastermind of Mars—Edgar Rice Burroughs; c-Krenkel	1.20	3.60	6.00	SF
F182	The Monster Men—Edgar Rice Burroughs; c-Frazetta	1.00	3.00	5.00	SF
F183	The Defiant Agents—Andre Norton	.80	2.40	4.00	SF
F184	The Kid From Lincoln County—Nelson Nye				W
	Death Valley Slim—Nelson Nye	.50	1.50	2.50	W
F185	The Dragon Masters—Jack Vance				SF
	The Five Gold Bands—Jack Vance	1.60	4.80	8.00	SF
F186	The High Hander—William O. Turner				W
	Wild Horse Range—Louis Trimble	.50	1.50	2.50	W
F187	Alpha Centauri—or Die!—Leigh Brackett				SF
	Legend of Lost Earth—G. McDonald Wallis	.40	1.20	2.00	SF
F188	Armageddon 2419 A.D.—Philip Francis Nowlan	.80	2.40	4.00	SF
F189	Tarzan the Invincible—Edgar Rice Burroughs; c-Krenkel	1.20	3.60	6.00	SF
F190	A Fighting Man of Mars—Edgar Rice Burroughs; c-Krenkel	1.20	3.60	6.00	SF
F191	Journey to the Center of the Earth—Jules Verne	.40	1.20	2.00	SF
F192	Star Born—Andre Norton; 1963	.80	2.40	4.00	SF
F193	The Son of Tarzan—Edgar Rice Burroughs; c-Frazetta	1.20	3.60	6.00	SF
F194	Tarzan Triumphant—Edgar Rice Burroughs; c-Krenkel	1.20	3.60	6.00	SF
F195	The Silent Invaders—Robert Silverberg				SF
	Battle on Venus—William F. Temple	.40	1.20	2.00	SF
F196	Prairie Raiders—Harry Whittington				W
	Drygulch Town—Harry Whittington	.80	2.40	4.00	W
F197	Witch World—Andre Norton; 1963	.80	2.40	4.00	SF
F198	The Short Cases of Inspector Maigret—Georges Simenon	1.00	3.00	5.00	M
F199	Captives of the Flame—Samuel R. Delany	1.00	3.00	5.00	SF

		Good	Fine	N/Mint	
	The Psionic Menace—Samuel R. Delany	1.00	3.00	5.00	SF
F200	Triggering Texan—Tom West				W
	The Big Snow—Frank Wynne	.50	1.50	2.50	W
F201	Doomsday, 1999—Paul MacTyre	.40	1.20	2.00	SF
F202	The Hovering Darkness—Evelyn Berckman	.40	1.20	2.00	R
F203	The Beasts of Tarzan—Edgar Rice Burroughs; c-Frazetta	1.20	3.60	6.00	SF
F204	Tarzan and the Jewels of Opar—Edgar Rice Burroughs; c-Frazetta	1.20	3.60	6.00	SF
F205	Tarzan and the City of Gold—Edgar Rice Burroughs; c-Frazetta	1.20	3.60	6.00	SF
F206	Jungle Tales of Tarzan—Edgar Rice Burroughs; c-Frazetta	1.20	3.60	6.00	SF
F207	The Stars Are Ours!—Andre Norton	.80	2.40	4.00	SF
F208	Side Me at Sundown—L. P. Holmes				W
	The Buzzards of Rocky Pass—L. P. Holmes	.50	1.50	2.50	W
F209	Let the Spacemen Beware—Poul Anderson				SF
	The Wizard of Starship Poseidon—Kenneth Bulmer	.40	1.20	2.00	SF
F210	Red Alert—Peter Bryant	.40	1.20	2.00	SF
F211	Planet of Peril—Otis Adelbert Kline; c-Frazetta	1.00	3.00	5.00	SF
F212	Tarzan and the Lion Man—Edgar Rice Burroughs; c-Frazetta	1.20	3.60	6.00	SF
F213	The Land That Time Forgot—Edgar Rice Burroughs—c-Krenkel	.80	2.40	4.00	SF
F214	The Wildcatters—Bill Burchardt				W
	The Man From Colorado—Louis Trimble	.50	1.50	2.50	W
F215	Listen! the Stars!—John Brunner				SF
	The Rebellers—Jane Roberts	.40	1.20	2.00	SF
F216	The Man Who Upset the Universe—Isaac Asimov	.80	2.40	4.00	SF
F217	The Best From Fantasy and Science Fiction, 8th Series—ed. Anthony Boucher	.80	2.40	4.00	NF
F218	They Never Came Back—Churchill	.50	1.50	2.50	NF
F219	Ask Henry—Henry Makow	.50	1.50	2.50	H
F220	The People That Time Forgot—Edgar Rice Burroughs; c-Krenkel	.80	2.40	4.00	SF
F221	Lost on Venus—Edgar Rice Burroughs; c-Frazetta	.80	2.40	4.00	SF
F222	First on the Moon—Jeff Sutton	.40	1.20	2.00	SF
F223	Envoy to New Worlds—Keith Laumer				SF
	Flight From Yesterday—Robert Moore Williams	.80	2.40	4.00	SF
F224	The Seven Six-Gunners—Nelson Nye				W
	Bancroft's Banco—Nelson Nye	.50	1.50	2.50	W
F225	Space Viking—H. Beam Piper	1.60	4.80	8.00	SF
F226	Huon of the Horn—Andre Norton; 1963	.80	2.40	4.00	F
F227	The Astronauts Must Not Land—John Brunner				SF
	The Space-Time Juggler—John Brunner	.40	1.20	2.00	SF
F228					
F229	The Dead and the Deadly—Louis Trimble; 1963				M
	Homicide Handicap—Bob McKnight	.50	1.50	2.50	M
F230	Lobo Lawman—Tom West				W
	Trail of the Fresno Kid—Ray Hogan	.50	1.50	2.50	W
F231	Star Gate—Andre Norton	.80	2.40	4.00	SF
F232	The Land of Hidden Men—Edgar Rice Burroughs; c-Krenkel	.80	2.40	4.00	SF
F233	Out of Time's Abyss—Edgar Rice Burroughs; c-Krenkel	.80	2.40	4.00	SF
F234	The Eternal Savage—Edgar Rice Burroughs; c-Krenkel	.80	2.40	4.00	SF
F235	The Lost Continent—Edgar Rice Burroughs; c-Frazetta	.80	2.40	4.00	SF
F236	The Time Traders—Andre Norton	.80	2.40	4.00	SF
F237	Beyond the Galactic Rim—A. Bertram Chandler				SF
	The Ship From Outside—A. Bertram Chandler	1.20	3.60	6.00	SF
F238	Brand Him Outlaw—Stephen Payne; 1963				W
	Quicktrigger—Gordon D. Shirreffs	.50	1.50	2.50	W
F239	Time and Again—Clifford D. Simak	.40	1.20	2.00	SF
F240	When the Sleeper Wakes—H. G. Wells	.80	2.40	4.00	SF
F241	Star Bridge—James E. Gunn & Jack Williamson	.80	2.40	4.00	SF
F242	Castaways' World—John Brunner				SF
	The Rites of Ohe—John Brunner	1.00	3.00	5.00	SF
F243	Lord of Thunder—Andre Norton; 1963, c-Schomburg	.80	2.40	4.00	SF

Ace F198, © Ace

Ace F211, © Ace

Ace F232, © Ace

Ace F265, © Ace   Ace F281, © Ace   Ace F305, © Ace

		Good	Fine	N/Mint	
(ACE F-SERIES, continued)					
F244	Last Gun at Cabresto—Ray Hogan				W
	Valley of Violence—Edwin Booth	.50	1.50	2.50	W
F245	Back to the Stone Age—Edgar Rice Burroughs; c-Krenkel	.80	2.40	4.00	SF
F246	Metropolis—Thea von Harbou	.80	2.40	4.00	SF
F247	Carson of Venus—Edgar Rice Burroughs; c-Frazetta	.80	2.40	4.00	SF
F248	Beyond the Stars—Ray Cummings	.80	2.40	4.00	SF
F249	The Hand of Zei—L. Sprague de Camp				SF
	The Search for Zei—L. Sprague de Camp	1.20	3.60	6.00	SF
F250	Gallows Gulch—Tom West				W
	The Masked Gun—Barry Cord	.50	1.50	2.50	W
F251	The Game-Players of Titan—Philip K. Dick	.80	2.40	4.00	SF
F252	The Shooting of Storey James—John Clifford	.50	1.50	2.50	W
F253	One of Our Asteroids Is Missing—Calvin M. Knox				SF
	The Twisted Men—A. E. Van Vogt	.40	1.20	2.00	SF
F254	Hardcase Halloran—William Heuman				W
	The Ghost Riders—Philip Ketchum	.50	1.50	2.50	W
F255	The Prodigal Sun—Philip E. High	.40	1.20	2.00	SF
F256	Land of Terror—Edgar Rice Burroughs; c-Frazetta	.80	2.40	4.00	SF
F257	Alien Planet—Fletcher Pratt	.40	1.20	2.00	SF
F258	The Cave Girl—Edgar Rice Burroughs; c-Krenkel	.80	2.40	4.00	SF
F259	Prince of Peril—Otis Adelbert Kline; c-Krenkel	1.00	3.00	5.00	SF
F260	Trail Drive—Brian Garfield; 1964				W
	Trouble at Gunsight—Louis Trimble	.50	1.50	2.50	W
F261	The Towers of Toron—Samuel R. Delany				SF
	The Lunar Eye—Robert Moore Williams	.40	1.20	2.00	SF
F262	Reckless Men—Clifton Adams	.50	1.50	2.50	W
F263	Web of the Witch World—Andre Norton; 1964	.80	2.40	4.00	SF
F264	Don't Cross My Line—Tom West; 1964				W
	Contract in Cartridges—Ben Elliott	.50	1.50	2.50	W
F265	The Houses of Iszm—Jack Vance				SF
	Son of the Tree—Jack Vance	1.60	4.80	8.00	SF
F266	Roundup on the Yellowstone—Allan Vaughan Elston	.50	1.50	2.50	W
F267	The Best From Fantasy and Science Fiction, 9th Series—ed. Robert P. Mills	.80	2.40	4.00	SF
F268	Escape on Venus—Edgar Rice Burroughs; c-Frazetta	.80	2.40	4.00	SF
F269	Quest of the Dawn Man—J. H. Rosny	.80	2.40	4.00	SF
F270	The Mad King—Edgar Rice Burroughs; c-Frazetta	.80	2.40	4.00	SF
F271	Outside the Universe—Edmond Hamilton	1.00	3.00	5.00	SF
F272	No Job for a Cowboy—Stephen Payne				W
	The Man From Barranca Negra—Ray Hogan	.50	1.50	2.50	W
F273	The Dark Intruder—Marion Zimmer Bradley				SF
	Falcons of Narabedla—Marion Zimmer Bradley	1.00	3.00	5.00	SF
F274	The Cosmic Computer—H. Beam Piper	1.20	3.60	6.00	SF
F275	No Truce With Terra—Philip E. High				SF
	The Duplicators—Murray Leinster	.40	1.20	2.00	SF
F276	The Wolf Slayer—William E. Vance				W
	Mr. Sixgun—Brian Wynne	.50	1.50	2.50	W
F277	To Conquer Chaos—John Brunner	1.00	3.00	5.00	SF
F278	Patty Goes to Washington—Frances Spatz Leighton; TV tie-in	.40	1.20	2.00	
F279	Sargasso of Space—Andre Norton; 1964	.80	2.40	4.00	SF
F280	Savage Pellucidar—Edgar Rice Burroughs; c-Frazetta	.80	2.40	4.00	SF
F281	Atlantida—Pierre Benoit	1.00	3.00	5.00	F
F282	Beyond the Farthest Star—Edgar Rice Burroughs; c-Frazetta	.80	2.40	4.00	SF
F283	The Day the World Ended—Sax Rohmer	1.00	3.00	5.00	SF
F284	Border Passage—Lin Searles				W
	The Homesteader—Ben Smith	.50	1.50	2.50	W
F285	The Million Year Hunt—Kenneth Bulmer				SF
	Ships to the Stars—Fritz Leiber	.40	1.20	2.00	SF
F286	The Long Way North—Jim Bosworth	.50	1.50	2.50	W

		Good	Fine	N/Mint	
F287	Key Out of Time—Andre Norton	.80	2.40	4.00	SF
F288					
F289	Demons' World—Kenneth Bulmer				SF
	I Want the Stars—Tom Purdom	.40	1.20	2.00	SF
F290	The Night of the Bowstring—D. B. Olsen	.50	1.50	2.50	W
F291	Plague Ship—Andre Norton; 1964	.80	2.40	4.00	SF
F292	The Man at Rope's End—Tom West				W
	The Hidden Rider of Dark Mountain—Gordon D. Shirreffs	.50	1.50	2.50	W
F293	Moon Base—E. C. Tubb	.80	2.40	4.00	SF
F294	The Port of Peril—Otis Adelbert Kline; c-Frazetta	1.00	3.00	5.00	SF
F295	The World of Null-A—A. E. Van Vogt	.80	2.40	4.00	SF
F296	Gulliver of Mars—Edwin L. Arnold	.80	2.40	4.00	SF
F297	Valley of the Flame—Henry Kuttner	2.00	6.00	10.00	SF
F298	Treasure Trail From Tucson—Nelson Nye				W
	Sudden Country—Nelson Nye	.50	1.50	2.50	W
F299	Endless Shadow—John Brunner				SF
	The Arsenal of Miracles—Gardner F. Fox	1.00	3.00	5.00	SF
F300	Vultures in the Sun—Brian Garfield	.50	1.50	2.50	W
F301	The Simulacra—Philip K. Dick	.80	2.40	4.00	SF
F302	Dragoon Pass—Frank Wynne	.50	1.50	2.50	W
F303	The Bloody Sun—Marion Zimmer Bradley	.40	1.20	2.00	SF
F304	The Radio Beasts—Ralph Milne Farley	.80	2.40	4.00	SF
F305	Almuric—Robert E. Howard	2.00	6.00	10.00	SF
F306	Earth's Last Citadel—C. L. Moore & Henry Kuttner; c-Schomburg	1.20	3.60	6.00	SF
F307	Warrior of Llarn—Gardner F. Fox; c-Frazetta	1.00	3.00	5.00	SF
F308	Judgement on Janus—Andre Norton; 1964	.80	2.40	4.00	SF
F309	Clans of the Alphane Moon—Philip K. Dick	.80	2.40	4.00	SF
F310	Galactic Derelict—Andre Norton	.80	2.40	4.00	SF
F311	Swordsmen in the Sky—Donald A. Wollheim	1.00	3.00	5.00	SF
F312	The Radio Planet—Ralph Milne Farley	.80	2.40	4.00	SF
F313	A Brand New World—Ray Cummings	.80	2.40	4.00	SF
F314	The Universe Against Her—James H. Schmitz	1.00	3.00	5.00	SF
F315	The Beast Master—Andre Norton; 1964	.80	2.40	4.00	SF
F316	The Burntwood Men—Robert McCaig	.50	1.50	2.50	W
F317	The Escape Orbit—James White	.80	2.40	4.00	SF
F318	The Spot of Life—Austin Hall & Homer Eon Flint	.80	2.40	4.00	SF
F319	Crashing Suns—Edmond Hamilton	.80	2.40	4.00	SF
F320	The Martian Sphinx—Keith Woodcott	.80	2.40	4.00	SF
F321	Maza of the Moon—Otis Adelbert Kline; c-Frazetta	1.00	3.00	5.00	SF
F322	City of a Thousand Suns—Samuel R. Delany	.80	2.40	4.00	SF
F323	Daybreak 2250 A.D.—Andre Norton; 1965	.40	1.20	2.00	SF
F324	Apache Canyon—Brian Garfield	.50	1.50	2.50	W
F325	Ordeal in Otherwhere—Andre Norton; 1965	.80	2.40	4.00	SF
F326	The Wizard of Lemuria—Lin Carter; c-Morrow	.80	2.40	4.00	SF
F327	The Dark World—Henry Kuttner	2.00	6.00	10.00	SF
F328	The Galaxy Primes—Edward E. 'Doc' Smith	.80	2.40	4.00	SF
F329	Storm Over Warlock—Andre Norton	.80	2.40	4.00	SF
F330	What Strange Stars and Skies—Avram Davidson	.40	1.20	2.00	SF
F331	Gravestone Manor—Gahan Wilson	1.00	3.00	5.00	
F332	Three Against the Witch World—Andre Norton; 1965	.80	2.40	4.00	SF
F333	Rogue Queen—L. Sprague de Camp	.80	2.40	4.00	SF
F334	The Insect Warriors—Rex Dean Levie	1.00	3.00	5.00	SF
F335	The Second Atlantis—Robert Moore Williams	.40	1.20	2.00	SF
F337	Dr. Bloodmoney, or, How We Got Along After the Bomb—Philip K. Dick	.40	1.20	2.00	SF
F338	Ace Crossword Puzzle Book No. 1	1.00	3.00	5.00	NF
F339	Private Duty for Nurse Scott—Arlene Hale	.40	1.20	2.00	R
340					
F341	A Prize for Nurse Darci—Suzanne Roberts	.40	1.20	2.00	R
F342	Lord Kalvan of Otherwhen—H. Beam Piper	1.20	3.60	6.00	SF
F343	The Exile of Time—Ray Cummings	.40	1.20	2.00	SF
F344	The Well of the Worlds—Henry Kuttner; c-Schomburg	1.60	4.80	8.00	SF
F345	The Lord of Death and the Queen of Life—Homer Eon Flint	.80	2.40	4.00	SF
F346	The Black Star Passes—John W. Campbell	.80	2.40	4.00	SF
F347	The Last Hope of Earth—Lan Wright	.80	2.40	4.00	SF
F348	Guns of Horse Prairie—Nelson Nye	.50	1.50	2.50	W
F349	Celebrity Suite Nurse—Suzanne Roberts	.40	1.20	2.00	R
F350	Star of Danger—Marion Zimmer Bradley	.80	2.40	4.00	SF
F351	The Holdout in the Diablos—Louis Trimble	.50	1.50	2.50	W
F352	Nurse on Leave—Arlene Hale	.40	1.20	2.00	R
F353	Rogue Dragon—Avram Davidson	1.00	3.00	5.00	SF
F354	Hunter Out of Time—Gardner F. Fox; frontis by Frazetta	1.00	3.00	5.00	SF
F355	The Devolutionist and the Emancipatrix—Homer Eon Flint	.80	2.40	4.00	SF
F356	The Time Axis—Henry Kuttner	1.00	3.00	5.00	SF
F357	Year of the Unicorn—Andre Norton; 1965	.80	2.40	4.00	SF
F358					W
F359	Jungle Nurse—Sharon Heath	.40	1.20	2.00	R
F360	Rawhiders of the Brasada—L. L. Foreman	.50	1.50	2.50	W

		Good	Fine	N/Mint	
F361	The Day of the Star Cities—John Brunner	.80	2.40	4.00	SF
F362	The Two Dr. Barlowes—Suzanne Roberts	.40	1.20	2.00	R
F363	Tama of the Light Country—Ray Cummings	.80	2.40	4.00	SF
F364	The Mightiest Machine—John W. Campbell	.80	2.40	4.00	SF
F365	Night of Masks—Andre Norton	.80	2.40	4.00	SF
F366	The Last Planet—Andre Norton; 1965	.80	2.40	4.00	SF
F367	Maker of Universes—Philip Jose Farmer	1.20	3.60	6.00	SF
F368	Chicago Nurse—Arlene Hale	.40	1.20	2.00	R
F369	The Lobo Horseman—Samuel Anthony Peeples	.50	1.50	2.50	W
F370	The Man From Andersonville—Brad Ward	.50	1.50	2.50	W
F371	Camp Nurse—Arlene Hale	.40	1.20	2.00	R
F372	Spacehounds of IPC—Edward E. 'Doc' Smith	.80	2.40	4.00	SF
F373	The Sword of Lankor—Howard L. Cory	.80	2.40	4.00	SF
F374	The Atom Conspiracy—Jeff Sutton	.80	2.40	4.00	SF
F375	The Worlds of Robert A. Heinlein—Robert A. Heinlein	1.00	3.00	5.00	SF
F376	The Odds Against Circle L—Lewis B. Patten	.50	1.50	2.50	W
F377	The Crack in Space—Philip K. Dick	.80	2.40	4.00	SF
F378	Danger - Nurse at Work—Mary Mann Fletcher	.40	1.20	2.00	R
F379	The Green Brain—Frank Herbert	.80	2.40	4.00	SF
F380	The Legend of Blackjack Sam—Lee Hoffman	.50	1.50	2.50	W
F381					
F382	Bow Down to Null—Brian W. Aldiss	.80	2.40	4.00	SF
F383	Thongor of Lemuria—Lin Carter; c-Morrow	1.00	3.00	5.00	SF
F384					
F385	Emergency for Nurse Selena—Arlene Hale	.40	1.20	2.00	R
F386	The Time Traders—Andre Norton	.80	2.40	4.00	SF
F387	Mountain Nurse—Arlene Hale	.40	1.20	2.00	R
F388	Babel-17—Samuel R. Delany	.50	1.50	2.50	SF
F389	Shoot Him on Sight!—William Colt MacDonald	.50	1.50	2.50	W
F390	The Languages of Pao—Jack Vance	1.20	3.60	6.00	SF
F391	Crossroads of Time—Andre Norton	.80	2.40	4.00	SF
F392	Saga of Lost Earths—Emil Petaja	.80	2.40	4.00	SF
F393	This Immortal—Roger Zelazny	.80	2.40	4.00	SF
F394	Journey for a Nurse—Gail Everett	.40	1.20	2.00	R
F395	Iron Hand—Nelson Nye	.50	1.50	2.50	W
F396	Worlds for the Taking—Kenneth Bulmer	.80	2.40	4.00	SF
F397	Nurse Kay's Conquest—Willo Davis Roberts	.40	1.20	2.00	R
F398	Somewhere a Voice—Eric Frank Russell	1.00	3.00	5.00	SF
F399	Thief of Llara—Gardner F. Fox; c-Morrow	.80	2.40	4.00	SF
F400	Jan of the Jungle—Otis Adelbert Kline	1.00	3.00	5.00	SF-A
F401	Outrage at Bearskin Forks—Merle Constiner	.50	1.50	2.50	W
F402	Quest of the Three Worlds—Cordwainer Smith	1.00	3.00	5.00	SF
F403	The Dream Master—Roger Zelazny	.80	2.40	4.00	SF
F404	The Grabhorn Bounty—Clifton Adams	.80	2.40	4.00	W
F405	Vietnam Nurse—Suzanne Roberts	.40	1.20	2.00	R
F406	Tama, Princess of Mercury—Ray Cummings	.80	2.40	4.00	SF
F407	Day of the Minotaur—Thomas Burnett Swann	1.00	3.00	5.00	SF
F408	The Sioux Spaceman—Andre Norton; 1966	.80	2.40	4.00	SF
F409	Cliff Rider—Lin Searles	.50	1.50	2.50	W
F410	Lake Resort Nurse—Arlene Hale	.40	1.20	2.00	R
F411	The Mustang Trail—L. L. Foreman	.50	1.50	2.50	W
F412	The Gates of Creation—Philip Jose Farmer	1.20	3.60	6.00	SF
F413	A Vacation for Nurse Dean—Sharon Heath	.40	1.20	2.00	R
F414	The Star Mill—Emil Petaja; 1966	.80	2.40	4.00	SF
F415	The Bravos—Brian Wynne	.50	1.50	2.50	W
F416	Utopia Minus X—Rex Gordon	.40	1.20	2.00	SF
F417	Once a Nurse—Willo Davis Roberts	.40	1.20	2.00	R
F418	Single Action—Nelson Nye	.50	1.50	2.50	W
F419	Rangeland Nurse—Suzanne Roberts	.40	1.20	2.00	R
F420	Planet of the Double Sun—Neil R. Jones	.40	1.20	2.00	SF
F421	Anarchaos—Curt Clark (Donald Westlake)	.80	2.40	4.00	SF
F422	The Sword of Rhiannon—Leigh Brackett	.80	2.40	4.00	SF
F423	Giant on Horseback—Lewis B. Patten	.50	1.50	2.50	W
F424	Community Nurse—Arlene Hale	.40	1.20	2.00	R
F425	World Without Stars—Poul Anderson	1.00	3.00	5.00	SF
F426	The Genetic General—Gordon R. Dickson	1.00	3.00	5.00	SF
F427	The Einstein Intersection—Samuel R. Delany	.80	2.40	4.00	SF
F428	Mascarada Pass—William Colt MacDonald	.50	1.50	2.50	W
F429	The World Jones Made—Philip K. Dick; 1967	.80	2.40	4.00	SF
F430	Nurse on the Beach—Arlene Hale; 1967	.40	1.20	2.00	R

ADVENTURE NOVEL CLASSIC
Hillman Periodicals, Inc./Novel Selections, Inc.

Digest Size

		Good	Fine	N/Mint	
1	The Blanket of the Dark—John Buchan	.80	2.40	4.00	A
2	Bardelys the Magnificent—Rafael Sabatini	.80	2.40	4.00	A
4	House of the Four Winds—John Buchan	.80	2.40	4.00	A
5	The Queen's Messenger—Rafael Sabatini	.80	2.40	4.00	A
6	Big Timber—Robert Ormond Chase	.80	2.40	4.00	A
7	Hands Up!—A. Treynor	.80	2.40	4.00	A
10	Connie Morgan Hits the Trail—James Hendryx	.80	2.40	4.00	A
11	The Vengeance of Hurricane Williams—Gordon Young	.80	2.40	4.00	A
12	The Trampling of the Lilies—Raphael Sabatini	.80	2.40	4.00	A
13	Gone North—Charles Alden Seltzer	.80	2.40	4.00	W
14	Rivermen Die Broke	.80	2.40	4.00	A
15	The Courage of Marge O'Doone—James Oliver Curwood	.80	2.40	4.00	A
16	Out From Shanghai—Sydney Parkman	.80	2.40	4.00	A
17	Death Heads North—James Hendryx	.80	2.40	4.00	A
18	River of Fear	.80	2.40	4.00	A
21	Hawk of the Desert—A. Treynor	.80	2.40	4.00	A
22	Secret Command—John & Ward Hawkins	.80	2.40	4.00	A
23	Hard Money—Luke Short	.80	2.40	4.00	A
24	Jungle Murder—Alan Amos; aka Pray for a Miracle	.80	2.40	4.00	A
26	Montana Rides—Evan Evans	.80	2.40	4.00	W
27	North to Danger—Tom Gill	.80	2.40	4.00	A
28	Riot at Red Water—Frederick R. Bechdolt	.80	2.40	4.00	W
29	Broken River—John & Ward Hawkins	.80	2.40	4.00	A
30	Arizona—Clarence Budington Kelland	.80	2.40	4.00	W
31	Death Charter—Eustace L. Adams	.80	2.40	4.00	A
32	Montana Rides Again—Evan Evans	.80	2.40	4.00	W
33	Stagecoach Kingdom—Harry Sinclair Drago	.80	2.40	4.00	W
34	Journey to Murder—Robert Portner Koehler	.80	2.40	4.00	M
35	Devil on His Trail—John & Ward Hawkins	.80	2.40	4.00	A
39	Flame in the Forest—Harold Titus	.80	2.40	4.00	A
40	Ship Ashore—Sydney Parkman	.80	2.40	4.00	A
41	Hard Rock Man—James Hendryx	.80	2.40	4.00	A
42	Vanishing Ships—Philip M. Fisher	.80	2.40	4.00	A

ALL-PICTURE MYSTERY
St. John Publishing Company

Digest Size

nn	The Case of the Winking Buddha—Manning Lee Stokes; orig., 1950, comic book style	4.00	12.00	20.00	M
nn	It Rhymes With Lust; orig., 1951, comic book style with Matt Baker art	5.00	15.00	25.00	M

AMAZING STORIES SCIENCE FICTION NOVEL
Ziff-Davis Publishing Company

Digest Size

nn	20 Million Miles to Earth—Henry Slesar; 1957, movie tie-in	6.00	18.00	30.00	SF

AMERICAN FOLK-LORE AND HUMOR
Atomic Books, Inc.

Digest Size

nn(1)	The True Story of Billy the Kid: The Outlaw	2.00	6.00	10.00	B
nn(2)	The True Story of "Wild Bill" Hickok: Gun Fighter—J. W. Buel; 1946	2.00	6.00	10.00	B

Adv. Novel Classic 22, © Hill

All-Picture Mystery nn, © Stj

Amazing Stories SF Novel nn, © ZD

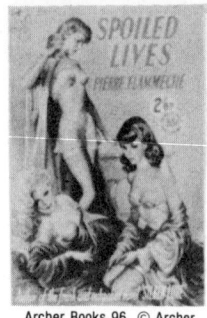

Archer Books 51, © Archer	Archer Books 96, © Archer		Argyle nn, © Argyle

(AMERICAN FOLK-LORE AND HUMOR, continued)

		Good	Fine	N/Mint	
nn(3)	The True Story of Jesse James: King of Robbers	2.00	6.00	10.00	B

AMERICAN LIBRARY
David McKay Company

Digest Size

		Good	Fine	N/Mint	
1	Silent Witness—John Stephen Strange	1.20	3.60	6.00	M
2	Acts of Black Night—Kathleen Moore Knight	1.20	3.60	6.00	M
3	Dead Man Control—Helen Reilly	1.20	3.60	6.00	M
4	The Case of the Constant God—Rufus King	1.20	3.60	6.00	M

ARCHER BOOKS
Kaywin Publishers, Inc./Archer Press Ltd.

		Good	Fine	N/Mint	
2	Dames Are No Dice	2.00	6.00	10.00	E
3	Take It, and Like It—Spike Morelli; 1951; c-Heade	3.00	9.00	15.00	E
4	This Thing Called ''Sin''	2.00	6.00	10.00	E
5	Dame in My Bed—Michael Storme; 1951, c-Heade	4.00	12.00	20.00	E
6	Satan's Sister—Tony Angelo; c-Heade	4.00	12.00	20.00	M
8	You'll Never Get Me—Spike Morelli; 1952, c-Heade	4.00	12.00	20.00	E
10	The Body Ran Home	2.00	6.00	10.00	M
11	Coffin for a Cutie	3.00	9.00	15.00	M
12	Sinner's Shroud—Tony Angelo	3.00	9.00	15.00	E
13	The Worms Have Eaten Them	3.00	9.00	15.00	E
14	Shipwreck Passion	3.00	9.00	15.00	E
15	Lost Souls of Bohemia	4.00	12.00	20.00	E
28	Girl From Tiger Bay	4.00	12.00	20.00	E
31	Two Smart Dames	3.00	9.00	15.00	E
33	Come Into My Parlor	3.00	9.00	15.00	E
35	Vice Rackets of Soho—Roland Vane	12.50	37.50	60.00	E
36	Flame—Paul Renin	4.00	12.00	20.00	E
37	Willing Sinner—Roland Vane	3.00	9.00	15.00	
38	Where They Breed	3.00	9.00	15.00	E
39	Black Mistress	3.00	9.00	15.00	E
40	Sin Stained	3.00	9.00	15.00	E
42	Eternal Conflict	3.00	9.00	15.00	E
44	Pleasure's Price—Paul Renin	3.00	9.00	15.00	E
45	When Passion Rules	3.00	9.00	15.00	E
47	Double Life	2.00	6.00	10.00	E
48	Passionate Puritan	3.00	9.00	15.00	E
49	Sultry Love	3.00	9.00	15.00	E
50	Sex—Paul Renin; 1951	2.00	6.00	10.00	E
51	Night Haunts of Paris—Roland Vane; 1951	2.00	6.00	10.00	E
52	Sinful Sisters—Roland Vane; 1951, c-Heade	4.00	12.00	20.00	E
53	Love—Paul Renin	2.00	6.00	10.00	E
54	Fortnight's Folly—Paul Renin	3.00	9.00	15.00	E
57	Plaything of Passion—Jeanette Revere; 1951, c-Heade	4.00	12.00	20.00	E
68	White Slaves of New Orleans—Roland Vane; c-Heade	6.00	18.00	30.00	E
69	Ladies of the Red Lamp—Roland Vane; c-Heade	4.00	12.00	20.00	E
70	The Silken Lure—Pierre Flammeche; c-Heade	4.00	12.00	20.00	E
71	Unlucky Virgin—Michael Storme	3.00	9.00	15.00	E
72	Ladies Sleep Alone—Lew Della; 1951	2.00	6.00	10.00	E
81	Outrage	2.00	6.00	10.00	E
82	Virtue	3.00	9.00	15.00	E
83	Men Women Love	2.00	6.00	10.00	E
84	Make Mine a Harlot—Michael Storme	3.00	9.00	15.00	E

(ARCHER BOOKS, continued)

		Good	Fine	N/Mint	
96	Spoiled Lives—Pierre Flammeche; 1952, c-Heade	4.00	12.00	20.00	E

ARGYLE
Argyle Press

Digest Size

nn	Germany Must Perish!—Theodore N. Kaufman; anti-Nazi war propaganda	2.00	6.00	10.00

ARMED SERVICES EDITIONS
Editions for the Armed Services, Inc.

		Good	Fine	N/Mint	
A- 1	The Education of Hyman Kaplan—L. Q. Ross; 1943	1.20	3.60	6.00	
A- 2	Report From Tokyo—J. C. Grew	1.20	3.60	6.00	
A- 3	Good Intentions—Ogden Nash	1.20	3.60	6.00	
A- 4	Mama's Bank Account—K. Forbes	1.20	3.60	6.00	
A- 5	There Go the Ships—Robert Carse	1.20	3.60	6.00	
A- 6	Sophie Halenczik, American—R. C. Field	1.20	3.60	6.00	
A- 7	Mr. Winkle Goes to War—Theodore Pratt	1.20	3.60	6.00	
A- 8	Oliver Twist—Charles Dickens	2.00	6.00	10.00	
A- 9	Tortilla Flat—John Steinbeck	2.00	6.00	10.00	
A-10	World Series—John R. Tunis	1.20	3.60	6.00	B
A-11	My World and Welcome to It—James Thurber	2.00	6.00	10.00	H
A-12	Peace Marshal—Frank Gruber	1.20	3.60	6.00	W
A-13	Heathen Days—H. L. Mencken	1.20	3.60	6.00	
A-14	The Ship—C. S. Forester	1.20	3.60	6.00	A
A-15	The Human Comedy—William Saroyan	1.20	3.60	6.00	
A-16	Wind, Sand and Stars—Antoine De Saint-Exupery	1.60	4.80	8.00	
A-17	The Making of Modern Britain—J. B. Brebner	1.00	3.00	5.00	NF
A-18	The Arabs—P. K. Hitti	1.20	3.60	6.00	
A-19	The Unvanquished—Howard Fast	1.20	3.60	6.00	
A-20	Miracles of Military Medicine	1.00	3.00	5.00	NF
A-21	A Time for Greatness—H. Agar	1.20	3.60	6.00	
A-22	The Ministry of Fear—Graham Greene	1.20	3.60	6.00	M
A-23	Happy Landings—M. J. Herzberg	1.20	3.60	6.00	
A-24	Typee—Herman Melville.........................	1.60	4.80	8.00	A
A-25	George Washington Carver—R. Holt	1.20	3.60	6.00	B
A-26	Lord Jim—Joseph Conrad	1.60	4.80	8.00	A
A-27	Storm Over the Land—Carl Sandburg	1.60	4.80	8.00	A
A-28	Action at Aquila—Hervey Allen	1.20	3.60	6.00	
A-29	Reprisal—Grace Zaring Stone	1.20	3.60	6.00	
A-30	The Fireside Book of Dog Stories—J. Goodman	1.20	3.60	6.00	A
B-31	Let the Hurricane Roar—R. W. Lane; 1943	1.20	3.60	6.00	
B-32	Dynamite Cargo—F. Herman	1.20	3.60	6.00	A
B-33	Come In—Robert Frost	1.60	4.80	8.00	
B-34	Ethan Frome—Edith Wharton	1.60	4.80	8.00	
B-35	Suds in Your Eye—M. Lasswell	1.20	3.60	6.00	
B-36	Fight for Powder Valley!—Peter Field	1.20	3.60	6.00	W
B-37	Our Hearts Were Young and Gay—C. O. Skinner	1.20	3.60	6.00	
B-38	Gentle Annie—MacKinlay Kantor	1.20	3.60	6.00	
B-39	Benchley Beside Himself—Robert Benchley	1.60	4.80	8.00	H
B-40	To Walk the Night—William Sloane	1.20	3.60	6.00	
B-41	The Gaunt Woman—E. Gilligan	1.20	3.60	6.00	
B-42	Winter Range—Alan LeMay	1.20	3.60	6.00	W
B-43	Painted Buttes—A. H. Gooden	1.60	4.80	8.00	W
B-44	Chicken Every Sunday—R. Taylor	1.20	3.60	6.00	
B-45	Father and Glorious Descendant—P. Lowe	1.20	3.60	6.00	
B-46	Life in a Putty Knife Factory—H. Allen Smith	1.20	3.60	6.00	H
B-47	Lightship—A. Binns	1.20	3.60	6.00	
B-48	Get Thee Behind Me—H. Spence	1.20	3.60	6.00	
B-49	My Friend Flicka—M. O'Hara	1.20	3.60	6.00	A
B-50	Moscow Dateline—H. C. Cassidy	1.20	3.60	6.00	
B-51	The Uninvited—D. Macardle	1.60	4.80	8.00	
B-52	Rome Haul—Walter D. Edmonds	1.20	3.60	6.00	
B-53	Powder River—S. Burt	1.20	3.60	6.00	W
B-54	The Natives Return—L. Adamic	1.20	3.60	6.00	
B-55	The Yearling—M. K. Rawlings	1.60	4.80	8.00	
B-56	Hostages—S. Heym	1.20	3.60	6.00	
B-57	Good Neighbors—H. Herring	1.20	3.60	6.00	
B-58	Klondike Mike—M. Denison	1.20	3.60	6.00	
B-59	Delilah—M. Goodrich	1.20	3.60	6.00	
B-60	Arctic Adventure—Peter Freuchen	1.60	4.80	8.00	A
C-61	North Africa—A. H. Brodrick; 1944	1.20	3.60	6.00	
C-62	The Sea of Grass—Conrad Richter	1.60	4.80	8.00	A
C-63	The Mind in the Making—J. H. Robinson	1.20	3.60	6.00	

		Good	Fine	N/Mint	
C-64	Candide—Voltaire	1.60	4.80	8.00	
C-65	The Forest—S. E. White	1.20	3.60	6.00	
C-66	Pistols for Hire—Nelson E. Nye	1.20	3.60	6.00	W
C-67	Seven Men—M. Beerbohm	1.20	3.60	6.00	
C-68	Swamp Water—V. Bell	1.20	3.60	6.00	
C-69	Unlocking Adventure—C. Courtney	1.20	3.60	6.00	A
C-70	Penrod—Booth Tarkington	1.60	4.80	8.00	
C-71	Green Mansions—W. H. Hudson	3.00	9.00	15.00	F
D-72	Hopalong Cassidy Serves a Writ—Clarence E. Mulford	1.60	4.80	8.00	W
C-73	U. S. Foreign Policy—Walter Lippman	1.00	3.00	5.00	NF
C-74	Star Spangled Virgin—D. B. Heyward	1.20	3.60	6.00	
C-75	Black-out in Gretley—J. B. Priestley	1.60	4.80	8.00	
C-76	The Adventures of Tom Sawyer—Mark Twain	2.00	6.00	10.00	A
C-77	The Short Stories of Stephen Vincent Benet—Stephen Vincent Benet	1.60	4.80	8.00	F
C-78	Miracle in Hellas—B. Wason	1.20	3.60	6.00	
C-79	Fathoms—F. Meier	1.20	3.60	6.00	A
C-80	Australian Frontier—E. Hill	1.20	3.60	6.00	
C-81	Storm—G. R. Stewart	1.20	3.60	6.00	A
C-82	Kabloona—G. DePoncins	1.20	3.60	6.00	
C-83	The Forest and the Fort—Hervey Allen	1.20	3.60	6.00	A
C-84	The Hawkeye—H. Quick	1.20	3.60	6.00	
C-85	. . .and a Few Marines—J. W. Thomason	1.20	3.60	6.00	
C-86	Starbuck—J. Selby	1.20	3.60	6.00	
C-87	Great Smith—Edison Marshall	1.20	3.60	6.00	A
C-88	Paul Revere—Edith Forbes	1.20	3.60	6.00	A
C-89	Coronet—M. Komroff	1.20	3.60	6.00	
C-90	The Grapes of Wrath—J. Steinbeck	2.00	6.00	10.00	
D-91	The Story of Dr. Wassell—James Hilton; 1944	1.20	3.60	6.00	
D-92	Love at First Flight—C. Spalding	1.20	3.60	6.00	
D-93	Blazed Trail Stories—S. E. White	1.20	3.60	6.00	A
D-94	Tumbling River Range—W. C. Tuttle	1.20	3.60	6.00	W
D-95	Colonel Effingham's Raid—B. Fleming	1.20	3.60	6.00	A
D-96	Without Orders—M. Albrand	1.20	3.60	6.00	
D-97	Death Comes for the Archbishop—Willa Cather	1.60	4.80	8.00	M
D-98	The Trees—Conrad Richter	1.20	3.60	6.00	A
D-99	The Night of the Summer Solstice—M. Van Doren	1.20	3.60	6.00	
D-100	Valley of the Sun—Clarence Buddington Kelland	1.20	3.60	6.00	W
D-101	Evidence of Things Seen—Elizabeth Daly	1.60	4.80	8.00	M
D-102	Java Head—J. Hergesheimer	1.20	3.60	6.00	
D-103	Mystery Ship—G. S. Bryan	1.20	3.60	6.00	
D-104	Burma Surgeon—G. S. Seagrave	1.20	3.60	6.00	
D-105	On Being a Real Person—H. E. Fosdick	1.20	3.60	6.00	
D-106	Rats, Lice and History—H. Zinsser	1.20	3.60	6.00	NF
D-107	R. F. D.—C. A. Smart	1.20	3.60	6.00	
D-108	McSorley's Wonderful Saloon—J. Mitchell	1.20	3.60	6.00	
D-109	Country Lawyer—B. Partridge	1.20	3.60	6.00	
D-110	The Adventures of Huckleberry Finn—Mark Twain	2.00	6.00	10.00	A
D-111	Blanche Fury—J. Shearing	1.20	3.60	6.00	
D-112	Cross Creek—M. K. Rawlings	1.20	3.60	6.00	
D-113	The Keys of the Kingdom—A. J. Cronin	1.20	3.60	6.00	
D-114	We Cannot Escape History—J. T. Whitaker	1.20	3.60	6.00	NF
D-115	Slim—W. W. Haines	1.20	3.60	6.00	
D-116	The Best American Short Stories of 1942—M. Foley	1.20	3.60	6.00	
D-117	A Tree Grows in Brooklyn—B. Smith	1.20	3.60	6.00	
D-118	The Robe—Lloyd C. Douglas	1.60	4.80	8.00	
D-119	Rivers of Glory—F. VanWyck Mason	1.20	3.60	6.00	
D-120	So Little Time—J. P. Marquand	1.20	3.60	6.00	
E-121	State Fair—P. Stong; 1944	1.20	3.60	6.00	
E-122	Seven Essays—R. W. Emerson	1.20	3.60	6.00	
E-123	Ghost Trails—W. C. Tuttle	1.20	3.60	6.00	W
E-124	The Range Hawk—A. H. Gooden	1.60	4.80	8.00	W
E-125	The Mountain Divide—F. H. Spearman	1.20	3.60	6.00	
E-126	A Sense of Humus—B. Damon	1.20	3.60	6.00	
E-127	Bushido—Alexandre Pernikoff	1.60	4.80	8.00	E
E-128	The Moon and Sixpence—W. Somerset Maugham	1.60	4.80	8.00	
E-129	Saddle and Ride—Ernest Haycox	1.60	4.80	8.00	W
E-130	Seven Keys to Baldpate—Earl Derr Biggers	2.00	6.00	10.00	M
E-131	Science Year Book of 1943—J. D. Ratcliff	1.20	3.60	6.00	NF
E-132	Green Hell—J. Duguid	1.60	4.80	8.00	
E-133	Ship of the Line—C. S. Forester	1.20	3.60	6.00	A
E-134	Ordeal by Hunger—G. R. Stewart, Jr.	1.20	3.60	6.00	
E-135	The Gambler Takes a Wife—M. Brinig	1.20	3.60	6.00	
E-136	Stories for Men—C. Grayson	1.20	3.60	6.00	
E-137	Jamaica Inn—Daphne DuMaurier	1.20	3.60	6.00	
E-138	Random Harvest—James Hilton	1.60	4.80	8.00	
E-139	A Connecticut Yankee in King Arthur's Court—Mark Twain	2.00	6.00	10.00	F
E-140	Cimarron—Edna Ferber	2.00	6.00	10.00	W

		Good	Fine	N/Mint	
E-141	I Married Adventure—Ona Johnson	1.20	3.60	6.00	
E-142	Windswept—M. E. Chase	1.20	3.60	6.00	
E-143	Roughly Speaking—L. R. Pierson	1.20	3.60	6.00	
E-144	Hell on Ice—C. E. Ellsberg	1.20	3.60	6.00	
E-145	Doctors on Horseback—J. T. Flexner	1.20	3.60	6.00	
E-146	The Late George Apley—J. P. Marquand	1.20	3.60	6.00	
E-147	Selected Short Stories—Stephen Crane	1.60	4.80	8.00	
E-148	One Man's West—D. Lavender	1.20	3.60	6.00	
E-149	Drums Along the Mohawk—Walter D. Edmonds	1.60	4.80	8.00	A
E-150	King's Row—H. Bellamann	1.20	3.60	6.00	
F-151	Messer Marco Polo—D. Byrne; 1944	1.20	3.60	6.00	
F-152	Night Flight—Antoine DeSaint—Exupery	1.20	3.60	6.00	
F-153	The Selected Writings—Abraham Lincoln	1.60	4.80	8.00	
F-154	Black Majesty—John W. Vandercook	1.20	3.60	6.00	A
F-155	Going Fishing—N. Farson	1.20	3.60	6.00	
F-156	Lassie Come Home—Eric Knight	1.20	3.60	6.00	
F-157	Flying Colours—C. S. Forester	1.20	3.60	6.00	A
F-158	Clear the Tracks—J. Bromley	1.20	3.60	6.00	
F-159	Happy Days—H. L. Mencken	1.20	3.60	6.00	
F-160	Border Breed—William MacLeod Raine	1.20	3.60	6.00	W
F-161	Jungle Peace—W. Beebe	1.20	3.60	6.00	
F-162	Selected Short Stories—Bret Harte	1.20	3.60	6.00	
F-163	The Bar 20 Rides Again—Clarence E. Mulford	1.60	4.80	8.00	W
F-164	The Border Trumpet—Ernest Haycox	1.20	3.60	6.00	W
F-165	So Big—Edna Ferber	1.20	3.60	6.00	
F-166	West With the Night—B. Markham	1.20	3.60	6.00	
F-167	Land Below the Wind—A. N. Keith	1.20	3.60	6.00	
F-168	Under a Lucky Star—R. C. Andrews	1.20	3.60	6.00	
F-169	The Horse and Buggy Doctor—A. E. Hertzler	1.20	3.60	6.00	
F-170	Here Is Your War—Ernie Pyle	1.20	3.60	6.00	NF
F-171	The Blazed Trail—S. E. White	1.20	3.60	6.00	W
F-172	Round Up—Ring Lardner	1.20	3.60	6.00	
F-173	Old Jules—Mari Sandoz	1.20	3.60	6.00	W
F-174	Life on the Mississippi—Mark Twain	2.00	6.00	10.00	
F-175	The Essays of Charles Lamb—Charles Lamb	1.20	3.60	6.00	
F-176	A Subtreasury of American Humor—E. B. White	1.20	3.60	6.00	
F-177	Wellington—P. Guedalla	1.20	3.60	6.00	
F-178	Casuals of the Sea—W. McFee	1.20	3.60	6.00	
F-179	Dr. Dogbody's Leg—J. N. Hall	1.60	4.80	8.00	
F-180	The Sea-wolf—Jack London	2.00	6.00	10.00	A
G-181	The Glorious Pool—Thorne Smith; 1944	1.60	4.80	8.00	H
G-182	White Fang—Jack London	2.00	6.00	10.00	A
G-183	Low Man on a Totem Pole—H. Allen Smith	1.20	3.60	6.00	A
G-184	Trail's End—William MacLeod Raine	1.20	3.60	6.00	W
G-185	My Antonia—Willa Cather	1.20	3.60	6.00	
G-186	Long, Long Ago—Alexander Woolcott	1.20	3.60	6.00	
G-187	Sam Small Flies Again—E. Knight	1.20	3.60	6.00	
G-188	Taps for Private Tussie—J. Stuart	1.20	3.60	6.00	
G-189	Kamongo—H. W. Smith	1.20	3.60	6.00	
G-190	The Trusty Knaves—E. M. Rhodes	1.20	3.60	6.00	W
G-191	Little Caesar—W. R. Burnett	2.00	6.00	10.00	M
G-192	Inside Benchley—Robert Benchley	1.20	3.60	6.00	H
G-193	How to Think Straight—R. H. Thouless	1.20	3.60	6.00	
G-194	The Mirror of the Sea—Joseph Conrad	1.60	4.80	8.00	
G-195	Raiders of the Rimrock—Luke Short	1.20	3.60	6.00	W
G-196	A Crystal Age—W. H. Hudson	1.20	3.60	6.00	
G-197	Laught With Leacock—S. Leacock	1.20	3.60	6.00	H
G-198	Kim—Rudyard Kipling	1.60	4.80	8.00	A

Armed Services Editions F-180

Armed Services Editions G-182

Armed Services Editions G-198

		Good	Fine	N/Mint	
G-199	Journey Into America—D. C. Peattie	1.20	3.60	6.00	
G-200	As the Earth Turns—G. H. Carroll	1.20	3.60	6.00	
G-201	Young Man of Caracas—T. R. Ybarra	1.20	3.60	6.00	
G-202	Arouse and Beware—MacKinlay Kantor	1.20	3.60	6.00	A
G-203	This Chemical Age—W. Haynes	1.20	3.60	6.00	NF
G-204	Thunderhead—M. O'Hara	1.20	3.60	6.00	A
G-205	The Fleet in the Forest—C. D. Lane	1.20	3.60	6.00	
G-206	The Best American Short Stories of 1943—ed. M. Foley	1.20	3.60	6.00	
G-207	Rogues' Company—H. H. Kroll	1.20	3.60	6.00	
G-208	H. M. Pulham, Esq.—J. P. Marquand	1.20	3.60	6.00	
G-209	Moby Dick—Herman Melville	2.00	6.00	10.00	
G-210	East of the Giants—G. R. Stewart	1.20	3.60	6.00	
H-211	C/O Postmaster—Corp. T. R. St. George; 1944	1.20	3.60	6.00	
H-212	Beyond the Desert—Eugene Manlove Rhodes	1.20	3.60	6.00	W
H-213	Payment Deferred—C. S. Forester	1.20	3.60	6.00	A
H-214	Buried Alive—A. Bennett	1.20	3.60	6.00	
H-215	Westen Star—Stephen Vincent Benet	1.20	3.60	6.00	
H-216	Laughing Boy—O. LaFarge	1.20	3.60	6.00	
H-217	The Republic of Plato—I. A. Richard	1.20	3.60	6.00	
H-218	Forward the Nation—D. C. Peattie	1.20	3.60	6.00	
H-219	Three Times I Bow—C. Glick	1.20	3.60	6.00	
H-220	Night Over Fitch's Pond—C. Jarrett	1.20	3.60	6.00	
H-221	The Cruise of the Snark—Jack London	1.60	4.80	8.00	
H-222	Riders of the Night—Eugene Cunningham	1.20	3.60	6.00	W
H-223	Danger in the Cards—M. MacDougall	1.20	3.60	6.00	
H-224	Burning an Empire—Stewart H. Holbrook	1.20	3.60	6.00	
H-225	Animal Reveille—R. Dempewolff	1.20	3.60	6.00	
H-226	Red Raskall—C. McMeekin	1.20	3.60	6.00	
H-227	Corson of the J C—Clarence E. Mulford	1.20	3.60	6.00	W
H-228	Captain Caution—K. Roberts	1.20	3.60	6.00	
H-229	The Cold Journey—G. Z. Stone	1.20	3.60	6.00	
H-230	The Bishop's Jaegers—Thorne Smith	1.60	4.80	8.00	H
H-231	Innocent Merriment—F. P. Adams	1.20	3.60	6.00	
H-232	Carmen of the Rancho—F. H. Spearman	1.20	3.60	6.00	
H-233	Cardigan—R. W. Chambers	1.20	3.60	6.00	
H-234	Box Office—M. Barrows	1.20	3.60	6.00	
H-235	The Pacific Ocean—F. Riesenberg	1.20	3.60	6.00	
H-236	The Travels of Marco Polo—Manuel Komroff	1.20	3.60	6.00	A
H-237	The Ringed Horizon—E. Gilligan	1.20	3.60	6.00	
H-238	Botany Bay—Charles Nordhoff	1.60	4.80	8.00	A
H-239	How Green Was My Valley—R. Liewellyn	1.20	3.60	6.00	
H-240	Chad Hanna—Walter D. Edmonds	1.20	3.60	6.00	
I-241	Avalanche—K. Boyle; 1944	1.20	3.60	6.00	
I-242	Semper Fidelis—K. Ayling	1.20	3.60	6.00	
I-243	Mr. and Mrs. Cugat—I. S. Rorick	1.20	3.60	6.00	
I-244	Ol' Man Adam an' His Chillun—R. Bradford	1.20	3.60	6.00	
I-245	The Mystery of the Red Triangle—W. C. Tuttle	1.20	3.60	6.00	
I-246	We Followed Our Hearts to Hollywood—E. Kimbrough	1.20	3.60	6.00	
I-247	Deserts on the March—P. B. Sears	1.20	3.60	6.00	
I-248	Rogue Male—Geoffrey Household	1.60	4.80	8.00	M
I-249	High Tension—W. W. Haines	1.20	3.60	6.00	
I-250	The Book Nobody Knows—Bruce Barton	1.20	3.60	6.00	
I-251	Stage Coach Kingdom—Harry Sinclair Drago	1.20	3.60	6.00	W
I-252	Selected Short Stories—K. Mansfield	1.20	3.60	6.00	
I-253	The Middle-aged Man on the Flying Trapeze—James Thurber	1.60	4.80	8.00	
I-254	Deep West—Ernest Haycox	1.20	3.60	6.00	W
I-255	Arizona—Clarence Buddington Kelland	1.20	3.60	6.00	W
I-256	Cow by the Tail—J. J. Benton	1.20	3.60	6.00	
I-257	Hopalong Cassidy's Protege—Clarence E. Mulford	1.60	4.80	8.00	W
I-258	Coast Guard to the Rescue—K. Baarslag	1.20	3.60	6.00	
I-259	On the Bottom—E. Ellsberg	1.20	3.60	6.00	
I-260	Ashenden—Somerset Maugham	1.20	3.60	6.00	M
I-261	Queen Victoria—L. Strachey	1.20	3.60	6.00	
I-262	The Tides of Malvern—F. Griswold	1.20	3.60	6.00	
I-263	Ten. . .and Out—A. Johnston	1.20	3.60	6.00	
I-264	Victory—Joseph Conrad	1.60	4.80	8.00	
I-265	Mrs. Parkington—L. Bromfield	1.20	3.60	6.00	
I-266	The Sea-Hawk—Rafael Sabatini	1.60	4.80	8.00	A
I-267	Honey in the Horn—H. L. Davis	1.20	3.60	6.00	
I-268	Jane Eyre—Charlotte Bronte	1.20	3.60	6.00	
I-269	Paradise—Edith Forbes	1.20	3.60	6.00	
I-270	My Son, My Son!—H. Spring	1.20	3.60	6.00	
J-271	The Proud Sheriff—Eugene Manlove Rhodes; 1944	1.20	3.60	6.00	W
J-272	My Name Is Aram—William Saroyan	1.20	3.60	6.00	
J-273	The Shadow Line—Joseph Conrad	1.60	4.80	8.00	
J-274	Tree Toad—B. Davis	1.20	3.60	6.00	

		Good	Fine	N/Mint	
J-275	Riot at Red Water—F. R. Bechdolt	1.20	3.60	6.00	W
J-276	Past the End of the Pavement—C. J. Finney	1.20	3.60	6.00	
J-277	Lou Gehrig—F. Graham	1.20	3.60	6.00	B
J-278	You Know Me, Al—Ring Lardner	1.20	3.60	6.00	
J-279	The Phantom Filly—G. A. Chamberlain	1.20	3.60	6.00	
J-280	Sheriff of Yavisa—C. H. Snow	1.20	3.60	6.00	
J-281	Davy Crockett—C. Rourke	1.20	3.60	6.00	B
J-282	A High Wind in Jamaica—R. Hughes	1.20	3.60	6.00	
J-283	The Gangs All Here—H. Smith	1.20	3.60	6.00	
J-284	Skin and Bones—Thorne Smith	1.60	4.80	8.00	H
J-285	The Last Adam—J. G. Cozzens	1.20	3.60	6.00	
J-286	South of Rio Grande—Max Brand	1.20	3.60	6.00	W
J-287	George M. Cohan—W. Morehouse	1.20	3.60	6.00	B
J-288	The Golden Fleece—N. Lofts	1.20	3.60	6.00	
J-289	End of Track—Ward Weaver (Van Wyck Mason)	1.20	3.60	6.00	
J-290	Selected Stories—Paul Gallico	1.20	3.60	6.00	
J-291	February Hill—V. Lincoln	1.20	3.60	6.00	
J-292	The Sea and the Jungle—H. M. Tomlinson	1.20	3.60	6.00	A
J-293	No Life for a Lady—A. M. Cleaveland	1.20	3.60	6.00	
J-294	The Bayous of Louisiana—H. T. Kane	1.20	3.60	6.00	
J-295	The Wake of the Prairie Schooner—I. D. Paden	1.20	3.60	6.00	
J-296	Vanity Fair—W. M. Thackery	1.20	3.60	6.00	
J-297	Selected Stories—Edgar Allan Poe	2.00	6.00	10.00	
J-298	Young Ames—Walter D. Edmonds	1.20	3.60	6.00	A
J-299	The Apostle—Sholem Asch	1.20	3.60	6.00	
J-300	Good Night, Sweet Prince—G. Fowler	1.20	3.60	6.00	
J-301	Forty-niners—A. B. Hulbert	1.20	3.60	6.00	
J-302	Indians Abroad—C. T. Foreman	1.20	3.60	6.00	
K- 1	This Simian World—Clarence Day; 1944	1.20	3.60	6.00	
K- 2	The Old Soak—D. Marquis	1.20	3.60	6.00	
K- 3	The Call of the Wild—Jack London	2.00	6.00	10.00	A
K- 4	The Dark Gentleman—G. B. Stern	1.20	3.60	6.00	
K- 5	The Secret of Dr. Kildare—Max Brand	1.20	3.60	6.00	
K- 6	The Noise of Their Wings—MacKinlay Kantor	1.20	3.60	6.00	
K- 7	Bounty of the Wayside—W. B. Wilder	1.20	3.60	6.00	
K- 8	Stepsons of Light—Eugene Manlove Rhodes	1.20	3.60	6.00	W
K- 9	Selected Short Stories—Ernest Hemingway	2.00	6.00	10.00	
K-10	The Life and Death of Little Jo—R. Bright	1.20	3.60	6.00	
K-11	Rebel of Ronde Valley—C. H. Snow	1.20	3.60	6.00	
K-12	The St. Lawrence—H. Beston	1.20	3.60	6.00	
K-13	Ethan Allen—Stewart H. Holbrook	1.20	3.60	6.00	A
K-14	The Wild Bunch—Ernest Haycox	1.20	3.60	6.00	W
K-15	The Stray Lamb—Thorne Smith	1.60	4.80	8.00	H
K-16	Selected Short Stories—O. Henry	1.60	4.80	8.00	
K-17	The Eight Million—M. Berger	1.20	3.60	6.00	
K-18	Moon Tide—W. Robertson	1.20	3.60	6.00	
K-19	The Journey of the Flame—A. D. F. Blanco	1.20	3.60	6.00	
K-20	Young Man of the World—T. R. Ybarra	1.20	3.60	6.00	
K-21	Winter Wheat—M. Walker	1.20	3.60	6.00	
K-22	Walt Whitman—H. S. Canby	1.20	3.60	6.00	B
K-23	Andrew Jackson: The Border Captain—M. James	1.20	3.60	6.00	B
K-24	Babbitt—Sinclair Lewis	2.00	6.00	10.00	
K-25	The Autobiography of a Yankee Lawyer—E. Tutt	1.20	3.60	6.00	
K-26	Suckers Progress—H. Asbury	1.20	3.60	6.00	
K-27	The Robe—L. C. Douglas	1.20	3.60	6.00	
K-28	A Tree Grows in Brooklyn—B. Smith	1.20	3.60	6.00	
K-29	AP: The Story of News—O. Gramling	1.20	3.60	6.00	NF
K-30	Benjamin Franklin—Carl Van Doren	1.20	3.60	6.00	B
K-31	Tristram Shandy—Laurence Sterne	1.20	3.60	6.00	
K-32	Rise to Follow—A. Spalding	1.20	3.60	6.00	
L- 1	A Book of Americans—R & S. V. Benet; 1944	1.20	3.60	6.00	B
L- 2	My Life and Hart Times—James Thurber	1.60	4.80	8.00	H
L- 3	Kilgour's Mare—H. G. Lamond	1.20	3.60	6.00	
L- 4	Etched in Moonlight—J. Stephens	1.20	3.60	6.00	
L- 5	Porgy—D. B. Heyward	1.20	3.60	6.00	
L- 6	Great Poems From Chaucer to Whitman—L. Untermeyer	1.20	3.60	6.00	
L- 7	What Became of Anna Bolton—Louis Bromfield	1.20	3.60	6.00	
L- 8	Montana Rides Again—Evan Evans (Max Brand)	1.20	3.60	6.00	W
L- 9	The Sheriff's Son—William MacLeod Raine	1.20	3.60	6.00	W
L-10	Happy Stories Just to Laugh At—Stephen Leacock	1.20	3.60	6.00	H
L-11	Roaring River Range—A. H. Gooden	1.60	4.80	8.00	W
L-12	There's One in Every Family—F. Eisenberg	1.20	3.60	6.00	
L-13	The King Bird Rides—Max Brand	1.20	3.60	6.00	W
L-14	The Sea Is So Wide—E. Eaton	1.20	3.60	6.00	
L-15	Omoo—Hermen Melville	1.60	4.80	8.00	A
L-16	Hackberry Cavalier—G. S. Perry	1.20	3.60	6.00	

Armed Services Editions G-209

Armed Services Editions M-2

Armed Services Editions S-20

(ARMED SERVICES EDITIONS, continued)

		Good	Fine	N/Mint	
L-17	Turnabout—Thorne Smith	1.60	4.80	8.00	
L-18	400 Million Customers—C. Crow	1.20	3.60	6.00	
L-19	Fish and Tin Fish—Philip Wylie	1.20	3.60	6.00	
L-20	Eminent Victorians—L. Strachey	1.20	3.60	6.00	
L-21	Country Cured—Homer Croy	1.20	3.60	6.00	
L-22	Science at War—G. W. Gray	1.20	3.60	6.00	NF
L-23	Bedford Village—Hervey Allen	1.20	3.60	6.00	
L-24	The Lady and the Arsenic—J. Shearing	1.20	3.60	6.00	
L-25	Dracula—Bram Stoker	7.00	21.00	35.00	HO
L-26	Wickford Point—J. P. Marquand	1.20	3.60	6.00	
L-27	I, Claudius—Robert Graves	1.20	3.60	6.00	B
L-28	Selected Short Stories—Thomas Mann	1.20	3.60	6.00	
L-29	Lust for Life—Irving Stone	1.20	3.60	6.00	B
L-30	Of Human Bondage—W. Somerset Maugham	1.60	4.80	8.00	
L-31	The Land Is Bright—A. Binns	1.20	3.60	6.00	
L-32	Four Years in Paradise—Ona Johnson	1.20	3.60	6.00	
M- 1	Selected Poems—A. E. Houseman; 1944	1.20	3.60	6.00	
M- 2	Is Sex Necessary—James Thurber	1.60	4.80	8.00	H
M- 3	Selected Short Stories of ''Saki''—H. H. Munro	1.60	4.80	8.00	
M- 4	20,000 Leagues Under the Sea or David Copperfield—Robert Benchley	1.60	4.80	8.00	
M- 5	Pere Marquette—A. Repplier	1.20	3.60	6.00	
M- 6	Copper Streak Trail—Eugene Manlove Rhodes	1.20	3.60	6.00	W
M- 7	Dune Boy—E. W. Teale	1.20	3.60	6.00	
M- 8	Paul Bunyon—J. Stevens	1.20	3.60	6.00	
M- 9	Science Yearbook of 1944—J. D. Ratcliff	1.20	3.60	6.00	NF
M-10	The Chicken-wagon Family—B. Benefield	1.20	3.60	6.00	
M-11	The Big Ones Get Away—Philip Wylie	1.20	3.60	6.00	
M-12	Old McDonald Had a Farm—A. McDonald	1.20	3.60	6.00	
M-13	Action by Night—Ernest Haycox	1.20	3.60	6.00	W
M-14	The Border Kid—Max Brand	1.20	3.60	6.00	W
M-15	Fighting Men of the West—Dane Coolidge	1.20	3.60	6.00	W
M-16	Tarzan of the Apes—Edgar Rice Burroughs	10.00	30.00	50.00	A
M-17	The Boomer—H. Bedwell	1.20	3.60	6.00	
M-18	Such Interesting People—R. J. Casey	1.20	3.60	6.00	
M-19	Call Her Rosie—E. Bruce	1.20	3.60	6.00	
M-20	Larrish Hundred—A. R. B. Giddings	1.20	3.60	6.00	
M-21	Country Editor—H. B. Hough	1.20	3.60	6.00	
M-22	With a Dutch Accent—D. C. DeJong	1.20	3.60	6.00	
M-23	Four Modern American Plays—Hellman, Thurber, Nugent, Chodorov, Fields, & Kingsley	1.20	3.60	6.00	
M-24	A Treasury of the Worlds Great Letters—M. L. Schuster	1.20	3.60	6.00	
M-25	Indigo—C. Weston	1.20	3.60	6.00	
M-26	Barnum—M. R. Werner	1.20	3.60	6.00	
M-27	Show Me a Land—M. R. McMeekin	1.20	3.60	6.00	
M-28	New Stories for Men—Capt. C. Grayson	1.20	3.60	6.00	
M-29	The Moonstone—Wilkie Collins	1.60	4.80	8.00	M
M-30	Der Fuehrer—K. Heiden	1.20	3.60	6.00	
M-31	Stars on the Sea—F. Van Wyck Mason	1.20	3.60	6.00	
M-32	While Still We Live—Helen MacInnes	1.20	3.60	6.00	
N- 1	The Mysterious Stranger—Mark Twain; 1944	2.00	6.00	10.00	
N- 2	The Dream Department—S. J. Perelman	1.20	3.60	6.00	H
N- 3	America—Stephen Vincent Benet	1.20	3.60	6.00	
N- 4	The Man Nobody Knows—Bruce Barton	1.20	3.60	6.00	
N- 5	The Crock of Gold—J. Stevens	1.20	3.60	6.00	
N- 6	Selected Poems—Carl Sandburg	1.60	4.80	8.00	
N- 7	Let Your Mind Alone—James Thurber	1.60	4.80	8.00	
N- 8	We Pointed Them North—E. C. Abbot	1.20	3.60	6.00	
N- 9	Rim of the Desert—Ernest Haycox	1.20	3.60	6.00	W

		Good	Fine	N/Mint	
N-10	Useless Cowboy—Alan Lemay	1.20	3.60	6.00	W
N-11	The Fallen Sparrow—Dorothy B. Hughes	1.60	4.80	8.00	M
N-12	Snow Above Town—D. Hough	1.20	3.60	6.00	
N-13	Kidnapped—Robert Louis Stevenson	2.00	6.00	10.00	A
N-14	The Summing Up—W. Somerset Maugham	1.20	3.60	6.00	
N-15	The Iron Trail—Max Brand	1.20	3.60	6.00	W
N-16	Riata and Spurs—Charles A. Siringo	1.20	3.60	6.00	W
N-17	Duel in the Sun—Niven Busch	1.20	3.60	6.00	W
N-18	Thunder Mountain—Theodore Pratt	1.20	3.60	6.00	
N-19	I Dive for Treasure—H. E. Riesenberg	1.20	3.60	6.00	
N-20	Prophet by Experience—Jack Iams	1.20	3.60	6.00	
N-21	Hangman's House—D. Byrne	1.20	3.60	6.00	
N-22	The Great American Novel—C. B. Davis	1.20	3.60	6.00	
N-23	Fire Bell in the Night—C. Robertson	1.20	3.60	6.00	
N-24	Bonin—R. Standish	1.20	3.60	6.00	
N-25	Mathematics and the Imagination—J. Newman	1.20	3.60	6.00	
N-26	Magnus Merriman—E. Linklater	1.20	3.60	6.00	
N-27	Look Away, Look Away—L. T. White	1.20	3.60	6.00	
N-28	Martin Eden—Jack London	1.60	4.80	8.00	A
N-29	The Turning Wheels—Stuart Cloete	1.20	3.60	6.00	
N-30	Perilous Journey—C. M. Sublette	1.20	3.60	6.00	
N-31	David Copperfield—Charles Dickens	2.00	6.00	10.00	
N-32	The Big Rock Candy Mountain—Wallace Stegner	1.20	3.60	6.00	
O- 1	Selected Poems—Percy Bysshe Shelley; 1945	1.20	3.60	6.00	
O- 2	The Prophet—Kahlil Gibran	1.60	4.80	8.00	
O- 3	The Art of Illusion—J. Mulholland	1.20	3.60	6.00	
O- 4	They Played the Game—H. Grayson	1.20	3.60	6.00	
O- 5	Tales of the Pampas—W. H. Hudson	1.20	3.60	6.00	A
O- 6	Plowmans Folly—E. H. Faulkner	1.20	3.60	6.00	
O- 7	Mr. Glencannon Ignores the War—Guy Gilpatric	1.20	3.60	6.00	
O- 8	My Dear Bella—A. Kober	1.20	3.60	6.00	
O- 9	Donovan's Brain—Curt Siodmak	4.00	12.00	20.00	SF
O-10	Wild Horse Shorty—C. Nelson Nye	1.20	3.60	6.00	
O-11	Journey Into the Fog—C. Goodhue	1.20	3.60	6.00	
O-12	The African Queen—C. S. Forester	1.20	3.60	6.00	A
O-13	Lost Worlds—A. T. White	1.20	3.60	6.00	
O-14	I Never Left Home—B. Hope	1.20	3.60	6.00	
O-15	Island in the Sky—Ernest K. Gann	1.60	4.80	8.00	A
O-16	Crazy Weather—C. L. McNichols	1.20	3.60	6.00	
O-17	Nobody Lives Forever—W. R. Burnett	2.00	6.00	10.00	M
O-18	Runyon A La Carte—Damon Runyon	1.60	4.80	8.00	
O-19	The Lost Weekend—Charles Jackson	1.60	4.80	8.00	
O-20	Selected Short Stories—John Russell	1.60	4.80	8.00	
O-21	On the Danger Line—Georges Simenon	1.60	4.80	8.00	M
O-22	The Return of Tarzan—Edgar Rice Burroughs	10.00	30.00	50.00	A
O-23	Men Like Gods—R. Sturgis	1.20	3.60	6.00	
O-24	The Three Black Pennies—J. Hergesheimer	1.20	3.60	6.00	
O-25	Selwood of Sleepy Cat—Frank Spearman	1.20	3.60	6.00	W
O-26	We Live in Alaska—C. Helmericks	1.20	3.60	6.00	
O-27	The Red Cock Crows—F. Gaither	1.20	3.60	6.00	
O-28	Selected Short Stories—M. R. James	1.60	4.80	8.00	
O-29	Leave Her to Heaven—B. A. Williams	1.20	3.60	6.00	
O-30	Blessed Are the Meek—Z. Kozzak	1.20	3.60	6.00	
O-31	Look Homeward Angel—Thomas Wolfe	1.60	4.80	8.00	
O-32	Look to the Mountain—L. Cannon, Jr.	1.20	3.60	6.00	
P- 1	Lady Into Fox—D. Garnett; 1945	1.20	3.60	6.00	
P- 2	Boomerang—W. Chambliss	1.20	3.60	6.00	C
P- 3	Rookie of the Year—John R. Tunis	1.20	3.60	6.00	S
P- 4	Hotel Splendide—L. Bemelmans	1.20	3.60	6.00	
P- 5	Lost Island—James Norman Hall	1.60	4.80	8.00	A
P- 6	Not Quite Dead Enough—Rex Stout	2.00	6.00	10.00	M
P- 7	The Great Bustard and Other People—Will Cuppy	1.20	3.60	6.00	
P- 8	The Fighting Four—Max Brand	1.20	3.60	6.00	W
P- 9	Valley of the Sky—H. D. Skidmore	1.20	3.60	6.00	
P-10	The Kingdom of Swing—Goodman & Kolodin	1.20	3.60	6.00	NF
P-11	Lie Down in Darkness—H. R. Hays	1.20	3.60	6.00	
P-12	The Valley of Silent Men—James Oliver Curwood	1.20	3.60	6.00	A
P-13	Mother Wore Tights—M. Young	1.20	3.60	6.00	
P-14	Pilotin' Come Natural—F. Way, Jr.	1.20	3.60	6.00	
P-15	Starlight Pass—Tom Gill	1.20	3.60	6.00	W
P-16	Trail Town—Ernest Haycox	1.20	3.60	6.00	W
P-17	Blood Upon the Snow—Hilda Lawrence	1.60	4.80	8.00	M
P-18	Many Happy Days I've Squandered—A. Loveridge	1.20	3.60	6.00	
P-19	Stories by Erskine Caldwell—Erskine Caldwell	1.20	3.60	6.00	
P-20	Danger Is My Business—Capt. J. D. Craig	1.20	3.60	6.00	
P-21	Botts in War, Botts in Peace—W. H. Upson	1.20	3.60	6.00	
P-22	World's Great Humorous Stories—I. S. Cobb	1.20	3.60	6.00	

		Good	Fine	N/Mint	
P-23	Aunt Beardie—J. Shearing	1.20	3.60	6.00	
P-24	Rebellion of Leo McGuire—C. B. Davis	1.20	3.60	6.00	
P-25	O. Henry Prize Stories—H. Brickell	1.20	3.60	6.00	
P-26	One Mans Meat—E. B. White	1.20	3.60	6.00	
P-27	Dragonwyck—Anna Seton	1.20	3.60	6.00	
P-28	Slogum House—Mari Sandoz	1.20	3.60	6.00	
P-29	The Republic—C. A. Beard	1.20	3.60	6.00	
P-30	Brave Men—Ernie Pyle	1.20	3.60	6.00	NF
P-31	A Treasury of Science—H. Shapley	1.20	3.60	6.00	NF
P-32	Yankee From Olympus—C. D. Bowen	1.20	3.60	6.00	
Q- 1	Excuse It, Please!—Cornelia Otis Skinner; 1945	1.20	3.60	6.00	
Q- 2	The Postman Always Rings Twice—James M. Cain	1.60	4.80	8.00	M
Q- 3	The Story of George Gershwin—D. Ewen	1.20	3.60	6.00	B
Q- 4	The Education of T. C. Mits—L. R. Lieber & H. Gray	1.20	3.60	6.00	
Q- 5	The Feather Merchants—Max Shulman	1.20	3.60	6.00	
Q- 6	The World Ends at Hoboken—M. Heimer	1.20	3.60	6.00	
Q- 7	High Time—M. Lasswell	1.20	3.60	6.00	
Q- 8	Keystone Kids—John R. Tunis	1.20	3.60	6.00	S
Q- 9	Selected Short Stories—S. Anderson	1.20	3.60	6.00	
Q-10	Give 'em the Ax—A. A. Fair	1.60	4.80	8.00	M
Q-11	Prairie Guns—E. E. Halleran	1.20	3.60	6.00	W
Q-12	Watch Out for Willie Carter—T. Naidish	1.20	3.60	6.00	
Q-13	The Passionate Witch—Thorne Smith	1.60	4.80	8.00	H
Q-14	Guerrilla—Lord Dunsany	3.00	9.00	15.00	
Q-15	The Corpse Without a Clue—R. A. J. Walling	1.60	4.80	8.00	M
Q-16	Man in the Saddle—Ernest Haycox	1.20	3.60	6.00	W
Q-17	The Amethyst Spectacles—Frances Crane	1.60	4.80	8.00	M
Q-18	Beat to Quarters—C. S. Forester	1.20	3.60	6.00	A
Q-19	The Heritage of the Desert—Zane Grey	1.20	3.60	6.00	W
Q-20	Devil on His Trail—John & Ward Hawkins	1.20	3.60	6.00	W
Q-21	Salt Water Daffy—Philip Wylie	1.20	3.60	6.00	
Q-22	The House of Cobwebs—M. Reisner	1.20	3.60	6.00	
Q-23	Luck in All Weather—D. H. Haines	1.20	3.60	6.00	
Q-24	Happy Jack—Max Brand	1.20	3.60	6.00	W
Q-25	Mom Counted Six—M. Gardner	1.20	3.60	6.00	
Q-26	Take Them Up Tenderly—M. C. Harriman	1.20	3.60	6.00	
Q-27	The Green Years—A. J. Cronin	1.20	3.60	6.00	
Q-28	The Saddle and the Plow—R. M. Taylor	1.20	3.60	6.00	
Q-29	The Lively Lady—K. Roberts	1.20	3.60	6.00	
Q-30	Reckon With the River—C. McMeekin	1.20	3.60	6.00	
Q-31	The Razor's Edge—W. Somerset Maugham	1.60	4.80	8.00	
Q-32	Strange Fruit—Lillian Smith	1.20	3.60	6.00	
Q-33	The Seventh Cross—A. Seghers	1.20	3.60	6.00	
Q-34	Wild Is the River—Louis Bromfield	1.20	3.60	6.00	
Q-35	Selected Plays—Eugene O'Neill	1.20	3.60	6.00	
Q-36	The Shadow and the Glory—John Jennings	1.60	4.80	8.00	
Q-37	Time Out of Mind—R. Field	1.20	3.60	6.00	
Q-38	The Sea Witch—A. Laing	1.20	3.60	6.00	
Q-39	The Strange Woman—B. A. Williams	1.20	3.60	6.00	
Q-40	The Education of Henry Adams—Henry Adams	1.20	3.60	6.00	
R- 1	The Ugly Dachshund—G. B. Stern; 1945	1.20	3.60	6.00	
R- 2	Selected Poems—John Keats	1.20	3.60	6.00	
R- 3	One More Spring—Robert Nathan	1.20	3.60	6.00	
R- 4	Selected Short Stories—Dorothy Parker	1.20	3.60	6.00	
R- 5	After 1903 - What?—Robert Benchley	1.20	3.60	6.00	
R- 6	Psychology You Can Use—W. H. Roberts	1.20	3.60	6.00	NF
R- 7	Selected Radio Plays—N. Corwin	1.20	3.60	6.00	
R- 8	You Wouldn't Know Me From Adam—Col. Stoopnagle	1.20	3.60	6.00	
R- 9	Sea Duty—J. Marmur	1.20	3.60	6.00	
R-10	The Dark Page—S. M. Fuller	1.20	3.60	6.00	
R-11	War on the Cimarron—Luke Short	1.20	3.60	6.00	W
R-12	Geography in Human Destiny—R. Peattie	1.20	3.60	6.00	NF
R-13	Bermuda Calling—David Garth	1.20	3.60	6.00	
R-14	A Shorter History of Science—Sir W. C. Dampier	1.20	3.60	6.00	NF
R-15	Crime on My Hands—G. Sanders	1.60	4.80	8.00	
R-16	The American Character—D. W. Brogan	1.20	3.60	6.00	
R-17	Our Hearts Were Young and Gay—Kimbrough & Skinner	1.20	3.60	6.00	
R-18	Winter Range—Alan LeMay	1.20	3.60	6.00	W
R-19	The Gaunt Woman—E. Gilligan	1.20	3.60	6.00	
R-20	Painted Buttes—A. H. Gooden	1.60	4.80	8.00	W
R-21	Selected Short Stories—K. A. Porter	1.20	3.60	6.00	
R-22	Cluny Brown—M. Sharp	1.20	3.60	6.00	
R-23	Of Men and Music—Deems Taylor	1.20	3.60	6.00	NF
R-24	The Long Chance—Max Brand	1.20	3.60	6.00	W
R-25	Kitty Foyle—Christopher Morley	1.20	3.60	6.00	
R-26	Combustion on Wheels—D. L. Cohn	1.20	3.60	6.00	
R-27	Earth and High Heaven—G. Graham	1.20	3.60	6.00	

		Good	Fine	N/Mint	
R-28	Young 'Un—H. Best	1.20	3.60	6.00	
R-29	Gamble's Hundred—C. Dowdey	1.20	3.60	6.00	
R-30	The Bridal Wreath—S. Undset	1.20	3.60	6.00	
R-31	Try and Stop Me—Bennett Cerf	1.20	3.60	6.00	
R-32	Captain Blood—Rafael Sabatini	1.60	4.80	8.00	A
R-33	Sleep No More—August Derleth	3.00	9.00	15.00	
R-34	Of Smiling Peace—S. Heym	1.20	3.60	6.00	
R-35	The Time for Decision—S. Welles	1.20	3.60	6.00	
R-36	For My Great Folly—Thomas B. Costain	1.20	3.60	6.00	
R-37	Disputed Passage—Lloyd C. Douglas	1.20	3.60	6.00	
R-38	The Way Our People Lived—W. E. Woodward	1.20	3.60	6.00	
R-39	Deep River—H. Buckmaster	1.20	3.60	6.00	
R-40	Canal Town—S. H. Adams	1.20	3.60	6.00	
S- 1	A Wartime Whitman—Maj. W. A. Aiken; 1945	1.20	3.60	6.00	
S- 2	Dear Baby—William Saroyan	1.20	3.60	6.00	
S- 3	I Love You, I Love You, I Love You—L. Bemelmans	1.20	3.60	6.00	
S- 4	Castaway—J. G. Cozzens	1.20	3.60	6.00	
S- 5	My World and Welcome to It—James Thurber	1.60	4.80	8.00	H
S- 6	Peace Marshal—Frank Gruber	1.20	3.60	6.00	W
S- 7	Not Too Narrow, Not Too Deep—Richard Sale	1.60	4.80	8.00	M
S- 8	Selected Short Stories—Philip Wylie	1.20	3.60	6.00	
S- 9	Selected Short Stories—Mark Twain	2.00	6.00	10.00	
S-10	Young Man With a Horn—D. Baker	1.20	3.60	6.00	
S-11	A Pearl in Every Oyster—F. Sullivan	1.20	3.60	6.00	
S-12	Unexpected Uncle—Eric Hatch	1.20	3.60	6.00	
S-13	The Mauve Decade—T. Beer	1.20	3.60	6.00	
S-14	In What Torn Ship—E. Eaton	1.20	3.60	6.00	
S-15	Clipper Ship Men—A. Laing	1.20	3.60	6.00	
S-16	Alarum and Excursion—V. Perdue	1.20	3.60	6.00	
S-17	Captain Retread—D. Hough	1.20	3.60	6.00	
S-18	Guns of the Frontier—William MacLeod Raine	1.20	3.60	6.00	W
S-19	Your Kids and Mine—J. E. Brown	1.20	3.60	6.00	
S-20	After-dinner Story—William Irish	2.00	6.00	10.00	M
S-21	The Case of the Black-eyed Blonde—Erle Stanley Gardner	1.60	4.80	8.00	M
S-22	Lost in the Horse Latitudes—H. Allen Smith	1.20	3.60	6.00	H
S-23	Hunted Riders—Max Brand	1.20	3.60	6.00	W
S-24	The Ox-bow Incident—W. Van Tillburg Clark	2.00	6.00	10.00	
S-25	The St. Louis Cardinals—F. G. Lieb	1.20	3.60	6.00	S
S-26	Selected Short Stories—Algernon Blackwood	2.00	6.00	10.00	
S-27	An Almanac for Moderns—D. C. Peattie	1.20	3.60	6.00	
S-28	The Night Life of the Gods—Thorne Smith	1.60	4.80	8.00	H
S-29	People on Our Side—E. Snow	1.20	3.60	6.00	
S-30	The Great Lakes—H. Hatcher	1.20	3.60	6.00	
S-31	The Farm—Louis Bromfield	1.20	3.60	6.00	
S-32	The Bolinvars—M. F. Bayliss	1.20	3.60	6.00	
S-33	The Yearling—M. K. Rawlings	1.20	3.60	6.00	
S-34	Klondike Mike—M. Denison	1.20	3.60	6.00	
S-35	Henry Esmond—W. M. Thackery	1.20	3.60	6.00	
S-36	The History of Rome Hanks—J. S. Pennell	1.20	3.60	6.00	
S-37	Henry the Eighth—F. Hackett	1.20	3.60	6.00	
S-38	Arundel—Kenneth Roberts	1.20	3.60	6.00	
S-39	Green Dolphin Street—E. Goudge	1.20	3.60	6.00	
S-40	Boston Adventure—J. Stafford	1.20	3.60	6.00	
T- 1	Dithers and Jitters—C. O. Skinner; 1945	1.20	3.60	6.00	
T- 2	The Time Machine—H. G. Wells	5.00	15.00	25.00	SF
T- 3	Anything Can Happen—G. & H. Papashvily	1.20	3.60	6.00	
T- 4	Men of Popular Music—D. Ewen	1.20	3.60	6.00	NF
T- 5	Cannery Row—John Steinbeck	2.00	6.00	10.00	
T- 6	This Is Murder—T. Fuller	1.20	3.60	6.00	
T- 7	A Smattering of Ignorance—Oscar Levant	1.20	3.60	6.00	H
T- 8	The Fireside Book of Verse—Louis Untermeyer	1.20	3.60	6.00	
T- 9	Coming, Major!—W. & Stone E. Melick	1.20	3.60	6.00	
T-10	Men Against the Sea—Charles Nordhoff & James Norman Hall	2.00	6.00	10.00	A
T-11	We Farm for a Hobby and Make It Pay—H. Tetlow	1.20	3.60	6.00	
T-12	The Stone of Chastity—M. Sharp	1.20	3.60	6.00	
T-13	Benchley Beside Himself—Robert Benchley	1.60	4.80	8.00	H
T-14	Gentle Annie—MacKinlay Kantor	1.20	3.60	6.00	
T-15	The Outlaw Years—R. M. Coates	1.20	3.60	6.00	
T-16	The Range Boss—Charles Alden Seltzer	1.20	3.60	6.00	W
T-17	Puzzle for Puppets—Patrick Quentin	1.60	4.80	8.00	M
T-18	Daisy Miller and Other Stories—Henry James	1.20	3.60	6.00	
T-19	Ridin' the Rainbow—R. Taylor	1.20	3.60	6.00	
T-20	Pistol Passport—Eugene Cunningham	1.20	3.60	6.00	W
T-21	Riders of the Plains—Max Brand	1.20	3.60	6.00	W
T-22	Tunnel From Calais—D. Rame	1.20	3.60	6.00	
T-23	The Edge of Running Water—William Sloane	1.20	3.60	6.00	
T-24	The New York Yankees—F. Graham	1.20	3.60	6.00	S

		Good	Fine	N/Mint	
T-25	The Best Plays of 1943-44—B. Mantle	1.20	3.60	6.00	
T-26	Freedom Road—Howard Fast	1.20	3.60	6.00	
T-27	Blow for a Landing—B. L. Burman	1.20	3.60	6.00	
T-28	Wolf Law and Three Other Stories—Nafziger Foster	1.20	3.60	6.00	
T-29	The General's Lady—E. Forbes	1.20	3.60	6.00	
T-30	Genesee Fever—C. Carmer	1.20	3.60	6.00	
T-31	Battle Report—Karig & Kelley	1.20	3.60	6.00	C
T-32	The World We Live In—Louis Bromfield	1.20	3.60	6.00	
T-33	The Citadel—A. J. Cronin	1.20	3.60	6.00	
T-34	Whistle Stop—M. M. Wolff	1.20	3.60	6.00	
T-35	The Loon Feather—I. Fuller	1.20	3.60	6.00	
T-36	Rebecca—Daphne DuMaurier	1.20	3.60	6.00	
T-37	Delilah—M. Goodrich	1.20	3.60	6.00	
T-38	Arctic Adventure—Peter Freuchen	1.20	3.60	6.00	A
T-39	Forever Amber—K. Winsor	1.60	4.80	8.00	
T-40	Anna and the King of Siam—Margaret Landon	1.60	4.80	8.00	
655	Portrait of Jenny—R. Nathan; 1945	1.20	3.60	6.00	
656	Adventures of Superman—George Lowther	15.00	45.00	75.00	A
657	Barefoot Boy With Cheek—Max Shulman	1.20	3.60	6.00	H
658	The Charge of the Light Brigade—Alfred Lord Tennyson	1.60	4.80	8.00	
659	What's on Your Mind?—J. Dunninger	1.20	3.60	6.00	
660	The Outermost House—H. Beston	1.20	3.60	6.00	
661	Look to the Frontiers—R. Peattie	1.20	3.60	6.00	
662	My Family, Right or Wrong—J. P. Sousa, III	1.20	3.60	6.00	
663	Murder and the Married Virgin—Brett Halliday	1.60	4.80	8.00	M
664	Where Away—Perry & Leighton	1.20	3.60	6.00	
665	The Old Dark House—J. B. Priestley	1.60	4.80	8.00	
666	Laura—Vera Caspary	1.20	3.60	6.00	
667	To Have and Have Not—Ernest Hemingway	1.60	4.80	8.00	
668	Mrs. Egg and Other Barbarians—T. Beer	1.20	3.60	6.00	
669	Mademoiselle Fifi and Other Stories—Guy de Maupassant	1.20	3.60	6.00	
670	Gunman's Chance—Luke Short	1.20	3.60	6.00	W
671	The Glorious Pool—Thorne Smith	1.60	4.80	8.00	F
672	White Fang—Jack London	2.00	6.00	10.00	A
673	Low Man on a Totem Pole—H. Allen Smith	1.20	3.60	6.00	
674	Trail's End—William MacLeod Raine	1.20	3.60	6.00	W
675	The 17th Letter—D. C. Disney	1.20	3.60	6.00	
676	Esquire's Jazz Book 1944—P. E. Miller	1.20	3.60	6.00	
677	Selected Short Stories—Walter D. Edmonds	1.20	3.60	6.00	
678	Western Union—Zane Grey	1.20	3.60	6.00	W
679	The Captain From Connecticut—C. S. Forester	1.20	3.60	6.00	A
680	Calamity Town—Ellery Queen	1.60	4.80	8.00	M
681	Tomorrow Will Sing—E. Arnold	1.20	3.60	6.00	
682	Science Remakes the World—J. Stokley	1.20	3.60	6.00	
683	Bugles in the Afternoon—Ernest Haycox	1.60	4.80	8.00	W
684	Prodigal Genius—J. J. O'Neill	1.20	3.60	6.00	
685	The Cadavar of Gideon Wyck—A. Laing	1.20	3.60	6.00	
686	Western Story Omnibus—W. Targ	1.20	3.60	6.00	W
687	Seven Gothic Tales—I. Dinesen	1.20	3.60	6.00	
688	Barren Ground—E. Glasgow	1.20	3.60	6.00	
689	Great Smith—Edison Marshall	1.20	3.60	6.00	A
690	The Grapes of Wrath—John Steinbeck	2.00	6.00	10.00	
691	Pickwick Papers—Charles Dickens	2.00	6.00	10.00	
692	Lock, Stock and Barrel—D. & E. Rigby	1.20	3.60	6.00	
693	Immortal Wife—Irving Stone	1.20	3.60	6.00	
694	Journey in the Dark—M. Flavin	1.20	3.60	6.00	
695	The McKenneys Carry On—R. McKenney; 1945	1.20	3.60	6.00	
696	Quo Vadimus?—E. B. White	1.20	3.60	6.00	
697	Thunder Over the Bronx—A. Kober	1.20	3.60	6.00	
698	The Island of Dr. Moreau—H. G. Wells	6.00	18.00	30.00	HO
699	Meet Me in St. Louis—S. Benson	1.20	3.60	6.00	
700	A Home in the Century—F. F. Vam de Water	1.20	3.60	6.00	
701	Another Claudia—R. Franken	1.20	3.60	6.00	
702	I Am Gazing Into My 8-Ball—Earl Wilson	1.20	3.60	6.00	
703	The Pastures of Heaven—John Steinbeck	2.00	6.00	10.00	
704	Paul Revere's Ride and Other Poems—H. W. Longfellow	1.20	3.60	6.00	
705	The Middle-Aged Man on the Flying Trapeze—James Thurber	1.60	4.80	8.00	
706	Deep West—Ernest Haycox	1.20	3.60	6.00	W
707	Arizona—Clarence Buddington Kelland	1.20	3.60	6.00	W
708	Cow by the Tail—J. J. Benton	1.20	3.60	6.00	
709	To the Indies—C. S. Forester	1.20	3.60	6.00	A
710	Eddie and the Archangel Mike—B. Benefield	1.20	3.60	6.00	
711	Wings of Fear—Mignon G. Eberhart	1.60	4.80	8.00	M
712	The Three Mesqueteers—William Colt MacDonald	1.60	4.80	8.00	W
713	The Golden Rooms—V. Fisher	1.20	3.60	6.00	
714	Lad: A Dog—A. P. Terhune	1.20	3.60	6.00	

		Good	Fine	N/Mint	
715	Gunman's Gold—Max Brand	1.20	3.60	6.00	
716	Tall Tale America—W. Blair	1.20	3.60	6.00	
717	Webster's New Handy Dictionary—A. Merriam Webster	1.20	3.60	6.00	NF
718	Webster's New Handy Dictionary—A. Merriam Webster	1.20	3.60	6.00	NF
719	The Sad Sack—Sgt. George Baker	6.00	18.00	30.00	H
720	Voyage of the Golden Hind—E. Gilligan	1.20	3.60	6.00	
721	The Purple Land—W. H. Hudson	1.20	3.60	6.00	
722	Sunset Pass—Zane Grey	1.20	3.60	6.00	W
723	The Woman in the Window—J. H. Wallis; aka Once Off Guard	1.60	4.80	8.00	
724	South Moon Under—M. K. Rawlings	1.20	3.60	6.00	
725	Pitcairn's Island—Charles Nordhoff & James Norman Hall	2.00	6.00	10.00	A
726	Jazzmen—Ramsey & Smith	1.20	3.60	6.00	NF
727	Death and the Dancing Footman—Ngaio Marsh	1.60	4.80	8.00	M
728	Farewell to Sport—Paul Gallico	1.20	3.60	6.00	
729	Mankind So Far—W. Howells	1.20	3.60	6.00	
730	The Dunwich Horror and Other Weird Tales—H. P. Lovecraft	10.00	30.00	50.00	SF
731	...and a Few Marines—Col. J. W. Thomason	1.20	3.60	6.00	
732	Starbuck—J. Selby	1.20	3.60	6.00	
733	The Cross and the Arrow—A. Maltz	1.20	3.60	6.00	
734	Lower Than the Angels—Walter Karig	1.20	3.60	6.00	
735	A Little Night Music—G. W. Johnson; 1945	1.20	3.60	6.00	
736	My Heart Leaps Up and Other Poems—Williams Wordsworth	1.20	3.60	6.00	
737	The Enchanted Voyage—Robert Nathan	1.20	3.60	6.00	F
738	Lives—G. Eckstein	1.20	3.60	6.00	
739	Prize Winners in Special Services Art Contest	1.20	3.60	6.00	
740	Cartoons for Fighters—Sgt. F. Brandt	1.60	4.80	8.00	H
741	Pipe Night—John O'Hara	1.20	3.60	6.00	
742	Joe, the Wounded Tennis Player—M. Thompson	1.20	3.60	6.00	
743	Brag Dog and Other Stories—V. Bell	1.20	3.60	6.00	
744	Harvard Has a Homicide—T. Fuller	1.20	3.60	6.00	M
745	The War of the Worlds—H. G. Wells	6.00	18.00	30.00	SF
746	Kid Galahad—F. Wallace	1.20	3.60	6.00	
747	Death on the Aisle—Frances & Richard Lockridge	1.60	4.80	8.00	M
748	Starlight Rider—Ernest Haycox	1.20	3.60	6.00	W
749	Looking for a Bluebird—J. Wechsberg	1.20	3.60	6.00	
750	Cup of Gold—John Steinbeck	2.00	6.00	10.00	A
751	The Big Sleep—Raymond Chandler	10.00	30.00	50.00	M
752	The Valley of Dry Bones—A. H. Gooden	1.60	4.80	8.00	W
753	Diamond River Man—Eugene Cunningham	1.20	3.60	6.00	W
754	Adventures of Hiram Holliday—Paul Gallico	1.20	3.60	6.00	
755	Let Your Mind Alone—James Thurber	1.20	3.60	6.00	H
756	We Pointed Them North—Smith & Abbott	1.20	3.60	6.00	
757	The Eight Million—M. Berger	1.20	3.60	6.00	
758	Moon Tide—W. Robertson	1.20	3.60	6.00	
759	Buck Peters, Ranchman—Clarence E. Mulford	1.20	3.60	6.00	W
760	Died in the Wool—Ngaio Marsh	1.60	4.80	8.00	M
761	Keep 'em Crawling—W. H. Upson	1.20	3.60	6.00	
762	Joseph Lister—R. Truax	1.20	3.60	6.00	
763	Listen for a Lonesome Drum—C. Carmer	1.20	3.60	6.00	
764	The Asiatics—F. Prokosch	1.20	3.60	6.00	
765	Worlds Great Tales of the Sea—W. McFee	1.20	3.60	6.00	A
766	Double Indemnity and Two Other Stories—James M. Cain	1.60	4.80	8.00	M
767	Selected Stories—Edgar Allan Poe	1.60	4.80	8.00	
768	Young Ames—Walter D. Edmonds	1.20	3.60	6.00	A
769	Life With Father and Mother—Clarence Day	1.60	4.80	8.00	
770	Quietly My Captain Waits—E. Eaton	1.20	3.60	6.00	
771	Myths After Lincoln—L. Lewis	1.20	3.60	6.00	
772	The Years—V. Woolf	1.20	3.60	6.00	
773	Timber Line—G. Fowler	1.20	3.60	6.00	
774	Night Unto Night—Philip Wylie	1.20	3.60	6.00	
775	Some Like Them Short—W. March; 1945	1.20	3.60	6.00	
776	The Collected Poems—R. Brooke	1.20	3.60	6.00	
777	Canary—G. Eckstein	1.20	3.60	6.00	
778	A Genius in the Family—H. P. Maxim	1.20	3.60	6.00	
779	On Borrowed Time—L. E. Watkin	1.20	3.60	6.00	
780	Horsethief Creek—Bliss Lomax (H. S. Drago)	1.20	3.60	6.00	W
781	Lou Gehrig—F. Graham	1.20	3.60	6.00	B
782	You Know Me Al—Ring Lardner	1.20	3.60	6.00	
783	The Phantom Filly—G. Chamberlain	1.20	3.60	6.00	
784	Sheriff of Yavisa—C. H. Snow	1.20	3.60	6.00	W
785	The So Blue Marble—Dorothy B. Hughes	1.20	3.60	6.00	M
786	Blind Man's Bluff—Baynard Kendrick	1.60	4.80	8.00	M
787	Patrick Henry and the Frigate's Keel—Howard Fast	1.20	3.60	6.00	
788	The Bruiser—E. L. McKenna	1.20	3.60	6.00	
789	Payoff for the Banker—Frances & Richard Lockridge	1.60	4.80	8.00	M
790	This Is Our World—P. B. Sears	1.20	3.60	6.00	

Armed Services Editions 789

Armed Services Editions 801

Armed Services Editions 909

(ARMED SERVICES EDITIONS, continued)

		Good	Fine	N/Mint	
791	Trail Smoke—Ernest Haycox	1.20	3.60	6.00	W
792	Apartment in Athens—G. Wescott	1.20	3.60	6.00	
793	The Barefoot Mailman—Theodore Pratt	1.20	3.60	6.00	
794	The Long Valley—John Steinbeck	2.00	6.00	10.00	
795	King Solomon's Mines—H. Rider Haggard	5.00	15.00	25.00	A
796	Mr. Tutt Finds a Way—Arthur Train	1.20	3.60	6.00	
797	Forlorn River—Zane Grey	1.20	3.60	6.00	W
798	Pattern for Murder—I. S. Shriber	1.20	3.60	6.00	M
799	Butterfield 8—John O'Hara	1.60	4.80	8.00	
800	The Bishop's Wife and Two Other Novels—Robert Nathan	1.20	3.60	6.00	
801	When Worlds Collide—Edwin Balmer & Philip Wylie	4.00	12.00	20.00	SF
802	Winter's Tales—I. Dinesen	1.20	3.60	6.00	
803	Five Western Stories—Coburn, Foster, Ranger, McCulley & Wilson	1.20	3.60	6.00	W
804	Commodore Hornblower—C. S. Forester	1.20	3.60	6.00	A
805	Yankee Woman—E. Baume	1.20	3.60	6.00	
806	The Hudson—C. Carmer	1.20	3.60	6.00	
807	Sun in Their Eyes—M. Barrett	1.20	3.60	6.00	
808	Men Against Death—P. de Kruif	1.20	3.60	6.00	
809	Men of Science in America—B. Jaffe	1.20	3.60	6.00	
810	Great Stories From Great Lives—H. V. Prochnow	1.20	3.60	6.00	
811	Mrs. Parkington—Louis Bromfield	1.20	3.60	6.00	
812	The Sea Hawk—Rafael Sabatini	1.20	3.60	6.00	A
813	Author's Choice—MacKinlay Kantor	1.20	3.60	6.00	
814	Ride With Me—Thomas B. Costain	1.20	3.60	6.00	
815	The Voice of the Turtle—J. Van Druten; 1945	1.20	3.60	6.00	
816	In the Fog—R. H. Davis	1.20	3.60	6.00	
817	Pal Joey—John O'Hara	1.20	3.60	6.00	
818	Rackety Rax—J. Sayre	1.20	3.60	6.00	
819	The New Yorker's Baedeker	1.20	3.60	6.00	
820	Selected Poems—John Masefield	1.20	3.60	6.00	
821	The Half-Haunted Saloon—R. Shattuck	1.20	3.60	6.00	
822	Up Front—Bill Mauldin	1.20	3.60	6.00	H
823	O Pioneers!—Willa Cather	1.20	3.60	6.00	
824	Electronics Today and Tomorrow—J. Mills	1.20	3.60	6.00	NF
825	A Rose for Emily and Other Stories—William Faulkner	1.20	3.60	6.00	
826	Coming of Age in Samoa—Margaret Mead	1.20	3.60	6.00	NF
827	The Indigo Necklace—Frances Crane	1.60	4.80	8.00	M
828	The Delicate Ape—Dorothy B. Hughes	1.60	4.80	8.00	M
829	Payment Deferred—C. S. Forester	1.20	3.60	6.00	A
830	Buried Alive—A. Bennett	1.20	3.60	6.00	
831	Virgin With Butterflies—T. Powers	1.20	3.60	6.00	
832	The Sporting Gesture—T. L. Stix	1.20	3.60	6.00	
833	Square Deal Sanderson—Charles Alden Seltzer	1.20	3.60	6.00	W
834	Bar 20 Days—Clarence E. Mulford	1.20	3.60	6.00	W
835	American Guerilla in the Phillipines—Ira Wolfert	1.20	3.60	6.00	C
836	Claudia and David—Rose Franken	1.20	3.60	6.00	
837	Sundown Jim—Ernest Haycox	1.20	3.60	6.00	W
838	The Lady in the Lake—Raymond Chandler	10.00	30.00	50.00	M
839	River Song—H. Hamilton	1.20	3.60	6.00	
840	The Biscuit Eater and Other Stories—J. Street	1.20	3.60	6.00	
841	The Upstart—Edison Marshall	1.20	3.60	6.00	A
842	Twin Sombreros—Zane Grey	1.20	3.60	6.00	
843	Young Bess—M. Irwin	1.20	3.60	6.00	
844	Little Orvie—Booth Tarkington	1.20	3.60	6.00	
845	Pleasant Valley—Louis Bromfield	1.20	3.60	6.00	
846	McGraw of the Giants—F. Graham	1.20	3.60	6.00	
847	Cuckoo Time—R. Temple	1.20	3.60	6.00	S
848	Time to Be Young—W. Burnett	1.60	4.80	8.00	

35

		Good	Fine	N/Mint	
849	Bedford Village—Hervey Allen	1.20	3.60	6.00	
850	The Lady and the Arsenic—J. Shearing	1.20	3.60	6.00	
851	Dracula—Bram Stoker	6.00	18.00	30.00	HO
852	Wickford Point—John P. Marquand	1.20	3.60	6.00	
853	A Lion Is in the Streets—A. L. Langley	1.20	3.60	6.00	
854	Captain From Castile—Samuel Shellabarger	1.20	3.60	6.00	A
855	A Book of Americans—Stephen Vincent Benet	1.20	3.60	6.00	
856	My Life and Hard Times—James Thurber	1.60	4.80	8.00	
857	Lyrics and Sonnets—Edna St. Vincent Millay	1.20	3.60	6.00	
858	The Rumelhearts of Rampler Ave.—M. S. Delavan	1.20	3.60	6.00	
859	Tacey Cromwell—Conrad Richter	1.20	3.60	6.00	
860	The Royal Game—S. Zweig	1.20	3.60	6.00	
861	The Pearl Lagoon—Charles Nordhoff	1.60	4.80	8.00	A
862	The Great Gatsby—F. Scott Fitzgerald	2.00	6.00	10.00	
863	The Gray Champion and Other Tales—Nathaniel Hawthorne	1.60	4.80	8.00	
864	Ariel: The Life of Shelley—A. Maurois	1.20	3.60	6.00	
865	My Ten Years in a Quandry—Robert Benchley	1.60	4.80	8.00	H
866	Tragic Ground—Erskine Caldwell	1.20	3.60	6.00	
867	Rim of the Desert—Ernest Haycox	1.20	3.60	6.00	W
868	Useless Cowboy—Alan LeMay	1.20	3.60	6.00	W
869	The Fallen Sparrow—Dorothy B. Hughes	1.20	3.60	6.00	M
870	Snow Above Town—D. Hough	1.20	3.60	6.00	
871	Green Thoughts and Other Strange Tales—John Collier	3.00	9.00	15.00	F
872	Crazy Like a Fox—S. J. Perelman	1.20	3.60	6.00	H
873	The Confidential Agent—Grahan Greene	1.20	3.60	6.00	M
874	Ramrod—Luke Short	1.20	3.60	6.00	W
875	Mostly Canallers—Walter D. Edmonds	1.20	3.60	6.00	
876	The Countess to Boot—Jack Iams	1.20	3.60	6.00	M
877	Danger Trail—Max Brand	1.20	3.60	6.00	W
878	Deadline at Dawn—William Irish	2.00	6.00	10.00	M
879	Wind Before Rain—J. D. Weaver	1.20	3.60	6.00	
880	Walden—H. David Thoreau	1.60	4.80	8.00	
881	She—H. Rider Haggard	5.00	15.00	25.00	A
882	Colour Scheme—Ngaio Marsh	1.60	4.80	8.00	M
883	Desert Gold—Zane Grey	1.20	3.60	6.00	W
884	Ruggles of Red Gap—H. L. Wilson	1.20	3.60	6.00	
885	The Strange Case of Dr. Jekyll and Mr. Hyde—Robert Louis Stevenson	6.00	18.00	30.00	SF
886	White Sales Crowding—E. Gilligan	1.20	3.60	6.00	
887	The Virginian—Owen Wister	2.00	6.00	10.00	W
888	Head O'W-Hollow—J. Stuart	1.20	3.60	6.00	·
889	Five Acres and Independence—M. G. Kains	1.20	3.60	6.00	
890	Busman's Honeymoon—Dorothy L. Sayers	1.60	4.80	8.00	M
891	Hatter's Castle—A. J. Cronin	1.20	3.60	6.00	
892	The Sky's the Limit—B. A. Botkin	1.20	3.60	6.00	
893	The Loom of Language—F. Bodmer	1.20	3.60	6.00	
894	Reveille in Washington—M. Leach	1.20	3.60	6.00	
895	Dear Sir and Dumb-belles Letters—Juliet Lowell; 1946	1.20	3.60	6.00	H
896	How to Do Practically Anything—Goodman & Green	1.20	3.60	6.00	
897	Bowleg Bill—J. Digges	1.20	3.60	6.00	
898	Walls Rise Up—G. S. Perry	1.20	3.60	6.00	
899	Mr. Wilmer—R. Lawson	1.20	3.60	6.00	
900	The Full Life and Other Stories—D. D. Beauchamp	1.20	3.60	6.00	
901	The Daniel Jazz and Other Poems—V. Lindsay	1.20	3.60	6.00	
902	My Bitter Half and Other Stories—J. Weaver	1.20	3.60	6.00	
903	Keep Your Head Down—W. Bernstein	1.20	3.60	6.00	
904	The Story of Penicillin—B. Sokoloff, M.D.	1.20	3.60	6.00	
905	Lost Island—James Norman Hall	1.60	4.80	8.00	A
906	Not Quite Dead Enough—Rex Stout	1.60	4.80	8.00	
907	The Great Bustard and Other People—Will Cuppy	1.20	3.60	6.00	
908	The Fighting Four—Max Brand	1.20	3.60	6.00	
909	Frankenstein—Mary Wollstonecraft Shelley	7.00	21.00	35.00	SF
910	The Happy Time—R. Fontaine	1.20	3.60	6.00	
911	Mantrap—Sinclair Lewis	1.20	3.60	6.00	
912	Ironies—R. Connell	1.20	3.60	6.00	
913	Best Sport Stories of 1944—Marsh & Ehre	1.20	3.60	6.00	S
914	The Lucky Stiff—Craig Rice	1.60	4.80	8.00	M
915	The Case of the Golddiggers Purse—Erle Stanley Gardner	1.60	4.80	8.00	M
916	Canyon Passage—Ernest Haycox	1.20	3.60	6.00	W
917	The Trail Horde—Charles Alden Seltzer	1.20	3.60	6.00	W
918	''Tex''—Clarence E. Mulford	1.20	3.60	6.00	
919	The Folded Leaf—W. Maxwell	1.20	3.60	6.00	
920	Jazz—R. Goffin	1.20	3.60	6.00	NF
921	Concerning a Woman of Sin and Other Stories—Ben Hecht	1.20	3.60	6.00	
922	Rain in the Doorway—Thorne Smith	1.60	4.80	8.00	H
923	Aunt Beardie—J. Shearing	1.20	3.60	6.00	
924	Rebellion of Leo McGuire—C. B. Davis	1.20	3.60	6.00	
925	The Odyssey of Homer—T. E. Shaw	1.60	4.80	8.00	

		Good	Fine	N/Mint	
926	The Giaconda Smile and Other Stories—Aldous Huxley	1.20	3.60	6.00	
927	The Last Time I Saw Paris—E. Paul	1.20	3.60	6.00	
928	Fortitude—Hugh Walpole	1.20	3.60	6.00	
929	Names on the Land—G. R. Stewart	1.20	3.60	6.00	
930	God's Angry Man—L. Ehrlich	1.20	3.60	6.00	
931	A Woollcott—S. H. Adams	1.20	3.60	6.00	B
932	Two Solitudes—H. MacLennan	1.20	3.60	6.00	
933	The Bedside Tables—Peter Arno	1.20	3.60	6.00	H
934	The Best From Yank—Editors of Yank	1.20	3.60	6.00	
935	Dear Ruth—N. Krasna; 1946	1.20	3.60	6.00	
936	Set 'Em Up—J. Madden	1.20	3.60	6.00	
937	The Deadly Dove—Rufus King	1.60	4.80	8.00	M
938	Admirals of the Caribbean—F. R. Hart	1.20	3.60	6.00	
939	Love Poems—Robert & Elizabeth Barrett Browning	1.20	3.60	6.00	
940	The Great God Pan and Other Weird Stories—Arthur Machen	3.00	9.00	15.00	HO
941	Artie Greengroin, Pfc.—H. Brown	1.20	3.60	6.00	
942	The World, the Flesh and Father Smith—B. Marshall	1.20	3.60	6.00	
943	Bedelia—Vera Caspary	1.20	3.60	6.00	
944	The Ransom of Red Chief and Other Stories—O. Henry	1.60	4.80	8.00	
945	God's Little Acres—Erskine Caldwell	1.20	3.60	6.00	
946	Deadlier Than the Male—J. Gunn	1.20	3.60	6.00	
947	Comanche Kid—E. B. Mann	1.20	3.60	6.00	
948	Laugh It Off—M. E. Derrickson	1.20	3.60	6.00	
949	The Boss of the Lazy Y—Charles Alden Seltzer	1.20	3.60	6.00	W
950	Killing the Goose—Frances & Richard Lockridge	1.60	4.80	8.00	M
951	Prairie Guns—E. E. Halleran	1.20	3.60	6.00	W
952	Watch Out for Willie Carter—T. Naidish	1.20	3.60	6.00	
953	The Passionate Witch—Thorne Smith	1.60	4.80	8.00	H
954	Guerrilla—Lord Dunsany	2.00	6.00	10.00	
955	The New Yorker Profiles	1.20	3.60	6.00	
956	Cartridge Carnival—William Colt MacDonald	1.20	3.60	6.00	W
957	Winds, Blow Gently—R. Kirkbride	1.20	3.60	6.00	
958	The Food of the Gods—H. G. Wells	6.00	18.00	30.00	SF
959	Great Son—Edna Ferber	1.20	3.60	6.00	
960	Rockets and Jets—H. S. Zim	1.20	3.60	6.00	
961	Marta of Moscovy—P. Stong	1.20	3.60	6.00	
962	Science Yearbook of 1945—J. D. Ratcliff	1.20	3.60	6.00	NF
963	The Brooklyn Dodgers—F. Graham	1.20	3.60	6.00	B
964	Trail of the Money Bird—D. Ripley	1.20	3.60	6.00	S
965	Esquire's First Sports Reader—H. Graffis	1.20	3.60	6.00	S
966	So Well Remembered—J. Hilton	1.20	3.60	6.00	
967	There's Laughter in the Air!—Gaver & Stanley	1.20	3.60	6.00	
968	Rickshaw Boy—L. Shaw	1.20	3.60	6.00	
969	Cass Timberlane—Sinclair Lewis	1.60	4.80	8.00	
970	The Thurber Carnival—James Thurber	1.60	4.80	8.00	H
971	The Razor's Edge—W. Somerset Maugham	1.60	4.80	8.00	
972	Strange Fruit—Lillian Smith	1.20	3.60	6.00	
973	Against These Three—Stuart Cloete	1.20	3.60	6.00	
974	The City of Trembling Leaves—W. Van Tillburg Clark	1.20	3.60	6.00	
975	Gentlemen Overboard—H. C. Lewis; 1946	1.20	3.60	6.00	
976	My Remarkable Uncle and Other Sketches—Stewart Leacock	1.20	3.60	6.00	
977	Buy and Acre—P. Corey	1.20	3.60	6.00	
978	The Helicopters Are Coming—C. B. Macauley	1.20	3.60	6.00	
979	The Doctor's Son and Other Stories—John O'Hara	1.20	3.60	6.00	
980	Silversides—R. Trumbull	1.20	3.60	6.00	
981	i'm a Stranger Here Myself—Ogden Nash	1.20	3.60	6.00	
982	Silvertip's Search—Max Brand	1.20	3.60	6.00	W
983	An Eye for an Eye—W. Bayer	1.20	3.60	6.00	
984	The Man Who Was Thursday—G. K. Chesterton	3.00	9.00	15.00	F
985	Slow Train to Yesterday—A. Robertson	1.20	3.60	6.00	
986	Our United States Secret Service—Irving Crump	1.20	3.60	6.00	
987	''Beau'' Rand—Charles Alden Seltzer	1.20	3.60	6.00	W
988	Lay That Pistol Down—R. Powell	1.20	3.60	6.00	
989	Who Wants to Live Forever?—William MacLeod Raine	1.20	3.60	6.00	W
990	Louis Beretti—Donald Henderson Clarke	1.60	4.80	8.00	M
991	The Curse of the Bronze Lamp—Carter Dickson	2.00	6.00	10.00	M
992	Chicago Murders—S. P. Wright	1.20	3.60	6.00	
993	Sports Extra—S. Frank	1.20	3.60	6.00	
994	The Private Life of Helen of Troy—John Erskine	1.20	3.60	6.00	A
995	The Amethyst Spectacles—Frances Crane	1.60	4.80	8.00	M
996	Beat to Quarters—C. S. Forester	1.20	3.60	6.00	A
997	The Heritage of the Desert—Zane Grey	1.20	3.60	6.00	W
998	Devil on His Trail—John & Ward Hawkins	1.20	3.60	6.00	
999	Rooster Crows for a Day—P. E. Burman	1.20	3.60	6.00	
1000	Esquire's 1945 Jazz Book—P. E. Miller	1.20	3.60	6.00	NF
1001	Black Moon—C. McMeekin	1.20	3.60	6.00	

(ARMED SERVICES EDITIONS, continued)

		Good	Fine	N/Mint	
1002	Twenty Careers of Tomorrow—D. & F. Huff	1.20	3.60	6.00	
1003	Dan Sickles—E. Pinchon	1.20	3.60	6.00	
1004	January Thaw—B. Partridge	1.20	3.60	6.00	
1005	Arms and the Man and Two Other Plays—G. B. Shaw	1.20	3.60	6.00	
1006	The Birth of Mischief—Rafael Sabatini	1.20	3.60	6.00	
1007	All Brides Are Beautiful—T. Bell	1.20	3.60	6.00	
1008	Atoms in Action—G. R. Harrison	1.20	3.60	6.00	
1009	The Green Years—A. J. Cronin	1.20	3.60	6.00	
1010	The Saddle and the Plow—R. M. Taylor	1.20	3.60	6.00	
1011	Best Short Stories—Jack London	1.60	4.80	8.00	
1012	Some of These Days—S. Tucker	1.20	3.60	6.00	
1013	Of Time and the River—T. Wolfe	1.60	4.80	8.00	
1014	Northwest Passage—Kenneth Roberts	1.20	3.60	6.00	
1015	Selected Poems—A. E. Housman; 1946	1.20	3.60	6.00	
1016	Is Sex Necessary—Thurber & White	1.60	4.80	8.00	H
1017	I'll Try Anything Twice—F. Russell	1.20	3.60	6.00	
1018	Your Personal Plane—J. P. Andrews	1.20	3.60	6.00	
1019	Parlor, Bedlam and Bath—Perelman & Reynolds	1.20	3.60	6.00	H
1020	Till I Come Back to You—T. Bell	1.20	3.60	6.00	
1021	The Wolf Pack of Lobo Butte—W. C. Tuttle	1.20	3.60	6.00	W
1022	Rusty Guns—Bliss Lomax	1.20	3.60	6.00	W
1023	The State of Music—V. Thomson	1.20	3.60	6.00	NF
1024	Liberal Education—M. Van Doren	1.20	3.60	6.00	NF
1025	Dreamland—Clarence Buddington Kelland	1.20	3.60	6.00	
1026	The King Is Dead on Queen Street—F. Bonnamy	1.20	3.60	6.00	
1027	Big Ben—E. S. Miers	1.20	3.60	6.00	
1028	Red Sand—T. S. Stribling	1.20	3.60	6.00	
1029	Is It Anyone We Know?—G. Price	1.20	3.60	6.00	
1030	"Drag" Harlan—Charles Alden Seltzer	1.20	3.60	6.00	W
1031	The Corpse in the Snowman—N. Blake	1.20	3.60	6.00	
1032	Make the Most of Your Life—D. E. Lurton	1.20	3.60	6.00	
1033	O Genteel Lady!—E. Forbes	1.20	3.60	6.00	
1034	Panic—H. McCloy	1.20	3.60	6.00	
1035	Mahogany—A. Segre	1.20	3.60	6.00	
1036	Buckaroo—Eugene Cunningham	1.20	3.60	6.00	W
1037	Frank Leahy and the Fighting Irish—A. Ward	1.20	3.60	6.00	S
1038	They Tell No Tales—Manning Coles	1.60	4.80	8.00	
1039	The Case of the Half-Wakened Wife—Erle Stanley Gardner	1.60	4.80	8.00	M
1040	The Japanese Nation—J. F. Embree	1.20	3.60	6.00	NF
1041	The Lost Weekend—Charles Jackson	2.00	6.00	10.00	
1042	Selected Short Stories—J. Russell	1.20	3.60	6.00	
1043	The Diamond As Big As the Ritz and Others—F. Scott Fitzgerald	1.20	3.60	6.00	
1044	New World of Machines—H. Manchester	1.20	3.60	6.00	
1045	Storm—G. Stewart	1.20	3.60	6.00	
1046	Kabloona—G. de Poncins	1.20	3.60	6.00	
1047	Three O'Clock Dinner—J. Pinckney	1.20	3.60	6.00	
1048	Trelawny—M. Armstrong	1.20	3.60	6.00	
1049	Oil for the Lamps of China—A. T. Hobart	1.20	3.60	6.00	
1050	Modern American Short Stories—Bennett Cerf	1.20	3.60	6.00	
1051	The Builders of the Bridge—D. B. Steinman	1.20	3.60	6.00	
1052	Saints and Strangers—G. F. Willison	1.20	3.60	6.00	
1053	The White Tower—J. R. Ullman	1.20	3.60	6.00	
1054	The Stars Look Down—A. J. Cronin	1.20	3.60	6.00	
1055	Hunter's Moon and Other Stories—E. Gilligan; 1946	1.20	3.60	6.00	
1056	The Love Poems of Robert Herrick—Louis Untermeyer	1.20	3.60	6.00	
1057	Excuse It, Please!—C. O. Skinner	1.20	3.60	6.00	
1058	The Postman Always Rings Twice—James M. Cain	1.60	4.80	8.00	M
1059	The Story of George Gershwin—D. Ewen	1.20	3.60	6.00	
1060	The Education of T. C. Mits—Gray & Lieber	1.20	3.60	6.00	

Armed Services Editions 950

Armed Services Editions 1042

Armed Services Editions 1093

		Good	Fine	N/Mint	
1061	One Day on Beetle Rock—S. Carrighar	1.20	3.60	6.00	
1062	Jumper—N. Kalashnikoff	1.20	3.60	6.00	
1063	Atomic Energy in the Coming Era—David Dietz	1.20	3.60	6.00	NF
1064	Block That Bride and Other Stories—C. S. Brooks	1.20	3.60	6.00	
1065	Kazan—James Oliver Curwood	1.20	3.60	6.00	A
1066	The New Yorker Reporter at Large	1.20	3.60	6.00	
1067	Hold Autumn in Your Hand—G. S. Perry	1.20	3.60	6.00	
1068	Inside the F. B. I.—J. J. Floherty	1.20	3.60	6.00	NF
1069	The Department of Queer Complaints—Carter Dickson	3.00	9.00	15.00	M
1070	Enrico Caruso—D. Caruson	1.20	3.60	6.00	B
1071	The Vengeance of Jefferson Gawne—Charles Alden Seltzer	1.20	3.60	6.00	W
1072	The Man From Bar-20—Clarence E. Mulford	1.20	3.60	6.00	W
1073	Gold and Guns on Halfaday Creek—James B. Hendryx	1.20	3.60	6.00	W
1074	The Sunday Pigeon Murders—Craig Rice	1.60	4.80	8.00	M
1075	The Murder That Had Everything—Hulbert Footner	1.60	4.80	8.00	M
1076	Comic Relief—R. N. Linscott	1.20	3.60	6.00	H
1077	We Took to the Woods—L. D. Rich	1.20	3.60	6.00	
1078	My True Love—D. L. Teilhet	1.20	3.60	6.00	
1079	The Story of the Great Geologists—Fenton & Fenton	1.20	3.60	6.00	NF
1080	Tales by Tolstoy—Leo Tolstoy	1.60	4.80	8.00	
1081	You and Your Future Job—Campbell & Bedford	1.20	3.60	6.00	NF
1082	The Black Rose—Thomas B. Costain	1.20	3.60	6.00	A
1083	Baseball Recorder—W. Tulley; 1946	1.20	3.60	6.00	
1084	Repent in Haste—J. P. Marquand	1.20	3.60	6.00	
1085	Best Cartoons of the Year 1945—Lawrence Lariar	1.20	3.60	6.00	H
1086	The Lunatic at Large—J. S. Clouston	1.20	3.60	6.00	
1087	Biography of the Earth—G. Gamow	1.20	3.60	6.00	
1088	The Double Take—Roy Huggins	1.60	4.80	8.00	M
1089	If the Prospect Pleases—L. Haystead	1.20	3.60	6.00	
1090	Straight, Place and Show—R. S. Dowst	1.20	3.60	6.00	
1091	The War of the Worlds—H. G. Wells	4.00	12.00	20.00	SF
1092	Kid Galahad—F. Wallace	1.20	3.60	6.00	
1093	Death on the Aisle—Frances & Richard Lockridge	1.60	4.80	8.00	M
1094	Starlight Rider—Ernest Haycox	1.20	3.60	6.00	W
1095	A Small Store and Independence—Greenberg & Schindall	1.20	3.60	6.00	
1096	Steamboat Round the Bend—B. L. Burman	1.20	3.60	6.00	
1097	Out of Control—Baynard Kendrick	1.60	4.80	8.00	
1098	V As in Victim—Lawrence Treat	1.60	4.80	8.00	M
1099	Typhoon and the End of the Tether—Joseph Conrad	1.60	4.80	8.00	
1100	The Egg and I—Betty MacDonald	1.20	3.60	6.00	H
1101	The Ranchman—Charles Alden Seltzer	1.20	3.60	6.00	W
1102	My Three Years With Eisenhower—Capt. H. C. Butcher	1.20	3.60	6.00	
1103	The Well-Tempered Listener—Deems Taylor	1.20	3.60	6.00	NF
1104	The Manatee—N. Bruff	1.20	3.60	6.00	
1105	The Theory and Practice of Earning a Living—J. F. Wharton	1.20	3.60	6.00	
1106	The Big Midget Murders—Craig Rice	1.60	4.80	8.00	M
1107	The Border Legion—Zane Grey	1.20	3.60	6.00	W
1108	The Saga of Billy the Kid—Walter Noble Burns	1.20	3.60	6.00	B
1109	Mr. Digby—D. Welch	1.20	3.60	6.00	
1110	White Water and Black Magic—R. C. Gill	1.20	3.60	6.00	
1111	Saratoga Trunk—Edna Ferber	1.20	3.60	6.00	
1112	Radio's 100 Men of Science—O. E. Dunlap, Jr.	1.20	3.60	6.00	
1113	Days and Nights—K. Simonov	1.20	3.60	6.00	
1114	John Brown's Body—Stephen Vincent Benet	1.60	4.80	8.00	
1115	Prater Violet—Christopher Isherwood; 1946	1.20	3.60	6.00	
1116	The Wolf—Sgt. L. Sansone	1.20	3.60	6.00	
1117	Come in Like a Yankee and Other Stories—H. V. Dixon	1.20	3.60	6.00	
1118	Joe Louis: American—M. Miller	1.20	3.60	6.00	B
1119	The Zebra Derby—Max Shulman	1.20	3.60	6.00	
1120	Dingo—H. G. Lamond	1.20	3.60	6.00	
1121	The Crock of Gold—J. Stephens	1.20	3.60	6.00	
1122	Selected Poems—Carl Sandburg	1.60	4.80	8.00	
1123	Port of Seven Strangers—K. M. Knight	1.60	4.80	8.00	
1124	Safari—M. Johnson	1.20	3.60	6.00	
1125	The Bitter Tea of General Yen—Grace Zaring Stone	1.20	3.60	6.00	
1126	The Great American Customer—C. Crow	1.20	3.60	6.00	
1127	Valiant Is the Word for Carrie—Barry Benefield	1.20	3.60	6.00	
1128	My Greatest Day in Baseball—J. P. Carmichael	1.20	3.60	6.00	
1129	Courage Stout—William MacLeod Raine	1.20	3.60	6.00	W
1130	The Noose Is Drawn—Barber & Schabelitz	1.20	3.60	6.00	
1131	The Case of the Black-eyed Blonde—Erle Stanley Gardner	1.60	4.80	8.00	M
1132	Lost in the Horse Latitudes—H. Allen Smith	1.20	3.60	6.00	H
1133	Hunted Riders—Max Brand	1.20	3.60	6.00	W
1134	The Ox-bow Incident—Van Tilburg Clark	1.60	4.80	8.00	W
1135	Troopers West—F. Parkhill	1.20	3.60	6.00	W
1136	Woman at Bay—George Harmon Coxe	1.60	4.80	8.00	M

		Good	Fine	N/Mint	
1137	Tales for Males—E. Fitzgerald	1.20	3.60	6.00	
1138	The Small General—R. Standish	1.20	3.60	6.00	
1139	Caribbean Treasure—I. T. Sanderson	1.20	3.60	6.00	
1140	Miracles Ahead—Carlisie & Latham	1.20	3.60	6.00	
1141	The Bar-20 Three—Clarence E. Mulford	1.20	3.60	6.00	W
1142	Shakespeare—M. Van Doren	1.20	3.60	6.00	
1143	Where Do People Take Their Troubles?—L. R. Steiner	1.20	3.60	6.00	
1144	The Cherokee Strip—M. James	1.20	3.60	6.00	
1145	Modern Woman in Love—Stead & Blake	1.20	3.60	6.00	
1146	That Girl From Memphis—W. D. Steele	1.20	3.60	6.00	
1147	Pal Joey—John O'Hara; 1946	1.20	3.60	6.00	
1148	Rackety Rax—J. Sayre	1.20	3.60	6.00	
1149	Anything Can Happen—G. & H. Papashvily	1.20	3.60	6.00	
1150	Men of Popular Music—D. Ewen	1.20	3.60	6.00	NF
1151	Many Long Years Ago—Ogden Nash	1.20	3.60	6.00	
1152	Winter Meeting—Grace Zaring Stone	1.20	3.60	6.00	
1153	Wheels in His Head—M. M. Musselman	1.20	3.60	6.00	
1154	The End of the Trail—Peter Field	1.20	3.60	6.00	
1155	The Owl in the Cellar—Margaret Scherf	1.60	4.80	8.00	
1156	The Dark Ship and Other Selections From the New Yorker	1.20	3.60	6.00	
1157	The Story of the Moon—C. Fisher	1.20	3.60	6.00	
1158	The Tenderfoot—W. H. B. Kent	1.20	3.60	6.00	W
1159	It's Still Maloney—R. Maloney	1.20	3.60	6.00	
1160	Meet Your Ancestors—R. C. Andrews	1.20	3.60	6.00	
1161	Tomorrow's Another Day—W. R. Burnett	1.60	4.80	8.00	
1162	Murder Within Murder—Frances & Richard Lockridge	1.60	4.80	8.00	M
1163	Starlight Pass—Tom Gill	1.20	3.60	6.00	W
1164	Trail Town—Ernest Haycox	1.20	3.60	6.00	W
1165	The Salvation of Pisco Gabar and Other Stories—Geoffrey Household	1.60	4.80	8.00	
1166	She Came Back—P. Wentworth	1.20	3.60	6.00	
1167	Your Servant the Molecule—W. S. Landis	1.20	3.60	6.00	NF
1168	Treasure Below—E. Comm. Ellsberg	1.20	3.60	6.00	
1169	The Edge of Running Water—W. Sloane	1.20	3.60	6.00	
1170	The New York Yankees—F. Graham	1.20	3.60	6.00	S
1171	Top Stuff—H. Hart	1.20	3.60	6.00	
1172	The Gashouse Gang—J. R. Stockton	1.20	3.60	6.00	S
1173	I Wouldn't Be in Your Shoes—William Irish	2.00	6.00	10.00	M
1174	Green Fire—P. W. Ranier	1.60	4.80	8.00	
1175	Cobb's Cavalcade—B. D. Zevin	1.20	3.60	6.00	
1176	The King's General—Daphne du Maurier	1.20	3.60	6.00	
1177	Arch of Triumph—Erich Marie Remarque	1.20	3.60	6.00	C
1178	While You Were Gone—J. Goodman	1.20	3.60	6.00	
1179	Last Chapter—Ernie Pyle; 1946	1.20	3.60	6.00	C
1180	Third Avenue, New York—J. McNulty	1.20	3.60	6.00	
1181	Ravaged Range—Peter Field	1.20	3.60	6.00	W
1182	Williwaw—Gore Vidal	1.20	3.60	6.00	
1183	Outlaw on Horseback—Will Ermine	1.20	3.60	6.00	W
1184	Coroner Creek—Luke Short	1.20	3.60	6.00	W
1185	The Unforeseen—D. Macardle	2.00	6.00	10.00	F
1186	Let's Kill George—L. Cores	1.20	3.60	6.00	
1187	Lord Hornblower—C. S. Forester	1.20	3.60	6.00	A
1188	With Bated Breath—A. Campbell	1.20	3.60	6.00	
1189	A Solo in Tom-Toms—G. Fowler	1.20	3.60	6.00	
1190	The Saturday Evening Post Stories 1942-1945	1.20	3.60	6.00	
1191	Denver Murders—L. Casey; 1946	1.20	3.60	6.00	M
1192	By Way of Wyoming—C. Bishop	1.20	3.60	6.00	
1193	A Rock in Every Snowball—F. Sullivan	1.20	3.60	6.00	
1194	Death's Old Sweet Song—Jonathan Stagge	2.00	6.00	10.00	
1195	The World in His Arms—Rex Beach	1.20	3.60	6.00	A
1196	Clattering Hoofs—William MacLeod Raine	1.20	3.60	6.00	W
1197	The Chicago Cubs—W. Brown	1.20	3.60	6.00	S
1198	Man-eaters of Kumaon—James Corbett	1.20	3.60	6.00	A
1199	Jim Bridger, Mountain Man—Stanley Vestal	1.20	3.60	6.00	B
1200	Blaze of Noon—Ernest K. Gann	1.20	3.60	6.00	
1201	All the King's Men—R. P. Warren	1.60	4.80	8.00	
1202	Tell Your Sons—W. Gibbs	1.20	3.60	6.00	
1203	Mister Roberts—T. Heggen; 1946	1.20	3.60	6.00	
1204	Football Coach—A. Sampson	1.20	3.60	6.00	
1205	Benefit Performance—Richard Sale	1.60	4.80	8.00	M
1206	Double Cross Trail—E. E. Halleran	1.20	3.60	6.00	W
1207	Pikes Peek or Bust—Earl Wilson	1.20	3.60	6.00	
1208	Thunderbird Trail—William Colt MacDonald	1.20	3.60	6.00	W
1209	Stranger Than Truth—Vera Caspary	1.20	3.60	6.00	
1210	Companions of the Left Hand—G. Tabori	1.20	3.60	6.00	
1211	Green Grass of Wyoming—Mary O'Hara	1.20	3.60	6.00	
1212	Driftwood Valley—T. C. S. Fletcher	1.20	3.60	6.00	

		Good	Fine	N/Mint	
1213	The Best Stories of W. D. Steele—W. D. Steele	1.20	3.60	6.00	
1214	Under the Red Sea Sun—Com. E. Ellsworth	1.20	3.60	6.00	
1215	The Big Clock—K. Fearing; 1947	1.60	4.80	8.00	
1216	Mountain Riders—Max Brand	1.20	3.60	6.00	W
1217	Mr. Adam—Pat Frank	1.60	4.80	8.00	SF
1218	The Case of the Borrowed Brunette—Erle Stanley Gardner	1.60	4.80	8.00	M
1219	The Sudden Guest—C. LaFarge	1.20	3.60	6.00	
1220	White Man—Peter Freuchen	1.20	3.60	6.00	
1221	Frontier on the Potomac—J. Daniels	1.20	3.60	6.00	
1222	The Silent Speaker—Rex Stout	1.60	4.80	8.00	M
1223	Strange and Fantastic Stories—J. A. Margolies	1.60	4.80	8.00	
1224	Holdfast Gaines—Shepard & Shepard	1.20	3.60	6.00	
1225	B. F.'s Daughter—J. P. Marquand	1.20	3.60	6.00	
1226	The Salem Frigate—John Jennings	1.60	4.80	8.00	A
1227	Boy From Nebraska—R. G. Martin; 1947	1.20	3.60	6.00	
1228	Francis—D. Stern	1.20	3.60	6.00	H
1229	Surreptitious Entry—W. George	1.20	3.60	6.00	
1230	Courage of the North—James B. Hendryx	1.20	3.60	6.00	W
1231	Death of a Tall Man—Frances & Richard Lockridge	1.60	4.80	8.00	M
1232	The Wayward Bus—John Steinbeck	2.00	6.00	10.00	
1233	But Look, the Morn—MacKinlay Kantor	1.20	3.60	6.00	
1234	Saigon Singer—Van Wyck Mason	1.20	3.60	6.00	
1235	Fabulous Empire—F. Gibson	1.20	3.60	6.00	
1236	The Colorado—F. Waters	1.20	3.60	6.00	
1237	Eagles Fly West—E. Ainsworth	1.20	3.60	6.00	
1238	Toil of the Brave—I. Fletcher	1.20	3.60	6.00	
1239	Treasure of the Brasada—Les Savage, Jr.; 1947	1.20	3.60	6.00	W
1240	Six Gun Showdown—T. West	1.20	3.60	6.00	W
1241	The Silver Leopard—Helen Reilly	1.60	4.80	8.00	M
1242	The Face of the Clam—L. Whiteman	1.20	3:60	6.00	
1243	Command Decision—W. W. Haines	1.20	3.60	6.00	
1244	The Shadowed Trail—A. H. Gooden	1.60	4.80	8.00	W
1245	The Natural History of Nonsense—B. Evans	1.20	3.60	6.00	H
1246	My Late Wives—Carter Dickson	2.00	6.00	10.00	M
1247	The Quarry—M. Walker	1.20	3.60	6.00	
1248	Tales of the South Pacific—J. A. Michener	2.00	6.00	10.00	
1249	Look South to the Polar Star—H. Cahill	1.20	3.60	6.00	
1250	Not So Wild a Dream—Eric Sevareid	1.20	3.60	6.00	
1251	The Barber of Tubac—Nelson C. Nye; 1947	1.20	3.60	6.00	W
1252	The Magnificent Barb—D. Faralla	1.20	3.60	6.00	
1253	Mixture for Men—ed. Fred Feldkamp	1.20	3.60	6.00	
1254	Buckaroo's Code—Wayne D. Overholser	1.20	3.60	6.00	W
1255	Pick Your Victim—P. McGerr	1.60	4.80	8.00	M
1256	The Widow-Makers—M. Blankfort	1.20	3.60	6.00	
1257	The Border Bandit—Evan Evans (Max Brand)	1.20	3.60	6.00	W
1258	The Middle of Midnight—W. G. Beymer	1.20	3.60	6.00	
1259	Jeremy Bell—C. B. Davis	1.20	3.60	6.00	
1260	The Detroit Tigers—F. G. Lieb	1.20	3.60	6.00	B
1261	Wake of the Red Witch—Garland Roark	1.20	3.60	6.00	A
1262	The Walls of Jericho—Paul I. Wellman	1.20	3.60	6.00	
1263	Valley of Vanishing Men—Max Brand; 1947	1.20	3.60	6.00	W
1264	Gambler's Gold—Peter Field	1.20	3.60	6.00	W
1265	Aurora Dawn—Herman Wouk	1.20	3.60	6.00	
1266	The Strumpet Wind—G. Merrick	1.20	3.60	6.00	
1267	Long Storm—Ernest Haycox	1.20	3.60	6.00	W
1268	Gentleman's Agreement—L. Z. Hobson	1.20	3.60	6.00	
1269	Final Curtain—Ngaio Marsh	1.60	4.80	8.00	M
1270	Death of a Doll—Hilda Lawrence	1.60	4.80	8.00	M
1271	The Boston Red Sox—F. G. Lieb	1.20	3.60	6.00	S
1272	9 Lives Before Thirty—M. Manus	1.20	3.60	6.00	
1273	Blood Brother—E. Arnold	1.20	3.60	6.00	
1274	This Is the Story—D. L. Cohn	1.20	3.60	6.00	
1275	Shadow Range—C. Bishop; 1947	1.20	3.60	6.00	
1276	So Long at the Fair—A. Thorne	1.20	3.60	6.00	
1277	Silver Spurs—M. Layton	1.20	3.60	6.00	
1278	Alaska: Land of Tomorrow—E. A. Herron	1.20	3.60	6.00	
1279	With Intent to Deceive—Manning Coles	1.60	4.80	8.00	
1280	The Sleeping Sphinx—John Dickson Carr	1.60	4.80	8.00	
1281	Mr. On Loong—Robert Standish	1.20	3.60	6.00	
1282	Go-devil—M. Eyssen	1.20	3.60	6.00	
1283	There Was Once a Slave—S. Graham	1.20	3.60	6.00	
1284	My Name Is Christopher Nagel—C. W. Grafton	1.20	3.60	6.00	
1285	The Wild Yazoo—J. M. Myers	1.20	3.60	6.00	
1286	Jed Blaine's Woman—E. Wells	1.20	3.60	6.00	
1287	Within the Ropes—H. Rice; 1947	1.20	3.60	6.00	
1288	Trail Dust—Bliss Lomax	1.20	3.60	6.00	W
1289	How Green Was My Father—David Dodge	1.60	4.80	8.00	

(ARMED SERVICES EDITIONS, continued)		Good	Fine	N/Mint	
1290	The Drifting Kid—Will Ermine	1.20	3.60	6.00	W
1291	Puzzle for Pilgrims—Patrick Quentin	1.60	4.80	8.00	M
1292	Ghost of a Chance—Roos Kelley	1.20	3.60	6.00	
1293	Think of Death—Richard & Frances Lockridge	1.60	4.80	8.00	M
1294	Valley of Wild Horses—Zane Grey	1.20	3.60	6.00	W
1295	Mrs. Mike—B. & N. Freedman	1.20	3.60	6.00	
1296	Little Gate—A. Ewing	1.20	3.60	6.00	
1297	The Big Sky—A. B. Guthrie, Jr.	1.60	4.80	8.00	W
1298	Famous Stories of Code and Cipher—R. T. Bond	1.20	3.60	6.00	
1299	Hang and Rattle—A. R. Bosworth	1.20	3.60	6.00	
1300	Trail From Needle Rock—Peter Field	1.20	3.60	6.00	W
1301	Flannigan's Folly—G. Milburn	1.20	3.60	6.00	
1302	The Case of the Fan-Dancers Horse—Erle Stanley Gardner	1.60	4.80	8.00	M
1303	Blood Money—R. Bellamy	1.20	3.60	6.00	
1304	Master of the Mesa—William Colt MacDonald	1.20	3.60	6.00	W
1305	Tomorrow's a Holiday—A. Loveridge	1.20	3.60	6.00	
1306	Boston: Cradle of Liberty—John Jennings	1.20	3.60	6.00	
1307	Comrade Forest—M. Leigh	1.20	3.60	6.00	
1308	The Side of the Angels—R. McLaughlin	1.20	3.60	6.00	
1309	The Thresher—H. Krause	1.20	3.60	6.00	
1310	Vermilion—I. Jones	1.20	3.60	6.00	
1311	The False Rider—Max Brand; 1947	1.20	3.60	6.00	W
1312	The Blue Horse of Taxco—Kathleen Moore Knight	1.20	3.60	6.00	
1313	Los Angeles Murders—Craig Rice	1.60	4.80	8.00	M
1314	Passing By—E. Merrick	1.20	3.60	6.00	
1315	On My Way Home—R. Phenix	1.20	3.60	6.00	
1316	Strikeout Story—Bob Feller	1.20	3.60	6.00	S
1317	The Harder They Fall—Budd Schulberg	1.20	3.60	6.00	
1318	Raw North—C. E. Gillham	1.20	3.60	6.00	
1319	The Story of Mrs. Murphy—N. A. Scott	1.20	3.60	6.00	
1320	The Moneyman—Thomas B. Costain	1.20	3.60	6.00	
1321	Prince of Foxes—Samuel Shellabarger	1.20	3.60	6.00	A
1322	Home Country—Ernie Pyle	1.20	3.60	6.00	

ARROW MYSTERY
Arrow Publishers

Digest Size

5	Murder on High Heels—Richard Burke	1.20	3.60	6.00	M
6	Murder on Friday—Harriette Ashbrook; aka The Purple Onion Mystery	1.20	3.60	6.00	M
7	Death Takes a Redhead—Anthony Gilbert; 1944, aka Dear Dead Woman	1.20	3.60	6.00	M
8	The Kissed Corpse—Asa Baker (Brett Halliday)	1.20	3.60	6.00	M
9	Invitation to Murder—Manning Long; aka False Alarm	1.20	3.60	6.00	M
10	Death Hides a Mask—M. E. Corne	1.20	3.60	6.00	M
11	Design for Murder—Frederic Arnold Kummer	1.20	3.60	6.00	M

ASTRO
Astro Distributing Corporation

Digest Size

1	Part-Time Virgin—James Clayford	.80	2.40	4.00	E
2	Week-end Girl—James Clayford; c-Rodewald	.80	2.40	4.00	E
4	Any Man's Girl	.80	2.40	4.00	E
5	Divorce Bait	.80	2.40	4.00	E
9	Unwilling Bride—Ethel Owen; aka Romance in the Rain	.80	2.40	4.00	E

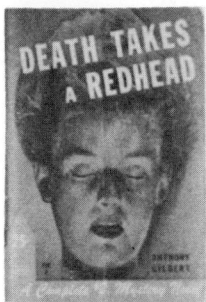

Arrow Mystery 7, © Arrow

Astro 12, © Astro

Atlas Mystery nn, © Bard Publ.

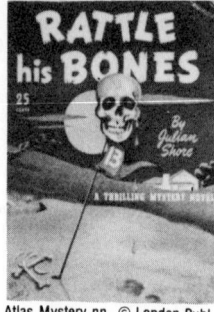

Atlas Mystery nn, © Cornell Publ.   Atlas Mystery nn, © Hercules Publ.   Atlas Mystery nn, © London Publ.

(ASTRO, continued)

		Good	Fine	N/Mint	
10	Confessions of a Good-Time Girl—Ethel Owen	.80	2.40	4.00	E
11	Confessions of a Party Wife—Helen Ahern	.80	2.40	4.00	E
12	Shakedown Dame—Dorothy Herzog; 1948, aka Undercover Woman	.80	2.40	4.00	E
14	Shameless Virgin—Peggy Gaddis; 1948, aka One More Woman	.80	2.40	4.00	E
15	Illicit Wife—James Clayford; aka Respectable? Note: Same cover as Quarter Book 69	.80	2.40	4.00	E
16	Wedding Night Confession—James Clayford; aka Wedding Night	.80	2.40	4.00	E
17	Careless Virgin—James Clayford; c-Rodewald	.80	2.40	4.00	E
18	Strange Mistress—James Clayford	.80	2.40	4.00	E
31	Overnight Girl—Joan Sherman (Peggy Gaddis); aka Overnight Cabins	.80	2.40	4.00	E

ATLAS MYSTERY
Bard Publishing Corporation

Digest Size

nn	The Corpse and the Three Ex-Husbands—Sue McVeigh	1.60	4.80	8.00	M
nn	The Singing Widow—Veronica Parker Johns; 1945	1.60	4.80	8.00	M

ATLAS MYSTERY
Cornell Publishing Corporation

Digest Size

nn	H As in Hangman—Lawrence Treat	1.60	4.80	8.00	M
nn	Murder Goes to College—Kurt Steel; 1944	1.60	4.80	8.00	M

ATLAS MYSTERY
Euclid Publishing Company

Digest Size

nn	Murder RFD—Herman Peterson	1.60	4.80	8.00	M
nn	Hush Gabriel—Veronica Parker Johns; 1944	1.60	4.80	8.00	M

ATLAS MYSTERY
Gem Publishing Company

Digest Size

nn	Murder Will In—Carolyn Wells	1.60	4.80	8.00	M
nn	Death Goes Native—Max Long; 1944	1.60	4.80	8.00	M

ATLAS MYSTERY
Hercules Publishing Corporation

Digest Size

nn	The Lisping Man—Frank Rawlings; 1944	1.60	4.80	8.00	M

ATLAS MYSTERY
London Publishing Corporation

Digest Size

		Good	Fine	N/Mint	
nn	Rattle His Bones—Julian Shore; 1944	1.60	4.80	8.00	M

ATLAS MYSTERY
Margood Publishing Company

Digest Size

nn	Murder in the House With the Blue Eyes—J. N. Darby; 1944	1.60	4.80	8.00	M

ATLAS MYSTERY
Mohawk Publishing Corporation

Digest Size

nn	Kill One, Kill Two—W. W. Anderson; 1944	1.60	4.80	8.00	M

ATLAS MYSTERY
Select Publications, Inc.

Digest Size

nn	The Golden Dress—Ione Montgomery; 1944	1.60	4.80	8.00	M
nn	Midsummer Night's Murder—Lee Crosby	1.60	4.80	8.00	M
nn	Shady Doings—Veronica Parker Johns	1.60	4.80	8.00	M

ATLAS MYSTERY
Sphere Publishing Company

Digest Size

nn	Final Appearance—Jeannette Covert Nolan	1.60	4.80	8.00	M

ATLAS MYSTERY
Vital Publications, Inc./Current Detective Stories, Inc.

Digest Size

1	Rendezvous With Dead Men—Nick Carter (John Chambliss); 1948, aka Murder on Skull Island	3.00	9.00	15.00	M
2	A Blonde for Murder—Walter B. Gibson; orig., 1948	5.00	15.00	25.00	M
3	The Yellow Disk Murder—Nick Carter (T. C. McClary); 1948, aka Power	3.00	9.00	15.00	M
5	Looks That Kill—Walter B. Gibson; orig., 1948	5.00	15.00	25.00	M

ATLAS MYSTERY
Zenith Publishing Corporation

Digest Size

nn	Murder With Long Hair—H. Donald Spatz; 1944	1.60	4.80	8.00	M
nn	The Corpse Comes Ashore—John Merserau; 1945	1.60	4.80	8.00	M

ATOMIC BOOKS
Atomic Books, Inc.

Atlas Mystery nn, © Mohawk Publ.

Atlas Mystery nn, © Select Publ.

Atlas Mystery 1, © Vital Publ.

Atomic Books nn, © Atomic   Avon 1, © Avon   Avon 3, © Avon

(ATOMIC BOOKS, continued)
Digest Size

		Good	Fine	N/Mint	
nn	The Case of the Golden Blonde—Maurice LeBlanc; 1946, Sherlock Holmes pastiche	6.00	18.00	30.00	M

AVON
Avon Book Company/New Avon Library/Avon Publishing Co., Inc./Avon Publications, Inc./Avon Book Division—Hearst Corporation

nn(1)	Elmer Gantry—Sinclair Lewis; 1941	12.50	37.50	60.00	
nn(2)	The Rubiyat of Omar Khayam—Edward Fitzgerald	5.00	15.00	25.00	
nn(3)	The Big Four—Agatha Christie	9.00	27.00	45.00	M
nn(4)	Ill Wind—James Hilton	4.00	12.00	20.00	
nn(5)	Dr. Priestly Investigates—John Rhode	6.00	18.00	30.00	M
nn(6)	The Haunted Hotel and 25 Other Ghost Stories—Wilkie Collins (ed. W. Bob Holland)	5.00	15.00	25.00	M/HO
nn(7)	The Plague Court Murders—Carter Dickson	4.00	12.00	20.00	M
nn(8)	The Corpse in the Green Pajamas—R. A. J. Walling	4.00	12.00	20.00	M
nn(9)	Willful and Premeditated—Freeman Wills Crofts	3.00	9.00	15.00	M
nn(10)	Dr. Thorndyke's Discovery—R. Austin Freeman	5.00	15.00	25.00	M
nn(11)	Count Bruga—Ben Hecht	3.00	9.00	15.00	M
nn(12)	Mosquitoes—William Faulkner	4.00	12.00	20.00	
nn(13)	Mystery at Spanish Hacienda—Jackson Gregory; 1942	3.00	9.00	15.00	M
nn(14)	Call Her Savage—Tiffany Thayer	5.00	15.00	25.00	E
nn(15)	The Avon Book of Modern Short Stories; aka My Best Story	3.00	9.00	15.00	
nn(16)	Murder at Midnight—R. A. J. Walling	4.00	12.00	20.00	M
nn(17)	The Agony Column—Earl Derr Biggers	4.00	12.00	20.00	M
nn(18)	The Man Who Murdered Himself—Geoffrey Holmes	4.00	12.00	20.00	M
nn(19)	48 Saroyan Stories—William Saroyan	3.00	9.00	15.00	
nn(20)	The League of Frightened Men—Rex Stout	5.00	15.00	25.00	M
nn(21)	The Avon Book of Modern Crime Stories—John Rhode; aka Line Up, aka Detection Medley. Note: This number was reprinted as The Avon Book of Crime and Detective Stories, and still later an abridged edition was released as The Avon Book of Detective and Crime Stories.	6.00	18.00	30.00	M
nn(22)	The Red Headed Woman—Katharine Brush	3.00	9.00	15.00	
nn(23)	Suspicious Characters—Dorothy L. Sayers; 1943	5.00	15.00	25.00	M
nn(24)	Ashenden, or the British Agent—W. Somerset Maugham	3.00	9.00	15.00	M
nn(25)	Trumpet in the Dust—Gene Fowler	3.00	9.00	15.00	
nn(26)	Seven Footprints to Satan—A. A. Merritt	8.00	24.00	40.00	SF
nn(27)	The Avon Book of Puzzles	10.00	30.00	50.00	NF
nn(28)	Tonight at 8:30—Noel Coward	4.00	12.00	20.00	

Avon 12, © Avon   Avon 21, © Avon   Avon 26, © Avon

Avon 35, © Avon

Avon 38, © Avon

Avon 44, © Avon

(AVON, continued)

		Good	Fine	N/Mint	
nn(29)	The Sabotage Murder Mystery—Margery Allingham	4.00	12.00	20.00	M
nn(30)	Gorgeous Ghoul Murder Case—Dwight V. Babcock	4.00	12.00	20.00	M
nn(31)	Doctor's Son—John O'Hara	1.60	4.80	8.00	
nn(32)	Stage Door Canteen—Delmer Daves; movie tie-in	3.00	9.00	15.00	C
nn(33)	Corpse in the Waxworks—John Dickson Carr	4.00	12.00	20.00	M
nn(34)	The Saint Goes On—Leslie Charteris	4.00	12.00	20.00	M
nn(35)	Poison for One—John Rhode	6.00	18.00	30.00	M
nn(36)	The Avon Book of Great Mystery Stories. Note: This book apparently does not exist. It was later released as No. 86 in the series.				
nn(37)	Coffin for One—Francis Beeding	4.00	12.00	20.00	M
nn(38)	The Big Sleep—Raymond Chandler	10.00	30.00	50.00	M
nn(39)	Rage in Heaven—James Hilton	1.60	4.80	8.00	
nn(40)	In the Teeth of the Evidence—Dorothy L. Sayers	3.00	9.00	15.00	M
41	The Narrow Corner—W. Somerset Maugham; 1944	2.00	6.00	10.00	
42	The Passionate Year—James Hilton	1.60	4.80	8.00	
43	Burn Witch Burn—A. A. Merritt	8.00	24.00	40.00	SF
44	The Saint in New York—Leslie Charteris	4.00	12.00	20.00	M
45	Germany - Past, Present and Future—Lord Vansittart	3.00	9.00	15.00	NF
46	Death on the Nile—Agatha Christie	4.00	12.00	20.00	M
47	Shoe the Wild Mare—Gene Fowler	1.60	4.80	8.00	
48	The Road to Victory—Cardinal Francis J. Spellman	1.60	4.80	8.00	
49	The London Spy Murders—Peter Cheyney; aka The Stars Are Dark	4.00	12.00	20.00	M
50	Cakes and Ale—W. Somerset Maugham	1.60	4.80	8.00	
51	Nobody's in Town—Edna Ferber	1.60	4.80	8.00	
52	The Man Who Had Everything—Louis Bromfield	1.60	4.80	8.00	
53	Mystery of the Red Triangle—W. C. Tuttle	2.00	6.00	10.00	W
54	See What I Mean?—Lewis Browne	3.00	9.00	15.00	C
55	Presenting Lily Mars—Booth Tarkington	1.60	4.80	8.00	
56	Theatre—W. Somerset Maugham	1.60	4.80	8.00	
57	The Hills Beyond—Thomas Wolfe	1.60	4.80	8.00	
58	Winged Victory—Moss Hart	1.60	4.80	8.00	C
59	Heaven's My Destination—Thornton Wilder; 1945	1.60	4.80	8.00	
60	Double Indemnity—James M. Cain	2.00	6.00	10.00	M
61	Murder in Three Acts—Agatha Christie	3.00	9.00	15.00	M
62	Over My Dead Body—Rex Stout	3.00	9.00	15.00	M
63	Five Murderers—Raymond Chandler	10.00	30.00	50.00	M
64	Back Stage—Vicki Baum	1.60	4.80	8.00	
65	Now I'll Tell One—Harry Hershfield	2.00	6.00	10.00	H
66	Little Caesar—W. R. Burnett; Note: Same cover as the comic Famous Gangsters No. 3	5.00	15.00	25.00	M

Avon 46, © Avon

Avon 61, © Avon

Avon 63, © Avon

Avon 68, © Avon

Avon 76, © Avon

Avon 83, © Avon

(AVON, continued)

		Good	Fine	N/Mint	
67	Action This Day—Bishop Francis J. Spellman	1.60	4.80	8.00	
68	A Homicide for Hannah—Dwight V. Babcock	2.00	6.00	10.00	M
69	The Stray Lamb—Thorne Smith	1.60	4.80	8.00	H
70	Poirot Loses a Client—Agatha Christie	3.00	9.00	15.00	M
71	The Saint Intervenes—Leslie Charteris	2.00	6.00	10.00	M
72	The Avon Story Teller; orig., 1945. Note: Includes Merritt, Chandler, others	1.60	4.80	8.00	
73	A Goodly Heritage—Mary Ellen Chase	1.60	4.80	8.00	
74	The Ghost Patrol and Other Stories—Sinclair Lewis	1.60	4.80	8.00	
75	The Mysterious Affair at Styles—Agatha Christie	3.00	9.00	15.00	M
76	Atomic Energy in the Coming Era—David Dietz	1.60	4.80	8.00	NF
77	The Long Valley—John Steinbeck	2.00	6.00	10.00	
78	To Step Aside—Noel Coward; 1946	1.60	4.80	8.00	
79	Catherine Herself—James Hilton	1.60	4.80	8.00	
80	You Can't Keep the Change—Peter Cheyney	3.00	9.00	15.00	M
81	Bad Girl—Vina Delmar	1.60	4.80	8.00	E
82	The Red Box—Rex Stout	3.00	9.00	15.00	M
83	Sight Unseen and the Confession—Mary Roberts Rinehart	2.00	6.00	10.00	
84	Mistress Wilding—Rafael Sabatini; Note: Same cover as Modern Short Story Monthly No. 36	1.60	4.80	8.00	A
85	The Regatta Mystery—Agatha Christie	3.00	9.00	15.00	M
86	Avon Mystery Story Teller—anthology; Note: Includes Irish, Wallace, Carr, Christie	3.00	9.00	15.00	M
87	The Private Affairs of Bel Ami—Guy de Maupassant; movie tie-in	1.60	4.80	8.00	
88	Five Sinister Characters—Raymond Chandler	10.00	30.00	50.00	M
89	Death in the Air—Agatha Christie	3.00	9.00	15.00	M
90	Avon Ghost Reader—ed. Herbert Williams; Note: Includes Merritt, Lovecraft, Derleth, Stoker	8.00	24.00	40.00	SF
91	The French Key Mystery—Frank Gruber	2.00	6.00	10.00	M
92	Loose Ladies—Vina Delmar	1.60	4.80	8.00	E
93	The Dark Street Murders—Peter Cheyney	3.00	9.00	15.00	M
94	Butterfield 8—John O'Hara	1.60	4.80	8.00	
95	Black Orchids—Rex Stout	3.00	9.00	15.00	M
96	Black Angel—Cornell Woolrich	4.00	12.00	20.00	M
97	Wedding Ring—Beth Brown	1.60	4.80	8.00	R
98	The Virgin and the Gypsy—D. H. Lawrence	1.60	4.80	8.00	E
99	The Embezzler—James M. Cain	1.60	4.80	8.00	
100	The Secret Adversary—Agatha Christie	3.00	9.00	15.00	M
101	Avon Improved Cook Book—Pearl V. Metzelthin	4.00	12.00	20.00	
102	The Three Wise Guys and Other Stories—Damon Runyon	1.60	4.80	8.00	
103	Where There's a Will—Rex Stout	3.00	9.00	15.00	M

Avon 85, © Avon

Avon 93, © Avon

Avon 101, © Avon

Avon 104, © Avon

Avon 110, © Avon

Avon 124, © Avon

(AVON, continued)

		Good	Fine	N/Mint	
104	If I Should Die Before I Wake—William Irish; Note: Same cover as Murder Mystery Monthly No. 13 and Avon Detective Mystery No. 2.	8.00	24.00	40.00	M
105	Lady Ann—Donald Henderson Clarke; Note: Same cover as Avon No. 78.	1.20	3.60	6.00	E
106	The Black Path of Fear—Cornell Woolrich	3.00	9.00	15.00	M
107	The Marriage Racket—Vina Delmar	1.60	4.80	8.00	
108	A Taste for Honey—H. F. Heard	2.00	6.00	10.00	M
109	Avon Bedside Companion; 1947	1.60	4.80	8.00	
110	Terror at Night	7.00	21.00	35.00	SF
111	The Imperial Orgy—Edgar Saltus	2.00	6.00	10.00	E
112	The Squealer—Edgar Wallace; Note: Same cover as Avon No. 17.	2.00	6.00	10.00	M
113	Aphrodite—Pierre Louys	2.00	6.00	10.00	E
114	Sinister Errand—Peter Cheyney; Note: Same cover as the comic Parole Breakers No. 2.	3.00	9.00	15.00	M
115	The Avon Book of W. Somerset Maugham	1.60	4.80	8.00	
116	Kelly—Donald Henderson Clarke	1.20	3.60	6.00	E
117	Creep Shadow Creep—A. A. Merritt	8.00	24.00	40.00	SF
118	The Saint in Action—Leslie Charteris; aka The Ace of Knaves. Note: Same cover as the comic Saint No. 7.	2.00	6.00	10.00	M
119	The Better Taylors—Richard Taylor	2.00	6.00	10.00	
120	Alabam—Donald Henderson Clarke	1.20	3.60	6.00	E
121	Kept Woman—Vina Delmar; Note: Same cover as the comic book Intimate Confessions No. 6.	1.60	4.80	8.00	R
122	Unconscious Witness—R. Austin Freeman; Note: Same cover as the pulp magazine Private Detective Stories October, 1944, and Avon Detective Mysteries No. 3.	2.00	6.00	10.00	M
123	The Case of the Dark Hero—Peter Cheyney; Note: Same cover as the comic Saint No. 12.	2.00	6.00	10.00	A
124	Holiday for Murder—Agatha Christie	3.00	9.00	15.00	M
125	The Door With Seven Locks—Edgar Wallace	1.60	4.80	8.00	M
126	Cold Blooded Murder—Freeman Wills Crofts	3.00	9.00	15.00	M
127	Eastern Shame Girl	8.00	24.00	40.00	E
128	Ten Nights of Love	1.20	3.60	6.00	E
129	The Gentleman in the Parlour—W. Somerset Maugham	1.20	3.60	6.00	
130	The Saint Goes West—Leslie Charteris; 1948	1.60	4.80	8.00	M
131	Death Takes a Bow—Frances & Richard Lockridge	2.00	6.00	10.00	M
132	14 Great Short Stories From the Long Valley—John Steinbeck	1.60	4.80	8.00	
133	Naughty 90's Joke Book—Harold Meyers	3.00	9.00	15.00	H
134	Georgia Boy—Erskine Caldwell	1.20	3.60	6.00	E
135	The Woman and the Puppet—Pierre Louys	1.20	3.60	6.00	E
136	The Lurking Fear—H. P. Lovecraft	10.00	30.00	50.00	SF
137	Double Indemnity—James M. Cain	1.60	4.80	8.00	M
138	The Hard-Boiled Virgin—Jack Woodford; aka Lady Killer	1.20	3.60	6.00	E

Avon 125, © Avon

Avon 127, © Avon

Avon 131, © Avon

Avon 142, © Avon

Avon 143, © Avon

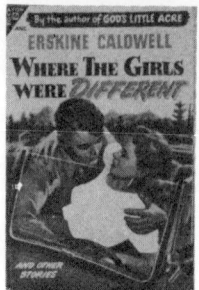

Avon 151, © Avon

(AVON, continued)

		Good	Fine	N/Mint	
139	Liza of Lambeth—W. Somerset Maugham	1.20	3.60	6.00	E
140	In Bed We Cry—Ilka Chase	1.20	3.60	6.00	
141	Career in C Major—James M. Cain	1.20	3.60	6.00	
142	Killing the Goose—Frances & Richard Lockridge; 1948	2.00	6.00	10.00	M
143	Casey - Hard Boiled Detective—George Harmon Coxe	4.00	12.00	20.00	M
144	Hope of Heaven—John O'Hara	1.20	3.60	6.00	E
145	The Restless Passion—Vina Delmar; aka Women Live Too Long	1.20	3.60	6.00	E
146	The Abortive Hussy—Jack Woodford	1.20	3.60	6.00	E
147	The Avenging Saint—Leslie Charteris	2.00	6.00	10.00	M
148	Love, Health, and Marriage—John Cowan & Arthur Rose Guerard	1.60	4.80	8.00	NF
149	John Bartel Jr.—Donald Henderson Clarke	1.20	3.60	6.00	E
150	A Love Episode—Emile Zola	1.20	3.60	6.00	E
151	Where the Girls Were Different—Erskine Caldwell; Note: Same cover as the comic Campus Romances No. 2	1.20	3.60	6.00	E
152	Georgie May—Maxwell Bodenheim	1.20	3.60	6.00	E
153	Valley Vixen—Ben Ames Williams; aka Hostile Valley	1.20	3.60	6.00	E
154	When She Was Bad . . .—Katherine Brush; aka You Go Your Way	1.20	3.60	6.00	E
155	The Unfaithful Lady—Charles Pettit	2.00	6.00	10.00	E
156	Pardners of the Badlands—Bliss Lomax	1.60	4.80	8.00	W
157	Yesterday's Love—James T. Farrell	1.20	3.60	6.00	
158	Now I'll Tell One—Harry Hershfield	2.00	6.00	10.00	H
159	This Is Murder, Mr. Herbert—Day Keene; 1st ed., 1948	4.00	12.00	20.00	M
160	Casanova's Homecoming—Arthur Schnitzler	1.20	3.60	6.00	E
161	Love's Lovely Counterfeit—James M. Cain	1.60	4.80	8.00	
162	The Avon Book of Complete Crosswords and Cryptograms—Clark Kinnaird	10.00	30.00	50.00	NF
163	Love in the Latin Quarter—Henri Murger	1.60	4.80	8.00	E
164	The Moving Finger—Agatha Christie	3.00	9.00	15.00	M
165	The Stone of Chastity—Margery Sharp; Note: Same cover as the comic Women to Love	1.20	3.60	6.00	F
166	Psyche—Pierre Louys	1.20	3.60	6.00	E
167	Piping Hot—Emile Zola	1.60	4.80	8.00	E
168	A Virtuous Girl—Maxwell Bodenheim	1.60	4.80	8.00	E
169	The Amboy Dukes—Irving Shulman; Note: Three cover variations exist on this number, one of which is a movie tie-in	2.00	6.00	10.00	E
170	Bronc Buckaroo—J. Edward Leithead	1.60	4.80	8.00	W
171	Amorous Philandre—Jean-Galli De Bibiena	2.00	6.00	10.00	F
172	Bubu of Montparnasse—Charles-Louis Philippe	2.00	6.00	10.00	E
173	On the Spot—Edgar Wallace	1.60	4.80	8.00	
174	Sinful Woman—James M. Cain	1.20	3.60	6.00	
175	A Woman's Heart—Guy De Maupassant	1.20	3.60	6.00	E

Avon 155, © Avon

Avon 159, © Avon

Avon 170, © Avon

Avon 176, © Avon

Avon 187, © Avon

Avon 189, © Avon

(AVON, continued)

		Good	Fine	N/Mint	
176	Whose Body?—Dorothy L. Sayers	3.00	9.00	15.00	M
177	Midsummer Passion—Erskine Caldwell	1.60	4.80	8.00	E
178	Fast One—Paul Cain	5.00	15.00	25.00	M
179	Blondie Iscariot—Edgar Lustgarten; Note: Same cover as the comic Prison Break No. 3.	3.00	9.00	15.00	E
180	French Summer—Guy Gilpatric	1.60	4.80	8.00	E
181	Her Private Passions—Marty Holland; aka The Glass Heart	1.60	4.80	8.00	E
182	New Avon Bedside Companion; 1949	1.60	4.80	8.00	
183	Burial of the Fruit—David Dortort	2.00	6.00	10.00	E
184	The Girl With the Hungry Eyes—ed. Don Wollheim; 1st ed., 1949	10.00	30.00	50.00	SF
185	Never Come Morning—Nelson Algren	2.00	6.00	10.00	E
186	Night Cry—William L. Stuart	3.00	9.00	15.00	M
187	Love Trap—Vina Delmar	2.00	6.00	10.00	E
188	Fools and Their Folly—W. Somerset Maugham; aka Then and Now	1.60	4.80	8.00	
189	The Daughter of Fu Manchu—Sax Rohmer	12.50	37.50	60.00	M
190	The Life and Loves of a Modern Mr. Bluebeard—Ward Greene; aka Ride the Nightmare	3.00	9.00	15.00	E
191	Replenishing Jessica—Maxwell Bodenheim	1.60	4.80	8.00	E
192	Young Man of Manhattan—Katharine Brush	1.60	4.80	8.00	
193	The Impatient Virgin—Donald Henderson Clarke	1.60	4.80	8.00	E
194	Avon Book of New Stories of the Great Wild West—Don Wollheim	4.00	12.00	20.00	W
195	Out of the Silent Planet—C. S. Lewis	10.00	30.00	50.00	SF
196	Memory of Love—Bessie Breuer	1.60	4.80	8.00	
197	The Son of the Grand Eunuch—Charles Pettit	2.00	6.00	10.00	E
198	Yvette and Other Stories—Guy de Maupassant	1.60	4.80	8.00	
199	The Miller and the Mayor's Wife—Pedro DeAlarcon	1.60	4.80	8.00	E
200	Your Most Intimate Problems—Lawrence Gould	3.00	9.00	15.00	NF
201	Strange Desires—Len Zinberg; aka What D'ya Know for Sure; Note: Same cover as the comic Campus Romances No. 3.	1.60	4.80	8.00	E
202	From Gags to Riches—Joey Adams	3.00	9.00	15.00	H
203	Quartet—W. Somerset Maugham	1.60	4.80	8.00	
204	Portrait of a Man With Red Hair—Hugh Walpole	2.00	6.00	10.00	HO
205	The Last Frontier—Howard Fast	1.60	4.80	8.00	W
206	The Palace of Pleasure—Jacques-Rochette de la Morliere	1.60	4.80	8.00	E
207	Virgie, Goodbye—Nathan Rothman; Note: Same cover as the comic Romantic Love No. 6 and Avon Monthly Novel No. 8.	3.00	9.00	15.00	E
208	The Devil Thumbs a Ride—Robert C. Du Soe	3.00	9.00	15.00	E
209	New Orleans Lady—Vina Delmar	1.60	4.80	8.00	
210	Wicked Sister—Helen Topping Miller	1.60	4.80	8.00	E
211	Scarf of Passion—Robert Bloch; Note: Same cover as Avon Monthly Novel No. 9 and				

Avon 194, © Avon

Avon 195, © Avon

Avon 200, © Avon

Avon 214, © Avon

Avon 216, © Avon

Avon 220, © Avon

(AVON, continued)

		Good	Fine	N/Mint	
	the comic book Realistic Romances No. 1.	4.00	12.00	20.00	HO
212	Iron Man—W. R. Burnett; Note: Same cover as the comic Romantic Love No. 10.	4.00	12.00	20.00	
213	Nina—Donald Henderson Clarke	1.60	4.80	8.00	E
214	The Fox Woman and Other Stories—A. A. Merritt; 1st ed., 1949	10.00	30.00	50.00	SF
215	All the Brothers Were Valiant—Ben Ames Williams	1.60	4.80	8.00	
216	Gladiator—Philip Wylie	9.00	27.00	45.00	SF
217	Miss Jill From Shanghai—Emily Hahn	1.60	4.80	8.00	E
218	Anyone Can Win at Gin Rummy and Canasta—Alfred Drake	1.20	3.60	6.00	NF
219	Finger Man—Raymond Chandler	9.00	27.00	45.00	M
220	I Married a Dead Man—Wiliam Irish	9.00	27.00	45.00	M
221	Don Juan—Ludwig Lewisohn	1.60	4.80	8.00	E
222	Neon Wilderness—Nelson Algren; Note: Same cover as the comic Intimate Confessions No. 1.	7.00	21.00	35.00	
223	Three Loves Had Margaret—James Hilton	1.60	4.80	8.00	
224	Port Afrique—Bernard Victor Dryer	1.60	4.80	8.00	E
225	Anyone Can Have a Great Vocabulary—J. L. Stephenson	160	4.80	8.00	NF
226	I Can Get It for You Wholesale!—Jerome Weidman	2.00	6.00	10.00	
227	Just What the Doctor Ordered—Dr. Anthony Bassler	2.00	6.00	10.00	H
228	Gilbert and Sullivan Operas—William Schwenck Gilbert & Arthur Sullivan; 1950	1.60	4.80	8.00	
229	All About Girls	2.00	6.00	10.00	H
230	The Big Fights—Harold Meyers; orig., 1950	3.00	9.00	15.00	S
231	Butterfield 8—John O'Hara	1.60	4.80	8.00	
232	Alabam—Donald Henderson Clarke	1.00	3.00	5.00	E
233	The Servant—Robin Maugham	1.60	4.80	8.00	E
234	The Old Goat—Tiffany Thayer	1.20	3.60	6.00	E
235	Seven Footprints to Satan—A. A. Merritt	8.00	24.00	40.00	SF
236	Venus of the Counting House—Emile Zola	3.00	9.00	15.00	E
237	Tawny—Donald Henderson Clarke	1.60	4.80	8.00	E
238	The First Lady Chatterley—D. H. Lawrence	1.60	4.80	8.00	E
239	Bad Girl From Maine—Katharine Brush	1.60	4.80	8.00	
240	End As a Man—Calder Willingham	1.60	4.80	8.00	
241	What's in It for Me?—Jerome Weidman	1.00	3.00	5.00	E
242	The Case of the Untidy Murder—Frances & Richard Lockridge	3.00	9.00	15.00	M
243	Mysterious Mickey Finn—Elliot Paul	3.00	9.00	15.00	M
244	Cry Tough!—Irving Shulman	1.60	4.80	8.00	E
245	The Big Four—Agatha Christie	5.00	15.00	25.00	M
246	A Shropshire Lad—Housman	1.60	4.80	8.00	
247	The Midsummer Fires—James Aswell	1.60	4.80	8.00	E
248	Love Among the Haystacks—D. H. Lawrence	1.60	4.80	8.00	E
249	It Happens Every Spring—Valentine Davies	1.60	4.80	8.00	F

Avon 235, © Avon

Avon 239, © Avon

Avon 249, © Avon

Avon 261, © Avon   Avon 268, © Avon   Avon 272 (girl by map), © Avon

(AVON, continued)

		Good	Fine	N/Mint	
250	Carlotta—Robert Briffault; aka Fandango; Note: Same cover as the comic Intimate Confessions No. 3 and Avon Monthly Novel No. 13	3.00	9.00	15.00	E
251	Sonnets From the Portuguese—Elizabeth Barrett Browning	1.20	3.60	6.00	
252	A Hell of a Good Time—James T. Farrell; Note: Same cover as the comic Romantic Love No. 1.	1.60	4.80	8.00	
253	Confidential—Donald Henderson Clarke; Note: Same cover as the comic book Realistic Romances No. 4.	2.00	6.00	10.00	E
254	Flame Vine—Helen Topping Miller	2.00	6.00	10.00	E
255	Tropical Passions—anthology; Note: Same cover as Avon Book Dividend 7 and basically the same as Avon Modern Short Story Monthly 44.	2.00	6.00	10.00	E
256	The Case of the Black Orchids—Rex Stout	4.00	12.00	20.00	M
257	Aphrodite—Pierre Louys	3.00	9.00	15.00	E
258	Hope of Heaven—John O'Hara	1.60	4.80	8.00	E
259	For a Night of Love—Emile Zola	1.60	4.80	8.00	E
260	Yesterday's Love—James T. Farrell	1.60	4.80	8.00	E
261	Avon Improved Cook Book—P. V. Metzelthin	4.00	12.00	20.00	NF
262	The Rubiyat of Omar Khayam—Edward Fitzgerald	1.60	4.80	8.00	
263	The Gangs of New York—Herbert Asbury	2.00	6.00	10.00	NF
264	Six Deadly Dames—Frederick Nebel; 1st ed., 1950	6.00	18.00	30.00	M
265	Mortgage on Life—Vicki Baum	2.00	6.00	10.00	E
266	Death in the Deep South—Ward Greene	5.00	15.00	25.00	E
267	A Bullet for Billy the Kid—Nelson Nye	2.00	6.00	10.00	W
268	Seven Slayers—Paul Cain	8.00	24.00	40.00	M
269	Jadie Greenway—I. S. Young	1.60	4.80	8.00	E
270	The Chastity of Gloria Boyd—Donald Henderson Clarke	2.00	6.00	10.00	E
271	Nana's Mother—Emile Zola	1.60	4.80	8.00	E
272	Europa—Robert Briffault; Note: Two cover variants noted:				
	Girl by map	2.00	6.00	10.00	
	Girl in bondage	8.00	24.00	40.00	
273	Imperial City—Elmer Rice	1.60	4.80	8.00	E
274	T As in Trapped—Lawrence Treat	2.00	6.00	10.00	M
275	My Bride in the Storm—Theodore Pratt	2.00	6.00	10.00	E
276	Madwoman?—Emily Harvin	4.00	12.00	20.00	
277	Perelandra—C. S. Lewis	8.00	24.00	40.00	SF
278	A Killer Is Loose Among Us—Robert Terrall	2.00	6.00	10.00	M
279	The Price Is Right—Jerome Weidman	1.60	4.80	8.00	E
280	Dangerous Love—Jack Woodford; aka Temptress	3.00	9.00	15.00	E
281	Into Plutonian Depths—Stanton A. Coblentz	10.00	30.00	50.00	SF
282	Lovely Lady, Pity Me—Roy Huggins	2.00	6.00	10.00	M

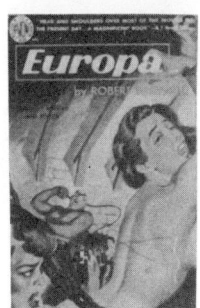

Avon 272 (girl in bondage), © Avon   Avon 276, © Avon   Avon 277, © Avon

Avon 288, © Avon

Avon 302, © Avon

Avon 307, © Avon

(AVON, continued)

		Good	Fine	N/Mint	
283	She Posed for Death—Russell Gordon; aka Dead Level. Note: Same cover as the comic Parole Breakers No. 1.	2.00	6.00	10.00	M
284	Madam Is Dead—Robert Terrell; 1951	2.00	6.00	10.00	M
285	An Earthman on Venus—Ralph Milne Farley; aka The Radio Man	12.50	37.50	60.00	SF
286	Kept Woman—Vina Delmar	1.60	4.80	8.00	E
287	How to Play Samba Canasta—Richard L. Frey; 1951	1.00	3.00	5.00	NF
288	Front for Murder—Guy Emery.	3.00	9.00	15.00	M
289	Friday for Death—Lawrence Lariar; Note: Same cover as the comic The Saint No. 10.	2.00	6.00	10.00	M
290	Gas-House McGinty—James T. Farrell	2.00	6.00	10.00	
291	Call Her Savage—Tiffany Thayer	2.00	6.00	10.00	E
292	Four Boys, a Girl and a Gun—Willard Wiener; aka Four Boys and a Gun. Note: Same cover as the comic Gangsters and Gun Molls No. 1.	2.00	6.00	10.00	JD
293	Hellbox—John O'Hara	2.00	6.00	10.00	
294	Sappho—Alphonse Daudet	2.00	6.00	10.00	
295	Avon Book of Puzzles for Everybody—John Paul Adams	10.00	30.00	50.00	NF
296	A Modern Lover—D. H. Lawrence	2.00	6.00	10.00	E
297	Untamed Darling—Jack Woodford; aka Iris	3.00	9.00	15.00	IE
298	House of Fury—Felice Swados; Note: Later titled Reform School Girl and adapted into a very rare and popular comic book of the same name.	10.00	30.00	50.00	E
299	The Round-Up—Oscar J. Friend	2.00	6.00	10.00	W
300	The Amboy Dukes—Irving Shulman; Note: Two cover variants exist of this number.	2.00	6.00	10.00	E
301	We Are Not Alone—James Hilton	1.60	4.80	8.00	
302	Perversity—Francis Carco	2.00	6.00	10.00	E
303	Dream Street—Robert Sylvester	1.60	4.80	8.00	E
304	Song Without Sermon—James Woolf; Note: Same cover as the comic Intimate Confessions No. 4.	2.00	6.00	10.00	
305	God Wears a Bow Tie—Lyle Stuart	3.00	9.00	15.00	E
306	Gone to Texas—John W. Thomason, Jr.	2.00	6.00	10.00	W
307	Big League Baseball	3.00	9.00	15.00	S
308	Musk, Hashish, and Blood—Hector France	8.00	24.00	40.00	E
309	Midsummer Passion—Erskine Caldwell	2.00	6.00	10.00	E
310	Bubu of Montparnasse—Charles-Louis Phillippe	2.00	6.00	10.00	E
311	The Saturday Evening Post Western Stories—ed. Barthold Fles	3.00	9.00	15.00	W
312	The Mysterious Affair at Styles—Agatha Christie	3.00	9.00	15.00	M
313	The Ugly Duchess—Lion Feuchtwanger	2.00	6.00	10.00	E
314	Nigger Heaven—Carl Van Vechten	8.00	24.00	40.00	E
315	The Metal Monster—A. A. Merritt	8.00	24.00	40.00	SF
316	Murder in Three Acts—Agatha Christie	3.00	9.00	15.00	M
317	Death on the Nile—Agatha Christie	3.00	9.00	15.00	M
318	Dear Sir—Juliet Lowell	1.60	4.80	8.00	H

Avon 311, © Avon

Avon 314, © Avon

Avon 315, © Avon

Avon 324, © Avon

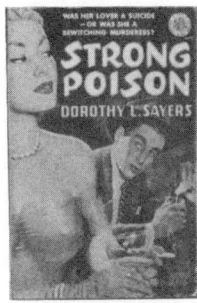

Avon 328, © Avon

Avon 330, © Avon

(AVON, continued)

		Good	Fine	N/Mint	
319	Along the Broadway Beat—Louis Sobol	2.00	6.00	10.00	E
320	Gorgeous Ghoul Murder Case—Dwight V. Babcock	4.00	12.00	20.00	M
321	The Saint in New York—Leslie Charteris	2.00	6.00	10.00	M
322	Slipping Beauty—Jerome Weidman; aka The Horse That Could Whistle 'Dixie'	2.00	6.00	10.00	E
323	The Furies in Her Body; aka Methinks the Lady	2.00	6.00	10.00	F
324	The Ship of Ishtar—A. A. Merritt	9.00	27.00	45.00	SF
325	Ill Wind—James Hilton	1.60	4.80	8.00	
326	Burial of the Fruit—David Dortort	2.00	6.00	10.00	E
327	One Man Show—Tiffany Thayer	2.00	6.00	10.00	F
328	Strong Poison—Dorothy L. Sayers	3.00	9.00	15.00	M
329	Little Caesar—W. R. Burnett; Note: Same cover as the comic Police Line-Up No. 2.	4.00	12.00	20.00	M
330	Desperate Men—James D. Horan	3.00	9.00	15.00	NF
331	Trio—W. Somerset Maugham	1.60	4.80	8.00	
332	A Homicide for Hannah—Dwight V. Babcock	2.00	6.00	10.00	M
333	Line on Ginger—Robin Maugham	2.00	6.00	10.00	E
334	Red Bone Woman—Carlyle Tillery	1.60	4.80	8.00	E
335	In the Teeth of the Evidence—Dorothy L. Sayers	3.00	9.00	15.00	M
336	The Housekeeper's Daughter—Donald Henderson Clarke	1.60	4.80	8.00	E
337	The Agony Column—Earl Derr Biggers	2.00	6.00	10.00	M
338	Hollywood Bedside Reader	3.00	9.00	15.00	
339	The Terror of the Leopard Men—Juba Kennerley; 1st American edition, 1951	8.00	24.00	40.00	NF
340	Midsummer Passion—Erskine Caldwell	2.00	6.00	10.00	E
341	The Saint Sees It Through—Leslie Charteris	2.00	6.00	10.00	M
342	The Woman Aroused—Ed Lacy	5.00	15.00	25.00	E
343	Six-Gun Melody—William Colt MacDonald	2.00	6.00	10.00	W
344	The Chinese Parrot—Earl Derr Biggers	8.00	24.00	40.00	M
345	I Lost My Girlish Laughter—Jane Allen	2.00	6.00	10.00	E
346	Possess Me Not—Fan Nichols	3.00	9.00	15.00	E
347	The Saint at the Thieve's Picnic—Leslie Charteris	2.00	6.00	10.00	M
348	Jealous Woman—James M. Cain; Note: Same cover as the comic Campus Romance No. 1.	2.00	6.00	10.00	M
349	Mistress Murder—Peter Cheyney	3.00	9.00	15.00	M
350	Charlie Chan Carries On—Earl Derr Biggers	8.00	24.00	40.00	M
351	Millie's Daughter—Donald Henderson Clarke	1.60	4.80	8.00	E
352	Ninth Avenue—Maxwell Bodenheim	1.60	4.80	8.00	E
353	Poirot Loses a Client—Agatha Christie	2.00	6.00	10.00	M
354	The Werewolf of Paris—Guy Endore	5.00	15.00	25.00	HO
355	No Orchids for Miss Blandish—James Hadley Chase	4.00	12.00	20.00	M
356	I Can Get It for You Wholesale!—Jerome Weidman; movie tie-in	2.00	6.00	10.00	E
357	All About Girls	2.00	6.00	10.00	H

Avon 339, © Avon

Avon 344, © Avon

Avon 354, © Avon

Avon 370, © Avon

Avon 373, © Avon

Avon 376, © Avon

(AVON, continued)

		Good	Fine	N/Mint	
358	Woman and the Puppet—Pierre Louys	1.60	4.80	8.00	E
359	Can Can Americana—Harold Meyers; 1st ed., 1951	3.00	9.00	15.00	NF
360	As They Reveled—Philip Wylie; Note: Same cover as the comic Realistic Romance No. 7.	2.00	6.00	10.00	E
361	Does not exist				
362	Calamity Jane of Deadwood Gulch—Ethel Hueston	4.00	12.00	20.00	W
363	Murder Is Served—Frances & Richard Lockridge	2.00	6.00	10.00	M
364	The Point of Honour—W. Somerset Maugham	1.60	4.80	8.00	
365	The Impatient Virgin—Donald Henderson Clarke	2.00	6.00	10.00	E
366	They'll Do It Every Time—Jimmy Hatlo	2.00	6.00	10.00	H
367	Outlaw Guns—E. E. Halleran	2.00	6.00	10.00	W
368	All the Girls He Wanted—John O'Hara	2.00	6.00	10.00	
369	The Dishonest Murderer—Francis & Richard Lockridge	2.00	6.00	10.00	M
370	The Moon Pool—A. A. Merritt	8.00	24.00	40.00	SF
371	The Regatta Mystery—Agatha Christie	3.00	9.00	15.00	M
372	Cry Tough!—Irving Shulman	1.60	4.80	8.00	E
373	The Blue Negro—Robert Payne	7.00	21.00	35.00	E
374	Gun Fight at Horsethief Range—B. M. Bower	1.60	4.80	8.00	W
375	Babes and Sucklings—Philip Wylie; Note: Same cover as the comic Intimate Confessions No. 8.	2.00	6.00	10.00	E
376	Home to Harlem—Claude McKay	8.00	24.00	40.00	E
377	Taffy—Philip B. Kaye	6.00	18.00	30.00	E
378	Marshal of Deer Creek—Al Cody	1.60	4.80	8.00	W
379	Death in the Air—Agatha Christie	3.00	9.00	15.00	M
380	If This Be Sin—Loren Wahl	1.60	4.80	8.00	E
381	Nothing So Strange—James Hilton	1.60	4.80	8.00	M
382	Tough Kid From Brooklyn—Robert Mende	1.60	4.80	8.00	
383	The Untamed Wife of Louis Scott—W. Carroll Munro; aka The Gift of Glory	1.60	4.80	8.00	E
384	Louis Beretti—Donald Henderson Clarke	2.00	6.00	10.00	M
385	Cat and Mouse—Christianna Brand; 1952	2.00	6.00	10.00	M
386	Does not exist. Note: Announced as The Face in the Abyss by A. Merritt but instead was released as Murder Mystery Monthly No. 29.				
387	Maniac Rendezvous—Marc Brandel; aka Rain Before Seven	4.00	12.00	20.00	M
388	Does not exist. Note: Announced as After Many a Summer Dies the Swan—Aldous Huxley and later released as Avon AT435.				
389	The Saturday Evening Post Fantasy Stories	3.00	9.00	15.00	SF
390	The Savage Gentleman—Philip Wylie	4.00	12.00	20.00	F
391	Maidens in the Midden—Oliver Anderson; aka In for a Penny	2.00	6.00	10.00	E
392	Burn, Witch, Burn—A. A. Merritt	8.00	24.00	40.00	SF
393	The Moron—Marc Brandel; aka The Choice	3.00	9.00	15.00	M

Avon 379, © Avon

Avon 387, © Avon

Avon 390, © Avon

Avon 396, © Avon

Avon 398, © Avon

Avon 403, © Avon

(AVON, continued)

		Good	Fine	N/Mint	
394	Murderer's Holiday—Donald Henderson Clarke	2.00	6.00	10.00	M
395	The Drunk, the Damned, and the Bedeviled—Terence Ford; aka He Feeds the Birds	2.00	6.00	10.00	E
396	His First Million Women—George Weston	3.00	9.00	15.00	SF
397	Nina—Donald Henderson Clarke; Note: Same cover as the comic book Realistic Romances No. 8.	2.00	6.00	10.00	
398	Element of Shame—Cicely Schiller	2.00	6.00	10.00	E
399	. . . Plus Blood in Their Veins—Robert Paul Smith; 1952, aka So It Doesn't Whistle	3.00	9.00	15.00	E
400	Jule: Alabama Boy in Harlem—George Wylie Henderson	3.00	9.00	15.00	E
401	Perversity—Francis Carco	2.00	6.00	10.00	E
402	Dangerous Love—Jack Woodford	2.00	6.00	10.00	E
403	Untamed Darling—Jack Woodford; aka Iris	2.00	6.00	10.00	E
404	The Blackmailer—Ernst Klein; orig., 1952	1.60	4.80	8.00	
405	How Brave We Live—Paul Monash	1.60	4.80	8.00	E
406	Two Beds for Roxane—Stephen Longstreet; aka The Sound of an American	1.60	4.80	8.00	E
407	Strange Brother—Blair Niles	1.60	4.80	8.00	
408	Tawny—Donald Henderson Clarke	1.60	4.80	8.00	E
409	Does not exist. Note: Announced as The Rites of Love by Jack Woodford.				
410	The Secret Adversary—Agatha Christie	2.00	6.00	10.00	M
411	Hospital Happy—Bob Dunn	2.00	6.00	10.00	H
412	Waiting for Willy—Jack Houston	1.60	4.80	8.00	
413	Dwellers in the Mirage—A. A. Herritt	8.00	24.00	40.00	SF
414	The Gringo Bandit—William Hopson	2.00	6.00	10.00	W
415	Musk, Hashish, and Blood—Hector France	7.00	21.00	35.00	E
416	The Frenchman in Mohammed's Harem—Mario Uchard	5.00	15.00	25.00	E
417	Star Lust—Jack Hanley	2.00	6.00	10.00	E
418	Call Her Savage—Tiffany Thayer	2.00	6.00	10.00	E
419	Never Come Morning—Nelson Algren	1.60	4.80	8.00	E
420	The Saint Goes West—Leslie Charteris	1.60	4.80	8.00	M
421	Love's Lovely Counterfeit—James M. Cain	1.60	4.80	8.00	
422	Butterfield 8—John O'Hara	1.60	4.80	8.00	
423	Love Among the Haystacks—D. H. Lawrence	1.60	4.80	8.00	E
424	The Neon Wilderness—Nelson Algren; Note: Same cover as the comic Intimate Confessions No. 1.	5.00	15.00	25.00	E
425	The Tragedy of X—Ellery Queen	1.60	4.80	8.00	M
426	Guns Blaze at Sundown—Al Cody	1.60	4.80	8.00	W
427	Georgie May—Maxwell Bodenheim	1.20	3.60	6.00	E
428	The Servant—Robin Maugham	1.20	3.60	6.00	E
429	The Price Is Right—Jerome Weidman	1.20	3.60	6.00	E
430	House of Fury—Felice Swados	7.00	21.00	35.00	E
431	That Mrs. Renney—Donald Henderson Clarke	1.20	3.60	6.00	E

Avon 411, © Avon

Avon 413, © Avon

Avon 432, © Avon

Avon A436, © Avon

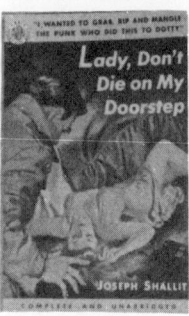

Avon 461, © Avon

Avon 485, © Avon

(AVON, continued)

		Good	Fine	N/Mint	
432	Saint Overboard—Leslie Charteris	1.60	4.80	8.00	M
433	Juvenile Delinquents—Leonard Kaufman; aka The Lower Part of the Sky	1.60	4.80	8.00	E
434	Murder Comes First—Frances & Richard Lockridge	1.60	4.80	8.00	M
AT435	After Many a Summer Dies the Swan—Aldous Huxley	1.60	4.80	8.00	SF
A436	Too Dangerous to Be Free—James Hadley Chase	1.60	4.80	8.00	M
437	The Battle at Apache Pass—Harold Conrad; orig., 1952, movie tie-in	1.20	3.60	6.00	W
438	Confidential—Donald Henderson Clarke; Note: Same cover as the comic book Realistic Romances No. 4.	1.20	3.60	6.00	E
439	Diplomatic Corpse—Phoebe Atwood Taylor	1.20	3.60	6.00	M
440	The Saint at the Thieves' Picnic—Leslie Charteris	1.20	3.60	6.00	M
441	A Mouse Is Born—Anita Loos	1.20	3.60	6.00	H
442	Slipping Beauty—Jerome Weidman; aka The Horse That Could Whistle 'Dixie'	1.60	4.80	8.00	E
443	A Holiday for Murder—Agatha Christie	1.60	4.80	8.00	M
444	Four Boys, a Girl and a Gun—Willard Wiener; aka Four Boys and a Gun. Note: Same cover as the comic Gangsters and Gun Molls No. 1.	1.20	3.60	6.00	E
AT445	End As a Man—Calder Willingham	1.20	3.60	6.00	E
446	The Outcasts of Poker Flat—Bret Harte; movie tie-in	1.20	3.60	6.00	W
AT447	Red Canvas—Marcel Wallenstein	1.20	3.60	6.00	E
448	The Last of Mr. Norris—Christopher Isherwood	1.60	4.80	8.00	E
449	The Virgin and the Gypsy—D. H. Lawrence	1.20	3.60	6.00	E
450	The Tragedy of Y—Ellery Queen	1.20	3.60	6.00	M
451	Gone to Texas—John W. Thomason, Jr.	1.20	3.60	6.00	W
452	Red Bone Woman—Carlyle Tillery	1.20	3.60	6.00	E
453	Glamor Girls—Don Flowers	1.60	4.80	8.00	H
454	The Challenge of Smoke Wade—Robert J. Hogan	1.20	3.60	6.00	W
455	The Root of His Evil—James M. Cain	1.20	3.60	6.00	
456	The Chastity of Gloria Boyd—Donald Henderson Clarke	1.20	3.60	6.00	E
457	Bimini Run—Howard Hunt	1.20	3.60	6.00	
458	Because of My Love—Robert Paul Smith	1.20	3.60	6.00	E
459	Mademoiselle Fifi and Other Stories—Guy de Maupassant	1.20	3.60	6.00	
460	Outlaw Justice at Hangman's Coulee—Al Cody	1.20	3.60	6.00	W
461	Lady, Don't Die on My Doorstep—Joseph Shallit	1.60	4.80	8.00	M
462	Pardners of the Badlands—Bliss Lomax (H. S. Drago)	1.20	3.60	6.00	W
463	The Saint in Action—Leslie Charteris; aka The Ace of Knaves	1.20	3.60	6.00	M
464	The Rough and the Smooth—Robin Maugham	1.20	3.60	6.00	E
465	The Tragedy of Z—Ellery Queen	1.20	3.60	6.00	M
466	Gas-House McGinty—James T. Farrell	1.20	3.60	6.00	
467	Hell-Bent With Jake—Russell LaDue; aka No More With Me	1.20	3.60	6.00	E
468	A Hell of a Good Time—James T. Farrell	1.20	3.60	6.00	
469	Roaring Guns at Apache Landing—Robert J. Hogan	1.20	3.60	6.00	W
470	Low Company—Mark Benney	1.20	3.60	6.00	
471	Mr. and Mrs. North Meet Murder—Frances & Richard Lockridge	1.20	3.60	6.00	M
472	The Headstrong Young Man—Donald Henderson Clarke; aka Regards to Broadway	1.20	3.60	6.00	E
473	The Saint's Getaway—Leslie Charteris	1.20	3.60	6.00	M
474	Outlaw Ambush on the Drumfire Trail—Tom J. Hopkins	1.20	3.60	6.00	W
475	Yesterday's Love—James T. Farrell	1.00	3.00	5.00	E
476	The Bride of Newgate—John Dickson Carr	1.60	4.80	8.00	M
477	The Saint Meets the Tiger—Leslie Charteris	1.20	3.60	6.00	M
478	A Bullet for Billy the Kid—Nelson C. Nye; aka Pistols for Hire	1.00	3.00	5.00	W
479	Jealous Woman—James M. Cain	1.00	3.00	5.00	
480	Millie—Donald Henderson Clarke	1.00	3.00	5.00	
481	The Hucksters—Frederic Wakeman	1.00	3.00	5.00	E
482	Avon Bedside Companion	1.00	3.00	5.00	
483	A Lady Named Lou—Donald Henderson Clarke	1.20	3.60	6.00	E
484	Murder in a Hurry—Frances & Richard Lockridge	1.00	3.00	5.00	M
485	12 Chinks and a Woman—James Hadley Chase	2.00	6.00	10.00	E
486	Bronc Buckaroo—J. Edward Leithead	1.00	3.00	5.00	W
487	Feud at Sundown—Robert Jasper; 1953	1.00	3.00	5.00	W

		Good	Fine	N/Mint	
488	Drury Lane's Last Case—Ellery Queen	1.00	3.00	5.00	M
489	The Saint Meets His Match—Leslie Charteris	1.00	3.00	5.00	M
490	Yell Bloody Murder—Joseph Shallit	1.20	3.60	6.00	M
491	Mesquiteer Mavericks—William Colt MacDonald	1.00	3.00	5.00	W
492	Waiting for Willy—Jack Houston	1.00	3.00	5.00	
493	Strange Brother—Blair Niles	1.00	3.00	5.00	
494	The Scarf—Robert Bloch	1.20	3.60	6.00	
495	Rebel's Roundup—W. Edmunds Claussen	1.00	3.00	5.00	W
496	Fast One—Paul Cain	2.00	6.00	10.00	M
497	A Night With Mr. Primrose—Whitfield Cook	1.00	3.00	5.00	
498	Six-Gun Melody—William Colt MacDonald	1.00	3.00	5.00	W
499	Chorus of Cuties—E. Simms Campbell	1.60	4.80	8.00	H
500	Colorado—William MacLeod Raine	1.00	3.00	5.00	W
501	The Untamed Wife of Louis Scott—W. Carroll Munro; aka The Gift of Glory	.80	2.40	4.00	E
502	Mr. and Mrs. North and a Pinch of Poison—Frances & Richard Lockridge	1.00	3.00	5.00	M
503	The Housekeeper's Daughter—Donald Henderson Clarke	.80	2.40	4.00	E
504	The Chase—Richard G. Huber	.80	2.40	4.00	E
505	Gun Fight at Horsethief Range—B. M. Bower; aka Five Furies of Leaning Ladder	.80	2.40	4.00	W
506	Nonce—Michael Brandon	1.00	3.00	5.00	E
507	Straw Boss—E. E. Halleran	.80	2.40	4.00	W
508	He Swung and He Missed—Eugene O'Brien	.80	2.40	4.00	
509	The Four of Hearts—Ellery Queen	1.20	3.60	6.00	M
510	The Thin Line—Edward Atiyah	.80	2.40	4.00	
511	Marshal of Deer Creek—Al Cody	.80	2.40	4.00	W
512	The Gifted—Roswell G. Ham, Jr.	.80	2.40	4.00	
513	Bachelor's Joke Book—Leo Guild	1.00	3.00	5.00	H
514	The Vanishing Gun Slinger—William Colt MacDonald	.80	2.40	4.00	W
515	Murder Out of Turn—Frances & Richard Lockridge	1.00	3.00	5.00	M
516	The Gringo Bandit—William Hopson	.80	2.40	4.00	W
517	The Fat Boy's Book—Elmer Wheeler	1.00	3.00	5.00	NF
518	The Avenging Saint—Leslie Charteris	.80	2.40	4.00	M
519	Dennis the Menace—Hank Ketcham	1.60	4.80	8.00	H
520	Scratch the Surface—Edmund Schiddel	.80	2.40	4.00	E
521	The Prisoner Ate a Hearty Breakfast—Jerome Ellison	.80	2.40	4.00	E
522	Outlaw Guns—E. E. Halleran	.80	2.40	4.00	W
523	The American Gun Mystery—Ellery Queen	.80	2.40	4.00	M
524	The New Jimmy Hatlo Book—Jimmy Hatlo; 1st ed., 1953	1.20	3.60	6.00	H
525	Guns Blaze at Sundown—Al Cody	.80	2.40	4.00	W
526	Call for the Saint—Leslie Charteris	.80	2.40	4.00	M
527	All About Girls	1.20	3.60	6.00	
528	Kiss the Killer—Joseph Shallit	.80	2.40	4.00	M
529	Gunshot Empire—Lee E. Wells	.80	2.40	4.00	W
530	Impatient Virgin—Donald Henderson Clarke	1.00	3.00	5.00	E
531	The Wages of Fear—Georges Arnaud	.80	2.40	4.00	
532	Trouble in the Saddle—Arthur Henry Gooden	.80	2.40	4.00	W
533	Follow the Saint—Leslie Charteris	.80	2.40	4.00	M
534	The Time and the Place—Robert Paul Smith	.80	2.40	4.00	E
535	Dead As a Dinosaur—Frances & Richard Lockridge	.80	2.40	4.00	M
536	Three-Notch Cameron—William Colt MacDonald	.80	2.40	4.00	W
537	The Innocent Villa—Barnaby Conrad	.80	2.40	4.00	
538	Dope, Inc.—Joachim Joesten; orig., 1953	3.00	9.00	15.00	
539	Hardcase—Matt Kinkaid	.80	2.40	4.00	
540	Pistols on the Pecos—Paul Evan Lehman	.80	2.40	4.00	W
541	Burial of the Fruit—David Dortort	1.00	3.00	5.00	E
542	Call Me Killer—Max Carter	1.00	3.00	5.00	
543	Millie's Daughter—Donald Henderson Clarke	.80	2.40	4.00	
544	The Saint and the Last Hero—Leslie Charteris	.80	2.40	4.00	M
545	Circle of Desire—Robert Paul Smith; aka The Journey	.80	2.40	4.00	E

Avon 511, © Avon

Avon A538, © Avon

Avon 567, © Avon

		Good	Fine	N/Mint	
546	The Hoodlums—John Eagle; orig., 1953	.80	2.40	4.00	E
547	Southern Daughter—Daniel White	.80	2.40	4.00	
548	Away & Beyond—A. E. Van Vogt	1.00	3.00	5.00	
A549	Tales of Love and Fury—anthology; 1st ed., 1953	1.00	3.00	5.00	E
550	Renegade Guns—Robert J. Hogan	.80	2.40	4.00	W
551	Stool Pigeon—Louis Malley	.80	2.40	4.00	M
552	Man on the Tightrope—Neil Paterson	.80	2.40	4.00	E
553	Rusty Desmond—Steve January; 1954	.80	2.40	4.00	E
554	I'll Call Every Monday—Orrie Hitt	.80	2.40	4.00	
555	Rue Pigalle—Francis Carco	.80	2.40	4.00	E
556	Guns of Circle 8—Jeff Cochran	.80	2.40	4.00	W
557	Glamor Girls—Don Flowers	1.20	3.60	6.00	H
558	Case of the Billion Dollar Body—Joseph Shallit	.80	2.40	4.00	M
559	A Cartoon Guide to the Kinsey Report—Charles Preston	1.20	3.60	6.00	H
560	Gang Girl—Wenzell Brown	1.00	3.00	5.00	JD
561	Enter Without Desire—Ed Lacy	.80	2.40	4.00	
562	Call of the Range—Arthur Henry Gooden	.80	2.40	4.00	W
563	The Creepers—John Creasey	.80	2.40	4.00	M
564	Every Bet's a Sure Thing—Thomas B. Dewey	.80	2.40	4.00	M
565	Thunder Below—Thomas Rourke	.80	2.40	4.00	E
566	Go for the Body—Ed Lacy	.80	2.40	4.00	
567	Ship Ahoy	1.20	3.60	6.00	H
568	I Worked for Lucky Luciano—anonymous	1.00	3.00	5.00	NF
569	Gunhead From Texas—William Heuman	.80	2.40	4.00	W
570	Devil's Daughter—Floyd Shaw	.80	2.40	4.00	
571	As They Reveled—Philip Wylie	.80	2.40	4.00	E
572	Laughter Came Screaming—Henry Kane	.80	2.40	4.00	M
573	The Long Noose—Lee E. Wells	.80	2.40	4.00	W
574	Make My Bed in Hell—John B. Sanford; aka Seventy Times Seven	.80	2.40	4.00	E
575	Louis Beretti - New York Hoodlum—Donald Henderson Clarke	.80	2.40	4.00	M
576	Forbidden—Leo Brattes	.80	2.40	4.00	
577	Jule: Alabama Boy in Harlem—George Wylie Henderson	1.00	3.00	5.00	
578	The Girl on the Left Bank—Joan Shepherd	.80	2.40	4.00	
579	Rebel Ranger—William Colt MacDonald	.80	2.40	4.00	W
580	The Guy From Coney Island—Jack Hanley	.80	2.40	4.00	E
581	Love's Lovely Counterfeit—James M. Cain	.80	2.40	4.00	
582	How Rough Can It Get?—Joe Weiss	.80	2.40	4.00	
583	Death Has a Small Voice—Frances & Richard Lockridge	.80	2.40	4.00	M
584	Few Die Well—Sterling Noel	.80	2.40	4.00	
585	Keeping Women in Line—Mischa Richter	.80	2.40	4.00	
586	The Riddle of Ramrod Ridge—William Colt MacDonald	.80	2.40	4.00	W
587	The Virgin and the Gypsy—D. H. Lawrence	.80	2.40	4.00	E
588	Saint Errant—Leslie Charteris	.80	2.40	4.00	
589	The Other Side of the Night—Edmund Schiddel	.80	2.40	4.00	
590	The Figure in the Dusk—John Creasey	.50	1.50	2.50	M
591	The Wrong Turn—Daniel Harper	.80	2.40	4.00	
592	The Phantom Pass—William Colt MacDonald	.80	2.40	4.00	W
593	Nina—Donald Henderson Clarke	.50	1.50	2.50	
594	The Pennycross Murders—Maurice Proctor	.80	2.40	4.00	M
595	How Brave We Live—Paul Monash	.50	1.50	2.50	
596	Gun Feud at Stampede Valley—Samuel A. Peeples	.80	2.40	4.00	W
597	Night Cry—William L. Stuart	1.00	3.00	5.00	M
598	More All About Girls	1.20	3.60	6.00	H
599	Sinful Woman—James M. Cain	.80	2.40	4.00	
600	More Dennis the Menace—Hank Ketcham	1.60	4.80	8.00	H
601	Love for a Stranger—John Pleasant McCoy	.80	2.40	4.00	
602	My Business Is Murder—Henry Kane	.80	2.40	4.00	M
603	Avon Bedside Companion—ed. Wollheim	.80	2.40	4.00	
604	The Case of the Burning Bride—Alan Hynd; aka Alan Hynd's Murder	.50	1.50	2.50	M
605	Death Hits the Jackpot—John Tiger	.80	2.40	4.00	
606	The Kansan—Richard Brister	.80	2.40	4.00	W
607	Bubu of Montparnasse—Charles-Louis Philippe	.80	2.40	4.00	E
608	Curtain for a Jester—Frances & Richard Lockridge	.80	2.40	4.00	M
609	French Postcards	1.20	3.60	6.00	H
610	The Saint Steps In—Leslie Charteris	.80	2.40	4.00	M
611	The Saint in Europe—Leslie Charteris	.80	2.40	4.00	M
612	The New Jimmy Hatlo Book—Jimmy Hatlo	1.20	3.60	6.00	H
613	Break-Up—Edmund Schiddel	.80	2.40	4.00	E
614	And Dream of Evil—Tedd Thomey	.80	2.40	4.00	
615	Tawny—Donald Henderson Clarke	.80	2.40	4.00	
616	A Holiday for Murder—Agatha Christie	.80	2.40	4.00	M
617	Battle of the Sexes—Charles Preston	1.20	3.60	6.00	H
618	Trinity in Violence—Henry Kane	.80	2.40	4.00	M
619	The Saint Sees It Through—Leslie Charteris	.80	2.40	4.00	M
620	Death in the Desert—Lee E. Wells	.80	2.40	4.00	W
621	It Walks by Night—John Dickson Carr	.80	2.40	4.00	M
622	Hellbound—Paul Monash	.80	2.40	4.00	E

(AVON, continued)

		Good	Fine	N/Mint	
623	Beat Not the Bones—Charlotte Jay	.80	2.40	4.00	
624	The Stone of Chastity—Margery Sharp	.80	2.40	4.00	F
625	A Taste for Murder—H. F. Heard	.80	2.40	4.00	M
626	The Case of the Murdered Model—Thomas B. Dewey	.80	2.40	4.00	M
627	Caveman Cartoons—Harold Meyers	1.20	3.60	6.00	H
628	The Monk and the Hangman's Daughter—Ambrose Bierce	1.00	3.00	5.00	
629	The Saint and Mr. Teal—Leslie Charteris	.80	2.40	4.00	M
630	20 Great Ghost Stories	1.60	4.80	8.00	HO
631	Murderer's Holiday—Donald Henderson Clarke	.80	2.40	4.00	M
632	Jet Pilot—Tedd Thomey	.80	2.40	4.00	
633	Klever Kid Kartoons—Harold Meyers	1.00	3.00	5.00	H
634	Miss Lonelyhearts—Nathanel West	.80	2.40	4.00	
635	The Saint Goes West—Leslie Charteris	.80	2.40	4.00	M
636	The Moving Finger—Agatha Christie	.80	2.40	4.00	M
637	Animals Are Funnier Than People—Harold Meyers	1.20	3.60	6.00	H
638	Tropical Passions—anthology	1.00	3.00	5.00	E
639	Cartoons by Jimmy Hatlo; 1st ed., 1955	1.20	3.60	6.00	H
640	The Man Who Never Was—Ewen Montague	.80	2.40	4.00	
641	The Case of the Acid Throwers—John Creasey	.50	1.50	2.50	M
642	The Fighting Texan—Paul Evan Lehman	.80	2.40	4.00	W
643	South Sea Cartoons—Harold Meyers; c-Ward	1.20	3.60	6.00	H
644	Stories for Tonight—anthology; 1st ed., 1955	1.00	3.00	5.00	
645	Puzzles for Everybody—John Paul Adams	1.00	3.00	5.00	NF
646	The Case of the Murdered Madam—Henry Kane	.80	2.40	4.00	M
647	Unfaithful—John Baxter	.80	2.40	4.00	
648	Murder in Three Acts—Agatha Christie	.80	2.40	4.00	M
649	Nudist Cartoons—Harold Meyers	1.20	3.60	6.00	H
650	Confidential—Donald Henderson Clarke	.80	2.40	4.00	
651	Murder in Las Vegas—Jack Waer	.80	2.40	4.00	M
652	Hatlo's Inferno—Jimmy Hatlo; 1st ed., 1955	2.00	6.00	10.00	H
653	The Saint Goes On—Leslie Charteris	.80	2.40	4.00	M
654	Bloody Kansas—Chuck Martin; 1st ed., 1955	.80	2.40	4.00	W
655	Seven Who Were Hanged—Leonid Andreyev	.80	2.40	4.00	
656	Impatient Virgin—Donald Henderson Clarke	1.20	3.60	6.00	
657	The Doctor's Woman—H. P. Koenig	.80	2.40	4.00	
658	Death in the Air—Agatha Christie	.80	2.40	4.00	M
659	Hell-town in Texas—Leslie Ernenwein	.80	2.40	4.00	W
660	Wake Up to Murder—Day Keene	.80	2.40	4.00	M
661	Stories of Venial Sin—John O'Hara	.80	2.40	4.00	
662	Teen-age Cartoons and Jokes—Harold Meyers	1.20	3.60	6.00	H
663	The Ace of Knaves—Leslie Charteris	.80	2.40	4.00	M
664	Desire in the Deep South—Ward Greene	1.20	3.60	6.00	E
665	Dennis the Menace—Hank Ketcham	1.20	3.60	6.00	H
666	A Key to Death—Frances & Richard Lockridge	.80	2.40	4.00	M
667	The Range Bum—Kenneth Fowler	.80	2.40	4.00	W
668	Woman and the Puppet—Pierre Louys	.80	2.40	4.00	E
669	Sensualite—Georges de La Fouchardiere	.80	2.40	4.00	E
670	The Fugitive Eye—Charlotte Jay	.80	2.40	4.00	
671	A Lady Named Lou—Donald Henderson Clarke	.80	2.40	4.00	E
672	Too French and Too Deadly—Henry Kane	.80	2.40	4.00	
673	Henry Morgan's Joke Book—Henry Morgan	1.00	3.00	5.00	H
674	The Challenge of Smoke Wade—Robert J. Hogan	.80	2.40	4.00	W
675	A Room in Berlin—Gunther Birkenfeld	.80	2.40	4.00	
676	White Barrier—Noel Clad	.80	2.40	4.00	
677	Case of the Black, Black Hearse—Frederic Freyer	.80	2.40	4.00	M
678	The Fighting Kid From Eldorado—William Colt MacDonald	.80	2.40	4.00	W
679	Hellbox—John O'Hara	.80	2.40	4.00	
680	The Saint - The Happy Highwayman—Leslie Charteris	.80	2.40	4.00	M

Avon 585, © Avon

Avon 652, © Avon

Avon 656, © Avon

Avon 682, © Avon   Avon 705, © Avon   Avon 707, © Avon

(AVON, continued)	Good	Fine	N/Mint	
681 Showgirl Cartoons, Photographs, Stories—Harold Meyers	1.20	3.60	6.00	H
682 Chinese Love Tales—Edward Powys Mathers	1.60	4.80	8.00	
683 Coming, Aphrodite!	1.00	3.00	5.00	
684 The Passion Murders—Day Keene	1.00	3.00	5.00	M
685 Alibi Baby—Stewart Sterling	.80	2.40	4.00	M
686 The Hungering Shame—R. V. Cassill; orig., 1956	.80	2.40	4.00	E
687 Vegas, Gunman Marshal—William Hopson	.80	2.40	4.00	W
688 The Art Studio Murders—Edward Ronns	.80	2.40	4.00	M
689 Riders of the Whistling Skull—William Colt MacDonald	.80	2.40	4.00	W
690 The Big Four—Agatha Christie; c-Kinstler	1.60	4.80	8.00	M
691 Sappho—Alphonse Daudet	.80	2.40	4.00	E
692 The Counterfeit General Montgomery—M. E. Clifton James	.80	2.40	4.00	
693 The Hotshot—Fletcher Flora	.80	2.40	4.00	
694 The Saint - Wanted for Murder—Leslie Charteris; aka Wanted for Murder	.80	2.40	4.00	M
695 The Jungle of Love—Robin Maugham; aka Behind the Mirror	.80	2.40	4.00	
696 Murder Somewhere in This City—Maurice Procter; aka Hell in a City	.80	2.40	4.00	M
697 The Girl With the Golden Eyes—Honore De Balzac	.80	2.40	4.00	E
698 Smoking-room Jokebook—Harold Meyers	1.00	3.00	5.00	H
699 Counterspy Murders—Peter Cheyney	.80	2.40	4.00	M
700 Mirror of Your Mind—Joseph Whitney; orig., 1956	.80	2.40	4.00	NF
701 The Anatomy of a Crime—Joseph F. Dinneen	.80	2.40	4.00	
702 The Room in the Dragon Inn—Joseph Sheridan LeFanu; aka The Room in the Dragon Volant	.80	2.40	4.00	A
703 Armchair in Hell—Henry Kane	.80	2.40	4.00	
704 Whiplash War—Al Cody	.80	2.40	4.00	W
705 Hunt the Killer—Day Keene	1.00	3.00	5.00	
706 Operation Intrigue—Walter Hermann	.80	2.40	4.00	
707 Jimmy Hatlo Cartoons of 1956—Jimmy Hatlo; 1st ed., 1956	1.20	3.60	6.00	H
708 Arrest the Saint!—Leslie Charteris	.80	2.40	4.00	M
709 Montana Gunslinger—William Hopson	.80	2.40	4.00	W
710 The Wound of Love—R. V. Cassill	.80	2.40	4.00	
711 Experiment in Crime—Philip Wylie	.80	2.40	4.00	
712 The Man Nobody Saw—Peter Cheyney; c-Kinstler	1.00	3.00	5.00	M
713 The Outraged Sect—Jada M. Davis; orig., 1956	.80	2.40	4.00	E
714 The Case of the Black Orchids—Rex Stout	1.00	3.00	5.00	M
715 The Vengeance Trail—Paul Evan Lehman	.80	2.40	4.00	W
716 Poirot Investigates—Agatha Christie	.80	2.40	4.00	M
717 How Rough Can It Get?—Joe Weiss	.80	2.40	4.00	
718 Enter the Saint—Leslie Charteris	.80	2.40	4.00	M
719 Few Die Well—Sterling Noel	.80	2.40	4.00	
720 Give a Man a Gun—John Creasey; aka A Gun for Inspector West	.50	1.50	2.50	M
721 Lilly's Story—Ethel Wilson	.80	2.40	4.00	
722 Gang Girl—Wenzell Brown	1.00	3.00	5.00	JD
723 Yucca City Outlaw—William Hopson	.80	2.40	4.00	W
724 Empty Saddles—Al Cody	.80	2.40	4.00	W
725 The Case of the Bludgeoned Teacher—Jim Hollis	.80	2.40	4.00	M
726 The Tragedy of Z—Ellery Queen	.80	2.40	4.00	M
727 The Smuggled Atom Bomb—Philip Wylie	1.00	3.00	5.00	
728 Safari to Dishonor—Edmund Schiddel	.80	2.40	4.00	
729 The Battle at Apache Pass—Harold Conrad	.80	2.40	4.00	W
730 The Case of the Hypnotized Virgin—John Roeburt	.80	2.40	4.00	M
731 Operation Tokyo—Ted Middleton	.80	2.40	4.00	
732 The Kansan—Richard Brister	.80	2.40	4.00	W
733 Who Killed Sweet Sue?—Henry Kane	1.00	3.00	5.00	M
734 The Case of the Dark Hero—Peter Cheyney	1.00	3.00	5.00	M
735 The Hoodlums—John Eagle	.80	2.40	4.00	
736 The Yellow Turban—Charlotte Jay	.80	2.40	4.00	M
737 And Dream of Evil—Tedd Thomey	.80	2.40	4.00	

			Good	Fine	N/Mint	
738	Invitation to Murder—Rex Stout		1.00	3.00	5.00	M
739	Hired Gun—Archie Joscelyn		.80	2.40	4.00	W
740	Park Avenue Girl—Floyd Shaw		.80	2.40	4.00	
741	Outlaw Loot—Paul Evan Lehman		.80	2.40	4.00	W
742	KKK—Paul E. Walsh; orig., 1956		1.60	4.80	8.00	
743	Love Affair—William Russell		.80	2.40	4.00	
744	The Saint and the Sizzling Saboteur—Leslie Charteris		.80	2.40	4.00	M
745	Martinis and Murder—Henry Kane		.80	2.40	4.00	M
746	The Girl With the Frightened Eyes—Lawrence Lariar		.80	2.40	4.00	
747	Tawny—Donald Henderson Clarke		.80	2.40	4.00	E
748	Gunsight Showdown—Johnston McCulley		.80	2.40	4.00	
749	Violent Maverick—Walt Coburn		.80	2.40	4.00	W
750	Southern Daughter—Daniel White		.80	2.40	4.00	
751	Murder of the Park Avenue Playgirl—Henry Kane; 1957		.80	2.40	4.00	M
752	Death by Moonlight—Michael Innes; aka The Man From the Sea		.80	2.40	4.00	M
753	The Passionate Seekers—Peter Matthiessen		.80	2.40	4.00	
754	The Long Noose—Lee E. Wells		.80	2.40	4.00	W
755	A Spy in the House of Love—Anais Nin		.80	2.40	4.00	
756	The Saint - The Brighter Buccaneer—Leslie Charteris		.80	2.40	4.00	M
757	Inspector Maigret & the Dead Girl—Georges Simenon; c-Kinstler		1.20	3.60	6.00	M
758	Arizona Dead-shot—Nelson Nye		.80	2.40	4.00	W
759	Fighting Buckaroo—Paul Evan Lehman		.80	2.40	4.00	W
760	Love of Seven Dolls—Paul Gallico		.80	2.40	4.00	
761	Death on the Double—Henry Kane		.80	2.40	4.00	M
762	The Hotel Murders—Stewart Sterling		.80	2.40	4.00	M
763	Vice Squad Cop—Michael Carey		.80	2.40	4.00	
764	The Dark Street Murders—Peter Cheyney		1.00	3.00	5.00	M
765	California Gunman—William Colt MacDonald		.80	2.40	4.00	W
766	Mr. & Mrs. North and the Poisoned Playboy—Frances & Richard Lockridge; aka Death of an Angel		.80	2.40	4.00	M
767	The Murder Room—Paul Walsh		.80	2.40	4.00	M
768	Sinful Woman—James M. Cain		.80	2.40	4.00	
769	The Phantom Pass—William Colt MacDonald		.80	2.40	4.00	W
770	Outlaw Fury—Burt Arthur		.80	2.40	4.00	W
771	The Saint on the Spanish Main—Leslie Charteris		.80	2.40	4.00	M
772	Murder in Manhattan—John Roeburt		.80	2.40	4.00	M
773	The Woman and the Prowler—Stuart Friedman		.80	2.40	4.00	
774	Gunfight at the O. K. Corral; movie tie-in		1.20	3.60	6.00	W
775	The Tall T—Elmore Leonard; movie tie-in		1.20	3.60	6.00	W
776	Sinister Murders—Peter Cheyney		1.00	3.00	5.00	M
777	Kiss and Kill—Reed McCary; aka Sleep With the Devil		1.00	3.00	5.00	
778	Tales of Midsummer Passion—anthology		1.00	3.00	5.00	
779	Gunsmoke Vengeance—Johnston McCulley; aka South of the Pass, c-Kinstler		1.00	3.00	5.00	W
780	The Lonely Man—Robert Turner; movie tie-in		1.20	3.60	6.00	W
781	The Calypso Murders—P. J. Mulholland; Note: Same cover as Avon No. 506.		1.00	3.00	5.00	M
782	Gun Feud at Stampede Valley—Samuel A. Peeples		.80	2.40	4.00	
783	Hot Rod Gang Rumble—Meyer Dolinsky		1.20	3.60	6.00	JD
784	Murder in Las Vegas—Jack Waer		.80	2.40	4.00	M
785	Gun Play at the X-Bar-X—Burt Arthur		.80	2.40	4.00	W
786	Murder, My Love—Edward Atiyah		.80	2.40	4.00	M
787	The Case of the Murdered Model—Thomas B. Dewey		.50	1.50	2.50	M
788	Six-gun Sawbones—Archie Joscelyn		.80	2.40	4.00	W
789	More They'll Do It Every Time—Jimmy Hatlo; 1st ed., 1957		1.20	3.60	6.00	H
790	My Business Is Murder—Henry Kane		.80	2.40	4.00	M
791	Texas Revenge—Archie Joscelyn		.80	2.40	4.00	W
792	Murder in Lima—Robert A. Levey		.80	2.40	4.00	M
793	The Moving Finger—Agatha Christie		.80	2.40	4.00	M
794	The Ripper Murders—Maurice Proctor		.80	2.40	4.00	M
795	Blood on the Saddle—Johnston McCulley		.80	2.40	4.00	W

Avon 742, © Avon

Avon 783, © Avon

Avon 795, © Avon

		Good	Fine	N/Mint	
796	A Mask for Murder—Henry Kane	.80	2.40	4.00	M
797	Cocktails and the Killer—Peter Cheyney	.80	2.40	4.00	M
798	Outlaw—Archie Joscelyn; 1958	.80	2.40	4.00	W
799	Powdersmoke Range—William Colt MacDonald	.80	2.40	4.00	W
800	Case of the Murdered Redhead—Frances & Richard Lockridge	.80	2.40	4.00	M
801	Night Cry—William L. Stuart	.80	2.40	4.00	M
802	Murder in Baracoa—Paul Walsh	.80	2.40	4.00	M
803	Featuring the Saint—Leslie Charteris	.80	2.40	4.00	M
804	Flesh and Fire—Georges Arnaud	.80	2.40	4.00	
805	The Tough Texan—Paul Evan Lehman	.80	2.40	4.00	W
806	Bandit in Black—Paul Evan Lehman	.80	2.40	4.00	W
807	Wine, Women and Murder—John Roeburt	.80	2.40	4.00	M
808	A Taste for Murder—H. F. Heard	.80	2.40	4.00	M
809	The Vice Net—Michael Carey	.80	2.40	4.00	
810	Montana Helltown—Al Cody	.80	2.40	4.00	W
811	Let Me Kill You, Sweetheart—Fletcher Flora	.80	2.40	4.00	M
812	Bloody Wyoming—Al Cody	.80	2.40	4.00	W
813	Fighting Kid From Texas—Archie Joscelyn	.80	2.40	4.00	W
814	It's a Sin to Kill—Day Keene; orig., 1958	1.00	3.00	5.00	M
815	Bachelor's Guide to the Opposite Sex—Max Lieg & Georges Pichard	1.00	3.00	5.00	H
816	Thunderbolt Range—Paul Evan Lehman; aka The Sheep Killers	.80	2.40	4.00	W
817	The Doctor's Woman—H. P. Koenig	.80	2.40	4.00	
818	Alias the Saint—Leslie Charteris	.50	1.50	2.50	M
819	Cheyenne Kid—Archie Joscelyn	.80	2.40	4.00	W
820	Stampede Canyon—Robert J. Hogan	.80	2.40	4.00	W
821	Guns Blaze on Spiderweb Range—Walt Coburn	.80	2.40	4.00	W
822	Montana Dead-Shot—Chuck Martin	.80	2.40	4.00	W
823	Cry Killer!—Kenneth Fearing	.50	1.50	2.50	M
824	Notched Guns—William Hopson	.80	2.40	4.00	W
825	Gun-Whipped!—Paul Evan Lehman; orig., 1958	.80	2.40	4.00	W
826	Another New Jimmy Hatlo Book—Jimmy Hatlo; 1st ed., 1958	1.20	3.60	6.00	H
827	The Saint on Guard—Leslie Charteris	.50	1.50	2.50	M
828	Tall in the Saddle—Chuck Martin	.80	2.40	4.00	W
829	Hell Range in Texas—J. E. Grinstead	.80	2.40	4.00	W
830	The Bitch—Gil Brewer	.80	2.40	4.00	
831	Renegade Marshal—Paul Evan Lehman; aka Devil's Doorstep, c-Abbett	.80	2.40	4.00	W
832	Disaster Trail—Al Cody	.80	2.40	4.00	W
833	The Wolf Streak—Richard Brister	.80	2.40	4.00	W
834	Concerning the Saint—Leslie Charteris	.50	1.50	2.50	M
835	Too Hot to Kill—Stewart Sterling	.80	2.40	4.00	M
836	Unfaithful—John Baxter; Note: Basically the same cover as Avon No. 114.	.80	2.40	4.00	
837	Long Ride to Abilene—William Hopson	.80	2.40	4.00	W
838	The Dead Ride Hard—Lynn Westland	.80	2.40	4.00	W
839	Leave Her to Hell!—Fletcher Flora	.50	1.50	2.50	
841	Day of Vengeance—Chuck Martin	.50	1.50	2.50	W
842	Wyoming Ambush—Al Cody	.50	1.50	2.50	W
843	Gunsmoke at Buffalo Basin—Paul Evan Lehman	.80	2.40	4.00	W
844	Deadly Draw—Lee Floren	.50	1.50	2.50	W
845	The Man From the Badlands—Paul Evan Lehman	.80	2.40	4.00	W
846	Born Reckless—Milton Rogers	.50	1.50	2.50	
847	My Name Is Violence—John D. Matthews & Jeffrey Roche	.50	1.50	2.50	
848	The Saint Cleans Up—Leslie Charteris	.50	1.50	2.50	M
849	It Happened at Thunder River—Bliss Lomax (H. S. Drago)	.80	2.40	4.00	W
850	The Manhunter—Paul Evan Lehman; aka Law of the Forty-five	.50	1.50	2.50	W
851	Ship Ahoy	1.00	3.00	5.00	H
852	Fast Gun—Walt Coburn	.50	1.50	2.50	W
853	French Postcards	1.00	3.00	5.00	H
854	Make Mine Vengeance—Robert Colby	.50	1.50	2.50	
855	Then Came Mulvane—William Heuman	.50	1.50	2.50	W
856	Bullet Law—Johnston McCulley	.80	2.40	4.00	W
857	The Newest Jimmy Hatlo Cartoon Book—Jimmy Hatlo; 1st ed., 1959	1.20	3.60	6.00	H
858	Branded—Walt Coburn	.50	1.50	2.50	W
859	More All About Girls	1.00	3.00	5.00	H
860	Caveman Cartoons—Harold Meyers	1.00	3.00	5.00	H
861	Six Bullets Left—Barry Cord	.50	1.50	2.50	W
862	Renegade Lawman—Gordon D. Shirreffs	.50	1.50	2.50	W
863	Bloody Kansas—Chuck Martin	.50	1.50	2.50	W
864	The Deadly Game—Norman Daniels; c-Abbett	.80	2.40	4.00	M
1001	Jew Suss—Lion Feuchtwanger; 1951, interior illos-Kinstler	4.00	12.00	20.00	E
1002	The Avon All-American Fiction Reader; 1951	3.00	9.00	15.00	

AVON ANNUAL
Avon Book Company

Digest Size

(AVON ANNUAL, continued)	Good	Fine	N/Mint	
nn(1) Avon Annual; 1944	1.60	4.80	8.00	
nn(2) Avon Annual; 1945	2.00	6.00	10.00	
nn(3) Avon Annual; 1946	2.00	6.00	10.00	
nn(4) Avon Annual; 1947	1.60	4.80	8.00	

AVON BARD
Avon Publications, Inc./Avon Book Division—Hearst Corporation

		Good	Fine	N/Mint	
Bard 1	The Rubaiyat of Omar Khayyam; 1955	.40	1.20	2.00	
Bard 2	The Meaning and Psychology of Dreams—Wilheim Stekel	.40	1.20	2.00	NF
Bard 3	Anyone Can Have a Great Vocabulary—S. L. Stephenson	.40	1.20	2.00	NF
Bard 4	Favorite Stories—W. Somerset Maugham	.40	1.20	2.00	
Bard 5	(T 05) My Lord What a Morning—Marian Anderson; 1958	.40	1.20	2.00	
Bard 6	(T 06) You and the Atom—Gerald Wendt	.40	1.20	2.00	NF
Bard11	(T 11) Sonnets From the Portuguese—Elizabeth Barrett Browning	.40	1.20	2.00	

AVON BEDSIDE NOVELS
Avon Publishing Company, Inc.

Digest Size

		Good	Fine	N/Mint	
1	The Rites of Love—Jack Woodford	3.00	9.00	15.00	E
2	The Hard-boiled Virgin—Jack Woodford; 1950	3.00	9.00	15.00	E
3	Queer Patterns—Lilyan Brock	3.00	9.00	15.00	E
4	Bedroom Eyes—Maurice Dekobra	3.00	9.00	15.00	E
5	Male and Female—Jack Woodford	3.00	9.00	15.00	E
6	The Passionate Princess—Jack Woodford; aka Proxy Princess	3.00	9.00	15.00	E

AVON BOOK DIVIDEND
Avon Publishing Company, Inc.

Digest Size

		Good	Fine	N/Mint	
1	The Abortive Hussy—Jack Woodford	3.00	9.00	15.00	E
2	Star Lust—Jack Hanley	3.00	9.00	15.00	E
3	New York Madness—Maxwell Bodenheim	3.00	9.00	15.00	E
4	Grounds for Divorce—Jack Woodford	3.00	9.00	15.00	E
5	Her Private Passions—Marty Holland	3.00	9.00	15.00	E
6	Teach Me to Love—Jack Woodford	3.00	9.00	15.00	E
7	Tropical Passions—anthology; Note: Same cover as Avon No. 255 and basically the same as Avon Modern Short Story Monthly No. 44.	3.00	9.00	15.00	E

AVON DETECTIVE MYSTERIES
Avon Detective - Mysteries, Inc.

Digest Size

		Good	Fine	N/Mint	
1	Includes Woolrich, Starrett, Christie, others; 1947	3.00	9.00	15.00	M
2	Includes Carter Dickson, Eberhart, others; 1947. Note: Same cover as Avon No. 104 and Murder Mystery Monthly No. 13.	3.00	9.00	15.00	M
3	Includes Gruber, Rohmer, Brown, others; 1947. Note: Partially the same cover as Avon No. 122 and the pulp Private Detective Stories, October 1944	3.00	9.00	15.00	M

Avon Annual 2, © Avon

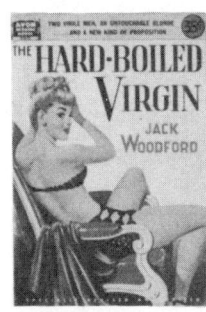

Avon Bedside Novels 2, © Avon

Avon Book Dividend 2, © Avon

Avon Fantasy Reader 4, © Avon   Avon Fantasy Reader 13, © Avon   Avon G1035, © Avon

AVON FANTASY NOVELS
Avon Publishing Company

		Good	Fine	N/Mint	
1	Princess of the Atom—Ray Cummings; 1950	5.00	15.00	25.00	SF
2	The Green Girl—Jack Williamson; 1950	10.00	30.00	50.00	SF

Note: Coblentz' Into Plutonian Depths and Farley's Earthman on Venus were planned as No. 3 and No. 4 of the series but instead became No. 281 and No. 285 of the regular Avon series.

AVON FANTASY READER
Avon Book Company/Avon Novels, Inc.

Digest Size

1	Includes Leinster, Derleth, Merritt, Smith, others; 1947	4.00	12.00	20.00	SF
2	Includes Pratt, Howard, Endore, Keller; 1947	2.00	6.00	10.00	SF
3	Includes Merritt, Lovecraft, Moore, Bradbury, others; 1947	3.00	9.00	15.00	SF
4	Includes Miller, Bradbury, Smith, Van Vogt, others; 1947	2.00	6.00	10.00	SF
5	Includes Moore, Bloch, Jacobi, Kornbluth; 1947	2.00	6.00	10.00	SF
6	Includes Lovecraft, Merritt, Hamilton, McClusky, others; 1948	3.00	9.00	15.00	SF
7	Includes Moore, Rohmer, Howard, Merritt, others; 1948	3.00	9.00	15.00	SF
8	Includes Howard, Bradbury, Lovecraft, Bierce, others; 1948	3.00	9.00	15.00	SF
9	Includes Smith, Leiber, Kline, Bloch, others; 1949	2.00	6.00	10.00	SF
10	Includes Howard, Lovecraft, Breuer, Wollheim, others; 1949	2.00	6.00	10.00	SF
11	Includes Quinn, Bond, Stribling, Bradbury, others; 1949	2.00	6.00	10.00	SF
12	Includes Howard, Smith, Rohmer, Wellman, others	2.00	6.00	10.00	SF
13	Includes Long, Cummings, Derleth, Wandrei; 1950	2.00	6.00	10.00	SF
14	Includes Howard, Bradbury, Cummings, Keller, others; 1950, c-Wood	3.00	9.00	15.00	SF
15	Includes Weinbaum, Smith, Kornbluth, Miller, others; 1951	2.00	6.00	10.00	SF
16	Includes Bloch, Shiel, Wandrei, Long, others; 1951	2.00	6.00	10.00	SF
17	Includes Bradbury, Lovecraft, Price, Chesterton, others; 1951	3.00	9.00	15.00	SF
18	Includes Howard, Hodgson, Blackwood, Clark, others; 1952	4.00	12.00	20.00	SF

AVON G-SERIES
Avon Publishing Company, Inc.

G1003	The Collected Works of Pierre Louys; 1951	4.00	12.00	20.00	E
G1004	Giant Mystery Reader	5.00	15.00	25.00	M
G1005	Geraldine Bradshaw—Calder Willingham	3.00	9.00	15.00	E
G1006	Men at War—Ernest Hemingway; 1952	3.00	9.00	15.00	A
G1007	Avon Webster English Dictionary	3.00	9.00	15.00	NF
G1008	Temptation—John Pen	5.00	15.00	25.00	E
G1009	The Big Brokers—Irving Shulman; 1953	3.00	9.00	15.00	
G1010	Out of This World to Forbidden Tibet—Lowell Thomas; 1954	.80	2.40	4.00	NF
G1011	Master of the World—Cothburn O'Neal	.80	2.40	4.00	A
G1012	Send Me Down—Henry Steig	.80	2.40	4.00	
G1013	The Human Beast—Emile Zola	.80	2.40	4.00	
G1014	Journey to the End of the Night—Louis-Ferdinand Celine	.80	2.40	4.00	
G1015	Queen's Caprice—George Preedy	.80	2.40	4.00	A
G1016	Avon Book of Modern Writing No. 2—William Phillips & Philip Rahr	.50	1.50	2.50	
G1017	The Third Angel—Jerome Weldman; 1955	.80	2.40	4.00	E
G1018	The Collected Works of Pierre Louys; 1955	1.00	3.00	5.00	E
G1019	Temptation—John Pen	1.00	3.00	5.00	E
G1020	Point Counter Point—Aldous Huxley	1.00	3.00	5.00	
G1021	Women in Love—D. H. Lawrence	1.00	3.00	5.00	E
G1022	Death on the Installment Plan—Louis-Ferdinand Celine	.80	2.40	4.00	
G1023	The Big Brokers—Irving Shulman	.80	2.40	4.00	
G1024	Crime and Punishment—Fyodor Dostoyevsky; 1956	.80	2.40	4.00	
G1025	Aaron's Rod—D. H. Lawrence	.80	2.40	4.00	E

(AVON G-SERIES, continued)		Good	Fine	N/Mint	
G1026	Your Daughter Iris—Jerome Weidman	.50	1.50	2.50	
G1027	Those Barren Leaves—Aldous Huxley	.80	2.40	4.00	
G1028	The Rainbow—D. H. Lawrence	.80	2.40	4.00	E
G1029	Dishonored Flesh—Joseph Pennell	.50	1.50	2.50	IE
G1030	Conquests of Tamerlane—Cothburn O'Neal; 1957	.50	1.50	2.50	A
G1031	Point Counter Point—Aldous Huxley	.80	2.40	4.00	
G1032	The Third Angel—Jerome Weidman; 1958	.50	1.50	2.50	
G1033	Temptation—John Penn; 1959	.80	2.40	4.00	E
G1034	A Death in the Family—James Agee	.50	1.50	2.50	
G1035	Maggie Cassidy—Jack Kerouac; 1st ed., 1959	3.00	9.00	15.00	
G1036	Last Summer—Boris Pasternak	.80	2.40	4.00	
G1037	They Hanged My Saintly Billy—Robert Graves	.50	1.50	2.50	
G1038	The Rainbow—D. H. Lawrence	.80	2.40	4.00	E
G1039	Aaron's Rod—D. H. Lawrence	.50	1.50	2.50	E
G1040	Great Short Stories by Soviet Authors	.50	1.50	2.50	
G2001	After Many a Summer Dies the Swan—Aldous Huxley	.50	1.50	2.50	SF
G2002	Butterfield 8—John O'Hara	.50	1.50	2.50	

AVON LOVE BOOK MONTHLY
Avon Publishing Company, Inc.

Digest Size

		Good	Fine	N/Mint	
1	Blonde Baggage—Marty Holland	3.00	9.00	15.00	E
2	Chorus Girl—Thyra Samter Winslow	3.00	9.00	15.00	E

AVON MODERN SHORT STORY MONTHLY
Avon Publishing Company, Inc.

Digest Size

		Good	Fine	N/Mint
1	Cosmopolitans: 29 Short Stories—John O'Hara	1.20	3.60	6.00
2	Files on Parade—John O'Hara	1.20	3.60	6.00
3	To Step Aside—Noel Coward	1.20	3.60	6.00
4	Inhale and Exhale—William Saroyan	1.20	3.60	6.00
5	Ill Wind—James Hilton	1.20	3.60	6.00
6	Selected Short Stories—Sinclair Lewis	1.20	3.60	6.00
7	14 Great Stories—anthology	1.20	3.60	6.00
8	First Person Singular—W. S. Maugham	1.20	3.60	6.00
9	13 Great Stories—John Steinbeck; 1943	1.20	3.60	6.00
10	15 Selected Stories—James T. Farrell	1.20	3.60	6.00
11	Selected Great Stories—Ben Hecht	1.20	3.60	6.00
12	34 More Great Stories—William Saroyan	1.20	3.60	6.00
13	Three Short Novels—Louis Bromfield	1.20	3.60	6.00
14	22 Modern Stories—Erskine Caldwell	1.20	3.60	6.00
15	13 Great Modern Stories—anthology	1.20	3.60	6.00
16	Eight Long Short Stories—Fannie Hurst	1.20	3.60	6.00
17	Selected Stories—Thomas Wolfe	1.20	3.60	6.00
18	Ah King—W. S. Maugham	1.20	3.60	6.00
19	They Brought Their Women—Edna Ferber	1.20	3.60	6.00
20	Twelve Selected Modern Stories—anthology	1.20	3.60	6.00
21	12 Great Modern Short Stories—James T. Farrell	1.20	3.60	6.00
22	Career in C Major—J. M. Cain	1.20	3.60	6.00
23	Great Stories of China—Pearl S. Buck	1.20	3.60	6.00
24	Five Long Short Stories—Louis Bromfield	1.20	3.60	6.00
25	The Bottle Collectors—Kenneth Roberts	1.20	3.60	6.00
26	A Thousand and One Afternoons in New York—Ben Hecht	1.20	3.60	6.00

Avon Modern Short Story 1, © Avon

Avon Modern Short Story 3, © Avon

Avon Modern Short Story 5, © Avon

Avon Modern Short Story 47, © Avon

Avon Monthly Novel 8, © Avon

Avon Monthly Novel 9, © Avon

(AVON MODERN SHORT STORY MONTHLY, continued)

		Good	Fine	N/Mint	
27	Ten Hilarious Stories—Damon Runyon	1.20	3.60	6.00	
28	Too Bad—Dorothy Parker	1.20	3.60	6.00	
29	Hope of Heaven—John O'Hara	1.20	3.60	6.00	
30	Georgia Boy—Erskine Caldwell	1.20	3.60	6.00	
31	Everybody Was Nice—Stephen Vincent Benet	1.20	3.60	6.00	
32	Welcome to the City—Irwin Shaw	1.20	3.60	6.00	
33	The Road to Recovery—Budd Shulberg	1.20	3.60	6.00	
34	Great Stories by Louis Bromfield	1.20	3.60	6.00	
35	Trembling of a Leaf—W. S. Maugham	1.20	3.60	6.00	
36	Stories of Love and Adventure—Rafael Sabatini; Note: Same cover as Avon No. 84	1.20	3.60	6.00	A
37	Another Selection of Ben Hecht's Sparkling Stories	1.20	3.60	6.00	
38	Stories of Intrigue—W. S. Maugham	1.20	3.60	6.00	
39	Stories of Venial Sin—John O'Hara	1.20	3.60	6.00	
40	Marianne in India and Other Stories—Lion Feuchtwanger	1.20	3.60	6.00	
41	Ten Selected Stories—James T. Farrell	1.20	3.60	6.00	
42	Hollywood Love Clinic—anthology	1.60	4.80	8.00	
43	East of Suez/Great Stories of the Tropics—W. S. Maugham	1.20	3.60	6.00	
44	Tropical Passions—anthology; Note: Basically the same cover as Avon No. 255 and Avon Book Dividend No. 7.	1.60	4.80	8.00	
45	Hellbox—John O'Hara	1.60	4.80	8.00	
46	Love Among the Haystacks—D. H. Lawrence	1.60	4.80	8.00	
47	Love in Greenwich Village—Floyd Dell	1.60	4.80	8.00	
48	Night Club—Katharine Brush	1.60	4.80	8.00	
49	A Modern Lover—D. H. Lawrence	1.60	4.80	8.00	
50	All the Girls He Wanted—John O'Hara	1.60	4.80	8.00	

AVON MONTHLY NOVEL
Avon Publishing Co., Inc.

Digest Size

1	Sinful Woman—James M. Cain; orig., 1947	2.00	6.00	10.00	E
2	Her Private Passions—Marty Holland	2.00	6.00	10.00	E
3	The Regenerate Lover—D. H. Clarke	2.00	6.00	10.00	E
4	The Villain and the Virgin—J. H. Chase	2.00	6.00	10.00	E
5	Uneasy Virtue—Dana Wilson; 1948, aka Make With the Brains, Pierre	2.00	6.00	10.00	E
6	Strange Desires—Len Zinberg; aka What D'ya Know for Sure	2.00	6.00	10.00	E
7	12 Chinks and a Woman—J. H. Chase	7.00	21.00	35.00	E
8	Virgie, Goodbye—Nathan Rothman; Note: Same cover as the comic Romantic Love No. 7.	3.00	9.00	15.00	E
9	The Scarf of Passion—Robert Bloch; aka The Scarf. Note: Same cover as Avon No. 211 and an unnumbered Avon Special of the same name.	3.00	9.00	15.00	E
10	The Lady Said Yes—G. V. Martin	2.00	6.00	10.00	E
11	The Devil Is Loneliness—Elma K. Lobaugh	2.00	6.00	10.00	E
12	Little Sins—Katharine Brush	2.00	6.00	10.00	E
13	Carlotta—Robert Briffault	2.00	6.00	10.00	E
14	The Man Who Drove Girls Wild—M. H. Hanline	2.00	6.00	10.00	E
15	The Darling of Paris—Marty Holland; orig., 1949	2.00	6.00	10.00	E
16	Millie's Daughter—D. H. Clarke	2.00	6.00	10.00	E
17	Jealous Woman—J. M. Cain	2.00	6.00	10.00	E
18	I'll Get You for This—J. H. Chase	3.00	9.00	15.00	E
19					
20	Ecstasy Girl—Jack Woodford	2.00	6.00	10.00	E
21	Tomcat in Tights—Jack Hanley	2.00	6.00	10.00	E

AVON MURDER MYSTERY MONTHLY
Avon Book Company/Avon Publishing Company, Inc.

Digest Size

(Continuation of Avon Murder of the Month)

		Good	Fine	N/Mint	
3	Silinski - Master Criminal—Edgar Wallace	4.00	12.00	20.00	M
4	The French Key Mystery—Frank Gruber	4.00	12.00	20.00	M
5	Burn, Witch, Burn—A. A. Merritt	3.00	9.00	15.00	SF
6	The Postman Always Rings Twice—J. M. Cain	4.00	12.00	20.00	M
7	The Big Sleep—Raymond Chandler	12.50	37.50	60.00	M
8	Maigret Aboard—Georges Simenon; 1943	5.00	15.00	25.00	M
9	The Red Box—Rex Stout	9.00	27.00	45.00	M
10	Homicide for Hannah—Dwight V. Babcock	3.00	9.00	15.00	M
11	Creep Shadow Creep—A. A. Merritt	3.00	9.00	15.00	SF
12	Hungry Dog Murders—Frank Gruber	5.00	15.00	25.00	M
13	If the Shroud Fits—Kelley Roos	3.00	9.00	15.00	M
14	Whose Body?—Dorothy L. Sayers	4.00	12.00	20.00	M
15	Premeditated Murder—Peter Cheyney; aka A Trap for Bellamy	5.00	15.00	25.00	M
16	Double Indemnity—James M. Cain; 1st ed., 1943	6.00	18.00	30.00	M
17	Who Killed Chloe?—Margery Allingham; aka Dancers in Mourning	3.00	9.00	15.00	M
18	The Moon Pool—A. A. Merritt; 1944	3.00	9.00	15.00	SF
19	5 Murderers—Raymond Chandler; 1st ed., 1944	16.50	50.00	80.00	M
20	The Embezzler—J. M. Cain	5.00	15.00	25.00	M
21	Counter Spy Murders—Peter Cheyney; aka Dark Duet	5.00	15.00	25.00	M
22	Ace of Knaves—Leslie Charteris; aka The Saint Goes Into Action	5.00	15.00	25.00	M
23	Simon Lash, Private Detective—Frank Gruber	6.00	18.00	30.00	M
24	Dwellers in the Mirage—A. A. Merritt	3.00	9.00	15.00	SF
25	About the Murder of a Startled Lady—Anthony Abbot	5.00	15.00	25.00	M
26	The Mysterious Affair at Styles—Agatha Christie	5.00	15.00	25.00	M
27	The Black Angel—Cornell Woolrich	9.00	27.00	45.00	M
28	Five Criminals—Raymond Chandler; 1st ed. 1945	16.50	50.00	80.00	M
29	The Face in the Abyss—A. A. Merritt	3.00	9.00	15.00	SF
30	Farewell to the Admiral—Peter Cheyney	5.00	15.00	25.00	M
31	If I Should Die Before I Wake—William Irish; 1st ed., 1945	15.00	45.00	75.00	M
32	The Saint Vs. Scotland Yard—Leslie Charteris	5.00	15.00	25.00	M
33	Nobody Lives Forever—W. R. Burnett	5.00	15.00	25.00	M
34	The Ship of Ishtar—A. A. Merritt; Note: Uses retouched cover from the pulp magazine Argosy, May 10, 1930.	3.00	9.00	15.00	SF
35	Flowers for the Judge—Margery Allingham; 1946	4.00	12.00	20.00	M
36	They Never Say When—Peter Cheyney	5.00	15.00	25.00	M
37	Orchids to Murder—Hulbert Footner	5.00	15.00	25.00	M
38	Hannah Says Foul Play—Dwight V. Babcock; 1st ed., 1946	3.00	9.00	15.00	M
39	Flash Casey - Detective—George Harmon Coxe; 1st ed., 1946	8.00	24.00	40.00	M
40	High Sierra—W. R. Burnett	5.00	15.00	25.00	M
41	The Metal Monster—A. A. Merritt	3.00	9.00	15.00	SF
42	Borrowed Crime—William Irish; 1st ed., 1946	15.00	45.00	75.00	M
43	Finger Man—Raymond Chandler; 1st ed., 1946.	16.50	50.00	80.00	M
44	Love's Lovely Counterfeit—J. M. Cain; 1947	5.00	15.00	25.00	M
45	On the Spot—Edgar Wallace	5.00	15.00	25.00	M
46	Green Ice Murders—Raoul Whitfield; 1947	6.00	18.00	30.00	M
47	The Blonde, the Gangster and the Private Eye—Dale Clark; 1950, aka The Red Rods.	8.00	24.00	40.00	M
48	Murder in Her Big Blue Eyes—Julius Long; aka Keep the Coffins Coming	7.00	21.00	35.00	M
49	Lady, the Guy is Dead—Edward Ronns; 1950, aka No Place to Live. Note: Same cover as the comic The Saint No. 10.	7.00	21.00	35.00	M

AVON MURDER OF THE MONTH
Avon Book Company

Digest Size

Avon Murder Mystery 5, © Avon

Avon Murder Mystery 31, © Avon

Avon Murder Mystery 46, © Avon

Avon Murder of the Month 1, © Avon   Avon Romance Novel 1, © Avon   Avon Science Fiction Reader 1, © Avon

(AVON MURDER OF THE MONTH, continued)
(Continued as Avon Murder Mystery Monthly)

		Good	Fine	N/Mint	
1	Seven Footprints to Satan—A. A. Merritt; 1942	5.00	15.00	25.00	SF
2	Mysterious Mickey Finn—Elliott Paul; 1942	4.00	12.00	20.00	M

AVON ROMANCE NOVEL MONTHLY
Avon Publishing Co., Inc.

Digest Size

1	The Little Sinner—Ruby M. Ayers; 1949	3.00	9.00	15.00	E
2	Love Should Be Laughter—Frances S. Moore	3.00	9.00	15.00	E
3	Help Yourself to Love—Peggy Dern; 1950	3.00	9.00	15.00	E

AVON SCIENCE FICTION AND FANTASY READER
Avon Novels, Inc./Stratford Novels, Inc.

Digest Size

1	Includes Clarke, Christopher, Jakes, others; 1953	2.00	6.00	10.00	SF
2	Includes Vance, Clarke, Jakes, others; 1953	1.60	4.80	8.00	SF

AVON SCIENCE FICTION READER
Avon Novels, Inc.

Digest Size

1	Includes Hamilton, Merritt, Williamson, Smith, others; 1951	3.00	9.00	15.00	SF
2	Includes Wandrei, Smith, Cummings, Dunsany, others; 1951	3.00	9.00	15.00	SF
3	Includes Long, Wright, Lovecraft, Bok, others; 1952	3.00	9.00	15.00	SF

AVON SPECIALS
Avon Publishing Company, Inc.

Digest Size

nn	Seduction—Leo Guild	3.00	9.00	15.00	E
nn	A Lady Named Lou—D. H. Clarke	3.00	9.00	15.00	E
nn	Peeping Tom—Woodford	3.00	9.00	15.00	E
nn	Night Club Girl—John Wilstach; 1951, aka Fiddler's Fee	3.00	9.00	15.00	E
nn	Three Gorgeous Hussies—Woodford	3.00	9.00	15.00	E
nn	Free Lovers—Woodford	3.00	9.00	15.00	E
nn	Scarf of Passion—Robert Bloch; Note: Same cover as Avon No. 211 and Avon Monthly Novel No. 9.	3.00	9.00	15.00	E

AVON T/AT-SERIES
Avon Book Company/Avon Publishing Co., Inc.

T- 2	Aaron's Rod—D. H. Lawrence	.50	1.50	2.50	E
AT-51	Bad Girl—Vina Delmar; 1953	.50	1.50	2.50	E
AT-52	The Night Air—Harrison Dowd	.50	1.50	2.50	E
AT-53	The Second Oldest Profession—Robert Sylvester	.50	1.50	2.50	E
AT-54	Madame Serpent—Jean Plaidy	.50	1.50	2.50	A
AT-55	The Rake's Progress—Philip Lindsay	.50	1.50	2.50	A
AT-57	Jessamy John—Phil Stong	.50	1.50	2.50	

(AVON T/AT-SERIES, continued)		Good	Fine	N/Mint
AT-58	The Scorpion—Anna Elisabet Weirauch	.50	1.50	2.50	E
AT-59	The Rose and the Flame—Jonreed Lauritzen	.50	1.50	2.50
AT-60	Kings Mountain—Florette Henri	.50	1.50	2.50
AT-61	Stories in the Modern Manner	.40	1.20	2.00
AT-62	Powder Mission—Herbert E. Stover	.50	1.50	2.50
AT-63	The Hand of the Hunter—Jerome Weidman	.50	1.50	2.50	E
AT-64	Son of Egypt—James Busbee, Jr.	.50	1.50	2.50	A
AT-65	Sex Habits of American Women—Dr. Fritz Wittels	.50	1.50	2.50	NF
AT-66	The Avon Book of Modern Writing—ed. William Phillips & Philip Rahr	.40	1.20	2.00
AT-67	Dark Passions Subdue—Douglas Sanderson	.50	1.50	2.50
AT-68	I, Claudius—Robert Graves	.50	1.50	2.50	A
AT-69	Intimacy—Jean-Paul Sartre	.50	1.50	2.50
AT-70	Turn Back the River—W. G. Hardy	.50	1.50	2.50
T-71	Painted Veils—James Huneker	.50	1.50	2.50	E
T-72	Tide of Empire—Bates Baldwin	.50	1.50	2.50	A
T-73	Yankee Mariner—James Busbee, Jr.; 1954	.50	1.50	2.50
T-74	Never Leave Me—Harold Robbins	.50	1.50	2.50	E
T-75	After Many a Summer Dies the Swan—Aldous Huxley	.50	1.50	2.50	SF
T-76	Blade of Conquest—Jonreed Lauritzen	.50	1.50	2.50	A
T-77	More Stories in the Modern Manner	.40	1.20	2.00
T-78	A Foreign Affair—John Baxter	.50	1.50	2.50
T-79	The Scarlet Petticoat—Nard Jones	.50	1.50	2.50	A
T-80	No Time Like the Future—Nelson Bond	.50	1.50	2.50	SF
T-81	Captain Adam—Donald Barr Chidsey	.50	1.50	2.50	A
T-82	I'll Never Go There Any More—Jerome Weidman	.50	1.50	2.50
T-83	The Bitterweed Path—Thomas Hal Phillips	.50	1.50	2.50
T-84	Naked Acre—Francis Mitchell; aka The Wing and the Yoke	.50	1.50	2.50	E
T-85	Gone to Texas—John W. Thomason, Jr.	.50	1.50	2.50	W
T-86	Savage Holiday—Richard Wright	1.00	3.00	5.00
T-87	Dawn on Our Darkness—Emmanuel Robles	.50	1.50	2.50
T-88	Send Them Summer—Hansford Martin	.50	1.50	2.50
T-89	The Merry Mistress—Philip Lindsay	.50	1.50	2.50
T-90	Nine Days to Mukalla—Frederic Prokosch	.50	1.50	2.50	A
T-91	The Dark Journey—Julian Green	.50	1.50	2.50
T-92	Belly Laughs Annual—Harold Meyers	.50	1.50	2.50	H
T-93	What D'ya Know for Sure?—Len Zinberg	.50	1.50	2.50
T-94	Diary of a Chambermaid—Octave Mirbeau	.80	2.40	4.00	E
T-95	Honeymoon Guide—Harold Meyers	1.00	3.00	5.00	H
T-96	Lord of the Isles—Donald Barr Chidsey	.50	1.50	2.50	A
T-97	I Can Get It for You Wholesale!—Jerome Weidman	.50	1.50	2.50
T-98	Chattels of Eldorado—Edgar Jean Bracco; c-Kinstler	1.00	3.00	5.00	A
T-99	Tough Kid From Brooklyn—Robert Mende	.50	1.50	2.50
T-100	The Flesh and the Sea—John Dobbin	.50	1.50	2.50
T-101	Life and Death of a Tough Guy—Benjamin Appel; 1st ed., 1955	.50	1.50	2.50	M
T-102	Droll Stories—Honore de Balzac	.50	1.50	2.50
T-103	What's in It for Me?—Jerome Weidman	.50	1.50	2.50	E
T-104	Love in the Shadows—John Evans	.50	1.50	2.50	E
T-105	Juvenile Delinquents—Lenard Kaufman	.80	2.40	4.00	JD
T-106	Confessions of a Princess—H. R. H.	.50	1.50	2.50	A
T-107	Butterfield 8—John O'Hara	.50	1.50	2.50
T-108	Never Come Morning—Nelson Algren	.50	1.50	2.50	E
T-109	Various Temptations—anthology	.80	2.40	4.00
T-110	Royal Scandal—Philip Lindsay; c-Kinstler	1.00	3.00	5.00	A
T-111	Dishonor—Gerald Kersh; aka Night and the City	.50	1.50	2.50
T-112	An Artist in Love—Philip Lindsay; c-Kinstler	1.00	3.00	5.00
T-113	Stories of Scarlet Women	.50	1.50	2.50	E
T-114	The First Lady Chatterley—D. H. Lawrence	.50	1.50	2.50	E
T-115	Seven Footprints to Satan—A. A. Merritt; 1956	1.20	3.60	6.00	SF

Avon AT-54, © Avon

Avon T-94, © Avon

Avon T-98, © Avon

Avon T-118, © Avon

Avon T-127, © Avon

Avon T-152, © Avon

(AVON T/AT-SERIES, continued)

		Good	Fine	N/Mint	
T-116	Suzanne, Savage Vixen—Jonreed Lauritzen	.50	1.50	2.50	
T-117	Typee: A Peep at Polynesian Life—Herman Melville; c-Gauguin	.80	2.40	4.00	E
T-118	The Loves of Liberace—Leo Guild	1.20	3.60	6.00	NF
T-119	Ashenden, or the British Agent—W. Somerset Maugham; c-Kinstler	1.00	3.00	5.00	M
T-120	The Kiss and the Duel—Anton Chekhov	.50	1.50	2.50	
T-121	Down and Out in Paris and London—George Orwell	.50	1.50	2.50	
T-122	To Love by Candlelight—Philip Lindsay; aka A Piece for Candlelight	.50	1.50	2.50	
T-123	Girls - for Men Only—John Paul Adams	1.00	3.00	5.00	H
T-124	Cry Tough!—Irving Shulman	.50	1.50	2.50	
T-125	The Neon Wilderness—Nelson Algren	.50	1.50	2.50	E
T-126	Gold for the Gay Masters—Harriet Gray	.50	1.50	2.50	
T-127	Out of the Silent Planet—C. S. Lewis; c-Kinstler	1.00	3.00	5.00	SF
T-128	Emma: My Lord Admiral's Mistress—F. W. Kenyon	.50	1.50	2.50	
T-129	The Gin Palace—Emile Zola	.50	1.50	2.50	
T-130	The Savage Soldiers—Harold Waters & Aubrey Wisberg	.50	1.50	2.50	
T-131	Slipping Beauty—Jerome Weidman	.50	1.50	2.50	E
T-132	Naked Acre—Francis Mitchell	.50	1.50	2.50	E
T-133	Polikushka and Two Hussars—Leo Tolstoy	.50	1.50	2.50	
T-134	Captain Adam—Donald Barr Chidsey	.50	1.50	2.50	A
T-135	The Moon Pool—A. A. Merritt	.80	2.40	4.00	SF
T-136	Sir Naked Blade—Philip Lindsay	.50	1.50	2.50	A
T-137	The Bride Comes to Yellow Sky—Stephen Crane	.50	1.50	2.50	W
T-138	The Amboy Dukes—Irving Shulman	.50	1.50	2.50	
T-139	The Gifted Sinners—Roswell G. Ham, Jr.	.50	1.50	2.50	E
T-140	Temptation in Paris—Honore De Balzac; aka Illusions Perdues	.50	1.50	2.50	E
T-141	The Tragedy of X—Ellery Queen	.50	1.50	2.50	
T-142	Murder in Port Afrique—Bernard Dryer	.50	1.50	2.50	
T-143	Burial of the Fruit—David Dortort	.50	1.50	2.50	E
T-144	Coming Up for Air—George Orwell	.50	1.50	2.50	
T-145	Diary of a Chambermaid—Octave Mirbeau	.50	1.50	2.50	E
T-146	21st Century Sub—Frank Herbert; aka The Dragon in the Sea	.50	1.50	2.50	SF
T-147	Money, Money, Money—David Wagoner	.50	1.50	2.50	
T-148	Around the World in 80 Days—Jules Verne; movie tie-in	1.00	3.00	5.00	SF
T-149	Death on the Nile—Agatha Christie	.50	1.50	2.50	M
T-150	Zarak—A. J. Beran; movie tie-in	1.00	3.00	5.00	A
T-151	Hannibal: Scourge of Imperial Rome—Mary Dolan; 1957, aka Hannibal of Carthage	.50	1.50	2.50	A
T-152	The Ship of Ishtar—A. A. Merritt	.80	2.40	4.00	SF
T-153	I'll Never Go There Any More—Jerome Weidman	.50	1.50	2.50	
T-154	26 Men and a Girl—Maxim Gorky	.80	2.40	4.00	
T-155	Gladiator—Philip Wylie	.80	2.40	4.00	SF
T-156	Bride of Violence—Harriet Gray	.50	1.50	2.50	E
T-157	Perelandra—C. S. Lewis	.80	2.40	4.00	SF
T-158	A Man Can Love Twice—Robert Paul Smith	.50	1.50	2.50	
T-159	Intrigue in Paris—Sterling Noel	.50	1.50	2.50	
T-160	After the Fireworks and Other Stories—Aldous Huxley; aka Brief Candles	.50	1.50	2.50	E
T-161	Face in the Abyss—A. A. Merritt	.80	2.40	4.00	SF
T-162	Teen-age Mobster—Benjamin Appel; aka Life and Death of a Tough Guy	.80	2.40	4.00	JD
T-163	Love Among the Haystacks—D. H. Lawrence	.50	1.50	2.50	E
T-164	The Scarlet Petticoat—Nard Jones	.50	1.50	2.50	
T-165	Boy on a Dolphin—David Divine; movie tie-in	2.00	6.00	10.00	A
T-166	Josephine, the Great Lover—N. P. Nezelof	.50	1.50	2.50	E
T-167	7 Dials Mystery—Agatha Christie	.50	1.50	2.50	M
T-168	Tomorrow Plus X—Wilson Tucker; aka Time Bomb	.50	1.50	2.50	SF
T-169	The Unholy Wife—John Roeburt; movie tie-in	2.00	6.00	10.00	E
T-170	Juvenile Hoods—Joseph Shallit	1.00	3.00	5.00	JD
T-171	The Duke's Temptation—Paula Batchelor	.50	1.50	2.50	
T-172	The Metal Monster—A. A. Merritt	.80	2.40	4.00	SF
T-173	Naked Morning—R. V. Cassill	.50	1.50	2.50	

		Good	Fine	N/Mint	
T-174	The Young Killers—Willard Wiener	.50	1.50	2.50	JD
T-175	From Outer Space—Hal Clement	.50	1.50	2.50	SF
T-176	A Holiday for Murder—Agatha Christie	.50	1.50	2.50	M
T-177	Man on Fire—Owen Aherne; movie tie-in	.80	2.40	4.00	
T-178	Beyond Mombasa—Joseph Hilton; movie tie-in	1.00	3.00	5.00	A
T-179	Cry Slaughter!—E. K. Tiempo	.50	1.50	2.50	
T-180	The Space Plague—George O. Smith	.50	1.50	2.50	SF
T-181	Pickup Alley—Edward Ronns; movie tie-in	1.00	3.00	5.00	E
T-182	An Affair to Remember—Owen Aherne; movie tie-in	.80	2.40	4.00	
T-183	Butterfield 8—John O'Hara	.50	1.50	2.50	
T-184	Drury Lane's Last Case—Ellery Queen	.50	1.50	2.50	M
T-185	The Jungle—Nelson Algren	.50	1.50	2.50	
T-186	The Time Dissolver—Jerry Sohl	.50	1.50	2.50	SF
T-187	Temptations of Valerie—Harry Whittington; movie tie-in	2.00	6.00	10.00	E
T-188	Action of the Tiger—James Wellard; movie tie-in	.80	2.40	4.00	A
T-189	Make My Bed in Hell—John B. Sanford	.50	1.50	2.50	
T-190	The Hunchback of Notre Dame—Victor Hugo; movie tie-in	2.00	6.00	10.00	HO
T-191	Bomber Crew—Joseph Landon	.50	1.50	2.50	C
T-192	Poirot Loses a Client—Agatha Christie	.50	1.50	2.50	M
T-193	Year 2018!—James Blish	.50	1.50	2.50	SF
T-194	The Wild One—Bonnie Golightly	.80	2.40	4.00	
T-195	The Flesh Agents—Jean Bosquet	.50	1.50	2.50	
T-196	Man in the Shadow—Harry Whittington; movie tie-in	1.20	3.60	6.00	
T-197	Panzer Ghost Division—Thomas Goethals	.50	1.50	2.50	C
T-198	Ride Out for Revenge—Burt Arthur	.50	1.50	2.50	W
T-199	The Saint Vs. Scotland Yard—Leslie Charteris	.50	1.50	2.50	M
T-200	Diary of a 16-year Old French Girl—Sidonie Colette	.50	1.50	2.50	
T-201	The Long Haul—Mervyn Mills; movie tie-in	.80	2.40	4.00	
T-202	The Planet Explorer—Murray Leinster	.50	1.50	2.50	SF
T-203	Les Girls—Constance Tomkinson; movie tie-in	.80	2.40	4.00	
T-204	The Mysterious Affair at Styles—Agatha Christie	.50	1.50	2.50	M
T-205	U-Boat Killer—Donald MacIntyre	.50	1.50	2.50	E
T-206	Soldier's Weekend—Hansford Martin	.50	1.50	2.50	
T-207	The Price is Right—Jerome Weidman	.50	1.50	2.50	E
T-208	Seven Footprints to Satan—A. A. Merritt	.50	1.50	2.50	SF
T-209	Don Gastone and the Women—Geoffredo Parise; aka Don Gastone and the Ladies	.50	1.50	2.50	E
T-210	The Secret Adversary—Agatha Christie; 1958	.50	1.50	2.50	M
T-211	The Tortured Planet—C. S. Lewis	.50	1.50	2.50	SF
T-212	Case of the Dark Wanton—Peter Cheyney	.50	1.50	2.50	M
T-213	I Survived Hitler's Ovens—Olga Lengyel	.50	1.50	2.50	NF
T-214	Hot Spell—Lonnie Coleman; movie tie-in	1.00	3.00	5.00	E
T-215	Tobruk Commando—Gordon Landsborough	.50	1.50	2.50	C
T-216	Case of the Red Box—Rex Stout	.50	1.50	2.50	M
T-217	Juvenile Delinquents—Lenard Kaufman; aka The Lower Part of the Sky	.80	2.40	4.00	JD
T-218	A Modern Lover—D. H. Lawrence	.50	1.50	2.50	E
T-219	Juvenile Jungle—Firth Counsel	.50	1.50	2.50	JD
T-220	The Regatta Mystery—Agatha Christie	.50	1.50	2.50	M
T-221	Children of the Atom—Wilmar H. Shiras	.50	1.50	2.50	SF
T-222	Officers' Plot to Kill Hitler—Constantine Fitzgibbon	.50	1.50	2.50	NF
T-223	Never Come Morning—Nelson Algren	.50	1.50	2.50	
T-224	Passiontide—Wirt Williams	.50	1.50	2.50	
T-225	Earthman, Come Home—James Blish	.50	1.50	2.50	SF
T-226	Raid at Dieppe—Quentin Reynolds	.50	1.50	2.50	C
T-227	Belly Laughs Annual—Harold Meyers	.50	1.50	2.50	H
T-228	The Lady Takes a Flyer—Edward Ronns; movie tie-in	.80	2.40	4.00	M
T-229	Young and Wild—Morton Cooper	.50	1.50	2.50	
T-230	Cry Baby Killer—Joseph Hilton; movie tie-in	1.00	3.00	5.00	
T-231	Rogue's March—Maristan Chapman	.50	1.50	2.50	A
T-232	2nd Foundation: Galactic Empire—Isaac Asimov	.50	1.50	2.50	SF

Avon T-187, © Avon

Avon T-190, © Avon

Avon T-219, © Avon

Avon T-246, © Avon

Avon T-287, © Avon

Avon T-310, © Avon

		Good	Fine	N/Mint	
(AVON T/AT-SERIES, continued)					
T-233	Impatient Virgin—Donald Henderson Clarke	.50	1.50	2.50	
T-234	The Saint in Miami—Leslie Charteris	.50	1.50	2.50	M
T-235	Gang Girl—Wenzell Brown	.80	2.40	4.00	JD
T-236	The Secret Raiders—David Woodward	.50	1.50	2.50	
T-237	High Cost of Loving—Bonnie Golightly; movie tie-in	1.00	3.00	5.00	
T-238	VOR—James Blish	.50	1.50	2.50	SF
T-239	D-Day—John Gunther	.50	1.50	2.50	C
T-240	I Can Get It for You Wholesale!—Jerome Weidman	.50	1.50	2.50	
T-241	Teen-age Jungle—Harry Whittington	.80	2.40	4.00	JD
T-242	The Four of Hearts—Ellery Queen	.50	1.50	2.50	M
T-243	Murder in Three Acts—Agatha Christie	.50	1.50	2.50	M
T-244	Naked Sin—Gordon Clark; orig., 1958	.50	1.50	2.50	E
T-245	The Tuesday Club Murders—Agatha Christie	.50	1.50	2.50	M
T-246	Sunk!—Mochitsura Hashimoto	.50	1.50	2.50	C
T-247	Delinquent!—Morton Cooper; orig., 1958	.80	2.40	4.00	JD
T-248	Chattels of Eldorado—Edgar Jean Bracco	.50	1.50	2.50	A
T-249	Worlds Apart—J. T. McIntosh	.50	1.50	2.50	SF
T-250	The Saint in England—Leslie Charteris	.40	1.20	2.00	M
T-251	The Young Who Sin—John Haase	.50	1.50	2.50	
T-252	The Mind Cage—A. E. Van Vogt	.50	1.50	2.50	SF
T-253	Breathe No More, My Lady—Ed Lacy	.50	1.50	2.50	
T-254	Death of a Fool—Ngaio Marsh	.50	1.50	2.50	M
T-255	Of All My Sins—Thomas Rourke	.40	1.20	2.00	
T-256	Jet Ace—Tedd Thomey	.50	1.50	2.50	C
T-257	High School Confidential—Morton Cooper; movie tie-in	1.20	3.60	6.00	
T-258	The G-String Murders—Gypsy Rose Lee; Note: Actually written by Craig Rice	.50	1.50	2.50	M
T-259	Hiroshima Diary—Michihiko Hachiya	.50	1.50	2.50	C
T-260	Painted Veils—James Huneker	.50	1.50	2.50	
T-261	Waldo: Genius in Orbit—Robert A. Heinlein	.50	1.50	2.50	SF
T-262	Gang Rumble—Edward Ronns	.80	2.40	4.00	JD
T-263	Love in the Shadows—John Evans; aka Shadows Flying	.50	1.50	2.50	E
T-264	Trinity in Violence—Henry Kane	.50	1.50	2.50	M
T-265	Cry Attack!—John Burgan	.50	1.50	2.50	C
T-266	The Vice Trap—Elliott Gilbert	.50	1.50	2.50	
T-267	Naked Tide—Roderic Hastings	.50	1.50	2.50	
T-268	ESPer—James Blish	.50	1.50	2.50	SF
T-269	Mitsou—Sidonie Colette	.40	1.20	2.00	
T-270	Run for Your Life!—Sterling Noel; orig., 1958	.50	1.50	2.50	M
T-271	Raw Wind in Eden—Ed Robinson; movie tie-in	1.00	3.00	5.00	
T-272	I Am a Marked Woman—anonymous	.50	1.50	2.50	E
T-273	The Bitterweed Path—Thomas Hal Phillips	.50	1.50	2.50	
T-274	West of the Law—Al Cody	.50	1.50	2.50	W
T-275	Destination: Infinity—Henry Kuttner	.50	1.50	2.50	SF
T-276	Fistful of Death—Henry Kane	.50	1.50	2.50	M
T-277	Sinful—Bart Frame	.50	1.50	2.50	
T-278	Out for a Killing—John W. Vandercook	.50	1.50	2.50	
T-279	The Triumph of Time—James Blish	.50	1.50	2.50	SF
T-280	Death Hits the Jackpot—Walter Wager	.50	1.50	2.50	M
T-281	Lustful Summer—R. V. Cassill; orig., 1958	.50	1.50	2.50	E
T-282	Honeymoon Guide—Harold Meyers	.80	2.40	4.00	H
T-283	A Hell of a Murder—Warren Carrier	.50	1.50	2.50	M
T-284	Horror!—H. P. Lovecraft	.80	2.40	4.00	HO
T-285	Shameless—James M. Cain	.50	1.50	2.50	
T-286	The Merry Mistress—Philip Lindsay	.50	1.50	2.50	
T-287	The Death Dealers—Isaac Asimov	.80	2.40	4.00	M
T-288	Shakedown for Murder—Ed Lacy	.50	1.50	2.50	
T-289	BR-R-R!—ed. Groff Conklin; 1959	.50	1.50	2.50	SF
T-290	Prelude to Murder—Sterling Noel	.50	1.50	2.50	

		Good	Fine	N/Mint	
T-291	Death Is the Last Lover—Henry Kane	.50	1.50	2.50	M
T-292	The American Gun Mystery—Ellery Queen	.50	1.50	2.50	M
T-293	The Buccaneer—R. V. Cassill; movie tie-in	.80	2.40	4.00	A
T-294	Waiting for Willy—Jack Houston	.40	1.20	2.00	
T-295	The Hot Half Hour—Robert L. Foreman	.40	1.20	2.00	
T-296	Over My Dead Body—Rex Stout	.50	1.50	2.50	M
T-297	Doomsday Morning—C. L. Moore	.50	1.50	2.50	SF
T-298	Break-up—Edmund Schiddel	.50	1.50	2.50	
T-299	Halfway to Hell—Harry Whittington	.80	2.40	4.00	
T-300	Confidential—Donald Henderson Clarke	.40	1.20	2.00	
T-301	Claudine—Sidonie Colette	.50	1.50	2.50	
T-302	The Subterraneans—Jack Kerouac; Note: Original preface by Henry Miller	1.00	3.00	5.00	
T-303	Cry Tough!—Irving Shulman; movie tie-in	1.00	3.00	5.00	
T-304	Aliens 4—Theodore Sturgeon	.50	1.50	2.50	SF
T-305	The Naked Sword—Donald Barr Chidsey	.50	1.50	2.50	A
T-306	The Night Was Made for Murder—Will Cotton	.50	1.50	2.50	M
T-307	Doorway to Death—Dan Marlowe	.80	2.40	4.00	M
T-308	And Sin No More—H. P. Koenig	.50	1.50	2.50	
T-309	Mark It for Murder—Douglas Sanderson	.50	1.50	2.50	M
T-310	Beat Girl—Bonnie Golightly	.80	2.40	4.00	
T-311	Anything for Kicks—Morton Cooper	.50	1.50	2.50	
T-312	The Lonely Gun—Gordon D. Shirreffs	.50	1.50	2.50	W
T-313	Diary of a Geisha Girl—Kimiko Omura & William Vaneer	.50	1.50	2.50	E
T-314	Undressed to Kill—Peter Cheyney	.50	1.50	2.50	M
T-315	Death in the Desert—Lee E. Wells	.50	1.50	2.50	W
T-316	Ginny—Morton Cooper	.50	1.50	2.50	
T-317	The Saint in New York—Leslie Charteris	.40	1.20	2.00	M
T-318	Lord of the Isles—Donald Barr Chidsey	.40	1.20	2.00	A
T-319	Too Innocent to Kill—Doris Miles Disney	.40	1.20	2.00	M
T-320	The Blonde in Suite 14—Stewart Sterling	.40	1.20	2.00	M
T-321	They Who Sin—John Roeburt	.40	1.20	2.00	E
T-322	The Hard Man—Philip Ketchum	.50	1.50	2.50	W
T-323	Pnin—Vladimir Nabokov	.40	1.20	2.00	
T-324	The Jungle—Nelson Algren	.40	1.20	2.00	
T-325	The Savage Warriors—Henry Treece; aka The Dark Island	.50	1.50	2.50	A
T-326	Never Leave Me—Harold Robbins	.40	1.20	2.00	E
T-327	Gun for Sale—Lee E. Wells	.40	1.20	2.00	W
T-328	The Real Cool Killers—Chester Himes	.40	1.20	2.00	
T-329	The Shame—Richard Himmel	.40	1.20	2.00	
T-330	Blonde Bait—Stephen Marlowe	.50	1.50	2.50	M
T-331	Savage Star—Lewis B. Patten	.40	1.20	2.00	W
T-332	How Rough Can It Get?—Joe Weiss	.40	1.20	2.00	
T-333	The Devil's Bride—Carter A. Vaughan	.40	1.20	2.00	A
T-334	The Amboy Dukes—Irving Shulman	.40	1.20	2.00	
T-335	Sugar—Gil Brewer; orig., 1959	.50	1.50	2.50	E
T-336	The Strange Co-ed—Bart Frame	.40	1.20	2.00	
T-337	The Tragedy of Y—Ellery Queen	.40	1.20	2.00	M
T-338	Nadia—Assia Djebar	.40	1.20	2.00	
T-339	The Man Who Rode Alone—Lewis B. Patten	.40	1.20	2.00	W
T-340	The Subterraneans—Jack Kerouac	.50	1.50	2.50	
T-341	Iron Lover—Gardner F. Fox	.80	2.40	4.00	A
T-342	The Unholy Lovers—Paul Monash	.40	1.20	2.00	E
T-343	Find Eileen Hardin - Alive!—Andrew Frazer	.40	1.20	2.00	
T-344	Three Loves Had She—Mark Schorer	.40	1.20	2.00	
T-345	Monsters and Such—Murray Leinster	.50	1.50	2.50	SF
T-346	Bachelor's Joke Book—Leo Guild	.50	1.50	2.50	H
T-347	Strange Bargain—Harry Whittington	.80	2.40	4.00	
T-348	This Range Is Mine—Dean Owen	.40	1.20	2.00	W
T-349	Killer With a Key—Dan Marlowe	.80	2.40	4.00	M
T-350	Love for a Stranger—John Pleasant McCoy	.40	1.20	2.00	
T-351	Murder Is an Art—Michael Innes; aka One Man Show	.40	1.20	2.00	M
T-352	Fort Suicide—Gordon D. Shirreffs	.40	1.20	2.00	W
T-353	The Town That God Forgot—William Colt MacDonald	.40	1.20	2.00	W
T-354	Beyond the Night—Cornell Woolrich; orig., 1959	2.00	6.00	10.00	M
T-355	Bachelor Summer—Herbert D. Kastle	.40	1.20	2.00	
T-356	Girl in a Jam—James Savage	.40	1.20	2.00	
T-357	The Crazy Kill—Chester Himes	.40	1.20	2.00	
T-358	The Mistress—Theodora Keogh	.80	2.40	4.00	
T-359	Rusty Desmond—Steve January	.50	1.50	2.50	JD
T-360	We Who Survived...the Fifth Ice Age—Sterling Noel	1.60	4.80	8.00	SF
T-361	Run, Killer, Run!—Lionel White; orig., 1959	1.00	3.00	5.00	
T-362	The Man Who Could Cheat Death—Barre Lyndon & Jimmy Sangster; movie tie-in	1.20	3.60	6.00	SF
T-363	The Pagan Queen—Henry Treece; aka Red Queen, White Queen	.80	2.40	4.00	A
T-364	Young Awakening—Robert Fontaine	.40	1.20	2.00	
T-365	The Terrible Night—Peter Cheyney	.50	1.50	2.50	M
T-366	The Figure in the Dusk—John Creasey	.40	1.20	2.00	M

Avon Western Novel Monthly 2, © Avon

Avon Western Reader 1, © Avon

Ballantine Books 2, © BB

		Good	Fine	N/Mint	
(AVON T/AT-SERIES, continued)					
T-367	Avon Bedside Companion	.40	1.20	2.00	
T-368	Cheyenne War Cry—Noel M. Loomis	.40	1.20	2.00	W
T-369	Ambush at Scorpion Valley—William Colt MacDonald	.40	1.20	2.00	W
T-370	The Captive—Norman Daniels; orig., 1959	.80	2.40	4.00	E
T-371	Planet in Peril—John Christopher	.50	1.50	2.50	SF
T-372	The Long Night—Ovid Demaris	.40	1.20	2.00	
T-373	Law Killer—Richard Brister	.40	1.20	2.00	W
T-374	Where There's a Will—Rex Stout	.50	1.50	2.50	M
T-375	I, Barbarian—Jay Scotland (John Jakes); orig., 1959	1.20	3.60	6.00	A
T-376	Beat Not the Bones—Charlotte Jay	.40	1.20	2.00	
T-377	McHugh—Jay Flynn	.40	1.20	2.00	M
T-378	The Naked Land—Lee E. Wells	.40	1.20	2.00	W
T-379	The Blockhouse—Jean-Paul Clebert; 1960	.40	1.20	2.00	NF

AVON UN-NUMBERED
Avon Publishing Company, Inc.

Digest Size

nn	Book of Jokes—Harry Hershfield	3.00	9.00	15.00	H
nn	Cuties—E. Simms Campbell; 1945	4.00	12.00	20.00	H
nn	Cartoons From Colliers	3.00	9.00	15.00	H

AVON WESTERN NOVEL MONTHLY
Avon Publishing Co., Inc.

Digest Size

1	The Gun-Wolf of Tubac—Nelson C. Nye; 1949, aka The Barber of Tubac	3.00	9.00	15.00	W
2	Cattle War Buckaroo—William Hopson; 1950, aka The Laughing Vaquero	3.00	9.00	15.00	W
3	Arizona Roundup—William Hopson	3.00	9.00	15.00	W
4	Great Stories of the Golden West—anthology	3.00	9.00	15.00	W

AVON WESTERN READER
Avon Book Company

Digest Size

1	Includes Coburn, Raine, Haycox, others	3.00	9.00	15.00	W
2	Includes White, Drago, Haycox, others	3.00	9.00	15.00	W
3	Includes Woolrich, Gruber, Haycox, Raine, others	3.00	9.00	15.00	W
4	Includes Gruber, Raine, Tuttle, others	3.00	9.00	15.00	W

BALLANTINE BOOKS
Ballantine Books, Inc.

1	Executive Suite—Cameron Hawley; 1952	1.20	3.60	6.00	
2	The Golden Spike—Hal Ellson; orig., 1952	2.00	6.00	10.00	E
3	All My Enemies—Stanley Baron	1.20	3.60	6.00	
4	Saddle by Starlight—Luke Short; c-Saunders	1.60	4.80	8.00	W
5	The Witch's Thorn—Ruth Park	1.20	3.60	6.00	
6	Tides of Time—Emile Danoen; 1st ed., 1952, aka Dust in the Wind	1.20	3.60	6.00	E
7	Blood on the Land—Frank Bonham	1.20	3.60	6.00	W
8	The World of Li'l Abner—Al Capp	4.00	12.00	20.00	H
9	The Red Gate—LaSelle Gilman	1.20	3.60	6.00	

(BALLANTINE BOOKS, continued)

		Good	Fine	N/Mint	
10	Concannon—Frank O'Rourke; c-Saunders	1.60	4.80	8.00	W
	With dust jacket	10.00	30.00	50.00	
11	War Bonnet—Clay Fisher	1.20	3.60	6.00	W
12	Heyday—W. M. Spackman; orig., 1953	1.00	3.00	5.00	
13	First Blood—Jack Schaefer; orig., 1953	1.60	4.80	8.00	W
14	Why Did They Kill?—John Bartlow Martin	1.00	3.00	5.00	NF
15	The Wheel and the Hearth—Lucia B. Moore	.80	2.40	4.00	
16	Star Science Fiction Stories—Frederik Pohl	3.00	9.00	15.00	SF
17	The Racer—Hans Ruesch	1.20	3.60	6.00	
18	Kingdom of the Spur—Gene Markey	1.20	3.60	6.00	W
19	Stories of Sudden Truth—Elizabeth Abell & Joseph I. Green	1.20	3.60	6.00	
20	I Though of Daisy—Edmund Wilson	1.00	3.00	5.00	
21	The Space Merchants—F. Pohl & C. M. Kornbluth; orig., 1953, c-Powers	3.00	9.00	15.00	SF
22	The Big Range—Jack Schaefer	1.60	4.80	8.00	W
23	Patrol—Fred Majdalany	1.20	3.60	6.00	
24	Desert Passage—Richard Poole	1.20	3.60	6.00	W
25	The Undying Fire—Fletcher Pratt; orig., 1953, c-Powers	2.00	6.00	10.00	SF
26	The City of Anger—William Manchester; orig., 1953	1.20	3.60	6.00	
27	Summer Street—Hal Ellson; orig., 1953, c-Maguire	1.60	4.80	8.00	
28	The Secret Masters—Gerald Kersh; orig., 1953, aka The Great Wash, c-Powers	2.00	6.00	10.00	SF
29	Indian Country—Dorothy M. Johnson	1.60	4.80	8.00	
30	Ahead of Time—Henry Kuttner	2.00	6.00	10.00	SF
31	A Gradual Joy—Alma Routsong	1.00	3.00	5.00	
32	The Far Command—Elinor Chamberlain	1.20	3.60	6.00	
33	Childhood's End—Arthur C. Clarke; c-Powers	2.00	6.00	10.00	SF
34	The Best Short Stories of 1953	1.20	3.60	6.00	
35	Gun Hand—Frank O'Rourke	1.20	3.60	6.00	
36	Earthly Creatures—Charles Jackson	2.00	6.00	10.00	
37	Silent Army—Chin Kee Onn	1.20	3.60	6.00	C
38	Bring the Jubilee—Ward Moore	1.20	3.60	6.00	SF
39	New Poems by American Poets—Rolfe Humphries	1.00	3.00	5.00	
40	Yellow Hair—Clay Fisher	1.20	3.60	6.00	W
41	Fahrenheit 451—Ray Bradbury; c-Powers	5.00	15.00	25.00	SF
42	Ratoons—Daphne Rooke	1.20	3.60	6.00	A
43	Silver Rock—Luke Short	1.20	3.60	6.00	W
44	The Valiant Virginians—James Warner Bellah	1.20	3.60	6.00	W
45	The Canyon—Jack Schaefer	1.20	3.60	6.00	W
46	More Than Human—Theodore Sturgeon; c-Powers	2.00	6.00	10.00	SF
47	King of Abilene—Thomas Thompson	1.20	3.60	6.00	W
48	The Burl Ives Song Book—Burl Ives	1.00	3.00	5.00	NF
49	Ride West—Frank O'Rourke	1.20	3.60	6.00	W
50	Out of the Deeps—John Wyndham; orig., 1953, aka The Kraken Wakes	2.00	6.00	10.00	SF
51	Law Man—Lee Leighton	1.20	3.60	6.00	W
52	Expedition to Earth—Arthur C. Clarke	2.00	6.00	10.00	SF
53	Edge of the World—Vincent McHugh	1.00	3.00	5.00	
54	The Bounty Hunters—Elmore Leonard	1.00	3.00	5.00	W
55	Star Science Fiction Stories No. 2—Frederik Pohl	2.00	6.00	10.00	SF
56	Dark Dominion—David Duncan; orig., 1954	2.00	6.00	10.00	SF
57	Brandon's Empire—Dave Hardin	1.00	3.00	5.00	W
58	Riders to the Stars—Curt Siodmak	1.60	4.80	8.00	SF
59	The Tall Men—Clay Fisher	1.20	3.60	6.00	W
60	The Peacemaker—Richard Poole; orig., 1954	1.20	3.60	6.00	W
61	Search the Sky—Frederik Pohl & C. M. Kornbluth; orig., 1954, c-Powers	2.00	6.00	10.00	SF
62	The Night Winds—Brian Talbot Cleeve	1.00	3.00	5.00	
63	New Short Novels—Mary Louise Aswell; orig., 1954	1.00	3.00	5.00	
64	Night Raid—Frank Bonham	1.20	3.60	6.00	W
65	West of Justice—John Hunter; orig., 1954	1.00	3.00	5.00	W
66	The Coasts of the Earth—Harold E. Livingston; orig., 1954	.80	2.40	4.00	

Ballantine Books 13, © BB

Ballantine Books 35, © BB

Ballantine Books 46, © BB

Ballantine Books 78, © BB

Ballantine Books 99, © BB

Ballantine Books 108, © BB

(BALLANTINE BOOKS, continued)

		Good	Fine	N/Mint	
67	Aircraft Carrier—Joseph Bryan III	1.00	3.00	5.00	NF
68	Prelude to Space—Arthur C. Clarke	1.60	4.80	8.00	SF
69	Thunder in the Sun—Frank O'Rourke	1.00	3.00	5.00	W
70	Broken Wagon—Norman A. Fox	1.00	3.00	5.00	W
71	Hero's Walk—Robert Crane; orig., 1954	2.00	6.00	10.00	SF
72	Prize Articles 1954—Llewellyn Miller; orig., 1954. Note: Contains first book appearance of a Ray Bradbury story.	1.60	4.80	8.00	
73	Untouched by Human Hands—Robert Sheckley; orig., 1954	2.00	6.00	10.00	SF
74	Trouble Rider—Thomas Thompson; orig., 1954	1.00	3.00	5.00	W
75	American Accent—Elizabeth Abell	.80	2.40	4.00	
76	Trumpets of Company K—William Chamberlain; orig., 1954	1.00	3.00	5.00	W
F77	Break Down the Walls—John Bartlow Martin	.80	2.40	4.00	NF
78	The Real Story of Lucille Ball—Eleanor Harris	2.00	6.00	10.00	B
79					
80	Brain Wave—Poul Anderson; c-Powers	1.60	4.80	8.00	SF
81					
82	High Vengeance—Frank O'Rourke	1.00	3.00	5.00	W
83					
84	They Brought Their Guns—Thomas Thompson	1.00	3.00	5.00	W
85	The Feud at Spanish Ford—Frank Bonham	1.00	3.00	5.00	W
86	The Explorers—C. M. Kornbluth; orig., 1954	1.60	4.80	8.00	SF
87	Fire in the Desert—Ford Logan	1.00	3.00	5.00	
88	Strange Conquest—Alfred Neumann	1.00	3.00	5.00	
89	Star Short Novels—Frederik Pohl	1.60	4.80	8.00	SF
90	Security and the Middle East	1.00	3.00	5.00	NF
91	Shadows in the Sun—Chad Oliver; orig., 1954	1.60	4.80	8.00	SF
92	A Life for a Life—Horst Fanyer; c-Maguire	1.00	3.00	5.00	
93	The Mad Reader—Harvey Kurtzman	2.00	6.00	10.00	H
94	Messiah—Gore Vidal; 1954, c-Powers	2.00	6.00	10.00	SF
95	Brave Harvest—Richard Cargoe; orig., 1954	1.00	3.00	5.00	W
96	Star Science Fiction Stories No. 3—Frederik Pohl	1.20	3.60	6.00	SF
97	Earthlight—Arthur C. Clarke; c-Powers	1.20	3.60	6.00	SF
98	Violence at Sundown—Frank O'Rourke	1.00	3.00	5.00	W
99	Of All Possible Worlds—William Tenn; orig., 1955, c-Powers	2.00	6.00	10.00	SF
100	Young—Miriam Colwell	1.00	3.00	5.00	
101	The Dam Busters—Paul Brickhill	.80	2.40	4.00	NF
102	Beyond Eden—David Duncan; orig., 1955, c-Powers	1.60	4.80	8.00	SF
103	Rock—Hal Ellson	1.60	4.80	8.00	
104	Re-Birth—John Wyndham; orig., 1955, c-Powers	1.60	4.80	8.00	SF
105	How to Play With Your Child—A. F. Arnold	1.00	3.00	5.00	NF
106	Mad Strikes Back—Harvey Kurtzman	2.00	6.00	10.00	H
107	Gladiator-at-Law—Frederik Pohl & C. M. Kornbluth; c-Powers	2.00	6.00	10.00	SF
108	Marilyn Monroe As the Girl—Sam Shaw; movie tie-in	4.00	12.00	20.00	
109	Far and Away—Anthony Boucher; orig., 1955	2.00	6.00	10.00	SF
110	The Mackenzie Raid—Red Reeder	1.00	3.00	5.00	W
111	Car Deal!—Frank O'Rourke; orig., 1955	.80	2.40	4.00	
112	My Lady Greensleaves—Constance Beresford-Howe	1.00	3.00	5.00	A
113	Another Kind—Chad Oliver; orig., 1955, c-Powers	1.60	4.80	8.00	SF
114	The Guests of Faine—Daniel Stern	1.00	3.00	5.00	
115	The Power of Negative Thinking—Charles Preston	1.00	3.00	5.00	H
116	Jet—Frank Harvey	1.00	3.00	5.00	C
117	The Girls From Planet 5—Richard Wilson; orig., 1955, c-Powers	1.60	4.80	8.00	SF
118	Great Dog Stories—Stanley Kaufmann	1.60	4.80	8.00	
119	Caviar—Theodore Sturgeon; orig., 1955	2.00	6.00	10.00	
120	U-Boats at War—Harald Busch	1.00	3.00	5.00	NF
121	Lone Gun—Clark Brooker	1.00	3.00	5.00	W
122	No Boundaries—Henry Kuttner & C. L. Moore; orig., 1955	2.00	6.00	10.00	
123	A Town Is Drowning—C. M. Kornbluth & Frederik Pohl	3.00	9.00	15.00	

		Good	Fine	N/Mint	
124	Inside Mad—Harvey Kurtzman	2.00	6.00	10.00	H
125	North to Texas—Noel M. Loomis	1.00	3.00	5.00	W
126	Citizen in Space—Robert Sheckley; orig., 1955	1.60	4.80	8.00	SF
127	How to Succeed in Business Without Really Trying—Shepherd Mead; 1956	1.00	3.00	5.00	H
128	Hot Iron—Elmer Kelton	1.20	3.60	6.00	W
129	Tell Them Nothing—Hal Ellson	1.20	3.60	6.00	
130	Alternating Currents—Frederik Pohl; c-Powers	1.60	4.80	8.00	SF
F131	A Woman of Bangkok—Jack Reynolds	1.00	3.00	5.00	
132	In One Head and Out the Other—Roger Price	.80	2.40	4.00	H
F133	The Best Short Stories of 1955—Martha Foley	1.00	3.00	5.00	
134	Beyond Courage—Clay Blair, Jr.	1.00	3.00	5.00	NF
135	Reach for Tomorrow—Arthur C. Clarke	1.20	3.60	6.00	SF
136	The Pioneers—Jack Schaefer	1.20	3.60	6.00	W
137	The God of Channel 1—Donald Stacy with Frederik Pohl	2.00	6.00	10.00	
138	My First 10,000,000 Sponsors—Frank Edwards	1.00	3.00	5.00	
F139	The October Country—Ray Bradbury	6.00	18.00	30.00	SF
140	New Short Novels II; orig., 1956, c-Powers. Note: Contains Norman Mailer	1.20	3.60	6.00	
141	Never Plead Guilty—Bernard Averbuch & John Wesley Noble	1.00	3.00	5.00	NF
142	Devil's Canyon—E. E. Halleran	1.00	3.00	5.00	W
143	Flood—David Dempsey	1.00	3.00	5.00	
144	Presidential Year—C. M. Kornbluth & Frederik Pohl	3.00	9.00	15.00	
145	God Is My Co-Pilot—Gen. Robert L. Scott, Jr.	.80	2.40	4.00	C
146	Sea Songs of Sailing, Whaling and Fishing—Burl Ives	1.00	3.00	5.00	
147	Bright Phoenix—Harold Mead	1.60	4.80	8.00	SF
148	Beyond the Pass—Lee Leighton	1.00	3.00	5.00	W
149	Hard Men—Frank O'Rourke	1.00	3.00	5.00	W
F150	The Power and the Prize—Howard Swiggett	.80	2.40	4.00	
151	Nerves—Lester del Ray	1.60	4.80	8.00	SF
152	I'm for Me First—Roger Price; orig., 1956	.80	2.40	4.00	H
153	Blazing Border—E. E. Halleran	1.00	3.00	5.00	W
154					
155	The Wright Brothers—Fred C. Kelly	1.00	3.00	5.00	
156					
157	Fight for Control—David Karr	1.00	3.00	5.00	
158	The Night of the Coyotes—Philip Ketchum	1.00	3.00	5.00	W
159	The Human Angle—William Tenn	2.00	6.00	10.00	SF
160	Best Television Plays—Gore Vidal	1.20	3.60	6.00	
161	Olympic Cavalcade of Sports—John V. Grombach; orig., 1956	.80	2.40	4.00	NF
F162	The Cruiser—Warren Tute	.80	2.40	4.00	
163	Grab Your Socks—Shel Silverstein	.80	2.40	4.00	
164	Frontier—Marvin De Vries	1.00	3.00	5.00	W
165	I, Libertine—Frederick R. Ewing (Theodore Sturgeon & Jean Shepherd); orig., 1956, c-Freas	5.00	15.00	25.00	H
166	Scout—R. M. Roberts; orig., 1956	1.00	3.00	5.00	W
167	To Live Forever—Jack Vance; c-Powers	3.00	9.00	15.00	SF
168	The Road to Stalingrad—Benno Zeiser	1.00	3.00	5.00	NF
F169	The Scourge of the Swastika—Lord Russell of Liverpool	1.60	4.80	8.00	NF
170	Wagon Captain—E. E. Halleran	1.00	3.00	5.00	W
171	The Wild Reader—Bernard W. Shir-Cliff	1.00	3.00	5.00	
172	The World of Li'l Abner—Al Capp	1.00	3.00	5.00	H
173	Turn the Tigers Loose—Col. Walt Lasly with Frederik Pohl	1.60	4.80	8.00	W
174	The Big Ball of Wax—Shepherd Mead	1.00	3.00	5.00	H
175	Fish the Strong Waters—N. C. McDonald; orig., 1956	1.00	3.00	5.00	A
176	Kansas Trail—Hascal Giles	1.00	3.00	5.00	W
177	I Drive the Turnpikes - and Survive—Paul Kearney	1.00	3.00	5.00	NF
178	Utterly Mad—William M. Gaines	1.60	4.80	8.00	H
179	E Pluribus Unicorn—Theodore Sturgeon	2.00	6.00	10.00	SF
180	James Dean: A Biography—William Bast	1.20	3.60	6.00	B
181	Hangtown—Les Savage, Jr.	1.00	3.00	5.00	W

Ballantine Books 129, © BB

Ballantine Books 167, © BB

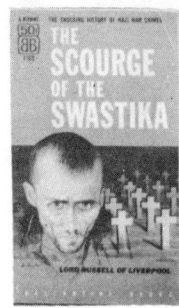

Ballantine Books F169, © BB

Ballantine Books 186, © BB

Ballantine Books 220, © BB

Ballantine Books 229, © BB

(BALLANTINE BOOKS, continued)

		Good	Fine	N/Mint	
182	Tales of Gooseflesh & Laughter—John Wyndham; orig., 1956, c-Powers	2.00	6.00	10.00	SF
183	Defeat at Sea—C. D. Bekker	1.00	3.00	5.00	NF
184	The German Raider Atlantis—Wolfgang Frank & Bernhard Rogge; 1957	1.00	3.00	5.00	NF
185	Shadow on the Border—George C. Appell	1.00	3.00	5.00	W
186	Tales From the White Hart—Arthur C. Clarke	1.60	4.80	8.00	SF
187	Buffalo Wagons—Elmer Kelton	1.20	3.60	6.00	W
188	Cavalry Raid—Sydney E. Whitman	1.00	3.00	5.00	W
189	Fire Mission—William P. Mulvihill	1.00	3.00	5.00	
190	The Battle of the Bulge—Robert E. Merriam	1.00	3.00	5.00	NF
191	Halfway to Heaven—Terrance Flair	1.00	3.00	5.00	
192	Slave Ship—Frederik Pohl	1.60	4.80	8.00	SF
F193	The First and the Last—Adolf Galland	1.00	3.00	5.00	
194	The Spotted Horse—Jack Dillon	1.00	3.00	5.00	
F195	Wing Leader—Capt. J. E. Johnson	.80	2.40	4.00	NF
196	The Lonely Women—Gerda Rhoads	.80	2.40	4.00	
197	The Frozen Year—James Blish	1.60	4.80	8.00	SF
198	Fight at Sun Mountain—Clark Brooker	1.00	3.00	5.00	W
199	Edge of the City—Frederik Pohl	3.00	9.00	15.00	
200	Cycle of Fire—Hal Clement	.80	2.40	4.00	SF
F201	Zero—Okumiya Horikoshi & Martin Caidin	1.00	3.00	5.00	NF
202	Yellowhorse—Dee Brown	.80	2.40	4.00	W
203	Paris Blues—Harold Flender	1.00	3.00	5.00	
F204	The Best American Short Stories of 1956—Martha Foley	.80	2.40	4.00	
205	The Hostile Hills—E. E. Halleran	1.00	3.00	5.00	W
206	The Case Against Tomorrow—Frederik Pohl	1.60	4.80	8.00	SF
207	U-Boat 977—Heinz Schaeffer	1.00	3.00	5.00	NF
208	Lawman's Pay—Frank C. Robertson	1.00	3.00	5.00	W
209	Commando Extraordinary—Charles Foley	.50	1.50	2.50	
210	The Green Odyssey—Philip Jose Farmer; orig., 1957	5.00	15.00	25.00	SF
211	Legend in the Dust—Frank O'Rourke	1.00	3.00	5.00	W
212	Gun Hand—Frank O'Rourke	1.00	3.00	5.00	W
213	Violence at Sundown—Frank O'Rourke	1.00	3.00	5.00	W
214	High Vengeance—Frank O'Rourke	1.00	3.00	5.00	W
215	Sometime, Never—John Wyndham, William Golding & Mervyn Peake	1.20	3.60	6.00	SF
216	Serenade to the Big Bird—Bert Stiles	.80	2.40	4.00	
217	Between the Elephant's Eyes—Robert L. Scott, Jr.	.80	2.40	4.00	A
218	High Vacuum—Charles Eric Maine	.80	2.40	4.00	SF
219	Spanish Ridge—E. E. Halleran	.80	2.40	4.00	W
220	The Deep South Says Never—John Bartlow Martin	.80	2.40	4.00	NF
221	The Password Is Courage—John Castle	.50	1.50	2.50	NF
222	One Minute to Ditch—Cornelius Ryan	.80	2.40	4.00	
223	A Woman in Berlin	1.00	3.00	5.00	
F224	Midway—Mitsuo Fuchida & Masatake Okumiya	1.00	3.00	5.00	NF
F225	Panzer Leader—Heinz Guderian	1.00	3.00	5.00	NF
226	New Poems by American Poets No. 2—Rolfe Humphries	.80	2.40	4.00	
227	The Battle for Leyte Gulf—C. Vann Woodward	.80	2.40	4.00	NF
228	Aircraft Carrier—Joseph Bryan III	.50	1.50	2.50	NF
229	Sergeant Bilko—Nat Hiken; TV tie-in	1.00	3.00	5.00	H
230	Occam's Razor—David Duncan	.50	1.50	2.50	SF
F231	The 85 Days—R. W. Thompson	.80	2.40	4.00	NF
232	Disaster Valley—Frank C. Robertson	1.00	3.00	5.00	W
233	The Crack in the Picture Window—John Keats	.50	1.50	2.50	
F234	The Bridge at Remagen—Ken Hechler	.80	2.40	4.00	
235	Best TV Humor of 1957—Irving Settel	.80	2.40	4.00	H
236	Gunsmoke—Don Ward; orig., 1957, TV tie-in	1.00	3.00	5.00	W
237	Those Idiots From Earth—Richard Wilson	1.20	3.60	6.00	SF
238	Best TV Plays: 1957—Florence Britton	.50	1.50	2.50	
239	The Wild Sweet Wine—Don Congdon; orig., 1958	1.00	3.00	5.00	

		Good	Fine	N/Mint	
240	Chain Link—Owen Evens	.80	2.40	4.00	
241	Indian Country—Dorothy M. Johnson	.80	2.40	4.00	W
242	The Humbug Digest—Harvey Kurtzman	1.20	3.60	6.00	H
243	Man of Earth—Algis Budrys	1.00	3.00	5.00	SF
244	Kamikaze—Gordon T. Allred & Yasuo Kuwahara	.80	2.40	4.00	NF
245	The Dam Busters—Paul Brickhill	.80	2.40	4.00	NF
246	Robots and Changelings—Lester del Rey	1.20	3.60	6.00	SF
247	Barbed Wire—Elmer Kelton	1.00	3.00	5.00	W
F248	Samurai!—Martin Caidin & others	.80	2.40	4.00	
249	Earthlight—Arthur C. Clarke	1.20	3.60	6.00	SF
250	The Big Boxcar—Alfred Maund	1.00	3.00	5.00	
251	Sun Dance—Fred Grove	.80	2.40	4.00	W
F252	The Battle of Cassino—Fred Majdalany	.50	1.50	2.50	NF
253	Patrol—Fred Majdalany	.50	1.50	2.50	
254	Blood on the Land—Frank Bonham	.50	1.50	2.50	W
255	Tomahawk—Lee Leighton	.80	2.40	4.00	W
256	A Case of Conscience—James Blish	1.00	3.00	5.00	SF
257	The Graveyard Reader—Groff Conklin	1.20	3.60	6.00	HO
F258	The Sea Wolves—Wolfgang Frank	.50	1.50	2.50	
259	The Return of the Texan—L. L. Foreman; orig., 1958	.50	1.50	2.50	W
260	Deadly Image—Edmund Cooper	.50	1.50	2.50	SF
F261	The Big Show—Pierre Clostermann	.50	1.50	2.50	
F262	The One That Got Away—Kendal Burt & James Leasor	.50	1.50	2.50	
263	The Mad Reader—Harvey Kurtzman	.80	2.40	4.00	H
264	Mad Strikes Back—Harvey Kurtzman	.80	2.40	4.00	H
265K	Inside Mad—Harvey Kurtzman	.80	2.40	4.00	H
266K	Utterly Mad—William M. Gaines	.80	2.40	4.00	H
267K	The Brothers Mad—William M. Gaines	.80	2.40	4.00	H
268	On an Odd Note—Gerald Kersh	1.00	3.00	5.00	SF
269K	Hardrock—Frank Bonham	.80	2.40	4.00	W
270K					
271K					
272K	Star Science Fiction Stories No. 4—Frederik Pohl	.80	2.40	4.00	SF
F273K	V-2: The Nazi Rocket—Walter Dornberger	1.20	3.60	6.00	NF
274K	The Hanging Tree—Dorothy M. Johnson	1.00	3.00	5.00	W
275K	Those About to Die—Daniel P. Mannix	.80	2.40	4.00	NF
F276K	Stuka Pilot—Hans Ulrich Rudel	.50	1.50	2.50	NF
F277K	This Woman—Pietro di Donato	1.20	3.60	6.00	
278K	Count Five and Die—Barry Wynne	.50	1.50	2.50	
279K	Tomorrow's Gift—Edmund Cooper	.50	1.50	2.50	SF
F280K	The Call Girl—Harold Greenwald	.50	1.50	2.50	NF
281K	The Old Copper Collar—Dan Cushman	.80	2.40	4.00	
282K	Colorado Gold—Lee Leighton & Chad Merriman	.50	1.50	2.50	W
283K	The Sledge Patrol—David Howarth	.50	1.50	2.50	
284K	After the Rain—John Bowen	.50	1.50	2.50	SF
285K	Rebel Ranger—S. E. Whitman	.50	1.50	2.50	W
286K	Ingenue—Millicent Brower	.50	1.50	2.50	
287K	How to Succeed With Women Without Really Trying—Shepherd Mead	.80	2.40	4.00	H
288K	The Bright Road to Fear—Richard Martin Stern	.50	1.50	2.50	M
289K	Sergeant Bilko Joke Book; TV tie-in	1.00	3.00	5.00	H
290K	The Tide Went Out—Charles Eric Maine	.50	1.50	2.50	SF
F291K	Battle for the Rhine—R. W. Thompson	.50	1.50	2.50	NF
292K	Brain Surgeon—William Sharpe	.50	1.50	2.50	
293K	Heat Wave—Caesar Smith	.50	1.50	2.50	
294K	Apache Wells—Robert Steelman	.50	1.50	2.50	
F295K	The Burl Ives Song Book—Burl Ives	.50	1.50	2.50	NF
296K	The Mad Reader—Harvey Kurtzman	.50	1.50	2.50	H
297K	Mad Strikes Back—Harvey Kurtzman	.50	1.50	2.50	H
298K	The Avengers—Chad Merriman	.50	1.50	2.50	W

Ballantine Books 250, © BB

Ballantine Books F273K, © BB

Ballantine Books 289K, © BB

Ballantine Books 302K, © BB

Ballantine Books 340K, © BB

Ballantine Books 354K, © BB

		Good	Fine	N/Mint	
(BALLANTINE BOOKS, continued)					
299K	The Midwich Cuckoos—John Wyndham	1.60	4.80	8.00	SF
300K	End of a War—Edward Loomis	.50	1.50	2.50	
301K	Ride the Nightmare—Richard Matheson	2.00	6.00	10.00	M
302K	The Beast—Daniel P. Mannix	1.20	3.60	6.00	NF
303K	The Marching Morons—C. M. Kornbluth	1.20	3.60	6.00	SF
304K	Shadow of a Star—Elmer Kelton	1.00	3.00	5.00	W
305K	Sensual Love—Don Congdon	.80	2.40	4.00	
306K	Tiger in the Sky—Robert L. Scott, Jr.	.50	1.50	2.50	
F307K	Air Spy—Constance Babington-Smith	.50	1.50	2.50	NF
308K	Star Science Fiction Stories No. 5—Frederik Pohl	1.00	3.00	5.00	SF
309K	Fort Starke—Wade Everett	.50	1.50	2.50	
310K	False Witness—Helen Nielsen	.50	1.50	2.50	
311K	Sex, Vice and Business—Monroe Fry	.50	1.50	2.50	NF
312K	Witch Doctor—N. C. McDonald	.80	2.40	4.00	
F313K	Who Dares, Wins—Virginia Cowles	.50	1.50	2.50	
314K	God Is My Co-Pilot—Gen. Robert L. Scott, Jr.	.50	1.50	2.50	
315K	Bunch Quitter—Chad Merriman	.50	1.50	2.50	W
316K	The Fourth ''R''—George O. Smith	.50	1.50	2.50	SF
317K	Kamikaze—Gordon T. Allred & Yasuo Kuwahara	.50	1.50	2.50	NF
F318K	The Coast Watchers—Eric D. Feldt	.50	1.50	2.50	
319K	Stairway to Nowhere—Hal Ellson	1.00	3.00	5.00	
320K	The Chemical Elements—Helen Miles Davis	.50	1.50	2.50	NF
321K					
F322K	Boing 707—Martin Caidin	.50	1.50	2.50	NF
F323K	Thunderbolt!—Martin Caidin & Robert S. Johnson	.50	1.50	2.50	NF
324K	No Bugles, No Glory—Fred Grove	.50	1.50	2.50	W
325K	Tomorrow Times Seven—Frederik Pohl	.80	2.40	4.00	SF
326K	Deals With the Devil—ed. Basil Davenport; c-Powers	1.00	3.00	5.00	HO
327K	Seed of Light—Edmund Cooper	.50	1.50	2.50	SF
328K	Black Rock Valley—S. E. Whitman	.50	1.50	2.50	W
329K	Air Force!—Frank Harvey	.50	1.50	2.50	C
330K					
331K	Suspense—Richard Martin Stern	.50	1.50	2.50	
F332K	Zeebrugge—Barrie Pitt	.50	1.50	2.50	NF
F333K	Great Cases in Psychoanalysis—Harold Greenwald	.50	1.50	2.50	
334K	Winter of the Sioux—Robert Steelman	.50	1.50	2.50	W
335K	Wolfbane—Frederik Pohl & C. M. Kornbluth; orig., 1959, c-Powers	1.20	3.60	6.00	SF
F336K	Defeat in the East—Jurgen Thorwald	.50	1.50	2.50	NF
337K	Life Among the Savages—Shirley Jackson	.50	1.50	2.50	H
338K	Harvey Kurtzman's Jungle Book—Harvey Kurtzman	1.60	4.80	8.00	H
F339K	To Live and Kill—Stefan Gazel	.50	1.50	2.50	
340K	Cartoon Countdown—Bernard Wiseman	1.20	3.60	6.00	H
341K	The Outward Urge—John Wyndham & Lucas Parkes	.50	1.50	2.50	SF
342K	Raising Demons—Shirley Jackson	.50	1.50	2.50	H
343K	Stampede—Chad Merriman	.50	1.50	2.50	W
344K	First Command—Wade Everett	.50	1.50	2.50	
345K	The Funhouse—Benjamin Appel	1.00	3.00	5.00	SF
S346K	Pornography and the Law—Drs. Eberhard & Phyllis Kronhausen	.50	1.50	2.50	NF
347K	Rumor, Fear and the Madness of Crowds—J. P. Chaplin	1.00	3.00	5.00	NF
348K	Eagle in the Bathtub—Jule Mannix	.50	1.50	2.50	NF
F349K	American Aces—Edward H. Sims	.50	1.50	2.50	NF
350K	The World of Li'l Abner—Al Capp; movie tie-in	1.20	3.60	6.00	H
351					
352K	Ordeal at Blood River—James Warner Bellah; orig., 1959	.50	1.50	2.50	W
353K	Star Science Fiction Stories No. 6—Frederik Pohl	.80	2.40	4.00	SF
354K	The Hell Fire Club—Daniel P. Mannix	1.20	3.60	6.00	NF
355K	Those About to Die—Daniel P. Mannix	.50	1.50	2.50	
F356K	The Plague and I—Betty MacDonald	.50	1.50	2.50	H

(BALLANTINE BOOKS, continued)

		Good	Fine	N/Mint	
365K	Unearthly Neighbors—Chad Oliver; 1960	.50	1.50	2.50	SF
370K	Zacherly's Midnight Snacks—ed. Zacherly; c-Powers	1.00	3.00	5.00	HO
377K	The Sound of His Horn—Sarban	1.00	3.00	5.00	SF
380K	Tales to Be Told in the Dark—ed. Basil Davenport; c-Powers	.80	2.40	4.00	SF
388K	The Unexpected Dimension—Algis Budrys	.80	2.40	4.00	SF
391K	Strange Relations—Philip Jose Farmer; 1st ed., 1960	3.00	9.00	15.00	SF
397K	The Man Who Ate the World—Frederik Pohl	.80	2.40	4.00	SF
401K	Invisible Men—ed. Basil Davenport; c-Powers	1.00	3.00	5.00	SF
406K	The Climacticon—Harold Livingston; c-Powers	.50	1.50	2.50	SF
S414K	Stories of H. G. Wells—H. G. Wells	.80	2.40	4.00	SF
417K	Zacherly's Vulture Stew—ed. Zacherly; c-Powers	1.20	3.60	6.00	HO
422K	Guardians of Time—Poul Anderson	.80	2.40	4.00	SF
431K	The Doll Maker—Sarban	1.00	3.00	5.00	SF
434K	30 Day Wonder—Richard Wilson	.80	2.40	4.00	SF
439K	Drunkard's Walk—Frederik Pohl	.80	2.40	4.00	SF
441K	The Victorian Chaise Lounge—Marghanita Laski	.80	2.40	4.00	SF
449K	Trouble With Lichen—John Wyndham	.80	2.40	4.00	SF
453K	Village of the Damned—John Wyndham; aka The Midwich Cuckoos, movie tie-in	.80	2.40	4.00	SF
458K	Some of Your Blood—Theodore Sturgeon	1.20	3.60	6.00	M
465K	So Close to Home—James Blish; 1961	1.00	3.00	5.00	SF
466K	Things With Claws—ed. Whit & Hallie Burnett; c-Powers	.80	2.40	4.00	SF
476K	Turn Left at Thursday—Frederik Pohl	1.00	3.00	5.00	SF
479K	New Maps of Hell—Kingsley Amis; c-Powers. Note: History of science fiction writing	1.00	3.00	5.00	NF
480K	The Other Passenger—John Keir Cross	.80	2.40	4.00	SF
483K	Strangers From Earth—Poul Anderson	.80	2.40	4.00	SF
497K	Bypass to Otherness—Henry Kuttner	1.00	3.00	5.00	SF
498K	Ringstones—Sarban	1.00	3.00	5.00	SF
506K	Not Without Sorcery—Theodore Sturgeon	1.00	3.00	5.00	SF
507K	The Lovers—Philip Jose Farmer; 1st ed., 1961	3.00	9.00	15.00	SF
508K	Night's Black Agents—Fritz Leiber	1.00	3.00	5.00	SF
511K	Slan—A. E. Van Vogt; c-Powers	.80	2.40	4.00	SF
519K	A Cupful of Space—Mildred Clingerman	.80	2.40	4.00	SF
522K	Tales of Love and Horror—ed. Don Congdon	.80	2.40	4.00	SF
527	Greener Than You Think—Ward Moore	.50	1.50	2.50	SF
F528	The Challenge of the Spaceship—Arthur C. Clarke	.80	2.40	4.00	SF
531	The Clock Strikes 12—H. R. Wakefield	.80	2.40	4.00	SF
540	Sardonicus and Other Stories—Ray Russell	1.00	3.00	5.00	SF
542	Not Long for This World—August Derleth	1.00	3.00	5.00	SF
546	The Infinite Moment—John Wyndham	.80	2.40	4.00	SF
552	And Some Were Human—Lester del Rey	.80	2.40	4.00	SF
F555	The Primal Urge—Brian Aldiss	.80	2.40	4.00	SF
F561	The Silver Eggheads—Fritz Leiber	1.00	3.00	5.00	SF
563	Alone by Night—ed. Don & Michael Congdon	.80	2.40	4.00	SF
F571	The Unsleep—Diana & Meir Gillon; 1962	1.00	3.00	5.00	SF
577	Shadows With Eyes—Fritz Leiber	1.00	3.00	5.00	SF
579	After Doomsday—Poul Anderson	.80	2.40	4.00	SF
587	Nine Horrors and a Dream—Joseph Payne	.80	2.40	4.00	SF
F588	The Alley God—Philip Jose Farmer	3.00	9.00	15.00	SF
F595	Hospital Station—James White	1.00	3.00	5.00	SF
F602	The Day the Earth Caught Fire—Barry Wells	.50	1.50	2.50	SF
F609	The Telepath—Arthur Sellings	.50	1.50	2.50	SF
F619	Return to Otherness—Henry Kuttner	1.00	3.00	5.00	SF
F626	Conditionally Human—Walter M. Miller, Jr.	.80	2.40	4.00	SF
629	The Survivor and Others—H. P. Lovecraft & August Derleth	1.00	3.00	5.00	SF
F638	The Wonder Effect—Frederik Pohl & C. M. Kornbluth	.80	2.40	4.00	SF
F639	Eight Keys to Eden—Mark Clifton	.80	2.40	4.00	SF
F641	The Fiend in You—ed. Charles Beaumont	.80	2.40	4.00	SF

Ballantine Books 417K, © BB

Ballantine Books 507K, © BB

Ballantine Books F701, © BB

(BALLANTINE BOOKS, continued)

		Good	Fine	N/Mint	
F647	The Night Shapes—James Blish	.80	2.40	4.00	SF
F658	Time Out for Tomorrow—Richard Wilson	.80	2.40	4.00	SF
F680	The Frankenstein Reader—ed. Calvin T. Beck	1.20	3.60	6.00	HO
F685	The Abominable Earthman—Frederik Pohl; 1963	1.00	3.00	5.00	SF
F687	The First Men in the Moon—H. G. Wells	.80	2.40	4.00	SF
F701	A Princess of Mars—Edgar Rice Burroughs; c-Abbett	1.00	3.00	5.00	SF
F702	The Gods of Mars—Edgar Rice Burroughs; c-Abbett	1.00	3.00	5.00	SF
F703	A Handful of Time—Rosel George Brown	.80	2.40	4.00	SF
F709	Star Surgeon—James White	1.00	3.00	5.00	SF
F711	The Warlord of Mars—Edgar Rice Burroughs; c-Abbett	1.00	3.00	5.00	SF
F724	Mutant—Henry Kuttner	1.00	3.00	5.00	SF
F725	Food of the Gods—H. G. Wells	.80	2.40	4.00	SF
F728	Swords of Mars—Edgar Rice Burroughs; c-Abbett	1.00	3.00	5.00	SF
F739	Synthetic Men of Mars—Edgar Rice Burroughs; c-Abbett	1.00	3.00	5.00	SF
F745	Tarzan of the Apes—Edgar Rice Burroughs; 1963, c-Powers	1.00	3.00	5.00	A
F746	The Return of Tarzan—Edgar Rice Burroughs; c-Powers	1.00	3.00	5.00	A
F747	The Beasts of Tarzan—Edgar Rice Burroughs; c-Powers	1.00	3.00	5.00	A
F748	The Son of Tarzan—Edgar Rice Burroughs; c-Powers	1.00	3.00	5.00	A
F749	Tarzan and the Jewels of Opar—Edgar Rice Burroughs; c-Powers	1.00	3.00	5.00	A
F750	Jungle Tales of Tarzan—Edgar Rice Burroughs; c-Powers	1.00	3.00	5.00	A
F751	Tarzan the Untamed—Edgar Rice Burroughs; c-Powers	1.00	3.00	5.00	A
F752	Tarzan the Terrible—Edgar Rice Burroughs; c-Powers	1.00	3.00	5.00	A
F753	Tarzan and the Golden Lion—Edgar Rice Burroughs; c-Powers	1.00	3.00	5.00	A
F754	Tarzan and the Ant-Men—Edgar Rice Burroughs; c-Powers	1.00	3.00	5.00	A
F761	The Island of Dr. Moreau—H. G. Wells	.80	2.40	4.00	HO
F762	Llana of Gathol—Edgar Rice Burroughs; c-Abbett	1.00	3.00	5.00	SF
F770	Thuvia, Maid of Mars—Edgar Rice Burroughs; c-Abbett	1.00	3.00	5.00	SF
F772	Tarzan, Lord of the Jungle—Edgar Rice Burroughs; c-Powers	1.00	3.00	5.00	A
F776	The Chessmen of Mars—Edgar Rice Burroughs; c-Abbett	1.00	3.00	5.00	SF
F777	Tarzan and the Lost Empire—Edgar Rice Burroughs; c-Powers	1.00	3.00	5.00	A

BALLANTINE ADULT FANTASY
Ballantine Books, Inc.

		Good	Fine	N/Mint	
01602	The Blue Star—Fletcher Pratt; 1969	1.20	3.60	6.00	SF
01628	The King of Elfland's Daughter—Lord Dunsany	1.00	3.00	5.00	SF
01652	The Wood Beyond the World—William Morris	1.20	3.60	6.00	SF
01678	The Silver Stallion—James Branch Cabell	1.20	3.60	6.00	SF
01711	Lilith—George MacDonald	1.20	3.60	6.00	SF
01730	The Young Magicians—ed. Lin Carter	1.00	3.00	5.00	SF
01731	Dragons, Elves and Heroes—ed. Lin Carter	1.00	3.00	5.00	SF
01763	Figures of Earth—James Branch Cabell	1.20	3.60	6.00	SF
01795	The Sorceror's Ship—Hannes Bok	1.20	3.60	6.00	SF
01814	Land of Unreason—L. Sprague de Camp; 1970	1.00	3.00	5.00	SF
01855	The High Place—James Branch Cabell	1.20	3.60	6.00	SF
01879	At the Edge of the World—Lord Dunsany	1.00	3.00	5.00	SF
01880	Lud-in-the-Mist—Hope Mirrlees	1.00	3.00	5.00	SF
01902	Phantastes—George MacDonald	1.20	3.60	6.00	SF
01923	The Dream Quest of Unknown Kadath—H. P. Lovecraft	1.00	3.00	5.00	SF
01938	Zothique—Clark Ashton Smith	1.20	3.60	6.00	SF
01958	The Shaving of Shagpat—George Meredith	1.00	3.00	5.00	SF
01959	The Island of the Mighty—Evangeline Walton	1.00	3.00	5.00	SF
01981	Deryni Rising—Katharine Kurtz	1.00	3.00	5.00	SF
01982	The Well at World's End, Vol. 1—William Morris	1.00	3.00	5.00	SF
02015	The Well at World's End, Vol. 2—William Morris	1.00	3.00	5.00	SF
02045	Golden Cities, Far—ed. Lin Carter	1.00	3.00	5.00	SF
02067	Something About Eve—James Branch Cabell	1.20	3.60	6.00	SF
02093	Beyond the Golden Stair—Hannes Bok	1.20	3.60	6.00	SF
02107	The Broken Sword—Poul Anderson; 1971	1.20	3.60	6.00	SF
02145	The Boats of the 'Glen Carrig'—William Hope Hodgson	1.00	3.00	5.00	SF
02146	The Doom That Came to Sarnath—H. P. Lovecraft	1.00	3.00	5.00	SF
02178	Red Moon and Black Mountain—Joy Chant	1.00	3.00	5.00	SF
02206	Hyperborea—Clark Ashton Smith	1.20	3.60	6.00	SF
02244	Don Rodriguez: Chronicles of Shadow Valley—Lord Dunsany	1.20	3.60	6.00	SF
02279	Vathek—William Beckford	1.20	3.60	6.00	SF
02305	The Man Who Was Thursday—G. K. Chesterton	3.00	9.00	15.00	F
02332	The Children of Llyr—Evangeline Walton	1.00	3.00	5.00	SF
02364	The Cream of the Jest—James Branch Cabell	1.20	3.60	6.00	SF
02365	New Worlds for Old—ed. Lin Carter	1.00	3.00	5.00	SF
02394	The Spawn of Cthulu—ed. Lin Carter	1.00	3.00	5.00	SF
02420	Double Phoenix—Edmund Cooper & Roger L. Green	1.20	3.60	6.00	SF
02421	The Water of the Wondrous Isles—William Morris	1.00	3.00	5.00	SF
02445	The Tsaddik of the Seven Wonders—Isadore Haiblum	1.20	3.60	6.00	F
02446	Khaled—F. Marion Crawford	1.00	3.00	5.00	F
02467	The World's Desire—H. Rider Haggard; 1972	1.00	3.00	5.00	F
02501	Xiccarph—Clark Ashton Smith	1.20	3.60	6.00	SF

		Good	Fine	N/Mint	
02502	The Lost Continent—C. J. Cutliffe-Hyne	.80	2.40	4.00	SF
02545	Domnei—James Branch Cabell	1.20	3.60	6.00	SF
02546	Discoveries in Fantasy—ed. Lin Carter	1.00	3.00	5.00	F
02574	Kai Lung's Golden Hours—Ernest Bramah	1.20	3.60	6.00	SF
02598	Deryni Checkmate—Katharine Kurtz	1.00	3.00	5.00	SF
02599	Beyond the Fields We Know—Lord Dunsany	1.00	3.00	5.00	SF
02643	The Three Imposters—Arthur Machen	1.00	3.00	5.00	SF
02669	The Night Land, Vol. 1—William Hope Hodgson	1.00	3.00	5.00	SF
02670	The Night Land, Vol. 2—William Hope Hodgson	1.00	3.00	5.00	SF
02773	The Song of Rhiannon—Evangeline Walton	1.00	3.00	5.00	SF
02789	Great Short Novels of Adult Fantasy, Vol. 1—ed. Lin Carter	1.00	3.00	5.00	F
02874	Evenor—George MacDonald	1.20	3.60	6.00	SF
02892	The Last Unicorn—Peter Beagle	.40	1.20	2.00	F
02995	The Well at World's End, Vol. 1—William Morris	.80	2.40	4.00	SF
02996	The Well at World's End, Vol. 2—William Morris	.80	2.40	4.00	SF
03057	Orlando Furioso, Vol. 1—Ludovico Ariosto; 1973	1.00	3.00	5.00	SF
03085	The Charwoman's Shadow—Lord Dunsany	1.00	3.00	5.00	SF
03162	Great Short Novels of Adult Fantasy, Vol. 2—ed. Lin Carter	1.00	3.00	5.00	F
03261	The Sundering Flood—William Morris	.80	2.40	4.00	SF
03309	Imaginary Worlds—ed. Lin Carter	1.00	3.00	5.00	SF
03353	Poseidonis—Clark Ashton Smith	1.20	3.60	6.00	SF
23416	Excalibur—Sanders Anne Laubenthal	1.00	3.00	5.00	SF
23485	High Deryni—Katharine Kurtz	1.00	3.00	5.00	SF
23515	The Well at World's End, Vol. 1—William Morris	.50	1.50	2.50	SF
23516	The Well at World's End, Vol. 2—William Morris	.50	1.50	2.50	SF
23517	The King of Elfland's Daughter—Lord Dunsany	1.00	3.00	5.00	SF
23518	Titus Groan—Mervyn Peake	1.00	3.00	5.00	SF
23519	Gormenghast—Mervyn Peake	1.00	3.00	5.00	SF
23520	Titus Alone—Mervyn Peake	1.00	3.00	5.00	SF
23526	The Broken Sword—Poul Anderson	.50	1.50	2.50	SF
23527	The Dream Quest of Unknown Kadath—H. P. Lovecraft	.80	2.40	4.00	SF
23528	Lilith—George MacDonald	.80	2.40	4.00	SF
23562	Hrolf Kraki's Saga—Poul Anderson	1.00	3.00	5.00	SF
23611	Red Moon and Black Mountain—Joy Chant	.50	1.50	2.50	SF
23660	The People of the Mist—H. Rider Haggard	.80	2.40	4.00	F
23730	The Wood Beyond the World—William Morris; 1974	.80	2.40	4.00	SF
23787	Kai Lung Unrolls His Mat—Ernest Bramah	1.00	3.00	5.00	SF
23886	Over the Hills and Far Away—Lord Dunsany	1.00	3.00	5.00	SF
23927	The People of the Mist—H. Rider Haggard	.50	1.50	2.50	F
24010	Merlin's Ring—H. Warner Munn	1.20	3.60	6.00	SF
24209	The Song of Rhiannon—Evangeline Walton	1.00	3.00	5.00	SF
24233	Prince of Annwn—Evangeline Walton	1.00	3.00	5.00	SF

BALLANTINE U-SERIES
Ballantine Books, Inc.

U2001	Tarzan of the Apes—Edgar Rice Burroughs; Note: The 3rd printing is a TV tie-in	.80	2.40	4.00	A
U2002	The Return of Tarzan—Edgar Rice Burroughs; Note: The 3rd printing is a TV tie-in	.80	2.40	4.00	A
U2003	The Beasts of Tarzan—Edgar Rice Burroughs	.80	2.40	4.00	A
U2004	The Son of Tarzan—Edgar Rice Burroughs	.80	2.40	4.00	A
U2005	Tarzan and the Jewels of Opar—Edgar Rice Burroughs	.80	2.40	4.00	A
U2006	Jungle Tales of Tarzan—Edgar Rice Burroughs	.80	2.40	4.00	A
U2007	Tarzan the Untamed—Edgar Rice Burroughs	.80	2.40	4.00	A
U2008	Tarzan the Terrible—Edgar Rice Burroughs	.80	2.40	4.00	A
U2009	Tarzan and the Golden Lion—Edgar Rice Burroughs	.80	2.40	4.00	A
U2010	Tarzan and the Ant-Man—Edgar Rice Burroughs	.80	2.40	4.00	A
U2011	Tarzan, Lord of the Jungle—Edgar Rice Burroughs	.80	2.40	4.00	A

Ballantine Books F746, © BB

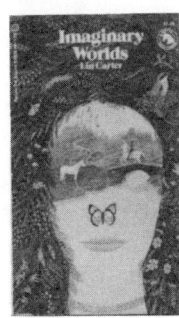

Ballantine Adult Fantasy 03309, © BB

Ballantine U2106, © BB

Ballantine U2141, © BB

Banner Mysteries 1, © Banner

Bantam A2, © Bantam

(BALLANTINE U-SERIES, continued)

		Good	Fine	N/Mint	
U2012	Tarzan and the Lost Empire—Edgar Rice Burroughs	.80	2.40	4.00	A
U2013	Tarzan at the Earth's Core—Edgar Rice Burroughs; 1964, c-Powers	1.00	3.00	5.00	A
U2014	Tarzan the Invincible—Edgar Rice Burroughs; c-Powers	1.00	3.00	5.00	A
U2015	Tarzan Triumphant—Edgar Rice Burroughs; c-Powers	1.00	3.00	5.00	A
U2016	Tarzan and the City of Gold—Edgar Rice Burroughs; c-Powers	1.00	3.00	5.00	A
U2017	Tarzan and the Lion Man—Edgar Rice Burroughs; c-Powers	1.00	3.00	5.00	A
U2018	Tarzan and the Leopard Men—Edgar Rice Burroughs; c-Powers	1.00	3.00	5.00	A
U2019	Tarzan's Quest—Edgar Rice Burroughs; c-Powers	1.00	3.00	5.00	A
U2020	Tarzan and the Forbidden City—Edgar Rice Burroughs; c-Powers	1.00	3.00	5.00	A
U2021	Tarzan the Magnificent—Edgar Rice Burroughs; c-Powers	1.00	3.00	5.00	A
U2022	Tarzan and the 'Foreign Legion'—Edgar Rice Burroughs; c-Powers	1.00	3.00	5.00	A
U2023	Tarzan and the Madman—Edgar Rice Burroughs; 1965, c-Abbett	1.00	3.00	5.00	A
U2024	Tarzan and the Castaways—Edgar Rice Burroughs; c-Abbett	1.00	3.00	5.00	A
U2031	A Princess of Mars—Edgar Rice Burroughs	.80	2.40	4.00	SF
U2032	The Gods of Mars—Edgar Rice Burroughs	.80	2.40	4.00	SF
U2033	The Warlord of Mars—Edgar Rice Burroughs	.80	2.40	4.00	SF
U2034	Thuvia, Maid of Mars—Edgar Rice Burroughs	.80	2.40	4.00	SF
U2036	The Mastermind of Mars—Edgar Rice Burroughs	.80	2.40	4.00	SF
U2037	A Fighting Man of Mars—Edgar Rice Burroughs	.80	2.40	4.00	SF
U2038	Swords of Mars—Edgar Rice Burroughs	.80	2.40	4.00	SF
U2039	Synthetic Men of Mars—Edgar Rice Burroughs	.80	2.40	4.00	SF
U2040	Llana of Gathol—Edgar Rice Burroughs	.80	2.40	4.00	SF
U2041	John Carter of Mars—Edgar Rice Burroughs; c-Abbett	1.00	3.00	5.00	SF
U2045	The War Chief—Edgar Rice Burroughs	1.20	3.60	6.00	W
U2046	Apache Devil—Edgar Rice Burroughs	1.20	3.60	6.00	W
U2048	The Lad and the Lion—Edgar Rice Burroughs; c-Abbett	1.00	3.00	5.00	A
U2106	Tales From the Crypt; c-Frazetta. Note: Contains EC comic reprints	2.00	6.00	10.00	HO
U2107	The Vault of Horror; 1965, c-Frazetta. Note: Contains EC comic reprints	2.00	6.00	10.00	HO
U2140	Tales From the Incredible; c-Frazetta. Note: Contains EC comic reprints	2.00	6.00	10.00	SF
U2141	The Autumn People—Ray Bradbury; c-Frazetta. Note: Contains EC comic adaptation reprints	2.00	6.00	10.00	SF
U2142	Tomorrow Midnight—Ray Bradbury; 1966, c-Frazetta. Note: Contains EC comic adaptation reprints	2.00	6.00	10.00	SF
U2271	Dracula—Bram Stoker, adapted by Otto Binder and Craig Tennis. Note: Comic book style, art by Al McWilliams	1.60	4.80	8.00	HO
U6039	The Mucker—Edgar Rice Burroughs; c-Abbett	1.00	3.00	5.00	A
U6035	Treasure of the Black Falcon—John Coleman Burroughs; orig., 1967	1.00	3.00	5.00	SF
U6125	Tarzan and the Valley of Gold—Fritz Lieber; orig., 1966, movie tie-in	1.20	3.60	6.00	A

BANNER MYSTERIES
Fact and Fiction Publications

Digest Size

1	The Sunday Pigeon Murders—Craig Rice; 1945, c-Raboy	4.00	12.00	20.00	M
2	Death Goes to School—Q. Patrick; 1945, c-Raboy	4.00	12.00	20.00	M

BANTAM A-SERIES
Bantam Books, Inc.

(See Bantam Books for other A volumes)

A1	Men and Volts at War—John A. Miller; 1948	.80	2.40	4.00	NF
A2	Model Railroading; 1950	.50	1.50	2.50	NF
A3	Main Street Merchant—Norman Beasley; 1950	.50	1.50	2.50	B
A4	How to Use Premiums in Your Business to Increase Your Sales and Profits; 1950	.50	1.50	2.50	NF
A5	The Power of People—Charles P. McCormick; 1952	.50	1.50	2.50	NF

BANTAM BIOGRAPHIES
Bantam Books, Inc.

		Good	Fine	N/Mint	
FB400	Cleopatra—Emil Ludwig; 1956	.50	1.50	2.50	B
FB401	Henry the Eighth—Francis Hackett	.50	1.50	2.50	B
FB402	The Great Pierpont Morgan—Frederick Lewis Allen	.50	1.50	2.50	B
FB403	Venetian Adventurer: Marco Polo—Henry Hart	.80	2.40	4.00	B
FB404	Autobiography of Benvenuto Cellini	.50	1.50	2.50	B
FB405	The Last Billionaire, Henry Ford—William C. Richards	.50	1.50	2.50	B
FB406	Up From Slavery—Booker T. Washington	.50	1.50	2.50	B
FB407	The Borgias—J. Lucas-Dubreton	.80	2.40	4.00	B
FB408	Andrew Jackson—Gerald Johnson	.50	1.50	2.50	B
FB409	Madame de Pompadour—Nancy Mitford; 1957	.50	1.50	2.50	B
FB410	The Memoirs of Catherine the Great; 1957	.50	1.50	2.50	B
FB411	Yankee From Olympus—Catherine Drinker Bowen	.50	1.50	2.50	B
FB412	Genghis Khan—Harold Lamb	.80	2.40	4.00	B
FB413	The Life and Time of Rembrandt—Hendrik Willem Van Loon	.80	2.40	4.00	B
FB414	Five and Ten—John K. Winkler	.50	1.50	2.50	B
FB415	The Memoirs of Casanova—Giacomo Casanova; 1958	.80	2.40	4.00	B
FB416	Charlemagne—Harold Lamb; 1958	.80	2.40	4.00	B
FB417	Ashurbanipal—Washington Young	.80	2.40	4.00	B
FB418	Clarence Darrow for the Defense—Irving Stone	.50	1.50	2.50	B

BANTAM BOOKS
Bantam Books, Inc.

		Good	Fine	N/Mint	
1	Life on the Mississippi—Mark Twain; 1945	2.00	6.00	10.00	
2	The Gift Horse—Frank Gruber	.80	2.40	4.00	M
3	Nevada—Zane Grey	.80	2.40	4.00	W
4	Evidence of Things Seen—Elizabeth Daly	.80	2.40	4.00	M
5	Scaramouche—Rafael Sabatini	.80	2.40	4.00	A
6	A Murder by Marriage—Robert George Dean	.80	2.40	4.00	M
7	The Grapes of Wrath—John Steinbeck	2.00	6.00	10.00	
	with dust jacket	10.00	30.00	50.00	
8	The Great Gatsby—F. Scott Fitzgerald	1.60	4.80	8.00	
	with dust jacket	10.00	30.00	50.00	
9	Rogue Male—Geoffrey Household	.80	2.40	4.00	A
	with dust jacket	10.00	30.00	50.00	
10	South Moon Under—Marjorie Kinnan Rawlings	.80	2.40	4.00	E
11	Mr. and Mrs. Cugat—Isabel Scott Rorick	.80	2.40	4.00	B
12	Then There Were Three—Geoffrey Homes	.80	2.40	4.00	
13	The Last Time I Saw Paris—Elliot Paul	.80	2.40	4.00	
14	Wind, Sand, and Stars—Antoine de Saint-Exupery	.80	2.40	4.00	A
15	Meet Me in St. Louis—Sally Benson	.80	2.40	4.00	H
16	The Town Cried Murder—Leslie Ford	.80	2.40	4.00	M
17	Seventeen—Booth Tarkington	.80	2.40	4.00	H
18	What Makes Sammy Run?—Budd Schulberg	.80	2.40	4.00	
19	One More Spring—Robert Nathan	.80	2.40	4.00	
	with dust jacket	10.00	30.00	50.00	
20	Oil for the Lamps of China—Alice Tisdale Hobart	.80	2.40	4.00	
21	Men, Women, and Dogs—James Thurber; 1946	1.20	3.60	6.00	H
22	Babbitt—Sinclair Lewis	1.60	4.80	8.00	
	with dust jacket	10.00	30.00	50.00	
23	The Fog Comes—Mary Collins	.80	2.40	4.00	M
24	Valiant Is the Word for Carrie—Barry Benefield	.80	2.40	4.00	
	with dust jacket	10.00	30.00	50.00	
25	Bugles in the Afternoon—Ernest Haycox; 1946	1.00	3.00	5.00	W
26	Net of Cobwebs—Elisabeth Sanxay Holding	.80	2.40	4.00	M
	with dust jacket	10.00	30.00	50.00	
27	Only Yesterday—Frederick Lewis Allen	.80	2.40	4.00	

Bantam Biographies FB415, © Bantam

Bantam Books 1, © Bantam

Bantam Books 26 (w/dj), © Bantam

Bantam Books 37, © Bantam	Bantam Books 71, © Bantam	Bantam Books 81, © Bantam

(BANTAM BOOKS, continued)

		Good	Fine	N/Mint	
28	Night in Bombay—Louis Bromfield	.80	2.40	4.00	
29	Was It Murder?—James Hilton	.80	2.40	4.00	M
30	Citizen Tom Paine—Howard Fast	.80	2.40	4.00	B
31	The Three Hostages—John Buchan	.80	2.40	4.00	A
32	The Great Mouthpiece—Gene Fowler	.80	2.40	4.00	B
33	The Prisoner of Zenda—Anthony Hope	.80	2.40	4.00	A
34	First Come, First Kill—Francis Allan	.80	2.40	4.00	M
35	My Dear Bella—Arthur Kober	.80	2.40	4.00	H
36	Trail Boss—Peter Dawson	1.00	3.00	5.00	W
37	Drawn and Quartered—Charles Addams	3.00	9.00	15.00	H
38	Anything for a Quiet Life—A. A. Avery	.80	2.40	4.00	M
39	Long, Long Ago—Alexander Woollcott	.80	2.40	4.00	
40	Captain From Connecticut—C. S. Forester	.80	2.40	4.00	A
41	David Harum—Edward Noyes Westcott	.80	2.40	4.00	
42	Road to Folly—Leslie Ford	.80	2.40	4.00	M
43	The Lives of a Bengal Lancer—Francis Yeats-Brown	.80	2.40	4.00	A
44	The Cold Journey—Grace Zaring Stone	.80	2.40	4.00	
	with dust jacket	10.00	30.00	50.00	
45	A Bell for Adano—John Hersey	.80	2.40	4.00	
46	Escape the Night—Mignon G. Eberhart	.80	2.40	4.00	M
47	Home Ranch—Will James	1.00	3.00	5.00	NF
48	The Laughter of My Father—Carlos Bulosan	.80	2.40	4.00	H
49	The Amethyst Spectacles—Frances Crane	.80	2.40	4.00	M
50	The Buffalo Box—Frank Gruber	1.00	3.00	5.00	M
51	Death in the Blackout—Anthony Gilbert	.80	2.40	4.00	M
52	No Hands on the Clock—Geoffrey Homes	.80	2.40	4.00	M
53	Nothing Can Rescue Me—Elizabeth Daly	.80	2.40	4.00	M
54	The Love Letters—Chris Massie	.80	2.40	4.00	R
55	Tutt and Mr. Tutt—Arthur Train	.80	2.40	4.00	H
56	The Tonto Kid—Henry Herbert Knibbs	.80	2.40	4.00	W
57	Anything for a Laugh—Bennett Cerf	.80	2.40	4.00	H
58	''Captains Courageous''—Rudyard Kipling	1.60	4.80	8.00	A
59	Wild Animals I Have Known—E. Thompson Seton	.80	2.40	4.00	NF
60	The Kennel Murder Case—S. S. Van Dine	1.20	3.60	6.00	M
61	The Bantam Concise Dictionary	.80	2.40	4.00	
62	Dead Center—Mary Collins	.80	2.40	4.00	M
63	Green Mansions—W. H. Hudson	1.20	3.60	6.00	F
64	Harriet—Elizabeth Jenkins	.80	2.40	4.00	
65	South Wind—Norman Douglas	.80	2.40	4.00	A
66	She Loves Me Not—Edward Hope	.80	2.40	4.00	H
67	The Bruiser—Jim Tully	.80	2.40	4.00	S
	with dust jacket	10.00	30.00	50.00	
68	Guns From Powder Valley—Peter Field	1.00	3.00	5.00	W
69	The Grandmothers—Glenway Wescott	.80	2.40	4.00	
70	Lay That Pistol Down—Richard Powell	.80	2.40	4.00	M
71	Mountain Meadow—John Buchan	.80	2.40	4.00	A
72	No Bones About It—Ruth Sawtell Wallis	.80	2.40	4.00	
73	The Last of the Plainsman—Zane Grey	.80	2.40	4.00	W
74	Halo in Blood—John Evans	.40	2.40	4.00	M
75	Cannery Row—John Steinbeck; 1947	1.60	4.80	8.00	
	with dust jacket	10.00	30.00	50.00	
76	Drink to Yesterday—Manning Coles	.80	2.40	4.00	
77	Pistol Passport—Eugene Cunningham	1.00	3.00	5.00	W
78	Deadly Nightshade—Elizabeth Daly	.80	2.40	4.00	M
79	A Tree Grows in Brooklyn—Betty Smith	.80	2.40	4.00	
80	False to Any Man—Leslie Ford	.80	2.40	4.00	M
81	Puzzles, Quizzes, and Games—Phyllis Fraser & Edith Young	1.20	3.60	6.00	NF
82	Ride the Man Down—Luke Short	1.00	3.00	5.00	W

		Good	Fine	N/Mint	
83	Up Front—Bill Mauldin	.80	2.40	4.00	H
84	The World, the Flesh and Father Smith—Bruce Marshall	.80	2.40	4.00	
85	Death at the Door—Anthony Gilbert; aka He Came by Night	.80	2.40	4.00	M
86	Border Roundup—Allan R. Bosworth	1.00	3.00	5.00	W
87	Apartment in Athens—Glenway Wescott	1.00	3.00	5.00	
88	Trigger Kid—Bennett Foster; aka The Maverick	1.00	3.00	5.00	W
89	Finders Keepers—Geoffrey Homes	.80	2.40	4.00	M
90	The Uninvited—Dorothy Macardle	1.00	3.00	5.00	F
91	The 17th Letter—Dorothy Cameron Disney	.80	2.40	4.00	M
92	My Life and Hard Times—James Thurber	1.20	3.60	6.00	H
93	Dagger of the Mind—Kenneth Fearing	.80	2.40	4.00	M
94	The Crimson Horseshoe—Peter Dawson	1.00	3.00	5.00	W
95	Assignment Without Glory—Marcos Spinelli	.80	2.40	4.00	M
96	The Scarab Murder Case—S. S. Van Dine	1.20	3.60	6.00	M
97	Swamp Water—Vereen Bell	.80	2.40	4.00	
98	Cry Wolf—Marjorie Carleton	.80	2.40	4.00	
99	Comanche Chaser—Dane Coolidge	1.00	3.00	5.00	W
100	The Cautious Amorist—Norman Lindsay; 1947	.80	2.40	4.00	
101	The Problem of the Green Capsule—J. D. Carr	1.60	4.80	8.00	M
102	Range Rider—W. H. B. Kent	1.00	3.00	5.00	W
103	The Bells of St. Mary's—George Victor Martin; movie tie-in	1.20	3.60	6.00	
104	Powder Valley Pay-Off—Peter Field	1.00	3.00	5.00	W
105	Our Hearts Were Young and Gay—Cornelia Otis Skinner & Emily Kimbrough	.80	2.40	4.00	
106	Asylum—William Seabrook	.80	2.40	4.00	
107	Murder in Brass—Lewis Padgett	2.00	6.00	10.00	M
108	Quick Draw—Curtis Bishop	1.00	3.00	5.00	
109	Blood From a Stone—Ruth Sawtell Wallis	.80	2.40	4.00	M
110	Romance for Sale—Maysie Greig	.80	2.40	4.00	R
111	Trouble Shooter—Robert Travor	.80	2.40	4.00	
112	Hardcase—Luke Short	.80	2.40	4.00	W
113	Riders of the Night—Eugene Cunningham	.80	2.40	4.00	W
114	Old Lover's Ghost—Leslie Ford	.80	2.40	4.00	M
115	Women Will Be Doctors—Hannah Lees	.80	2.40	4.00	R
116	Great Stories From the Saturday Evening Post	1.00	3.00	5.00	
117	Stiffs Don't Vote—Geoffrey Homes; aka Forty Whacks	.80	2.40	4.00	M
118	A Toast to Tomorrow—Manning Coles	.80	2.40	4.00	
119	Double Deal—Allan R. Bosworth; aka Hang and Rattle	1.00	3.00	5.00	W
120	Secret Beyond the Door—Rufus King; movie tie-in	1.00	3.00	5.00	
121	My Man Godfrey—Eric Hatch; aka Irene, the Stubborn Girl	.80	2.40	4.00	E
122	A Certain Doctor French—Elizabeth Seifert	.80	2.40	4.00	R
123	A Treasury of Folk Songs—Sylvia & John Kolb	1.20	3.60	6.00	NF
124	To Mary With Love—Richard Sherman	.80	2.40	4.00	
125	February Hill—Victoria Lincoln; 1947	.80	2.40	4.00	E
126	Quality—Cid Ricketts Sumner	.80	2.40	4.00	E
127	Chicago Murders—Sewell Peaslee Wright	1.00	3.00	5.00	NF
128	Six-Gun Outcast—Charles N. Heckelmann	1.00	3.00	5.00	W
129	"Whip" Ryder's Way—Grant Taylor	1.00	3.00	5.00	W
130	The Cinnamon Murder—Frances Crane	1.00	3.00	5.00	M
131	The Pearl—John Steinbeck	1.60	4.80	8.00	
132	Date With Death—Eaton K. Goldthwaite	1.00	3.00	5.00	M
133	Kid Galahad—Francis Wallace	.80	2.40	4.00	
134	Hell for Breakfast—Alan LeMay	1.00	3.00	5.00	W
135	Mama's Bank Account—Kathryn Forbes; movie tie-in	1.00	3.00	5.00	
136	Up at the Villa—W. Somerset Maugham	1.00	3.00	5.00	
137	Wings of Fear—Mignon G. Eberhart; 1948	.80	2.40	4.00	M
138	Murder Cheats the Bride—Anthony Gilbert	.80	2.40	4.00	M
139	Station West—Luke Short; movie tie-in	1.00	3.00	5.00	W
140	Coroner Creek—Luke Short	1.00	3.00	5.00	W

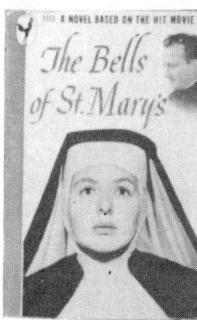

Bantam Books 103, © Bantam

Bantam Books 116, © Bantam

Bantam Books 131, © Bantam

Bantam Books 156 (w/dj), © Bantam   Bantam Books 205, © Bantam   Bantam Books 255, © Bantam

(BANTAM BOOKS, continued)

		Good	Fine	N/Mint	
141	Scandals of Clochemerie—Gabriel Chevallier	.80	2.40	4.00	
142	Treasure Island—Robert Louis Stevenson	1.60	4.80	8.00	A
143	The She-Wolf—H. H. Munro; aka A Saki Sampler. Note: Exists only as a Bantam dust jacket on Superior M656	10.00	30.00	50.00	F
144	The Mighty Blockhead—Frank Gruber; Note: Exists only as a Bantam dust jacket on Superior M655.	10.00	30.00	50.00	
145	The Love Nest—Ring Lardner; Note: Exists only as a Bantam dust jacket on Superior M646.	10.00	30.00	50.00	H
146	The Rynox Murder Mystery—Philip MacDonald; Note: Exists only as a Bantam dust jacket on Superior M642.	10.00	30.00	50.00	M
147	Only the Good—Mary Collins	.80	2.40	4.00	
148	On Ice—Robert George Dean; Note: Exists only as a Bantam dust jacket on Superior M654.	10.00	30.00	50.00	M
149	Good Night, Sheriff—Harrison R. Steeves; Note: Exists only as a Bantam dust jacket on Superior M657.	10.00	30.00	50.00	
150	The Informer—Liam O'Flaherty; 1948. Note: Exists only as a Bantam dust jacket on Superior M650.	10.00	30.00	50.00	
151	The Navy Colt—Frank Gruber; Note: Exists only as a Bantam dust jacket on Superior M649	10.00	30.00	50.00	
152	Mrs. Mike—Benedict & Nancy Freedman	.80	2.40	4.00	
153					
154	Twenty Grand Short Stories—Ernest Taggard	.80	2.40	4.00	
155	Storm—George R. Stewart; Note: Exists only as a Bantam dust jacket on Penguin Special s238.	10.00	30.00	50.00	
156	Boomerang!—William C. Chambliss; Note: Exists only as a Bantam dust jacket on Infantry Journal J101.	10.00	30.00	50.00	
157					
158	The Sign of the Ram—Margaret Ferguson; movie tie-in	1.00	3.00	5.00	E
200	Western Triggers—Arnold Hano; 1948	1.00	3.00	5.00	W
201	Trail South From Powder Valley—Peter Field	1.00	3.00	5.00	W
202	The Tenderfoot—W. H. B. Kent	1.00	3.00	5.00	W
203	Sugarfoot!—Clarence Budington Kelland	.80	2.40	4.00	W
204	Blood on the Moon—Luke Short; aka Gunman's Chance	1.00	3.00	5.00	W
205	Red River—Borden Chase; aka Blazing Guns on the Chisholm Trail, movie tie-in	1.20	3.60	6.00	W
206	Deputy Marshal—Charles N. Heckelmann; c-Saunders	1.00	3.00	5.00	W
207	Short Grass—Thomas W. Blackburn; c-Saunders	1.00	3.00	5.00	W
208	Dead Man's Range—Tom J. Hopkins; aka Bullets Over Broken Leg	1.00	3.00	5.00	W
209	Hard Money—Luke Short; 1949, c-Saunders	1.00	3.00	5.00	W
210	The Land Grabber—Peter Field; aka Fight for Powder Valley	1.00	3.00	5.00	W
211	The Rescue of Broken Arrow—Evan Evans	1.00	3.00	5.00	W
212	Fighting Man—Frank Gruber	1.00	3.00	5.00	W
213	Hell or High Water—Dick Pearce; aka Desert Steel	1.00	3.00	5.00	W
214	Rio Grande Kid—R. M. Hankins; aka Lonesome River Justice, c-Saunders	1.00	3.00	5.00	W
227	American Sexual Behaviour & the Kinsey Report—Morris L. Ernst & David Loth	1.00	3.00	5.00	NF
250	The Stagline Feud—Peter Dawson; 1948	1.00	3.00	5.00	W
251	Relentless—Kenneth Perkins; aka Three Were Thoroughbreds	1.00	3.00	5.00	W
252	Barbed Wire—Bennett Foster; aka Powdersmoke Fence	1.00	3.00	5.00	W
	with dust jacket	10.00	30.00	50.00	
253	Wild Justice—Alan LeMay; aka The Smoky Years	1.00	3.00	5.00	W
254	Border Bandit—Evan Evans	1.00	3.00	5.00	W
255	Badlands—Bennett Foster; c-Saunders	1.00	3.00	5.00	W
256	Western Roundup—Arnold Hano	1.00	3.00	5.00	W
257	Arizona—Clarence Budington Kelland	.80	2.40	4.00	W
258	Raiders of the Rimrock—Luke Short; 1949	1.00	3.00	5.00	W
259	The Man From Wyoming—R. M. Hankins	1.00	3.00	5.00	W
260	Pay-off at Ladron—Bennett Foster	1.00	3.00	5.00	
261	The Wild Bunch—Ernest Haycox; c-Saunders	1.00	3.00	5.00	W
262	A Ghost Town on the Yellowstone—Elliot Paul	.80	2.40	4.00	W

(BANTAM BOOKS, continued)

		Good	Fine	N/Mint	
300	The Kidnap Murder Case—S. S. Van Dine	1.20	3.60	6.00	M
301	Headlined for Murder—Edwin Lanham	.80	2.40	4.00	M
302	The Fabulous Clipjoint—Fredric Brown	2.00	6.00	10.00	M
	with dust jacket	10.00	30.00	50.00	
303	Siren in the Night—Leslie Ford	.80	2.40	4.00	
304	The Problem of the Wire Cage—John Dickson Carr	1.20	3.60	6.00	M
305	Hanged for a Sheep—Richard & Francis Lockridge	1.20	3.60	6.00	M
306	The Day He Died—Lewis Padgett	2.00	6.00	10.00	M
307	The Bride Saw Red—Robert Carson	.80	2.40	4.00	
308	The Silent Speaker—Rex Stout	1.00	3.00	5.00	M
309	The Case of the Mexican Knife; aka Street of the Crying Woman	.80	2.40	4.00	M
310	Murder in the Glass Room—Edwin Rolfe & Lester Fuller	.80	2.40	4.00	M
311	Saigon Singer—F. Van Wyck Mason	.80	2.40	4.00	
312	The Indigo Necklace Murders—Frances Crane	.80	2.40	4.00	M
313	The Chasm—Victor Canning	.80	2.40	4.00	
	with dust jacket	10.00	30.00	50.00	
314	The Yellow Room—Mary Roberts Rinehart	.80	2.40	4.00	M
315	Brighton Rock—Graham Greene	.80	2.40	4.00	M
	with dust jacket	10.00	30.00	50.00	
316					
317	Murder Is Cheap—Anthony Gilbert	.80	2.40	4.00	M
320	As Long As I Live—Ione Sandberg Shriber	.80	2.40	4.00	
350	Your Red Wagon—Edward Anderson; movie tie-in	1.00	3.00	5.00	
	with dust jacket	10.00	30.00	50.00	
351	The Lying Ladies—Robert Finnegan	1.00	3.00	5.00	
352	Miss Agatha Doubles for Death—H. L. V. Fletcher	.80	2.40	4.00	M
353	The Book of the Dead—Elizabeth Daly	1.00	3.00	5.00	M
354	San Francisco Murders—Joseph Henry Jackson	.80	2.40	4.00	NF
355	The Man Within—Graham Greene	.80	2.40	4.00	M
	with dust jacket	10.00	30.00	50.00	
356	Sorry, Wrong Number—Lucille Fletcher & Allan Ullman; movie tie-in	1.00	3.00	5.00	
357	The Sealed Verdict—Lionel Shapiro	.80	2.40	4.00	
358	The Voice of the Corpse—Max Murray	1.00	3.00	5.00	M
359	All for the Love of a Lady—Leslie Ford; 1949	.80	2.40	4.00	M
360	One More Unfortunate—Edgar Lustgarten	.80	2.40	4.00	M
	with dust jacket	10.00	30.00	50.00	
361	The Dead Ringer—Fredric Brown	3.00	9.00	15.00	M
362	The Dragon Murder Case—S. S. Van Dine	1.20	3.60	6.00	M
363	Many a Monster—Robert Finnegan	.80	2.40	4.00	
364	Fire in the Snow—Hammond Innes	1.00	3.00	5.00	
365	The Man Who Could Not Shudder—John Dickson Carr	1.00	3.00	5.00	M
366	The Hound of the Baskervilles—Sir Arthur Conan Doyle	3.00	9.00	15.00	M
400	Winter Meeting—Ethel Vance	1.00	3.00	5.00	
401	Yesterday's Madness—Marian Cockrell; movie tie-in	.80	2.40	4.00	
402	The Red Pony—John Steinbeck	1.60	4.80	8.00	
403	Beggar's Choice—George Axelrod	.80	2.40	4.00	
404	Hiroshima—John Hersey	1.20	3.60	6.00	
405	The Hucksters—Frederic Wakeman	.50	1.50	2.50	
406	Mickey—Peggy Goodin; aka Clementine, movie tie-in	1.00	3.00	5.00	
407	Behold This Woman—David Goodis	1.20	3.60	6.00	
408	Doctor Kim—Lucy Agnes Hancock	.80	2.40	4.00	E
409	Low Man on a Totem Pole—H. Allen Smith	.50	1.50	2.50	
410	The Grass Is Always Greener—George Malcolm-Smith	.80	2.40	4.00	F
411	Hotel Hostess—Faith Baldwin	.80	2.40	4.00	R
412	Encore for Love—Katharine Dunlop	.80	2.40	4.00	R
413	Family Honeymoon—Homer Croy; movie tie-in	1.00	3.00	5.00	
414	Spendthrift—Eric Hatch	.80	2.40	4.00	E
415	Something Wonderful to Happen—Darwin L. Teilhet	.80	2.40	4.00	

Bantam Books 302, © Bantam

Bantam Books 361, © Bantam

Bantam Books 366, © Bantam

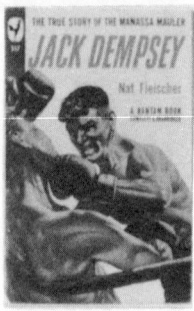

Bantam Books 421 (w/dj), © Bantam   Bantam Books 469, © Bantam   Bantam Books 557, © Bantam

(BANTAM BOOKS, continued)

		Good	Fine	N/Mint	
416	Miss Dilly Says No—Theodore Pratt	.80	2.40	4.00	
417	Confession—Dorothy Les Tina	.80	2.40	4.00	
418	Someone Called Maggie Lane—Frances Shelley Wees	.80	2.40	4.00	
419	My Flag Is Down—James Maresca	.50	1.50	2.50	
420	Illusion—Allane Corliss; aka Marry for Love	.80	2.40	4.00	E
421	No Place to Hide—David Bradley	1.20	3.60	6.00	
	with dust jacket	10.00	30.00	50.00	
422	Office Nurse—Adelaide Humphries	.80	2.40	4.00	R
423	Stranger in Paris—W. Somerset Maugham	.80	2.40	4.00	
424					
425	My Sister, My Bride—Merriam Modell	.80	2.40	4.00	
426	The Stranger—Lillian Bos Ross	.80	2.40	4.00	W
427	Prison Nurse—Louis Berg	1.20	3.60	6.00	
450	Moonlit Voyage—Elizabeth Dunn; 1948	.80	2.40	4.00	
451	Love Is the Winner—Natalie Shipman; aka Who Wins His Love	.80	2.40	4.00	
452	Cabbage Holiday—Anthony Thorne	.80	2.40	4.00	E
453	Five Nights—Eric Hatch; aka Five Days	.80	2.40	4.00	
454	The Chinese Room—Vivian Connell	.50	1.50	2.50	
455	Love Is a Surprise!—Faith Baldwin	.80	2.40	4.00	R
456	Yankee Storekeeper—R. E. Gould	.80	2.40	4.00	
457					
458	Dr. Woodward's Ambition—Elizabeth Seifert	.80	2.40	4.00	E
459	Joan of Arc—Frances Winwar; movie tie-in	1.00	3.00	5.00	A
460	Earth and High Heaven—Gwethalyn Graham	.80	2.40	4.00	E
461	Back Home—Bill Mauldin	.80	2.40	4.00	
462	What Became of Anna Bolton?—Louis Bromfield	.80	2.40	4.00	
	with dust jacket	10.00	30.00	50.00	
463	The Other Room—Worth Tuttle Hedden	.80	2.40	4.00	E
464	Nurse Into Woman—Marguerite Mooers Marshall	.80	2.40	4.00	R
465	Bitter Forfeit—Mabel Louise Robinson	.80	2.40	4.00	E
466	The Big Town—Ring Lardner	.80	2.40	4.00	H
467	A Farewell to Arms—Ernest Hemingway	1.60	4.80	8.00	
468					
469	Lady Godiva and Master Tom—Raoul C. Faure	2.00	6.00	10.00	E
470	The Men in Her Life—Edith Roberts	.80	2.40	4.00	
471	Marry for Money—Faith Baldwin	.80	2.40	4.00	R
473	Danger Trail—Theodore Pratt	1.00	3.00	5.00	
474	Hazard—Roy Chanslor	.80	2.40	4.00	E
475					
476	Road Show—Eric Hatch	.50	1.50	2.50	
477	The Fascination—Jean Pedrick	.80	2.40	4.00	E
500	My Greatest Day in Baseball—J. P. Carmichael	1.00	3.00	5.00	S
501	Strikeout Story—Bob Feller	1.00	3.00	5.00	S
502	The Unexpected—Bennett Cerf	1.00	3.00	5.00	SF
503	First Love—Elizabeth Abell & Joseph I. Greene	.80	2.40	4.00	R
504	Kick-Off—Ed Fitzgerald	1.00	3.00	5.00	S
505	Babe Ruth—Tom Meany	1.00	3.00	5.00	B
506	Lucky to Be a Yankee—Joe DiMaggio; 1949	1.20	3.60	6.00	S
507	Clowning Through Baseball—Al Schacht	1.00	3.00	5.00	S
550	Out of My Trunk—Milton Berle	.80	2.40	4.00	H
551	The ABC of Horseracing—Dan Parker	.80	2.40	4.00	NF
552	The Gashouse Gang—J. Roy Stockton	1.00	3.00	5.00	S
553	The Big Bet—Edward Harris Heth	.80	2.40	4.00	E
554	Hot Leather—Beulah Marie Dix & Bertram Millhauser	.80	2.40	4.00	
555	Great Stories From the Saturday Evening Post, 1947—ed. Ben Hibbs	1.00	3.00	5.00	
556	The Story of the Brooklyn Dodgers—Ed Fitzgerald	1.00	3.00	5.00	S
557	Jack Dempsey—Nat Fleischer	1.00	3.00	5.00	B
700	Blackjack—Joseph E. Kelleam; 1949	.80	2.40	4.00	W

(BANTAM BOOKS, continued)	Good	Fine	N/Mint	
701 Dead As a Dummy—Geoffrey Homes	1.00	3.00	5.00	M
702 The Rustlers—Luke Short	1.00	3.00	5.00	W
703 Hands Off!—Luke Short	1.00	3.00	5.00	W
704 The Memoirs of Sherlock Holmes—Sir Arthur Conan Doyle	2.00	6.00	10.00	M
705 Kingsblood Royal—Sinclair Lewis	.80	2.40	4.00	
706 The Other Woman—Isabel Moore	.80	2.40	4.00	
707 The Harder They Fall—Budd Schulberg	.80	2.40	4.00	
708 The Captive Women—Walter D. Edmonds; aka In the Hands of the Senecas	1.00	3.00	5.00	A
709 The Web of Days—Edna Lee	.50	1.50	2.50	E
710 The Pitfall—Jay J. Dratler	.80	2.40	4.00	E
711 Summer Lightning—Allene Corliss	.80	2.40	4.00	E
712 The African Queen—C. S. Forester	1.60	4.80	8.00	
713 Murder Listens In—Elizabeth Daly; aka Arrow Pointing Nowhere	.80	2.40	4.00	M
714 The Gilded Rooster—Richard Emery Roberts	.80	2.40	4.00	
715 My Greatest Day in Football—Murray Goodman & Leonard Lewin; c-Saunders	1.00	3.00	5.00	S
716 High Pressure—Ahmad Kamal; aka Full Fathom Five	1.00	3.00	5.00	E
717 The Sun Also Rises—Ernest Hemingway	1.60	4.80	8.00	
718 Death Warmed Over—Mary Collins	.80	2.40	4.00	M
720 Action at Three Peaks—Frank O'Rourke	1.00	3.00	5.00	W
721 Hollywood Without Makeup—Pete Martin	1.00	3.00	5.00	NF
722 Too Many Women—Rex Stout	1.00	3.00	5.00	M
723 The Dark Wood—Christine Weston	.80	2.40	4.00	E
724 The Heller—William E. Henning	.80	2.40	4.00	E
725 Blackleg Range—Bennett Foster	1.00	3.00	5.00	W
726 Desert Law—Clarence Budington Kelland; c-Saunders	1.00	3.00	5.00	W
727 City Limits—Hollis Summers	.80	2.40	4.00	JD
728 I Escaped From Devil's Island—Rene Belbenoit; aka Dry Guillotine	1.00	3.00	5.00	NF
729 Belvedere—Gwen Davenport	.80	2.40	4.00	H
730 Dark Interlude—Peter Cheyney	1.00	3.00	5.00	M
731 Sheriff's Revenge—Peter Field; c-Saunders	1.00	3.00	5.00	W
732 Valley of the Shadow—Charles M. Warren	1.00	3.00	5.00	
733 The Valley of Fear—Sir Arthur Conan Doyle	2.00	6.00	10.00	M
734 Panther's Moon—Victor Canning; movie tie-in	.50	1.50	2.50	M
735 A Plot for Murder—Fredric Brown	3.00	9.00	15.00	M
736 The Wine of Astonishment—Martha Gellhorn	.80	2.40	4.00	
737 The Darker Brother—Bucklin Moon	1.20	3.60	6.00	
738 The Big Clock—Kenneth Fearing	.80	2.40	4.00	M
739 The White Dress—Mignon G. Eberhart	.80	2.40	4.00	M
740 Bullet Breed—Leslie Ernenwein; c-Saunders	1.00	3.00	5.00	W
741 Gale Warning—Hammond Innes	1.00	3.00	5.00	
742 Husbands and Lovers—Joseph I. Greene & Elizabeth Abell	.80	2.40	4.00	E
743 Twelve O'Clock High—Sy Bartlett & Beirne Lay, Jr.; movie tie-in	1.20	3.60	6.00	C
744 The Spring Begins—Helen Rich	.80	2.40	4.00	E
745 Camille—Alexandre Dumas	.80	2.40	4.00	E
746 Politics Is Murder—Edwin Lanham; 1950	.80	2.40	4.00	M
747 Bull-Whip—Luke Short	.80	2.40	4.00	W
748 And the Wind Blows Free—Luke Short	.80	2.40	4.00	W
749 The Angry Woman—James Ronald	.80	2.40	4.00	
750 Thieves' Market—A. I. Bezzerides	.50	1.50	2.50	
751 Shot in the Dark—Judith Merril	3.00	9.00	15.00	SF
752 The Wayward Bus—John Steinbeck	1.60	4.80	8.00	
753 Midnight Lace—MacKinlay Kantor	.80	2.40	4.00	E
754 The Hour of Truth—David Davidson	.80	2.40	4.00	
755 Wayward Angel—Verne Chute	.80	2.40	4.00	M
756 The Smell of Murder—S. S. Van Dine	1.20	3.60	6.00	M
757 Ace-in-the-Hole Haggarty—R. M. Hankins	.80	2.40	4.00	W
758 Desperate Choice—Dorothy Speare	.80	2.40	4.00	
759 Tacey Cromwell—Conrad Richter	.80	2.40	4.00	W

Bantam Books 704, © Bantam

Bantam Books 733, © Bantam

Bantam Books 737, © Bantam

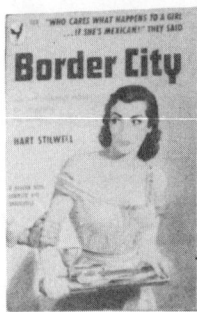

Bantam Books 765, © Bantam

Bantam Books 769, © Bantam

Bantam Books 817, © Bantam

(BANTAM BOOKS, continued)

		Good	Fine	N/Mint	
A760	This Side of Innocence—Taylor Caldwell	1.00	3.00	5.00	
761	Explosion—Dorothy Cameron Disney	.80	2.40	4.00	M
762	Seven Slash Range—Bennett Foster	1.00	3.00	5.00	W
763	Baseball's Greatest Teams—Tom Meany	1.00	3.00	5.00	S
764	Range Drifter—Thomas Thompson	.80	2.40	4.00	W
765	Border City—Hart Stilwell	1.60	4.80	8.00	
766	Jassy—Norah Lofts	.50	1.50	2.50	E
767	No Marriage in Paradise—Myron Brinig	.80	2.40	4.00	E
768	Death Lifts the Latch—Anthony Gilbert	.80	2.40	4.00	M
769	Valley of Violence—Louis Trimble	.80	2.40	4.00	
770	The Whip—Sara Elizabeth Mason	.80	2.40	4.00	
A771	Leave Her to Heaven—Ben Ames Williams	.80	2.40	4.00	
772	Flying Colors—C. S. Forester	.80	2.40	4.00	A
773	Come Clean, My Love—Rosemary Taylor	.80	2.40	4.00	
774	Heritage of the River—Muriel Elwood	.80	2.40	4.00	
775	Hell's Corner—Peter Field	.80	2.40	4.00	W
776	Only the Valiant—Charles M. Warren	.80	2.40	4.00	
777	The Furies—Niven Busch	.50	1.50	2.50	
778	Irene—Ronald Marsh	.50	1.50	2.50	
779	The Case of the Unhappy Angels—Geoffrey Homes	.80	2.40	4.00	M
780	Walk the Dark Streets—William Krasner	.80	2.40	4.00	
781	The Enchanted Heart—Marjorie Worthington	.80	2.40	4.00	
782	The Keys of the Kingdom—A. J. Cronin	.80	2.40	4.00	
783	The Bloody Moonlight—Fredric Brown	3.00	9.00	15.00	M
784	Gunman's Legacy—Evan Evans	.80	2.40	4.00	W
785	Pleasure Island—William Maier	.80	2.40	4.00	E
786	Sins of New York—Milton Crane	.80	2.40	4.00	
787	The Sister of Cain—Mary Collins	.80	2.40	4.00	M
788	Long Storm—Ernest Haycox	.80	2.40	4.00	W
789	Mary Hallam—Susan Ertz	.80	2.40	4.00	
790	The Blazing Land—Norman Collins; aka Flames Coming Out of the Top	.80	2.40	4.00	
791	The Feud at Single Shot—Luke Short	.80	2.40	4.00	W
792	War on the Cimarron—Luke Short	.80	2.40	4.00	W
793	Till Death Do Us Part—John Dickson Carr	1.00	3.00	5.00	M
794	Angels Camp—Kay Morrison	1.00	3.00	5.00	JD
795	My Sister, Goodnight—Gordon McDonell	.80	2.40	4.00	
796	Lord and Master—Robert Standish; aka Elephant Walk	.80	2.40	4.00	
797	The Third Man—Graham Greene	.80	2.40	4.00	
A798	The Underworld—Ira Wolfert; aka Tucker's People	.50	1.50	2.50	E
799	Thunder on the Buckhorn—Frank O'Rourke; c-Saunders	1.00	3.00	5.00	
800	Halo for Satan—John Evans	.50	1.50	2.50	M
801	The Steeper Cliff—David Davidson	.80	2.40	4.00	
802	Fire—George R. Stewart	.80	2.40	4.00	
803	Killer by Proxy—Selwyn Jepson	.80	2.40	4.00	
A804	Drums Along the Mohawk—Walter D. Edmonds	1.00	3.00	5.00	A
A805	H. M. Pulham Esquire—John P. Marquand	.80	2.40	4.00	
A806	Woman of Property—Mabel Seeley	.80	2.40	4.00	E
A807	The Gallery—John Horne Burns	.80	2.40	4.00	
808	The Owl Hoot Trail—Bennett Foster	.80	2.40	4.00	W
809	Wicked Water—MacKinlay Kantor	.80	2.40	4.00	
810	The Moon and Sixpence—W. Somerset Maugham	1.00	3.00	5.00	E
811	Any Shape or Form—Elizabeth Daly	.80	2.40	4.00	M
812	Cotton Country—Hubert Creekmore; aka The Fingers of Night	.80	2.40	4.00	E
813	Sailor Town—Paul Fox	.50	1.50	2.50	
A814	Never Love a Stranger—Harold Robbins	.80	2.40	4.00	
A815	A Lion Is in the Street—Adria Locke Langley	.50	1.50	2.50	
816	Payment Deferred—C. S. Forester	.80	2.40	4.00	M
817	The Whipping—Roy Flannagan	2.00	6.00	10.00	E

		Good	Fine	N/Mint	
A818	The Black Rose—Thomas B. Costain; movie tie-in	2.00	6.00	10.00	A
819	Donovan's Brain—Curt Siodmak	2.00	6.00	10.00	SF
820	The Purple Plain—H. E. Bates	.80	2.40	4.00	
821	Reflections in a Golden Eye—Carson McCullers	.50	1.50	2.50	
822	The Member of the Wedding—Carson McCullers	.80	2.40	4.00	
823	Range Pirate—L. P. Holmes	.80	2.40	4.00	W
824	And Be a Villain—Rex Stout	1.00	3.00	5.00	M
825	A Private Killing—James Benet	.80	2.40	4.00	M
826	High Sierra—W. R. Burnett	1.20	3.60	6.00	
827	Thunder on the River—Charlton Laird	.80	2.40	4.00	
828	American Guerrilla in the Philippines—Ira Wolfert	.80	2.40	4.00	
829	An Affair of State—Pat Frank	.50	1.50	2.50	
830	Anna Becker—Max White	.80	2.40	4.00	E
831	The Screaming Mimi—Fredric Brown	2.00	6.00	10.00	M
832	Six-gun Doctor—Paul S. Powers	.80	2.40	4.00	W
833	Shane—Jack Schaefer	1.60	4.80	8.00	W
834	The Golden Salamander—Victor Canning	.50	1.50	2.50	
835	What Mad Universe—Fredric Brown	1.60	4.80	8.00	SF
836	Long Hunt—James Boyd	.80	2.40	4.00	
837	The Green Flames—Marcos Spinelli; aka From Jungle Roots	1.00	3.00	5.00	
838	The Rebellion of Leo McGuire—Clyde Brion Davis	.50	1.50	2.50	
839	Mission: Danger—Dod Orsborne; aka Master of the Girl Pat	.50	1.50	2.50	
840	Bold New Program—Willard R. Espy	.50	1.50	2.50	
841	Rider of the Rifle Rock—Bennett Foster	.80	2.40	4.00	W
842	The Wooden Horse—Eric Williams	.50	1.50	2.50	
843	Ordeal by Slander—Owen Lattimore	.50	1.50	2.50	
844	Brazos—Ross McLaury Taylor	.50	1.50	2.50	
845	How to Survive an Atomic Bomb—Richard Gerstell	1.20	3.60	6.00	NF
846	This Is My Story—Eleanor Roosevelt	.50	1.50	2.50	B
A847	The Strange Woman—Ben Ames Williams	.50	1.50	2.50	
848	The Queen Bee—Edna Lee	.50	1.50	2.50	E
849	Another Woman's House—Mignon Eberhart	.50	1.50	2.50	
850	Mayhem in B-Flat—Elliot Paul	.80	2.40	4.00	
851	The Innocent Bottle—Anthony Gilbert	.50	1.50	2.50	M
852	Catalina—W. Somerset Maugham	.80	2.40	4.00	
853	Ambush—Luke Short	.80	2.40	4.00	W
854	Fiddlefoot—Luke Short	.80	2.40	4.00	W
855	A Sort of a Saga—Bill Mauldin	.80	2.40	4.00	
856	The Rim of Terror—Hildegarde Tolman Teilhet	.80	2.40	4.00	
857	The Haters—Theodore Strauss	.80	2.40	4.00	
858	With Naked Foot—Emily Hahn	.50	1.50	2.50	
859	Cyrano de Bergerac—Edmond Rostand; movie tie-in	1.20	3.60	6.00	
A860	Captain From Castile—Samuel Shellabarger	1.00	3.00	5.00	
861	Verdict in Dispute—Edgar Lustgarten	.80	2.40	4.00	M
862	The Mesh—Lucie Marchal	.50	1.50	2.50	E
863	The Hangman's Tree—Dorothy Cameron Disney	.50	1.50	2.50	M
864	Broken Valley—Thomas Thompson	.80	2.40	4.00	W
865	The Hunter—Hugh Fosburgh	.50	1.50	2.50	
A866	Bright Feather—Robert Wilder; 1950	.50	1.50	2.50	A
A867	Tender Is the Night—F. Scott Fitzgerald; 1951	1.20	3.60	6.00	
A868	The Grapes of Wrath—John Steinbeck	1.20	3.60	6.00	
A869	Night in Bombay—Louis Bromfield	.50	1.50	2.50	
870	Evered—Ben Ames Williams	.50	1.50	2.50	
A871	Bridal Journey—Dale Van Every	.50	1.50	2.50	
872	The Passionate Pilgrim—Charles Terrot	.50	1.50	2.50	
873	The Cow Thief Trail—Bennett Foster	.80	2.40	4.00	W
874	Murder on the Purple Water—Frances Crane	.80	2.40	4.00	M
875	Something for Nothing—H. Vernor Dixon	1.00	3.00	5.00	E
876	Compliments of a Fiend—Fredric Brown	3.00	9.00	15.00	M
877	Dog Eat Dog—Mary Collins	.50	1.50	2.50	M
878	Ticket to Oblivion—Robert Parker	.50	1.50	2.50	
879	Low Down—Reynolds Packard; aka The Kansas City Milkman	.50	1.50	2.50	E
880	Tasker Martin—Diana Gaines	.50	1.50	2.50	
881	Repent in Haste—John P. Marquand	.50	1.50	2.50	E
882	Lone Hand—Evan Evans	.80	2.40	4.00	W
A883	For Whom the Bell Tolls—Ernest Hemingway	2.00	6.00	10.00	
A884	The Fires of Spring—James A. Michener	1.00	3.00	5.00	
885	House of Storm—Mignon G. Eberhart	.50	1.50	2.50	M
886	The Martian Chronicles—Ray Bradbury	2.00	6.00	10.00	SF
887	The Husband Who Ran Away—Hildegarde Dolson	.80	2.40	4.00	
888	Nobody Lives Forever—W. R. Burnett	1.60	4.80	8.00	
889	Dark Hunger—Theodore Strauss	.50	1.50	2.50	
890	Run by Night—Hammond Innes	.50	1.50	2.50	
891	Wolf Song—Harvey Fergusson	.80	2.40	4.00	
892	Gunsmoke Justice—Louis Trimble	.80	2.40	4.00	W
A893	Cass Timberlane—Sinclair Lewis	1.00	3.00	5.00	
A894	The Courts of the Lion—Robert W. Krepps	.80	2.40	4.00	A

Bantam Books 923, © Bantam

Bantam Books 945, © Bantam

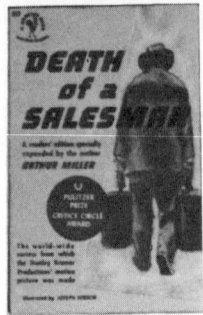

Bantam Books 952, © Bantam

(BANTAM BOOKS, continued)

		Good	Fine	N/Mint	
895	Nightmare in Manhattan—Thomas Walsh	.50	1.50	2.50	
896	He Who Whispers—John Dickson Carr	1.00	3.00	5.00	M
897	Death Has a Past—Anita Boutell	.80	2.40	4.00	M
898	Black Sage—L. P. Holmes	.80	2.40	4.00	W
899	The Pastures of Heaven—John Steinbeck	1.60	4.80	8.00	
900	Arouse and Beware—MacKinlay Kantor	1.00	3.00	5.00	C
901	Shake Well Before Using—Bennett Cerf	.40	1.20	2.00	H
A902	The Flames of Time—Baynard Kendrick	1.20	3.60	6.00	E
A903	The Burnished Blade—Lawrence Schoonover	1.00	3.00	5.00	A
A904	The Great Mouthpiece—Gene Fowler	.40	1.20	2.00	B
905	Strangers in a Train—Patricia Highsmith	1.00	3.00	5.00	M
906	Bend of the Snake—Bill Gulick	.80	2.40	4.00	W
907	The Case Against Myself—Gregory Tree	.80	2.40	4.00	M
908	So Many Doors—Oakley Hall	.50	1.50	2.50	E
909	The Narrow Corner—W. Somerset Maugham	.50	1.50	2.50	
A910	Wild Is the River—Louis Bromfield	.40	1.20	2.00	C
911	Vengeance Valley—Luke Short	.50	1.50	2.50	W
A912	Captain Horatio Hornblower—C. S. Forester; movie tie-in	1.60	4.80	8.00	A
913	The Saturday Review Reader	.40	1.20	2.00	
A914	Stories for Here and Now—Elizabeth Abell & Joseph I. Green	.40	1.20	2.00	
915	The Unforseen—Dorothy Macardle	.50	1.50	2.50	F
916	Blackwater—Frank O'Rourke	.50	1.50	2.50	W
917	To the Indies—C. S. Forester	.50	1.50	2.50	A
A918	Blood Brother—Elliott Arnold	.80	2.40	4.00	
A919	B. F.'s Daughter—John P. Marquand	.40	1.20	2.00	
920	Scottsboro Boy—Earl Conrad & Haywood Patterson	.50	1.50	2.50	NF
921	12 Against Crime—Edward D. Radin	.50	1.50	2.50	
922	Apache—Will Levington Comfort	.80	2.40	4.00	W
923	Hot Rod—Henry Gregor Felsen	1.00	3.00	5.00	
924	Saddle-man—Matt Stuart	.80	2.40	4.00	W
925	Trouble in Triplicate—Rex Stout	1.00	3.00	5.00	M
926	Night Without Sleep—Elick Moll	.80	2.40	4.00	
927	The Judas Cat—Dorothy Salisbury Davis	.50	1.50	2.50	M
A928	Flamingo Road—Robert Wilder	.80	2.40	4.00	
929	Steel to the Sunset—Allan R. Bosworth	.80	2.40	4.00	W
A930	The Citadel—A. J. Cronin	.50	1.50	2.50	
931	Louisville Saturday—Margaret Long	.50	1.50	2.50	E
932	Torch for a Long Journey—Lionel Shapiro	.50	1.50	2.50	
A933	Look to the Mountain—Le Grand Cannon, Jr.	.40	1.20	2.00	
934	Blues for the Prince—Bart Spicer	.40	1.20	2.00	
F935	A Rage to Live—John O'Hara	.50	1.50	2.50	
936	Previews of Entertainment—Gilbert Seldes	.50	1.50	2.50	NF
937	Bright Victory—Baynard Kendrick	.50	1.50	2.50	
A938	W. C. Fields: His Follies and His Fortunes	1.00	3.00	5.00	B
A939	All the King's Men—Robert Penn Warren	1.00	3.00	5.00	
940	Apache Gold and Yaqui Silver—J. Frank Dobie	.80	2.40	4.00	NF
941	Sundown Riders—Thomas Thompson	.50	1.50	2.50	W
942	Romelle—W. R. Burnett	1.20	3.60	6.00	
943	Here Comes a Candle—Fredric Brown	3.00	9.00	15.00	M
A944	Timeless Stories for Today and Tomorrow—Ray Bradbury	1.60	4.80	8.00	SF
945	Tomboy—Hal Ellson; intro. by F. Wertham	2.00	6.00	10.00	E
946	No Survivors—Will Henry	.50	1.50	2.50	W
947	A Room on the Route—Godfrey Blunder	.40	1.20	2.00	
948	A Forest of Eyes—Victor Canning	.40	1.20	2.00	
949	Woman of the World—W. Somerset Maugham	.50	1.50	2.50	
A950	Fifty Great Short Stories—Milton Crane	.40	1.20	2.00	
A951	For My Great Folly—Thomas B. Costain	.50	1.50	2.50	A
952	Death of a Salesman—Arthur Miller	1.60	4.80	8.00	

			Good	Fine	N/Mint	
953	Burning Bright—John Steinbeck		1.60	4.80	8.00	
A954	Grant of Land—Lucile Finlay		.50	1.50	2.50	
A955	The Dream Merchants—Harold Robbins		.50	1.50	2.50	
A956	The Earth Is the Lords—Taylor Caldwell; 1952		.50	1.50	2.50	A
957	Colorado—Louis Bromfield		.50	1.50	2.50	
958	Raton Pass—Thomas W. Blackburn		.50	1.50	2.50	W
959	The Best Go First—Frank O'Malley		.50	1.50	2.50	M
960	Cheaper by the Dozen—Ernestine Carey & Frank B. Gilbreth, Jr.		.50	1.50	2.50	
961	What a Man Wants—Harvey Fergusson; aka The Life of Riley		.50	1.50	2.50	E
962	The Trees—Conrad Richter		.50	1.50	2.50	
963	The God That Failed—Richard Crossman		.40	1.20	2.00	
A964	Terror in the Streets—Howard Whitman; c-Maguire		1.00	3.00	5.00	
A965	Signal Thirty-two—MacKinlay Kantor		.40	1.20	2.00	
966	Sawdust and Sixguns—Evan Evans		.50	1.50	2.50	W
967	A Man Without Friends—Margaret Echard		.40	1.20	2.00	
968	Dig Me a Grave—John Spain		.50	1.50	2.50	M
969	The Little Princesses—Marion Crawford		.40	1.20	2.00	B
970	Jackson Mahaffey—Fred Ross		.40	1.20	2.00	
971	The Confidential Agent—Graham Greene		.50	1.50	2.50	
972	Dollar Cotton—John Faulkner		.40	1.20	2.00	
A973	The Prince of Foxes—Samuel Shellabarger		.50	1.50	2.50	A
974	The Outlaw of Longbow—Peter Dawson		.50	1.50	2.50	W
975	The Golden Door—Bart Spicer		.50	1.50	2.50	
976	The Gambler—William Krasner		.50	1.50	2.50	
977	The Silver Hook—John Mortimer		.50	1.50	2.50	E
978	Mima—Tom Hanlin; aka Yesterday Will Return		.50	1.50	2.50	E
A979	Model Railroading		.80	2.40	4.00	NF
A980	Bugles in the Afternoon—Ernest Haycox		1.00	3.00	5.00	W
A981	The Shining Mountains—Dale Van Every		.40	1.20	2.00	
982	Operation Cicero—L. C. Moyzisch		.50	1.50	2.50	C
A983	God Has a Long Face—Robert Wilder		.40	1.20	2.00	
A984	Ride With Me—Thomas B. Costain		.50	1.50	2.50	A
A985	His Eye Is on the Sparrow—Ethel Waters with Charles Samuels		.40	1.20	2.00	B
A986	Wyatt Earp, Frontier Marshal—Stuart N. Lake		.50	1.50	2.50	NF
A987	Point of No Return—John P. Marquand		.50	1.50	2.50	
988	Dead Man's Saddle—L. P. Holmes		.50	1.50	2.50	W
989	Johnny Christmas—Forrester Blake		.50	1.50	2.50	
990	Night of the Jabberwock—Fredric Brown		3.00	9.00	15.00	M
991	The Illustrated Man—Ray Bradbury		2.00	6.00	10.00	SF
992	Circus Doctor—J. Y. Henderson & Richard Taplinger		.50	1.50	2.50	NF
993	The Gun—C. S. Forester		.50	1.50	2.50	A
A994	The Gentle Infidel—Lawrence Schoonover		.50	1.50	2.50	A
A995	The Witch Diggers—Jessamyn West		.50	1.50	2.50	
996	The Sleeping Sphinx—John Dickson Carr		1.00	3.00	5.00	M
997	12 Against the Law—Edward D. Radin		.50	1.50	2.50	
998	Tomorrow's Another Day—W. R. Burnett		1.60	4.80	8.00	
A999	Return to Paradise—James A. Michener		.80	2.40	4.00	
A1000	The Voice of Asia—James A. Michener		.40	1.20	2.00	NF
1001	Stormy Range—Dwight Bennett		.50	1.50	2.50	W
A1002	Web of Destiny—Muriel Elwood		.50	1.50	2.50	
A1003	Far From Home—Raymond Mason		.50	1.50	2.50	
1004	High Prairie—E. E. Halleran		.50	1.50	2.50	W
1005	Warbonnet Law—Frank O'Rourke		.50	1.50	2.50	W
1006	Step Right Up!—Daniel P. Mannix		1.00	3.00	5.00	NF
1007	Castaway—James Gould Cozzens		.50	1.50	2.50	
A1008	Long Remember—MacKinlay Kantor		.50	1.50	2.50	
A1009	The Devil in Velvet—John Dickson Carr		2.00	6.00	10.00	M
1010	Laughter, Incorporated—Bennett Cerf		.40	1.20	2.00	H
1011	Rifleman Dodd—C. S. Forester		.50	1.50	2.50	A
1012	Murder on the West Bank—Elliot Paul		.50	1.50	2.50	M
1013	The Clay Hand—Dorothy Salisbury Davis		.50	1.50	2.50	M
1014	Alibi at Dusk—Ben Benson		.50	1.50	2.50	M
A1016	The Judas Tree—Neil H. Swanson		.50	1.50	2.50	
A1017	Ann Carmeny—Hoffman Birney		.50	1.50	2.50	
1018	Gun Law at Vermillion—Matt Stuart		.50	1.50	2.50	W
1019	A Rough Shoot—Geoffrey Household		.50	1.50	2.50	
1020	Theresa—Emile Zola		.50	1.50	2.50	
F1021	Soldier of Democracy—Kenneth S. Davis		.50	1.50	2.50	
A1022	Scaramouche—Rafael Sabatini		1.00	3.00	5.00	A
1023	Men Working—John Faulkner		.50	1.50	2.50	
1024	The Survivors—Hammond Innes		.80	2.40	4.00	
1025	Dark Madonna—Richard Summers		.50	1.50	2.50	E
1026	Big Shot—Lawrence Trent		.50	1.50	2.50	M
A1027	High Towers—Thomas B. Costain		.50	1.50	2.50	A
A1028	Written on the Wind—Robert Wilder		.50	1.50	2.50	
1029	Angel of Gaiety—Joseph Hitrec		.50	1.50	2.50	
1030	The Frightened Dove—Peter Hardin		.50	1.50	2.50	M

Bantam Books A1071, © Bantam

Bantam Books 1077, © Bantam

Bantam Books A1138, © Bantam

(BANTAM BOOKS, continued)

		Good	Fine	N/Mint	
1031	West of Abilene—Vingie Roe	.50	1.50	2.50	W
1032	The Second Confession—Rex Stout	1.00	3.00	5.00	M
A1033	Inside U. S. A., Volume 1—John Gunther	.50	1.50	2.50	NF
A1034	Inside U. S. A., Volume 2—John Gunther	.50	1.50	2.50	NF
A1035	Live With Lightning—Mitchell Wilson	.50	1.50	2.50	
A1036	The Grand Portage—Walter O'Meara	.50	1.50	2.50	
A1037	Harper's Magazine Reader	.50	1.50	2.50	
1038	Don'tTouch Me—MacKinlay Kantor	.50	1.50	2.50	E
1039	The Desert of Love—Francois Muriac	.50	1.50	2.50	
1040	Death Has Many Doors—Frederic Brown	1.60	4.80	8.00	M
F1041	The Silent Drum—Neil H. Swanson	.50	1.50	2.50	
F1042	The Stars Look Down—A. J. Cronin	.50	1.50	2.50	
A1043	Fighting Men of the West—Dane Coolidge	.50	1.50	2.50	NF
A1044	The Affairs of Flavie—Gabriel Chevallier	.50	1.50	2.50	E
1045	The Grass Is Singing—Doris Lessing	.50	1.50	2.50	
1046	The Farmers Hotel—John O'Hara	.50	1.50	2.50	
1047	The End of My Life—Vance Bourjaily	.50	1.50	2.50	E
1048	Summer Range—L. P. Holmes	.50	1.50	2.50	W
1049	Black Sheep, Run—Bart Spicer	.50	1.50	2.50	
A1050	Grand Canary—A. J. Cronin	.50	1.50	2.50	
A1051	The Disenchanted—Budd Schulberg	.50	1.50	2.50	
A1052	The Last Englishman—Hebe Weenolsen	1.00	3.00	5.00	A
A1053	No People Like Show People—Maurice Zolotow	.50	1.50	2.50	NF
1054	Cage of Darkness—Rene Masson	.50	1.50	2.50	
1055	Pagoda—James Atlee Phillips	.50	1.50	2.50	
1056	The Lonesome Quarter—Richard Wormser	.50	1.50	2.50	W
1057	Cimarron Crossing—Michael Carder	.50	1.50	2.50	W
1058	The Angry Mountain—Hammond Innes	.50	1.50	2.50	
1059	The 31st of February—Julian Symons	.50	1.50	2.50	M
A1060	The Keys of the Kingdom—A. J. Cronin	.40	1.20	2.00	
1061	Arizona—Clarence Budington Kelland	.50	1.50	2.50	W
1062	The Tonto Kid—Henry Herbert Knibbs	.50	1.50	2.50	W
1063	Ride the Man Down—Luke Short	.50	1.50	2.50	W
1064	Trail Boss—Peter Dawson	.50	1.50	2.50	W
1065	Cannery Row—John Steinbeck	.80	2.40	4.00	
1066	The Pastures of Heaven—John Steinbeck	.80	2.40	4.00	
1067	Nevada—Zane Grey	.50	1.50	2.50	W
1068	Valley of the Shadow—Charles M. Warren	.50	1.50	2.50	
A1069	Only Yesterday—Frederick Lewis Allen; 1953	.40	1.20	2.00	
1070	Beware the Pale Horse—Ben Benson	.50	1.50	2.50	M
A1071	Brave New World—Aldous Huxley	2.00	6.00	10.00	SF
A1072	Nightrunners of Bengal—John Masters	.50	1.50	2.50	
A1073	An Unfound Door—Al Hine	.50	1.50	2.50	
1074	Berenstain's Baby Book—Janice & Stanley Berenstain	.50	1.50	2.50	
1075	Play a Lone Hand—Luke Short	.50	1.50	2.50	W
1076	Final Copy—Jay Barbette	.50	1.50	2.50	M
1077	Space on My Hands—Fredric Brown	2.00	6.00	10.00	SF
1078	Hold Back the Night—Pat Frank	.50	1.50	2.50	
1079	Is Another World Watching?—H. F. Heard	1.60	4.80	8.00	UFO
1080	Single-handed—C. S. Forester	.50	1.50	2.50	A
1081	Harbin's Ridge—Henry Giles	.50	1.50	2.50	E
1082	Gunman Brand—Thomas Thompson	.50	1.50	2.50	W
1083	A Gentle Murderer—Dorothy Salisbury Davis	.50	1.50	2.50	M
A1084	The Looking Glass—William March	.50	1.50	2.50	E
A1085	Storm Centre—Robert Standish	.50	1.50	2.50	E
A1086	Green Fire—Peter Rainier	.50	1.50	2.50	
F1087	So Little Time—John P. Marquand	.50	1.50	2.50	
A1088	Delilah—Marcus Goodrich	.50	1.50	2.50	

		Good	Fine	N/Mint	
A1089	Coronado's Children—J. Frank Dobie	.80	2.40	4.00	NF
A1090	The Captive Witch—Dale Van Every	.50	1.50	2.50	
A1091	The Heart Is a Lonely Hunter—Carson McCullers	.50	1.50	2.50	
1092	Parole Chief—David Dressler	.50	1.50	2.50	
1093	The Day of the Locust—Nathanael West	.50	1.50	2.50	
1094	A Drum Calls West—Bill Gulick	.50	1.50	2.50	W
1095	The Smoky Trail—Matt Stuart	.50	1.50	2.50	W
1096	Spin the Glass Web—Max Ehrlich	.50	1.50	2.50	
A1097	Come Fill the Cup—Harlan Ware	.50	1.50	2.50	
A1098	The Story of Ernie Pyle—Lee Miller	.50	1.50	2.50	B
A1099	Rome Haul—Walter D. Edmonds	.50	1.50	2.50	
A1100	Roger Sudden—Thomas H. Raddall	.80	2.40	4.00	
1101	The Mountains Have No Shadow—Owen Cameron	.50	1.50	2.50	
1102	Strange Courage—Evan Evans	.50	1.50	2.50	W
1103	Black Sage—L. P. Holmes	.80	2.40	4.00	W
1104	Ambush—Luke Short	.50	1.50	2.50	W
1105	Fiddlefoot—Luke Short	.50	1.50	2.50	W
A1106	Fancies and Goodnights—John Collier	3.00	9.00	15.00	SF
A1107	Sunrise to Sunset—Samuel Hopkins Adams	.50	1.50	2.50	A
1108	Full of Life—John Fante	.50	1.50	2.50	
1109	Clara—Lonnie Coleman	.50	1.50	2.50	
1110	Road Kid—Howard Pease	.80	2.40	4.00	
1111	Brazos—Ross McLaury Taylor	.50	1.50	2.50	W
1112	Badlands—Bennett Foster	.50	1.50	2.50	W
1113	The Crimson Horseshoe—Peter Dawson	.50	1.50	2.50	W
1114					
1115	The Wild Bunch—Ernest Haycox	.50	1.50	2.50	W
1116	Trigger Kid—Bennett Foster	.50	1.50	2.50	W
1117	The Last Apaches—William Hopson	.50	1.50	2.50	W
1118	Saturday Review Reader No. 2	.50	1.50	2.50	
1119	Below Suspicion—John Dickson Carr	1.00	3.00	5.00	M
1120	Gaptown Law—Louis Trimble	.50	1.50	2.50	W
A1121	The Golden Exile—Lawrence Schoonover	1.00	3.00	5.00	A
1122					
A1123	Of Former Love—Emma Laird	.50	1.50	2.50	E
1124	Little Men, Big World—W. R. Burnett	1.60	4.80	8.00	
1125	Air Bridge—Hammond Innes	.50	1.50	2.50	
1126	The Long Green—Bart Spicer	.50	1.50	2.50	
1127	Genghis Khan—Harold Lamb	.80	2.40	4.00	B
1128	Thin Edge of Violence—William O'Farrell	.50	1.50	2.50	
1129					
F1130	Green Centuries—Caroline Gordon	.50	1.50	2.50	
A1131	The King's Cavalier—Samuel Shellabarger	1.00	3.00	5.00	A
1132	Rim of the Caprock—Noel M. Loomis	.50	1.50	2.50	W
1133	The Far Cry—Fredric Brown	3.00	9.00	15.00	M
1134	The Fabulous Clipjoint—Fredric Brown	1.60	4.80	8.00	M
1135	Rock Bottom—Earl Conrad	.50	1.50	2.50	
A1136	Lament for Four Virgins—Lael Tucker	.50	1.50	2.50	
A1137	The Lute Player—Norah Lofts	.50	1.50	2.50	
A1138	Hill of the Hawk—Scott O'Dell	1.00	3.00	5.00	
A1139	Melissa—Taylor Caldwell	.50	1.50	2.50	
1140	Night Man—Lucille Fletcher & Allan Ullman	.50	1.50	2.50	
1141	Lost Wolf River—Dwight Bennett	.50	1.50	2.50	W
1142	Antic Hay—Aldous Huxley	1.00	3.00	5.00	
1143	Mountain Meadow—John Buchan	.50	1.50	2.50	A
A1144	Westward the River—Dale Van Every	.80	2.40	4.00	
A1145	The Great Rascal—Jay Monaghan	.80	2.40	4.00	
A1146	The Gallery—John Horne Burns	.50	1.50	2.50	
1147	A Cry of Children—John Horne Burns	.50	1.50	2.50	
1148	The Price of Salt—Claire Morgan	.50	1.50	2.50	
1149	Gold Under Skull Peak—Frank O'Rourke	.50	1.50	2.50	
1150	The Night Watch—Thomas Walsh	.50	1.50	2.50	
A1151	Paradise—Esther Forbes	.50	1.50	2.50	
F1152	Model Railroading	.80	2.40	4.00	NF
1153	A Worthy Man—Robert Standish	.50	1.50	2.50	
1154	Man Drowning—Henry Kuttner	3.00	9.00	15.00	
A1155					
A1156	Reflections in a Golden Eye—Carson McCullers	.50	1.50	2.50	
A1157	Empress of Byzantium—Helen A. Mahler	1.00	3.00	5.00	A
A1158	Argosy Book of Adventure Stories—Rogers Terrill	.80	2.40	4.00	A
A1159	The Forbidden Ground—Neil H. Swanson	.50	1.50	2.50	
A1160	Juan Belmonte: Killer of Bulls—Juan Belmonte Y Garcia & Manuel Chaves Nogales	.80	2.40	4.00	B
1161	Missing—Egon Hostovsky	.50	1.50	2.50	
A1162	And Ride a Tiger—Robert Wilder	.50	1.50	2.50	
F1163	What to Wear Where	.50	1.50	2.50	NF
1164	Short Grass—Thomas W. Blackburn	.80	2.40	4.00	W
F1165	Flee the Angry Strangers—George Mandel	.50	1.50	2.50	

		Good	Fine	N/Mint	
1166	Laughter, Incorporated—Bennett Cerf	.50	1.50	2.50	H
1167	Southwest—John Houghton Allen	.50	1.50	2.50	
1168	No Survivors—Will Henry	.80	2.40	4.00	W
1169	The Paradise Below the Stairs—Andre Brincourt	.50	1.50	2.50	
1170	The General—C. S. Forester	.50	1.50	2.50	A
F1171	50 Great Artists—Bernard Myers	.80	2.40	4.00	NF
A1172	Bright Feather—Robert Wilder	.80	2.40	4.00	
1173	In the Best Families—Rex Stout	1.20	3.60	6.00	M
A1174	My Brother, My Enemy—Mitchell Wilson	.50	1.50	2.50	
1175	Warwhoop—MacKinlay Kantor	.80	2.40	4.00	
1176	We All Killed Grandma—Fredric Brown	4.00	12.00	20.00	M
1177	Bird of Prey—Victor Canning	.50	1.50	2.50	
1178	The Quick Brown Fox—Lawrence Schoonover	1.00	3.00	5.00	
1179	Four Steps to the Wall—Jon Edgar Webb	.50	1.50	2.50	
1180	Gunfighters Pay—William Hopson	.50	1.50	2.50	W
A1181	Wait for Tomorrow—Robert Wilder	.50	1.50	2.50	E
A1182	The Bizarre Sisters—Jay & Audrey Walz	.50	1.50	2.50	
A1183	The Weight of the Cross—Robert O. Bowen	.80	2.40	4.00	
1184	Cup of Gold—John Steinbeck	.80	2.40	4.00	
A1185	Dance to the Piper—Agnes deMille; 1954	.50	1.50	2.50	
F1186	The Moneyman—Thomas B. Costain	.50	1.50	2.50	
1187	The Deceivers—John Masters	.80	2.40	4.00	
1188	Dead Pigeon—Robert P. Hanson	.50	1.50	2.50	M
1189	Gunflame—John S. Daniels	.50	1.50	2.50	W
A1190	The Wonderful Country—Tom Lea	.50	1.50	2.50	
1191	Son of Haman—Louis Cochran	.50	1.50	2.50	
A1192	The Other Room—Worth Tuttle Hedden	.50	1.50	2.50	E
A1193	Here Comes Joe Mungin—Chalmers S. Murray	.50	1.50	2.50	
1194	Ask the Dust—John Fante	.50	1.50	2.50	
1195	Catch a Tiger—Owen Cameron	.50	1.50	2.50	
A1196	The Ship—C. S. Forester	.50	1.50	2.50	A
1197	Dead on Arrival—George Bagby	.50	1.50	2.50	M
1198	Broken Lance—Frank Gruber	.50	1.50	2.50	W
1199					
F1200	Melville Goodwin, USA—John P. Marquand	.50	1.50	2.50	
A1201	Manhattan—Seymour Krim	.50	1.50	2.50	
1202					
F1203	The Kings of the Road—Ken W. Purdy	1.20	3.60	6.00	NF
A1204	The Hate Merchant—Niven Busch	.50	1.50	2.50	
A1205	The Man From Brazil—E. B. Garside	.50	1.50	2.50	
1206	Royal Gorge—Peter Dawson	.50	1.50	2.50	W
1207	The Burning Court—John Dickson Carr	1.60	4.80	8.00	M
1208	The Sea of Grass—Conrad Richter	.50	1.50	2.50	A
A1209	Gal Young 'Un—Marjorie Kinnan Rawlings	.50	1.50	2.50	
A1210	Our American Government—Wright Patman	.50	1.50	2.50	NF
A1211	The Wild Ohio—Bart Spicer	.50	1.50	2.50	
A1212	The Mustangs—J. Frank Dobie	.80	2.40	4.00	NF
A1213	Some Faces in the Crowd—Budd Schulberg	.50	1.50	2.50	
A1214	Someday, Boy—Sam Ross	.50	1.50	2.50	
1215	The Deep End—Fredric Brown	2.00	6.00	10.00	M
1216	The Dead Ringer—Fredric Brown	1.60	4.80	8.00	M
A1217	The Power and the Glory—Graham Greene	.50	1.50	2.50	
1218					
1219	Hiroshima—John Hersey	.50	1.50	2.50	
A1220	Picaroon—Ernest Dudley	.50	1.50	2.50	
A1221	Troubling of a Star—Walt Sheldon	.80	2.40	4.00	
1222					
1223					
1224					
1225	Swamp Water—Vereen Bell	.50	1.50	2.50	
1226	Blood Will Tell—George Bagby	.50	1.50	2.50	M
A1227	A Treasury of Folk Songs—Sylvia & John Kolb	.80	2.40	4.00	NF
A1228	The Great Gatsby—F. Scott Fitzgerald	.80	2.40	4.00	
A1229	The God That Failed—Richard Crossman	.50	1.50	2.50	
A1230	Cyrano de Bergerac—Edmond Rostand	.80	2.40	4.00	A
A1231	Good for a Laugh—Bennett Cerf	.50	1.50	2.50	H
1232	A Man Gets Around—John McNulty	.50	1.50	2.50	
F1233	Eyeless in Gaza—Aldous Huxley	1.00	3.00	5.00	
A1234	Suleiman the Magnificent—Harold Lamb	.80	2.40	4.00	A
A1235	Seven—Carson McCullers	.50	1.50	2.50	
A1236	Wait, Son, October Is Near—John Bell Clayton	.50	1.50	2.50	
1237	The Daughter of Bugle Ann—MacKinlay Kantor	.50	1.50	2.50	
1238	Wicked Water—MacKinlay Kantor	.50	1.50	2.50	
A1239	The Restless Border—Dick Pearce	.50	1.50	2.50	W
A1240	A Farewell to Arms—Ernest Hemingway	1.00	3.00	5.00	
A1241	The Golden Apples of the Sun—Ray Bradbury	1.20	3.60	6.00	SF
A1242	The Saturday Review Reader No. 3	.50	1.50	2.50	

(BANTAM BOOKS, continued)

		Good	Fine	N/Mint	
1243	Sword and Candle—Sidney Herschel Small	.80	2.40	4.00	A
A1244	Restless House—Emile Zola	.50	1.50	2.50	
A1245	A Good Man—Jefferson Young	.50	1.50	2.50	
A1246	Billy the Kid—Edwin Corle	.80	2.40	4.00	
1247	Man Alone—William Doyle & Scott O'Dell	.50	1.50	2.50	
1248					
A1249	The Sun Also Rises—Ernest Hemingway	1.00	3.00	5.00	
A1250	The Trembling Earth—Dale Van Every	.50	1.50	2.50	
1251	Line to Tomorrow—Lewis Padgett	1.20	3.60	6.00	SF
1252	Murder by the Book—Rex Stout	1.00	3.00	5.00	M
1253	What Mad Universe—Fredric Brown	1.20	3.60	6.00	SF
A1254	The Boyds of Black River—Walter D. Edmonds	.80	2.40	4.00	
A1255	The Woods Colt—Thames Williamson	.50	1.50	2.50	
1256					
A1257	Sea Struck—Bennett Stanley	.50	1.50	2.50	
A1258	Autumn Thunder—Robert Wilder	.50	1.50	2.50	
1259					
A1260	Crome Yellow—Aldous Huxley	.80	2.40	4.00	
1261	The Martian Chronicles—Ray Bradbury	1.00	3.00	5.00	SF
A1262	Utopia 14—Kurt Vonnegut, Jr.	2.00	6.00	10.00	SF
1263					
1264	The Light in the Forest—Conrad Richter	.50	1.50	2.50	
1265					
1266	Cannery Row—John Steinbeck	.80	2.40	4.00	
F1267	East of Eden—John Steinbeck	2.00	6.00	10.00	
A1268	The Chinese Room—Vivian Connell	.50	1.50	2.50	E
1269	The Bridges of Toko-ri—James A. Michener	1.00	3.00	5.00	C
1270					
1271	The Venus Death—Ben Benson	.80	2.40	4.00	M
1272	Crazy Weather—Charles L. McNichols	.50	1.50	2.50	
1273	Case File: FBI—the Gordons	.50	1.50	2.50	M
F1274	Best of the Bedside Esquire—Arnold Gingrich	.80	2.40	4.00	
A1275	In the Years of Our Lord—Manuel Komroff	.50	1.50	2.50	
A1276	The Streak—Paul Darcy Boles	.50	1.50	2.50	
1277	The Stagline Feud—Peter Dawson	.50	1.50	2.50	W
1278	Costigan's Needle—Jerry Sohl	.80	2.40	4.00	SF
F1279	Battle Cry—Leon Uris	.50	1.50	2.50	C
1280					
A1281	White Hunter, Black Heart—Peter Viertel	.50	1.50	2.50	
1282	The Illustrated Man—Ray Bradbury	1.00	3.00	5.00	SF
1283	Sailor Town—Paul Fox	.50	1.50	2.50	
F1284	Lord Vanity—Samuel Shellabarger; 1955	1.00	3.00	5.00	A
1285	The Lights in the Sky Are Stars—Fredric Brown	1.20	3.60	6.00	SF
1286	Shakedown—Richard Ellington	.50	1.50	2.50	M
1287	Bitter Sage—Frank Gruber	.50	1.50	2.50	W
1288	The Cautious Amorist—Norman Lindsay	.50	1.50	2.50	
A1289	The Undaunted—John Harris	.50	1.50	2.50	
A1290	The Kill—Emile Zola	.50	1.50	2.50	
A1291	Tamerlane—Harold Lamb	.80	2.40	4.00	A
A1292	War With the Newts—Karel Capek	1.00	3.00	5.00	SF
1293	And the Wind Blows Free—Luke Short	.50	1.50	2.50	W
1294	Third From the Sun—Richard Matheson	1.20	3.60	6.00	SF
1295	The Name Is Archer—John Ross MacDonald	1.00	3.00	5.00	M
A1296	How to Buy Stocks—Louis Engel	.50	1.50	2.50	NF
1297	Shane—Jack Schaefer	.80	2.40	4.00	W
1298	Nevada—Zane Grey	.50	1.50	2.50	W
F1299	The Thorndike-Barnhart Handy Pocket Dictionary—Clarence Barnhart	.50	1.50	2.50	NF
A1300	Never Love a Stranger—Harold Robbins	.50	1.50	2.50	

Bantam Books A1234, © Bantam

Bantam Books A1262, © Bantam

Bantam Books 1371, © Bantam

		Good	Fine	N/Mint	
F1301	The Grapes of Wrath—John Steinbeck	.80	2.40	4.00	
F1302	Fifty Great Short Stories—Milton Crane	.50	1.50	2.50	
A1303	Twenty Grand Short Stories—Ernestine Taggard	.50	1.50	2.50	
A1304	Far From Customary Skies—Warren Eyster	.50	1.50	2.50	
A1305	Mr. Midshipman Hornblower—C. S. Forester	.50	1.50	2.50	A
A1306	The End of the Affair—Graham Greene	.50	1.50	2.50	
A1307	Man Without a Star—Dee Linford	.80	2.40	4.00	
1308	Drop Dead—George Bagby	.50	1.50	2.50	M
1309	1001 Valuable Things You Can Get Free—Mort Weisinger	.40	1.20	2.00	NF
1310	More Adventures in Time and Space—Raymond J. Healy & J. Francis McComas	.50	1.50	2.50	SF
1311	The Natural Way to Better Golf—Jack Burke	.40	1.20	2.00	NF
1312	The Screaming Mimi—Fredric Brown	1.00	3.00	5.00	M
1313	High Gear—Evan Jones	.50	1.50	2.50	
A1314	To the Indies—C. S. Forester	.50	1.50	2.50	A
1315	Murder Points a Finger—David Alexander	.50	1.50	2.50	M
1316	This Gun for Hire—Graham Greene	.50	1.50	2.50	
1317	The Syndic—C. M. Kornbluth	.80	2.40	4.00	SF
A1318	Sayonara—James A. Michener	1.00	3.00	5.00	
A1319	The Enchanted Cup—Dorothy James Roberts	.50	1.50	2.50	
A1320	Peace of Mind—Joshua Loth Liebman	.50	1.50	2.50	
F1321	Beyond This Place—A. J. Cronin	.50	1.50	2.50	
A1322	Death of a Salesman—Arthur Miller	.80	2.40	4.00	
1323	Target in Taffeta—Ben Benson	.50	1.50	2.50	M
A1324	To a God Unknown—John Steinbeck	1.00	3.00	5.00	
1325	The Nine Wrong Answers—John Dickson Carr	.80	2.40	4.00	
1326	Prisoner's Base—Rex Stout	1.00	3.00	5.00	
1327	The Schirmer Inheritance—Eric Ambler; mentioned in *Parade of Pleasure*, pg. 174	.80	2.40	4.00	M
1328	Frontiers in Space—Everett F. Bleiler & T. E. Dikty	.80	2.40	4.00	SF
A1329	Of Mice and Men—John Steinbeck	1.20	3.60	6.00	
1330	But That's Unprintable—Dave Breger	.50	1.50	2.50	
A1331	Captain Lightfoot—W. R. Burnett	1.00	3.00	5.00	A
A1332	The Time of the Fire—Marc Brandel	.80	2.40	4.00	
1333	Orient Express—Graham Greene	.50	1.50	2.50	M
1334	Strange As It Seems—Elsie Hix	.50	1.50	2.50	
A1335	The Lotus and the Wind—John Masters	.80	2.40	4.00	
A1336	The Kentuckians—Janice Holt Giles	.80	2.40	4.00	
F1337	The Cobweb—William Gibson	.50	1.50	2.50	
F1338	All the King's Men—Robert Penn Warren	.80	2.40	4.00	
A1339	The Moon and Sixpence—W. Somerset Maugham	.80	2.40	4.00	
A1340	Don't Tread on Me—Horace V. Bird & Walter Karig	.50	1.50	2.50	
1341					
A1342	Laughter, Incorporated—Bennett Cerf	.50	1.50	2.50	H
1343	The Man From Tomorrow—Wilson Tucker	1.00	3.00	5.00	SF
1344	High Dive—Frank O'Rourke	.50	1.50	2.50	
1345	The Far Shore—Gordon Webber	.50	1.50	2.50	
1346	Cattle, Guns and Men—Luke Short	.50	1.50	2.50	W
1347	Johnny Vengeance—Frank Gruber	.50	1.50	2.50	W
1348	F. B. I. Story—The Gordons	.50	1.50	2.50	M
1349	Death's Long Shadow—Jay Barbette	.50	1.50	2.50	M
F1350	The Fires of Spring—James A. Michener	.50	1.50	2.50	
1351	God and My Country—MacKinlay Kantor	.50	1.50	2.50	
1352	Science Fiction Thinking Machines—ed. Groff Conklin	.80	2.40	4.00	SF
A1353	Alexander of Macedon—Harold Lamb	.80	2.40	4.00	A
A1354					
A1355	View From the Air—Hugh Fosburgh	.50	1.50	2.50	
1356	Station West—Luke Short	.50	1.50	2.50	W
A1357	The Informer—Liam O'Flaherty	.50	1.50	2.50	
A1358	Women and Children First—Paul Steiner	.50	1.50	2.50	H
1359	The Girl in the Cage—Ben Benson	.50	1.50	2.50	M
1360	Find a Victim—John Ross MacDonald	.50	1.50	2.50	
1361	The Big Outfit—Peter Dawson	.50	1.50	2.50	W
1362	Deep Space—Eric Frank Russell	.80	2.40	4.00	SF
1363	The Killers—Peter Dawson	.50	1.50	2.50	W
1364	Honey, I'm Home—Marione R. Nickles	.50	1.50	2.50	
F1365	The Complete Book of First Aid—John Henderson	.40	1.20	2.00	NF
F1366	The Spider King—Lawrence Schoonover	.80	2.40	4.00	A
F1367	New Campus Writing—Nolan Miller	.40	1.20	2.00	
A1368	The Second Happiest Day—John Philips	.50	1.50	2.50	
A1369	Brave New World—Aldous Huxley	.80	2.40	4.00	SF
A1370	Port Royal—Noel B. Gerson	.80	2.40	4.00	A
1371	The Seven Year Itch—George Axelrod; movie tie-in	1.20	3.60	6.00	
1372	Tears for the Bride—Robert Martin	.50	1.50	2.50	
1373	Hardcase—Luke Short	.50	1.50	2.50	W
A1374	The Case for the UFO—M. K. Jessup	.50	1.50	2.50	UFO
A1375	They Went Wrong—Croswell Bowen	.40	1.20	2.00	
1376	Giveaway—Steve Fisher	.80	2.40	4.00	
1377	Scandals of Clochemerle—Gabriel Chevallier	.40	1.20	2.00	

(BANTAM BOOKS, continued)		Good	Fine	N/Mint	
A1378	The Art of Italian Cooking—Maria Lo Pinto & Milo Miloradovich	.40	1.20	2.00	NF
F1379	The Time of the Gringo—Elliott Arnold	.50	1.50	2.50	
1380					
F1381	Bhowani Junction—John Masters	.50	1.50	2.50	
A1382	Genghis Khan—Harold Lamb	.50	1.50	2.50	A
1383	The Sands of Karakorum—James Ramsey Ullman	.50	1.50	2.50	
1384	Delta Deputy—L. P. Holmes	.50	1.50	2.50	W
1385	Winter Ambush—E. E. Halleran	.50	1.50	2.50	W
1386	The Black Mountain—Rex Stout	.50	1.50	2.50	M
1387	The Golden Spiders—Rex Stout	.50	1.50	2.50	M
1388	Three Men Out—Rex Stout	.50	1.50	2.50	M
1389	The Howls of Ivy—Henry Boltinoff	.40	1.20	2.00	H
1390	Guns of the Timberlands—Louis L'Amour	.80	2.40	4.00	W
A1391	Hunter—J. A. Hunter	.50	1.50	2.50	A
A1392	The Do-It-Yourself Gadget Hunter's Guide—William Manners	.40	1.20	2.00	NF
F1393	The Alaskan—Robert Lund	.50	1.50	2.50	
1394	Trouble in Triplicate—Rex Stout	.50	1.50	2.50	M
1395	Too Many Women—Rex Stout	.50	1.50	2.50	M
1396	Dead Man Pass—Peter Dawson	.50	1.50	2.50	W
1397	The Widow and the Web—Robert Martin	.40	1.20	2.00	
1398	Pagan in Paradise—Susanne McConnaughey	.40	1.20	2.00	
A1399	Stranger in Paris—W. Somerset Maugham	.40	1.20	2.00	
1400	Time: X—Wilson Tucker	.50	1.50	2.50	SF
A1401	Frontier: 150 Years of the West—Luke Short	.80	2.40	4.00	NF
A1402	King's Rebel—James D. Horan	.80	2.40	4.00	
A1403	Best Loved Books of the Twentieth Century—Vincent Starrett	.80	2.40	4.00	NF
1404	Hazel—Ted Key	.80	2.40	4.00	H
A1405	Hotel Tallegrand—Paul Hyde Donner	.40	1.20	2.00	
1406	The Red Pony—John Steinbeck	.50	1.50	2.50	
1407	The Steel Web—Thomas Thompson; 1956	.50	1.50	2.50	W
1408	Terror on Broadway—David Alexander	.50	1.50	2.50	M
1409	The Taming of Carney Wilde—Bart Spicer	.40	1.20	2.00	
A1410	The Courts of the Lion—Robert W. Krepps	.40	1.20	2.00	A
A1411	Who Rides With Wyatt—Will Henry	.50	1.50	2.50	W
A1412	Sweet Thursday—John Steinbeck	.80	2.40	4.00	
A1413	The Fifty-Minute Hour—Robert Lindner	.40	1.20	2.00	
A1414	3 Weeks to a Better Memory—Brendan Byrne	.40	1.20	2.00	NF
F1415	Away All Boats—Kenneth Dodson	.40	1.20	2.00	C
F1416	Coromandel!—John Masters	.40	1.20	2.00	
F1417	Three Complete Western Novels—Luke Short	.50	1.50	2.50	W
A1418	The Complete Book of Roses—Dorothy H. Jenkins	.40	1.20	2.00	NF
1419	Deep Hills—Matt Stuart	.40	1.20	2.00	W
1420	Dead Fall—Dale Wilmer	.40	1.20	2.00	
1421	The Burning Fuse—Ben Benson	.40	1.20	2.00	M
1422	Hope of Heaven—John O'Hara	.40	1.20	2.00	
1423	Star Shine—Fredric Brown	.80	2.40	4.00	SF
A1424	The Heart of the Matter—Graham Greene	.40	1.20	2.00	
A1425	The Long Swords—Edward Franklin	.50	1.50	2.50	A
A1426	Last Frontier—Richard Emery Roberts	.50	1.50	2.50	
A1427	The Round-the-World Cookbook—Myra Waldo	.40	1.20	2.00	NF
F1428	The Day Lincoln Was Shot—Jim Bishop; Note: a ''Special Tab Club Edition'' exists of this title	.40	1.20	2.00	
F1429	The Citadel—A. J. Cronin	.40	1.20	2.00	
F1430	Model Railroading	.40	1.20	2.00	NF
F1431	The Dream Merchants—Harold Robbins	.40	1.20	2.00	
1432	Woman Doctor—Hannah Lees	.40	1.20	2.00	R
1433	Graduate Nurse—Lucy Agnes Hancock	.40	1.20	2.00	R
1434	Ward Nurse—Marguerite Mooers Marshall	.40	1.20	2.00	R
1435	Haywire Town—Robert McCaig	.40	1.20	2.00	W
1436	His Name Was Death—Fredric Brown	1.60	4.80	8.00	M
1437	Street Rod—Henry Gregor Felsen	.50	1.50	2.50	
1438	Violent Saturday—William L. Heath	.40	1.20	2.00	
A1439	The Four Lives of Mundy Tolliver—Ben Lucien Burman	.40	1.20	2.00	
A1440	Rap Sheet—My Forty Years Outside the Law—Blackie Audett	.40	1.20	2.00	
F1441	The Golden Argosy—Van H. Cartmell & Charles Grayson	.40	1.20	2.00	
F1442	The Inspirational Reader—William Oliver Stevens	.40	1.20	2.00	
A1443	Forbidden Planet—W. J. Stuart	3.00	9.00	15.00	SF
F1444	For My Great Folly—Thomas B. Costain	.40	1.20	2.00	A
F1445	Life on the Mississippi—Mark Twain	.50	1.50	2.50	
1446	High Vermilion—Luke Short	.40	1.20	2.00	W
1447	The Third Bullet—John Dickson Carr	.40	1.20	2.00	M
1448	Million Dollar Murder—Thomas Black	.40	1.20	2.00	
1449					
A1450	Ben-Hur—Lew Wallace	.40	1.20	2.00	
1451	Crossfire—Louis Trimble	.40	1.20	2.00	W
A1452	Man Against Nature—Charles Neider	.40	1.20	2.00	
F1453	Sincerely, Willis Wayde—John P. Marquand	.40	1.20	2.00	

Bantam Books A1411, © Bantam   Bantam Books A1493, © Bantam   Bantam Books 1518, © Bantam

(BANTAM BOOKS, continued)

			Good	Fine	N/Mint	
F1454	Point of No Return—John P. Marquand		.40	1.20	2.00	
1455	The Case of the Talking Bug—The Gordons		.40	1.20	2.00	M
F1456	The Burnished Blade—Lawrence Schoonover		.50	1.50	2.50	A
1457	Picnic—William Inge; movie tie-in		.80	2.40	4.00	
A1458	Cyrano de Bergerac—Edmund Rostand		.40	1.20	2.00	A
F1459	The Sixth of June—Lionel Shapiro		.40	1.20	2.00	
1460	Why the Long Puss?—Reamer Keller		.40	1.20	2.00	
1461	Cry Viva!—William Hopson		.40	1.20	2.00	W
A1462	So Help Me God—Felix Jackson		.40	1.20	2.00	
A1463	The Harder They Fall—Budd Schulberg		.40	1.20	2.00	
A1464	A Wonderful World for Children—Peter Cardozo		.40	1.20	2.00	NF
A1465	Tiger of the Snows—Tenzing Norgay & James Ramsey Ullman		.40	1.20	2.00	
1466	Rimrock—Luke Short		.40	1.20	2.00	W
1467	The Renegade—John Prescott		.40	1.20	2.00	W
1468	The Silver Cobweb—Ben Benson		.40	1.20	2.00	M
1469	Trouble Comes Double—Robert P. Hansen		.40	1.20	2.00	M
A1470	Timeliner—Charles Eric Maine		.80	2.40	4.00	SF
1471	My Flag Is Down—James Maresca		.30	.90	1.50	
A1472	Captain Cut-Throat—John Dickson Carr		.50	1.50	2.50	M
F1473	The Wine of Youth—Robert Wilder		.30	.90	1.50	
F1474	The Keys of the Kingdom—A. J. Cronin		.30	.90	1.50	
1475	Campaign Train—The Gordons		.40	1.20	2.00	M
1476	Some Die Slow—William E. Heber		.30	.90	1.50	
1477	Here's Hazel—Ted Key		.50	1.50	2.50	H
A1478	The Pastures of Heaven—John Steinbeck		.50	1.50	2.50	
1479	With Naked Foot—Emily Hahn		.30	.90	1.50	
A1480	The Shipwrecked—Graham Greene		.40	1.20	2.00	
A1481	The Raiders—Will Henry		.40	1.20	2.00	W
A1482	The Fourth Horseman—Will Henry		.40	1.20	2.00	
A1483	Pillars of the Sky—Will Henry		.40	1.20	2.00	
A1484	The Great Short Stories of John O'Hara		.30	.90	1.50	
1485	Vengeance Valley—Luke Short		.40	1.20	2.00	W
1486	The Burning Hills—Louis L'Amour		.80	2.40	4.00	W
1487	A Cry in the Night—Whit Masterson		.40	1.20	2.00	M
1488	The Limping Goose—Frank Gruber		.40	1.20	2.00	
1489	Up at the Villa—W. Somerset Maugham		.30	.90	1.50	
A1490	The Genius and the Goddess—Aldous Huxley		.50	1.50	2.50	
A1491	Guns of Chickamauga—Richard O'Connor		.40	1.20	2.00	C
A1492	Not This August—C. M. Kornbluth		.80	2.40	4.00	SF
A1493	Analyze Yourself—William Gerhardi & Leopold Loewenstein		.80	2.40	4.00	NF
F1494	Lost Pony Tracks—Ross Santee		.40	1.20	2.00	W
F1495	Apache Land—Ross Santee		.40	1.20	2.00	W
1496	Nurse Landon's Challenge—Adelaide Humphries		.30	.90	1.50	R
S1497	War and Peace—Leo Tolstoy		.40	1.20	2.00	C
1498	Doctor Jane—Adeline McElfresh		.30	.90	1.50	R
A1499	Dining Out in Any Language—Myra Waldo		.30	.90	1.50	NF
F1500	Blood Brother—Elliott Arnold		.50	1.50	2.50	W
1501						
1502	Follow the New Grass—Cliff Farrell		.40	1.20	2.00	
1503	The Problem of the Wire Cage—John Dickson Carr		.50	1.50	2.50	M
1504	The Man Who Could Not Shudder—John Dickson Carr		.50	1.50	2.50	M
1505	The Problem of the Green Capsule—John Dickson Carr		.50	1.50	2.50	M
1506	Hammer Me Home—Richard R. Werry		.50	1.50	2.50	
1507	Reincarnation - the Whole Startling Story—R. DeWitt Miller		.40	1.20	2.00	NF
A1508	The Green Cockade—Frederic F. Van de Water		.50	1.50	2.50	A
A1509	"Captains Courageous"—Rudyard Kipling		.50	1.50	2.50	A
F1510	Waterfront—Budd Schulberg		.40	1.20	2.00	
1511	Hold Back the Night—Pat Frank		.40	1.20	2.00	

		Good	Fine	N/Mint	
1512					
1513	Mama's Bank Account—Kathryn Forbes	.40	1.20	2.00	
1514	Somewhere They Die—L. P. Holmes	.50	1.50	2.50	W
1515	The Buscadero—Noel M. Loomis	.40	1.20	2.00	W
1516	Campbell's Kingdom—Hammond Innes	.40	1.20	2.00	
1517	Satan's Rock—Carl D. Burton	.40	1.20	2.00	
1518	Bus Stop—William Inge; movie tie-in	1.60	4.80	8.00	
A1519	The Circus of Dr. Lao and Other Improbable Stories—Ray Bradbury	1.20	3.60	6.00	SF
F1520	The Count of Monte Cristo—Alexandre Dumas	.50	1.50	2.50	A
1521					
1522					
1523	Sex Rears Its Lovely Head—Jerome Beatty, Jr.	.40	1.20	2.00	
1524					
A1525	Royalist—Edward Grierson	.50	1.50	2.50	
F1526	The Hunchback of Notre Dame—Victor Hugo	.50	1.50	2.50	A
1527	Bitter Sage—Frank Gruber	.40	1.20	2.00	
A1528	Common Sense Book of Puppy and Dog Care—Harry Miller	.40	1.20	2.00	NF
1529	Hiroshima—John Hersey	.40	1.20	2.00	
1530					
1531	Sunset Graze—Luke Short	.40	1.20	2.00	W
1532	Gunman's Chance—Luke Short	.40	1.20	2.00	W
1533	Coroner Creek—Luke Short	.40	1.20	2.00	W
1534	Paint the Town Black—David Alexander	.40	1.20	2.00	M
1535	The Pale Door—Lee Roberts	.40	1.20	2.00	
F1536	The Green Years—A. J. Cronin	.30	.90	1.50	
F1537	Shannon's Way—A. J. Cronin	.30	.90	1.50	
1538	Rag Top—Henry Gregor Felsen	.40	1.20	2.00	
1539	A Night to Remember—Walter Lord	.40	1.20	2.00	NF
A1540	Written on the Wind—Robert Wilder	.30	.90	1.50	
1541	The Age of the Tail—H. Allen Smith	.30	.90	1.50	H
1542	Beast in View—Margaret Millar	.30	.90	1.50	M
1543	Dead, She Was Beautiful—Whit Masterson	.50	1.50	2.50	M
1544	The Pearl—John Steinbeck	.40	1.20	2.00	
A1545	Omar Khayyam—Harold Lamb	.50	1.50	2.50	A
A1546	Martians, Go Home—Fredric Brown	.80	2.40	4.00	SF
1547	Adobe Walls—W. R. Burnett	.80	2.40	4.00	W
1548					
1549	Latigo—Frank O'Rourke	.40	1.20	2.00	W
A1550	19 Tales of Terror—Whit & Hallie Burnett	.50	1.50	2.50	HO
1551	The Boss of Broken Spur—Nick Sumner	.40	1.20	2.00	W
1552	Broken Shield—Ben Benson	.40	1.20	2.00	M
A1553	Forbidden Area—Pat Frank	.40	1.20	2.00	SF
F1554	Ten North Frederick—John O'Hara	.30	.90	1.50	
A1555	The Wayward Bus—John Steinbeck	.80	2.40	4.00	
F1556	A New Southern Harvest—Albert Erskine & Robert Penn Warren	1.00	3.00	5.00	
A1557	The Siege—Jay Williams	.50	1.50	2.50	
F1558	Cartoon Treasury—Lucy Black & Pyke Johnson, Jr.	.50	1.50	2.50	H
1559	The Rainmaker—N. Richard Nash; movie tie-in	1.20	3.60	6.00	
A1560	Antic Hay—Aldous Huxley	.40	1.20	2.00	
1561	Tomboy—Hal Ellson	.40	1.20	2.00	JD
1562	Nurse Fairchild's Decision—Zillah K. MacDonald	.30	.90	1.50	R
1563					
1564	Dead Freight for Piute—Luke Short	.40	1.20	2.00	W
1565	The Wench Is Dead—Fredric Brown	2.00	6.00	10.00	M
1566	The Fabulous Clipjoint—Fredric Brown	1.20	3.60	6.00	M
1567	Death Has Many Doors—Fredric Brown	1.20	3.60	6.00	M
F1568	Island in the Sun—Alec Waugh	.40	1.20	2.00	
A1569	Dragoon—Nelson & Shirley Wolford	.50	1.50	2.50	
A1570	Your Own Beloved Sons—Thomas Anderson	.30	.90	1.50	
A1571	The Shores of Space—Richard Matheson	.80	2.40	4.00	
F1572	Cass Timberlane—Sinclair Lewis	.40	1.20	2.00	
1573					
1574	Full of Life—John Fante	.30	.90	1.50	
1575	Nurse With Wings—Marguerite Mooers Marshall	.30	.90	1.50	R
1576	Tejas Country—Frank Miller	.40	1.20	2.00	
1577	The Tough Die Hard—Robert Martin	.40	1.20	2.00	
A1578	The Year of the Tempest—Peter Matthiessen	.50	1.50	2.50	
F1579	Bitter Creek—James Boyd	.40	1.20	2.00	
F1580	Native Stone—Edwin Gilbert	.30	.90	1.50	
S1581	The Boston Cooking School Cook Book—Fannie Farmer	.30	.90	1.50	NF
A1582	Fear Strikes Out—Al Hirshberg & Jim Piersall	.50	1.50	2.50	B
F1583	A Rage to Live—John O'Hara	.40	1.20	2.00	
1584	Captain McRae—William Herman	.40	1.20	2.00	
1585	Dr. Woodward's Ambition—Elizabeth Seifert	.30	.90	1.50	E
A1586	Seventeen—Booth Tarkington	.40	1.20	2.00	H
A1587	The Good Shepherd—C. S. Forester	.40	1.20	2.00	
1588	The Feud at Single Shot—Luke Short	.40	1.20	2.00	W

(BANTAM BOOKS, continued)	Good	Fine	N/Mint	
1589 Live Bait for Murder—William E. Herber	.40	1.20	2.00	
1590 The Sound of White Water—Hugh Fosburgh	.40	1.20	2.00	
F1591 A Crossbowman's Story—George Millar	.50	1.50	2.50	A
1592 Stop Dieting! Start Losing!—Ruth West	.30	.90	1.50	NF
A1593 The Power—Frank M. Robinson	.40	1.20	2.00	SF
1594 The Farmers Hotel—John O'Hara	.30	.90	1.50	
1595 The Bells of St. Mary's—George Victor Martin	.40	1.20	2.00	
1596 The Baron of Boot Hill—Brad Ward	.40	1.20	2.00	W
F1597 Lord Jim—Joseph Conrad	.50	1.50	2.50	A
A1598 The Big Land—Frank Gruber	.40	1.20	2.00	W
F1599 The Cross of Iron—Willi Heinrich	.50	1.50	2.50	C
A1600 The Package Deal—W. T. Ballard	1.00	3.00	5.00	
1601 Shoot a Sitting Duck—David Alexander	.40	1.20	2.00	M
1602 Square in the Middle—William Campbell Gault	.40	1.20	2.00	M
A1603 West of the River—Charlton Laird	.40	1.20	2.00	
F1604 Harry of Monmouth—A. M. Maughan	.50	1.50	2.50	A
1605				
1606 1001 Valuable Things You Can Get Free, No. 2—Mort Weisinger	.30	.90	1.50	NF
1607 Nora Meade, M.D.—Elizabeth Weslery	.30	.90	1.50	
A1608 The Pass—Thomas Savage	.40	1.20	2.00	
S1609 A Treasury of Short Stories—Rudyard Kipling	.50	1.50	2.50	
1610 The Gun—C. S. Forester	.40	1.20	2.00	A
A1611 Randall and the River of Time—C. S. Forester	.30	.90	1.50	A
1612 Starlight Basin—Giff Cheshire	.40	1.20	2.00	W
1613 The Barbarous Coast—John Ross MacDonald	.40	1.20	2.00	
1614 Visiting Nurse—Jeanne Judson	.30	.90	1.50	R
A1615 Science Fiction Carnival—Fredric Brown & Mack Reynolds	.80	2.40	4.00	SF
F1616 Amy Vanderbilt's Everyday Etiquette—Amy Vanderbilt	.30	.90	1.50	NF
A1617 What Makes Sammy Run?—Budd Schulberg	.40	1.20	2.00	
1618 For All Your Life—Emilie Loring	.30	.90	1.50	
A1619 The Ship—C. S. Forester	.30	.90	1.50	A
F1620 Only Yesterday—Frederick Lewis Allen	.30	.90	1.50	
A1621 The Chinese Room—Vivian Connell	.30	.90	1.50	E
F1622 Eyeless in Gaza—Aldous Huxley	.30	.90	1.50	
1623 Mating Manual—Reamer Keller	.30	.90	1.50	
F1624 A Thing of Beauty—A. J. Cronin	.30	.90	1.50	
A1625 Arouse and Beware—MacKinlay Kantor	.30	.90	1.50	C
A1626 Beau James—Gene Fowler	.40	1.20	2.00	
A1627 Long Storm—Ernest Haycox	.40	1.20	2.00	W
1628 The Wild Bunch—Ernest Haycox	.40	1.20	2.00	W
1629				
A1630 Chocolates for Breakfast—Pamela Moore	.30	.90	1.50	
A1631 Triple Jeopardy—Rex Stout	.50	1.50	2.50	M
A1632 Before Midnight—Rex Stout	.50	1.50	2.50	M
A1633 Three Witnesses—Rex Stout	.50	1.50	2.50	M
A1634 The Golden Princess—Alexander Baron	.50	1.50	2.50	
A1635 A Face in the Crowd—Bud Schulberg	.30	.90	1.50	
A1636 Goodbye, Mr. Chips—James Hilton	.40	1.20	2.00	
F1637 God Has a Long Face—Robert Wilder	.30	.90	1.50	
1638 Day of the Ram—William Campbell Gault	.30	.90	1.50	M
1639 Return of the Outlaw—Michael Carder	.40	1.20	2.00	W
1640 A Family Party—John O'Hara	.30	.90	1.50	
A1641 Sayonara—James A. Michener	.50	1.50	2.50	
1642 Man on the Buckskin—Peter Dawson	.40	1.20	2.00	W
F1643 Jonathan Eagle—Alexander Laing	.40	1.20	2.40	
1644				
1645 Her Soul to Keep—Marguerite Mooers Marshall	.30	.90	1.50	R
A1646 Pebble in the Sky—Isaac Asimov	.50	1.50	2.50	SF
F1647 The Joker Is Wild—Art Cohn	.30	.90	1.50	
F1648 Drums Along the Mohawk—Walter D. Edmonds	.40	1.20	2.00	A
F1649 New Campus Writing, No. 2—Nolan Miller	.40	1.20	2.00	
A1650 The Bridge at Andau—James A. Michener	.40	1.20	2.00	C
A1651 How to Buy Stocks—Louis Engel	.30	.90	1.50	NF
1652 Raiders of the Rimrock—Luke Short	.40	1.20	2.00	W
A1653 Will Success Spoil Rock Hunter?—George Axelrod; movie tie-in	1.20	3.60	6.00	
1654 Wagon Train—John Prescott	.50	1.50	2.50	W
1655 Die, Little Goose—David Alexander	.40	1.20	2.00	M
A1656 The Man Who Paid His Way—Walt Sheldon	.30	.90	1.50	
A1657 The Scimitar—Samuel Edwards	.50	1.50	2.50	A
A1658 100 Stories of Business Success	.30	.90	1.50	
F1659 The Last Hurrah—Edwin O'Connor	.40	1.20	2.00	
F1660 The Strange Woman—Ben Ames Williams	.40	1.20	2.00	
F1661 Indian-Fighting Army—Fairfax Downey	.50	1.50	2.50	
F1662 The Old Santa Fe Trail—Stanley Vestal	.80	2.40	4.00	
S1663 Model Railroading	.40	1.20	2.00	NF

(BANTAM BOOKS, continued)

		Good	Fine	N/Mint	
A1664	Flamingo Road—Robert Wilder	.40	1.20	2.00	
F1665	A Parent's Guide to Children's Illnesses—John Henderson	.30	.90	1.50	NF
1666	Bugles West—Frank Gruber	.40	1.20	2.00	W
1667	Carol Trent, Air Stewardess—Jeanne Judson	.30	.90	1.50	R
1668	The Whip—Luke Short	.40	1.20	2.00	W
A1669	The Quiet American—Graham Greene	.40	1.20	2.00	
A1670	The Frozen Jungle—Lawrence Earl	.40	1.20	2.00	
A1671	State of Siege—Eric Ambler	.40	1.20	2.00	
A1672	Pilgrimage to Earth—Robert Sheckley	.80	2.40	4.00	SF
F1673	The Queen's Cross—Lawrence Schoonover	.50	1.50	2.50	A
F1674	Return to Paradise—James A. Michener	.40	1.20	2.00	
F1675	H. M. Pulham, Esq.—John P. Marquand	.30	.90	1.50	
A1676	Wild Animals I Have Known—Ernest Thompson Seton	.40	1.20	2.00	NF
A1677	The Bridge Over the River Kwai—Pierre Boulle	.50	1.50	2.50	C
F1678	The Hunchback of Notre Dame—Victor Hugo	.40	1.20	2.00	A
1679	Pal Joey—John O'Hara; movie tie-in	1.00	3.00	5.00	
1680	Colt's Law—Luke Short	.40	1.20	2.00	W
1681	Silver Canyon—Louis L'Amour	.80	2.40	4.00	W
1682	Patrick Butler for the Defense—John Dickson Carr	.50	1.50	2.50	M
1683	Till Death Do Us Part—John Dickson Carr	.50	1.50	2.50	M
1684	He Who Whispers—John Dickson Carr	.50	1.50	2.50	M
A1685	Wagons to Tucson—Ed Newsom	.40	1.20	2.00	W
1686					
F1687	Dodge City: Queen of Cowtowns—Stanley Vestal	.80	2.40	4.00	NF
F1688	The Art of Mixing Drinks—Frederic A. Birmingham	.30	.90	1.50	
A1689	Porgy—Du Bose Heyward	.40	1.20	2.00	
A1690	Stopover: Tokyo—John P. Marquand	.40	1.20	2.00	
A1691	Thank You, Mr. Moto—John P. Marquand	.40	1.20	2.00	M
S1692	50 Great Artists—Bernard Myers	.40	1.20	2.00	NF
A1693	Death of a Man—Lael Tucker Wertenbaker	.40	1.20	2.00	
1694	My Man Godfrey—Eric Hatch	.30	.90	1.50	E
1695	Trail Boss—Peter Dawson	.40	1.20	2.00	W
1696	Gun Smoke Showdown—Matt Stuart	.40	1.20	2.00	W
1697	The Secret World of Roy Williams—Roy Williams	1.20	3.60	6.00	
A1698	The Ninth Hour—Ben Benson	.40	1.20	2.00	M
A1699	Touch of Evil—Whit Masterson	.40	1.20	2.00	M
A1700	The Hunters—James Salter	.40	1.20	2.00	
A1701	Rogue in Space—Fredric Brown	.80	2.40	4.00	SF
F1702	The Earth Is the Lord's—Taylor Caldwell	.40	1.20	2.00	A
A1703	Fancies and Goodnights—John Collier	.80	2.40	4.00	SF
A1704	The Day of the Locust—Nathanael West	.40	1.20	2.00	
F1705	The Fires of Spring—James A. Michener	.40	1.20	2.00	
A1706	Knock and Wait Awhile—William Rawle Weeks; 1958	.30	.90	1.50	
F1707	The Big War—Anton Myrer	.40	1.20	2.00	C
A1708	The Heller—William E. Henning	.40	1.20	2.00	
1709	Outlaw's Code—Evan Evans	.40	1.20	2.00	W
1710	Ambush—Luke Short	.40	1.20	2.00	W
1711	Special Nurse—Margaret Howe	.30	.90	1.50	R
1712	The Lenient Beast—Fredric Brown	1.60	4.80	8.00	M
A1713	Sitka—Louis L'Amour	1.20	3.60	6.00	W
F1714	Bugles and a Tiger—John Masters	.40	1.20	2.00	
F1715	Day of Infamy—Walter Lord	.40	1.20	2.00	NF
1716					
A1717	Nevada—Zane Grey	.40	1.20	2.00	W

Bantam Books 1584, © Bantam

Bantam Books A1676, © Bantam

Bantam Books 1681, © Bantam

(BANTAM BOOKS, continued)		Good	Fine	N/Mint	
A1718	The Last of the Plainsmen—Zane Grey	.40	1.20	2.00	W
A1719	The Spanish Gardener—A. J. Cronin	.30	.90	1.50	
F1720	Tolbecken—Samuel Shellabarger	.40	1.20	2.00	
A1721	The Big Nickelodeon—Maritta Wolff	.40	1.20	2.00	
F1722	The Great World and Timothy Colt—Louis Auchincloss	.30	.90	1.50	
F1723	Rachel Cade—Charles Mercer	.30	.90	1.50	
A1724	Captain Ironhand—Rosamond Marshall	.40	1.20	2.00	A
1725	Red River—Borden Chase	.40	1.20	2.00	W
1726	Tales of Wells Fargo—Frank Gruber; TV tie-in	.80	2.40	4.00	W
1727	Halo in Brass—John Evans	.40	1.20	2.00	M
1728	Halo in Blood—John Evans	.40	1.20	2.00	M
1729	Halo for Satan—John Evans	.40	1.20	2.00	M
A1730	Reprieve—John Resko	.40	1.20	2.00	
A1731	The Naked Sun—Isaac Asimov	.50	1.50	2.50	SF
A1732	The Life of the Party—Bennett Cerf	.30	.90	1.50	H
1733					
S1734	The Red and the Black—Stendahl	.40	1.20	2.00	
F1735	Crime and Punishment—Fyodor Dostoyevsky	.40	1.20	2.00	
1736	The Murder of Whistler's Brother—David Alexander	.40	1.20	2.00	M
1737	The Light in the Forest—Conrad Richter	.40	1.20	2.00	A
F1738	Lancet—Garet Rogers	.30	.90	1.50	
A1739	An End to Dying—Sam Astrachan	.40	1.20	2.00	
F1740	Say, Darling—Richard Bissell	.30	.90	1.50	
1741	Peace Marshal—Frank Gruber	.40	1.20	2.00	W
1742	Lonesome River—Frank Gruber	.40	1.20	2.00	W
1743	Fighting Man—Frank Gruber	.40	1.20	2.00	W
F1744	Our Valiant Few—F. Van Wyck Mason	.30	.90	1.50	
A1746	Miracle Gardening—Samm Sinclair Baker	.30	.90	1.50	NF
F1747	The Bantam Book of Correct Letter Writing—Lilian E. Watson	.30	.90	1.50	NF
A1748	The Lives of a Bengal Lancer—Francis Yeats-Brown	.40	1.20	2.00	A
F1749	Cowhand: The Story of a Working Cowboy—Fred Gipson	.40	1.20	2.00	NF
1750					
1751	Nancy Ross, Private Secretary—Jeanne Judson	.30	.90	1.50	R
A1752	Never Love a Stranger—Harold Robbins	.30	.90	1.50	
A1753	The Short Reign of Pippin IV—John Steinbeck	1.20	3.60	6.00	
A1754	Cimarron—Edna Ferber	.40	1.20	2.00	W
1755	Fiddlefoot—Luke Short	.40	1.20	2.00	W
1756	Mr. Taxicab—James Maresca	.30	.90	1.50	
1757	The Screaming Mimi—Fredric Brown; movie tie-in	1.00	3.00	5.00	M
1758	Riddle of a Lady—Anthony Gilbert	.40	1.20	2.00	M
A1759	Yonder—Charles Beaumont	.80	2.40	4.00	SF
A1760	The Invisible Curtain—Joseph Anthony	.30	.90	1.50	
F1761	The Member of the Wedding—Carson McCullers	.30	.90	1.50	
F1762	The Heart Is a Lonely Hunter—Carson McCullers	.30	.90	1.50	
F1763	Reflections in a Golden Eye—Carson McCullers	.30	.90	1.50	
F1764	Ballad of the Sad Cafe—Carson McCullers	.30	.90	1.50	
A1765	Satellite!—William Beller & Erik Bergaust	.30	.90	1.50	NF
A1766	Satellite E One—Jeffrey Lloyd Castle	.50	1.50	2.50	SF
F1767	Silver Spoon—Edwin Gilbert	.30	.90	1.50	
A1768	Thieves' Market—A. I. Bezzerides	.30	.90	1.50	
1769	The Land Grabbers—John S. Daniels	.40	1.20	2.00	W
A1770	Rescue!—Elliott Arnold	.30	.90	1.50	
1771	Sorry, Wrong Number—Lucille Fletcher & Allan Ullman	.30	.90	1.50	
A1772	Epitaph for a Spy—Eric Ambler	.40	1.20	2.00	
A1773	The Confidential Agent—Graham Greene	.40	1.20	2.00	
A1774	The Tyrant of Bagdad—Glenn Pierce	.40	1.20	2.00	A
F1775	The Art of Barbecue and Outdoor Cooking	.30	.90	1.50	NF
1776	Calling Doctor Jane—Adeline McElfresh	.30	.90	1.50	R
F1777	South Wind—Norman Douglas	.30	.90	1.50	A
F1778	The Mustangs—J. Frank Dobie	.40	1.20	2.00	NF
A1779	The Wind Cannot Read—Raymond Mason	.30	.90	1.50	
1780	Teacher's Pet—Michael & Fay Kanin	.30	.90	1.50	
A1781	Life at Happy Knoll—John P. Marquand	.30	.90	1.50	
1782	The Big Frame—The Gordons	.40	1.20	2.00	M
F1783	Alabama Empire—Welbaurn Kelley	.40	1.20	2.00	
A1784	The Teen-age Diet Book—Ruth West	.30	.90	1.50	NF
A1785	They Fought for the Sky—Quentin Reynolds	.40	1.20	2.00	C
A1786	Time in Advance—William Tenn	.50	1.50	2.50	SF
1787	What, Then, Is Love—Emilie Loring	.30	.90	1.50	R
F1788	Folk Songs of the Caribbean—James Morse	.50	1.50	2.50	NF
F1789	Three Plays—Thornton Wilder	.40	1.20	2.00	
A1790	A Wonderful World for Children, No. 2—Peter Cardoze & Lilli Taylor	.30	.90	1.50	NF-A
F1791	Rally Round the Flag, Boys!—Max Shulman	.30	.90	1.50	H
A1792	The Lady—Conrad Richter	.30	.90	1.50	
A1793	Ape and Essence—Aldous Huxley	.50	1.50	2.50	
1794	The Lawbringers—William Porter	.40	1.20	2.00	
A1795	Might As Well Be Dead—Rex Stout	.50	1.50	2.50	M

		Good	Fine	N/Mint	
A1796	Three for the Chair—Rex Stout	.50	1.50	2.50	M
A1797	The Silent Speaker—Rex Stout	.50	1.50	2.50	M
A1798	Sierra Baron—Thomas W. Blackburn	.40	1.20	2.00	W
1799	Eve Cameron, M.D.—Ann Rush	.30	.90	1.50	R
A1800	The Inn of the Sixth Happiness—Alan Burgess; movie tie-in	.50	1.50	2.50	
A1801	Getting Along in French—John Fisher & Mario Pei	.30	.90	1.50	NF
A1802	Getting Along in Italian—Mario Pei	.30	.90	1.50	NF
F1803	Typee—Herman Melville	.50	1.50	2.50	A
F1804	Tales of Fair and Gallant Ladies—Abbe de Brantome	.50	1.50	2.50	
F1805	Far, Far the Mountain Peak—John Masters	.40	1.20	2.00	
1806	Gidget—Frederick Kohner	.40	1.20	2.00	R
F1807	Home Before Dark—Eileen Bassing	.30	.90	1.50	
A1808	Wilderness Passage—Forrester Blake	.40	1.20	2.00	
A1809	Johnny Christmas—Forrester Blake	.40	1.20	2.00	
1810	Think Fast, Mr. Moto—John P. Marquand	.40	1.20	2.00	M
A1811	Lieutenant Hornblower—C. S. Forester	.40	1.20	2.00	A
A1812	Honeymoon in Hell—Fredric Brown	1.60	4.80	8.00	SF
1813	If You Like Hazel—Ted Key	.80	2.40	4.00	H
F1814	The New Art of Selling—Elmer G. Leterman	.30	.90	1.50	NF
A1815	Mr. Midshipman Hornblower—C. S. Forester	.40	1.20	2.00	A
A1816	Beat to Quarters—C. S. Forester	.40	1.20	2.00	A
F1817	The Philadelphian—Richard Powell	.30	.90	1.50	
F1818	The Drummond Tradition—Charles Mercer	.30	.90	1.50	
A1819	Underdog—W. R. Burnett	1.00	3.00	5.00	
A1820	Great Circle—Robert Carse	.40	1.20	2.00	
1821	Play a Lone Hand—Luke Short	.40	1.20	2.00	W
1822	The Plunders—L. P. Holmes	.40	1.20	2.00	W
1823	The Stag Party—William Krasner	.30	.90	1.50	
A1824	Echo of a Bomb—Mark Derby	.30	.90	1.50	
A1825	Station in Space—James E. Gunn	.40	1.20	2.00	SF
A1826	Helmet for My Pillow—Robert Leckie	.30	.90	1.50	
A1827	The Art of French Cooking—Fernande Silve Garvin	.30	.90	1.50	NF
A1828	Harry Black—David Walker	.30	.90	1.50	
1829					
1830					
A1831	The Price of Salt—Claire Morgan	.30	.90	1.50	
F1832	Patterns—Rod Serling	.50	1.50	2.50	
F1833	The Wapshot Chronicle—John Cheever	.40	1.20	2.00	
A1834	The Temple of Gold—William Goldman	.40	1.20	2.00	
A1835	The Killing Ground—Elleston Trevor	.30	.90	1.50	
A1836	Tubie's Monument—Peter Keveson	.30	.90	1.50	
1837	Outlaw Valley—Evan Evans	.40	1.20	2.00	W
1838	The Trail From Texas—Dale Homer	.40	1.20	2.00	W
1839	Blue City—John Ross MacDonald	.40	1.20	2.00	
1840	The Dark Window—Thomas Walsh	.30	.90	1.50	
1841	A Nurse for Galleon Key—Ethel Hamill	.30	.90	1.50	R
A1842	Bell, Book and Candle—John van Druten	.30	.90	1.50	
S1843	One Basket—Edna Ferber	.30	.90	1.50	
F1844	Rascals in Paradise—James A. Michener & A. Grove Day	.30	.90	1.50	
A1845	The Blue Chips—Jay Deiss	.30	.90	1.50	
F1846	The Spiral Road—Jan de Hartog	.40	1.20	2.00	
A1847	Fire, Burn!—John Dickson Carr	.50	1.50	2.50	M
A1848	Louisville Saturday—Margaret Long	.40	1.20	2.00	E
A1849	The Sleeping Sphinx—John Dickson Carr	.50	1.50	2.50	M
A1850	The Fields—Conrad Richter	.30	.90	1.50	
F1851	The Town—Conrad Richter	.30	.90	1.50	
A1852	The Trees—Conrad Richter	.30	.90	1.50	
1853	Radigan—Louis L'Amour	.80	2.40	4.00	W
F1854	1000 Ways to Make $1,000—Helen Hoke	.30	.90	1.50	NF
1855	The North Star—Will Henry	.40	1.20	2.00	
1856	The Outlaw of Longbow—Peter Dawson	.40	1.20	2.00	W
A1857	Proud Land—Logan Forster	.40	1.20	2.00	
1858	The Canvas Dagger—Helen Reilly	.40	1.20	2.00	M
A1859	First Train to Batylon—Max Ehrlich	.30	.90	1.50	
A1860	The Big Eye—Max Ehrlich	.40	1.20	2.00	SF
1861	Write Me a Poem, Baby—H. Allen Smith	.30	.90	1.50	
F1862	Pigboats—Theodore Roscoe	.40	1.20	2.00	
1863					
A1864	Jaina—Mazo de la Roche	.30	.90	1.50	
1865	Rawhide and Bob-wire—ed. Luke Short	.50	1.50	2.50	W
1866	Summer of the Smoke—Luke Short	.40	1.20	2.00	W
A1867	A Stranger in My Arms—Robert Wilder	.30	.90	1.50	
A1868	The Journey—George Tabori	.30	.90	1.50	
F1869	Zoomar—Ernie Kovacs	.30	.90	1.50	
F1870	The Prisoners of Combine D—Len Giovannitti	.30	.90	1.50	
A1871	Little Caesar—W. R. Burnett	.50	1.50	2.50	
F1872	The Earthbreakers—Ernest Haycox	.40	1.20	2.00	W

		Good	Fine	N/Mint	
	(BANTAM BOOKS, continued)				
1873	Modoc, the Last Sundown—L. P. Holmes	.40	1.20	2.00	W
1874					
1875	No Vacation for Maigret—Georges Simenon	.40	1.20	2.00	M
1876	Rival to My Heart—Ann Pinchot	.30	.90	1.50	
F1877	TV Movie Almanac and Ratings, 1958-1959—Steven H. Schever	.50	1.50	2.50	NF
F1878	Green Mansions—W. H. Hudson	.40	1.20	2.00	F
S1879	The Sound of Thunder—Taylor Caldwell	.30	.90	1.50	
A1880	My Face for the World to See—Alfred Hayes	.30	.90	1.50	
1881					
1882					
1883	Death of a Postman—John Creasey	.30	.90	1.50	M
1884	The Gelignite Gang—John Creasey	.30	.90	1.50	M
A1885	The Martian Chronicles—Ray Bradbury	.40	1.20	2.00	SF
F1886	The Tall Captains—Bart Spicer	.40	1.20	2.00	
1887					
A1888	Bat Masterson—Richard O'Connor; TV tie-in	.80	2.40	4.00	W
A1890	Across the Everglades—Budd Schulberg	.30	.90	1.50	
A1891	Meet Me in St. Louis—Sally Benson	.30	.90	1.50	H
A1892	Hot Rod—Henry Gregor Felsen	.30	.90	1.50	
1893	Rio Bravo—Leigh Brackett; movie tie-in	2.00	6.00	10.00	W
A1894	Our Hearts Were Young and Gay—Cornelia Otis Skinner & Emily Kimbrough	.30	.90	1.50	
F1895	East of Eden—John Steinbeck	.40	1.20	2.00	
F1896	Hitler, a Study in Tyranny—Alan Bullock	.40	1.20	2.00	B
A1897	The Betty Bissell Book of Home Cleaning—Betty Bissell; 1959	.30	.90	1.50	NF
A1898	So Many Doors—Oakley Hall	.30	.90	1.50	E
A1899	Cry for Happy—George Campbell	.30	.90	1.50	
F1900	Maggie Now—Betty Smith	.30	.90	1.50	
A1901	The Hon. Rocky Slade—William Wister Haines	.30	.90	1.50	
F1902	Slim—William Wister Haines	.30	.90	1.50	
F1903	Ben-Hur—Lew Wallace	.30	.90	1.50	
A1904	Mrs. Mike—Benedict & Nancy Freedman	.30	.90	1.50	
1905	The First Fast Draw—Louis L'Amour	.80	2.40	4.00	W
1906					
1907	Nurse Howard's Assignment—Virginia Roberts	.30	.90	1.50	R
A1908	The Price of Courage—Curt Anders	.30	.90	1.50	
1909	The Black Mirror—Ben Benson	.40	1.20	2.00	M
1910	The Running Man—Ben Benson	.40	1.20	2.00	M
1911	I Take This Man—Emilie Loring	.30	.90	1.50	
F1912	Ice Palace—Edna Ferber	.30	.90	1.50	
F1913	Crack of Doom—Willis Heinrich	.30	.90	1.50	
A1914	Love Me Little—Amanda Vail	.30	.90	1.50	
F1915	Ride the Red Earth—Paul I. Wellman	.40	1.20	2.00	
1916	And the Wind Blows Free—Luke Short	.40	1.20	2.00	W
A1917	The Hunger and Other Stories—Charles Beaumont	.80	2.40	4.00	SF
1918					
A1919	The Red Knight of Germany—Floyd Gibbons	.40	1.20	2.00	B
G1920	And Save Them for Pallbearers—James Garrett	.40	1.20	2.00	
A1921	The Hard Sell—David Delman	.30	.90	1.50	
A1922	Dandelion Wine—Ray Bradbury	.80	2.40	4.00	
1923	The Mesh—Lucie Marchal	.30	.90	1.50	E
A1924	The Teen-age Diet Book—Ruth West	.30	.90	1.50	NF
1925	Silent River—Wayne Roberts	.30	.90	1.50	
1926	Barbed Wire Kingdom—C. William Harrison	.40	1.20	2.00	W
1927	The Convertible Hearse—William Campbell Gault	.40	1.20	2.00	M
1928					
1929	Young Doctor Randall—Adeline McElfresh	.30	.90	1.50	R
A1930	Theatre—W. Somerset Maugham	.30	.90	1.50	
A1931	The Narrow Corner—W. Somerset Maugham	.30	.90	1.50	
F1932	The Disenchanted—Bud Schulberg	.30	.90	1.50	
1933					
1934	Outlaw—Frank Gruber	.40	1.20	2.00	W
A1935	Reckoning at Yankee Flat—Will Henry	.40	1.20	2.00	W
1936	The Doctor Is a Lady—Beth Myers	.30	.90	1.50	
A1937	The Witches—Jay Williams	.40	1.20	2.00	
1938	My Dearest Love—Emilie Loring	.30	.90	1.50	
A1939	Barefoot Boy With Cheek—Max Shulman	.30	.90	1.50	H
A1940	The Feather Merchants—Max Shulman	.30	.90	1.50	H
A1941	The Naked Maja—Samuel Edwards	.40	1.20	2.00	
A1942	Night of the Quarter Moon—Franklin Coen	.30	.90	1.50	
A1943	Getting Along in Spanish—Mario Pei & Eloy Vaquero	.30	.90	1.50	NF
A1944	Getting Along in German—Mario Pei & Robert Politzer	.30	.90	1.50	NF
1945	A Night to Remember—Walter Lord	.40	1.20	2.00	NF
F1946	The Image Makers—Bernard Dryer	.30	.90	1.50	
F1947	The Northern Light—A. J. Cronin	.30	.90	1.50	
1948	The Hours After Midnight—Joseph Hayes	.30	.90	1.50	
1949	Gunfighter's Return—Ben Smith	.40	1.20	2.00	W
1950					

		Good	Fine	N/Mint	
1951	Hill Country Nurse—Adeline McElfresh	.30	.90	1.50	R
A1952	Point Ultimate—Jerry Sohl	.40	1.20	2.00	SF
A1953	Goren Presents the Italian Bridge System—Charles H. Goren	.30	.90	1.50	NF
A1954	The Summer Lovers—Hollis Alpert	.30	.90	1.50	
F1955	The Violated—Vance Bourjaily	.30	.90	1.50	
F1956	The Wonderful Country—Tom Lea	.40	1.20	2.00	A
A1957	Blue Denim—James Leo Herlihy & William Noble	.30	.90	1.50	
A1958	Solomon and Sheba—Jay Williams; movie tie-in	.50	1.50	2.50	A
A1959	Hard Money—Luke Short	.40	1.20	2.00	W
1960					
A1961	If Death Ever Slept—Rex Stout	.50	1.50	2.50	M
1962					
1963					
A1964	Command Decision—William Wister Haines	.40	1.20	2.00	
1965	The Beat Generation—Albert Zugsmith; orig., 1959, movie tie-in				JD
A1966	Middle of the Night—Paddy Chayefsky	.40	1.20	2.00	
1967					
F1968	The Bramble Bush—Charles Mergendahl	.30	.90	1.50	
1969					
A1970	Nothing But the Night—James Yaffe	.30	.90	1.50	
A1971	The Transcendent Man—Jerry Sohl	.50	1.50	2.50	SF
F1972	Hoof Trails and Wagon Tracks	.50	1.50	2.50	
1973	Bitter Ground—W. R. Burnett	.50	1.50	2.50	
1974	The Blonde in Black—Ben Benson	.40	1.20	2.00	M
1975	Nurse on Location—Virginia Roberts	.30	.90	1.50	R
F1976	His Eye Is on the Sparrow—Ethel Waters & Charles Samuels	.30	.90	1.50	B
1977	Taggart—Louis L'Amour	.80	2.40	4.00	W
A1978	Earth Is Room Enough—Isaac Asimov	.40	1.20	2.00	SF
1979					
F1980	Warlock—Oakley Hall	.40	1.20	2.00	W
A1981	Sports Shorts—Mac Davis	.40	1.20	2.00	S
A1982	The Mouse That Roared—Leonard Wibberley	.40	1.20	2.00	H
A1983	Ask Any Girl—Winifred Wolfe	.30	.90	1.50	
1984	The Savages—Peter Dawson	.40	1.20	2.00	W
1985					
A1986	The Fume of Poppies—Jonathan Kozol	.40	1.20	2.00	
F1987	The Detroiters—Harold Livingston	.30	.90	1.50	
F1988	The Voyagers—Dale Van Every	.30	.90	1.50	
A1989	War on the Cimarron—Luke Short	.40	1.20	2.00	W
1990	One for the Road—Fredric Brown	1.60	4.80	8.00	M
A1991	Immortality, Inc.—Robert Sheckley	.50	1.50	2.50	SF
A1992	Dr. John's Decision—Dorothy Worley	.30	.90	1.50	
1993					
1994					
S1995	Exodus—Leon Uris	.30	.90	1.50	C
F1996	Battle Cry—Leon Uris	.30	.90	1.50	C
1997					
A1998	Town Tamer—Frank Gruber	.40	1.20	2.00	W
A1999	The Crimson Horseshow—Peter Dawson	.40	1.20	2.00	W
A2000	Fear Is the Same—Carter Dickson	2.00	6.00	10.00	M
2001	The Affair of the Exotic Dancer—Ben Benson	.40	1.20	2.00	M
2002	Debutante Nurse—Margaret Howe	.30	.90	1.50	R
A2003	Notions Unlimited—Robert Scheckley	.50	1.50	2.50	SF
F2004	The End of the Affair—Graham Greene	.30	.90	1.50	
2005					
A2006	Silver Rock—Luke Short	.40	1.20	2.00	W
F2007	The Shining Mountains—Dale Van Every	.30	.90	1.50	
A2008	Prison Nurse—Louis Berg	.30	.90	1.50	

Bantam Books 1977, © Bantam   Bantam Books A2000, © Bantam   Bantam Books E3016, © Bantam

Bantam Books F3569, © Bantam Bantam Books F3667, © Bantam Bantam Books H4463, © Bantam

(BANTAM BOOKS, continued)

		Good	Fine	N/Mint	
A2009	Irene—Ronald Marsh	.30	.90	1.50	
A2010	The Forest Lord—Noel B. Gerson	.40	1.20	2.00	
F2011	The God That Failed—Richard Crossman	.30	.90	1.50	
A2012	Sleep Till Noon—Max Shulman	.30	.90	1.50	H
S2013	Women and Thomas Harrow—John P. Marquand	.30	.90	1.50	
2014					
F2015	Wyatt Earp, Frontier Marshal—Stuart N. Lake	.40	1.20	2.00	NF
A2016	And Four to Go—Rex Stout	.50	1.50	2.50	M
A2017	1001 Valuable Things You Can Get Free, No. 3—Mort Weisinger	.30	.90	1.50	NF
A2020	Rock—David Wagoner	.50	1.50	2.50	
A2021	The Marshal—Frank Gruber	.40	.1.20	2.00	W
A2024	The Doomsters—John Ross MacDonald	.40	1.20	2.00	
2031	Hill Smoke—L. P. Holmes	.40	1.20	2.00	W
F2033	Beloved Infidel—Gerold Frank & Sheilah Graham	.30	.90	1.50	
A2034	Look Back in Anger—John Osborne	.30	.90	1.50	
F2035	The Day Lincoln Was Shot—Jim Bishop	.30	.90	1.50	NF
A2036	Saddle by Starlight—Luke Short	.40	1.20	2.00	W
A2042	On the Line—Harvey Swados	.40	1.20	2.00	
A2060	Sink the Bismarck!—C. S. Forester	.40	1.20	2.00	C
A2063	The Methods of Maigret—Georges Simenon	.40	1.20	2.00	M
F2070	The Russian Revolution—Alan Moorehead	.30	.90	1.50	
A2073	Cheaper by the Dozen—Ernestine Carey & Frank B. Gilbreth, Jr.	.30	.90	1.50	H
E2853	The Man of Bronze—Kenneth Robeson; 1964	1.00	3.00	5.00	A
E2854	The Thousand-Headed Man—Kenneth Robeson	1.00	3.00	5.00	A
E2855	Meteor Menace—Kenneth Robeson	1.00	3.00	5.00	A
E3015	The Polar Treasure—Kenneth Robeson; 1965	1.00	3.00	5.00	A
E3016	Brand of the Werewolf—Kenneth Robeson	1.00	3.00	5.00	A
E3017	The Lost Oasis—Kenneth Robeson	1.00	3.00	5.00	A
E3033	The Monsters—Kenneth Robeson	1.00	3.00	5.00	A
E3042	The Land of Terror—Kenneth Robeson	1.00	3.00	5.00	A
E3047	The Phantom City—Kenneth Robeson	1.00	3.00	5.00	A
F3093	King Kong—Edgar Wallace, Merian C. Cooper, & Delos W. Lovelace	1.00	3.00	5.00	HO
E3110	Quest of Qui—Kenneth Robeson; 1966	1.00	3.00	5.00	A
E3115	The Mystic Mullah—Kenneth Robeson	1.00	3.00	5.00	A
E3146	Fear Cay—Kenneth Robeson	1.00	3.00	5.00	A
E3202	Land of Always-Night—Kenneth Robeson	1.00	3.00	5.00	A
E3269	The Fantastic Island—Kenneth Robeson	1.00	3.00	5.00	A
E3296	Murder Melody—Kenneth Robeson; 1967	1.00	3.00	5.00	A
F3340	The Spook Legion—Kenneth Robeson	1.00	3.00	5.00	A
F3387	The Red Skull—Kenneth Robeson	1.00	3.00	5.00	A
F3441	The Sargasso Ogre—Kenneth Robeson	1.00	3.00	5.00	A
F3486	Pirate of the Pacific—Kenneth Robeson	1.00	3.00	5.00	A
F3533	The Secret in the Sky—Kenneth Robeson	1.00	3.00	5.00	A
F3569	The Avengers Battle the Earth-Wrecker—Otto Binder	1.20	3.60	6.00	A
F3584	Cold Death—Kenneth Robeson	1.00	3.00	5.00	A
F3667	The Czar of Fear—Kenneth Robeson	1.00	3.00	5.00	A
F3716	Fortress of Solitude—Kenneth Robeson	1.00	3.00	5.00	A
F3755	Mystery Under the Sea—Kenneth Robeson	1.00	3.00	5.00	A
F3780	The Great Gold Steal—Ted White; 1968	1.00	3.00	5.00	A
F3782	The Green Eagle—Kenneth Robeson	1.00	3.00	5.00	A
F3805	Death in Silver—Kenneth Robeson	1.00	3.00	5.00	A
F3839	The Deadly Dwarf—Kenneth Robeson	1.00	3.00	5.00	A
F3841	The Devil's Playground—Kenneth Robeson	1.00	3.00	5.00	A
F3877	The Other World—Kenneth Robeson	1.20	3.60	6.00	A
F3885	The Annihilist—Kenneth Robeson	1.20	3.60	6.00	A
F3897	The Flaming Falcons—Kenneth Robeson	1.20	3.60	6.00	A
F3937	Dust of Death—Kenneth Robeson; 1969	1.20	3.60	6.00	A
F3969	The Terror in the Navy—Kenneth Robeson	1.20	3.60	6.00	A

		Good	Fine	N/Mint	
F3986	Mad Eyes—Kenneth Robeson	1.20	3.60	6.00	A
H4056	Eyes of the Shadow—Maxwell Grant	1.00	3.00	5.00	M
H4065	Red Snow—Kenneth Robeson	1.20	3.60	6.00	A
F4362	The Squeaking Goblin—Kenneth Robeson	1.20	3.60	6.00	A
F4403	Resurrection Day—Kenneth Robeson	1.20	3.60	6.00	A
H4463	The Living Shadow—Maxwell Grant	1.00	3.00	5.00	M
H4624	The Dagger in the Sky—Kenneth Robeson	1.20	3.60	6.00	A
H4688	The Shadow Laughs!—Maxwell Grant	1.00	3.00	5.00	M
H4689	Merchants of Disaster—Kenneth Robeson	1.20	3.60	6.00	A
H4707	Hex—Kenneth Robeson	1.20	3.60	6.00	A
H4721	World's Fair Goblin—Kenneth Robeson	1.20	3.60	6.00	A
H4730	The Gold Ogre—Kenneth Robeson	1.20	3.60	6.00	A
H4761	The Man Who Shook the Earth—Kenneth Robeson	1.20	3.60	6.00	A
H4770	The Death Tower—Maxwell Grant	1.00	3.00	5.00	M
H4810	The Sea Magician—Kenneth Robeson	1.20	3.60	6.00	A
H4875	The Men Who Smiled No More—Kenneth Robeson	1.20	3.60	6.00	A
H4884	Hidden Death—Maxwell Grant	1.00	3.00	5.00	M
H5217	The Midas Man—Kenneth Robeson; 1970	1.20	3.60	6.00	A
H5309	Land of Long Ju Ju—Kenneth Robeson	1.20	3.60	6.00	A
H5366	Mad Eyes—Kenneth Robeson	1.20	3.60	6.00	A
H5367	The Feathered Octopus—Kenneth Robeson	1.20	3.60	6.00	A
H5406	The Sea Angel—Kenneth Robeson	1.20	3.60	6.00	A
H5413	Gangdom's Doom—Maxwell Grant	1.00	3.00	5.00	M
H5422	The Squeaking Goblins—Kenneth Robeson; 1971	1.20	3.60	6.00	A
H5482	Haunted Ocean—Kenneth Robeson	1.20	3.60	6.00	A
H5556	The Mental Wizard—Kenneth Robeson	1.20	3.60	6.00	A
H5743	Poison Island—Kenneth Robeson	1.20	3.60	6.00	A
S5788	The Munitions Master—Kenneth Robeson	1.20	3.60	6.00	A
Y5869	Deadbone Erotica—Vaughn Bode; 1st ed., 1971. Note: Oversize 5-1/8''x8¼'' volume of collected comic strip reprints from Cavalier.	6.00	18.00	30.00	F
S5871	Blackmark—Gil Kane; orig., 1971. Note: A comic art novel	1.20	3.60	6.00	F
S5909	The Majii—Kenneth Robeson	1.00	3.00	5.00	A

BANTAM BOOKS (LOS ANGELES)
Bantam Publications

Note: Later printings of 21, 22, 23, 26, 27 (and probably others) have pictorial covers whereas first printings do not. Later variants are equal in value and desirability with first printings.

			Good	Fine	N/Mint	
A	1	The Red Threads—Rex Stout	12.50	37.50	60.00	M
	1	The Spanish Cape Mystery—Ellery Queen	10.00	30.00	50.00	M
	2	Little Known Facts About Famous People—Dale Carnegie	7.00	21.00	35.00	NF
	3	Your Health Questions—M. M. D. Fishbein	7.00	21.00	35.00	NF
	4	Everybody's Dream Book, Your Dreams Explained	7.00	21.00	35.00	NF
	5	How to Make Friends Easily—S. Currie	7.00	21.00	35.00	NF
	6	Everybody's Book of Jokes and Wisecracks—J. Gregory	7.00	21.00	35.00	H
	7	The Voice of Experience	7.00	21.00	35.00	
	8	Favorite Poems: Popular Selections From the World's Literature	7.00	21.00	35.00	
	9	Enter the G-Men—William Engle	10.00	30.00	50.00	M
	10	1000 Facts Worth Knowing	7.00	21.00	35.00	NF
	11	How to Win and Hold a Husband—L. Martin	7.00	21.00	35.00	NF
	12	The World's Great Love Affairs—Hendrik Willem Van Loon	7.00	21.00	35.00	
	13	Poems of Passion—Ella Wheeler Wilcox	7.00	21.00	35.00	
	14	The Lone Ranger and the Secret of Thunder Mountain—Fran Striker; aka Heigh-Yo Silver: A Story of the Lone Ranger	12.50	37.50	60.00	W
	15	Children's Favorite Stories	9.00	27.00	45.00	
	16	Grimm's Fairy Tales	9.00	27.00	45.00	
	17	Private Lives of the Movie Stars—Eleanor Packer	9.00	27.00	45.00	NF
	18	Love on the Run—Fred Macisaac	8.00	24.00	40.00	

Bantam Books H5309, © Bantam

Bantam Books (L. A.) 14, © Bantam

Bantam Books (L. A.) 21, © Bantam

(BANTAM BOOKS (LOS ANGELES), continued)

		Good	Fine	N/Mint	
19	The Tower of Flame/Jaragu of the Lost Islands—Rex Beach	9.00	27.00	45.00	A
20	The Story of Rabelais and Voltaire—Hendrik Willem Van Loon	7.00	21.00	35.00	
21	The Shadow and the Voice of Murder—Maxwell Grant	20.00	60.00	100.00	M
22	The Green Death—Brett Hutton	10.00	30.00	50.00	M
23	Tarzan in the Forbidden City—Edgar Rice Burroughs; 1940	20.00	60.00	100.00	A
24	Humorous Anecdotes and Funny Stories	7.00	21.00	35.00	H
25	Nobody Heard the Shot—Donald Barr Chidsey	9.00	27.00	45.00	M
26	Mystery of the Blue Geranium and Other Tuesday Club Murders—Agatha Christie	10.00	30.00	50.00	M
27	Danger Mansion—Philip Wylie	8.00	24.00	40.00	M
28	Stranger in Flight—Mignon G. Eberhart	8.00	24.00	40.00	M

BANTAM CLASSICS
Bantam Books, Inc.

		Good	Fine	N/Mint	
AC 1	Brave New World—Aldous Huxley	.80	2.40	4.00	SF
FC 2	Four Great Comedies of the Restoration and Eighteenth Century	.50	1.50	2.50	
SC 3	The Complete Short Stories of Mark Twain	.80	2.40	4.00	
SC 4	The Idiot—Fyodor Dostoyevsky	.50	1.50	2.50	
FC 5	Four Great Plays—Anton Chekhov	.50	1.50	2.50	
FC 6	Sister Carrie—Theodore Dreiser	.50	1.50	2.50	
FC 7	Lord Jim—Joseph Conrad	.80	2.40	4.00	
FC 8	The Octopus—Frank Norris	.50	1.50	2.50	
FC 9	Henry the Eighth—Francis Hackett	.50	1.50	2.50	B
FC10	Emma—Jane Austen	.50	1.50	2.50	
FC11	The Voyage of the Beagle—Charles Darwin	.50	1.50	2.50	NF
AC12	Of Mice and Men—John Steinbeck	.50	1.50	2.50	
FC13	Penguin Island—Anatole France	.50	1.50	2.50	
AC14	The Day of the Locust—Nathanael West	.50	1.50	2.50	
FC15	Only Yesterday—Frederick Lewis Allen	.50	1.50	2.50	
FC16	Four Short Novels—Herman Melville	.50	1.50	2.50	
AC17	Eugenie Grandet—Honore de Balzac	.50	1.50	2.50	
AC18	Cannery Row—John Steinbeck	.50	1.50	2.50	
AC19	Cyrano de Bergerac—Edmond Rostand	.50	1.50	2.50	
FC20	Two Years Before the Mast—Richard Henry Dana	.50	1.50	2.50	A
FC21	Barchester Towers—Anthony Trollope	.50	1.50	2.50	
AC22	Crome Yellow—Aldous Huxley	.50	1.50	2.50	
FC23	Four Great Plays by Ibsen—Henrik Ibsen	.50	1.50	2.50	
FC24	Canterbury Tales—Geoffrey Chaucer	.50	1.50	2.50	
AC25	The Moon and Sixpence—W. Somerset Maugham; 1959	.50	1.50	2.50	
AC26	Hiroshima—John Hersey	.50	1.50	2.50	
FC27	Cleopatra—Emil Ludwig	.50	1.50	2.50	B
FC28	Manhattan Transfer—John Dos Passos	.50	1.50	2.50	
FC29	Fifty Great Short Stories—Milton Crane	.50	1.50	2.50	
FC30	Crime and Punishment—Fyodor Dostoyevsky	.50	1.50	2.50	
AC31	The Crucible—Arthur Miller	.50	1.50	2.50	
FC32	Marriage and Morals—Bertrand Russell	.50	1.50	2.50	
NC33	50 Great Artists—Bernard Myers	.50	1.50	2.50	
FC34	All the King's Men—Robert Penn Warren	.50	1.50	2.50	
AC35	Madame Bovary—Gustave Flaubert	.50	1.50	2.50	
36					
FC37	Up From Slavery—Booker T. Washington	.50	1.50	2.50	B
AC38	Washington Square—Henry James	.50	1.50	2.50	
FC39	Life on the Mississippi—Mark Twain	.50	1.50	2.50	
SC40	The Red and the Black—Stendhal	.50	1.50	2.50	
FC41	Fathers and Sons—Ivan Turgenev	.50	1.50	2.50	
AC42	Rashomon and Other Stories—Ryunosuke Akutagawa	.50	1.50	2.50	
SC43	The Age of Reason—Jean-Paul Sartre	.50	1.50	2.50	
FC44	Citizen Tom Paine—Howard Fast	.50	1.50	2.50	B
45					
FC46	War With the Newts—Karel Capek	.50	1.50	2.50	SF
FC47	The Finest Stories of Sean O'Faolain—Sean O'Faolain	.50	1.50	2.50	
AC48	Seventeen—Booth Tarkington	.50	1.50	2.50	H
FC49	Beyond the Pleasure Principle—Sigmund Freud	.50	1.50	2.50	
AC50	Pudd'nhead Wilson—Mark Twain; 1959	.50	1.50	2.50	
AC51	Candide—Voltaire	.50	1.50	2.50	
FC52	Man and Superman—George Bernard Shaw	.50	1.50	2.50	

BANTAM UN-NUMBERED
Bantam Books, Inc.

		Good	Fine	N/Mint	
nn	Roosevelt and Hopkins, Volume 1—Robert E. Sherwood; 1950	.40	1.20	2.00	NF
nn	Roosevelt and Hopkins, Volume 2—Robert E. Sherwood; 1950	.40	1.20	2.00	NF

BARD
Bard Publishing Corporation

Digest Size

		Good	Fine	N/Mint	
nn	Dead Giveaway—Dorothy Wheelock; 1944	1.20	3.60	6.00	M

BARNES
A. S. Barnes Company

		Good	Fine	N/Mint	
nn	The Encyclopedia of Sports—Frank G. Menke; 1955	1.00	3.00	5.00	S
nn	Official 1957-58 Automobile Handbook—ed. Charles N. Barnard; 1957	1.00	3.00	5.00	NF

BART HOUSE
Bartholomew House, Inc.

		Good	Fine	N/Mint	
nn(1)	The Hand in the Cobbler's Safe—Seth Bailey; 1944	3.00	9.00	15.00	M
nn(2)	The Delinquent Ghost—Eric Hatch	2.00	6.00	10.00	M
3	The Spy Trap—William Gilman	2.00	6.00	10.00	
4	Weird Shadow Over Innsmouth—H. P. Lovecraft	12.50	37.50	60.00	SF
5	John Smith Hears Death Walking—Wyatt Blassingame	4.00	12.00	20.00	
6	Rebirth—Thomas Calvert McClary	7.00	21.00	35.00	SF
7	The Shivering Bough—Noel Burke	2.00	6.00	10.00	M
8	The Blue Geranium—Dolan Birkley	2.00	6.00	10.00	M
9	The Waltz of Death—P. B. Maxon	3.00	9.00	15.00	M
10	The Devil Drives—Virgil Markham	2.00	6.00	10.00	M
11	Murder Meets Mephisto—Queena Mario; 1945	1.60	4.80	8.00	M
12	The Dunwich Horror—H. P. Lovecraft	12.50	37.50	60.00	SF
13	4 Feet in the Grave—Amelia Reynolds Long	1.60	4.80	8.00	M
14	The Wheelchair Corpse—Will Levinrew; aka Murder on the Palisades	1.60	4.80	8.00	M
15	Three Short Biers—Jimmy Starr	1.60	4.80	8.00	M
16	Murder Is Out—Lee Thayer	1.60	4.80	8.00	M
17	The Deaths of Lora Karen—Roman McDougald	1.60	4.80	8.00	M
18	Terry—Harriet T. Comstock	1.60	4.80	8.00	E
19	Said With Flowers—Anne Nash	1.60	4.80	8.00	M
20	Motionless Shadows—Kathleen Norris; aka Come Back to Me, Beloved	1.20	3.60	6.00	R
21	The Promise—Pearl S. Buck; 1946	1.20	3.60	6.00	
22	Checkmate to Murder—E. C. R. Lorac	1.60	4.80	8.00	M
23	Roughly Speaking—Louise Randall Pierson	1.20	3.60	6.00	H
24	Murder Secretary—William Beyer; aka Eenie, Meenie, Minie - Murder!	1.60	4.80	8.00	M
25	Hollywood Mystery—Ben Hecht; aka I Hate Actors	1.60	4.80	8.00	M
26	Bury the Hatchet—Manning Long	1.60	4.80	8.00	M
27	Design for Dying—Louis Trimble	1.60	4.80	8.00	M
28	Grand Hotel—Vicki Baum	1.20	3.60	6.00	
29	Puzzle in Porcelain—Robin Grey	1.60	4.80	8.00	M
30	The Lion's Skin—Rafael Sabatini	1.60	4.80	8.00	A
31	The Blue Cloak—Temple Bailey	1.20	3.60	6.00	R
32	Hangman's Tie—Christopher Hale	1.60	4.80	8.00	M
33	A Smattering of Ignorance—Oscar Levant	1.20	3.60	6.00	H
34	Death in the Cards—Ann T. Smith	1.60	4.80	8.00	M
35	The Clue in the Clay—D. B. Olsen	1.60	4.80	8.00	M
36	Murder Among Friends—Lange Lewis	1.60	4.80	8.00	M
39	Can You Top This?—Senator Ed Ford, Harry Hershfield & Joe Laurie, Jr.	1.20	3.60	6.00	H
101	Mr. Ace—Helen Christy; 1946, movie tie-in	1.20	3.60	6.00	M
102	The Sin of Harold Diddlebock—Harry Hershfield; 1947, movie tie-in	1.60	4.80	8.00	H
103	Honeymoon—Elizabeth Ogilvie; movie tie-in	1.60	4.80	8.00	R
nn	The Defendant in the Case—ed. Henry Lieferant; 1946	2.00	6.00	10.00	NF

BEACON
Universal Publishing and Distributing Corporation

Barnes nn, © A. S. Barnes Co.   Bart House 4, © Bart   Bart House 30, © Bart

Beacon B101, © Univ

Beacon B105, © Univ

Beacon B108, © Univ

(BEACON, continued)

		Good	Fine	N/Mint	
B101	She Got What She Wanted—Orrie Hitt; orig., 1954	1.20	3.60	6.00	E
B102	Pawn—Fan Nichols	1.00	3.00	5.00	E
B103	Rooming House—Fred Malloy; orig., 1954	1.00	3.00	5.00	E
B104	Shabby Street—Orrie Hitt; orig., 1954	1.00	3.00	5.00	E
B105	King of the Khyber Rifles—Talbot Mundy	3.00	9.00	15.00	A
B106	Walk in Darkness—Hans Habe	1.20	3.60	6.00	E
B107	Stable Boy—Adam Rebel	1.20	3.60	6.00	E
B108	Gutter Gang—Jay de Bekker	3.00	9.00	15.00	JD
B109	Pick-up—Charles Willeford; Note: Same cover as Royal Giant No. 21	1.20	3.60	6.00	E
B110	Keyhole Peeper—Jay de Bekker	1.00	3.00	5.00	E
B111	Liz—Frank Kane	1.00	3.00	5.00	E
B112	Lady Cop—J. T. Pritchard	1.00	3.00	5.00	E
B113	Highlights From Yank—The Army Weekly	1.60	4.80	8.00	C
B114	Scandalous Lady—Fan Nichols	1.00	3.00	5.00	E
B115	Gonzaga's Woman—John Jakes	2.00	6.00	10.00	E
B116	Hired Girl—Valerie Taylor	1.20	3.60	6.00	E
B117	The Hussy—Idabel Williams	1.00	3.00	5.00	E
B118	The Woman He Wanted—Daoma Winston	1.00	3.00	5.00	E
B119	Forbidden Fruit—Curtis Lucas	1.00	3.00	5.00	E
B120	Confessions of a Psychiatrist—Henry Lewis Nixon	1.60	4.80	8.00	E
B121	Warped Women—Janet Pritchard	1.60	4.80	8.00	E
B122	Dolly—Fan Nichols	1.00	3.00	5.00	E
B123	Passion in the Pines—Jack Woodford & John B. Thompson	1.00	3.00	5.00	E
B124	Honey—Jack Woodford & John B. Thompson	1.00	3.00	5.00	E
B125	Swamp Hoyden—Jack Woodford & John B. Thompson	1.00	3.00	5.00	E
B126	Unfaithful Wives—Orrie Hitt	1.00	3.00	5.00	E
B127	Savage Eve—Jack Woodford & John B. Thompson	1.00	3.00	5.00	E
B128	Witch on Wheels—William Boltin	1.00	3.00	5.00	E
B129	Bayou Girl—John Thompson	1.20	3.60	6.00	E
B130	High Priest of California—Charles Willeford	1.60	4.80	8.00	E
B131	Rock'N Roll Gal—Ernie Weatherall	2.00	6.00	10.00	E
B132	The Sucker—Orrie Hitt	1.00	3.00	5.00	E
B133	French Model—Cecil Barr	1.00	3.00	5.00	E
B134	Twisted—George Jones; c-Gross. Note: Same cover as Intimate No. 19	1.00	3.00	5.00	E
B135	Queer Affair—Carol Emery	1.00	3.00	5.00	E
B136	Shack Baby—Lon Williams	1.00	3.00	5.00	E
B137	Nudist Camp—Orrie Hitt	1.00	3.00	5.00	E
B138	Hitch-Hike Hussy—John B. Thompson & Jack Woodford	1.00	3.00	5.00	E
B139	Pushover—Orrie Hitt	1.00	3.00	5.00	E
B140	Sugar Doll—Jack Woodford & John B. Thompson	1.00	3.00	5.00	E

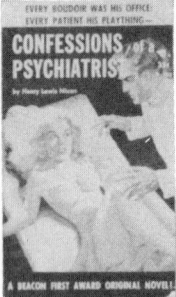
Beacon B120, © Univ

Beacon B121, © Univ

Beacon B139, © Univ

		Good	Fine	N/Mint	
B141	Love Peddler—Joe Weiss	1.00	3.00	5.00	E
B144	Girls of the French Quarter—John B. Thompson	1.00	3.00	5.00	E
B145	Passion Blues—Joe Weiss	1.00	3.00	5.00	E
B146	Ladies Man—Orrie Hitt	1.00	3.00	5.00	E
B147	Footloose Fraulein—Hans Habe	1.00	3.00	5.00	E
B148	Love Fraud—Joe Weiss	1.00	3.00	5.00	E
B149	Call Her Wanton—Lon Williams	1.00	3.00	5.00	E
B150	Blonde Trap—Ernie Weatherall	1.00	3.00	5.00	E
B151	Dolls and Dues—Orrie Hitt	1.00	3.00	5.00	E
B152	Adam and Two Eves—anonymous	1.00	3.00	5.00	E
B153	Trailer Tramp—Orrie Hitt	1.00	3.00	5.00	E
B154	Sinful Virgin—John B. Thompson	1.00	3.00	5.00	E
B155	Gang Girl—Joe Weiss	1.60	4.80	8.00	E
B156	Twilight Women—Les Scott; Note: Same cover as Universal Giant No. 9	1.00	3.00	5.00	E
B157	Paprika—Eric Von Stroheim; Note: Same cover as Universal Giant No. 2	2.00	6.00	10.00	E
B158	Teaser—Orrie Hitt	1.00	3.00	5.00	E
B159	Ellie's Shack—Orrie Hitt	1.00	3.00	5.00	E
B160	Honey Gal—Charles Willeford	1.00	3.00	5.00	E
B161	Back of Town—Herbert Pruett	1.00	3.00	5.00	E
B162	Hill Hoyden—Lon Williams	1.00	3.00	5.00	E
B163	Hell Bent—H. P. Ames	1.00	3.00	5.00	E
B164	Suburban Wife—Orrie Hitt	1.00	3.00	5.00	E
B165	Gutter Gang—Jay de Bekker	1.20	3.60	6.00	E
B166	The Private Pleasures of Mary Linton—William Arthur	.80	2.40	4.00	E
B167	Play for Pay—Wright Williams	.80	2.40	4.00	E
B168	Summer Hotel—Orrie Hitt	.80	2.40	4.00	E
B169	Wild Oats—Orrie Hitt	1.00	3.00	5.00	E
B170	Side Street—Wright Williams	.80	2.40	4.00	E
B171	Wild Hunger—Fred Malloy	.80	2.40	4.00	E
B172	Woman He Wanted—Daoma Winston	.80	2.40	4.00	E
B173	Forbidden Fruit—Curtis Lucas	1.00	3.00	5.00	E
B174	Affairs of a Beauty Queen—Orrie Hitt	.80	2.40	4.00	E
B175	Lust Is a Woman—Charles Willeford	.80	2.40	4.00	E
B176	Call South 3300: Ask for Molly!—Orrie Hitt	.80	2.40	4.00	E
B177	Hill Hellion!—Lon Williams	.80	2.40	4.00	E
B178	Fair Game—Clement Wood	.80	2.40	4.00	E
B179	The Girl in the Black Chemise—Les Scott	1.20	3.60	6.00	E
B180	Burlesque Queen—Orrie Hitt	.80	2.40	4.00	E
B181	Back Alley—Frank Smith	.80	2.40	4.00	E
B182	Fast Girl—Token West	.80	2.40	4.00	E
B183	The Naked and the Fair—Hal Moore	.80	2.40	4.00	E
B184	Confessions of a Psychiatrist—Henry Lewis Nixon; Note: Same cover as Uni-Book No. 31	1.00	3.00	5.00	E
B185	Rooming House—Fred Malloy	.80	2.40	4.00	E
B186	Trapped—Orrie Hitt	1.00	3.00	5.00	E
B187	The Lusting Breed—Mary S. Gooch	.80	2.40	4.00	E
B188	I Made My Bed—Celia Hye	.80	2.40	4.00	E
B189	Studio Affair—Clement Wood	.80	2.40	4.00	E
B190	Three Women—March Hastings	.80	2.40	4.00	E
B192	Forbidden—J. C. Priest	.80	2.40	4.00	E
B193	The Other Stranger—Daoma Winston	.80	2.40	4.00	E
B194	Shabby Street—Orrie Hitt	.80	2.40	4.00	E
B195	She Got What She Wanted—Orrie Hitt	.80	2.40	4.00	E
B198	Shame—March Hastings	.80	2.40	4.00	E
B200	Pick-up—Charles Willeford; Note: Same cover as Royal Giant No. 21	.80	2.40	4.00	E
B203	Hot Cargo—Orrie Hitt; 1958	1.00	3.00	5.00	E
B204	Surabaya—James Fox	.80	2.40	4.00	A
B205	Red Curtain—Duncan Taylor; 1959	.80	2.40	4.00	E

Beacon B144, © Univ

Beacon B157, © Univ

Beacon B164, © Univ

Beacon 236, © Univ

Beacon 242, © Univ

Beacon 256, © Univ

(BEACON, continued)

		Good	Fine	N/Mint	
B207	Circle of Sin—March Hastings	.80	2.40	4.00	E
B208	Spawn of the Bayou—John B. Thompson	1.00	3.00	5.00	E
B209	Rotten to the Core—Orrie Hitt	.80	2.40	4.00	E
B210	The Dispossessed—Geoffrey Wagner	.80	2.40	4.00	E
B211	Sheba—Orrie Hitt	.80	2.40	4.00	E
B212	Nudist Camp—Orrie Hitt	.80	2.40	4.00	E
B213	Hitch-Hike Hussy—John B. Thompson & Jack Woodford	.80	2.40	4.00	E
B214	Adulteress—Lon Williams	.80	2.40	4.00	E
B215	Passionate Land—Geoffrey Wagner	.80	2.40	4.00	E
B216	Steffi—Eunice Gray	.80	2.40	4.00	E
B217	Slave Ship—H. B. Drake	1.00	3.00	5.00	E
B218	Strumpet's Seed—Fred Malloy	.80	2.40	4.00	E
B219	Tabasco—John B. Thompson	.80	2.40	4.00	E
B220	Scandalous Lady—Fan Nichols	.80	2.40	4.00	E
B221	The Hussy—Idabel Williams	.80	2.40	4.00	E
B222	The Widow—Orrie Hitt	.80	2.40	4.00	E
B223	Chris—Randy Salem	.80	2.40	4.00	E
B224	Half-caste—John B. Thompson	.80	2.40	4.00	E
B226	The Strange Ones—Ben Travis	.80	2.40	4.00	E
B227	Add Flesh to the Fire—Orrie Hitt	.80	2.40	4.00	E
B228	Nude in the Mirror—George Viereck	.80	2.40	4.00	E
B229	Alcoholic Woman—Ruth M. Walsh	.80	2.40	4.00	E
B230	Odd Girl—Artemis Smith	1.00	3.00	5.00	E
B231	Tap Softly on My Bedroom Door—Roswell Lewis	.80	2.40	4.00	E
B232	Private Club—Orrie Hitt	.80	2.40	4.00	E
B233	Turncoat—Richard Fox	.80	2.40	4.00	E
B234	Night of Shame—Lewis Lester	.80	2.40	4.00	E
B235	Lita—Fred Malloy	.80	2.40	4.00	E
236	Odd John—Olaf Stapledon; 1959	4.00	12.00	20.00	SF
B237	The Needle—Sloane M. Britain	2.00	6.00	10.00	E
B238	Carnival Girl—Orrie Hitt	.80	2.40	4.00	E
B239	The Peeper—Orrie Hitt	.80	2.40	4.00	E
B240	Temple of Lust—John Burton Thompson	.80	2.40	4.00	E
B241	Street Walker—E. S. Seeley	.80	2.40	4.00	E
242	The Deviates—Raymond F. Jones	3.00	9.00	15.00	SF
B243	Hellcat—Dorine Clark	.80	2.40	4.00	E
B244	The Virgin—Don Morro	.80	2.40	4.00	E
B245	The Young Hoods—Joe Castro	1.00	3.00	5.00	JD
B246	The Divorcees—Scott Stone	.80	2.40	4.00	E
B247	Too Many Women—Barry Devlin	.80	2.40	4.00	E
B248	Margo—Scott Stone	.80	2.40	4.00	E
249	Thirty One Short Stories From Colliers—anthology; Note: Includes some fantasy	1.60	4.80	8.00	
B250	Too Hot to Handle—Orrie Hitt	.80	2.40	4.00	E
B251	One-Kind of Woman—Ralph Dean	.80	2.40	4.00	E
B252	Cheating Wives—Barry Devlin	.80	2.40	4.00	E
B253	Nude in the Sand—John Burton Thompson	.80	2.40	4.00	E
B254	Sin Doll—Orrie Hitt	.80	2.40	4.00	E
B255	Make Sure I Win—Barry Devlin	.80	2.40	4.00	E
256	Troubled Star—George O. Smith; 1959	2.00	6.00	10.00	SF
B257	Shack Woman—Kathie Reed	.80	2.40	4.00	E
B258	Wild Blonde—Jack Kelly	.80	2.40	4.00	E
B260	Basement Gang—David Williams; 1959. Note: Virtually the same cover as Intimate No. 32 and Stallion No. 213	1.60	4.80	8.00	JD
B261	Tawny—Orrie Hill	.80	2.40	4.00	E
B262	Danielle—Joseph Foster	.80	2.40	4.00	E
263	Pagan Passions—Randall Garrett & Larry M. Harris; 1st ed., 1959	3.00	9.00	15.00	SF
B264	Strange Thirsts—Michael Norday	.80	2.40	4.00	E
B265	Hot Blood—John B. Thompson	.80	2.40	4.00	E

(BEACON, continued)

		Good	Fine	N/Mint	
B266	Strip-Tease Girl—Cal Anton	.80	2.40	4.00	E
B267	Ex-Virgin—Orrie Hitt	.80	2.40	4.00	E
B268	The Third Sex—Artemis Smith	.80	2.40	4.00	E
B269	Private School—J. C. Priest	.80	2.40	4.00	E
270	Virgin Planet—Poul Anderson; 1960	3.00	9.00	15.00	SF
B271	Naked Desire—Henry Louis Nixon	.80	2.40	4.00	E
B272	Golden Tramp—Daoma Winston	.80	2.40	4.00	E
B273	Of G-Strings and Strippers—Mark Tryon	.80	2.40	4.00	E
B274	Suburban Sin—Orrie Hitt	.80	2.40	4.00	E
B275	Mimi—Lee Morell	.80	2.40	4.00	E
B276	Triangle of Sin—Manning	.80	2.40	4.00	E
277	Flesh—Philip Jose Farmer; 1st ed., 1960	10.00	30.00	50.00	SF
B278	Sorority Sin—E. S. Seeley	.80	2.40	4.00	E
B279	Convention Girl—Rick Lucas	.80	2.40	4.00	E
B280	Warped—Michael Norday	.80	2.40	4.00	E
B281	Strange Circle—Gale Sydney	.80	2.40	4.00	E
B282	Mavis—Justin Kent	.80	2.40	4.00	E
B283	Night of the Lash—Barry Devlin	.80	2.40	4.00	E
284	The Sex War—Sam Merwin; 1960, aka The White Widows	3.00	9.00	15.00	SF
B285	Ex-Mistress—Thomas Stone	.80	2.40	4.00	E
B286	Helena's House—Kim Savage	.80	2.40	4.00	E
B287	Pound of Flesh—Simms Albert	.80	2.40	4.00	E
B288	Wayward Girl—Orrie Hitt	.80	2.40	4.00	E
B289	Warped Desire—Kay Addams	.80	2.40	4.00	E
B290	Scarlet City—Winchell Barry	.80	2.40	4.00	E
291	A Woman a day—Philip Jose Farmer; 1st ed., 1960	10.00	30.00	50.00	SF
B292	Male Virgin—Jack Woodford & John Burton Thompson	.80	2.40	4.00	E
B293	Station Wagon Wives—Janet Pritchard	.80	2.40	4.00	E
B294	The Torrid Teens—Orrie Hitt	.80	2.40	4.00	E
B295	Song of the Whip—Barry Devlin	.80	2.40	4.00	E
B296	Very Private Secretary—Jack Hanley	.80	2.40	4.00	E
B297	Summer Resort Women—Gordon Semple	.80	2.40	4.00	E
298	The Mating Cry—A. E. Van Vogt; 1960, aka The House That Stood Still	7.00	21.00	35.00	SF
B299	Ask for Therese—Evans Wall	.80	2.40	4.00	E
B300	Lingerie Limited—Ralph Dean	.80	2.40	4.00	E
B301	One More for the Road—John Burton Thompson	.80	2.40	4.00	E
B302	Doctor Prescott's Secret—Peggy Gaddis	.80	2.40	4.00	E
B303	Restless Women—Rick Lucas	.80	2.40	4.00	E
B304	From Door to Door—Orrie Hitt; 1960	.80	2.40	4.00	E
305	The Male Response—Brian Aldiss; 1st ed., 1961	2.00	6.00	10.00	SF
B306	Gutter Girl—Leo Rifkin & Tony Norman	1.00	3.00	5.00	JD
B307	Pleasure Alley—Ralph Carter; Note: Same cover as Intimate No. 20 and Falcon 43	.80	2.40	4.00	E
B308	Lucy—Kay Addams	.80	2.40	4.00	E
B309	Hucksters' Women—Rick Lucas	.80	2.40	4.00	E
B310	Infidelity—Fred Malloy	.80	2.40	4.00	E
B311	Different—Dorene Clark	.80	2.40	4.00	E
312	Sin in Space—Cyril Judd (Judith Merril & C. M. Kornbluth); 1961, aka Outpost Mars	2.00	6.00	10.00	SF
B313	Private Chauffeur—N. R. DeMexico	.80	2.40	4.00	E
B315	She Learned the Hard Way—Scott Stone	.80	2.40	4.00	E
B317	Trailer Camp Woman—Doug Duperrault	.80	2.40	4.00	E
B318	Philanderer's Women—Lewis Lester	.80	2.40	4.00	E
B321	Lust for Love—Florence Stonebreaker	.80	2.40	4.00	E
B322	Intimate Physician—Florenz Branch	.80	2.40	4.00	E
B323	Wanton—Ben Smith	.80	2.40	4.00	E
B324	She Made Her Bed—Evans McKnight	.80	2.40	4.00	E
B325	Tell Them Anything—Orrie Hitt	.80	2.40	4.00	E
B327	Play Girl—Barney DeForest	.80	2.40	4.00	E
B328	Marijuana Girl—N. R. DeMexico	3.00	9.00	15.00	E

Beacon 277, © Univ

Beacon 284, © Univ

Beacon 312, © Univ

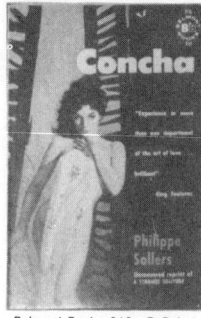

Belmont Books 204, © Belmt   Belmont Books 216, © Belmt   Belmont Books 239, © Belmt

		Good	Fine	N/Mint	
(BEACON, continued)					
B329	The Eager Ones—John Burton Thompson	.80	2.40	4.00	E
B330	Alcoholic Wife—G. G. Revelle	.80	2.40	4.00	E

BEARMAN
Samuel Bearman

Digest Size

nn	Past Sin—Eliot Brewster	.80	2.40	4.00	E

BELMONT BOOKS
Belmont Productions, Inc.

201	Temptress—Andre Maurois; 1960, aka September Roses	.80	2.40	4.00	E
202	The Question—Henri Alleg	.80	2.40	4.00	NF
203	Payola Woman—Carson Bingham	.50	1.50	2.50	E
204	Johnny Havoc—John Jakes	1.20	3.60	6.00	M
205	Who Live in Shadow—Judge John Murtagh & Sara Harris	.80	2.40	4.00	NF
206	Bloody Precinct—Bill Douglas	.50	1.50	2.50	M
207	The Cruel City—Joe Mackey	.50	1.50	2.50	E
208	The Slave—Micheline Maurel; aka An Ordinary Camp	.80	2.40	4.00	NF
209	Hong Kong Kill—Bryan Peters	.50	1.50	2.50	E
210	The Oldest Profession—Jean Campbell	.50	1.50	2.50	E
211	Cage of Passion—Isa Mari; movie tie-in	.80	2.40	4.00	E
212	Something Wild—Alex Karmel; aka Mary Ann, movie tie-in	1.00	3.00	5.00	E
213	The Blanket—A. A. Murray	.50	1.50	2.50	
214	Come-on Girl—Stuart Friedman	.50	1.50	2.50	E
215	Lights, Camera, Murder—John Shepherd	.50	1.50	2.50	M
216	Concha—Philippe Sollers; aka A Strange Solitude	1.00	3.00	5.00	E
217	Sugar Shannon—Adam Knight	.50	1.50	2.50	M
218	Sex-Clusive—Jack Heller	.80	2.40	4.00	H
219	Hitler's Woman—Antoni Gronowicz; aka Hitler's Wife	.80	2.40	4.00	B
220	South Pacific Affair—Ed Lacy; 1961	.50	1.50	2.50	E
221	Vice Cop—Richard Deming	.50	1.50	2.50	M
222	A Wind Is Rising—William Russell	.50	1.50	2.50	E
223	Skid Row U.S.A.—Sara Harris	.50	1.50	2.50	NF
224	Lonely Boy Blues—Alan Kapelner	.50	1.50	2.50	
225	Foxhole in Cairo—Leonard Mosley	.50	1.50	2.50	
226	Neither Sin nor Shame—Ann Marie & Michael Burgess	.50	1.50	2.50	
227	The Borgia Blade—Gardner F. Fox	1.00	3.00	5.00	A
228	The Ladies Man—Carl Winston; movie tie-in	.80	2.40	4.00	
229	Ten Against the Third Reich—Stan Smith	.80	2.40	4.00	NF
230	Creeps by Night—Dashiell Hammett	1.20	3.60	6.00	HO
231	My Life and Loves in Greenwich Village—Maxwell Bodenheim	1.00	3.00	5.00	B
232	The Day the War Ends—Irwin Shaw	.80	2.40	4.00	NF
233	Nightmares—Robert Bloch	1.20	3.60	6.00	HO
234	Love Doctor—Florence Stonebraker	.50	1.50	2.50	E
235	A Gun for Cantrell—Harry Sinclair Drago	.50	1.50	2.50	W
236	Markham—Lawrence Block; TV tie-in	1.00	3.00	5.00	M
237	Stronger Than Fear—Richard Tregaskis	.50	1.50	2.50	C
238	13 Against the Rising Sun—Stanley E. Smith	.80	2.40	4.00	NF
239	The Red Brain—Dashiell Hammett	1.20	3.60	6.00	HO
240	Lover Boy—John B. Flint	.50	1.50	2.50	E
241	The Trail of Johnny Dice—Harry Sinclair Drago	.50	1.50	2.50	W
242	The Back of the Tiger—Richard Cargoe	.50	1.50	2.50	E
243	The Love Mill—Louis Malley	.50	1.50	2.50	E
244	Nurse Durand's Affair—Peggy Gaddis	.50	1.50	2.50	R

		Good	Fine	N/Mint	
245					
246	The Horror Expert—Frank B. Long	1.60	4.80	8.00	HO

BELMONT BOOKS L-SERIES
Belmont Productions, Inc.

		Good	Fine	N/Mint	
L501	Varieties of Love—Herbert Kubly	.50	1.50	2.50	
L502	The Incorrigibles—William Wiegand; aka The Treatment Man	.50	1.50	2.50	
L503	Sex Life of the Modern Adult—Dr. Leland E. Glover	.50	1.50	2.50	NF
L504	The Brigitte Bardot Story—George Carpozi, Jr.	2.00	6.00	10.00	B
L505	The Cheat—Charles Jackson; aka Earthly Creatures	.80	2.40	4.00	
L506	The Secret Agent's Badge of Courage—ed. Ernest Hemingway	.50	1.50	2.50	
L507	Meet the Mob—Detective Mullady & Bill Kofoed	.50	1.50	2.50	NF
L508	Marilyn Monroe: ''Her Own Story''—George Carpori, Jr.	3.00	9.00	15.00	B
L509	The Battle of Leyte Gulf—Stan Smith	.50	1.50	2.50	NF
L510	Most Likely to Succeed—John Dos Passos	.50	1.50	2.50	
L511	The Traitor—W. Somerset Maugham	.50	1.50	2.50	
L512	The Shadow in the Rose Garden—D. H. Lawrence	.80	2.40	4.00	E
L513	How to Get Rich Buying Stocks—Ira U. Cobleigh	.40	1.20	2.00	NF
L514	Sinatra and His Rat Pack—Richard Gehman	1.60	4.80	8.00	B
L515	Memoirs—Admiral Karl Doenitz	1.00	3.00	5.00	NF
L516	The Ambassador—Aldous Huxley	.50	1.50	2.50	
L517	Eat Your Troubles Away—Dr. Lelord Kordel	.40	1.20	2.00	NF
L518	Come Into My Parlor—Charles Washburn	.40	1.20	2.00	E
L519	Khrushchev's ''Mein Kampf''—Harrison E. Salisbury	.50	1.50	2.50	NF
L520	Black-Shirt—Graham Fisher & Michael McNair-Wilson	1.00	3.00	5.00	NF
L521	The Integration of Maybelle Brown—Bonnie Golightly	.80	2.40	4.00	E
L522	Behind Every Door—Julius Horwitz	.40	1.20	2.00	
L523	Sex Life of the Modern Teen-ager—Dr. Leland E. Glover	.40	1.20	2.00	NF
L524	Berlin Betrayal—Willi Frischaver	.50	1.50	2.50	NF

BELMONT BOOKS - POST 1959
Belmont Productions, Inc.

		Good	Fine	N/Mint	
90-298	Return of the Shadow—Walter B. Gibson; orig., 1963	2.00	6.00	10.00	M
92-602	The Shadow Strikes—Maxwell Grant (Dennis Lynds); orig., 1964	1.60	4.80	8.00	M
92-615	Shadow Beware—Maxwell Grant (Dennis Lynds); orig., 1965	1.60	4.80	8.00	M
92-624	Cry Shadow—Maxwell Grant (Dennis Lynds); orig., 1965	1.60	4.80	8.00	M
B50-647	The Shadow's Revenge—Maxwell Grant (Dennis Lynds); orig., 1965	1.60	4.80	8.00	M
B50-683	Mark of the Shadow—Maxwell Grant (Dennis Lynds); orig., 1966	1.60	4.80	8.00	M
B50-695	High Camp Superheroes—Jerry Siegel; 1st ed., 1966. Note: Contains comic book reprints	1.00	3.00	5.00	A
B50-709	Shadow - Go Mad!—Maxwell Grant (Dennis Lynds); orig., 1966	1.60	4.80	8.00	M
B50-725	Night of the Shadow—Maxwell Grant (Dennis Lynds); orig., 1966	1.60	4.80	8.00	M
B50-737	The Shadow: Destination Moon—Maxwell Grant (Dennis Lynds); orig., 1967	1.60	4.80	8.00	M

BELMONT BOOKS X-SERIES
Belmont Productions, Inc.

		Good	Fine	N/Mint	
X201	The Family Survival Handbook—Martin A. Smith & William E. Eliason	.40	1.20	2.00	NF

BERKLEY
Berkley Publishing Corporation

		Good	Fine	N/Mint	
101	The Pleasures of the Jazz Age—William Hodapp; 1955	1.20	3.60	6.00	NF
102	Loveliest of Friends—G. Sheila Donisthorpe	.80	2.40	4.00	

Belmont Books L508, © Belmt

Belmont Books 90-298, © Belmt

Belmont Books B50-695, © Belmt

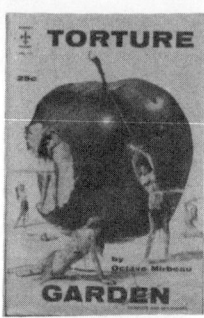
Berkley 111, © Berk

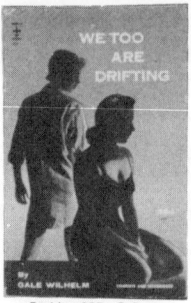
Berkley 327, © Berk

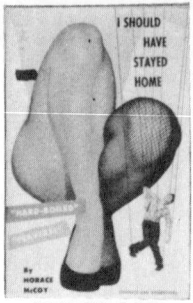
Berkley 328, © Berk

(BERKLEY, continued)

		Good	Fine	N/Mint	
103	S. S. San Pedro—James Gould Cozzens	.80	2.40	4.00	
104	Fever Pitch—Frank Waters	.80	2.40	4.00	
105	Death of an Ad Man—Alfred Eichler	.80	2.40	4.00	
106	Three Day Pass - to Kill—James Wakefield Burke & Edward Grace	1.00	3.00	5.00	
107	Border Raider—William Hopson	.80	2.40	4.00	W
108	They Shoot Horses, Don't They?—Horace McCoy	1.20	3.60	6.00	
109	So It Doesn't Whistle—Robert Paul Smith	1.00	3.00	5.00	
110	All the Girls We Loved—Prudencio DePereda	1.00	3.00	5.00	
111	Torture Garden—Octave Mirbeav	2.00	6.00	10.00	
112	Mask of Glass—Holly Roth	1.00	3.00	5.00	
313	Saddle Hawks—Bliss Lomax (H. S. Drago)	1.00	3.00	5.00	W
314	Andrew's Harvest—John Evans	.80	2.40	4.00	
315	Eleven Blue Men—Berton Roueche	.40	1.20	2.00	
316	Pattern for Panic—Richard S. Prather	1.00	3.00	5.00	M
317	Roadside Motel—Arthur Herbert Bryant	.80	2.40	4.00	
318	White Hell—Don Tracy	1.00	3.00	5.00	
319	Portrait of a Woman—John Hyde Preston	.80	2.40	4.00	
320	Sweetie Pie—Nadine Seltzer	1.00	3.00	5.00	H
321	Gunfighter Breed—Nelson Nye	.80	2.40	4.00	W
322	Danger at Sea—Georges Simenon	1.00	3.00	5.00	M
323	The Temptation of Roger Heriott—Edward Newhouse	.80	2.40	4.00	
324	Cowpoke Justice—William Hopson	.80	2.40	4.00	W
325	Oh, Doctor!—Charles Preston; 1955	.80	2.40	4.00	H
326	The Velvet Whip—Leonard Snyder	1.00	3.00	5.00	
327	We Too Are Drifting—Gale Wilhelm	1.20	3.60	6.00	
328	I Should Have Stayed Home—Horace McCoy	1.20	3.60	6.00	
329	Who's in Charge Here?—George Price	.80	2.40	4.00	H
330	Cartridge - Case Law—Nelson Nye	.80	2.40	4.00	W
331	Joe and Jennie—Donald Henderson Clarke	.80	2.40	4.00	
332	The Twisted Trail—Paul Evan Lehman	.80	2.40	4.00	W
333	Cue for Murder—Matt Bryant	.80	2.40	4.00	M
334	Manhunt—Philip Van Doren Stern	.80	2.40	4.00	
335	Powder Burns—Al Cody	.80	2.40	4.00	W
336	Mopsy—Gladys Parker	.80	2.40	4.00	H
337	Only a Woman—Francis Carco	.80	2.40	4.00	
338	The Man With My Face—Samuel W. Taylor	.80	2.40	4.00	M
339	The Girl With the Golden Yo-Yo—Edmund Schiddel	.80	2.40	4.00	
340	Danger Ashore—Georges Simenon	1.00	3.00	5.00	M
341	Outlaw of Hidden Valley—William Hopson	.80	2.40	4.00	W
342	The Postman—Roger Martin du Gard	.80	2.40	4.00	
343	Gunshot Trail—Nelson Nye	.80	2.40	4.00	W
344	Mission to the Stars—A. E. Van Vogt	1.00	3.00	5.00	SF
345	Cruel Is the Night—Howard Hunt	.80	2.40	4.00	
346	The $64,000,000 Answer—Charles Preston	.80	2.40	4.00	H
347	Tombstone Stage—William Hopson; 1956	.80	2.40	4.00	W
348	Dupree Blues—Dale Curran	.80	2.40	4.00	
349	Strictly Business—Dale McFeatters	.80	2.40	4.00	
350	Saddle Bow Slim—Nelson Nye; 1956	.80	2.40	4.00	W
351	The Magician—Georges Simenon	1.00	3.00	5.00	M
352					
353	Forbidden River—Al Cody	.80	2.40	4.00	W
354	The Narrowing Circle—Julian Symons	.80	2.40	4.00	M
355					
356	Outlaws of Lost River—Paul Evan Lehman	.80	2.40	4.00	W
357					
358	Bailey's Daughters—John De Meyer	.80	2.40	4.00	
359	Loveliest of Friends—G. Sheila Donisthorpe	.80	2.40	4.00	
360	Sweetie Pie—Nadine Seltzer	1.00	3.00	5.00	H

		Good	Fine	N/Mint	
361	Seven Men From Now—Burt Kennedy; movie tie-in	1.00	3.00	5.00	W
362	Pattern for Panic—Richard S. Prather	1.00	3.00	5.00	M
363	Ranger's Revenge—Nelson Nye	.80	2.40	4.00	W
364	Pistol Law—Paul Evan Lehman; aka Vengeance Valley	.80	2.40	4.00	W
365	No Money Down - 36 Months to Pay!—Charles Preston; 1957	.80	2.40	4.00	H
366	Ramrod Vengeance—William Hopson	.80	2.40	4.00	W
357	We Too Are Drifting—Gale Wilhelm	1.20	3.60	6.00	
368	Kinkaid of Red Butte—Leslie Ernenwein	.80	2.40	4.00	W
369	Only a Woman—Francis Carco	.80	2.40	4.00	
370	Texas Vengeance—Paul Evan Lehman	.80	2.40	4.00	W
371	Bubu of Montparnasse—Charles-Louis Philippe	.80	2.40	4.00	E
372	Rustlers of the Rio Grande—Paul Evan Lehman	.80	2.40	4.00	W
373	The Devil His Due—William O'Farrell	.80	2.40	4.00	
374	Red Man's Range—Al Cody	.80	2.40	4.00	W
375	The Lost and the Damned—Warren Carrier; 1957	.80	2.40	4.00	
376	We Dare You to Solve This!—John Paul Adams	.80	2.40	4.00	P
377	Twist of the Knife—Victor Canning	.80	2.40	4.00	M
378	Brand of Iron—Al Cody	.80	2.40	4.00	W
379	The Burial of Monsieur Bouvet—Georges Simenon	1.00	3.00	5.00	M
380	The Time Machine—H. G. Wells	1.00	3.00	5.00	SF
381	More Sweetie Pie—Nadine Seltzer	1.00	3.00	5.00	H
382	Tizzy—Kate Osann; 1958	.80	2.40	4.00	
383	Will-Yum—Fred Neher	.80	2.40	4.00	H
384	Baby Sitter's Guide—Mary Furlong Moore; 1959	.80	2.40	4.00	NF
385	Hi-teens—Fred Neher	.80	2.40	4.00	H
386	Phyllis—Ted Key	.80	2.40	4.00	H

BERKLEY DIAMOND
Berkley Publishing Corporation

		Good	Fine	N/Mint	
D2001	Cruel Is the Night—Howard Hunt; 1959	.80	2.40	4.00	
D2002	Guns Along the Arrowhead—Lee Floren	.80	2.40	4.00	W
D2003	The Big Kiss-off—Day Keene	1.00	3.00	5.00	M
D2004	Shack Road Girl—Harry Whittington	1.00	3.00	5.00	E
D2005	Descent to Darkness—Fritz Peters	.80	2.40	4.00	
D2006	Wildcats of Tonto Basin—Nelson Nye	.80	2.40	4.00	W
D2007	Dressed to Kill—Milton K. Ozaki	.80	2.40	4.00	M
D2008	Hideaway—Fan Nichols	.80	2.40	4.00	
D2009	Rifle Law—Lee Floren	.80	2.40	4.00	W
D2010	Kill Me in Shimbashi—Earl Norman; c-Maguire	1.00	3.00	5.00	M
D2011	Vengeance Trail—Charles M. Martin	.80	2.40	4.00	W
D2012	Messalina—Vivian Crockett; c-Maguire	1.20	3.60	6.00	E
D2013	Drift Fence—Walt Coburn	.80	2.40	4.00	W
D2014	Twin Mavericks—William Hopson	.80	2.40	4.00	W
D2015	Renegade Cop—Jonathan Craig	.80	2.40	4.00	
D2016	Murder Doll—Milton K. Ozaki	.80	2.40	4.00	M
D2017	Guns Along the Pecos—Lee Floren	.80	2.40	4.00	W
D2018	Desert Desperados—Nelson Nye	.80	2.40	4.00	W
D2019	Married to Murder—Harry Whittington	1.00	3.00	5.00	M
D2020	Naked Fury—Day Keene	1.00	3.00	5.00	E

BERKLEY G/BG-SERIES
Berkley Publishing Corporation

		Good	Fine	N/Mint	
G 1	The Lost Weekend—Charles Jackson; 1955	1.00	3.00	5.00	
G 2	Sexual Conduct of the Teen-ager—Jules Archer & S. V. Lawton	.80	2.40	4.00	NF
G 3	Possible Worlds of Science Fiction—ed. Groff Conklin	.80	2.40	4.00	SF
G 4	South Street—William Gardner Smith	.80	2.40	4.00	

Berkley Diamond D2012, © Berk

Berkley G1, © Berk

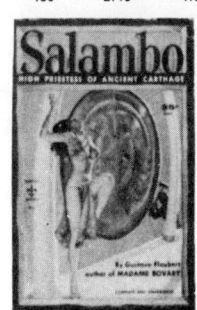

Berkley G5, © Berk

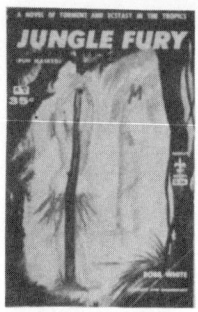

Berkley G12, © Berk   Berkley G56, © Berk   Berkley G60, © Berk

(BERKLEY G/BG-SERIES, continued)

		Good	Fine	N/Mint	
G 5	Salambo—Gustave Flaubert	1.20	3.60	6.00	
G 6	If He Hollers Let Him Go—Chester Himes	.50	1.50	2.50	
G 7	A Seed Upon the Wind—William Michelfelder	.50	1.50	2.50	
G 8	The Devil's Brigadier—Don Ryan	.50	1.50	2.50	
G 9	Naked Hollywood—Mel Harris, Weegee	.50	1.50	2.50	H
G10	Lone Star Preacher—J. W. Thomason, Jr.	.80	2.40	4.00	W
G11	Diana—Diana Fredericks	.50	1.50	2.50	
G12	Crazy Mixed-Up Kids—William Hodapp	.80	2.40	4.00	
G13	The Sign of Eros—Paul Bodin	.50	1.50	2.50	
G14	Messalina—Vivian Crockett	.80	2.40	4.00	
G15	A Lust to Live—E. B. Garside; 1956, aka Whirligig	.50	1.50	2.50	
G16	Jungle Fury—Robb White	1.20	3.60	6.00	E
G17	The Thorn in the Flesh—D. H. Lawrence	.80	2.40	4.00	
BG18	Modern Writing No. 3—William Phillips & Philip Rahv	.40	1.20	2.00	
G19	The Rat Race—Alfred Bester	1.00	3.00	5.00	
G20	Paris, My Love—Henry Calet	.40	1.20	2.00	
G21	Bessie Cotter—Wallace Smith	.50	1.50	2.50	
G22	Renee—H. R. Lenormand	.50	1.50	2.50	
G23	The Place of Jackals—Ronald Hardy	.50	1.50	2.50	
G24	Adios, O'Shaughnessy—Robert Tallman	1.00	3.00	5.00	
G25	A Girl in Every Port—Donald R. Morris; 1956	.50	1.50	2.50	
G26	Love on the Rocks—Elliott Chaze; aka The Golden Tag	.50	1.50	2.50	
G27	The Blaze of Noon—Rayner Heppenstall	.50	1.50	2.50	
G28	Young Man of Paris—Henri Calet	.50	1.50	2.50	
G29	Hypnotism Comes of Age—Raymond Rosenthal & Bernard Wolfe	.40	1.20	2.00	
G30	Intimacy—Jean-Paul Sartre	.50	1.50	2.50	
G31	Science Fiction Omnibus—ed. Groff Conklin	.80	2.40	4.00	SF
G32	Six Days in Marapore—Paul Scott	.50	1.50	2.50	
G33	Perversity—Francis Carco	.80	2.40	4.00	
G34	Alabam—Donald Henderson Clarke	.50	1.50	2.50	
BG35	Night Rider—Robert Penn Warren	.50	1.50	2.50	
G36	The Strange Case of Miss Annie Spragg—Louis Bromfield	.80	2.40	4.00	SF
G37	Virgie, Goodbye—Nathan Rothman	.80	2.40	4.00	
G38	Escape From Colditz—P. R. Reid	.50	1.50	2.50	NF
G39	Torture Garden—Octave Mirbeau	1.60	4.80	8.00	E
G40	Daughters of Eve; c-Maguire	1.00	3.00	5.00	
G41	Astounding Science Fiction Anthology—ed. John W. Campbell, Jr.	.80	2.40	4.00	SF
G42	To Wake the Dead—John Dickson Carr	1.00	3.00	5.00	M
G43	The Captain's Doll—D. H. Lawrence	.80	2.40	4.00	
G44	My Sister, My Beloved—Edwina Mark; 1957	.50	1.50	2.50	
G45	Scratch the Surface—Edmund Schiddel	.50	1.50	2.50	
G46	Aphrodite—Pierre Louys	1.00	3.00	5.00	
G47	Astounding Tales of Space and Time—John W. Campbell, Jr.	.80	2.40	4.00	SF
G48	The Eight of Swords—John Dickson Carr; c-Maguire	1.20	3.60	6.00	M
G49	A Dime a Throw—Jerome Weidman	.50	1.50	2.50	
G50	Diana—Diana Fredericks; 1957	.50	1.50	2.50	
G51	The Body of Love—Charles Keats	.50	1.50	2.50	
G52	The Virgin and the Gypsy—D. H. Lawrence	.80	2.40	4.00	
G53	The Big Book of Science Fiction—ed. Groff Conklin	.80	2.40	4.00	SF
G54	The Sign of Eros—Paul Bodin	.50	1.50	2.50	
G55	Love in a Hot Climate—Edmund Schiddel	.50	1.50	2.50	
G56	Jungle Fury—Robb White	1.00	3.00	5.00	
G57	Take Me As I Am—Loren Wahl	.80	2.40	4.00	
G58	How Cheap Can You Get?—Martin Abzug; aka Seventh Avenue Story	.80	2.40	4.00	E
G59	The Woman Who Rode Away—D. H. Lawrence	.80	2.40	4.00	
G60	The Case of the Constant Suicides—John Dickson Carr; c-Maguire	1.20	3.60	6.00	M
G61	Andrew's Harvest—John Evans	.80	2.40	4.00	
G62	The Most Dangerous Game	.80	2.40	4.00	

		Good	Fine	N/Mint	
G63	A Treasury of Science Fiction—ed. Groff Conklin	.80	2.40	4.00	SF
G64	The Tirpitz—David Woodward	.50	1.50	2.50	NF
G65	A Seed Upon the Wind—William Michelfelder	.40	1.20	2.00	
BG66	Time Must Have a Stop—Aldous Huxley; c-Maguire	1.00	3.00	5.00	
G67	Spy Catcher—Oreste Pinto	.50	1.50	2.50	
G68	This Is My Body	.40	1.20	2.00	
G69	Affair in Capri—Mario Soldati	.40	1.20	2.00	
BG70	The Last Days of Hitler—H. R. Trevor-Roper	.50	1.50	2.50	NF
G71	Strangers in the Universe—Cifford D. Simak	.80	2.40	4.00	SF
G72	Poison in Jest—John Dickson Carr; c-Maguire	1.20	3.60	6.00	
BG73	Salambo—Gustave Flaubert; c-Maguire	4.00	12.00	20.00	E
G74	Olivia—Olivia	.50	1.50	2.50	
G75	The Case of the Lady Who Took a Bath—Alan Hynd; 1957	.50	1.50	2.50	
G76	The Chastity of Gloria Boyd—Donald Henderson Clarke	.50	1.50	2.50	
G77	Beachheads in Space—August Derleth	.80	2.40	4.00	SF
G78	Harlem Is My Heaven—Ian Gordon	.80	2.40	4.00	
G79	Gun-Quick—Nelson Nye	.50	1.50	2.50	W
G80	The Blind Barber—John Dickson Carr	1.20	3.60	6.00	M
G81	Depravity—Francis Carco	.80	2.40	4.00	
BG82	Graf Spee—Dudley Pope	.50	1.50	2.50	NF
G83	Martha Crane—Charles Gorham	.40	1.20	2.00	
G84	The Corpse With Sticky Fingers—George Bagby	.50	1.50	2.50	M
G85	Three of a Kind—P. J. Wolfson	.50	1.50	2.50	
G86	Juvenile Jungle	.80	2.40	4.00	
G87	Gunthrower—William Hopson	.50	1.50	2.50	W
G88	Trish—Margaret Maze Craig	.40	1.20	2.00	
G89	Great Sports Stories—Herman L. Masin	.40	1.20	2.00	S
BG90	Drive to Victory—Robert S. Allen	.50	1.50	2.50	
G91	The Four False Weapons—John Dickson Carr; c-Maguire	1.20	3.60	6.00	M
G92	Legend of the Lost—Bonnie Golightly; movie tie-in	1.60	4.80	8.00	
G93	All Woman's Flesh—Paul Bodin	.40	1.20	2.00	
G94	The Tunnel Escape—Eric Williams; 1958	.50	1.50	2.50	
G95	Such Is My Beloved—Carol Hales	.40	1.20	2.00	
BG96	Rommel, the Desert Fox—Desmond Young	.50	1.50	2.50	NF
G97	Nude Croquet	1.00	3.00	5.00	
G98	Pattern for Panic—Richard S. Prather	.80	2.40	4.00	M
G99	G Stands for Gun—Nelson Nye	.50	1.50	2.50	W
BG100	Finnley Wren—Philip Wylie; 1958	.80	2.40	4.00	
G101	Death Watch—John Dickson Carr	1.20	3.60	6.00	M
BG102	Stalingrad—Theodor Plievier	.50	1.50	2.50	NF
G103	Forbid Me Not—Blair Fuller	.50	1.50	2.50	
G104	Beyond Time and Space—August Derleth	.80	2.40	4.00	SF
G105	Intimacy—Jean-Paul Sartre	.80	2.40	4.00	
G106	S. S. San Pedro—James Gould Cozzens	.50	1.50	2.50	
G107	Escape From Colditz—P. R. Reid	.50	1.50	2.50	NF
BG108	The Exurbanites—A. C. Spectorsky	.40	1.20	2.00	H
G109	Marsha—Margaret Maze Craig	.40	1.20	2.00	
BG110	The Theory and Practice of Hell—Eugen Kogon	.80	2.40	4.00	NF
G111	The Strange Path—Gale Wilhelm	1.00	3.00	5.00	
G112	Bessie Cotter—Wallace Smith	.40	1.20	2.00	
G113	The Girl of the Roman Night—Dante Arfelli; aka The Unwanted	.40	1.20	2.00	
G114	The End of the Track—Andrew Garve	.40	1.20	2.00	
G115	Holocaust at Sea; the Drama of the Scharnhorst—Fritz-Otto Busch	.40	1.20	2.00	NF
G116	The Outer Reaches—August Derleth	.80	2.40	4.00	SF
G117	The Mad Hatter Mystery—John Dickson Carr	1.20	3.60	6.00	M
G118	Guns of Arizona—Nelson Nye	.50	1.50	2.50	W
G119	The Enormous Radio and Other Stories—John Cheever	3.00	9.00	15.00	SF
G120	Black Opium—Claude Farrere; c-Maguire	15.00	45.00	75.00	E

Berkley BG73, © Berk

Berkley G91, © Berk

Berkley G120, © Berk

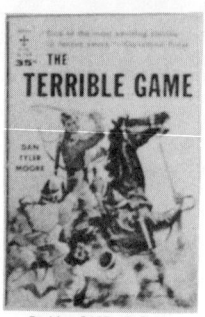

Berkley G129, © Berk   Berkley G169, © Berk   Berkley G180, © Berk

(BERKLEY G/BG-SERIES, continued)

		Good	Fine	N/Mint	
BG121	The Fatal Decisions—Seymour Freidin & William Richardson	.40	1.20	2.00	
G122	Gideon of Scotland Yard—J. J. Marric; movie tie-in	.80	2.40	4.00	M
G123	To Whom It May Concern—Juliet Lowell	.40	1.20	2.00	
G124	Joe and Jennie—Donald Henderson Clarke	.40	1.20	2.00	
G125	So It Doesn't Whistle—Robert Paul Smith; 1958, c-Maguire	1.20	3.60	6.00	
G126	Naomi Martin—Clarkson Crane	.50	1.50	2.50	
S127	Men at War—Ernest Hemingway	1.00	3.00	5.00	
BG128	Sex in Our Changing World—John McPartland	.50	1.50	2.50	NF
G129	Hag's Nook—John Dickson Clarke; c-Maguire	1.20	3.60	6.00	
G130	Thieves Like Us—Edward Anderson	.50	1.50	2.50	
G131	Strange Ports of Call—August Derleth	1.00	3.00	5.00	SF
G132	Tormented—Carolyn Weston	.50	1.50	2.50	
G133	Tropic Moon—Georges Simenon	1.00	3.00	5.00	M
G134	I Should Have Stayed Home—Horace McCoy	1.20	3.60	6.00	
BG135	The German Generals Talk—B. H. Liddell Hart	.50	1.50	2.50	NF
G136	China Doll—Edgar Jean Bracco	.50	1.50	2.50	
G137	The 31st of February—Julian Symons; c-Maguire	1.00	3.00	5.00	M
G138	Gunfighter Brand—Nelson Nye	.50	1.50	2.50	W
G139	If He Hollers Let Him Go—Chester Himes	.50	1.50	2.50	
G140	Infamy—Frances Carco	.50	1.50	2.50	
G141	My Sister, My Beloved—Edwina Mark	1.00	3.00	5.00	
G142	Low Level Mission—Leon Wolff	.50	1.50	2.50	
G143	The Corpse in the Waxworks—John Dickson Carr	1.20	3.60	6.00	M
G144	Proud Youth—Alexander Eliot	.50	1.50	2.50	
G145	The Man Who Watched the Train Go By—Georges Simenon	1.00	3.00	5.00	M
G146	The Man Within—Graham Greene	.50	1.50	2.50	
G147	Bailey's Daughters—John DeMeyer	.50	1.50	2.50	
G148	Men, Martians and Machines—Eric Frank Russell	.50	1.50	2.50	SF
BG149	Ah King—W. Somerset Maugham	1.00	3.00	5.00	
BG150	The First Lady Chatterley—D. H. Lawrence; 1958	.80	2.40	4.00	
G151	The Golden Jungle—William Howard Harris	.50	1.50	2.50	
G152	Hell's Kitchen—Benjamin Appel	1.00	3.00	5.00	
G153	The Last of Mr. Norris—Christopher Isherwood; c-Maguire	1.00	3.00	5.00	
G154	Gunshot Trail—Nelson Nye	.50	1.50	2.50	W
G155	Perversity—Francis Carco	.50	1.50	2.50	
G156	Laughter in the Dark—Vladimir Nabokov	.50	1.50	2.50	
G157	The Crooked Hinge—John Dickson Carr	1.00	3.00	5.00	M
G158	Mystery Walks the Campus—Annette Turngren	.50	1.50	2.50	M
G159	Marcia, Private Secretary—Zillah K. MacDonald	.50	1.50	2.50	R
G160	Desire and Other Stories—Clement Wood	.50	1.50	2.50	
G161	The Wicked and the Warped—Max Alth	.50	1.50	2.50	
G162	The Evil That Men Do—George Victor Martin	.50	1.50	2.50	
G163	Worlds of Tomorrow—August Derleth	.80	2.40	4.00	SF
G164	Three Day Pass - to Kill—James Wakefield Burke & Edward Grace	.50	1.50	2.50	
G165	The Pub Crawler—Maurice Procter	.50	1.50	2.50	M
G166	Morning, Winter and Night—John Nairne Michaelson	.40	1.20	2.00	
G167	Adam and Evil—John Carlova	.40	1.20	2.00	
G168	Renee—H. R. Lenormand	.40	1.20	2.00	
G169	The Terrible Game—Dan Tyler Moore	.50	1.50	2.50	A
G170	Devil's Holiday—Fred Malloy	.50	1.50	2.50	
G171	Stag Stripper—Jack Hanley	.50	1.50	2.50	
G172	Loveliest of Friends—G. Sheila Donisthorpe	.40	1.20	2.00	
G173	We Too Are Drifting—Gale Wilhelm	1.00	3.00	5.00	
G174	Only a Woman—Francis Carco	.50	1.50	2.50	
G175	Olivia; 1958	.40	1.20	2.00	
G176	Mystery on Graveyard Head—Edith Dorian	.50	1.50	2.50	M
BG177	Pocket Battleship—H. J. Brennecke & Theodor Krancke	.50	1.50	2.50	
BG178	The Hucksters—Frederic Wakeman	.40	1.20	2.00	

		Good	Fine	N/Mint	
G179	No Bed of Her Own—Cicely Schiller	.50	1.50	2.50	
G180	Boots and Saddles—Edgar Jean Braco; TV tie-in	1.00	3.00	5.00	W
G181	Is My Flesh of Brass?—P. J. Wolfson	.50	1.50	2.50	
G182	Too Many Girls—Don Tracy	.50	1.50	2.50	
G183	Virgie, Goodbye—Nathan Rothman	.80	2.40	4.00	
G184	The Shameless Ones—Uberto Quintavalle	.50	1.50	2.50	
G185	Wicked Woman—Fred Malloy	.50	1.50	2.50	
G186	Scarlet Angel—Dorene Clark	.50	1.50	2.50	
G187	The Big Wheel—John Brooks	.50	1.50	2.50	
G188	The Incurable Wound—Berton Roueche	.30	.90	1.50	
G189	Time to Come—August Derleth	.80	2.40	4.00	SF
G190	The Judge and His Hangman—Friedrich Durrenmatt	.50	1.50	2.50	
G191	Awakening—Jean-Baptiste Rossi	.50	1.50	2.50	
G192	Kill Me in Tokyo—Earl Norman	.50	1.50	2.50	
G193	South Street—William Gardner Smith	.40	1.20	2.00	
G194	The Postman—Roger Martin duGard	.40	1.20	2.00	
G195	Hot Money Girl—Arlo Wayne	.40	1.20	2.00	
G196	Passion in Panama—Richard Marshe	.40	1.20	2.00	
BG197	The Professional—W. C. Heinz	.40	1.20	2.00	
G198	Early to Rise—Arnold E. Grisman	.40	1.20	2.00	
G199	Make Me an Offer—Charles Gorham	.50	1.50	2.50	
G200	Sexual Conduct of the Teen-ager—Jules Archer & S. V. Lawton; 1954	.50	1.50	2.50	NF
G201	Smoke Wagon Kid—Clem Colt	.50	1.50	2.50	W
BG202	Last in Convoy—James Pattinson	.50	1.50	2.50	
G203	Love Around the World	.50	1.50	2.50	
G204	The Blaze of Noon—Rayner Heppenstall	.40	1.20	2.00	
G205	Forbidden Pleasures—B. Devlin	.50	1.50	2.50	
G206	The Sinning Lens—Mark Tryon	.50	1.50	2.50	
G207	The Home Encyclopedia of Moving Your Family—Margaret Randall	.30	.90	1.50	NF
G208	Mystery in Blue—Gertrude E. Mallette	.40	1.20	2.00	M
G209	The Singing Heart—Elizabeth Cadell; 1959	.40	1.20	2.00	
G210	How to Make Your Emotions Work for You—Dorothy C. Finkelhor	.30	.90	1.50	NF
BG211	73 North—Dudley Pope	.40	1.20	2.00	
BG212	Prettiest Girl in Town—Thomas Fall	.40	1.20	2.00	
BG213	First Person Singular—W. Somerset Maugham	.40	1.20	2.00	
G214	The Bowstring Murders—Carter Dickson	1.20	3.60	6.00	
G215	Away and Beyond—A. E. Van Vogt	.80	2.40	4.00	SF
G216	The Sign of Eros—Paul Bodin	.50	1.50	2.50	
G217	Love on the Rocks—Elliott Chaze; aka The Golden Tag	.50	1.50	2.50	E
G218	Jule—George Wylie Henderson	.40	1.20	2.00	E
G219	Sandy—John B. Thompson	.40	1.20	2.00	
G220	The Fire That Burns—Mark Tryon	.40	1.20	2.00	
G221	I'll Find My Love—Joan Dirksen	.40	1.20	2.00	
G222	The Big Book of Horse Stories—Page Cooper	.50	1.50	2.50	
G223	Beany Malone—Lenora Mattingly Weber	.40	1.20	2.00	
G224	I Flew for the Fuhrer—Heinz Knoke	.50	1.50	2.50	NF
G225	What D'ya Know for Sure?—Len Zinberg; 1959	.40	1.20	2.00	
G226	All Woman's Flesh—Paul Bodin	.40	1.20	2.00	
G227	Blaze—Scott Stone	.40	1.20	2.00	
G228	Dreamboat—Rick Lucas	.40	1.20	2.00	
G229	Easy Living—Terence Ford	.40	1.20	2.00	
G230	Rambling Top Hand—William Hopson	.40	1.20	2.00	W
BG231	Dateline: Paris—Reynolds Packard	.40	1.20	2.00	
G232	Deadlier Than the Male—James E. Gunn	1.00	3.00	5.00	M
G233	Imagination Unlimited—T. E. Dikty & Everett F. Bleiler	.50	1.50	2.50	SF
G234	Guns of Horse Prairie—Nelson Nye	.50	1.50	2.50	W
G235	Channel Dash—Terence Robertson	.50	1.50	2.50	
G236	A Woman Called Desire—Richard Marshe	.50	1.50	2.50	
G237	Showroom Girls—Token West	.50	1.50	2.50	
BG238	The Lessons of Love—W. Carroll Munro	.50	1.50	2.50	
BG239	The Wooden Horse—Eric Williams	.50	1.50	2.50	
G240	House of Fury—Felice Swados	2.00	6.00	10.00	E
G241	Pattern for Panic—Richard S. Prather	.80	2.40	4.00	M
G242	Duel on the Range—Burt Arthur	.40	1.20	2.00	W
G243	Count Me In—Fan Nichols	.40	1.20	2.00	
G244	Vice Girl—Sim Albert	.40	1.20	2.00	
G245	The Odd Ones—Edwina Mark	1.00	3.00	5.00	E
G246	The Frogmen—James Gleeson & T. J. Waldron	.40	1.20	2.00	
G247	Box Star Buckaroo—Charles M. Martin	.40	1.20	2.00	W
G248	Three of a Kind—P. J. Wolfson	.40	1.20	2.00	
G249	The Other Side of the Moon—August Derleth	.80	2.40	4.00	SF
G250	Native Girl—Harry Whittington; 1959	.80	2.40	4.00	
G251	Affairs of Marie-Odette—Cecil Saint-Laurent	.40	1.20	2.00	
G252	Immoral Woman—Jack Hanley	.40	1.20	2.00	
G253	Devil Take Her—Fan Nichols	.40	1.20	2.00	
BG254	A Man Escaped—Andre Devigny	.40	1.20	2.00	

Berkley BG263, © Berk   Berkley Medallion X1735, © Berk   Berkley Medallion X2058, © Berk

(BERKLEY G/BG-SERIES, continued)	Good	Fine	N/Mint	
G255 Hangman's Range—Lee Floren	.40	1.20	2.00	W
G256 The Incredible Truth—Chris Massie	.40	1.20	2.00	
G257 Woman of the Night—Robert Carse	.40	1.20	2.00	
G258 Wake Up to Murder—Day Keene	.80	2.40	4.00	M
G259 Harlem Is My Heaven—Ian Gordon	.80	2.40	4.00	
G260 Shanty Boat Girl—Kirk Westley	.50	1.50	2.50	
G261 Strip Street—Jack Hanley	.40	1.20	2.00	
G262 Down and Out in Paris and London—George Orwell	.50	1.50	2.50	
BG263 The Knights of Bushido—Lord Russell	1.00	3.00	5.00	NF
BG264 The Ginger Man—J. P. Donleavy	.40	1.20	2.00	
G265 The Daughter of Time—Josephine Tey	.40	1.20	2.00	M
G266 The Girl Beneath the Lion—Andre Pieyre de Mandiargues	.40	1.20	2.00	
G267 The Plague Court Murders—Carter Dickson	1.00	3.00	5.00	M
G268 Cosmopolitans—W. Somerset Maugham	.50	1.50	2.50	
G269 Money, Marbles and Chalk—Douglas Fairbairn	.40	1.20	2.00	
G270 Thomas Alva Edison—G. Glenwood Clark	.40	1.20	2.00	B
G271 Deliver Us From Evil—Thomas A. Dooley	.40	1.20	2.00	
G272 The Edge of Tomorrow—Thomas A. Dooley	.40	1.20	2.00	
G273 Something Foolish, Something Gay—Jane & Glen Sire	.40	1.20	2.00	
G274 Francie Comes Home—Emily Hahn	.40	1.20	2.00	
G275 Comanche of the 7th—Margaret Leighton; 1959	.50	1.50	2.50	W
G276 Sharon—Harriett H. Carr	.30	.90	1.50	
G277 Desert Love—Henry de Montheriant	.30	.90	1.50	
G278 Gideon's Month—J. J. Marric	.40	1.20	2.00	M
G279 Altars of the Heart—Richard Lebherz	.30	.90	1.50	
G280 A Touch of Strange—Theodore Sturgeon	.50	1.50	2.50	SF
G281 Death Turns the Tables—John Dickson Carr	1.00	3.00	5.00	M
G282 The Other Side of the Night—Edmund Schiddel	.40	1.20	2.00	
G283 Aphrodite—Pierre Louys	.80	2.40	4.00	E
G284 My Sister Eileen—Ruth McKenney	.30	.90	1.50	
G285 Blue Ribbon Romance—Jane S. McIlvaine	.30	.90	1.50	R
G286 Mystery of Hidden Village—Annette Turngren	.40	1.20	2.00	M
G287 The Emperor's Snuff Box—John Dickson Carr	1.00	3.00	5.00	M
G288 Flight Nurse—Adelaide Humphries	.30	.90	1.50	R
G289 The Enemy Stars—Poul Anderson	.50	1.50	2.50	SF
G290 The Thorn in the Flesh—D. H. Lawrence	.50	1.50	2.50	
G291 Flight—Edgar Jean Bracco	.30	.90	1.50	
G292 Laughs Around the World	.40	1.20	2.00	H
G293 Meet the Malones—Lenora Mattingly Weber	.30	.90	1.50	
G294 Step to the Music—Phyllis A. Whitney	.30	.90	1.50	

BERKLEY MEDALLION
Berkley Publishing Corporation

X1734 The Bat Staffel—Robert J. Hogan; 1969, c-Steranko	1.00	3.00	5.00	C
X1735 The Spider Strikes—R. T. M. Scott	.80	2.40	4.00	M
X1746 Purple Aces—Robert J. Hogan; c-Steranko	1.00	3.00	5.00	C
X1764 Ace of the White Death—Robert J. Hogan; 1970, c-Steranko	1.00	3.00	5.00	C
nn (1774) The Wheel of Death—R. T. M. Scott; Note: Was distributed as a free bonus with X1735	.80	2.40	4.00	M
X1782 Wings of the Black Death—Grant Stockbridge	.80	2.40	4.00	M
X2002 Bombs From the Murder Wolves—Robert J. Hogan; 1971	1.00	3.00	5.00	C
X2004 Vultures of the White Death—Robert J. Hogan	1.00	3.00	5.00	C
X2023 Flight From the Grave—Robert J. Hogan	1.00	3.00	5.00	C
X2043 Fangs of the Sky Leopard—Robert J. Hogan	1.00	3.00	5.00	C
X2058 The Mark of the Vulture—Robert J. Hogan	1.00	3.00	5.00	C

BEST DETECTIVE NOVEL OF THE MONTH
Select Publications, Inc.

Digest Size

(Also see Best Detective Selection of the Month)

		Good	Fine	N/Mint	
1	Come and Be Killed—Dorothy Bennett	1.60	4.80	8.00	M
2	$1,000,000 in Corpses—Edward Ronns; 1942	1.60	4.80	8.00	M

BEST DETECTIVE SELECTION OF THE MONTH
Select Publications, Inc.

Digest Size

(Also see Best Detective Novel of the Month)

3	Death Goes to a Party—Michael Jaffe	1.60	4.80	8.00	M
4	The Bloody Wig Murders—George Bagby	1.60	4.80	8.00	M
5	Pool of Death—Keats Patrick; aka Death Is a Tory	1.60	4.80	8.00	M
6	Wail for the Corpse—Lawrence Treat; aka B As in Banshee	1.60	4.80	8.00	M
8	Modeled in Murder—Manning Long; 1943	1.60	4.80	8.00	M
9	Say Yes to Murder—W. T. Ballard	1.60	4.80	8.00	M
nn	The Corpse Hangs High—Edward Ronns; 1943	1.60	4.80	8.00	M
nn	Murder RFD—Herman Petersen	1.60	4.80	8.00	M

BESTSELLER LIBRARY/MYSTERY
The American Mercury, Inc./Mercury Publications

Digest Size

nn(1)	The Adventures of Ellery Queen—Ellery Queen	1.20	3.60	6.00	M
B 2	One More Spring—Robert Nathan	.40	1.20	2.00	
B 3	More Adventures of Ellery Queen—Ellery Queen	.80	2.40	4.00	M
B 4	Life Begins at Forty—Walter B. Pitkin	.40	1.20	2.00	
B 5	Tobacco Road—Jack Kirkland (Erskine Caldwell)	.40	1.20	2.00	E
B 6	Twenty-Four Hours—Louis Bromfield	.40	1.20	2.00	
B 7	The Bellamy Trial—Frances Noyes Hart	.40	1.20	2.00	M
B 8	The Devil to Pay—Ellery Queen	.50	1.50	2.50	M
B 9	The Mysterious Mr. Quin—Agatha Christie	.50	1.50	2.50	M
B10	The Case of the Curious Bride—Erle Stanley Gardner	.40	1.20	2.00	M
B11	The Spanish Cape Mystery—Ellery Queen	.50	1.50	2.50	M
B12	Thank You, Mr. Moto—John P. Marquand	.50	1.50	2.50	M
B13	Lord Peter Views the Body—Dorothy L. Sayers	.50	1.50	2.50	M
B14	The Greek Coffin Mystery—Ellery Queen	.50	1.50	2.50	M
B15	Inquest—Percival Wilde	.40	1.20	2.00	M
B16	Murder in Stained Glass—Margaret Armstrong	.40	1.20	2.00	M
B17	The Egyptian Cross Mystery—Ellery Queen	.50	1.50	2.50	M
B18	Dead Man's Mirror—Agatha Christie	.50	1.50	2.50	M
B19	The Case of the Sleepwalker's Niece—Erle Stanley Gardner	.40	1.20	2.00	M
B20	In the Teeth of the Evidence—Dorothy L. Sayers	.50	1.50	2.50	M
B21	Murder in Three Acts—Agatha Christie	.50	1.50	2.50	M
B22	The D. A. Holds a Candle—Erle Stanley Gardner	.40	1.20	2.00	M
B23	Death in Ecstacy—Ngaio Marsh	.50	1.50	2.50	M
B24	A Face for a Clue—Georges Simenon	.50	1.50	2.50	M
B25	Partners in Crime—Agatha Christie	.50	1.50	2.50	M
B26	Does not exist				
B27	The Cairo Garter Murders—Van Wyck Mason	.40	1.20	2.00	M

Best Detective Novel/Month 2, © Select

Best Detective Selection 6, © Select

Bestseller Library/Mystery nn(1), © Merc

Bestseller Library/Mystery B40, © Merc   Bestseller Library/Mystery B50, © Merc   Bestseller Library/Mystery B62, © Merc

(BESTSELLER LIBRARY/MYSTERY, continued)

		Good	Fine	N/Mint	
B28	The Tragedy of Y—Ellery Queen	.50	1.50	2.50	M
B29	Murder up My Sleeve—Erle Stanley Gardner	.40	1.20	2.00	M
B30	The Man With No Face—Margaret Armstrong	.40	1.20	2.00	M
B31	Some Buried Caesar—Rex Stout	.50	1.50	2.50	M
B32	The Seven Dials Mystery—Agatha Christie	.50	1.50	2.50	M
B33	Black Plumes—Margery Allingham	.40	1.20	2.00	M
B34	The Department of Queer Complaints—Carter Dickson	1.60	4.80	8.00	M
B35	This Is Murder—Erle Stanley Gardner	.40	1.20	2.00	M
B36	The Regatta Mystery—Agatha Christie	.50	1.50	2.50	M
B37	The Whispering Cup—Mabel Seeley	.40	1.20	2.00	M
B38	Hangman's Holiday—Dorothy L. Sayers	.50	1.50	2.50	M
B39	The Boomerang Clue—Agatha Christie	.50	1.50	2.50	M
B40	$106,000 Blood Money—Dashiell Hammett; 1st ed., 1943	16.50	50.00	80.00	M
B41	The Flemish Shop—Georges Simenon	.50	1.50	2.50	M
B42	The G-String Murders—Gypsy Rose Lee; Note: Actually written by Craig Rice	.40	1.20	2.00	M
B43	Poirot Investigates—Agatha Christie	.50	1.50	2.50	M
B44	Where There's a Will—Rex Stout	.50	1.50	2.50	M
B45	Death in Five Boxes—Carter Dickson	.50	1.50	2.50	M
B46	Death in the Doll's House—Hannah Lees & Lawrence Bachmann	.40	1.20	2.00	M
B47	The Three Coffins—John Dickson Carr	.50	1.50	2.50	M
B48	The Secret Adversary—Agatha Christie	.50	1.50	2.50	M
B49	Dark Garden—Mignon G. Eberhart	.40	1.20	2.00	M
B50	The Adventures of Sam Spade—Dashiell Hammett; 1st ed., 1944	20.00	60.00	100.00	M
B51	Police at the Funeral—Margery Allingham	.40	1.20	2.00	M
B52	The Man in the Brown Suit—Agatha Christie	.50	1.50	2.50	M
B53	Thirty Days Hath September—Dorothy Cameron Disney & George Sessions Perry	.40	1.20	2.00	M
B54	Sad Cypress—Agatha Christie	.50	1.50	2.50	M
B55	The Pattern—Mignon G. Eberhart	.40	1.20	2.00	M
B56	Kingdom of Death—Margery Allingham	.40	1.20	2.00	M
B57	The Washington Legation Murders—Van Wyck Mason	.40	1.20	2.00	M
B58	Appointment With Death—Agatha Christie	.50	1.50	2.50	M
B59	The Case Book of Ellery Queen—Ellery Queen; orig., 1945	10.00	30.00	50.00	M
B60	Hangman's Whip—Mignon G. Eberhart	.40	1.20	2.00	M
B61	Murder at Hazelmoor—Agatha Christie	.50	1.50	2.50	M
B62	The Continental Op—Dashiell Hammett; 1st ed., 1945	16.50	50.00	80.00	M
B63	The Budapest Parade Murders—Van Wyck Mason	.40	1.20	2.00	M
B64	Artists in Crime—Ngaio Marsh	.50	1.50	2.50	M
B65	Compound for Death—Doris Miles Disney	.40	1.20	2.00	M
B66	Alarm of the Black Cat—D. B. Olsen	.40	1.20	2.00	M
B67	Dagger of the Mind—Kenneth Fearing	.40	1.20	2.00	M
B68	Vintage Murder—Ngaio Marsh	.50	1.50	2.50	M
B69	The Patience of Maigret—Georges Simenon; aka Battle of Nerves	.50	1.50	2.50	M
B70	Deadly Nightshade—Elizabeth Daly	.40	1.20	2.00	M
B71	The Crimson Circle—Edgar Wallace	.50	1.50	2.50	M
B72	The Parchment Key—Stanley Hopkins	.40	1.20	2.00	M
B73	The Affair of the Crimson Gull—Clifford Knight	.40	1.20	2.00	M
B74	Laura—Vera Caspary	.40	1.20	2.00	M
B75	Miss Silver Deals With Death—Patricia Wentworth	.40	1.20	2.00	M
B76	The Pricking Thumb—H. C. Branson	.40	1.20	2.00	M
B77	While She Sleeps—Ethel Lina White	.40	1.20	2.00	M
B78	Death Watch—John Dickson Carr	.50	1.50	2.50	M
B79	Mr. Parker Pyne, Detective—Agatha Christie	.50	1.50	2.50	M
B80	The Chuckling Fingers—Mabel Seeley	.40	1.20	2.00	M
B81	Hammett Homicides—Dashiell Hammett; 1st ed., 1946	16.50	50.00	80.00	M
B82	Quoth the Raven—Bruno Fischer	.50	1.50	2.50	M
B83	She Fell Among Actors—James Warren	.40	1.20	2.00	M
B84	Sinners Never Die—A. E. Martin	.40	1.20	2.00	M
B85	The Black Honeymoon—Constance & Gwenyth Little	.40	1.20	2.00	M

(BESTSELLER LIBRARY/MYSTERY, continued)	Good	Fine	N/Mint	
B86 Murder in the Calais Coach—Agatha Christie	.50	1.50	2.50	M
B87 The Corpse With Purple Thighs—George Bagby	.40	1.20	2.00	M
B88 Whisper Murder—Vera Kelsey	.40	1.20	2.00	M
B89 The Blonde Died First—Dana Chambers	.40	1.20	2.00	M
B90 Deadline at Dawn—William Irish	.50	1.50	2.50	M
B91 The Department of Dead Ends—Roy Vickers	.40	1.20	2.00	M
B92 The Book of the Dead—Elizabeth Daly	.40	1.20	2.00	M
B93 One Alone—Van Siller	.40	1.20	2.00	M
B94 Cops and Robbers—O. Henry	.40	1.20	2.00	M
B95 The Yellow Room—Mary Roberts Rinehart	.30	.90	1.50	M
B96 Dead at the Take-Off—Lester Dent	1.00	3.00	5.00	M
B97 The Man Who Slept All Day—Michael Venning	.40	1.20	2.00	M
B98 Stranger at Home—George Sanders	.40	1.20	2.00	M
B99 Cats Don't Need Coffins—D. B. Olsen	.40	1.20	2.00	M
B100 The Hawk—Roy Vickers	.40	1.20	2.00	M
B101 Lady to Kill—Lester Dent	1.00	3.00	5.00	M
B102 Kiss the Blonde Goodbye—Finlay McDermid; aka Ghost Wanted	.40	1.20	2.00	M
B103 Rope for an Ape—Dana Chambers	.40	1.20	2.00	M
B104 Fear No More—Leslie Edgley	.40	1.20	2.00	M
B105 So Deadly Fair—Gertrude Walker	.40	1.20	2.00	M
B106 The Bleeding Scissors—Bruno Fischer	.50	1.50	2.50	M
B107 Make My Bed Soon—John Stephen Strange	.40	1.20	2.00	M
108 Murder Picks the Jury—Harrison Hunt	.40	1.20	2.00	M
B109 The Angry Heart—Leslie Edgley	.40	1.20	2.00	M
B110 Bullets for a Blonde—Will Oursler; aka Departure Delayed	.40	1.20	2.00	M
B111 Death for My Beloved—Doris Miles Disney; aka Enduring Old Charms	.40	1.20	2.00	M
B112 The Book of the Lion—Elizabeth Daly	.40	1.20	2.00	M
B113 In Cold Blood—George Bagby	.40	1.20	2.00	M
B114 The Blue Horse of Taxco—Kathleen Moore Knight	.40	1.20	2.00	M
B115 Lady Afraid—Lester Dent	1.00	3.00	5.00	M
B116 Fountain of Death—Hugh Lawrence Nelson	.40	1.20	2.00	M
B117 Death Has Four Hands—Hilda Lawrence; aka Composition for Four Hands	.40	1.20	2.00	M
B118 Short Shrift—Manning Long	.40	1.20	2.00	M
B119 The Dark River—Philip Clark	.40	1.20	2.00	M
B120 Devious Design—D. B. Olsen	.40	1.20	2.00	M
B121 Nightfall—David Goodis	.50	1.50	2.50	M
B122 The Bleeding House—Hilda Lawrence; aka The House	.40	1.20	2.00	M
B123 Bait for Murder—Kathleen Moore Knight	.40	1.20	2.00	M
B124 Think Fast, Mr. Moto—John P. Marquand	.40	1.20	2.00	M
B125 Shark River—Richard Powell	.40	1.20	2.00	M
B126 For the Love of Murder—Margaret Scherf; aka Gilbert's Last Toothache	.40	1.20	2.00	M
B127 The Dark Light—Bart Spicer	.40	1.20	2.00	M
B128 The Monkey Murder—Stuart Palmer	.80	2.40	4.00	M
B129 Place for a Poisoner—E. C. R. Lorac	.40	1.20	2.00	M
B130 Kill to Fit—Bruno Fischer	.50	1.50	2.50	M
B131 Kill 'Em With Kindness—Fred Dickenson	.40	1.20	2.00	M
B132 Days of Misfortune—Aaron Marc Stein	.40	1.20	2.00	M
B133 Too Like the Dead—Dana Chambers; aka Too Like the Lightning	.40	1.20	2.00	M
B134 A Lonely Way to Die—Hal Debrett	.40	1.20	2.00	M
B135 Murder for Millions—Nancy Rutledge; aka Emily Will Know	.40	1.20	2.00	M
B136 Blood on My Shoes—Jean Leslie; aka Shoes for My Love	.40	1.20	2.00	M
B137 He Didn't Mind Danger—Michael Gilbert	.40	1.20	2.00	M
B138 The Whitebird Murders—Thomas B. Black	.40	1.20	2.00	M
B139 Death of a Big Shot—Clifford Knight	.40	1.20	2.00	M
B140 Rather Cool for Mayhem—Lawrence G. Blochman	.40	1.20	2.00	M
B141 Sinister Shelter—Charles L. Leonard	.40	1.20	2.00	M
B142 Hot Tip—Jack Dolph	.40	1.20	2.00	M
B143 Murder Makes a Deadline—Samuel M. Fuller; aka The Dark Page	.40	1.20	2.00	M
B144 Mr. Blessington's Imperialist Plot—John Sherwood	.40	1.20	2.00	M
B145 Half-Past Mortem—John Saxon	.40	1.20	2.00	M
B146 The Knife Behind You—James Benet	.40	1.20	2.00	M
B147 The Man in the Mist—Francis Bonnamy	.40	1.20	2.00	M
B148 Smallbone Deceased—Michael Gilbert	.40	1.20	2.00	M
B149 These Arrows Point to Death—William O'Farrell	.40	1.20	2.00	M
B150 The Kahuna Killer—Juanita Sheridan	.40	1.20	2.00	M
B151 The 3-13 Murders—Thomas B. Black	.40	1.20	2.00	M
B152 Alias Basil Willing—Helen McCloy	.40	1.20	2.00	M
B153 FBI Story—The Gordons	.40	1.20	2.00	M
B154 Fatal Lover—Van Siller; aka The Last Resort	.40	1.20	2.00	M
B155 The Mamo Murders—Juanita Sheridan	.40	1.20	2.00	M
B156 Don't Kill, My Love—Rae Foley; aka Wake the Sleeping Wolf	.40	1.20	2.00	M
B157 F As in Flight—Lawrence Treat	.40	1.20	2.00	M
B158 Mask for Murder—Aaron Marc Stein	.40	1.20	2.00	M
B159 Divine and Deadly—Margaret Scherf; aka The Curious Custard Pie	.40	1.20	2.00	M
B160 Dead Ringer—Ferguson Findley; aka The Man in the Middle	.40	1.20	2.00	M
B161 The Fair and the Dead—John Stephen Strange; aka Reasonable Doubt	.40	1.20	2.00	M

Bestseller Library/Mystery B165, © Merc   Big Green Detective Novel 2, © Green   Big Green Publication 5, © Green

(BESTSELLER LIBRARY/MYSTERY, continued)

		Good	Fine	N/Mint	
B162	Murder Is a Gamble—Glenn Barns	.40	1.20	2.00	M
B163	Lust for Vengeance—Robert Bloomfield; aka Vengeance Streets	.40	1.20	2.00	M
B164	Death My Darling Daughters—Jonathan Stagge	1.00	3.00	5.00	M
B165	Vice Squad—Leslie T. White; aka Harness Bull, movie tie-in	1.00	3.00	5.00	M
B166	Dance of Death—Veronica Parker	.50	1.50	2.50	M
B167	The Virgin Huntress—Elizabeth Sanxay Holding	.40	1.20	2.00	M
B168	Dead Yesterday—Ruth Fenisong	.40	1.20	2.00	M
B169	One Murder Too Many—Edwin Lanham	.40	1.20	2.00	M
B170	Make Haste to Live—The Gordons	.40	1.20	2.00	M
B171	One Blonde Died—Leslie Edgley; aka The Runaway Pigeon	.40	1.20	2.00	M
B172	Killer Loose!—Genevieve Holden	.40	1.20	2.00	M
B173	The Corpse Who Had Too Many Friends—Hampton Stone	.40	1.20	2.00	M
B174	This Year's Death—John Godey	.40	1.20	2.00	M
B175	Lawyers Don't Hang—Glenn Barns	.40	1.20	2.00	M
B176	The Passionate Victims—Lange Lewis	.40	1.20	2.00	M
B177	Terror Lurks in Darkness—Dolores Hitchens	.40	1.20	2.00	M
B178	V As in Victim—Lawrence Treat	.40	1.20	2.00	M
B179	Lovely in Death—William O'Farrell; aka The Snakes of St. Cyr	.40	1.20	2.00	M
B180	Killer at His Back—John Godey; aka The Blue Hour	.40	1.20	2.00	M
B181	You'll Fry Tomorrow—M. V. Heberden; aka Exit This Way	.40	1.20	2.00	M
B182	The Case of the Missing Corpse—Edwin Lanham; aka Death of a Corinthian	.40	1.20	2.00	M
B183	Embrace of Death—Carroll Cox Estes; aka The Moon Gate	.40	1.20	2.00	M
B184	The Fatal Flirt—Dolores Hitchens; aka Beat Back the Tide	.40	1.20	2.00	M
B185	Too Lovely Too Live—Ruth Fenisong; aka Miscast for Murder	.40	1.20	2.00	M
B186	They All Bleed Red—Richard Sted	.40	1.20	2.00	M
B187	Buried for Pleasure—Edmund Crispin	.40	1.20	2.00	M
B188	The Blonde Betrayer—John Godey; aka The Man in Question	.40	1.20	2.00	M
B189	Trap for a Redhead—Stuart Palmer; aka Nipped in the Bud	.80	2.40	4.00	M
B190	Trial and Terror—Lawrence Treat	.40	1.20	2.00	M
B191	Shroud for a Lady—Elizabeth Daly; aka The Wrong Way Down	.40	1.20	2.00	M
B192	Another Morgue Heard From—Frederick C. Davis	.40	1.20	2.00	M
B193	Catch and Kill—Nicholas Blake; aka The Whisper in the Gloom	.40	1.20	2.00	M
B194	Network of Fear—Alvin Yudkoff; aka Circumstances Beyond Control	.40	1.20	2.00	M
B195	No Time for Terror—Philip MacDonald; aka Guest in the House	.40	1.20	2.00	M
B196	Murder Muscles In—Max Franklin; aka Justice Has No Sword	.40	1.20	2.00	M
B197	Murder Makes an Entrance—Clarence Budington Kelland	.40	1.20	2.00	M
B198	Black Alibi—Cornell Woolrich	.50	1.50	2.50	M
B199	The Book of the Crime—Elizabeth Daly	.40	1.20	2.00	M
B200	A Dirty Way to Die—George Bagby	.40	1.20	2.00	M
B201	Tell Her It's Murder—Helen Reilly	.40	1.20	2.00	M
B202	Take One for Murder—M. E. Chaber; aka As Old As Cain	.50	1.50	2.50	M
B203	The Long Body—Helen McCloy	.40	1.20	2.00	M
B204	I Wake Up Screaming—Steve Fisher	.50	1.50	2.50	M
B205	Don't Look Back—Miriam Borgenicht	.40	1.20	2.00	M
B206	The Black Angel—Cornell Woolrich	.50	1.50	2.50	M
B207	Hang the Man High—Geoffrey Household; aka Fellow Passenger	.40	1.20	2.00	M
B208	The Deadly Truth—Helen McCloy	.40	1.20	2.00	M
B209	Bridge to Vengeance—Winston Graham; aka The Little Walls. Note: After No. 209, the series became Bestseller Mystery Magazine.				

BIG GREEN DETECTIVE NOVEL
Green Publishing Company

Digest Size

2	Hot Bullets for Love—Gentry Nyland; aka Mr. South Burned His Mouth. Note: Same cover as Double Action Detective No. 2	1.60	4.80	8.00	M

		Good	Fine	N/Mint	
3	Run Corpse Run—Guy Pember-Hiller; Note: Same cover as Double Action Detective No. 3	1.20	3.60	6.00	M
4	Murder With Love—Garland Lord	1.20	3.60	6.00	M
5	Target for Murder—Guy Elwyn Giles	1.20	3.60	6.00	M

BIG GREEN PUBLICATION
Green Publishing Company

Digest Size

		Good	Fine	N/Mint	
5	The Little Dog Barked—Anne Rowe	1.00	3.00	5.00	M

BLACK CAT DETECTIVE
Crestwood Publishing Co., Inc.

Digest Size

		Good	Fine	N/Mint	
1	3 Died Variously—Guy Elwyn Giles	1.20	3.60	6.00	M
2	Bait for a Tiger—Bayard Veiller	1.20	3.60	6.00	M
3	Curtains for the Judge—Thomas Polsky	1.20	3.60	6.00	M
5	The Case of the Cheating Bride—Milton Propper; 1943	1.20	3.60	6.00	M
6	Death Thumbs a Ride—Jean Lilly	1.20	3.60	6.00	M
7	The Beast Must Die—Nicholas Blake	1.60	4.80	8.00	M
8	The Body in the Road—Moray Dalton; 1944	1.20	3.60	6.00	M
9	It Takes a Thief—Dan Billany	1.20	3.60	6.00	M
10	Crazy to Kill—Ann Cardwell	1.20	3.60	6.00	M
11	John Doe - Murderer—William Dale	1.20	3.60	6.00	M
12	6 Were to Die—Kirk Wales	1.20	3.60	6.00	M
13	Murder As Usual—Owen Fox Jerome	1.20	3.60	6.00	M
14	Dark Power—Elizabeth Sanxay Holding	1.20	3.60	6.00	M
15	Head Long for Murder—Merlda Mace; 1945	1.20	3.60	6.00	M
16	The Crooked Circle—Gerald Verner	1.20	3.60	6.00	M
17	Motto for Murder—Merlda Mace	1.20	3.60	6.00	M
18	Murder Trouble—Louis Trimble	1.60	4.80	8.00	M
19	Murder in Miniatures—Sam Merwin, Jr.	1.60	4.80	8.00	M
20	Murder in Plain Sight—Gerlad Brown; 1946	1.20	3.60	6.00	M
21	The Voodoo Goat—Audrey Gaines	1.20	3.60	6.00	M
23	Judge Robinson Murdered!—R. L. Goldman	1.20	3.60	6.00	M
24	Death in the State House—Timothy Knox	1.20	3.60	6.00	M
25	Dear Dead Professor—K. Alison LaRoche	1.20	3.60	6.00	M
27	The Bright Face of Danger—Julius Fast; 1947	1.20	3.60	6.00	M
28	Blondes Don't Cry—Merlda Mace	1.20	3.60	6.00	M

BLACK CAT WESTERN
Crestwood Publishing Co., Inc.

Digest Size

		Good	Fine	N/Mint	
29	The Outlaw of Antler—Frank C. Robertson	1.00	3.00	5.00	W
30	Prairie Pioneers—Lynn Westland	1.00	3.00	5.00	W
33	Gunsmoke in Paradise—Burt Arthur	1.00	3.00	5.00	W
34	The Silver Cayuse—Lynn Westland	1.00	3.00	5.00	W
38	Saddle River Spread—Lynn Westland	1.00	3.00	5.00	W
39	Nighthawk's Gold—Kim Knight	1.00	3.00	5.00	W
40	The Faceless Riders—Archie Joscelyn	1.00	3.00	5.00	W
41	Smoke in the West—Archie Joscelyn	1.00	3.00	5.00	W

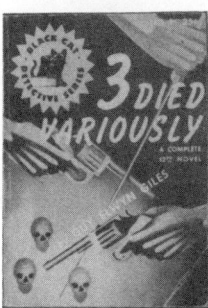

Black Cat Detective 1, © Crest

Black Cat Detective 19, © Crest

Black Cat Western 40, © Crest

Black Knight 26, © Ideal

Black Knight 27, © Ideal

Black Knight 29, © Ideal

		Good	Fine	N/Mint	
(BLACK CAT WESTERN, continued)					
42	Gunslammer—Lee Floren	1.00	3.00	5.00	W
43	Renegade Guns—James L. Rubel	1.00	3.00	5.00	W
44	Mad River Guns—Lee Floren	1.00	3.00	5.00	W
45	Outcast Law—Archie Joscelyn	1.00	3.00	5.00	W

BLACK KNIGHT
Ideal Distributing Company

Some Digest Size

		Good	Fine	N/Mint	
15	Corpse in the Wind—Robert Portner Koehler; digest size	1.20	3.60	6.00	M
16	Last Year's Snow—Don Tracey; digest size	1.20	3.60	6.00	M
17	Death to Drumbeat—Jeremy Lane; digest size	1.20	3.60	6.00	M
18	Murder Behind the Mike—R. L. Goldman; digest size	1.20	3.60	6.00	M
19	Death by Dynamite—Joseph L. Bonney; digest size	1.20	3.60	6.00	M
22	Murder's Coming—Donald Clough Cameron	1.20	3.60	6.00	M
25	Come Dwell With Death—M. W. Glidden; digest size	1.20	3.60	6.00	M
26	Death Is No Lady—M. E. Corne; aka Death Is a Masquerade	2.00	6.00	10.00	M
27	The Psychiatric Murders—M. Scott Michel	2.00	6.00	10.00	M
28	The Kidnappers—Albert E. Ullman	2.00	6.00	10.00	M
29	Green for a Grave—Manning Lee Stokes	2.00	6.00	10.00	M
30	Make Mine Murder—R. Sidney Bowen	2.00	6.00	10.00	M
31	Dead Weight—Addison Simmons	2.00	6.00	10.00	M
32	Kill Him Tonight—Jeremy Lane	2.00	6.00	10.00	M
33	Stop Press - Murder!—Peter Stirling	2.00	6.00	10.00	M
34	Puzzle in Petticoats—Kootz	2.00	6.00	10.00	M

BLEAK HOUSE
Parsee Publications

Some Digest Size

		Good	Fine	N/Mint	
12	Design for Dying—Albert Jeffers; aka Screen for Murder, digest size	1.20	3.60	6.00	M
13	Murder Wore Green—Robert Portner Koehler; digest size	1.20	3.60	6.00	M
14	The Case of the Blood-stained Dime—Minna Barton; aka Murder Does Light Housekeeping	2.00	6.00	10.00	M
15	The Case of the Missing Corpse—Joan Langar	2.00	6.00	10.00	M
16	The Corpse in the Guest Room—Clement Wood	2.00	6.00	10.00	M
17	The Skyscraper Murder—Samuel Spewack	2.00	6.00	10.00	M

Black Knight 32, © Ideal

Bleak House 12, © Par

Bleak House 15, © Par

Bleak House 19, © Par | Bleak House 21, © Par | Boblin Book nn, © Boblin Sales Co.

		Good	Fine	N/Mint	
(BLEAK HOUSE, continued)					
18	Murder Menagerie—Jeremy Lane	2.00	6.00	10.00	M
19	If I Should Murder—Patrick Laing	2.00	6.00	10.00	M
20	The Terror of the Headless Corpse—William Dale	2.00	6.00	10.00	M
21	Here Come the Dead—Robert Portner Koehler	2.00	6.00	10.00	M
22	White for a Shroud—Donald Clough Cameron	2.00	6.00	10.00	

BOBLEY BOOKS
Robert Edwards Publishing Co.

Digest Size

B4	Best Read Short Stories—anthology; 1946	.80	2.40	4.00

BOBLIN BOOK
Boblin Sales Company

Digest Size

		Good	Fine	N/Mint	
nn	The Adventures of Buffalo Bill—William F. Cody; movie tie-in	3.00	9.00	15.00	W
nn	The Jumping Frog and Sixteen Other Stories—Mark Twain	2.00	6.00	10.00	H
nn	Was It Murder?—James Hilton	2.00	6.00	10.00	W
nn	Judge Priest Turns Detective—Irvin S. Cobb	2.00	6.00	10.00	M

BONDED
Bond-Charteris/Black/Jacobs/Shaw

Digest Size

		Good	Fine	N/Mint	
1	The Saint Meets the Tiger—Leslie Charteris	1.60	4.80	8.00	M
2	Featuring the Saint—Leslie Charteris; 1945	1.20	3.60	6.00	M
3	The Saint's Getaway—Leslie Charteris	1.60	4.80	8.00	M
4	The Saint's Choice of English Crime—ed. Leslie Charteris	1.60	4.80	8.00	M
5	Alias the Saint—Leslie Charteris	1.20	3.60	6.00	M
6	The Saint's Choice of American Crime—ed. Leslie Charteris	1.60	4.80	8.00	M
7	Paging the Saint—Leslie Charteris; aka Wanted for Murder	1.60	4.80	8.00	M
8	The Saint's Choice of True Crimes—ed. Leslie Charteris	1.60	4.80	8.00	M
9	The Saint's Choice of Humorous Crime Stories—ed. Leslie Charteris	1.60	4.80	8.00	M
10	Fast One—Paul Cain	4.00	12.00	20.00	M

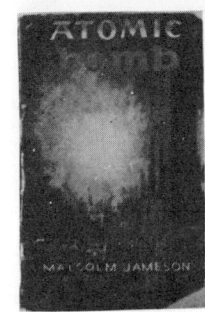

Bonded 2, © Bonded-Charteris | Bonded 5, © Bonded-Charteris | Bonded 10A, © Bonded-Charteris

Bonded 10B, © Bonded-Charteris

Bonded 11, © Bonded-Charteris

Bonded nn, © Bonded-Charteris

		Good	Fine	N/Mint	
(BONDED, continued)					
10A	Atomic Bomb—Malcolm Jameson	3.00	9.00	15.00	SF
10B	Guns of Powder River—Oscar J. Friend	2.00	6.00	10.00	W
11	The Saint's Choice of Impossible Crime—ed. Leslie Charteris; 1st ed., 1945	5.00	15.00	25.00	SF
12	The Craig Rice Mystery Digest—ed. Craig Rice	2.00	6.00	10.00	M
13	8 Faces at 3—Craig Rice	1.60	4.80	8.00	M
14	The Saint Meets His Match—Leslie Charteris	1.60	4.80	8.00	M
15	Crime on My Hands—George Sanders	1.60	4.80	8.00	M
16	I'll Hate Myself in the Morning—Elliot Paul	1.20	3.60	6.00	M
nn	Lady on a Train—Leslie Charteris; movie tie-in	2.00	6.00	10.00	M

BONDED MYSTERY
Anson Bond Publications, Inc.

Some Digest Size

		Good	Fine	N/Mint	
1	The Goose Is Cooked—Emnett Hogarth; digest size	2.00	6.00	10.00	M
2	Murder of a Novelist—Sally Wood; digest size	1.60	4.80	8.00	M
3	The Hungry House—Lilian Lauferty; digest size	1.60	4.80	8.00	M
4	Murder Strikes Thrice—Charles G. Booth; digest size	1.60	4.80	8.00	M
5	I'll Eat You Last—H. C. Branson	2.00	6.00	10.00	M
6	The Thing in the Brook—Peter Storme	2.00	6.00	10.00	M
7	Death Blew Out the Match—Kathleen Moore Knight	2.00	6.00	10.00	M
8	Twittering Bird Mystery—H. C. Bailey	2.00	6.00	10.00	M
9	Murder Needs a Name—Ruth Fenisong	2.00	6.00	10.00	M
10	''B'' As in Banshee—Lawrence Treat	2.00	6.00	10.00	M
11	Johnnie—Dorothy B. Hughes	2.00	6.00	10.00	M
12	Kingdom of Death—Margery Allingham	2.00	6.00	10.00	M
13	Harbour—Philip MacDonald	2.00	6.00	10.00	M
14	Who's Afraid?—Elisabeth Sanxay Holding	2.00	6.00	10.00	M
15	Footsteps in the Air—Susan Wells	2.00	6.00	10.00	M
16	This Is Mr. Fortune—H. C. Bailey	2.00	6.00	10.00	M

BOOKS INC.
Books, Inc.

		Good	Fine	N/Mint	
107	Webster's New Handy Pocket Dictionary—ed. Noah Webster & Edward N. Teall; 1952	.40	1.20	2.00	NF

Bonded Mystery 10, © Anson

Bonded Mystery 11, © Anson

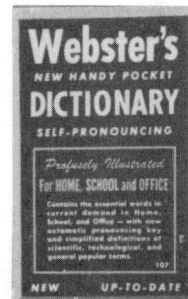

Books Inc. 107, © Books, Inc.

BOWKER
R. R. Bowker Company

		Good	Fine	N/Mint	
nn	Banned Books—Anne Lyon Haight; 1955	3.00	9.00	15.00	NF

Note: Contains interesting information on the banning of some paperback books either as pornography or because of lurid covers.

BROADWAY NOVEL MONTHLY
Diversey Periodicals, Inc.

Digest Size

1	Infidelity—Arthur Weigal	4.00	12.00	20.00	E
2	Venus on Wheels—Maurice Dekobra	4.00	12.00	20.00	E
3	Ladies of the Evening—Milton Herbert Gropper; 1949	3.00	9.00	15.00	E
4	Tom's Temptations—Don Prince	4.00	12.00	20.00	E
5	Night Boat—Timothy Trent	4.00	12.00	20.00	E
6	Three Loose Ladies—M. H. Gropper	4.00	12.00	20.00	E
7	Fleshpots of Malibu—Carroll & Garrett Graham; aka Queer People	4.00	12.00	20.00	E
8	Blonde Baby—Wilson Collison	4.00	12.00	20.00	E
9	Dangerous Love—Jack Woodford	4.00	12.00	20.00	E
10	Untamed Darling—Jack Woodford	4.00	12.00	20.00	E

BRONZE BOOKS
Designs Publishing Company

Digest Size

1	Harlem Model—Luke Roberts; orig., 1952	6.00	18.00	30.00	E
2	Hot Chocolate—Jesse Lee Carter; orig., 1952	6.00	18.00	30.00	E

BRUSSEL
J. Brussel

Digest Size

nn	Murder in the Bedroom—Gaston Leroux; 1945	2.00	6.00	10.00	M

BULL'S-EYE DETECTIVE NOVELS
Duchess Printing and Publishing Co., Ltd.

Digest Size

(Canadian)

1	Silent Terror—T. C. H. Jacobs; 1944	1.20	3.60	6.00	M
2	Death by Desire—Richard Goyne	1.20	3.60	6.00	M

CAMEO
Detective House, Inc.

Digest Size

300	No Man of Her Own—Florence Stonebraker	1.00	3.00	5.00	E
301	The Loves of Alice Brandt—Gene Harvey; orig., 1951	1.00	3.00	5.00	E
302	Night of Ecstasy—William Arnold	1.00	3.00	5.00	E
303	Conquest of Margie—Norman Bligh	1.00	3.00	5.00	E

Broadway Novel Monthly 2, © Div

Bronze Books 2, © Designs

Bull's-Eye Detective Novels 1, ©Duch

Cameo 308, © Det   Candid Love Novels 21, © Crest   Candid Love Novels 22, © Crest

(CAMEO, continued)		Good	Fine	N/Mint	
304	Naughty Blonde—Florence Stonebraker	1.00	3.00	5.00	E
305	Pick-Up at Midnight—Gene Harvey	1.00	3.00	5.00	E
306	Passion C. O. D.—Albert L. Quandt	1.00	3.00	5.00	E
307	Sin Preferred—Kermit Welles	1.00	3.00	5.00	E
308	Secret Affair—Amos Hatter; orig., 1951	1.00	3.00	5.00	E
309	A Girl Called Joy—Gene Harvey	1.00	3.00	5.00	E
310	Pleasure Bound—Kermit Welles	1.00	3.00	5.00	E
311	The Affairs of a Country Girl—Gail Jordan & Peggy Gaddis	1.00	3.00	5.00	E
312	Crossroads of Desire—Amos Hatter	1.00	3.00	5.00	E
313	Three-time Sinner—Norman Bligh	1.00	3.00	5.00	E
314	The Big Tease—William Arnold; orig., 1952	1.00	3.00	5.00	E
315	Passion's Harvest—Florence Stonebraker; c-Gross	1.00	3.00	5.00	E
316	Soft Shoulders—Norman Bligh	1.00	3.00	5.00	E
317	Woman of Fire—Peggy Gaddis	1.00	3.00	5.00	E
318	Island Ecstasy—Amos Hatter	1.00	3.00	5.00	E
319	Beach Party—Ralph Douglas	1.00	3.00	5.00	E
320	Girl of the Midway—Amos Hatter	1.00	3.00	5.00	E
321	Tight Skirt—Frederic Spencer	1.00	3.00	5.00	E
322	Loose Women—Robert E. Reynolds; orig., 1952	1.00	3.00	5.00	E
323	Wild Girl—L. Dixon; c-Belarski	1.00	3.00	5.00	E
324	Young Nurse—Sylvia Erskine	1.00	3.00	5.00	E
325	Mountain Girl—Peggy Gaddis	1.00	3.00	5.00	E
326	At Ruby's Place—Jean Tucker	1.00	3.00	5.00	E
327	Cleo—Frederic Spencer; orig., 1953	1.00	3.00	5.00	E
328	Country Girl—Gail Jordan & Peggy Gaddis	1.00	3.00	5.00	E
329	Backwoods Bride—Robert E. Reynolds; c-Gross	1.00	3.00	5.00	E
331	House of Lost Women—Frank Haskell	1.00	3.00	5.00	E
332	Nurse's Quarters	1.00	3.00	5.00	E
333	Young Sinner—Elisabeth Gill; orig., 1953	1.00	3.00	5.00	E
334	Office Sinner—Gene Harvey; aka The Loves of Alice Brandt	1.00	3.00	5.00	E
335	Wild Girl—Lewis Dixon; c-Belarski	1.00	3.00	5.00	E
336	Doctor's Nurse—Gene Harvey; aka A Girl Called Joy	1.00	3.00	5.00	E
337	Mountain Bride—Peggy Gaddis	1.00	3.00	5.00	E
339	French Maid—M. Cooper	1.00	3.00	5.00	E
341	Country Girl—Gail Jordan & Peggy Gaddis	1.00	3.00	5.00	E
342	Shanty Girl—Jean Tucker; c-Belarski	1.00	3.00	5.00	E
343	Slum Doctor—Matthew Clay	1.00	3.00	5.00	E
344	Woman of Passion—Norman Bligh	1.00	3.00	5.00	E
345	Lost Women—Robert E. Reynolds	1.00	3.00	5.00	E
346	Backwoods Bride—Robert E. Reynolds	1.00	3.00	5.00	E
351	French Maid	1.00	3.00	5.00	E
357	Woman of Passion—Norman Bligh; aka 3-Time Sinner	1.00	3.00	5.00	E
359	Boy-Chaser—Nickerson	1.00	3.00	5.00	E
362	Mountain Bride—Peggy Gaddis	1.00	3.00	5.00	E
364	Island Girl	1.00	3.00	5.00	E
365	Boarding House—Frank Haskell; aka House of Lost Women, c-Gross	1.00	3.00	5.00	E
367	Lost Women—Robert E. Reynolds	1.00	3.00	5.00	E

CANDID LOVE NOVELS
Crestwood Publishing Co., Inc.

Digest Size

20	Love for Sale—Gladys Sloan; aka Single Bed	1.00	3.00	5.00	E
21	Wild Weekend—Gene Harvey; 1949, aka Pack Up Your Sins, c-Wenzel	1.00	3.00	5.00	E
22	Notorious Woman—James Harlow	1.00	3.00	5.00	E
23	Lessons in Love—Florence Stonebraker	1.00	3.00	5.00	E
26	For Men Only—Beth Brown	1.00	3.00	5.00	E

CARDINAL EDITIONS
Pocket Books, Inc.

		Good	Fine	N/Mint	
C 1	Four Great Historical Plays—William Shakespeare	.40	1.20	2.00	
C 2	Kings Row—Henry Bellamann	.40	1.20	2.00	
C 3	In Tragic Life—Vardis Fisher	.40	1.20	2.00	
C 4	Cutlass Empire—F. Van Wyck Mason	.40	1.20	2.00	A
C 5	The Merriam—Webster Pocket Dictionary	.30	.90	1.50	NF
C 6	Hungry Hill—Daphne du Maurier	.30	.90	1.50	
C 7	A Short History of the Civil War—Fletcher Pratt	.50	1.50	2.50	NF
C 8	Prince of Egypt—Dorothy Clarke Wilson	.40	1.20	2.00	A
C 9	The Pocket Bible	.40	1.20	2.00	NF
C10	Lust for Life—Irving Stone	.30	.90	1.50	
C11	The Pocket Book of Verse—M. E. Speare	.40	1.20	2.00	
C12	The Pocket Book of Short Stories—M. E. Speare	.40	1.20	2.00	
C13	Roget's Pocket Thesaurus—Christopher Mawson, Katharine Whiting	.30	.90	1.50	NF
C14	Four Great Tragedies—William Shakespeare	.40	1.20	2.00	
C15	Four Great Comedies—William Shakespeare	.40	1.20	2.00	
C16	The Pocket Book of Quotations—Henry Davidoff	.30	.90	1.50	
C17	Tales From the Arabian Nights	.50	1.50	2.50	
C18	Honey in the Horn—H. L. Davis	.40	1.20	2.00	
C19	Cakes and Ale and Other Favorites—W. Somerset Maugham	.40	1.20	2.00	
C20	Rand McNally - Pocket World Atlas; 1952	.30	.90	1.50	NF
C21	Pride's Castle—Frank Yerby	.40	1.20	2.00	A
C22	The Pepper Tree—John Jennings	.50	1.50	2.50	
C23	Rivers of Glory—F. Van Wyck Mason	.40	1.20	2.00	
C24	The 100 Most Important People in the World Today—Donald Robinson	.30	.90	1.50	NF
C25	A Short History of the American Revolution—John Hyde Preston; 1952	.50	1.50	2.50	NF
C26	Tap Roots—James Street	.40	1.20	2.00	
C27	The Confessions of St. Augustine—Aurelius Augustinus	.30	.90	1.50	
C28	Lives of Famous French Painters—Herman J. Wechsler	.40	1.20	2.00	NF
C29	The Pocket Book of Baby and Child Care—Benjamin Spock	.30	.90	1.50	NF
C30	The Way West—A. B. Guthrie, Jr.	.40	1.20	2.00	W
C31	The Man With the Golden Arm—Nelson Algren	.50	1.50	2.50	
	with dust jacket	10.00	30.00	50.00	
C32	The Loyalty of Free Men—Alan Barth	.40	1.20	2.00	
C33	Wuthering Heights—Emily Bronte	.40	1.20	2.00	
C34	Mutiny on the Bounty—James Norman Hall & Charles Nordhoff	.40	1.20	2.00	A
C35	A Tale of Two Cities—Charles Dickins	.40	1.20	2.00	
C36	Famous Chinese Short Stories—Lin Yutang	.40	1.20	2.00	
C37	Pride and Prejudice—Jane Austen	.40	1.20	2.00	
C38	The Witching Pool—Robert Presnell, Jr.	.40	1.20	2.00	
C39	Hour of Glory—Robert Lund	.40	1.20	2.00	
C40	The Disappearance—Philip Wylie	.40	1.20	2.00	
C41	The Conqueror—John Tebbel	.40	1.20	2.00	A
C42	The Return of the Native—Thomas Hardy	.40	1.20	2.00	
C43	Dawn's Early Light—Elswyth Thane	.40	1.20	2.00	
C44	Moll Flanders—Daniel Defoe	.40	1.20	2.00	
C45	Great Tales and Poems—Edgar Allan Poe	.40	1.20	2.00	
C46	Kinfolk—Pearl S. Buck	.40	1.20	2.00	
C47	Tess of the D'Urbervilles—Thomas Hardy	.40	1.20	2.00	
C48	The Great Short Stories of Robert Louis Stevenson	.40	1.20	2.00	
C49	Jubilee Trail—Gwen Bristow	.40	1.20	2.00	
C50	Immortal Poems of the English Language—Oscar Williams; 1952	.40	1.20	2.00	
C51	Abraham Lincoln—Lord Charnwood	.40	1.20	2.00	NF
C52	The Big Sky—A. B. Guthrie, Jr.	.40	1.20	2.00	W
C53	Rebecca—Daphne du Maurier	.30	.90	1.50	
C54	The Golden Hawk—Frank Yerby	.40	1.20	2.00	A
C55	The Complete Sonnets, Songs and Poems of Shakespeare—William Shakespeare	.40	1.20	2.00	
C56	Caroline Hicks—Walter Karig	.40	1.20	2.00	
C57	Three Harbours—F. Van Wyck Mason	.40	1.20	2.00	
C58	River of the Sun—James Ramsey Ullman	.40	1.20	2.00	
C59	Madame Bovary—Gustave Flaubert	.40	1.20	2.00	
C60	Buddenbrooks—Thomas Mann	.40	1.20	2.00	
C61	Questions and Answers From the Book of Knowledge—E. U. McLoughlin	.40	1.20	2.00	NF
C62	The Golden Ass of Apuleius—Madaurensis Apuleius	.40	1.20	2.00	
C63	Of Human Bondage—W. Somerset Maugham	.40	1.20	2.00	
C64	The Turquoise—Anya Seton	.40	1.20	2.00	
C65	The Scarlet Letter—Nathaniel Hawthorne	.40	1.20	2.00	
C66	Dialogues of Plato	.40	1.20	2.00	
C67	The Song of Bernadette—Franz Werfel	.40	1.20	2.00	
C68	The Parasites—Daphne du Maurier	.30	.90	1.50	
C69	The Foundling—Francis J. Spellman	.30	.90	1.50	
C70	Morning Journey—James Hilton	.40	1.20	2.00	
C71	The Cardinal—Henry Morton Robinson	.30	.90	1.50	
C72	The 42nd Parallel—John Dos Passos	.40	1.20	2.00	
C73	Passions Spin the Plot—Vardis Fisher; 1953	.40	1.20	2.00	

Cardinal Editions C31 (w/dj), © Pkb   Cardinal Editions C77, © Pkb   Cardinal Editions C226, © Pkb

(CARDINAL EDITIONS, continued)

		Good	Fine	N/Mint	
C74	Tomorrow We Reap—James Childers & James Street	.40	1.20	2.00	
C75	English Through Pictures - Book 1—Christine Gibson & I. A. Richards; 1953	.30	.90	1.50	NF
C76	The White Tower—James Ramsey Ullman	.40	1.20	2.00	
C77	My Six Convicts—Donald Powell Wilson	.40	1.20	2.00	
C78	French Through Pictures—I. A. Richards, others	.30	.90	1.50	NF
C79	Ivanhoe—Walter Scott	.40	1.20	2.00	A
C80	Discovery No. 1—John W. Aldridge & Vance Bourjaily	.30	.90	1.50	
C81	Dinner at Belmont—Alfred Leland Crabb	.40	1.20	2.00	
C82	Fight Against Fears—Lucy Freeman	.40	1.20	2.00	
C83	Spanish Through Pictures—I. A. Richards, others	.30	.90	1.50	NF
C84	The Producer—Richard Brooks	.40	1.20	2.00	
C85	The Southern Cook Book—Marion Brown	.30	.90	1.50	NF
C86	The 100 Most Important People of 1953—Donald Robinson	.30	.90	1.50	NF
C87	Floodtide—Frank Yerby	.40	1.20	2.00	A
C88	Jane Eyre—Charlotte Bronte	.40	1.20	2.00	
C89	The Ragged Ones—Burke Davis	.40	1.20	2.00	
C90	The Pocket Household Encyclopedia—N. H. Mager & S. K. Mager	.30	.90	1.50	NF
C91	A Stone for Danny Fisher—Harold Robbins	.30	.90	1.50	
C92	Look Away, Look Away—Leslie Turner White	.40	1.20	2.00	
C93	A Pocket Guide to the Trees—Rutherford Platt	.40	1.20	2.00	NF
C94	The Pocket Book of Robert Frost's Poems	.40	1.20	2.00	
C95	German Through Pictures—I. A. Richards, others	.30	.90	1.50	NF
C96	The Iron Mistress—Paul I. Wellman	.40	1.20	2.00	A
C97	The Earthbreakers—Ernest Haycox	.40	1.20	2.00	W
C98	The Pedlocks—Stephen Longstreet	.40	1.20	2.00	
C99	The King's General—Daphne du Maurier	.30	.90	1.50	
C100	Flesh and the Dream—George Williams; 1953	.30	.90	1.50	
C101	Devils, Drugs and Doctors—Howard H. Haggard	.30	.90	1.50	NF
C102	A Woman Called Fancy—Frank Yerby	.40	1.20	2.00	
C103	Yankee Stranger—Elswyth Thane	.40	1.20	2.00	
C104	The Imitation of Christ—Thomas A. Kempis	.40	1.20	2.00	
C105	Pavilion of Women—Pearl S. Buck	.40	1.20	2.00	
C106	Tales From the Decameron—Giovanni Boccaccio	.40	1.20	2.00	
C107	A Connecticut Yankee in King Arthur's Court—Mark Twain; 1954	.40	1.20	2.00	
C108	Come, My Beloved—Pearl S. Buck	.40	1.20	2.00	
C109	The Pocket Book of American Poems—Louis Untermeyer	.40	1.20	2.00	
C110	Lincoln McKeever—Eleazar Lipsky	.30	.90	1.50	
C111	The Good Earth—Pearl S. Buck	.40	1.20	2.00	
C112	How to Stop Worrying and Start Living—Dale Carnegie	.30	.90	1.50	NF
C113	Great Essays—Houston Peterson	.40	1.20	2.00	
C114	God's Men—Pearl S. Buck	.40	1.20	2.00	
C115	Discovery No. 2—Vance Bourjaily	.30	.90	1.50	
C116	Matthew Steel—Mildred Masterson McNeilly	.40	1.20	2.00	
C117	Captain Marooner—Louis B. Davidson & Eddie Doherty	.40	1.20	2.00	A
C118	Great Escapes—Basil Davenport	.40	1.20	2.00	
C119	We Are Betrayed—Vardis Fisher	.40	1.20	2.00	
C120	Giant—Edna Ferber; movie tie-in	.50	1.50	2.50	
C121	Young Ames—Walter D. Edmonds	.30	.90	1.50	
C122	The University of Chicago Spanish-English, English-Spanish Dictionary—Carlos Castillo	.30	.90	1.50	NF
C123	Yorktown—Burke Davis	.40	1.20	2.00	
C124	The Saracen Blade—Frank Yerby	.40	1.20	2.00	A
C125	Carol Curtis' Complete Book of Knitting and Crocheting—Carol Curtis; 1954	.30	.90	1.50	NF
C126	The Court of Last Resort—Erle Stanley Gardner	.30	.90	1.50	M
C127	Crimson Is the Eastern Shore—Don Tracy	.40	1.20	2.00	
C128	God's Angry Man—Leonard Ehrlich	.40	1.20	2.00	
C129	Marye Dahnke's Salad Book—Marye Dahnke	.30	.90	1.50	NF
C130	Discovery No. 3—Vance Bourjaily	.30	.90	1.50	

139

		Good	Fine	N/Mint	
C131	1919—John Dos Passos	.40	1.20	2.00	
C132	The Science Book of Wonder Drugs—Donald G. Cooley	.30	.90	1.50	NF
C133	Winston Churchill—Robert Lewis Taylor	.30	.90	1.50	NF
C134	Nana—Emile Zola	.30	.90	1.50	
C135	The Exploration of Space—Arthur C. Clarke	.40	1.20	2.00	NF
C136	The Border Lord—Jan Westcott	.40	1.20	2.00	
C137	The Strange Brigade—John Jennings	.50	1.50	2.50	A
C138	Pleasant Valley—Louis Bromfield	.40	1.20	2.00	
C139	The Adventures of Huckleberry Finn—Mark Twain	.40	1.20	2.00	
C140	The Smoldering Sea—U. S. Anderson	.40	1.20	2.00	
C141	Jubal Troop—Paul I. Wellman	.40	1.20	2.00	W
C142	The Devil's Laughter—Frank Yerby	.40	1.20	2.00	A
C143	Discovery No. 4—Vance Bourjaily	.30	.90	1.50	
C144	Night Light—Douglass Wallop	.40	1.20	2.00	
C145	Six Minutes a Day to Perfect Spelling—Harry Shefter	.30	.90	1.50	NF
C146	Call Me Lucky—Bing Crosby	.40	1.20	2.00	NF
C147	Hope for the Troubled—Lucy Freeman	.30	.90	1.50	
C148	Drawing Self-Taught—Arthur Zaidenberg	.30	.90	1.50	NF
C149	The Bandit and the Priest—Audrey Erskine Lindop	.40	1.20	2.00	
C150	Freud: His Dream and Sex Theories; 1954	.30	.90	1.50	NF
C151	The Chieftain—Robert Payne	.40	1.20	2.00	A
C152	The Pocket Book Magazine—Franklin Watts	.30	.90	1.50	
C153	My Cousin Rachel—Daphne du Maurier	.30	.90	1.50	
C154	The Story of the World—John van Duyn Southworth	.30	.90	1.50	NF
C155	A Minute of Prayer—Christopher Cross	.30	.90	1.50	
C156	Great Tales of Fantasy and Imagination—Philip Van Doren Stern	1.00	3.00	5.00	SF
C157	The Walsingham Woman—Jan Westcott; 1955	.40	1.20	2.00	
C158	The Pocket Book of Ogden Nash—Ogden Nash	.30	.90	1.50	
C159	Discovery No. 5—Vance Bourjaily	.30	.90	1.50	
C160	The Pocket Book Magazine No. 2—Franklin Watts	.30	.90	1.50	
C161	The Razor's Edge—W. Somerset Maugham	.40	1.20	2.00	
C162	The Kingpin—Tom Wickes	.40	1.20	2.00	
C163	The Silent World—Jacques-Yves Cousteau & Frederic Dumas	.40	1.20	2.00	NF
C164	Ever After—Elswyth Thane	.40	1.20	2.00	
C165	Golden Admiral—F. Van Wyck Mason	.40	1.20	2.00	A
C166	Six Weeks to Words of Power—Wilfred Funk	.40	1.20	2.00	NF
C167	The 1955 Baseball Almanac—Hy Turkin	.50	1.50	2.50	S
C168	Kiss Me Again, Stranger—Daphne du Maurier	.30	.90	1.50	
C169	Sex and the Nature of Things—N. J. Berrill	.30	.90	1.50	NF
C170	Hebrew Through Pictures—I. A. Richards	.40	1.20	2.00	NF
C171	Hebrew Reader—I. A. Richards, others	.40	1.20	2.00	NF
C172	Silver Street Woman—Les Savage, Jr.	.40	1.20	2.00	
C173	N. Y., N. Y.—Will Oursler	.30	.90	1.50	
C174	The Science Book of the Human Body—Edith E. Sproul	.30	.90	1.50	NF
C175	The Vixens—Frank Yerby; 1955	.40	1.20	2.00	
C176	Disputed Passage—Lloyd C. Douglas	.40	1.20	2.00	
C177	No Villain Need Be—Vardis Fisher	.40	1.20	2.00	
C178	Sir Rogue—Leslie Turner White	.50	1.50	2.50	A
C179	A Marriage Manual—Hannah Stone & Abraham Stone	.30	.90	1.50	NF
C180	Your Own Book of Camp Craft—Catherine T. Hammett	.30	.90	1.50	NF
C181	The Pocket Cook Book—Elizabeth Woody	.30	.90	1.50	NF
C182	Sign of the Pagan—Roger Fuller	.40	1.20	2.00	A
C183	A Subtreasury of American Humor—E. B. White & Katherine S. White	.40	1.20	2.00	
C184	Diane—Herbert Best	.30	.90	1.50	
C185	Discovery No. 6—Vance Bourjaily	.30	.90	1.50	
C186	How to Make More Money—Marvin Small	.30	.90	1.50	NF
C187	The Blackboard Jungle—Evan Hunter	.50	1.50	2.50	
C188	The Duncan Hines Dessert Book—Duncan Hines	.30	.90	1.50	NF
C189	Roanoke Renegade—Don Tracy	.40	1.20	2.00	
C190	Short Cuts to Effective English—Harry Shefter	.30	.90	1.50	NF
C191	Aboard the Flying Swan—Stanley Wolpert	.40	1.20	2.00	
C192	Lord Grizzly—Frederick Manfred	.40	1.20	2.00	W
C193	Best-Seller Digest No. 1	.30	.90	1.50	
C194	American Captain—Edison Marshall	.40	1.20	2.00	A
C195	The French Quarter—Herbert Asbury	.50	1.50	2.50	
C196	The Compact Treasury of Inspiration—Kenneth S. Giniger	.30	.90	1.50	
C197	Buccaneer Surgeon—C. V. Terry	.40	1.20	2.00	A
C198	The Gown of Glory—Agnes Sligh Turnball	.40	1.20	2.00	
C199	The Toastmaster's and Speaker's Handbook—Herbert V. Prochnow	.30	.90	1.50	NF
C200	The Pocket Book Magazine No. 3—Franklin Watts; 1955	.30	.90	1.50	
C201	Italian Through Pictures—I. A. Richards; 1956	.30	.90	1.50	NF
C202	Never Victorious, Never Defeated—Taylor Caldwell	.40	1.20	2.00	
C203	The Last Hunt—Milton Lott	.40	1.20	2.00	W
C204	The Adventures—Ernest Haycox	.40	1.20	2.00	W
C205	Have Tux, Will Travel—Bob Hope	.30	.90	1.50	H
C206	Ann Pillsbury's Baking Book—Ann Pillsbury	.30	.90	1.50	NF

		Good	Fine	N/Mint	
C207	The Science Book of Space Travel—Harold Leland Goodwin	.40	1.20	2.00	NF
C208	Benton's Row—Frank Yerby	.40	1.20	2.00	A
C209	The Virginian—Owen Wister	.40	1.20	2.00	W
C210	Somebody Up There Likes Me—Rowland Barber & Rocky Graziano	.50	1.50	2.50	
C211	Blue Hurricane—F. Van Wyck Mason	.40	1.20	2.00	
C212	The 1956 Baseball Almanac—Don Schiffer	.50	1.50	2.50	S
C213	The Long Goodbye—Raymond Chandler	.50	1.50	2.50	M
C214	Bless This House—Norah Lofts	.40	1.20	2.00	
C215	The Gadget Maker—Maxwell Griffith	.40	1.20	2.00	
C216	Mary Anne—Daphne du Maurier	.30	.90	1.50	
C217	Big Business: A New Era—David E. Lilienthal	.30	.90	1.50	NF
C218	The Man From Mesabi—Sarah Lockwood	.40	1.20	2.00	
C219	79 Park Avenue—Harold Robbins	.30	.90	1.50	
C220	Katrina—Jeramie Price	.40	1.20	2.00	
C221	"Before I Kill More. . ."—Lucy Freeman	.40	1.20	2.00	
C222	Anna and the King of Siam—Margaret Landon	.40	1.20	2.00	
C223	The Great Man—Al Morgan	.40	1.20	2.00	
C224	My Brother's Keeper—Marcia Davenport	.40	1.20	2.00	
C225	The Lost Eagles—Ralph Graves; 1956	.40	1.20	2.00	
C226	Tales of the South Pacific—James A. Michener	.40	1.20	2.00	
C227	Roxana—Marian Castle	.40	1.20	2.00	
C228	Carolina Corsair—Don Tracy	.40	1.20	2.00	A
C229	The View From Pompey's Head—Hamilton Basso	.30	.90	1.50	
C230	The Man in the Gray Flannel Suit—Sloan Wilson	.30	.90	1.50	
C231	The U. P. Trail—Zane Grey	.40	1.20	2.00	W
C232	The Complete Guide to Home Sewing—S. K. Mager; 1957	.30	.90	1.50	NF
C233	The Gentleman—Edison Marshall	.40	1.20	2.00	A
C234	The Last Temptation—Joseph Viertel	.40	1.20	2.00	
C235	Heritage—Anthony West	.40	1.20	2.00	
C236	Quartet in "H"—Evan Hunter	.40	1.20	2.00	
C237	How to Develop Self-Confidence—Dale Carnegie	.30	.90	1.50	NF
C238	Profiles in Courage—John F. Kennedy	.40	1.20	2.00	NF
C239	The Border Legion—Zane Grey	.40	1.20	2.00	W
C240	Forgive Us Our Trespasses—Lloyd C. Douglas	.40	1.20	2.00	
C241	The Golden Journey—Agnes Sligh Turnbull	.40	1.20	2.00	
C242	Silver Leopard—F. Van Wyck Mason	.40	1.20	2.00	
C243	The Quick Cook Book—Lois S. Kellogg	.30	.90	1.50	NF
C244	The Wanderer—Mika Waltari	.40	1.20	2.00	
C245	Tender Victory—Taylor Caldwell	.40	1.20	2.00	
C246	The Winged Sword—Leslie Turner White	.40	1.20	2.00	
C247	The Sudden Strangers—William E. Barrett	.40	1.20	2.00	
C248	Will Acting Spoil Marilyn Monroe?—Pete Martin	4.00	12.00	20.00	NF
C249	Captain Rebel—Frank Yerby	.40	1.20	2.00	A
C250	Hilda Manning—Allan Seager; 1957	.40	1.20	2.00	
C251	The Barbary Coast—Herbert Asbury	.50	1.50	2.50	
C252	Dynasty of Death—Taylor Caldwell	.40	1.20	2.00	
C253	Pemmican—Vardis Fisher	.40	1.20	2.00	A
C254	Deluxe Tour—Frederic Wakeman	.40	1.20	2.00	
C255	Mary—Sholem Asch	.30	.90	1.50	
C256	First Steps in Reading English—Christine Gibson & I. A. Richards	.30	.90	1.50	NF
C257	Magnificent Obsession—Lloyd C. Douglas	.40	1.20	2.00	
C258	English Through Pictures - Book 2—Christine Gibson & I. A. Richards	.30	.90	1.50	NF
C259	A First Workbook of French—I. A. Richards	.30	.90	1.50	NF
C260	How to Work With Tools & Wood—Fred Gross	.40	1.20	2.00	NF
C261	The Painted Veil—W. Somerset Maugham	.40	1.20	2.00	
C262	The Swordsman—Jefferson Cooper	.50	1.50	2.50	A
C263	The Dark Angel—Mika Waltari	.40	1.20	2.00	
C264	The Drift Fence—Zane Grey	.40	1.20	2.00	W
C265	The World's Best Recipes—Marvin Small	.30	.90	1.50	NF
C266	Jenny—Ada Cook Lewis	.30	.90	1.50	
C267	These Thousand Hills—A. B. Guthrie, Jr.	.40	1.20	2.00	
C268	The Case of the Sun-Bather's Diary—Erle Stanley Gardner	.30	.90	1.50	M
C269	Green Light—Lloyd C. Douglas	.30	.90	1.50	
C270	The Pocket Book of Erskine Caldwell Stories—E. Caldwell	.40	1.20	2.00	
C271	Canton Barrier—Andrew Geer; 1958	.40	1.20	2.00	
C272	The Voice at the Back Door—Elizabeth Spencer	.40	1.20	2.00	
C273	The Magician—W. Somerset Maugham	.40	1.20	2.00	
C274	The Strong City—Taylor Caldwell	.40	1.20	2.00	
C275	The Case of the Terrified Typist—Erle Stanley Gardner; 1958	.30	.90	1.50	M
C276	The Scapegoat—Daphne du Maurier	.30	.90	1.50	
C277	Chance Elson—W. T. Ballard	.50	1.50	2.50	
C278	Jericho's Daughters—Paul I. Wellman	.40	1.20	2.00	
C279	The Prosecuter—Bernard Botein	.40	1.20	2.00	
C280	The Innocent Ambassadors—Philip Wylie	.40	1.20	2.00	
C281	The Case of the Runaway Corpse—Erle Stanley Gardner	.30	.90	1.50	M
C282	The Case of the Glamorous Ghost—Erle Stanley Gardner	.30	.90	1.50	M

		Good	Fine	N/Mint	
C283	The Case of the Half-Wakened Wife—Erle Stanley Gardner	.30	.90	1.50	M
C284	The Case of the Empty Tin—Erle Stanley Gardner	.30	.90	1.50	M
C285	The Case of the Lazy Lover—Erle Stanley Gardner	.30	.90	1.50	M
C286	Cast the First Stone—Sara Harris & John M. Murtagh	.30	.90	1.50	
C287	The Etruscan—Mika Waltari	.40	1.20	2.00	A
C288	The Hidden Persuaders—Vance Packard	.30	.90	1.50	
C289	Basketball—Arnold ''Red'' Auerbach	.50	1.50	2.50	S
C290	The Promoters—Stephen Longstreet	.40	1.20	2.00	
C291	The D.A. Calls a Turn—Erle Stanley Gardner	.30	.90	1.50	M
C292	The D.A. Breaks a Seal—Erle Stanley Gardner	.30	.90	1.50	M
C293	The D.A. Takes a Chance—Erle Stanley Gardner	.30	.90	1.50	M
C294	The D.A. Breaks an Egg—Erle Stanley Gardner	.30	.90	1.50	M
C295	The D.A. Calls It Murder—Erle Stanley Gardner	.30	.90	1.50	M
C296	Halfway Down the Stairs—Charles Thompson	.40	1.20	2.00	
C297	The Case of the Nervous Accomplice—Erle Stanley Gardner	.30	.90	1.50	M
C298	No Down Payment—John McPartland	.40	1.20	2.00	
C299	The Case of the Careless Kitten—Erle Stanley Gardner	.30	.90	1.50	M
C300	Cherokee—Don Tracy; 1958	.40	1.20	2.00	
C301	Riders of Judgement—Frederick Manfred	.40	1.20	2.00	
C302	The Case of the Crooked Candle—Erle Stanley Gardner	.30	.90	1.50	M
C303	How to Win Friends and Influence People—Dale Carnegie	.30	.90	1.50	NF
C304	Care and Training of Dogs—Arthur Frederick Jones	.40	1.20	2.00	NF
C305	Monsieur Yankee—Leslie Turner White	.40	1.20	2.00	A
C306	Cast of Characters—Al Morgan	.40	1.20	2.00	
C307	The Case of the Forgotten Murder—Erle Stanley Gardner	.30	.90	1.50	M
C308	Letter From Peking—Pearl S. Buck	.40	1.20	2.00	
C309	The Case of the Sulky Girl—Erle Stanley Gardner	.30	.90	1.50	M
C310	Fairoaks—Frank Yerby	.40	1.20	2.00	
C311	The Final Hour—Taylor Caldwell	.40	1.20	2.00	
C312	Remembered Death—Agatha Christie	.40	1.20	2.00	M
C313	Cash McCall—Cameron Hawley	.40	1.20	2.00	
C314	A Parent's Guide to Children's Reading—Nancy Larrick	.30	.90	1.50	NF
C315	Kings Go Forth—Joe David Brown	.40	1.20	2.00	
C316	Odds Against Tomorrow—William P. McGivern	.40	1.20	2.00	
C317	The Diary of a Young Girl—Anne Frank	.30	.90	1.50	
C318	What Mrs. McGillicuddy Saw!—Agatha Christie	.40	1.20	2.00	M
C319	New Tales of Space and Time—Raymond J. Healy; 1959	.40	1.20	2.00	NF
C320	The Case of the One-Eyed Witness—Erle Stanley Gardner	.30	.90	1.50	M
C321	On the Midnight Tide—Don Tracy	.40	1.20	2.00	
C322	To Have and to Hold—Mary Johnston	.40	1.20	2.00	
C323	The Case of the Demure Defendant—Erle Stanley Gardner	.30	.90	1.50	M
C324	The Case of the Curious Bride—Erle Stanley Gardner	.30	.90	1.50	M
C325	The Case of the Haunted Husband—Erle Stanley Gardner; 1959	.30	.90	1.50	M
C326	Jamaica Inn—Daphne du Maurier	.30	.90	1.50	
C327	''Where Did Yoo Go?'' ''Out'' ''What Did You Do?'' ''Nothing''—Robert Paul Smith	.30	.90	1.50	
C328	The Year the Yankees Lost the Pennant—Douglass Wallop	.30	.90	1.50	
C329	The Case of the Lucky Legs—Erle Stanley Gardner	.30	.90	1.50	M
C330	Kids Say the Darndest Things!—Art Linkletter	.30	.90	1.50	H
C331	The Pocket Book of Esquire Cartoons	1.60	4.80	8.00	H
C332	The Case of the Cautious Coquette—Erle Stanley Gardner	.30	.90	1.50	M
C333	The Trail Driver—Zane Grey	.40	1.20	2.00	W
C334	The Angry Wife—Pearl S. Buck	.40	1.20	2.00	
C335	Death Comes As the End—Agatha Christie	.40	1.20	2.00	M
C336	White Banners—Lloyd C. Douglas	.30	.90	1.50	
C337	The Case of the Gilded Lily—Erle Stanley Gardner	.30	.90	1.50	M
C338	The Immortal—Walter Ross	.40	1.20	2.00	
C339	Dragonwyck—Anya Seton	.40	1.20	2.00	
C340	The Man Who Broke Things—John Brooks	.40	1.20	2.00	
C341	Case of the Lucky Loser—Erle Stanley Gardner	.30	.90	1.50	M
C342	Young Mr. Keefe—Stephen Birmingham	.40	1.20	2.00	
C343	The Finishing Stroke—Ellery Queen	.40	1.20	2.00	M
C344	The Lady in the Lake—Raymond Chandler	.50	1.50	2.50	M
C345	The D.A. Cooks a Goose—Erle Stanley Gardner	.30	.90	1.50	M
C346	The D.A. Draws a Circle—Erle Stanley Gardner	.30	.90	1.50	M
C347	The D.A. Goes to Trial—Erle Stanley Gardner	.30	.90	1.50	M
C348	The D.A. Holds a Candle—Erle Stanley Gardner	.30	.90	1.50	M
C349	Peril at End House—Agatha Christie	.40	1.20	2.00	M
C350	A Gift From the Boys—Art Buchwald; 1959	.30	.90	1.50	
C351	Valley of Wild Horses—Zane Grey	.40	1.20	2.00	W
C352	The Serpent and the Staff—Frank Yerby	.40	1.20	2.00	A
C353	The Nine Lives of Michael Todd—Art Cohn	.40	1.20	2.00	NF
C354					
C355	The Case of the Vagabond Virgin—Erle Stanley Gardner	.30	.90	1.50	M
C356	Dear Abby—Abigail Van Buren	.30	.90	1.50	NF
C357	Cat of Many Tails—Ellery Queen	.40	1.20	2.00	M
C358	Power Golf—Ben Hogan	.30	.90	1.50	S

		Good	Fine	N/Mint	
	(CARDINAL EDITIONS, continued)				
C359	The Low Calorie Diet—Marvin Small	.30	.90	1.50	NF
C360	And Then There Were None—Agatha Christie	.40	1.20	2.00	M
C361	Towards Zero—Agatha Christie	.40	1.20	2.00	M
C362	A Murder Is Announced—Agatha Christie	.40	1.20	2.00	M
C363	Lady Chatterley's Lover—D. H. Lawrence	.40	1.20	2.00	
C364	The 1959 Pro Football Handbook—Don Schiffer	.50	1.50	2.50	S
C365	Return of the Eagles—F. Van Wyck Mason	.30	.90	1.50	
C366					
C367	The Foxes of Harrow—Frank Yerby	.30	.90	1.50	
C368	Lucky Larribee—Max Brand	.40	1.20	2.00	W
C369	Lady L—Romain Gary	.40	1.20	2.00	
C370	Action by Night—Ernest Haycox	.40	1.20	2.00	W
C371	Gazella—Stuart Cloete	.30	.90	1.50	
C372	The Long Love—Pearl S. Buck	.40	1.20	2.00	
C373	The Crossing—Clay Fisher	.40	1.20	2.00	W
C374	The Scientists—Eleazar Lipsky	.30	.90	1.50	NF
C375	Playback—Raymond Chandler	.50	1.50	2.50	M
C376	The Case of the Dubious Bridegroom—Erle Stanley Gardner	.30	.90	1.50	M
C391	Third Man on the Mountain—James R. Ullman; 1959	.40	1.20	2.00	A

CARDINAL EDITIONS GC-SERIES
Pocket Books, Inc.

		Good	Fine	N/Mint	
GC 1	The Cardinal—Henry Morton Robinson; 1953	.30	.90	1.50	
GC 2	Three Harbours—F. Van Wyck Mason	.40	1.20	2.00	
GC 3	Buddenbrooks—Thomas Mann	.40	1.20	2.00	
GC 4	The Story of Philosophy—Will Durant	.30	.90	1.50	NF
GC 5	The Story of Mankind—Hendrik Willem Van Loon	.30	.90	1.50	NF
GC 6	Stars on the Sea—F. Van Wyck Mason	.40	1.20	2.00	
GC 7	Langenscheidt's German-English, English-German Dictionary	.30	.90	1.50	NF
GC 8	Oh, Promised Land—James Street	.40	1.20	2.00	
GC 9	Eagle in the Sky—F. Van Wyck Mason	.40	1.20	2.00	
GC10	The Cruel Sea—Nicholas Monsarrat	.40	1.20	2.00	
GC11	Napoleon—Emil Ludwig; 1954	.40	1.20	2.00	NF
GC12	The Wall—John Hersey	.40	1.20	2.00	
GC13	The Office Encyclopedia—N. H. Mager & S. K. Mager	.30	.90	1.50	NF
GC14	The Devil Rides Outside—John Howard Griffin	.40	1.20	2.00	
GC15	Immortal Poems of the English Language—Oscar Williams	.40	1.20	2.00	
GC16	The Pocket Book of Modern Verse—Oscar Williams	.40	1.20	2.00	
GC17	Proud New Flags—F. Van Wyck Mason	.40	1.20	2.00	
GC18	The Pocket Guide to Birds—Allen D. Cruickshank	.50	1.50	2.50	NF
GC19	The Pocket Household Encyclopedia—N. H. Mager & S. K. Mager	.30	.90	1.50	NF
GC20	The Female—Paul I. Wellman	.40	1.20	2.00	
GC21	Marie Antoinette—Stefan Zweig	.40	1.20	2.00	
GC22	Desiree—Annemarie Selinko	.40	1.20	2.00	
GC23	The Lincoln Reader—Abraham Lincoln; 1955	.40	1.20	2.00	
GC24	Larousse's French-English, English-French Dictionary	.30	.90	1.50	NF
GC25	The Whitman Reader—Walt Whitman; 1955	.40	1.20	2.00	
GC26	The Big Money—John Dos Passos	.40	1.20	2.00	
GC27	Understanding Surgery—Robert E. Rothenberg	.40	1.20	2.00	NF
GC28	Youngblood—John O. Killens	.40	1.20	2.00	
GC29	An Act of Love—Ira Wolfert	.40	1.20	2.00	
GC30	The Doctors Mayo—Helen Clapesattle; 1956	.30	.90	1.50	NF
GC31	The Egyptian—Mika Waltari	.40	1.20	2.00	A
GC32	Love Is Eternal—Irving Stone	.30	.90	1.50	
GC33	A Baby's First Year—Benjamin Spock	.30	.90	1.50	NF
GC34	The Adventurer—Mika Waltari	.40	1.20	2.00	
GC35	My Several Worlds—Pearl S. Buck	.40	1.20	2.00	
GC36	The Nazarene—Sholem Asch	.40	1.20	2.00	
GC37	The Search for Bridey Murphy—Morey Bernstein	.40	1.20	2.00	
GC38	The Apostle—Sholem Asch	.40	1.20	2.00	
GC39	Masters of Deceit—J. Edgar Hoover	.30	.90	1.50	
GC40	Baby and Child Care—Benjamin Spock	.30	.90	1.50	NF
GC41	Imperial Woman—Pearl S. Buck; 1958	.40	1.20	2.00	
GC42	King of Paris—Guy Endore	.40	1.20	2.00	A
GC43	Moses—Sholem Asch	.40	1.20	2.00	
GC44	Language for Everybody—Mario Pei	.40	1.20	2.00	NF
GC45	The FBI Story—Don Whitehead; movie tie-in	.40	1.20	2.00	
GC46	The Townsman—Pearl S. Buck	.40	1.20	2.00	
GC47	Mondadori's Pocket Italian-English, English-Italian Dictionary—Alberto Tedeschi	.30	.90	1.50	NF
GC48	A Stillness at Appomattox—Bruce Catton	.40	1.20	2.00	NF
GC49	The Prophet—Sholem Asch	.40	1.20	2.00	
GC50	Faster Reading Self-Taught—Harry Shefter; 1958	.30	.90	1.50	NF
GC51	The Family of Man—Edward Steichen	.40	1.20	2.00	
GC52	Baruch: My Own Story—Bernard Baruch	.30	.90	1.50	NF
GC53	The Robe—Lloyd C. Douglas	.40	1.20	2.00	

		Good	Fine	N/Mint	
GC54	The Nun's Story—Kathryn Hulme	.30	.90	1.50	
GC55	Kings Row—Henry Bellamann	.40	1.20	2.00	
GC56	Strangers When We Meet—Evan Hunter; 1959	.40	1.20	2.00	
GC57	Madame Curie—Eve Curie	.40	1.20	2.00	NF
GC58	The Kodak Camera Guide	.40	1.20	2.00	NF
GC59	The Big Fisherman—Lloyd C. Douglas	.40	1.20	2.00	
GC60	Diccionario del Idiona Espanol—Edwin B. Williams	.30	.90	1.50	NF
GC61	The Roots of Heaven—Romain Gary	.40	1.20	2.00	
GC62	Generation of Vipers—Philip Wylie	.30	.90	1.50	
GC63	Justine—Lawrence Durrell	.40	1.20	2.00	
GC64	Sailor on Horseback—Jack London	.40	1.20	2.00	A
GC65	A Summer Place—Sloan Wilson	.40	1.20	2.00	
GC66	Madison Avenue, U.S.A.—Martin Mayer	.30	.90	1.50	
GC67	High-Speed Math Self-Taught—Lester Meyers	.30	.90	1.50	NF
GC68	The Best of Everything—Rona Jaffe	.30	.90	1.50	
GC69	The Stars in the Making—Cecilia Payne-Gaposchkin	.40	1.20	2.00	
GC70	Devils, Drugs and Doctors—Howard W. Haggard	.30	.90	1.50	NF
GC71					
GC72	Parrish—Mildred Savage	.40	1.20	2.00	
GC73	The Day Christ Died—Jim Bishop	.40	1.20	2.00	
GC74	Compulsion—Meyer Levin	.40	1.20	2.00	
GC75	Ben-Hur—Lew Wallace; 1959	.40	1.20	2.00	A
GC76	Microbe Hunters—Paul De Kruif	.30	.90	1.50	NF
GC77	The Winthrop Woman—Anya Seton; 1953	.40	1.20	2.00	
GC81	Tale of Valor—Vardis Fisher	.40	1.20	2.00	A
GC99	Balthazar—Lawrence Durrell	.40	1.20	2.00	
nn	The 1954 Pocket Almanac; 1954	.30	.90	1.50	NF
GC1955	The 1955 Pocket Almanac; 1955	.30	.90	1.50	NF
GC1956	The 1956 Pocket Almanac; 1956	.30	.90	1.50	NF
GC750	The English-Portuguese Pocket Dictionary—Hygino Aliandro	.30	.90	1.50	NF
GC751	Cash McCall—Cameron Hawley; 1957	.40	1.20	2.00	
GC752	Katherine—Anya Seton	.40	1.20	2.00	
GC753	Something of Value—Robert Ruark	.40	1.20	2.00	
GC754	1958	.40	1.20	2.00	
GC755	The Tribe That Lost Its Head—Nicholas Monsarrat	.30	.90	1.50	
GC756	Compulsion—Meyer Levin; 1959	.30	.90	1.50	
GC757	The Last Angry Man—Gerald Green	.40	1.20	2.00	

CARNIVAL
Hanro Corporation

Digest Size

901	A Body to Own—Robert W. Harmon; 1952, aka Pickup, aka Sacrifice	1.00	3.00	5.00	E
902	Midnight Sinners—John Caldwall	1.00	3.00	5.00	E
903	Lovers Bewitched—William E. Gordon; aka Frenchy	1.00	3.00	5.00	E
904	Borrowed Ecstasy—Watkins E. Wright; aka Wild Passion	1.00	3.00	5.00	E
905	Strangers in the Dark—Peggy Gaddis; aka Pushover, c-Gross	1.00	3.00	5.00	E
906	A Lover for Anne—Sylvia Erskine; aka Men Call Her "Tramp," c-Gross	1.00	3.00	5.00	E
907	Tempting Tigress—John Underwood; aka Bedtime Blonde	1.00	3.00	5.00	E
908	Girl-Hungry—William E. Gordon; aka The Transgressor	1.00	3.00	5.00	E
909	The Girl From Mimi's—Joan Tucker; aka Girl on the Make	1.00	3.00	5.00	E
910	Pick-Up—Albert L. Quandt; aka Ticket to Passion	1.00	3.00	5.00	E
911	Affairs of a Ward Nurse—Mitchell Coleman; aka Born to Be Bad	1.00	3.00	5.00	E
912	Wild Party—Frederic Spencer	1.00	3.00	5.00	E
913	Affairs of a Career Girl—Mitchell Coleman; 1953, aka Fast, Loose, and Lovely, c-Gross	1.00	3.00	5.00	E
914	Girl of the Slums—Raymond Blair	1.00	3.00	5.00	E

Carnival 904, © Hanro

Carnival 914, © Hanro

Carnival 918, © Hanro

Cavalcade 2, © Delta

Century 26, © Cen

Century 29, © Cen

(CARNIVAL, continued)		Good	Fine	N/Mint	
915	Lost to Desire—Peggy Gaddis	1.00	3.00	5.00	E
916	Passion's Harvest—Peggy Gaddis; aka Woman of Fire, c-Gross	1.00	3.00	5.00	E
917	Frenchie	1.00	3.00	5.00	E
918	Rapture Alley—Whit Harrison (Harry Whittington); 1953	2.00	6.00	10.00	E
919	City Hotel	1.00	3.00	5.00	E
920	Hotel Waitress—Gene Harvey	1.00	3.00	5.00	E
922	City of Sin—Robert O. Saber	1.00	3.00	5.00	E
923	Sinners Club—Harry Whittington; aka Teenage Jungle	1.00	3.00	5.00	E
924	Pick-Up—Albert L. Quandt; 1954, aka Ticket to Passion	1.00	3.00	5.00	E
925	Reckless!—Kermit Welles; aka Pleasure Bound	1.00	3.00	5.00	E
928	Frenchie—David Charlson	1.00	3.00	5.00	E
930	Social Club—Albert L. Quandt	1.00	3.00	5.00	E
931	Backwoods Shack—Hallam Whitney (Harry Whittington)	1.00	3.00	5.00	E
935	Girl-Hungry—William E. Gordon; aka The Transgressor	1.00	3.00	5.00	E
937	Boy Chaser—Kate Nickerson	1.00	3.00	5.00	E
942	City of Sin—Robert O. Saber	1.00	3.00	5.00	E
956	Big-Town Hellcat—Amos Hatter; aka On Borrowed Love	1.00	3.00	5.00	E
957	Boy Chaser—Kate Nickerson	1.00	3.00	5.00	E

CAVALCADE
Delta Library, Inc.

Digest Size

nn	Madman on a Drum	.80	2.40	4.00	M
1	Men Are Molehills—Ruth S. Livingston; 1946	.80	2.40	4.00	R
2	Magic for Murder—Armstrong Livingston	.80	2.40	4.00	M

CENTURY
Century Publications

Some Digest Size

10	The Man Who Murdered Himself—Geoffrey Holmes; digest size	1.60	4.80	8.00	M
11	Outlaws Three	1.20	3.60	6.00	W
12	Murder Without Makeup—Elda Benjamin; digest size	1.20	3.60	6.00	M
13	Here Comes the Corpse—George Bagby; digest size	1.20	3.60	6.00	M
14	Diagnosis: Murder—Rufus King; digest size	1.60	4.80	8.00	M
15	Ghost Trails—W. C. Tuttle; digest size	1.20	3.60	6.00	W
16	Renegade Roundup—William Colt MacDonald; digest size	1.20	3.60	6.00	W
17	As Good As Murdered—James O'Hanlon	1.20	3.60	6.00	M
18	Stab in the Back—Philip Wylie				
	Bottom Deal—Judson Philips; digest size	1.60	4.80	8.00	M
19	Fair Warning—Mignon G. Eberhart	1.60	4.80	8.00	M
20	Gun Bulldogger—Eugene Cunningham; digest size	1.20	3.60	6.00	M
21	The Sulu Sea Murders—Van Wyck Mason; digest size	1.60	4.80	8.00	M
22	Trigger Vengeance—John Trace	1.20	3.60	6.00	W
23	Death Came Dancing—Kathleen Moore Knight; digest size	1.60	4.80	8.00	M
24	The Trail of Gold—Dane Coolidge	1.20	3.60	6.00	W
25	Time Off for Murder—Zelda Popkin	1.20	3.60	6.00	M
26	Fallen Angel—Marty Holland; movie tie-in	1.60	4.80	8.00	E
27	Picture of the Victim—John S. Strange; digest size	1.60	4.80	8.00	M
28	Bad for Business—Rex Stout	1.60	4.80	8.00	M
29	All Concerned Notified—Helen Reilly	1.20	3.60	6.00	M
30	Weekend to Kill—Frederick Nebel				
	Secret Corridors—Hugh Pentecost; digest size	1.60	4.80	8.00	M
31	The Dark Corner—Leonard Q. Ross; movie tie-in	1.60	4.80	8.00	M

Century 32, © Cen

Century 50, © Cen

Century 51, © Cen

(CENTURY, continued)

		Good	Fine	N/Mint	
32	The Shanghai Bund Murders—Van Wyck Mason; digest size	3.00	9.00	15.00	M
33	Corpses at Indian Stone—Philip Wylie; digest size	1.20	3.60	6.00	M
34	Red Gardenias—Jonathan Latimer; digest size	1.20	3.60	6.00	M
35	The Glass Slipper—Mignon Eberhardt; digest size	1.20	3.60	6.00	M
37	Singapore—William Bogert; movie tie-in, digest size	2.00	6.00	10.00	M
50	Dead Freight for Piute—Luke Short	1.00	3.00	5.00	W
51	Dust of the Trail—Bennett Foster	1.00	3.00	5.00	W
52	No Nice Girl—Perry Lindsay (Peggy Gaddis)	1.00	3.00	5.00	E
52	Danger on the Border—Frederick R. Bechdolt	1.00	3.00	5.00	W
53	Death Rides the Mesa—Tom Gill	1.00	3.00	5.00	W
54	Scarlet Sin—John Saxon	1.00	3.00	5.00	E
55	Love Business—William Arthur	1.00	3.00	5.00	E
55	Don Desperado—L. L. Foreman	1.00	3.00	5.00	W
56	The Phantom Pass—William Colt MacDonald	1.00	3.00	5.00	W
56	Cue for Passion—Gordon Semple	1.00	3.00	5.00	E
57	Buckskin Empire—H. S. Drago	1.00	3.00	5.00	W
58	Gringo Gunfire—Bliss Lomax (H. S. Drago); digest size	1.00	3.00	5.00	W
59	Secret of the Wasteland—Bliss Lomax	1.00	3.00	5.00	W
nn(60)	Peace Marshal—Frank Gruber	1.00	3.00	5.00	W
61	One More Lover—Thomas Stone	1.00	3.00	5.00	E
61	Roaring Lead—William Colt MacDonald	1.00	3.00	5.00	W
62	Colt Comrades—Bliss Lomax (H. S. Drago)	1.00	3.00	5.00	W
nn(63)	Body and Soul—Sam Merwin, Jr.; movie tie-in, digest size	2.00	6.00	10.00	
64	Outlaw—Frank Gruber	1.00	3.00	5.00	W
66	Sleep My Love—Leonard Q. Ross; movie tie-in	1.00	3.00	5.00	E
67	No Nice Girl—Perry Lindsay (Peggy Gaddis)	1.00	3.00	5.00	E
68	A Double Life—Manly Wade Wellman; movie tie-in	3.00	9.00	15.00	
69	California Caballero—William Colt MacDonald	1.00	3.00	5.00	W
nn(70)	Cairo Garter Murders—Van Wyck Mason	1.00	3.00	5.00	M
71	Sign of the Gun—Archie Joscelyn	1.00	3.00	5.00	W
72	Gunsight—Frank Gruber	1.00	3.00	5.00	W
73	Saddles West—H. B. Hickey	1.00	3.00	5.00	W
74	Notched Guns—William Hopson	1.00	3.00	5.00	W
75	Scarlet Sin—John Saxon	1.00	3.00	5.00	E
76	Powdersmoke Range—W. C. MacDonald	1.00	3.00	5.00	W
77	Blonde Trouble—Perry Lindsay (Peggy Gaddis)	1.00	3.00	5.00	E
78	Gunsmoke—Lee Floren	1.00	3.00	5.00	W
79	Love Business—William Arthur	1.00	3.00	5.00	E
80	Cue for Passion—Gordon Semple	1.00	3.00	5.00	E
81	Drygulch Canyon—F. M. Bechdolt; digest size	1.00	3.00	5.00	W

Century 55, © Cen

Century 58, © Cen

Century 102, © Cen

Century 116, © Cen

Century 120, © Cen

Century 135, © Cen

(CENTURY, continued)

		Good	Fine	N/Mint	
82	Ranger Justice—J. E. Grinstead	1.00	3.00	5.00	W
83	Ripe for Love—Carmen Snow	1.00	3.00	5.00	E
84	Marriage Is for Two—Phyllis Arthur	1.00	3.00	5.00	E
85	Unashamed—Perry Lindsay	1.00	3.00	5.00	E
86	Bad Company—Gordon Semple	1.00	3.00	5.00	E
87	One More Lover—Thomas Stone	1.00	3.00	5.00	E
89	Common Passion—John Saxon	1.00	3.00	5.00	E
90	Too Loose—Carlotta Baker	1.00	3.00	5.00	E
91	Scandalous—Ralph Carter	1.00	3.00	5.00	E
92	Outlaw Justice—Leigh Carder	1.00	3.00	5.00	W
93	Fleshpots—Florenz Branch	1.00	3.00	5.00	E
94	Passion's Way—Gordon Semple	1.00	3.00	5.00	E
95	Teaser—Craig Shepard	1.00	3.00	5.00	E
96	Body for Sale—Eliot Brewster	1.00	3.00	5.00	E
97	Call It Love—Hall Bennett	1.00	3.00	5.00	E
98	Quick Passion—Ralph Carter	1.00	3.00	5.00	E
99	Nice and Naughty—Gordon Semple	1.00	3.00	5.00	E
99	Trigger Vengeance—John Trace	1.00	3.00	5.00	W
100	Dark Memory—Jonathan Latimer; digest size	1.00	3.00	5.00	E
101	Bright Star of Danger—W. C. Chambers	1.20	3.60	6.00	
102	Hot Gold—Frederick R. Bechdolt; digest size	1.20	3.60	6.00	W
103	Without Reservations—Jane Allen and Mae Livingston; movie tie-in; digest size	1.60	4.80	8.00	E
104	The Green Man—Harold Sherman; digest size	2.00	6.00	10.00	SF
105	Man-Handled—Eliot Brewster	1.00	3.00	5.00	E
106	Marriage Later—William Arthur	1.00	3.00	5.00	E
107	Inherited Husband—Cecile Gilmore	1.00	3.00	5.00	E
108	Kept Woman—John Saxon	1.00	3.00	5.00	E
109	Passion's Lesson—Gordon Semple	1.00	3.00	5.00	E
110	Three Time Sin—Thomas Stone	1.00	3.00	5.00	E
111	Sinner Take All—William Arthur	1.00	3.00	5.00	E
112	Profane—Ralph Carter	1.00	3.00	5.00	E
113	Sinful Lady—Gordon Semple	1.00	3.00	5.00	E
114	Passion's Program—Florenz Branch	1.00	3.00	5.00	E
115	Two Time Lover—William Arthur	1.00	3.00	5.00	E
116	Time Trap—Rog Phillips; 1949	3.00	9.00	15.00	SF
117	Red for Passion—Thomas Stone	1.00	3.00	5.00	E
118	Desperato—William Hopson	1.00	3.00	5.00	W
119	Love Slave—Gail Jordan	1.00	3.00	5.00	E
120	Forbidden Sin—William Arthur; aka Burlesque Girl	1.00	3.00	5.00	E
121	Voluptueous—Charles Thornton	1.00	3.00	5.00	E
122	Passion's Sin—Ralph Carter; aka The Quiet Passion	1.00	3.00	5.00	E
123	Past Folly—Florenz Branch	1.00	3.00	5.00	E
124	Worlds Within—Rog Phillips	2.00	6.00	10.00	SF
125	Trigger Trails—Hamilton Craigie	1.00	3.00	5.00	W
126	Street Girl—Eliot Brewster	1.00	3.00	5.00	E
127	Charming Sinner—Barry DeForest; aka Partners in Sin	1.00	3.00	5.00	E
128	Bullet Trail—Burt Arthur	1.00	3.00	5.00	W
129	Tombstone Stage—William Hopson	1.00	3.00	5.00	W
130	Sinful Love—William Arthur; aka Redhead	1.00	3.00	5.00	E
131	Reckless Range—Johnston McCulley	1.00	3.00	5.00	W
132	Six Gun Stampede—Jackson Cole	1.00	3.00	5.00	W
133	California Trail—H. Bedford Jones	1.00	3.00	5.00	W
135	Saddle Wolves—Allan K. Echols	1.00	3.00	5.00	W
136	Headed for a Hearse—Jonathan Latimer	1.20	3.60	6.00	M

CHARTERED
Bond-Charteris Pub./Saint Enterprises, Inc.

Chartered 26, © Bond-Charteris

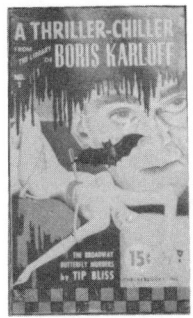
Checker Books 2, © Check

Checker Books 3, © Check

(CHARTERED, continued)
Digest Size

		Good	Fine	N/Mint	
17	The Saint's Choice of Hollywood Crime Stories—ed. Leslie Charteris	1.60	4.80	8.00	M
18	Deadlier Than the Male—James Gunn	1.20	3.60	6.00	M
19					
20					
21	Seven Slayers—Paul Cain; 1st ed. 1946	7.00	21.00	35.00	M
22	The Man Who Limped—Otis Adelbert Kline; 1st ed., 1946	6.00	18.00	30.00	SF
23					
24					
25	The Last Door Bell—Frank Gruber	1.20	3.60	6.00	M
26	The Brighter Buccaneer—Leslie Charteris	1.20	3.60	6.00	M
27	The Saint's Choice of Radio Thrillers—ed. Leslie Charteris	1.60	4.80	8.00	M
28	A Pocketful of Clues—James R. Langham	1.20	3.60	6.00	M

CHECKER BOOKS
Checker Books, Inc.

		Good	Fine	N/Mint	
1	Terry and the Pirates: The Jewels of Jade—Edward J. Boylan, Jr.; 1949, c-Wenzel	8.00	24.00	40.00	A
2	The Broadway Butterfly Murders—Tip Bliss	5.00	15.00	25.00	M
3	Make Mine Murder—Robert Bowen	5.00	15.00	25.00	M
4	Lost River Buckaroos—Charles M. Martin	3.00	9.00	15.00	W
5	Horror and Homicide—anthology; 1949	5.00	15.00	25.00	M
6	Duke Herring—Maxwell Bodenheim; 1949, c-Wenzell	3.00	9.00	15.00	M
7	Master-at-Arms—Rafael Sabatini; 1949	3.00	9.00	15.00	A
8	Taxi—Abraham Bernstein	3.00	9.00	15.00	
9	The Florentine Dagger—Ben Hecht; 1949	3.00	9.00	15.00	M
10	Lady, Mind That Corpse—Hank Janson; 1949, c-Heade	5.00	15.00	25.00	M
11	The Practical Party Guide and Cook Book—Dorothy & Fifi Bannett	2.00	6.00	10.00	NF
12	Over 100 Best Cartoons—Patricia Fulford; 1949	3.00	9.00	15.00	NF
nn	From Pearl Harbor Into Tokyo; orig., 1945	1.20	3.60	6.00	NF
nn	From D-Day Through Victory in Europe—ed. Paul Hollister and Robert Strunsky; orig., 1945	1.20	3.60	6.00	NF

COLUMBIA BROADCASTING SYSTEM
Columbia Broadcasting System

		Good	Fine	N/Mint	
nn	From Pearl Harbor Into Tokyo—orig., 1945	1.20	3.60	6.00	NF
nn	From D-Day Through Victory in Europe—ed. Paul Hollister and Robert Strunsky; orig., 1945	1.20	3.60	6.00	NF

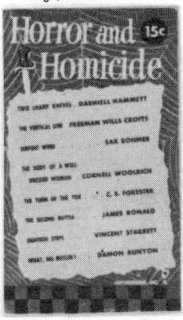
Checker Books 5, © Check

Checker Books 10, © Check

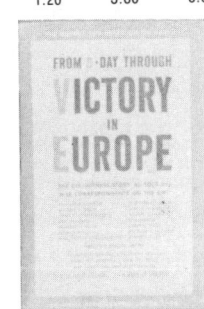
Columbia Broadcasting Sys. nn, © CBS

Comet Books 1, © Pkb

Comet Books 4, © Pkb

Comet Books 28, © Pkb

COMET BOOKS
Pocket Books, Inc.

(Most are digest size) (See Pocket Book Jr.)

		Good	Fine	N/Mint	
1	Wagons Westward—Armstrong Sperry; 1948	.50	1.50	2.50	W
2	Batter Up—Jackson Scholz	.50	1.50	2.50	S
3	Star Spangled Summer—Janet Lambert	.50	1.50	2.50	R
4	Tawny—Thomas C. Hinkle; standard paperback size	.50	1.50	2.50	A
5	300 Tricks You Can Do—Howard Thurston	.50	1.50	2.50	NF
6	Peggy Covers the News—Emma Bugbee	.50	1.50	2.50	
7	Winged Mystery—Alan Gregg	.50	1.50	2.50	M
8	Your Own Joke Book—Gertrude Crampton	.50	1.50	2.50	H
9	Sue Barton, Student Nurse—Helen Boylston; standard paperback size	.50	1.50	2.50	
10	The Tatooed Man—Howard Pease	.50	1.50	2.50	A
11	Skycruiser—Howard M. Brier	.50	1.50	2.50	
12	The Spanish Cave—Geoffrey Household	.50	1.50	2.50	M
13	The Green Turtle Mystery—Ellery Queen Jr.; 1949, c-Powers	.50	1.50	2.50	M
14	Silver—Thomas C. Hinkle; c-Powers	.50	1.50	2.50	W
15	Strangers in the Desert—Alice Russell	.50	1.50	2.50	
16	The Southpaw—Donal Hamilton Haines	.50	1.50	2.50	S
17	Bat Boy of the Giants—Garth Garreau	.50	1.50	2.50	S
18	Big Red—Jim Kjelgaard	.50	1.50	2.50	
19	The Mystery of the Empty Room—Augusta Seaman	.50	1.50	2.50	M
20	Husky: Co-Pilot of the Pilgrim; Rutherford Montgomery	.50	1.50	2.50	
21	Starbuck Valley Winter—Roderick Haig-Brown	.50	1.50	2.50	
22	Hobby Horse Hill—Lavinia R. Davis	.50	1.50	2.50	
23	Your Own Party Book—Gertrude Crampton	.50	1.50	2.50	NF
24	Gray Wolf—Rutherford Montgomery	.50	1.50	2.50	
25	Fighting Coach—Jackson Scholz; 1949, c-Powers	.50	1.50	2.50	
26	Midnight—Rutherford Montgomery	.50	1.50	2.50	
27	Forest Patrol—Jim Kjelgaard	.50	1.50	2.50	
28	Scarface—Andre Norton	1.60	4.80	8.00	A
29	Lightning on Ice—Philip Harkins	.50	1.50	2.50	S
30	No Other White Men—Julia Davis; interior illustrations-Powers	.50	1.50	2.50	
31	Indian Paint—Glen Balch	.50	1.50	2.50	
32	Puppy Stakes—Betty Cavanna	.50	1.50	2.50	
33	Long Wharf—Howard Pease	.50	1.50	2.50	A
34	Fun With Puzzles—Joseph Leeming	.50	1.50	2.50	NF

CORINTH (REGENCY) SUSPENSE
Corinth Publications, Inc.

CR101	Phantom Detective/The Vampire Murders—Robert Wallace; 1965	1.60	4.80	8.00	M
CR102	Phantom Detective/The Dancing Doll Murders—Robert Wallace	1.60	4.80	8.00	M
CR103	Phantom Detective/The Beast-King Murders—Robert Wallace	1.60	4.80	8.00	M
CR104	Phantom Detective/Tycoon of Crime—Robert Wallace	1.60	4.80	8.00	M
CR105	Phantom Detective/The Broadway Murders—Robert Wallace	1.60	4.80	8.00	M
CR106	Phantom Detective/The Daggers of Kali—Robert Wallace	1.60	4.80	8.00	M
CR107	Phantom Detective/Murder Under the Big Top—Robert Wallace	1.60	4.80	8.00	M
CR108	Phantom Detective/The Trail of Death—Robert Wallace	1.60	4.80	8.00	M
CR109	Phantom Detective/Yellow Shadows of Death—Robert Wallace	1.60	4.80	8.00	M
CR110	Phantom Detective/Murder Trail—Robert Wallace	1.60	4.80	8.00	M
CR111	Phantom Detective/The Green Glare Murders—Robert Wallace	1.60	4.80	8.00	M
CR112	Phantom Detective/Fangs of Murder—Robert Wallace	1.60	4.80	8.00	M
CR113	Phantom Detective/The Curio Murders—Robert Wallace	1.60	4.80	8.00	M
CR114	Phantom Detective/Murder Stalks a Billion—Robert Wallace	1.60	4.80	8.00	M
CR115	Phantom Detective/Murder Money—Robert Wallace	1.60	4.80	8.00	M
CR116	Operator #5/Legions of the Death Master—Curtis Steele	2.00	6.00	10.00	A

(CORINTH (REGENCY) SUSPENSE, continued)		Good	Fine	N/Mint	
CR117	Phantom Detective/Death Glow—Robert Wallace	1.60	4.80	8.00	M
CR118	Doctor Death/12 Must Die—Zorro	3.00	9.00	15.00	HO
CR119	Phantom Detective/Stones of Satan—Robert Wallace	1.60	4.80	8.00	M
CR120	Operator #5/The Army of the Dead—Curtis Steele	2.00	6.00	10.00	A
CR121	Doctor Death/The Gray Creatures—Zorro	3.00	9.00	15.00	HO
CR122	Secret Agent X/The Torture Trust—Brant House	2.00	6.00	10.00	A
CR123	Phantom Detective/The Melody Murders—Robert Wallace	1.60	4.80	8.00	M
CR124	Operator #5/The Invisible Empire—Curtis Steele	2.00	6.00	10.00	A
CR125	Doctor Death/The Shriveling Murders—Zorro	3.00	9.00	15.00	HO
CR126	Secret Agent X/Servants of the Skull—Brant House	2.00	6.00	10.00	A
CR127	Phantom Detective/The Uniformed Killers—Robert Wallace	1.60	4.80	8.00	M
CR128	Operator #5/Master of Broken Men—Curtis Steele	2.00	6.00	10.00	A
CR129	Doctor Death/Doctor Death and Other Terror Tales—Zorro	3.00	9.00	15.00	HO
CR130	Secret Agent X/Curse of the Mandarin's Fan—Brant House	2.00	6.00	10.00	A
CR131	Phantom Detective/The Forty Thieves—Robert Wallace	1.60	4.80	8.00	M
CR132	Operator #5/Hosts of the Flaming Death—Curtis Steele	2.00	6.00	10.00	A
CR133	Dusty Ayres/Black Lightning—Robert Sidney Bowen	1.60	4.80	8.00	C
CR134	Secret Agent X/City of the Living Dead—Brant House	2.00	6.00	10.00	A
CR135	Phantom Detective/Death Under Contract—Robert Wallace	1.60	4.80	8.00	M
CR136	Operator #5/Blood Reign of the Dictator—Curtis Steele	2.00	6.00	10.00	A
CR137	Dusty Ayres/Crimson Doom—Robert Sidney Bowen	1.60	4.80	8.00	C
CR138	Secret Agent X/The Death-Torch Terror—Brant House	2.00	6.00	10.00	A
CR139	Phantom Detective/The Corpse Parade—Robert Wallace	1.60	4.80	8.00	M
CR140	Operator #5/March of the Flame Marauders—Curtis Steele	2.00	6.00	10.00	A
CR141	Dusty Ayres/Purple Tornado—Robert Sidney Bowen	1.60	4.80	8.00	C
CR142	Secret Agent X/Octopus of Crime—Brant House	2.00	6.00	10.00	A
CR143	The House of Living Death and Other Terror Tales—anthology	2.00	6.00	10.00	HO
CR144	Operator #5/Invasion of the Yellow Warlords—Curtis Steele	2.00	6.00	10.00	A
CR145	Dusty Ayres/The Telsa Raiders—Robert Sidney Bowen	1.60	4.80	8.00	C
CR146	Secret Agent X/The Sinister Scourge—Brant House	2.00	6.00	10.00	A
CR147	Death's Loving Arms and Other Terror Tales—anthology	2.00	6.00	10.00	HO
CR148	Dusty Ayres/Black Invaders vs. the Battle Birds—Robert Sidney Bowen	1.60	4.80	8.00	C

CREST BOOKS
Fawcett Publications, Inc.

		Good	Fine	N/Mint	
114	Best Cartoons From True; 1955	.80	2.40	4.00	H
115	Run, Thief, Run—Frank Gruber	.50	1.50	2.50	M
116	Top Hand With a Gun—Harry Sinclair Drago	.50	1.50	2.50	W
117	Stranger at the Door—Gil Meynier	.50	1.50	2.50	
118	The Best From Captain Billy's Whizbang—Lester Grady	1.00	3.00	5.00	H
119	Love in Dishevelment—David Greenhood	.40	1.20	2.00	
120	Avenger From Texas—Will Ermine	.50	1.50	2.50	W
121	Affair—Emily Hahn	.40	1.20	2.00	
122	A Journey With Love—Denys Val Baker; 1956	.40	1.20	2.00	
123	Riders by Night—Nelson Nye	.50	1.50	2.50	W
s124	The Golden Hussy—Octavus Roy Cohen	.50	1.50	2.50	
125	So Sweet, So Cruel—Julian Farren	.50	1.50	2.50	
126	Captive in the Night—Donald Stokes	.50	1.50	2.50	
127	The Education of a French Model—Kiki	.40	1.20	2.00	E
128	The Thundering Trail—Norman A. Fox	.50	1.50	2.50	W
s129	Son of the Giant—Stuart Engstrand	.50	1.50	2.50	
130	Jadie—I. S. Young	.50	1.50	2.50	E
131	Gunsmoke on the Mesa—Davis Dresser	.50	1.50	2.50	W
132	Lie Down, Killer—Richard S. Prather	.50	1.50	2.50	M
s133	All My Sins—Norbert Estey	.50	1.50	2.50	E
134	Destination, Danger—William Colt MacDonald	.50	1.50	2.50	W
135	A Man's Affair—Dawn Powell	.50	1.50	2.50	

Corinth Suspense CR121, © Cor

Corinth Suspense CR146, © Cor

Crest Books 118, © Faw

Crest Books 193, © Faw

Crest Books 210, © Faw

Crest Books s307, © Faw

(CREST BOOKS, continued)

		Good	Fine	N/Mint	
136	Down Through the Night—Julius Fast	.50	1.50	2.50	
137	War on the Range—Norman A. Fox	.50	1.50	2.50	W
138	The Memoirs of Maisie—Maude Hutchins; 1956	.40	1.20	2.00	
139	So Nude, So Dead—Richard Marsten	.50	1.50	2.50	M
s140	Of Sin and the Flesh—Robert De Vries	.50	1.50	2.50	
141	Sex Without Tears—Norman Lockridge & Virgil Partch	.50	1.50	2.50	H
142	Dagger of Flesh—Richard S. Prather	.50	1.50	2.50	M
s143	Hypnotism and the Power Within—S. J. VanPelt	.40	1.20	2.00	NF
s144	Come Desire Me—Anton Fereva	.40	1.20	2.00	
s145	You Can Live After Death—Harold Sherman	.50	1.50	2.50	
146	Code of the Gun—Gordon D. Shirreffs	.50	1.50	2.50	W
147	And the Girl Screamed—Gil Brewer	.50	1.50	2.50	E
s148	My First Two Thousand Years—Paul Eldridge & George Sylvester Viereck	.80	2.40	4.00	F
149	The Comanche Scalp—William Colt MacDonald	.50	1.50	2.50	W
150	The Rule of the Pagbeasts—J. T. McIntosh; aka The Fittest	1.20	3.60	6.00	SF
151	Saturday Night Town—Harry Whittington	.50	1.50	2.50	
152	Ambush at Buffalo Wallow—T. D. Allen	.50	1.50	2.50	W
153	The Golden Lure—Michael Barrett	.50	1.50	2.50	
154	Six-gun Vengeance—Dudley Dean	.50	1.50	2.50	W
155	Crazy Cartoons by VIP—Virgil Partch	.80	2.40	4.00	H
s156	The Trumpet Unblown—William Hoffman; 1957	.50	1.50	2.50	W
d157	A Walk on the Wild Side—Nelson Algren	.80	2.40	4.00	
158	Badge for a Gunfighter—Clair Huffaker	.50	1.50	2.50	W
159	Office Laffs—Charles Preston	.80	2.40	4.00	H
d160	A Dream of Kings—Davis Grubb	.50	1.50	2.50	
161	Last Stand at Anvil Pass—Merle Constiner	.50	1.50	2.50	W
162	Seawife—J. M. Scott; movie tie-in	.50	1.50	2.50	
s163	The Empire - and Martin Brill—George deMare; 1957	.50	1.50	2.50	
164	Gunswift—Stewart Gordon	.50	1.50	2.50	
165	The Right to Love—Markoosha Fischer	.50	1.50	2.50	
166	The Conquering Prince—Gardner F. Fox	1.00	3.00	5.00	A
167	Badman—Clair Huffaker; movie tie-in	1.00	3.00	5.00	W
s168	Way to Happiness—Fulton J. Sheen	.30	.90	1.50	
169	Evil in the Night—Erico Verissimo	.50	1.50	2.50	
170	Fury Trail—Giles A. Lutz	.50	1.50	2.50	W
s171	Strangers in Paradise—Howard Otway	.50	1.50	2.50	
172	Case of the Brunette Bombshell—Hillary Waugh	.50	1.50	2.50	M
173	Little Tramp—Gil Brewer	.50	1.50	2.50	E
174	Valley of Violent Men—Lewis B. Patten	.50	1.50	2.50	W
s175	The Loving and the Lost—James Lord	.50	1.50	2.50	
d176	Tom Jones—Henry Fielding	.40	1.20	2.00	
177	Border Renegade—Dudley Dean	.50	1.50	2.50	W
s178	The Spiked Heel—Richard Marsten	.50	1.50	2.50	
179	Walk With Evil—Robert Wilder	.50	1.50	2.50	
d180	According to Hoyle—Richard Frey	.30	.90	1.50	NF
181	Gun the Man Down—Giles A. Lutz	.50	1.50	2.50	W
s182	Seed of Violence—Williams Forrest	.50	1.50	2.50	
s183	The Home Book of Italian Cooking—Angela Catanzaro	.30	.90	1.50	NF
s184	City at World's End—Edmond Hamilton	.80	2.40	4.00	SF
185	Top Gun—Gordon Donalds	.50	1.50	2.50	W
186	The Heart Has Its Reasons—Duchess of Windsor	.30	.90	1.50	
187	Whisper Their Love—Valerie Taylor	1.00	3.00	5.00	E
s188	Beyond Defeat—Hans Werner Richter; 1957	.50	1.50	2.50	
189	The Hell-Fire Kid—Steve Shannon	.50	1.50	2.50	W
s190	Sweepings—Lester Cohen	.50	1.50	2.50	
191	A Dram of Poison—Charlotte Armstrong	.50	1.50	2.50	M
192	Mantrap—Duane Yarnell	.50	1.50	2.50	E
193	Rider From Thunder Mountain—Clair Huffaker	.50	1.50	2.50	W

		Good	Fine	N/Mint	
s194	And Come Back a Man—John Bell Clayton	.50	1.50	2.50	
195	Meet Morocco Jones—Jack Baynes	.50	1.50	2.50	M
196	The New Crest Crossword Puzzle Book—James Freeman	.50	1.50	2.50	NF
s197	Five Tales From Tomorrow—T. E. Dikty	.40	1.20	2.00	SF
198	West of Devil's Canyon—Richard Poole; 1958	.50	1.50	2.50	
d199	Eastern Love—Edward Powys Mathers	.80	2.40	4.00	
s200	Gas-House McGinty—James T. Farrell	.40	1.20	2.00	
s201	The Hungry Years—Annabel Johnson	.50	1.50	2.50	
t202	Mandingo—Kyle Onstott	.40	1.20	2.00	E
s203	House in Shanghai—Emily Hahn	.50	1.50	2.50	
s204	The Home Book of French Cooking—Anita Abbott & Lisa Andors	.30	.90	1.50	NF
205	Texas Fury—John Callahan	.50	1.50	2.50	W
206	Baby Moll—Steve Brackeen	.50	1.50	2.50	
s207	Off Limits—Hans Habe	.50	1.50	2.50	
s208	The Magnificent Rascal—Thomas Sancton	.50	1.50	2.50	
s209	The 27th Day—John Mantley	.80	2.40	4.00	SF
210	Swamp Babe—Robert Faherty	.80	2.40	4.00	E
211	High Hell—Steve Frazee	.50	1.50	2.50	W
s212	Night of Fire and Snow—Alfred Coppel; 1958	.50	1.50	2.50	
213	Did You Kill Mona Leeds?—John Roeburt; aka The Lunatic Time	.40	1.20	2.00	M
s214	Of Love Forbidden—Anna Elisabet Weirauch	.50	1.50	2.50	
s215	All Quiet on the Western Front—Erich Maria Remarque	.50	1.50	2.50	
s216	From the Earth to the Moon and Round the Moon—Jules Verne	.50	1.50	2.50	SF
s217	The Legion of the Damned—Sven Hassel	.50	1.50	2.50	
s218	A Fool There Was—John Manson	.50	1.50	2.50	
219	Dr. Anders' Dilemma—Henry & Sylvia Lieferaut	.30	.90	1.50	
s220	The Best of Balzac—Honore de Balzac	.40	1.20	2.00	
s221	Yanqui's Woman—George McKenna	.50	1.50	2.50	
222	Posse From Hell—Clair Huffaker	.50	1.50	2.50	W
s223	How You Can Take Better Photos—Simon Nathan	.30	.90	1.50	NF
224	Hand of the Mafia—Jack Baynes	.50	1.50	2.50	M
225	Root of Evil—James Cross	.50	1.50	2.50	
s226	Ralph 124C41+—Hugo Gernsback	1.00	3.00	5.00	SF
s227	The Pink Hotel—Patrick Dennis & Dorothy Erskine	.40	1.20	2.00	
d228	The Durable Fire—Howard Swiggett	.40	1.20	2.00	
229	Wild—Gil Brewer	.50	1.50	2.50	E
230	The Widow Wore Red—Richard Wormser	.40	1.20	2.00	M
s231	Awake Monique—Astrid Van Royen	.40	1.20	2.00	
d232	Blue Camellia—Frances Parkinson Keyes	.30	.90	1.50	
s233	Small Town D.A.—Robert Traver	.40	1.20	2.00	
234	The Peeping Tom Murders—Jack Baynes	.50	1.50	2.50	M
235	The Red Sombrero—Nelson Nye	.40	1.20	2.00	W
s236	Stigma for Valor—Williams Forest	.40	1.20	2.00	
s237	Ten Seconds to Hell—Lawrence Bachmann	.40	1.20	2.00	
238	The Vengeful Virgin—Gil Brewer; 1958	.50	1.50	2.50	E
239	Cartoon Laffs From True—Bill McIntyre	.50	1.50	2.50	H
s240	The Best of Crunch and Des—Philip Wylie	.40	1.20	2.00	
s241	The Power of Positive Living—Douglas Lurton	.30	.90	1.50	NF
242	The Wind River Kid—Will Cook	.40	1.20	2.00	W
s243	The Dangerous Games—Tereska Torres	.80	2.40	4.00	
s244	The Unforgiven—J. Edward Leithead; movie tie-in	.80	2.40	4.00	W
s245	Race to the Stars—Oscar J. Friend & Leo Margulies	.40	1.20	2.00	SF
246	The Long Nightmare—John Roeburt	.40	1.20	2.00	
247	Mask of Evil—Charlotte Armstrong	.40	1.20	2.00	M
248	End of a Call Girl—William Campbell Gault	.40	1.20	2.00	M
d249	The Black Obelisk—Erich Maria Remarque	.40	1.20	2.00	
s250	The Grand Seduction—Marcel Ayme	.40	1.20	2.00	
s251	The Doctor's Husband—Elizabeth Seifert	.30	.90	1.50	R
s252	The House on the Beach—E. L. Withers; c-Powers	.50	1.50	2.50	
253	Murder Bait—Duane Yarnell	.40	1.20	2.00	M
s254	Bad Girls—Leo Margulies	.40	1.20	2.00	
255	Lie Down, Killer—Richard S. Prather	.40	1.20	2.00	M
d256	A Treasury of True—Charles N. Barnard	.40	1.20	2.00	
s257	Pappy's Women—Jack Gotshall	.40	1.20	2.00	E
s258	Six From Worlds Beyond—T. E. Dikty	.30	.90	1.50	SF
s259	Devil's Prize—Samuel Edwards	.40	1.20	2.00	
260	Night Lady—William Campbell Gault	.40	1.20	2.00	
261	Gold at Kansas Gulch—Steve Frazee	.40	1.20	2.00	W
d262	Fun With Mathematics—Jerome S. Meyer	.30	.90	1.50	NF
s263	Please Don't Eat the Daisies—Jean Kerr; 1959	.30	.90	1.50	
d264	The Silver Mountain—Dan Cushman	.50	1.50	2.50	
s265	The Great Captains—Henry Treece	.40	1.20	2.00	A
266	Clementine Cherie—Jean Bellus	.30	.90	1.50	
s267	Edge of Twilight—Paula Christian	1.20	3.60	6.00	
268	The Vanishing Vixen—Roy B. Sparkia	.40	1.20	2.00	
s269	The Great Religions by Which Men Live—Tynette Hills & Floyd H. Ross	.30	.90	1.50	

		Good	Fine	N/Mint	
s270	The Devil's Agent—Hans Habe	.40	1.20	2.00	
d271	Seven Keys to Koptic Court—Herbert D. Kastle	.40	1.20	2.00	
s272	Young and Deadly—Leo Margulies	.40	1.20	2.00	
s273	The Caves of Night—John Christoper	.50	1.50	2.50	
274	Fighting Rawhide—Lewis B. Patten	.40	1.20	2.00	W
s275	How to Retire and Enjoy It—Ray Giles	.30	.90	1.50	NF
d276	The World's Ten Greatest Novels—W. Somerset Maugham	.30	.90	1.50	
277	Dagger of Flesh—Richard S. Prather	.40	1.20	2.00	M
d278	Days in the Yellow Leaf—William Hoffman	.40	1.20	2.00	
s279	Enter Laughing—Carl Reiner	.30	.90	1.50	B
s280	The Damned Wear Wings—David Camerer	.40	1.20	2.00	
281	The Wayward Widow—William Campbell Gault	.40	1.20	2.00	E
s282	Three From Out There—Leo Margulies	.30	.90	1.50	SF
s283	The Way to Inner Peace—Fulton J. Sheen	.30	.90	1.50	
s284	How to Write and Speak Effective English—Edward Frank Allen	.30	.90	1.50	NF
d285	Wine of Life—Charles Gorham	.30	.90	1.50	
286	Dead Dolls Don't Talk—Day Keene; orig., 1959	.50	1.50	2.50	M
287	The Cautious Bachelor—Sarel Eimerl	.30	.90	1.50	
s288	Legacy of a Spy—Henry S. Maxfield	.40	1.20	2.00	
s289	Handsome's Seven Women—Theodore Pratt	.40	1.20	2.00	
s290	The Girls in 3-B—Valerie Taylor	1.00	3.00	5.00	
s291	The Sergeant—Dennis Murphy	.40	1.20	2.00	
292	The Eighth Mrs. Bluebeard—Hillary Waugh	.40	1.20	2.00	M
d293	Steamboat Gothic—Frances Parkinson Keyes	.30	.90	1.50	
294	Pardon My Blooper—Kermit Schafer	.30	.90	1.50	H
s295	The Executioners—John D. MacDonald	.40	1.20	2.00	M
296	Passport to Peril—Stephen Marlowe	.40	1.20	2.00	M
297	Doctor's Temptation—Henry & Sylvia Lieferant	.30	.90	1.50	
298	In This Corner - Dennis the Menace—Hank Ketcham	.40	1.20	2.00	H
s299	The Way We Live Now—Warren Miller	.40	1.20	2.00	
d300	North From Rome—Helen MacInnes	.30	.90	1.50	
s301	Shake Hands With the Devil—Rearden Conner	.40	1.20	2.00	
s302	The Girl Cage—Charles Mergendahl	.40	1.20	2.00	
303	Night of Violence—Louis Charbonneau	.40	1.20	2.00	
304	Creole Woman—Gardner F. Fox	1.00	3.00	5.00	E
d305	The Old Blood—Edgar Mittelholzer	.40	1.20	2.00	
s306	Sun in the Hunter's Eyes—Mark Derby	.40	1.20	2.00	
s307	The Horn—Clellon Holmes	1.60	4.80	8.00	
s308	A Stir of Echoes—Richard Matheson	.50	1.50	2.50	SF
309	Sweet Wild Wench—William Campbell Gault	.40	1.20	2.00	E
310	The Red Scarf—Gil Brewer	.40	1.20	2.00	
311	Crazy Cartoons by VIP—Virgil Partch	.50	1.50	2.50	H
d312	Showcase—Martin Dibner	.40	1.20	2.00	
313					
d314	Joy Street—Frances Parkinson Keyes	.30	.90	1.50	
315	Rendezvous—Steve Frazee	.40	1.20	2.00	W
316	Danger in My Blood—Steve Brackeen	.40	1.20	2.00	
s317	The Insolent Chariots—John Keats	.40	1.20	2.00	H
s318	The Enjoyment of Love in Marriage—LeMon Clark	.30	.90	1.50	NF
d319	Lost Summer—Christopher Davis	.30	.90	1.50	
s320	Venus in Sparta—Louis Auchircloss	.30	.90	1.50	
s321	The Shook-up Generation—Harrison S. Salisbury	.40	1.20	2.00	
s322	The Passionate City—Ian Stuart Black	.40	1.20	2.00	
323	You've Got Him Cold—Thomas B. Dewey	.40	1.20	2.00	
s324	Treasure Book of Fairy Tales—Ann McGovern	.50	1.50	2.50	
325	Morocco Jones in the Case of the Golden Angel—Jack Baynes	.50	1.50	2.50	M
t326	By Love Possessed—James Gould Cozzens	.40	1.20	2.00	
s327	Murder on the Mistral—Vincent Gaspard Malo	.40	1.20	2.00	M
s328	The Bystander—Albert Guerard	.40	1.20	2.00	
s329	The Star of Life—Edmond Hamilton	.40	1.20	2.00	SF
d330	Tom Jones—Henry Fielding	.40	1.20	2.00	
s331	Drink and Be Merry—Lester Grady	.40	1.20	2.00	H
s332	Someone From the Past—Margot Bennett	.40	1.20	2.00	
d333	Victorine—Frances Parkinson Keyes	.30	.90	1.50	
334	Kill My Love—Kyle Hunt	.40	1.20	2.00	M
s335	A Little Revolution—Paul Edmondson	.40	1.20	2.00	
s336	Strange Are the Ways of Love—Lesley Evans	.30	.90	1.50	
s337	All Quiet on the Western Front—Erich Maria Remarque	.40	1.20	2.00	
d338	Lolita—Vladimir Nabokov; 1959	.50	1.50	2.50	
339	Lyn Darling, M.D.—Ray Dorien	.30	.90	1.50	
340	Jimmy Hoffa's Hot—John Bartlow Martin	.40	1.20	2.00	
s341	The Badge—Jack Webb	.40	1.20	2.00	M
s342	No Place on Earth—Louis Charbonneau	.50	1.50	2.50	SF
s343	The Ruling Passion—George deMare	.40	1.20	2.00	
344	Meet Morocco Jones—Jack Baynes	.50	1.50	2.50	M

CRIME NOVEL SELECTION
Red Circle Magazines, Inc.

Digest Size

		Good	Fine	N/Mint	
1	Strangler's Holiday—Kurt Steel; 1942, aka Murder in G-Sharp, c-Saunders	2.00	6.00	10.00	M
2	The Travelling Corpses—Kurt Steel	1.60	4.80	8.00	M
3	The Submarine Signaled . . . Murder—Allan R. Bosworth	1.60	4.80	8.00	M
4	Murder for What?—Kurt Steel	1.60	4.80	8.00	M
5	3 Girls and a Killer—H. Donald Spatz	1.60	4.80	8.00	M
nn	Death Is the Host—Lawrence Lariar; 1943, aka Death Paints the Picture	1.60	4.80	8.00	M

CRIMES OF LOVE AND PASSION
Louellen Publishing Company

Digest Size

		Good	Fine	N/Mint	
1	The Secret Lover of Madeleine Smith—ed. Paul Renin; 1945	1.60	4.80	8.00	E
2	The Crimes of Belle Gunness—ed. Paul Renin	1.60	4.80	8.00	E
3	Dorothy Jordan, the Siren of Old Drury—ed. Paul Renin	1.60	4.80	8.00	E
4	Bela Kiss—ed. Paul Renin	1.60	4.80	8.00	E

CROSSWORD PLEASURE
Crossword Pleasure, Inc.

		Good	Fine	N/Mint	
nn	Collector's Crosswords - With a Medical Twist—Jesse Jacobs; 1st ed., 1961	.80	2.40	4.00	NF
nn	Today's New, Enlarged Crossword Dictionary—Davis Shulman	.40	1.20	2.00	NF

CROW EDITIONS
Alval Publishers of Canada, Ltd.

(Canadian)

		Good	Fine	N/Mint	
nn	Careless Virgin—James Clayford; 1949	.80	2.40	4.00	E
nn	Overnight Girl—Joan Sherman (Peggy Gaddis); aka Overnight Cabins	.80	2.40	4.00	E
22	Red Moon of Desire—Darryl X. Dexter	.80	2.40	4.00	E
24	Overnight Girl—Joan Sherman (Peggy Gaddis)	.80	2.40	4.00	E
25	Reckless Maiden—Peggy Gaddis	.80	2.40	4.00	E
27	Impatient Temptress—James Clayford	.80	2.40	4.00	E
32	Illicit Honeymoon—James Clayford	.80	2.40	4.00	E
37	Desirable—Luther Gordon	.80	2.40	4.00	E
40	Sideshow Girl—James Clayford	.80	2.40	4.00	E

CROYDON
Croydon Publishing Co./Star Publications, Inc.

Digest Size unless noted

		Good	Fine	N/Mint	
nn	Vicious Circle—Manning Long; 1945, c-Cole	1.60	4.80	8.00	M
nn	Many a Murder—Delia Van Deusen; 1945, aka Murder Bicarb, c-Cole	1.60	4.80	8.00	M
nn	Murders I've Seen—Philip Mechem; 1945, aka And Not for Love	1.60	4.80	8.00	M
nn	Slave of Desire—Gordon Semple; orig., 1951	1.60	4.80	8.00	E
nn	Here Lies Blood—M. M. Mannon; c-Cole	1.60	4.80	8.00	M
nn	Have You Seen This Man?—Gene Hurley; c-Cole	1.60	4.80	8.00	M
nn	Murder on the Mountain—Christine Noble Govan; c-Cole	1.60	4.80	8.00	M
6	Murder Makes a Villain—Dennis Scott; c-Cole	1.60	4.80	8.00	M

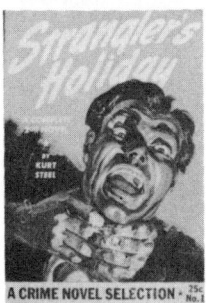

Crime Novel Selection 1, © Red Circle

Crimes of Love & Passion 1, © Louellen

Croydon nn, © Croy

Croydon 14, © Croy

Croydon 73, © Croy

Croydon 94, © Croy

(CROYDON, continued)	Good	Fine	N/Mint	
9 The Dead Take No Bows—Richard Burke; c-Cole, small size	3.00	9.00	15.00	M
11 Cheaters at Love—Wright Williams; c-Cole	3.00	9.00	15.00	E
12 Love Hungry—E. D. Jerome; aka Cute Kid, c-Cole, small size	3.00	9.00	15.00	M
13 Reckless Virgin—Glen Watkins; c-Cole, small size	3.00	9.00	15.00	E
14 Shadows of Lust—Ralph Carter; c-Cole, small size	3.00	9.00	15.00	E
15 Fool for Love—Wright Williams; c-Cole, small size	3.00	9.00	15.00	E
16 Sinner—Gordon Semple; 1950, aka Life of Passion, c-Cole, small size	3.00	9.00	15.00	E
17 Street of Sin—Wright Williams	.80	2.40	4.00	E
19 Restless Wife—Gail Jordan (Peggy Gaddis); aka Passionate Lover	.80	2.40	4.00	E
20 The Shame at Vanna Gilbert—Glenn Watkins; aka Sinful Life	.80	2.40	4.00	E
21 Shameless Sue—Gordon Semple	.80	2.40	4.00	E
22 Strange Desires—Richard Himmel	.80	2.40	4.00	E
23 Sins of a Private Secretary—Gail Jordan (Peggy Gaddis)	.80	2.40	4.00	E
24 Love-Hungry Doctor—Florence Stonebraker; 1953	.80	2.40	4.00	E
25 Spotlight on Sin—Doug Duperrault	.80	2.40	4.00	E
26 Immoral Models—Joan Sherman (Peggy Gaddis); orig., 1952	.80	2.40	4.00	E
31 Army Mistress—David Williams; orig., 1953	.80	2.40	4.00	E
33 High Priced Party Girl—Bart Frame	.80	2.40	4.00	E
34 Gang Mistress—Doug Duperault	1.00	3.00	5.00	E
35 Vengeful Sinner—Harry Whittington; aka Die Lover	.80	2.40	4.00	E
36 Blonde Temptress—Gordon Semple; orig., 1953	.80	2.40	4.00	E
37 Strange Passions—Florence Stonebraker	.80	2.40	4.00	E
38 Part-time Wife—Gerald Foster	.80	2.40	4.00	E
39 Indiscretions of a French Model	.80	2.40	4.00	E
40 Cellar Club Girl—Alan Bennett	1.20	3.60	6.00	E
43 Love Hungry Boss—Peggy Gaddis	.80	2.40	4.00	E
44 Confessions of a B-Girl—Sim Albert; orig., 1953	.80	2.40	4.00	E
45 Man-Hungry Widow—Peggy Gaddis	.80	2.40	4.00	E
49 Sinful Island Vacation—William Vaneer	.80	2.40	4.00	E
52 Love Cult—William Vaneer	1.00	3.00	5.00	E
54 Scandalous French Doctor—Jean Calvert; orig., 1954	.80	2.40	4.00	E
56 Confessions of a Pick-up Girl—Sim Albert; orig., 1954	.80	2.40	4.00	E
59 Scandals at a Country Club—Bart Frame; orig., 1954	.80	2.40	4.00	E
60 Forbidden Passions—Wright Williams; aka Lust for Love	.80	2.40	4.00	E
62 Night Club Sinner—Harry Whittington; aka Vengeful Sinner	.80	2.40	4.00	E
63 Man-Crazy Hussy—Gordon Semple	.80	2.40	4.00	E
65 Indiscretions of a TV Sinner—Gordon Semple; orig., 1954	.80	2.40	4.00	E
66 Joy Girl—Delmar Kingsland; orig., 1954	.80	2.40	4.00	E
68 Lady of Many Sins—Gerald Foster	.80	2.40	4.00	E
69 Scandalous Nurse—Peggy Gaddis; orig., 1954	.80	2.40	4.00	E
70 Confessions of a Ladie's Chauffeur—Florence Stonebraker	.80	2.40	4.00	E
71 Bad Girls' Club—William Davids	.80	2.40	4.00	E
72 Hoyden of the Mountains—D. Kingsland	.80	2.40	4.00	E
73 Woman-Crazy Doctor—S. Albert	.80	2.40	4.00	E
78 Stag-Party Girl—Bart Frame	.80	2.40	4.00	E
80 Lonely Soldiers—William David; aka Army Mistress	.80	2.40	4.00	E
82 Thrill-Hungry Girl—Peggy Gaddis	.80	2.40	4.00	E
83 Affairs of a Party Girl—Bart Frame	.80	2.40	4.00	E
87 Wild Bride—Sim Albert; orig., 1954	.80	2.40	4.00	E
88 Maybelle - Georgia Girl in Harlem—Bart Frame; orig., 1954	1.60	4.80	8.00	E
89 Shanty-Town Tease—Florence Stonebraker	.80	2.40	4.00	E
90 Man-Crazy Nurse—Peggy Gaddis	.80	2.40	4.00	E
91 Waterfront Girl—Gordon Semple	.80	2.40	4.00	E
92 Warped Desires—Gordon Semple	.80	2.40	4.00	E
93 Confessions of a B-Girl—S. Albert	.80	2.40	4.00	E
94 Tenement Girl—Alan Bennett; 1955, aka Cellar Club Girl	1.20	3.60	6.00	E
101 She Lived in Sin	.80	2.40	4.00	E
102 Shameful Love—Thomas Stone	.80	2.40	4.00	E

Croydon 107, © Croy

Daggar House Mystery 26, © Daggar

Death House nn, © Wm. H. Wise

		Good	Fine	N/Mint	
(CROYDON, continued)					
103	Sinner—Gordon Semple; aka Life of Passion	.80	2.40	4.00	E
107	Intimate Affairs of a Sinful Model—Joan Sherman (Peggy Gaddis)	.80	2.40	4.00	E
108	Sins of an Aspiring Actress	.80	2.40	4.00	E
110	Scandalous Career Girl—Gordon Semple	.80	2.40	4.00	E

CROYDON HOW-TO BOOKS
Croydon Publishing Company

Digest Size

		Good	Fine	N/Mint	
11	The Giant Hobby Handbook; 1953, c-Cole	1.00	3.00	5.00	NF

DAGGER HOUSE MYSTERY
Dagger House, Inc.

Digest Size

		Good	Fine	N/Mint	
20	Murder at Lover's Lake—Margaretta Brucker	1.20	3.60	6.00	M
24	If a Body Kill a Body—Peter Mortimer	1.20	3.60	6.00	M
26	You Can't Kill a Corpse—Louis Trimble; 1947	1.20	3.60	6.00	M
28	Murder Makes a Marriage—Schuyler Broocks; 1947	1.20	3.60	6.00	M

DEATH HOUSE
William H. Wise & Co., Inc.

Digest Size

		Good	Fine	N/Mint	
nn	Vengeance Pulls the Trigger—Sturges Mason Schley; aka Who'd Shoot a Genius?	2.00	6.00	10.00	M
nn	Death Springs the Trap—Eaton K. Goldthwaite; aka You Dit It	2.00	6.00	10.00	M
3	Murder on the Downbeat—Robert Avery	1.60	4.80	8.00	M
4	The Case of the Nameless Corpse—Eaton K. Goldthwaite	1.60	4.80	8.00	M
5	Dead Reckoning—Francis Bonnamy	1.60	4.80	8.00	M
6	Full Crash Dive—Allan R. Bosworth; aka Murder Goes to Sea	1.60	4.80	8.00	M

DELL
Dell Publishing Company, Inc.

		Good	Fine	N/Mint	
1	Death in the Library—Philip Ketchum; 1943	15.00	45.00	75.00	M
2	Dead or Alive—Patricia Wentworth	2.00	6.00	10.00	M

Death House nn, © Wm. H. Wise

Dell 1, © Dell

Dell 2, © Dell

Dell 13, © Dell

Dell 20, © Dell

Dell 21, © Dell

(DELL, continued)

		Good	Fine	N/Mint	
3	Murder-on-Hudson—Jennifer Jones	4.00	12.00	20.00	M
4	The American Gun Mystery—Ellery Queen; aka Death at the Rodeo	2.00	6.00	10.00	M
5	Four Frightened Women—George Harmon Coxe	3.00	9.00	15.00	M
6	Ill Met by Moonlight—Leslie Ford	2.00	6.00	10.00	M
7	See You at the Morgue—Lawrence G. Blochman	3.00	9.00	15.00	M
8	The Tuesday Club Murders—Agatha Christie	3.00	9.00	15.00	M
9	Double for Death—Rex Stout	3.00	9.00	15.00	M
10	The Lone Wolf—Louis Joseph Vance	3.00	9.00	15.00	M
11	Hearses Don't Hurry—Stephen Ransome	3.00	9.00	15.00	M
12	Wife vs. Secretary—Faith Baldwin	2.00	6.00	10.00	R
13	Death Wears a White Gardenia—Zelda Popkin	2.00	6.00	10.00	M
14	The Doctor Died at Dusk—Geoffrey Homes	3.00	9.00	15.00	M
15	The Golden Swan Murder—Dorothy Cameron Disney	3.00	9.00	15.00	M
16	The Unicorn Murders—Carter Dickson	4.00	12.00	20.00	M
17	The Dead Can Tell—Helen Reilly	3.00	9.00	15.00	M
18	The Puzzle of the Silver Persian—Stuart Palmer	3.00	9.00	15.00	M
19	Death Over Sunday—James Francis Bonnell	2.00	6.00	10.00	M
20	Tambay Gold—Samuel Hopkins Adams	3.00	9.00	15.00	R
21	I Was a Nazi Flyer—Gottfried Leske	12.50	37.50	60.00	C
22	Holiday Homicide—Rufus King	2.00	6.00	10.00	M
23	The Private Practice of Michael Shayne—Bret Halliday	2.00	6.00	10.00	M
24	The Phantom of the Opera—Gaston Leroux	8.00	24.00	40.00	M
25	Speak No Evil—Mignon G. Eberhart	2.00	6.00	10.00	M
26	The Raft—Robert Trumbull	2.00	6.00	10.00	A
27	The Camera Clue—George Harmon Coxe	3.00	9.00	15.00	M
28	The Mountain Cat Murders—Rex Stout	2.00	6.00	10.00	M
29	Curtains for the Copper—Thomas Polsky	3.00	9.00	15.00	M
30	Memo to a Firing Squad—Frederick Hazlitt Brennan	3.00	9.00	15.00	C
31	The Fallen Sparrow—Dorothy B. Hughes	2.00	6.00	10.00	M
32	This Time for Keeps—John MacCormac	2.00	6.00	10.00	NF
33	Dance of Death—Helen McCloy; 1944	2.00	6.00	10.00	M
34	Crime Hound—Mary Semple Scott	2.00	6.00	10.00	M
35	The Cat Saw Murder—D. B. Olsen	2.00	6.00	10.00	M
36	The Hammersmith Murders—David Frome	2.00	6.00	10.00	M
37	Queen of the Flat-tops—Stanley Johnston	1.60	4.80	8.00	C
38	Liberty Laughs—Frances Cavanah & Ruth Weir	7.00	21.00	35.00	H
39	Murder Challenges Valcour—Rufus King	2.00	6.00	10.00	M
40	The Case of Jennie Brice—Mary Roberts Rinehart	1.60	4.80	8.00	M
41	The Man Who Didn't Exist—Geoffrey Homes	2.00	6.00	10.00	M
42	Murder at Scandal House—Peter Hunt	2.00	6.00	10.00	M

Dell 24, © Dell

Dell 29, © Dell

Dell 33, © Dell

Dell 47, © Dell

Dell 53, © Dell

Dell 56, © Dell

	Good	Fine	N/Mint	
(DELL, continued)				
43 Midnight Sailing—Lawrence G. Blochman	2.00	6.00	10.00	M
44 Reply Paid—H. F. Heard	1.60	4.80	8.00	M
45 Too Many Cooks—Rex Stout	3.00	9.00	15.00	M
46 The Boomerang Clue—Agatha Christie	2.00	6.00	10.00	M
47 Keeper of the Keys—Earl Derr Biggers	4.00	12.00	20.00	M
48 The Cross-Eyed Bear Murders—Dorothy B. Hughes	2.00	6.00	10.00	M
49 The Feathered Serpent—Edgar Wallace	2.00	6.00	10.00	M
50 The Iron Spiders—Baynard Kendrick; 1944	2.00	6.00	10.00	M
51 While the Wind Howled—Audrey Gaines	2.00	6.00	10.00	M
52 The Body That Wasn't Uncle—George Worthing Yates	2.00	6.00	10.00	M
53 Blood Money—Dashiell Hammett	10.00	30.00	50.00	M
54 Harvard Has a Homicide—Timothy Fuller	1.60	4.80	8.00	M
55 The D.A.'s Daughter—Herman Petersen	2.00	6.00	10.00	M
56 The Frightened Stiff—Kelley Roos	1.60	4.80	8.00	M
57 Murder at the White Cat—Mary Roberts Rinehart	1.60	4.80	8.00	M
58 Murder for the Asking—George Harmon Coxe	2.00	6.00	10.00	M
59 Turn on the Heat—A. A. Fair	2.00	6.00	10.00	M
60 Thirteen at Dinner—Agatha Christie	2.00	6.00	10.00	M
61 The Clue of the Judas Tree—Leslie Ford	1.60	4.80	8.00	M
62 The Strawstack Murder—Dorothy Cameron Disney	2.00	6.00	10.00	M
63 Mourned on Sunday—Helen Reilly	2.00	6.00	10.00	M
64 Blood on the Black Market—Brett Halliday	2.00	6.00	10.00	M
65 Scotland Yard Department of Queer Complaints—Carter Dickson	5.00	15.00	25.00	M
66 A Talent for Murder—Anna Mary Wells	2.00	6.00	10.00	
67 Hidden Ways—Frederic F. Van de Water	2.00	6.00	10.00	M
68 Juliet Dies Twice—Lange Lewis	2.00	6.00	10.00	M
69 Death From a Top Hat—Clayton Rawson; 1945	3.00	9.00	15.00	M
70 The Red Bull—Rex Stout; aka Some Buried Caesar	2.00	6.00	10.00	M
71 Murder in the Mist—Zelda Popkin	2.00	6.00	10.00	M
72 The Man in the Moonlight—Helen McCloy	2.00	6.00	10.00	M
73 Week-end Marriage—Faith Baldwin	1.60	4.80	8.00	R
74 The Murder That Had Everything—Hulbert Footner	2.00	6.00	10.00	M
75 The Affair of the Scarlet Crab—Clifford Knight; 1945	2.00	6.00	10.00	M
76 Death in the Back Seat—Dorothy Cameron Disney	1.60	4.80	8.00	M
77 G. I. Jokes—Lou Nielsen	7.00	21.00	35.00	H
78 Murder Wears a Mummer's Mask—Brett Halliday	2.00	6.00	10.00	M
79 The Hornet's Nest—Bruno Fischer	2.00	6.00	10.00	M
80 Prescription for Murder—Hannah Lees	1.60	4.80	8.00	M
81 The Glass Triangle—George Harmon Coxe	2.00	6.00	10.00	M
82 Curtains for the Editor—Thomas Polsky	2.00	6.00	10.00	M

Dell 65, © Dell

Dell 69, © Dell

Dell 75, © Dell

Dell 88, © Dell

Dell 111, © Dell

Dell 117, © Dell

(DELL, continued)

		Good	Fine	N/Mint	
83	With This Ring—Mignon G. Eberhart	1.60	4.80	8.00	M
84	Gold Comes in Brick—A. A. Fair	1.60	4.80	8.00	M
85	The Savage Gentleman—Philip Wylie	4.00	12.00	20.00	A
86	The Man Who Murdered Goliath—Geoffrey Homes	2.00	6.00	10.00	M
87	Painted for the Kill—Lucy Cores	2.00	6.00	10.00	M
88	The Creeps—Anthony Abbot	3.00	9.00	15.00	M
89	Dell Book of Jokes—Frances Cavanah & Ruth Weir	7.00	21.00	35.00	H
90	A Man Called Spade—Dashiell Hammett	10.00	30.00	50.00	M
91	The Case of the Constant Suicides—John Dickson Carr	3.00	9.00	15.00	M
92	Suspense Stories—Alfred Hitchcock	6.00	18.00	30.00	M
93	Beyond the Dark—Kieran Abbey	2.00	6.00	10.00	
94	No Crime for a Lady—Zelda Popkin	2.00	6.00	10.00	
95	The Last Express—Baynard Kendrick	2.00	6.00	10.00	M
96	Skeleton Key—Lenore Glen Offord	2.00	6.00	10.00	
97	Trail Boss of Indian Beef—Harold Channing Wire; 1946, aka Indian Beef	1.60	4.80	8.00	W
98	Spring Harrowing—Phoebe Atwood Taylor	1.20	3.60	6.00	R
99	Now, Voyager—Olive Higgins Prouty	1.20	3.60	6.00	
100	The So Blue Marble—Dorothy B. Hughes; 1946	1.20	3.60	6.00	M
101	Murder With Pictures—George Harmon Coxe	1.60	4.80	8.00	
102	You Only Hang Once—H. W. Roden	2.00	6.00	10.00	M
103	Murder Is a Kill-Joy—Elisabeth Sanxay Holding	1.60	4.80	8.00	M
104	The Crooking Finger—Cleve F. Adams	2.00	6.00	10.00	M
105	Appointment With Death—Agatha Christie	2.00	6.00	10.00	M
106	Made Up to Kill—Kelley Roos	1.60	4.80	8.00	M
107	The Deadly Truth—Helen McCloy	1.60	4.80	8.00	M
108	Death in Five Boxes—Carter Dickson	2.00	6.00	10.00	M
109	Spill the Jackpot—A. A. Fair	1.60	4.80	8.00	M
110	Wall of Eyes—Margaret Millar	1.60	4.80	8.00	M
111	Greenmask—Jefferson Farjeon	1.60	4.80	8.00	M
112	Michael Shayne's Long Chance—Brett Halliday	1.60	4.80	8.00	M
113	The Whistling Hangman—Baynard Kendrick	1.60	4.80	8.00	M
114	Three Women in Black—Helen Reilly	1.60	4.80	8.00	M
115	The Broken Vase—Rex Stout	2.00	6.00	10.00	M
116	Honor Bound—Faith Baldwin	1.20	3.60	6.00	R
117	Women Are Like That—Alice Elinor Lambert	1.20	3.60	6.00	R
118	Half Angel—Fanny Heaslip Lea	1.20	3.60	6.00	R
119	Robin Hill—Lida Larrimore	1.20	3.60	6.00	R
120	Man in the Saddle—Ernest Haycox	1.20	3.60	6.00	W
121	Footprints on the Ceiling—Clayton Rawson	2.00	6.00	10.00	M
122	Death in the Doll's House—Lawrence Bachmann & Hannah Lees	1.20	3.60	6.00	M
123	Too Many Bones—Ruth Sawtell Wallace	1.60	4.80	8.00	M
124	The Man in Lower Ten—Mary Roberts Rinehart	1.60	4.80	8.00	M
125	Dreadful Hollow—Irina Karlova; 1946	1.60	4.80	8.00	M
126	Murderer's Choice—Anna Mary Wells	1.60	4.80	8.00	M
127	Old Bones—Herman Petersen	1.60	4.80	8.00	M
128	Murder and the Married Virgin—Brett Halliday	1.60	4.80	8.00	M
129	The Continental Op—Dashiell Hammett	8.00	24.00	40.00	M
130	The Harvey Girls—Samuel Hopkins Adams	1.60	4.80	8.00	
131	The Red Lamp—Mary Roberts Rinehart	1.60	4.80	8.00	
132	The Visitor—Carl Randau & Leane Zugsmith	1.60	4.80	8.00	
133	Cobweb House—Elizabeth Holloway	1.60	4.80	8.00	
134	Wives to Burn—Lawrence G. Blochman	1.60	4.80	8.00	M
135	Meat for Murder—Lange Lewis	1.60	4.80	8.00	M
136	Wolf in Man's Clothing—Mignon G. Eberhart	1.60	4.80	8.00	M
137	Crimson Friday—Dorothy Cameron Disney	1.20	3.60	6.00	M
138	Men Are Such Fools—Faith Baldwin	1.20	3.60	6.00	R
139	Love - and the Countess to Boot—Jack Iams	1.20	3.60	6.00	R
140	Footprint of Cinderella—Philip Wylie	1.60	4.80	8.00	

	(DELL, continued)	Good	Fine	N/Mint	
141	The Swift Hour—Harriett Thurman	1.60	4.80	8.00	
142	Cold Steal—Alice Tilton	1.60	4.80	8.00	M
143	Bar the Doors!—Alfred Hitchcock	5.00	15.00	25.00	M
144	The White Brigand—Edison Marshall; 1947	1.20	3.60	6.00	A
145	Murder in Mesopotamia—Agatha Christie	1.60	4.80	8.00	M
146	Alphabet Hicks—Rex Stout	2.00	6.00	10.00	M
147	The Lady Is Afraid—George Harmon Coxe	1.60	4.80	8.00	M
148	Name Your Poison—Helen Reilly	1.60	4.80	8.00	M
149	The Blackbirder—Dorothy B. Hughes	1.60	4.80	8.00	M
150	Midsummer Nightmare—Christopher Hale; 1947	1.60	4.80	8.00	M
151	Who's Calling?—Helen McCloy	1.60	4.80	8.00	M
152	Jokes, Gags and Wisecracks—Ted Shane	7.00	21.00	35.00	H
153	Western Stories—Gene Autry	2.00	6.00	10.00	W
154	Return of the Continental Op—Dashiell Hammett	9.00	27.00	45.00	M
155	Sailor, Take Warning!—Kelley Roos	1.60	4.80	8.00	M
156	Blow-down—Lawrence G. Blochman	1.60	4.80	8.00	M
157	Fire Will Freeze—Margaret Millar	1.60	4.80	8.00	M
158	The Devil in the Bush—Matthew Head	1.60	4.80	8.00	M
159	If a Body—George Worthing Yates	1.60	4.80	8.00	M
160	Double or Quits—A. A. Fair	1.60	4.80	8.00	M
161	The Man Next Door—Mignon G. Eberhart	1.60	4.80	8.00	M
162	Odor of Violets—Baynard Kendrick	1.60	4.80	8.00	M
163	Self-made Woman—Faith Baldwin	1.20	3.60	6.00	R
164	The Left Leg—Alice Tilton	1.20	3.60	6.00	M
165	Wiped Out—John D. Newsom	1.60	4.80	8.00	A
166	The Wall—Mary Roberts Rinehart	1.20	3.60	6.00	M
167	White Fawn—Olive Higgins Prouty	1.60	4.80	8.00	
168	The Corpse Came Calling—Brett Halliday	1.60	4.80	8.00	M
169	Murdock's Acid Test—George Harmon Coxe; aka The Barotique Mystery	1.60	4.80	8.00	M
170	Reluctant Millionaire—Maysie Greig	1.20	3.60	6.00	
171	Octagon House—Phoebe Atwood Taylor	1.60	4.80	8.00	M
172	Sad Cypress—Agatha Christie	2.00	6.00	10.00	M
173	Rim of the Pit—Hake Talbot	1.60	4.80	8.00	M
174	The Sheik—E. M. Hull	2.00	6.00	10.00	A
175	And So to Murder—Carter Dickson; 1947	2.00	6.00	10.00	M
176	The Headless Lady—Clayton Rawson	3.00	9.00	15.00	M
177	The Hand in the Glove—Rex Stout	2.00	6.00	10.00	M
178	The Pink Camellia—Temple Bailey	1.20	3.60	6.00	R
179	Trail's End—William MacLeod Raine	1.20	3.60	6.00	W
180	The Rat Began to Gnaw the Rope—C. W. Grafton	1.20	3.60	6.00	M
181	Great Black Kanba—Gwenyth & Constance Little	1.20	3.60	6.00	M
182	No Time to Kill—George Harmon Coxe	1.60	4.80	8.00	M
183	American Acres—Louise Redfield Peattie	1.20	3.60	6.00	R
184	Murder Is My Business—Brett Halliday	1.60	4.80	8.00	M
185	Too Busy to Die—H. W. Roden	2.00	6.00	10.00	M
186	She Ate Her Cake—Blair Treynor	1.00	3.00	5.00	M
187	N or M?—Agatha Christie	1.20	3.60	6.00	M
188	Splendid Quest—Edison Marshall	1.20	3.60	6.00	
189	Kind Are Her Answers—Mary Renault	1.20	3.60	6.00	R
190	Dead Man's Gift—Zelda Popkin	1.20	3.60	6.00	M
191	The Lady in the Tower—Katherine Newlin Burt	1.60	4.80	8.00	
192	Tugboat Annie—Norman Reilly Raine	1.60	4.80	8.00	
193	Scarecrow—Eaton K. Goldthwaite	1.60	4.80	8.00	M
194	The Innocent Mrs. Duff—Elisabeth Sanxay Holding	1.20	3.60	6.00	M
195	Beam Ends—Errol Flynn	1.20	3.60	6.00	A
196	Rich Girl, Poor Girl—Faith Baldwin	1.20	3.60	6.00	R
197	Kiss the Blood Off My Hands—Gerald Butler	1.60	4.80	8.00	M
198	The Glass Mask—Lenore Glen Offord	1.60	4.80	8.00	

Dell 143, © Dell

Dell 174, © Dell

Dell 193, © Dell

Dell 205, © Dell   Dell 223, © Dell   Dell 235, © Dell

(DELL, continued)

		Good	Fine	N/Mint	
199	The Secret of Chimneys—Agatha Christie	1.60	4.80	8.00	M
200	The Opening Door—Helen Reilly; 1947	1.60	4.80	8.00	M
201	The First Men in the Moon—H. G. Wells	6.00	18.00	30.00	SF
202	Mrs. Murdock Takes a Case—George Harmon Coxe	1.60	4.80	8.00	M
203	The State vs. Elinor Norton—Mary Roberts Rinehart	1.20	3.60	6.00	
204	The Frightened Pigeon—Richard Burke	1.20	3.60	6.00	M
205	Dell Book of Crossword Puzzles—Kathleen Rafferty	6.00	18.00	30.00	NF
206	Hold Your Breath—Alfred Hitchcock	5.00	15.00	25.00	M
207	The Crimson Feather—Sara Elizabeth Mason	1.60	4.80	8.00	M
208	The Black Curtain—Cornell Woolrich	2.00	6.00	10.00	M
209	The Iron Gates—Margaret Millar	1.60	4.80	8.00	M
210	Ride the Pink Horse—Dorothy B. Hughes; 1948	1.20	3.60	6.00	M
211	Owls Don't Blink—A. A. Fair	1.60	4.80	8.00	M
212	Cue for Murder—Helen McCloy	1.60	4.80	8.00	M
213	Unidentified Woman—Mignon G. Eberhart	1.60	4.80	8.00	M
214	The Birthday Murder—Lange Lewis	1.60	4.80	8.00	M
215	Dr. Parrish, Resident—Sydney Thompson	1.20	3.60	6.00	R
216	Golden Earrings—Yolanda Foldes	1.20	3.60	6.00	
217	Gun Smoke Yarns—Gene Autry	1.20	3.60	6.00	W
218	H As in Hunted—Lawrence Treat	1.60	4.80	8.00	M
219	The Smell of Money—Matthew Head	1.60	4.80	8.00	
220	Hospital Nocturne—Alice Elinor Lambert	1.20	3.60	6.00	R
221	Dark Passage—David Goodis	1.60	4.80	8.00	
222	Marked for Murder—Brett Halliday	1.60	4.80	8.00	M
223	Hammett Homicides—Dashiell Hammett	8.00	24.00	40.00	M
224	How to Pick a Mate—Clifford Adams & Vance Packard	1.20	3.60	6.00	NF
225	Silent Are the Dead—George Harmon Coxe; 1948	1.20	3.60	6.00	M
226	Murder at the Vicarage—Agatha Christie	1.20	3.60	6.00	M
227	Trail Town—Ernest Haycox	1.00	3.00	5.00	W
228	Murder on Angler's Island—Helen Reilly	1.20	3.60	6.00	M
229	Murder Within Murder—Richard & Frances Lockridge	1.20	3.60	6.00	M
230	Blind Man's Bluff—Baynard Kendrick	1.20	3.60	6.00	M
231	A Halo for Nobody—Henry Kane	1.20	3.60	6.00	M
232	The Rope Began to Hang the Butcher—C. W. Grafton	1.20	3.60	6.00	M
233	The Upstart—Edison Marshall	1.20	3.60	6.00	A
234	Student Nurse—Renee Shann	1.00	3.00	5.00	R
235	Red Threads—Rex Stout	1.60	4.80	8.00	M
236	Skyscraper—Faith Baldwin	1.00	3.00	5.00	R
237	House of Darkness—Allan MacKinnon	1.20	3.60	6.00	
238	Gunsight Pass—William MacLeod Raine	1.00	3.00	5.00	W
239	Candidate for Love—Maysie Greig	1.00	3.00	5.00	R
240	The Charred Witness—George Harmon Coxe	1.20	3.60	6.00	M
241	The Bat—Mary Roberts Rinehart	1.20	3.60	6.00	M
242	The Unafraid—Gerald Butler; movie tie-in	1.00	3.00	5.00	M
243	Owls Don't Blink—A. A. Fair	1.20	3.60	6.00	M
244	Judas, Incorporated—Kurt Steel	1.20	3.60	6.00	M
245	Wallflowers—Temple Bailey	1.00	3.00	5.00	R
246	Bar-20 Days—Clarence E. Mulford	1.20	3.60	6.00	W
247	One Angel Less—H. W. Roden	1.20	3.60	6.00	M
248	Dangerous Ground—Francis Wickware	1.20	3.60	6.00	M
249	Stars Still Shine—Lida Larrimore	1.00	3.00	5.00	R
250	Skyline Riders—Francis W. Hilton; 1948	1.00	3.00	5.00	W
251	Banbury Bog—Phoebe Atwood Taylor	1.20	3.60	6.00	M
252	Benefit Performance—Richard Sale	1.20	3.60	6.00	
253	Treasure of the Brasada—Les Savage, Jr.	1.00	3.00	5.00	W
254	Bats Fly at Dusk—A. A. Fair	1.20	3.60	6.00	M
255	Enchanted Oasis—Faith Baldwin	1.20	3.60	6.00	R
256	Madonna of the Sleeping Cars—Maurice Dekobra	1.00	3.00	5.00	

(DELL, continued)

		Good	Fine	N/Mint	
257	Murder in Retrospect—Agatha Christie	1.20	3.60	6.00	M
258	No Coffin for the Corpse—Clayton Rawson	2.00	6.00	10.00	M
259	Murder Wears Mukluks—Eunice Mays Boyd	1.20	3.60	6.00	M
260	Chinese Red—Richard Burke	1.00	3.00	5.00	M
261	Do Not Disturb—Helen McCloy	1.20	3.60	6.00	M
262	Rope—AlfredHitchcock; movie tie-in. Note: Actually written by Don Ward	6.00	18.00	30.00	M
263	The Panic-Stricken—Mitchell Wilson	1.20	3.60	6.00	M
264	Fear and Trembling—Alfred Hitchcock	5.00	15.00	25.00	M
265	Men Under the Sea—Frank Meier	1.20	3.60	6.00	A
266	Ghost of a Chance—Kelley Roos	1.20	3.60	6.00	M
267	Not Quite Dead Enough—Rex Stout	1.60	4.80	8.00	M
268	Blood on Biscayne Bay—Brett Halliday	1.60	4.80	8.00	M
269	The Invisible Man—H. G. Wells	6.00	18.00	30.00	SF
270	It Ain't Hay—David Dodge; 1949	5.00	15.00	25.00	M
271	Gunsmoke and Trail Dust—Bliss Lomax; aka Trail Dust	1.00	3.00	5.00	W
272	The Velvet Fleece—Lois Eby & John C. Fleming	1.00	3.00	5.00	M
273	Death Knell—Baynard Kendrick	1.20	3.60	6.00	M
274	The Body Missed the Boat—Jack Iams	1.20	3.60	6.00	M
275	Where There's Smoke—Stewart Sterling; 1949	1.20	3.60	6.00	M
276	Murder for Two—George Harmon Coxe	1.20	3.60	6.00	M
277	Ex-Wife—Ursula Parott	1.20	3.60	6.00	R
278	Second Dell Book of Crossword Puzzles—Kathleen Rafferty	8.00	24.00	40.00	NF
279	Sons of the Shiek—E. M. Hull	1.20	3.60	6.00	M
280	Counterfeit Wife—Brett Halliday	1.20	3.60	6.00	M
281	Anthony Adverse in Italy—Hervey Allen	1.00	3.00	5.00	A
282	Western Stories—William MacLeod Raine	3.00	9.00	15.00	W
283	Anthony Adverse in Africa—Hervey Allen	1.00	3.00	5.00	A
284	Outlaw on Horseback—Will Ermine	1.00	3.00	5.00	W
285	Anthony Adverse in America—Hervey Allen	1.00	3.00	5.00	A
286	Eisenhower Was My Boss—Kay Summersby	1.20	3.60	6.00	NF
287	The Silver Leopard—Helen Reilly	3.00	9.00	15.00	M
288	The Heart Remembers—Faith Baldwin	1.00	3.00	5.00	R
289	Bitter Ending—Alexander Irving	1.20	3.60	6.00	
290	The Pioneers—Courtney Ryley Cooper	1.00	3.00	5.00	
291	So Dear to My Heart—Sterling North; movie tie-in	2.00	6.00	10.00	
292	Hits, Runs, & Errors—Robert Smith	1.20	3.60	6.00	S
293	Cards on the Table—Agatha Christie	1.20	3.60	6.00	M
294	Jim the Conqueror—Peter B. Kyne	1.00	3.00	5.00	W
295	The Goblin Market—Helen McCloy	1.00	3.00	5.00	M
296	Little Women—Louisa May Alcott & Jean Francis Webb; movie tie-in	1.20	3.60	6.00	
297	The Great Mistake—Mary Roberts Rinehart	1.00	3.00	5.00	M
298	Promise of Love—Mary Renault	1.00	3.00	5.00	R
299	Bad for Business—Rex Stout	1.60	4.80	8.00	M
300	The Paintin' Pistoleer—Walker A. Thompkins; 1949	1.20	3.60	6.00	W
301	'Q' as in Quicksand—Lawrence Treat	1.20	3.60	6.00	M
302	The Dark Device—Hannah Lees	1.20	3.60	6.00	
303	The Mirabilis Diamond—Jerome Odlum	1.20	3.60	6.00	M
304	Doctor Hudson's Secret Journal—Lloyd C. Douglas	1.00	3.00	5.00	
305	Invasion From Mars—Orson Welles	4.00	12.00	20.00	SF
306	Brandy for a Hero—William O'Farrell	1.20	3.60	6.00	
307	Pick Your Victim—Pat McGerr	1.60	4.80	8.00	M
308	Dead Yellow Women—Dashiell Hammett	9.00	27.00	45.00	M
309	Satin Straps—Maysie Greig	1.00	3.00	5.00	R
310	West of Texas Law—Walker A. Tompkins	1.00	3.00	5.00	W
311	Bengal Fire—Lawrence G. Blochman	1.00	3.00	5.00	A
312	The Gaunt Woman—Edmund Gilligan	1.00	3.00	5.00	
313	Death of a Bullionaire—A. B. Cunningham	1.00	3.00	5.00	M
314	Dead Wrong—Stewart Sterling	1.00	3.00	5.00	M

Dell 268, © Dell

Dell 287, © Dell

Dell 308, © Dell

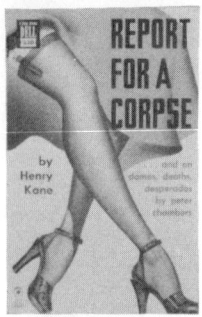

Dell 330, © Dell   Dell 343, © Dell   Dell 371, © Dell

(DELL, continued)

		Good	Fine	N/Mint	
315	Cats Prowl at Night—A. A. Fair	1.00	3.00	5.00	M
316	Armchair in Hell—Henry Kane	1.20	3.60	6.00	M
317	Alder Gulch—Ernest Haycox	1.00	3.00	5.00	W
318	Alimony—Faith Baldwin	1.20	3.60	6.00	R
319	The Man in the Brown Suit—Agatha Christie	1.20	3.60	6.00	M
320	The Cave Girl—Edgar Rice Burroughs	5.00	15.00	25.00	A
321	Assignment in Guiana—George Harmon Coxe	1.00	3.00	5.00	M
322	Death of a Tall Man—Richard & Frances Lockridge	1.20	3.60	6.00	M
323	Murder and the Married Virgin—Brett Halliday	1.00	3.00	5.00	M
324	The Corpse Came Calling—Brett Halliday	1.00	3.00	5.00	M
325	Michael Shayne's Long Chance—Brett Halliday; 1949	1.00	3.00	5.00	M
326	Murder Is My Business—Brett Halliday	1.00	3.00	5.00	M
327	Leave Cancelled—Nicholas Monsarrat	1.00	3.00	5.00	R
328	Cream of the Crop—Ed Fort	1.00	3.00	5.00	
329	Young Doctor Kildare—Max Brand	1.00	3.00	5.00	
330	Report for a Corpse—Henry Kane	1.00	3.00	5.00	M
331	Anna Lucasta—Jean Francis Webb; movie tie-in	1.00	3.00	5.00	
332	Fact Detective Mysteries—W. A. Swanberg; 1st ed., 1949	1.20	3.60	6.00	
333	Stampede—E. B. Mann	1.00	3.00	5.00	
334	The Case of the Seven Sneezes—Anthony Boucher	1.60	4.80	8.00	M
335	Double Treasure—Clarence Budington Kelland	1.00	3.00	5.00	W
336	Afterglow—Ruby M. Ayers	1.00	3.00	5.00	
337	Just Around the Corner—Stuart Brock	1.00	3.00	5.00	M
338	The Lady Regrets—James M. Fox	1.00	3.00	5.00	M
339	She—H. Rider Haggard; Note: Retold by Don Ward	5.00	15.00	25.00	F
340	The Care of Your Child From Infancy to Six—William Rosenson & Bela Schick	1.00	3.00	5.00	NF
341	The Upstart—Edison Marshall	1.00	3.00	5.00	
342	Sons of the Sheik—E. M. Hull	1.20	3.60	6.00	
343	The Chinese Doll—Wilson Tucker	1.60	4.80	8.00	M
344	Bedeviled—Libbie Block	1.00	3.00	5.00	
345	Wake for a Lady—H. W. Roden	1.00	3.00	5.00	M
356	The Accomplice—Matthew Head	1.00	3.00	5.00	
347	Trail Town—Ernest Haycox	1.00	3.00	5.00	W
348	A Halo for Nobody—Henry Kane	1.00	3.00	5.00	M
349	Too Busy to Die—H. W. Roden	1.20	3.60	6.00	M
350	It Ain't Hay—David Dodge; 1949	3.00	9.00	15.00	
351	Showdown—Errol Flynn	1.00	3.00	5.00	A
352	Gunsmoke Graze—Peter Dawson	1.00	3.00	5.00	W
353	Yankee Pasha—Edison Marshall	2.00	6.00	10.00	A
354	The Philadelphia Murder Story—Leslie Ford	1.00	3.00	5.00	M
355	The One That Got Away—Helen McCloy	1.00	3.00	5.00	M
356	Death in the Doll's House—Lawrence Bachmann & Hannah Lees	1.00	3.00	5.00	M
357	Leave It to Psmith—P. G. Wodehouse	1.20	3.60	6.00	H
358	To a God Unknown—John Steinbeck	1.20	3.60	6.00	
359	Trail's End—William MacLeod Raine	1.00	3.00	5.00	W
360	Don Lorenzo's Bride—Juanita Savage	1.20	3.60	6.00	
361	Haunted Lady—Mary Roberts Rinehart	1.00	3.00	5.00	M
362	Silent in the Saddle—Norman A. Fox	1.00	3.00	5.00	W
363	Blue City—Kenneth Millar	1.00	3.00	5.00	
364	Forlorn Island—Edison Marshall	1.20	3.60	6.00	A
365	The Death of a Worldly Woman—A. B. Cunningham	1.00	3.00	5.00	M
366	Unfinished Business—Cary Lucas	1.00	3.00	5.00	M
367	Suspense Stories—Alfred Hitchcock	3.00	9.00	15.00	M
368	The Moon's Our Home—Faith Baldwin; 1950	1.00	3.00	5.00	R
369	Panic—Helen McCloy	1.00	3.00	5.00	M
370	He Wouldn't Kill Patience—Carter Dickson	1.60	4.80	8.00	M
371	Wisteria Cottage—Robert M. Coates	1.60	4.80	8.00	
372	Buckaroo's Code—Wayne D. Overholser	1.00	3.00	5.00	W

		Good	Fine	N/Mint	
373	The Heart Has April Too—Gladys Taber	1.00	3.00	5.00	R
374	Night and the City—Gerald Kersh; movie tie-in	1.00	3.00	5.00	M
375	Date With Darkness—Donald Hamilton; 1950	1.20	3.60	6.00	
376	Out of Control—Baynard Kendrick	1.20	3.60	6.00	M
377	Alias the Dead—George Harmon Coxe	1.00	3.00	5.00	M
378	Last of the Longhorns—Will Ermine	1.00	3.00	5.00	W
379	Nightmare Town—Dashiell Hammett	5.00	15.00	25.00	M
380	Invitation to Live—Lloyd C. Douglas	1.00	3.00	5.00	
381	The Clever Sister—Margaret Culkin Banning	1.00	3.00	5.00	R
382	Celeste...the Gold Coast Virgin—Rosamond Marshall	3.00	9.00	15.00	E
383	Rutledge Trails the Ace of Spades—William MacLeod Raine	1.00	3.00	5.00	W
384	Girl Meets Body—Jack Iams	1.00	3.00	5.00	M
385	Blood on the Stars—Brett Halliday	1.00	3.00	5.00	M
386	The Uncomplaining Corpses—Brett Halliday	1.00	3.00	5.00	M
387	Tickets for Death—Brett Halliday	1.00	3.00	5.00	M
388	Murder Wears a Mummer's Mask—Brett Halliday	1.00	3.00	5.00	M
389	Give 'Em the Ax—A. A. Fair	1.00	3.00	5.00	M
390	The Cabinda Affair—Matthew Head	1.00	3.00	5.00	M
391	Murder at Hazelmoor—Agatha Christie	1.00	3.00	5.00	M
392	Virgin With Butterflies—Tom Powers	1.00	3.00	5.00	
393	The Code of the Woosters—P. G. Wodehouse	1.20	3.60	6.00	H
394	Return to Night—Mary Renault	1.00	3.00	5.00	
395	Devil's Stronghold—Leslie Ford	1.00	3.00	5.00	M
396	After Midnight—Martha Albrand	1.00	3.00	5.00	
397	The Farmhouse—Helen Reilly	1.00	3.00	5.00	M
398	Murder in Any Language—Kelley Roos	1.00	3.00	5.00	M
399	The Ridin' Kid From Powder River—Henry Herbert Knibbs	.80	2.40	4.00	W
400	Big City After Dark—Jack Lait & Lee Mortimer; 1950	1.00	3.00	5.00	
401	They Can't All Be Guilty—M. V. Heberden	1.00	3.00	5.00	M
402	The Captive of the Sahara—E. M. Hull	1.00	3.00	5.00	A
403	The Man in Lower Ten—Mary Roberts Rinehart	1.00	3.00	5.00	M
404	The Case of Jennie Brice—Mary Roberts Rinehart	1.00	3.00	5.00	M
405	The Long Escape—David Dodge	1.00	3.00	5.00	
406	Cactus Cavalier—Norman A. Fox	1.00	3.00	5.00	W
407	To a God Unknown—John Steinbeck	1.00	3.00	5.00	
408	Blue City—Kenneth Millar	.80	2.40	4.00	
409	Strangers May Kiss—Ursula Parrott	1.00	3.00	5.00	R
410	The Affair at the Boat Landing—A. G. Cunningham	1.00	3.00	5.00	M
411	A Man Called Spade—Dashiell Hammett	5.00	15.00	25.00	M
412	Seven Deadly Sisters—Pat McGerr	1.00	3.00	5.00	M
413	Arizona Feud—Frank R. Adams	1.00	3.00	5.00	W
414	Cleopatra's Nights—Allan Barnard	3.00	9.00	15.00	A
415	Ladies in Hades—Frederic Arnold Kummer	2.00	6.00	10.00	F
416	They Drive by Night—A. I. Bezzenides	1.00	3.00	5.00	
417	Tell Me About Women—Harry Reasoner	1.00	3.00	5.00	
418	Gunsmoke and Trail Dust—Bliss Lomax	1.00	3.00	5.00	W
419	Murder Is Mutual—Jack Dolph	1.00	3.00	5.00	M
420	Dead Sure—Stewart Sterling	1.00	3.00	5.00	M
421	Dead Yellow Women—Dashiell Hammett	8.00	24.00	40.00	M
422	Yankee Pasha—Edison Marshall	2.00	6.00	10.00	A
423	Murder in Havana—George Harmon Coxe	1.00	3.00	5.00	M
424	The Bandit Trail—William MacLeod Raine	1.00	3.00	5.00	W
425	Breakdown—Louis Paul; 1950	1.00	3.00	5.00	
426	A Taste for Violence—Brett Halliday	1.00	3.00	5.00	M
427	Dead Man's Diary and Dinner at Dupre's—Brett Halliday	1.00	3.00	5.00	M
428	Call for Michael Shayne—Brett Halliday	1.00	3.00	5.00	M
429	The Private Practice of Michael Shayne—Brett Halliday	1.00	3.00	5.00	M
430	She Walks Alone—Helen McCloy	1.00	3.00	5.00	M

Dell 382, © Dell

Dell 414, © Dell

Dell 415, © Dell

Dell 441, © Dell

Dell 452, © Dell

Dell 457, © Dell

(DELL, continued)

		Good	Fine	N/Mint	
431	Benjamin Blake, Son of Fury—Edison Marshall	1.00	3.00	5.00	A
432	Stag Night—Phillips Rogers	1.20	3.60	6.00	
433	King Solomon's Mines—H. Rider Haggard; movie tie-in. Note: Actually written by Jean Francis Webb	2.00	6.00	10.00	A
434	Dell Crossword Puzzle Dictionary—Kathleen Rafferty	2.00	6.00	10.00	NF
435	Their Ancient Grudge—Harry Harrison Kroll	1.00	3.00	5.00	
436	Gone to Earth—Mary Webb	1.00	3.00	5.00	
437	Gunpowder Lightning—Bertrand W. Sinclair	1.00	3.00	5.00	W
438	All Men Are Liars—John Stephen Strange	1.00	3.00	5.00	
439	The Border Lord—Jan Westcott	1.00	3.00	5.00	
440	New York Confidential—Jack Lait & Lee Mortimer	.80	2.40	4.00	NF
441	Murder With Pictures—George Harmon Coxe	1.00	3.00	5.00	M
442	Root of Evil—Eaton K. Goldthwaite	1.00	3.00	5.00	M
443	Dinner at Antoine's—Frances Parkinson Keyes	.80	2.40	4.00	
444	Tender Mercy—Lenard Kaufman	1.00	3.00	5.00	E
445	The High Road—Faith Baldwin	1.00	3.00	5.00	R
446	Yours Ever—Maysie Greig	.80	2.40	4.00	R
447	The Woman in Black—Leslie Ford	1.00	3.00	5.00	M
448	Flaming Canyon—Walker A. Tompkins	1.00	3.00	5.00	W
449	West of Texas Law—Walker A. Tompkins; aka Hang-Rope Harvest	1.00	3.00	5.00	W
450	Alder Gulch—Ernest Haycox; 1950	1.00	3.00	5.00	W
451	The Long Rope—Francis W. Hilton	1.00	3.00	5.00	W
452	A Man Called Spade—Dashiell Hammett	4.00	12.00	20.00	M
453	The Camera Clue—George Harmon Coxe	1.00	3.00	5.00	M
454	Murder on the Links—Agatha Christie	1.00	3.00	5.00	M
455	Hang by Your Neck—Henry Kane	1.00	3.00	5.00	M
456	Gentlemen of the Jungle—Tom Gill	1.00	3.00	5.00	E
457	Death Draws the Line—Jack Iams	1.00	3.00	5.00	M
458	A Taste for Violence—Brett Halliday	1.00	3.00	5.00	M
459	Blood on Biscayne Bay—Brett Halliday	1.00	3.00	5.00	M
460	Give 'Em the Ax—A. A. Fair	1.00	3.00	5.00	M
461	Innocent Bystander—Craig Rice	1.00	3.00	5.00	M
462	Desperate Angel—Helen Topping Miller	1.00	3.00	5.00	
463	The Inconvenient Bride—James M. Fox	1.00	3.00	5.00	M
464	The Corpse in the Corner Saloon—Hampton Stone	1.00	3.00	5.00	M
465	Death Haunts the Dark Lane—A. B. Cunningham	1.00	3.00	5.00	M
466	Pirates of the Range—B. M. Bower	1.00	3.00	5.00	W
467	Money to Burn—Peter B. Kyne	1.00	3.00	5.00	
468	Jungle Hunting Thrills—Edison Marshall	1.00	3.00	5.00	A
469	Uncle Dynamite—P. G. Wodehouse	1.20	3.60	6.00	H
470	Flight of an Angel—Verne Chute; 1951	1.00	3.00	5.00	
471	Vigilante—Richard Summers	1.00	3.00	5.00	
472	Crows Can't Count—A. A. Fair	1.00	3.00	5.00	M
473	The Steel Mirror—Donald Hamilton	1.00	3.00	5.00	
474	The Miracle of the Bells—Russell Janney; movie tie-in	.80	2.40	4.00	
475	Manhattan Nights—Faith Baldwin; 1951	1.00	3.00	5.00	R
476	My True Love Lies—Lenore Glen Offord	.80	2.40	4.00	
477	Crosstown—John Held, Jr.	1.00	3.00	5.00	
478	Plunder of the Sun—David Dodge	.80	2.40	4.00	A
479	The Web of Evil—Lucille Emerick	1.00	3.00	5.00	
480	The Thirsty Land—Norman A. Fox	.80	2.40	4.00	W
481	The Skeleton in the Clock—Carter Dickson	1.20	3.60	6.00	M
482	Women Must Weep—Ruth Adams Knight	.80	2.40	4.00	
483	What a Body!—Alan Green	1.00	3.00	5.00	
484	Untamed—Helga Moray	1.00	3.00	5.00	
485	The Queen and the Corpse—Max Murray	.80	2.40	4.00	M
486	Blood Money—Dashiell Hammett	5.00	15.00	25.00	M
487	Castle in the Swamp—Edison Marshall	1.00	3.00	5.00	

			Good	Fine	N/Mint	
488	Bombay Mail—Lawrence C. Blochman		1.00	3.00	5.00	
489	My Chinese Wife—Karl Eskelund		1.00	3.00	5.00	
490	The Stirrup Boss—Peter Dawson		.80	2.40	4.00	W
491	The Labors of Hercules—Agatha Christie		1.00	3.00	5.00	M
492	Blood of the Lamb—Charles Baker, Jr.		1.00	3.00	5.00	
493	She Shall Have Murder—Delano Ames		1.00	3.00	5.00	M
494	Miss Pinkerton—Mary Roberts Rinehart		.80	2.40	4.00	M
495	Double for Death—Rex Stout		1.20	3.60	6.00	M
496	Whispers in the Sun—Maysie Greig		.80	2.40	4.00	R
497	The Three Roads—Kenneth Millar		.80	2.40	4.00	
498	Staircase 4—Helen Reilly		.80	2.40	4.00	M
499	West of the Rimrock—Wayne D. Overholser		.80	2.40	4.00	W
500	Blood and Sand—Vincente Blasco Ibanez; 1951		.80	2.40	4.00	
501	The Demon Caravan—Georges Surdez		1.20	3.60	6.00	
502	The Groom Lay Dead—George Harmon Coxe		1.00	3.00	5.00	M
503	Marked for Murder—Brett Halliday		.80	2.40	4.00	M
504	The Sunnier Side—Charles Jackson		.80	2.40	4.00	
505	Murder With Southern Hospitality—Leslie Ford		.80	2.40	4.00	M
506	The Window at the White Cat—Mary Roberts Rinehart		.80	2.40	4.00	M
507	Francis—David Stern; movie tie-in		1.00	3.00	5.00	H
508	The Baited Blonde—Robinson MacLean		1.00	3.00	5.00	
509	Blazing Trails—Francis W. Hilton		.80	2.40	4.00	W
510	You Play the Black and the Red Comes Up—Richard Hallas		.80	2.40	4.00	
511	Slippery Hitch—Gerald Butler		.80	2.40	4.00	M
512	The Robbed Heart—Clifton Cuthbert		.80	2.40	4.00	
513	Alarm in the Night—Stewart Sterling		.80	2.40	4.00	M
514	Do Not Murder Before Christmas—Jack Iams		.80	2.40	4.00	M
515	Message From a Stranger—Marya Mannes		.80	2.40	4.00	
516	No Highway—Nevil Shute; movie tie-in		.80	2.40	4.00	
517	The Sagebrush Bandit—Bliss Lomax (H. S. Drago)		.80	2.40	4.00	W
518	Shell Game—Richard Powell		.80	2.40	4.00	M
519	Through a Glass, Darkly—Helen McCloy		.80	2.40	4.00	M
520	Dead Giveaway—Hugh Lawrence Nelson		.80	2.40	4.00	
521	Hell Cat—Idabel Williams		1.60	4.80	8.00	
522	The Glass Triangle—George Harmon Coxe		.80	2.40	4.00	M
523	Zane Grey Western Award Stories		1.00	3.00	5.00	W
524	Once in Vienna—Vicki Baum		.80	2.40	4.00	
525	Diamond Lil—Mae West; 1951		2.00	6.00	10.00	E
526	The Gentle Hangman—James M. Fox		1.60	4.80	8.00	M
527	Trouble Valley—Ward West		.80	2.40	4.00	W
528	Young Claudia—Rose Franken		.80	2.40	4.00	
529	Sad Cypress—Agatha Christie		1.00	3.00	5.00	M
530	Love Stories of India—Edison Marshall		.80	2.40	4.00	A
531	Death in Four Colors—Brandon Bird		.80	2.40	4.00	M
532	The Incredible Year—Faith Baldwin		.80	2.40	4.00	R
533	This Is It, Michael Shayne—Brett Halliday		.80	2.40	4.00	M
534	New York Confidential—Jack Lait & Lee Mortimer		.80	2.40	4.00	NF
535	Edge of Panic—Henry Kane		.80	2.40	4.00	M
536	Tarzan and the Lost Empire—Edgar Rice Burroughs		3.00	9.00	15.00	A
537	Hag's Nook—John Dickson Carr		1.00	3.00	5.00	M
538	The Creeping Siamese—Dashiell Hammett		6.00	18.00	30.00	M
539	Shadow on the Range—Norman A. Fox		.80	2.40	4.00	W
540	Too Many Cooks—Rex Stout		1.00	3.00	5.00	M
541	Episode of the Wandering Knife—Mary Roberts Rinehart		.80	2.40	4.00	M
542	Fools Die on Friday—A. A. Fair		.80	2.40	4.00	M
543	A Graveyard to Let—Carter Dickson		1.00	3.00	5.00	M
544	Wait for the Dawn—Martha Albrand		.80	2.40	4.00	
545	The Sheriff of San Miguel—Allan Vaughan Elston		.80	2.40	4.00	W

Dell 501, © Dell

Dell 536, © Dell

Dell 538, © Dell

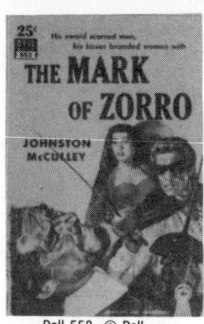

Dell 553, © Dell   Dell 600, © Dell   Dell 601, © Dell

(DELL, continued)

		Good	Fine	N/Mint	
546	Hunt With the Hounds—Mignon G. Eberhart	.80	2.40	4.00	M
547	Date With Death—Leslie Ford	.80	2.40	4.00	M
548	That Girl From Memphis—Wilbur Daniel Steele	.80	2.40	4.00	
549	The Jade Venus—George Harmon Coxe	.80	2.40	4.00	M
550	Mr. Parker Pyne, Detective—Agatha Christie; 1951	.80	2.40	4.00	M
551	Manhunt West—Walker A. Tomkins	.80	2.40	4.00	W
552	Murder Begins at Home—Delano Ames	.80	2.40	4.00	M
553	The Mark of Zorro—Johnston McCulley	2.00	6.00	10.00	W
554	Letter to Five Wives—John Klempner	.80	2.40	4.00	
555	Causeway to the Past—William O'Farrell	.80	2.40	4.00	
556	Draw of Drag—Wayne D. Overholser	.80	2.40	4.00	W
557	Backwoods Woman—Jack Boone	.80	2.40	4.00	E
558	Do Evil in Return—Margaret Millar	.80	2.40	4.00	M
559	Renegade Canyon—Peter Dawson	.80	2.40	4.00	W
560	The Neat Little Corpse—Max Murray	.80	2.40	4.00	M
561	Crescent Carnival—Frances Parkinson Keyes; 1952	.80	2.40	4.00	
562	Raw Land—Luke Short	.80	2.40	4.00	W
563	The King's Choice—Margaret Campbell Barnes	.80	2.40	4.00	A
564	Death-watch—John Dickson Carr	1.00	3.00	5.00	M
565	The Red Tassel—David Dodge	.80	2.40	4.00	
566	The Happy Time—Robert Fontaine	.80	2.40	4.00	
567	The Harem—Louis-Charles Royer	1.20	3.60	6.00	E
568	Passport to Peril—Robert Parker	.80	2.40	4.00	
569	Stormy in the West—Norman A. Fox	.80	2.40	4.00	W
570	The Mysterious Mr. Quin—Agatha Christie	.80	2.40	4.00	M
571	No Mask for Murder—Andrew Grave	.80	2.40	4.00	M
572	Dark Moon of March—Emmett Gowen	.80	2.40	4.00	
573	The Wheel Is Fixed—James M. Fox	.80	2.40	4.00	M
574	For Richer, for Poorer. . .—Faith Baldwin	.80	2.40	4.00	R
575	Montana, Here I Be!—Dan Cushman; 1952	1.00	3.00	5.00	W
576	Murder at Arroways—Helen Reilly	.80	2.40	4.00	M
577	Murder Twice Told—Donald Hamilton	.80	2.40	4.00	M
578	Framed in Blood—Brett Halliday	.80	2.40	4.00	M
579	Nobody Wore Black—Delano Ames	.80	2.40	4.00	
580	Until You Are Dead—Henry Kane	.80	2.40	4.00	M
581	The Lost Buckaroo—Bliss Lomax (H. S. Drago)	.80	2.40	4.00	W
582	Trial by Marriage—Vereen Bell	.80	2.40	4.00	
583	Dead of Night—Stewart Sterling	.80	2.40	4.00	M
584	Proceed at Will—Burke Wilkinson	.80	2.40	4.00	
585	The Circular Staircase—Mary Roberts Rinehart	.80	2.40	4.00	M
586	Dangerous Legacy—George Harmon Coxe	.80	2.40	4.00	M
587	The Stampeders—James B. Hendryx	.80	2.40	4.00	W
588	The Unknown Path—Anne Meredith	.80	2.40	4.00	
589	The Cabin in the Cotton—Harry Harrison Kroll	.80	2.40	4.00	
590	Counterfeit Wife—Brett Halliday	.80	2.40	4.00	M
591	Rocket to the Morgue—Anthony Boucher	2.00	6.00	10.00	M
592	Rustlers' Bend—Will Ermine	.80	2.40	4.00	W
593	Too Hot to Handle—Frank G. Presnell	.80	2.40	4.00	M
594	Keep Cool, Mr. Jones—Timothy Fuller	.80	2.40	4.00	M
595	My Enemy, My Wife—Allen Haden	.80	2.40	4.00	
596	A Taste of Murder—Joanna Cannan	.80	2.40	4.00	M
597	Georgia Girl—Margaret Rebecca Lay; c-Gross	.80	2.40	4.00	
598	Return of a Fighter—Ernest Haycox	.80	2.40	4.00	W
599	Heaven Ran Last—William P. McGivern	.80	2.40	4.00	
600	Rogue Queen—L. Sprague de Camp; 1952	5.00	15.00	25.00	SF
601	Before It's Too Late—Stuart Palmer	1.20	3.60	6.00	M
602	Tequila—Margaret Page Hood	.80	2.40	4.00	
603	Bedrooms Have Windows—A. A. Fair	.80	2.40	4.00	M

			Good	Fine	N/Mint	
604	Sudden Fear—Edna Sherry		.80	2.40	4.00	M
605	The Congo Venus—Matthew Head		.80	2.40	4.00	
606	Savage Range—Luke Short		.80	2.40	4.00	W
607	Funny Side Up—James E. Gunn		.80	2.40	4.00	H
608	The Human Beast—George Milburn & Emile Zola		1.00	3.00	5.00	
609	Brother Death—John Lodwick		.80	2.40	4.00	
610	Dr. Norton's Wife—Mildred Walker		.80	2.40	4.00	
611	How to Get Rich in Washington—Blair Bolles		.80	2.40	4.00	
612	Follow, as the Night—Pat McGerr		.80	2.40	4.00	M
613	Saddlebum—William MacLeod Raine		.80	2.40	4.00	W
614	Jewels for a Shroud—Walter de Steiguer		.80	2.40	4.00	M
615	The Sea Is a Woman—Lonnie Coleman		.80	2.40	4.00	
616	No Range Is Free—E. E. Halleran		.80	2.40	4.00	W
617	Dividend on Death—Brett Halliday		.80	2.40	4.00	M
618	Man in the Saddle—Ernest Haycox		.80	2.40	4.00	W
619	Spill the Jackpot—A. A. Fair		.80	2.40	4.00	M
620	Turn on the Heat—A. A. Fair		.80	2.40	4.00	M
621	Lament for the Bride—Helen Reilly		.80	2.40	4.00	M
622	Age of Consent—Clem Yore		.80	2.40	4.00	
623	Fatal in Furs—James M. Fox		.80	2.40	4.00	M
624	Steel to the South—Wayne D. Overholser		.80	2.40	4.00	W
625	Border Town—Carroll Graham; 1952		.80	2.40	4.00	
626	Three Doors to Death—Rex Stout		.80	2.40	4.00	M
627	When Worlds Collide—Philip Wylie & Edwin Balmer		2.00	6.00	10.00	SF
628	Speak No Evil—Mignon G. Eberhart		.80	2.40	4.00	M
629	Gunsight Pass—William MacLeod Raine		.80	2.40	4.00	W
630	Untamed—Helga Moray		1.20	3.60	6.00	
631	What Rhymes With Murder?—Jack Iams		.80	2.40	4.00	M
632	Border Ambush—Walker A. Tompkins		.80	2.40	4.00	W
633	Three Blind Mice—Agatha Christie		.80	2.40	4.00	M
634	Two If by Sea—Roger Bax; c-McCarthy		.80	2.40	4.00	
635	To Wake the Dead—John Dickson Carr		1.00	3.00	5.00	M
636	Triggerman—Frank Austin		.80	2.40	4.00	
637	Indian Beef—Harold Channing Wire		.80	2.40	4.00	W
638	See You at the Morgue—Lawrence G. Blochman		.80	2.40	4.00	M
639	Good Luck to the Corpse—Max Murray		.80	2.40	4.00	M
640	The Life and Death of the Wicked Lady Skelton—Magdalen King-Hall		.80	2.40	4.00	
641	Carry My Coffin Slowly—Lee Herrington		.80	2.40	4.00	M
642	Tall Man Riding—Norman A. Fox		.80	2.40	4.00	W
643	Deadline at Durango—Allan Vaughan Elston		.80	2.40	4.00	W
644	The Fifth Key—George Harmon Coxe		.80	2.40	4.00	M
645	The Body That Wasn't Uncle—George Worthing Yates		.80	2.40	4.00	M
646	No Mourners Present—Frank G. Presnell		.80	2.40	4.00	
647	King Colt—Luke Short		.80	2.40	4.00	W
648	Fabia—Olive Higgins Prouty		.80	2.40	4.00	
649	The Kind Man—Helen Nielsen		.80	2.40	4.00	
650	Night at the Mocking Widow—Carter Dickson; 1953		1.00	3.00	5.00	M
651	Desperate Moment—Martha Albrand		.80	2.40	4.00	
652	The Bat—Mary Roberts Rinehart		.50	1.50	2.50	M
653	Outlaw on Horseback—Will Ermine		.80	2.40	4.00	W
654	Dell Crossword Puzzles—Kathleen Rafferty		1.60	4.80	8.00	NF
655	No Tears for Hilda—Andrew Garve		.80	2.40	4.00	M
656	Badlands Justice—Dan Cushman		1.00	3.00	5.00	W
657	The Hunter—James Aldridge		.80	2.40	4.00	
658	To Catch a Thief—David Dodge		.80	2.40	4.00	
659	Stairway to an Empty Room—Dolores Hitchens		.50	1.50	2.50	M
660	Buckskin Empire—Harry Sinclair Drago		.80	2.40	4.00	W
661	Stormy Present—Hope Field		.80	2.40	4.00	
662	Murder Leaves a Ring—Fay Grissom Stanley		.80	2.40	4.00	M
663	The Arms of Venus—John Appleby		.80	2.40	4.00	
664	The Boomerang Clue—Agatha Christie		.80	2.40	4.00	M
665	Dead Weight—Frank Kane		1.00	3.00	5.00	M
666	The Law Busters—Bliss Lomax (H. S. Drago)		.80	2.40	4.00	W
667	Four Fallen Women—anthology		.80	2.40	4.00	E
668	Bodies Are Where You Find Them—Brett Halliday		.80	2.40	4.00	M
669	Never Look Back—Mignon G. Eberhart		.80	2.40	4.00	M
670	The Witching Night—C. S. Cody		.80	2.40	4.00	
671	1953 Racing Almanac—Rowland Barber & John I. Day		.80	2.40	4.00	NF
672	Don't Cry for Me—William Campbell Gault		.80	2.40	4.00	M
673	Treasure of the Brasada—Les Savage, Jr.		.50	1.50	2.50	W
674	The Broken Vase—Rex Stout		.80	2.40	4.00	M
675	Hardly a Man Is Now Alive—Herbert Brean; 1953		.80	2.40	4.00	
676	All Over Town—George Milburn		.80	2.40	4.00	
677	Texas Fury—John Callahan		.80	2.40	4.00	W
678	Fashioned for Murder—George Harmon Coxe		.80	2.40	4.00	M
679	Night Has a Thousand Eyes—William Irish		2.00	6.00	10.00	M

| Dell 676, © Dell | Dell 715, © Dell | Dell 722, © Dell |

		Good	Fine	N/Mint	
	(DELL, continued)				
680	First He Died—Clifford D. Simak	1.20	3.60	6.00	SF
681	The Picture of Dorian Grey—Oscar Wilde	1.60	4.80	8.00	H
682	The Gallows in My Garden—Richard Deming	.80	2.40	4.00	M
683	An Overdose of Death—Agatha Christie	.80	2.40	4.00	M
684	The Silver Star—Will Ermine	.80	2.40	4.00	W
685	The Scarlet Slippers—James M. Fox	.80	2.40	4.00	M
686	The Juggler—Michael Blankfort	.80	2.40	4.00	
687	The Frightened Stiff—Kelley Roos	.80	2.40	4.00	M
688	The Proud Sheriff—Eugene Manlove Rhodes	.80	2.40	4.00	W
689	The Bahamas Murder Case—Leslie Ford	.50	1.50	2.50	M
690	Behind the Crimson Blind—Carter Dickson	1.00	3.00	5.00	M
691	Bats Fly at Dusk—A. A. Fair	.80	2.40	4.00	M
692	The River Road—Frances Parkinson Keyes	.50	1.50	2.50	
693	Nightmare at Noon—Stewart Sterling	.80	2.40	4.00	M
694	Roughshod—Norman A. Fox	.80	2.40	4.00	W
695	The Other One—Catherine Turney	.80	2.40	4.00	M
696	Slan—A. E. Van Vogt	2.00	6.00	10.00	SF
697	At Last, Mr. Tolliver—William Wiegand; c-Powers	.80	2.40	4.00	
698	The Big Fist—Clyde Ragsdale	.80	2.40	4.00	
699	Buckaroo's Code—Wayne D. Overholser	.80	2.40	4.00	W
700	Curtains for the Copper—Thomas Polsky; 1953	.80	2.40	4.00	M
701	They Died Laughing—Alan Green	.80	2.40	4.00	
702	Bounty Guns—Luke Short	.80	2.40	4.00	W
703	The Stockade—Kenneth Lamott	.80	2.40	4.00	E
704	The Chill—E. C. Bentley	.80	2.40	4.00	M
705	Brutally With Love—Edith Pope	.80	2.40	4.00	
706	The Mad Hatter Mystery—John Dickson Carr	1.00	3.00	5.00	M
707	Gold Brick Range—Allan Vaughan Elston	.80	2.40	4.00	W
708	Mosquitoes—William Faulkner	.80	2.40	4.00	
709	Three Women in Black—Helen Reilly	.50	1.50	2.50	M
710	The Follower—Patrick Quentin	.80	2.40	4.00	M
711	Challenge to Danger—William MacLeod Raine	.50	1.50	2.50	W
712	The Natural—Bernard Malamud	.50	1.50	2.50	
713	Strangle Hold—Mary McMullen	.50	1.50	2.50	
714	Matador—Barnaby Conrad	.50	1.50	2.50	A
715	Four Lost Ladies—Stuart Palmer	1.20	3.60	6.00	
716	Gunsmoke Graze—Peter Dawson	.50	1.50	2.50	
717	Trial by Terror—Paul Gallico	.50	1.50	2.50	
718	Double or Quits—A. A. Fair	.50	1.50	2.50	M
719	The Iron Virgin—James M. Fox	.50	1.50	2.50	M
720	The Ripper From Rawhide—Dan Cushman	.80	2.40	4.00	W
721	Mercy Island—Theodore Pratt	.50	1.50	2.50	
722	A Shot of Murder—Jack Iams	.50	1.50	2.50	M
723	When Dorinda Dances—Brett Halliday	.50	1.50	2.50	M
724	Guns Along the Yellowstone—Bliss Lomax (H. S. Drago)	.50	1.50	2.50	W
725	Seeds of Contemplation—Thomas Merton; 1953	.50	1.50	2.50	
726	Blow Hot, Blow Cold—Gerald Butler	.50	1.50	2.50	M
727	The Burden of Guilt—Ian Gordon	.50	1.50	2.50	
728	The Dell Bowling Handbook—Joe Falcaro & Murray Goodman	.50	1.50	2.50	NF
729	Fabulous Gunman—Wayne D. Overholser	.50	1.50	2.50	W
730	Vanish in an Instant—Margaret Millar	.50	1.50	2.50	M
731	Fetish—Christine Garnier	.50	1.50	2.50	
732	The Double Man—Helen Reilly	.50	1.50	2.50	M
733	The Fatal Caress—Richard Barker	.50	1.50	2.50	M
734	The Lady Is Afraid—George Harmon Coxe	.50	1.50	2.50	M
735	A Corpse for Christmas—Henry Kane	.50	1.50	2.50	M
736	The Cumberland Rifles—Noel B. Gerson	.50	1.50	2.50	A
737	Ghostly Hoofbeats—Norman A. Fox	.50	1.50	2.50	W

		Good	Fine	N/Mint	
738	Nothing More Than Murder—Jim Thompson	1.20	3.60	6.00	M
739	Hurry the Darkness—Maurice Procter	.50	1.50	2.50	M
740	Blow-down—Lawrence B. Blochman	.50	1.50	2.50	
741	Dr. Gatskill's Blue Shoes—Paul Conant	.50	1.50	2.50	
742	Colorado Showdown—Allan Vaughan Elston	.50	1.50	2.50	W
743	Mum's the Word for Murder—Brett Halliday	.50	1.50	2.50	M
744	Death Has Deep Roots—Michael Gilbert	.50	1.50	2.50	
745	Venturous Lady—George Harmon Coxe	.50	1.50	2.50	M
746	The Bloody Bokhara—William Campbell Gault	.50	1.50	2.50	M
747	Dead on the Level—Helen Nielsen; 1954	.50	1.50	2.50	M
748	Trail Town—Ernest Haycox	.50	1.50	2.50	W
749	Bare Trap—Frank Kane	.50	1.50	2.50	M
750	The Gabriel Horn—Felix Holt; 1954	.50	1.50	2.50	
751	Barbary Hoard—John Appleby	.50	1.50	2.50	
752	The Spider Lily—Bruno Fischer	.80	2.40	4.00	M
753	Murder After Hours—Agatha Christie	.50	1.50	2.50	M
754	Laughing on the Inside—Bill Yates	.50	1.50	2.50	H
755	Smoky Range—E. E. Halleran	.50	1.50	2.50	W
756	Whomsoever I Shall Kiss—Curt Siodmak	.80	2.40	4.00	
757	The Hollow Needle—George Harmon Coxe	.50	1.50	2.50	M
758	The Clock Strikes 13—Herbert Brean	.50	1.50	2.50	
759	Black Widow—Patrick Quentin	.80	2.40	4.00	M
760	Outpost Mars—Cyril Judd	.80	2.40	4.00	SF
761	Sex After Forty—John Gilmore & S. A. Lewin	.50	1.50	2.50	NF
762	Silver Doll—Blair Treynor	.50	1.50	2.50	M
763	The Key to Nicholas Street—Stanley Ellin	.50	1.50	2.50	
764	Prairie Marshal—Walker A. Tompkins	.50	1.50	2.50	W
765	By-line for Murder—Andrew Garve	.50	1.50	2.50	M
766	Nell Gwyn: Royal Mistress—John H. Wilson	.50	1.50	2.50	A
767	Dead Man's Plans—Mignon G. Eberhart; c-Powers	.50	1.50	2.50	M
768	What Really Happened—Brett Halliday	.50	1.50	2.50	M
769	Brand of Empire—Luke Short	.50	1.50	2.50	W
770	Thirteen at Dinner—Agatha Christie	.50	1.50	2.50	M
771	The Loved One—Evelyn Waugh	.50	1.50	2.50	
772	Top of the Heap—A. A. Fair	.50	1.50	2.50	M
773	Evil Became Them—Pat Root	.50	1.50	2.50	
774	Sam Snead's Natural Golf—Sam Snead	.50	1.50	2.50	S
775	The Corpse in the Waxworks—John Dickson Carr; 1954, c-Powers	.80	2.40	4.00	M
776	Gun Bulldogger—Eugene Cunningham	.50	1.50	2.50	W
777	The Tiger in the Smoke—Margery Allingham; c-Powers	.50	1.50	2.50	M
778	Crows Can't Count—A. A. Fair	.50	1.50	2.50	M
779	Widow's Won't Wait—Dolores Hitchens	.50	1.50	2.50	M
780	Tall in the Saddle—Gordon Young	.50	1.50	2.50	W
781	Beyond Infinity—Robert Spencer Carr	.80	2.40	4.00	SF
782	The Red Lamp—Mary Roberts Rinehart	.50	1.50	2.50	M
783	Long Lightning—Norman A. Fox	.50	1.50	2.50	W
784	Dead Babes in the Woods—D. B. Olsen	.50	1.50	2.50	M
785	Bullet Proof—Frank Kane	.50	1.50	2.50	M
786	Hold It, Florence—Whitney Darrow, Jr.	.50	1.50	2.50	
787	The Long Memory—Howard Clewes	.50	1.50	2.50	
788	Murder Is the Pay-off—Leslie Ford	.50	1.50	2.50	M
789	Stagecoach Kingdom—Harry Sinclair Drago	.50	1.50	2.50	W
790	The Corpse That Refused to Stay Dead—Hampton Stone	.50	1.50	2.50	M
791	The Long Loud Silence—Wilson Tucker	1.60	4.80	8.00	SF
792	The Evil Men Do—Benedict Kiely; aka Honey Seems Bitter	.50	1.50	2.50	
793	The Bandit Trail—William MacLeod Raine	.50	1.50	2.50	W
794	Sleep, My Love—Robert Martin	.50	1.50	2.50	
795	The Canvas Coffin—William Campbell Gault	.50	1.50	2.50	M
796	West of the Rimrock—Wayne D. Overholser	.50	1.50	2.50	W
797	The Harlot Killer—Allan Barnard	.50	1.50	2.50	
798	Cooking for Two—Janet McKenzie Hill	.40	1.20	2.00	NF
799	Inland Passage—George Harmon Coxe	.50	1.50	2.50	M
800	Daisy Miller and the Turn of the Screw—Henry James; 1954	.30	.90	1.50	
801	Riders of the Buffalo Grass—Bliss Lomax (H. S. Drago)	.50	1.50	2.50	W
802	Asylum—William Seabrook; c-Powers	.50	1.50	2.50	
803	One Night With Nora—Brett Halliday	.50	1.50	2.50	M
804	Wide Loop—Nelson Nye	.50	1.50	2.50	W
805	Murder in Mesopotamia—Agatha Christie	.50	1.50	2.50	M
806	Obit Delayed—Helen Nielsen	.50	1.50	2.50	M
807	Vile Bodies—Evelyn Waugh	.50	1.50	2.50	
808	Deadlock—Ruth Fenisong	.50	1.50	2.50	M
809	Some Women Won't Wait—A. A. Fair	.50	1.50	2.50	M
810	Roundup on the Picketwire—Allan Vaughan Elston	.50	1.50	2.50	W
811	The Unknown Quantity—Mignon G. Eberhart	.50	1.50	2.50	M
812	Deep Is the Night—James Wellard	.50	1.50	2.50	
813	My Name Is Michael Sibley—John Bingham	.50	1.50	2.50	M

		Good	Fine	N/Mint	
814	Haunted Lady—Mary Roberts Rinehart	.40	1.20	2.00	M
815	Valley of Guns—Wayne D. Overholser	.50	1.50	2.50	W
816	Five Alarm Funeral—Stewart Sterling	.50	1.50	2.50	M
817	The Pigskin Bag—Bruno Fischer; 1955	.80	2.40	4.00	
818	The Golden Violet—Joseph Shearing	.50	1.50	2.50	
819	The Amazing Adventures of Father Brown—G. K. Chesterton	.80	2.40	4.00	M
820	Is Sex Necessary?—James Thurber & E. B. White	.80	2.40	4.00	H
821	Riders of Buck River—William MacLeod Raine	.50	1.50	2.50	W
822	Poisons Unknown—Frank Kane	.50	1.50	2.50	M
823	A Town of Masks—Dorothy Salisbury Davis	.50	1.50	2.50	M
824	The Company She Keeps—Mary McCarthy	.50	1.50	2.50	
825	Gunfire Men—L. L. Foreman; 1955	.50	1.50	2.50	W
826	Savage Range—Luke Short	.50	1.50	2.50	W
827	Murder Through the Looking Glass—Andrew Garve	.40	1.20	2.00	M
828	Strawberry Roan—Clem Colt	.50	1.50	2.50	W
829	Before I Wake—Brett Halliday	.50	1.50	2.50	M
830	There Is a Tide—Agatha Christie	.50	1.50	2.50	M
831	The Rawhide Years—Norman A. Fox	.50	1.50	2.50	W
832	The Stirrup Boss—Peter Dawson	.50	1.50	2.50	W
833	Recipe for Homicide—Lawrence G. Blochman	.50	1.50	2.50	M
834	The Strangers—William E. Wilson	.50	1.50	2.50	
835	Blood on the Boards—William Campbell Gault	.50	1.50	2.50	M
836	Gold Comes in Bricks—A. A. Fair	.50	1.50	2.50	M
837	Detour to Death—Helen Nielsen	.50	1.50	2.50	M
838	The Frightened Fiancee—George Harmon Coxe	.50	1.50	2.50	M
839	Baseball's Greatest Players—Tom Meany	.50	1.50	2.50	S
840	The Bridal Bed Murders—A. E. Martin	.50	1.50	2.50	M
841	The Evil of Time—Evelyn Berckman	.50	1.50	2.50	
842	The Corpse Came Calling—Brett Halliday	.50	1.50	2.50	M
843	Man the Beast and the Wild, Wild Women—Virgil Partch	1.20	3.60	6.00	H
844	The Proud Diggers—William O. Turner	.50	1.50	2.50	W
845	Death Commits Bigamy—James M. Fox	.50	1.50	2.50	M
846	Tough Hand—Wayne D. Overholser	.50	1.50	2.50	W
847	The Bad Seed—William March	.50	1.50	2.50	
848	Give the Little Corpse a Great Big Hand—George Bagby	.50	1.50	2.50	M
849	Wyoming Gun—Tom Roan	.50	1.50	2.50	W
850	The Shocking Secret—Holly Roth; 1955	.50	1.50	2.50	M
851	Run to Death—Patrick Quentin	.50	1.50	2.50	M
852	The Affairs of Caroline Cherie—Cecil Saint-Laurent	.50	1.50	2.50	
853	The Body on the Bench—Dorothy B. Hughes	.50	1.50	2.50	M
854	Heather Mary—J. M. Scott	.80	2.40	4.00	
855	The Witness for the Prosecution—Agatha Christie	.50	1.50	2.50	M
856	To Walk the Night—William Sloane	.40	1.20	2.00	M
857	Dead and Gone—Brandon Bird	.50	1.50	2.50	M
858	Bury Me Not—Allan R. Bosworth	.50	1.50	2.50	M
859	The Crooked Hinge—John Dickson Carr	.80	2.40	4.00	M
860	Seeing Red—Theodora DuBois	.50	1.50	2.50	
861	Saddle Up for Sunlight—Allan Vaughan Elston	.50	1.50	2.50	W
862	My Favorite Football Stories—Red Grange	.40	1.20	2.00	S
863	The Law at Randado—Elmore Leonard	.50	1.50	2.50	W
864	The Thirsty Land—Norman A. Fox	.50	1.50	2.50	W
865	Death Has Three Lives—Brett Halliday	.50	1.50	2.50	M
866	Michael Shayne's Long Chance—Brett Halliday	.50	1.50	2.50	M
867	She Woke to Darkness—Brett Halliday	.50	1.50	2.50	M
868	Run, Killer, Run—William Campbell Gault	.50	1.50	2.50	M
869	Bounty Guns—Luke Short	.50	1.50	2.50	W
870	The Danger Within—Michael Gilbert	.50	1.50	2.50	
871	Murder in Retrospect—Agatha Christie	.50	1.50	2.50	M
872	Grin and Bear It—George Lichty	.50	1.50	2.50	H
873	The Tender Poisoner—John Bingham	.50	1.50	2.50	M
874	The Big Money—Harold Q. Masur	.50	1.50	2.50	M
875	The Violent Land—Wayne D. Overholser; 1955	.50	1.50	2.50	W
876	The Long Chase—James B. Hendryx	.50	1.50	2.50	W
877	Man Missing—Mignon G. Eberhart	.50	1.50	2.50	M
878	The Border Jumpers—Will C. Brown	.50	1.50	2.50	W
879	Gold on the Hoof—Walker A. Tompkins	.50	1.50	2.50	W
880	The Silent Women—Margaret Page Hood	.50	1:50	2.50	
881	Fog of Doubt—Christianna Brand; 1956	.50	1.50	2.50	
882	The High Passes—John Reese	.50	1.50	2.50	
883	The Murder That Wouldn't Stay Solved—Hampton Stone	.50	1.50	2.50	M
884	Danger West!—Robert McCaig	.50	1.50	2.50	W
885	Straw Man—Doris Miles Disney	.50	1.50	2.50	M
886	Grave Danger—Frank Kane	.50	1.50	2.50	
887	The Ponder Heart—Eudora Welty	.50	1.50	2.50	
888	Murder at the Vicarage—Agatha Christie	.50	1.50	2.50	M
889	Trail's End—William MacLeod Raine	.50	1.50	2.50	W

		Good	Fine	N/Mint	
890	My Son, the Murderer—Patrick Quentin	.50	1.50	2.50	M
891	Blood on the Stars—Brett Halliday	.50	1.50	2.50	M
892	Quick on the Shoot—George C. Appell	.50	1.50	2.50	
893	The Frightened Fingers—Spencer Dean	.50	1.50	2.50	M
894	Thin Air—Howard Browne	.40	1.20	2.00	
895	Raw Land—Luke Short	.50	1.50	2.50	W
896	The Butcher's Wife—Owen Cameron	.50	1.50	2.50	
897	The Twilighters—Noel M. Loomis	.50	1.50	2.50	W
898	Gulf Coast Girl—Charles Williams; c-Maguire	1.00	3.00	5.00	
899	Cats Prowl at Night—A. A. Fair	.50	1.50	2.50	M
900	The Woman on the Roof—Helen Nielsen; 1956	.50	1.50	2.50	M
901	Red Hot Ice—Frank Kane	.50	1.50	2.50	M
902	Eye Witness—George Harmon Coxe	.50	1.50	2.50	M
903	Draw or Drag—Wayne D. Overholser	.50	1.50	2.50	W
904	The Body in the Basket—George Bagby	.50	1.50	2.50	M
905	In a Deadly Vein—Brett Halliday	.50	1.50	2.50	M
906	Day of the Outlaw—Lee E. Wells	.50	1.50	2.50	W
907	Shadow on the Range—Norman A. Fox	.50	1.50	2.50	W
908	Washington Whispers Murder—Leslie Ford	.50	1.50	2.50	M
909	Day of the Dead—Bart Spicer	.50	1.50	2.50	
910	The Restless Hands—Bruno Fischer	.50	1.50	2.50	
911	Lazy H Feud—Ed LaVanway	.50	1.50	2.50	W
912	Cards on the Table—Agatha Christie	.50	1.50	2.50	M
913	Goodbye to Gunsmoke—Ralph Catlin	.50	1.50	2.50	W
914	Stranger in Town—Brett Halliday	.50	1.50	2.50	M
915	Masterpiece in Murder—Richard Powell	.50	1.50	2.50	M
916	Last of the Longhorns—Will Ermine	.50	1.50	2.50	W
917	The Opening Door—Helen Reilly	.50	1.50	2.50	M
918	Green Light for Death—Frank Kane	.50	1.50	2.50	M
919	Their Guns Were Fast—Harry Sinclair Drago	.50	1.50	2.50	W
920	The Lively Corpse—Margaret Millar	.50	1.50	2.50	M
921	The Cautious Maiden—Cecil Saint-Laurent	.50	1.50	2.50	
922	The Hidden Grave—Peter Hardin	.50	1.50	2.50	
923	Scout Commander—S. E. Whitman	.50	1.50	2.50	
924	Cast a Long Shadow—Wayne D. Overholser	.50	1.50	2.50	W
925	The Tall Dark Man—Anne Chamberlain; 1956	.50	1.50	2.50	
926	Murder in the Raw—William Campbell Gault	.50	1.50	2.50	M
927	Stormy in the West—Norman A. Fox	.50	1.50	2.50	W
928	The Unquiet Corpse—William Sloane	.50	1.50	2.50	M
929	Dead Stop—Doris Miles Disney	.50	1.50	2.50	M
930	The Texas Pistol—James Keene; 1957	.50	1.50	2.50	
931	Never Bet Your Life—George Harmon Coxe	.50	1.50	2.50	M
932	Rustlers' Bend—Will Ermine	.50	1.50	2.50	W
933	Murder at Nightfall—Edna Sherry	.50	1.50	2.50	M
934	A Taste for Violence—Brett Halliday	.50	1.50	2.50	M
935	Border Guns—Eugene Cunningham	.50	1.50	2.50	W
936	Worse Than Murder—Evelyn Berckman	.50	1.50	2.50	
937	Murder at Hazelmoor—Agatha Christie	.50	1.50	2.50	M
938	Renegade Canyon—Peter Dawson	.50	1.50	2.50	W
939	Fools Die on Friday—A. A. Fair	.50	1.50	2.50	M
940	Escape From Five Shadows—Elmore Leonard	.50	1.50	2.50	
941	Murder Is a Witch—John Bingham; c-Powers	.50	1.50	2.50	M
942	The Sagebrush Bandit—Bliss Lomax (H. S. Drago)	.50	1.50	2.50	W
943	The Man Who Had Too Much to Lose—Hampton Stone	.50	1.50	2.50	M
944	Bury Me Deep—Harold Q. Masur	.40	1.20	2.00	M
945	Alder Gulch—Ernest Haycox	.50	1.50	2.50	W
946	The Blonde Cried Murder—Brett Halliday	.50	1.50	2.50	M
947	The Settler—William O. Turner	.50	1.50	2.50	W
948	Steel to the South—Wayne D. Overholser	.50	1.50	2.50	W
949	Dead Storage—George Bagby	.50	1.50	2.50	M
950	Night Passage—Norman A. Fox; 1957	.50	1.50	2.50	W
951	Murder in a Nunnery—Eric Shepherd	.50	1.50	2.50	M
952	Man in the Saddle—Ernest Haycox	.50	1.50	2.50	W
953	Dead of Summer—Dana Mosely	.50	1.50	2.50	
954	To Ride the River With—William MacLeod Raine	.50	1.50	2.50	W
955	Postmark Murder—Mignon G. Eberhart	.50	1.50	2.50	M
956	Riding Gun—Eugene Cunningham	.50	1.50	2.50	W
957	This Is It, Michael Shayne—Brett Halliday	.50	1.50	2.50	M
958	Framed in Blood—Brett Halliday	.50	1.50	2.50	M
959	The Brass and the Blue—James Keene	.50	1.50	2.50	
960	Murder and the Married Virgin—Brett Halliday	.50	1.50	2.50	M
961	Mr. Parker Pyne, Detective—Agatha Christie	.50	1.50	2.50	M
962	King Colt—Luke Short	.50	1.50	2.50	W
963	Savage Range—Luke Short	.50	1.50	2.50	W
964	Inspector Maigret and the Burglar's Wife—Georges Simenon	.80	2.40	4.00	M
965	Murder Is My Business—Brett Halliday; 1958	.50	1.50	2.50	M

		Good	Fine	N/Mint	
966	The Diamond Hitch—Frank O'Rourke	.50	1.50	2.50	
967	Secret of the Wastelands—Bliss Lomax	.50	1.50	2.50	W
968	The Blonde Died Dancing—Kelley Roos	.50	1.50	2.50	M
969	Stranger From Arizona—Norman A. Fox	.50	1.50	2.50	W
970	Focus on Murder—George Harmon Coxe	.50	1.50	2.50	M
971	Seven Days Before Dying—Helen Nielsen	.50	1.50	2.50	M
972	Gunlock—Wayne D. Overholser	.50	1.50	2.50	W
973	The Fatal Foursome—Frank Kane	.50	1.50	2.50	
974	Stampede at Blue Springs—Gene Olson	.50	1.50	2.50	
975	Return of a Fighter—Ernest Haycox; 1958	.50	1.50	2.50	W
976	Dear Doctor—Juliet Lowell	.40	1.20	2.00	H
977	Vertigo—Pierre Boileau & Thomas Narcejac; movie tie-in	1.00	3.00	5.00	
978	Weep for a Blonde—Brett Halliday	.50	1.50	2.50	M
979	Bullet Brand—Nick Sumner	.50	1.50	2.50	W
980	Tall Man Riding—Norman A. Fox	.50	1.50	2.50	W
981	The Uncomplaining Corpses—Brett Halliday	.50	1.50	2.50	M
982	The Diehard—Jean Potts	.40	1.20	2.00	
983	The Demon Stirs—Owen Cameron	.50	1.50	2.50	
984	Man on a Rope—George Harmon Coxe	.50	1.50	2.50	M
985	So Young, So Cold, So Fair—John Creasey	.50	1.50	2.50	M
986	Man of the West—Will C. Brown; movie tie-in	.80	2.40	4.00	W
987	Heads You Lose—Brett Halliday	.50	1.50	2.50	M
988	Shoot the Works—Brett Halliday	.50	1.50	2.50	M
989	Tickets for Death—Brett Halliday	.50	1.50	2.50	M
990	Here We Go Again and Bottle Fatigue—Virgil Partch	1.00	3.00	5.00	H
991	Deadly Beloved—William Ard	.50	1.50	2.50	
992	Don't Count the Corpses—Christopher Monig	.50	1.50	2.50	M
993	Desperate Man—Wayne D. Overholser	.50	1.50	2.50	W
994	Grounds for Murder—John Appleby	.50	1.50	2.50	M
995	Lady Killer—William M. Hardy	.50	1.50	2.50	
996	Now, Will You Try for Murder?—Harry Olesker; 1959	.50	1.50	2.50	M
997	Cop Killer—George Bagby	.50	1.50	2.50	M
998	Lover Boy—Janice Berenstain & Stanley Berenstain	.80	2.40	4.00	H
999	The Trouble With Fidelity—George Malcolm-Smith	.50	1.50	2.50	
1000	Justice, My Brother!—James Keene; 1959	.50	1.50	2.50	
1001	Dear Hollywood—Juliet Lowell	.50	1.50	2.50	
1002	The Badlands Beyond—Norman A. Fox	.50	1.50	2.50	W
1003	Once a Widow—Lee Roberts	.50	1.50	2.50	
1004	She Asked for Murder—Edna Sherry	.50	1.50	2.50	M
1005	Stranger With a Gun—Bliss Lomax (H. S. Drago)	.50	1.50	2.50	W
1006	Trapped!—Jean Hougron	.50	1.50	2.50	
1007	A Gem of a Murder—Carleton Keith	.50	1.50	2.50	
1008	The Lone Deputy—Wayne D. Overholser	.50	1.50	2.50	W

DELL D-SERIES
Dell Publishing Company

		Good	Fine	N/Mint	
D101	Chicago Confidential—Jack Lait & Lee Mortimer; 1952	.30	.90	1.50	NF
D102	The Great Smith—Edison Marshall	1.00	3.00	5.00	A
D103	Gypsy Sixpence—Edison Marshall	.50	1.50	2.50	
D104	Tomorrow Will Be Better—Betty Smith	.40	1.20	2.00	
D105	The Natchez Woman—Alice Walworth Graham	.50	1.50	2.50	
D106	Mrs. Craddock—W. Somerset Maugham	.50	1.50	2.50	
D107	Rivers Parting—Shirley Barker	.50	1.50	2.50	
D108	Washington Confidential—Jack Lait & Lee Mortimer	.40	1.20	2.00	NF
D109	The Chequer Board—Nevil Shute	.50	1.50	2.50	
D110	The Forest and the Fort—Hervey Allen	.50	1.50	2.50	
D111	Gold for My Fair Lady—Sidney H. Courtier	.40	1.20	2.00	
D112	Three Hundred Pillsbury Prize Recipes	.30	.90	1.50	NF
D113	The Phantom Emperor—Neil H. Swanson	.40	1.20	2.00	
D114	Go Down to Glory—Richard Warren Hatch	.50	1.50	2.50	
	with dust jacket	10.00	30.00	50.00	
D115	The Circle of the Day—Helen Howe	.40	1.20	2.00	
D116	Slogum House—Mari Sandoz	.50	1.50	2.50	
D117	Across the River and Into the Trees—Ernest Hemingway; 1953	.50	1.50	2.50	
D118	Really the Blues—Mezz Mezzrow & Bernard Wolfe	.50	1.50	2.50	
D119	Castle in the Swamp—Edison Marshall	.50	1.50	2.50	
D120	Snowslide—Carl Jonas	.40	1.20	2.00	
D121	Caroline Cherie—Cecil Saint-Laurent	.40	1.20	2.00	
D122	The Infinite Woman—Edison Marshall	.40	1.20	2.00	
D123	The Legacy—Nevil Shute	.40	1.20	2.00	
D124	Jefferson Selleck—Carl Jonas	.40	1.20	2.00	
D125	Captain Ebony—Hamilton Cochran; 1953	.50	1.50	2.50	
D126	The Swimming Pool—Mary Roberts Rinehart	.40	1.20	2.00	M
D127	Diamond Head—Houston Branch & Frank Waters	.40	1.20	2.00	
D128	Bedford Village—Hervey Allen	.40	1.20	2.00	

		Good	Fine	N/Mint	
D129	Boom Town—Jack O'Connor	.40	1.20	2.00	
D130	Round the Bend—Nevil Shute	.30	.90	1.50	
D131	Gina—George Albert Glay	.40	1.20	2.00	
D132	Tallulah—Tallulah Bankhead; 1954	.50	1.50	2.50	B
D133	Caroline Coquette—Cecil Saint-Laurent	.40	1.20	2.00	
D134	Fresh Water Fishing—Arthur Carhart	.40	1.20	2.00	NF
D135	Reap the Whirlwind—Jean Hougron	.40	1.20	2.00	
D136	The Rogue From Padua—Jay Williams	.50	1.50	2.50	
D137	The Bold Sabouteurs—Chandler Brossard	.40	1.20	2.00	
D138	Daughter of Strangers—Elizabeth Boatwright Coker	.40	1.20	2.00	
D139	The Viking—Edison Marshall	.50	1.50	2.50	A
D140	This Side of Paradise—F. Scott Fitzgerald	.50	1.50	2.50	
D141	Three to Get Married—Fulton J. Sheen	.30	.90	1.50	
D142	The Story of America—Hendrik Willem Van Loon	.40	1.20	2.00	NF
D143	The Doctor of Bean Street—Simon Kent	.50	1.50	2.50	
D144	Rogue's Holiday—Hamilton Cochran	.50	1.50	2.50	
D145	The Magnificent Bastards—Lucy Herndon Crockett; 1955	.40	1.20	2.00	
D146	How to Help Your Doctor Help You—Walter C. Alvarez	.30	.90	1.50	NF
D147	The Long Rifle—Steward Edward White	.50	1.50	2.50	A
D148	Fresh and Salt Water Spinning—Eugene Burns	.40	1.20	2.00	NF
D149	The Night of the Hunter—Davis Grubb	.40	1.20	2.00	
D150	Who Goes There?—John W. Campbell, Jr.; 1955	1.00	3.00	5.00	SF
D151	Sylvia—Edgar Mittelholzer	.40	1.20	2.00	
D152	Sunset Land—Eugene Manlove Rhodes	.50	1.50	2.50	W
D153	Herself Surprised—Joyce Cary	.40	1.20	2.00	
D154	The Frightened Wife—Mary Roberts Rinehart	.30	.90	1.50	M
D155	Guns and Hunting—Pete Brown	.40	1.20	2.00	NF
D156	Tell It on the Drums—Robert Krepps	.50	1.50	2.50	A
D157	Caravan to Xanadu—Edison Marshall	.50	1.50	2.50	A
D158	Indigo—Christine Weston	.40	1.20	2.00	
D159	The Man Who Killed Lincoln—Philip Van Doren Stern	.50	1.50	2.50	
D160	Trial—Don M. Mankiewicz; 1956	.40	1.20	2.00	
D161	The Tumult and the Shouting—Grantland Rice	.40	1.20	2.00	
D162	The Drinker—Hans Fallada	.40	1.20	2.00	
D163	Brideshead Revisited—Evelyn Waugh	.40	1.20	2.00	
D164	The Dark Arena—Mario Puzo	.40	1.20	2.00	
D165	The Wall—Mary Roberts Rinehart	.30	.90	1.50	M
D166	Bonjour Tristesse—Francoise Sagan	.30	.90	1.50	
D167	The Picture of Dorian Grey—Oscar Wilde	.50	1.50	2.50	
D168	Mosquitoes—William Faulkner	.40	1.20	2.00	
D169	Roads From the Fort—Arvid Shulenberger	.40	1.20	2.00	
D170	The Young Lovers—Julian Halevy	.40	1.20	2.00	
D171	The Steep Ascent—Anne Morrow Lindbergh	.40	1.20	2.00	
D172	Fourteen for Tonight—Steve Allen	.40	1.20	2.00	
D173	Benjamin Blake—Edison Marshall	.40	1.20	2.00	A
D174	An Affair of Dishonor—Louis A. Brennan	.40	1.20	2.00	
D175	The Far Country—Nevil Shute; 1956	.40	1.20	2.00	
D176	Mrs. Craddock—W. Somerset Maugham	.40	1.20	2.00	
D177	Warhorse—John Cunningham	.50	1.50	2.50	
D178	The Golden Kazoo—John G. Schneider	.40	1.20	2.00	F
D179	The Yellow Room—Mary Roberts Rinehart	.30	.90	1.50	M
D180	Child Behavior: Gesell Institute—Louis Bates Ames & Frances L. Ilg	.30	.90	1.50	NF
D181	Daisy Miller and the Turn of the Screw—Henry James	.30	.90	1.50	
D182	Listen! The Wind—Anne Morrow Lindbergh	.40	1.20	2.00	
D183	Nightmare—Guy Endore	.40	1.20	2.00	
D184	The Company She Keeps—Mary McCarthy	.40	1.20	2.00	
D185	Ship's Company—Lonnie Coleman; 1957	.40	1.20	2.00	
D186	The Bride Wore Black—Cornell Woolrich	.80	2.40	4.00	M

Dell D147, © Dell

Dell D204, © Dell

Dell D266, © Dell

		Good	Fine	N/Mint	
D187	Trial by Fury—Craig Rice	.40	1.20	2.00	M
D188	Laura—Vera Caspary	.40	1.20	2.00	M
D189	No Man Is an Island—Thomas Merton	.40	1.20	2.00	
D190	Blaze of the Sun—Jean Hougren	.40	1.20	2.00	
D191	Winter's Tales—Isak Dinesen	.40	1.20	2.00	F
D192	A Puzzle for Fools—Patrick Quentin	.40	1.20	2.00	M
D193	Aspects of Love—David Garnett	.40	1.20	2.00	
D194	Warrant for X—Philip MacDonald	.40	1.20	2.00	M
D195	The Wicked Village—Gabriel Chevallier	.40	1.20	2.00	
D196	Headed for a Hearse—Jonathan Latimer	.40	1.20	2.00	M
D197	The Circular Staircase—Mary Roberts Rinehart	.30	.90	1.50	M
D198	The Loved and the Unloved—Thomas Hal Phillips	.40	1.20	2.00	
D199	Love in the South Seas—Bengt Danielsson	.50	1.50	2.50	
D200	Dell Crossword Puzzle Dictionary—Kathleen Rafferty; 1957	.40	1.20	2.00	NF
D201	A Coffin for Dimitrios—Eric Ambler	.40	1.20	2.00	M
D202	Mountain Boy—Felix Holt	.40	1.20	2.00	
D203	The Red Right Hand—Joel Townsley Rogers	.40	1.20	2.00	M
D204	The Mark of Zorro—Johnston McCulley; TV tie-in	1.20	3.60	6.00	A
D205	The Lonely Passion of Judith Hearne—Brian Moore	.40	1.20	2.00	
D206	A Certain Smile—Francoise Sagan	.30	.90	1.50	
D207	Phantom Lady—William Irish	.80	2.40	4.00	M
D208	Seeds of Contemplation—Thomas Merton; 1958	.30	.90	1.50	
D209	Paths of Glory—Humphrey Cobb	.40	1.20	2.00	
D210	Owls Don't Blink—A. A. Fair	.40	1.20	2.00	M
D211	Spill the Jackpot—A. A. Fair	.40	1.20	2.00	M
D212	Bedrooms Have Windows—A. A. Fair	.40	1.20	2.00	M
D213	Give 'Em the Ax—A. A. Fair	.40	1.20	2.00	M
D214	A Charmed Life—Mary McCarthy	.40	1.20	2.00	
D215	Before the Fact—Frances Iles	.40	1.20	2.00	M
D216	The Long Rifle—Stewart Edward White	.50	1.50	2.50	A
D217	Sad Cypress—Agatha Christie	.40	1.20	2.00	M
D218	The Witness for the Prosecution—Agatha Christie	.40	1.20	2.00	M
D219	House Party—Virginia Rowans	.40	1.20	2.00	
D220	The Door—Mary Roberts Rinehart	.30	.90	1.50	M
D221	Dead Sure—Herbert Brean	.40	1.20	2.00	M
D222	The Loved One—Evelyn Waugh	.40	1.20	2.00	
D223	Fer-de-lance—Rex Stout	.40	1.20	2.00	M
D224	No Time at All—Charles Einstein	.40	1.20	2.00	
D225	Ride the Pink Horse—Dorothy B. Hughes; 1958	.40	1.20	2.00	M
D226	A Real Gone Guy—Frank Kane	.40	1.20	2.00	M
D227	The Beast Must Die—Nicholas Blake	.40	1.20	2.00	M
D228	Two-thirds of a Ghost—Helen McCloy	.40	1.20	2.00	M
D229	A Houseful of Love—Marjorie Housepian	.40	1.20	2.00	
D230	The Amazing Adventures of Father Brown—G. K. Chesterton	.50	1.50	2.50	M
D231	12 Stories They Wouldn't Let Me Do on TV—Alfred Hitchcock	.50	1.50	2.50	M
D232	Tall, Dark and Deadly—Harold Q. Masur	.40	1.20	2.00	M
D233	The Bellamy Trial—Frances Noyes Hart	.40	1.20	2.00	M
D234	Death of a Ghost—Margery Allingham	.40	1.20	2.00	M
D235	Dead Man's Mirror—Agatha Christie	.40	1.20	2.00	M
D236	Appointment With Death—Agatha Christie	.40	1.20	2.00	M
D237	The Brain Pickers—Hallie Burnett	.40	1.20	2.00	
D238	Background to Danger—Eric Ambler	.40	1.20	2.00	M
D239	Grand Hotel—Vicki Baum	.40	1.20	2.00	
D240	Rage of Desire—Charles Mergendahl	.40	1.20	2.00	
D241	The Flower Drum Song—C. Y. Lee; movie tie-in	.50	1.50	2.50	
D242	Miss Pinkerton—Mary Roberts Rinehart	.30	.90	1.50	M
D243	Secrets of Successful Selling—John D. Murphy	.30	.90	1.50	NF
D244	Falling Through Space—Richard Hillary	.40	1.20	2.00	
D245	Corner Boy—Herbert Simmons	.40	1.20	2.00	
D246	A Mirror for Observers—Edgar Pangborn	.50	1.50	2.50	
D247	The Mystery of the Dead Police—Philip MacDonald	.40	1.20	2.00	M
D248	The Private Practice of Michael Shayne—Brett Halliday	.40	1.20	2.00	M
D249	The Man in the Brown Suit—Agatha Christie	.40	1.20	2.00	M
D250	Suddenly a Corpse—Harold Q. Masur; 1958	.40	1.20	2.00	M
D251	The Great Mistake—Mary Roberts Rinehart	.30	.90	1.50	M
D252	The Mountain Cat Murders—Rex Stout	.40	1.20	2.00	M
D253	Turn on the Heat—A. A. Fair	.40	1.20	2.00	M
D254	The Secrets of Caroline Cherie—Cecil Saint-Laurent; 1959	.40	1.20	2.00	
D255	The Main in the Queue—Josephine Tey	.40	1.20	2.00	M
D256	The Living Bread—Thomas Merton	.40	1.20	2.00	
D257	The Decline and Fall of Practically Everybody—Will Cuppy	.40	1.20	2.00	H
D258	The Camp Followers—Ugo Pirro	.40	1.20	2.00	
D259	Another Man's Murder—Mignon G. Eberhart	.40	1.20	2.00	M
D260	Student Nurse—Renee Shann	.30	.90	1.50	
D261	The Man in the Net—Patrick Quentin	.40	1.20	2.00	M
D262	The Secret of Chimneys—Agatha Christie	.40	1.20	2.00	M
D263	Into the Valley—John Hersey	.40	1.20	2.00	

		Good	Fine	N/Mint	
D264	Slay Ride—Frank Kane	.40	1.20	2.00	M
D265	The Doctor's Secret—Hans Kades	.40	1.20	2.00	
D266	The Story of Walt Disney—Pete Martin & Diane Disney Miller	1.20	3.60	6.00	B
D267	The Golden Eagle—John Jennings	.50	1.50	2.50	A
D268	The Strange Bedfellow—Evelyn Berckman	.40	1.20	2.00	
D269	Call for Michael Shayne—Brett Halliday	.40	1.20	2.00	M
D270	Murder in Venice—Thomas Sterling	.40	1.20	2.00	M
D271	Murder on Their Minds—George Harmon Coxe	.40	1.20	2.00	M
D272	Shadow of a Killer—William Mole	.40	1.20	2.00	
D273	Focus—Arthur Miller	.40	1.20	2.00	
D274	The Third Level—Jack Finney	.50	1.50	2.50	
D275	A Hole in the Ground—Andrew Garve; 1959	.40	1.20	2.00	M
D276	The Man in Lower Ten—Mary Roberts Rinehart	.30	.90	1.50	M
D277	Those Without Shadows—Francoise Sagan	.30	.90	1.50	
D278	The Girl Who Kept Knocking Them Dead—Hampton Stone	.40	1.20	2.00	M
D279	In Case of Emergency—Georges Simenon	.50	1.50	2.50	M
D280	Trigger Mortis—Frank Kane	.40	1.20	2.00	M
D281	13 More Stories They Wouldn't Let Me Do on TV—Alfred Hitchcock	.50	1.50	2.50	M
D282	The Talented Mr. Ripley—Patricia Highsmith	.50	1.50	2.50	
D283	Murder and the Wanton Bride—Brett Halliday	.40	1.20	2.00	M
D284	Earthshaker—Robert W. Krepps	.50	1.50	2.50	A
D285	Lover's Point—C. Y. Lee	.40	1.20	2.00	
D286	The Gentle Murderer—Dorothy Salisbury Davis	.40	1.20	2.00	M
D287	The Meaning of Dreams—Calvin S. Hall	.40	1.20	2.00	NF
D288	Murder on the Links—Agatha Christie	.40	1.20	2.00	M
D289	Brand of Empire—Luke Short	.40	1.20	2.00	W
D290	Trail Town—Ernest Haycox	.40	1.20	2.00	W
D291	Marked for Murder—Brett Halliday	.40	1.20	2.00	M
D292	Dead Man's Diary and a Taste for Cognac—Brett Halliday	.40	1.20	2.00	M
D293	Dividend on Death—Brett Halliday	.40	1.20	2.00	M
D294	The Sensualists—Ben Hecht	.30	.90	1.50	
D295					
D296	The Color of Murder—Julian Symons	.30	.90	1.50	M
D297	Sophie—Geoffrey Wagner	.40	1.20	2.00	
D298	Murder on Broadway—Harold Q. Masur	.40	1.20	2.00	M
D299	One More Unfortunate—Edgar Lustgarten	.40	1.20	2.00	
D300	Long Shot—David Mark; 1959	.40	1.20	2.00	
D301	The Woman in the Woods—Lee Blackstock	.40	1.20	2.00	
D302	The Hound of the Baskervilles—Arthur Conan Doyle	.50	1.50	2.50	M
D303	Only Akiko—Duncan Thorp	.40	1.20	2.00	
D304	Angel's Ransom—David Dodge	.40	1.20	2.00	
D305	The Labors of Hercules—Agatha Christie	.40	1.20	2.00	M
D306	The April Robin Murders—Ed McBain & Craig Rice	.40	1.20	2.00	M
D307	Gypsy—Gypsy Rose Lee	.40	1.20	2.00	B
D308	Kind Are Her Answers—Mary Renault	.30	.90	1.50	R
D309	Top of the Heap—A. A. Fair	.40	1.20	2.00	M
D310	Boulevard—Robert Sabatier	.40	1.20	2.00	
D311	The Eighth Circle—Stanley Ellin	.40	1.20	2.00	
D312	Twixt Twelve and Twenty—Pat Boone	.30	.90	1.50	
D313	The Silent Life—Thomas Merton	.40	1.20	2.00	
D314	Fit to Kill—Brett Halliday	.40	1.20	2.00	M
D315	The Search—Myrick Land	.40	1.20	2.00	
D316	The Confession and Sight Unseen—Mary Roberts Rinehart	.30	.90	1.50	M
D317	The Heart Remembers—Faith Baldwin	.30	.90	1.50	R
D318	The Shrew Is Dead—Shelley Smith	.40	1.20	2.00	
D319	Child of Our Time—Michael del Castillo	.30	.90	1.50	
D320	The Sunlit Ambush—Mark Derby	.40	1.20	2.00	
D321	The Red House Mystery—A. A. Milne	.40	1.20	2.00	M
D322	The Man With Two Wives—Patrick Quentin	.40	1.20	2.00	M
D323	The Three Coffins—John Dickson Carr	.40	1.20	2.00	M
D324	Mrs. Bridge—Evan S. Connell, Jr.	.40	1.20	2.00	
D325	Quiet Horror—Stanley Ellin	.40	1.20	2.00	
D326	The Mysterious Mr. Quinn—Agatha Christie	.40	1.20	2.00	M
D327	Bodies Are Where You Find Them—Brett Halliday	.40	1.20	2.00	M
D328	Moment of Danger—Donald MacKenzie	.40	1.20	2.00	
D329	You Can't Live Forever—Harold Q. Masur	.40	1.20	2.00	M
D330	The Bat—Mary Roberts Rinehart	.30	.90	1.50	M
D331	Murder in Miami—Brett Halliday	.40	1.20	2.00	M
D333	Bare Trap—Frank Kane	.40	1.20	2.00	M
D336	Scarface—Armitage Trail; 1959	.40	1.20	2.00	

DELL F-SERIES
Dell Publishing Company

		Good	Fine	N/Mint	
F50	Gus the Great—Thomas W. Duncan; 1953	.40	1.20	2.00	
F51	Canal Town—Samuel Hopkins Adams	.40	1.20	2.00	

Dell F67, © Dell

Dell F85, © Dell

Dell First Editions 7, © Dell

(DELL F-SERIES, continued)

		Good	Fine	N/Mint	
F52	Wake of the Red Witch—Garland Roark	.40	1.20	2.00	A
F53	War and Peace—Leo Tolstoy; 1955	.40	1.20	2.00	
F54					
F55	The Brothers Karamazov—Fyodor Dostoyevsky	.40	1.20	2.00	
F56	The Story of Edgar Cayce—Thomas Sugrue	.30	.90	1.50	B
F57	Bedside Book of Famous French Stories—Belle Becker & Robert N. Linscott	.50	1.50	2.50	
F58	Raintree County—Ross Lockridge, Jr.; 1957	.50	1.50	2.50	A
F59	Life of Christ—Giovanni Papini	.40	1.20	2.00	B
F60	The Ninth Wave—Eugene Burdick	.40	1.20	2.00	
F61	Peyton Place—Grace Metalious	.30	.90	1.50	
F62	How to Take Better Pictures—Joseph C. Keeley	.30	.90	1.50	NF
F63	Dodsworth—Sinclair Lewis	.40	1.20	2.00	
F64	The Savage Place—Leon Arden; 1958	.40	1.20	2.00	
F65	Make Each Day Count—James Keller	.40	1.20	2.00	NF
F66	Maybe I'm Dead—Joe Klaas	.40	1.20	2.00	
F67	The Viking—Edison Marshall; movie tie-in	.50	1.50	2.50	A
F68	Brideshead Revisited—Evelyn Waugh	.40	1.20	2.00	
F69	Beloved—Vina Delmar	.40	1.20	2.00	
F70	David Copperfield—Charles Dickens	.40	1.20	2.00	
F71	The Bounty Lands—William Ellis	.40	1.20	2.00	
F72	The Upstart—Edison Marshall; 1959	.40	1.20	2.00	A
F73	Sharks and Little Fish—Wolfgang Ott	.40	1.20	2.00	NF
F74	A Handful of Dust and Decline and Fall—Evelyn Waugh	.40	1.20	2.00	
F75	Anatomy of a Murder—Robert Traver; 1959	.30	.90	1.50	M
F76	The Horse Soldiers—Harold Sinclair; movie tie-in	1.20	3.60	6.00	A
F77	The Fiery Trial—Carl Sandburg	.40	1.20	2.00	
F78	Embezzled Heaven—Franz Werfel	.30	.90	1.50	
F79	Ben-Hur—Lew Wallace	.40	1.20	2.00	A
F80	This Earth Is Mine—Alice Tisdale Hobart	.30	.90	1.50	
F81	The Raw Edge—Benjamin Appel	.30	.90	1.50	
F82	The Circus in the Attic—Robert Penn Warren	.40	1.20	2.00	
F83	Theme for Ballet—Vicki Baum	.30	.90	1.50	
F84	The Beat Generation and the Angry Young Men—Gene Feldman & Max Gartenberg	1.00	3.00	5.00	
F85	Ranchero—Stewart Edward White	.50	1.50	2.50	W
F86	On My Own—Eleanor Roosevelt	.30	.90	1.50	
F87	Yankee Pasha—Edison Marshall	.40	1.20	2.00	A
F88	Baa Baa Black Sheep—Pappy Boyington	.40	1.20	2.00	NF
F89	Great True Adventures—Lowell Thomas	.40	1.20	2.00	NF
F90	Harrison High—John Farris	.40	1.20	2.00	
F91	Return to Peyton Place—Grace Metalious	.30	.90	1.50	
F92					
F93					
F94	The Intruder—Charles Beaumont	.50	1.50	2.50	
F95	The Magnificent Bastards—Lucy Herndon Crockett	.40	1.20	2.00	

DELL FIRST EDITIONS
Dell Publishing Company

1E	Down—Walt Grove; 1953	.40	1.20	2.00	
2E	Madball—Frederic Brown; 1st ed., 1953	3.00	9.00	15.00	
D3	Women—A. M. Krich	.40	1.20	2.00	
4	Girl on the Beach—George Sumner Albee	.40	1.20	2.00	
5	The Bloody Spur—Charles Einstein	.40	1.20	2.00	M
6	Next Time Is for Life—Paul Warren	.40	1.20	2.00	
7	Bold Rider—Luke Short	.50	1.50	2.50	W
8	Back Country—William Fuller; 1954	.40	1.20	2.00	
D9	6 Great Short Novels of Science Fiction—ed. Groff Conklin; c-Powers	.50	1.50	2.50	SF
F10	The Ribald Reader—ed. A. M. Krich	.40	1.20	2.00	

		Good	Fine	N/Mint	
11	Arrow in the Dust—L. L. Foreman	.40	1.20	2.00	W
12	Area of Suspicion—John D. MacDonald; 1st ed., 1954	1.20	3.60	6.00	M
13	Fever Heat—Angus Vicker	.40	1.20	2.00	
14	The Man From Laramie—T. T. Flynn	.40	1.20	2.00	W
D15	Men—A. M. Krich	.40	1.20	2.00	
F16	Short Story Masterpieces—ed. Albert Erskine, Robert Penn Warren	.40	1.20	2.00	
17	The Crooked City—Robert Kyle	.40	1.20	2.00	
18	Smoky Valley—Donald Hamilton	.50	1.50	2.50	W
19	Conduct Unbecoming—Charles Fenton	.40	1.20	2.00	
D20	I Detest All My Sins—Jack Weeks	.40	1.20	2.00	
21	French Cartoons—William Cole & Douglas McKee	.50	1.50	2.50	H
22	The Nothing Man—Jim Thompson; 1st ed., 1954	1.20	3.60	6.00	
23	Teresa—Les Savage, Jr.	.40	1.20	2.00	W
24	The Joys She Chose—Matthew Peters	.40	1.20	2.00	
25	Trouble on Big Cat—Glenn Corbin; 1954	.40	1.20	2.00	
26	The Deadly Mermaid—James Atlee Phillips	.40	1.20	2.00	
27	Night Walker—Donald Hamilton	.50	1.50	2.50	
28	Goat Island—William Fuller	.40	1.20	2.00	
29	Sole Survivor—Louis Falstein	.40	1.20	2.00	
30	Plain Murder—C. S. Forester	.40	1.20	2.00	
31	The Man on the Blue—Luke Short	.50	1.50	2.50	W
32	Year of Consent—Kendell Foster Crossen	.40	1.20	2.00	SF
33	Two Faces West—T. T. Flynn	.40	1.20	2.00	W
34	The Calm Man—David Cort	.40	1.20	2.00	
F35	Six Great Modern Short Novels	.40	1.20	2.00	
36	The Golden Urge—Robert Kyle	.40	1.20	2.00	
37	Last of the Breed—Les Savage, Jr.	.40	1.20	2.00	W
38	The Book of Prayers—Elfrieda & Leon McCauley	.40	1.20	2.00	
39	Too Funny for Words—Bill Yates	.40	1.20	2.00	H
D40	The Handbook of Beauty—Constance Hart	.30	.90	1.50	NF
41	Dakota Rifle—Frank O'Rourke	.40	1.20	2.00	W
42	The Body Snatchers—Jack Finney; 1st ed., 1955, aka Invasion of the Body Snatchers	3.00	9.00	15.00	SF
43	New Ways to Greater Word Power—Roger B. Goodman & David Lewin	.30	.90	1.50	NF
44	Now Is the Time—Lillian Smith	.40	1.20	2.00	
45	City of Love—Daniel Talbot	.40	1.20	2.00	
46	Line of Fire—Donald Hamilton	.50	1.50	2.50	
47	The Only Game in Town—Charles Einstein	.40	1.20	2.00	
F48	The Complete Book of Gardening—W. W. Goodpasture	.40	1.20	2.00	NF
49	A Gun for Billy Reo—C. Hall Thompson; 1955	.40	1.20	2.00	W
50	Marital Blitz—Janice & Stanley Berenstain	.50	1.50	2.50	H
51	Nice Guys Finish Last—Robert Kyle	.40	1.20	2.00	
52	Fort Sun Dance—Manly Wade Wellman	.50	1.50	2.50	
D53	Everybody's Book of Modern Diet and Nutrition—Henrietta Fleck & Elizabeth Munves	.30	.90	1.50	NF
FE54	How to Draw and Paint—Henry Gasser	.30	.90	1.50	NF
55	What, When, Where and How to Drink—David Meyers & Richard L. Williams	.40	1.20	2.00	NF
D56	Too Near the Sun—Gordon Forbes	.40	1.20	2.00	
57	Women of the Avalon—L. L. Foreman	.40	1.20	2.00	W
58	After Innocence—Ian Gordon	.40	1.20	2.00	
59	The Big Fifty—Frank O'Rourke	.40	1.20	2.00	W
60	Dell Crossword Puzzles—Rosalind Moore & Kathleen Rafferty	.50	1.50	2.50	NF
61	The Dirty Shame—John R. Humphries	.40	1.20	2.00	
62	A Bullet for Cinderella—John D. MacDonald; 1st ed., 1955, aka On the Make	1.20	3.60	6.00	M
63	Hunger Mountain—William R. Scott	.40	1.20	2.00	
64	More French Cartoons—William Cole & Douglas McKee	.50	1.50	2.50	H
65	Return to Warbow—Les Savage, Jr.	.40	1.20	2.00	W
66	A Tiger in the Night—Robert Kyle	.40	1.20	2.00	
67	The Fastest Gun—Dan Cushman	.50	1.50	2.50	W
68	Bought With a Gun—Luke Short	.40	1.20	2.00	W
FE69	Six Centuries of Great Poetry—ed. Albert Erskine, Robert Penn Warren	.40	1.20	2.00	
70	Marauder's Moon—Luke Short	.50	1.50	2.50	W
71	Local Color—John Andrew Rice	.40	1.20	2.00	
D72	How to Build and Operate a Model Railroad—Marshall McClintock	.40	1.20	2.00	NF
73	In His Blood—Harold R. Daniels	.40	1.20	2.00	
74	Queen's Own—George C. Appell	.40	1.20	2.00	A
FE75	The Long Playing Record Guide—Warren de Motte; 1955	.40	1.20	2.00	NF
76	Wiretap!—Charles Einstein	.40	1.20	2.00	
77	Dangerous Dames—Mike Shayne	.40	1.20	2.00	M
78	Little Iodine—Jimmy Hatlo	1.60	4.80	8.00	H
79	The $64,000 Question Quiz Book	.40	1.20	2.00	NF
D80	Short Stories, Short Plays and Songs by Noel Coward	.40	1.20	2.00	
D81	Down—Walt Grove	.40	1.20	2.00	
82	Texas, Blood Red—Shepard Rifkin; 1956	.40	1.20	2.00	W
83	Night Fell on Georgia—Louise & Charles Samuels	.40	1.20	2.00	
FE84	The New Hammond-Dell World Atlas	.30	.90	1.50	NF
85	April Evil—John D. MacDonald; 1st ed., 1956	1.20	3.60	6.00	M

Dell First Editions 62, © Dell   Dell First Editions 78, © Dell   Dell First Editions A110, © Dell

(DELL FIRST EDITIONS, continued)

		Good	Fine	N/Mint	
D86	While the City Sleeps—Charles Einstein	.40	1.20	2.00	
87	The Loner—Bliss Lomax (H. S. Drago)	.40	1.20	2.00	W
88	Intent to Kill—Michael Bryan	.40	1.20	2.00	M
89	Battle Royal—Frank O'Rourke; c-Gross	.40	1.20	2.00	A
D90	The Last Enemy—Berton Roueche	.40	1.20	2.00	
91	Mad River—Donald Hamilton	.50	1.50	2.50	
92	Night Boat to Paris—Richard Jessup	.40	1.20	2.00	
93	Forever Funny—Bill Yates	.50	1.50	2.50	H
94	Atlantic Avenue—Albert Halper	.40	1.20	2.00	
95	The Devil's Spawn—Robert Carse	.50	1.50	2.50	
96	The Great Locomotive Chase—MacLennan Roberts; movie tie-in	.80	2.40	4.00	A
97	Juvenile Delinquency—Charles Preston	.50	1.50	2.50	NF
FE98	Modern French Painting, 1855-1956—Samuel Hunter	.40	1.20	2.00	NF
D99	Thirteen Great Stories—Daniel Talbot	.40	1.20	2.00	
FE100	Six Great Modern Plays—ed. Edward Parone; 1956	.40	1.20	2.00	
103	The Angry Man—T. T. Flynn	.40	1.20	2.00	W
104	The Last Chance—Frank O'Rourke	.40	1.20	2.00	
105	The Pace That Kills—William Fuller	.40	1.20	2.00	
106	Be My Victim—Robert Dietrich	.40	1.20	2.00	M
107	Singapore Passage—Donald Barr Chidsey	.40	1.20	2.00	A
108	Segundo—Frank O'Rourke	.40	1.20	2.00	
109	Cry Passion—Richard Jessup	.40	1.20	2.00	
A110	Riders West—anthology	.40	1.20	2.00	W
A111	The Big Success—Ian Gordon	.40	1.20	2.00	
A112	The Girl in 304—Harold R. Daniels	.40	1.20	2.00	
A113	Murder in the Wind—John D. MacDonald; 1st ed., 1956	1.20	3.60	6.00	
A114	The Big Bite—Charles Williams	.40	1.20	2.00	
A115	Maverick—Verne Athanas	.40	1.20	2.00	W
A116	Kundu—Morris L. West	.40	1.20	2.00	
A117	Johnny Liddell's Morgue—Frank Kane	.40	1.20	2.00	M
A118	The Race of Giants—Matt Kinkaid	.40	1.20	2.00	
A119	Cimarron Trace—James Norman	.40	1.20	2.00	
A120	Wetback—William O'Farrell	.40	1.20	2.00	
A121	The Last Laugh—Charles Einstein	.40	1.20	2.00	
A122	The Branded Man—Luke Short	.50	1.50	2.50	W
A123	Assignment: Murder—Donald Hamilton	.50	1.50	2.50	M
A124	Rebel Gun—Arthur Stever	.40	1.20	2.00	W
A125	This Is Little Lulu—Marge	2.00	6.00	10.00	H
A126	Key Witness—Frank Kane	.50	1.50	2.50	M
A127	Lone Hand—L. L. Foreman	.50	1.50	2.50	W
A128	The King and Four Queens—Theodore Sturgeon; 1st ed., 1956	2.00	6.00	10.00	W
A129	Bottoms Up!—Charles Preston	.40	1.20	2.00	H
A130	Death Trap—John D. MacDonald; 1st ed., 1957	1.20	3.60	6.00	M
A131	The Bravados—Frank O'Rourke	.40	1.20	2.00	
A132	Under the Badge—C. Hall Thompson	.40	1.20	2.00	W
A133	The Girl in the Frame—William Fuller	.40	1.20	2.00	
A134	Bold Rider—Luke Short	.50	1.50	2.50	W
A135	Desert Guns—Steve Frazee	.40	1.20	2.00	W
A136	A Taste of Brass—Robert Donald Locke	.40	1.20	2.00	
A137	A Shady Place to Die—John Savage	.40	1.20	2.00	
A138	Showdown at Stony Crest—Joseph Wayne	.40	1.20	2.00	W
A139	The House of Numbers—Jack Finney	.50	1.50	2.50	
A140	Tall Wyoming—Dan Cushman	.50	1.50	2.50	W
A141	Murder on the Rocks—Robert Dietrich	.40	1.20	2.00	M
A142	The Living End—Frank Kane	.40	1.20	2.00	M
A143	The Outcast—Richard Ferber	.40	1.20	2.00	
A144	Death for Sale—Henry Kane	.40	1.20	2.00	M
A145	Murder in Majorca—Michael Bryan	.40	1.20	2.00	M

		Good	Fine	N/Mint	
A146	The Dice Spelled Murder—Al Fray	.40	1.20	2.00	M
A147	Year of the Gun—Giff Cheshive	.40	1.20	2.00	W
A148	Treachery at Rock Point—Peter Dawson	.40	1.20	2.00	W
A149	Death at Flood Tide—Louis A. Brennan	.40	1.20	2.00	
A150	Tough Country—Frank Bonham; 1958	.40	1.20	2.00	W
A151	The Man on the Blue—Luke Short	.40	1.20	2.00	W
A152	The Price of Murder—John D. MacDonald; 1st ed., 1957	1.20	3.60	6.00	M
A153	Brad Dolan's Blonde Cargo—William Fuller	.40	1.20	2.00	
A154	Bought With a Gun—Luke Short; 1958	.50	1.50	2.50	W
A155	Blackmail, Inc.—Robert Kyle	.40	1.20	2.00	
A156	The Body Looks Familiar—Richard Wormser	.40	1.20	2.00	M
A157	The Bravados—Frank O'Rourke	.40	1.20	2.00	
A158	Brad Dolan's Miami Manhunt—William Fuller	.40	1.20	2.00	
A159	The Perfect Victim—James McKimmey	.40	1.20	2.00	
A160	A Bullet for a Blonde—Paul Kruger	.40	1.20	2.00	M
A161	Come Back for More—Al Fray	.40	1.20	2.00	M
A162	The Hostiles—Richard Ferber	.40	1.20	2.00	
A163	Under Cover of Night—Manning Lee Stokes	.40	1.20	2.00	M
A164	Talk of the Town—Charles Williams	.40	1.20	2.00	
A165	All the Way—Charles Williams	.40	1.20	2.00	
A166	Man From Nowhere—T. T. Flynn	.40	1.20	2.00	W
A167	Built for Trouble—Al Fray	.40	1.20	2.00	M
A168	Revenge—Jack Ehrlich	.40	1.20	2.00	
A169	The Concubine—Michael East	.50	1.50	2.50	
A170	The Snatch—Harold R. Daniels	.40	1.20	2.00	
A171	Buckskin Man—Thomas W. Blackburn	.40	1.20	2.00	W
A172	The Long Rope—Hal G. Evarts	.40	1.20	2.00	W
A173	Nellie the Nurse—Kaz	.50	1.50	2.50	H
A174	The Raiders—Richard Ferber; 1959	.40	1.20	2.00	
A175	The House on Q Street—Robert Dietrich	.40	1.20	2.00	M
A176	77 Sunset Strip—Roy Huggins; TV tie-in	1.00	3.00	5.00	M
A177	Sound of Gunfire—Frank Bonham	.40	1.20	2.00	W
A178	The Other Woman—Bill Yates	.40	1.20	2.00	H
A179	On Becoming a Woman—Irene Kane & Mary McGee Williams	.30	.90	1.50	NF
A180	The Naked City—Sterling Silliphant; TV tie-in	1.00	3.00	5.00	
A181	Darby O'Gill and the Little People—Lawrence Edward Watkin; movie tie-in	1.00	3.00	5.00	
A182	Sweet Cheat—Peter Duncan	.40	1.20	2.00	
A183	Laredo Road—Will C. Brown	.40	1.20	2.00	W
A184	Last Stand at Saber River—Elmore Leonard	.40	1.20	2.00	
A185	Winner Take All—James McKimmey	.40	1.20	2.00	
A186	Last Stage West—Frank Bonham	.40	1.20	2.00	W
A187	Kay Manion, M.D.—Adeline McElfresh	.30	.90	1.50	R
A188	Corruption City—Horace McCoy	1.20	3.60	6.00	JD
A189	Tight Squeeze—William Fuller	.40	1.20	2.00	
A190	McCracken in Command—James Keene	.40	1.20	2.00	
A191	Texas Heller—E. M. Parsons	.40	1.20	2.00	W
A192	Model for Murder—Robert Kyle	.40	1.20	2.00	M
A193	Epitaph for a Tramp—David Markson	.40	1.20	2.00	
A194	The Deadly Duo—Richard Jessup; 1959	.40	1.20	2.00	
B101	The Official American Medical Association Book of Health—W. W. Bauer; 1957	.30	.90	1.50	NF
B102	New Worlds of Modern Science—Leonard Engel	.30	.90	1.50	NF
B103	SF: The Year's Greatest Science-Fiction and Fantasy—ed. Judith Merril	.50	1.50	2.50	SF
B104	The Walt Disney Story of Our Friend the Atom—Heinz Haber	.80	2.40	4.00	NF
B105	Moses and the Ten Commandments—Paul Ilton & MacLennan Roberts	.50	1.50	2.50	
B106	A Treasury of Faith—Leon McCauley	.40	1.20	2.00	
B107	Stories for the Dead of Night—ed. Don Congdon	.50	1.50	2.50	
B108	More Than Flesh—Louis A. Brennan	.40	1.20	2.00	
B109	The Fabulous Buccaneer—Robert Carse	.50	1.50	2.50	A

Dell First Editions A125, © Dell

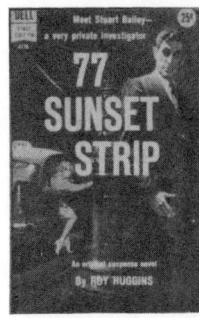

Dell First Editions A176, © Dell

Dell First Editions A188, © Dell

Dell First Editions B113, © Dell

Dell First Editions B135, © Dell

Dell First Editions C107, © Dell

(DELL FIRST EDITIONS, continued)

		Good	Fine	N/Mint	
B110	SF: The Year's Greatest Science-Fiction and Fantasy, 2nd Annual Volume—ed. Judith Merril	.50	1.50	2.50	SF
B111	By Appointment Only—Russell Boltar	.40	1.20	2.00	
B112	A Man of Affairs—John D. MacDonald; 1st ed., 1957	1.20	3.60	6.00	M
B113	Sea Avenger—Jack Beater & MacLennan Roberts	.50	1.50	2.50	A
B114	Girl Out Back—Charles Williams	.40	1.20	2.00	
B115	The Big Country—Donald Hamilton	.50	1.50	2.50	W
B116	The Accused—Harold R. Daniels	.40	1.20	2.00	
B117	The Deceivers—John D. MacDonald; 1st ed., 1958	1.20	3.60	6.00	M
B118	Lowdown—Richard Jessup	.40	1.20	2.00	
B119	SF: The Year's Greatest Science-Fiction and Fantasy, 3rd Annual Volume—ed. Judith Merril	.50	1.50	2.50	SF
B120	The Cosmic Rape—Theodore Sturgeon	.50	1.50	2.50	SF
B121	Soft Touch—John D. MacDonald; 1st ed., 1958, aka Man-Trap	1.20	3.60	6.00	M
B122	Untamed—Warner Hall	.40	1.20	2.00	
B123	Syndicate Girl—Frank Kane; 1959	.40	1.20	2.00	M
B124	The Two Lives of Dr. Stratton—Russell Boltar	.40	1.20	2.00	
B125	The Lineup—Frank Kane	.40	1.20	2.00	M
B126	The Strain—Kenneth E. Shiflet	.40	1.20	2.00	
B127	Deadly Welcome—John D. MacDonald; 1st ed., 1959	1.20	3.60	6.00	M
B128	The Five Pennies—Grady Johnson	.40	1.20	2.00	
B129	SF: The Year's Greatest Science-Fiction and Fantasy, 4th Annual Volume—ed. Judith Merril	.50	1.50	2.50	SF
B130	Marauders' Moon—Luke Short	.40	1.20	2.00	W
B131	Girl on the Beach—George Sumner Albee	.40	1.20	2.00	
B132	Paula—Don Kingery	.40	1.20	2.00	
B133	The Flesh Merchants—Bob Thomas	.40	1.20	2.00	
B134	On the Make—John D. MacDonald; aka A Bullet for Cinderella	.40	1.20	2.00	M
B135	The Witch Finder—Thomas L. O'Brien	.50	1.50	2.50	
B136	The Joy Boys—Walt Grove	.40	1.20	2.00	
B137	Juke Box King—Frank Kane	.40	1.20	2.00	
B138	The Sirens of Titan—Kurt Vonnegut, Jr.; orig., 1959	6.00	18.00	30.00	SF
B139	Sin Street—Bob Bristow	.40	1.20	2.00	
B140	Montana!—C. Hall Thompson	.40	1.20	2.00	
B141	The Lethal Sex—John D. MacDonald	1.00	3.00	5.00	M
B142	Poker According to Maverick; TV tie-in. Note: Two premium variants also exist, for Willys Motors and the Drackett Company.	.50	1.50	2.50	NF
B143	Marital Blitz—Janice & Stanley Berenstain	.50	1.50	2.50	H
B145	When She Was Bad—William Ard	.40	1.20	2.00	
B148	Career—Victor Chapin	.40	1.20	2.00	
B152	Scent of Mystery—Kelley Roos	.40	1.20	2.00	M
C101	The American Heritage Reader	.40	1.20	2.00	
C102	A Popular History of Music—Carter Harman	.40	1.20	2.00	NF
C103	From Medicine Man to Freud—Jan Ehrenwald; 1956	.40	1.20	2.00	NF
C104	The Second Ribald Reader—ed. A. M. Krich	.50	1.50	2.50	
C105	Great Scenes From Great Novels—ed. Robert Terrall	.40	1.20	2.00	
C106	The Handbook of Beauty—Constance Hart	.30	.90	1.50	NF
C107	Combat: European Theater - World War II—Don Congdon	.40	1.20	2.00	NF
C108	Combat: Pacific Theater - World War II—Don Congdon	.40	1.20	2.00	NF

DELL LAUREL EDITIONS
Dell Publishing Company

LB110	New Ways to Greater Word Power—Roger B. Goodman & David Lewin	.30	.90	1.50	NF
LB111	The World in Space—Alexander Marshack	.40	1.20	2.00	NF
LB112	Hamlet—William Shakespeare	.30	.90	1.50	
LB113	The Taming of the Shrew—William Shakespeare	.30	.90	1.50	
LB114	Romeo and Juliet—William Shakespeare	.30	.90	1.50	

		Good	Fine	N/Mint	
LB115	Richard III—William Shakespeare	.30	.90	1.50	
LB116	Great Flying Stories—Frank W. Anderson, Jr.	.40	1.20	2.00	
LB117	The Walt Disney Story of Our Friend the Atom—Heinz Haber	.80	2.40	4.00	NF
LB118	The Merchant of Venice—William Shakespeare	.30	.90	1.50	
LB119	Julius Caesar—William Shakespeare	.30	.90	1.50	
LB120	Poe—Edgar Allan Poe	.40	1.20	2.00	
LB121	Whitman—Walt Whitman	.40	1.20	2.00	
LB122	Coleridge—Samuel Taylor Coleridge	.40	1.20	2.00	
LB123	Wordsworth—William Wordsworth	.40	1.20	2.00	
LB124	Macbeth—William Shakespeare	.30	.90	1.50	
LB125	Twelfth Night—William Shakespeare	.30	.90	1.50	
LB126	Great Tales of Action and Adventure—George Bennett; c-Powers	.40	1.20	2.00	
LB127	Great Sea Stories—Alan Villiers	.40	1.20	2.00	
LB128	Kim—Rudyard Kipling	.40	1.20	2.00	A
LB129	Othello—William Shakespeare	.30	.90	1.50	
LB130	As You Like It—William Shakespeare	.30	.90	1.50	
LB131	Keats—John Keats	.40	1.20	2.00	
LB132	Longfellow—Henry Wadsworth Longfellow	.40	1.20	2.00	
LB133	The Winter's Tale—William Shakespeare	.30	.90	1.50	
LB134	Henry IV, Part 1—William Shakespeare; 1959	.30	.90	1.50	
LC101	Four Plays—George Bernard Shaw	.40	1.20	2.00	
LC102	Great English Short Stories—ed. Christopher Isherwood	.40	1.20	2.00	
LC103	Great American Short Stories—ed. Mary & Wallace Stegner	.40	1.20	2.00	
LC104	The New Dell Modern American Dictionary—Jess Stein	.30	.90	1.50	NF
LC105	Common Wild Animals and Their Young—Rita and William Vandivert	.40	1.20	2.00	NF
LC106	The Modern Meat Cookbook—Jeannette Frank	.30	.90	1.50	NF
LC107	Panorama: The Laurel Reader No. 1—ed. R. F. Tannenbaum	.40	1.20	2.00	
LC108	Lincoln and the Civil War—Courtlandt Canby	.50	1.50	2.50	NF
LC109	Six Centuries of Great Poetry—Albert Erskine & Robert Penn Warren	.40	1.20	2.00	
LC110	Great Russian Short Stories—ed. Norris Houghton	.40	1.20	2.00	
LC111	Mark Twain—Mark Twain	.40	1.20	2.00	
LC112	A Catholic Prayer Book—Dale Francis	.30	.90	1.50	
LC113	Jean-Christophe—Romain Rolland	.40	1.20	2.00	
LC114	Martin Eden—Jack London	.40	1.20	2.00	
LC115	How to Draw the Human Figure—John R. Grabach	.40	1.20	2.00	NF
LC116	Emerson—Ralph Waldo Emerson	.40	1.20	2.00	
LC117	The Wings of the Dove—Henry James	.40	1.20	2.00	
LC118	Madame Bovary—Gustave Flaubert	.40	1.20	2.00	
LC119	Elmer Gantry—Sinclair Lewis	.40	1.20	2.00	
LC120	Child Behavior: Gesell Institute—Louise Bates Ames & Frances L. Ilg	.30	.90	1.50	NF
LC121	The Aspern Papers and the Spoils of Poynton—Henry James	.40	1.20	2.00	
LC122	Pride and Prejudice—Jane Austen	.40	1.20	2.00	
LC123	Three Plays by Ibsen—Henrik Ibsen	.40	1.20	2.00	
LC124	Everybody's Book of Modern Diet and Nutrition—Henrietta Fleck & Elizabeth Munves	.30	.90	1.50	NF
LC125	How to Draw and Paint—Henry Gasser; 1959	.40	1.20	2.00	NF
LC126	Great Stories by Chekhov—Anton Chekhov	.40	1.20	2.00	
LC127	Great Italian Short Stories—ed. Pier Pasinetti	.40	1.20	2.00	
LC128	Sense and Sensibility—Jane Austen	.40	1.20	2.00	
LC129					
LC130	Poetry: A Modern Guide to Its Understanding and Enjoyment—Elizabeth Drew	.40	1.20	2.00	
LC131	The House of the Dead—Fyodor Dostoyevsky	.40	1.20	2.00	
LC132	Six Great Modern Short Novels	.40	1.20	2.00	
LC133	Four Great Russian Short Novels	.40	1.20	2.00	
LC134	Voltaire—Voltaire	.40	1.20	2.00	
LC135	Maupassant—Guy de Maupassant	.40	1.20	2.00	
LC136	Washington Square and the Europeans—Henry James	.40	1.20	2.00	
LC137	Freud: His Life and His Mind—Helen W. Puner	.40	1.20	2.00	B
LC138	Lives of the Noble Greeks—Plutarchus	.40	1.20	2.00	B
LC139	Lives of the Noble Romans—Plutarchus	.40	1.20	2.00	B
LC140	Stevenson—Robert Louis Stevenson	.40	1.20	2.00	
LX101	A History of the United States—William Miller	.40	1.20	2.00	NF
LX102	Short Story Masterpieces—ed. Albert Erskine & Robert Penn Warren	.40	1.20	2.00	
LX103	Six Great Modern Plays—ed. Edward Parone	.40	1.20	2.00	
LX104	Brideshead Revisited—Evelyn Waugh	.40	1.20	2.00	
LX105	Moby Dick—Herman Mellville	.40	1.20	2.00	A
LX106	Crime and Punishment—Fyodor Dostoyevsky	.40	1.20	2.00	
LX107					
LX108	Jude the Obscure—Thomas Hardy	.40	1.20	2.00	
LX109	The Titan—Theodore Dreiser	.40	1.20	2.00	
LX110	Six Centuries of Great Poetry—ed. Albert Erskine & Robert Penn Warren	.40	1.20	2.00	
LX111	Bulfinch's Mythology—Thomas Bulfinch	.40	1.20	2.00	
LX112	Ballet: A New Guide to the Liveliest Art—Walter Terry	.30	.90	1.50	NF
LX113	Abraham Lincoln: The Prairie Years—Carl Sandburg	.50	1.50	2.50	B
LX114	Abraham Lincoln: The War Years, 1861-1864—Carl Sandburg	.50	1.50	2.50	B
LX115	Abraham Lincoln: The War Years, 1864-1865—Carl Sandburg	.50	1.50	2.50	B
LX116	Famous American Plays of the 20's—ed. Kenneth MacGowan	.40	1.20	2.00	

Dell Mystery Novels 1, © Dell

Dell 10-Cent Books 1, © Dell

Dell 10-Cent Books 5, © Dell

		Good	Fine	N/Mint	
(DELL LAUREL EDITIONS, continued)					
LX117					
LX120	How to Draw the Human Figure—John R. Grabach	.40	1.20	2.00	NF
LY101	An American Tragedy—Theodore Dreiser	.40	1.20	2.00	
LY102	Modern American Painting and Sculpture—Samuel Hunter	.40	1.20	2.00	NF

DELL M-SERIES
Dell Publishing Company, Inc.

M101	The Complete Book of Plastic Model Kits—Advisory Board, Aurora Plastics Corporation; 1961	1.20	3.60	6.00	NF

DELL MYSTERY NOVELS
Dell Publishing Company, Inc.

Digest Size

1	Includes Brett Halliday, Gault, Fischer; 1955	1.60	4.80	8.00	M

DELL 10-CENT BOOKS
Dell Publishing Company, Inc.

		Good	Fine	N/Mint	
1	Trumpets West—Luke Short; 1951	2.00	6.00	10.00	W
2	Rain—W. S. Maugham	2.00	6.00	10.00	
3	Night Bus—Samuel H. Adams	2.00	6.00	10.00	
4	Locked Doors—Mary Roberts Rinehart	2.00	6.00	10.00	M
5	Bride From Broadway—Faith Baldwin	2.00	6.00	10.00	R
6	The Wedding Journey—Walter D. Edmonds	1.60	4.80	8.00	
7	Deadly is the Diamond—Mignon G. Eberhart	2.00	6.00	10.00	M
8	Journey for Life—Pearl S. Buck	2.00	6.00	10.00	
9	Strangers in Love—Vina Delmar	2.00	6.00	10.00	R
10	Trees Die at the Top—Edna Ferber	1.60	4.80	8.00	
11	Marihuana—William Irish	25.00	75.00	125.00	M
12	The Longhorn Legion—Norman A. Fox; 1st ed., 1951	2.00	6.00	10.00	W
13	Sun, Sea and Sand—John P. Marquand	2.00	6.00	10.00	
14	The Name Is Mary—Fannie Hurst	2.00	6.00	10.00	R
15	A Taste for Cognac—Brett Halliday	3.00	9.00	15.00	M
16	The Beachcomber—W. S. Maugham	2.00	6.00	10.00	
17	Remembering Laughter—Wallace Stegner	2.00	6.00	10.00	

Dell 10-Cent Books 9, © Dell

Dell 10-Cent Books 11, © Dell

Dell 10-Cent Books 15, © Dell

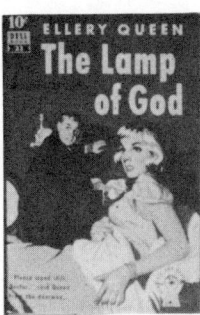

Dell 10-Cent Books 23, © Dell

Dell 10-Cent Books 26, © Dell

Dell 10-Cent Books 33, © Dell

(DELL 10-CENT BOOKS, continued)

		Good	Fine	N/Mint	
18	Free Woman—Katharine Brush	2.00	6.00	10.00	
19	Death Walks in Marble Halls—Lawrence Blochman; 1st ed., 1951	3.00	9.00	15.00	M
20	Broken Arrow Range—Thomas W. Blackburn; 1st ed., 1951	2.00	6.00	10.00	W
21	Door to Death—Rex Stout	4.00	12.00	20.00	M
22	Alibi for Israel—Mary Roberts Rinehart	2.00	6.00	10.00	M
23	The Lamp of God—Ellery Queen	4.00	12.00	20.00	M
24	Pal Joey—John O'Hara	1.60	4.80	8.00	
25	South of Cancer—John Hersey	2.00	6.00	10.00	
26	You'll Never See Me Again—William Irish; 1st ed., 1951	10.00	30.00	50.00	M
27	Thief Is an Ugly Word—Paul Gallico	3.00	9.00	15.00	
28	Beauty Marks the Spot—Kelley Roos	3.00	9.00	15.00	M
29	Delilah of the Back Stairs—Geoffrey Household	3.00	9.00	15.00	
30	Wife vs. Secretary—Faith Baldwin	3.00	9.00	15.00	R
31	Chinese Nightmare—Hugh Pentecost; 1st ed., 1951	4.00	12.00	20.00	M
32	The Murderer Who Wanted More—Baynard Kendrick	3.00	9.00	15.00	M
33	The Case of the Dancing Sandwiches—Frederic Brown; 1st ed., 1951	15.00	45.00	75.00	M
34	Better Off Dead—Helen McCloy; 1st ed., 1951	3.00	9.00	15.00	M
35	Superstition Farm—Perry Stowe	4.00	12.00	20.00	
36	Universe—Robert Heinlein; 1st ed., 1951	7.00	21.00	35.00	SF

DELL TOLD IN PICTURES
Dell Publishing Company

Digest Size, All Comic Book Style

1	Twice Loved; 1950	9.00	27.00	45.00	R
2	Four Frightened Women—George Harmon Coxe; 1950	10.00	30.00	50.00	M

DELL UNNUMBERED
Dell Publishing Company

Some Digest Size

nn	Blondie and Dagwood in Footlight Folly—Chic Young; 1947	9.00	27.00	45.00	H
nn	Dick Tracy and the Woo-Woo Sisters—Chester Gould; 1947	12.50	37.50	60.00	M
nn	Hopalong Cassidy—Clarence E. Mulford; nd, movie tie-in, digest size	6.00	18.00	30.00	W
nn	Jungle Belles—	5.00	15.00	25.00	

Dell 10-Cent Books 36, © Dell

Dell Told in Pictures 1, © Dell

Dell Unnumbered nn, © Dell

Detective Novel Classic 3, © Hill   Detective Novel Classic 21, © Hill   Detective Novel Classic 40, © Hill

DELL X-SERIES
Dell Publishing Company

		Good	Fine	N/Mint	
X1	The James Beard Cookbook—James A. Beard & Isabel E. Callvert	.40	1.20	2.00	NF

DERBY BOOKS
Derby Publishing Company

Canadian

3	Passion or Kingdom—Claude Anet; 1949, aka Idyll's End	.80	2.40	4.00	E
7	Men to Burn—William Arthur; 1950	.80	2.40	4.00	E
9	Body Betrays—Wayne Way	.80	2.40	4.00	E
12	Borrowed Husband—Florenz Branch	.80	2.40	4.00	E

DETECTIVE NOVEL CLASSIC
Hillman Periodicals/Novel Selections, Inc.

Digest Size

2	The Pedigreed Murder Case—J. S. Fletcher	.80	2.40	4.00	M
3	Death by Remote Control—Emmett Hogarth	1.20	3.60	6.00	M
4	The Case Is Closed—Patricia Wentworth	.80	2.40	4.00	M
5	The Radio Studio Murder—Caroline Wells	.80	2.40	4.00	M
6	The Scarecrow Murders—Frederic Arnold Kummer	.80	2.40	4.00	M
7	The Case of the Rusted Room—John Donavan	.80	2.40	4.00	M
8	Murder Will Out—Jeanette Covert Nolan	.80	2.40	4.00	M
9	Hong-Kong Airbase Murders—Van Wyck Mason	.80	2.40	4.00	M
10	The Clue of the Twisted Face—Frederic Arnold Kummer	1.00	3.00	5.00	M
11	The Bathtub Murder Case—E. R. Punshon	.80	2.40	4.00	M
12	The Blue Santo Murder Mystery—Margaret Armstrong	.80	2.40	4.00	M
13	Gone North—Charles Alden Seltzer	.80	2.40	4.00	W
14	Murder in the Morning—Anthony Wynnes	.80	2.40	4.00	M
15	The Strange Death of Manny Square—A. B. Cunningham	.80	2.40	4.00	M
16	Death of a Greek—John Brandon	.80	2.40	4.00	M
17	Murder on Stilts—Gregory Dean	.80	2.40	4.00	M
18	The Penguin Pool Murder—Stuart Palmer	1.00	3.00	5.00	M
19	The Case of the Headless Corpse—Dennis Allan	.80	2.40	4.00	M
20	Death at "the Bottoms"—A. B. Cunningham	.80	2.40	4.00	M
21	Tickets for Death—Brett Halliday	.80	2.40	4.00	M
22	Murder for a Wanton—Whitman Chambers	.80	2.40	4.00	M
23	Murder in the Mews—Helen Reilly	.80	2.40	4.00	M
24	Little Hercules—F. Wallace	.80	2.40	4.00	M
25	The Bancock Murder Case—A. B. Cunningham	.80	2.40	4.00	M
26	The Uncomplaining Corpses—Brett Halliday	.80	2.40	4.00	M
27	Steps to Murder—Robert Portner Koehler	.80	2.40	4.00	M
28	Dead Men Leave No Fingerprints—Whitman Chambers	.80	2.40	4.00	M
29	Death Over Hollywood—Charles Saxby & Louis Molnar	.80	2.40	4.00	M
30	The Affair at the Boat Landing—A. B. Cunningham	.80	2.40	4.00	M
31	Bodies Are Where You Find Them—Brett Halliday	.80	2.40	4.00	M
32	The Eight of Swords—John Dickson Carr	1.00	3.00	5.00	M
33	Murder by Latitude—Rufus King	.80	2.40	4.00	M
34	Exit Screaming—Christopher Hale	.80	2.40	4.00	M
35	Death Is Like That—John Spain	.80	2.40	4.00	M
36	Death and Bitters—Kit Christian	.80	2.40	4.00	M
37	The Great Yant Mystery—A. B. Cunningham	.80	2.40	4.00	M
38	A Murderer in This House—Rufus King; aka Somewhere in This House	.80	2.40	4.00	M
39	Dead of Winter—Christopher Hale	.80	2.40	4.00	M

		Good	Fine	N/Mint	
40	The 4 False Weapons—John Dickson Carr	1.00	3.00	5.00	M
41	The Gull Cove Murders—Eli Colter	.80	2.40	4.00	M
42	The Cane-Patch Mystery—A. B. Cunningham	.80	2.40	4.00	M
43	The Cat Wears a Noose—D. B. Olsen	.80	2.40	4.00	M
44	The Evil Star—John Spain	.80	2.40	4.00	M
45	Down Among the Dead Men—Stewart Sterling	.80	2.40	4.00	M
46	Death Visits the Apple Hole—A. B. Cunningham	.80	2.40	4.00	M
47	Blood on Nassau's Moon—Walbridge McCully	.80	2.40	4.00	M
48	Murder Makes a Racket—M. V. Heberden	.80	2.40	4.00	M
49	I Can't Die Here—Jeannette Covert Nolan	.80	2.40	4.00	M
51	Rumor Hath It—Christopher Hale	.80	2.40	4.00	M
52	Murder Before Midnight—A. B. Cunningham	.80	2.40	4.00	M
53	Doctors Beware!—Walbridge McCully	.80	2.40	4.00	M
54	Neck in a Noose—E. X. Ferrars	.80	2.40	4.00	M

DIAMOND LIBRARY
The Diamond Library

Digest Size

		Good	Fine	N/Mint	
nn	Murder by Mandate—Elston & Beam; 1945	1.20	3.60	6.00	M
nn	Murder Goes Fishing—Theodore Pratt	1.20	3.60	6.00	M

DIVERSEY LOVE BOOK MONTHLY
Diversey Publishing Corporation

Digest Size

		Good	Fine	N/Mint	
1	Bedroom Eyes—Maurice De Kobra	3.00	9.00	15.00	E
2	One Night With Nancy—Wilson Collison; 1948; Note: Same cover as Novel Library No. 20	3.00	9.00	15.00	E

DIVERSEY POPULAR NOVELS
Diversey Periodicals, Inc.

Digest Size

		Good	Fine	N/Mint	
1	Broadway Virgin—Lois Bull; 1949	4.00	12.00	20.00	E
2	Naked on Roller Skates—Maxwell Bodenheim; Note: Same cover as Novel Library No. 46	8.00	24.00	40.00	E

DIVERSEY PRIZE NOVELS
Diversey Periodicals, Inc.

Digest Size

		Good	Fine	N/Mint	
3	The Passions of Linda Lane—Frances Marion; 1949, aka Minnie Flynn	3.00	9.00	15.00	E
4	Fast Woman—Marty Holland	3.00	9.00	15.00	E
5	Love for Sale—John Wilstach; 1949, aka The Fate of Fay Delroy	3.00	9.00	15.00	E
6	The Amorous Interne—Edward Reltid	3.00	9.00	15.00	E

DIVERSEY ROMANCE NOVELS
Diversey Publishing Corporation

Digest Size

Diamond Library nn, © Diamond Library

Diversey Popular Novels 2, © Div

Diversey Prize Novels 5, © Div

Diversey Romance Novels 1, © Div

Docket Series 3, © Oceana Publ.

Docket Series 5, © Oceana Publ.

(DIVERSEY ROMANCE NOVELS, continued)

		Good	Fine	N/Mint	
1	Reform School Girl—Felice Swados; 1948, aka House of Fury. Note: Same cover as Reform School Girl comic book	70.00	210.00	350.00	E

NOTE: *Prices can vary widely on this book.*

DOCKET SERIES
Oceana Publications

		Good	Fine	N/Mint
1	The Holmes Reader—ed. Julius J. Marke; 1955	.80	2.40	4.00
2	The Freedom Reader—ed. Edwin S. Newman	.80	2.40	4.00
3	The Marshall Reader—ed. Erwin C. Surrency	.80	2.40	4.00
4	The Wilson Reader—ed. Frances Farmer; 1956	.80	2.40	4.00
5	The Daniel Webster Reader—ed. Bertha Rothe	.80	2.40	4.00
6	The Medico-Legal Reader—ed. Samuel Polsky	.80	2.40	4.00
7	The Brandeis Reader—ed. Ervin Pollack	.80	2.40	4.00
8	The American Jurisprudence Reader—ed. T. A. Cowan	.80	2.40	4.00

DOMINO MYSTERIES
Duchess Printing and Publishing Co., Ltd.

Digest Size

		Good	Fine	N/Mint	
1	The ''Q'' Squad—Gerald Verner; 1944	2.00	6.00	10.00	M
2	Gentleman of Crime—Arthur Gask	1.60	4.80	8.00	M

DOUBLE ACTION DETECTIVE
Close-Up, Inc.

Digest Size

		Good	Fine	N/Mint	
1	Run, Corpse, Run—Guy Pember-Hiller	1.60	4.80	8.00	M
2	Hot Bullets for Love—Gentry Nyland; 1943, aka Mr. South Burned His Mouth. Note: Same cover as Big Green Detective Novel No. 2	2.00	6.00	10.00	M
3	Jealousy Pulls the Trigger—M. E. Corne; 1943, aka A Magnet for Murder. Note: Same cover as Big Green Detective Novel No. 3	1.60	4.80	8.00	M

DOUBLE-ACTION POCKETBOOK
Columbia Publications, Inc.

Domino Mysteries 1, © Duch

Double Action Detective 2, © Close

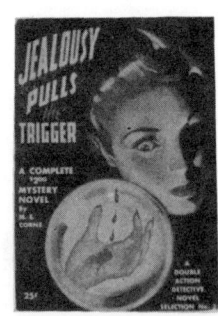
Double Action Detective 3, © Close

Double-Action Pocketbook nn, © Col · Doubleday nn, © DD · Doubleday Doran nn, © DD

(DOUBLE-ACTION POCKETBOOK, continued)

Digest Size

		Good	Fine	N/Mint	
nn	City of Glass—Noel Loomis; 1955	2.00	6.00	10.00	SF

DOUBLEDAY
Doubleday and Company, Inc.

nn	The Farmer Takes a Hand—Marquis Childs; orig., 1952	.40	1.20	2.00	NF
nn	The Caine Mutiny—Herman Wouk; 1954, movie and theatrical tie-in	2.00	6.00	10.00	

DOUBLEDAY DORAN
Doubleday, Doran and Company, Inc.

Digest Size

nn	Come Wind, Come Weather—Daphne Du Maurier; 1941	.50	1.50	2.50	

DOUGLAS
Douglas Publishing, Inc.

nn	Today's Business Market—John Garris; 1954	.50	1.50	2.50	NF

DUCHESS
Duchess Printing and Publishing Co., Ltd.

Canadian

nn	Brigands of the Moon—John Campbell; nd. Note: Miscredited, actually written by Ray Cummings	2.00	6.00	10.00	SF
nn	Bait for a Tiger—Bayard Veiller	1.20	3.60	6.00	M
nn	Murder at the Mike—Charles Saxby	1.20	3.60	6.00	M
nn	Run, Corpse, Run—Guy Pember-Hiller	1.20	3.60	6.00	M

EAGLE BOOKS
Eagle Books, Inc./New American Library

nn(1)	Dear Sir—Juliet Lowell; 1943	1.00	3.00	5.00	H

Duchess nn, © Duch · Eagle Books E3, © New American Library · Ecstasy Novel 2, © Falcon

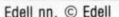

Edell nn, © Edell

Eerie Series 1, © Eerie

Eton Books ET106, © Eton

		Good	Fine	N/Mint	
(EAGLE BOOKS, continued)					
nn(2)	Kitty—Rosamond Marshall; 1945	1.00	3.00	5.00	E
E3	Duchess Hotspur—Rosamond Marshall; 1947	.50	1.50	2.50	E

ECSTASY NOVEL
Falcon Books, Inc.
Digest Size

		Good	Fine	N/Mint	
nn	Intimate Confessions of an Artist's Model—Norman Bligh; 1950	1.00	3.00	5.00	E
nn	Bed Time Angel—Norman Bligh	1.00	3.00	5.00	E
nn	Confessions of a Dime a Dance Queen—Douglas Duperault; c-Gross	1.00	3.00	5.00	E
12	Web of Sin—Anthony Scott; aka Virgin's Holiday	1.00	3.00	5.00	E
15	Wanton by Night—James Clayford (Norman Daniels)	1.00	3.00	5.00	E
16	They Call Her ''Easy''—Gwen Lyons; 1951	1.00	3.00	5.00	E
17	Come Night, Come Desire—David Wade (Norman Daniels)	1.00	3.00	5.00	E

EDELL
The Edell Company
Digest Size

		Good	Fine	N/Mint	
nn	The Case of the Deadly Drops—Gerald Benedict	1.20	3.60	6.00	M

EERIE SERIES
Eerie Publishing Co./Spotlight Publishers
Digest Size

		Good	Fine	N/Mint	
1	The Case of the Curious Heel—Ken Crossen; nd	3.00	9.00	15.00	M
2	Murder in Mocking Valley—Will Crowell	2.00	6.00	10.00	M
3	The Corpse Wore No Shoes—Donald Thompson	2.00	6.00	10.00	M
4	Satan Comes Across—Bennett Barlay; 1945	2.00	6.00	10.00	M
5	Murder in the Radio Department—Alfred Eichler	2.00	6.00	10.00	M
6	The Pleasure Primer	1.60	4.80	8.00	
7	A Spy in the Room—Denison Clift	1.60	4.80	8.00	M
8	Homicide Johnny—Stephen Gould	1.60	4.80	8.00	M
9	Haunted Harbor—Dayle Douglas; 1945	2.00	6.00	10.00	M

ETON BOOKS
Eton Books, Inc.

		Good	Fine	N/Mint	
ET 51	Sex Habits of American Women—Fritz Wittels, M.D.	1.20	3.60	6.00	NF
101	United States Book of Baby & Child Care; 1951	1.20	3.60	6.00	NF
102	Sex Habits of American Women—Fritz Wittels, M.D.	1.20	3.60	6.00	NF
103	The Hygiene of Marriage—Millard Spencer Everett	1.20	3.60	6.00	NF
ET104	Control Blood Pressure—Herman Pomeranz, M.D.	1.20	3.60	6.00	NF
ET105	How to Understand Your Dreams—Wilhelm Stekel	1.20	3.60	6.00	NF
ET106	The Show of Violence—Fredric Wertham	3.00	9.00	15.00	NF
ET107	Authentic Librettos of the Grand Opera	1.20	3.60	6.00	NF
ET108	This Is Russia Un-Censored!—Edmund Stevens	1.20	3.60	6.00	NF
E109	Self-Mastery Through Psycho-Analysis—William J. Fielding; 1952	1.20	3.60	6.00	NF
E110	I Killed Stalin—Sterling Noel	1.60	4.80	8.00	SF
E111	Sin in Their Blood—Ed Lacy; orig., 1952	1.60	4.80	8.00	M
E112	Kiss My Fist!—James Hadley Chase	2.00	6.00	10.00	M
E113	The Renegade Hills—Allan K. Echols; orig., 1952	1.60	4.80	8.00	W
E114	Give Me Your Love—Jerome Weidman; orig., 1952	1.60	4.80	8.00	E

		Good	Fine	N/Mint	
	(ETON BOOKS, continued)				
E115	I'll Bring Her Back—Peter Cheyney; aka Dark Bahama	1.60	4.80	8.00	
E116	The Marijuana Mob—James Hadley Chase	10.00	30.00	50.00	M
E117	Invitation to Dishonor—Eric Arthur	1.60	4.80	8.00	E
E118	Gun-Play in Killer Canyon—Tevis Miller	1.60	4.80	8.00	W
E119	I Killed Stalin—Sterling Noel; illo in *Parade of Pleasure*	3.00	9.00	15.00	SF
E120	Mark It With a Stone—George Victor Martin	1.20	3.60	6.00	E
E121	Queer Patterns—Lilyan Brock	1.60	4.80	8.00	E
E122	Paris Escort—Daniel Harper; orig., 1953	1.20	3.60	6.00	E
E123	Strip for Violence—Ed Lacy; orig., 1953	1.60	4.80	8.00	M
E124	Tuck's Girl—Marcel Wallenstein; orig., 1953	1.20	3.60	6.00	
E125	Gunfighter—Paul Craig	1.20	3.60	6.00	W
E126					
E127	Stir Up the Dust—William Colt MacDonald; orig., 1953	1.20	3.60	6.00	W
E128	Stagecoach to Hellfire Pass—Paul Evan Lehman	1.20	3.60	6.00	W
E129	Wit From Overseas—Roy Hoopes, Jr.	1.20	3.60	6.00	
E130					
E131	Vengeance Valley—Allan K. Echols	1.20	3.60	6.00	W
E132	Hide-out—Larry Holden	1.20	3.60	6.00	M

EUGENICS
Eugenics Publishing Co., Inc.

101	The Torch of Life, a Key to Sex Harmony—Frederick M. Rossiter, M.D.; 1952	1.00	3.00	5.00	NF

EXOTIC NOVELS
Falcon Books, Inc.

Digest Size

5	Buy My Love!—Perry Lindsay (Peggy Gaddis); 1949, c-Rodewald	1.00	3.00	5.00	E
17	Ten Toes Up—Anthony Scott; 1951	1.20	3.60	6.00	E
18	Give Me Ecstasy—Mark Reed (Norman Daniels)	1.00	3.00	5.00	E
20	Lovers Don't Sleep—Laura Hale	1.00	3.00	5.00	E
nn	Three Men and a Mistress—Florence Stonebraker; 1950	1.00	3.00	5.00	E

FALCON BOOKS
Falcon Books, Inc.

Digest Size

21	Season for Sin—Anthony Scott	1.00	3.00	5.00	E
22	The Scarlet Bride—M. Reed (Norman Daniels)	1.00	3.00	5.00	E
24	Three for Passion—Hodge Evens	1.00	3.00	5.00	E
25	Case of the Cancelled Redhead—Hamlin Daly	1.00	3.00	5.00	E
26	Lay Down and Die—Mark Reed (Norman Daniels)	1.00	3.00	5.00	E
27	Lida Lynn - Daughter of Passion—Norma Dann (Norman Daniels)	1.00	3.00	5.00	E
29	Mistress on a Deathbed!—Norman A. Daniels; orig., 1952	1.00	3.00	5.00	M
31	Slave Girl—Tom Roan	1.00	3.00	5.00	E
32	Sins of the Flesh—Mark Reed (Norman Daniels)	1.00	3.00	5.00	E
33	Yellow-Head!—Hodge Evens; orig., 1952	1.00	3.00	5.00	E
34	Shack Girl—Norma Dann (Norman Daniels)	1.00	3.00	5.00	E
35	Raise the Devil—David Wade (Norman Daniels)	1.00	3.00	5.00	E
36	Junkie—Johnathan Craig; orig., 1952	1.20	3.60	6.00	E
37	Woman Hunter—Laura Hale	1.00	3.00	5.00	E
38	Sweet Savage—Norma Dann (Norman Daniels)	1.00	3.00	5.00	E
39	Joy Street—	1.00	3.00	5.00	E

Eton Books E116, © Eton

Eton Books E119, © Eton

Falcon Books 28, © Falcon

Famous Mystery Series 1, © How   Femack Publications nn, © Fem   Fiesta Books 2, © Rio

		Good	Fine	N/Mint	
(FALCON BOOKS, continued)					
40	Whip - Hand!—Hodge Evens; orig., 1952	1.00	3.00	5.00	E
41	The Evil Sleep!—Evan Hunter; orig., 1952	1.20	3.60	6.00	M
42	The Long Night—Bryce Walton	1.00	3.00	5.00	E
43	House of 1,000 Desires—Mark Reed (Norman Daniels); orig., 1953. Note: Same cover as Intimate No. 20 and Beacon B307.	1.00	3.00	5.00	E

FAMOUS MYSTERY SERIES
Howard Publications

Digest Size

(Canadian)

1	Murder Takes a Honeymoon—Edith Fleming; 1940	1.20	3.60	6.00	M
2	The Pay-off—Joe Barry	1.00	3.00	5.00	M

FAWCETT PUBLICATIONS, FAWCETT-GOLD MEDAL — See GOLD MEDAL

FEDERAL
Federal Publishing Company

(Canadian)

1	Marjorie—Tex Lane; 1950	.80	2.40	4.00	E
2	Room Girl—Beth Brown; 1951	.80	2.40	4.00	E
3	Variety's the Life—Frank E. Kane	.80	2.40	4.00	E
4	Jetsam Journey—Frank E. Kane; 1952	.80	2.40	4.00	E

FEINER
J. P. Feiner

Digest Size

nn	The Greatest Adventure Stories Ever Told—Arnold Shaw; 1945	.50	1.50	2.50	A

FEMACK PUBLICATIONS
The Femack Company

Digest Size

nn	He Died Laughing—Lawrence Lariar	.80	2.40	4.00	M

FIESTA BOOKS
Rio Publishing Corporation

Digest Size

1	The Lady Was a Tramp—Nick Baroni	.80	2.40	4.00	E
2	Ask for Therese—Evans Wall (Peggy Gaddis); orig., 1952	.80	2.40	4.00	E
3	Love Fetish—Evans Wall (Peggy Gaddis)	.80	2.40	4.00	E
6	Unwanted Wife—Ben Smith	.80	2.40	4.00	E

FIGHTING FORCES SERIES
The Infantry Journal

Some Are Digest Size

NOTE: Some Fighting Forces Series titles are also Penguin Specials and are listed under that imprint.

		Good	Fine	N/Mint	
F14	Report on the Army, 1939-1943—George C. Marshall	.80	2.40	4.00	NF
nn	World War II—Roger W. Shugg and H. A. DeWeerd	.80	2.40	4.00	NF
nn	Selected Speeches and Statements—George C. Marshall	.80	2.40	4.00	NF
nn	Fishes and Shells of the Pacific World	.80	2.40	4.00	NF
nn	Plant Life of the Pacific World—Merrill	.80	2.40	4.00	NF
nn	Native Peoples of the Pacific World—Keesing	1.00	3.00	5.00	NF
nn	Japan and the Japanese	1.00	3.00	5.00	NF
nn	Japan's Military Masters—Hillis Lory	1.00	3.00	5.00	NF
nn	Survival	1.00	3.00	5.00	
nn	We Cannot Escape History—John Whitaker	.50	1.50	2.50	NF
nn	America's Navy in World War II—Gilbert Cant	.80	2.40	4.00	NF
nn	Abraham Lincoln and the Fifth Column—George Fort Milton; 1943	.80	2.40	4.00	NF
nn	America in Arms—John McA. Palmer	.80	2.40	4.00	
nn	Animals of the Pacific World—Hill, Carter, & Tate	.80	2.40	4.00	NF
nn	The Battle Is the Pay-off—Major Ingersoll	.80	2.40	4.00	
nn	Blitzkrieg: Armies on Wheels—S. L. A. Marshall	.80	2.40	4.00	NF
nn	Burma Surgeon—Gordon Seagrave	.80	2.40	4.00	NF
nn	The Capture of Attu	.80	2.40	4.00	NF
nn	Combat First Aid: How to Save Lives in Battle	.80	2.40	4.00	NF
nn	Conflict: The American Civil War—George Fort Milton	.80	2.40	4.00	NF
nn	Defense Against Chemical War	2.00	6.00	10.00	NF
nn	Fear in Battle—John Dollard	.80	2.40	4.00	
nn	Freedom Speaks: Ideals of Democracy in Poetry and Prose	.80	2.40	4.00	
nn	Fundamentals of Electricity—Mott-Smith	.50	1.50	2.50	NF
nn	Fundamentals of Mathematics—Mott-Smith & Van de Water	.50	1.50	2.50	NF
nn	Gas Warfare—Alden H. Waitt	1.60	4.80	8.00	NF
nn	The German Soldier: How He Is Trained	1.00	3.00	5.00	NF
nn	Great Soldiers of the First World War—H. A. DeWeerd	.80	2.40	4.00	NF
nn	The Gun—C. S. Forester	.50	1.50	2.50	A
nn	Hitler's Second Army—Alfred Vagts	.80	2.40	4.00	NF
nn	How to Abandon Ship—Richards & Banigan	1.00	3.00	5.00	NF
nn	How to Shoot the U. S. Army Rifle	.80	2.40	4.00	NF
nn	Island Victory: How Kwajalein Was Won	.80	2.40	4.00	NF
nn	The Jap Soldier: How He Is Trained	1.00	3.00	5.00	NF
nn	Leadership for American Army Leaders—E. L. Munson	.80	2.40	4.00	NF
nn	The Living Thoughts of Clausewitz	.50	1.50	2.50	
nn	The Lost Battalion—Thomas M. Johnson & Fletcher Pratt; 1943	.80	2.40	4.00	NF
nn	Machine Warfare—J. F. C. Fuller	1.00	3.00	5.00	NF
nn	The Making of Modern China—Owen & Eleanor Lattimore	.50	1.50	2.50	NF
nn	The Nazi State—William Ebenstein	1.00	3.00	5.00	NF
nn	Our Enemy Japan—Wilfrid Fleisher	1.00	3.00	5.00	NF
nn	Reptiles of the Pacific World—A. Loveridge	.80	2.40	4.00	NF
nn	Patriot Battles, 1775-1782—A. C. M. Azoy	.80	2.40	4.00	NF
nn	Report on India—T. A. Raman	.50	1.50	2.50	NF
nn	Rifleman Dodd—C. S. Forester	.50	1.50	2.50	A
nn	Rifles and Machine Guns of the World's Armies—Johnson	.80	2.40	4.00	NF
nn	The Russian Army—Walter Kerr	.80	2.40	4.00	NF
nn	Scouting and Patrolling	.80	2.40	4.00	NF
nn	Sergeant Terry Bull: His Ideas on War and Fighting—Terry Bull	.50	1.50	2.50	
nn	Short History of the Army and Navy—Fletcher Pratt	.50	1.50	2.50	NF
nn	So You're Going Overseas—R. S. Barker	.80	2.40	4.00	NF
nn	The Story of West Point, 1802-1943—R. E. Dupuy	.80	2.40	4.00	NF
nn	Studies on War	.80	2.40	4.00	NF

Fighting Forces Series F14, © Infan

Fighting Forces Series nn, © Infan

Fighting Forces Series nn, © Infan

Fighting Western Novel 12, © Hill   Fighting Western Novel 22, © Hill   Fighting Western Novel 33, © Hill

			Good	Fine	N/Mint	
(FIGHTING FORCES SERIES, continued)						
nn	Tank-Fighter Team—R. M. Gerard		.80	2.40	4.00	NF
nn	Thesaurus of Humor		.80	2.40	4.00	H
nn	Weapons for the Future—Johnson and Haven		1.00	3.00	5.00	NF
nn	What to Do Aboard the Transport; Note: Co-publication with Science Service		.80	2.40	4.00	NF
nn	Modern Battle: Campaigns of 1939-1941—P. W. Thompson		.80	2.40	4.00	NF
nn	New Ways of War—Tom Wintringham		.80	2.40	4.00	NF
nn	Warships at Work—T. A. Hardy		.80	2.40	4.00	NF
nn	Pipeline to Battle: Campaigns in Africa—Major Rainier		.80	2.40	4.00	NF
nn	Engineer Training Notebook		.50	1.50	2.50	NF
nn	Company Duties: A Checklist		.80	2.40	4.00	NF
nn	Machine Gunner's Handbook—C. H. Coates		.80	2.40	4.00	NF
nn	Driver Training: Handbook for Instructors		.80	2.40	4.00	NF
nn	Keep 'em Rolling: Handbook for Drivers		.80	2.40	4.00	NF
nn	You Must Be Fit		.80	2.40	4.00	
nn	Platoon Record Book		.80	2.40	4.00	NF
nn	Squad Record Book		.80	2.40	4.00	NF
nn	Our Armed Forces: A Complete Description		.80	2.40	4.00	NF
nn	Spanish Dictionary for the Soldier—Frank Henius		.50	1.50	2.50	NF
nn	French Dictionary for the Soldier—Frank Henius		.50	1.50	2.50	NF
nn	German Dictionary for the Soldier—Frank Henius		.50	1.50	2.50	NF
nn	Italian Dictionary for the Soldier—Frank Henius		.50	1.50	2.50	NF
nn	Italian Sentence Book for the Soldier—Frank Henius		.50	1.50	2.50	NF

FIGHTING WESTERN NOVEL
Novel Selections, Inc./Hillman

Digest Size

		Good	Fine	N/Mint	
2	Under the Mesa Rim—Chandler Whipple	.80	2.40	4.00	W
3	Two-Gun Texan—Herbert Shappiro	.80	2.40	4.00	W
4	Rope Neckties—John Wilstach	.80	2.40	4.00	W
5	Coyote Hunter—Denver Bardwell	.80	2.40	4.00	W
6	Silver Spurs—Charles Alden Seltzer	.80	2.40	4.00	W
7	Stranger at Storm Ranch—Dan James	.80	2.40	4.00	W
8	South of the Pass—Johnston McCulley	.80	2.40	4.00	W
9	Coyote Song—Clem Colt	.80	2.40	4.00	W
12	Ghost Bullet Range—Johnson McCulley	.80	2.40	4.00	W
14	Law of the Trail—J. E. Grinstead	.80	2.40	4.00	W
15	Kincaid of Red Butte—Leslie Ernenwein	.80	2.40	4.00	W
16	Trigger Trail—Roy Manning	.80	2.40	4.00	W
20	Spectre Spread—Tom West	.80	2.40	4.00	W
21	Prairie Smoke—Will Ermine	.80	2.40	4.00	W
22	The Cougar of Canyon Caballo—Paul Evan Lehman	.80	2.40	4.00	W
23	The Bar D Boss—Ranger Lee	.80	2.40	4.00	W
24	Painted Post Roundup—Tom Dunn	.80	2.40	4.00	W
25	The Drifting Kid—Will Ermine	.80	2.40	4.00	W
26	Prairie Pinto—Lynn Westland	.80	2.40	4.00	W
27	Wolves of the Chaperral—Paul Evan Lehman	.80	2.40	4.00	W
28	Prentiss of the Box 8—Lynn Westland	.80	2.40	4.00	W
30	Tall in the Saddle—Gordon Young	.80	2.40	4.00	W
33	Black Creek Buckaroo—Anson Piper	.80	2.40	4.00	W
34	Rustlers of Table Butte—Ernie Phillips	.80	2.40	4.00	W
38	Wild Horse Shorty—Nelson Nye	.80	2.40	4.00	W
39	Brand of the Open Hand—Frank C. Robertson	1.00	3.00	5.00	W
40	Return to the Range—Lynn Westland	.80	2.40	4.00	W
41	Blood of Kings—Nelson C. Nye	.80	2.40	4.00	W

Fingerprint Mystery nn, © Readers Det. Five Star Mystery 1, © Green Five Star Mystery 3, © Green

FINGERPRINT MYSTERY
Readers Detective Book Service

Digest Size

		Good	Fine	N/Mint	
nn	Murder Rings Twice—Helen Joan Hultman; aka Murder on Route 40	1.00	3.00	5.00	M
nn	The Man Without a Head—Joseph Bowen.	1.00	3.00	5.00	M

FIVE STAR MYSTERY
Green Publishing Company

Digest Size

1	The Dress Circle Murders—Peter Yates; orig., 1945	1.60	4.80	8.00	M
3	You'll Die Laughing—Bruce Elliott; orig., 1945	1.20	3.60	6.00	M
4	Death Comes to Dinner—Peter Yates; orig., 1945.	1.60	4.80	8.00	M
5	The Invisible Man Murders—Richard Foster; orlg., 1945.	2.00	6.00	10.00	M
13	The Laughing Buddha Murders—Richard Foster (Kendell Foster Crossen).	1.60	4.80	8.00	M
15	The Case of the Phantom Fingerprints—Kendell Foster Crossen	1.60	4.80	8.00	M
16	Curtain Call for Murder—Peter Yates; orig., 1945	1.60	4.80	8.00	M
21	The Dress Circle Murders—Peter Yates	1.20	3.60	6.00	M
22	Murder Out of Mind—Kendell Foster Crossen; orig., 1945	2.00	6.00	10.00	M
26	You'll Die Laughing—Bruce Elliott	1.00	3.00	5.00	M
28	Death Comes to Dinner—Peter Yates	1.20	3.60	6.00	M
35	Curtain Call for Murder—Peter Yates	1.20	3.60	6.00	M
36	The Invisible Man Murders—Richard Foster (Kendell Foster Crossen)	1.60	4.80	8.00	M
37	Death in the Hands of Talent—Peter Yates; orig., 1945	1.60	4.80	8.00	M
38	Murder Seeks an Agent—Wenzell Brown; orig., 1945	1.60	4.80	8.00	M
41	Death's Long Shadow—Katharine Wolffe; orig., 1946	1.20	3.60	6.00	M
42	Death Wears a Green Hat—Will Creed; orig., 1946	1.60	4.80	8.00	M
43	Crime Is of the Essence—Joe Csida; orig., 1946	1.20	3.60	6.00	M
44	The Corpse Is Indignant—Douglas Stapleton and Helen A. Carey; orig., 1946	1.20	3.60	6.00	M
45	Murder in the Rough—Leslie Allen (Horace Brown); orig., 1946	1.20	3.60	6.00	M
46	Kill to Fit—Bruno Fischer	1.60	4.80	8.00	M
47	Death Comes Grinning—Will Creed	1.20	3.60	6.00	M

GALAXY SCIENCE FICTION NOVELS
Galaxy Publishing Corporation

1 - 31 Are Digest Size

Five Star Mystery 42, © Green Five Star Mystery 46, © Green Galaxy S/F Novels 11, © Glxy

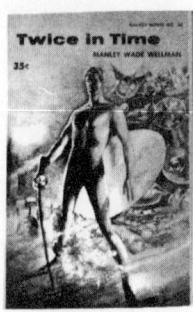

Galaxy S/F Novels 34, © Glxy

Golden Willow 52, © GW

Golden Willow 55, © GW

(GALAXY SCIENCE FICTION NOVELS, continued)

		Good	Fine	N/Mint	
1	Sinister Barrier—Eric Frank Russell	1.20	3.60	6.00	SF
2	Legion of Space—Jack Williamson	1.20	3.60	6.00	SF
3	Prelude to Space—Arthur C. Clarke; 1st ed., 1951	1.60	4.80	8.00	SF
4	The Amphibians—S. Fowler Wright	1.20	3.60	6.00	SF
5	The World Below—S. Fowler Wright	1.20	3.60	6.00	SF
6	The Alien—Raymond F. Jones; 1st ed., 1951	1.20	3.60	6.00	SF
7	Empire—Clifford D. Simak; 1st ed., 1951	1.60	4.80	8.00	SF
8	Odd John—Olaf Stapledon	1.20	3.60	6.00	SF
9	Four Sided Triangle—William F. Temple	1.20	3.60	6.00	SF
10	Rat Race—Jay Franklin	1.20	3.60	6.00	SF
11	City in the Sea—Wilson Tucker	1.20	3.60	6.00	SF
12	The House of Many Worlds—Sam Merwin, Jr.	1.20	3.60	6.00	SF
13	Seeds of Life—John Taine	1.20	3.60	6.00	SF
14	Pebble in the Sky—Isaac Asimov	1.20	3.60	6.00	SF
15	Three Go Back—J. Leslie Mitchell	1.20	3.60	6.00	SF
16	The Warriors of Day—James Blish; 1st ed., 1953	1.20	3.60	6.00	SF
17	Well of the Worlds—Lewis Padgett	1.20	3.60	6.00	SF
18	City at World's End—Edmond Hamilton	1.20	3.60	6.00	SF
19	Jack of Eagles—James Blish	1.20	3.60	6.00	SF
20	The Black Galaxy—Murray Leinster	1.20	3.60	6.00	SF
21	The Humanoids—Jack Williamson	1.20	3.60	6.00	SF
22	Killer to Come—Sam Merwin, Jr.	1.20	3.60	6.00	SF
23	Murder in Space—David V. Reed	1.20	3.60	6.00	SF
24	Lest Darkness Fall—L. Sprague de Camp	1.60	4.80	8.00	SF
25	The Last Spaceship—Murray Leinster; 1955	1.60	4.80	8.00	SF
26	Chessboard Planet—Lewis Padgett (Henry Kuttner & C. L. Moore); aka The Fairy Chessman	3.00	9.00	15.00	SF
27	Tarnished Utopia—Malcolm Jameson	2.00	6.00	10.00	SF
28	Destiny Times Three—Fritz Leiber	3.00	9.00	15.00	SF
29	Fear—L. Ron Hubbard	3.00	9.00	15.00	SF
30	Double Jeopardy—Fletcher Pratt	1.60	4.80	8.00	SF
31	Shambleau—C. L. Moore	1.60	4.80	8.00	SF
32	Address: Centauri—F. L. Wallace; c-Wood	1.60	4.80	8.00	SF
33	Mission of Gravity—Hal Clement; c-Wood	1.60	4.80	8.00	SF
34	Twice in Time—Manly Wade Wellman; c-Wood	1.60	4.80	8.00	SF
35	The Forever Machine—Mark Clifton & Frank Riley; c-Wood	1.60	4.80	8.00	SF

GEM BOOKS
Gem Books, Inc.

Digest Size

		Good	Fine	N/Mint	
101	She Lived in Sin—Ralph Carter; 1952 aka The Sins of Donna Kenyon	.80	2.40	4.00	E
102	Shameful Love—Thomas Stone aka Raging Passions	.80	2.40	4.00	E

GOLDEN WILLOW
Golden Willow Press, Inc.

Digest Size

		Good	Fine	N/Mint	
51	Rampage in the Rockies—Shoshone Green; 1945	.80	2.40	4.00	W
52	So Much Blood—Bruno Fischer; 1946	1.00	3.00	5.00	M
54	Steel to the Sunset—Allan R. Bosworth	.80	2.40	4.00	W
55	Murder by Schedule—Julian Hinckley; 1946, aka The Letter in His Throat	.80	2.40	4.00	M

Gold Medal 100, © Faw

Gold Medal 102, © Faw

Gold Medal 105, © Faw

GOLD MEDAL
Fawcett Publications, Inc.

		Good	Fine	N/Mint	
nn(99)	The Best From True, the Man's Magazine; 1949	6.00	18.00	30.00	
nn(100)	What Today's Woman Should Know About Marriage and Sex—editiors of Today's Woman	3.00	9.00	15.00	NF
101	We Are the Public Enemies—Alan Hynd; orig., 1950	2.00	6.00	10.00	NF
102	Man Story—anthology; 1st ed., 1950.	1.60	4.80	8.00	A
103	The Persian Cat—John Flagg	1.20	3.60	6.00	M
104	I'll Find You—Richard Himmel	1.20	3.60	6.00	M
105	Nude in Mink—Sax Rohmer; orig., 1950	4.00	12.00	20.00	M
106	Stretch Dawson—W. R. Burnett	3.00	9.00	15.00	W
107	The Flying Saucers Are Real—Donald Keyhoe	1.00	3.00	5.00	UFO
108	Devil May Care—Wade Miller	1.20	3.60	6.00	M
109	The Awakening of Jenny—Lillian Colter	1.00	3.00	5.00	E
110	Million Dollar Murder—Edward Ronns	1.20	3.60	6.00	M
111	The Wild Horse—Les Savage, Jr.; aka Black Horse Canyon	1.20	3.60	6.00	W
112	Your Child and You—Sidonie Matsner Gruenberg, ed. Frances Ullman	1.20	3.60	6.00	NF
113	The Violent Ones—Howard Hunt	1.20	3.60	6.00	M
114	No Business for a Lady—James Rubel	1.20	3.60	6.00	M
115	Help Wanted - for Murder—William L. Rohde	1.20	3.60	6.00	M
116	The Slaughtered Lovelies—Don Stanford	1.20	3.60	6.00	M
117	State Department Murders—Edward Ronns	1.20	3.60	6.00	M
118	The Goldfish Murders—Will Mitchell	1.20	3.60	6.00	M
119	The Tormented—Theodore Pratt	1.20	3.60	6.00	E
120	The Man Who Said No—Walt Grove	1.00	3.00	5.00	
121	The Desperado—Clifton Adams	1.20	3.60	6.00	W
122	One Wild Oat—MacKinlay Kantor	1.00	3.00	5.00	E
123	House of Flesh—Bruno Fischer; orig., 1950.	1.60	4.80	8.00	M
124	The Brass Cupcake—John D. MacDonald; orig., 1950	5.00	15.00	25.00	M
125	The Obsessed—Gertrude Schweitzer; 1950	1.00	3.00	5.00	
126	Dallas—Will F. Jenkins (Murray Leinster); orig., 1950, movie tie-in	3.00	9.00	15.00	W
127	Case of the Vanishing Beauty—Richard S. Prather	1.20	3.60	6.00	M
128	Three Secrets—Margaret Lee Runbeck	1.00	3.00	5.00	
129	Mansion of Evil—Joseph Millard; orig., 1950. Note: Comic book format	10.00	30.00	50.00	M
130	A Man of Parts—Vivian Connell	1.00	3.00	5.00	
131	Guns at Broken Bow—William Heuman	1.20	3.60	6.00	W
132	Women's Barracks—Tereska Torres	1.60	4.80	8.00	E
133	Catspaw Ordeal—Edward Ronns	1.00	3.00	5.00	
134	Hell-bent for Danger—Walt Grove	1.20	3.60	6.00	

Gold Medal 114, © Faw

Gold Medal 126, © Faw

Gold Medal 129, © Faw

Gold Medal 142, © Faw

Gold Medal 160, © Faw

Gold Medal 170, © Faw

(GOLD MEDAL, continued)

		Good	Fine	N/Mint	
135	Bar Guide—Virgil Partch & Ted Shane	1.20	3.60	6.00	H
136	Savage Bride—Cornell Woolrich; orig., 1951	4.00	12.00	20.00	M
137	War Bonnet Pass—Logan Stewart	1.20	3.60	6.00	W
138	The Corpse That Walked—Octavus Roy Cohen	1.20	3.60	6.00	M
139	Stolen Woman—Wade Miller	1.20	3.60	6.00	E
140	Gunfighter's Return—Leslie Ernenwein	1.20	3.60	6.00	W
141	Hill Girl—Charles Williams; orig., 1951	1.20	3.60	6.00	E
142	Jewel of the Java Sea—Dan Cushman	1.00	3.00	5.00	A
143	The Chinese Keyhole—Richard Himmel	1.00	3.00	5.00	M
144	Winchester Cut—Mark Sabin	1.00	3.00	5.00	W
145	High Red for Dead—William L. Rohde; orig., 1951	1.00	3.00	5.00	M
146	Roll the Wagons—William Heuman	1.20	3.60	6.00	W
147	Bodies in Bedlam—Richard S. Prather	1.20	3.60	6.00	M
148	The Lady Kills—Bruno Fischer; orig., 1951	1.20	3.60	6.00	E
149	Gunsmoke Reckoning—Joseph Chadwick	1.20	3.60	6.00	W
150	Come Murder Me—James Kieran; 1951	1.20	3.60	6.00	M
151	Death and the Naked Lady—John Flagg	1.20	3.60	6.00	
152	The Killer—Wade Miller; orig., 1951	1.20	3.60	6.00	M
153	Cocotte—Theodore Pratt	1.00	3.00	5.00	E
154	A Gun in His Hand—Victor Rosen	1.20	3.60	6.00	
155	The Apache—James Warner Bellah	1.20	3.60	6.00	W
156	The Texas Gun—Leslie Ernenwein	1.20	3.60	6.00	W
157	Westport Landing—Homer Hatten	1.20	3.60	6.00	
158	Naked Ebony—Dan Cushman	1.20	3.60	6.00	
159	Barren Land Murders—Luke Short	1.20	3.60	6.00	W
160	Catnips at Love and Marriage—Walter Chandoh & Rhar Dee	1.20	3.60	6.00	H
161	Son of the Flying Y—Will F. Jenkins (Murray Leinster); orig., 1951	1.60	4.80	8.00	
162	Bargain in Blood—Don Stanford; orig., 1951	1.20	3.60	6.00	M
163	Big City Girl—Charles Williams; orig., 1951	1.00	3.00	5.00	E
164	Murder for the Bride—John D. MacDonald	2.00	6.00	10.00	M
165	Everybody Had a Gun—Richard S. Prather	1.20	3.60	6.00	M
166	I Can't Stop Running—Edward Ronns; orig., 1951	1.00	3.00	5.00	
167	The Judas Hour—Howard Hunt	1.20	3.60	6.00	M
168	A Noose for the Desperado—Clifton Adams	1.20	3.60	6.00	W
169	Satan Is a Woman—Gil Brewer	1.20	3.60	6.00	E
170	Death on a Ferris Wheel—Aylwin Lee Martin	1.00	3.00	5.00	M
171	I, Mobster—anonymous	1.20	3.60	6.00	
172	Lost Lady—Octavus Roy Cohen	1.20	3.60	6.00	M
173	The Tiger's Wife—Wade Miller	1.00	3.00	5.00	
174	Rider From Nowhere—Joseph Chadwick	1.20	3.60	6.00	W
175	Gay Ghastly Holiday—Sebastian Blayne; 1951	1.20	3.60	6.00	
176	Crockett's Woman—Eric Hatch	1.00	3.00	5.00	
177	This Is Costello—Norton Mockridge & Robert H. Prall	1.20	3.60	6.00	NF
178	Cabin Road—John Faulkner	1.00	3.00	5.00	E
179	I Have Gloria Kirby—Richard Himmel; orig., 1951	1.00	3.00	5.00	M
180	The Girl in the Stateroom—Charles Boswell & Lewis Thompson	1.20	3.60	6.00	NF
181	Shanghai Flame—A. S. Fleischman; orig., 1951	1.20	3.60	6.00	E
182	They Died Healthy—Logan Stewart	1.20	3.60	6.00	
183	. . .and Be My Love—Ledru Baker, Jr.; orig., 1951	1.20	3.60	6.00	E
184	Thunderclap—Jack Sheridan; orig., 1951	1.20	3.60	6.00	E
185	We Never Called Him Henry—Harry Bennett & Paul Marcus	.80	2.40	4.00	B
186	Judge Me Not—John D. MacDonald; orig., 1951	2.00	6.00	10.00	M
187	Hunt the Man Down—William Heuman	1.20	3.60	6.00	W
188	Get Out of Town—Paul Connolly	1.20	3.60	6.00	
189	Cassidy's Girl—David Goodis; orig., 1951	1.20	3.60	6.00	E
190	Fires That Destroy—Harry Whittington	1.60	4.80	8.00	
191	It's Your Money - Come and Get It—Sidney Margolius	1.20	3.60	6.00	NF
192	The Devil's Mistress—Kenneth Thomas	1.20	3.60	6.00	

		Good	Fine	N/Mint	
193	The Trail—Logan Stewart	1.20	3.60	6.00	W
194	The Decoy—Edward Ronns	1.20	3.60	6.00	M
195	Saratoga Mantrap—Dexter St. Clare	1.20	3.60	6.00	
196	So Rich, So Dead—Gil Brewer	1.20	3.60	6.00	
197	The Lady and the Cheetah—John Flagg	1.20	3.60	6.00	
198	To Hell Together—H. Vernor Dixon	1.20	3.60	6.00	E
199	Sumuru—Sax Rohmer; orig., 1951	5.00	15.00	25.00	A
200	Weep for Me—John D. MacDonald; orig., 1951	5.00	15.00	25.00	M
201	Stampede—Yukon Miles	1.20	3.60	6.00	W
202	The Unpossessed—William H. Fielding	1.00	3.00	5.00	
203	Find This Woman—Richard S. Prather	1.20	3.60	6.00	M
204	Death for Mr. Big—John Gonzales	1.00	3.00	5.00	
G205	Handsome—Theodore Pratt	1.00	3.00	5.00	
206	To Kiss or Kill—Day Keene; orig., 1951	1.20	3.60	6.00	E
G207	River Girl—Charles Williams; orig., 1951	1.20	3.60	6.00	E
208	Wild Blood—A. C. Abbott	1.20	3.60	6.00	W
209	Fools Walk In—Bruno Fischer	1.20	3.60	6.00	M
210	Don't Get Caught—Carter Cullen	1.20	3.60	6.00	
211	13 French Street—Gil Brewer; orig., 1951	1.20	3.60	6.00	E
s212	Deep Is the Pit—H. Vernor Dixon; orig., 1952	1.20	3.60	6.00	E
213	The Golden Woman—Eric Hatch	1.00	3.00	5.00	
214	Fear Comes Calling—Aylwin Lee Martin	1.20	3.60	6.00	M
215	Conquest—Homer Hatten	1.20	3.60	6.00	
216	Red Runs the River—William Heuman	1.20	3.60	6.00	W
217	Passage to Terror—Edward Ronns; orig., 1952	1.20	3.60	6.00	E
218	Here Is My Body—Booth Mooney	1.20	3.60	6.00	
219	The Sheltering Night—Steve Fisher; orig., 1952	1.60	4.80	8.00	
220	Give a Man a Gun—Leslie Ernenwein	1.20	3.60	6.00	W
221	The Forbidden Room—Jaclen Steele	1.20	3.60	6.00	
222	Spring Fire—Vin Packer; orig., 1952	1.20	3.60	6.00	E
223	Look Behind You, Lady—A. S. Fleischman	1.00	3.00	5.00	
224	Tears Are for Angels—Paul Connolly; orig., 1952	1.20	3.60	6.00	
225	Home Is the Sailor—Day Keene; orig., 1952	1.20	3.60	6.00	
226	Of Tender Sin—David Goodis; orig., 1952	1.20	3.60	6.00	
227	The Creeping Shadow—Sam Merwin, Jr.	1.20	3.60	6.00	
228	Appointment in Paris—Fay Adams	1.00	3.00	5.00	
229	Little Sister—Lee Roberts; orig., 1952	1.20	3.60	6.00	E
230	The Colonel's Lady—Clifton Adams	1.20	3.60	6.00	W
231	The Road's End—Albert Conroy; orig., 1952	1.20	3.60	6.00	E
232	Woman Soldier—Arnold Rodin; orig., 1952	1.60	4.80	8.00	C
233	Way of a Wanton—Richard S. Prather	1.20	3.60	6.00	M
234	The Sharp Edge—Richard Himmel	1.20	3.60	6.00	
235	The Avenger—Matthew Blood	1.00	3.00	5.00	M
236	Lone Star—Borden Chase	1.20	3.60	6.00	W
237	Terror in the Sun—Richard Glendinning; orig., 1952	1.20	3.60	6.00	E
238	Uncle Good's Girls—John Faulkner	1.00	3.00	5.00	E
239	Don't Cry, Beloved—Edward Ronns	1.20	3.60	6.00	M
240	The Damned—John D. MacDonald; orig., 1952	2.00	6.00	10.00	M
241	Savage Interlude—Dan Cushman	1.60	4.80	8.00	A
242	Trapped—Richard Hayward; orig., 1952	1.20	3.60	6.00	M
243	The Secret Rider—Logan Stewart	1.20	3.60	6.00	W
244	The Cheaters—Ledru Baker, Jr.	1.20	3.60	6.00	
245	Double Cross—Joseph Chadwick; orig., 1952	1.20	3.60	6.00	W
246	The Scarlet Venus—Chalmers Green; orig., 1952	1.00	3.00	5.00	E
247	Cry at Dusk—Lester Dent; orig., 1952	3.00	9.00	15.00	M
248	Blackmailer—George Axelrod	1.20	3.60	6.00	
249	Cartoon Laffs From True—ed. Clyde Carley	1.20	3.60	6.00	H
250	Dark Intruder—Vin Packer; 1952	1.00	3.00	5.00	

Gold Medal 199, © Faw   Gold Medal 200, © Faw   Gold Medal 230, © Faw

Gold Medal 273, © Faw

Gold Medal 283, © Faw

Gold Medal 307, © Faw

(GOLD MEDAL, continued)

		Good	Fine	N/Mint	
251	The Caged—Fan Nichols	1.00	3.00	5.00	
252	Satan Takes the Helm—Calvin Clements	1.20	3.60	6.00	
253	The Crimson Frame—Aylwin Lee Martin	1.00	3.00	5.00	M
254	About Doctor Ferrel—Day Keene; orig., 1952	1.20	3.60	6.00	E
255	The White Squaw—Larabie Sutter	1.20	3.60	6.00	W
256	Street of the Lost—David Goodis; orig., 1952	1.20	3.60	6.00	E
257	Branded Woman—Wade Miller	1.20	3.60	6.00	
258	Escape to Love—Edward S. Aarons	1.00	3.00	5.00	
259	Walk in Fear—W. T. Ballard; aka I Could Kill You	1.60	4.80	8.00	
260	Men Into Beasts—George Sylvester Viereck	1.00	3.00	5.00	M
261	Devil's Legacy—Joseph Chadwick	1.00	3.00	5.00	W
262	Who Evil Thinks—Richard Glendinning	1.00	3.00	5.00	
263	Love Me Now—John McPartland; orig., 1952	1.00	3.00	5.00	E
264	Brenda—Lehi Zane; orig., 1952	1.00	3.00	5.00	E
265	Darling, It's Death—Richard S. Prather	1.00	3.00	5.00	M
266	Plunder—Benjamin Appel	1.00	3.00	5.00	C
267	Secret of Death Valley—William Heuman	1.00	3.00	5.00	W
268	Whisper Her Name—Howard Hunt	1.00	3.00	5.00	
269	The Devil Drives—Robert Ames	1.00	3.00	5.00	
270	The Fast Buck—Bruno Fischer; orig., 1952	1.20	3.60	6.00	M
271	Blood on the Sun—Chad Merriman	1.00	3.00	5.00	
272	Take Me As I Am—William H. Fielding	1.00	3.00	5.00	
273	Unholy Flame—Olga Rosmanith; orig., 1952	1.20	3.60	6.00	E
274	Beyond Desire—Richard Himmel	.80	2.40	4.00	
275	Move Along, Stranger—Frank Castle; 1953	1.00	3.00	5.00	
276	Mountain Girl—Cord Wainer; orig., 1952	1.00	3.00	5.00	E
277	Flight to Darkness—Gil Brewer	1.00	3.00	5.00	
278	That French Girl—Joseph Hilton	1.00	3.00	5.00	
279	The Big Guy—Wade Miller	1.00	3.00	5.00	
280	The Sinners—Edward S. Aarons	.80	2.40	4.00	M
281	Swamp Brat—Allen O'Quinn	1.20	3.60	6.00	E
282	Woman of Cairo—John Flagg	1.00	3.00	5.00	
283	The Fire Goddess—Sax Rohmer; orig., 1952, aka Virgin in Flames	5.00	15.00	25.00	A
284	Whip Hand—Joseph Chadwick	1.00	3.00	5.00	W
285	Too Rich to Die—H. Vernor Dixon	1.00	3.00	5.00	
286	Hell Hath No Fury—Charles Williams; orig., 1953	1.00	3.00	5.00	E
287	On to Santa Fe—William Heuman	1.00	3.00	5.00	W
288	Maggie - Her Marriage—Taylor Caldwell; orig., 1953	.80	2.40	4.00	E
289	The Chislers—Albert Conroy; orig., 1953	1.00	3.00	5.00	E
290	Jungle She—Dan Cushman; orig., 1953	1.20	3.60	6.00	
291	Whom Gods Destroy—Clifton Adams	.80	2.40	4.00	
292	Run, Chico, Run—Wenzell Brown; orig., 1953	1.00	3.00	5.00	JD
293	Mystery Raider—Leslie Ernenwein	1.00	3.00	5.00	W
294	The Girl in the Red Velvet Swing—Charles Samuels	1.00	3.00	5.00	
295	Danger in Paradise—A. S. Fleischman	1.00	3.00	5.00	
296	Black Wings Has My Angel—Elliott Chaze	1.00	3.00	5.00	
297	Lovers Are Losers—Howard Hunt	1.00	3.00	5.00	
298	Dead Low Tide—John D. MacDonald; orig., 1953	1.60	4.80	8.00	M
299	Six-gun Code—Perry Westwood	1.00	3.00	5.00	W
300	The Borgia Blade—Gardner F. Fox; 1953	1.20	3.60	6.00	A
301	Leave Her to God—O. O. Osborne	1.00	3.00	5.00	
302	Masquerade Into Madness—Russ Meservey	1.00	3.00	5.00	
303	Barge Girl—Calvin Clements	1.00	3.00	5.00	E
304	The Snatchers—Lionel White; orig., 1953	1.60	4.80	8.00	
305	Ridge Runner—Chad Merriman	1.00	3.00	5.00	W
306	The Girl in the Death Cell—Fred J. Cook	1.00	3.00	5.00	NF
307	Witch of Salem—Benjamin Siegel; orig., 1953	1.20	3.60	6.00	E
308	Hideaway—Nikki Content	1.00	3.00	5.00	

		Good	Fine	N/Mint	
309	Sword in His Hand—John Vail	1.20	3.60	6.00	A
310	Keelboats North—William Heuman	1.00	3.00	5.00	W
311	Thieves Fall Out—Cameron Kay	1.00	3.00	5.00	
s312	Gold Medal Treasury of American Verse—ed. John Gilland Brunini	1.00	3.00	5.00	
313	War Bonnet Pass—Logan Stewart	1.00	3.00	5.00	W
314	Gunsmoke Reckoning—Joseph Chadwick	1.00	3.00	5.00	W
315	Saturday's Harvest—Paul Shelley	1.00	3.00	5.00	
316	Up a Winding Stair—H. Vernor Dixon	.80	2.40	4.00	
317	Come Feed on Me—Morton Cooper	.80	2.40	4.00	
318	Ambush at Rincon—Dudley Dean	1.00	3.00	5.00	W
319	The Crooked Mile—Norbert Fagan	1.00	3.00	5.00	
320	Escape From Morales—Virginia Myers	1.00	3.00	5.00	
321	Nude in Mink—Sax Rohmer	1.20	3.60	6.00	M
322	Guns at Broken Bow—William Heuman	1.00	3.00	5.00	
323	The Neon Jungle—John D. MacDonald; orig., 1953	4.00	12.00	20.00	M
324	Look Back to Love—Vin Packer	1.00	3.00	5.00	
325	Terror in the Night—Sebastian Blayne; 1953; aka Until Death Do Us	1.00	3.00	5.00	
326	Moment of Truth—Arnold Rodin	1.00	3.00	5.00	
327	Savage Stronghold—Logan Stewart	1.00	3.00	5.00	W
328	Madame Buccaneer—Gardner F. Fox; orig., 1953	1.20	3.60	6.00	A
329	Gunfighter's Return—Leslie Ernenwein	1.00	3.00	5.00	W
330	Roll the Wagons—William Heuman	1.00	3.00	5.00	W
331	South of the Sun—Wade Miller	1.00	3.00	5.00	
332	Timberjack—Dan Cushman	1.20	3.60	6.00	
333	To Love to Hate—Fay Adams	1.00	3.00	5.00	
334	The Girl in Lover's Lane—Charles Boswell & Lewis Thompson	1.00	3.00	5.00	NF
335	Valley of Angry Men—Matthew Gant	1.00	3.00	5.00	
336	Tokyo Doll—John McPartland	1.00	3.00	5.00	
337	Bar Guide—Virgil Partch & Ted Shane	1.00	3.00	5.00	H
338	Rider From Nowhere—Joseph Chadwick	1.00	3.00	5.00	W
s339	Escape to Eden—Theodore Pratt	.80	2.40	4.00	
340	Nothing in Her Way—Charles Williams	1.00	3.00	5.00	
341	Ride a High Horse—Richard S. Prather	1.00	3.00	5.00	
342	Belle Bradley, Her Story—anonymous	1.00	3.00	5.00	
343	Run for Your Life—Bruno Fischer	1.00	3.00	5.00	M
344	Wagon Train Woman—Alan Henry	1.00	3.00	5.00	W
345	Hell's Our Destination—Gil Brewer	1.00	3.00	5.00	
346	Son of the Flyng Y—Will F. Jenkins (Murray Leinster)	1.00	3.00	5.00	W
347	Hondo—Louis L'Amour; orig., 1953, movie tie-in	1.60	4.80	8.00	W
348	The Moon in the Gutter—David Goodis; orig., 1953	1.20	3.60	6.00	
349	I Came to Kill—Gordon Davis	1.00	3.00	5.00	M
350	Rage in Texas—Howard Rigsby; 1953	1.00	3.00	5.00	W
351	The Girl in Poison Cottage—Jim Bishop & H. Hoffmann	1.0	3.00	5.00	NF
352	Eagle on His Wrist—Homer Hatten	1.00	3.00	5.00	
353	The Fall of Suzanne Swift—V. A. McMillen	1.00	3.00	5.00	E
354	Big Red's Daughter—John McPartland	.80	2.40	4.00	E
355	Big Stan—John Monahan; 1954	.80	2.40	4.00	
356	Paradise Motel—Jack Sheridan	1.00	3.00	5.00	
357	Guns Along the Wickiup—D. B. Newton	1.00	3.00	5.00	W
358	Pappy - and the Promised Land—Jack Gotshall	1.00	3.00	5.00	
359	The Girl in the House of Hate—Charles Samuels & Louise Samuels	1.00	3.00	5.00	NF
360	One Sword for Love—Gardner F. Fox	1.20	3.60	6.00	A
361	Rampage—Leslie Ernenwein	1.00	3.00	5.00	W
362	Come Back, My Love—Edward S. Aarons; orig., 1954	1.00	3.00	5.00	M
363	Come Destroy Me—Vin Packer	1.00	3.00	5.00	
364	Gold Brick Cassie—David Loth	1.00	3.00	5.00	NF
365	Monte Carlo Mission—Vivian Connell	.80	2.40	4.00	
366	This Woman Is Mine—Harry Whittington	1.60	4.80	8.00	
367	Rails West—Logan Stewart	1.00	3.00	5.00	W
368	Malay Woman—A. S. Fleischman	1.00	3.00	5.00	A
369	Seminole—Theodore Pratt	2.00	6.00	10.00	A
370	A Lover for Cindy—H. Vernon Dixon	1.00	3.00	5.00	
371	Go Home, Stranger—Charles Williams	1.00	3.00	5.00	
372	Notorious—Day Keene; orig., 1954	1.20	3.60	6.00	
373	Two Deaths Must Die—Richard Himmel	1.00	3.00	5.00	
374	Come Out Shooting—Joseph Chadwick	1.00	3.00	5.00	W
375	As a Man Falls—Howard Rigsby; 1954	1.00	3.00	5.00	
376	Take Your Last Look—Matt Brady	1.00	3.00	5.00	
377	The Range Grabbers—Sidney Stewart	1.00	3.00	5.00	
378	Let Them Eat Bullets—Howard Schoenfeld	1.00	3.00	5.00	M
379	Women's Barracks—Tereska Torres	1.00	3.00	5.00	E
380	A Killer Is Loose—Gil Brewer	1.00	3.00	5.00	
381	Fury on the Plains—Chad Merriman	1.00	3.00	5.00	W
382	One Against the Odds—Norbert Fagan	1.00	3.00	5.00	
383	Cartoon Fun From True	1.00	3.00	5.00	H
384	The Girl With the Scarlet Brand—Charles Boswell & Lewis Thompson	1.00	3.00	5.00	NF

Gold Medal 411, © Faw   Gold Medal 417, © Faw   Gold Medal 438, © Faw

(GOLD MEDAL, continued)

		Good	Fine	N/Mint	
385	Sweet Money Girl—Benjamin Appel	1.00	3.00	5.00	
386	The Beautiful and Dead—Ross MacRoss	1.00	3.00	5.00	
d387	Driven—Richard Gehman	1.00	3.00	5.00	
388	I'll Take What's Mine—Nard Jones	1.00	3.00	5.00	
389	Retreat Into Night—Richard Glendinning	1.00	3.00	5.00	
390	Renegade Gun—Joseph Chadwick	1.00	3.00	5.00	
391	Dear, Deadly Beloved—John Flagg	1.00	3.00	5.00	
392	The Fabulous Finn—Don Cushman	1.20	3.60	6.00	M
393	The Face of Evil—John McPartland	1.00	3.00	5.00	
394	The Gentleman Rogue—Gardner F. Fox	1.20	3.60	6.00	A
395	And Two Shall Meet—Raymond Mason	1.00	3.00	5.00	
396	The Dark Throne—John Vail	1.00	3.00	5.00	A
397	The Girl on the Gallows—Q. Patrick	1.20	3.60	6.00	M
398	Spring Fire—Vin Packer	1.00	3.00	5.00	E
399	A Woman for Henry—Allen O'Quinn	1.00	3.00	5.00	
400	Lucinda—Howard Rigsby; 1954	1.00	3.00	5.00	
401	Saddle the Storm—Harry Whittington	1.60	4.80	8.00	
402	French for Murder—Bernard Mara	1.20	3.60	6.00	M
s403	Portrait of Lisa—William Brothers	1.00	3.00	5.00	
404	The Wickedest Man—Joseph Millard	1.20	3.60	6.00	
405	There Was a Crooked Man—Day Keene; orig., 1954	1.20	3.60	6.00	
406	Affair in Tokyo—John McPartland	1.00	3.00	5.00	
407	Man Divided—Dean Douglas	1.00	3.00	5.00	
408	Return of Sumuru—Sax Rohmer; orig., 1954	4.00	12.00	20.00	A
409	Some Must Die—Gil Brewer	1.00	3.00	5.00	
410	Uncle Good's Girls—John Faulkner	1.00	3.00	5.00	E
411	Black Horse Canyon—Les Savage, Jr.; aka The Wild Horse, movie tie-in	1.20	3.60	6.00	W
412	Hell Ship to Kuma—Calvin Clements	1.20	3.60	6.00	
413	Always Leave 'em Dying—Richard S. Prather	1.00	3.00	5.00	M
414	Ride for Texas—William Heuman	1.00	3.00	5.00	W
415	Runaway Black—Richard Marsten	1.00	3.00	5.00	
416	Jezebel in Crinoline—Homer Hatten	1.00	3.00	5.00	E
417	I Am Legend—Richard Matheson; orig., 1954	3.00	9.00	15.00	SF
418	13 French Street—Gil Brewer	1.00	3.00	5.00	
419	Come Murder Me—James Kieran	1.00	3.00	5.00	M
420	All These Condemned—John D. MacDonald	1.20	3.60	6.00	M
421	Smash-up—Theodore Pratt	1.00	3.00	5.00	
422	Two-Gun Law—Clifton Adams	1.00	3.00	5.00	W
423	Death Is a Lovely Dame—Matthew Blood	1.00	3.00	5.00	M
424	Girl on the Run—Edward S. Aarons	1.00	3.00	5.00	M
425	Case of the Vanishing Beauty—Richard S. Prather; 1954	1.00	3.00	5.00	M
426	Whisper His Sin—Vin Packer	1.00	3.00	5.00	
427	Cry Down the Lonely Night—Milton White	1.00	3.00	5.00	
428	Street of No Return—David Goodis; orig., 1954	1.20	3.60	6.00	
429	The Range Buster—William Heuman	1.00	3.00	5.00	W
430	Beautiful Humbug—William H. Fielding	1.00	3.00	5.00	
431	The Girl on the Lonely Beach—Fred J. Cook	1.00	3.00	5.00	NF
s432	Handsome—Theodore Pratt	1.00	3.00	5.00	
433	Somebody Loves Me—Nancy Morgan	1.00	3.00	5.00	
434	A Touch of Death—Charles Williams; aka And Share Alike	1.00	3.00	5.00	
435	The Dangerous One—Robert Ames	1.00	3.00	5.00	
436	The Man From Riondo—Dudley Dean	1.00	3.00	5.00	W
437	So Wicked My Love—Bruno Fischer; aka Incident at Coney Island	1.00	3.00	5.00	M
438	Women of Kali—Gardner F. Fox	2.00	6.00	10.00	A
439	Cabin Road—John Faulkner	1.00	3.00	5.00	E
s440	The Cunning and the Haunted—Richard Jessup	1.00	3.00	5.00	
441	Sow the Wild Wind—John Vail	1.00	3.00	5.00	A
442	Rebel Raider—Joseph Chadwick	1.00	3.00	5.00	W

		Good	Fine	N/Mint	
443	Wild Breed—Ted Stratton	1.00	3.00	5.00	
444	Mission to Murder—Richard Glendinning	1.00	3.00	5.00	M
445	Funny Cartoons by VIP—Virgil Partch; 1955	1.00	3.00	5.00	H
446	Hill Girl—Charles Williams	.80	2.40	4.00	
447	Make My Coffin Strong—William R. Cox	1.00	3.00	5.00	
448	77 Rue Paradise—Gil Brewer	1.00	3.00	5.00	
449	The Mating Cry—Frank Daniels	1.00	3.00	5.00	
450	Strange But True—ed. Mee Morningside; 1955	1.00	3.00	5.00	NF
451	Bad Day at Black Rock—Michael Niall; movie tie-in	1.60	4.80	8.00	W
452	Outcast of Murder Mesa—Kenneth Fowler	1.00	3.00	5.00	W
s453	City of Women—Nancy Morgan	1.00	3.00	5.00	E
s454	The Hunger and the Hate—H. Vernor Dixon	1.00	3.00	5.00	
455	The Sin Shouter of Cabin Road—John Faulkner	1.00	3.00	5.00	E
456	Shanghai Incident—Steve Dodge	1.00	3.00	5.00	
457	Many Rivers to Cross—Steve Frazee	1.00	3.00	5.00	W
458	The Girl in Murder Flat—Mel Heimer	1.00	3.00	5.00	NF
459	Lady in Dread—Ryerson Johnson	1.00	3.00	5.00	
460	I'll Find You—Richard Himmel	.80	2.40	4.00	
461	The Glitter and the Greed—Robert W. Taylor; c-Maguire	1.00	3.00	5.00	
462	Funny Business—Charlest Preston	1.00	3.00	5.00	H
463	Strangers in My Bed—Allen O'Quinn	1.00	3.00	5.00	
464	Bullet Barricade—Leslie Ernenwein	1.00	3.00	5.00	W
465	A New Way to Eat and Get Slim—Donald G. Cooley	1.00	3.00	5.00	NF
466	Death Was the Bridegroom—Charles Samuels	1.00	3.00	5.00	
s467	River Girl—Charles Williams	1.00	3.00	5.00	E
468	Forever Is Today—Raymond Mason	1.00	3.00	5.00	
469	Mad Baxter—Wade Miller	1.00	3.00	5.00	M
470	The Big Caper—Lionel White; orig., 1955	1.60	4.80	8.00	M
471	Song of the Gun—Dudley Dean	1.00	3.00	5.00	W
472	A Bullet for My Lady—Bernard Mara	1.20	3.60	6.00	M
473	Violence in the Night—Alan Hynd	1.00	3.00	5.00	
s474	The Tormented—Theodore Pratt	1.00	3.00	5.00	
475	Angels in the Gutter—Joseph Hilton; 1955	1.60	4.80	8.00	JD
476	Blonde Savage—John Vail	1.20	3.60	6.00	A
477	Prey by Night—Malcolm Douglas	1.00	3.00	5.00	
478	Heller With a Gun—Louis L'Amour	2.00	6.00	10.00	W
479	The Soft Arms of Death—Richard Hayward	1.00	3.00	5.00	
480	The Girls in Nightmare House—Charles Boswell & Lewis Thompson	1.00	3.00	5.00	NF
481	The Damned—John D. MacDonald	1.00	3.00	5.00	
482	The Brass Cupcake—John D. MacDonald	1.00	3.00	5.00	M
483	Death's Sweet Song—Clifton Adams	1.00	3.00	5.00	
484	Rebel Wench—Gardner F. Fox	1.20	3.60	6.00	A
485	West to the Sun—Noel M. Loomis	1.00	3.00	5.00	W
486	Dark Heritage—John Foster	1.00	3.00	5.00	
487	The Truth About Belle Gunness—Lillian de la Torre	1.00	3.00	5.00	
488	Cry of the Flesh—Richard Himmel	1.00	3.00	5.00	
489	Find This Woman—Richard S. Prather	1.00	3.00	5.00	M
490	Mine to Avenge—Thomas Wills	1.00	3.00	5.00	
491	Assignment to Disaster—Edward S. Aarons	1.00	3.00	5.00	M
492	Plunder Range—Homer Hatten	1.00	3.00	5.00	
493	The Golden Frame—Joseph Chadwick	1.00	3.00	5.00	
494	Who Has Wilma Lathrop?—Day Keene; orig., 1955	1.20	3.60	6.00	M
495	Hell Strip—Lee Richards	1.00	3.00	5.00	
496	Bodies in Bedlam—Richard S. Prather	1.00	3.00	5.00	M
497	Way of a Wanton—Richard S. Prather	1.00	3.00	5.00	M
498	One of Our H-Bombs Is Missing—Frederick Hazlitt Brennan	1.60	4.80	8.00	M
499	Blood Alley—A. S. Fleischman; movie tie-in	1.60	4.80	8.00	A
500	So Fair, So Evil—Paul Connolly; 1955	1.00	3.00	5.00	

Gold Medal 455, © Faw

Gold Medal 498, © Faw

Gold Medal 509, © Faw

		Good	Fine	N/Mint	
501	Trouble Rides Tall—William Hopson	1.00	3.00	5.00	W
502	Homicide Hussy—Atha McGuire	1.00	3.00	5.00	M
503	Death Lies Deep—William Guinn	1.00	3.00	5.00	M
504	Everybody Had a Gun—Richard S. Prather	1.00	3.00	5.00	M
505	Darling, It's Death—Richard S. Prather	1.00	3.00	5.00	M
506	Stop This Man—Peter Rabe	1.00	3.00	5.00	
507	Murder in the Navy—Richard Marsten	1.00	3.00	5.00	M
508	Strip for Murder—Richard S. Prather	1.00	3.00	5.00	M
509	We Walk Alone—Ann Aldrich; orig., 1955	2.00	6.00	10.00	E
510	The Thrill Kids—Vin Packer	1.00	3.00	5.00	
511	The Broken Spur—Dudley Dean	1.00	3.00	5.00	W
512	Ride the Dark Storm—Nard Jones	1.00	3.00	5.00	
513	Stolen Woman—Wade Miller	1.00	3.00	5.00	
514	Shanghai Flame—A. S. Fleischman	1.00	3.00	5.00	
s515	A Rage to Die—Richard Jessup	1.00	3.00	5.00	
516	To Tame a Land—Louis L'Amour	2.00	6.00	10.00	W
517	Journey Into Death—Jack Johnson	1.00	3.00	5.00	
518	Awake and Die—Robert Ames	1.00	3.00	5.00	M
519	Lie Down With Lions—Marvin H. Albert	1.00	3.00	5.00	
520	Benny Muscles In—Peter Rabe	1.00	3.00	5.00	
521	The Killer—Wade Miller	1.00	3.00	5.00	
s522	Run, Chico, Run—Wenzell Brown	1.00	3.00	5.00	JD
523	The Second Longest Night—Stephen Marlowe	1.00	3.00	5.00	M
524	My Deadly Angel—John Chelton	1.00	3.00	5.00	
525	Your Sins and Mine—Taylor Caldwell	1.00	3.00	5.00	
526	Gunsmoke Empire—Lewis B. Patten	1.00	3.00	5.00	W
527	Renegade Brand—Richard Brister	1.00	3.00	5.00	W
528	A Shroud for Jesso—Peter Rabe	1.00	3.00	5.00	
529	The Decoy—Edward Ronns	1.00	3.00	5.00	
530	The Wounded and the Slain—David Goodis; orig., 1955	1.20	3.60	6.00	
531	The Dead Darling—Jonathan Craig	1.00	3.00	5.00	M
532	The Neighbor's Kids—George Clark	1.00	3.00	5.00	
533	Gambling Man—Clifton Adams	1.00	3.00	5.00	
534	The Outlaw Breed—D. B. Newton	1.00	3.00	5.00	W
535	Port Orient—Dan Cushman	1.20	3.60	6.00	A
536	Cocotte—Theodore Pratt	.80	2.40	4.00	
537	House of Flesh—Bruno Fischer	1.00	3.00	5.00	M
538	Flesh - and Mr. Rawlie—Morton Cooper	1.00	3.00	5.00	
539	Rain of Terror—Malcolm Douglas; 1955	1.00	3.00	5.00	
540	Zowie! Girl Meets Boy—Charles Preston	1.20	3.60	6.00	H
541	Horsemen From Hell—Homer Hatten	1.00	3.00	5.00	
542	The Lone Gun—Howard Rigsby	1.00	3.00	5.00	
543	The Chinese Keyhole—Richard Himmel	.80	2.40	4.00	
544	Cassidy's Girl—David Goodis	1.20	3.60	6.00	E
545	Hell-bent for Danger—Walt Grove	1.00	3.00	5.00	
546	Killer in White—Tedd Thomey	1.00	3.00	5.00	
547	A House in Naples—Peter Rabe	1.00	3.00	5.00	
548	To Hell - and Texas—Giles A. Lutz	1.00	3.00	5.00	W
s549	Queen of Sheba—Gardner F. Fox; orig., 1956	2.00	6.00	10.00	A
s550	Down to Eternity—Richard O'Connor	1.00	3.00	5.00	
551	Too Many Crooks—Richard S. Prather; aka Ride a High Horse	1.00	3.00	5.00	M
552	Men Into Beasts—George Sylvester Viereck	1.00	3.00	5.00	
553	The Law and Jake Wade—Marvin H. Albert	1.00	3.00	5.00	W
554	The Violent Hours—Frank Castle	1.00	3.00	5.00	
555	Sinister Madonna—Sax Rohmer; orig., 1956	4.00	12.00	20.00	A
556	Hold Back the Sun—John Vail	1.00	3.00	5.00	A
557	Hot, Sweet and Blue—Jack Baird	1.00	3.00	5.00	
558	Trapped—Richard Hayward	1.00	3.00	5.00	
559	Woman Soldier—Arnold Rodin	1.00	3.00	5.00	C
560	The Guns of Fort Petticoat—C. William Harrison	1.20	3.60	6.00	W
561	Death Must Wait—Don Kingery	1.00	3.00	5.00	
562	This Gun for Gloria—Bernard Mara	1.20	3.60	6.00	M
563	Build My Gallows High—Roy Benard Sparkia	1.00	3.00	5.00	
s564	Cry Blood—H. Vernor Dixon	1.00	3.00	5.00	
565	Little Sister—Lee Roberts	.80	2.40	4.00	E
566	I Have Gloria Kirby—Richard Himmel	1.00	3.00	5.00	
567	The Golden Bawd—Giles A. Lutz	1.00	3.00	5.00	
568	Assignment - Treason—Edward S. Aarons	1.00	3.00	5.00	M
569	Gunfire at Salt Fork—William Hopson	1.00	3.00	5.00	W
570	My Mistress, Death—Robert Spafford	1.00	3.00	5.00	
571	I'll See You in Hell—John McPartland	1.00	3.00	5.00	
572	Look Behind You, Lady—A. S. Fleischman	1.00	3.00	5.00	
573	Rope Law—Lewis B. Patten	1.00	3.00	5.00	W
574	Danger for Breakfast—John McPartland	1.00	3.00	5.00	
575	Mecca for Murder—Stephen Marlowe; 1956	1.00	3.00	5.00	M
576	Catch a Falling Star—Reed Marr	1.00	3.00	5.00	
s577	The Shrinking Man—Richard Matheson	2.00	6.00	10.00	SF

		Good	Fine	N/Mint	
(GOLD MEDAL, continued)					
578	Dark Intruder—Vin Packer	1.00	3.00	5.00	
579	The Road's End—Albert Conroy	1.00	3.00	5.00	
580	Rio Bravo—Gordon D. Shirreffs	1.00	3.00	5.00	W
581	The Young and Violent—Vin Packer	1.00	3.00	5.00	
582	Morgue for Venus—Jonathan Craig	1.00	3.00	5.00	M
s583	Hypnosis and You—Ben Benson & Howard D. Tawney	1.00	3.00	5.00	NF
584	The Diehards—Dudley Dean	1.00	3.00	5.00	W
585	Swamp Brat—Allen O'Quinn	1.00	3.00	5.00	
586	Let Them Eat Bullets—Howard Schoenfeld	1.00	3.00	5.00	
s587	Johnny Concho—Noel M. Loomis; movie tie-in	1.20	3.60	6.00	W
s588	The Innocent and Willing—Morton Cooper	1.00	3.00	5.00	
589	Love After Five—Raymond Mason	1.00	3.00	5.00	
s590	Edgar Cayce - Mystery Man of Miracles—Joseph Millard	1.00	3.00	5.00	NF
591	Knee-deep in Death—Bruno Fischer	1.00	3.00	5.00	M
592	The Wailing Frail—Richard S. Prather	1.00	3.00	5.00	M
593	Law of the Trigger—Clifton Adams	1.00	3.00	5.00	W
594	Kill the Boss Good-bye—Peter Rabe	1.00	3.00	5.00	
595	Brute in Brass—Harry Whittington	1.20	3.60	6.00	
596	The Wild Party—John McPartland	1.00	3.00	5.00	
s597	The Women With Claws—Williams Forrest	1.00	3.00	5.00	
598	Always Leave 'em Dying—Richard S. Prather	.80	2.40	4.00	M
599	Mountain Girl—Cord Wainer	1.00	3.00	5.00	E
600	Fools Walk In—Bruno Fischer; 1956	1.00	3.00	5.00	M
601	Tough Hombre—Dudley Dean	1.00	3.00	5.00	W
602	White Warrior—Lewis B. Patten; c-McCarthy	1.00	3.00	5.00	W
603	Bring Him Back Dead—Day Keene; orig., 1956	1.20	3.60	6.00	
604	The Name's Buchanan—Jonas Ward	1.00	3.00	5.00	W
605	Dead and Kicking—Frank Castle	1.00	3.00	5.00	
606	Operation - Murder—Lionel White; orig., 1956	1.60	4.80	8.00	
s607	The Diamond Bikini—Charles Williams	1.00	3.00	5.00	
608	The Chiselers—Albert Conroy	1.00	3.00	5.00	E
609	The Borgia Blade—Gardner F. Fox	1.20	3.60	6.00	A
610	Don't Get Caught—Carter Cullen	1.00	3.00	5.00	
611	Desire in the Dust—Harry Whittington	1.60	4.80	8.00	
612	Dig My Grave Deep—Peter Rabe	1.20	3.60	6.00	
613	He Rode Alone—Steve Frazee	1.00	3.00	5.00	W
614	The Deadly Dames—Malcolm Douglas	1.00	3.00	5.00	
615	Three Violent People—Leonard Praskins & Barney Slater; movie tie-in	1.20	3.60	6.00	
s616	Killer in Silk—H. Vernor Dixon	1.00	3.00	5.00	
617	About Doctor Ferrel—Day Keene	1.20	3.60	6.00	
s618	Handsome—Theodore Pratt	1.00	3.00	5.00	
619	Prairie Reckoning—Paul Durst	1.00	3.00	5.00	W
620	High Gun—Leslie Ernenwein; c-McCarthy	1.00	3.00	5.00	W
621	Assignment - Suicide—Edward S. Aarons	1.00	3.00	5.00	M
622	Murder on the Side—Day Keene; orig., 1956	1.20	3.60	6.00	M
623	Down There—David Goodis; orig., 1956, aka Shoot the Piano Player	1.20	3.60	6.00	
s624	Dark Don't Catch Me—Vin Packer	1.00	3.00	5.00	
625	Go Home Stranger—Charles Williams; 1956	1.00	3.00	5.00	
626	Of Tender Sin—David Goodis	1.00	3.00	5.00	E
627	Trouble Is My Name—Stephen Marlowe	1.00	3.00	5.00	M
628	Murder in Monaco—John Flagg	1.00	3.00	5.00	M
629	The Deadly Chase—Carter Cullen	1.00	3.00	5.00	
630	The White Squaw—Larabie Sutter	1.00	3.00	5.00	
631	Violence Valley—William Heuman	1.00	3.00	5.00	W
s632	Search for Surrender—Borden Deal	1.00	3.00	5.00	
633	The Sin Shouter of Cabin Road—John Faulkner	.80	2.40	4.00	E
634	State Department Murders—Edward Ronns	1.00	3.00	5.00	M
635	Seminole—Theodore Pratt; 1957	1.20	3.60	6.00	A
636	Vengeance Under Law—Frank Castle	1.00	3.00	5.00	
637	Running Target—Steve Frazee	1.00	3.00	5.00	
638	Women Without Men—Reed Marr	1.00	3.00	5.00	
639	Bugles on the Prairie—Gordon D. Shirreffs; c-McCarthy	1.00	3.00	5.00	W
640	The Wicked Streets—Wenzell Brown	1.00	3.00	5.00	JD
s641	The Golden Sorrow—Theodore Pratt	1.00	3.00	5.00	
s642	Sweet Money Girl—Benjamin Appel	1.00	3.00	5.00	
643	I Am Legend—Richard Matheson	1.20	3.60	6.00	SF
644	Ride the Gold Mare—Ovid Demaris	1.00	3.00	5.00	
645	Case of the Cold Coquette—Jonathan Craig	1.00	3.00	5.00	M
646	The Reluctant Gun—Howard Rigsby	1.00	3.00	5.00	
647	Cheyenne Saturday—Richard Jessup	1.00	3.00	5.00	W
648	Terror Over London—Gardner F. Fox	1.20	3.60	6.00	M
s649	The Wings of Eagles—Walt Grove; movie tie-in	1.60	4.80	8.00	
650	The Corpse That Walked—Octavus Roy Cohen; 1957	.80	2.40	4.00	M
651	Big City Girl—Charles Williams	.80	2.40	4.00	E
652	Street of the Lost—David Goodis	1.00	3.00	5.00	
s653	Odd Girl Out—Ann Bannon	2.00	6.00	10.00	

Gold Medal s649, © Faw   Gold Medal 686, © Faw   Gold Medal 700, © Faw

(GOLD MEDAL, continued)

		Good	Fine	N/Mint	
654	Pure Sweet Hell—Malcolm Douglas	1.00	3.00	5.00	
655	Gun in the Valley—Dudley Dean	1.00	3.00	5.00	W
656	Westward the Drums—L. A. Hearne	1.00	3.00	5.00	
657	The Cut Is Death—Peter Rabe	1.00	3.00	5.00	
658	Murder Is My Dish—Stephen Marlowe	1.00	3.00	5.00	M
659	Hell Strip—Lee Richards	1.00	3.00	5.00	
s660	The Young Don't Cry—Richard Jessup	1.00	3.00	5.00	
s661	The Maricopa Trail—Noel M. Loomis	1.00	3.00	5.00	W
662	Buchanan Says No—Jonas Ward	1.00	3.00	5.00	W
663	Death Takes the Bus—Lionel White; orig., 1957	1.60	4.80	8.00	M
664	So I'm a Heel—Mike Heller	1.00	3.00	5.00	
665	Three's a Shroud—Richard S. Prather	1.00	3.00	5.00	M
666	Assignment - Stella Marni—Edward S. Aarons	1.00	3.00	5.00	M
667	Saddle Justice—Steven C. Lawrence	1.00	3.00	5.00	W
668	Don't Let Her Die—Tarn Scott	1.00	3.00	5.00	
669	So Young, So Wicked—Jonathan Craig	1.00	3.00	5.00	M
670	Agreement to Kill—Peter Rabe	1.00	3.00	5.00	
671	Lusty Conquest—Lee Richards	1.00	3.00	5.00	E
672	Long Ride West—Richard Jessup	1.00	3.00	5.00	W
s673	Women's Barracks—Tereska Torres	1.00	3.00	5.00	
674	Outlaw's Son—Clifton Adams	1.00	3.00	5.00	W
675	One Wild Oat—MacKinlay Kantor; 1957	1.00	3.00	5.00	
676	Nice Guys Finish Dead—Albert Conroy	1.00	3.00	5.00	
677	Have Gat - Will Travel—Richard S. Prather	1.00	3.00	5.00	M
678	It's My Funeral—Peter Rabe	1.00	3.00	5.00	M
679	Gun Talk at Yuma—Frank Castle	1.00	3.00	5.00	W
680	The Hoods Take Over—Ovid Demaris	1.00	3.00	5.00	JD
681	Heller From Texas—William Heuman	1.00	3.00	5.00	W
682	The Tiger's Wife—Wade Miller	.80	2.40	4.00	
683	A Noose for the Desperado—Clifton Adams	1.00	3.00	5.00	W
s684	Re-enter Fu Manchu—Sax Rohmer; orig., 1957	3.00	9.00	15.00	A
685	Sundown at Crazy Horse—Vechel Howard	1.00	3.00	5.00	W
686	Last Stand at Papago Wells—Louis L'Amour; orig., 1957, c-McCarthy	2.00	6.00	10.00	W
687	Hostage for a Hood—Lionel White	1.60	4.80	8.00	
s688	The Girl in the Belfry—Joseph Henry Jackson & Lenore Glen Offord	1.00	3.00	5.00	NF
689	Three-Day Terror—Vin Packer	1.00	3.00	5.00	
690	Crockett's Woman—Eric Hatch	1.00	3.00	5.00	
691	Fire in the Flesh—David Goodis; orig., 1957	1.20	3.60	6.00	
692	Harry the Men High—Noel M. Loomis & Paul Leslie Peil	1.00	3.00	5.00	
693	Killers Are My Meat—Stephen Marlowe	1.00	3.00	5.00	M
694	Murder in the Raw—Bruno Fischer	1.00	3.00	5.00	M
695	Lovely and Lethal—Frank Castle	1.00	3.00	5.00	
696	Apache Rising—Marvin H. Albert	1.00	3.00	5.00	W
697	Hill Girl—Charles Williams	.80	2.40	4.00	
698	The Baby Doll Murders—James O. Causey	1.00	3.00	5.00	M
699	Comanche Vengeance—Richard Jessup	1.00	3.00	5.00	W
700	The Tall Stranger—Louis L'Amour; orig., 1957, movie tie-in	2.00	6.00	10.00	W
701	Run From the Hunter—Keith Grantland	1.00	3.00	5.00	
702	The Case of the Beautiful Body—Jonathan Craig	1.00	3.00	5.00	M
703	The Voodoo Murders—Michael Avallone	1.20	3.60	6.00	M
s704	This Is Costello—Norton Mockridge & Robert Prall	1.00	3.00	5.00	NF
705	Stagecoach West—William Heuman	1.00	3.00	5.00	W
706	The Massacre at San Pablo—Lewis B. Patten	1.00	3.00	5.00	W
707	Assignment - Budapest—Edward S. Aarons	1.00	3.00	5.00	M
708	The Brat—Gil Brewer	1.00	3.00	5.00	E
709	Murder in Red—Frank Castle	1.00	3.00	5.00	
710	Journey Into Terror—Peter Rabe	1.00	3.00	5.00	
711	A Man of Parts—Vivian Connell	.80	2.40	4.00	

		Good	Fine	N/Mint	
712	The Wailing Frail—Richard S. Prather	1.00	3.00	5.00	M
713	Summons to Silverhorn—Kenneth Fowler	1.00	3.00	5.00	
714	Ambush on the Mesa—Gordon D. Shirreffs	1.00	3.00	5.00	W
715	Case of the Deadly Kiss—Milton K. Ozaki	1.00	3.00	5.00	M
716	Come Night, Come Evil—Jonathan Craig	1.00	3.00	5.00	M
717	For Love of Imabelle—Chester Himes	1.00	3.00	5.00	
718	The Crazy Mixed-Up Corpse—Michael Avallone; orig., 1957	1.20	3.60	6.00	W
719	Savage Bride—Cornell Woolrich	1.00	3.00	5.00	M
720	Barren Land Showdown—Luke Short; aka Barren Land Murders	1.00	3.00	5.00	W
721	Murder on the Line—William L. Rohde	1.00	3.00	5.00	M
722	A Town to Tame—Joseph Chadwick	1.00	3.00	5.00	W
723	Five Rode West—Lewis B. Patten	1.00	3.00	5.00	W
724	The Damned—John D. MacDonald	1.00	3.00	5.00	M
s725	The Great Debauch—Williams Forrest; 1958	1.00	3.00	5.00	E
s726	Three Times Infinity—Leo Margulies	.50	1.50	2.50	SF
s727	We Too Must Love—Ann Aldrich; orig., 1958	2.00	6.00	10.00	E
728	Heller With a Gun—Louis L'Amour	1.00	3.00	5.00	W
729	Uncle Good's Girls—John Faulkner	.80	2.40	4.00	E
730	Cabin Road—John Faulkner	.80	2.40	4.00	E
s731	5:45 to Suburbia—Vin Packer	1.00	3.00	5.00	
732	Ripe Fruit—John McPartland	1.00	3.00	5.00	
733	Guns of Rio Conchos—Clair Huffaker	1.20	3.60	6.00	W
s734	Teen-age Terror—Wenzell Brown	1.20	3.60	6.00	JD
s735	The Rich and the Damned—Richard Himmel	1.00	3.00	5.00	
736	Cowboy—Clair Huffaker; movie tie-in	1.20	3.60	6.00	W
737	Dead Low Tide—John D. MacDonald	1.20	3.60	6.00	M
738	The Violent Ones—Howard Hunt	1.00	3.00	5.00	
739	I, Mobster	1.00	3.00	5.00	
740	Web of Murder—Harry Whittington	1.20	3.60	6.00	
741	Outcast Gun—Giles A. Lutz	1.00	3.00	5.00	W
742	One-man Massacre—Jonas Ward	1.00	3.00	5.00	W
743	I Like 'em Tough—Curt Cannon	1.20	3.60	6.00	
744	The Secret of Sylvia—Lee Borden	1.00	3.00	5.00	
745	Take a Murder, Darling—Richard S. Prather	1.00	3.00	5.00	M
s746	River Girl—Charles Williams	1.00	3.00	5.00	E
747	The Hoods Come Calling—Nick Quany	1.00	3.00	5.00	JD
748	Badman's Holiday—Will Cook	1.00	3.00	5.00	W
749	Assignment - Angelina—Edward S. Aarons	1.00	3.00	5.00	M
750	The Lusting Drive—Ovid Demaris; 1958	1.00	3.00	5.00	
s751	War With the Gizmos—Murray Leinster	1.20	3.60	6.00	SF
752	Dakota Boomtown—Frank Castle	1.00	3.00	5.00	W
753	So Wicked My Love—Bruno Fischer	.50	1.50	2.50	M
754	The Obsessed—Gertrude Schweitzer	.50	1.50	2.50	
755	The Lady Kills—Bruno Fischer	.50	1.50	2.50	M
756	The Law and Jake Wade—Marvin H. Albert	1.00	3.00	5.00	W
s757	Sumuru—Sax Rohmer	1.00	3.00	5.00	A
758	Devil May Come—Wade Miller	.80	2.40	4.00	
759	Wyoming Jones—Richard Telfair	.80	2.40	4.00	
760	The Bounty Killer—Marvin H. Albert	.80	2.40	4.00	W
761	Park Avenue Tramp—Fletcher Flora	.50	1.50	2.50	E
s762	The Tycoon and the Tigress—William R. Cox	.50	1.50	2.50	
763	Stop This Man—Peter Rabe	1.00	3.00	5.00	
s764	The Rise and Fall of Dr. Carey—O. O. Osborne	.50	1.50	2.50	
765	No Business for a Lady—James Rubel	.80	2.40	4.00	
766	Catspaw Ordeal—Edward Ronns	.80	2.40	4.00	
767	Murder for the Bride—John D. MacDonald	.80	2.40	4.00	M
d768	The Lost Years of Jesus Revealed—Rev. Dr. Charles Francis Potter	1.00	3.00	5.00	NF
769	Violence Is My Business—Stephen Marlowe	1.00	3.00	5.00	M

Gold Medal 728, © Faw

Gold Medal 736, © Faw

Gold Medal 768, © Faw

770	The Scrambled Yeggs—Richard S. Prather	1.60	4.80	8.00	M
771	Texas Outlaw—Richard Jessup	.80	2.40	4.00	W
772	Feud at Forked River—Philip Ketchum	.80	2.40	4.00	W
s773	Mission for Vengeance—Peter Rabe	1.00	3.00	5.00	
s774	We Walk Alone—Ann Aldrich	1.20	3.60	6.00	
775	Coffin for a Hood—Lionel White; orig., 1958	1.60	4.80	8.00	
776	Murder Comes Calling—Malcolm Douglas	.80	2.40	4.00	
s777	Clemmie—John D. MacDonald	1.20	3.60	6.00	
778	Home Is the Outlaw—Lewis B. Patten	.80	2.40	4.00	W
779	Tucson—Paul Leslie Peil	.80	2.40	4.00	
780	The Mob Says Murder—Albert Conroy	.80	2.40	4.00	
781	Here Is My Body—Booth Mooney	.50	1.50	2.50	
782	Judge Me Not—John D. MacDonald	.80	2.40	4.00	M
s783	The Fast Buck—Bruno Fischer	.80	2.40	4.00	M
784	Case of the Petticoat Murder—Jonathan Craig	.50	1.50	2.50	M
785	The Forbidden Land—Dan Cushman	1.00	3.00	5.00	
786	Too Young to Die—Lionel White; orig., 1958	1.60	4.80	8.00	
787	Death's Lovely Mask—John Flagg	.50	1.50	2.50	M
788	Brand of a Texan—Steven C. Lawrence	.80	2.40	4.00	W
789	Tall in the West—Vechel Howard; c-Abbett	.80	2.40	4.00	W
s790	The Neon Jungle—John D. MacDonald	.80	2.40	4.00	M
s791	Branded Woman—Wade Miller	.50	1.50	2.50	
792	The Brass Cupcake—John D. MacDonald	.80	2.40	4.00	M
s793	Spring Fire—Vin Packer	.80	2.40	4.00	
794	Trouble at Borrasca Rim—Mark Owen	.80	2.40	4.00	
795	Case of the Cop's Wife—Milton K. Ozaki	.50	1.50	2.50	M
s796	Self-made Widow—Philip Race	.50	1.50	2.50	M
s797	The Evil Friendship—Vin Packer	.80	2.40	4.00	
798	Guns of North Texas—Will Cook	.80	2.40	4.00	W
799	Assignment - Madeline—Edward S. Aarons	.50	1.50	2.50	M
800	Two Deaths Must Die—Richard Himmel	.50	1.50	2.50	M
s801	The Man Who Said No—Walt Grove; 1958	.50	1.50	2.50	
s802	The Devil's Mistress—Kenneth Thomas	.50	1.50	2.50	
803	Buchanan Gets Mad—Jonas Ward	.80	2.40	4.00	W
804	Relentless Gun—Giles A. Lutz	.80	2.40	4.00	W
805	The Deadly Pay-off—William H. Duhart	.50	1.50	2.50	
806	Murder in Room 13—Albert Conroy	.50	1.50	2.50	
807	Death Takes an Option—Neil MacNeil	.50	1.50	2.50	
808	Party Girl—Marvin H. Albert	.40	1.20	2.00	
s809	Plunder—Benjamin Appel	.40	1.20	2.00	C
810	The Killer—Wade Miller	.40	1.20	2.00	
811	Take Your Last Look—Matt Brady	.40	1.20	2.00	
s812	The Ungilded Lily—Morton Cooper	.40	1.20	2.00	
813	Terror Is My Trade—Stephen Marlowe	.80	2.40	4.00	M
814	I'm Cannon - for Hire—Curt Cannon	.80	2.40	4.00	
815	Showdown at War Cloud—Lewis B. Patten	.50	1.50	2.50	W
816	Fort Desperation—Frank Castle	.50	1.50	2.50	W
s817	Slab Happy—Richard S. Prather	.50	1.50	2.50	M
818	Everybody Had a Gun—Richard S. Prather	.50	1.50	2.50	M
819	Bodies in Bedlam—Richard S. Prather	.50	1.50	2.50	M
820	Case of the Vanishing Beauty—Richard S. Prather	.50	1.50	2.50	M
821	Find This Woman—Richard S. Prather	.50	1.50	2.50	M
822	Man on the Run—Charles Williams	.50	1.50	2.50	
823	Passage to Samoa—Day Keene; orig., 1958	1.00	3.00	5.00	
824	Trail of a Tramp—Nick Quarry	.50	1.50	2.50	
s825	Blood on the Desert—Peter Rabe; 1958; c-Powers	.80	2.40	4.00	
826	Renegade Posse—Marvin H. Albert	.50	1.50	2.50	W
827	Day of the Gun—Richard Telfair	.50	1.50	2.50	
s828	Naked Ebony—Dan Cushman	.50	1.50	2.50	A
s829	The Awakening of Jenny—Lillian Colter	.40	1.20	2.00	E
830	Way of a Wanton—Richard S. Prather	.40	1.20	2.00	M
831	Fires That Destroy—Harry Whittington	.50	1.50	2.50	
s832	The Monster From World's End—Murray Leinster	1.00	3.00	5.00	SF
d833	I Am a Woman—Ann Bannon	2.00	6.00	10.00	
834	Assignment - Carlotta Cortez—Edward S. Aarons	.50	1.50	2.50	M
835	The Captain Must Die—Robert Colby	.50	1.50	2.50	
s836	Smoke in the Valley—Steve Frazee	.50	1.50	2.50	W
837	Outcast of Cripple Creek—Will Cook	.50	1.50	2.50	W
838	Darling, It's Death—Richard S. Prather	.40	1.20	2.00	M
d839	City of Women—Nancy Morgan	.40	1.20	2.00	
s840	Jewel of the Java Sea—Dan Cushman	.40	1.20	2.00	
841	...and Be My Love—Ledru Baker, Jr.	.40	1.20	2.00	
842	Wagon Train West—William Heuman	.40	1.20	2.00	W
843	Outlaw Marshal—Ray Hogan	.40	1.20	2.00	W
s844	Third on a Seesaw—Neil MacNeil	.40	1.20	2.00	
s845	Kitten With a Whip—Wade Miller	.50	1.50	2.50	

		Good	Fine	N/Mint	
846	That Jane From Maine—Marvin H. Albert; 1959, movie tie-in	.40	1.20	2.00	
847	The Bloody Medallion—Richard Telfair	.40	1.20	2.00	M
848	Strip for Murder—Richard S. Prather	.40	1.20	2.00	M
849	Always Leave 'em Dying—Richard S. Prather	.40	1.20	2.00	M
850	Too Many Crooks—Richard S. Prather; 1959	.40	1.20	2.00	M
851	The Wailing Frail—Richard S. Prather	.40	1.20	2.00	M
d852	Tempest—R. V. Cassill; movie tie-in	.40	1.20	2.00	A
s853	The Rest Must Die—Richard Foster (K. F. Crossen); orig., 1959, c-Powers	1.20	3.60	6.00	SF
854	Murder With Love—Vechel Howard	.50	1.50	2.50	
855	Secret of the Second Door—Robert Colby	.50	1.50	2.50	
856	The Reformed Gun—Marvin H. Albert	.50	1.50	2.50	
857	Savage Breed—Joseph Chadwick	.50	1.50	2.50	W
858	13 French Street—Gil Brewer	.40	1.20	2.00	E
s859	Beyond Desire—Richard Himmel	.40	1.20	2.00	E
860	Have Gat - Will Travel—Richard S. Prather	.40	1.20	2.00	M
s861	The Twisted Ones—Vin Packer	.40	1.20	2.00	
862	A Ticket to Hell—Harry Whittington	.50	1.50	2.50	
863	Assignment - Helene—Edward S. Aarons	.40	1.20	2.00	M
864	Bring Me Another Corpse—Peter Rabe	.80	2.40	4.00	M
865	Above the Palo Duro—Noel M. Loomis	.40	1.20	2.00	W
866	The Ruthless Men—Lewis B. Patten	.40	1.20	2.00	W
867	Smash-up—Theodore Pratt	.40	1.20	2.00	
868	Return of Sumuru—Sax Rohmer	.80	2.40	4.00	A
s869	The Judas Hour—Howard Hunt	.40	1.20	2.00	
870	Let Them Eat Bullets—Howard Schoenfeld	.40	1.20	2.00	
871	Strangers in My Bed—Allen O'Quinn	.40	1.20	2.00	
872	Case of the Nervous Nude—Jonathan Craig	.50	1.50	2.50	M
873	Prowler in the Night—Jack Matcha	.40	1.20	2.00	
874	Take a Step to Murder—Day Keene; orig., 1959	1.00	3.00	5.00	M
875	Armande—Daniel May; 1959	.40	1.20	2.00	
876	The Brave Rifles—Gordon D. Shirreffs	.40	1.20	2.00	W
877	The Homing Bullet—Giles A. Lutz	.40	1.20	2.00	W
878	Murder on Her Mind—Vechel Howard	.40	1.20	2.00	
879	Wake Up and Scream—Milton K. Ozaki	.40	1.20	2.00	M
880	Homicide Is My Game—Stephen Marlowe	.80	2.40	4.00	M
881	The Kingdom of Johnny Cool—John McPartland	.40	1.20	2.00	M
882	Lawless Guns—Dudley Dean	.40	1.20	2.00	W
883	Wyoming Jones for Hire—Richard Telfair	.40	1.20	2.00	
884	Weep for Me—John D. MacDonald	1.60	4.80	8.00	M
885	The Mating Cry—Frank Daniels	.40	1.20	2.00	M
886	House of Flesh—Bruno Fischer	.40	1.20	2.00	M
s887	Over Her Dead Body—Richard S. Prather	.40	1.20	2.00	M
888	Killer Take All—Philip Race	.40	1.20	2.00	M
889	Backwoods Tramp—Harry Whittington	.80	2.40	4.00	E
890	The Corpse That Talked—Richard Telfair	.40	1.20	2.00	M
891	A Hole in the Head—Arnold Schulman	.40	1.20	2.00	
892	Marshal Without a Badge—Ray Hogan	.40	1.20	2.00	W
893	To Tame a Land—Louis L'Amour	.80	2.40	4.00	W
894	All These Condemned—John D. MacDonald	.40	1.20	2.00	M
895	Assignment to Disaster—Edward S. Aarons	.40	1.20	2.00	M
896	Three's a Shroud—Richard S. Prather	.40	1.20	2.00	M
s897	Cry Kill—Wenzell Brown	.80	2.40	4.00	
898	Two Guns for Hire—Neil MacNeil	.50	1.50	2.50	
899	Bier for a Chaser—Richard Foster (K. F. Crossen); orig., 1959	1.00	3.00	5.00	
900	Return to Vikki—John Tomerlin; 1959	.40	1.20	2.00	
901	The Lustful Ape—Bruno Fischer	.50	1.50	2.50	
902	Rider From Wind River—Marvin H. Albert	.40	1.20	2.00	W
s903	The Thrill Kids—Vin Packer	.50	1.50	2.50	

Gold Medal s832, © Faw

Gold Medal 848, © Faw

Gold Medal 899, © Faw

Gold Medal 913, © Faw

Gold Medal 928, © Faw

Gold Medal 929, © Faw

(GOLD MEDAL, continued)

		Good	Fine	N/Mint	
904	Cartoon Fun From True	.50	1.50	2.50	H
905	Hondo—Louis L'Amour	.50	1.50	2.50	W
906	Assignment - Stella Marni—Edward S. Aarons	.40	1.20	2.00	M
s907	The Beach Girls—John D. MacDonald	.40	1.20	2.00	M
s908	Uncle Sagamore and His Girls—Charles Williams	.50	1.50	2.50	E
909	The Last Night—John McPartland	.40	1.20	2.00	
s910	The Slasher—Ovid Demaris	.50	1.50	2.50	
s911	Assignment - Lili Lamaris—Edward S. Aarons	.40	1.20	2.00	M
912	Gun Shy—Dudley Dean & Les Savage, Jr.	.40	1.20	2.00	W
s913	Angels in the Gutter—Joseph Hilton	.80	2.40	4.00	JD
914	Trouble Is My Name—Stephen Marlowe	.80	2.40	4.00	M
915	It's My Funeral—Peter Rabe	.80	2.40	4.00	
916	Bullet Barricade—Leslie Ernenwein	.40	1.20	2.00	W
s917	Teen-age Mafia—Wenzell Brown	.80	2.40	4.00	JD
918	Pillow Talk—Marvin H. Albert; movie tie-in	.80	2.40	4.00	
s919	Women in the Shadows—Ann Bannon	1.20	3.60	6.00	
920	Top Man With a Gun—Lewis B. Patten	.40	1.20	2.00	W
921	The Wife Next Door—R. V. Cassill	.40	1.20	2.00	
s922	To Hell Together—H. Vernor Dixon	.40	1.20	2.00	
923	Assignment - Suicide—Edward S. Aarons	.40	1.20	2.00	
924	The Avenger—Matthew Blood	.40	1.20	2.00	M
925	Song of the Gun—Dudley Dean	.40	1.20	2.00	W
d926	Double in Trouble—Stephen Marlowe & Richard S. Prather	.40	1.20	2.00	M
927	Ain't Gonna Rain No More—John Faulkner	.40	1.20	2.00	E
928	Second-hand Nude—Bruno Fischer	.40	1.20	2.00	M
s929	Emperor Fu Manchu—Sax Rohmer; orig., 1959	2.00	6.00	10.00	A
930	Case of the Village Tramp—Jonathan Craig	.40	1.20	2.00	M
931	Too Hot to Hold—Day Keene; orig., 1959	.80	2.40	4.00	
932	The Secret of Apache Canyon—Richard Telfair	.40	1.20	2.00	W
s933	The Tormented—Theodore Pratt	.40	1.20	2.00	
934	Little Sister—Lee Roberts	.40	1.20	2.00	E
935	Many Rivers to Cross—Steve Frazee	.40	1.20	2.00	W
s936	The Big Guy—Wade Miller	.40	1.20	2.00	
s937	Four From Planet 5—Murray Leinster; orig., 1959	.80	2.40	4.00	SF
938	The Girl With No Place to Hide—Nick Quarry	.40	1.20	2.00	
939	Time Enough to Die—Peter Rabe	.80	2.40	4.00	
940	The Deadly Desire—Robert Colby	.40	1.20	2.00	
s941	The Young and Violent—Vin Packer	.40	1.20	2.00	
942	Witness This Woman—Gardner F. Fox	1.00	3.00	5.00	
943	Stage to Painted Creek—Vechel Howard	.40	1.20	2.00	W
944	The Range Buster—William Heuman	.40	1.20	2.00	W
945	The Tiger's Wife—Wade Miller	.40	1.20	2.00	
s946	Thunderclap—Jack Sheridan	.40	1.20	2.00	

GOLD MEDAL (BRITISH)
Fawcett Publications, Inc.

1	No Business for a Lady—James L. Rubel	.80	2.40	4.00	M
2	Million Dollar Murder—Edward Ronns	.80	2.40	4.00	M
3	Stretch Dawson—W. R. Burnett	1.00	3.00	5.00	W
4	Dallas—Will F. Jenkins (Murray Leinster); movie tie-in	1.00	3.00	5.00	W
5	The Desperado—Clifton Adams	.80	2.40	4.00	W
6	High Red for Dead—William L. Rohde	.80	2.40	4.00	M
7	To Kiss or Kill—Day Keene	.80	2.40	4.00	M
8	Lost Lady—Octavus Roy Cohen	.80	2.40	4.00	M
12	Help Wanted - for Murder—William L. Rohde	.80	2.40	4.00	M
13	Crockett's Woman—Eric Hatch	.50	1.50	2.50	
15	Look Behind You Lady—A. S. Fleischman	.50	1.50	2.50	

		Good	Fine	N/Mint	
16	A Noose for the Desperado—Clifton Adams	.80	2.40	4.00	W
17	Stampede—Yukon Miles	.80	2.40	4.00	W
18	Everybody Had a Gun—Richard S. Prather	.80	2.40	4.00	M
19	Death and the Naked Lady—John Flagg	.80	2.40	4.00	M
20	The Secret Rider—Logan Stewart	.80	2.40	4.00	W
21	Give a Man a Gun—Leslie Ernenwein	.80	2.40	4.00	W
22	I Have Gloria Kirby—Richard Himmel	.80	2.40	4.00	M
23	The Judas Hour—Howard Hunt	.80	2.40	4.00	
24	Naked Ebony—Dan Cushman	.80	2.40	4.00	
25	Maggie - Her Marriage—Taylor Caldwell	.80	2.40	4.00	E
26	Woman of Cairo—John Flagg	.80	2.40	4.00	
27	Hunt the Man Down—William Heumann	.80	2.40	4.00	W
28	Death on a Ferris Wheel—Alwin Lee Martin	.80	2.40	4.00	M
29	The Texas Gun—Leslie Ernenwein	.80	2.40	4.00	W
30	The Man Who Said No—Walt Grove	.80	2.40	4.00	M
31	Red Runs the River—William Heumann	.80	2.40	4.00	W
32	Wild Blood—A. C. Abbott	.80	2.40	4.00	W
33	Jungle She—Dan Cushman	1.00	3.00	5.00	A
34	Take Me As I Am—William Fielding	.80	2.40	4.00	M
35	The Trail—Logan Stewart	.80	2.40	4.00	W
36	The Sinners—Edward S. Aarons	.80	2.40	4.00	M
37	Hondo—Louis L'Amour	1.00	3.00	5.00	W
38	Witch of Salem—Benjamin Siegal	1.00	3.00	5.00	
39	Barren Land Murders—Luke Short	.80	2.40	4.00	W
40	Rider From Nowhere—Joseph Chadwick	.80	2.40	4.00	W
41	Murder for the Bride—John D. MacDonald	1.00	3.00	5.00	M
42	Run for Your Life—Bruno Fischer	.80	2.40	4.00	M
43	Mystery Raider—Leslie Ernenwein	.80	2.40	4.00	W
44	Madame Buccaneer—Gardner F. Fox	1.00	3.00	5.00	A
45	Come Feed on Me—Morton Cooper	.80	2.40	4.00	
46	Terror in the Night—Sebastian Blayne	.80	2.40	4.00	M
47	Up a Winding Stair—H. Vernor Dixon	.80	2.40	4.00	
48	Move Along, Stranger—Frank Castle	.80	2.40	4.00	W
49	Double Cross—Joseph Chadwick	.80	2.40	4.00	W
50	Gunsmoke Reckoning—Joseph Chadwick	.80	2.40	4.00	W
51	The Lady and the Cheetah—John Flagg	.80	2.40	4.00	
52	Come Back My Love—Edward S. Aaron	.80	2.40	4.00	M
53	The White Squaw—Larabie Sutter	.80	2.40	4.00	W
54	Nothing in Her Way—Charles Williams	.80	2.40	4.00	M
55	Branded Woman—Wade Miller	.80	2.40	4.00	
56	Whip Hand—Joseph Chadwick	.80	2.40	4.00	W
57	The Neon Jungle—John D. MacDonald	1.00	3.00	5.00	M
58	Hideaway—Nikki Content	.80	2.40	4.00	M
59	Keelboats North—William Heumann	.80	2.40	4.00	W
60	Tokyo Doll—John McPartland	.80	2.40	4.00	
61	Secret of Death Valley—William Heumann	.80	2.40	4.00	W
62	Devil's Legacy—Joseph Chadwick	.80	2.40	4.00	
63	Danger in Paradise—A. S. Fleischman	.80	2.40	4.00	A
64	Moment of Truth—Arnold Rodin	.80	2.40	4.00	
65	Barge Girl—Calvin Clements	.80	2.40	4.00	E
66	Savage Stronghold—Logan Stewart	.80	2.40	4.00	W
67	The Borgia Blade—Gardner F. Fox	1.00	3.00	5.00	A
68	The Girl in the Death Cell—Fred J. Cook	.80	2.40	4.00	M
69	Big Red's Daughter—John McPartland	.80	2.40	4.00	M
70	Gunfighter's Return—Leslie Ernenwein	.80	2.40	4.00	W
71	Saturday's Harvest—Paul Shelley	.80	2.40	4.00	
72	The Brass Cupcake—John D. MacDonald	1.00	3.00	5.00	M
81	The Crooked Mile—Norbert Fagan	.80	2.40	4.00	

GOLD STAR BOOKS
New International Library, Inc.

IL7-42	Tarzan & the Silver Globe—Barton Werper; orig., 1964	3.00	9.00	15.00	SF
IL7-49	Tarzan & the Cave City—Barton Werper; orig., 1964	3.00	9.00	15.00	A
IL7-54	Tarzan & the Snake People—Barton Werper; orig., 1964	3.00	9.00	15.00	SF
IL7-60	Tarzan & the Abominable Snowman—Barton Werper; orig., 1965	3.00	9.00	15.00	SF
IL7-65	Tarzan & the Winged Invaders—Barton Werper; orig., 1965	4.00	12.00	20.00	SF

NOTE: Barton Werper was the pseudonym of Peter and Peggy O'Neill Scott and this series, known as The New Tarzan Series, was unauthorized and stopped by legal action shortly after No. 5 was printed, with unsold copies being destroyed.

GRAPHIC
Graphic Publishing Company, Inc.

11	Murder - Queen High—Bill Miller & Bob Wade; 1949	1.20	3.60	6.00	M
12	If I Live to Dine—Hillary Waugh	1.00	3.00	5.00	M

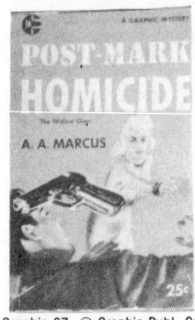

Gold Star Books IL7-54, © New   Graphic 52, © Graphic Publ. Co.   Graphic 67, © Graphic Publ. Co.

(GRAPHIC, continued)

		Good	Fine	N/Mint	
13	Flash - Hold for Murder—Paul Whelton	1.00	3.00	5.00	M
14	Death Commits Bigamy—James M. Fox	1.00	3.00	5.00	M
15	Tex—Clarence E. Mulford	1.20	3.60	6.00	W
16	Deadline at Dawn—William Irish	1.60	4.80	8.00	M
17	Call the Lady Indiscreet—Paul Whelton	1.00	3.00	5.00	
18	Dealing Out Death—W. T. Ballard	1.20	3.60	6.00	M
19	Lures of Death—Paul Whelton; 1950	1.20	3.60	6.00	
20	Dilemma of the Dead Lady—William Irish	1.60	4.80	8.00	M
21	The Widow Gay—A. A. Marcus	1.00	3.00	5.00	M
22	Tough Cop—John Roeburt	1.00	3.00	5.00	M
23	The Man From Bar 20—Clarence E. Mulford	1.20	3.60	6.00	W
24	Uninvited Corpse—Paul Whelton	1.00	3.00	5.00	M
25	The Singing Scorpion—William Colt MacDonald	1.00	3.00	5.00	W
26	Murder Can't Stop—W. T. Ballard	1.20	3.60	6.00	M
27	Corpse on the Town—John Roeburt	1.00	3.00	5.00	M
28	Tex—Clarence E. Mulford; 1951	1.00	3.00	5.00	W
29	Memo for Murder—Dal Wilmer; orig., 1951	1.00	3.00	5.00	M
30	Runyon First and Last—Damon Runyon	1.00	3.00	5.00	
31	Deadly Night Call—William Irish	1.20	3.60	6.00	M
32	Hangover House—Sax Rohmer	1.20	3.60	6.00	M
33	The Dummy Murder Case—Milton K. Ozaki; orig., 1951	1.00	3.00	5.00	M
34	Texas Men—Paul Evan Lehman	1.00	3.00	5.00	W
35	Walk the Bloody Boulevard—A. A. Marcus	1.00	3.00	5.00	M
36	Call Me Killer—Harry Whittington; orig., 1951	1.60	4.80	8.00	M
37	Pardon My Blood—Paul Whelton	1.00	3.00	5.00	M
38	Tough Cop—John Roeburt	1.00	3.00	5.00	M
39	Vultures of Paradise Valley—Paul Evan Lehman	1.00	3.00	5.00	W
40	The Crooked Circle—Manning Lee Stokes	1.00	3.00	5.00	M
41	Murder Is My Mistress—Harry Whittington; orig., 1951	1.60	4.80	8.00	M
42	There Are Dead Men in Manhattan—John Roeburt	1.00	3.00	5.00	M
43	If the Coffin Fits—Day Keene; 1952	1.20	3.60	6.00	M
44	Gun Hawk—Leslie Ernenwein	1.00	3.00	5.00	W
45	Death for a Hussy—Aylwin Lee Martin	1.00	3.00	5.00	M
46	Mourn the Hangman—Harry Whittington; orig., 1952	1.60	4.80	8.00	M
47	Faces in the Dust—Paul Evan Lehman	1.00	3.00	5.00	W
48	Pattern for Murder—David Knight	1.00	3.00	5.00	M
49	In Comes Death—Paul Whelton	1.00	3.00	5.00	M
50	The Singing Scorpion—William Colt MacDonald	1.00	3.00	5.00	W
51	Framed in Guilt—Day Keene	1.20	3.60	6.00	M
52	There Oughta Be a Law!—Al Fagaly & Harry Shorten	1.20	3.60	6.00	H
53	Tex—Clarence E. Mulford	1.00	3.00	5.00	W
54	Murder - Queen High—Bill Miller & Bob Wade	1.00	3.00	5.00	M
55	A Shot in the Dark—Richard Powell	1.00	3.00	5.00	M
56	Texas Men—Paul Evan Lehman	1.00	3.00	5.00	M
57	The Deadly Pick-up—Milton K. Ozaki; 1953	1.00	3.00	5.00	M
58	Strange Witness—Day Keene; orig., 1953	1.20	3.60	6.00	M
59	Dark Destiny—Edward Ronns	1.00	3.00	5.00	M
60	Dead Man's Tide—William Richards; orig., 1953	1.00	3.00	5.00	M
61	There Oughta Be a Law!—Al Fagaly & Harry Shorten	1.20	3.60	6.00	H
62	Gun Hawk—Leslie Ernenwein	1.00	3.00	5.00	W
63	Tough Cop—John Roeburt	1.00	3.00	5.00	M
64	Walk the Bloody Boulevard—A. A. Marcus	1.00	3.00	5.00	M
65	Murder Can't Stop—W. T. Ballard	1.20	3.60	6.00	M
66	Vultures of Paradise Valley—Paul Evan Lehman	1.00	3.00	5.00	W
67	Post-mark Homicide—A. A. Marcus; aka The Widow Gay. Note: Same cover as Harlequin 90	1.00	3.00	5.00	M
68	The Net—Edward Ronns	1.00	3.00	5.00	M
69	Runyon First and Last—Damon Runyon	1.00	3.00	5.00	

(GRAPHIC, continued)

		Good	Fine	N/Mint	
70	Late Last Night—James Reach	1.00	3.00	5.00	M
71	Pardon My Blood—Paul Whelton; 1954	1.00	3.00	5.00	M
72	Dealing Out Death—W. T. Ballard	1.20	3.60	6.00	M
73	Handle With Fear—Thomas B. Dewey	1.00	3.00	5.00	M
74	Two-gun Fury—Charles M. Martin	1.00	3.00	5.00	W
75	The Big Kiss-off—Day Keene; orig., 1954	1.20	3.60	6.00	M
76	Say It With Murder—Edward Ronns	1.00	3.00	5.00	M
77	Gunman's Creed—L. P. Holmes	1.00	3.00	5.00	W
78	Hangover House—Sax Rohmer	1.20	3.60	6.00	M
79	Dressed to Kill—Milton Ozaki	1.00	3.00	5.00	M
80	Blood on the Range—Eli Colter	1.00	3.00	5.00	W
81	Deadly Night Call—William Irish	1.20	3.60	6.00	M
82	Stand Up and Die—Frances & Richard Lockridge	1.00	3.00	5.00	M
83	The Fatal Cast—Curtiss T. Gardner	1.00	3.00	5.00	M
84	Your Shot, Darling—Lillian Bergquist & Irving Moore	1.00	3.00	5.00	H
85	More There Oughta Be a Law!—Al Fagaly & Harry Shorten	1.20	3.60	6.00	H
86	Texas Pride—Charles M. Martin	1.00	3.00	5.00	W
87	Homicidal Lady—Day Keene; orig., 1954	1.20	3.60	6.00	M
88	Outlaw Justice—Ford Pendleton	1.00	3.00	5.00	W
89	The Scarab Murder Case—S. S. Van Dine	1.60	4.80	8.00	M
90	Too Young to Die—Robert O. Saber	1.00	3.00	5.00	M
91	Tex—Clarence E. Mulford	1.00	3.00	5.00	W
92	The Deadly Pick-up—Milton K. Ozaki	1.00	3.00	5.00	M
93	Say It With Bullets—Richard Powell	1.00	3.00	5.00	M
94	Model for Murder—Stephen Marlowe; 1955	1.00	3.00	5.00	M
95	Call the Lady Indiscreet—Paul Whelton	1.00	3.00	5.00	M
96	Gun Lightning!—Steve Thurman	1.00	3.00	5.00	W
97	One Touch of Blood—Samm Sinclair Baker	1.00	3.00	5.00	M
98	Too Many Murderers—Manning Lee Stokes	1.00	3.00	5.00	M
99	Sucker Bait—Robert O. Saber	1.00	3.00	5.00	M
100	Faces in the Dust—Paul Evan Lehman	1.00	3.00	5.00	W
101	Cry Torment—Victor H. Johnson	1.00	3.00	5.00	M
102	Die by Night—M. S. Marble	1.00	3.00	5.00	M
103	Girl in the Red Dress—Richard Cargoe	1.00	3.00	5.00	
104	Mugs, Molls and Dr. Harvey—George Malcolm-Smith	1.00	3.00	5.00	H
105	Murder Has Many Faces—William Grew	1.00	3.00	5.00	M
106	Trap—George E. Jones	1.00	3.00	5.00	M
107	The Adventures of Ferd'nand—Mik	1.00	3.00	5.00	
108	Phantom Lady—William Irish	1.60	4.80	8.00	M
109	More There Oughta Be a Law!—Al Fagaly & Harry Shorten	1.20	3.60	6.00	H
110	The Hollow Man—John Roeburt	1.00	3.00	5.00	M
111	A Dame Called Murder—Robert O. Saber	1.00	3.00	5.00	M
112	Gun Hawk—Leslie Ernenwein	1.00	3.00	5.00	W
113	Unfinished Crime—Helen McCloy	1.00	3.00	5.00	M
114	They All Ran Away—Edward Ronns	1.00	3.00	5.00	M
115	Make Way for Murder—A. A. Marcus	1.00	3.00	5.00	M
116	Hell Rider—Ford Pendleton	1.00	3.00	5.00	W
117	Murder Can't Wait—Manning Lee Stokes	1.00	3.00	5.00	M
118	And Kill Once More—Al Fray	1.00	3.00	5.00	M
119	Mood for Murder—Frank Gruber; 1956	1.00	3.00	5.00	M
120	Texas Guns—Leslie Ernenwein	1.00	3.00	5.00	W
121	Tough Cop—John Roeburt	1.00	3.00	5.00	M
122	Homicide Lost—William E. Vance	1.00	3.00	5.00	M
123	A Time for Murder—Robert O. Saber	1.00	3.00	5.00	M
124	Gunpoint!—John L. Shelley	1.00	3.00	5.00	
125	The Intruder—Octavus Roy Cohen	1.00	3.00	5.00	M
126	Murder's End—Robert Kelston; c-Maguire	1.20	3.60	6.00	M
127	So Lovely to Kill—Harrison Wade	1.00	3.00	5.00	M

Graphic 81, © Graphic Publ. Co.

Graphic 104, © Graphic Publ. Co.

Graphic 108, © Graphic Publ. Co.

Graphic 151, © Graphic Publ. Co.　　Graphic G206, © Graphic Publ. Co.　　Graphic G216, © Graphic Publ. Co.

(GRAPHIC, continued)

		Good	Fine	N/Mint	
128	Two-gun Fury—Charles M. Martin	1.00	3.00	5.00	W
129	Six-gun Heritage—Brad Ward	1.00	3.00	5.00	W
130	Late Last Night—James Reach	1.00	3.00	5.00	M
131	This Kill Is Mine—Dean Evans	1.00	3.00	5.00	M
132	I Prefer Murder—Charles A. Landolf & Browning Norton	1.00	3.00	5.00	M
133	Gunmaster—Ford Pendleton	1.00	3.00	5.00	M
134	Who Dies There?—James Duff; orig., 1956	1.00	3.00	5.00	W
135	Murder - Very Dry—Samm Sinclair Baker	1.00	3.00	5.00	M
136	Killer's Choice—Stuart Brock	1.00	3.00	5.00	M
137	Blood on the Range—Eli Colter	1.00	3.00	5.00	W
138	The Corpse Next Door—John Farris; orig., 1956	1.00	3.00	5.00	M
139	Some Die Young—James Duff	1.00	3.00	5.00	M
140	Gun Trail—Mack Saunders	1.00	3.00	5.00	W
141	Dressed to Kill—Milton Ozaki	.80	2.40	4.00	M
142	Fair Prey—Will Duke	1.00	3.00	5.00	M
143	Three Must Die!—Dan Gregory	1.00	3.00	5.00	M
144	Gunman's Creed—L. P. Holmes; 1957	1.00	3.00	5.00	W
145	While Murder Waits—Bruce Cassiday	1.00	3.00	5.00	M
146	Six-guns Wild—Gene Thompson	1.00	3.00	5.00	W
147	Killer, Take All!—James O. Causey	1.00	3.00	5.00	M
148	Say It With Bullets—Richard Powell	1.00	3.00	5.00	M
149	Murder Without Tears—Leonard Lupton	1.00	3.00	5.00	M
150	Too Young to Die—Robert O. Saber	1.00	3.00	5.00	M
151	Gun Proud—Lewis B. Patten	1.00	3.00	5.00	M
152	Call Me Deadly—Hal Braham	1.00	3.00	5.00	M
153	Gun Lightning!—Steve Thurman	1.00	3.00	5.00	W
154	Outlaw Justice—Ford Pendleton	1.00	3.00	5.00	W
155	Gun Chance—Ford Pendleton	1.00	3.00	5.00	W
156	Sucker Bait—Robert O. Saber	1.00	3.00	5.00	M
157	Hell Rider—Ford Pendleton	1.00	3.00	5.00	W

GRAPHIC G-SERIES
Graphic Publishing Company, Inc.

G101	Captain for Elizabeth—Jan Westcott; 1952	1.00	3.00	5.00	A
G201	Captain for Elizabeth—Jan Westcott; 1953	.80	2.40	4.00	A
G202	River Queen—Charles N. Heckelmann	1.20	3.60	6.00	A
G203	45 Murderers—Craig Rice	1.20	3.60	6.00	M
G204	How to Live With Your Heart—Peter J. Stein Crohn; 1954	1.00	3.00	5.00	NF
G205	King's Rogue—Max Peacock	1.00	3.00	5.00	A
G206	The Gladiators—Arthur Koestler	1.00	3.00	5.00	A
G207	Great Sea Stories of Modern Times—William McFee	1.00	3.00	5.00	A
G208	Swords for Charlemagne—Mario Pei; 1955	.80	2.40	4.00	A
G209	The Golden Blade—John Clou	1.00	3.00	5.00	A
G210	Gunman's Spawn—Ben Thompson	1.00	3.00	5.00	W
G211	Captain for Elizabeth—Jan Westcott	.80	2.40	4.00	A
G212	Rogue Royal—Donn O'Hara; 1956, c-Maguire	1.20	3.60	6.00	A
G213	The Gladiators—Arthur Koestler	1.00	3.00	5.00	A
G214	Captain Bashful—Donald Barr Chidsey	1.00	3.00	5.00	A
G215	Call Me Duke—Harry Grey	1.00	3.00	5.00	M
G216	The Private Life of Helen of Troy—John Erskine	1.20	3.60	6.00	A
G217	Eve's Daughters—Laurette Pizer; 1957	1.00	3.00	5.00	A
G218	Guns of Hell Valley—John Prescott	1.00	3.00	5.00	W
G219	Swords for Charlemagne—Mario Pei	.80	2.40	4.00	A
G220	The Golden Blade—John Clou; c-Maguire	1.00	3.00	5.00	A
G221	River Queen—Charles N. Heckelmann	.80	2.40	4.00	A
G222	The Fair and the Bold—Donn O'Hara	.80	2.40	4.00	A
G223	Gunman's Spawn—Ben Thompson	.80	2.40	4.00	W

GREAT AMERICAN PUBLICATIONS, INC.
Great American Publications, Inc.

		Good	Fine	N/Mint	
nn	Economy Driving—ed. Peter Bowman; orig., 1956	1.00	3.00	5.00	NF

GREEN
Green Publishing Company
Digest Size

6	Some Like It Hot—Sidney Marshall	1.00	3.00	5.00	M
7	11 True Crimes—Joseph Gollomb	1.00	3.00	5.00	NF
8	The Laughing Loon—Josiah E. Greene	1.00	3.00	5.00	M
9	The Owl's Warning—Herman Landon	1.00	3.00	5.00	M
10	Death in the Sun—Charles Saxby; Note: Incorrectly says '1st edition'	1.00	3.00	5.00	M
11	A Dagger in the Dark—Walter E. Eberhardt............................	1.00	3.00	5.00	M
12	Kill or Cure—William Francis	1.00	3.00	5.00	M
13	Murder Stalks the Mayor—R. T. M. Scott	1.00	3.00	5.00	M
14	The Backstage Mystery—Octavus Roy Cohen	1.00	3.00	5.00	M

GREEN
Larkin, Roosevelt, and Larkin, Ltd.
Digest Size

1	Rough on Rats—William Francis.....................................	1.00	3.00	5.00	M

GREEN
R. W. Voigt
Digest Size

2	The Back Seat Murder—Herman Landon	1.00	3.00	5.00	M

GREEN DRAGON
Ideal Distributing Company/W. H. Wise & Company
Some Digest Size

1	Murder Makes By-Lines—Kelliher Secrist; digest size	1.20	3.60	6.00	M
2	The Mausoleum Key—Norman A. Daniels; digest size	1.20	3.60	6.00	M
3	Johnny on the Spot—Amen Dell; digest size.............................	1.20	3.60	6.00	M
4	A Murder a Day—Robert Avery; digest size	1.20	3.60	6.00	M
5	The Moscow Mystery—Iry Litrinoff; digest size	1.20	3.60	6.00	M
6	The Snatch—R. L. Goldman; digest size	1.20	3.60	6.00	M
7	Murder of the Night Club Lady—Anthony Abbot; aka About the Murder of the Night Club Lady; digest size..	1.20	3.60	6.00	M
8	A Most Immoral Murder—H. Ashbrook; digest size.......................	1.20	3.60	6.00	M
9	Murder Moves On—Jack Dall; digest size	1.20	3.60	6.00	M
10	Death Plays Solitaire—R. L. Goldman; digest size	1.20	3.60	6.00	M
11	Too Many Murderers—George Childerness; digest size	1.20	3.60	6.00	M
12	Grave Without Grass—Donald Clough Cameron; digest size	1.20	3.60	6.00	M
13	Ten Words of Poison—Barry Perowne; digest size	1.20	3.60	6.00	M
14	Talent for Murder—John L. Benton; digest size	1.20	3.60	6.00	M
16	Murder Without Clues—Joseph L. Bonney; digest size	1.20	3.60	6.00	M
17	...and Death Drove On—Robert Fleming; digest size	1.20	3.60	6.00	M
18	Murder Comes Back—H. Ashbrook; digest size..........................	1.20	3.60	6.00	M

Great American Publ. nn, © Great

Green 11, © Green

Green Dragon 3, © W. H. Wise & Co.

Green Dragon 30, © W. H. Wise & Co.

Griffin Books nn, © Griffin Books

Gunfire Western Novel 25, © Hill

(GREEN DRAGON, continued)

		Good	Fine	N/Mint	
19	Death Defies the Doctor—Denis Muir; digest size	1.20	3.60	6.00	M
20	Death at Her Elbow—Donald Clough Cameron; digest size	1.20	3.60	6.00	M
21	The Man Who Was Murdered Twice—Robert H. Leitfred; digest size	1.20	3.60	6.00	M
23	I Thought I'd Die—David V. Reed; 1st ed., aka The Metal Monster Murders, digest size	1.20	3.60	6.00	M
24	If I Die, It's Murder—Mari Ervin	2.00	6.00	10.00	M
25	She Screamed Blue Murder—Kelliher Secrist	2.00	6.00	10.00	M
26	Stone Dead—Patrick Laing	2.00	6.00	10.00	M
28	Headsman's Holiday—Dean Hawkins	2.00	6.00	10.00	M
29	The Late Lamented Lady—Marie Blizard	2.00	6.00	10.00	M
30	A Matter of Policy—Sam Merwin, Jr.	2.00	6.00	10.00	M
31	Murder by Magic—Amelia Reynolds Long	2.00	6.00	10.00	M
32	The Men in Her Death—Marie Blizard	2.00	6.00	10.00	M
33	Death Is Thy Neighbor—Laurence Dwight Smith	2.00	6.00	10.00	M
nn	The Corpse With the Listening Ear—Laurence Dwight Smith	1.20	3.60	6.00	M

GRIFFIN BOOKS
Griffin Books

Digest Size

nn	Love on Call—John Saxon	1.00	3.00	5.00	E
nn	Confessions of a Hat Check Girl—Carl Sturdy	1.00	3.00	5.00	E
nn	Hotel Love—W. McClellan	1.00	3.00	5.00	E
nn	Stolen Love—Thomas Stone; aka Too Much Love	1.00	3.00	5.00	E
nn	Easy Virtue—Carl Sturdy; aka Professional Model	1.00	3.00	5.00	E
nn	Wronged Virgin—Gladys Sloan; aka Professional Passion	1.00	3.00	5.00	E
nn	Office Playgirl—Eliot Brewster; aka Hard	1.00	3.00	5.00	E

GUNFIRE WESTERN NOVEL
Novel Selections, Inc./Hillman

Digest Size

6	The Morgan Trail—W. C. Tuttle	1.00	3.00	5.00	W
7	The Deputy Sheriff—Clarence E. Mulford	1.00	3.00	5.00	W
9	Vigilante War in Buena Vista—Frank C. Robertson	1.00	3.00	5.00	W
10	Prairie Fire—D. Bardwell	.80	2.40	4.00	W
11	Rebel Ranger—William Colt MacDonald	.80	2.40	4.00	W
12	Cowman's Jack-Pot—Frank C. Robertson	1.00	3.00	5.00	W
14	Six-Gun Melody—William Colt MacDonald	.80	2.40	4.00	W
15	Getley's Gold—Frank C. Robertson; c-Saunders	1.00	3.00	5.00	W
16	Smoke Tree Range—Arthur Henry Gooden	1.00	3.00	5.00	W
17	Thunderbird Trail—William Colt MacDonald	.80	2.40	4.00	W
18	Dangerous Dust—Kim Knight	.80	2.40	4.00	W
19	The Vanishing Gunslinger—William Colt MacDonald	.80	2.40	4.00	W
20	Grizzly Meadows—Frank C. Robertson	1.00	3.00	5.00	W
21	The Phantom Corral—Bliss Lomax (H. S. Drago)	.80	2.40	4.00	W
22	The Three Mesquiteers—William Colt MacDonald	1.00	3.00	5.00	W
23	Dunn of the Double D—N. M. Newland	.80	2.40	4.00	W
24	The Range Rebellion—W. D. Hoffman	.80	2.40	4.00	W
25	Boss of the OK—Brett Rider	.80	2.40	4.00	W
28	Outlaw Guns—E. E. Halleran	.80	2.40	4.00	W
30	Miracle at Gopher Creek—Hardy	.80	2.40	4.00	W
32	Desert Water—Harry Sinclair Drago	.80	2.40	4.00	W
33	Rope Crazy—Frank C. Robertson	1.00	3.00	5.00	W
34	Outlaw of Hidden Valley—John Sims	.80	2.40	4.00	W

Gunfire Western Novel 45, © Hill

Handi Books 1, © Quinn

Handi Books 3, © Quinn

(GUNFIRE WESTERN NOVEL, continued)

		Good	Fine	N/Mint	
35	Botched Brand—Tom West	.80	2.40	4.00	W
36	Feud at Silver Bend—J. E. Grinstead	.80	2.40	4.00	W
41	Milk River Range—Lee Floren	.80	2.40	4.00	W
42	Guns Along the Border—Charles H. Snow	.80	2.40	4.00	W
43	The Long S—Lee Floren	.80	2.40	4.00	W
45	Rebel on the Range—Ranger Lee	.80	2.40	4.00	W
46	The Pride of Pine Creek—Frank C. Robertson	1.00	3.00	5.00	W
50	Silver Gulch—	.80	2.40	4.00	W
51	Smuggler's Range—Lee Floren	.80	2.40	4.00	W
53	Dusty Boots—	.80	2.40	4.00	W

HANDI BOOKS
Quinn Publishing Co., Inc.

		Good	Fine	N/Mint	
nn(1)	Odds on the Hot Seat—Judson Phillips; 1941	3.00	9.00	15.00	M
nn(2)	Decoy—Cleve F. Adams	2.00	6.00	10.00	M
nn(3)	12 Chinks and a Woman—James Hadley Chase; 1942	5.00	15.00	25.00	M
nn(4)	Seven Men—Theodore Roscoe	2.00	6.00	10.00	M
nn(5)	Curtains for the Copper—Thomas Polsky	2.00	6.00	10.00	M
nn(6)	A Bullet in His Cap—Robert Fleming	2.00	6.00	10.00	M
nn(7)	The Black Door—Cleve Adams	2.00	6.00	10.00	M
8	She Got What She Asked For—James Ronald	2.00	6.00	10.00	M
9	Vicious Circle—Manning Long	2.00	6.00	10.00	M
10	The Case of the Vanishing Women—Robert Archer	2.00	6.00	10.00	M
11	The Nine Dark Hours—Lenore Glen Offord	2.00	6.00	10.00	M
12	The Big Frame—Sam Merwin, Jr.; 1943	2.00	6.00	10.00	M
13	Lazarus No. 7—Richard Sale	5.00	15.00	25.00	SF
14	Black Alibi—Cornell Woolrich	3.00	9.00	15.00	M
15	The Case of the Walking Corpse—Brett Halliday	2.00	6.00	10.00	M
16	The 14th Trump—Judson Phillips	2.00	6.00	10.00	M
17	Footsteps Behind Her—Mitchell Wilson	2.00	6.00	10.00	M
18	The Unscrupulous Mr. Callaghan—Peter Cheyney	2.00	6.00	10.00	M
19	Passing Strange—Richard Sale	2.00	6.00	10.00	M
20	To a Blindfold Lady—Joseph Purtell	2.00	6.00	10.00	M
21	The Case of the Shivering Chorus Girls—James Atlee Phillips	2.00	6.00	10.00	M
22	The Blonde Died First—Dana Chambers; 1944	2.00	6.00	10.00	M
23	Five Alarm Funeral—Stewart Sterling	2.00	6.00	10.00	M
24	Murder in Marble—Judson Phillips	2.00	6.00	10.00	M
25	Court of Shadows—Giles Jackson	2.00	6.00	10.00	M
26	To Catch a Thief—Daphne Sanders	1.60	4.80	8.00	M

Handi Books 8, © Quinn

Handi Books 13, © Quinn

Handi Books 19, © Quinn

Handi Books 27, © Quinn   Handi Books 62, © Quinn   Handi Books 84, © Quinn

(HANDI BOOKS, continued)

		Good	Fine	N/Mint	
27	I Wake Up Screaming—Steve Fisher	1.60	4.80	8.00	M
28	The Frightened Man—Dana Chambers	2.00	6.00	10.00	M
29	The Woman in Red—Anthony Gilbert	2.00	6.00	10.00	M
30	The X-Ray Murders—M. Scott Michel	2.00	6.00	10.00	M
31	The Case of the Curious Chair—Richard Power	2.00	6.00	10.00	M
32	No Good From a Corpse—Leigh Brackett	3.00	9.00	15.00	M
33	Up Jumped the Devil—Cleve Adams	2.00	6.00	10.00	M
34	The Last Secret—Dana Chambers; 1945	3.00	9.00	15.00	SF
35	The Snake in the Grass—James Howard Wellard	1.20	3.60	6.00	M
36	The Walls Came Tumbling Down—Jo Eisinger	1.20	3.60	6.00	M
37	The Dark Voyage—Hugh Addis	1.60	4.80	8.00	M
38	The Man With the Lumpy Nose—Lawrence Lariar	1.60	4.80	8.00	M
39	Send Another Coffin—F. G. Presnell	1.60	4.80	8.00	M
40	Dead Little Rich Girl—Norbert Davis	2.00	6.00	10.00	M
41	If I Kill Him—John & Ward Hawkins	1.60	4.80	8.00	M
42	The Fall Guy—Joe Barry	1.60	4.80	8.00	M
43	The Body on the Pavement—Gordon Meyrick	1.60	4.80	8.00	M
44	Knife in My Back—Sam Merwin, Jr.	1.60	4.80	8.00	M
45	The Blonde Is Dead—John Dow; aka The Little Boy Laughed	1.60	4.80	8.00	M
46	The Case of the Tearless Widow—John Roeburt; 1946	1.60	4.80	8.00	M
47	Sweet Murder—M. Scott Michel	1.60	4.80	8.00	M
48	The Body Next Door—Eaton K. Goldthwaite	1.20	3.60	6.00	M
49	The Corpse Who Wouldn't Die—Ed Doherty	1.60	4.80	8.00	M
50	The Dangerous Dead—William Brandon	1.20	3.60	6.00	M
51	Darling, This Is Death—Dana Chambers	1.20	3.60	6.00	M
52	The Triple Cross—Joe Barry	1.60	4.80	8.00	M
53	Puzzle for Players—Patrick Quentin	1.20	3.60	6.00	M
54	O, Murder Mine—Norbert Davis	2.00	6.00	10.00	M
55	Blood on the Cat—Nancy Rutledge	1.20	3.60	6.00	M
56	Lady With the Dice—Joel Townsley Rogers	1.60	4.80	8.00	M
57	Death Against Venus—Dana Chambers	1.60	4.80	8.00	M
58	The Corpse Awaits—Owen Fox Jerome; 1947	1.60	4.80	8.00	M
59	One of These Seven—Carolynne & Malcolm Logan	1.20	3.60	6.00	M
60	The Black Key—M. Scott Michel	1.60	4.80	8.00	M
61	The Gloved Hand—Leigh Bryson	1.60	4.80	8.00	M
62	The Murder of the U. S. A.—Will F. Jenkins (Murray Leinster)	4.00	12.00	20.00	SF
63	The Clean-Up—Joe Barry	1.20	3.60	6.00	M
64	The Fourth Star—Richard Burke	1.20	3.60	6.00	M
65	Guilty Bystander—Wade Miller	1.60	4.80	8.00	M
66					
67					
68	Killers Play Rough—Adam Ring	1.60	4.80	8.00	M
69	Bullet Breed—Leslie Ernenwein	1.60	4.80	8.00	W
70	Run for Your Life—Michael Stark; 1948	1.60	4.80	8.00	M
71	The Range Maverick—Oscar J. Friend	1.60	4.80	8.00	W
72	Death About Face—Frank Kane	1.60	4.80	8.00	M
73	Only the Brave—Paul Evan Lehman	1.60	4.80	8.00	W
74	If You Have Tears—John Evans	1.60	4.80	8.00	M
75	Boss of Panamint—Leslie Ernenwein	1.60	4.80	8.00	W
76	Cargo of Fear—Jay L. Currier	1.60	4.80	8.00	M
77	Calamity Range—Paul Evan Lehman	1.60	4.80	8.00	W
78	This Deadly Dark—Lee Wilson	1.60	4.80	8.00	M
79	Gun Harvest—Oscar J. Friend	1.60	4.80	8.00	W
80	Not With My Neck—Tom Van Dycke & Ben Kerner	1.60	4.80	8.00	M
81	Empty Saddles—Al Cody	1.60	4.80	8.00	W
82	Witch's Moon—Giles Jackson; 1949	1.60	4.80	8.00	M
83	The Faro Kid—Leslie Ernenwein; Note: Same cover as Harlequin 89	1.20	3.60	6.00	W
84	Yaller Gal—Carolina Lee	1.20	3.60	6.00	E

(HANDI BOOKS, continued)

		Good	Fine	N/Mint	
85	The Great I Am—Lewis Graham	1.20	3.60	6.00	E
86	Dig Another Grave—Don Cameron	1.20	3.60	6.00	M
87	Idaho—Paul Evan Lehman	1.20	3.60	6.00	W
88	Hope to Die—Hillary Waugh	1.20	3.60	6.00	M
89	The King of Thunder Valley—Archie Joscelyn	1.20	3.60	6.00	W
90	Love to Burn—Peggy Gaddis	1.20	3.60	6.00	E
91	Lulie—Joan Sherman	1.20	3.60	6.00	E
92	The Girl With the Frightened Eyes—Lawrence Lariar	1.20	3.60	6.00	M
93	Rebel Yell—Leslie Ernenwein	1.60	4.80	8.00	W
94	They All Died Young—Charles Boswell; orig., 1949	1.20	3.60	6.00	M
95	The Outcast of Lazy S—Eli Colter	1.20	3.60	6.00	W
96	The Black Dark Murders—Robert O. Saber	1.20	3.60	6.00	M
97	A Lover Would Be Nice—Hugh Herbert	1.20	3.60	6.00	E
98	Spider House—Van Wyck Mason	1.20	3.60	6.00	M
99	The Cold Trail—Paul Evan Lehman	1.20	3.60	6.00	W
100	Too Many Women—Milton K. Ozaki; 1950	1.20	3.60	6.00	
101	The Range Doctor—Oscar J. Friend	1.20	3.60	6.00	W
102	Satan's Gal—Carolina Lee	1.20	3.60	6.00	E
103	Maverick Guns—J. E. Grinstead	1.20	3.60	6.00	W
104	The Restless Corpse—Alan Pruitt	1.20	3.60	6.00	M
105	The Rider From Yonder—Norman A. Fox	1.20	3.60	6.00	M
106	Three for the Money—Joe Barry	1.20	3.60	6.00	M
107	The Siren of Silver Valley—Paul Evan Lehman	1.20	3.60	6.00	W
108	The Affair of the Frigid Blonde—Robert O. Saber	1.20	3.60	6.00	M
109	Shannahan's Feud—Archie Joscelyn	1.20	3.60	6.00	W
110	The Glass Ladder—Paul W. Fairman	1.20	3.60	6.00	M
111	Renegade Ramrod—Leslie Ernenwein	1.20	3.60	6.00	W
112	No Wings on a Cop—Cleve Adams	1.20	3.60	6.00	M
113	Barricade—Oscar J. Friend	1.20	3.60	6.00	W
114	False Face—Leslie Edgley	1.20	3.60	6.00	M
115	Range King—J. E. Grinstead	1.20	3.60	6.00	W
116	A Fiend in Need—Milton K. Ozaki	1.00	3.00	5.00	M
117	Thunder of Hoofs—Tex Holt	1.20	3.60	6.00	W
118	Window With the Sleeping Nude—Robert Leslie Bellem	1.20	3.60	6.00	M
119	Vengeance Valley—Paul Evan Lehman	1.20	3.60	6.00	W
120	Slay Ride for a Lady—Harry Whittington; orig., 1950	1.60	4.80	8.00	W
121	Rawhide Summons—Brett Austin	1.20	3.60	6.00	W
122	Dark Memory—Edward Ronns	1.20	3.60	6.00	M
123	When Texans Rode—J. E. Grinstead	1.20	3.60	6.00	W
124	The Scented Flesh—Robert O. Saber; 1951	1.20	3.60	6.00	M
125	Valley of the Tyrant—Dick Pearce	1.20	3.60	6.00	W
126	Yaller Gal—Carolina Lee	1.20	3.60	6.00	E
127	The Faro Kid—Leslie Ernenwein	1.20	3.60	6.00	W
128	Pursuit—Lawrence G. Blochman; orig., 1951	1.20	3.60	6.00	M
129	The Heiress of Copper Butte—Paul W. Fairman; aka The Montana Vixen	1.60	4.80	8.00	W
130	The Dove—Robert O. Saber; orig., 1951	1.20	3.60	6.00	M
131	The Lady Was a Tramp—Harry Whittington; orig., 1951	1.60	4.80	8.00	W
132	Trail Rider—Lynn Westland	1.20	3.60	6.00	W
133	Boot Hill—Clay Weston	1.20	3.60	6.00	W
134	Murder Is Dangerous—Saul Levinson; c-Saunders	1.20	3.60	6.00	M
135	Typed for a Corpse—Alan Pruitt; c-Saunders	1.20	3.60	6.00	M
136	Dark Canyon—Tex Holt; c-Saunders	1.20	3.60	6.00	W
137	Yucca City Outlaw—William Hopson; c-Saunders. Note: Same cover as Harlequin No. 158.	1.20	3.60	6.00	W
138	The Brass Monkey—Harry Whittington; orig., 1951	1.60	4.80	8.00	M
139	The Lady Killers—William T. Brannon; 1951	1.20	3.60	6.00	M

Handi Books 118, © Quinn

Handi Books 129, © Quinn

Handi·Books 137, © Quinn

Handi-Books Western 4, © Quinn

Hangman's House 1, © Par

Hangman's House 14, © Par

HANDI-BOOKS WESTERN
Quinn Publishing Co., Inc.

		Good	Fine	N/Mint	
1	The Cow Kingdom—Paul Evan Lehman; 1947	1.60	4.80	8.00	W
2	Rio Renegade—Leslie Ernenwein	1.60	4.80	8.00	W
3	The Long Noose—Oscar J. Friend	1.60	4.80	8.00	W
4	West of the Wolverine—Paul Evan Lehman	1.60	4.80	8.00	W

HANGMAN'S HOUSE
Parsee Publications

Some Digest Size

1	Murder on the Pike—Arville Nonweiler; digest size	1.20	3.60	6.00	M
2	Puzzle in Paint—Kootz (Samuel Melvin); digest size	1.20	3.60	6.00	M
3	Murder in False Face—George Childerness; digest size	1.20	3.60	6.00	M
4	The Man Who Feared—Will F. Jenkins (Murray Leinster); digest size	1.60	4.80	8.00	M
5	Death Gets a Head—A. R. McKenzie; digest size	1.20	3.60	6.00	M
6	Fit to Kill—Hans C. Owen; digest size	1.20	3.60	6.00	M
7	Murder on Beacon Hill—Gerald Brown; digest size	1.20	3.60	6.00	M
8	Death Like Thunder—Hugh Holman; digest size	1.20	3.60	6.00	M
9	The Corpse in the Cab—Aldin Vinton; aka Mystery in Green, digest size	1.20	3.60	6.00	M
10	Murder in Odd Sizes—Helen Joan Hultman; digest size	1.20	3.60	6.00	M
11	Murder Wore Green—Robert Portner Koehler; digest size	1.20	3.60	6.00	M
13	The Cowl of Doom—Edward Ronns; aka Death in a Lighthouse	2.00	6.00	10.00	M
14	The Corpse That Spoke—Robert H. Leitfred	2.00	6.00	10.00	M
15	The Cipher of Death—F. L. Gregory	2.00	6.00	10.00	M
16	Thereby Hangs a Corpse—Clarence Mullen	2.00	6.00	10.00	M
17	The Road House Murders—Robert Portner Koehler	2.00	6.00	10.00	M
18	Memory of a Scream—David X. Manners	2.00	6.00	10.00	M
19	Death in 1 - 2 - 3—Robert D. Abrahams	2.00	6.00	10.00	M
20	Murder Steals the Show—Lee Hirsch	2.00	6.00	10.00	M
21	Lady That's My Skull—Carl Shannon	2.00	6.00	10.00	M

HANRO
Hanro Corporation

Digest Size

1	Careless Hussy—Thomas Stone	.80	2.40	4.00	E

Hangman's House 18, © Par

Hangman's House 19, © Par

Hanro 1, © Hanro

(HANRO, continued)
| 2 | Shady Lady—Perry Lindsay (Peggy Gaddis) | .80 | 2.40 | 4.00 | E |
| 4 | Confessions of a Part-Time Bride—Hall Bennett; aka Make the Man Pay | .80 | 2.40 | 4.00 | E |

HARLEQUIN
Harlequin Books, Ltd.

(Canadian)

		Good	Fine	N/Mint	
1	The Manatee—Nancy Bruff; 1949	4.00	12.00	20.00	A
2	Lost House—Frances Shelly Wees	4.00	12.00	20.00	
3	Maelstrom—Howard Hunt	4.00	12.00	20.00	
4	Double Image—Arthur Herbert Bryant	4.00	12.00	20.00	
5	Close to My Heart—Margaret Nichols	4.00	12.00	20.00	
6	Wolf of the Mesas—Charles H. Snow	4.00	12.00	20.00	W
7	The House on Craig Street—Ronald J. Cooke	4.00	12.00	20.00	
8	Honeymoon Mountain—Frances Shelley Wees	4.00	12.00	20.00	R
9	The Dark Page—Samuel Michael Fuller	4.00	12.00	20.00	
10	Here's Blood in Your Eye—Manning Long	4.00	12.00	20.00	M
11	The Wicked Lady Skelton—Magdalen King-Hall	4.00	12.00	20.00	
12	A Killer Is Loose Among Us—Robert Terrall	3.00	9.00	15.00	M
13	His Wife the Doctor—Joseph McCord	4.00	12.00	20.00	
14	Six-Guns of Sandoval—Charles H. Snow	4.00	12.00	20.00	W
15	Virgin With Butterflies—Tom Powers	4.00	12.00	20.00	E
16	No Nice Girl—Perry Lindsay (Peggy Gaddis)	4.00	12.00	20.00	E
17	The D.A.'s Daughter—Herman Petersen	4.00	12.00	20.00	
18	Rebel of Ronde Valley—Charles H. Snow	4.00	12.00	20.00	W
19	Gina—George Albert Glay	4.00	12.00	20.00	E
20	Flame Vine—Helen Topping Miller	4.00	12.00	20.00	E
21	Renegade Ranger—Charles H. Snow	4.00	12.00	20.00	W
22	Crazy to Kill—Ann Cardwell	4.00	12.00	20.00	M
23	City for Conquest—Aben Kandel	4.00	12.00	20.00	
24	Painted Post Outlaws—Tom Gunn	4.00	12.00	20.00	W
25	Blondes Don't Cry—Merlda Mace	4.00	12.00	20.00	
26	Gambling on Love—Gale Jordan (Peggy Gaddis); 1950	4.00	12.00	20.00	R
27	Kiss Your Elbow—Alan Handley	4.00	12.00	20.00	
28	One Year With Grace—Martin Mooney	4.00	12.00	20.00	
29	Gunfighter Breed—Nelson C. Nye	4.00	12.00	20.00	W
30	Portrait of Love—Margaret Nichols	4.00	12.00	20.00	R
31	The Golden Feather—Theda Kenyon	4.00	12.00	20.00	
32	The Hollywood Mystery—Ben Hecht	4.00	12.00	20.00	M
33	Candle in the Morning—Helen Topping Miller	4.00	12.00	20.00	
34	Mobtown Clipper—S. S. Rabl	4.00	12.00	20.00	
35	Lush Valley—Patricia Campbell	4.00	12.00	20.00	
36	Murder Over Broadway—Fred Malina	4.00	12.00	20.00	M
37	Amaru—R. D. Frisbie	4.00	12.00	20.00	
38	Sheriff of Yavisa—Charles H. Snow	4.00	12.00	20.00	W
39	Be Still My Love—June Truesdell	4.00	12.00	20.00	R
40	Pass Key to Murder—Blair Reed	4.00	12.00	20.00	M
41	Panthers' Moon—Victor Canning	4.00	12.00	20.00	
42	House in Harlem—M. Scott Michel	4.00	12.00	20.00	E
43	The Clean-Up—Joe Barry	4.00	12.00	20.00	M
44	The So Blue Marble—Dorothy B. Hughes	4.00	12.00	20.00	M
45	Night and the City—Gerald Kersh	4.00	12.00	20.00	M
46	Fair Stranger—Cecile Gilmore	4.00	12.00	20.00	
47	Registered Nurse—Carl Sturdy	4.00	12.00	20.00	R
48	Poldrate Street—Garnett Weston	4.00	12.00	20.00	
49	Weep Not Fair Lady—John Evans	4.00	12.00	20.00	
50	One Way Street—Joseph McCord; 1950	4.00	12.00	20.00	

Harlequin 12, © HB

Harlequin 42, © HB

Harlequin 45, © HB

Harlequin 86, © HB   Harlequin 89, © HB   Harlequin 99, © HB

(HARLEQUIN, continued)

		Good	Fine	N/Mint	
51	The Pocket Purity Cook Book	3.00	9.00	15.00	NF
52	Livre de Cuisine Purity, Petit Format	3.00	9.00	15.00	NF
53	Pale Blonde of Sands Street—William C. White	4.00	12.00	20.00	
54	Speak of the Devil—Elizabeth Sanxay Holding	4.00	12.00	20.00	M
55	Mr. Sandeman Loses His Life—Eugene Healy	4.00	12.00	20.00	
56	The Mayor of Cote St. Paul—Ronald J. Cooke	4.00	12.00	20.00	
57	Murder Man—William Bogart	4.00	12.00	20.00	M
58	Outposts of Vengeance—E. E. Halleran	4.00	12.00	20.00	W
59	Cardinal Rock—Richard Sale	4.00	12.00	20.00	
60	Lady Killer—Elizabeth Sanxay Holding	4.00	12.00	20.00	M
61	Shadow of the Badlands—E. E. Halleran	4.00	12.00	20.00	W
62	Message From a Corpse—Sam Merwin, Jr.	4.00	12.00	20.00	M
63	The Dangerous Dead—William Brandon	4.00	12.00	20.00	M
64	Sinister Warning—M. Scott Michel	4.00	12.00	20.00	
65	Bridewell Beauty—H. M. E. Clamp	4.00	12.00	20.00	R
66	Royce of the Royal Mounted—Ames Moore	4.00	12.00	20.00	A
67	Criss Cross—Don Tracy	4.00	12.00	20.00	M
68	The Queen City Murder Case—William G. Bogart	4.00	12.00	20.00	M
69	Payoff in Black—William G. Schofield	4.00	12.00	20.00	M
70	Knife in My Back—Sam Merwin, Jr.	4.00	12.00	20.00	M
71	Bouquet Knitter's Guide	3.00	9.00	15.00	NF
72	Night of Terror—Joy Brown	4.00	12.00	20.00	M
73	The King of Thunder Valley—Archie Joscelyn	4.00	12.00	20.00	W
74	Spider House—Van Wyck Mason	4.00	12.00	20.00	
75	Maverick Guns—J. E. Grinstead; 1950	4.00	12.00	20.00	W
76	The Corpse Came Back—Amelia Reynolds Long	4.00	12.00	20.00	M
77	A Night at Club Bagdad—Owen Fox Jerome	4.00	12.00	20.00	
78	Rink Rat—Don MacMillan	4.00	12.00	20.00	
79	Lazarus No. 7—Richard Sale	7.00	21.00	35.00	SF
80	The Case of the Six Bullets—R. M. Laurenson	4.00	12.00	20.00	M
81	Idaho—Paul E. Lehman	4.00	12.00	20.00	W
82	The Cold Trail—Paul E. Lehman	4.00	12.00	20.00	W
83	The Fall Guy—Joe Barry	4.00	12.00	20.00	M
84	The Triple Cross—Joe Barry	4.00	12.00	20.00	M
85	She Died on the Stairway—Knight Rhoades	4.00	12.00	20.00	M
86	Double Life—Owen Fox Jerome	4.00	12.00	20.00	
87	Murder in Miniatures—Sam Merwin, Jr.	4.00	12.00	20.00	M
88	Renegade Ramrod—Leslie Ernenwein	4.00	12.00	20.00	W
89	The Faro Kid—Leslie Ernenwein; Note: Same cover as Handi-Book No. 83.	4.00	12.00	20.00	W
90	The Widow Gay—A. A. Marcus; aka Post-Mark Homicide. Note: Same cover as Graphic No. 67	4.00	12.00	20.00	M
91	Lady, That's My Skull—Carl Shannon; 1951	4.00	12.00	20.00	M
92	Dig Another Grave—Don Cameron	4.00	12.00	20.00	M
93	Empty Saddles—Al Cody	4.00	12.00	20.00	W
94	The Range Doctor—Oscar J. Friend	4.00	12.00	20.00	
95	You're Lonely When You're Dead—James Hadley Chase	4.00	12.00	20.00	M
96	The Rider From Yonder—Norman A. Fox	4.00	12.00	20.00	W
97	My Old Man's Badge—Ferguson Findley	4.00	12.00	20.00	
98	Jigger Moran—John Roeburt	4.00	12.00	20.00	M
99	Murder - Queen High—Bob Wade & Bill Miller	3.00	9.00	15.00	M
100	Black Rider—Jackson Cole; 1951	4.00	12.00	20.00	W
101	Three for the Money—Joe Barry	4.00	12.00	20.00	M
102	Wreath for a Redhead—Brian Moore	4.00	12.00	20.00	M
103	Wanton City—O. M. Hall	4.00	12.00	20.00	E
104	Tough Cop—John Roeburt	4.00	12.00	20.00	M
105	Vengeance Valley—Paul Evan Lehman	4.00	12.00	20.00	W
106	The Window With the Sleeping Nude—Robert Leslie Bellem	4.00	12.00	20.00	M
107	The Man From Bar-20—Clarence E. Mulford	4.00	12.00	20.00	W

(HARLEQUIN, continued)

	Good	Fine	N/Mint	
108 No Orchids for Miss Blandish—James Hadley Chase	5.00	15.00	25.00	M
109 Corpse on the Town—John Roeburt	4.00	12.00	20.00	M
110 Tombstone Stage—William Hopson	4.00	12.00	20.00	W
111 The Flesh of the Orchid—James Hadley Chase	4.00	12.00	20.00	M
112 Gina—George Albert Glay	4.00	12.00	20.00	E
113 Beyond the Blue Mountains—Jean Plaidy	3.00	9.00	15.00	
114 Johnny Saxon—William G. Bogart	4.00	12.00	20.00	
115 Manhattan Underworld—John Roeburt	4.00	12.00	20.00	M
116 Kill the Toff—John Creasey	4.00	12.00	20.00	M
117 The Executioners—Brian Moore	4.00	12.00	20.00	
118 Range Justice—Paul Evan Lehman	4.00	12.00	20.00	W
119 When Texans Ride—J. E. Grinstead	4.00	12.00	20.00	W
120 Slay Ride for a Lady—Harry Whittington	4.00	12.00	20.00	M
121 Run for Your Life—Michael Stark	4.00	12.00	20.00	M
122 A Matter of Policy—Sam Merwin, Jr.	4.00	12.00	20.00	M
123 Saddle Wolves—Allan K. Echols	4.00	12.00	20.00	W
124 The Dead Stay Dumb—James Hadley Chase	4.00	12.00	20.00	M
125 The Hidden Portal—Garnett Weston; 1951	4.00	12.00	20.00	
126 Death About Face—Frank Kane	4.00	12.00	20.00	M
127 Dark Memory—Edward Ronns	4.00	12.00	20.00	M
128 Law of the '45—Paul Evan Lehman	4.00	12.00	20.00	W
129 Hire This Killer—Ferguson Findley	4.00	12.00	20.00	M
130 Figure It Out for Yourself—James Hadley Chase	4.00	12.00	20.00	M
131 Tex—Clarence E. Mulford	4.00	12.00	20.00	W
132 False Face—Leslie Edgley	4.00	12.00	20.00	
133 Frontier Doctor—Bradford Scott	4.00	12.00	20.00	W
134 The Killers—George C. Henderson	4.00	12.00	20.00	
135 Lay Her Among the Lilies—James Hadley Chase	4.00	12.00	20.00	M
136 Boot Hill—Weston Clay	4.00	12.00	20.00	W
137 Berlin of Midnight—Robert Joseph	4.00	12.00	20.00	
138 Emma Hart—Lozania Prole	3.00	9.00	15.00	
139 The Glass Ladder—Paul W. Fairman	4.00	12.00	20.00	
140 The Lady Was a Tramp—Harry Whittington	4.00	12.00	20.00	M
141 Roger Sudden—Thomas H. Raddall	4.00	12.00	20.00	A
142 Doctor by Day—Thomas Stone	4.00	12.00	20.00	
143 Rebel Yell—Leslie Ernenwein	4.00	12.00	20.00	W
144 City for Conquest—Aben Kandel	4.00	12.00	20.00	
145 Rio Renegade—Leslie Ernenwein	4.00	12.00	20.00	W
146 Trail Rider—Lynn Westland	4.00	12.00	20.00	W
147 Pardon My Body—Dale Bogard	4.00	12.00	20.00	M
148 Wagon Train Westward—Lynn Westland; 1952	4.00	12.00	20.00	W
149 Remembering Laughter—Wallace Stegner	4.00	12.00	20.00	
150 Paprika—Erich Von Stroheim; 1952	4.00	12.00	20.00	E
151 The Great I Am—Lewis Graham	4.00	12.00	20.00	
152 Great Oaks—Ben Ames Williams	4.00	12.00	20.00	
153 Outlaw Valley—Al Cody	4.00	12.00	20.00	W
154 Rasputin and Crimes That Shook the World—Richard Hirsch	4.00	12.00	20.00	NF
155 Canyon of the Damned—Tex Holt	4.00	12.00	20.00	W
156 Blood of the North—James B. Hendryx	4.00	12.00	20.00	A
157 The Bizarre Sisters—Jay and Audrey Walz	4.00	12.00	20.00	E
158 Yucca City Outlaw—William Hopson; c-Saunders. Note: Same cover as Handi-Book No. 137	4.00	12.00	20.00	W
159 The Smiling Tiger—Glen Offord	4.00	12.00	20.00	
160 Twelve Chinks and a Woman—James Hadley Chase	20.00	60.00	100.00	E
161 Health, Sex and Birth Control—Percy E. Ryberg, M.D.	3.00	9.00	15.00	NF
162 The River's End—James Oliver Curwood	4.00	12.00	20.00	
163 Guntown—Dan Carew	4.00	12.00	20.00	W
164 Captain for Elizabeth—Jan Westcott	4.00	12.00	20.00	A

Harlequin 109, © HB

Harlequin 120, © HB

Harlequin 160, © HB

Harlequin 185, © HB   Harlequin 187, © HB   Harlequin 209, © HB

(HARLEQUIN, continued)

		Good	Fine	N/Mint	
165	Rats With Baby Faces—W. Stanley Moss	4.00	12.00	20.00	M
166	The Big Fist—Clyde B. Ragsdale	4.00	12.00	20.00	
167	Love Me - and Die!—Day Keene	4.00	12.00	20.00	M
168	Hunt the Killer—Day Keene	4.00	12.00	20.00	M
169	Lady of Cleves—Margaret Campbell Barnes	4.00	12.00	20.00	
170	The Sea Is So Wide—Evelyn Eaton	4.00	12.00	20.00	A
171	Savage Justice—Leslie Ernenwein	4.00	12.00	20.00	W
172	Gun Law—Paul Evan Lehman	4.00	12.00	20.00	W
173	Anna—Anneke de Lange	3.00	9.00	15.00	
174	Murder Is My Racket—Robert H. Leitfred	4.00	12.00	20.00	M
175	The Commandos—Elliot Arnold; 1952	4.00	12.00	20.00	C
176	The Valley of Silent Men—James Oliver Curwood	4.00	12.00	20.00	A
177	The House That Stood Still—A. E. van Vogt	12.50	37.50	60.00	SF
178	The Goldsmith's Wife—Jean Plaidy	4.00	12.00	20.00	
179	Madame Serpent—Jean Plaidy	4.00	12.00	20.00	E
180	If the Coffin Fits—Day Keene	4.00	12.00	20.00	M
181	The Wicked Lady Skelton—Magdalen King-Hall	3.00	9.00	15.00	
182	Crime on My Hands—Carl G. Hodges	4.00	12.00	20.00	M
183	Evening Street—Katrina Johnson	4.00	12.00	20.00	
184	Black Jade—Angeline Taylor	4.00	12.00	20.00	
185	Naked Fury—Day Keene	4.00	12.00	20.00	
186	Why Be a Sucker?—D. M. LeBourdais	4.00	12.00	20.00	NF
187	Shanghai Jezebel—Mark Corrigan	4.00	12.00	20.00	E
188	Beggars Might Ride—George Albert Glay	4.00	12.00	20.00	
189	The Nymph and the Lamp—Thomas H. Raddall	4.00	12.00	20.00	E
190	Slave Ship—H. B. Drake	4.00	12.00	20.00	A
191	Prison Doctor—Louis Berg, M.D.	4.00	12.00	20.00	
192	Swamp Willow—Edwina Elroy	4.00	12.00	20.00	E
193	The Firebrand—George Challis	4.00	12.00	20.00	A
194	Triggerman—Abel Shott	4.00	12.00	20.00	
195	Nine to Five—Harvey Smith	4.00	12.00	20.00	
196	His Majesty's Yankees—Thomas H. Raddall	4.00	12.00	20.00	A
197	Strictly for Cash—James Hadley Chase	4.00	12.00	20.00	M
198	The Rawhider—Charles N. Heckelmann	4.00	12.00	20.00	W
199	The Double Shuffle—James Hadley Chase	4.00	12.00	20.00	M
200	Doctor of Lonesome River—Edison Marshall; 1952	4.00	12.00	20.00	A
201	The Unfulfilled—W. G. Hardy	4.00	12.00	20.00	
202	Copper Town—Paul W. Fairman	4.00	12.00	20.00	W
203	Daughter of Satan—Jean Plaidy	5.00	15.00	25.00	E
204	Gun Hawk—Leslie Ernenwein; 1953	4.00	12.00	20.00	W
205	The Black Flame—Stanley G. Weinbaum	12.50	37.50	60.00	SF
206	You Never Know With Women—James Hadley Chase	4.00	12.00	20.00	E
207	Three Ships West—Harry Symons	4.00	12.00	20.00	
208	Pillar of Fire—George Borodin	4.00	12.00	20.00	
209	The Rock Cried Out—Edward Stanley	4.00	12.00	20.00	
210	McSorley's Wonderful Saloon—Joseph Mitchell	4.00	12.00	20.00	
211	The Cautious Amorist—Norman Lindsay	4.00	12.00	20.00	
212	Shooting Valley—Lynn Westland	4.00	12.00	20.00	W
213	The Royal Story—Richard J. Doyle	3.00	9.00	15.00	NF
214	Paprika—Erich von Stroheim	4.00	12.00	20.00	E
215	Turn Back the River—W. G. Hardy	4.00	12.00	20.00	
216	No Mean City—A. McArthur & H. Kingsley Long	4.00	12.00	20.00	
217	The Sea Hawk—Rafael Sabatini	4.00	12.00	20.00	A
218	The Golden Amazon—John Russell Fearn	12.50	37.50	60.00	SF
219	Girls in White—Rona Randall	4.00	12.00	20.00	
220	Masked Rider—Will Garth	4.00	12.00	20.00	W
221	The Great Impersonation—E. Phillips Oppenheim	3.00	9.00	15.00	A
222	Mad Mike—George Goodchild	4.00	12.00	20.00	

		Good	Fine	N/Mint	
223	The Wages of Virtue—P. C. Wren	4.00	12.00	20.00	A
224	Lady Hobo—Beth Brown	4.00	12.00	20.00	E
225	Sir Rusty Sword—Phillip Lindsay; 1953	4.00	12.00	20.00	A
226	The Owlhoot Trail—Buck Billings	4.00	12.00	20.00	W
227	We Too Can Die—Paul Le Butt	4.00	12.00	20.00	
228	Drums of Dambala—H. Bedford Jones	5.00	15.00	25.00	A
229	Framed in Guilt—Day Keene	4.00	12.00	20.00	M
230	Women Spies—Kurt Singer	5.00	15.00	25.00	E
231	Legionnaire—John Robb	4.00	12.00	20.00	A
232	Malay Gold—H. Bedford Jones	5.00	15.00	25.00	A
233	Die With Me Lady—Ronald Cocking	4.00	12.00	20.00	M
234	Rebound—Dick Diespecker	4.00	12.00	20.00	
235	General Duty Nurse—Lucy Agnes Hancock	4.00	12.00	20.00	R
236	Gun Thrower—William L. Hopson	4.00	12.00	20.00	W
237	Island of Escape—Alexander Key	4.00	12.00	20.00	
238	The Lost World—Sir Arthur Conan Doyle	10.00	30.00	50.00	SF
239	Mission of Revenge—Edison Marshall	4.00	12.00	20.00	
240	Violent Night—Whit Harrison	4.00	12.00	20.00	M
241	Son of the Gods—Rex Beach	4.00	12.00	20.00	A
242	The Murder on the Links—Agatha Christie	4.00	12.00	20.00	M
243	School for Love—Oliver Anderson	4.00	12.00	20.00	
244	Hostage—Archie Joscelyn	4.00	12.00	20.00	W
245	The Soft Touch—James Hadley Chase	4.00	12.00	20.00	M
246	The Law's Outlaw—Arnold Smith	4.00	12.00	20.00	
247	Dark Surgery—Ben Ames Williams	4.00	12.00	20.00	
248	Legion of the Lawless—Lynn Westland	4.00	12.00	20.00	
249	Come Blonde, Come Murder—Peter George	4.00	12.00	20.00	M
250	The Man in the Middle—Ferguson Findley; 1953	4.00	12.00	20.00	
251	Doctor in Buckskin—T. D. Allen	4.00	12.00	20.00	
252	Legion of Dishonor—Ivan Lebedeff	4.00	12.00	20.00	A
253	Wake Up to Murder—Day Keene	4.00	12.00	20.00	M
254	Mesquite Johnny—Barry Cord	4.00	12.00	20.00	W
255	Lady, Here's Your Wreath—Raymond Marshall	4.00	12.00	20.00	M
256	No Wings on a Cop—Cleve F. Adams	4.00	12.00	20.00	M
257	One Man Front—George Murdoch Rennie	4.00	12.00	20.00	
258	World Behind Bars—Louis Berg, M.D.	4.00	12.00	20.00	NF
259	Silver City—Bradford Scott	4.00	12.00	20.00	W
260	The Outlaw Trail—Johnston McCulley	4.00	12.00	20.00	W
261	Light in the Wilderness—E. B. Osler	4.00	12.00	20.00	
262	The Body on Mount Royal—David Montrose	4.00	12.00	20.00	
263	Texas Showdown—Archie Joscelyn	4.00	12.00	20.00	W
264	Community Nurse—Lucy Agnes Hancock	3.00	9.00	15.00	R
265	The Paw in the Bottle—Raymond Marshall; 1954	4.00	12.00	20.00	
266	Catalina—W. Somerset Maugham	4.00	12.00	20.00	
267	I'll Bury My Dead—James Hadley Chase	4.00	12.00	20.00	M
268	The Unholy Woman—Jean Plaidy	4.00	12.00	20.00	E
269	Queen Jezebel—Jean Plaidy	4.00	12.00	20.00	E
270	Fighting Buckaroo—Paul Evan Lehman	4.00	12.00	20.00	W
271	Mind Your Manners—Claire Wallace	3.00	9.00	15.00	
272	The Fabulous Nell Gwynne—Lozania Prole	3.00	9.00	15.00	
273	Holy Deadlock—A. P. Herbert	4.00	12.00	20.00	
274	Lost Valley—Al Cody	4.00	12.00	20.00	W
275	Hell's Horseman—William Hopson; 1954	4.00	12.00	20.00	W
276	Conflict—E. V. Timms	4.00	12.00	20.00	A
277	Lady of China Street—Mark Corrigan	4.00	12.00	20.00	A
278	The Bait and the Trap—George Challis	4.00	12.00	20.00	A
279	Crime on My Hands—Carl G. Hodges	4.00	12.00	20.00	M
280	The Nut Brown Maid—Philip Lindsay	4.00	12.00	20.00	E

Harlequin 232, © HB

Harlequin 240, © HB

Harlequin 269, © HB

Harlequin 281, © HB

Harlequin 286, © HB

Harlequin 330, © HB

(HARLEQUIN, continued)

		Good	Fine	N/Mint	
281	Outlaw Deputy—Murray Leinster	6.00	18.00	30.00	W
282	Frozen Frontier—Walter W. Liggett	4.00	12.00	20.00	
283	A Body for a Blonde—Ken McLeod	4.00	12.00	20.00	M
284	Calling Nurse Blair—Lucy Agnes Hancock	3.00	9.00	15.00	R
285	Texas Outlaw—Al Cody	4.00	12.00	20.00	W
286	Colonel Blood—Max Peacock	4.00	12.00	20.00	A
287	Gina—George Albert Glay	4.00	12.00	20.00	E
288	Bright Path to Adventure—Gordon Sinclair	3.00	9.00	15.00	A
289	The Black Donellys—Thomas P. Kelley	3.00	9.00	15.00	NF
290	The Violet Years—E. V. Timms	4.00	12.00	20.00	
291	Heart of Asia—Roy Chapman Andrews	3.00	9.00	15.00	NF
292	Nurse Barlow—Lucy Agnes Hancock	3.00	9.00	15.00	R
293	Mona—M. Coates Webster	4.00	12.00	20.00	
294	Girls in White—Rona Randall	4.00	12.00	20.00	
295	The Lost House—Frances Shelley Wees	4.00	12.00	20.00	
296	Half-Caste—Eric Baume	4.00	12.00	20.00	E
297	The Vice Merchants—Reed McCary	4.00	12.00	20.00	
298	Pride's Fancy—Thomas H. Raddall	4.00	12.00	20.00	A
299	Copper—Lieut. Tom McGrath	4.00	12.00	20.00	
300	Mallory—Raymond Marshall; 1954	4.00	12.00	20.00	
301	Mary Read, Buccaneer—Philip Rush	4.00	12.00	20.00	A
302	The Nurse—Lucy Agnes Hancock	3.00	9.00	15.00	R
303	Captain Gentleman—Verne Fletcher	4.00	12.00	20.00	
304	High Saddle—William Hopson	4.00	12.00	20.00	W
305	Out of the Night—Robert O. Saber	4.00	12.00	20.00	M
306	Fabian of the Yard—Robert Fabian	3.00	9.00	15.00	NF
307	The Cage—Sydney Horler	5.00	15.00	25.00	E
308	Doctor Paul—Bette Allan	3.00	9.00	15.00	R
309	Notched Guns—William Hopson	4.00	12.00	20.00	W
310	Why Pick on Me—Raymond Marshall	4.00	12.00	20.00	
311	Convicted—David Goodis	4.00	12.00	20.00	
312	The Seeker—Thomas Burtis	4.00	12.00	20.00	
313	Hospital Nurse—Lucy Agnes Hancock	3.00	9.00	15.00	R
314	Forbidden—Lois Bull	4.00	12.00	20.00	
315	The Black Eagle—Thomas Burtis	4.00	12.00	20.00	
316	This Way for a Shroud—James Hadley Chase	4.00	12.00	20.00	M
317	Blonde's Requiem—Raymond Marshall	4.00	12.00	20.00	
318	The Half-Breed—M. Constantin-Weyer	4.00	12.00	20.00	
319	Woman Doctor—Dorothy Pierce Walker	3.00	9.00	15.00	
320	The Deathless Amazon—John Russell Fearn	12.50	37.50	60.00	SF
321	London After Dark—Robert Fabian	4.00	12.00	20.00	NF
322	The Web—Sydney Horler	4.00	12.00	20.00	M
323	Tiger by the Tail—James Hadley Chase; 1955	4.00	12.00	20.00	M
324	West End Nurse—Lucy Agnes Hancock	3.00	9.00	15.00	R
325	Satan's Range—Al Cody; 1955	4.00	12.00	20.00	W
326	Girl Intern—Elizabeth Seifert	3.00	9.00	15.00	R
327	The World's Worst Women—Bernard O'Donnell	5.00	15.00	25.00	E
328	The Wife Traders—Arthur Stringer	4.00	12.00	20.00	
329	People of the Night—Victor Russell	4.00	12.00	20.00	
330	Convict Town—E. V. Timms	4.00	12.00	20.00	E
331	Women in Chains—E. V. Timms	7.00	21.00	35.00	E
332	Staff Nurse—Lucy Agnes Hancock	3.00	9.00	15.00	R
333	Resident Nurse—Lucy Agnes Hancock	3.00	9.00	15.00	R
334	The Square Emerald—Edgar Wallace	4.00	12.00	20.00	M
335	Hoodlum Alley—Albert E. Ullman	4.00	12.00	20.00	M
336	The Good and the Bad—John Fleming	3.00	9.00	15.00	R
337	The Man in the Brown Suit—Agatha Christie	4.00	12.00	20.00	M
338	District Nurse—Lucy Agnes Hancock	3.00	9.00	15.00	R

		Good	Fine	N/Mint	
339	Nurses Are People—Lucy Agnes Hancock	3.00	9.00	15.00	R
340	The Pick-Up—Raymond Marshall	4.00	12.00	20.00	
341	Ruthless—Raymond Marshall	4.00	12.00	20.00	
342	Nancy Craig, R.N.—Marcia Ford	3.00	9.00	15.00	R
343	Gun Thunder Valley—Al Cody	4.00	12.00	20.00	W
344	Village Doctor—Lucy Agnes Hancock	3.00	9.00	15.00	R
345	The Gunman—Al Cody	4.00	12.00	20.00	W
346	Doctor Bill—Lucy Agnes Hancock	3.00	9.00	15.00	R
347	Pat Whitney, R.N.—Lucy Agnes Hancock	3.00	9.00	15.00	R
348	The Doctor on Elm Street—Kay Hamilton; 1956	3.00	9.00	15.00	R
349	The Four Just Men—Edgar Wallace	4.00	12.00	20.00	M
350	The Renegade—Walt Coburn; 1956	4.00	12.00	20.00	W
351	Dr. Parrish, Resident—Sydney Thompson	3.00	9.00	15.00	R
352	The India-Rubber Men—Edgar Wallace	4.00	12.00	20.00	M
353	Gun Law—Paul Evan Lehman	4.00	12.00	20.00	W
354	Dark Bahama—Peter Cheyney	4.00	12.00	20.00	
355	Savage Justice—Leslie Ernenwein	4.00	12.00	20.00	W
356	Nurse's Aide—Lucy Agnes Hancock	3.00	9.00	15.00	R
357	Young Doctor Glenn—Kay Hamilton	3.00	9.00	15.00	R
358	Redrock Gold—Paul Evan Lehman	4.00	12.00	20.00	W
359	The Secret Adversary—Agatha Christie	4.00	12.00	20.00	M
360	Yucca City Outlaw—William Hopson	4.00	12.00	20.00	W
361	The Clue of the Silver Key—Edgar Wallace	4.00	12.00	20.00	M
362	Nora Was a Nurse—Peggy Dern	3.00	9.00	15.00	R
363	Doctor Alice's Daughter—Kay Hamilton	3.00	9.00	15.00	R
364	Surgeon in Charge—Elizabeth Seifert	3.00	9.00	15.00	R
365	Doctors Are Different—Dorothy Pierce Walker	3.00	9.00	15.00	R
366	The Brass Monkey—Harry Whittington	4.00	12.00	20.00	M
367	Hickory House—Kenneth Orvis	4.00	12.00	20.00	
368	Meredith Blake, M.D.—Peggy Gaddis	3.00	9.00	15.00	R
369	Three Doctors—Elizabeth Seifert	3.00	9.00	15.00	R
370	Appointment With Venus—Jerrard Tickell	4.00	12.00	20.00	
371	Renegade Ramrod—Leslie Ernenwein	4.00	12.00	20.00	W
372	Meet the Warrens—Lucy Agnes Hancock	3.00	9.00	15.00	R
373	Tonight, Josephine—Lozania Prole	3.00	9.00	15.00	
374	Valley of the Sun—Archie Joscelyn	4.00	12.00	20.00	W
375	Miss Doctor—Elizabeth Seifert	3.00	9.00	15.00	R
376	Blake Hospital—Dorothy Worley; 1957	3.00	9.00	15.00	R
377	The Secret of Chimneys—Agatha Christie	4.00	12.00	20.00	M
378	The Ringer—Edgar Wallace	4.00	12.00	20.00	M
379	The Doctor Takes a Wife—Elizabeth Seifert	3.00	9.00	15.00	R
380	The River's End—James Oliver Curwood	4.00	12.00	20.00	A
381	Doctor Joel—Watkins E. Wright	3.00	9.00	15.00	R
382	Never Trust a Woman—Raymond Marshall	3.00	9.00	15.00	
383	Valley of Silent Men—James Oliver Curwood	4.00	12.00	20.00	A
384	Nurse Ellen—Peggy Dern	3.00	9.00	15.00	R
385	Eve—James Hadley Chase	4.00	12.00	20.00	
386	The Faro Kid—Leslie Ernenwein	4.00	12.00	20.00	W
387	White Face—Edgar Wallace	4.00	12.00	20.00	M
388	Doctor Scott—Peggy Dern	3.00	9.00	15.00	R
389	Circle F Cowboy—Chuck Martin	4.00	12.00	20.00	W
390	Adopted Derelicts—Bluebell S. Phillips	4.00	12.00	20.00	
391	How to Get More From Your Car—W. J. Young & E. R. McCrea	3.00	9.00	15.00	NF
392	Doctor of Mercy—Elizabeth Seifert	3.00	9.00	15.00	R
393	A Forest of Eyes—Victor Canning	4.00	12.00	20.00	
394	Lady Doctor—Peggy Gaddis	3.00	9.00	15.00	R
395	The Angel of Terror—Edgar Wallace	4.00	12.00	20.00	M
396	Double Cross Ranch—Will Watson	4.00	12.00	20.00	W
397	The Shorn Lamb—Lucy Agnes Hancock	3.00	9.00	15.00	R
398	Sagebrush—Wade Hamilton	4.00	12.00	20.00	W
399	Royce of the Royal Mounted—Amos Moore	4.00	12.00	20.00	W
400	The Cage—Sydney Horter; 1957	4.00	12.00	20.00	M
401	The Doctor Disagrees—Elizabeth Seifert	3.00	9.00	15.00	R
402	The Football Gravy Train—Frank O'Rourke	4.00	12.00	20.00	S
403	Next of Kin—George Goodchild	3.00	9.00	15.00	R
404	Law in the Saddle—Paul Evan Lehman	4.00	12.00	20.00	W
405	City Nurse—Peggy Gaddis	3.00	9.00	15.00	R
406	The Flaming Forest—James Oliver Curwood	4.00	12.00	20.00	A
407	The Hospital in Buwambo—Anne Vinton	3.00	9.00	15.00	R
408	Rink Rat—Don MacMillan	4.00	12.00	20.00	
409	Hospital Corridors—Mary Burchell; 1958	3.00	9.00	15.00	R
410	Dark Journey—Sydney Horler	4.00	12.00	20.00	
411	Range King—J. E. Grinstead	4.00	12.00	20.00	W
412	Nurse Trenton—Caroline Trench	3.00	9.00	15.00	R
413	I'll Get You for This—James Hadley Chase	4.00	12.00	20.00	M
414	Devil's Portage—Charles Stoddard	4.00	12.00	20.00	

		Good	Fine	N/Mint	
415	The Normal Child—Alan Brown, M.D.	3.00	9.00	15.00	NF
416	Doctor Lucy—Barbara Allen	3.00	9.00	15.00	R
417	Maverick Guns—J. E. Grinstead	4.00	12.00	20.00	W
418	The Feathered Serpent—Edgar Wallace	4.00	12.00	20.00	M
419	Nurse Warding Takes Charge—Caroline Trench	3.00	9.00	15.00	R
420	The Squeaker—Edgar Wallace	4.00	12.00	20.00	M
421	The Golden Amazon's Triumph—John Russell Fearn	12.50	37.50	60.00	SF
422	Then Come Kiss Me—Mary Burchell	3.00	9.00	15.00	R
423	Nurse Greve—Jane Arbor	3.00	9.00	15.00	R
424	Flashing Spikes—Frank O'Rourke	4.00	12.00	20.00	S
425	The Return of the Nighthawk—Sydney Horler; 1958	4.00	12.00	20.00	
426	The World's Greatest Spy Stories—ed. Kurt Singer	4.00	12.00	20.00	
427	Nurse Brookes—Kate Norway	3.00	9.00	15.00	R
428	The Strange Countess—Edgar Wallace	4.00	12.00	20.00	M
429	Steele of the Royal Mounted—James Oliver Curwood	4.00	12.00	20.00	A
430	Ship's Nurse—Alex Stuart	3.00	9.00	15.00	R
431	The Silent Valley—Jean S. MacLeod	4.00	12.00	20.00	
432	The Lady Lost Her Head—Manning Lee Stokes	4.00	12.00	20.00	M
433	Because of Doctor Danville—Elizabeth Hoy	3.00	9.00	15.00	R
434	Dear Doctor Everett—Jean S. MacLeod	3.00	9.00	15.00	R
435	Canada's Greatest Crimes—Thomas P. Kelley	4.00	12.00	20.00	NF
436	Garrison Hospital—Alex Stuart	3.00	9.00	15.00	R
437	Saddlebag Surgeon—Robert Tyre	3.00	9.00	15.00	
438	Master of Surgery—Alex Stuart	3.00	9.00	15.00	
439	Hospital in Sudan—Anne Vinton	3.00	9.00	15.00	R
440	Pardon My Parka—Joan Walker	3.00	9.00	15.00	R
441	Murder on the Links—Agatha Christie	4.00	12.00	20.00	M
442	Curling With Ken Watson—Ken Watson	4.00	12.00	20.00	NF
443	Nurse on Call—Elizabeth Gilzean	3.00	9.00	15.00	R
444	Double Dan—Edgar Wallace	4.00	12.00	20.00	M
445	Nurse in the Tropics—Peggy Dern	3.00	9.00	15.00	R
446	To Please the Doctor—Marjorie Moore	3.00	9.00	15.00	R
447	The Crimson Circle—Edgar Wallace; 1959	4.00	12.00	20.00	M
448	Bridal Array—Elizabeth Cadell	3.00	9.00	15.00	R
449	Nurse in Training—Elizabeth Hoy	3.00	9.00	15.00	R
450	Gay Canadian Rogues—Frank Rasky; 1959	4.00	12.00	20.00	NF
451	Air Ambulance—Jean S. MacLeod	3.00	9.00	15.00	R
452	Crescent Dream Book and Fortune Teller	3.00	9.00	15.00	NF
453	Corner Cupboard—Carlyle Allison	3.00	9.00	15.00	R
454	Nurse in Love—Jane Arbor	3.00	9.00	15.00	R
455	Smoke Over Sikanaska—J. S. Gowland	4.00	12.00	20.00	A
456	The Yellow Snake—Edgar Wallace	4.00	12.00	20.00	M
457	Physical Fitness for All the Family—Lloyd Percival	3.00	9.00	15.00	NF
458	Next Patient, Doctor Anne—Elizabeth Gilzean	3.00	9.00	15.00	R
459	Ring for the Nurse—Marjorie Moore	3.00	9.00	15.00	R
460	At the Villa Rose—A. E. W. Mason	3.00	9.00	15.00	R
461	For Ever and Ever—Mary Burchell	3.00	9.00	15.00	R
462	Love From a Surgeon—Elizabeth Gilzean	3.00	9.00	15.00	R
463	Nurse Brodie—Kate Norway	3.00	9.00	15.00	R
464	The Captain's Table—Alex Stuart	3.00	9.00	15.00	
465	My Greatest Crime Story—ed. Kurt Singer	4.00	12.00	20.00	
466	The Traitor's Gate—Edgar Wallace	4.00	12.00	20.00	M
467	Nurse to the Island—Caroline Trench	3.00	9.00	15.00	R
468	Surgeon of Distinction—Mary Burchell	3.00	9.00	15.00	R
469	Maggy—Sara Seale	3.00	9.00	15.00	R
470	The Cat in the Convoy—William G. Schofield	4.00	12.00	20.00	
471	Nurse Hilary—Peggy Gaddis	3.00	9.00	15.00	R
472	Young Doctor Kirkdene—Elizabeth Hoy	3.00	9.00	15.00	R
473	The Cockoo in Spring—Elizabeth Cadell	3.00	9.00	15.00	R
474	Towards the Dawn—Jane Arbor	3.00	9.00	15.00	R
475	The Mind of Mr. J. G. Reeder—Edgar Wallace; 1959	4.00	12.00	20.00	M
476	Nurse Jess—Joyce Dingwell	3.00	9.00	15.00	R
477	Hospital Blue—Anne Vinton	3.00	9.00	15.00	R
478	Dear Trustee—Mary Burchell	3.00	9.00	15.00	R
479	The Case of the Ebony Queen—Cleo Adkins	4.00	12.00	20.00	
480	Grey Cup Cavalcade—Tony Allan	4.00	12.00	20.00	
481	Bachelor of Medicine—Alex Stuart	3.00	9.00	15.00	R
482	Nurse Harlowe—Jane Arbor	3.00	9.00	15.00	R
483	My Heart Has Wings—Elizabeth Hoy	3.00	9.00	15.00	R
484	The Northing Tramp—Edgar Wallace	4.00	12.00	20.00	M
485	Island Hospital—Elizabeth Houghton	3.00	9.00	15.00	R
486	Nurse Caril's New Post—Caroline Trench	3.00	9.00	15.00	R
487	The Happy Enterprise—Eleanor Farnes	3.00	9.00	15.00	
488	The Man Who Died Twice—Sydney Horler	4.00	12.00	20.00	
489	Consulting Surgeon—Jane Arbor	3.00	9.00	15.00	R
490	Nurse MacLean Goes West—Elizabeth Gilzean	3.00	9.00	15.00	R

	(HARLEQUIN, continued)	Good	Fine	N/Mint	
491	Nurse Tennant—Elizabeth Hoy	3.00	9.00	15.00	R
492	Hospital Pro—Marjorie Moore	3.00	9.00	15.00	R
493	The Man at the Carlton—Edgar Wallace	4.00	12.00	20.00	M
494	Love Is My Reason—Mary Burchell	3.00	9.00	15.00	R
495	Nurse With a Dream—Norrey Ford	3.00	9.00	15.00	R
496	Nurse in White—Lucy Agnes Hancock	3.00	9.00	15.00	R
497	Doctor Garth—Elizabeth Hoy	3.00	9.00	15.00	R
498	Nurse Atholl Returns—Jane Arbor	3.00	9.00	15.00	R
499	Junior Pro—Kate Norway	3.00	9.00	15.00	R
500	Honorary Surgeon—Marjorie Moore; 1959	3.00	9.00	15.00	R
501	Do Something Dangerous—Elizabeth Hoy	3.00	9.00	15.00	R

HART BOOKS
Horace Hart, Inc.

Digest Size

		Good	Fine	N/Mint	
K-1	The House of Creeping Horror—George F. Worts	.80	2.40	4.00	M
K-2	The Diamonds of Death—Borden Chase; aka Blue, White and Perfect	.80	2.40	4.00	M

HERCULES
Hercules Publishing Corporation

Digest Size

		Good	Fine	N/Mint	
nn	D - As in Dead—Lawrence Treat; 1943	1.20	3.60	6.00	M

HILLMAN BOOKS
Hillman Periodicals, Inc.

		Good	Fine	N/Mint	
nn(1)	Let's Make Mary—Jack Hanley; 1948	1.20	3.60	6.00	E
2	Tumbling River Range—W. C. Tuttle	1.60	4.80	8.00	W
3	Casanova's Memoirs—Giacomo Casanova	1.20	3.60	6.00	
4	Ironheart—William MacLeod Raine	1.60	4.80	8.00	W
5	Bluffer's Luck—W. C. Tuttle	1.60	4.80	8.00	W
6	Riders of Buck River—William MacLeod Raine	1.60	4.80	8.00	W
7	Sex and Marriage Problems—E. B. Taylor	1.60	4.80	8.00	
8	I Chose Freedom—Victor Kravchenko	1.60	4.80	8.00	NF
9	Guns on the High Mesa—Arthur Henry Gooden	1.60	4.80	8.00	W
10	Murder Under Construction—Sue MacVeigh	1.60	4.80	8.00	M
11	Steve Yeager—William MacLeod Raine	1.60	4.80	8.00	W
12	Ten Droll Tales—Honore de Balzac; includes some science fiction/fantasy	1.60	4.80	8.00	
13	Hell in the Saddle—Ed Earl Repp	1.60	4.80	8.00	W
14	The Physiology of Love—Remy de Gourmont; 1949	1.60	4.80	8.00	NF
15	Hanging Judge—Bruce Hamilton	1.60	4.80	8.00	M
16	Gold—Clarence Budington Kelland	1.20	3.60	6.00	W
17	Gun Hawk—Ed Earl Repp	1.60	4.80	8.00	W
18	Collusion—Theodore D. Irwin	1.60	4.80	8.00	NF
19	The Red Rider of Smoky Range—William Colt MacDonald	2.00	6.00	10.00	W
20	Dark Hazard—W. R. Burnett	2.00	6.00	10.00	M
21	Marriage, Sex, and Family Problems and How to Solve Them—John J. Anthony	1.60	4.80	8.00	NF
22	The Shadowed Trail—Arthur Henry Gooden	1.60	4.80	8.00	W
23	42 Days for Murder—Roger Torrey	1.20	3.60	6.00	M
24	The Trail of Danger—William MacLeod Raine	1.60	4.80	8.00	W
25	The Deputy of Carabina—William Colt MacDonald	1.60	4.80	8.00	W
26	Straws in the Wind—W. C. Tuttle	1.60	4.80	8.00	W
27	Dead on Arrival	1.20	3.60	6.00	

Hart Books K-1, © Hart

Hercules nn, © Hercules Publ.

Hillman Books 24, © Hill

Hillman Books 28, © Hill

Hillman Books 33, © Hill

Hillman Books 41, © Hill

(HILLMAN BOOKS, continued)

		Good	Fine	N/Mint	
28	The Redhead From Sun Dog—W. C. Tuttle; Note: Same cover as Western Novel Classic No. 89	1.60	4.80	8.00	W
29	Big-Town Round Up—William MacLeod Raine	1.60	4.80	8.00	W
30	Buzzard Tracks—Tom J. Hopkins	1.60	4.80	8.00	W
31	Wheels in the Dust—William Colt MacDonald	1.60	4.80	8.00	W
32	Bear Paw—Dane Coolidge	1.60	4.80	8.00	W
33	Rusty Guns—Bliss Lomax	1.60	4.80	8.00	W
34	King of Crazy River—William Colt MacDonald	1.60	4.80	8.00	W
35	Smoky River—Tom Roan	1.60	4.80	8.00	W
36	King of the Bush—William MacLeod Raine	1.60	4.80	8.00	W
37	Hashknife of Stormy River—W. C. Tuttle	1.60	4.80	8.00	W
38	Nothing More Than Murder—Jim Thompson	2.00	6.00	10.00	M
39	Meet Mr. Mulliner—P. G. Wodehouse	1.60	4.80	8.00	H
40	Trouble at the JHC—W. C. Tuttle	1.60	4.80	8.00	W
41	The Dying Earth—Jack Vance; 1st ed., 1950	30.00	90.00	150.00	SF
42	Roaring River—William MacLeod Raine	1.60	4.80	8.00	W
43	Arizona Nights—Stewart Edward White	1.60	4.80	8.00	W
44	The Trusty Knaves—Eugene Manlove Rhodes	1.60	4.80	8.00	W
45	Story of a Russian Spy—Alexander Foote; aka Handbook for Spies	1.60	4.80	8.00	B
46	Copper Streak Trail—Eugene Manlove Rhodes	1.60	4.80	8.00	W
47	Scattergun Ranch—Tom J. Hopkins	1.60	4.80	8.00	W
48	Father of the Bride—Edward Streeter; movie tie-in	2.00	6.00	10.00	
100	The Witness—Georges Simenon	1.00	3.00	5.00	M
101	Texas Man—William MacLeod Raine; 1957	1.00	3.00	5.00	W
102	Lightning Swift—William Colt MacDonald	1.00	3.00	5.00	W
103	The Short Night—Russell Turner; 1957	1.00	3.00	5.00	
104	Rimrock Town—William Heuman	1.00	3.00	5.00	W
105	The Watchmaker—Georges Simenon	1.00	3.00	5.00	M
106	Sex Without Guilt—Albert Ellis; 1959	1.00	3.00	5.00	NF
107	The Tormentors—Robert Payne	1.00	3.00	5.00	
108	Roy Bean: Law West of the Pecos—C. L. Sonnichsen	1.00	3.00	5.00	NF
109	Horses, Women and Guns—Nelson Nye	1.00	3.00	5.00	W
110	The Greatest Lover in the World—Alex Austin	1.00	3.00	5.00	
111	Morocco Episode—William Brothers; c-Maguire	1.00	3.00	5.00	M
112	The Sins of Skid Row—John White	1.00	3.00	5.00	
113	Soldier's Women—Stan Smith	1.00	3.00	5.00	
114	Temptation in a Southern Town—William L. Heath	1.00	3.00	5.00	E
115	Dead Warrior—John Myers Myers	1.20	3.60	6.00	
116	A Strange Innocence—Charles Mergendahl	1.00	3.00	5.00	
117	Cassandra—Frances Clippinger	1.00	3.00	5.00	E

Hillman Books 111, © Hill

Hillman Books 114, © Hill

Hillman Detective Novel 1, © Hill

		Good	Fine	N/Mint	
(HILLMAN BOOKS, continued)					
118	The Jayhawkers—Saul Cooper; movie tie-in	1.00	3.00	5.00	W
119	A Killer's Kiss—Hal Ellson	1.00	3.00	5.00	
120	Let's Make Mary—Jack Hanley	1.00	3.00	5.00	
121	The Sinful One—Edwina Mark	1.00	3.00	5.00	
122	Sixgun Helltown—Charles M. Martin; aka Sixgun Town	1.00	3.00	5.00	W
123	Savage Conqueror—Davenport Steward	1.00	3.00	5.00	
124	The Sinful Love—Calvin Turner	1.00	3.00	5.00	
125	Death Is Confidential—Lawrence Lariar	1.00	3.00	5.00	
126	And Then Murder—Julius Fast	1.00	3.00	5.00	
127	Maverick Gun—Barry Cord; aka Gun - Proddy Hombre	1.00	3.00	5.00	W
128	Elisa—Edmond de Goncourt	1.00	3.00	5.00	
129	The Moments Between—Robert Ackworth	1.00	3.00	5.00	
130	The Elvis Presley Story—James Gregory; 1st ed., 1960	6.00	18.00	30.00	B

HILLMAN DETECTIVE NOVEL
Hillman Periodicals, Inc.

		Good	Fine	N/Mint	
1	The Arabian Nights Murder—John Dickson Carr; 1943	5.00	15.00	25.00	M

HIP BOOKS
Hip Books, Inc.

		Good	Fine	N/Mint	
1	The Mystery of the Red Suitcase—Lula M. Day; 1946	5.00	15.00	25.00	M

HOWARD
F. E. Howard Publications

Digest Size

(Canadian)

		Good	Fine	N/Mint	
nn	I Hate You to Death—Keith Edgar; 1944	1.00	3.00	5.00	M
nn	True Mysteries and Murders—anthology	1.00	3.00	5.00	NF
nn	Honduras Double Cross—Keith Edgar	1.00	3.00	5.00	M
nn	The Incendiary Blonde—Keith Edgar	1.00	3.00	5.00	M

THE INFANTRY JOURNAL
The Infantry Journal

		Good	Fine	N/Mint	
J101	Boomerang—William C. Shambliss; 1945	.80	2.40	4.00	A
J102	The U. S. Marines on Iwo Jima; 1945	.80	2.40	4.00	NF

INTIMATE NOVELS
Design Publishing Company

Digest Size

		Good	Fine	N/Mint	
1	Wayward Bride—Paul Gaillard; 1950, aka One Unfaithful Year	1.00	3.00	5.00	E
2	French Model—Cecil Barr; aka Daffodil	.80	2.40	4.00	E
3	Cheap Hotel—Gerald Foster; aka Night Clerk	.80	2.40	4.00	E
4	Plaything—Gordon Semple	.80	2.40	4.00	E
5	Secrets of a Society Doctor—Jerry Cole	.80	2.40	4.00	E
6	Divorce Racket Girls—Jed Anthony	.80	2.40	4.00	E
7	Greenwich Village Girl—Robert Norcross	1.20	3.60	6.00	E
8	Gin Wedding—Ann Lawrence	.80	2.40	4.00	E

Howard nn, © How

Infantry Journal J102, © Infan

Intimate Novels 7, © Design

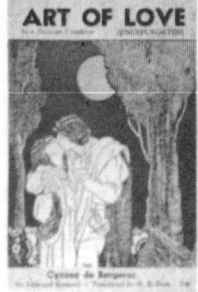

Intimate Novels 32, © Design　　　　Jacket Library nn(1), © NH　　　　Jacket Library nn, © NH

(INTIMATE NOVELS, continued)

		Good	Fine	N/Mint	
9	Temptress—Elliot Brewster	.80	2.40	4.00	E
10	Dangerous Trade—Charles Thornton	.80	2.40	4.00	E
11	Swamp Girl—Perry Lindsay (Peggy Gaddis)	1.20	3.60	6.00	E
12	Seventh Wife—Barry de Forest	.80	2.40	4.00	E
13	Local Talent—Florence Stonebraker	.80	2.40	4.00	E
14	Off Limits—Bruce Manning	.80	2.40	4.00	E
15	Private Chauffeur—N. R. De Mexico	.80	2.40	4.00	E
16	Lust for Love—Florence Stonebraker	.80	2.40	4.00	E
17	The Sins of Janet Benson, Showgirl—Ben West	.80	2.40	4.00	E
18	Hot Lips—Jack Hanley	.80	2.40	4.00	E
19	Mail-Order Passion—Hall Bennett; c-Gross. Note: Same cover as Beacon No. B134	.80	2.40	4.00	E
20	Pleasure Alley—Ralph Carter; orig., 1952. Note: Same cover as Beacon B307 and Falcon No. 43	.80	2.40	4.00	E
21	Dr. Randolph's Women—Thomas Stone	.80	2.40	4.00	E
22	Office Wife—Richard Grant; aka Teaser	.80	2.40	4.00	E
23	Ex-Mistress—Thomas Stone	.80	2.40	4.00	E
24	The Whipping Room—Florenz Branch	1.20	3.60	6.00	E
25	Triangle of Sin—Bruce Manning	.80	2.40	4.00	E
26	Very Private Secretary—Jack Hanley	.80	2.40	4.00	E
27	Tramp Girl—Thomas Stone	.80	2.40	4.00	E
28	Back Country Woman—Evans Wall; aka A Time to Sow	.80	2.40	4.00	E
29	Shameless Wife—Wayne Way	.80	2.40	4.00	E
30	Tent-Show Bride—Jack Hanley	.80	2.40	4.00	E
31	Naked Desire—Henry Lewis Nixon; orig., 1953	.80	2.40	4.00	E
32	Basement Gang—David Williams; orig., 1953. Note: Same cover as Stallion No. 213 and virtually identical to Beacon B260	2.00	6.00	10.00	E
33	Scarlet City—Winchell Barry	.80	2.40	4.00	E
34	Shack Woman—Kathie Keed	.80	2.40	4.00	E
35	Private Practice—Thomas Stone	.80	2.40	4.00	E
36	Waterfront Blonde—Gordon Semple	.80	2.40	4.00	E
37	New York Model—Jack Hanley	.80	2.40	4.00	E
38	Lily of New Orleans—Beth Brown; aka For Men Only	.80	2.40	4.00	E
39	Dr. Breyton's Wife—Florenz Branch	.80	2.40	4.00	E
40	Crusher's Girl—Gordon Semple	.80	2.40	4.00	E
42	Village Girl—Reed	.80	2.40	4.00	E
43	The Marriage Rite—Evans Wall	.80	2.40	4.00	E
44	Miami Widow—	.80	2.40	4.00	E
45	Pound of Flesh—Simms Albert	.80	2.40	4.00	E
47	Red-Headed Nurse—Thomas Stone	.80	2.40	4.00	E
48	Cafe Society Sinner—Bruce Manning; orig., 1953	.80	2.40	4.00	E
49	Strange Circle—Gale Sydney; orig., 1953	.80	2.40	4.00	E
51	Ship's Doctor—Henry Lewis Nixon; orig., 1954	.80	2.40	4.00	E
52	Gutter Star—Dorine B. Clark	.80	2.40	4.00	E
53	Girl Stowaway—Roy Booth	.80	2.40	4.00	E
54	Bachelor Girl—	.80	2.40	4.00	E
55	Secrets of Doctor's Bride—Henry Lewis Nixon	.80	2.40	4.00	E
56	Odd Girl—Hal R. Moore	1.00	3.00	5.00	E

JACKET LIBRARY
National Home Library Foundation

nn(1)	Treasure Island—R. L. Stevenson; 1932	1.60	4.80	8.00	A
nn(2)	The New Testament	1.20	3.60	6.00	
nn(3)	Green Mansions—W. H. Hudson	2.00	6.00	10.00	F
nn(4)	The Way of All Flesh—Samuel Butler	1.20	3.60	6.00	
nn(5)	The Merchant of Venice—William Shakespeare	1.20	3.60	6.00	
nn(6)	Emerson's Essays—Ralph Waldo Emerson	1.20	3.60	6.00	
nn(7)	Pierre Goriot—Honore de Balzac	1.20	3.60	6.00	

(JACKET LIBRARY, continued)

		Good	Fine	N/Mint	
nn(8)	Alice in Wonderland, Through the Looking Glass, Hunting of the Shark—Lewis Carroll	2.00	6.00	10.00	F
nn(9)	The Adventures of Tom Sawyer—Mark Twain	2.00	6.00	10.00	A
nn(10)	Tales of Sherlock Holmes—Arthur Conan Doyle	3.00	9.00	15.00	M
nn(11)	Under the Greenwood Tree—Thomas Hardy	1.20	3.60	6.00	
nn(12)	The Golden Treasury of Song and Verse	1.20	3.60	6.00	
nn(13)	Cyrano de Bergerac—Edmond Rostand; 1933	1.20	3.60	6.00	A
nn(14)	Other People's Money—Louis D. Brandeis	1.20	3.60	6.00	NF
nn	The Art of Love—a Parisian Casanova; Note: Ironically retitled reprint of Cyrano de Bergerac (No. 13).	1.60	4.80	8.00	A

JAMES
C. L. R. James

nn	Mariners, Renegades and Castaways—C. L. R. James; orig., 1953	2.00	6.00	10.00	B

JOE MOSS MYSTERY
Unknown publisher

Digest Size

nn	Murder on Both Sides—Abner Sideman; 1945	1.20	3.60	6.00	M

JONATHAN MYSTERY
The Jonathan Press, Inc.

Digest Size

J 1	The Chinese Orange Mystery—Ellery Queen	.50	1.50	2.50	M
J 2	Too Many Cooks—Rex Stout	.50	1.50	2.50	M
J 3	A Man Lay Dead—Ngaio Marsh	.50	1.50	2.50	M
J 4	The Bowstring Murders—Carter Dickson	.50	1.50	2.50	M
J 5	The French Powder Mystery—Ellery Queen	.50	1.50	2.50	M
J 6	Over My Dead Body—Rex Stout	.50	1.50	2.50	M
J 7	Murder for Christmas—Agatha Christie	.50	1.50	2.50	M
J 8	Maigret Sits It Out—Georges Simenon	.50	1.50	2.50	M
J 9	The Broken Vase—Rex Stout	.50	1.50	2.50	M
J10	Death in the Air—Agatha Christie	.50	1.50	2.50	M
J11	The Red Widow Murders—Carter Dickson	.50	1.50	2.50	M
J12	The Roman Hat Mystery—Ellery Queen	.50	1.50	2.50	M
J13	N or M?—Agatha Christie	.50	1.50	2.50	M
J14	The White Priory Murders—Carter Dickson	.50	1.50	2.50	M
J15	Cordially Invited to Meet Death—Rex Stout	.50	1.50	2.50	M
J16	Murder in Restrospect—Agatha Christie	.50	1.50	2.50	M
J17	The Return of the Continental Op—Dashiell Hammett; 1st ed., 1945	16.50	50.00	80.00	M
J18	Maigret Returns—Georges Simenon	.50	1.50	2.50	M
J19	The Plague Court Murders—Carter Dickson	.50	1.50	2.50	M
J20	Passing Strange—Richard Sale	.50	1.50	2.50	M
J21	Arrow Pointing Nowhere—Elizabeth Daly	.40	1.20	2.00	M
J22	Design for Murder—Percival Wilde	.40	1.20	2.00	M
J23	Black Alibi—Cornell Woolrich	.50	1.50	2.50	M
J24	Lazarus No. 7—Richard Sale	1.00	3.00	5.00	SF
J25	It Walks by Night—John Dickson	.50	1.50	2.50	M
J26	The Riddles of Hildegarde Withers—Stuart Palmer	.50	1.50	2.50	M
J27	Not Quite Dead Enough—Rex Stout	.50	1.50	2.50	M
J28	Jethro Hammer—Michael Venning	.40	1.20	2.00	M

James nn, © C. L. R. James

Jonathan Mystery J17, © Jon

Keep-Worthy Books 3, © KW

		Good	Fine	N/Mint	
J29	Dead Yellow Women—Dashiell Hammett; 1st ed., 1947	16.50	50.00	80.00	M
J30	The Glass Triangle—George Harmon Coxe	.50	1.50	2.50	M
J31	And So to Death—William Irish	.50	1.50	2.50	M
J32	Dancers in Mourning—Margery Allingham	.40	1.20	2.00	M
J33	The League of Frightened Men—Rex Stout	.50	1.50	2.50	M
J34	Dead, Dead Women—Dana Chambers; aka The Case of Caroline Animus	.40	1.20	2.00	M
J35	Build My Gallows High—Geoffrey Homes	.40	1.20	2.00	M
J36	The Big Knockover—Dashiell Hammett; 1948, aka $106,000 Blood Money	2.00	6.00	10.00	M
J37	The Pinball Murders—Thomas B. Black	.40	1.20	2.00	M
J38	The Frightened Man—Dana Chambers	.40	1.20	2.00	M
J39	With Intent to Deceive—Manning Coles	.40	1.20	2.00	M
J40	The Continental Op—Dashiell Hammett	2.00	6.00	10.00	M
J41	The 3-13 Murders—Thomas B. Black	.40	1.20	2.00	M
J42	The Billion Dollar Body—Joseph Shallit	.40	1.20	2.00	M
J43	Darling, This Is Death—Dana Chambers	.40	1.20	2.00	M
J44	Dead Level—Russell Gordon	.40	1.20	2.00	M
J45	The Spider Lily—Bruno Fischer	.50	1.50	2.50	M
J46	The Last Secret—Dana Chambers	.40	1.20	2.00	M
J47	Deadhead—Charles Marquis Warren	.40	1.20	2.00	M
J48	The Creeping Siamese—Dashiell Hammett; 1st ed., 1950	16.50	50.00	80.00	M
J49	Mr. Moto Is So Sorry—John P. Marquand	.40	1.20	2.00	M
J50	Death Against Venus—Dana Chambers	.40	1.20	2.00	M
J51	The Black Angel—Cornell Woolrich	.50	1.50	2.50	M
J52	No Hero—John P. Marquand	.40	1.20	2.00	M
J53	Dangerous Blondes—Kelley Roos; aka If the Shroud Fits	.40	1.20	2.00	M
J54	Ming Yellow—John P. Marquand	.40	1.20	2.00	M
J55	Blood on the Blonde—Dana Chambers; aka Witch's Moon	.40	1.20	2.00	M
J56	Dead Weight—Frank Kane	.40	1.20	2.00	M
J57	Dangerous by Nature—Manning Coles	.40	1.20	2.00	M
J58	The Blonde Died First—Dana Chambers	.40	1.20	2.00	M
J59	Woman in the Dark—Dashiell Hammett; 1st ed., 1951	16.50	50.00	80.00	M
J60	The Blue Ice—Hammond Innes	.40	1.20	2.00	M
J61	The Black Path of Fear—Cornell Woolrich	.50	1.50	2.50	M
J62	Now or Never—Manning Coles	.40	1.20	2.00	M
J63	Rope for an Ape—Dana Chambers	.40	1.20	2.00	M
J64	Bullet Proof—Frank Kane	.40	1.20	2.00	M
J65	The Fifth Grave—Jonathan Latimer	.40	1.20	2.00	M
J66	Die Like a Dog—Frank Gruber; aka The Hungry Dog	.40	1.20	2.00	M
J67	Scared to Death—George Bagby	.40	1.20	2.00	M
J68	Operation Manhunt—Manning Coles; aka Alias Uncle Hugo	.40	1.20	2.00	M
J69	Murder in the Madhouse—Jonathan Latimer	.40	1.20	2.00	M
J70	Kiss for a Killer—Dorothy B. Hughes; aka The Scarlet Imperial	.40	1.20	2.00	M
J71	A Body for the Bride—George Bagby; aka The Original Carcase	.40	1.20	2.00	M
J72	Too Tough to Die—Frank Gruber; aka The Lock and the Key	.40	1.20	2.00	M
J73	Dead Drunk—George Bagby	.40	1.20	2.00	M
J74	All That Glitters—Manning Coles	.40	1.20	2.00	M
J75	Layout for a Corpse—Gene Goldsmith	.40	1.20	2.00	M
J76	Fall Guy for a Killer—Frank Gruber; aka The Yellow Overcoat	.40	1.20	2.00	M
J77	Some Dames Are Deadly—Jonathan Latimer; aka Red Gardenias	.40	1.20	2.00	M
J78	Payoff in Blood—Hal Calin; aka Rocks and Ruin	.40	1.20	2.00	M
J79	Deadly Lure—Whitman Chambers	.40	1.20	2.00	M
J80	Death Rides a Painted Horse—Robert Patrick Wilmot	.40	1.20	2.00	M
J81	Lust to Kill—Edward Lee	.40	1.20	2.00	M
J82	Naked Fear—John Farr; aka Don't Feed the Animals	.40	1.20	2.00	M
J83	Give the Girl a Gun—Richard Deming; aka Whistle Past the Graveyard	.40	1.20	2.00	M
J84	Headed for a Hearse—Jonathan Latimer	.40	1.20	2.00	M
J85	The Long Arm of Murder—Frank Gruber	.40	1.20	2.00	M
J86	Hell Street—Max Franklin	.40	1.20	2.00	M
J87	Death Ain't Commercial—George Bagby	.40	1.20	2.00	M
J88	The Smell of Fear—Spencer Dean; aka The Scent of Fear	.40	1.20	2.00	M
J89	Once Over Deadly—Frank Gruber; aka The French Key Mystery	.40	1.20	2.00	M
J90	The Man in the Green Hat—Manning Coles	.40	1.20	2.00	M
J91	Hand-Picked to Die—Richard Deming; aka Tweak the Devil's Nose	.40	1.20	2.00	M
J92	A Shroud for Mr. Bundy—James M. Fox	.40	1.20	2.00	M
J93	The Basle Express—Manning Coles	.40	1.20	2.00	M
J94	Murder Is Insane—Glenn Barns	.40	1.20	2.00	M
J95	The Long Escape—David Dodge	.40	1.20	2.00	M
J96	Rites for a Killer—James M. Fox; aka The Bright Serpent	.40	1.20	2.00	M

KEEP-WORTHY BOOKS
Keep-Worthy Books, Inc.

		Good	Fine	N/Mint	
1	Twelve of the World's Famous Books—ed. Julius Muller	.50	1.50	2.50	
2	The Scarlet Letter—Nathaniel Hawthorne	.50	1.50	2.50	
3	Twelve of the World's Famous Adventure Books—ed. Julius Muller; 1946	.50	1.50	2.50	A
4	Twelve of the World's Famous Love Novels—ed. Julius Muller	.50	1.50	2.50	R

KNICKERBOCKER
Knickerbocker Publishing Co./Republic Publishing Co.

Digest Size

		Good	Fine	N/Mint	
1	Her First Sin—Jack Woodford	.50	1.50	2.50	E
15	Palm Beach Apartment—Gail Jordan (Peggy Gaddis)	.50	1.50	2.50	E
16	A Touch of Passion—John Saxon	.50	1.50	2.50	E
16	The Lost Virgin—Gail Jordan (Peggy Gaddis)	.50	1.50	2.50	E
24	The Sinful Sisters—Gladys Sloan	.50	1.50	2.50	E
nn	Death Has a Will—Amelia Reynolds Long	.50	1.50	2.50	M
nn	Confessions of a Studio Model—Gladys Sloan; aka Studio Apartment	.50	1.50	2.50	E
nn	Wayward Girl—Carlotta Baker	.50	1.50	2.50	E
nn	Love for Sale—Charles S. Strong	.50	1.50	2.50	E
nn	Pleasure After Hours—Florenz Branch	.50	1.50	2.50	E
nn	The Wife and the Wolf—Lee Jacquin	.50	1.50	2.50	E
nn	Excess Wife—Wright Williams	.50	1.50	2.50	E
nn	Professional Glamour Girl—Gail Jordan (Peggy Gaddis)	.50	1.50	2.50	E
nn	Careless Caresses—Thomas Stone	.50	1.50	2.50	E
nn	Marriage Later—William Arthur	.50	1.50	2.50	E
nn	Made for Love—Gail Jordan (Peggy Gaddis)	.50	1.50	2.50	E
nn	Tavern Girl—Glen Watkins	.50	1.50	2.50	E
nn	Small-Town Virgin—Gail Jordan (Peggy Gaddis)	.50	1.50	2.50	E
nn	A Talent for Love—Thomas Stone	.50	1.50	2.50	E
nn	Her Sacred Sin—H. A. Keller	.50	1.50	2.50	E
nn	Love at a Price—Robert Norcross	.50	1.50	2.50	E
nn	Torrid Love—Ralph Carter; aka Strictly a Wolf	.50	1.50	2.50	E
nn	Blonde Peril—Hall Bennett	.50	1.50	2.50	E
nn	Studio Lovers—Lee Jacquin	.50	1.50	2.50	E
nn	The Hard Boiled Blonde—Glen Watkins	.50	1.50	2.50	E
nn	Immoral Woman—Charles S. Strong	.50	1.50	2.50	E
nn	The Fallen Woman—Carlotta Baker	.50	1.50	2.50	E
nn	Born to Sin—H. L. Gates	.50	1.50	2.50	E
nn	The Wanton Blonde—Gail Jordan (Peggy Gaddis); aka Blonde and Beautiful	.50	1.50	2.50	E
nn	Shameless Woman—Perry Lindsay (Peggy Gaddis)	.50	1.50	2.50	E
nn	Hotel Wife—Glen Watkins	.50	1.50	2.50	E
nn	Her Day of Sin—H. A. Keller	.50	1.50	2.50	E
nn	Boarding House Blonde—Richard Grant	.50	1.50	2.50	E
nn	Two Time Girl—Thomas Stone	.50	1.50	2.50	E
nn	Love on the Run—Gail Jordan (Peggy Gaddis)	.50	1.50	2.50	E
nn	A Room for Love—Griffith James	.50	1.50	2.50	E
nn	Plenty of Love—Eliot Brewster	.50	1.50	2.50	E
nn	A Little Sin—Ralph Carter	.50	1.50	2.50	E
nn	Blonde Venus—Ralph Carter	.50	1.50	2.50	E
nn	Dangerous Loves—Griffith James; aka Ashes of Love	.50	1.50	2.50	E
nn	Carnival Girl—Wright Williams	.50	1.50	2.50	E
nn	Confessions of a Glamour Girl—Gail Jordan (Peggy Gaddis)	.50	1.50	2.50	E
nn	Shameless Woman—Perry Lindsay (Peggy Gaddis)	.50	1.50	2.50	E
nn	Illicit Passion—Carmen Gay; aka Strange Bed	.50	1.50	2.50	E
nn	The Passionate Widow—Perry Lindsay (Peggy Gaddis)	.50	1.50	2.50	E
nn	Once a Sinner—Gail Jordan (Peggy Gaddis)	.50	1.50	2.50	E
nn	Plenty of Love—	.50	1.50	2.50	E
nn	Unfaithful—Florenz Branch; aka This Year's Sin	.50	1.50	2.50	E
nn	Week-end Husband—Gail Jordan (Peggy Gaddis)	.50	1.50	2.50	E
nn	Pick-up Girl—Florenz Branch	.50	1.50	2.50	E
nn	Beautiful Body—Wright Williams	.50	1.50	2.50	E
nn	Forgotten Passion—John Saxon	.50	1.50	2.50	E
nn	The Wanton Blonde—Gail Jordan (Peggy Gaddis)	.50	1.50	2.50	E
nn	Part-Time Passion—Gail Jordan (Peggy Gaddis)	.50	1.50	2.50	E

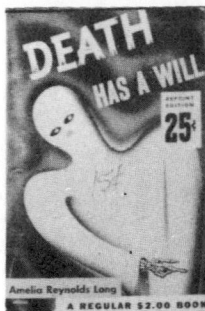

Knickerbocker nn, © Knic

Knickerbocker nn, © Knic

Knickerbocker nn, © Knic

Lancer Books 72-112, © Lancer   Lancer Books 72-125, © Lancer   Lancer Books 72-169, © Lancer

LADDER EDITION
Pocket Books, Inc.

		Good	Fine	N/Mint	
SP-10	My Nine Lives in the Red Army—Mikhael Soloviev; 1957	.80	2.40	4.00	NF

LANCER BOOKS
Lancer Books

		Good	Fine	N/Mint	
72-111	The Fantastic Four—Stan Lee; 1st ed., 1966	1.20	3.60	6.00	A
72-112	The Amazing Spider-Man—Stan Lee, 1st ed., 1966	1.20	3.60	6.00	A
72-124	The Incredible Hulk—Stan Lee; 1st ed., 1966	1.20	3.60	6.00	A
72-125	The Mighty Thor—Stan Lee; 1st ed., 1966	1.20	3.60	6.00	A
72-169	The Fantastic Four Return—Stan Lee; 1st ed., 1967	1.20	3.60	6.00	A

Note: All titles contain reprints from early issues of Marvel comics.

		Good	Fine	N/Mint	
72-732	The Beatle Book; 1964	1.20	3.60	6.00	NF

LARCH
Larch Publications

		Good	Fine	N/Mint	
1	Gag and Cartoon Book	1.00	3.00	5.00	H
2	Joke and Cartoon Book; 1944	1.00	3.00	5.00	H

LEISURE LIBRARY
Leisure Library, Inc.

Digest Size

		Good	Fine	N/Mint	
1	My Life Is My Own—Jules-Jean Morac; c-Heade	3.00	9.00	15.00	E
2	Death for a Doll—Spike Morelli; c-Heade	3.00	9.00	15.00	M
3	Pick-Up Girl—Roland Vane; c-Heade	3.00	9.00	15.00	E
4	Make Mine a Shroud—Michael Storme; c-Heade	3.00	9.00	15.00	M
5	Hot Dames on Cold Slabs—Michael Storme; c-Heade	4.00	12.00	20.00	M
6	No Prude—Jules-Jean Morac	3.00	9.00	15.00	E
7	This Way for Hell—Spike Morelli; 1952, c-Heade	4.00	12.00	20.00	M
8	White Slave Racket—Roland Vane; c-Heade	6.00	18.00	30.00	E
9	Two Smart Dames—Gene Ross; c-Heade	3.00	9.00	15.00	E
10	Midnight Sinner—Paul Renin; c-Heade	3.00	9.00	15.00	E
11	Curtains for Carla—Michael Storme	2.00	6.00	10.00	M

Larch 2, © Larch   Leisure Library 5, © Leisure   Leisure Library 8, © Leisure

(LEISURE LIBRARY, continued)

		Good	Fine	N/Mint	
12	Bertrand and the Blondes—Jules-Jean Morac; 1952, c-Heade	3.00	9.00	15.00	E
13	Sorry for You, Beautiful—Gene Ross; 1952, c-Heade	3.00	9.00	15.00	E
14	Wedding Night—Paul Renin; 1952, c-Heade	3.00	9.00	15.00	E
15	Carmen Was a Virgin—Michael Storme; c-Heade	3.00	9.00	15.00	E
16	Amorous Adventuress—Roland Vane; 1952, c-Heade	2.00	6.00	10.00	E
17	Honey, Hold That Scream!—Tony Angelo; c-Heade	3.00	9.00	15.00	M
18	She Who Hesitates . . . . —Paul Renin; c-Heade	3.00	9.00	15.00	E
19	A Corpse Spells Danger—Michael Storme; 1953	2.00	6.00	10.00	M
20	Pagan Interlude—Rosalind Brett	2.00	6.00	10.00	E
21	Curves Cause Trouble—Gene Ross; 1953, c-Heade	2.00	6.00	10.00	E
22	Thou Shalt Not—Paul Renin	2.00	6.00	10.00	E
23	This Woman Is Death—Michael Storme; c-Heade	3.00	9.00	15.00	M
24	White Man's Slave—Mary Clare; c-Heade	3.00	9.00	15.00	E

LEV GLEASON LIBRARY
Lev Gleason Publications, Inc.

Digest Size

101	Hotel Wife—Ruth Lyons	1.00	3.00	5.00	E
102	Devil-May-Care Girl—John Saxon; aka Something Like Passion	1.00	3.00	5.00	E
103	The Wench Is Willing—Griffith James; 1949	1.00	3.00	5.00	E
104	Passion's Darling—Thomas Stone	1.00	3.00	5.00	E
105	Scandal Girl—Doris Knight; aka Infamous Woman	1.00	3.00	5.00	E
106	Dishonorable Lady—Richard Lee	1.00	3.00	5.00	E

LION
Lion Books, Inc.

(Also see Red Circle)

8	Hungry Men--Edward Anderson; 1949	2.00	6.00	10.00	
9	Anniversary—Ludwig Lewisohn	2.00	6.00	10.00	E
10	Canyon Hell—Peter Dawson; aka High Country	1.60	4.80	8.00	W
11	The Blonde Body—Michael Morgan	2.00	6.00	10.00	M
14	The Lottery—Shirley Jackson	5.00	15.00	25.00	SF
15	Soft Shoulders—Peter Shelley	1.60	4.80	8.00	E
16	The Devil's Daughter—Peter Marsh	2.00	6.00	10.00	E
17	Dust of the Trail—Bennett Foster; 1950	1.60	4.80	8.00	W
18	Christ in Concrete—Pietro di Donato; movie tie-in	1.60	4.80	8.00	
19	He Ran All the Way—Sam Ross	1.60	4.80	8.00	M
20	Gambler's Gun Luck—Brett Austin	1.60	4.80	8.00	W
21	To Keep or Kill—Wilson Tucker	3.00	9.00	15.00	M
22	The French Touch—Jack Iams	1.60	4.80	8.00	
23	Baseball Stars of 1950—Bruce Jacobs; orig., 1950	2.00	6.00	10.00	S
24	Twilight Men—Andre Tellier	1.60	4.80	8.00	
25	The Intimate Stranger—William Lynch; 1950	1.60	4.80	8.00	E
26	The Outward Room—Millen Brand	1.60	4.80	8.00	
27	Dead Man's Gorge—E. B. Mann	1.60	4.80	8.00	W
28	Gun Devil!—W. Edmunds Claussen	1.60	4.80	8.00	W
29	Walk Hard - Talk Loud—Len Zinberg	1.60	4.80	8.00	
30	The Indiscreet Confessions of a Nice Girl—anonymous	1.60	4.80	8.00	E
31	The Small Back Room—Nigel Balchin	1.60	4.80	8.00	E
32	Ceylon—Margaret Rebecca Lay	1.60	4.80	8.00	E
33	The Continental Touch—Josef Wechsberg	1.60	4.80	8.00	
34	Guns of Arizona—Charles N. Heckelmann	1.60	4.80	8.00	W
35	Man Tracks—Bennett Foster	1.60	4.80	8.00	W

Lev Gleason Library 101, © Lev Gleason

Lion 21, © Lion

Lion 28, © Lion

Lion 42, © Lion

Lion 44, © Lion

Lion 53, © Lion

(LION, continued)

		Good	Fine	N/Mint	
36	The Road Through the Wall—Shirley Jackson	2.00	6.00	10.00	M
37	Guns on the Santa Fe—Peter Dawson	1.60	4.80	8.00	W
38	The Lustful Ape—Russell Gray (Bruno Fischer); orig., 1950	3.00	9.00	15.00	
39	Brain Guy—Benjamin Appel	1.20	3.60	6.00	M
40	All Thy Conquests—Alfred Hayes	1.60	4.80	8.00	
41	The Big Night—Stanley Ellin; aka Dreadful Summit	1.60	4.80	8.00	E
42	Spring Riot—Jay Presson	1.20	3.60	6.00	E
43	Massacre—James Warner Bellah	1.60	4.80	8.00	W
44	His Dead Wife—Elizabeth Eastman	1.60	4.80	8.00	
45	Now Sleeps the Beast—Don Tracy	1.60	4.80	8.00	
46	A Slight Case of Scandal—Jack Iams; aka Prematurely Gay	1.20	3.60	6.00	E
47	Trouble Follows Me—Kenneth Millar	1.60	4.80	8.00	M
48	The Dark Tunnel—Kenneth Millar	1.60	4.80	8.00	M
49	All Quiet on the Western Front—Erich Maria Remarque	1.60	4.80	8.00	C
50	Oregon Trunk—Dan J. Stevens; 1951	1.20	3.60	6.00	W
51	Tall, Dark and Dead—Kermit Jaediker	1.20	3.60	6.00	
52	No Letters for the Dead—Gale Wilhelm	1.60	4.80	8.00	E
53	Arena of Love—Helene Eliat	1.60	4.80	8.00	E
54	Joy Street—Clifton Cuthbert	1.60	4.80	8.00	
55	El Paso—W. Edmunds Claussen	1.60	4.80	8.00	W
56	The Glass Lady—Asa Bordages	1.20	3.60	6.00	E
57	Affair—Emily Hahn	1.20	3.60	6.00	
58	Art Colony—Clifton Cuthbert	1.60	4.80	8.00	E
59	Border Woman—Richard Carroll & Gregory Mason; aka Mexican Gallop	1.60	4.80	8.00	W
60	Murders in Silk—Mike Teagle	1.20	3.60	6.00	M
61	Wolf Dog Range—Will Watson	1.20	3.60	6.00	W
62	Blondes Are Skin Deep—Louis Trimble	1.60	4.80	8.00	M
63	Cage Me a Peacock—Noel Langley	1.20	3.60	6.00	E
64	The Savage—Mikhail Artzybasheff	1.20	3.60	6.00	E
65	Killers Five—William Hopson; aka Sunset Ranch	1.20	3.60	6.00	W
66	The Ranch Cat—William Hopson; aka Straight From Boot Hill	1.60	4.80	8.00	E
67	MacArthur - Man of Action—Frank Kelley & Cornelius Ryan	1.20	3.60	6.00	B
68	My Flesh Is Sweet—Day Keene; orig., 1951	1.60	4.80	8.00	E
69	The Cheat—Don Tracy; aka Criss-Cross	1.20	3.60	6.00	E
70	We Too Are Drifting—Gale Wilhelm	1.60	4.80	8.00	E
71	America's Cities of Sin—ed. Noah Sarlat	1.60	4.80	8.00	NF
72	The Tigress—Jeff Bogar; aka Payoff for Paula	1.60	4.80	8.00	E
73	Innocent Madame—Eleanore Browne; 1952	1.20	3.60	6.00	E
74	Either Is Love—Elisabeth Craigin	1.20	3.60	6.00	E
75	Die, Damn You!—Paul Durst	1.60	4.80	8.00	W

Lion 66, © Lion

Lion 70, © Lion

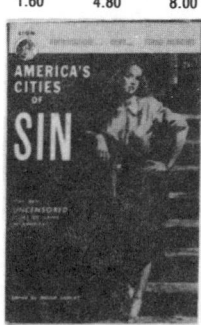

Lion 71, © Lion

(LION, continued)

		Good	Fine	N/Mint	
76	A Walk in the Sun—Harry Brown	1.20	3.60	6.00	C
77	The Lust of Private Cooper—James Gordon	1.20	3.60	6.00	E
78	Nevada Killing—Duke Montana; aka Lynch Law in Perdition	1.20	3.60	6.00	W
79	My Gun, Her Body—Jeff Bogar; aka Dinah for Danger	1.20	3.60	6.00	E
80	Third Ward - Newark—Curtis Lucas	1.20	3.60	6.00	
81	The Lurking Man—Gerald Butler; aka Mad With Much Heart	1.20	3.60	6.00	E
82	War in Korea—Marguerite Higgins	1.20	3.60	6.00	C
83	Bodies Are Dust—P. J. Wolfson	1.20	3.60	6.00	
84	Earth Woman—Edwin J. Becker; aka Coble Hill	1.20	3.60	6.00	E
85	Lie Down, Killer—Richard S. Prather; orig., 1952	1.60	4.80	8.00	M
86	Tough Kid—William Attaway; aka Let Me Breathe Thunder	1.20	3.60	6.00	E
87	You'll Get Yours—Thomas Wills	1.20	3.60	6.00	
88	The Missouri Maiden—C. William Harrison; orig., 1952	1.20	3.60	6.00	
89	Route 28—Ward Greene	1.20	3.60	6.00	E
90	Pistolman—Steve Frazee	1.20	3.60	6.00	W
91	So Low, So Lovely—Curtis Lucas	1.20	3.60	6.00	
92	South Sea Tales—Jack London	1.60	4.80	8.00	A
93	The Big Feeling—Daniel Karp; orig., 1952	1.20	3.60	6.00	E
94	Lona—John Evans; aka If You Have Tears, c-Bergey	1.20	3.60	6.00	E
95	Hell's Kitchen—Benjamin Appel	1.20	3.60	6.00	M
96	Utah Hell Guns—Steve Frazee	1.20	3.60	6.00	W
97	America's Cities of Sin—ed. Noah Sarlat	1.60	4.80	8.00	NF
98	Prelude to a Certain Midnight—Gerald Kersh	1.60	4.80	8.00	
99	The Killer Inside Me—Jim Thompson; orig., 1952	1.60	4.80	8.00	
100	One Is a Lonely Number—Bruce Elliot; c-Bergey	1.20	3.60	6.00	E
101	Joy Street—Clifton Cuthbert	1.20	3.60	6.00	E
102	Bailey's Daughters—John DeMeyer	1.20	3.60	6.00	E
103	Eat Dog or Die!—C. William Harrison	1.20	3.60	6.00	W
104	Little Killer—Gene Paul; orig., 1952	1.20	3.60	6.00	
105	The Brotherhood of Velvet—David Karp	1.20	3.60	6.00	E
106	Sintown, U. S. A.—Noah Sarlat	1.60	4.80	8.00	E
107	Candide—Voltaire	1.20	3.60	6.00	
108	Cropper's Cabin—Jim Thompson; orig., 1952	1.60	4.80	8.00	E
109	The Naked Storm—Simon Eisner (C. M. Kornbluth)	6.00	18.00	30.00	E
110	The Peddlers—Douglas Ring	1.20	3.60	6.00	
111	Company K—William March	1.20	3.60	6.00	C
112	The Man I Killed—Shel Walker	1.20	3.60	6.00	E
113	The Montana Vixen—Paul W. Fairman; aka The Heiress of Copper Butte	1.20	3.60	6.00	W
114	Luther—Roy Flannagan	1.60	4.80	8.00	E
115	Cora Potts—Ward Greene	1.20	3.60	6.00	E
116	Saskia—Claude Marais	1.20	3.60	6.00	E
117	Run the Wild River—D. L. Champion; 1953	1.20	3.60	6.00	
118	The Haploids—Jerry Sohl	1.60	4.80	8.00	SF
119	Hardman—David Karp; orig., 1953	1.20	3.60	6.00	
120	Recoil—Jim Thompson; orig., 1953	1.60	4.80	8.00	
121	The Strange Path—Gale Wilhelm	1.60	4.80	8.00	E
122	Life and Death in Soviet Russia—El Campesino (Valentin Gonzalez & Julian Gorkin)	1.20	3.60	6.00	NF
123	Don't Dig Deeper—William Francis	1.20	3.60	6.00	E
124	The Burglar—David Goodis; orig., 1953	1.60	4.80	8.00	M
125	Baseball Stars of 1953—Bruce Jacobs; orig., 1953	1.60	4.80	8.00	S
126	Mojave Guns—Roe Richmond	1.20	3.60	6.00	W
127	The Alcoholics—Jim Thompson; orig., 1953	1.60	4.80	8.00	
128	His Great Journey—Manuel Komroff	1.20	3.60	6.00	
129	.44—J. A. DeRosso	1.20	3.60	6.00	W
130	Sharp the Bugle Calls—Steve Frazee; orig., 1953	1.20	3.60	6.00	W
131	Bourbon Street—G. H. Otis; orig., 1953	1.20	3.60	6.00	M
132	Cry, Flesh—David Karp	1.20	3.60	6.00	E
133	The Dark Chase—David Goodis; aka Nightfall	1.20	3.60	6.00	M

Lion 82, © Lion

Lion 116, © Lion

Lion 125, © Lion

Lion 137, © Lion

Lion 147, © Lion

Lion 179, © Lion

(LION, continued)

		Good	Fine	N/Mint	
134	Colorado Creek—E. E. Halleran	1.20	3.60	6.00	W
135	Half—Jordan Park (C. M. Kornbluth); orig., 1953	6.00	18.00	30.00	E
136	Fighting Man—Mark Morgan	1.20	3.60	6.00	
137	Someone Is Bleeding—Richard Matheson; orig., 1953	6.00	18.00	30.00	M
138	Dark the Summer Dies—Walter Untermeyer, Jr.; orig., 1953	1.20	3.60	6.00	E
139	Gunman's Grudge—George C. Appell	1.20	3.60	6.00	W
140	Cockpit—Warwick Scott	1.20	3.60	6.00	
141	Rooming House—Berton Roueche; aka Black Weather	1.20	3.60	6.00	E
142	''I Was There''—Ken Jones; orig., 1953	1.20	3.60	6.00	NF
143	The Wild Bunch—Peter Dawson	1.20	3.60	6.00	W
144	A Tent on Corsica—Martin Quigley	1.20	3.60	6.00	
145	Malenkov—Robert Frazier; orig., 1953	1.20	3.60	6.00	NF
146	Frankenstein—Mary Wollstonecraft Shelley	5.00	15.00	25.00	SF
147	The Wench and the Flame—Robert L. Timnell	1.20	3.60	6.00	
148	Doomsday—Warwick Scott; orig., 1953	1.60	4.80	8.00	SF
149	Bad Boy—Jim Thompson; orig., 1953	1.60	4.80	8.00	
150	Lawman's Feud—Steve Frazee	1.20	3.60	6.00	W
151	Slaughter Street—Louis Falstein; orig., 1953	1.20	3.60	6.00	E
152	A Rage at Sea—Frederick Lorenz; orig., 1953	1.20	3.60	6.00	E
153	Tough Guy—A. I. Bezzerides; aka Long Haul	1.20	3.60	6.00	
154	Naked in the Dark—Gene Paul	1.20	3.60	6.00	E
155	Savage Night—Jim Thompson; orig., 1953	1.60	4.80	8.00	
156	Hero's Lust—Kermit Jaedicker	1.20	3.60	6.00	
157	The Lone Gunhawk—Frank Gruber	1.20	3.60	6.00	W
158	The Utah Kid—Roe Richmond	1.20	3.60	6.00	W
159	Sin People—George Milburn; aka Oklahoma Town	1.20	3.60	6.00	E
160	Sexual Practices of American Women—Christopher Gerould; orig., 1953	1.60	4.80	8.00	NF
161	The Hoodlum—Eleazar Lipsky	1.20	3.60	6.00	
162	Angel—Curtis Lucas	1.20	3.60	6.00	
163	Gunsight—Frank Gruber	1.20	3.60	6.00	W
164	Platoon—Adam Singer	1.20	3.60	6.00	
165	The Big Lure—William Manners	1.20	3.60	6.00	
166	Dock Walloper—Benjamin Appel	1.20	3.60	6.00	M
167	Every Man's Bible—Manuel Komroff	1.20	3.60	6.00	
168	Killer's Crossing—Burt Arthur	1.20	3.60	6.00	W
169	The Gunslammer—Lee Floren	1.20	3.60	6.00	W
170	Sailor's Luck—Basil Heatter	1.20	3.60	6.00	
171	Hot Cargo—Gitt Otis	1.20	3.60	6.00	
172	Korea's Heroes—Bruce Jacobs	1.20	3.60	6.00	NF
173	The Dream and the Flesh—Vivian Connell; aka The Peacock Is a Gentleman	1.00	3.00	5.00	
174	The Corrupters—William Francis; orig., 1953	1.20	3.60	6.00	E
175	The Gun Trail—H. A. DeRosso	1.20	3.60	6.00	W
176	Valerie—Jordan Park (C. M. Kornbluth); orig., 1953, c-Maguire	6.00	18.00	30.00	E
177	Men and Women—William Kozlenko; orig., 1953	1.20	3.60	6.00	
178	Bloody River—Paul Durst	1.20	3.60	6.00	W
179	Conjure Wife—Fritz Leiber; c-Maguire	5.00	15.00	25.00	F
180	Fury on Sunday—Richard Matheson; orig., 1953	6.00	18.00	30.00	
181	The Oxbow Kill—C. William Harrison	1.20	3.60	6.00	
182	O'Mara—Laurence Greene	1.20	3.60	6.00	
183	Trouble on Crazyman—Sam Allison	1.20	3.60	6.00	W
184	The Criminal—Jim Thompson; orig., 1953	1.60	4.80	8.00	M
185	The Kidnapper—Robert Bloch; orig., 1954	5.00	15.00	25.00	
186	The Blonde on the Street Corner—David Goodis; orig., 1954	1.60	4.80	8.00	
187	The Dakota Deal—Riley Ryan	1.20	3.60	6.00	W
188	The Naked Year—Philip Atlee; aka The Inheritors	1.20	3.60	6.00	E
189	Two-Gun Texan—Burt Arthur	1.20	3.60	6.00	W
190	The Joy Wheel—Paul W. Fairman	1.00	3.00	5.00	
191	Strange Desires—J. Vernon Shea	1.20	3.60	6.00	

Lion 192, © Lion

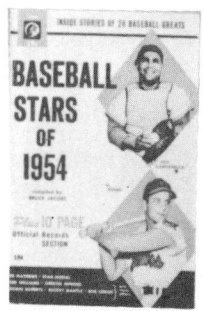

Lion 194, © Lion

Lion 196, © Lion

(LION, continued)

		Good	Fine	N/Mint	
192	The Golden Gizmo—Jim Thompson; orig., 1954	1.60	4.80	8.00	
193	Night Never Ends—Frederick Lorenz	1.20	3.60	6.00	
194	Baseball Stars of 1954—Bruce Jacobs; orig., 1954	1.60	4.80	8.00	S
195	Apache Greed—William Hopson	1.20	3.60	6.00	W
196	A Dog's Head—Jean Dutourd	2.00	6.00	10.00	F
197	The Naked Night—Dan Brennan	1.60	4.80	8.00	
198	Sin Pit—Paul Meskil	1.20	3.60	6.00	
199	Ambush Hell—George C. Appell	1.20	3.60	6.00	W
200	The Long Thrill—Olga Rosmanith; orig., 1954	1.20	3.60	6.00	
201	Roughneck—Jim Thompson; orig., 1954	1.60	4.80	8.00	
202	Hoboes and Harlots—George Milburn; orig., 1954	1.20	3.60	6.00	E
203	Whip Hand—Rod Patterson	1.20	3.60	6.00	W
204	Sleep With the Devil—Day Keene; orig., 1954	1.60	4.80	8.00	E
205	Human?—Judith Merril	2.00	6.00	10.00	SF
206	Alley Girl—Jonathan Craig; orig., 1954	1.20	3.60	6.00	M
207	Tiger Street—Elleston Treror	1.20	3.60	6.00	
208	Win - or Else!—D. J. Michael; orig., 1954	1.20	3.60	6.00	S
209	A Way With Women—William Gwinn	1.20	3.60	6.00	
210	Joy House—Day Keene; orig., 1954	1.60	4.80	8.00	
211	Boss Man—Roy B. Sparkia	1.20	3.60	6.00	E
212	A Swell-Looking Babe—Jim Thompson; orig., 1954	1.60	4.80	8.00	
213	Stag Gag—Sandy Nelkin & Pat Untermeyer	1.20	3.60	6.00	H
214	Fully Dressed and in His Right Mind—Michael Fessier	1.60	4.80	8.00	SF
215	Strange Sisters—Fletcher Flora	1.60	4.80	8.00	
216	Dormitory Women—R. V. Cassill	1.60	4.80	8.00	E
217	The Gunthrowers—Steve Frazee	1.20	3.60	6.00	W
218	A Hell of a Woman—Jim Thompson; orig., 1954	1.60	4.80	8.00	
219	Wharf Girl—William Manners	1.20	3.60	6.00	
220	Me an' You—Jay Thomas Caldwell	1.20	3.60	6.00	
221	The Naked and the Lost—Franklin M. Davis, Jr.	1.20	3.60	6.00	
222	Evil Roots—Walter Untermeyer, Jr.; orig., 1954	1.20	3.60	6.00	E
223	The Savage Chase—Frederick Lorenz; orig., 1954	1.20	3.60	6.00	
224	Black Friday—David Goodis; orig., 1954	1.60	4.80	8.00	M
225	Jazz Bum—William Gwinn	1.20	3.60	6.00	
226	Tina—Robert Bruce	1.20	3.60	6.00	E
227	Sinner's Game—Linton Baldwin	1.20	3.60	6.00	E
228	Act of Violence—Basil Heatter	1.20	3.60	6.00	
229	Champs and Bums—Bucklin Moon	1.20	3.60	6.00	
230	False Night—Algis Budrys	2.00	6.00	10.00	SF
231	House of Evil—Clayre Lipman & Michel Lipman	1.20	3.60	6.00	E

Lion 214, © Lion

Lion 216, © Lion

Lion 233, © Lion

Lion Library LL1, © Lion

Lion Library LL6, © Lion

Lion Library LL8, © Lion

		Good	Fine	N/Mint	
(LION, continued)					
232	Room for a Stranger—Constantine Fitzgibbon; 1955	1.20	3.60	6.00	
233	The Deluge—Leonardo da Vinci (ed. Robert Payne)	2.00	6.00	10.00	SF

LION LIBRARY/LION BOOK
Lion Books, Inc.

		Good	Fine	N/Mint	
LL 1	Number One—John Dos Passos; 1954	1.00	3.00	5.00	
LL 2	A Woman's Life—Guy de Maupassant	1.00	3.00	5.00	
LL 3	The Sky Block—Steve Frazee	1.20	3.60	6.00	SF
LL 4	The Flesh Baron—P. J. Wolfson; aka Is My Flesh of Brass	1.00	3.00	5.00	
LL 5	The Sin and the Flesh—Lloyd S. Thompson	1.00	3.00	5.00	
LL 6	The Damned—Daniel Talbot	1.20	3.60	6.00	
LL 7	The Green Millenium—Fritz Leiber	1.60	4.80	8.00	SF
LL 8	Gods and Demons—Manuel Komroff	1.00	3.00	5.00	
LL 9	Passage to Violence—Stetson Kennedy; orig., 1954	1.00	3.00	5.00	
LL10	Escape to Nowhere—David Karp; 1955	1.00	3.00	5.00	SF
LL11	Dark Plunder—Victor Rosen	1.00	3.00	5.00	E
LL12	Baseball Stars of 1955—Bruce Jacobs; orig., 1955	1.20	3.60	6.00	S
LL13	Hell's Pavement—Damon Knight	1.60	4.80	8.00	SF
LL14	Lila—Curtis Lucas; orig., 1955	1.00	3.00	5.00	E
LL15	The Unleashed Will—Christopher Clark	1.00	3.00	5.00	E
LL16	The Passionate Season—Victor Wolfson	1.00	3.00	5.00	
LL17	The Best Cartoons From France—Edna Bennett	1.20	3.60	6.00	H
LL18	The Lost Men—Benedict Thielen	1.00	3.00	5.00	
LL19	The Hills Beyond—Thomas Wolfe	1.00	3.00	5.00	
LL20	Net of Outrage—William Derby	1.00	3.00	5.00	
LL21	How I Made a Million—Noah Sarlat	1.00	3.00	5.00	
LL22	The Wild Place—Bogart Carlaw	1.00	3.00	5.00	
LL23	How Like a God—Rex Stout	1.60	4.80	8.00	
LL24	For Stags Only—Sandy Nelkin & Pat Untermeyer, Jr.	1.00	3.00	5.00	H
LL25	Galaxy of Ghouls—Judith Merril	2.00	6.00	10.00	SF
LL26	The Stork Didn't Bring You—Louis Pemberton	1.00	3.00	5.00	NF
LL27	A Mask of Guilt—Sigrid de Lima	1.00	3.00	5.00	
LL28	Don't You Weep, Don't You Moan—Richard Coleman	1.00	3.00	5.00	
LL29	Curve Ball Laughs—Herman L. Masin; orig., 1955	1.00	3.00	5.00	SH
LL30	Great Tales of the Deep South	1.00	3.00	5.00	
LL31	Nineteen Stories—Graham Green	1.00	3.00	5.00	
LL32	Whipsaw—William MacLeod Raine	1.00	3.00	5.00	W
LL33	The Storm and the Silence—David Walker	1.00	3.00	5.00	
LL34	The Tunnel of Love—Peter DeVries	1.00	3.00	5.00	

Lion Library LL12, © Lion

Lion Library LL25, © Lion

Lion Book LB152, © Lion

		Good	Fine	N/Mint	
LL35	The Fall of Valor—Charles Jackson	1.00	3.00	5.00	
LL36	Oregon Trunk—Dan J. Stevens	1.00	3.00	5.00	
LL37	Fruit of Desire—Willa Gibbs	1.00	3.00	5.00	
LL38	Cartoons the French Way—Rene Goscinny	1.20	3.60	6.00	H
LL39	Parent's Magazine Book of Baby Care—Eleanor S. Duncan	.80	2.40	4.00	NF
LL40	Trouble Follows Me—Kenneth Millar	1.00	3.00	5.00	E
LL41	Collision—James Gordon	1.00	3.00	5.00	
LL42	Adventures of a Young Man—John Dos Passos	.80	2.40	4.00	
LL43	The Kid From Dodge City—Bennett Foster	1.00	3.00	5.00	W
LL44	Desperate Asylum—Fletcher Flora	1.00	3.00	5.00	
LL45	The Night Before Dying—Robert M. Coates	1.00	3.00	5.00	
LL46	The Flesh Painter—Ad Gordon; orig., 1955, c-Gauguin	1.20	3.60	6.00	B
LL47	Strange Barriers—J. Vernon Shea	1.20	3.60	6.00	
LL48	The Naked and the Guilty—Ralph Ingersoll	1.00	3.00	5.00	
LL49	The Outward Room—Miller Brand	1.00	3.00	5.00	
LL50	Roberta Cowell's Story—Roberta Cowell	1.60	4.80	8.00	
LL51	Hungry Men—Edward Anderson	1.00	3.00	5.00	
LL52	I Die Slowly—Kenneth Millar	1.00	3.00	5.00	
LL53	Great Tales of City Dwellers—Alex Austin; c-Maguire	1.00	3.00	5.00	
LL54	The Wild Breed—Frank Bonham	1.00	3.00	5.00	
LL55	Cora Potts—Ward Green	1.00	3.00	5.00	
LL56	Love—William Saroyan	1.00	3.00	5.00	
LL57	Ramrod—George C. Appell	1.00	3.00	5.00	W
LL58	The Saturday Evening Post Cartoons—John Bailey	1.20	3.60	6.00	H
LL59	He Ran All the Way—Sam Ross	1.00	3.00	5.00	
LL60	The Sins of Joy Monson—Ludwig Lewisohn	1.00	3.00	5.00	
LB61	Leashed Guns—Peter Dawson	1.00	3.00	5.00	W
LB62	Company K—William March	1.00	3.00	5.00	
LL63	A Party Everynight—Frederick Lorenz; 1956	1.00	3.00	5.00	
LL64	Kill the Beloved—Lane Kauffmann; aka The Perfectionist	1.00	3.00	5.00	M
LL65	Two Thieves—Manuel Komroff	1.00	3.00	5.00	
LL66	The Naked Year—Philip Atlee	1.00	3.00	5.00	
LL67	Pius XII: Eugenio Pacelli, Pope of Peace—Oscar Haleck & James F. Murray, Jr.	1.00	3.00	5.00	B
LL68	All Thy Conquests—Alfred Hayes	1.00	3.00	5.00	
LB69	Utah Hell Guns—Steve Frazee	1.00	3.00	5.00	W
LB70	Fighting Man—Mark Morgan	1.00	3.00	5.00	E
LL71	Cage Me a Peacock—Noel Langley	1.00	3.00	5.00	
LL72	Gunman's Land	1.00	3.00	5.00	W
LL73	A Handful of Hell—Noah Sarlat	1.00	3.00	5.00	
LL74	Baseball Stars of 1956—Bruce Jacobs; orig., 1956	1.00	3.00	5.00	S
LL75	Joy Street—Clifton Cuthbert	1.00	3.00	5.00	E
LL76	The Heart in Exile—Rodney Garland	1.00	3.00	5.00	
LB77	Tough Kid—William Attaway; aka Let Me Breathe Thunder	1.00	3.00	5.00	E
LB78	Pistolman—Steve Frazee	1.00	3.00	5.00	W
LL79	Slade—Ad Gordpn	1.00	3.00	5.00	
LL80	Art Buchwald's Paris—Art Buchwald	1.00	3.00	5.00	
LL81	All Quiet on the Western Front—Erich Maria Remarque	1.00	3.00	5.00	C
LL82	Julie—George Milburn	1.00	3.00	5.00	
LL83	Rogues and Lovers—Noah Sarlat	1.00	3.00	5.00	E
LL84	To Keep or Kill—Wilson Tucker; c-Maguire	1.20	3.60	6.00	M
LB85	Two-Gun Texan—Burt Arthur	1.00	3.00	5.00	W
LB86	The Girl on Crown Street—David Karp	1.00	3.00	5.00	
LB87	The Brass Bed—Fletcher Flora	1.00	3.00	5.00	
LL88	Great Tales of the Far West—Alex Austin	1.00	3.00	5.00	
LL89	The Gunslingers—Harry Widmer	1.00	3.00	5.00	W
LL90	Around the World in 80 Days—Jules Verne	1.00	3.00	5.00	A
LL91	A Knife Is Silent—David Keaf	1.00	3.00	5.00	M
LB92	Lonely Boy Blues—Allan Kapelner	1.00	3.00	5.00	
LB93	Gunsight—Frank Gruber	1.00	3.00	5.00	W
LB94	Luther—Roy Flannagan	1.20	3.60	6.00	
LL95	Stories for Stags—Eddie Davis	1.00	3.00	5.00	H
LL96	Kiss Her Goodbye—Wade Miller	1.00	3.00	5.00	M
LL97	Sorority House—Jordan Park (C. M. Kornbluth & Frederick Pohl)	4.00	12.00	20.00	E
LL98	Art Colony—Clifton Cuthbert	1.00	3.00	5.00	E
LB99	French and Frisky—Rene Goscinny	1.20	3.60	6.00	H
LB100	Gun Hell—Riley Ryan	1.00	3.00	5.00	W
LB101	The Utah Kid—Roe Richmond; aka Conestoga Cowboy	1.00	3.00	5.00	W
LL102	The Oracle—Edwin O'Connor	1.00	3.00	5.00	
LL103	Sports Laughs—Herman Le Masin; orig., 1956, c-Powers	1.00	3.00	5.00	SH
LL104	Ruby—Frederick Lorenz	1.00	3.00	5.00	
LL105	Bedtime Laughs—Paul Steiner	1.00	3.00	5.00	H
LL106	House of Dolls—Ka-tzetnik 135633	1.20	3.60	6.00	NF
LB107	Candide—Voltaire	1.00	3.00	5.00	
LB108	Lawman's Feud—Steve Frazee	1.00	3.00	5.00	W
LB109	Platoon—Adam Singer	1.00	3.00	5.00	
LL110	His Great Journey—Manuel Komroff	1.00	3.00	5.00	

		Good	Fine	N/Mint	
LL111	Wives and Lovers—Alex Austin	1.00	3.00	5.00	
LL112	The Dream and the Flesh—Vivian Connell	1.00	3.00	5.00	
LL113	World So Wide—Sinclair Lewis	1.00	3.00	5.00	
LL114	Quintet—W. Somerset Maugham	1.00	3.00	5.00	
LB115	Paula—Gale Wilhelm; aka No Letters for the Dead	1.20	3.60	6.00	
LB116	Alley Kids—Benjamin Appel; aka Hell's Kitchen	1.00	3.00	5.00	E
LB117	The Lone Gunhawk—Frank Gruber; aka Smoky Road	1.00	3.00	5.00	W
LL118	The Cheat—Don Tracy	1.00	3.00	5.00	
LL119	College Humor—Sandy Nelkin	1.00	3.00	5.00	H
LL120	My Old Man—Richard B. Erno	1.00	3.00	5.00	
LL121	Desire and Damnation—William March; aka Come in at the Door	1.00	3.00	5.00	
LB122	Either Is Love—Elisabeth Craigin	1.00	3.00	5.00	
LB123	The Oxbow Kill—C. William Harrison	1.00	3.00	5.00	
LB124	Recoil—Jim Thompson; c-Maguire	1.20	3.60	6.00	
LL125	The Naked Storm—Simon Eisner (C. M. Kornbluth)	3.00	9.00	15.00	
LB126	Gil Paust's Gun Book—Gil Paust	1.00	3.00	5.00	NF
LL127	Combat!—Noah Sarlat	1.00	3.00	5.00	C
LL128	The Troubled Midnight—Rodney Garland	1.00	3.00	5.00	
LB129	You'll Get Yours—Thomas Wills	1.00	3.00	5.00	
LB130	The Hardboiled Lineup—ed. Harry Widmer	1.60	4.80	8.00	
LB131	Nightfall—David Goodis; aka The Dark Chase	1.20	3.60	6.00	M
LB132	Logan—Evan Hall; aka Colorado Creek	1.00	3.00	5.00	
LL133	Rooming House—Berton Roueche	1.00	3.00	5.00	
LL134	Raft of Despair—Ensio Tiira	1.00	3.00	5.00	A
LL135	The Big Rape—James Wakefield Burke	1.00	3.00	5.00	
LL136	Leave Her to Heaven—Ben Ames Williams	1.00	3.00	5.00	
LL137	Killer's Game—Edward Hudiburg	1.00	3.00	5.00	
LB138	A Hell of a Woman—Jim Thompson	1.20	3.60	6.00	
LB139	Bloody River—Paul Durst	1.00	3.00	5.00	W
LL140	Bachelor's Anonymous—Vivian Connell	1.00	3.00	5.00	
LL141	Women Without Men—Alex Austin	1.00	3.00	5.00	
LL142	The Kill-Off—Jim Thompson; orig., 1957	1.60	4.80	8.00	
LL143	Thread of Evil—Charles Jackson	1.00	3.00	5.00	
LB144	Hot—Frederick Lorenz	1.00	3.00	5.00	
LB145	.44—H. A. DeRosso	1.00	3.00	5.00	W
LL146					
LB147	The Naked Night—Dan Brennan; 1957	1.20	3.60	6.00	
LL148	The Bedside Corpse—Stuart Friedman; aka The Gray Eyes	.80	2.40	4.00	M
LL149	A Killer Among Us—Ben Ames Williams	1.00	3.00	5.00	M
LL150	Baseball Stars of 1957—Bruce Jacobs; orig., 1957	1.00	3.00	5.00	S
LL151	Brain Guy—Benjamin Appel	1.00	3.00	5.00	
LB152	Dolls Are Murder—Harold Q. Masur	1.60	4.80	8.00	M
LB153	Valerie—Jordan Park (C. M. Kornbluth)	1.00	3.00	5.00	E
LB154	The Man From Texas—H. A. DeRosso; aka The Gun Trail	1.00	3.00	5.00	W
LL155	The Gun-Hung Men—Leslie Ernenwein; aka Rio Renegade	1.00	3.00	5.00	W
LB156	Hangtree Range—William Hopson	1.00	3.00	5.00	W
LB157	Wyoming War—Sam Allison; aka Trouble on Crazyman	1.00	3.00	5.00	W
LB158	The Big Make—Gene Paul; c-Maguire	1.00	3.00	5.00	
LL159					
LL160	Hoboes and Harlots—George Milburn	1.00	3.00	5.00	
LL161	Gunman's Grudge—George C. Appell	1.00	3.00	5.00	W
LL162					
LB163	LaSignora—Elio Bartolini	1.00	3.00	5.00	E
LB164	Whip Hard—Rod Patterson	1.00	3.00	5.00	W
LB165	A Rage at Sea—Frederick Lorenz	1.00	3.00	5.00	
LL166					
LL167	This Is It!—Noah Sarlat; c-Maguire	1.00	3.00	5.00	
LL168	The Bedside Bachelor—Paul Steiner	1.00	3.00	5.00	H
LL169					
LL170	The Red Lily—Anatole France	1.00	3.00	5.00	
LB171	The Sleeper—Holly Roth	1.00	3.00	5.00	
LB172	Slaughter Street—Louis Falstein; c-Maguire	1.00	3.00	5.00	
LB173	The Gunthrowers—Steve Frazee	1.00	3.00	5.00	W
LL174	The Seventh Trumpet—Peter Julian	1.00	3.00	5.00	
LL175	Five Who Vanished—Robert Levin	1.00	3.00	5.00	

LOVE ROMANCE SERIES
Palace Promotions

Digest Size

		Good	Fine	N/Mint	
11	Faithfully Yours—Eliot Brewster; c-Cole. Note: Although No. 11 is on the spine, No. 2 is on the cover	1.60	4.80	8.00	E
12	Love Above All—Eliot Brewster; c-Cole. Note: Although No. 12 is on the spine, No. 3 is on the cover	1.60	4.80	8.00	R

LUCOM
David Lucom, Publishers

Digest Size

		Good	Fine	N/Mint	
nn	The Case of the Walking Corpse—Armstrong Livingston; 1945	1.60	4.80	8.00	M

MACFADDEN BOOKS
MacFadden-Bartell Corporation

		Good	Fine	N/Mint	
50-114	Tops in Pops Plus a Rock 'n' Roll Roundup—Steve Kahn; orig., 1961	1.20	3.60	6.00	NF
50-159	The Executives Comic Book—Harvey Kurtzman & Will Elder; 1st ed., 1962.				
	Note: Comic story reprints from Help magazine..........................	1.60	4.80	8.00	H
50-210	All About the Beatles—Edward De Blasio; 1st ed., 1964	2.00	6.00	10.00	NF

MAGABOOKS
Galaxy Publishing Corporation

Digest Size

		Good	Fine	N/Mint	
1	Badge of Infamy				SF
	The Sky Is Falling—Lester del Rey	1.00	3.00	5.00	SF
2	After Worlds End				SF
	The Legion of Time—Jack Williamson.....................................	1.00	3.00	5.00	SF
3	Baby Is Three				SF
	. . .and My Fear Is Great—Theodore Sturgeon	1.00	3.00	5.00	SF

MAGAZINE VILLAGE
Magazine Village, Inc.

Digest Size

		Good	Fine	N/Mint	
5	Confessions of a Park Avenue Playgirl—Carl Sturdy; aka Society Doctor	1.00	3.00	5.00	E
6	Illicit Honeymoon—Lois Bull; 1948, aka Seven Make a Honeymoon	1.00	3.00	5.00	E
7	Hard Boiled Mistress—Lois Bull; 1948, aka Mating Woman. Note: Cover gives				
	E. T. Keating as author.	1.00	3.00	5.00	E

MANHATTAN
Manhattan Fiction Publishing

Digest Size

		Good	Fine	N/Mint	
nn	Harem Nights—B. J. Vaswani; 1947	1.20	3.60	6.00	E

MENTOR BOOKS
New American Library

		Good	Fine	N/Mint	
M26	American Essays—Charles B. Shaw; 1948.................................	.40	1.20	2.00	
M27	Biography of the Earth—George Gamow	.40	1.20	2.00	NF
M28	Science and the Modern World—Alfred North Whitehead	.30	.90	1.50	NF
M29	The Autobiography of an Ex-Coloured Man—James Weldon Johnson	.50	1.50	2.50	
M30	American in Perspective—Henry Steele Commager	.30	.90	1.50	
M31	Man in the Modern World—Julian Huxley.................................	.30	.90	1.50	
M32	The Greek Way to Western Civilization—Edith Hamilton	.40	1.20	2.00	NF
M33	Indians of the Americas—John Collier	.50	1.50	2.50	NF

Love Romance Series 11, © Palace

MacFadden Books 50-159, © MacFadden

Mentor Books M33, © New

		Good	Fine	N/Mint	
M34	The Law and You—Max Radin	.30	.90	1.50	NF
M35	The Limitations of Science—J. W. N. Sullivan; 1949	.30	.90	1.50	NF
M36	How to Know the Birds—Roger Tory Peterson	.50	1.50	2.50	NF
M37	Russia—Bernard Pares	.40	1.20	2.00	NF
	with dust jacket	6.00	18.00	30.00	
M38	The Age of Jackson—Arthur M. Schlesinger, Jr.	.40	1.20	2.00	NF
M39	Life on Other Worlds—H. Spencer Jones	.40	1.20	2.00	
M40	Arts and the Man—Irwin Edman	.40	1.20	2.00	NF
M41	The Aims of Education—Alfred North Whitehead	.30	.90	1.50	NF
M42	Ballet—George Amberg; aka Ballet in America	.40	1.20	2.00	NF
M43	Science and the Moral Life—Max Otto	.40	1.20	2.00	NF
M44	The Coming of Age in Samoa—Margaret Mead	.40	1.20	2.00	NF
M45	Beethoven—J. W. N. Sullivan	.40	1.20	2.00	B
M46	The Iliad—Homerus; 1950	.50	1.50	2.50	
M47	Music for the Millions—David Ewen	.40	1.20	2.00	NF
M48	How to Know the Wild Flowers—Alfred Stefferud	.50	1.50	2.50	NF
M49	The Revolt of the Masses—Jose Ortega y Gasset	.40	1.20	2.00	
M50	The Next Development in Man—Lancelot Law White; 1950	.40	1.20	2.00	
M51	The Oregon Trail—Francis Parkman	.50	1.50	2.50	W
M52	New Handbook of the Heavens—Hubert J. Bernhard	.40	1.20	2.00	NF
M53	Reconstruction in Philosophy—John Dewey	.40	1.20	2.00	NF
M54	100 Modern Poems—Selden Rodman	.40	1.20	2.00	
M55	Life Stories of Men Who Shaped History—Plutarchus	.40	1.20	2.00	B
M56	Sex and Temperament in Three Primitive Societies—Margaret Mead	.40	1.20	2.00	NF
M57	Lenia—David Shub	.40	1.20	2.00	B
M58	Introduction to Economic Science—George Soule; 1951	.30	.90	1.50	NF
M59	The Democratic Way of Life—Eduard C. Lindeman & T. V. Smith	.40	1.20	2.00	NF
M60	The Summing Up—W. Somerset Maugham	.40	1.20	2.00	
M61	A Gallery of Americans—Frank Luther Mott	.40	1.20	2.00	B
M62	How to Know American Antiques—Alice Winchester	.40	1.20	2.00	NF
M63	How to Know the American Mammals—Ivan T. Sanderson	.50	1.50	2.50	NF
M64	Man Makes Himself—V. Gordon Childe	.40	1.20	2.00	
M65	The World of Copernicus—Angus Armitage	.40	1.20	2.00	
M66	The Meaning of Evolution—George Gaylord Simpson	.40	1.20	2.00	NF
M67	Psychopathology in Everyday Life—Sigmund Freud	.40	1.20	2.00	NF
M68	On Understanding Science—James B. Conant	.30	.90	1.50	NF
M69	The Prince—Niccolo Machiavelli; 1952	.40	1.20	2.00	
M70	Jefferson—Saul K. Padover	.40	1.20	2.00	B
M71	The Universe and Dr. Einstein—Lincoln Barnett	.40	1.20	2.00	NF
M72	Greek Historical Thought—Arnold J. Toynbee	.40	1.20	2.00	NF
Ms73	New World Writing No. 1	.40	1.20	2.00	
M74	Heredity, Race and Society—Th. Dobzhansky & L. C. Dunn	.40	1.20	2.00	NF
M75	A World Apart—Gustaw Herling; 1952	.40	1.20	2.00	
M76	Good Reading	.30	.90	1.50	
M77	The Birth and Death of the Sun—George Gamow	.40	1.20	2.00	NF
M78	A Documentary History of the United States—Richard D. Heffner	.40	1.20	2.00	NF
Ms79	New World Writing No. 2	.40	1.20	2.00	
M80	American Diplomacy: 1900-1950—George F. Kennan	.40	1.20	2.00	NF
M81	What to Listen for in Music—Aaron Copland; 1953	.40	1.20	2.00	NF
M82	The Wonderful World of Books—Alfred Stefferud	.40	1.20	2.00	NF
M83	Out of My Life and Thought—Albert Schweitzer & Everett Skillings	.40	1.20	2.00	NF
M84	How to Know and Predict the Weather—Robert Moore Fisher	.40	1.20	2.00	NF
Ms85	New World Writing No. 3	.40	1.20	2.00	
Ms86	Mythology—Edith Hamilton	.50	1.50	2.50	
M87	Walden and Civil Disobedience—Henry David Thoreau	.40	1.20	2.00	
M88	A History of the World in 240 Pages—Rene Sedillot	.40	1.20	2.00	NF
M89	Patterns of Culture—Ruth Benedict	.40	1.20	2.00	NF
Ms90	The Golden Treasury—F. T. Palgrave & Oscar Williams	.40	1.20	2.00	
M91	Growing Up in New Guinea—Margaret Mead	.40	1.20	2.00	NF
M92	The Odyssey—Homerus	.50	1.50	2.50	
M93	The Theory of the Leisure Class	.40	1.20	2.00	NF
Ms94	The Meaning of the Glorious Koran—Mohammed Marmaduke Pickthall	.40	1.20	2.00	NF
M95	The Living U. S. Constitution—Saul K. Padover	.40	1.20	2.00	NF
Ms96	New World Writing No. 4	.40	1.20	2.00	
Ms97	One Two Three . . . Infinity—George Gamow	.40	1.20	2.00	
M98	The Shaping of the Modern Mind—Crane Brinton	.30	.90	1.50	NF
M99	Greek Civilization and Character—Arnold J. Toynbee	.40	1.20	2.00	NF
M100	The Sea Around Us—Rachel L. Carson; 1954	.40	1.20	2.00	NF
MD101	Philosophy in a New Key—Susanne K. Langer	.30	.90	1.50	NF
M102	Basic Selections From Emerson—Ralph Waldo Emerson	.40	1.20	2.00	
M103	The Song of God: Bhagavad-gita	.40	1.20	2.00	
M104	Highlights of Modern Literature—Francis Brown	.30	.90	1.50	
M105	The Life of the Spider—John Crompton	.30	.90	1.50	NF
Ms106	New World Writing No. 5	.40	1.20	2.00	
M107	Ethics in a Business Society—Douglass Cater & Marquis W. Childs	.30	.90	1.50	
Ms108	An Analysis of the Kinsey Reports on Sexual Behavior in the Human Male and Female—Donald Porter Geddes	.30	.90	1.50	NF

		Good	Fine	N/Mint	
(MENTOR BOOKS, continued)					
M109	The World of History—Courtlands Canby & Nancy E. Gross	.40	1.20	2.00	
Ms110	The Iliad—Homerus	.40	1.20	2.00	
M111	The Life of the Bee—Maurice Maeterlinck	.30	.90	1.50	NF
Ms112	The Uses of the Past—Herbert J. Muller	.40	1.20	2.00	
Ms113	The Inferno—Dante Alighieri	.40	1.20	2.00	
Ms114	New Handbook of the Heavens—Hubert J. Bernhard & others	.40	1.20	2.00	NF
M115	Men, Wages and Employment in the Modern U. S. Economy—George Soule	.30	.90	1.50	
Ms116	The Holy Bible in Brief—James Reeves	.40	1.20	2.00	NF
Ms117	Leaves of Grass—Walt Whitman	.40	1.20	2.00	
Ms118	New World Writing No. 6	.40	1.20	2.00	
Ms119	Psychology of Sex—Havelock Ellis	.40	1.20	2.00	NF
Ms120	The Birth and Death of the Sun—George Gamow	.40	1.20	2.00	NF
Ms121	The Dynamics of Soviet Society—W. W. Rostow	.40	1.20	2.00	NF
MD122	Good Listening—R. D. Darrell	.40	1.20	2.00	NF
Ms123	Ballet in America—George Amberg	.40	1.20	2.00	NF
Ms124	Good Reading	.30	.90	1.50	
M125	The Nature of the Universe—Fred Hoyle; 1955	.40	1.20	2.00	NF
Ms126	The Age of Belief—Anne Fremantle	.40	1.20	2.00	NF
MD127	Here I Stand—Roland H. Bainton	.30	.90	1.50	
M128	Under the Sea Wind—Rachel L. Carson	.40	1.20	2.00	NF
M129	The Way of Life—Lao-Tzu	.40	1.20	2.00	
MD130	New World Writing No. 7	.40	1.20	2.00	
MD131	The Teachings of the Compassionate Buddha—Edwin A. Burtt	.40	1.20	2.00	
MD132	The Creative Process—Brewster Ghiselin	.40	1.20	2.00	
MD133	Sex and Temperament in Three Primitive Societies—Margaret Mead	.40	1.20	2.00	NF
MD134	Cultural Patters and Technical Change—Margaret Mead	.40	1.20	2.00	NF
M135	The Law and You—Max Radin	.30	.90	1.50	NF
M136	Mohammedanism—H. A. R. Gibb	.40	1.20	2.00	NF
MD137	American Essays—Charles B. Shaw	.40	1.20	2.00	
MD138	Biography of the Earth—George Gamow	.40	1.20	2.00	NF
MD139	Science and the Moral Life—Max Otto	.40	1.20	2.00	NF
MD140	Lenin—David Shub	.40	1.20	2.00	B
MD141	Adventures of Ideas—Alfred North Whitehead	.30	.90	1.50	
MD142	The Age of Analysis—Morton White	.40	1.20	2.00	NF
M143	Ideas of the Great Economists—George Soule	.40	1.20	2.00	NF
MD144	Life on Other Worlds—H. Spencer Jones	.40	1.20	2.00	
MD145	The Age of Jackson—Arthur M. Schlesinger, Jr.	.40	1.20	2.00	NF
MD146	New World Writing No. 8	.40	1.20	2.00	
M147	A Primer of Freudian Psychology—Calvin S. Hall	.40	1.20	2.00	NF
MD148	Man in the Modern World—Julian Huxley	.30	.90	1.50	
MD149	The Oregon Trail—Francis Parkman	.40	1.20	2.00	W
MD150	Male and Female—Margaret Mead; 1955	.40	1.20	2.00	
M151	The Sayings of Confucius—Confucius	.40	1.20	2.00	
MD152	The Aims of Education—Alfred North Whitehead	.30	.90	1.50	NF
MD153	The Coming of Age in Samoa—Margaret Mead	.40	1.20	2.00	NF
MD154	Man Makes Himself—V. Gordon Childe	.30	.90	1.50	
M155	Scheherezade: Tales From the 1001 Nights	.40	1.20	2.00	
M156	Company Manners—Louis Kronenberger	.40	1.20	2.00	
MD157	The Wonderful World of Books—Alfred Stefferud	.40	1.20	2.00	NF
MD158	The Age of Reason—Stuart Hampshire	.40	1.20	2.00	NF
M159	The Painter's Eye—Maurice Grosser	.40	1.20	2.00	NF
MD160	Jefferson—Saul K. Padover	.40	1.20	2.00	B
MD161	Democracy in America—Alexis de Tocqueville	.30	.90	1.50	NF
MD162	Science and the Modern World—Alfred North Whitehead	.30	.90	1.50	NF
MD163	Religion and the Rise of Capitalism—R. H. Tawney	.40	1.20	2.00	NF
MD164	Greek Historical Thought—Arnold J. Toynbee	.40	1.20	2.00	NF
MD165	Human Destiny—Pierre Lecomte du Nouy	.30	.90	1.50	
MD166	Life Stories of Men Who Shaped History—Plutarchus	.40	1.20	2.00	B
MD167	Great Dialogues of Plato	.40	1.20	2.00	
M168	Books That Changed the World—Robert B. Downs	.40	1.20	2.00	
MD169	America in Perspective—Henry Steele Commager	.30	.90	1.50	
MD170	New World Writing No. 9	.40	1.20	2.00	
MD171	Indians of the Americas—John Collier	.40	1.20	2.00	NF
MD172	The Age of Enlightenment—Isaiah Berlin	.40	1.20	2.00	NF
MD173	The Shaping of the Modern Mind—Crane Brinton	.30	.90	1.50	
M174	The Public Philosophy—Walter Lippmann	.30	.90	1.50	
MD175	American Skyline—Henry Hope Reed & Christopher Tunnard	.30	.90	1.50	
MD176	Walden and Civil Disobedience—Henry David Thoreau	.40	1.20	2.00	
MD177	The Papal Encyclicals in Their Historical Context—Anne Fremantle	.40	1.20	2.00	NF
MD178	Good Reading	.30	.90	1.50	
MD179	The Reader's Companion to World Literature—Lillian Herlands Hornstein	.30	.90	1.50	
MD180	Dialogues of Alfred North Whitehead	.40	1.20	2.00	
M181	Christopher Columbus, Mariner—Samuel Eliot Morison	.40	1.20	2.00	B
MD182	Russia and America: Dangers and Prospects—Henry L. Roberts	.30	.90	1.50	
MD183	New World Writing No. 10	.40	1.20	2.00	
MD184	The Age of Adventure—Giorgio deSantillana	.40	1.20	2.00	NF
MD185	The Age of Ideology—Henry O. Aiken	.40	1.20	2.00	NF

		Good	Fine	N/Mint	
MD186	100 American Poems—Selden Rodman	.40	1.20	2.00	
MD187	100 Modern Poems—Selden Rodman	.40	1.20	2.00	
MD188	The Cycle of American Literature—Robert E. Spiller; 1957	.40	1.20	2.00	
MD189	The Mentor Book of Religious Verse—Horace Gregory & Marya Zaturenska	.40	1.20	2.00	
MD190	The Nature of the Non-Western World—Vera Micheles Dean	.30	.90	1.50	NF
MD191	On Life and Sex—Havelock Ellis	.40	1.20	2.00	NF
MD192	Realm of the Incas—Victor W. Von Hagen	.40	1.20	2.00	NF
MD193	Of the Imitation of Christ—Thomas a Kempis	.40	1.20	2.00	NF
M194	The Upanishads	.40	1.20	2.00	
MD195	Eight Great Tragedies—Sylvan Barnet & others	.40	1.20	2.00	
MD196	New World Writing No. 11	.40	1.20	2.00	
MD197	The Anvil of Civilization—Leonard Cottrell	.40	1.20	2.00	NF
M198	The Hedgehog and the Fox—Isaiah Berlin	.40	1.20	2.00	
MD199	The Living Talmud: the Wisdom of the Fathers	.40	1.20	2.00	
MD200	The Frontiers of Astronomy—Fred Hoyle	.30	.90	1.50	NF
MD201	The Silver Treasury of Light Verse—Oscar Williams	.40	1.20	2.00	
MD202	On Love, Family and the Good Life—Plutarchus	.40	1.20	2.00	
MD203	The Summing Up—W. Somerset Maugham	.40	1.20	2.00	
MD204	Evolution in Action—Julian Huxley	.40	1.20	2.00	
MD205	Three Great Irishmen—Arland Ussher	.40	1.20	2.00	
MD206	The Negro in American Culture—Margaret Just Butcher	.50	1.50	2.50	NF
MD207	Don Quixote—Miguel de Cervantes	.40	1.20	2.00	
MD208	Arms and Men—Walter Millis	.40	1.20	2.00	
MD209	Language—Joshua Whatmough	.30	.90	1.50	NF
MD210	New World Writing No. 12	.40	1.20	2.00	
MD211	Enjoying Modern Art—Sarah Newmeyer	.30	.90	1.50	NF
MD212	Modern Music—John Tasker Howard & James Lyons	.30	.90	1.50	NF
MD213	The Roman Way to Western Civilization—Edith Hamilton	.40	1.20	2.00	NF
MD214	The Creation of the Universe—George Gamow	.40	1.20	2.00	NF
MD215	The Authentic New Testament; 1958	.40	1.20	2.00	
MD216	Eight Great Comedies—Sylvan Barnet & others	.40	1.20	2.00	
MD217	Medicine and Man—Ritchie Calder	.30	.90	1.50	NF
MD218	The Theory of Business Enterprise—Thorstein Veblen	.30	.90	1.50	NF
MD219	The Meaning of the Dead Sea Scrolls—A. Powell Davies	.40	1.20	2.00	NF
MD220	The United Nations and How It Works—David Cushman Coyle	.30	.90	1.50	NF
MD221	The Varieties of Religious Experience—William James	.30	.90	1.50	NF
MD222	The Origin of the Species—Charles Darwin	.40	1.20	2.00	NF
MT223	The Meaning of the Glorious Koran—Mohammed Marmaduke Pickthall	.40	1.20	2.00	
MD224	A Short History of India and Pakistan—T. Walter Wallbank	.30	.90	1.50	NF
MD225	The Dark Ages—W. P. Ker; 1958	.40	1.20	2.00	NF
MD226	The Greek Philosophers—Rex Warner	.40	1.20	2.00	NF
MD227	Human Types—Raymond Firth	.30	.90	1.50	
MD228	The True Believer—Eric Hoffer	.30	.90	1.50	
MD229	Books That Changed the World—Robert B. Downs	.40	1.20	2.00	NF
MD230	Russia—Bernard Pares	.30	.90	1.50	
MD231	The Universe and Dr. Einstein—Lincoln Barnett	.40	1.20	2.00	NF
MT232	The Reader's Companion to World Literature—Lillian Herlands Horstein & others	.40	1.20	2.00	
MT233	New World Writing No. 13	.40	1.20	2.00	
MD234	Relativity for the Layman—James A. Coleman	.30	.90	1.50	
MT235	Great Writings of Goethe—Johann Wolfgang von Goethe	.40	1.20	2.00	
MD236	The Aztec: Man and Tribe—Victor W. Von Hagen	.40	1.20	2.00	NF
MD237	Bertrand Russell's Best—Bertrand Russell	.40	1.20	2.00	
MT238	The Oedipus Plays of Sophocles	.40	1.20	2.00	
MD239	Man: His First Million Years—Ashley Montagu	.40	1.20	2.00	NF
MD240	The Story of Jazz—Marshall Stearns	.40	1.20	2.00	NF
MT241	Three Great Plays of Euripides	.40	1.20	2.00	
MD242	The Edge of the Sea—Rachel L. Carson	.40	1.20	2.00	NF
MD243	A Treasury of Asian Literature—John D. Yohannan	.40	1.20	2.00	
MD244	Religion Without Revelation—Julian Huxley	.30	.90	1.50	
MT245	The Golden Treasury—F. T. Palgrave & Oscar Williams	.40	1.20	2.00	
MT246	New World Writing No. 14	.40	1.20	2.00	
MD247	Stories From Shakespeare—Marchette Chute; 1959	.30	.90	1.50	
MT248	Mainsprings of Civilization—Ellsworth Huntington	.40	1.20	2.00	
MT249	Rebels and Redcoats—Hugh F. Rankin & George Scheer	.40	1.20	2.00	NF
MD250	The Statesman—Henry Taylor	.40	1.20	2.00	
MD251	The Origins of Oriental Civilization—Walter A. Fairservis, Jr.	.40	1.20	2.00	NF
MD252	The First Christian—A. Powell Davies	.30	.90	1.50	
MD253	The Religions of Man—Huston Smith	.40	1.20	2.00	
MD254	The Young Caesar—Rex Warner	.40	1.20	2.00	B
MD255	Growing Up in New Guinea—Margaret Mead	.30	.90	1.50	NF
MT256	The Papal Encyclicals in Their Historical Context—Anne Fremantle	.40	1.20	2.00	
MT257	Stories From Shakespeare—Marchette Chute	.30	.90	1.50	
MD258	The ABC of Relativity—Bertrand Russell	.40	1.20	2.00	
MD259	The Undiscovered Self—C. G. Jung	.40	1.20	2.00	NF
MT260	New World Writing No. 15	.40	1.20	2.00	
MD261	Music and Imagination—Aaron Copland	.40	1.20	2.00	NF
MT262	The History of Western Art—Erwin O. Christenson	.40	1.20	2.00	NF

	(MENTOR BOOKS, continued)	Good	Fine	N/Mint	
MD263	The Liveliest Art—Arthur Knight	.30	.90	1.50	
MD264	The Crust of the Earth—Samuel Rapport & Helen Wright	.40	1.20	2.00	NF
MD265	The Renaissance—Walter Pater	.40	1.20	2.00	NF
M266					
MD267	The American Presidency—Clinton Rossiter	.30	.90	1.50	
MD268					
M269					
M270					
MD271	A Primer of Freudian Psychology—Calvin S. Hall	.40	1.20	2.00	NF
MD272	The Sea Around Us—Rachel L. Carson	.40	1.20	2.00	NF
MD273	The Way of Zen—Alan W. Watts	.40	1.20	2.00	
MD274	A History of the Western World—L. J. Cheney	.30	.90	1.50	
MD275	The Greek Experience—C. M. Bowra; 1959	.40	1.20	2.00	
MD276	Understanding Chemistry—Lawrence P. Lessing	.30	.90	1.50	NF
MD277	The Song of Songs	.40	1.20	2.00	
MD278	The March Up Country: Xenophon's Anabasis	.40	1.20	2.00	
MD279	Gestalt Psychology—Wolfgang Kohler	.40	1.20	2.00	NF
MT287	Eight Great Comedies—Sylvan Barnet & others	.40	1.20	2.00	

MENTOR GUIDES
New American Library of World Literature, Inc.

		Good	Fine	N/Mint	
G2	How to Know and Enjoy New York—Carl Maas; 1949	1.00	3.00	5.00	NF

MERCURY LIBRARY
The American Mercury, Inc.

Digest Size

		Good	Fine	N/Mint	
L1	Archie and Mehitabel—Don Marquis	1.60	4.80	8.00	H

MERCURY MYSTERY
The American Mercury, Inc./Mercury Publications

Digest Size

		Good	Fine	N/Mint	
1	The Postman Always Rings Twice—James M. Cain	.80	2.40	4.00	M
2	Everything Is Thunder—J. L. Hardy	.40	1.20	2.00	
3	Thirteen Steps—Whitman Chambers	.50	1.50	2.50	M
4	Company K—William March	.40	1.20	2.00	
5	Thieves Like Us—Edward Anderson	.40	1.20	2.00	M
6	Weeping Is for Women—Donald Barr Chidsey	.50	1.50	2.50	
7	Diamond Jim Brady—Parker Morell	.40	1.20	2.00	
8	Hot Saturday—Harvey Fergusson	.40	1.20	2.00	
9	Criss-Cross—Don Tracy	.50	1.50	2.50	M
10	The General—C. S. Forester	.40	1.20	2.00	A
11	Mantrap—Sinclair Lewis	.40	1.20	2.00	
12	I Cover the Waterfront—Max Miller	.40	1.20	2.00	NF
13	To the Vanquished—I. A. R. Wylie	.40	1.20	2.00	
14	Death in the Deep South—Ward Greene	.50	1.50	2.50	M
15	Indelible—Elliot H. Paul	.40	1.20	2.00	
16	Once Too Often—Whitman Chambers	.50	1.50	2.50	M
17	The Prodigal Parents—Sinclair Lewis	.40	1.20	2.00	
18	The Loving Spirit—Daphne du Maurier	.40	1.20	2.00	
19	East Wind; West Wind—Pearl S. Buck	.40	1.20	2.00	
20	Cup of Gold—John Steinbeck	.50	1.50	2.50	A

Mentor Books MD240, © New

Mentor Guides G2, © New

Mercury Library L1, © Merc

Mercury Mystery 41, © Merc   Mercury Mystery 89, © Merc   Mercury Mystery 120, © Merc

(MERCURY MYSTERY, continued)

		Good	Fine	N/Mint	
21	The Missing Miniature—Erich Kastner	.40	1.20	2.00	
22	County Court—Roy Flannagan	.40	1.20	2.00	
23	The Devil in Satin—Dornford Yates	.40	1.20	2.00	
24	Divide by Two—Mildred Gilman	.40	1.20	2.00	
25	The Light That Failed—Rudyard Kipling	.50	1.50	2.50	A
26	Never in Vain—J. L. Hardy	.40	1.20	2.00	
27	The Dutch Shoe Mystery—Ellery Queen	.50	1.50	2.50	M
28	Jamaica Inn—Daphne du Maurier	.40	1.20	2.00	
29	Class Reunion—Franz Werfel	.40	1.20	2.00	
30	Dr. Norton's Wife—Mildred Walker	.40	1.20	2.00	
31	The Death of M. Gallet—Georges Simenon	.50	1.50	2.50	M
32	The Door Between—Ellery Queen	.50	1.50	2.50	M
33	Fifty Roads to Town—Frederick Nebel	.50	1.50	2.50	M
34	Strawstack—Dorothy Cameron Disney	.40	1.20	2.00	M
35	Death of Lord Haw Haw—Brett Rutledge	.40	1.20	2.00	M
36	The Siamese Twin Mystery—Ellery Queen	.50	1.50	2.50	M
37	Meet Nero Wolfe—Rex Stout	.50	1.50	2.50	M
38	Headed for a Hearse—Jonathan Latimer	.50	1.50	2.50	M
39	Halfway House—Ellery Queen	.50	1.50	2.50	M
40	The D. A. Calls It Murder—Erle Stanley Gardner	.40	1.20	2.00	M
41	Poirot Loses a Client—Agatha Christie	.50	1.50	2.50	M
42	The American Gun Mystery—Ellery Queen	.40	1.20	2.00	M
43	Murder at the Vicarage—Agatha Christie	.50	1.50	2.50	M
44	The Norths Meet Murder—Richard & Frances Lockridge	.50	1.50	2.50	M
45	The Listening House—Mabel Seeley	.40	1.20	2.00	M
46	The Incredible Theft—Agatha Christie	.50	1.50	2.50	M
47	The Four of Hearts—Ellery Queen	.50	1.50	2.50	M
48	The League of Frightened Men—Rex Stout	.50	1.50	2.50	M
49	Mystery Mile—Margery Allingham	.40	1.20	2.00	M
50	Murder in Mesopotamia—Agatha Christie	.50	1.50	2.50	M
51	Hasty Wedding—Mignon G. Eberhart	.40	1.20	2.00	M
52	The Unicorn Murders—Carter Dickson	.50	1.50	2.50	M
53	Cards on the Table—Agatha Christie	.50	1.50	2.50	M
54	The Golden Swan Murder—Dorothy Cameron Disney	.40	1.20	2.00	M
55	Red Gardenias—Jonathan Latimer	.50	1.50	2.50	M
56	The D. A. Draws a Circle—Erle Stanley Gardner	.40	1.20	2.00	M
57	The Dragon's Teeth—Ellery Queen	.50	1.50	2.50	M
58	The Case of the Dangerous Dowager—Erle Stanley Gardner	.40	1.20	2.00	M
59	Thirteen at Dinner—Agatha Christie	.50	1.50	2.50	M
60	Good Night, Sheriff—Harrison R. Steeves	.40	1.20	2.00	M
61	The Singing Clock—Virginia Perdue	.40	1.20	2.00	M
62	The Clew of the Forgotten Murder—Erle Stanley Gardner	.40	1.20	2.00	M
63	A Toast to Tomorrow—Manning Coles	.40	1.20	2.00	M
64	The Black Curtain—Cornell Woolrich	.50	1.50	2.50	M
65	Verdict of Twelve—Raymond Postgate	.40	1.20	2.00	M
66	Death on the Nile—Agatha Christie	.50	1.50	2.50	M
67	Mystery in the Woodshed—Anthony Gilbert	.40	1.20	2.00	M
68	Challenge to the Reader—Ellery Queen	.50	1.50	2.50	M
69	The Secret of Chimneys—Agatha Christie	.50	1.50	2.50	M
70	A Taste for Honey—H. F. Heard	.40	1.20	2.00	M
71	Death in the Back Seat—Dorothy Cameron Disney	.40	1.20	2.00	M
72	Black Orchids—Rex Stout	.50	1.50	2.50	M
73	Keep It Quiet—Selwyn Jepson	.40	1.20	2.00	M
74	The Crying Sisters—Mabel Seeley	.40	1.20	2.00	M
75	The Case of the Haunted Brides—William DuBois	.40	1.20	2.00	M
76	Mystery Week-End—Percival Wilde	.40	1.20	2.00	M
77	Murder Out of Town—Frances & Richard Lockridge	.50	1.50	2.50	M
78	Folio on Florence White—Will Oursler	.40	1.20	2.00	M

		Good	Fine	N/Mint	
79	The Nursing Home Murder—Ngaio Marsh & Dr. Henry Jellett	.50	1.50	2.50	M
80	He Fell Down Dead—Virginia Perdue	.40	1.20	2.00	M
81	Once Off Guard—J. H. Wallis	.40	1.20	2.00	M
82	I Wouldn't Be in Your Shoes—William Irish	.50	1.50	2.50	M
83	Tinsley's Bones—Percival Wilde	.40	1.20	2.00	M
84	The Moving Finger—Agatha Christie	.50	1.50	2.50	M
85	The Case of the Weird Sisters—Charlotte Armstrong	.40	1.20	2.00	M
86	The Trial of Vincent Doon—Will Oursler	.40	1.20	2.00	M
87	Donovan's Brain—Curt Siodmak	1.20	3.60	6.00	SF
88	The White Cockatoo—Mignon G. Eberhart	.40	1.20	2.00	M
89	Maigret to the Rescue—Georges Simenon	.50	1.50	2.50	M
90	The Bach Festival Murders—Blanche Bloch	.40	1.20	2.00	M
91	The Woman in Red—Anthony Gilbert	.40	1.20	2.00	M
92	The Case of the Foster Father—Virginia Perdue	.40	1.20	2.00	M
93	The Bride Dined Alone—Vera Kelsey	.40	1.20	2.00	M
94	The Black Paw—Constance & Gwenyth Little	.40	1.20	2.00	M
95	Look Your Last—John Stephen Strange	.40	1.20	2.00	M
96	The Smell of Money—Matthew Head	.40	1.20	2.00	M
97	The Rat Began to Gnaw the Rope—C. W. Grafton	.40	1.20	2.00	M
98	Keep It Quiet—Richard Hull	.40	1.20	2.00	M
99	The Spectral Bride—Joseph Shearing	.40	1.20	2.00	M
100	Murder on the Links—Agatha Christie	.50	1.50	2.50	M
101	Mr. Bowling Buys a Newspaper—Donald Henderson	.40	1.20	2.00	M
102	Beware the Hoot Owl—Nancy Rutledge	.40	1.20	2.00	M
103	Murder Through the Looking Glass—Michael Venning	.40	1.20	2.00	M
104	Footsteps Behind Her—Mitchell Wilson	.40	1.20	2.00	M
105	There Was a Crooked Man—Kelley Roos	.40	1.20	2.00	M
106	The Undertaker Dies—Garnett Weston	.40	1.20	2.00	M
107	The Black Rustle—Constance & Gwenyth Little	.40	1.20	2.00	M
108	Thirty Days to Live—Anthony Gilbert	.40	1.20	2.00	M
109	Clues to Christabel—Mary Fitt	.40	1.20	2.00	M
110	Dr. Fell, Detective and Other Stories—John Dickson Carr; 1st ed., 1947	10.00	30.00	50.00	M
111	Payment Deferred—C. S. Forester	.40	1.20	2.00	M
112	The Case Book of Mr. Campion—Margery Allingham	.40	1.20	2.00	M
113	Pattern for Murder—Ione Sandberg Shriber	.40	1.20	2.00	M
114	Dark Road—Doris Miles Disney	.40	1.20	2.00	M
115	Too Many Suspects—John Rhode	.40	1.20	2.00	M
116	The Outsiders—A. E. Martin	.40	1.20	2.00	M
117	Case of the Giant Killer—H. S. Branson	.40	1.20	2.00	M
118	The Hangover Murders—Adam Hobhouse	.40	1.20	2.00	M
119	When Last I Died—Gladys Mitchell	.40	1.20	2.00	M
120	Nightmare Town—Dashiell Hammett; 1st ed., 1948	16.50	50.00	80.00	M
121	The Bandaged Nude—Robert Finnegan	.40	1.20	2.00	M
122	And Hope to Die—Richard Powell	.40	1.20	2.00	M
123	The Whitebird Murders—Thomas B. Black	.40	1.20	2.00	M
124	The Dying Room—Manning Lee Stokes	.40	1.20	2.00	M
125	Come and Be Killed—Shelley Smith	.40	1.20	2.00	M
126	Let the Tiger Die—Manning Coles	.40	1.20	2.00	M
127	The Pigskin Bag—Bruno Fischer	.50	1.50	2.50	M
128	Fatal Bride—Van Siller; aka The Curtain Between	.40	1.20	2.00	M
129	Death of a Tall Man—Frances & Richard Lockridge	.50	1.50	2.50	M
130	I Am the Cat—Rosemary Kutak	.40	1.20	2.00	M
131	They Can Only Hang You Once—Dashiell Hammett; aka The Adventures of Sam Spade	2.00	6.00	10.00	M
132	Legacy in Blood—Margery Allingham; aka Flowers for the Judge	.40	1.20	2.00	M
133	Untidy Murder—Frances & Richard Lockridge	.50	1.50	2.50	M
134	Sweet and Deadly—David Duncan; aka The Bramble Bush	.40	1.20	2.00	M
135	Dead Man Blues—William Irish	.50	1.50	2.50	M
136	Relative to Poison—E. C. R. Lorac	.40	1.20	2.00	M
137	I Want to Go Home—Richard & Frances Lockridge	.50	1.50	2.50	M
138	The King and the Corpse—Max Murray	.40	1.20	2.00	M
139	Last Laugh, Mr. Moto—John P. Marquand	.50	1.50	2.50	M
140	Murder Makes Me Nervous—Margaret Scherf	.40	1.20	2.00	M
141	Call for the Saint—Leslie Charteris	.50	1.50	2.50	M
142	Too Good to Be True—J. F. Hutton	.40	1.20	2.00	M
143	Nightmare—Edward S. Aarons	.40	1.20	2.00	M
144	Not Negotiable—Manning Coles	.40	1.20	2.00	M
145	Murder Is Served—Frances & Richard Lockridge	.50	1.50	2.50	M
146	Rogue's Coat—Theodora DuBois	.40	1.20	2.00	M
147	The Beast Must Die—Nicholas Blake	.50	1.50	2.50	M
148	The Bulldog Has the Key—F. W. Bronson	.40	1.20	2.00	M
149	The Girl With the Hole in Her Head—Hampton Stone	.40	1.20	2.00	M
150	The Stalking Man—Wilson Tucker	1.00	3.00	5.00	M
151	And Dangerous to Know—Elizabeth Daly	.40	1.20	2.00	M
152	Terror in the Town—Edward Ronns	.40	1.20	2.00	M
153	The Leaden Bubble—H. C. Branson	.40	1.20	2.00	M

		Good	Fine	N/Mint	
154	Spin Your Web, Lady!—Richard & Frances Lockridge	.50	1.50	2.50	M
155	Death From a Top Hat—Clayton Rawson	1.00	3.00	5.00	M
156	Drop Dead—George Bagby	.40	1.20	2.00	M
157	Dig Me Later—Miriam-Ann Hagen	.40	1.20	2.00	M
158	House on Telegraph Hill—Dana Lyon; aka The Frightened Child	.40	1.20	2.00	M
159	Sudden Vengeance—Edmind Crispin	.40	1.20	2.00	M
160	The Three Fears—Jonathan Stagge	1.00	3.00	5.00	M
161	Dr. Bruderstein Vanishes—John Sherwood	.40	1.20	2.00	M
162	Death of a Nymph—Evelyn Piper; aka The Motive	.40	1.20	2.00	M
163	Give Up the Ghost—Margaret Erskine	.40	1.20	2.00	M
164	Death at the Rodeo—Ellery Queen; aka The American Gun Mystery	.40	1.20	2.00	M
165	Death and Letters—Elizabeth Daly	.40	1.20	2.00	M
166	Skeleton in the Closet—A. B. Cunningham	.40	1.20	2.00	M
167	Ill Wind—Ruth Fenisong	.40	1.20	2.00	M
168	Murder Comes Home—Anthony Gilbert	.40	1.20	2.00	M
169	The House in the Forest—Marten Cumberland	.40	1.20	2.00	M
170	Murder Goes to Press—Cicely Cairns	.40	1.20	2.00	M
171	Never Fight a Lady—Seldon Truss	.40	1.20	2.00	M
172	The Murder in Gay Ladies—James Ronald; aka Murder in the Family	.40	1.20	2.00	M
173	The Sound of Murder—Kenneth Fearing; aka The Loneliest Girl in the World	.40	1.20	2.00	M
174	A Noose for Her—Edmund Crispin; aka The Long Divorce	.40	1.20	2.00	M
175	The Party Was a Payoff—Elizabeth Sanxay Holding; aka Too Many Bottles	.40	1.20	2.00	M
176	A Grave Case of Murder—Roger Bax	.40	1.20	2.00	M
177	Fish and Kill—MacDonald Hastings; aka Cork on the Water	.40	1.20	2.00	M
178	D As in Dead—Lawrence Treat	.40	1.20	2.00	M
179	Blood on Baker Street—Anthony Boucher; aka The Case of the Baker Street Irregulars	.80	2.40	4.00	M
180	The Body in the Bridal Bed—Richard Shattuck; aka The Wedding Guest Sat on a Stone	.40	1.20	2.00	M
181	Murder Gone Mad—Philip MacDonald	.40	1.20	2.00	M
182	The Dead Don't Care—Jonathan Latimer	.40	1.20	2.00	M
183	Lady Marked for Murder—Peggy Bacon; aka The Inward Eye	.40	1.20	2.00	M
184	Come Out Killing—Robert Reeves; aka No Love Lost	.40	1.20	2.00	M
185	The Widow-Makers—Michael Blankfort	.40	1.20	2.00	M
186	Clues to Burn—Lenore Glen Offord	.40	1.20	2.00	M
187	The Pinball Murders—Thomas B. Black	.40	1.20	2.00	M
188	Death Is a Lover—Nedra Tyre; aka Mouse in Eternity	.40	1.20	2.00	M
189	The Missing Heiress—Bernice Carey	.40	1.20	2.00	M
190	The Christmas Murder—Cyril Hare; aka An English Murder	.40	1.20	2.00	M
191	Kiss the Boss Goodbye—Frank Gruber; aka The Last Doorbell	.40	1.20	2.00	M
192	Trial by Terror—Frances & Richard Lockridge; aka Death by Association	.50	1.50	2.50	M
193	The Wrong Body—Anthony Gilbert	.40	1.20	2.00	M
194	With Blood and Kisses—Richard Shattuck; aka The Snark Was a Boojum	.40	1.20	2.00	M
195	The Screaming Bride—H. T. Teilhet; aka A Private Undertaking	.40	1.20	2.00	M
196	Baltimore Madame—Helen Knowland; aka Madame Baltimore	.40	1.20	2.00	M
197	Murder by the Day—Veronica Parker Johns	.40	1.20	2.00	M
198	Murder of a Mistress—John Sherwood; aka Ambush for Anatol	.40	1.20	2.00	M
199	Blood Runs Cold—A. B. Cunningham; aka The Hunter Is the Hunted	.40	1.20	2.00	M
200	Killer in the Crowd—Josephine Tey; aka The Man in the Queue	.40	1.20	2.00	M
201	The Deadly Chase—John M. Eshelman; aka The Long Chase	.40	1.20	2.00	M
202	The Frightened Widow—Bernice Carey; aka Their Nearest and Dearest	.40	1.20	2.00	M
203	The Bride of Death—Ngaio Marsh; aka Spinsters in Jeopardy	.40	1.20	2.00	M
204	They Buried a Man—Mildred Davis	.40	1.20	2.00	M
205	You Die Today—Baynard Kendrick	.40	1.20	2.00	M
206	Death of a Cheat—John M. Eshelman	.40	1.20	2.00	M
207	Savage Breast—Manning Long	.40	1.20	2.00	M
208	Killer in the Straw—Richard & Frances Lockridge; aka Death at the Gentle Bull	.50	1.50	2.50	M
209	The Blonde With the Deadly Past—Mabel Seeley; aka The Whistling Shadow	.40	1.20	2.00	M

NOTE: After No. 209, the series became Mercury Mystery Book-Magazine.

| 233 | A Man Named Thin—Dashiell Hammett; 1st ed., 1962 | 12.50 | 37.50 | 60.00 | M |

MERIT BOOKS
Century Publications

Digest Size

B-10	Operation Interstellar—George O. Smith; 1950	2.00	6.00	10.00	SF
B-13	World of IF—Rog Phillips; 1951	2.00	6.00	10.00	SF
B-14	Model for Love—Gerald Seton	1.20	3.60	6.00	E
B-16	The Tin Ear—A. J. Collins	1.20	3.60	6.00	

METRO
Metro Publications

Digest Size

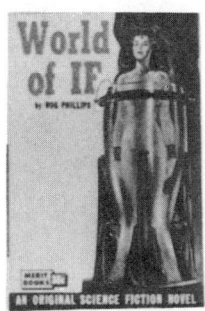

Merit Books B-13, © Cen   Metro nn, © Metro   Midwood nn(1), © Mid

(METRO, continued)

		Good	Fine	N/Mint	
nn	The Spy in the Room—Denison Clift	1.00	3.00	5.00	M
nn	Sabotage: The Secret War Against America—Sayers & Kahn	1.00	3.00	5.00	NF
7	Homicide Johnny—Stephen Gould	1.00	3.00	5.00	M

MIDWOOD
Midwood Enterprises, Inc.

nn(1)	There Oughta Be a Law—Al Fagaly & Harry Shorten; 1957	1.20	3.60	6.00	H
3	Call Me Mistress—Tomlin Rede	1.20	3.60	6.00	E
4	There Oughta Be a Law—Al Fagaly & Harry Shorten	1.20	3.60	6.00	H
nn(5)	I Take What I Want—Hal Ellson	1.60	4.80	8.00	JD
7	Love Nest—Loren Beauchamp (Robert Silverberg)	1.60	4.80	8.00	E
8	Carla—Sheldon Lord	1.20	3.60	6.00	E
9	A Strange Kind of Love—Sheldon Lord	1.20	3.60	6.00	E
11	Immoral Wife—Gordon Mitchell	1.20	3.60	6.00	E
12	Girl of the Streets—Orrie Hitt	1.20	3.60	6.00	E
13	Hired Lover—Fred Martin; orig., 1959	1.20	3.60	6.00	E
14	Born to Be Bad—Sheldon Lord; orig., 1959	1.20	3.60	6.00	E
15	All My Lovers—Alan Marshall	1.20	3.60	6.00	E
16	Summer Romance—Orrie Hitt; orig., 1959	1.20	3.60	6.00	E
18	Connie—Loren Beauchamp (Robert Silverberg); orig., 1959	1.60	4.80	8.00	E
23	As Bad As They Come—Orrie Hitt; orig., 1959	1.20	3.60.	6.00	E
24	69 Barrow Street—Sheldon Lord; orig., 1959	1.20	3.60	6.00	E
25	Sin School—Don Holliday; orig., 1959	1.20	3.60	6.00	E
26	Just Ask for Margaret—W. B. Tasker; orig., 1959	1.20	3.60	6.00	E
28	All the Girls Were Willing—Alan Marshall; orig., 1960	1.20	3.60	6.00	E
29	Another Night, Another Love—Loren Beauchamp (Robert Silverberg); orig., 1959	1.60	4.80	8.00	E
30	Meg—Loren Beauchamp (Robert Silverberg)	1.60	4.80	8.00	E
31	The Wife Next Door—Alan Marshall	1.20	3.60	6.00	E
32	Woman Hater—Dave Carson	1.20	3.60	6.00	E
33	A Woman Must Love—Sheldon Lord	1.20	3.60	6.00	E
34	The Cheaters—Orrie Hitt; orig., 1960	1.20	3.60	6.00	E
35	Kept—Sheldon Lord	1.20	3.60	6.00	E
36	Virgin's Summer—Alan Marshall	1.20	3.60	6.00	E
37	Anybody's Girl—March Hastings	1.20	3.60	6.00	E
38	A Doctor and His Mistress—Orrie Hitt	1.20	3.60	6.00	E
39	Sins of Martha Leslie—Don Holliday	1.20	3.60	6.00	E
40	Candy—Sheldon Lord	1.20	3.60	6.00	E
41	A Girl Called Honey—Sheldon Lord & Alan Marshall	1.20	3.60	6.00	E
42	Stag Model—James Harvey	1.20	3.60	6.00	E

Midwood 7, © Mid   Midwood 16, © Mid   Midwood 29, © Mid

		Good	Fine	N/Mint	
51	All About Annette—Alan Marshall	1.20	3.60	6.00	E
52	Meet Marilyn—Sloane Britain	1.20	3.60	6.00	E
53	The Unashamed—March Hastings—orig., 1960	1.20	3.60	6.00	E
54	Lana—Joan Ellis	1.20	3.60	6.00	E
55	21 Gay Street—Sheldon Lord	1.20	3.60	6.00	E
56	The Blonde—Peggy Swenson	1.20	3.60	6.00	E
57	Insatiable—Sloane Britain	1.20	3.60	6.00	E
58	Sabrina and the Senator—Nick Vendor	1.20	3.60	6.00	E
59	A Twilight Affair—James Harvey	1.20	3.60	6.00	E
60	All the Way—Michael Avallone	1.60	4.80	8.00	E
61	Flame—Joan Ellis	1.20	3.60	6.00	E
62	Sally—Alan Marshall	1.20	3.60	6.00	E
63	The Unfortunate Flesh—Randy Salem	1.20	3.60	6.00	E
64	Million Dollar Mistress—Clyde Allison	1.60	4.80	8.00	E
65	Nurse Carolyn—Loren Beauchamp (Robert Silverberg)	1.60	4.80	8.00	E
67	A Touch of Depravity—Paul Russo	1.20	3.60	6.00	E
69	Liza's Apartment—Joan Ellis	1.20	3.60	6.00	E
70	Sin on Wheels—Loren Beauchamp (Robert Silverberg)	1.60	4.80	8.00	E
71	A Woman—Bruce Elliot	1.20	3.60	6.00	E
72	The Path Between—Jay Warren	1.20	3.60	6.00	E

MODERN SHORT STORY MONTHLY (See AVON...)

MONARCH BOOKS
Monarch Books, Inc.

		Good	Fine	N/Mint	
101	Dark Hunger—Don James; 1958	.40	1.20	2.00	
102	Winter Range—Alan LeMay	.40	1.20	2.00	W
103	Love Me Now—Fan Nichols	.40	1.20	2.00	
104	Rawhider From Texas—Dean Owen	.40	1.20	2.00	W
105	Shadow of the Mafia—Louis Malley	.40	1.20	2.00	
106	Rogue Lover—Leon Phillips; 1959	.50	1.50	2.50	
107	Wild to Possess—Gil Brewer; c-Maguire	.50	1.50	2.50	
108	Brand Fires on the Ridge—Ernest Haycox	.40	1.20	2.00	W
109	Marmaduke Rides Again—Brad Anderson	.50	1.50	2.50	H
110	Touch Me Not—Brian Harwin; c-Maguire	.50	1.50	2.50	
111	Sword of Casanova—James Kendricks	.50	1.50	2.50	A
112	Spring of Desire—Louis Falstein	.40	1.20	2.00	
113	Thunderhead Range—Sam Bowie	.40	1.20	2.00	W
114	Killer Cop—Ferguson Findley	.40	1.20	2.00	
115	Madigan's Women—John Conway	.40	1.20	2.00	
116	Some Like It Tough—Jack Karney	.40	1.20	2.00	
117	Stronger Than Passion—George Byram	.40	1.20	2.00	
118	Way of the Wicked—William Woolfolk	.40	1.20	2.00	E
119	Occasion of Sin—Robert William Taylor	.40	1.20	2.00	E
120	Take Me Home—Fletcher Flora	.40	1.20	2.00	E
121	Kiss Me Quick—Karl Kramer; c-Maguire	.50	1.50	2.50	
122	Season for Love—Whitman Chambers	.40	1.20	2.00	
123	Beyond Our Pleasure—James Kendricks	.40	1.20	2.00	
124	All I Can Get—William Ard; c-Maguire	.50	1.50	2.50	
125	Nikki—Stuart Friedman; 1959, c-Maguire	.50	1.50	2.50	A
126	Law of the Gun—Max Brand	.40	1.20	2.00	W
127	Lust to Live—Peter W. Denzer	.40	1.20	2.00	
128	Hell Is My Destination—John Conway	.50	1.50	2.50	E
129	End to Innocence—Robert Carse	.40	1.20	2.00	
130	We Burn Like Fire—Will Cook	.40	1.20	2.00	
131	The Darkness of Love—Harry Olive	.40	1.20	2.00	
132	Save Them for Violence—James M. Fox	.40	1.20	2.00	
133	The Flesh Peddlers—Frank Boyd; c-Maguire	.50	1.50	2.50	E
134	Fury in the Heart—W. T. Ballard	.50	1.50	2.50	
135	Hangman's Mesa—Dan J. Sterens	.40	1.20	2.00	W
136	Not for a Curse—Karl Kramer	.40	1.20	2.00	
137	Jailbait Street—Hal Ellson	1.00	3.00	5.00	JD
138	Stephana—Joseph Foster	.40	1.20	2.00	
139	In Savage Surrender—Whitman Chambers	.40	1.20	2.00	
140	The Glory Jumpers—Delano Stagg	.40	1.20	2.00	
141	Falcons of France—James Norman Hall & Charles Nordhoff	.40	1.20	2.00	C
142	Night After Night—Steve Thurman	.40	1.20	2.00	
K50	Congo Song—Stuart Cloete; 1958	.40	1.20	2.00	
K51					
K52	This Naked Love—Helga Moray; 1959	.40	1.20	2.00	

MONARCH HUMAN BEHAVIOR SERIES
Monarch Books, Inc.

		Good	Fine	N/Mint	
MB501	Women in Trouble—James Donner; 1959, c-Maguire	.80	2.40	4.00	

	(MONARCH HUMAN BEHAVIOR SERIES, continued)	Good	Fine	N/Mint	
MB502	The Sexual Side of Love—Don James	.40	1.20	2.00	NF
MB503	Tormented Women—Edward J. McGoldrick, Jr.; c-Maguire	.80	2.40	4.00	

MURDER MYSTERY MONTHLY (See AVON...)

MYSTERY NOVEL CLASSIC
Novel Selections, Inc.

Digest Size

(Continuation of Mystery Novel of the Month)

		Good	Fine	N/Mint	
42	The Case of the Advertised Murders—Minna Bardon	.80	2.40	4.00	M
43	What Price Murder—Cleve. F. Adams	1.00	3.00	5.00	M
44	Murder Is Not Mute—Audrey Newell; 1943	.80	2.40	4.00	M
45	Mystery of the Hushing Pool—J. S. Fletcher	.80	2.40	4.00	M
46	The Jordans Murder—Sydney Fowler	.80	2.40	4.00	M
47	Fair Warning—Mignon G. Eberhart; 1943	.80	2.40	4.00	M
48	Date for Murder—Louis Trimble	.80	2.40	4.00	M
50	The Bride Brings Death—Darby St. John; 1943	.80	2.40	4.00	
51	Murder on Ghost Tree Island—K. S. Daiger	.80	2.40	4.00	M
52	The Death of a Celebrity—Hulbert Footner	.80	2.40	4.00	M
53	The Ballot Box Murders—John Stephen Strange	.80	2.40	4.00	M
54	Death Wears a Bridal Veil—Kathleen Moore Knight	.80	2.40	4.00	M
55	Murder Without Clues—Eleanor Pierson; aka The Defense Rests	.80	2.40	4.00	M
56	The Glass Slipper—Mignon G. Eberhart	.80	2.40	4.00	M
57	Death Writes an Ad—Marion Holbrook; aka Suitable for Framing	.80	2.40	4.00	M
58	Hostess to Murder—Elizabeth Sanxay Holding	.80	2.40	4.00	M
59	Murder at World's End—John Stephen Strange	.80	2.40	4.00	M
60	The Case of the Tainted Token—Kathleen Moore Knight	.80	2.40	4.00	M
61	Bring Me Another Murder—Whitman Chambers	.80	2.40	4.00	M
62	The Girl Died Laughing—Viola Paradise	.80	2.40	4.00	M
63	Wanted: A Murderess—Marion Holbrook	.80	2.40	4.00	M
64	O As in Omen—Lawrence Treat	.80	2.40	4.00	M
65	Echo of a Bomb—Van Siller	.80	2.40	4.00	M
66	Shadows on the Wall—Mary Reisner	.80	2.40	4.00	M
67	They Came to Kill—Margaret Scherf	.80	2.40	4.00	M
68	The Leather Man Murders—Lawrence Treat	.80	2.40	4.00	M
69	The Case of the Dowager's Etching—Rufus King	.80	2.40	4.00	M
70	Terror by Twilight—Kathleen Moore Knight	.80	2.40	4.00	M
71	The Corpse Grows a Beard—Margaret Scherf	.80	2.40	4.00	M
72	Escape While I Can—Melba Marlot	.80	2.40	4.00	M
73	The Case of the Copy-hook Killing—Royce Howes	.80	2.40	4.00	M
74	The Case of the Absent Corpse—Katharine Hill	.80	2.40	4.00	M
75	The Case of the Kippered Corpse—Margaret Scherf	.80	2.40	4.00	M
76	Acts of Black Knight—Kathleen Moore Knight	.80	2.40	4.00	M
77	Death Checks In—Stephen Ransome	.80	2.40	4.00	M
78	Let the Skeletons Rattle—Frederick C. Davis	.80	2.40	4.00	M
79	Clue of the Frightening Coin—Jessica Ryan	.80	2.40	4.00	M
80	Murder Goes Astray—M. V. Heberden	.80	2.40	4.00	M
81	Dead Man's Float—Amber Dean	.80	2.40	4.00	M
82	The Case of the Absent-minded Professor—Aaron Mark Stein	.80	2.40	4.00	M
83	The Cat's Cradle Murders—Jerome Barry; aka Leopard Cat's Cradle	.80	2.40	4.00	M
84	Death Rides Tandem—Walbridge McCully	.80	2.40	4.00	M
86	Lady of Night—Jerome Barry	.80	2.40	4.00	M
88	The Case of the Wicked Twin—Lois Eby & John C. Fleming	.80	2.40	4.00	M
89	The Blonde Is Dead—Amber Dean	.80	2.40	4.00	M

Mystery Novel Classic 56, © NS

Mystery Novel of the Month nn, © NS

Mystery Novel of the Month 22, © NS

Mystery Novel-of the Month 25, © NS   National Dairy nn, © Nat. Dairy Products   News Stand Library 141, © Export

(MYSTERY NOVEL CLASSIC, continued)

		Good	Fine	N/Mint	
90	One Man Must Die—A. B. Cunningham	.80	2.40	4.00	M
91	Stream Sinister—Kathleen Moore Knight	.80	2.40	4.00	M
92	Bells for the Dead—Kathleen Moore Knight	.80	2.40	4.00	M
96	Murder Strikes an Atomic Unit—Theodora DuBois	.80	2.40	4.00	M
97	The Butler Died in Brooklyn—Ruth Fenisong	.80	2.40	4.00	M

MYSTERY NOVEL OF THE MONTH
Novel Selections, Inc.

Digest Size

(Continued as Mystery Novel Classic)

nn	Murder by Proxy—Colver Harris; 1938	1.00	3.00	5.00	M
nn	42 Days for Murder—Roger Torrey; 1939	1.00	3.00	5.00	M
nn	The Merry-Go-Round of Murder—Joseph F. Dinneen; 1939	1.00	3.00	5.00	M
nn	Murder on the S-23—Steve Fisher	1.20	3.60	6.00	M
nn	Murders in Silk—Mike Teagle	1.00	3.00	5.00	M
nn	Death Is a Stowaway—Wesley Price	1.00	3.00	5.00	M
nn	The Case of the Severed Skull—H. Weiner; 1940	1.00	3.00	5.00	M
nn	Liar Dice—J. S. Mosher; 1941	1.00	3.00	5.00	M
nn	The Mussolini Murder Case—Bernard Newman; 1939	1.00	3.00	5.00	M
nn	The Clue of the Hungry Corpse—Inigo Jones	1.00	3.00	5.00	M
nn	If I Die Before I Wake—Sherwood King	1.00	3.00	5.00	M
nn	Death Takes a Dive—Eric Heath	1.00	3.00	5.00	M
nn	Murder in the Museum—Eric Heath	1.00	3.00	5.00	M
nn	The Case of the Crumpled Knave—Anthony Boucher	1.20	3.60	6.00	M
18	A Gentleman for the Gallows—Sydney Horler	.80	2.40	4.00	M
19	Cradled in Murder!—Rudd Fleming; 1941	.80	2.40	4.00	M
20	Clue in Two Flats—R. L. F. McCombs	.80	2.40	4.00	M
21	Murder Stops the Clock—Craig Rice	1.00	3.00	5.00	M
22	The Case of the Thing in the Brook—Peter Storme	1.00	3.00	5.00	M
23	Murder at Coney Island—James O'Hanlon	.80	2.40	4.00	M
25	Murder by Invitation—Richard Hull	.80	2.40	4.00	M
26	Death in the Chalk Pits—E. R. Punshon	.80	2.40	4.00	M
27	Grand Central Murder—Sue MacVeigh	.80	2.40	4.00	M
28	Murder on Stage—Sutherland Scott; 1941	.80	2.40	4.00	M
30	Death Took a Publisher—Norman Forrest; 1942	.80	2.40	4.00	M
31	Death Before Breakfast—Cleve F. Adams	1.00	3.00	5.00	M
32	Murder at the Schoolhouse—A. B. Cunningham	.80	2.40	4.00	M
33	The Albatross Murders—Inigo Jones	.80	2.40	4.00	M
34	I'll Kill You Last—H. C. Branson	.80	2.40	4.00	M
35	Murder at Deer Lick—A. B. Cunningham	.80	2.40	4.00	M
36	And Sudden Death—Cleve F. Adams	1.00	3.00	5.00	M
37	The Corpse in Company K—Robert Avery	.80	2.40	4.00	M
38	The Vice Czar Murders—Franklin Charles	.80	2.40	4.00	M
39	Murder on Every Floor—Ann Demarest	.80	2.40	4.00	M
40	The Clue of the Red Carnation—Burton Stevenson	.80	2.40	4.00	M
41	The Case of the Blue Lacquer Box—George F. Worts	.80	2.40	4.00	M

NATIONAL DAIRY
National Dairy Products Corp.

nn	641 Tested Recipes From the Sealtest Kitchens; 1954	.40	1.20	2.00	NF

NEWS STAND LIBRARY—1ST SERIES
Export Publishing Enterprises Limited

(Canadian)

		Good	Fine	N/Mint	
3	Ravager—David Lord	.80	2.40	4.00	E
4	Possess Me Not—Fan Nichols	.80	2.40	4.00	E
6	Broken Melody—Ronald Kirkbride	.80	2.40	4.00	E
14	Harlot—Cicely Schiller	.80	2.40	4.00	E
16	Pay for Her Passion—Gladys Stone	.80	2.40	4.00	E
22	Lost Virgin—Gail Jordan (Peggy Gaddis)	.80	2.40	4.00	E
23	Bed and the Blonde—Ian Peel	.80	2.40	4.00	E
25	Call House Madam—Serge C. Wolsey	.80	2.40	4.00	E
29	Lady of Lust—Carlotta Baker	.80	2.40	4.00	E
30	Room Service—Eliot Brewster	.80	2.40	4.00	E
33	Scream a Wanton Song—Wright Williams	.80	2.40	4.00	E
36	Limbo City—Edwin B. Self	.80	2.40	4.00	E
37	Red Rods—Dale Clark; aka The Blonde, the Gangster and the Private Eye	1.00	3.00	5.00	M
38	Two Time Doll—Gordon Semple	.80	2.40	4.00	E
39	Nightfall—David Goodis	1.00	3.00	5.00	M
40	Sligo—Brendon Wood	.80	2.40	4.00	E
42	Gloria—Glen Watkins; aka Fall Girl	.80	2.40	4.00	E
44	Bodies Are Dust—P. J. Wolfson	.80	2.40	4.00	E
53	Sin for Your Supper—Milton Douglas	.80	2.40	4.00	E
65	Love Goes Fast—Ursula Parrot	.80	2.40	4.00	E
67	Frustration—G. H. Henderson	.80	2.40	4.00	E
68	Chinatown Baby—Thomas Burke	1.00	3.00	5.00	E
71	Marriage a la Mode—Gustin Smith	.80	2.40	4.00	E
81	Office Girl—H. J. Krier	.80	2.40	4.00	E
88	Lover Boy—Julian Swift	.80	2.40	4.00	E
91	Round Moon—Genevieve Weinsott	.80	2.40	4.00	E
93	Daughter of Desire—Fletcher Knight	.80	2.40	4.00	E
95	Let Out the Beast—Leonard Fischer	3.00	9.00	15.00	SF
104	Never See the Sun—Moll Bennett	.80	2.40	4.00	E
114	The Evil Ear—G. A. Graeme	.80	2.40	4.00	E
117	Too Many Women—Gerry Martin	.80	2.40	4.00	E
128	A Killer Back Stage—Joshua Willard	1.00	3.00	5.00	M
137	Espionage Agent—Denison Clift	.80	2.40	4.00	
139	Reno Tramp—Florence Stonebraker	.80	2.40	4.00	E
141	Destroy the U. S. A.—Will F. Jenkins (Murray Leinster); aka Murder of the U. S. A.	3.00	9.00	15.00	SF
142	Worlds Within—Rog Phillips	3.00	9.00	15.00	SF
155	Harlot in Her Heart—Norman Bligh	.80	2.40	4.00	E

NEWS STAND LIBRARY—2ND SERIES
Export Publishing Enterprises Limited

(Canadian)

1A	Negligee—Gladys Sloan; 1949	.80	2.40	4.00	E
2A	The Long November—James Benson Nablo	.80	2.40	4.00	E
3A	Pay Her for Passion—P. J. Wolfson; aka Is My Flesh of Brass	.80	2.40	4.00	E
4A	Each Night a Black Desire—Bentz Plagemann	.80	2.40	4.00	E
5A	Sweet Surrender—George Willis; aka The Wild Faun	.80	2.40	4.00	E
6A	Sin for Your Supper—Milton Douglas	.80	2.40	4.00	E
7A	The Pagans—Jack Benedict	.80	2.40	4.00	E
8A	Dirty City—Michael Young	.80	2.40	4.00	E
9A	Touch of Violence—David Forrest	.80	2.40	4.00	M
10A	This Was Joanna—Grant R. Brooks	.80	2.40	4.00	E
11A	The House on Craig Street—Ronald J. Cooke	.80	2.40	4.00	E
12A	Frustration—Henry C. Clayton	.80	2.40	4.00	E
13A	No Place in Heaven—Laura Warren	.80	2.40	4.00	E

News Stand Library 1A, © Export

News Stand Library 14A, © Export

News Stand Library 15A, © Export

No Imprint nn, © Unknown

Novel Library 9, © Div

Novel Library 30, © Div

		Good	Fine	N/Mint	
	(NEWS STAND LIBRARY—2ND SERIES, continued)				
14A	Death Be My Destiny—Neil P. Perrin	1.00	3.00	5.00	M
	With dust jacket	12.50	37.50	60.00	
15A	Jesse James—Thomas P. Kelley	1.20	3.60	6.00	NF
16A	Daughters of Desire—Fletcher Knight	.80	2.40	4.00	E
17A	Penthouse Killings—Brown	.80	2.40	4.00	M
18A	Let Out the Beast—Leonard Fischer	3.00	9.00	15.00	SF
19A	In Passion's Fiery Pit—	.80	2.40	4.00	E
20A	Sugar Puss on Dorchester Street—Al Palmer	.80	2.40	4.00	E
21A	The Door Between—Neil P. Perrin	.80	2.40	4.00	E
23A	Pick-up—Leslie Scott	.80	2.40	4.00	E
24A	Overnight Escapade—Stephen Mark	.80	2.40	4.00	E
25A	Strange Desires—Alan Malston	.80	2.40	4.00	E
26A	He Learned About Women—Ted Greenshade	.80	2.40	4.00	E
27A	Waste No Tears—Jarvis Warwick (Hugh Garner)	5.00	15.00	25.00	E
28A	Too Many Women—Gerry Martin	.80	2.40	4.00	E

NO IMPRINT
Unknown publisher

D1920	How to Build and Operate a Model Railroad—Marshall McClintock; 1955	.40	1.20	2.00	NF

NO IMPRINT
Unknown publisher

Digest Size

nn	War Birds - Diary of an Unknown Aviator; 1951	1.60	4.80	8.00	C

NOVEL LIBRARY
Diversey Publishing Corporation

1	3 Gorgeous Hussies—Jack Woodford; 1948	5.00	15.00	25.00	E
2	Ecstasy Girl—Jack Woodford	3.00	9.00	15.00	E
3	Free Lovers—Jack Woodford; aka Fiddler's Fee	3.00	9.00	15.00	E
4	The Passionate Princess—Jack Woodford; aka Proxy Princess	3.00	9.00	15.00	E
5	Wanton Venus—Maurice LeBlanc	5.00	15.00	25.00	
6	Peeping Tom—Jack Woodford; aka Come Into My Parlor	7.00	21.00	35.00	E
7	Grounds for Divorce—Jack Woodford; aka Love at Last	3.00	9.00	15.00	E
8	The Regenerate Lover—D. H. Clarke; aka Young and Healthy, 1949	3.00	9.00	15.00	E
9	The Street of Painted Lips—Maurice DeKobra	5.00	15.00	25.00	E
10	Woman Without Love?—Roswell Williams	5.00	15.00	25.00	E
11	The Villain and the Virgin—J. H. Chase; aka No Orchids for Miss Blandish	5.00	15.00	25.00	E
12	Uneasy Virtue—Dana Wilson	4.00	12.00	20.00	E
13	A Good Time Man—E. P. Keating	4.00	12.00	20.00	E
14	Gold Diggers—Lois Bull	5.00	15.00	25.00	E
15	Playthings of Desire—J. Wesley Putnam	4.00	12.00	20.00	E
16	Women to Love—Sinclair Drago	5.00	15.00	25.00	E
17	Frisco Gal—Clarkson Crane; aka Naomi Martin. Note: Same cover as the comic Romantic Love No. 11	5.00	15.00	25.00	E
18	Bedroom Eyes—Maurice DeKobra	7.00	21.00	35.00	E
19	Louis Beretti—D. H. Clarke	5.00	15.00	25.00	E
20	One Night With Nancy—Wilson Collison; Note: Same cover as Diversey Love Book Monthly No. 2	5.00	15.00	25.00	E
21	The Love Toy—anonymous (H. S. Drago)	5.00	15.00	25.00	E
22	Mirabelle: Woman of Passion—Ellen Caren	3.00	9.00	15.00	E
23	Broadway Virgin—Lois Bull	4.00	12.00	20.00	E
24	Infidelity—Arthur Weigall; Note: Same cover as the comic Intimate Confessions 7	7.00	21.00	35.00	E

Novel Library 40, © Div

Novel Library 45, © Div

Novel Library 46, © Div

			Good	Fine	N/Mint	
(NOVEL LIBRARY, continued)						
25	Venus on Wheels—Maurice DeKobra; 1949		5.00	15.00	25.00	E
26	The Immodest Maidens—Eleanore Browne; aka Make Me Yours		5.00	15.00	25.00	E
27	Ladies of Chance—Anthony Scott		4.00	12.00	20.00	E
28	The Love Clinic—Maurice DeKobra		4.00	12.00	20.00	E
29	All Dames Are Dynamite—Timothy Trent		4.00	12.00	20.00	E
30	Diary of Death—Wilson Collison		4.00	12.00	20.00	E
31	Millions for Love—Colette Roberts		3.00	9.00	15.00	E
32	Dishonorable Darling—Wilson Collison; 1950, aka Farewell to Women		3.00	9.00	15.00	E
33	The Women in His Life—Eleanor Nash; aka Bachelors Are Made. Note: Same cover as the comic Romantic Love No. 7		4.00	12.00	20.00	E
34	Crystal Girl—Stephen Longstreet; Note: Same cover as the comic Romantic Love 5		4.00	12.00	20.00	E
35	The Lady Said Yes—George Martin		4.00	12.00	20.00	E
36	Male and Female—Jack Woodford		3.00	9.00	15.00	E
37	12 Chinamen and a Woman—J. H. Chase		6.00	18.00	30.00	E
38	Sixty Seconds—Maxwell Bodenheim		4.00	12.00	20.00	E
39	No Bed of Her Own—Val Lewton; Note: Same cover as the comic Realistic Romances No. 3		5.00	15.00	25.00	E
40	Wild Parties—Max Lief		5.00	15.00	25.00	E
41	Help Wanted - Male—Thomas Stone; Note: Same cover as the Avon comic Romantic Love No. 9		4.00	12.00	20.00	E
42	Lady for Love—Alan Brener Schultz		4.00	12.00	20.00	E
43	How to Play Canasta—Richard L. Frey		1.20	3.60	6.00	NF
44	Teach Me to Love—Jack Woodford		3.00	9.00	15.00	E
45	Blonde Baggage—Marty Holland		6.00	18.00	30.00	E
46	Naked on Roller Skates—Maxwell Bodenheim; Note: Same cover as Diversey Popular Novel No. 2		7.00	21.00	35.00	E

NOVEL SELECTIONS
Novel Selections, Inc.

			Good	Fine	N/Mint	
51	The Bastard—Erskine Caldwell		.80	2.40	4.00	E
52	Poor Fool—Erskine Caldwell		.80	2.40	4.00	E

NOVELS INC.
Novels Inc.

Digest Size

			Good	Fine	N/Mint	
nn	Made for Loving—William Arthur; c-Rodewald		.80	2.40	4.00	E

Novel Selections 51, © NS

Novels Inc. nn, © Novels, Inc.

Novels Inc. 10, © Novels, Inc.

Original Novels 700, © Orig

Original Novels 718, © Orig

Original Novels 720, © Orig

			Good	Fine	N/Mint	
(NOVELS, INC., continued)						
nn	Sinner in Gingham—Gail Jordan (Peggy Gaddis)		.80	2.40	4.00	E
10	The Tigress—John Saxon		.80	2.40	4.00	E

OMNIBUS
Omnibus Publishing Company
Digest Size

nn	Night of Crime—Armstrong Livingston		2.00	6.00	10.00	M

ORIGINAL NOVELS
Original Novels, Inc.

Digest Size

700	Women of the Night—Peggy Gaddis; orig., 1951, c-Gross		1.20	3.60	6.00	E
701	Backstage Affair—Amos Hatter		1.00	3.00	5.00	E
702	Strictly for Pleasure—Norman Bligh; orig., 1951		1.00	3.00	5.00	E
704	Gambler's Girl—Kermit Welles		1.00	3.00	5.00	E
707	Beyond Desire—Albert L. Quandt; orig., 1952		1.00	3.00	5.00	E
708	Forbidden Evil—Harry Whittington		1.20	3.60	6.00	E
709	Gang Moll—Albert L. Quandt		1.20	3.60	6.00	E
710	See No Evil—Kermit Welles		1.00	3.00	5.00	E
712	Farewell to Passion—Day Keene		1.00	3.00	5.00	E
713	Sleep With the Devil—Reed McCary		1.00	3.00	5.00	E
714	Body and Passion—White Harrison (Harry Whittington)		1.20	3.60	6.00	E
715	Wayward Nymph—Elisabeth Gill		1.00	3.00	5.00	E
716	Cellar Club—Albert L. Quandt		2.00	6.00	10.00	E
717	Sheila's Daughter—William Arnold		1.00	3.00	5.00	E
718	Savage Love—Whit Harrison (Harry Whittington); orig., 1952, c-Belarski		2.00	6.00	10.00	E
719	Harlem Woman—William Arnold		2.00	6.00	10.00	E
720	Baby Sitter—Albert L. Quandt; orig., 1952		1.20	3.60	6.00	E
721	Zip-Gun Angels—Albert L. Quandt; Note: Same cover as Star No. 750		2.00	6.00	10.00	JD
722	City of Sin—Robert O. Saber; orig., 1952		1.20	3.60	6.00	E
723	Backwoods Hussy—Hallam Whitney (Harry Whittington)		1.20	3.60	6.00	E
724	Runaway Girl—William Arnold		1.00	3.00	5.00	E
725	Ringside Jezebel—Kate Nickerson; orig., 1953		1.00	3.00	5.00	E
726	Dream Club—Albert L. Quandt; aka Beyond Desire		2.00	6.00	10.00	E
727	Visiting Nurse—Norman Bligh; orig., 1953		1.00	3.00	5.00	E

Original Novels 721, © Orig

Original Novels 726, © Orig

Original Novels 738, © Orig

	(ORIGINAL NOVELS, continued)	Good	Fine	N/Mint	
728	Baby Peddler—Albert L. Quandt	1.00	3.00	5.00	E
730	Waterfront Girl—Amos Hatter	1.00	3.00	5.00	E
731	Shack Road—Hallam Whitney (Harry Whittington); orig., 1953	1.20	3.60	6.00	E
732	Streets of Paris—Robert E. Reynolds	1.00	3.00	5.00	E
734	Runaway Girl—William Arnold	1.00	3.00	5.00	E
737	City Girl—Hallam Whitney (Harry Whittington)	1.20	3.60	6.00	E
738	Cellar Club—Albert L. Quandt	2.00	6.00	10.00	E
739	Ward Nurse—Mitchell Coleman; aka Born to be Bad, Affairs of a Ward Nurse	1.00	3.00	5.00	E
740	River Boat Girl—Norman Bligh; c-Belarski	1.00	3.00	5.00	E
741	Motel Mistress—Norman Bligh; aka Remembered Moment	1.00	3.00	5.00	E
742	Shanty Road—Whit Harrison (Harry Whittington)	1.20	3.60	6.00	E
743	Big City Nurse—Albert L. Quandt; aka Baby Peddler	1.00	3.00	5.00	E
744	City Streets—Gene Harvey	1.00	3.00	5.00	E
746	French Alley—Matthew Clay; orig., 1954	1.00	3.00	5.00	E

PADELL
Padell Book and Magazine Company

Digest Size

nn	Tales of French Love and Passion—Guy de Maupassant; 1943	1.00	3.00	5.00	
nn	From Dance Hall to White Slavery—John Dillon	4.00	12.00	20.00	E
nn	The Tragedies of the White Slaves—H. M. Lytle; 1945	4.00	12.00	20.00	E

PAPERBACK LIBRARY
Paperback Library, Inc.

52-290	The Best From Famous Monsters of Filmland—ed. Forrest J. Ackerman; 1st ed., 1964	1.00	3.00	5.00	NF
52-504	Son of Famous Monsters of Filmland—ed. Forrest J. Ackerman; 1st ed., 1964	1.00	3.00	5.00	NF
52-813	Famous Monsters of Filmland Strike Back!—ed. Forrest J. Ackerman; 1st ed., 1965	1.00	3.00	5.00	NF
64-729	Green Lantern and Green Arrow No. 1—Denny O'Neill; 1st ed., 1972. Note: Contains comic book reprints	1.00	3.00	5.00	A
64-755	Green Lantern and Green Arrow No. 2—Denny O'Neill; 1st ed., 1972. Note: Contains comic book reprints	1.00	3.00	5.00	A

PARENTS INSTITUTE
The Parents Institute, Inc.

Digest Size

nn	Best Stories for Boys and Girls—anthology; 1938, includes Mickey Mouse and Pluto	3.00	9.00	15.00	

PELICAN BOOKS
New American Library

(Also see Mentor)

P 1	Public Opinion—Walter Lippmann; 1946	.30	.90	1.50	NF
P 2	Patterns of Culture—Ruth Benedict	.30	.90	1.50	NF
P 3	You and Music—Christian Darnton	.30	.90	1.50	NF
P 4	The Birth and Death of the Sun—George Gamow	.40	1.20	2.00	NF
P 5	An Enemy of the People: Anti-Semitism—James Parkes	.40	1.20	2.00	NF
P 6	What Happened in History—V. Gordon Childe	.40	1.20	2.00	NF
P 7	The Physiology of Sex—Kenneth Walker	.30	.90	1.50	NF
P 8	Mathematician's Delight—W. W. Sawyer	.30	.90	1.50	NF
P 9	The Weather—Raymond Bush & George Kimble	.30	.90	1.50	NF

Padell nn, © Padell   Paperback Libr. 64-729, © Pprback. Lib.   Pelican Books P16, © NA

PELICAN BOOKS, continued)

		Good	Fine	N/Mint	
P10	America's Role in the World Economy—Alvin H. Hansen	.30	.90	1.50	NF
P11	Heredity, Race and Society—Th. Dobzhansky & L. C. Dunn	.30	.90	1.50	NF
P12	The Story of Human Birth—Alan F. Guttmacher; 1947	.30	.90	1.50	NF
P13	Thomas Jefferson on Democracy	.40	1.20	2.00	NF
P14	Introducing Shakespeare—G. B. Harrison	.30	.90	1.50	NF
P15	Emerson: The Basic Writings of America's Sage—Ralph Waldo Emerson	.40	1.20	2.00	NF
P16	The Personality of Animals—H. Munro Fox	.40	1.20	2.00	NF
P17	Human Breeding and Survival—Guy I. Burch & Elmer Pendell	.40	1.20	2.00	NF
P18	Is Marriage Necessary?—George H. Bartlett	.30	.90	1.50	NF
P19	Good Reading	.30	.90	1.50	NF
P20	An Introduction to Modern Architecture—Elizabeth B. Mock & J. M. Richards	.30	.90	1.50	NF
P21	The Odyssey—Homerus	.40	1.20	2.00	NF
P22	Religion and the Rise of Capitalism—R. H. Tawney	.40	1.20	2.00	NF
P23	Heredity, Race and Society—Th. Dobzhansky & L. C. Dunn	.40	1.20	2.00	NF
P24	Sweden: The Middle Way—Marquis W. Childs; 1948	.30	.90	1.50	NF
P25	Philosophy in a New Key—Susanne K. Langer	.30	.90	1.50	NF

PENGUIN

Penguin Books, Inc.

(Also see Signet; some issued as Penguin Signet)

		Good	Fine	N/Mint	
60	The Dark Invader—Captain von Rintelen	1.20	3.60	6.00	
79	The Rasp—Philip MacDonald	1.20	3.60	6.00	M
	With dust jacket	10.00	30.00	50.00	
239	Stealthy Terror—John Ferguson	1.20	3.60	6.00	M
276	The Case of the Late Pig—Margery Allingham	1.20	3.60	6.00	M
339	High Rising—Angela Thirkell	1.20	3.60	6.00	
501	Murder by an Aristocrat—Mignon G. Eberhart; 1942	1.20	3.60	6.00	M
502	Pygmalion—George Bernard Shaw	1.00	3.00	5.00	
503	Death of a Ghost—Margery Allingham	1.20	3.60	6.00	M
	With dust jacket	10.00	30.00	50.00	
504	All Concerned Notified—Helen Reilly	1.20	3.60	6.00	M
505	The Mother—Pearl S. Buck	1.20	3.60	6.00	
506	Two Survived—Guy Pearce Jones	1.20	3.60	6.00	
507	The Physiology of Sex—Kenneth Walker	1.20	3.60	6.00	
508	Walden—Henry David Thoreau	1.20	3.60	6.00	
509	The Pastures of Heaven—John Steinbeck	1.60	4.80	8.00	
510	Trent's Own Case—Warner H. Allen & E. C. Bentley	1.20	3.60	6.00	M
511	Cause for Alarm—Eric Ambler	1.00	3.00	5.00	M
512	The Strange Case of Miss Annie Spragg—Louis Bromfield	1.20	3.60	6.00	
513	The Catalyst Club—George Dyer	1.20	3.60	6.00	
514	Tombstone—Walter Noble Burns	1.20	3.60	6.00	NF
515	The Confidential Agent—Graham Greene; 1943	1.00	3.00	5.00	
516	Genghis Khan—Harold Lamb	.80	2.40	4.00	B
517	Philosopher's Holiday—Irwin Edman	1.20	3.60	6.00	
518	The Middle Temple Murder—J. S. Fletcher	1.20	3.60	6.00	M
519	A Blunt Instrument—Georgette Heyer	1.20	3.60	6.00	M
520	The Saga of Billy the Kid—Walter Noble Burns	1.00	3.00	5.00	B
521	The Ox-bow Incident—Walter Van Tilburg Clark	1.60	4.80	8.00	W
522	Sabotage—Cleve F. Adams	1.20	3.60	6.00	
523	Leaves of Grass—Walt Whitman	1.20	3.60	6.00	
524	Pencil Points to Murder—W. A. Barber & R. F. Schabelitz	1.20	3.60	6.00	M
525	The Penguin Book of Sonnets—Carl Withers	1.20	3.60	6.00	
526	My Own Murderer—Richard Hull	1.20	3.60	6.00	M
527	The Telephone Booth Indian—A. J. Liebling	1.20	3.60	6.00	
528	The Blind Barber—John Dickson Carr	1.60	4.80	8.00	M
529	Kitty Foyle—Christopher Morley; 1944	.80	2.40	4.00	
530	The Ministry of Fear—Graham Greene	1.20	3.60	6.00	
531	Drawn Conclusion—W. A. Barber & R. F. Schabelitz	1.20	3.60	6.00	M
532	Hag's Nook—John Dickson Carr	1.60	4.80	8.00	M
533	The Purple Sickle Murder—Freeman Wills Crofts	1.60	4.80	8.00	
534	Black Plumes—Margery Allingham	1.60	4.80	8.00	
535	The Old Dark House—J. B. Priestley	1.60	4.80	8.00	
536	In Hazard—Richard Hughes	.80	2.40	4.00	
537	Out of This World—Julius Fast	1.60	4.80	8.00	SF
538	The Laughing Fox—Frank Gruber	1.60	4.80	8.00	
	With dust jacket	10.00	30.00	50.00	
539	Laughing Boy—Oliver LaFarge	1.20	3.60	6.00	
540	My Name Is Aram—William Saroyan	.80	2.40	4.00	
541	Mr. Pinkerton Grows a Beard—David Frome	1.20	3.60	6.00	M
542	Murder Enters the Picture—W. A. Barber & R. F. Schabelitz	1.20	3.60	6.00	M
543	Shell of Death—Nicholas Blake	1.20	3.60	6.00	M
544	Ten Holy Horrors—Francis Beeding	1.20	3.60	6.00	M
545	The Talking Clock—Frank Gruber	1.60	4.80	8.00	
	With dust jacket	10.00	30.00	50.00	

		Good	Fine	N/Mint	
546	O'Halloran's Luck—Stephen Vincent Benet	1.20	3.60	6.00	
547	Death of My Aunt—C. H. B. Kitchin	1.20	3.60	6.00	M
548	Black-Out in Gretley—J. B. Priestley	1.20	3.60	6.00	
549	Murders in Volume II—Elizabeth Daly	1.20	3.60	6.00	M
550	To Walk the Night—William Sloane	1.20	3.60	6.00	
551	Mr. Littlejohn—Martin Flavin	1.00	3.00	5.00	
552	Murder in Trinidad—John W. Vandercook	1.20	3.60	6.00	M
553	Nine Times Nine—H. H. Holmes; 1945	3.00	9.00	15.00	M
554	Tales of Piracy, Crime and Ghosts—Daniel Defoe	1.20	3.60	6.00	A
555	Dr. Toby Finds Murder—Sturges Mason Schley	1.20	3.60	6.00	M
557	McSorley's Wonderful Saloon—Joseph Mitchell	1.00	3.00	5.00	
558	Porgy—Du Bose Heyward	1.00	3.00	5.00	
559	Death of a Saboteur—Hulbert Footner	1.20	3.60	6.00	
560	Murder in Fiji—John W. Vandercook	1.20	3.60	6.00	M
561	Young Man With a Horn—Dorothy Baker	1.00	3.00	5.00	
562	Simon Lash, Private Detective—Frank Gruber	1.60	4.80	8.00	M
563	Appointment in Samarra—John O'Hara	1.00	3.00	5.00	
564	Maigret Travels South—Georges Simenon	1.20	3.60	6.00	M
565	Step in the Dark—Ethel Lina White	1.00	3.00	5.00	M
566	Say Yes to Murder—W. T. Ballard	1.20	3.60	6.00	M
567	Trouble in July—Erskine Caldwell	1.00	3.00	5.00	
568	Night Flight—Antoine de Saint Exupery	1.00	3.00	5.00	
569	Conceived in Liberty—Howard Fast	1.00	3.00	5.00	
570	And Berry Came Too—Dornford Yates	1.00	3.00	5.00	
571	Death Down East—Eleanor Blake	1.20	3.60	6.00	M
572	The Good Soldier Schweik—Jaroslav Hasek; 1946	1.00	3.00	5.00	
573	The Turning Wheels—Stuart Cloete	1.00	3.00	5.00	
574	A Passage to India—E. M. Forster	1.00	3.00	5.00	
575	The Cask—Freeman Wills Crofts	1.00	3.00	5.00	M
576	The Lovely Lady—D. H. Lawrence	1.00	3.00	5.00	
577	Manhattan Transfer—John Dos Passos	1.00	3.00	5.00	
578	Bread and Wine—Ignazio Silone	1.00	3.00	5.00	
579	Patience of Maigret—Georges Simenon	1.20	3.60	6.00	M
580	Pal Joey—John O'Hara	1.00	3.00	5.00	
581	God's Little Acre—Erskine Caldwell	1.20	3.60	6.00	
582	Thunder on the Left—Christopher Morley	1.00	3.00	5.00	
583	Vein of Iron—Ellen Glasgow	1.00	3.00	5.00	
584	Dead Reckoning—Francis Bonnamy	1.00	3.00	5.00	M
585	Winesburg, Ohio—Sherwood Anderson	1.00	3.00	5.00	
586	The Rasp—Philip MacDonald	1.20	3.60	6.00	M
	With dust jacket	10.00	30.00	50.00	
587	Martin Eden—Jack London	1.20	3.60	6.00	
588	The Unvanquished—Howard Fast	1.00	3.00	5.00	
589	Back Street—Fannie Hurst	1.00	3.00	5.00	
590	Orlando—Virginia Woolf	1.00	3.00	5.00	
591	Mildred Pierce—James M. Cain	1.20	3.60	6.00	
592	Malice in Wonderland—Nicholas Blake	1.20	3.60	6.00	M
593	Handbook of Politics and Voters' Guide—Lowell Mellett	.80	2.40	4.00	
594	Heavenly Discourse—Charles Erskine Scott Wood	1.00	3.00	5.00	
595	Cabbages and Kings—O. Henry	.80	2.40	4.00	
596	The Heart Is a Lonely Hunter—Carson McCullers	.80	2.40	4.00	
597	The Summing Up—W. Somerset Maugham	1.00	3.00	5.00	
598	Put Out the Light—Ethel Lina White	1.00	3.00	5.00	M
599	Tortilla Flat—John Steinbeck	1.60	4.80	8.00	
600	Montana Rides!—Evan Evans (Max Brand)	1.00	3.00	5.00	W
601	Jurgen—James Branch Cabell	1.20	3.60	6.00	F
602	The New Veteran—Charles G. Bolte	1.00	3.00	5.00	
603	Short Stories of James T. Farrell	1.00	3.00	5.00	
604	Trio—Dorothy Baker	1.00	3.00	5.00	
605	Cimarron—Edna Ferber	1.60	4.80	8.00	
606	A Rope of Sand—Francis Bonnamy	1.00	3.00	5.00	M
607	Pygmalion—George Bernard Shaw	1.00	3.00	5.00	
608	Major Barbara—George Bernard Shaw	1.00	3.00	5.00	
609	Saint Joan—George Bernard Shaw	1.00	3.00	5.00	
610	Lady Chatterley's Lover—D. H. Lawrence	1.20	3.60	6.00	
611	Messer Marco Polo—Donn Byrne	1.00	3.00	5.00	
612	Christianity Takes a Stand—William Scarlett	.80	2.40	4.00	NF
613	The Odyssey—Homerus	.80	2.40	4.00	A
614	The Penguin Hoyle—Albert H. Morehead & Geoffrey Mott-Smith	.50	1.50	2.50	NF
615	Lady Into Fox and a Man in the Zoo—David Garnett	1.00	3.00	5.00	F
616	Eleven of Diamonds—Baynard Kendrick	1.00	3.00	5.00	M
617	Saratoga Trunk—Edna Ferber	1.00	3.00	5.00	
618	The Perennial Boarder—Phoebe Atwood Taylor	1.00	3.00	5.00	
	With dust jacket	10.00	30.00	50.00	
619	Almayer's Folly—Joseph Conrad	1.20	3.60	6.00	
620	Montana Rides Again—Evan Evans (Max Brand)	1.00	3.00	5.00	W

Penguin 528, © Pen

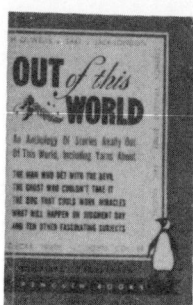

Penguin 537, © Pen

Penguin 641, © Pen

(PENGUIN, continued)

		Good	Fine	N/Mint	
621	Serenade—James M. Cain	1.00	3.00	5.00	
622	Looking for a Bluebird—Josef Wechsberg	1.00	3.00	5.00	
623	The Silver Jackass—Frank Gruber	1.20	3.60	6.00	
624	The Velvet Well—John Gearon	1.00	3.00	5.00	
625	Daisy Miller and an International Episode—Henry James	1.00	3.00	5.00	
626	The Purple Onion Mystery—Harriette Ashbrook	1.00	3.00	5.00	M
627	Tobacco Road—Erskine Caldwell	1.20	3.60	6.00	
628	The Innocent Voyage—Richard Hughes	1.00	3.00	5.00	
629	The King Is Dead on Queen Street—Francis Bonnamy	1.00	3.00	5.00	M
630	Mother Wore Tights—Miriam Young	1.00	3.00	5.00	
631	A Funeral in Eden—Paul McGuire	1.00	3.00	5.00	
632	Sanctuary—William Faulkner	1.00	3.00	5.00	
633	Great Son—Edna Ferber	1.00	3.00	5.00	
634	The Unbearable Bassington—Saki	1.00	3.00	5.00	
635	Blood on Lake Louisa—Baynard Kendrick	1.00	3.00	5.00	
636	The Voice of Bugle Ann and the Romance of Rosy Ridge—MacKinlay Kantor	.80	2.40	4.00	
637	Hotel Splendide—Ludwig Bemelmans	.80	2.40	4.00	
638	A Portrait of Jennie—Robert Nathan	.80	2.40	4.00	
639	So Big—Edna Ferber	.80	2.40	4.00	
640	Cartoons: All in Line—Saul Steinberg	1.00	3.00	5.00	H
641	Murder! Great True Crime Cases—Alan Hynd	1.20	3.60	6.00	NF
642	The Kiss of Death—Eleazar Lipsky	1.00	3.00	5.00	
643	Young Lonigan—James T. Farrell	1.00	3.00	5.00	
644	Short Stories of Thomas Wolfe	1.00	3.00	5.00	
645	Song of the Whip—Evan Evans (Max Brand)	1.00	3.00	5.00	W
646	Journeyman—Erskine Caldwell	1.00	3.00	5.00	E
647	Uncle Tom's Children—Richard Wright	1.00	3.00	5.00	
648	Deadly Weapon—Wade Miller	1.20	3.60	6.00	M
649	The Tyranny of Sex—Ludwig Lewisohn	.80	2.40	4.00	
650	American Beauty—Edna Ferber	.80	2.40	4.00	
651	Market for Murder—Frank Gruber	1.00	3.00	5.00	M
652	The New Quiz Book—Albert H. Morehead & Geoffrey Mott-Smith	1.00	3.00	5.00	NF
653	Show Boat—Edna Ferber	1.20	3.60	6.00	
654	Great Western Stories—William Targ	1.00	3.00	5.00	W
655	Great Murder Stories	1.20	3.60	6.00	M
656	Christ Stopped at Eboli—Carlo Levi	.80	2.40	4.00	
657	Desire Me—Leonhard Frank	.80	2.40	4.00	
658	Death of a Swagman—Arthur W. Upfield	1.20	3.60	6.00	M
659	The Wild Palms—William Faulkner	1.00	3.00	5.00	

Penguin 644, © Pen

Penguin 655, © Pen

Penguin 658, © Pen

PENGUIN GUIDES
Penguin Books, Inc.

		Good	Fine	N/Mint	
G1	The Penguin Guide to California—Carl Maas; 1947	1.00	3.00	5.00	NF

PENGUIN SPECIALS
Penguin Books, Inc./The Infantry Journal

		Good	Fine	N/Mint	
s75	New Ways of War—Tom Wintringham; 1940	.80	2.40	4.00	NF
	With dust jacket	2.00	6.00	10.00	
s81	Russia—Bernard Pares; 1943	.50	1.50	2.50	NF
s82	Aircraft Recognition—R. A. Saville-Sneath	.80	2.40	4.00	NF
s201	What's That Plane—Walter Pitkin, Jr.; 1942	.80	2.40	4.00	NF
s202	New Soldier's Handbook	.80	2.40	4.00	NF
s203	Guerrilla Warfare—''Yank'' Levy	.80	2.40	4.00	NF
s204	How the Jap Army Fights—Paul W. Thompson, others; 1942	1.00	3.00	5.00	NF
s206	How Russia Prepared—Maurice Edelman	.50	1.50	2.50	NF
s207	Christianity and Social Order—William Temple	.40	1.20	2.00	NF
s209	Americans vs. Germans; 1942	.80	2.40	4.00	NF
s210	Modern Battle—Paul W. Thompson	.80	2.40	4.00	NF
s211	The Good Soldier Schweik—Jaroslav Hasek	.80	2.40	4.00	
s212	Psychology for the Fighting Man; 1943	1.00	3.00	5.00	NF
s213	Empire in the Changing World—W. K. Hancock	.80	2.40	4.00	NF
s214	Hitler's Second Army—Alfred Hancock; 1943	1.00	3.00	5.00	NF
s215	Handbook for Army Wives and Mothers—Catherine Redmond	1.00	3.00	5.00	NF
s216	A History of the War—Rudolf Modley	.80	2.40	4.00	NF
s217	The Next Germany	.80	2.40	4.00	NF
s218	Shipyard Diary of a Woman Welder—Augusta H. Clawson	1.00	3.00	5.00	NF
s219	The Moon Is Down—John Steinbeck; 1943	1.00	3.00	5.00	
s220	Guadalcanal Diary—Richard Tregaskis; 1943	.50	1.50	2.50	C
s221	Thirty Seconds Over Tokyo—Ted W. Lawson; 1944	.50	1.50	2.50	C
s222	The British Navy's Air Arm—Owen Rutter	.80	2.40	4.00	NF
s223	They Were Expendable—W. L. White	.80	2.40	4.00	
s224	A Short History of the Army and Navy—Fletcher Pratt	.80	2.40	4.00	NF
s225	G. I. Sketch Book—Aimee Crane	.80	2.40	4.00	
s226	The Battle Is the Pay-off—Ralph Ingersoll; 1944	.80	2.40	4.00	
s227	This Is the Navy—Gilbert Cant	.50	1.50	2.50	NF
s229	Psychology for the Returning Serviceman—Marjorie van de Water; 1945	1.00	3.00	5.00	NF
s230	I Knew Your Soldier—Eleanor Stevenson & Pete Martin	.80	2.40	4.00	
s231	Cartoons for Fighters—Frank Brandt; 1945	.80	2.40	4.00	
s237	Pipeline to Battle—Peter W. Rainier	.80	2.40	4.00	
s238	Storm—George R. Stewart	.50	1.50	2.50	
s239	This Is the Navy—Gilbert Cant	.50	1.50	2.50	NF
s240	Island Victory—S. L. A. Marshall	.80	2.40	4.00	

PENNANT
Pennant Books/Bantam Books, Inc.

		Good	Fine	N/Mint	
P 1	Navajo Canyon—Thomas W. Blackburn; 1953	.80	2.40	4.00	W
P 2	The Last of the Plainsmen—Zane Grey	.50	1.50	2.50	W
P 3	Epitaph for a Spy—Eric Ambler	.50	1.50	2.50	M
P 4	Stamped for Murder—Ben Benson	.50	1.50	2.50	M
P 5	In Those Days—Harvey Fergusson	.50	1.50	2.50	W
P 6	Mojave—Edwin Corle	.50	1.50	2.50	W
P 7	Vanity Row—W. R. Burnett	.50	1.50	2.50	
P 8	Sunset Rider—Matt Stuart	.50	1.50	2.50	W
P 9	Ruler of the Range—Peter Dawson	.50	1.50	2.50	W
P10	Six-gun Boss—Clay Randall	.50	1.50	2.50	W

Penguin Specials s75, © Pen

Penguin Specials s218, © Pen

Pennant P1, © Bantam

Pennant P11, © Bantam

Pennant P20, © Bantam

Pennant P40, © Bantam

(PENNANT, continued)

		Good	Fine	N/Mint	
P11	A Time to Kill—Geoffrey Household	.50	1.50	2.50	M
P12	Warrant for a Wanton—Michael Gillian	.50	1.50	2.50	
P13	Apache Desert—L. P. Holmes	.50	1.50	2.50	W
P14	Action at War Bow Valley—Michael Carder	.50	1.50	2.50	W
P15	Takeoff—C. M. Kornbluth	1.00	3.00	5.00	SF
P16	Lily in Her Coffin—Ben Benson	.50	1.50	2.50	M
P17	Gunsmoke Over Big Muddy—Frank O'Rourke	.50	1.50	2.50	M
P18	Wire in the Wind—Matt Stuart	.50	1.50	2.50	W
P19	Reap the Wild Wind—Thelma Strabel	.50	1.50	2.50	A
P20	Two and the Town—Henry Gregor Felsen	.50	1.50	2.50	
P21	Border Graze—Dwight Bennett	.50	1.50	2.50	W
P22	Long Ride—Peter Dawson	.50	1.50	2.50	W
P23	Maneaters of Kumaon—Jim Corbett	.50	1.50	2.50	NF
P24	Murder Won't Out—Russel Crouse	.50	1.50	2.50	M
P25	High Starlight—L. P. Holmes	.50	1.50	2.50	W
P26	Santa Fe Passage—Clay Fisher	.50	1.50	2.50	W
P27	Burro Alley—Edwin Corle	.50	1.50	2.50	
P28	Blackcock's Feather—Maurice Walsh	.50	1.50	2.50	A
P29	The Naked Spur—Rolfe Bloom & Allan Ullman; 1954	.50	1.50	2.50	W
P30	Bold Raiders of the West—Frederick R. Bechdolt	.50	1.50	2.50	W
P31	The Outlaw Years—Robert M. Coates	.50	1.50	2.50	NF
P32	Walls Rise Up—George Sessions Perry	.50	1.50	2.50	
P33	Shadow of the Butte—Thomas Thompson	.50	1.50	2.50	W
P34	Dodge City: Queen of Cowtowns—Stanley Vestal	.80	2.40	4.00	NF
P35	Walk the Dark Bridge—William O'Farrell	.50	1.50	2.50	
P36	Elephant Bill—J. H. Williams	.50	1.50	2.50	NF
P37	Longhorn Empire—Will Ermine	.50	1.50	2.50	W
P38	Outlaw Valley—Evan Evans (Max Brand)	.50	1.50	2.50	W
P39	American Me—Beatrice Griffith	.50	1.50	2.50	
P40	Doubloons—Charles B. Driscoll	.50	1.50	2.50	A
P41	The Bronze Mermaid—Paul Ernst	.50	1.50	2.50	
P42	Saddle-man—Matt Stuart	.50	1.50	2.50	W
P43	Fort Starvation—Frank Gruber	.50	1.50	2.50	W
P44	Adventures in Time and Space—Raymond J. Healy & J. Francis McComas	.50	1.50	2.50	SF
P46	Guaracha Trail—George Parker	.50	1.50	2.50	
P47	Tombstone—Clarence Budington Kelland	.50	1.50	2.50	W
P48	When Oil Ran Red—Clay Randall	.50	1.50	2.50	W
P49	The Sixpenny Dame—Eaton K. Goldthwaite	.50	1.50	2.50	
P50	One Way Ticket—Eugene O'Brien	.50	1.50	2.50	
P51	A Vaquero of the Brush Country—J. Frank Dobie	.50	1.50	2.50	NF
P52	The Border Queen—Nick Sumner	.50	1.50	2.50	W
P53	Toll Mountain—Robert McCaig	.50	1.50	2.50	
P54	To the Last Man—William E. Barrett	.50	1.50	2.50	
P55	Repeat Performance—William O'Farrell	.50	1.50	2.50	
P56	Beyond Human Ken—Judith Merril	.80	2.40	4.00	SF
P57	Horse Thief Trail—Frederick R. Bechdolt	.50	1.50	2.50	W
P59	Mostly Murder—Fredric Brown	5.00	15.00	25.00	M
P61	The Argosy Book of Sports Stories—Rogers Terrill	.50	1.50	2.50	S
P62					
P64	The Stakes are High—Brent Ashabrannar	.50	1.50	2.50	
P65	In Winter Light—Edwin Corle	.50	1.50	2.50	
P67	Dry Bones in the Valley—William MacLeod Raine	.50	1.50	2.50	W
P69	The Nester—John S. Daniels	.50	1.50	2.50	W
P70					
P75	The Altered Ego—Jerry Sohl; 1955	.50	1.50	2.50	SF
P76	Whiplash—Brad Ward	.50	1.50	2.50	W
P77	High Country—Peter Dawson	.50	1.50	2.50	W
P78					
P79	Code Three—James M. Fox	.50	1.50	2.50	

PENNANT MYSTERY
Maco Publishing

Digest Size

		Good	Fine	N/Mint	
1	Death Out of Thin Air—Stuart Towne (Clayton Rawson)	2.00	6.00	10.00	M
2	The Six Iron Spiders—Phoebe Atwood Taylor	1.20	3.60	6.00	M
3	So Much Blood—Bruno Fischer	1.20	3.60	6.00	M
4	The Purple Parrot—C. B. Clason	1.20	3.60	6.00	M

PENNANT STUDENT EDITIONS
Bantam Books, Inc.

		Good	Fine	N/Mint
nn	Life on the Mississippi—Mark Twain	1.00	3.00	5.00

NOTE: Other titles exist in this series.

PERMA BOOKS
Pocket Books, Inc.

		Good	Fine	N/Mint	
M1000	Peace of Soul—Fulton J. Sheen; 1954	.30	.90	1.50	
M1600	The Greatest Book Ever Written—Fulton Oursler	.40	1.20	2.00	
M2001	Texan-Killer—Gene Austin; 1955	.50	1.50	2.50	W
M3002	Too Dead to Run—Jason Manor	.50	1.50	2.50	
M3003	Spur to the Smoke—Steve Frazee	.50	1.50	2.50	W
M3004	Life Among the Savages—Shirley Jackson	.30	.90	1.50	NF
M3005	Tender to Danger—Eliot Reed	.40	1.20	2.00	M
M3006	Boy Gang—Mark Kennedy	2.00	6.00	10.00	JD
M3007	The Desperate Hours—Joseph Hayes	.40	1.20	2.00	E
M3008	Horse Thief Crossing—Tom J. Hopkins	.50	1.50	2.50	W
M3009	Honky-tonk Woman—Bliss Lomax	.80	2.40	4.00	W
M3010	The Crimson Clue—George Harmon Coxe	.80	2.40	4.00	M
M3011	The Stainless Steel Kimono—Elliott Chaze	.40	1.20	2.00	H
M3012	Dead Game—Michael Avallone	1.20	3.60	6.00	
M3013	Massacre Trail—George C. Appell	.80	2.40	4.00	W
M3014	End of the Gun—H. A. DeRosso	.80	2.40	4.00	W
M3015	The Queen's Awards: Eighth Series—Ellery Queen	.80	2.40	4.00	M
M3016	The Secret Road—Bruce Lancaster	.50	1.50	2.50	
M3017	The Big Water—Mark Derby	.80	2.40	4.00	
M3018	Tejanos!—K. R. G. Granger	.80	2.40	4.00	
M3019	Doubles in Death—William Grew	.80	2.40	4.00	M
M3020	The Dreamers—J. Bigelow Clark	.80	2.40	4.00	
M3021	The Settling of the Sage—Hal G. Evarts	.80	2.40	4.00	W
M3022	The Big Boodle—Robert Sylvester	.80	2.40	4.00	
M3023	Top Hand—Dwight Bennett	.80	2.40	4.00	W
M3024	Frenchman's River—Will Ermine	.80	2.40	4.00	W
M3025	The Maras Affair—Eliot Reed	.50	1.50	2.50	M
M3026	Easy Money—Frank Peace; 1956	.80	2.40	4.00	
M3027	World Out of Mind—J. T. McIntosh; c-Powers	1.00	3.00	5.00	SF
M3028	The Bad Step—Mark Derby	.80	2.40	4.00	
M3029	Do It Yourself—Morris Brickman	.40	1.20	2.00	NF
M3030	Border Fever—C. William Harrison	.80	2.40	4.00	W
M3031	Fractured French—F. S. Pearson II & Richard Taylor	.80	2.40	4.00	H
M3032	The Mean Streets—Thomas B. Dewey	1.00	3.00	5.00	E
M3033	Blood Money—Dan J. Stevens	.80	2.40	4.00	
M3034	Snow Fury—Richard Holden	3.00	9.00	15.00	SF
M3035	Bar 4 Roundup of Best Western Stories—Scott Meredith	.80	2.40	4.00	W
M3036	Visa to Death—Ed Lacy; c-Maguire	.80	2.40	4.00	
M3037	Cop Hater—Ed McBain	.80	2.40	4.00	M

Pennant Mystery 2, © Maco Publ. ·   Perma Books M3006, © Pkb   Perma Books M3034, © Pkb

Perma Books M3046, © Pkb

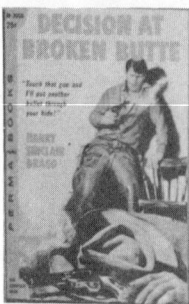

Perma Books M3068, © Pkb

Perma Books M3084, © Pkb

(PERMA BOOKS, continued)

		Good	Fine	N/Mint	
M3038	Pay-off at Black Hawk—Harry Sinclair Drago	.80	2.40	4.00	W
M3039	The Perma Quiz Book—Joseph Nathan Kane	.80	2.40	4.00	NF
M3040	Sleep With Strangers—Dolores Hitchens	.80	2.40	4.00	M
M3041	To Have and Have Not—Ernest Hemingway	.80	2.40	4.00	
M3042	From Here to Shimbashi—Jim Sack	.40	1.20	2.00	
M3043	Red Harvest—Dashiell Hammett	1.00	3.00	5.00	
M3044	Showdown Creek—Lucas Todd	.80	2.40	4.00	W
M3045	The Avenger—Dwight Bennett	.80	2.40	4.00	W
M3046	The Murder of Eleanor Pope—Henry Kuttner	2.00	6.00	10.00	M
M3047	Blessed Event—Bill O'Mally	.40	1.20	2.00	H
M3048	Live and Let Die—Ian Fleming	6.00	18.00	30.00	M
M3049	Tumbling Range Woman—Steve Frazee	.80	2.40	4.00	W
M3050	Droodles—Roger Price; 1956	.50	1.50	2.50	H
M3051	F. O. B. Murder—Bert & Dolores Hitchens	.50	1.50	2.50	M
M3052	The Brass Brigade—Frank Peace	.50	1.50	2.50	
M3053	Invasion of Privacy—Harry Kurnitz	.40	1.20	2.00	M
M3054	Play It Yourself—Jack Bassett & Norman Monath	.40	1.20	2.00	
M3055	The Con Man—Ed McBain	.80	2.40	4.00	M
M3056	Green Hills of Africa—Ernest Hemingway	.80	2.40	4.00	
M3057	The Perma X-Word Puzzle Book—Alexander Field	.80	2.40	4.00	NF
M3058	The Murder of Ann Avery—Henry Kuttner	1.60	4.80	8.00	M
M3059	Hot Town—Frank Malachy	.80	2.40	4.00	
M3060	Best Jokes for All Occasions—Jerry Lieberman & Powers Moulton	.40	1.20	2.00	H
M3061	The Mugger—Ed McBain	.80	2.40	4.00	M
M3062	The Pusher—Ed McBain	1.00	3.00	5.00	M
M3063	Die in the Saddle—Lincoln Drew	.80	2.40	4.00	W
M3064	The Bloody Sevens—Jefferson Cooper; 1957	.80	2.40	4.00	
M3065	Wilbert—Gill Fox	.50	1.50	2.50	
M3066	Murder Is Where You Find It—Robert P. Hansen	.80	2.40	4.00	M
M3067	Pets - Including Women—Charles Preston	.80	2.40	4.00	H
M3068	Decision at Broken Butte—Harry Sinclair Drago	.80	2.40	4.00	W
M3069	The Last Round—Frank O'Rourke	.80	2.40	4.00	W
M3070	Too Hot to Handle—Ian Fleming; aka Moonraker	5.00	15.00	25.00	M
M3071	Chronicle of the Calypso Clipper—John Jennings	.80	2.40	4.00	A
M3072	Death in the Wind—Edwin Lanham	.80	2.40	4.00	
M3073	The Wild Life—Herbert Gold	.80	2.40	4.00	
M3074	The Maltese Falcon—Dashiell Hammett	2.00	6.00	10.00	M
M3075	Oh, What a Wonderful Wedding—Virginia Rowans; 1957	.40	1.20	2.00	
M3076	Ellery Queen's Awards: Tenth Series—Ellery Queen	.80	2.40	4.00	M
M3077	Boomer—Clay Randall	.80	2.40	4.00	
M3078	Feeling No Pain—Bill O'Malley	.50	1.50	2.50	H
M3079	Unhappy Hooligan—Stuart Palmer	1.00	3.00	5.00	M
M3080	The Splintered Man—M. E. Chaber	1.60	4.80	8.00	M
M3081	The Wild West Joke Book—Oren Arnold	.80	2.40	4.00	H
M3082	Bar 5 Roundup of Best Western Stories—Scott Meredith	.80	2.40	4.00	W
M3083	Choice Cartoons From Sports Illustrated—Charles Preston	.50	1.50	2.50	H
M3084	Diamonds Are Forever—Ian Fleming	4.00	12.00	20.00	M
M3085	Wild Grass—Harry Sinclair Drago	.80	2.40	4.00	W
M3086	Montana Bad Man—Roe Richmond	.80	2.40	4.00	W
M3087	The Golden Widow—Floyd Mahannah	.80	2.40	4.00	
M3088	Pursuit—Lewis B. Patten	.80	2.40	4.00	W
M3089	The Brave, Bad Girls—Thomas B. Dewey	.50	1.50	2.50	
M3090	Don't Do It Yourself—Morris Brickman	.50	1.50	2.50	NF
M3091	The Men in Her Death—Stephen Ransome	.80	2.40	4.00	
M3092	Ride the Wind South—John Hunter	.80	2.40	4.00	
M3093	Unarmed Killer—William Harrison	.80	2.40	4.00	W
M3094	This Is My Funniest—Whit Burnett	.50	1.50	2.50	H
M3095	Shadow of the Rope—Ray Gaulden	.80	2.40	4.00	

		Good	Fine	N/Mint	
M3096	Widow's Pique—Blair Treynor	.80	2.40	4.00	M
M3097	Vanishing Ladies—Richard Marsten	.80	2.40	4.00	
M3098	Red—Richard Vincent	.50	1.50	2.50	
M3099	Nurse Kathy—Adeline McElfresh; 1958	.40	1.20	2.00	R
M3100	One-Way Ticket—Bert & Dolores Hitchens	.40	1.20	2.00	M
M3101	Cavalry Scout—Dee Brown	.80	2.40	4.00	W
M3102	Marcia Blake, Publicity Girl—Nancy Webb	.40	1.20	2.00	R
M3103	The Saint Around the World—Leslie Charteris	.50	1.50	2.50	M
M3104	Lash of Idaho—Roe Richmond	.50	1.50	2.50	W
M3105	O'Malley's Nuns—Bill O'Malley	.40	1.20	2.00	H
M3106	Lead With Your Left—Ed Lacy	.50	1.50	2.50	
M3107	Yellow Rope—Lincoln Drew	.50	1.50	2.50	W
M3108	Killer's Choice—Ed McBain	.50	1.50	2.50	M
M3109	The Lonely Law—Matt Stuart	.50	1.50	2.50	W
M3110	The Vengeful Men—Ray Gaulden	.50	1.50	2.50	
M3111	The Best From Manhunt—Scott Meredith & Sidney Meredith	1.00	3.00	5.00	
M3112	Three Trails—George C. Appell	.50	1.50	2.50	W
M3113	Killer's Payoff—Ed McBain	.50	1.50	2.50	M
M3114	Deadly Summer—Glenn M. Barns	.50	1.50	2.50	
M3115	Showdown at Sunset—Harry Sinclair Drago	.50	1.50	2.50	W
M3116	Bar 6 Roundup of Best Western Stories—Scott Meredith	.50	1.50	2.50	W
M3117	Even the Wicked—Richard Marsten	.50	1.50	2.50	
M3118	Spearhead—Franklin M. Davis, Jr.	.50	1.50	2.50	
M3119	Lady Killer—Ed McBain	.50	1.50	2.50	M
M3120	Rifle Ranch—Lincoln Drew	.50	1.50	2.50	W
M3121					
M3122	The Velvet Ape—David C. Holmes	.50	1.50	2.50	
M3123	The Marshal From Deadwood—John Hunter; 1958	.50	1.50	2.50	
M4001	Botany Bay—James Norman Hall & Charles Nordhoff; 1955	.40	1.20	2.00	
M4002	The High and the Mighty—Ernest K. Gann	.40	1.20	2.00	
M4003	Peace With God—Billy Graham	.30	.90	1.50	
M4004	Anyone's My Name—Seymour Shubin	.40	1.20	2.00	
M4005	The Velvet Doublet—James Street	.50	1.50	2.50	
M4006	Corpus of Joe Bailey—Oakley Hall	.30	.90	1.50	
M4007	The Time Is Noon—Hiram Haydn	.40	1.20	2.00	
M4008	Storm Haven—Frank G. Slaughter	.40	1.20	2.00	
M4009	The Art of Living—Norman Vincent Peale	.30	.90	1.50	
M4010	The Girl With the Glass Heart—Daniel Stern	.40	1.20	2.00	E
M4011	Stories of the Foreign Legion—Percival C. Wren	1.00	3.00	5.00	A
M4012	Sight Without Glasses—Harold M. Peppard	.40	1.20	2.00	NF
M4013	Be Glad You're Neurotic—Louis E. Bisch	.40	1.20	2.00	NF
M4014	Best Jokes—Powers Moulton	.40	1.20	2.00	H
M4015	Eat and Reduce—Victor H. Lindlahr	.40	1.20	2.00	NF
M4016	The Fundamentals of Contract Bridge—Charles H. Goren	.30	.90	1.50	NF
M4017	Modern Parables—Fulton Oursler	.30	.90	1.50	
M4018	New Standard Book of Model Letters for All Occasions—Leo J. Henkin	.30	.90	1.50	
M4019	Sex and the Love-Life—William J. Fielding	.30	.90	1.50	NF
M4020	Word Power Made Easy—Norman Lewis	.30	.90	1.50	NF
M4021	The Perma Cross Word Puzzle Dictionary—Frank Eaton Newman	.40	1.20	2.00	NF
M4022	Operation Future—Groff Conklin	.80	2.40	4.00	SF
M4023	Your Legal Advisor—Samuel G. Kling	.30	.90	1.50	NF
M4024	The Well of Loneliness—Radclyffe Hall	.40	1.20	2.00	
M4025	Spencer Brade, M.D.—Frank G. Slaughter; 1955	.30	.90	1.50	
M4026	That None Should Die—Frank G. Slaughter	.30	.90	1.50	
M4027	East Side General—Frank G. Slaughter	.30	.90	1.50	
M4028	The Deep Six—Martin Dibner	.40	1.20	2.00	
M4029	To Hell and Back—Audie Murphy	.50	1.50	2.50	B
M4030	The Standard Bartender's Guide—Patrick Gavin Duffy & James A. Beard	.40	1.20	2.00	NF

Perma Books M3111, © Pkb

Perma Books M3116, © Pkb

Perma Books M4011, © Pkb

Perma Books M4054, © Pkb

Perma Books M4061, © Pkb

Perma Books P15, © DD

(PERMA BOOKS, continued)

		Good	Fine	N/Mint	
M4031	The Song of Ruth—Frank G. Slaughter	.30	.90	1.50	
M4032	Captain of the Medici—John J. Pugh	.50	1.50	2.50	A
M4033	Lift Up Your Heart—Fulton J. Sheen	.30	.90	1.50	
M4034	Soldier of Fortune—Ernest K. Gann	.40	1.20	2.00	
M4035	Your Child From 2 to 5—Morton Edwards	.30	.90	1.50	
M4036	The Greatest Faith Ever Known—Fulton Oursler	.40	1.20	2.00	
M4037	The Cotton Road—Frank Feville	.40	1.20	2.00	
M4038	A Touch of Glory—Frank G. Slaughter; 1956	.30	.90	1.50	
M4039	Prisoner in Paradise—Garet Rogers	.40	1.20	2.00	
M4040	But We Were Born Free—Elmer Davis	.40	1.20	2.00	
M4041	Lights Along the Shore—Fulton Oursler	.30	.90	1.50	
M4042	Mardios Beach—Oakley Hall	.40	1.20	2.00	
M4043	The Silver Oar—Howard Breslin	.40	1.20	2.00	
M4044	Ceremony of Love—Thomas Williams	.40	1.20	2.00	
M4045	The Strongbox—Howard Swiggett	.40	1.20	2.00	
M4046	The Greatest Story Ever Told—Fulton Oursler	.40	1.20	2.00	
M4047	Divine Mistress—Frank G. Slaughter	.50	1.50	2.50	
M4048	Battle Surgeon—Frank G. Slaughter	.30	.90	1.50	C
M4049	The Galileans—Frank G. Slaughter	.30	.90	1.50	
M4050	Slattery's Hurricane—Herman Wouk; 1956	.30	.90	1.50	
M4051	The Healer—Frank G. Slaughter	.30	.90	1.50	
M4052	The Hound of Earth—Vance Bourjaily	.30	.90	1.50	
M4053	Air Surgeon—Frank G. Slaughter	.30	.90	1.50	C
M4054	Fort Everglades—Frank G. Slaughter	2.00	6.00	10.00	A
M4055	The Road to Bithynia—Frank G. Slaughter	.30	.90	1.50	
M4056	South Sea Stories—W. Somerset Maugham	.40	1.20	2.00	
M4057	Darien Venture—C. V. Terry	.40	1.20	2.00	
M4058	Shad Run—Howard Breslin	.40	1.20	2.00	
M4059	The Will to Live—Arnold A. Hutschnecker	.30	.90	1.50	
M4060	Science and Surgery—Frank G. Slaughter	.30	.90	1.50	
4061	Run Silent, Run Deep—Edward L. Beach	.50	1.50	2.50	C
M4062	Kon-Tiki—Thor Heyerdahl	.40	1.20	2.00	NF
M4063	Cell 2455, Death Row—Caryl Chessman	.80	2.40	4.00	B
M4064	Flight From Natchez—Frank G. Slaughter	.30	.90	1.50	
M4065	How to Eat Better for Less Money—Sam W. Aaron	.30	.90	1.50	NF
M4066	The Complete Letter Writer—N.,H. & S. K. Mayer	.30	.90	1.50	NF
M4067	H. M. S. Ulysses—Alistair MacLean	.50	1.50	2.50	A
M4068	Winter Harvest—Norah Lofts	.30	.90	1.50	
M4069	The Scarlet Cord—Frank G. Slaughter	.30	.90	1.50	
M4070	The Highwayman—Noel B. Gerson	.50	1.50	2.50	A
M4071	The Smiling Rebel—Harnett T. Kane	.40	1.20	2.00	
M4072	The Golden Isle—Frank G. Slaughter	.30	.90	1.50	
M4073	The Dice of God—Hoffman Birney	.30	.90	1.50	
M4074	How to Win and Hold a Mate—Samuel G. Kling	.30	.90	1.50	NF
M4075	Christopher Humble—Charles B. Judah; 1957	.40	1.20	2.00	
M4076	The Corsair—Madeleine Fabiola Kent	.50	1.50	2.50	A
M4077	The Loving Couple—Virginia Rowans	.40	1.20	2.00	
M4078	Kentucky Pride—Gene Markey	.40	1.20	2.00	
M4079	The Wreck of the Mary Deare—Hammond Innes	.40	1.20	2.00	
M4080	Breakaway—Wally Depew	.40	1.20	2.00	
M4081	Position Unknown—Ian Mackersey	.40	1.20	2.00	
M4082	Murder of a Mistress—Henry Kuttner	2.00	6.00	10.00	M
M4083	Bellevue Is My Home—S. R. Cutolo, others	.40	1.20	2.00	NF
M4084	Rate Yourself—Pauline Arnold	.30	.90	1.50	NF
M4085	Underworld U. S. A.—Joseph F. Dinneen	.40	1.20	2.00	NF
M4086	Diamond in the Sky—Mary Orr	.40	1.20	2.00	
M4087	The Warrior—Frank G. Slaughter	.40	1.20	2.00	
M4088	Dracula—Bram Stoker	1.00	3.00	5.00	HO

		Good	Fine	N/Mint	
M4089	The Guns of Navarone—Alistair MacLean	.40	1.20	2.00	C
M4090	The Calendar Epic—James Kubeck	.40	1.20	2.00	
M4091	Twilight for the Gods—Ernest K. Gann	.30	.90	1.50	
M4092	Sword and Scalpel—Frank G. Slaughter	.30	.90	1.50	
M4093	The Proving Flight—David Beaty	.40	1.20	2.00	
M4094	Star of Macedon—Karl V. Eiker	.40	1.20	2.00	
M4095	In the Wet—Nevil Shute	.30	.90	1.50	
M4096	Murder of a Wife—Henry Kuttner	2.00	6.00	10.00	M
M4097	The Midwife of Pont Clery—Flora Sandstrom	.40	1.20	2.00	
M4098	Till the Rafters Ring—Roswell G. Ham, Jr.	.40	1.20	2.00	
M4099	The Tortured Path—Kendell Foster Crossen	.80	2.40	4.00	
M4100	The Golden Ones—C. V. Terry; 1958	.40	1.20	2.00	
M4101	The Second Perma Quiz Book—Joseph Nathan Kane	.50	1.50	2.50	
M4102	The Mask—Stuart Cloete	.40	1.20	2.00	
M4103	The Royal Vultures—Hillel Black & Sam Kolman	.40	1.20	2.00	
M4104	The Success—Helen Howe	.40	1.20	2.00	
M4105	The Country Club Set—Otis Carney	.30	.90	1.50	
M4106	What to Tell Your Children About Sex—Adie Suehsdorf	.30	.90	1.50	NF
M4107	Doctor Pygmalion—Maxwell Maltz	.30	.90	1.50	
M4108	Give Me Possession—Paul Horgan	.40	1.20	2.00	
M4109	Flight Hostess—Emily Thorne	.30	.90	1.50	
M4110	Astrology and You—Carroll Righter	.30	.90	1.50	NF
M4111	The Mapmaker—Frank G. Slaughter	.40	1.20	2.00	
M4112	No Hiding Place—Beth Day	.30	.90	1.50	
M4113	The Questing Sword—Jefferson Cooper	.50	1.50	2.50	
M4114	The Bixby Girls—Rosamond Marshall; 1959	.40	1.20	2.00	
M4115	Pork Chop Hill—S. L. A. Marshall; movie tie-in	1.00	3.00	5.00	
M4116	South by Java Head—Alistair MacLean	.40	1.20	2.00	A
M4117	Veronica's Veil—Jefferson Cooper	.50	1.50	2.50	
M4118	The D. A.'s Man—Harold Danforth & James D. Horan	.40	1.20	2.00	
M4119	The Devil's Cross—Walter O'Meara	.40	1.20	2.00	
M4120	Wasp—Eric Frank Russell	.40	1.20	2.00	SF
M4121	The Forbidden Road—Victor Canning	.40	1.20	2.00	
M4122	The Counterfeit Traitor—Alexander Klein	.40	1.20	2.00	
M4123	Betty White's Teen-age Dance Book—Betty White	.30	.90	1.50	NF
M4124	Imitation of Life—Fannie Hurst	.30	.90	1.50	
M4125	10 Days to a Successful Memory—Joyce Brothers & Edward P. F. Eagan; 1959	.30	.90	1.50	NF
M4126	A Family Affair—Roger Eddy	.30	.90	1.50	
M4127	Scent of Cloves—Norah Lofts	.30	.90	1.50	
M4128	Home From the Hill—William Humphrey	.40	1.20	2.00	
M4129	His Majesty's Highwayman—Donald Barr Chidsey	.50	1.50	2.50	A
M4130	Daybreak—Frank G. Slaughter	.30	.90	1.50	
M4131	The Pocket Book of Household Hints—Holly Cantus	.30	.90	1.50	NF
M4132	Warm Bodies—Donald R. Morris	.40	1.20	2.00	
M4133	A Man Against Fate—Frank Canizio & Robert Markel	.30	.90	1.50	
M4134	Freud: His Dream and Sex Theories—Joseph Jastrow	.30	.90	1.50	NF
M4135	The Southern Cross—Peter French	.40	1.20	2.00	
M4136	The Fundamentals of Fishing and Hunting—Byron Dalrymple	.40	1.20	2.00	
M4137					
M4138	Fun for the Family—Jerome S. Meyer	.40	1.20	2.00	NF
M4139	The Captives of Mora Island—Victor Canning	.40	1.20	2.00	
M4140	All About Men—Joseph H. Peck	.30	.90	1.50	
M4141	The Cultured Man—Ashley Montagu	.40	1.20	2.00	NF
M4142	Top of the World—Hans Ruesch	.40	1.20	2.00	
M4143	Abondon Ship!—Richard F. Newcomb	.40	1.20	2.00	
M4145	The Widow's Tale—John Coates	.40	1.20	2.00	
M4146	Woman Obsessed—John Mantley; movie tie-in	.40	1.20	2.00	
M4147	AMF Guide to Natural Bowling—Victor Kalman	.30	.90	1.50	NF
M4148	A Guide to Better Living—N. H. & S. K. Mayer	.30	.90	1.50	NF
M4149	Sands of Mars—Arthur C. Clarke	.50	1.50	2.50	
M4150	Killer's Wedge—Ed McBain; 1959	.50	1.50	2.50	M
M4151	Tales Out of (Night) School—Hy Gardner	.40	1.20	2.00	H
M4152	The Savage—Noel Clad	.40	1.20	2.00	
M4153	Settlement Nurse—Rosie M. Banks	.30	.90	1.50	R
M4154	Pax—Middleton Kieffer	.40	1.20	2.00	
M4158	Five Galaxy Short Novels—ed. H. L. Gold	.40	1.20	2.00	SF
M4161	Journey to the Center of the Earth—Jules Verne; movie tie-in	1.00	3.00	5.00	SF
M4168	Hound-dog Man—Fred Gipson; movie tie-in	.50	1.50	2.50	
M4185	Starfire	.40	1.20	2.00	SF-H
M4201	Red Harvest—Dashiell Hammett	.50	1.50	2.50	M
M4203	Diminishing Returns—E. L. Withers	.40	1.20	2.00	
M5000	Son of a Hundred Kings—Thomas B. Costain; 1955	.40	1.20	2.00	A
M5001	A General Introduction to Psychoanalysis—Sigmund Freud	.30	.90	1.50	NF
M5002	The Shorter Bartlett's Familiar Quotations—John Bartlett	.40	1.20	2.00	NF
M5003	The Silver Chalice—Thomas B. Costain; 1956	.40	1.20	2.00	A
M5004	Stories of the Great Operas—Milton Cross	.40	1.20	2.00	NF
M5005	The Story of the Bible—Hendrik Willem van Loon	.40	1.20	2.00	NF

		Good	Fine	N/Mint	
M5006	A Complete Guide to Gardening—Montague Free; 1957	.30	.90	1.50	NF
M5007	The Concise Treasury of Great Poems—Louis Untermeyer; 1958	.40	1.20	2.00	
M5008	When Your Child Is Ill—Samuel Karelitz	.30	.90	1.50	NF
M5009	The Sexual Responsibility of Woman—Maxine Davis; 1959	.30	.90	1.50	
M5010	The Well of Loneliness—Radclyffe Hall	.40	1.20	2.00	
M5011	Only in America—Harry Golden	.30	.90	1.50	
M5012	The Legal Encyclopedia for Home and Business—Samuel G. Kling	.30	.90	1.50	NF
M5013	Schiffers' Family Medical Encyclopedia—Justus J. Schifferes	.30	.90	1.50	NF
M5014	The Greatest Book Ever Written—Fulton Oursler	.40	1.20	2.00	
M7500	Gone With the Wind—Margaret Mitchell; 1958	.50	1.50	2.50	

PERMA BOOKS (Hardbound)
Perma Books/Doubleday and Co., Inc.

[See Perma Books (Softbound)]

		Good	Fine	N/Mint	
P 1	Best Loved Poems—ed. MacKenzie	.50	1.50	2.50	
P 2	How to Write Letters for All Occasions—Alexander L. Sheff & Edna Ingalls	.40	1.20	2.00	NF
P 3	Best Quotations for All Occasions	.50	1.50	2.50	
P 4	Common Errors in English and How to Avoid Them—Alexander M. Witherspoon	.40	1.20	2.00	NF
P 5	The Standard Bartender's Guide—Patrick Duffy	.40	1.20	2.00	NF
P 6	Sex and the Love Life—William J. Fielding	.40	1.20	2.00	NF
P 7	Eat and Reduce!—Victor H. Lindlahr	.40	1.20	2.00	
P 8	Best Jokes for All Occasions—Moulton	.50	1.50	2.50	H
P 9	Ida Bailey Allen's Cook Book	.50	1.50	2.50	NF
P10	The Conquest of Fear—Basil King	.50	1.50	2.50	
P11	How Shall I Tell My Child?—Belle S. Mooney	.50	1.50	2.50	
P12	The Male Hormone—Paul de Kruif	.40	1.20	2.00	NF
P13	Something to Live By—Dorothea Kopplin	.50	1.50	2.50	
P14	Sight Without Glasses—Harold M. Peppard; 1948	.30	.90	1.50	NF
P15	Blackstone's Tricks Anyone Can Do	3.00	9.00	15.00	NF
P16	Fortune Telling for Fun and Popularity—Paul Showers	.50	1.50	2.50	NF
P17	Handy Encyclopedia of Useful Information	.50	1.50	2.50	NF
P18	Famous Sheriffs and Western Outlaws—William MacLeod Raine	1.20	3.60	6.00	NF
P19	Good English Made Easy—J. Milnor Dorey	.50	1.50	2.50	NF
P20	Mathematics for Home and Business	.40	1.20	2.00	NF
P21	Modern Sex Life—Edwin W. Hirsch	.40	1.20	2.00	NF
P22	Life With Mother—Clarence Day	.50	1.50	2.50	
P23	Strange Customs of Courtship and Marriage—William J. Fielding	.50	1.50	2.50	NF
P24	Brief Biographies of Famous Men and Women—W. Stuart Sewell	.50	1.50	2.50	NF
P25	Handy Legal Adviser for Home and Business—Samuel G. Kling	.40	1.20	2.00	NF
P26	What Your Dreams Mean—Herbert Hespro	.50	1.50	2.50	
P27	Handbook for House Repairs—Louis Gelders & Eugene O'Hare	.40	1.20	2.00	NF
P28	A Short History of the World—J. Milnor Dorey	.40	1.20	2.00	NF
P29	In His Steps—Charles M. Sheldon	.50	1.50	2.50	
P30	Stories for Men—Charles Grayson	.80	2.40	4.00	
P31	The Art of Enjoying Music—Sigmund Spaeth	.50	1.50	2.50	NF
P32	Photography As a Hobby—Fred B. Barton	.50	1.50	2.50	NF
P33	Winning Poker—Oswald Jacoby	.50	1.50	2.50	NF
P34	The Handy Book of Hobbies—Geoffrey Mott-Smith	.50	1.50	2.50	NF
P35	Dale Carnegie's Five Minute Biographies	.40	1.20	2.00	NF
P36	Astrology for Everyone—Evangeline Adams	.40	1.20	2.00	
P37	Numerology—Morris C. Goodman	.50	1.50	2.50	NF
P38	Three Famous French Novels	.50	1.50	2.50	
P39	Character Reading Made Easy—Meier	.50	1.50	2.50	
P40	Stop Me If You've Heard This One—Lehr, Tinney, & Bower	.50	1.50	2.50	H
P41	Best Short Stories of Jack London	1.00	3.00	5.00	
P42	The Art of Living—Norman Vincent Peale	.30	.90	1.50	
P43	The Human Body and How It Works—Tokay	.40	1.20	2.00	NF
P44	A Handy Illustrated Guide to Football	.50	1.50	2.50	NF
P45	The Golden Book of Prayer—D. B. Aldrich	.40	1.20	2.00	
P46	How to Control Worry—Matthew N. Chappell	.40	1.20	2.00	
P47	A Handy Illustrated Guide to Basketball	.50	1.50	2.50	NF
P48	Better Speech for You—Daniel P. Eginton	.40	1.20	2.00	NF
P49	The Man Nobody Knows—Bruce Barton	.50	1.50	2.50	
P50	Psychoanalysis and Love—Andre Tridon	.40	1.20	2.00	
P51	The Key to Your Personality—Charles B. Roth	.40	1.20	2.00	
P52	A Handy Illustrated Guide to Bowling	.40	1.20	2.00	NF
P53	A Handy Illustrated Guide to Boxing	.50	1.50	2.50	NF
P54	Magic Explained—Walter B. Gibson	7.00	21.00	35.00	NF
P55	The Handy Book of Indoor Games—Geoffrey Mott-Smith	.50	1.50	2.50	NF
P56					
P57	Understanding Human Nature—Alfred Adler	.40	1.20	2.00	
P58	Bridge Quiz Book—Charles H. Goren; 1st ed., 1949	.50	1.50	2.50	NF

		Good	Fine	N/Mint	
P59	Reading Handwriting for Fun and Popularity—Dorothy Sara	.50	1.50	2.50	NF
P60	Be Glad You're Neurotic—Louis E. Bisch	.40	1.20	2.00	
P61	Grammar Made Easy—Richard D. Mallery	.40	1.20	2.00	NF
P62	Permabook of Art Masterpieces—Ray Brock	.50	1.50	2.50	NF
P63	The Handy Book of Gardening—Wilkinson & Tiedjens	.40	1.20	2.00	NF
P64	The Meaning of Psychoanalysis—Martin W. Peck	.40	1.20	2.00	NF
P65	Know Your Real Abilities—C. V. & M. E. Broadley	.40	1.20	2.00	
P66	Stories of Famous Operas—Harold V. Milligan	.50	1.50	2.50	
P67	The Science Fiction Galaxy—Groff Conklin	1.60	4.80	8.00	SF
P68	How to Use Your Imagination to Make Money—C. B. Roth	.30	.90	1.50	
P69	Favorite Verse of Edgar A. Guest; 1950	.40	1.20	2.00	
P70	Perma Handy World Atlas	.30	.90	1.50	NF
P71	Goren's Canasta Up-to-Date—Charles H. Goren	.30	.90	1.50	NF
P72	Meditations and My Daily Strength—Preston Bradley	.30	.90	1.50	
P73	Personality Pointers—Jill Edwards	.40	1.20	2.00	
P74	South Sea Stories—W. Somerset Maugham	.50	1.50	2.50	
P75	Manners for Millions—Sophie C. Hadida	.30	.90	1.50	
P76	The Care and Handling of Dogs—Jack Baird	.40	1.20	2.00	NF
P77	A Handy Illustrated Guide to Baseball	.50	1.50	2.50	NF
P78	Buried Treasure—Ken Krippene	.40	1.20	2.00	NF
P79	Everyday Speech—Bess Sondel	.30	.90	1.50	NF
P80	The New Standard Ready Reckoner	.30	.90	1.50	
P81	How to Read Palms—Litzka Raymond	.50	1.50	2.50	
P82	The Perma Week-End Companion—E. Mitchell	.40	1.20	2.00	
P83	How to Travel for Fun—Helen Eva Tates	.40	1.20	2.00	NF
P84					
P85	Dictionary of First Aid for Emergencies—H. Pomeranz	.30	.90	1.50	NF
P86	The Perma Rhyming Dictionary—Langford Reed	.40	1.20	2.00	NF
P87	Famous Scenes From Shakespeare—Van H. Cartmell; 1950	.40	1.20	2.00	
P88	Reading for Enjoyment—Donald MacCampbell	.40	1.20	2.00	NF
P89	The Perma Crossword Puzzle Dictionary—Frank Eaton Newman	.40	1.20	2.00	NF
P90	Essentials of Arithmetic—Henry Sticker	.30	.90	1.50	NF
P91	The Perma Treasury of Love Poems—William Lord	.40	1.20	2.00	
P92	Favorite Stories From the Bible—S. E. Frost, Jr.	.40	1.20	2.00	
P93					
P94	Perma Book of Ghost Stories—W. Bob Holland	2.00	6.00	10.00	
P95	Strange Tales of Famous Frauds—Henry & Dana Lee Thomas	.50	1.50	2.50	NF
P96	Powdersmoke Justice—William Colt MacDonald	.50	1.50	2.50	W
P97	You Can Win—Norman Vincent Peale	.30	.90	1.50	
P99	Married Love—Marie Stopes	.30	.90	1.50	NF
P100	Fundamentals of Contract Bridge—Charles H. Goren	.30	.90	1.50	NF
P101	Careers That Change Your World—James Keller	.30	.90	1.50	

PERMA BOOKS (Softbound)
Perma Books Doubleday and Company, Inc.

[Also see Perma Books (Hardbound)]

P 5	The Standard Bartender's Guide—Patrick Gavin Duffy; 1951	.40	1.20	2.00	NF
P 7	Eat and Reduce—Victor H. Lindlahr; 1952	.30	.90	1.50	NF
P22	Life With Mother—Clarence Day	.40	1.20	2.00	
P25	Handy Legal Advisor for Home and Business—Samuel G. Kling; 1951	.30	.90	1.50	NF
P65	Know Your Real Abilities—Charles V. & Margaret E. Broadley; 1953	.30	.90	1.50	NF
P89	The Perma Cross-Word Puzzle Dictionary—Frank Eaton Newman; 1951	.40	1.20	2.00	NF
P98	New Standard Book of Model Letters for All Occasions—Leo J. Henkin; 1951	.40	1.20	2.00	NF
P102					
P103					
P104					

Perma Books P62, © DD

Perma Books P87, © DD

Perma Books P117, © DD

Perma Books P118, © DD

Perma Books P124, © DD

Perma Books P137, © DD

(PERMABOOKS (Softbound), continued)

		Good	Fine	N/Mint	
P105	Three Minutes a Day—James Keller	.30	.90	1.50	NF
P106	How to Overcome Nervous Stomach Trouble—Joseph F. Montague	.30	.90	1.50	NF
P107	In a Dark Garden—Frank G. Slaughter	.50	1.50	2.50	
P108	Unconquered—Neil H. Swanson	.50	1.50	2.50	
P109	One Tropical Night—Vicki Baum	.50	1.50	2.50	
P110.	Bell Timson—Marguerite Steen	.40	1.20	2.00	
P111	Castaway Island—William George Weekley	.50	1.50	2.50	
P112	The Well of Loneliness—Radclyffe Hall	.50	1.50	2.50	
P113	Poems for Men—Damon Runyon	.50	1.50	2.50	
P114	The Mudlark—Theodore Bonnet	.40	1.20	2.00	
P115	The Chain—Paul I. Wellman	.50	1.50	2.50	
P116	Fear Is the Hunter—Hildegarde Tolman Teilhet	.50	1.50	2.50	
P117	In the Grip of Terror—Groff Conklin	2.00	6.00	10.00	HO
P118	As Tough As They Come—ed. Will Oursler	2.00	6.00	10.00	
P119	To Hell and Back—Audie Murphy	1.20	3.60	6.00	B
P120	The Case of the Little Doctor—Hilda Lewis	.50	1.50	2.50	M
P121	The Golden Isle—Frank G. Slaughter	.80	2.40	4.00	A
P122	New Stories for Men—Charles Grayson	.50	1.50	2.50	
P123	The Beautiful and the Damned—F. Scott Fitzgerald	.80	2.40	4.00	
P124	Arrest the Saint!—Leslie Charteris	2.00	6.00	10.00	M
P125	The Salem Frigate—John Jennings; 1951	1.00	3.00	5.00	A
P126	Spurs West!—Joseph T. Shaw	1.20	3.60	6.00	W
P127	Fair Wind to Java—Garland Roark	1.00	3.00	5.00	
P128	Night Without Stars—Winston Graham	1.00	3.00	5.00	
P129	The Walls of Jericho—Paul I. Wellman	.80	2.40	4.00	
P130	The Thorndike-Barnhart Handy Pocket Dictionary—Clarence Barnhart	.50	1.50	2.50	NF
P131	You Can Change the World—James Keller	.50	1.50	2.50	NF
P132	Chad Hanna—Walter D. Edmonds	.80	2.40	4.00	
P133	The Sea Eagles—John Jennings	1.00	3.00	5.00	A
P134	The Raging Tide—Ernest K. Gann	.80	2.40	4.00	
P135	The Greatest Story Ever Told—Fulton Oursler	.80	2.40	4.00	
P136	Quietly My Captain Waits—Evelyn Eaton	.80	2.40	4.00	E
P137	Lusty Wind for Carolina—Inglis Fletcher	1.60	4.80	8.00	
P138	Black Judas—Burke Wilkinson; aka Run Mongoose	1.00	3.00	5.00	E
P139	Rainbow in the Royals—Garland Roark	1.00	3.00	5.00	E
P140	Divine Mistress—Frank G. Slaughter	1.00	3.00	5.00	
P141	Land of Vengeance—John Jennings; aka Call the New World	1.00	3.00	5.00	
P142	Angel With Spurs—Paul I. Wellman; 1952	1.00	3.00	5.00	
P143	Tidewater—Clifford Dowdey	1.00	3.00	5.00	E
P144	Scarlet Cockerel—Gerald Lagard	1.00	3.00	5.00	A
P145	Beyond the End of Time—Frederik Pohl	2.00	6.00	10.00	SF
P146	Tom Bone—Charles B. Judah	1.00	3.00	5.00	E
P147	The Turning Wheels—Stuart Cloete	1.00	3.00	5.00	E
P148	Guard of Honor—James Gould Cozzens	1.00	3.00	5.00	
P149	Phantom Fortress—Bruce Lancaster	1.00	3.00	5.00	
P150	The Man With One Talent—Josiah E. Greene; 1952	1.00	3.00	5.00	
P151	Roanoke Hundred—Inglis Fletcher	1.20	3.60	6.00	
P152	The Color of Blood—E. Ralph Rundell	1.00	3.00	5.00	
P153	Before the Sun Goes Down—Elizabeth Metzger Howard	1.00	3.00	5.00	
P154	Gentleman's Agreement—Laura Z. Hobson	1.00	3.00	5.00	
P155	Fort Everglades—Frank G. Slaughter	1.00	3.00	5.00	
P156	If a Man Be Mad—Harold Maine	1.00	3.00	5.00	
P157	River to the West—John Jennings	1.00	3.00	5.00	A
P158S	Crusade in Europe—Dwight D. Eisenhower	1.00	3.00	5.00	
P159	Bugles Blow No More—Clifford Dowdey	1.00	3.00	5.00	
P160	The Mission of Jeffery Tomaly—Darwin L. Teilhet	.80	2.40	4.00	
P161	Woman in Love—Lucy Cores	1.00	3.00	5.00	
P162	The Ironmaster—Anne Powers	1.00	3.00	5.00	

(PERMABOOKS (Softbound), continued)

		Good	Fine	N/Mint	
P163	Morning Time—Charles O'Neill	1.00	3.00	5.00	
P164	My Lord America—Alex Rackowe	1.00	3.00	5.00	
P165S	Lydia Bailey—Kenneth Roberts	1.00	3.00	5.00	
P166	The Plymouth Adventure—Ernest Gebler	1.00	3.00	5.00	
P167	Hear This Woman—Ann & Ben Pinchot	.80	2.40	4.00	
P168	Sir Pagan—Henry John Colyton	1.00	3.00	5.00	A
P169	Sing at My Wake—Jo Sinclair	1.00	3.00	5.00	
P170	Be My Love—Harriet Hinsdale	.80	2.40	4.00	E
P171	Bennett's Welcome—Inglis Fletcher	1.20	3.60	6.00	
P172	Government Is Your Business—James Keller	.50	1.50	2.50	NF
P173	Rogue's Honor—Anne Powers; aka Ride East! Ride West!	1.00	3.00	5.00	A
P174	Stronghold—Donald Barr Chidsey	1.00	3.00	5.00	A
P175	Victory in the Dust—Arthur Phillips; 1952	1.00	3.00	5.00	
P176	Trumpet to Arms—Bruce Lancaster	1.00	3.00	5.00	
P177	Modern Parables—Fulton Oursler	.40	1.20	2.00	
P178S	Green Dolphin Street—Elizabeth Goudge	.40	1.20	2.00	
P179	Big Old Sun—Robert Faherty	.50	1.50	2.50	
P180	That None Should Die—Frank G. Slaughter	.50	1.50	2.50	
P181	They Had a Glory—Davenport Steward	.50	1.50	2.50	
P182	King's Arrow—Joseph Patrick	1.00	3.00	5.00	A
P183	Some Thing to Live By—Dorothea S. Kopplin	.40	1.20	2.00	
P184	The Fundamentals of Contract Bridge—Charles H. Goren	.40	1.20	2.00	NF
P185	Journey to Nowhere—Martin Dibner; aka The Bachelor Seals	.50	1.50	2.50	
P186	Devil's Spawn—Wenzell Brown	2.00	6.00	10.00	A
P187S	Murder, Inc.—Sid Feder & Burton B. Turkus	.80	2.40	4.00	
P188	Restless Are the Sails—Evelyn Eaton	.80	2.40	4.00	
P189	Men of Albermarle—Inglis Fletcher	1.60	4.80	8.00	A
P190	The Celebrity—Laura Z. Hobson	.50	1.50	2.50	
P191	Beau Geste—Percival C. Wren	1.00	3.00	5.00	A
P192	Detour—Norma Ciraci	.50	1.50	2.50	E
P193	Silver Nutmeg—Norah Lofts; 1953	1.00	3.00	5.00	E
P194	Dark Memory—Jonathan Latimer	1.00	3.00	5.00	
P195	Battle Surgeon—Frank G. Slaughter	.50	1.50	2.50	C
P196	The Scarlet Patch—Bruce Lancaster	1.00	3.00	5.00	
P197	Port of Call—Maxwell Griffith	.80	2.40	4.00	
P198	Slant of the Wild Wind—Garland Roark	.80	2.40	4.00	E
P199S	The Prodigal Women—Nancy Hale	.50	1.50	2.50	
P200	Rogue Errant—Michael Leigh; 1953	1.00	3.00	5.00	A
P201S	The Story of the Bible—Hendrik Willem van Loon	.50	1.50	2.50	NF
P202S	A General Introduction to Psychoanalysis—Sigmund Freud	.30	.90	1.50	NF
P203	Music Out of Dixie—Harold Sinclair	1.00	3.00	5.00	
P204	The Wire—David Walker	.80	2.40	4.00	
P205S	The Shorter Bartlett's Familiar Quotations—John Bartlett	.40	1.20	2.00	NF
P206S	The Concise Treasury of Great Poems—Louis Untermeyer	.40	1.20	2.00	
P207	Raleigh's Eden—Inglis Fletcher	1.60	4.80	8.00	A
P208	Grand Hotel—Vicki Baum	1.00	3.00	5.00	
P209	Word Power Made Easy—Norman Lewis	.40	1.20	2.00	NF
P210	Schnozzola—Gene Fowler	1.20	3.60	6.00	B
P211	The Long Run—J. Bigelow Clark	.40	1.20	2.00	
P212S	7 Arts—Fernando Puma	.40	1.20	2.00	
P213S	New Voices: American Writing Today—Don M. Wolfe	.50	1.50	2.50	
P214	To Hell and Back—Audie Murphy	.50	1.50	2.50	B
P215	The Gladiator—Thames Williamson	1.00	3.00	5.00	S
P216	Toil of the Brave—Inglis Fletcher	1.20	3.60	6.00	
P217S	Show Biz—Abel Green & Joe Laurie, Jr.	.80	2.40	4.00	NF
P218	East Side General—Frank G. Slaughter	.40	1.20	2.00	
P219	Venture in the East—Bruce Lancaster	.80	2.40	4.00	
P220	In a Dark Garden—Frank G. Slaughter	.40	1.20	2.00	

Perma Books P207, © DD

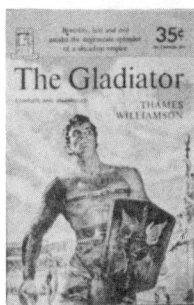

Perma Books P215, © DD

Perma Books P232, © DD

(PERMABOOKS (Softbound), continued)	Good	Fine	N/Mint	
P221 The Golden Isle—Frank G. Slaughter	.50	1.50	2.50	
P222 Touched in Fire—John Tebbel	.50	1.50	2.50	
P223 The Bengal Tiger—Hall Hunter	.50	1.50	2.50	A
P224 Summer in Rome—Paul Hyde Bonner	.40	1.20	2.00	
P225 Beyond the Blue Mountains—Jean Plaidy; 1953	.40	1.20	2.00	
P226 Spencer Brade, M.D.—Frank G. Slaughter	.40	1.20	2.00	
P227 Swing the Big-Eyed Rabbit—John Pleasant McCoy	.40	1.20	2.00	E
P228 Immortal Wife—Irving Stone	.40	1.20	2.00	
P229 Front Office—Herbert Lyons	.40	1.20	2.00	
P230 Indian Summer—Robert Sylvester	.40	1.20	2.00	
P231 The Golden Egg—James Pollak	.40	1.20	2.00	
P232 Beau Sabreur—Percival C. Wren	1.00	3.00	5.00	A
P233 Divine Mistress—Frank G. Slaughter	.50	1.50	2.50	
P234 No Bugles Tonight—Bruce Lancaster	.80	2.40	4.00	
P235 Yankee Woman—Eric Baume	.80	2.40	4.00	A
P236 Shadow of Tomorrow—Frederik Pohl	2.00	6.00	10.00	SF
P237 Salome, the Princess of Galilee—Henry Denker	1.20	3.60	6.00	A
238 Trail End—Tom J. Hopkins	1.00	3.00	5.00	W
239 Women in Prison—Joan Henry	1.20	3.60	6.00	
P240 The Bowl of Brass—Paul I. Wellman	.80	2.40	4.00	
P241 The Road to Bithynia—Frank G. Slaughter	.50	1.50	2.50	
P242 The Handy Home Medical Adviser—Morris Fishbein	.40	1.20	2.00	NF
P243 Kon Tiki—Thor Heyerdahl	.40	1.20	2.00	NF
244 The Tall Dolores—Michael Avallone	1.00	3.00	5.00	M
245 Memory of Love—Bessie Brever	.40	1.20	2.00	
P246 Coins in the Fountain—John H. Secondari	.40	1.20	2.00	
P247 My Love Must Wait—Ernestine Hill	.40	1.20	2.00	
P248 Panama Passage—Donald Barr Chidsey	.80	2.40	4.00	
P249 Big Beverage—William T. Campbell	.40	1.20	2.00	
P250S The Greatest Book Ever Written—Fulton Oursler; 1953	.40	1.20	2.00	
251 The Old Man's Place—John B. Sanford	.40	1.20	2.00	
252 The Face in the Shadows—Peter Ordway	.40	1.20	2.00	M
253 To Have and Have Not—Ernest Hemingway	1.00	3.00	5.00	
P254 Crossroads in Time—Groff Conklin	1.00	3.00	5.00	SF
P255 By Valour and Arms—James Street	.40	1.20	2.00	
P256 The Shadow and the Glory—John Jennings	.80	2.40	4.00	A
257 The Secret Brand—Gene Austin	.40	1.20	2.00	
258 The Assault—Allen R. Matthews	.40	1.20	2.00	
P259 Air Surgeon—Frank G. Slaughter	.40	1.20	2.00	C
P260 Thunder in the Wilderness—Harry Hamilton	.50	1.50	2.50	
P261 Baghdad-by-the-Bay—Herb Caen	.40	1.20	2.00	
P262S 7 Arts No. 2—Fernando Puma; 1954	.40	1.20	2.00	
263 The Comancheros—Paul I. Wellman	.80	2.40	4.00	W
264 City—Clifford D. Simak	1.00	3.00	5.00	SF
265 Element of Risk—Mark Derby	.50	1.50	2.50	
P266 Bright to the Wanderer—Bruce Lancaster	.50	1.50	2.50	
P267 Down and Out in Paris and London—George Orwell	.50	1.50	2.50	
P268 Queen's Gift—Inglis Fletcher	1.00	3.00	5.00	A
P269S The Celluloid Jungle—Robert Carson	.40	1.20	2.00	
270 Nine to Five—W. H. Prosser	.40	1.20	2.00	
271 Range War—Tom J. Hopkins	.50	1.50	2.50	W
272 Why I Know There Is a God—Fulton Oursler	.30	.90	1.50	
P273 The Sinner of Saint Ambrose—Robert Raynolds	.30	.90	1.50	E
P274 The Wreck of the Running Gale—Garland Roark	.50	1.50	2.50	
P275 The White Rabbit—Bruce Marshall; 1954	3.00	9.00	15.00	C
P276 The Will to Live—Arnold A. Hutschenecker	.40	1.20	2.00	
277 With Murder for Some—H. C. Huston	.50	1.50	2.50	M
278 The Intruders—Robert Bright	.40	1.20	2.00	
279 The Lost World—Arthur Conan Doyle	1.00	3.00	5.00	SF
P280 Seed of Mischief—Willa Gibbs	.40	1.20	2.00	
P281 Killers in Africa—Alexander Lake	.40	1.20	2.00	
P282 The Proud Retreat—Clifford Dowdey	.40	1.20	2.00	A
P283 The Rifleman—John Brick	.40	1.20	2.00	
P284S The Silver Chalice—Thomas B. Costain	.40	1.20	2.00	A
P285S Gardening—Montague Free	.30	.90	1.50	NF
286 The Condemned—Jo Pagano	.30	.90	1.50	
287 The Crooked Man—Shelley Smith	.40	1.20	2.00	
288 Destination Revenge—Jim Conroy	.40	1.20	2.00	
289 The Spitting Image—Michael Avallone	.80	2.40	4.00	
P290 The Galileans—Frank G. Slaughter	.40	1.20	2.00	
P291 Outsiders: Children of Wonder—William Tenn	2.00	6.00	10.00	SF
P292 Day of the Harvest—Helen Upshaw	.40	1.20	2.00	
P293 Gentleman Ranker—John Jennings	1.00	3.00	5.00	A
P294 Gone With the Wind—Margaret Mitchell	1.60	4.80	8.00	
295 Escape the Thunder—Lonnie Coleman; c-Maguire	.50	1.50	2.50	
P296 Green Hills of Africa—Ernest Hemingway	1.00	3.00	5.00	

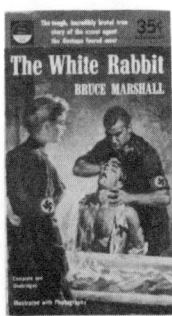

Perma Books P275, © DD

Phantom Books 502, © Hanro

Phantom Books 506, © Hanro

		Good	Fine	N/Mint	
(PERMABOOKS (Softbound), continued)					
297	Flying Saucers From Outer Space—Donald Keyhoe	.80	2.40	4.00	
P298	The Golden Eagle—Noel B. Gerson	.80	2.40	4.00	A
P299	The Southpaw—Mark Harris	.40	1.20	2.00	
P300	Father Divine: Holy Husband—Sara Harris; 1954	.30	.90	1.50	
P301	The High and the Mighty—Ernest K. Gann	.50	1.50	2.50	
P305	The Babylonians—Nathaniel Norsen Weinreb	.50	1.50	2.50	A
308	Tic-Polonga—Russ Anderton	.40	1.20	2.00	
310	Against the Fall of Night—Arthur C. Clarke	.80	2.40	4.00	SF
P311	The Deep Six—Martin Dibner	.40	1.20	2.00	
P313	He Hanged Them High—Homer Croy	1.00	3.00	5.00	NF

PHANTOM BOOKS
Hanro Corporation

Digest Size

500	Homicide Hotel—Joe Barry	2.00	6.00	10.00	M
501	Kisses Can Kill—Donnell Carey	1.60	4.80	8.00	M
502	The Deadly Lover—Robert O. Saber; orig., 1951	1.60	4.80	8.00	M
503	Married to Murder—Harry Whittington	2.00	6.00	10.00	M
504	Love Me and Die!—Day Keene	2.00	6.00	10.00	M
505	Satan's Widow	1.60	4.80	8.00	M
506	Crime on My Hands—Carl G. Hoges; c-Gross	1.60	4.80	8.00	M
507	Hunt the Killer—Day Keene; 1st ed., 1951	2.00	6.00	10.00	M
508	Swamp Kill—Whit Harrison (Harry Whittington); orig., 1952	2.00	6.00	10.00	M
509	Naked Fury—Day Keene; orig., 1952	2.00	6.00	10.00	M
510	Murder Doll—Robert O. Saber	1.60	4.80	8.00	M
511	Violent Night—Whit Harrison (Harry Whittington)	2.00	6.00	10.00	M
512	No Way Out—Robert O. Saber; orig., 1952	1.60	4.80	8.00	M
513	Wake Up to Murder—Day Keene; orig., 1952	2.00	6.00	10.00	M

PHANTOM MYSTERY
Unknown publisher

1	Rocket to the Morgue—H. H. Holmes (Anthony Boucher); 1st ed., 1942	15.00	45.00	75.00	M

PHOENIX
Phoenix Books

Phantom Books 507, © Hanro

Phantom Mystery 1, © Unknown

Phoenix nn, © Phoen

Pocket Book 1, © Pkb   Pocket Book 16, © Pkb   Pocket Book 34, © Pkb

		Good	Fine	N/Mint	
(PHOENIX, continued)					
nn	Tokyo Escapade—Shel Walker; orig., 1955	4.00	12.00	20.00	M

PITMAN EDITION
Pitman Publishing Corporation

		Good	Fine	N/Mint	
nn	Franklin Delano Roosevelt: A Memorial—ed. Donald Porter Geddes	.50	1.50	2.50	B

NOTE: Variant edition of Pocket Book No. 300.

POCKET BOOK
Pocket Books, Inc.

		Good	Fine	N/Mint	
nn	The Good Earth—Pearl S. Buck; 1938, introductory book of series	25.00	75.00	125.00	
1	Lost Horizon—James Hilton; 1939	20.00	60.00	100.00	
2	Wake Up and Live—Dorothea Brande	15.00	45.00	75.00	NF
3	Five Great Tragedies—William Shakespeare	15.00	45.00	75.00	
4	Topper—Thorne Smith	15.00	45.00	75.00	H
5	The Murder of Roger Ackroyd—Agatha Christie	16.50	50.00	80.00	M
6	Enough Rope—Dorothy Parker	15.00	45.00	75.00	
7	Wuthering Heights—Emily Bronte	15.00	45.00	75.00	
8	The Way of All Flesh—Samuel Butler	15.00	45.00	75.00	
9	The Bridge of San Luis Rey—Thornton Wilder	15.00	45.00	75.00	
10	Bambi—Felix Salten	15.00	45.00	75.00	
11	The Good Earth—Pearl S. Buck	3.00	9.00	15.00	
12	Great Short Stories—Guy de Maupassant	2.00	6.00	10.00	
13	Show Boat—Edna Ferber	2.00	6.00	10.00	
14	A Tale of Two Cities—Charles Dickens	2.00	6.00	10.00	
15	The Story of Mankind—Hendrik Willem Van Loon	1.60	4.80	8.00	NF
16	Green Mansions—W. H. Hudson	4.00	12.00	20.00	
17	The Chinese Orange Mystery—Ellery Queen	2.00	6.00	10.00	M
18	Pinocchio—Carlo Collodi	3.00	9.00	15.00	
19	Abraham Lincoln—Lord Charnwood	2.00	6.00	10.00	NF
20	The Return of the Native—Thomas Hardy	2.00	6.00	10.00	
21	Murder Must Advertise—Dorothy L. Sayers	3.00	9.00	15.00	M
22	The Swiss Family Robinson—Johann Wyss	3.00	9.00	15.00	A
23	The Autobiography of Benjamin Franklin—B. Franklin	1.60	4.80	8.00	NF
24	The Corpse With the Floating Foot—R. A. J. Walling	2.00	6.00	10.00	M
25	Treasure Island—Robert Louis Stevenson; 1939	3.00	9.00	15.00	A
26	Elizabeth and Essex—Lytton Strachey	1.60	4.80	8.00	
27	Appointment in Samarra—John O'Hara	2.00	6.00	10.00	
28	Jeeves—P. G. Wodehouse	2.00	6.00	10.00	
29	A Christmas Carol—Charles Dickens	3.00	9.00	15.00	
30	The Little French Girl—Anne Douglas Sedgwick	2.00	6.00	10.00	
31	The Hunchback of Notre Dame - Volume I—Victor Hugo	3.00	9.00	15.00	A
32	The Hunchback of Notre Dame - Volume II—Victor Hugo	3.00	9.00	15.00	A
33	The Watchman's Clock—Leslie Ford	2.00	6.00	10.00	M
34	Gulliver's Travels—Jonathan Swift; 1940, movie tie-in	4.00	12.00	20.00	A
35	Beau Geste—Percival C. Wren	3.00	9.00	15.00	
36	The Three Musketeers - Volume I—Alexandre Dumas	3.00	9.00	15.00	A
37	The Three Musketeers - Volume II—Alexandre Dumas	3.00	9.00	15.00	A
38	The Mystery of the Blue Train—Agatha Christie	3.00	9.00	15.00	M
39	Great Tales and Poems—Edgar Allan Poe	3.00	9.00	15.00	
40	The Man Nobody Knows—Bruce Barton	2.00	6.00	10.00	
41	The Constant Nymph—Margaret Kennedy	2.00	6.00	10.00	
42	Autobiography of Benvenuto Cellini—B. Cellini	2.00	6.00	10.00	NF
43	The Lodger—Marie Belloc Lowndes	2.00	6.00	10.00	
44	Mother—Kathleen Norris	2.00	6.00	10.00	
45	The Light That Failed—Rudyard Kipling	2.00	6.00	10.00	

(POCKET BOOK, continued)

		Good	Fine	N/Mint	
46	The Bowstring Murders—Carter Dickson	3.00	9.00	15.00	M
47	Bring 'Em Back Alive—Edward Anthony & Frank Buck	1.60	4.80	8.00	A
48	Scarlet Sister Mary—Julia Peterkin	2.00	6.00	10.00	
49	Dr. Ehrlich's Magic Bullet—Paul deKruif; (later editions retitled Microbe Hunters); movie tie-in	1.60	4.80	8.00	NF
50	The House Without a Key—Earl Derr Biggers; 1940	4.00	12.00	20.00	M
51	Thunder on the Left—Christopher Morley	2.00	6.00	10.00	
52	The House of the Seven Gables—Nathaniel Hawthorne	2.00	6.00	10.00	
53	The Best of Damon Runyon—D. Runyon	2.00	6.00	10.00	
54	The Great Prince Shan—E. Phillips Oppenheim	2.00	6.00	10.00	
55	Our Town—Thornton Wilder; movie tie-in	2.00	6.00	10.00	
56	The Green Bay Tree—Louis Bromfield	1.60	4.80	8.00	
57	After Such Pleasures—Dorothy Parker	1.60	4.80	8.00	
58	Tom Brown's School Days—Thomas Hughes	2.00	6.00	10.00	
59	Think Fast, Mr. Moto—John P. Marquand	4.00	12.00	20.00	M
60	The Scandal of Father Brown—G. K. Chesterton	4.00	12.00	20.00	M
61	Bob, Son of Battle—Alfred Ollivant	3.00	9.00	15.00	A
62	The Pocket Book of Verse—M. E. Speare	1.60	4.80	8.00	
63	Pride and Prejudice—Jane Austin	1.60	4.80	8.00	
64	While the Patient Slept—Mignon G. Eberhart	1.60	4.80	8.00	M
65	The Four Million—O. Henry	1.60	4.80	8.00	
66	National Velvet—Enid Bagnold	3.00	9.00	15.00	
67	Heidi—Johanna Spyri	3.00	9.00	15.00	
68	How to Win Friends and Influence People—Dale Carnegie	1.20	3.60	6.00	NF
69	The Thirty-nine Steps—John Buchan	2.00	6.00	10.00	
70	The Mystery of the Dead Police—Philip MacDonald	2.00	6.00	10.00	M
71	The French Powder Mystery—Ellery Queen	1.60	4.80	8.00	M
72	Anne of Windy Poplars—L. M. Montgomery	1.60	4.80	8.00	
73	The Case of the Velvet Claws—Erle Stanley Gardner	1.60	4.80	8.00	M
74	The Unpleasantness at the Bellona Club—Dorothy L. Sayers	2.00	6.00	10.00	M
75	Little Men—Louisa May Alcott; 1940	2.00	6.00	10.00	
76	Sunset Gun—Dorothy Parker	2.00	6.00	10.00	
77	The Roman Hat Mystery—Ellery Queen	1.60	4.80	8.00	M
78	Oh, You Tex!—William MacLeod Raine	2.00	6.00	10.00	W
79	Murder in the Calais Coach—Agatha Christie	2.00	6.00	10.00	M
80	Up From Slavery—Booker T. Washington	2.00	6.00	10.00	
81	The Red House Mystery—A. A. Milne	1.60	4.80	8.00	M
82	Captain Blood—Rafael Sabatini	2.00	6.00	10.00	A
83	A Puzzle for Fools—Patrick Quentin	2.00	6.00	10.00	M
84	The Riddle of the Sands—Erskine Childers	1.60	4.80	8.00	
85	Clouds of Witness—Dorothy L. Sayers	2.00	6.00	10.00	M
86	The Red Widow Murders—Carter Dickson	2.00	6.00	10.00	M
87	Mister Glencannon—Guy Gilpatric; 1941	1.60	4.80	8.00	
88	The ABC Murders—Agatha Christie	1.60	4.80	8.00	M
89	And Now Good-bye—James Hilton	1.60	4.80	8.00	
90	The Case of the Sulky Girl—Erle Stanley Gardner	1.60	4.80	8.00	M
91	The Pocket Book of Short Stories—M. E. Speare	1.60	4.80	8.00	
92	The Pocket Bible	2.00	6.00	10.00	
93	Goodbye, Mr. Chips—James Hilton	1.60	4.80	8.00	
94	Greenmantle—John Buchan	1.60	4.80	8.00	
95	The Sherlock Holmes Pocket Book—Arthur Conan Doyle	5.00	15.00	25.00	M
96	Believe It or Not—Robert Ripley	3.00	9.00	15.00	NF
97	The Werewolf of Paris—Guy Endore	10.00	30.00	50.00	HO
98	The Circular Staircase—Mary Roberts Rinehart	1.60	4.80	8.00	M
99	The Adventures of Ellery Queen—E. Queen	2.00	6.00	10.00	M
100	The General Died at Dawn—Charles G. Booth; 1941	2.00	6.00	10.00	
101	It Walks by Night—John Dickson Carr	4.00	12.00	20.00	M
102	The Philadelphia Story—Philip Barry; movie tie-in	2.00	6.00	10.00	

Pocket Book 55, © Pkb

Pocket Book 95, © Pkb

Pocket Book 100, © Pkb

Pocket Book 124, © Pkb

Pocket Book 133, © Pkb

Pocket Book 151, © Pkb

		Good	Fine	N/Mint	
(POCKET BOOK, continued)					
103	The Pocket Book of Great Detectives—Lee Wright	3.00	9.00	15.00	M
104	Nana—Emile Zola	1.60	4.80	8.00	
105	Sir John Magill's Last Journey—Freeman Wills Crofts	3.00	9.00	15.00	M
106	The Case of the Lucky Legs—Erle Stanley Gardner	1.60	4.80	8.00	M
107	The Pocket Book of Etiquette—Margery Wilson	1.60	4.80	8.00	NF
108	The Pocket Reader—Philip Van Doren Stern	1.60	4.80	8.00	
109	The Siamese Twin Mystery—Ellery Queen	2.00	6.00	10.00	M
110	The Pocket Book of Boners; interior illustrations-Dr. Suess	2.00	6.00	10.00	H
111	Mr. Pinkerton Finds a Body—David Frome	2.00	6.00	10.00	M
112	Fer-de-Lance—Rex Stout	2.00	6.00	10.00	M
113	Enter a Murderer—Ngaio Marsh	2.00	6.00	10.00	M
114	Five Great Comedies—William Shakespeare	1.20	3.60	6.00	
115	Dodsworth—Sinclair Lewis	1.60	4.80	8.00	
116	The Case of the Howling Dog—Erle Stanley Gardner	1.20	3.60	6.00	M
117	The Pocket Book of Mystery Stories—Lee Wright	2.00	6.00	10.00	M
118	We Are Not Alone—James Hilton	1.60	4.80	8.00	
119	The Pocket History of the World—H. G. Wells	1.60	4.80	8.00	NF
120	Life Begins at Forty—Walter B. Pitkin	1.60	4.80	8.00	
121	The Album—Mary Roberts Rinehart	1.60	4.80	8.00	M
122	The Simple Way of Poison—Leslie Ford	2.00	6.00	10.00	M
123	Dr. Jekyll and Mr. Hyde—Robert Louis Stevenson; movie tie-in	4.00	12.00	20.00	SF
124	Mr. Pinkerton Goes to Scotland Yard—David Frome	2.00	6.00	10.00	M
125	The Tragedy of X—Ellery Queen; 1941	1.60	4.80	8.00	M
126	Pocket Self-Pronouncing Dictionary and Vocabulary Builder—William J. Pelo	1.60	4.80	8.00	NF
127	The Pocket Book of the War—Quincy Howe	1.60	4.80	8.00	NF
128	The Rubaiyat of Omar Khayyam—Omar Khayyam	1.60	4.80	8.00	
129	The Singapore Exile Murders—F. van Wyck Mason	1.60	4.80	8.00	M
130	Strong Poison—Dorothy L. Sayers	2.00	6.00	10.00	M
131	While Rome Burns—Alexander Woollcott	1.60	4.80	8.00	
132	The Pocket Quiz Book—Louise Crittenden & Rosejeanne Slifer	1.60	4.80	8.00	NF
133	The Black Camel—Earl Derr Biggers	3.00	9.00	15.00	M
134	The New Adventures of Ellery Queen—E. Queen	2.00	6.00	10.00	M
135	Long Remember—MacKinlay Kantor	1.60	4.80	8.00	
136	Without Armor—James Hilton; 1942	1.60	4.80	8.00	
137	Death in a White Tie—Ngaio Marsh	1.60	4.80	8.00	M
138	The Case of the Caretaker's Cat—Erle Stanley Gardner	1.60	4.80	8.00	M
139	You Can't Do Business With Hitler—Douglas Miller	1.60	4.80	8.00	NF
140	The Door—Mary Roberts Rinehart	1.60	4.80	8.00	M
141	The Saint-Fiacre Affair—Georges Simenon	2.00	6.00	10.00	M
142	The Pocket Companion—Philip Van Doren Stern	1.20	3.60	6.00	
143	The Man Who Came to Dinner—Moss Hart & George S. Kaufman; movie tie-in	1.60	4.80	8.00	
144	Singing Guns—Max Brand	1.60	4.80	8.00	W
145	The Pocket Book of Modern American Plays—Bennett Cerf	1.60	4.80	8.00	
146	The Spanish Cape Mystery—Ellery Queen	2.00	6.00	10.00	M
147	The Royal Road to Romance—Richard Halliburton	2.00	6.00	10.00	
148	The Pocket Book of Vegetable Gardening—Charles Nissley	1.60	4.80	8.00	NF
149	Escape—Ethel Vance	1.60	4.80	8.00	
150	The Office Wife—Faith Baldwin; 1942	1.60	4.80	8.00	R
151	Hugger-Mugger in the Louvre—Elliot Paul	2.00	6.00	10.00	M
152	The Balcony—Dorothy Cameron Disney	1.60	4.80	8.00	M
153	The Man From Scotland Yard—David Frome	2.00	6.00	10.00	M
154	The Red Badge of Courage—Stephen Crane	2.00	6.00	10.00	
155	Hunger Fighters—Paul de Kruif	1.00	3.00	5.00	NF
156	The White Priory Murders—Carter Dickson	2.00	6.00	10.00	M
157	The Case of the Counterfeit Eye—Erle Stanley Gardner	1.20	3.60	6.00	M
158	Damon Runyon Favorites—D. Runyon	1.60	4.80	8.00	
159	Mrs. Miniver—Jan Struther	1.20	3.60	6.00	
160	The Art of Thinking—Ernest Dimnet	1.60	4.80	8.00	NF

		Good	Fine	N/Mint	
161	The Spirit of the Border—Zane Grey	1.60	4.80	8.00	W
162	Arrowsmith—Sinclair Lewis	1.60	4.80	8.00	
163	Have His Carcase—Dorothy L. Sayers	1.60	4.80	8.00	M
164	A Puzzle for Players—Patrick Quentin	1.60	4.80	8.00	M
165	The Pocket Entertainer—Shirley Cunningham	1.20	3.60	6.00	NF
166	The Norths Meet Murder—Richard & Frances Lockridge	2.00	6.00	10.00	M
167	Peril at End House—Agatha Christie	2.00	6.00	10.00	M
168	The Chinese Parrot—Earl Derr Biggers	3.00	9.00	15.00	M
169	The Nutmeg Tree—Margery Sharp; movie tie-in	1.60	4.80	8.00	
170	Defense Will Not Win the War—W. F. Kernan	1.60	4.80	8.00	NF
171	The Cape Cod Mystery—Phoebe Atwood Taylor	1.60	4.80	8.00	M
172	The Pocket Mystery Reader—Lee Wright	2.00	6.00	10.00	M
173	The Strategy of Terror—Edmond Taylor	2.00	6.00	10.00	NF
174	Beat to Quarters—C. S. Forester	1.60	4.80	8.00	
175	Green Light—Lloyd C. Douglas; 1942	1.20	3.60	6.00	
176	The Pocket Book of Quotations—Henry Davidoff	1.20	3.60	6.00	NF
177	The Case of the Curious Bride—Erle Stanley Gardner	1.20	3.60	6.00	M
178	I Saw It Happen—Lewis Gannett	1.60	4.80	8.00	
179	The Greek Coffin Mystery—Ellery Queen	1.60	4.80	8.00	M
180	The Peacock Feather Murders—Carter Dickson	2.00	6.00	10.00	M
181	The Pocket Cook Book—Elizabeth Woody	1.60	4.80	8.00	NF
182	The Pocket Book of America—Philip Van Doren Stern	1.60	4.80	8.00	
183	The Return to Religion—Henry C. Link	1.20	3.60	6.00	
184	A Silent Witness—R. Austin Freeman	2.00	6.00	10.00	M
185	The Nine Tailors—Dorothy L. Sayers	2.00	6.00	10.00	M
186	Above Suspicion—Helen MacInnes	1.60	4.80	8.00	
187	The Pocket Book of Dog Stories—Harold Berman	2.00	6.00	10.00	
188	The Hurricane—James Norman Hall & Charles Nordhoff	1.60	4.80	8.00	A
189	My Sister Eileen—Ruth McKenney	1.20	3.60	6.00	
190	The Best of Mr. Fortune Stories—H. C. Bailey	3.00	9.00	15.00	M
191	Behind That Curtain—Earl Derr Biggers	2.00	6.00	10.00	M
192	Prelude to Victory—James B. Reston	1.60	4.80	8.00	
193	Journey Into Fear—Eric Ambler	1.20	3.60	6.00	
194	The Coming Battle of Germany—William B. Ziff	1.60	4.80	8.00	NF
195	The Pocket History of the United States—Henry Steele Commager & Alan Nevius	1.20	3.60	6.00	NF
196	The Thin Man—Dashiell Hammett; 1943	5.00	15.00	25.00	M
197	The Pocket Book of War Humor—Bennett Cerf	1.60	4.80	8.00	H
198	The Human Body—Logan Clendening	1.20	3.60	6.00	NF
199	Arsenic and Old Lace—Joseph Kesselring	1.60	4.80	8.00	H
200	The Pocket Book of Flower Gardening; 1943	1.20	3.60	6.00	NF
201	The Case of the Stuttering Bishop—Erle Stanley Gardner	1.20	3.60	6.00	M
202	The Dutch Shoe Mystery—Ellery Queen	1.60	4.80	8.00	M
203	Mission to Moscow—Joseph E. Davies	1.20	3.60	6.00	NF
204	Death Lights a Candle—Phoebe Atwood Taylor	1.60	4.80	8.00	M
205	Rebecca—Daphne du Maurier	1.20	3.60	6.00	
206	See Here, Private Hargrove—Marion Hargrove	.30	.90	1.50	H
207	Charlie Chan Carries On—Earl Derr Biggers	3.00	9.00	15.00	M
208	The Rubber Band—Rex Stout	3.00	9.00	15.00	M
209	Topper Takes a Trip—Thorne Smith	2.00	6.00	10.00	H
210	The Pocket Book of Crossword Puzzles—Margaret Petherbridge	3.00	9.00	15.00	NF
211	The Glass Key—Dashiell Hammett; 1942	4.00	12.00	20.00	M
212	Farewell My Lovely—Raymond Chandler	4.00	12.00	20.00	M
213	The Pocket Book of True Crime Stories—Anthony Boucher; 1943	3.00	9.00	15.00	NF
214	The Pocket Book of Science Fiction—Donald A. Wollheim	6.00	18.00	30.00	SF
215	Magnificent Obsession—Lloyd C. Douglas	1.20	3.60	6.00	
216	Mutiny on the Bounty—James Norman Hall & Charles Nordhoff	1.60	4.80	8.00	A
217	The Pocket Book of Home Canning—Elizabeth Beveridge	1.20	3.60	6.00	NF
218	Claudia—Rose Franken	1.20	3.60	6.00	

Pocket Book 164, © Pkb

Pocket Book 212, © Pkb

Pocket Book 214, © Pkb

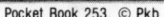

Pocket Book 253, © Pkb

Pocket Book 259, © Pkb

Pocket Book 268 (w/dj), © Pkb

(POCKET BOOK, continued)

		Good	Fine	N/Mint	
219	The Punch and Judy Murders—Carter Dickson	3.00	9.00	15.00	M
220	What to Do Till the Doctor Comes—Donald Armstrong & Grace T. Hallock	1.20	3.60	6.00	NF
221	Overture to Death—Ngaio Marsh	2.00	6.00	10.00	M
222	Fast Company—Marco Page	1.00	3.00	5.00	M
223	The Case of the Lame Canary—Erle Stanley Gardner	1.20	3.60	6.00	M
224	The Great Impersonation—E. Phillips Oppenheim	1.00	3.00	5.00	
225	Into the Valley—John Hersey; 1943	1.00	3.00	5.00	
226	The House of Exile—Nora Wain	1.20	3.60	6.00	
227	The Egyptian Cross Mystery—Ellery Queen	1.60	4.80	8.00	M
228	The Bigger They Come—A. A. Fair	1.20	3.60	6.00	M
229	One World—Wendell L. Willkie	1.00	3.00	5.00	
230	The Pocket Aviation Quiz Book—Milton Figen	1.60	4.80	8.00	NF
231	The Judas Window—Carter Dickson	3.00	9.00	15.00	M
232	A Coffin for Dimitrios—Eric Ambler	1.20	3.60	6.00	M
233	The Pocket Book of Cartoons—Bennett Cerf	1.60	4.80	8.00	H
234	Vogue's Pocket Book of Home Dressmaking	1.20	3.60	6.00	NF
235	Assignment in Brittany—Helen MacInnes	1.20	3.60	6.00	
236	The Pocket Book of Father Brown—G. K. Chesterton	3.00	9.00	15.00	M
237	Trial by Fury—Craig Rice	1.20	3.60	6.00	M
238	The Pocket Book of Modern American Short Stories—Philip Van Doren Stern	1.20	3.60	6.00	
239	How to Play Winning Checkers—Millard Hopper	1.20	3.60	6.00	NF
240	Madame Bovary—Gustave Flaubert; 1943	1.00	3.00	5.00	
241	Red Harvest—Dashiell Hammett	4.00	12.00	20.00	M
242	The Case of the Substitute Face—Erle Stanley Gardner	1.00	3.00	5.00	M
243	The Steinbeck Pocket Book—John Steinbeck	2.00	6.00	10.00	
244	U. S. Foreign Policy—Walter Lippmann; 1944	1.00	3.00	5.00	NF
245	The Four of Hearts—Ellery Queen	1.60	4.80	8.00	M
246	The Lady in the Morgue—Jonathan Latimer	2.00	6.00	10.00	M
247	No Surrender—Martha Albrand	1.20	3.60	6.00	
248	The Canary Murder Case—S. S. Van Dine	1.60	4.80	8.00	M
249	The Patriotic Murders—Agatha Christie	1.60	4.80	8.00	M
250	Destry Rides Again—Max Brand; 1944	1.20	3.60	6.00	W
251	The Ogden Nash Pocket Book—Ogden Nash	1.00	3.00	5.00	
252	The Case of the Dangerous Dowager—Erle Stanley Gardner	1.00	3.00	5.00	M
253	Phantom Lady—William Irish	2.00	6.00	10.00	M
254	The New Testament	1.60	4.80	8.00	
255	The New Pocket Quiz Book—Louise Crittenden & Rosejeanne Slifer	1.60	3.60	6.00	NF
256	The Greene Murder Case—S. S. Van Dine	1.60	4.80	8.00	M
257	Enter the Saint—Leslie Charteris	1.60	4.80	8.00	M
258	The Late George Apley—John P. Marquand	1.60	4.80	8.00	
259	Halfway House—Ellery Queen; Note: 1st printing was published in a unique oblong format, with the binding along the top.	4.00	12.00	20.00	M
260	The Pocket Book of Games—Albert H. Morehead	1.60	4.80	8.00	NF
261	And Then There Were None—Agatha Christie	1.60	4.80	8.00	M
262	The Somerset Maugham Pocket Book—W. S. Maugham	1.60	4.80	8.00	
263	The D. A. Calls It Murder—Erle Stanley Gardner	1.00	3.00	5.00	M
264	The Bellamy Trial—Frances Noyes Hart	1.00	3.00	5.00	
265	AAF: The Official Guide	1.20	3.60	6.00	NF
266	Lend-lease: Weapon for Victory—Edward R. Stettinius, Jr.	1.20	3.60	6.00	NF
267	Land Below the Wind—Agnes Newton Keith	1.20	3.60	6.00	
268	The Maltese Falcon—Dashiell Hammett	4.00	12.00	20.00	M
	With dust jacket	12.50	37.50	60.00	
269	Trent's Last Case—E. C. Benttey	1.60	4.80	8.00	M
270	The Devil to Pay—Ellery Queen	1.60	4.80	8.00	M
271	The Bride Wore Black—Cornell Woolrich	2.00	6.00	10.00	M
272	The Happy Highwayman—Leslie Charteris	1.60	4.80	8.00	M
273	Tarawa—Robert Sherrod	1.20	3.60	6.00	C
274	Here Is Your War—Ernie Pyle	1.20	3.60	6.00	NF

		Good	Fine	N/Mint	
275	Random Harvest—James Hilton; 1944	1.60	4.80	8.00	
276	The Story Pocket Book—ed. Whit Burnett	1.60	4.80	8.00	
277	The Case of the Sleepwalker's Niece—Erle Stanley Gardner	1.00	3.00	5.00	M
278	Experiment Perilous—Margaret Carpenter	1.20	3.60	6.00	
279	A Bell for Adano—John Hersey	1.00	3.00	5.00	
280	Life With Father—Clarence Day	1.60	4.80	8.00	H
281	Pastoral—Nevil Shute; 1945	1.00	3.00	5.00	
282	The Human Comedy—William Saroyan	1.00	3.00	5.00	
283	Calamity Town—Ellery Queen	1.60	4.80	8.00	M
284	The Pocket Book of Adventure Stories—Philip Van Doren Stern	1.60	4.80	8.00	A
285	Evil Under the Sun—Agatha Christie	1.60	4.80	8.00	M
286	Background to Danger—Eric Ambler	1.60	4.80	8.00	M
287	The D. A. Holds a Candle—Erle Stanley Gardner	1.00	3.00	5.00	M
288	TVA: Democracy on the March—David E. Lilienthal	1.00	3.00	5.00	NF
289	Having a Wonderful Crime—Craig Rice	1.60	4.80	8.00	M
290	Jalna—Mazo de la Roche	1.20	3.60	6.00	
291	The Complete Sayings of Jesus—Arthur Hinds	2.00	6.00	10.00	
292	Take It Easy—Damon Runyon	1.60	4.80	8.00	
293	The Pocket Book of Western Stories—Harry E. Manle	1.60	4.80	8.00	W
294	The Pocket Book of Jokes—Bennett Cerf	1.20	3.60	6.00	H
295	The Dain Curse—Dashiell Hammett	4.00	12.00	20.00	M
296	Claudia and David—Rose Franken	1.00	3.00	5.00	
297	Death at the Bar—Ngaio Marsh	1.60	4.80	8.00	M
298	They'll Do It Every Time—Jimmy Hatlo	2.00	6.00	10.00	H
299	The Pocket Book of Basic English—I. A. Richards	1.20	3.60	6.00	NF
300	Franklin Delano Roosevelt: A Memorial—Donald Porter Geddes; 1945	1.00	3.00	5.00	B
301	The Border Trumpet—Ernest Haycox	1.60	4.80	8.00	W
302	Young Doctor Galahad—Elizabeth Seifert	1.20	3.60	6.00	
303	The Reader Is Warned—Carter Dickson	2.00	6.00	10.00	M
304	Alexander Botts: Earthworm Tractors—William Hazlett Upson	2.00	6.00	10.00	
305	The Bishop Murder Case—S. S. Van Dine	1.60	4.80	8.00	M
306	Small Beer—Ludwig Bemelmans	1.60	4.80	8.00	
307	Trial and Error—Anthony Berkeley	1.20	3.60	6.00	M
	With dust jacket	9.00	27.00	45.00	
308	The Pocket Book of Modern Verse—Ted Malone	1.20	3.60	6.00	
309	Rats, Lice and History—Hans Zinsser	1.60	4.80	8.00	NF
310	The Whoop-up Trail—B. M. Bower	1.60	4.80	8.00	W
311	White Collar Girl—Faith Baldwin	1.60	4.80	8.00	R
312	The Case of the Shoplifter's Shoe—Erle Stanley Gardner	1.00	3.00	5.00	M
313	The Tragedy of Y—Ellery Queen	1.60	4.80	8.00	M
314	The Bishop's Jaegers—Thorne Smith	1.60	4.80	8.00	H
315	Stalk the Hunter—Mitchell Wilson	1.60	4.80	8.00	
316	Fightin' Fool—Max Brand	1.60	4.80	8.00	W
317	On Borrowed Time—Lawrence Edward Watkin	1.60	4.80	8.00	
318	Farewell to Sport—Paul Gallico	1.20	3.60	6.00	S
319	Easy to Kill—Agatha Christie	1.60	4.80	8.00	M
320	The High Window—Raymond Chandler	3.00	9.00	15.00	M
321	Chicken Every Sunday—Rosemary Taylor; movie tie-in	1.20	3.60	6.00	
	With dust jacket	10.00	30.00	50.00	
322	The Last Frontier—Howard Fast	1.60	4.80	8.00	W
323	400 Million Customers—Carl Crow	1.60	4.80	8.00	
324	Busman's Honeymoon—Dorothy L. Sayers	1.60	4.80	8.00	M
	With dust jacket	10.00	30.00	50.00	
325	The Sea-Wolf—Jack London; 1946	1.60	4.80	8.00	A
326	There Was an Old Woman—Ellery Queen	1.60	4.80	8.00	M
327	Country Lawyer—Bellamy Partridge	1.60	4.80	8.00	
328	Warrant for X—Philip MacDonald	1.60	4.80	8.00	M
329	The Fashion in Shrouds—Margery Allingham	1.60	4.80	8.00	M
330	You Must Relax—Edmund Jacobson	1.20	3.60	6.00	

Pocket Book 295, © Pkb

Pocket Book 307 (w/dj), © Pkb

Pocket Book 321 (w/dj), © Pkb

		Good	Fine	N/Mint	
331	Verdict of Twelve—Raymond Postgate	2.00	6.00	10.00	
332	Junior Miss—Sally Benson	1.20	3.60	6.00	
333	The Benson Murder Case—S. S. Van Dine	1.60	4.80	8.00	M
334	The D. A. Draws a Circle—Erle Stanley Gardner	1.00	3.00	5.00	M
335	Nine - and Death Makes Ten—Carter Dickson	1.60	4.80	8.00	M
336	Blood Upon the Snow—Hilda Lawrence	1.60	4.80	8.00	M
337	Hopalong Cassidy Returns—Clarence E. Mulford	1.60	4.80	8.00	W
338	The Pocket History of the Second World War—Henry Steele Commager	1.20	3.60	6.00	NF
339	Young Widow—Clarissa Fairchild Cushman	1.20	3.60	6.00	
340	The Atomic Age Opens—Donald Porter Geddes	1.20	3.60	6.00	NF
341	The Body in the Library—Agatha Christie	1.60	4.80	8.00	M
342	The Pocket Book of Story Poems—Louis Untermeyer	1.20	3.60	6.00	
343	First Aid for the Ailing House—Roger B. Whitman	1.20	3.60	6.00	NF
344	Lust for Life—Irving Stone	1.20	3.60	6.00	
345	Spiderweb Trail—Eugene Cunningham	1.60	4.80	8.00	W
346	A Pinch of Poison—Richard & Frances Lockridge	2.00	6.00	10.00	M
347	The Phantom Filly—George Agnew Chamberlain	1.60	4.80	8.00	
348	Gringo Guns—Peter Field	1.60	4.80	8.00	W
349	Fielding's Folly—Frances Parkinson Keyes	1.20	3.60	6.00	
350	Death Turns the Tables—John Dickson Carr; 1946	2.00	6.00	10.00	M
351	Color Scheme—Ngaio Marsh	1.20	3.60	6.00	M
352	Disputed Passage—Lloyd C. Douglas	1.00	3.00	5.00	
353	The Valley of Dry Bones—Arthur Henry Gooden	1.60	4.80	8.00	W
354	To Have and to Hold—Mary Johnston	1.20	3.60	6.00	
355	The Tragedy of Z—Ellery Queen	1.20	3.60	6.00	M
356	The Horse and Buggy Doctor—Arthur E. Hertzler	1.00	3.00	5.00	
357	Taps for Private Tussie—Jesse Stuart	1.20	3.60	6.00	
358	Men Against the Sea—James Norman Hall & Charles Nordhoff	1.20	3.60	6.00	A
359	Dragon Seed—Pearl S. Buck	1.20	3.60	6.00	
360	The Stephen Vincent Benet Pocketbook—Stephen Vincent Benet	1.20	3.60	6.00	
361	Home Sweet Homicide—Craig Rice	1.20	3.60	6.00	M
362	Steele of the Royal Mounted—James Oliver Curwood	1.20	3.60	6.00	A
363	Steamboat Round the Bend—Ben Lucien Burman	1.20	3.60	6.00	
364	The Journey Home—Zelda Popkin	1.20	3.60	6.00	
365	Dragonwyck—Anya Seton	1.20	3.60	6.00	
366	Barnaby—Crockett Johnson	1.20	3.60	6.00	
367	The Best-Loved Poems and Ballads of James Whitcomb Riley—J. W. Riley	1.20	3.60	6.00	
368	Murder up My Sleeve—Erle Stanley Gardner	1.00	3.00	5.00	M
369	Silvertip—Max Brand	1.20	3.60	6.00	W
370	Action at Aquila—Hervey Allen	1.20	3.60	6.00	
	With dust jacket	10.00	30.00	50.00	
371	The Last Trail—Zane Grey	1.20	3.60	6.00	W
372	The Emperor's Snuff Box—John Dickson Carr	1.60	4.80	8.00	M
373	Lad: A Dog—Albert Payson Terhune	1.20	3.60	6.00	
374	The Pocket Book of Robert Frost's Poems	1.20	3.60	6.00	
375	Whiteoaks of Jalna—Mazo de la Roche; 1947	1.00	3.00	5.00	
376	Murder Out of Town—Richard & Frances Lockridge	1.60	4.80	8.00	M
377	The Pocket Book of Baby & Child Care—Benjamin Spock	1.00	3.00	5.00	NF
378	The Case of the Perjured Parrot—Erle Stanley Gardner	1.00	3.00	5.00	M
379	Devils, Drugs and Doctors—Howard W. Haggard	1.00	3.00	5.00	
380	Medical Center—Faith Baldwin	1.00	3.00	5.00	R
381	The Murder of My Aunt—Richard Hull	1.20	3.60	6.00	M
382	Freedom Road—Howard Fast	1.20	3.60	6.00	
383	Roget's Pocket Thesaurus—Christopher Mawson & Katherine Whiting	1.00	3.00	5.00	NF
384	The Pocket Book of Ghost Stories—Philip Van Doren Stern	2.00	6.00	10.00	
385	The Red Right Hand—Joel Townsley Rogers	1.00	3.00	5.00	M
386	Seeing Is Believing—Carter Dickson	1.60	4.80	8.00	M
387	White Banners—Lloyd C. Douglas	1.00	3.00	5.00	
388	The Pocket Book of Humerous Verse—David McCord	1.20	3.60	6.00	H
389	The Lady in the Lake—Raymond Chandler	1.60	4.80	8.00	M
390	South of Rio Grande—Max Brand	1.20	3.60	6.00	W
391	The Lucky Stiff—Craig Rice	1.20	3.60	6.00	M
392	The Pocket Book of Erskine Caldwell Stories—E. Caldwell	1.20	3.60	6.00	
393	The Walsh Girls—Elizabeth Janeway	1.00	3.00	5.00	
394	The Bamboo Blonde—Dorothy B. Hughes	1.20	3.60	6.00	M
395	Cluny Brown—Margery Sharp	1.00	3.00	5.00	
396	Laugh With Leacock—Stephen Leacock	1.00	3.00	5.00	H
397	The Pocket Atlantic—Edward Weeks	1.20	3.60	6.00	
398	Towards Zero—Agatha Christie	1.20	3.60	6.00	M
399	The Fear Makers—Darwin L. Teilhet	1.20	3.60	6.00	
400	Madame Curie—Eve Curie; 1946	1.20	3.60	6.00	B
401	The Passionate Witch—Thorne Smith	1.20	3.60	6.00	H
402	Darkness of Slumber—Rosemary Kutak	1.20	3.60	6.00	
403	Jamaica Inn—Daphne du Maurier	1.00	3.00	5.00	
404	Past Imperfect—Ilka Chase	1.20	3.60	6.00	
405	Forgive Us Our Trespasses—Lloyd C. Douglas	1.00	3.00	5.00	
406	Runyon a la Carte—Damon Runyon	1.20	3.60	6.00	

		Good	Fine	N/Mint	
407	The D. A. Goes to Trial—Erle Stanley Gardner	1.00	3.00	5.00	M
408	The Lost God and Other Adventure Stories—John Russell	3.00	9.00	15.00	A
409	The Glorious Pool—Thorne Smith	1.20	3.60	6.00	H
410	The Covered Wagon—Emerson Hough	1.20	3.60	6.00	W
411	Death on the Aisle—Richard & Frances Lockridge	1.60	4.80	8.00	M
412	Slim—William Wister Haines	1.00	3.00	5.00	
413	The Sea of Grass—Conrad Richter; movie tie-in	1.00	3.00	5.00	
414	The Case of the Baited Hook—Erle Stanley Gardner	1.00	3.00	5.00	M
415	Frenchman's Creek—Daphne du Maurier	1.00	3.00	5.00	
416	Bill Stern's Favorite Boxing Stories—B. Stern	1.00	3.00	5.00	S
417	The Peter Arno Pocket Book—Peter Arno	1.00	3.00	5.00	H
418	The Razor's Edge—W. Somerset Maugham; 1947	1.00	3.00	5.00	
419	Before the Fact—Francis Iles	1.20	3.60	6.00	M
420	Puzzle for Puppets—Patrick Quentin	1.20	3.60	6.00	M
421	The Merriam Webster Pocket Dictionary	1.00	3.00	5.00	NF
422	The Delicate Ape—Dorothy B. Hughes	1.20	3.60	6.00	M
423	The Fighting Four—Max Brand	1.20	3.60	6.00	W
424	The Pocket Treasury—Louis Untermeyer	1.00	3.00	5.00	
425	The G-String Murders—Gypsy Rose Lee; 1947	1.00	3.00	5.00	M
426	The Second Believe It or Not—Robert Ripley	1.60	4.80	8.00	NF
427	The Innocent Flower—Charlotte Armstrong	1.20	3.60	6.00	M
428	The Night Life of the Gods—Thorne Smith	1.20	3.60	6.00	H
429	North of 36—Emerson Hough	1.20	3.60	6.00	W
430	Good Night, Sweet Prince—Gene Fowler	1.00	3.00	5.00	
431	The Pocket Book of Famous French Short Stories—Eric Swenson	1.00	3.00	5.00	
432	Malice Aforethought—Francis Iles	1.60	4.80	8.00	M
433	The Song of Bernadette—Franz Werfel	1.00	3.00	5.00	
434	The Sunday Pigeon Murders—Craig Rice	1.20	3.60	6.00	M
435	Father Malachy's Miracle—Bruce Marshall	1.00	3.00	5.00	F
436	The Lost Gallows—John Dickson Carr	1.60	4.80	8.00	M
437	Death and the Dancing Footman—Ngaio Marsh	1.20	3.60	6.00	M
438	The Clue of the Forgotten Murder—Erle Stanley Gardner	1.00	3.00	5.00	M
439	A Time to Die—Hilda Lawrence	1.20	3.60	6.00	M
440	Wife for Sale—Kathleen Norris	1.20	3.60	6.00	
441	The Shepherd of the Hills—Harold Bell Wright	1.20	3.60	6.00	W
442	Daisy Kenyon—Elizabeth Joneway	1.00	3.00	5.00	
443	The Postman Always Rings Twice—James M. Cain	1.20	3.60	6.00	M
444	The Unsuspected—Charlotte Armstrong; movie tie-in	1.00	3.00	5.00	M
445	Private Duty—Faith Baldwin	1.00	3.00	5.00	R
446	The Pocket Book of O. Henry Prize Stories—Herschel Brickell	1.00	3.00	5.00	
447	Turnabout—Thorne Smith	1.20	3.60	6.00	H
448	Castle Skull—John Dickson Carr	2.00	6.00	10.00	M
449	My Ten Years in a Quandry—Robert Benchley	1.20	3.60	6.00	H
450	The 2nd Pocket Book of Crossword Puzzles—Margaret Petherbridge; 1947	1.60	4.80	8.00	NF
451	Remembered Death—Agatha Christie	1.20	3.60	6.00	M
452	Dracula—Bram Stoker	6.00	18.00	30.00	HO
453	Mystery House—Kathleen Norris	1.00	3.00	5.00	
454	Dread Journey—Dorothy B. Hughes	1.20	3.60	6.00	M
455	The Treasure of the Sierra Madre—B. Traven; movie tie-in	1.60	4.80	8.00	A
456	District Nurse—Faith Baldwin	1.00	3.00	5.00	R
457	Pitcairn's Island—James Norman Hall & Charles Nordhoff	1.20	3.60	6.00	A
458	Win, Place and Show—Robert Dowst	1.00	3.00	5.00	
459	Dragon's Teeth—Ellery Queen; 1948	2.00	6.00	10.00	M
460	Slay the Loose Ladies—Patrick Quentin	1.60	4.80	8.00	M
461	The Thursday Turkey Murders—Craig Rice	1.60	4.80	8.00	M
462	How Green Was My Valley—Richard Llewellyn	1.20	3.60	6.00	
463	Doctor's Wife—Maysie Greig	1.00	3.00	5.00	
464	The Case of the Rolling Bones—Erle Stanley Gardner	1.00	3.00	5.00	M

Pocket Book 408, © Pkb

Pocket Book 426, © Pkb

Pocket Book 452, © Pkb

Pocket Book 465, © Pkb   Pocket Book 472, © Pkb   Pocket Book 495, © Pkb

(POCKET BOOK, continued)

		Good	Fine	N/Mint	
465	Death Comes As the End—Agatha Christie	1.20	3.60	6.00	M
466	Rim of the Desert—Ernest Haycox	1.20	3.60	6.00	W
467	Circle C Moves In—Brett Rider	1.20	3.60	6.00	W
468	The Case of the Silent Partner—Erle Stanley Gardner	1.00	3.00	5.00	M
469	Kitty—Rosamond Marshall	1.00	3.00	5.00	
470	A Lantern in Her Hand—Bess Streeter Aldrich	1.00	3.00	5.00	
471	The Door Between—Ellery Queen	1.20	3.60	6.00	M
472	Odd Man Out—F. L. Green; movie tie-in	1.20	3.60	6.00	
473	Under Northern Stars—William MacLeod Raine	1.20	3.60	6.00	W
474	The Barbary Coast—Herbert Asbury	1.60	4.80	8.00	NF
475	Death of a Peer—Ngaio Marsh; 1947	1.20	3.60	6.00	M
476	The Corpse Steps Out—Craig Rice	1.20	3.60	6.00	M
477	Tales From the Decameron—Giovanni Boccaccio	1.20	3.60	6.00	
478	Death - and the Gilded Man—Carter Dickson	1.60	4.80	8.00	M
479	Did She Fall?—Thorne Smith	1.00	3.00	5.00	H
480	Passion Flower—Kathleen Norris	1.00	3.00	5.00	
481	The Emperor's Physician—J. R. Perkins	1.00	3.00	5.00	
482	Deep Summer—Gwen Bristow; 1948	1.00	3.00	5.00	
483	The King's General—Daphne du Maurier	1.00	3.00	5.00	
484	The Chair for Martin Rome—Henry Edward Helseth; movie tie-in	1.00	3.00	5.00	
485	The Hollow—Agatha Christie	1.20	3.60	6.00	M
486	If Winter Comes—A. S. M. Hutchinson; movie tie-in	1.00	3.00	5.00	
487	The Yukon Trail—William MacLeod Raine	1.20	3.60	6.00	W
488	Walls of Gold—Kathleen Norris	1.00	3.00	5.00	
489	I Am Gazing Into My 8-Ball—Earl Wilson	1.00	3.00	5.00	H
490	Skin and Bones—Thorne Smith	1.00	3.00	5.00	H
491	The Border Kid—Max Brand	1.00	3.00	5.00	W
492	The Deadly Pavilion—Hilda Lawrence	1.00	3.00	5.00	M
493	The Flying Yorkshireman—Eric Knight	1.20	3.60	6.00	F
494	My Favorite Sports Stories—Bill Stern	1.00	3.00	5.00	S
495	Carry On, Jeeves!—P. G. Wodehouse	1.60	4.80	8.00	H
496	Farmer Takes a Wife—John Gould	1.00	3.00	5.00	
497	A Connecticut Yankee in King Arthur's Court—Mark Twain	1.20	3.60	6.00	F
498	Mr. Adam—Pat Frank	1.00	3.00	5.00	SF
499	Another Claudia—Rose Franken	1.00	3.00	5.00	
500	The Sexual Side of Marriage—M. J. Exner; 1948				NF
501	Payoff for the Banker—Richard & Frances Lockridge	1.60	4.80	8.00	M
502	High Tension—William Wister Haines	1.20	3.60	6.00	
503	Peabody's Mermaid—Guy Pearce & Constance Jones; movie tie-in	1.00	3.00	5.00	F
504	Fun in Bed—Frank Scully	1.00	3.00	5.00	H
505	Mr. Blandings Builds His Dream House—Eric Hodgins; movie tie-in	1.20	3.60	6.00	
506	The Pursuit of Love—Nancy Mitford	1.00	3.00	5.00	
507	She Died a Lady—Carter Dickson	1.60	4.80	8.00	M
508	Deep Waters—Ruth Moore; movie tie-in	1.00	3.00	5.00	
509	The Stolen Stallion—Max Brand	1.00	3.00	5.00	W
510	The Pocket Book of O. Henry Stories—O. Henry	1.00	3.00	5.00	
511	We Took to the Woods—Louise Dickinson Rich	1.00	3.00	5.00	
512	This Is Murder—Erle Stanley Gardner	1.00	3.00	5.00	M
513	Rehersal for Love—Faith Baldwin	1.00	3.00	5.00	R
514	Flame of Sunset—L. P. Holmes	1.20	3.60	6.00	W
515	Anna Karenina—Leo Tolstoy; movie tie-in	1.20	3.60	6.00	
516	Tales of the South Pacific—James A. Michener	1.20	3.60	6.00	
517	The Murderer Is a Fox—Ellery Queen	1.20	3.60	6.00	M
518	The Stray Lamb—Thorne Smith	1.00	3.00	5.00	H
519	Oliver Twist—Charles Dickens	1.20	3.60	6.00	
520	Student Nurse—Lucy Agnes Hancock	1.00	3.00	5.00	
521	More Deaths Than One—Bruno Fischer	1.20	3.60	6.00	M
522	Freud: His Dream and Sex Theories—Joseph Jastrow	1.00	3.00	5.00	NF

(POCKET BOOK, continued)

		Good	Fine	N/Mint	
523	The Longhorn Feud—Max Brand	1.00	3.00	5.00	W
524	The Double Take—Roy Huggins	1.20	3.60	6.00	M
525	The Foolish Virgin—Kathleen Norris; 1948	1.00	3.00	5.00	
526	Desert Town—Ramona Stewart	1.00	3.00	5.00	
527	Final Curtain—Ngaio Marsh	1.20	3.60	6.00	M
528	The Big Midget Murders—Craig Rice	1.20	3.60	6.00	M
529	The Pocket Book of American Poems—Louis Untermeyer	1.00	3.00	5.00	
530	Guns on the Cimarron—Allan Vaughan Elston	1.00	3.00	5.00	W
531	Saddle and Ride—Ernest Haycox	1.00	3.00	5.00	W
532	Four Great Tragedies—William Shakespeare	1.00	3.00	5.00	
533	Four Great Comedies—William Shakespeare	1.00	3.00	5.00	
534	The Turquoise—Anya Seton	1.00	3.00	5.00	
535	Precious Bane—Mary Webb	1.00	3.00	5.00	
536	The Ballad and the Source—Rosamond Lehmann	1.00	3.00	5.00	
537	The Shadowy Third—Marco Page	1.00	3.00	5.00	M
538	You Got to Stay Happy—Robert Carson	.80	2.40	4.00	
539	Age of Consent—Norman Lindsay	1.00	3.00	5.00	E
540	Death of a Doll—Hilda Lawrence	1.20	3.60	6.00	M
541	Professional Lover—Maysie Greig	1.00	3.00	5.00	
542	Death Stalks the Range—Brett Rider	1.00	3.00	5.00	W
543	Five Acres and Independence—M. G. Kains	.80	2.40	4.00	
544	The Case of the Turning Tide—Erle Stanley Gardner	1.00	3.00	5.00	M
545	The Pocket Book of True Stories—Ernest Heyn	1.60	4.80	8.00	
546	Rain in the Doorway—Thorne Smith	1.00	3.00	5.00	H
547	Silvertips Strike—Max Brand	1.00	3.00	5.00	W
548	Minute for Murder—Nicholas Blake	1.20	3.60	6.00	M
549	Younger Sister—Kathleen Norris	.80	2.40	4.00	
550	Mister Roberts—Thomas Heggen; 1948	1.20	3.60	6.00	
551	The Scarlet Letter—Nathaniel Hawthorne	1.20	3.60	6.00	
552	Silas Marner—George Eliot	1.20	3.60	6.00	
553	Economics in One Lesson—Henry Hazlitt	.80	2.40	4.00	NF
554	Texas Triggers—Eugene Cunningham	1.00	3.00	5.00	
555	Bill Stern's Favorite Football Stories—B. Stern	.80	2.40	4.00	S
556	Anything Can Happen—George & Helen Papashvily	.80	2.40	4.00	
557	The Horizontal Man—Helen Eustis	1.00	3.00	5.00	
558	Bury Me Deep—Harold Q. Masur	1.20	3.60	6.00	M
559	Carmen and Other Stories—Prosper Merimee; movie tie-in	1.00	3.00	5.00	
560	So Evil My Love—Joseph Shearing; 1949	1.00	3.00	5.00	
561	The D. A. Cooks a Goose—Erle Stanley Gardner	1.00	3.00	5.00	M
562	The Babe Ruth Story—Bob Considine & Babe Ruth	1.60	4.80	8.00	B
563	Range Boss—D. B. Newton	1.00	3.00	5.00	W
564	A City of Bells—Elizabeth Goudge	1.00	3.00	5.00	
565	The French Quarter—Herbert Asbury	1.20	3.60	6.00	NF
566	The Egg and I—Betty MacDonald	1.00	3.00	5.00	H
567	Outlaws Three—Peter Field	1.00	3.00	5.00	W
568	The Curse of the Bronze Lamp—Carter Dickson	1.60	4.80	8.00	M
569	30 Days to a More Powerful Vocabulary—Wilfred Funk & Norman Lewis	.80	2.40	4.00	NF
570	Rendezvous in Black—Cornell Woolrich	1.60	4.80	8.00	M
571	Command Decision—William Wister Haines	1.00	3.00	5.00	
572	Favorite Baseball Stories—Bill Stern	.80	2.40	4.00	S
573	Sundown Jim—Ernest Haycox	1.00	3.00	5.00	W
574	Unmarried Couple—Maysie Greig	1.00	3.00	5.00	
575	The Chocolate Cobweb—Charlotte Armstrong; 1949	1.00	3.00	5.00	M
576	Anna and the King of Siam—Margaret Landon	1.20	3.60	6.00	
577	The Foxes of Harrow—Frank Yerby	1.00	3.00	5.00	
578	The Pocket Book of Old Masters—Herman J. Wechsler	2.00	6.00	10.00	NF
579	Famous Artists and Their Models—Thomas Craven	2.00	6.00	10.00	NF
580	Fun for the Family—Jerome S. Meyer	1.20	3.60	6.00	NF

Pocket Book 528, © Pkb

Pocket Book 545, © Pkb

Pocket Book 580, © Pkb

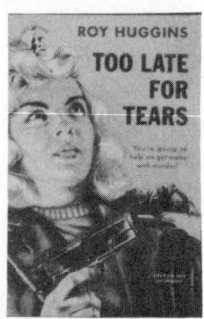

Pocket Book 602, © Pkb

Pocket Book 633, © Pkb

Pocket Book 647, © Pkb

(POCKET BOOK, continued)	Good	Fine	N/Mint	
581 The Painted Veil—W. Somerset Maugham	.80	2.40	4.00	
582 Wilders Walk Away—Herbert Brean	1.00	3.00	5.00	
583 Dr. Whitney's Secretary—Dorothy Pierce Walker	1.00	3.00	5.00	
584 King of the Range—Max Brand	1.00	3.00	5.00	W
585 Hit the Saddle—Allan Vaughan Elston	1.00	3.00	5.00	W
586 The Pocket Weekend Book—Philip Van Doren Stern	1.00	3.00	5.00	
587 In a Lonely Place—Dorothy B. Hughes; c-Frank McCarthy	1.20	3.60	6.00	M
588 Conspirator—Humphrey Slater	1.00	3.00	5.00	
589 The Handsome Road—Gwen Bristow	1.00	3.00	5.00	
590 The Case of the Haunted Husband—Erle Stanley Gardner	.80	2.40	4.00	M
591 Alexandra—Gladys Schmitt	1.00	3.00	5.00	
592 The Strange Case of Lucile Clery—Joseph Shearing	.80	2.40	4.00	
593 The Call of the Wild—Jack London	1.20	3.60	6.00	A
594 Deep West—Ernest Haycox	1.00	3.00	5.00	W
595 The D. A. Calls a Turn—Erle Stanley Gardner	.80	2.40	4.00	M
596 Try and Stop Me—Bennett Cerf	.80	2.40	4.00	H
597 The Story of Mrs. Murphy—Natalie Anderson Scott	.80	2.40	4.00	
598 Let's Explore Your Mind—Albert Edward Wiggam	.80	2.40	4.00	
599 Secret Marriage—Kathleen Norris	.80	2.40	4.00	
600 The Big Sky—A. B. Guthrie, Jr.; 1949	1.20	3.60	6.00	W
601 Lani—Margaret Widdemer	1.00	3.00	5.00	
602 Too Late for Tears—Roy Huggins	1.60	4.80	8.00	M
603 Woman in Her Way—Faith Baldwin	.80	2.40	4.00	R
604 Lost Stage Valley—Frank Bonham	1.00	3.00	5.00	W
605 Burned Fingers—Kathleen Norris	.80	2.40	4.00	
606 Disposing of Henry—Roger Bax	1.00	3.00	5.00	M
607 Seven Short Novels From the Woman's Home Companion—Barthold Fles	1.00	3.00	5.00	
608 Action by Night—Ernest Haycox	1.00	3.00	5.00	W
609 Valley of Vanishing Men—Max Brand	1.00	3.00	5.00	W
610 West of the Law—Al Cody	1.00	3.00	5.00	W
611 Square Shooter—William MacLeod Raine	1.00	3.00	5.00	W
612 Moby Dick—Herman Melville	1.60	4.80	8.00	A
613 No Private Heaven—Faith Baldwin	.80	2.40	4.00	R
614 Love Is a Deadly Weapon—Patrick Quentin; aka Puzzle for Friends, c-Frank McCarthy	1.20	3.60	6.00	M
615 Desert Island Decameron—H. Allen Smith	.80	2.40	4.00	H
616 Kim—Rudyard Kipling	1.00	3.00	5.00	A
617 There Is a Tide—Agatha Christie	1.00	3.00	5.00	M
618 The Big Con—David W. Maurer	1.00	3.00	5.00	
619 The Case of the Empty Tin—Erle Stanley Gardner	.80	2.40	4.00	M
620 Circle C Carries On—Brett Rider; c-Frank McCarthy	1.00	3.00	5.00	W
621 The Life and Times of the Shmoo—Al Capp	4.00	12.00	20.00	H
622 The Pocket Book of Great Operas—Henry Simon & Abraham Veinus	1.00	3.00	5.00	NF
623 Red Rust—Cornelia James Cannon	1.00	3.00	5.00	
624 Shoot the Works—Richard Ellington	1.00	3.00	5.00	M
625 Mink Coat—Kathleen Norris; 1949	.80	2.40	4.00	
626 Died in the Wool—Ngaio Marsh	1.00	3.00	5.00	M
627 The Renegade—L. L. Foreman	1.00	3.00	5.00	W
628 The Best of Wodehouse—P. G. Wodehouse; 1st ed., 1949	3.00	9.00	15.00	H
629 Care and Training of Dogs—Arthur Frederick Jones	1.00	3.00	5.00	NF
630 So Well Remembered—James Hilton	1.00	3.00	5.00	
631 Jean-Christophe—Romain Rolland	1.00	3.00	5.00	
632 Black Ivory—Norman Collins	1.20	3.60	6.00	
633 My Late Wives—Carter Dickson	1.60	4.80	8.00	M
634 Silvertips Chase—Max Brand	1.00	3.00	5.00	W
635 Black Jade—Angeline Taylor	1.00	3.00	5.00	
636 What Are the Odds?—Leo Guild	1.00	3.00	5.00	NF
637 Jed Blaine's Woman—Evelyn Wells	.80	2.40	4.00	

(POCKET BOOK, continued)

		Good	Fine	N/Mint	
638	The Room Upstairs—Mildred Davis	1.00	3.00	5.00	
639	The Man With My Face—Samuel W. Taylor	1.00	3.00	5.00	M
640	Canyon Passage—Ernest Haycox	1.00	3.00	5.00	W
641	Minute Mysteries—Austin Ripley	1.20	3.60	6.00	M
642	Pavilion of Women—Pearl S. Buck	1.00	3.00	5.00	
643	The Case of the Drowning Duck—Erle Stanley Gardner	.80	2.40	4.00	M
644	Sister Carrie—Theodore Dreiser	.80	2.40	4.00	
645	Stars in My Crown—Joe David Brown	1.00	3.00	5.00	
646	They Died With Their Boots On—Thomas Ripley	1.00	3.00	5.00	W
647	The Trial of Mary Dugan—Bayard Veiller & William Almon Wolff; 1950	1.00	3.00	5.00	
648	Disaster Trail—Al Cody	1.00	3.00	5.00	W
649	The Saturday Evening Post Sports Stories—Red Smith	1.00	3.00	5.00	S
650	French Taught With Pictures—I. A. Richards; 1950	.80	2.40	4.00	NF
651	The Fourth Postman—Craig Rice	1.20	3.60	6.00	M
652	The Sea Chase—Andrew Geer	1.20	3.60	6.00	
653	Spotlight—Helen Topping Miller	.80	2.40	4.00	
654	Consultation Room—Frederic Loomis	.80	2.40	4.00	
655	The Vixens—Frank Yerby	1.00	3.00	5.00	
656	Man-size—William MacLeod Raine	1.00	3.00	5.00	W
657	The Bishop's Mantle—Agnes Sligh Turnbull	.80	2.40	4.00	
658	Give Love the Air—Faith Baldwin	.80	2.40	4.00	R
659	Voice Out of Darkness—Ursula Curtiss	1.00	3.00	5.00	M
660	Return of the Rio Kid—Don Davis	1.00	3.00	5.00	W
661	Gods and Goddesses in Art and Legend—Herman J. Wechsler	2.00	6.00	10.00	NF
662	The Blank Wall—Elisabeth Sanxay Holding	1.00	3.00	5.00	M
663	Renegade Ranch—Roy Manning	1.00	3.00	5.00	W
664	No Trumpet Before Him—Nelia Gardner White	1.00	3.00	5.00	
665	More Work for the Undertaker—Margery Allingham	1.00	3.00	5.00	M
666	The Girl on the Via Flaminia—Alfred Hayes	1.00	3.00	5.00	
667	The Case of the Smoking Chimney—Erle Stanley Gardner	.80	2.40	4.00	M
668	Valley Thieves—Max Brand	1.00	3.00	5.00	W
669	Drury Lane's Last Case—Ellery Queen	1.00	3.00	5.00	M
670	The Casebook of Sherlock Holmes—Arthur Conan Doyle	2.00	6.00	10.00	M
671	The Franchise Affair—Josephine Tey	1.00	3.00	5.00	
672	Pilgrim's Inn—Elizabeth Goudge	1.00	3.00	5.00	
673	One Woman—Tiffany Thayer	1.00	3.00	5.00	
674	All You Need to Know About Fishing, Hunting and Camping—Byron Dalrymple	1.20	3.60	6.00	NF
675	Desert Rails—L. P. Holmes; 1950	1.00	3.00	5.00	W
676	The Fate of the Immodest Blonde—Patrick Quentin	1.00	3.00	5.00	M
677	The Pocket Book of Greek Art—Thomas Craven	2.00	6.00	10.00	NF
678	The Case of the Buried Clock—Erle Stanley Gardner	.80	2.40	4.00	M
679	Peony—Pearl S. Buck	1.00	3.00	5.00	
680	The Moving Target—John Ross MacDonald	1.20	3.60	6.00	M
681	Rampart Street—Everett & Olga Webber	1.20	3.60	6.00	
682	Small Talk—Syms	1.00	3.00	5.00	H
683	The Boss of the Lazy 9—Peter Field	1.00	3.00	5.00	W
684	The Pocket Treasury of American Folklore—B. A. Botkin	1.20	3.60	6.00	
685	Wine, Women and Words—Billy Rose	1.00	3.00	5.00	B
686	Five O'Clock Surgeon—Dorothy Pierce Walker	1.00	3.00	5.00	
687	Flaming Irons—Max Brand	1.00	3.00	5.00	W
688	Three Men and Diana—Kathleen Norris	.80	2.40	4.00	
689	The Case of the Drowsy Mosquito—Erle Stanley Gardner	.80	2.40	4.00	M
690	Annie Jordan—Mary Brinker Post	.80	2.40	4.00	
691	The Fighting Edge—William MacLeod Raine	1.00	3.00	5.00	W
692	Special Nurse—Lucy Agnes Hancock	.80	2.40	4.00	
693	The Whispering Corpse—William P. McGivern	1.00	3.00	5.00	M
694	Killer's Range—E. B. Mann	1.00	3.00	5.00	W
695	Rhubarb—H. Allen Smith	2.00	6.00	10.00	H

Pocket Book 677, © Pkb

Pocket Book 695, © Pkb

Pocket Book 788, © Pkb

		Good	Fine	N/Mint	
696	The Big Sleep—Raymond Chandler	3.00	9.00	15.00	M
697	Without Magnolias—Bucklin Moon	1.00	3.00	5.00	
698	The Darker the Night—Herbert Brean	1.00	3.00	5.00	
699	No Benefit of Law—Brett Rider	1.00	3.00	5.00	W
700	Of Human Bondage—W. Somerset Maugham; 1950	1.60	4.80	8.00	
701	Big Sol—Henry Von Rhau	1.00	3.00	5.00	
702	Desperado's Gold—L. L. Foreman	1.00	3.00	5.00	W
703	Rustlers' Canyon—E. E. Halleran	1.00	3.00	5.00	W
704	Suddenly a Corpse—Harold Q. Masur	1.00	3.00	5.00	M
705	Hired Guns—Max Brand	1.00	3.00	5.00	W
706	Death Rides the Pecos—Davis Dresser	1.00	3.00	5.00	W
707	The Girl From Nowhere—Rae Foley	1.00	3.00	5.00	
708	The Pocket History of American Painting—James Thomas Flexner	2.00	6.00	10.00	NF
709	Halo in Brass—John Evans	1.20	3.60	6.00	
710	An Apple for Eye—Kathleen Norris	.80	2.40	4.00	
711	Midnight Round-up—Peter Field	1.00	3.00	5.00	W
712	The Doctor at Coffin Gap—Les Savage, Jr.	1.00	3.00	5.00	W
713	Hound-dog Man—Fred Gipson	1.00	3.00	5.00	
714	The Asphalt Jungle—W. R. Burnett	2.00	6.00	10.00	JD
715	The University of Chicago Spanish-English, English-Spanish Dictionary—Carlos Castillo & others	.80	2.40	4.00	NF
716	The Trouble With Murder—Roger Bax	1.00	3.00	5.00	M
717	The Bandit of the Black Hills—Max Brand	1.00	3.00	5.00	W
718	Great American Sports Humor—Mac Davis	1.00	3.00	5.00	SH
719	Singing Lariat—Will Ermine	1.00	3.00	5.00	W
720	Spanish Through Pictures—I. A. Richards	.80	2.40	4.00	NF
721	Border Breed—William MacLeod Raine	1.00	3.00	5.00	W
722	Opus 21—Philip Wylie	.80	2.40	4.00	
723	The Hearth and the Eagle—Anya Seton	.80	2.40	4.00	
724	The Case of the Careless Kitten—Erle Stanley Gardner	.80	2.40	4.00	M
725	Suitable for Framing—James Atlee Phillips; 1950	1.00	3.00	5.00	M
726	Dusty Wagons—Matt Stuart	1.00	3.00	5.00	W
727	Perilous Passage—Arthur Mayse	1.00	3.00	5.00	
728	The Feather Merchants—Max Shulman	.80	2.40	4.00	
729	Chesapeake Cavalier—Don Tracy	1.00	3.00	5.00	A
730	This Is America—Max Herzberg	.80	2.40	4.00	
731	The 3rd Pocket Book of Crossword Puzzles—Margaret Petherbridge	1.20	3.60	6.00	NF
732	Cowboy—Ross Santee	1.00	3.00	5.00	W
733	Ghost Gold—Tom West	.80	2.40	4.00	W
734	The Red Dress—John Watson	1.00	3.00	5.00	
735	The March Hare Murders—E. X. Ferrars	1.00	3.00	5.00	M
736	Coffin Corner—George Bagby	1.00	3.00	5.00	M
737	Murder One—Eleazar Lipsky	1.00	3.00	5.00	M
738	Dead Lion—Emery Bonett, John Bonett	1.00	3.00	5.00	
739	The Man Who Held Five Aces—Jean Leslie	1.00	3.00	5.00	
740	Ten Day's Wonder—Ellery Queen	1.00	3.00	5.00	M
741	The Case of the Journeying Boy—Michael Innes	1.00	3.00	5.00	M
742	Head of a Traveller—Nicholas Blake	2.00	6.00	10.00	M
743	On the Dodge—William MacLeod Raine	1.00	3.00	5.00	W
744	Hunted Riders—Max Brand	1.00	3.00	5.00	W
745	Lord Johnnie—Leslie Turner White	1.00	3.00	5.00	
746	Wilderness Nurse—Marguerite Mooers Marshall	.80	2.40	4.00	R
747	Combat—Van Van Praag	.80	2.40	4.00	C
748	Call It Treason—George Howe; 1951, movie tie-in	1.00	3.00	5.00	
749	The Golden Hawk—Frank Yerby	1.00	3.00	5.00	A
750	The Little Sister—Raymond Chandler	2.00	6.00	10.00	M
751	The Perfect Hostess—Maureen Daly	.80	2.40	4.00	
752	Beyond a Reasonable Doubt—C. W. Grafton	1.00	3.00	5.00	M
753	Crooked House—Agatha Christie	1.00	3.00	5.00	M
754	Riders by Night—Nelson Nye	1.00	3.00	5.00	W
755	The Human Side of Animals—Vance Packard	1.00	3.00	5.00	NF
756	It's a Crime—Richard Ellington	1.00	3.00	5.00	M
757	The Man With the Golden Arm—Nelson Algren	1.20	3.60	6.00	
758	The Case of the Crooked Candle—Erle Stanley Gardner	.80	2.40	4.00	M
759	The Tenderfoot Kid—Peter Field	1.00	3.00	5.00	W
760	Outlaw Vengeance—Samuel A. Peeples	1.20	3.60	6.00	W
761	Rustlers' Moon—Will Ermine	1.00	3.00	5.00	W
762	Swing, Brother, Swing—Ngaio Marsh	1.00	3.00	5.00	M
763	All the Ship's at Sea—William J. Lederer	1.00	3.00	5.00	
764	Laughing Boy—Oliver LaFarge	1.00	3.00	5.00	
765	The Pocket Book of Great Drawings—Paul J. Sachs	2.00	6.00	10.00	NF
766	Law of the Gun—Brett Rider	1.00	3.00	5.00	W
767	The Big Wheel—John Brooks	1.00	3.00	5.00	
768	The Fight for the Sweetwater—Bliss Lomax	1.00	3.00	5.00	W
769	Bitter Creek—Al Cody	1.00	3.00	5.00	W
770	The Naked Eye—Gita Lewis & Henriette Martin	1.00	3.00	5.00	

		Good	Fine	N/Mint	
771	The Brave Bulls—Tom Lea	1.00	3.00	5.00	
772	Ruggles of Red Gap—Harry Leon Wilson	.80	2.40	4.00	H
773	My Dead Wife—William Worley	1.60	4.80	8.00	M
774	The House Without a Door—Thomas Sterling	1.00	3.00	5.00	
775	The 22 Brothers—Dana Sage; 1951	1.00	3.00	5.00	
776	The End Is Known—Geoffrey Holiday Hall	1.00	3.00	5.00	
777	So Young a Body—Frank Bunce	1.00	3.00	5.00	
778	Top of the World—Hans Ruesch	1.00	3.00	5.00	
779	And When She Was Bad She Was Murdered—Richard Starnes	1.20	3.60	6.00	M
780	The Way West—A. B. Guthrie, Jr.	1.20	3.60	6.00	W
781	Rustlers of Beacon Creek—Max Brand	1.00	3.00	5.00	W
782	Dialogues of Plato	1.00	3.00	5.00	
783	Outlaw Trail—E. E. Halleran	1.00	3.00	5.00	W
784	Come and Kill Me—Josephine Tey	1.00	3.00	5.00	
785	The Golden Fury—Marian Castle	1.00	3.00	5.00	
786	Very Cold for May—William P. McGivern	1.00	3.00	5.00	
787	Ranger's Luck—William MacLeod Raine	1.00	3.00	5.00	W
788	The Pocket Guide to the Wildflowers—Samuel Gottscho	1.20	3.60	6.00	NF
789	Ann Pillsbury's Baking Book—Ann Pillsbury	1.00	3.00	5.00	NF
790	Rough Justice—Ernest Haycox	1.00	3.00	5.00	W
791	Red Range—Eugene Cunningham	1.00	3.00	5.00	W
792	The Case of the Black-eyed Blonde—Erle Stanley Gardner	.80	2.40	4.00	M
793	Diagnosis: Homicide—Lawrence G. Blochman	1.20	3.60	6.00	M
794	Broncho Apache—Paul I. Wellman	1.20	3.60	6.00	W
795	Hold Autumn in Your Hand—George Sessions Perry	.80	2.40	4.00	
796	For Doctors Only—Francis Leo Golden	1.00	3.00	5.00	H
797	The Outlaw—Max Brand	1.00	3.00	5.00	W
798	Under the Skin—Phyllis Bottome	1.00	3.00	5.00	
799	Dardanelles Derelict—F. Van Wyck Mason	1.00	3.00	5.00	
800	Conception, Pregnancy and Birth—J. D. Ratcliff; 1951	1.00	3.00	5.00	NF
801	Reprisal—Arthur Gordon	1.00	3.00	5.00	
802	Big As Life—John Pleasant McCoy	1.00	3.00	5.00	
803	The Hide Rustlers—Les Savage, Jr.	1.00	3.00	5.00	W
804	The Deadly Miss Ashley—Frederick C. Davis	1.00	3.00	5.00	M
805	Mischief—Charlotte Armstrong	1.00	3.00	5.00	M
806	Murder's Web—Dorothy Dunn	1.00	3.00	5.00	M
807	Bullets for a Badman—Bennett Foster	1.00	3.00	5.00	W
808	The Sheriff of Painted Post—Tom Gunn	1.00	3.00	5.00	W
809	Colt Comrades—Bliss Lomax	1.00	3.00	5.00	W
810	The Freeholder—Joe David Brown	1.00	3.00	5.00	A
811	The Witch of Spring—William Shore	1.60	4.80	8.00	E
812	The Case of the Golddigger's Purse—Erle Stanley Gardner	.80	2.40	4.00	M
813	Stone Cold Dead—Richard Ellington	1.20	3.60	6.00	M
814	The Poisoned Chocolates Case—Anthony Berkeley	1.20	3.60	6.00	M
815	The Sheriff's Son—William MacLeod Raine	1.00	3.00	5.00	W
816	Wall of Guns—Jim O'Mara	1.00	3.00	5.00	W
817	Something About Midnight—D. B. Olsen	1.00	3.00	5.00	M
818	High Valley—Charmian Clift & George Henry Johnston	1.00	3.00	5.00	
819	Mingo Dabney—James Street	1.00	3.00	5.00	A
820	A Murder Is Announced—Agatha Christie	1.00	3.00	5.00	M
821	The Drowning Pool—John Ross MacDonald	1.20	3.60	6.00	M
822	Cat of Many Tails—Ellery Queen	1.00	3.00	5.00	M
823	Trouble Is My Business—Raymond Chandler	3.00	9.00	15.00	M
824	The Road to San Jacinto—L. L. Foreman	1.60	4.80	8.00	W
825	Sexual Feeling in Married Men and Women—G. Lombard Kelly; 1951	1.00	3.00	5.00	NF
826	Face of a Hero—Louis Falstein	1.00	3.00	5.00	
827	The Hepburn—Jan Westcott	1.00	3.00	5.00	
828	Murder City—Oakley Hall	1.20	3.60	6.00	M
829	Murder of a Nymph—Margot Neville	1.20	3.60	6.00	M
830	Homeward Borne—Ruth Chatterton	1.00	3.00	5.00	
831	The San Quentin—Clinton T. Duffy & Dean Jennings	1.00	3.00	5.00	NF
832	The Case of the Half-Wakened Wife—Erle Stanley Gardner	.80	2.40	4.00	M
833	Off Missing Persons—David Goodis	1.20	3.60	6.00	
834	Signal Guns at Sunup—John Jo Carpenter	1.00	3.00	5.00	
835	Alice in Wonderland and Other Favorites—Lewis Carroll	2.00	6.00	10.00	F
836	Attack—Perry Wolff; 1952	1.00	3.00	5.00	C
837	The Golden Herd—Curt Carroll	1.00	3.00	5.00	
838	About Mrs. Leslie—Vina Delmar	.80	2.40	4.00	E
839	Walk With the Devil—Elliott Arnold	1.00	3.00	5.00	
840	The Zebra Derby—Max Shulman	.80	2.40	4.00	
841	Painted Post Law—Tom Gunn	1.00	3.00	5.00	W
842	Gun Showdown—William MacLeod Raine	1.00	3.00	5.00	W
843	The Great Snow—Henry Morton Robinson	1.00	3.00	5.00	
844	Each Bright River—Mildred Masterson McNeilly	1.00	3.00	5.00	
845	The Candy Kid—Dorothy B. Hughes	1.20	3.60	6.00	
846	Pick-up on Noon Street—Raymond Chandler	2.00	6.00	10.00	M

Pocket Book 845, © Pkb

Pocket Book 872, © Pkb

Pocket Book 903, © Pkb

(POCKET BOOK, continued)

		Good	Fine	N/Mint	
847	The Smoking Iron—Peter Field	1.00	3.00	5.00	W
848	Danger Trail—Max Brand	1.00	3.00	5.00	W
849	The Build-up Boys—Jeremy Kirk	.80	2.40	4.00	
850	Foxfire—Anya Seton; 1952	.80	2.40	4.00	
851	White Witch Doctor—Louise A. Stinetorf	1.00	3.00	5.00	
852	Martha Logan's Meat Cook Book—Thora Campbell & Beth Bailey McLean	.80	2.40	4.00	NF
853	Death on Treasure Trail—Don Davis	1.00	3.00	5.00	W
854	Why Slug a Postman?—Seldon Truss	1.00	3.00	5.00	
855	The Case of the Backward Mule—Erle Stanley Gardner	.80	2.40	4.00	M
856	The Case of the Borrowed Brunette—Erle Stanley Gardner	.80	2.40	4.00	M
857	Black Majesty—John W. Vandercook	1.00	3.00	5.00	A
858	Another Mug for the Bier—Ricard Starnes	1.00	3.00	5.00	M
859	Bold Passage—Frank Bonham	1.00	3.00	5.00	W
860	You Can't Live Forever—Harold Q. Masur	1.00	3.00	5.00	M
861	Grant of Kingdom—Harvey Fergusson	1.00	3.00	5.00	
862	The Beckoning Door—Mabel Seeley	1.00	3.00	5.00	M
863	The People Against O'Hara—Eleazar Lipsky	1.00	3.00	5.00	
864	By Rope and Lead—Ernest Haycox	1.00	3.00	5.00	W
865	Tonto Riley—Lee E. Wells	1.00	3.00	5.00	W
866	The Story of My Psychoanalysis—John Knight	2.00	6.00	10.00	NF
867	The Raid—John Brick	1.00	3.00	5.00	
868	Strumpet City—Don Tracy; aka Streets of Askelon	1.00	3.00	5.00	
869	The D. A. Breaks a Seal—Erle Stanley Gardner	.80	2.40	4.00	M
870	Shield for Murder—William P. McGivern	1.00	3.00	5.00	M
871	The Hangman of Sleepy Valley—Davis Dresser; c-Frank McCarthy	1.00	3.00	5.00	W
872	What the Doctor Ordered—Francis Leo Golden	1.00	3.00	5.00	H
873	Magnus the Magnificent—Leslie Turner White	1.00	3.00	5.00	A
874	Double, Double—Ellery Queen	1.00	3.00	5.00	M
875	The Hard-Boiled Omnibus—Joseph T. Shaw; 1952	3.00	9.00	15.00	M
876	Double Cross Trail—E. E. Halleran	1.00	3.00	5.00	W
877	Gunman's Gold—Max Brand	1.00	3.00	5.00	W
878	Dark Laughter—Sherwood Anderson	1.00	3.00	5.00	
879	New York 22—Ilka Chase	1.00	3.00	5.00	
880	The Black-Eyed Stranger—Charlotte Armstrong	1.00	3.00	5.00	
881	The Eleventh Hour—Robert B. Sinclair	1.00	3.00	5.00	
882	Death Rides the Night—Peter Field	1.00	3.00	5.00	W
883	The Captain—Russell Thacher	1.00	3.00	5.00	
884	The Sultan's Warrior—Bates Baldwin	1.20	3.60	6.00	A
885	Southern Territory—Robert Tallant	1.00	3.00	5.00	
886	The Case of the Fan-Dancer's Horse—Erle Stanley Gardner; c-Bergey. Note: A special Libby-Owens-Ford premium variant exists of this title.	1.20	3.60	6.00	M
887	Judgement on Deltchev—Eric Ambler	.80	2.40	4.00	
888	Shadow Riders of the Yellowstone—Les Savage, Jr.	1.00	3.00	5.00	W
889	Beulah Land—H. L. Davis	1.00	3.00	5.00	
890	A Complete Guide to Home Sewing—Sylvia K. Mager	.80	2.40	4.00	NF
891	The Unknown Lincoln—Dale Carnegie	1.20	3.60	6.00	NF
892	The Pocket Stamp Album—H. E. Harris	1.20	3.60	6.00	NF
893	Your Own Book of Campcraft—Catherine T. Hammett	1.00	3.00	5.00	NF
894	Horns for the Devil—Louis Malley	1.00	3.00	5.00	M
895	Mystery Ranch—Max Brand	1.00	3.00	5.00	W
896	Miami Murder-Go-Round—Marston LaFrance	1.00	3.00	5.00	M
897	They Come to Baghdad—Agatha Christie	1.00	3.00	5.00	M
898	Cop—Jack Karney	1.00	3.00	5.00	
899	Cobean's Naked Eye—Samuel E. Cobean	1.00	3.00	5.00	
900	Scirocco—Romualdo Romano; 1952, c-Belarski	1.20	3.60	6.00	
901	Murder for the Holidays—Howard Rigsby	1.00	3.00	5.00	M
902	The End of the Trail—Peter Field	1.00	3.00	5.00	W
903	Miracle on 34th Street—Valentine Davies	4.00	12.00	20.00	F

(POCKET BOOK, continued)

		Good	Fine	N/Mint	
904	Fear in the Night—Irving Schwartz	1.00	3.00	5.00	
905	The Women of Champion City—Doris Davis	1.60	4.80	8.00	E
906	Lynch-Rope Law—Davis Dresser	1.00	3.00	5.00	W
907	The Way Some People Die—John Ross MacDonald	1.00	3.00	5.00	M
908	New Tales of Space and Time—Raymond J. Healy	1.00	3.00	5.00	SF
909	The Case of the Lazy Lover—Erle Stanley Gardner; 1953	.80	2.40	4.00	M
910	The Streak—Max Brand	1.00	3.00	5.00	W
911	My Gun Is My Law—Will Ermine	1.00	3.00	5.00	W
912	...And to My Beloved Husband—Philip Loraine	1.00	3.00	5.00	
913	Dark Dream—Robert Martin	1.00	3.00	5.00	
914	The Man From Thief River—Peter Field	1.00	3.00	5.00	W
915	Ruby—Vina Delmar; 1952	.80	2.40	4.00	
916	The Simple Art of Murder—Raymond Chandler	2.00	6.00	10.00	M
917	The Other Body in Grant's Tomb—Richard Starnes	1.00	3.00	5.00	M
918	Shadows More Among Them—Edgar Mittelholzer	1.00	3.00	5.00	
919	The Lord God of the Flesh—Jules Romains	1.00	3.00	5.00	
920	Space Platform—Murray Leinster; c-Bergey	1.60	4.80	8.00	SF
921	Rio Kid Justice—Don Davis	1.00	3.00	5.00	W
922	The Case of the Lonely Heiress—Erle Stanley Gardner	.80	2.40	4.00	M
923	Hangman's Hat—Paul Ernst	1.00	3.00	5.00	
924	The Left Hand of God—William E. Barrett	1.20	3.60	6.00	
925	Favorite Hymns—Albert H. Morehead & James Morehead; 1953	1.20	3.60	6.00	NF
926	The Origin of Evil—Ellery Queen	1.00	3.00	5.00	M
927	Red Blizzard—Clay Fisher	1.00	3.00	5.00	W
928	Power Golf—Ben Hogan	.80	2.40	4.00	NF
929	Himalayan Assignment—F. Van Wyck Mason	1.00	3.00	5.00	
930	The Hair-Trigger Kid—Max Brand	1.00	3.00	5.00	W
931	Reclining Figure—Marco Page	1.00	3.00	5.00	
932	Captain Barney—Jan Westcott	1.00	3.00	5.00	A
933	Basketball—Arnold ''Red'' Averbach	.80	2.40	4.00	NF
934	Kill and Tell—Howard Rigsby	1.00	3.00	5.00	M
935	Out From Eden—Victoria Lincoln	1.00	3.00	5.00	
936	The Proud Ones—Verne Athanas	1.00	3.00	5.00	W
937	Sheriff on the Spot—Peter Field	1.00	3.00	5.00	W
938	Candlemas Bay—Ruth Moore	1.00	3.00	5.00	
939	The Sundowners—Jon Cleary	1.00	3.00	5.00	
940	Catch a Killer—Ursula Curtiss	1.00	3.00	5.00	M
941	Exit for a Dame—Richard Ellington	1.00	3.00	5.00	M
942	Painted Post Range—Tom Gunn	1.00	3.00	5.00	W
943	Planet of the Dreamers—John D. MacDonald	2.00	6.00	10.00	SF
944	Winds of Morning—H. L. Davis	1.00	3.00	5.00	
945	Floodtide—Frank Yerby	1.00	3.00	5.00	
946	River of Rogues—A. R. Beverley-Giddings	1.20	3.60	6.00	
947	The War of the Worlds—H. G. Wells	2.00	6.00	10.00	SF
948	Laughter Is Legal—Francis Lea Golden	1.00	3.00	5.00	H
949	Two Clues—Erle Stanley Gardner	.80	2.40	4.00	M
950	Single Jack—Max Brand; 1953	1.00	3.00	5.00	W
951	Portrait of a Marriage—Pearl S. Buck	.80	2.40	4.00	
952	Stella—Jan de Hartog	.80	2.40	4.00	
953	The Sea—Jan de Hartog	.80	2.40	4.00	
954	Outlaw Thickets—Les Savage, Jr.	1.00	3.00	5.00	W
955	101 Best Loved Songs—Albert H. & James Morehead	.80	2.40	4.00	NF
956	Mrs. McGinty's Dead—Agatha Christie	1.00	3.00	5.00	M
957	Woman's Medical Problems—Maxine Davis	1.00	3.00	5.00	NF
958	Outside the Law—Philip Loraine	1.00	3.00	5.00	
959	The Man From Nazareth—Harry Emerson Fosdick	1.00	3.00	5.00	
960	Calendar of Crime—Ellery Queen; c-Richard Powers	1.00	3.00	5.00	M
961	The Crooked Frame—William P. McGivern	1.00	3.00	5.00	M

Pocket Book 920, © Pkb

Pocket Book 946, © Pkb

Pocket Book 961, © Pkb

		Good	Fine	N/Mint	
962	Canyon of Death—Peter Field	1.00	3.00	5.00	W
963	Excuse It, Please!—Cornelia Otis Skinner	1.00	3.00	5.00	
964	Trespass—Eugene Brown	1.00	3.00	5.00	
965	The Case of the Vagabond Virgin—Erle Stanley Gardner	.80	2.40	4.00	M
966	The 4th Pocket Book of Crossword Puzzles—Margaret Petherbridge Farrar	1.20	3.60	6.00	NF
967	Snaketrack—Frank Bonham	1.00	3.00	5.00	W
968	The Low Calorie Diet—Marvin Small	.80	2.40	4.00	NF
969	The Tender Age—Russell Thacher	1.00	3.00	5.00	
970	The Diary of a Young Girl—Anne Frank	.80	2.40	4.00	
971	Marked for Murder—John Ross MacDonald	1.00	3.00	5.00	M
972	Halfway to Timberline—Ward West	1.00	3.00	5.00	
973	Tough Company—Clem Colt	1.00	3.00	5.00	W
974	The Highland Hawk—Leslie Turner White	1.00	3.00	5.00	
975	Blood in Your Eye—Robert Patrick Wilmot; 1954	1.00	3.00	5.00	M
976	The Case of the Dubious Bridegroom—Erle Stanley Gardner	.80	2.40	4.00	M
977	Wild Drum Beat—F. Van Wyck Mason	1.00	3.00	5.00	
978	Land of the Lawless—Les Savage, Jr.	1.00	3.00	5.00	W
979	Vengeance Trail—Max Brand	1.00	3.00	5.00	W
980	A Great Time to Be Alive—Harry Emerson Fosdick	1.00	3.00	5.00	
981	The Big Heat—William P. McGivern	1.00	3.00	5.00	M
982	Doctor Two-Guns—Peter Field	1.00	3.00	5.00	W
983	Pioneer Loves—Ernest Haycox	1.00	3.00	5.00	W
984	The Shining Tides—Win Brooks	1.00	3.00	5.00	
985	Worse Than Murder—David Duncan	1.00	3.00	5.00	M
986	Watchdog of Thunder River—Will Ermine	1.00	3.00	5.00	W
987	The Whistler—E. B. Mann	1.00	3.00	5.00	W
988	Last Seen Wearing . . . —Hillary Waugh	1.00	3.00	5.00	M
989	Sands of Mars—Arthur C. Clarke	1.60	4.80	8.00	SF
990	Coyote Gulch—Peter Field	1.00	3.00	5.00	W
991	Border Guns—Max Brand	1.00	3.00	5.00	W
992	Ripley's New Believe It or Not!—Robert Ripley	1.60	4.80	8.00	NF
993	The Hidden Flower—Pearl S. Buck	.80	2.40	4.00	
994	April Snow—Lillian Budd	.80	2.40	4.00	
995	The Medicine Whip—John & Margaret Harris	.80	2.40	4.00	
996	Lyle Brown's Sports Quiz—Lyle Brown	.80	2.40	4.00	S
997	Murder on Monday—Robert Patrick Wilmont	1.00	3.00	5.00	M
998	So Rich, So Lovely, and So Dead—Harold Q. Masur	1.00	3.00	5.00	M
999	Rogue Valley—Verne Athanas	1.00	3.00	5.00	W
1000	The Little World of Don Camillo—Giovanni Guareschi; 1954	.80	2.40	4.00	
1001	Homer Crist—John Brick	1.00	3.00	5.00	
1002	Painted Post Gunplay—Tom Gunn	1.00	3.00	5.00	W
1003	Funerals Are Fatal—Agatha Christie	1.00	3.00	5.00	M
1004	The Big Deal—Selig Seligman	1.00	3.00	5.00	
1005	The King Is Dead—Ellery Queen	1.00	3.00	5.00	M
1006	The Amber Fire—Don Tracy	1.00	3.00	5.00	
1007	My Best Science Fiction Story—Leo Margulies & Oscar J. Friend	1.60	4.80	8.00	SF
1008	Windom's Way—James Ramsey Ullman	1.00	3.00	5.00	
1009	The Case of the Cautious Coquette—Erle Stanley Gardner	.80	2.40	4.00	M
1010	The D. A. Takes a Chance—Erle Stanley Gardner	.80	2.40	4.00	M
1011	Murder on the Frontier—Ernest Haycox	1.00	3.00	5.00	W
1012	Tale of Two Lovers—Henry Morton Robinson	1.00	3.00	5.00	
1013	Tales for Salesmen—Francis Leo Golden	.80	2.40	4.00	H
1014	The Covered Wagon—Emerson Hope	1.00	3.00	5.00	W
1015	The Girls of Sanfrediano—Vasco Prutolini	.80	2.40	4.00	
1016	Last Race—Jon Manchip White	1.00	3.00	5.00	
1017	Johnny Guitar—Roy Chanslor	1.00	3.00	5.00	
1018	The Gun Tamer—Max Brand	1.00	3.00	5.00	W
1019	In Love—Alfred Hayes	1.00	3.00	5.00	
1020	Meet Me at the Morgue—John Ross MacDonald	1.00	3.00	5.00	M
1021	Murder With Mirrors—Agatha Christie	1.00	3.00	5.00	M
1022	Troubled Range—E. B. Mann	1.00	3.00	5.00	W
1023	Two-Gun Rio Kid—Don Davis	1.00	3.00	5.00	W
1024	The Barbarians—F. Van Wyck Mason	1.00	3.00	5.00	A
1025	How to Stop Smoking—Herbert Brean; 1954	1.00	3.00	5.00	NF
1026	The Intruder—Helen Fowler	1.00	3.00	5.00	
1027	Law Badge—Peter Field	1.00	3.00	5.00	W
1028	Outlaw—Ernest Haycox	1.00	3.00	5.00	W
1029	The Case of the Negligent Nymph—Erle Stanley Gardner	.80	2.40	4.00	M
1030	Rogue Cop—William P. McGivern	1.00	3.00	5.00	M
1031	Busted Range—Will Ermine	1.00	3.00	5.00	W
1032	The Colors of the Day—Romain Gary	1.00	3.00	5.00	
1033	The Night Horseman—Max Brand	1.00	3.00	5.00	W
1034	Walk Out on Death—Charlotte Armstrong; 1955	1.00	3.00	5.00	M
1035	The Outlaw of Eagle's Nest—Peter Field	1.00	3.00	5.00	W
1036	A Pocket Full of Rye—Agatha Christie	1.00	3.00	5.00	M
1037	Space Tug—Murray Leinster	1.20	3.60	6.00	SF
1038	You Shall Know Them—Vercors	1.20	3.60	6.00	SF-M

		Good	Fine	N/Mint	
1039	The Beautiful Frame—William Pearson	1.00	3.00	5.00	
1040	Boss of the Plains—Will Ermine	1.00	3.00	5.00	W
1041	The Case of the One-eyed Witness—Erle Stanley Gardner	.80	2.40	4.00	M
1042	The Little Ark—Jan de Hartog	.80	2.40	4.00	
1043	The Story of Esther Costello—Nicholas Monsarrat	1.00	3.00	5.00	
1044	The Long Goodbye—Raymond Chandler	2.00	6.00	10.00	
1045	Science Fiction Terror Tales—Groff Conklin	2.00	6.00	10.00	SF
1046	Time and Time Again—James Hilton	1.00	3.00	5.00	
1047	Rogue's Yarn—John Jennings	1.20	3.60	6.00	A
1048	Ride the Dark Hills—W. Edmunds Claussen	1.00	3.00	5.00	W
1049	The Scarlet Letters—Ellery Queen	1.00	3.00	5.00	M
1050	Three for the Money—James McConnaughey; 1955	1.00	3.00	5.00	
1051	A Fair Wind Home—Ruth Moore	1.00	3.00	5.00	
1052	The D. A. Breaks an Egg—Erle Stanley Gardner	.80	2.40	4.00	M
1053	Crackers in Bed—Vic Fredericks	1.00	3.00	5.00	
1054	Gambler's Gold—Peter Field	1.00	3.00	5.00	W
1055	I Die Possessed—J. B. O'Sullivan	1.00	3.00	5.00	
1056	Seven Trails—Max Brand	1.00	3.00	5.00	
1057	How to Work With Tools and Wood—Fred Gross	.80	2.40	4.00	NF
1058	Murder's Nest—Charlotte Armstrong	1.00	3.00	5.00	M
1059	Hero Driver—Alfred Coppel	1.00	3.00	5.00	
1060	Hired Hand—Nelson Nye	1.00	3.00	5.00	W
1061	Arrow in the Moon—John & Margaret Harris	1.00	3.00	5.00	
1062	Margin of Terror—William P. McGivern	1.00	3.00	5.00	
1063	The Case of the Musical Cow—Erle Stanley Gardner	.80	2.40	4.00	M
1064	Stage Road to Denver—Allan Vaughan Elston	1.00	3.00	5.00	W
1065	The Tenderfoot—Max Brand	1.00	3.00	5.00	W
1066	The Conquest of Don Pedro—Harvey Fergusson	.80	2.40	4.00	
1067	Don Camillo and His Flock—Giovanni Guareschi	.80	2.40	4.00	
1068	Mustang Mesa—Peter Field	1.00	3.00	5.00	W
1069	Prairie Guns—Ernest Haycox	1.00	3.00	5.00	W
1070	The Victim Was Important—Joe Rayter	1.00	3.00	5.00	M
1071	Arrow in the Hill—Jefferson Cooper	1.00	3.00	5.00	
1072	The 5th Pocket Book of Crossword Puzzles—Margaret Petherbridge Farrar	1.20	3.60	6.00	NF
1073	Cress Delahanty—Jessamyn West	.80	2.40	4.00	
1074	Invaders of Earth—Groff Conklin	1.00	3.00	5.00	SF
1075	A Ray and a Bone—Hillary Waugh; 1955	1.00	3.00	5.00	
1076	Captain Judas—F. Van Wyck Mason	1.00	3.00	5.00	A
1077	The Deadly Climate—Ursula Curtiss	1.00	3.00	5.00	M
1078	Five Against the House—Jack Finney	1.20	3.60	6.00	
1079	The Fool Killer—Helen Eustis	1.00	3.00	5.00	
1080	Baby Sitter's Guide, by Dennis the Menace—Hank Ketcham & Bob Harmon	1.20	3.60	6.00	H
1081	Ravaged Range—Peter Field	1.00	3.00	5.00	W
1082	The Glass Village—Ellery Queen	1.00	3.00	5.00	M
1083	And Sometimes Death—J. Valentine	1.00	3.00	5.00	
1084	The Untamed—Max Brand	1.00	3.00	5.00	W
1085	The Under Dog and Other Mysteries—Agatha Christie	1.00	3.00	5.00	M
1086	Wagon Wheel Gap—Allan Vaughan Elston	1.00	3.00	5.00	W
1087	The New Peter Arno Pocket Book—Peter Arno; 1956	1.00	3.00	5.00	
1088	Guns in the Saddle—Peter Field	1.00	3.00	5.00	W
1089	The Case of the Fiery Fingers—Erle Stanley Gardner	.80	2.40	4.00	M
1090	The Devil Threw Dice—Amber Dean	1.00	3.00	5.00	
1091	Rider of the Midnight Range—Will Ermine	1.00	3.00	5.00	W
1092	The Case of the Angry Mourner—Erle Stanley Gardner	.80	2.40	4.00	M
1093	The Compleat Practical Joker—H. Allen Smith	.80	2.40	4.00	H
1094	Death Rides the Dondrino—Roe Richmond	1.00	3.00	5.00	W
1095	Alibi for Murder—Charlotte Armstrong	1.00	3.00	5.00	M
1096	Doctor Hudson's Secret Journal—Lloyd C. Douglas	.80	2.40	4.00	

Pocket Book 1028, © Pkb

Pocket Book 1062, © Pkb

Pocket Book 1078, © Pkb

Pocket Book 1120, © Pkb   Pocket Book 1140, © Pkb   Pocket Book 1178, © Pkb

(POCKET BOOK, continued)

		Good	Fine	N/Mint	
1097	Tragedy Trail—Max Brand	1.00	3.00	5.00	W
1098	Guys and Dolls—Damon Runyon	2.00	6.00	10.00	
1099	Good Morning, Miss Dove—Frances Gray Patton	.50	1.50	2.50	
1100	Off the Cuff—Jerry Lieberman; 1956	.80	2.40	4.00	H
1101	Cry, Coyote—Steve Frazee	.80	2.40	4.00	W
1102	A Most Contagious Game—Samuel Grafton	.80	2.40	4.00	
1103	Showdown—Allan Vaughan Elston	.80	2.40	4.00	W
1104	Once a Fighter . . .—Les Savage, Jr.	.80	2.40	4.00	W
1105	Waterfront Cop—William P. McGivern	.80	2.40	4.00	
1106	Feeding Your Baby and Child—Miriam E. Lowenberg & Benjamin Spock	.50	1.50	2.50	NF
1107	The Case of the Moth-eaten Mink—Erle Stanley Gardner	.50	1.50	2.50	M
1108	The Brass Command—Clay Fisher	.80	2.40	4.00	W
1109	Don't Hang Me Too High—J. B. O'Sullivan	.80	2.40	4.00	
1110	Governor's Choice—Martin Mayer	.50	1.50	2.50	
1111	The Big Store—Oscar Schisgall	.80	2.40	4.00	
1112	The Girl From Frisco—William Heuman	.80	2.40	4.00	W
1113	Man of the West—Philip Yordan	.80	2.40	4.00	
1114	So Many Steps to Death—Agatha Christie	.80	2.40	4.00	M
1115	Two Tickets for Tangier—F. Van Wyck Mason	.80	2.40	4.00	
1116	Forbidden Valley—Allan Vaughan Elston	.80	2.40	4.00	W
1117	The River Witch—Marjorie McIntyre	.80	2.40	4.00	
1118	Q. B. I.—Ellery Queen	.50	1.50	2.50	M
1119	Onions in the Stew—Betty MacDonald	.80	2.40	4.00	
1120	Dragnet: Case No. 561—David Knight; TV tie-in	1.00	3.00	5.00	M
1121	The Case of the Grinning Gorilla—Erle Stanley Gardner	.50	1.50	2.50	M
1122	The False Rider—Max Brand	.80	2.40	4.00	W
1123	The Road to Laramie—Peter Field	.80	2.40	4.00	W
1124	Cowboy, Say Your Prayers!—Will Ermine	.80	2.40	4.00	W
1125	Dennis the Menace Rides Again—Hank Ketcham; 1956	1.20	3.60	6.00	H
1126	The Jungle Kids—Evan Hunter	1.60	4.80	8.00	JD
1127	The Case of the Hesitant Hostess—Erle Stanley Gardner	.50	1.50	2.50	M
1128	The Guns of Witchwater—Colby Wolford	.80	2.40	4.00	
1129	The 6th Pocket Book of Crossword Puzzles—Margaret Petherbridge Farrar	1.00	3.00	5.00	NF
1130	Strictly for Laughs—Joey Adams	.80	2.40	4.00	H
1131	The Treasure of Pleasant Valley—Frank Yerby	.80	2.40	4.00	
1132	Asking for Trouble—Joe Rayter	.80	2.40	4.00	
1133	Galloping Broncos—Max Brand	.80	2.40	4.00	W
1134	The Iron Bronc—Will Ermine	.80	2.40	4.00	W
1135	The Parson of Gunbarrel Basin—Nelson Nye	.80	2.40	4.00	W
1136	Sinners and Shrouds—Jonathan Latimer	1.00	3.00	5.00	M
1137	The Big Pasture—Clay Fisher	.80	2.40	4.00	W
1138	The Case of the Fugitive Nurse—Erle Stanley Gardner	.50	1.50	2.50	M
1139	Castle Garac—Nicholas Monsarrat	.80	2.40	4.00	
1140	The Invisible Man—H. G. Wells	2.00	6.00	10.00	SF
1141	Hunt the Man Down—William Pearson; 1957	.50	1.50	2.50	
1142	The Lonely Grass—Nelson Nye	.80	2.40	4.00	W
1143	Lysander—F. Van Wyck Mason	.80	2.40	4.00	
1144	The Laff Parade—Jerry Lieberman	.80	2.40	4.00	H
1145	Stab in the Dark—Joe Rayter	.80	2.40	4.00	
1146	The Dangerous Years—Douglass Wallop	.80	2.40	4.00	
1147	Combat Nurse—Frieda K. Franklin	.50	1.50	2.50	R
1148	The Last Rodeo—Ernest Haycox	.80	2.40	4.00	W
1149	The Gambler—Max Brand	.80	2.40	4.00	W
1150	The Man on the Couch—Mischa Richter; 1957	.50	1.50	2.50	
1151	Hickory Dickory Death—Agatha Christie	.80	2.40	4.00	M
1152	The Men From the Boys—Ed Lacy	.80	2.40	4.00	
1153	Wanted: Dennis the Menace—Hank Ketcham	1.20	3.60	6.00	H
1154	The 7th Pocket Book of Crossword Puzzles—Margaret Petherbridge Farrar	1.00	3.00	5.00	NF

		Good	Fine	N/Mint	
1155	The Case of the Green-eyed Sister—Erle Stanley Gardner	.50	1.50	2.50	M
1156	The 7 File—William P. McGivern	.80	2.40	4.00	
1157	Widow's Web—Ursula Curtiss	.50	1.50	2.50	M
1158	Cakes and Ale—W. Somerset Maugham	.50	1.50	2.50	
1159	The Blue Mustang—Clay Fisher	.80	2.40	4.00	W
1160	Double Entendre—Newton Wilson Hoke	.80	2.40	4.00	
1161	Maverick's Return—Peter Field	.80	2.40	4.00	W
1162	Combat Mission—Joe David Brown	.50	1.50	2.50	
1163	The Wyoming Bubble—Allan Vaughan Elston	.80	2.40	4.00	W
1164	The Bulls and the Bees—Roger Eddy	.80	2.40	4.00	
1165	Ripley's Believe It or Not! 4th Series—Robert Ripley	1.20	3.60	6.00	NF
1166	Lone Wolf—Bennett Foster	.80	2.40	4.00	W
1167	Inspector Queen's Own Case—Ellery Queen	.80	2.40	4.00	M
1168	Smiling Desperado—Max Brand	.80	2.40	4.00	W
1169	War on the Saddle Rock—Will Ermine	.80	2.40	4.00	W
1170	The Case of the Restless Redhead—Erle Stanley Gardner	.50	1.50	2.50	M
1171	When Strangers Meet—Robert Bloomfield	.80	2.40	4.00	
1172	The Seven Islands—Jon Godden	.80	2.40	4.00	
1173	Sheriff Wanted!—Peter Field	.80	2.40	4.00	W
1174	Dead Man's Folly—Agatha Christie	.80	2.40	4.00	M
1175	The 8th Pocket Book of Crossword Puzzles—Margaret Petheridge Farrar; 1957	1.00	3.00	5.00	NF
1176	Captain Nemesis—F. Van Wyck Mason	.80	2.40	4.00	A
1177	Old Yeller—Fred Gipson	.80	2.40	4.00	A
1178	Rebecca's Pride—Donald McNutt Douglass	1.60	4.80	8.00	
1179	Dennis the Menace vs. Everybody—Hank Ketcham	1.20	3.60	6.00	H
1180	The Invisible Outlaw—Max Brand	.80	2.40	4.00	W
1181	The Marked Men—Allan Vaughan Elston	.80	2.40	4.00	W
1182	The 9th Pocket Book of Crossword Puzzles—Margaret Petheridge Farrar	1.00	3.00	5.00	NF
1183	No Blade of Grass—John Christopher	1.60	4.80	8.00	SF
1184	The NBC Book of Stars—Earl Wilson	1.60	4.80	8.00	NF
1185	The Brave Cowboy—Edward Abbey	.80	2.40	4.00	W
1186	Santa Fe Passage—Clay Fisher; 1958	.80	2.40	4.00	W
1187	Powder Valley Showdown—Peter Field	.80	2.40	4.00	W
1188	The Abode of Love—AuGray Menen	.50	1.50	2.50	
1189	My Kingdom for a Hearse—Craig Rice	1.00	3.00	5.00	M
1190	Outlaw Breed—Max Brand	.80	2.40	4.00	W
1191	Last Stage to Aspen—Allan Vaughan Elston	.80	2.40	4.00	W
1192	The Enemy Below—D. A. Rayner; movie tie-in	.80	2.40	4.00	
1193	Night Extra—William P. McGivern	.80	2.40	4.00	
1194	Shottin' Melody—E. B. Mann	.80	2.40	4.00	W
1195	Ripley's Believe It or Not! 5th Series—Robert Ripley	1.20	3.60	6.00	NF
1196	Wagonmaster—Robert Turner; TV tie-in	1.00	3.00	5.00	
1197	Hard Man—Leo Katcher	.80	2.40	4.00	
1198	Dragnet: The Case of the Courteous Killer—Richard Deming; TV tie-in	1.00	3.00	5.00	M
1199	The Day the Money Stopped—Brendan Gill	.80	2.40	4.00	
1200	Too Humorous to Mention—Charles Preston; 1958	.80	2.40	4.00	H
1201	The Sulu Sea Murders—F. Van Wyck Mason	.80	2.40	4.00	
1202	The Tank Destroyers—Lawrence H. Kahn	.80	2.40	4.00	C
1203	Trail Partners—Max Brand	.80	2.40	4.00	
1204	The O. S. S. and I—William J. Morgan	.80	2.40	4.00	
1205	Return to Powder Valley—Peter Field	.80	2.40	4.00	W
1206	The Murder of the Missing Link—Vercors; aka You Shall Know Them	1.20	3.60	6.00	SF-M
1207	The Assault—Allen R. Matthews	.80	2.40	4.00	C
1208	Ripley's Believe It or Not! 6th Series—Robert Ripley	1.20	3.60	6.00	NF
1209	Yellowstone Kelly—Clay Fisher; movie tie-in	1.00	3.00	5.00	W
1210	Betty Cornell's Glamour Guide for Teens—Betty Cornell	.50	1.50	2.50	NF
1211	Grand Mesa—Allan Vaughan Elston	.80	2.40	4.00	W
1212	Beyond the Call of Duty—Eugene Brown	.80	2.40	4.00	

Pocket Book 1184, © Pkb

Pocket Book 1196, © Pkb

Pocket Book 1222, © Pkb

(POCKET BOOK, continued)

		Good	Fine	N/Mint	
1213	Blacksnake Trail—Peter Field	.80	2.40	4.00	W
1214	Dragnet: The Case of the Crime King—Richard Deming; TV tie-in	.80	2.40	4.00	M
1215	Knocked for a Loop—Craig Rice	1.00	3.00	5.00	M
1216	The Scout—Robert Turner; TV tie-in	1.00	3.00	5.00	M
1217	Dennis the Menace: Household Hurricane—Hank Ketcham	1.20	3.60	6.00	H
1218	Ensign O'Toole and Me—William J. Lederer	.80	2.40	4.00	
1219	The China Sea Murders—F. Van Wyck Mason	.80	2.40	4.00	M
1220	Murder on Delivery—Spencer Dean	.80	2.40	4.00	M
1221	Speedy—Max Brand	.80	2.40	4.00	W
1222	The Winds of Time—Chad Oliver; c-Powers	1.00	3.00	5.00	SF
1223	The Gracious Lily Affair—F. Van Wyck Mason; 1959	.80	2.40	4.00	
1224	Brother Sebastian—Chon Day	.80	2.40	4.00	H
1225	A Roman Affair—Ercole Patti	.50	1.50	2.50	
1226	Wagons West!—Robert Turner	.80	2.40	4.00	
1227	The 10th Pocket Book of Crossword Puzzles—Margaret Petherbridge Farrar	.80	2.40	4.00	
1228	Blood on the Trail—Max Brand	.80	2.40	4.00	W
1229	The Hit—Julian Mayfield	.80	2.40	4.00	
1230	End of the Line—Bert Hitchens & Dolores Hitchens	.80	2.40	4.00	M
1231	The Broken Angel—Floyd Mahannah	1.00	3.00	5.00	M
1232	The Man Who Shot Quantrill—George Appell	.80	2.40	4.00	W
1233	Thanks to the Saint—Leslie Charteris	.80	2.40	4.00	M
1234	Stranger in the Land—Colby Wolford	.80	2.40	4.00	
1235	Big Man—Richard Marsten	.80	2.40	4.00	
1236	Visiting Nurse—Margaret Howe	.50	1.50	2.50	R
1237	Captain Seadog—Jefferson Cooper	.80	2.40	4.00	A
1238					
1239	Fool's Gold—Delores Hitchens	.80	2.40	4.00	
1240	The Lady Came to Kill—M. E. Chaber	1.00	3.00	5.00	M
1241	Outlaw Valley—Peter Field	.80	2.40	4.00	W
1242	Brother Juniper—Justin McCarthy	.80	2.40	4.00	H
1243	Surgical Nurse—Rosie M. Banks	.50	1.50	2.50	R
1244	Fire Brain—Max Brand	.80	2.40	4.00	W
1245	Substitute Doctor—Elizabeth Seifert	.50	1.50	2.50	
1246	The Mission—Dean Brelis	.80	2.40	4.00	
1247	The Angry Land—Frank Bass	.80	2.40	4.00	
1248	Dishonor Among Thieves—Spencer Dean	.80	2.40	4.00	M
1249	Badlands Buccaneer—John Hunter	.80	2.40	4.00	W
1250	The Killer Is Mine—Talmage Powell; 1959	.80	2.40	4.00	
1251	Beyond Wind River—Les Savage, Jr.	.80	2.40	4.00	W
1252	Cairo Intrigue—William Manchester	.80	2.40	4.00	
1253	Seventeen—Bernard Lansky	.50	1.50	2.50	H
1254	Rio Grande Deadline—Allan Vaughan Elston	.80	2.40	4.00	W
1255	Murder Takes a Wife—James Howard	.80	2.40	4.00	M
1256	Never Kill a Cop—Lee Costigan	.80	2.40	4.00	M
1257	Rebel Basin—Harry Sinclair Drago	.80	2.40	4.00	W
1258					
1259	A Hearse of Another Color—M. E. Chaber	.80	2.40	4.00	M
1260	Trail From Needle Rock—Peter Field	.80	2.40	4.00	W
1261	Mark Kilby Solves a Murder—Robert Caine Frazer	.50	1.50	2.50	M
1262	Reason for Murder—Jack Usher	.80	2.40	4.00	M
1263	A Butcher's Dozen of Wicked Women—ed. Lee Wright	.80	2.40	4.00	M
1264	Buckskin Affair—Harry Sinclair Drago	.80	2.40	4.00	M

POCKET BOOKS (BRITISH)
Jarrold and Sons Limited

		Good	Fine	N/Mint	
B 1	Ming Yellow—John P. Marquand; 1950	1.20	3.60	6.00	
B 2	Pro—Bruce Hamilton	1.20	3.60	6.00	
B 3	The Lost Weekend—Charles Jackson	1.20	3.60	6.00	
B 4	Mink Coat—Kathleen Morris; Note: Same cover as Pocket Book No. 625	1.20	3.60	6.00	
B 5	The Anatomy of Murder—Dorothy L. Sayers	1.20	3.60	6.00	M
B 6	Farewell Campo 12—Brigadier James Hargest	1.20	3.60	6.00	
B 7	The Hound of the Baskervilles—Sir Arthur Conan Doyle	2.00	6.00	10.00	M
B 8	The Other Day—Dorothy Whipple	1.20	3.60	6.00	
B 9	Circle C Moves On—Arthur Henry Gooden	1.20	3.60	6.00	W
B10	Outlaws Three—Peter Field	1.20	3.60	6.00	W
B11	Double Indemnity—James M. Cain	1.20	3.60	6.00	M
B12	Famous British Short Stories—ed. Lyle Blair	1.20	3.60	6.00	
B13	Maiden's Trip—Emma Smith	1.20	3.60	6.00	
B14	Lam to the Slaughter—A. A. Fair	1.20	3.60	6.00	M
B15	Tell Death to Wait—Anita Boutell	1.20	3.60	6.00	M
B16	Evensong—Beverly Nichols	1.20	3.60	6.00	
B17	The Dippers—Ben Travers	1.20	3.60	6.00	
B18	Pardners of the Badlands—Bliss Lomax (Harry Sinclair Drago)	1.20	3.60	6.00	W
B19	The Wind That Blows—F. W. Lister	1.20	3.60	6.00	
B20	Kid Galahad—Francis Wallace	1.20	3.60	6.00	S

		Good	Fine	N/Mint	
B21	The Selected Short Stories of H. E. Bates	1.20	3.60	6.00	
B22	The Mountain Village—Chun-Chan Yeh	1.20	3.60	6.00	
B23	The Whispering House—Margaret Erskine	1.20	3.60	6.00	
B24	The Jury—Gerald Bullett; 1951	1.20	3.60	6.00	
B25	Great Dramas and Poems From the Bible—ed. C. Lloyd-Jones	1.20	3.60	6.00	
B26	Give Up the Ghost—Margaret Erskine	1.20	3.60	6.00	
B27	Tenderfoot Boss—Arthur Henry Gooden	1.20	3.60	6.00	W
B28	Prairie Smoke—Will Ermine	1.20	3.60	6.00	W
B29	Let Him Have Judgement—Bruce Hamilton	1.20	3.60	6.00	
B30	Mildred Pierce—James M. Cain	1.20	3.60	6.00	
B31	The Bachelor of Arts—R. K. Narayan	1.20	3.60	6.00	
B32	The Pilgrim's Progress—John Bunyan	1.20	3.60	6.00	
B33	Blonde Iscariot—Edgar Lustgarten	1.20	3.60	6.00	
B34	"It's Loaded, Mr. Bauer"—John P. Marquand	1.20	3.60	6.00	
B35	Gallows Parade—George Charles	1.20	3.60	6.00	
B36	Stage Coach Kingdom—Harry Sinclair Drago	1.20	3.60	6.00	W
B37	Death of a Salesman—Arthur Miller	1.20	3.60	6.00	
B38	Pocket Book of Modern Cooking—Philip Harben	1.20	3.60	6.00	NF
B39	Famous Sporting Stories—ed. John Arlot	1.20	3.60	6.00	S
B40	Pocket Book of Popular Poetry—ed. John Pudney	1.20	3.60	6.00	
B41	Rehearsal for Love—Faith Baldwin; c-Heade	1.60	4.80	8.00	R
B42	Tropical Tales—Howard Jones	s1.20	3.60	6.00	
B43	You're Lonely When You're Dead—James Hadley Chase	1.60	4.80	8.00	M
B44	The Concertgoer's Handbook—Hubert Ross	1.20	3.60	6.00	NF
B45	No, Sir Jeremy—Anthony Weymouth	1.20	3.60	6.00	
B46	Spill the Jackpot—A. A. Fair; 1952	1.20	3.60	6.00	M
B47	Tempt Me Not—Anthony Weymouth	1.20	3.60	6.00	
B48	Before the Fact—Francis Iles	1.20	3.60	6.00	
B49	The Case of the Haunted Husband—Erle Stanley Gardner	1.20	3.60	6.00	M
B50	The Case of the Crooked Candle—Erle Stanley Gardner; Note: Same cover as Pocket Book No. 758	1.20	3.60	6.00	M
B51	Age Cannot Wither—Ursula Bloom	1.20	3.60	6.00	
B52	Turn on the Heat—A. A. Fair	1.20	3.60	6.00	M
B53	So Young a Body—Frank Bunce	1.20	3.60	6.00	
B54	High, Wild and Handsome—Lytle Shannon	1.20	3.60	6.00	
B55	How Stalin Knows—Justin Atholl	1.20	3.60	6.00	
B56	Black Jade—Angeline Taylor	1.20	3.60	6.00	
B57	Keeper of the Keys—Earl Derr Biggers	1.60	4.80	8.00	M
B58	Operation Cicero—L. C. Moyzisch	1.20	3.60	6.00	
B59	The Glittering Serpent—Emmeline Morrison	1.20	3.60	6.00	
B60	The 22 Brothers—Dana Sage; Note: Same cover as Pocket Book No. 775	1.20	3.60	6.00	
B61	Panama Is Burning—Philip Lindsay	1.20	3.60	6.00	
B62	The Case of the Golddigger's Purse—Erle Stanley Gardner	1.20	3.60	6.00	M
B64	One Dagger for Two—Philip Lindsay	1.20	3.60	6.00	
B65	The D. A. Holds a Candle—Erle Stanley Gardner	1.20	3.60	6.00	M
B66	The D. A. Goes to Trial—Erle Stanley Gardner	1.20	3.60	6.00	M
B67	The Case of the Baited Hook—Erle Stanley Gardner	1.20	3.60	6.00	M
B68	The Black Camel—Earl Derr Biggers	1.60	4.80	8.00	M
B69	Murder for Two—George Harmon Coxe	1.20	3.60	6.00	M
B70	Quo Vadis/The Story of the MGM Technicolor Film	2.00	6.00	10.00	
B71	Broncho Apache—Paul I. Wellman	1.20	3.60	6.00	W
B73	Wayne of the Flying W—Arthur Henry Gooden	1.20	3.60	6.00	W
B74	Here's Blood in Your Eye—Manning Long	1.20	3.60	6.00	M
B77	The Lives of Harry Lime—Orson Welles	1.20	3.60	6.00	
B78	The Purple Plain—H. E. Bates	1.20	3.60	6.00	
B79	Ivor Novello—Peter Noble	1.20	3.60	6.00	B
B80	Vicious Circle—Manning Long	1.20	3.60	6.00	M
B82	Rimrock Red—Lytle Shannon	1.20	3.60	6.00	W
B86	The D. A. Cooks a Goose—Erle Stanley Gardner	1.20	3.60	6.00	M
B88	Trailers of the Sage—J. K. Bassett	1.20	3.60	6.00	W
B89	The Ghost Knows His Greengages—R. B. Saxe	1.20	3.60	6.00	
B90	Murder in Havana—George Harmon Coxe	1.20	3.60	6.00	M
B92	The Ink Street Murder—Francis Grierson	1.20	3.60	6.00	M
B94	Short Shift—Manning Long	1.20	3.60	6.00	M
B100	Pickwick Papers—Charles Dickens	1.20	3.60	6.00	
B106	Arizona Justice—Stuart Hardy	1.20	3.60	6.00	W

POCKET BOOKS JR.
Pocket Books, Inc.

(Continuation of Comet Books)

J35	Ski Patrol—Montgomery Atwater	.50	1.50	2.50	A
J36	Long Lash—Bertrand Shurtleff	.50	1.50	2.50	
J37	Tom Sawyer—Mark Twain	1.00	3.00	5.00	A
J38	Baldy of Nome—Esther Birdsall Darling	.50	1.50	2.50	A

Pocket Books Jr. J39, © Pkb   Pocket Books Jr. J75, © Pkb   Pocket Book Special Ed. nn, © Pkb

(POCKET BOOKS JR., continued)

		Good	Fine	N/Mint	
J39	Sponger's Jinx—Bert Sackett	.50	1.50	2.50	A
J40	Mountain Pony—Henry V. Larom	.50	1.50	2.50	A
J41	Black Storm—Thomas C. Hinkle	.50	1.50	2.50	W
J42	Huckleberry Finn—Mark Twain	1.00	3.00	5.00	A
J43	Black Beauty—Anna Sewell	1.00	3.00	5.00	
J44	Popularity Plus—Sally S. Simpson	.50	1.50	2.50	
J45	Your Own Book of Funny Stories	.50	1.50	2.50	H
J46	Your Own Book of Campcraft—Catherine T. Hammett	.50	1.50	2.50	NF
J47	The Mystery of Batty Ridge—Allan Gregg	.50	1.50	2.50	M
J48	Buffalo Bill—Shannon Garst	.50	1.50	2.50	B
J49	Blue Treasure—Helen Girvan	.50	1.50	2.50	
J50	Tiger Roan—Glenn Balch	.50	1.50	2.50	
J51	Kingdom of Flying Men—Frederick Nelson Litten	.50	1.50	2.50	
J52	Gridiron Challenge—Jackson Scholz	.50	1.50	2.50	S
J53	Sue Barton, Senior Nurse—Helen Dore Boylston	.50	1.50	2.50	R
J54	Logging Chance—M. H. Lasher	.50	1.50	2.50	
J55	Touchdown Twins—Philip Harkins	.50	1.50	2.50	S
J56	Cowdog—Ned Andrews	.50	1.50	2.50	
J57	The Black Arrow—Robert Louis Stevenson	.80	2.40	4.00	A
J58	Mustang—Thomas C. Hinkle	.50	1.50	2.50	W
J59	Pirot Man—Dick Friendlich	.50	1.50	2.50	S
J60	Buckskin Brigade—Jim Kjelgaard; 1951	.50	1.50	2.50	A
J61	Black Spaniel Mystery—Betty Cavanna	.50	1.50	2.50	M
J62	Yellowstone Scout—William Marshall Rush	.50	1.50	2.50	W
J63	The Great Houdini—Samuel Stein & Beryl Williams	.50	1.50	2.50	B
J64	Secret Sea—Robb White	.50	1.50	2.50	
J65	Mountain Pony and the Pinto Calf—Henry V. Larom	.50	1.50	2.50	W
J66	High, Inside!—Guy Emery	.50	1.50	2.50	
J67	The Kid Comes Back—John R. Tunis	.50	1.50	2.50	S
J68	The Teen-age Manual—Edith Heal	.50	1.50	2.50	NF
J69	Back to Treasure Island—H. A. Calahan	.50	1.50	2.50	
J70	Shag—Thomas C. Hinkle	.50	1.50	2.50	
J71	The Jinx Ship—Howard Pease	.50	1.50	2.50	A
J72	Beyond Rope and Fence—David Grew	.50	1.50	2.50	
J73	The Wind in the Rigging—Howard Pease	.50	1.50	2.50	A
J74	Riders of the Gabilans—Graham Dean	.50	1.50	2.50	
J75	Wolf Dogs of the North—Jack Hines	.50	1.50	2.50	A
J76	The Ship Without a Crew—Howard Pease	.50	1.50	2.50	A
J77	Partners of Powder Hole—Robert Davis	.50	1.50	2.50	

POCKET BOOK—SPECIAL EDITION
Pocket Books, Inc.

		Good	Fine	N/Mint	
nn	Green Light—Lloyd C. Douglas; 1942. Note: Special edition of Pocket Book No. 175, issued for the American Red Cross	1.00	3.00	5.00	
nn	Official AAF Guide Book; 1944. Note: Special edition of Pocket Book No. 265, issued for the Army Air Forces	1.00	3.00	5.00	NF

POCKET LIBRARY
Pocket Books, Inc.

		Good	Fine	N/Mint	
PL 1	Man and State: The Political Philosophers—Saxe Commins & Robert N. Linscott; 1954	.40	1.20	2.00	NF
PL 2	Man and Man: The Social Philosophers—Saxe Commins & Robert N. Linscott	.40	1.20	2.00	NF
PL 3	Man and the Universe: The Philosophers of Science—Saxe Commins & Robert N. Linscott	.40	1.20	2.00	NF
PL 4	Man and Spirit: The Speculative Philosophers—Saxe Commins & Robert N. Linscott	.40	1.20	2.00	NF

		Good	Fine	N/Mint	
PL 5	The Imitation of Christ—Thomas A. Kempis	.40	1.20	2.00	
PL 6	The Golden Ass of Apuleius—Apuleius Madaurensis	.40	1.20	2.00	
PL 7	Dialogues of Plato	.40	1.20	2.00	
PL 8	Famous Chinese Short Stories—Lin Yutang	.50	1.50	2.50	
PL 9	Pride and Prejudice—Jane Austen	.50	1.50	2.50	
PL10	Wuthering Heights—Emily Bronte	.50	1.50	2.50	
PL11	The Story of Philosophy—Will Durant	.40	1.20	2.00	NF
PL12	The Story of Mankind—Hendrik Willem Van Loon	.40	1.20	2.00	NF
PL13	The Pocket Bible	.50	1.50	2.50	
PL14	The Great Short Stories of Robert Louis Stevenson	.50	1.50	2.50	
PL15	The House of the Seven Gables—Nathaniel Hawthorne	.50	1.50	2.50	
PL16	Tales From the Arabian Nights	.50	1.50	2.50	
PL17	The Way West—A. B. Guthrie, Jr.	.50	1.50	2.50	W
PL18	The Autobiography of Benjamin Franklin	.40	1.20	2.00	B
PL19	Ivanhoe—Walter Scott	.50	1.50	2.50	A
PL20	The Red Badge of Courage—Stephen Crane	.50	1.50	2.50	A
PL21	The Pocket Book of Great Operas—Henry Simon & Abraham Veinus	.40	1.20	2.00	
PL22	A Tale of Two Cities—Charles Dickens	.50	1.50	2.50	
PL23	The Return of the Native—Thomas Hardy	.50	1.50	2.50	
PL24	The Pocket Book of Modern American Short Stories—Philip van Doren Stern	.40	1.20	2.00	
PL25	Tess of the D'Urbervilles—Thomas Hardy	.50	1.50	2.50	
PL26	The Scarlet Letter—Nathaniel Hawthorne; 1955	.50	1.50	2.50	
PL27	Silas Marner—George Eliot	.50	1.50	2.50	
PL28	Moby Dick—Herman Melville	.50	1.50	2.50	
PL29	Great Short Stories—Guy de Maupassant	.40	1.20	2.00	
PL30	Four Great Tragedies—William Shakespeare	.40	1.20	2.00	
PL31	Four Great Comedies—William Shakespeare	.40	1.20	2.00	
PL32	German Stories and Tales—Robert Pick	.40	1.20	2.00	
PL33	The Basic Ideas of Alexander Hamilton	.40	1.20	2.00	
PL34	Kidnapped—Robert Louis Stevenson	.50	1.50	2.50	
PL35	The New Pocket Anthology of American Verse—Oscar Williams; 1955	.40	1.20	2.00	
PL36	The Bridge of San Luis Rey—Thornton Wilder	.50	1.50	2.50	
PL37	French Stories and Tales—Stanley Geist; 1956	.40	1.20	2.00	
PL38	The Pocket Book of O. Henry Stories	.40	1.20	2.00	
PL39	The Adventures of Tom Sawyer—Mark Twain	.50	1.50	2.50	
PL40	Spanish Stories and Tales—Harriet de Onis	.40	1.20	2.00	
PL41	The Pocket Book of Verse—M. E. Speare	.40	1.20	2.00	
PL42	The Adventures of Huckleberry Finn—Mark Twain	.50	1.50	2.50	
PL43	Tales From the Decameron—Giovanni Boccaccio	.40	1.20	2.00	
PL44	Jane Eyre—Charlotte Bronte	.50	1.50	2.50	
PL45	The Confessions of St. Augustine—Aurelius Augustinus	.40	1.20	2.00	
PL46	Great Tales and Poems—Edgar Allan Poe	.50	1.50	2.50	
PL47	The Pocket Book of Robert Frost's Poems	.40	1.20	2.00	
PL48	Irish Stories and Tales—Devin A. Garrity	.40	1.20	2.00	
PL49	Treasure Island—Robert Louis Stevenson	.50	1.50	2.50	
PL50	Great Expectations—Charles Dickens	.50	1.50	2.50	
PL51	Gulliver's Travels—Jonathan Swift; 1957	.50	1.50	2.50	
PL52	The Mayor of Casterbridge—Thomas Hardy	.40	1.20	2.00	
PL53	The Pilgrim's Progress—John Bunyan	.50	1.50	2.50	
PL54	The Vicar of Wakefield—Oliver Goldsmith	.40	1.20	2.00	
PL55	The Pocket Book of Short Stories—M. E. Speare	.40	1.20	2.00	
PL56	The Confessions of Jean—Jacques Rousseau	.40	1.20	2.00	
PL57	The Tragedy of King Lear—William Shakespeare	.40	1.20	2.00	
PL58	Great Essays in Science—Martin Gardner	.40	1.20	2.00	
PL59	The Marble Fawn—Nathaniel Hawthorne	.40	1.20	2.00	
PL60	The Merchant of Venice—William Shakespeare	.40	1.20	2.00	
PL61	The Tragedy of Othello, the Moor of Venice—William Shakespeare	.40	1.20	2.00	
PL62	The Last of the Mohicans—James Fenimore Cooper	.50	1.50	2.50	
PL63	Nana—Emile Zola; 1958	.40	1.20	2.00	
PL64	The Tragedy of Hamlet, Prince of Denmark—William Shakespeare	.40	1.20	2.00	
PL65	Mid-century—Orville Prescott	.40	1.20	2.00	
PL66	The Tragedy of Julius Caesar—William Shakespeare	.40	1.20	2.00	
PL67	A Midsummer's Night's Dream—William Shakespeare	.40	1.20	2.00	
PL68	A Christmas Carol—Charles Dickens	.50	1.50	2.50	
PL69	Madame Bovary—Gustave Flaubert	.40	1.20	2.00	
PL70	The Tragedy of Macbeth—William Shakespeare; 1959	.40	1.20	2.00	
PL71	Laughing Boy—Oliver La Farge	.40	1.20	2.00	
PL500	The Story of Philosophy—Will Durant	.40	1.20	2.00	
PL501	The Story of Mankind—Hendrik Willem Van Loon	.40	1.20	2.00	
PL502	Ivanhoe—Walter Scott	.40	1.20	2.00	
PL503	The New Pocket Anthology of American Verse—Oscar Williams	.40	1.20	2.00	
PL504	Immortal Poems of the English Language—Oscar Williams	.40	1.20	2.00	
PL505	The Pocket Book of Modern Verse—Oscar Williams	.40	1.20	2.00	
PL506	Tales From the Arabian Nights	.40	1.20	2.00	
PL507	Adam Bede—George Eliot; 1956	.40	1.20	2.00	
PL508	Lorna Doone—R. D. Blackmore	.40	1.20	2.00	

Pocket Library PL7, © Pkb   Pocket Library/Great Art A15, © Pkb   Pocket Library/Great Art A21, © Pkb

(POCKET LIBRARY, continued)

		Good	Fine	N/Mint
PL509	The Mill on the Floss—George Eliot	.40	1.20	2.00
PL510	Robinson Crusoe—Daniel Defoe	.40	1.20	2.00
PL511	The Life and Opinions of Tristram Shandy, Gentleman—Laurence Sterne	.40	1.20	2.00
PL512	The Pocket History of the United States—Henry Steele Commager & Allan Nevins	.40	1.20	2.00
PL513	The Way West—A. B. Guthrie, Jr.	.40	1.20	2.00
PL514	Oliver Twist—Charles Dickens; 1957	.40	1.20	2.00
PL515	The Pocket History of American Painting—James Thomas Flexner	.40	1.20	2.00
PL516	Story Poems—Louis Untermeyer	.40	1.20	2.00
PL517	Don Quixote—Miguel de Cervantes	.40	1.20	2.00
PL518	Essays in Philosophy—James Bayley & Houston Peterson	.40	1.20	2.00
PL519	The Pocket Aristotle—Aristotle	.40	1.20	2.00
PL520	The Selected Essays of Montaigne—Michel de Montaigne	.40	1.20	2.00
PL521				
PL522	A Tale of Two Cities—Charles Dickens	.40	1.20	2.00
PL523				
PL524				
PL525	Tess of the D'Urbervilles—Thomas Hardy	.40	1.20	2.00
PL544	Jane Eyre—Charlotte Bronte	.40	1.20	2.00
PL750	Vanity Fair—William Makepeace Thackeray	.40	1.20	2.00
PL751	David Copperfield—Charles Dickens	.40	1.20	2.00

POCKET LIBRARY OF GREAT ART
Pocket Books, Inc./N. Abrams, Inc.

A 1	Degas—Daniel Catton Rich; 1953	.50	1.50	2.50	NF
A 2	El Greco—John F. Matthews	.50	1.50	2.50	NF
A 3	Toulouse-Lautrec—Samuel Hunter	.50	1.50	2.50	NF
A 4	Cezanne—Theodore Rousseau, Jr.	.50	1.50	2.50	NF
A 5	Dufy—Alfred Werner	.50	1.50	2.50	NF
A 6	Van Gogh—Robert Goldwater	.50	1.50	2.50	NF
A 7	The French Impressionists and Their Circle—Herman J. Wechsler	.50	1.50	2.50	NF
A 8	Rembrandt—Wilhelm Koehler	.50	1.50	2.50	NF
A 9	Botticelli—Frederick Hartt	.50	1.50	2.50	NF
A10	Matisse—Clement Greenberg	.50	1.50	2.50	NF
A11	Renoir—Milton S. Fox	.50	1.50	2.50	NF
A12	Utrillo—Alfred Werner	.50	1.50	2.50	NF
A13	Manet—S. Lane Faison, Jr.; 1954	.50	1.50	2.50	NF
A14	Rouault—Jacques Maritain	.50	1.50	2.50	NF
A15	Gauguin—John Rewald	.50	1.50	2.50	NF
A16	Modigliani—Jacques Lipchitz	.50	1.50	2.50	NF
A17	Rubens—Julius S. Held	.50	1.50	2.50	NF
A18	Pissarro—John Rewald	.50	1.50	2.50	NF
A19	Velazquez—Margaretta Salinger	.50	1.50	2.50	NF
A20	Picasso (Blue and Rose Periods)—William S. Lieberman	.50	1.50	2.50	NF
A21	Bruegel—Wolfgang Stechow; 1955	.50	1.50	2.50	NF
A22	Goya—Frederick S. Wight	.50	1.50	2.50	NF
A23	Michelangelo—Margaretta Salinger	.50	1.50	2.50	NF
A24	Flower Painting by the Great Masters—Margaret Fairbanks Marcus	.50	1.50	2.50	NF

PONY BOOKS
Stamford House

45	Your Life in the Atom World—John Houston Craige; 1946	2.00	6.00	10.00	NF
46	The Singing Corpse—Bernard Dougall; 1945	2.00	6.00	10.00	M
47	The Orange Divan—Valentine Williams	2.00	6.00	10.00	M
48	The Narrow Cell—Dale Clark	2.00	6.00	10.00	M
49	The Corpse With the Red-Headed Friend—R. A. J. Walling	2.00	6.00	10.00	M

(PONY BOOKS, continued)

		Good	Fine	N/Mint	
50	The Wager and the House at Fernwood—Fulton Oursler; 1st ed., 1946	2.00	6.00	10.00	
51	The Heart Has Wings—Faith Baldwin	1.60	4.80	8.00	R
52	A Clue for Mr. Fortune—H. C. Bailey	2.00	6.00	10.00	M
53	Unhurrying Chase—Morris Markey; 1st ed., 1946	3.00	9.00	15.00	
54	Cellini Smith: Detective—Robert Reeves	2.00	6.00	10.00	M
55	Second Hand Wife—Kathleen Norris	2.00	6.00	10.00	
56	Wanted: Someone Innocent—Margery Allingham; 1st ed., 1946	3.00	9.00	15.00	M
57	The Stolen Squadron—Charles L. Leonard	1.20	3.60	6.00	C
58	Salt River Ranny—Nelson C. Nye	2.00	6.00	10.00	W
59	One Small Candle—Cecil Roberts	1.20	3.60	6.00	
60	The Bishop's Crime—H. C. Bailey	2.00	6.00	10.00	M
61	Fifty Famous Sports Stories—Caswell Adams; 1st ed., 1946	1.60	4.80	8.00	S
62	The Inconvenient Corpse—E. P. Fenwick	2.00	6.00	10.00	M
63	Death and the Devil—Paul Whelton	2.00	6.00	10.00	M
64	Mr. Fortune Wonders—H. C. Bailey	2.00	6.00	10.00	M
65	The Quiz Crossword Puzzle Book; orig., 1946	3.00	9.00	15.00	NF
66	Blood of the North—James B. Hendryx	2.00	6.00	10.00	A

PONY BOOKS
Weldun

(Canadian)

123	The Waltz of Death—P. B. Maxon	2.00	6.00	10.00	M
124	Hellcat—Isabel Williams	2.00	6.00	10.00	
125	Monkeys in the Mirror—Donald Bayne Hobart	2.00	6.00	10.00	
126	Orchids to You—Hank Janson	2.00	6.00	10.00	

POPULAR LIBRARY
Popular Library, Inc.

nn(1)	Saint Overboard—Leslie Charteris; 1943	12.50	37.50	60.00	M
nn(2)	Danger in the Dark—Mignon G. Eberhart	2.00	6.00	10.00	M
nn(3)	Crime of Violence—Rufus King	3.00	9.00	15.00	M
4	Murder in the Madhouse—Jonathan Latimer	3.00	9.00	15.00	M
5	Miss Pinkerton—Mary Roberts Rinehart	3.00	9.00	15.00	M
6	Three Bright Pebbles—Leslie Ford	2.00	6.00	10.00	M
7	Death Demands an Audience—Helen Reilly	3.00	9.00	15.00	M
8	Death for Dear Clara—Q. Patrick	3.00	9.00	15.00	M
9	The Eee Pie Murders—David Frome	2.00	6.00	10.00	M
10	To Wake the Dead—John Dickson Carr	6.00	18.00	30.00	M
11	The Stoneware Monkey—R. Austin Freeman	3.00	9.00	15.00	M
12	Death Sits on the Board—John Rhode	3.00	9.00	15.00	M
13	Valcour Meets Murder—Rufus King	2.00	6.00	10.00	M
14	The Criminal C. O. D.—Phoebe Atwood Taylor	3.00	9.00	15.00	M
15	The Third Eye—Ethel Lina White	2.00	6.00	10.00	M
16	The Dead Don't Care—Jonathan Latimer	3.00	9.00	15.00	M
17	The House on the Roof—Mignon G. Eberhart	2.00	6.00	10.00	M
18	Tragedy in the Hollow—Freeman Wills Crofts	2.00	6.00	10.00	M
19	The Crooked Hinge—John Dickson Carr	3.00	9.00	15.00	M
20	Murder in Shinbone Alley—Helen Reilly	2.00	6.00	10.00	M
21	The After House—Mary Roberts Rinehart; 1944	2.00	6.00	10.00	M
22	Murder Masks Miami—Rufus King	2.00	6.00	10.00	M
23	S. S. Murder—Q. Patrick	3.00	9.00	15.00	M
24	Reno Rendezvous—Leslie Ford	2.00	6.00	10.00	M
25	Out of Order—Phoebe Atwood Taylor; 1944	2.00	6.00	10.00	M
26	Mr. Pinkerton Has the Clue—David Frome	2.00	6.00	10.00	M

Pony Books 63, © SH

Popular Library 1, © Poplib

Popular Library 23, © Poplib

Popular Library 40, © Poplib   Popular Library 61, © Poplib   Popular Library 70, © Poplib

(POPULAR LIBRARY, continued)

		Good	Fine	N/Mint	
27	From This Dark Stairway—Mignon G. Eberhart	2.00	6.00	10.00	M
28	The Burning Court—John Dickson Carr	4.00	12.00	20.00	M
29	Weekend With Death—Patricia Wentworth	2.00	6.00	10.00	M
30	There's Trouble Brewing—Nicholas Blake	3.00	9.00	15.00	M
31	Murder by the Clock—Rufus King	2.00	6.00	10.00	M
32	The Wheel Spins—Ethel Lina White; movie tie-in	3.00	9.00	15.00	M
33	McKee of Centre Street—Helen Reilly	2.00	6.00	10.00	M
34	Mr. Pinkerton at the Old Angel—David Frome; aka Visitor in the Night	2.00	6.00	10.00	M
35	The Mystery of Hunting's End—Mignon G. Eberhart	2.00	6.00	10.00	M
36	Death and the Maiden—Q. Patrick	3.00	9.00	15.00	M
37	Mother Finds a Body—Gypsy Rose Lee	2.00	6.00	10.00	M
38	The Dark Ships—Hulbert Footner	2.00	6.00	10.00	
39	In the Balance—Patricia Wentworth	2.00	6.00	10.00	M
40	The Stars Spell Death—Jonathan Stagge	3.00	9.00	15.00	M
41	The Smiler With the Knife—Nicholas Blake	3.00	9.00	15.00	M
42	Murdered: One by One—Francis Beeding	2.00	6.00	10.00	M
43	The Fatal Kiss Mystery—Rufus King; 1945	2.00	6.00	10.00	M
44	The Brass Chills—Hugh Pentecost	2.00	6.00	10.00	M
45	The Wrong Murder—Craig Rice	2.00	6.00	10.00	M
46	Sound of Revelry—Octavus Roy Cohen	2.00	6.00	10.00	M
47	Return to the Scene—Q. Patrick; aka The Green Diary	3.00	9.00	15.00	M
48	Mr. Smith's Hat—Helen Reilly	2.00	6.00	10.00	M
49	Tiger Milk—David Garth	3.00	9.00	15.00	M
50	Green Shiver—Clyde B. Clason; 1945	2.00	6.00	10.00	
51	The Whispering Cup—Mabel Seeley	2.00	6.00	10.00	M
52	Murder by Prescription—Jonathan Stagge	3.00	9.00	15.00	M
53	Cancelled in Red—Hugh Pentecost	2.00	6.00	10.00	M
54	Her Heart in Her Throat—Ethel Lina White	2.00	6.00	10.00	M
55	Murder in the Willett Family—Rufus King	2.00	6.00	10.00	M
56	Dead for a Ducat—Helen Reilly	2.00	6.00	10.00	M
57	The Twelve Disguises—Francis Beeding	2.00	6.00	10.00	M
58	The Turquoise Shop—Frances Crane	2.00	6.00	10.00	M
59	The Case of the Solid Key—Anthony Boucher	3.00	9.00	15.00	M
60	The Corpse in the Snowman—Nicholas Blake	3.00	9.00	15.00	M
61	The Mad Hatter Mystery—John Dickson Carr	3.00	9.00	15.00	M
62	The Yellow Taxi—Jonathan Stagge	3.00	9.00	15.00	M
63	Sing a Song of Homicide—James R. Langham	2.00	6.00	10.00	M
64	They Can't Hang Me—James Ronald	2.00	6.00	10.00	M
65	The Woman in the Picture—John August	2.00	6.00	10.00	
66	The Blind Side—Patricia Wentworth	2.00	6.00	10.00	M
67	Murder on the Yacht—Rufus King	2.00	6.00	10.00	M
68	The Cat Screams—Todd Downing	1.60	4.80	8.00	M
69	The Listening House—Mabel Seeley; 1946	1.60	4.80	8.00	M
70	Mr. Polton Explains—R. Austin Freeman	3.00	9.00	15.00	M
71	Hell Let Loose—Francis Beeding	1.60	4.80	8.00	M
72	Who Killed Aunt Maggie?—Medora Field	2.00	6.00	10.00	M
73	Hasty Wedding—Mignon G. Eberhart	2.00	6.00	10.00	M
74	Murder in Season—Octavus Roy Cohen; aka Romance in Crimson	2.00	6.00	10.00	M
75	She Faded Into Air—Ethel Lina White; 1946	1.60	4.80	8.00	M
76	Fog—Valentine Williams & Dorothy Rice Sims	2.00	6.00	10.00	M
77	Buckaroo—Eugene Cunningham	1.60	4.80	8.00	W
78	Timbal Gulch Trail—Max Brand	1.60	4.80	8.00	W
79	Rolling Stone—Patricia Wentworth	1.60	4.80	8.00	M
80	The Golden Box—Frances Crane	1.60	4.80	8.00	M
81	Three Thirds of a Ghost—Timothy Fuller	1.60	4.80	8.00	M
82	The 24th Horse—Hugh Pentecost	1.60	4.80	8.00	M
83	The Black-Headed Pins—Constance & Gwenyth Little	1.60	4.80	8.00	M
84	Challenge for Three—David Garth	1.60	4.80	8.00	M

Popular Library 87, © Poplib

Popular Library 91, © Poplib

Popular Library 107, © Poplib

(POPULAR LIBRARY, continued)

		Good	Fine	N/Mint	
85	Trouble Shooter—Ernest Haycox	2.00	6.00	10.00	W
86	Bucky Follows a Cold Trail—William MacLeod Raine	2.00	6.00	10.00	W
87	Fatal Descent—John Rhode & Carter Dickson	4.00	12.00	20.00	M
88	Romance in the First Degree—Octavus Roy Cohen	2.00	6.00	10.00	M
89	The Right Murder—Craig Rice	2.00	6.00	10.00	M
90	The Scarlet Circle—Jonathan Stagge	3.00	9.00	15.00	M
91	The Sea-Hawk—Rafael Sabatini	3.00	9.00	15.00	A
92	All Over But the Shooting—Richard Powell	1.60	4.80	8.00	M
93	The Blue Lacquer Box—George F. Worts	1.60	4.80	8.00	M
94	The Mortal Storm—Phyllis Bottome	1.20	3.60	6.00	M
95	The Red Law—Jackson Gregory	1.60	4.80	8.00	W
96	Singing River—W. C. Tuttle	1.60	4.80	8.00	W
97	A Variety of Weapons—Rufus King	1.60	4.80	8.00	M
98	Dividend on Death—Brett Halliday	1.60	4.80	8.00	M
99	Dead of the Night—John Rhode	2.00	6.00	10.00	M
100	The African Poison Murders—Elspeth Huxley; 1947	1.60	4.80	8.00	M
101	Lummox—Fanny Hurst	1.20	3.60	6.00	
102	Duel in the Sun—Niven Busch; movie tie-in	1.60	4.80	8.00	W
103	The Phantom Canoe—William Byron Mowery; 1947	1.60	4.80	8.00	
104	Mesquite Jenkins, Tumbleweed—Clarence E. Mulford	1.60	4.80	8.00	W
105	The Case Is Closed—Patricia Wentworth	1.60	4.80	8.00	M
106	The Corpse With the Eerie Eye—R. A. J. Walling	1.60	4.80	8.00	M
107	Crossword Puzzles	8.00	24.00	40.00	NF
108	The Yellow Violet—Frances Crane	1.60	4.80	8.00	M
109	I'll Sing at Your Funeral—Hugh Pentecost	1.60	4.80	8.00	M
110	Congo Song—Stuart Cloete	2.00	6.00	10.00	E
111	Bedelia—Vera Caspary; movie tie-in	2.00	6.00	10.00	E
112	The Black Shrouds—Constance & Gwenyth Little	1.60	4.80	8.00	M
113	Crucible—Ben Ames Williams	1.60	4.80	8.00	
114	Ramrod—Luke Short; movie tie-in	1.60	4.80	8.00	W
115	Popular Book of Cartoons—Ned L. Pines	3.00	9.00	15.00	H
116	The Red House—George Agnew Chamberlain; movie tie-in	2.00	6.00	10.00	M
117	This Is Murder, Mr. Jones—Timothy Fuller	2.00	6.00	10.00	M
118	The Flying U's Last Stand—B. M. Bower	1.60	4.80	8.00	W
119	Firebrand—Tom Gill	1.60	4.80	8.00	W
120	The Spiral Staircase—Ethel Lina White	2.00	6.00	10.00	M
121	A Losing Game—Freeman Wills Crofts	2.00	6.00	10.00	M
122	The Adventures of Dr. Thorndyke—R. Austin Freeman; aka The Singing Bone	2.00	6.00	10.00	M
123	A Question of Proof—Nicholas Blake	2.00	6.00	10.00	M
124	Design in Evil—Rufus King	1.60	4.80	8.00	M

Popular Library 110, © Poplib

Popular Library 114, © Poplib

Popular Library 122, © Poplib

Popular Library 132, © Poplib

Popular Library 137, © Poplib

Popular Library 147, © Poplib

(POPULAR LIBRARY, continued)

		Good	Fine	N/Mint	
125	Said the Spider to the Fly—Richard Shattuck; 1947	1.60	4.80	8.00	M
126	The Deadly Sunshade—Phoebe Atwood Taylor	1.60	4.80	8.00	M
127	Paradise Trail—William Byron Mowery	1.60	4.80	8.00	W
128	The Voice of the Pack—Edison Marshall	1.60	4.80	8.00	W
129	I Wake Up Screaming—Steve Fisher	2.00	6.00	10.00	M
130	The Mystery Companion—ed. A. L. Furman	3.00	9.00	15.00	M
131	The Clock Strikes Twelve—Patricia Wentworth	1.60	4.80	8.00	M
132	Seven Keys to Baldpate—Earl Derr Biggers	3.00	9.00	15.00	M
133	Advance Agent—John August	1.60	4.80	8.00	
134	Fighting Blood—Gordon Young	1.60	4.80	8.00	W
135	Law Rides the Range—Walt Coburn	1.60	4.80	8.00	W
136	Appointment With Danger—David Garth; aka Road to Glenfairlie	1.60	4.80	8.00	M
137	Six Time Death—William Irish; aka After-dinner Story	3.00	9.00	15.00	M
138	The Case Against Mrs. Ames—Arthur Somers Roche; Note: Same cover as the pulp magazine Popular Detective, November 1945.	1.60	4.80	8.00	M
139	The Corpse With the Grimy Glove—R. A. J. Walling; 1948	1.60	4.80	8.00	M
140	Secret Valley—Jackson Gregory	1.60	4.80	8.00	W
141	Winter Range—Alan LeMay; Note: Same cover as the pulp magazine Range Riders Western, March 1947.	1.60	4.80	8.00	W
142	Guardians of the Desert—Tom Gill	1.60	4.80	8.00	W
143	Free Grass—Ernest Haycox	1.60	4.80	8.00	W
144	Danger in Paradise—Octavus Roy Cohen	2.00	6.00	10.00	M
145	Gunsmoke Trail—William MacLeod Raine; aka Moran Beats Back	1.60	4.80	8.00	W
146	Hopalong Cassidy Takes Cards—C. E. Mulford	2.00	6.00	10.00	W
147	The Private Life of Helen of Troy—John Erskine; c-Bergey	9.00	27.00	45.00	E
148	The Ranger Way—Eugene Cunningham	1.60	4.80	8.00	W
149	Hidden Blood—W. C. Tuttle; Note: Same cover as the pulp magazine Range Riders Western, Summer 1945.	2.00	6.00	10.00	W
150	Crossword Puzzles, Book Two; 1948	9.00	27.00	45.00	NF
151	Double Cross Ranch—Charles Alden Seltzer	1.60	4.80	8.00	W
152	Rancher's Revenge—Max Brand	1.60	4.80	8.00	W
153	The Secret of Father Brown—G. K. Chesterton	3.00	9.00	15.00	M
154	The Case of the Crumpled Knave—Anthony Boucher; c-Belarski	6.00	18.00	30.00	M
155	The Dreadful Night—Ben Ames Williams; c-Belarski	3.00	9.00	15.00	M
156	Popular Book of Western Stories—Leo Margulies	1.60	4.80	8.00	W
157	The Flying U Strikes—B. M. Bower	1.60	4.80	8.00	W
158	The Strangled Witness—Leslie Ford	3.00	9.00	15.00	M
159	About the Murder of the Circus Queen—Anthony Abbot	2.00	6.00	10.00	M
160	The Silver Star—Jackson Gregory	1.20	3.60	6.00	W
161	Thunder in the Dust—Alan LeMay	1.60	4.80	8.00	W

Popular Library 149, © Poplib

Popular Library 154, © Poplib

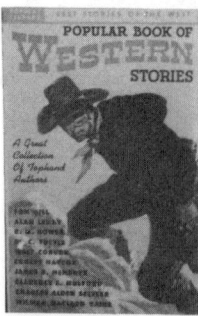

Popular Library 156, © Poplib

Popular Library 163, © Poplib

Popular Library 167, © Poplib

Popular Library 168, © Poplib

(POPULAR LIBRARY, continued)

		Good	Fine	N/Mint	
162	Love Has No Alibi—Octavus Roy Cohen; c-Belarski	2.00	6.00	10.00	M
163	Death at Sea—Richard Sale; aka Destination Unknown, c-Belarski	3.00	9.00	15.00	M
164	Lady in Peril—Ben Ames Williams; aka Money Musk, c-Belarski	2.00	6.00	10.00	M
165	Valley of Vanishing Herds—W. C. Tuttle	1.60	4.80	8.00	W
166	Sky-Pilot Cowboy—Walt Coburn	1.60	4.80	8.00	W
167	Pattern of Murder—Mignon G. Eberhart; aka The Pattern, c-Belarski	2.00	6.00	10.00	M
168	Death and Taxes—David Dodge	3.00	9.00	15.00	M
169	The Bitter Tea of General Yen—Grace Zaring Stone; 1949	3.00	9.00	15.00	E
170	Omnibus of American Humor—ed. Robert N. Linscott	1.60	4.80	8.00	H
171	Chaffee of Roaring Horse—Ernest Haycox; Note: Same cover as the pulp magazine Thrilling Western, November 1944.	1.20	3.60	6.00	W
172	Pistol Pardners—William MacLeod Raine; aka The Black Tolts	1.60	4.80	8.00	W
173	Death Is a Lovely Lady—Ruth Fenisong; aka Jenny Kissed Me	1.60	4.80	8.00	M
174	The Three Coffins—John Dickson Carr; c-Belarski	1.60	4.80	8.00	M
175	Roaring Guns—Gordon Young; 1949, aka Red Clark O'Tulluco	1.60	4.80	8.00	W
176	Diamond River Range—Eugene Cunningham; aka Diamond River Man. Note: Same cover as the pulp magazine Range Riders Western, September 1947.	1.20	3.60	6.00	W
177	Some Day I'll Kill You—Dana Chambers	1.60	4.80	8.00	M
178	Death Is Like That—John Spain	2.00	6.00	10.00	M
179	Outlaw Breed—William Byron Mowery; aka The Black Automatic	1.60	4.80	8.00	W
180	Wild West—Bertrand W. Sinclair	1.60	4.80	8.00	W
181	How I Pick Winners—Ken Kling	2.00	6.00	10.00	NF
182	Little Known Facts About Well Known People—Dale Carnegie	1.60	4.80	8.00	NF
183	Gentle Annie—MacKinlay Kantor; c-Belarski	1.20	3.60	6.00	
184	Marshal of Sundown—Jackson Gregory	1.20	3.60	6.00	W
185	Whispering Smith—Frank H. Sperman; movie tie-in	1.60	4.80	8.00	
186	Cartoon Fun—Ned L. Pines	8.00	24.00	40.00	H
187	Selected Western Stories—ed. Leo Margulies	1.60	4.80	8.00	W
188	The Yellow Overcoat—Frank Gruber. Note: Same cover as the pulp magazine Thrilling Detective, August 1947.	3.00	9.00	15.00	M
189	The Death Wish—Elisabeth Sanxay Holding	1.60	4.80	8.00	M
190	The Gay Bandit of the Border—Tom Gill	1.60	4.80	8.00	W
191	Barb Wire—Walt Coburn	1.20	3.60	6.00	W
192	Bodies Are Where You Find Them—Brett Halliday; c-Belarski	3.00	9.00	15.00	M
193	The Case of the Constant God—Rufus King; c-Belarski	2.00	6.00	10.00	M
194	Death on Scurvy Street—Ben Ames Williams; c-Belarski	2.00	6.00	10.00	M
195	Ward 20—James Warner Bellah; c-Belarski	1.60	4.80	8.00	E
196	There's Always Time to Die—Octavus Roy Cohen; aka I Love You Again	2.00	6.00	10.00	M
197	Pursuit of a Parcel—Patricia Wentworth	2.00	6.00	10.00	M

Popular Library 174, © Poplib

Popular Library 178, © Poplib

Popular Library 192, © Poplib

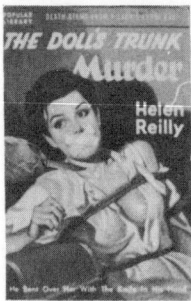

Popular Library 206, © Poplib   Popular Library 211, © Poplib   Popular Library 215, © Poplib

(POPULAR LIBRARY, continued)

		Good	Fine	N/Mint	
198	Hopalong Cassidy's Saddle Mate—Clarence E. Mulford; aka Hopalong Cassidy's Protege	1.60	4.80	8.00	W
199	Whispering Range—Ernest Haycox	1.60	4.80	8.00	W
200	Bats in the Belfry—Norman Matson; 1949	1.60	4.80	8.00	F
201	Blood on Her Shoe—Medora Field; c-Belarski	1.20	3.60	6.00	M
202	Shear the Black Sheep—David Dodge	1.60	4.80	8.00	M
203	Wild Horse Valley—W. C. Tuttle	1.20	3.60	6.00	W
204	Arizona Jim—Charles Alden Seltzer	1.20	3.60	6.00	W
205	Home Is the Hangman—Richard Sale; c-Belarski	2.00	6.00	10.00	M
206	The Grindle Nightmare—Q. Patrick; c-Belarski	3.00	9.00	15.00	M
207	Reunion With Murder—Timothy Fuller	2.00	6.00	10.00	M
208	The Deputy at Snow Mountain—Edison Marshall	1.20	3.60	6.00	W
209	Gunsight Trail—Alan LeMay	1.20	3.60	6.00	W
210	That Winter—Merle Miller	1.20	3.60	6.00	E
211	The Doll's Trunk Murder—Helen Reilly; c-Belarski	10.00	30.00	50.00	M
212	Awake to Darkness—Richard McMullen	1.00	3.00	5.00	E
213	Rustlers' Gap—William MacLeod Raine	1.20	3.60	6.00	W
214	Guns in the Valley—William Byron Mowery; aka The Village Beyond	1.20	3.60	6.00	W
215	The Silver Forest—Ben Ames Williams; c-Belarski	3.00	9.00	15.00	E
216	Cup of Gold—John Steinbeck	2.00	6.00	10.00	A
217	Tales of Chinatown—Sax Rohmer; c-Belarski	12.50	37.50	60.00	M
218	The Pink Umbrella Murder—Frances Crane; aka The Pink Umbrella, c-Belarski	2.00	6.00	10.00	M
219	Duke—Hal Ellson; c-Belarski	3.00	9.00	15.00	E
220	The Damon Runyon Story—Ed Weiner	1.20	3.60	6.00	B
221	Gentlemen Prefer Blondes—Anita Loos; c-Bergey	10.00	30.00	50.00	E
222	Something's Got to Give—Marion Hargrove	1.00	3.00	5.00	H
223	Picture Quiz Book—ed. John Paul Adams; 1950, c-Schomburg	10.00	30.00	50.00	NF
224	Sun in Their Eyes—Monte Barrett; c-Belarski	1.00	3.00	5.00	W
225	Fast on the Draw—Gordon Young; aka Red Clark Rides Alone	1.00	3.00	5.00	W
226	Sudden Bill Dorn—Jackson Gregory	1.00	3.00	5.00	W
227	The Illustrious Corpse—Tiffany Thayer; c-Belarski. Note: Same cover as the pulp magazine Popular Detective, September 1948	1.60	4.80	8.00	M
228	The Sex Machine—Shepherd Mead; aka The Magnificent MacInnes, c-Schomburg	2.00	6.00	10.00	SF
229	Homicide Johnny—Steve Fisher; c-Belarski	4.00	12.00	20.00	M
230	Focus—Arthur Miller; c-Belarski	1.20	3.60	6.00	
231	The Chuckling Fingers—Mabel Seeley	1.60	4.80	8.00	M
232	The Key—Patricia Wentworth	1.60	4.80	8.00	M
233	Macamba—Lilla Van Saher	1.60	4.80	8.00	E
234	Quick Triggers—Eugene Cunningham; 1950	1.20	3.60	6.00	W
235	Starlight Rider—Ernest Haycox	1.20	3.60	6.00	W

Popular Library 217, © Poplib   Popular Library 219, © Poplib   Popular Library 233, © Poplib

(POPULAR LIBRARY, continued)

		Good	Fine	N/Mint	
236	Pikes Peek or Bust—Earl Wilson; c-Schomburg	1.60	4.80	8.00	H
237	Drums of Destiny—Peter Bourne; c-Bergey	2.00	6.00	10.00	A
238	She'll Be Dead by Morning—Dana Chambers	1.60	4.80	8.00	M
239	The Evil Star—John Spain	2.00	6.00	10.00	M
240	Acres and Pains—S. J. Perelman	1.60	4.80	8.00	H
241	Fortunes of Captain Blood—Rafael Sabatini; c-Belarski, movie tie-in	2.00	6.00	10.00	A
242	Riders of the Smoky Land—Edison Marshall	1.20	3.60	6.00	W
243	Texas Breed—William MacLeod Raine	1.20	3.60	6.00	W
244	Find Me in Fire—Robert Lowry	5.00	15.00	25.00	E
245	Death Is a Gold Coin—Ruth Fenisong	1.60	4.80	8.00	M
246	Murder by Latitude—Rufus King	1.60	4.80	8.00	M
247	Not Too Narrow - Not Too Deep—Richard Sale	1.60	4.80	8.00	
248	The Great Ones—Ralph Ingersoll	1.20	3.60	6.00	E
249	Twisted Trails—W. C. Tuttle; aka The Santa Dolores Stage	1.20	3.60	6.00	W
250	Mavericks—Walt Coburn; 1950	1.20	3.60	6.00	W
251	Eagle at My Eyes—Norman Katkov	1.20	3.60	6.00	E
252	Bullets for the Bridegroom—David Dodge	1.60	4.80	8.00	M
253	Yesterday's Murder—Craig Rice; aka Telefair	1.60	4.80	8.00	M
254	The Pale Blonde of Sands Street—William Chapman White; c-Bergey	1.60	4.80	8.00	E
255	The Lone Rider—Jackson Gregory	1.20	3.60	6.00	W
256	Drygulch Trail—William MacLeod Raine	1.20	3.60	6.00	W
257	Whistle Stop—Maritta M. Wolff	1.60	4.80	8.00	E
258	Six Nights of Mystery—William Irish; 1st ed., 1950	10.00	30.00	50.00	M
259	Murder in the Mews—Helen Reilly	1.60	4.80	8.00	M
260	The Edge of Doom—Leo Brady; movie tie-in	1.20	3.60	6.00	M
261	Painted Ponies—Alan LeMay	1.20	3.60	6.00	W
262	Guns of the Arrowhead—Gordon Young; aka Red Clark of the Arrowhead. Note: Same cover as the pulp magazine Thrilling Western, November 1945.	1.20	3.60	6.00	
263	Murder at Cambridge—Q. Patrick	2.00	6.00	10.00	M
264	Dangerous Lady—Octavus Roy Cohen; c-Belarski	1.60	4.80	8.00	M
265	The Girl in the Spike-Heeled Shoes—Martin Yoseloff	1.20	3.60	6.00	
266	The Captain's Lady—Basil heatter; c-Belarski	1.60	4.80	8.00	E
267	Turn of the Table—Jonathan Stagge	2.00	6.00	10.00	
268	The Nine Waxed Faces—Francis Beeding; c-Belarski	1.60	4.80	8.00	M
269	Mirror, Mirror on the Wall—Mona Kent	1.20	3.60	6.00	E
270	Tempered Blade—Monte Barrett	1.20	3.60	6.00	A
271	Riders West—Ernest Haycox	1.20	3.60	6.00	W
272	Trail's End—Edison Marshall	1.20	3.60	6.00	W
273	The Big Eye—Max Ehrlich; c-Bergey	2.00	6.00	10.00	SF
274	They Move With the Sun—Daniel Taylor	1.60	4.80	8.00	E
275	Murder at Midnight—Richard Sale; 1950	2.00	6.00	10.00	M
276	Somewhere in This House—Rufus King; c-Belarski	1.60	4.80	8.00	M
277	The Sure Thing—Merle Miller	1.60	4.80	8.00	E
278	The Hero—Millard Lampell; c-Bergey	1.60	4.80	8.00	
279	Shortgrass—Hal G. Evarts	1.20	3.60	6.00	W
280	The River Bend Feud—William MacLeod Raine	1.20	3.60	6.00	W
281	That's My Baby—Josef A. Schneider	1.60	4.80	8.00	
282	The Four False Weapons—John Dickson Carr; c-Belarski	2.00	6.00	10.00	M
283	Silence in Court—Patricia Wentworth; Note: Same cover as the pulp magazine Detective Novel, August 1945.	1.60	4.80	8.00	M
284	Laura—Vera Caspary	1.20	3.60	6.00	
285	The Curtain Never Falls—Joey Adams; c-Bergey	1.60	4.80	8.00	E
286	Murder of the Clergyman's Mistress—Anthony Abbot	2.00	6.00	10.00	
287	Don't Look Behind You—Samuel Rogers	1.60	4.80	8.00	
288	The Leather Pushers—H. C. Witwer; c-Bergey	1.60	4.80	8.00	
289	Trail of the Macaw—Eugene Cunningham	1.20	3.60	6.00	W
290	The Ringtailed Rannyhans—Walt Coburn	1.20	3.60	6.00	W
291	The Wrath and the Wind—Alexander Key	1.60	4.80	8.00	A

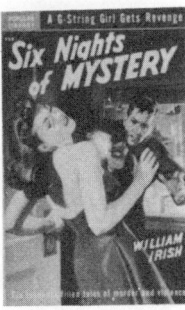

Popular Library 258, © Poplib

Popular Library 266, © Poplib

Popular Library 273, © Poplib

Popular Library 293, © Poplib

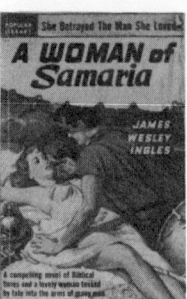

Popular Library 299, © Poplib

Popular Library 300, © Poplib

(POPULAR LIBRARY, continued)	Good	Fine	N/Mint	
292 Overboard—George F. Worts; c-Belarski	10.00	30.00	50.00	E
293 The Hangman's Whip—Mignon G. Eberhart; c-Belarski. Note: Same cover as the pulp magazine Mystery Book, Summer 1949.	6.00	18.00	30.00	M
294 The Two Worlds of Johnny Truro—George Sklar	1.00	3.00	5.00	E
295 The Wolf That Fed Us—Robert Lowry	1.20	3.60	6.00	E
296 The Dead Tree Gives No Shelter—Virgil Scott	1.00	3.00	5.00	E
297 Shotgun Gold—W. C. Tuttle	1.20	3.60	6.00	W
298 Guns of Mist River—Jackson Cole	1.20	3.60	6.00	W
299 A Woman of Samaria—James Wesley Ingles	5.00	15.00	25.00	E
300 The Winds of Fear—Hodding Carter; c-Belarski	6.00	18.00	30.00	E
301 The Fifth Grave—Jonathan Latimer; 1950, c-Belarski	1.60	4.80	8.00	M
302 The Old Battle Ax—Elisabeth Sanxay Holding; c-Belarski. Note: Same cover as the pulp magazine Detective Novel, Spring 1949.	3.00	9.00	15.00	M
303 Bound Girl—Everett & Olga Webber	2.00	6.00	10.00	E
304 This Spring of Love—Charles Mergendahl; 1951	1.00	3.00	5.00	
305 The Desert Hawk—Harry Sinclair Drago	1.20	3.60	6.00	W
306 The Haunted Hills—B. M. Bower	1.20	3.60	6.00	W
307 Her Life to Live—Oriana Atkinson; aka Big Eyes, c-Bergey	6.00	18.00	30.00	E
308 It's a Free Country—Ben Ames Williams	1.00	3.00	5.00	
309 The Dancing Detective—William Irish	5.00	15.00	25.00	M
310 Here Lies the Body—Richard Burke	2.00	6.00	10.00	M
311 Smoke Up the Valley—Monte Barrett	1.20	3.60	6.00	W
312 Mamie Brandon—Jack Sheridan	1.20	3.60	6.00	E
313 The Far Call—Jackson Gregory	1.20	3.60	6.00	W
314 Edge of Beyond—James B. Hendryx	1.20	3.60	6.00	
315 Check Your Wits—Jules Leopold	8.00	24.00	40.00	NF
316 Tuesday to Bed—Francis Sill Wickware	1.20	3.60	6.00	E
317 The Night Before Murder—Steve Fisher; c-Belarski	2.00	6.00	10.00	M
318 The Deadly Dove—Rufus King	2.00	6.00	10.00	M
319 My Forbidden Past—Polan Banks	1.60	4.80	8.00	E
320 Excuse My Dust—Bellamy Partridge	1.60	4.80	8.00	H
321 Trouble on the Border—Gordon Young	1.20	3.60	6.00	W
322 Hell and High Water—William MacLeod Raine	1.20	3.60	6.00	W
323 Home Guide to Repair, Upkeep and Remodeling—William H. Crouse	3.00	9.00	15.00	NF
324 My Old Man's Badge—Ferguson Findley	1.60	4.80	8.00	
325 Murder by the Dozen—Hugh Wiley; 1951	1.60	4.80	8.00	M
326 Behind the Flying Saucers—Frank Scully; c-Bergey	2.00	6.00	10.00	UFO
327 Stranger and Alone—J. Saunders Redding	1.60	4.80	8.00	
328 Soldiers' Daughters Never Cry—Audrey Erskine Lindop	1.20	3.60	6.00	E
329 Bullet Brand—Hal G. Evarts; aka Spanish Acres	1.20	3.60	6.00	W

Popular Library 307, © Poplib

Popular Library 318, © Poplib

Popular Library 326, © Poplib

Popular Library 331, © Poplib

Popular Library 332, © Poplib

Popular Library 334, © Poplib

(POPULAR LIBRARY, continued)

		Good	Fine	N/Mint	
330	The Trouble Trailer—W. C. Tuttle	1.20	3.60	6.00	W
331	Campus Town—Hart Stilwell	10.00	30.00	50.00	E
332	Don't Ever Love Me—Octavus Roy Cohen; Note: Same cover as the pulp magazine Mystery Book Magazine, Winter 1950.	3.00	9.00	15.00	M
333	Lonesome Road—Patricia Wentworth	1.60	4.80	8.00	M
334	The Magnificent Courtesan—Lozania Prole; c-Belarski	3.00	9.00	15.00	E
335	Shadow of a Hero—Allan Chase	1.00	3.00	5.00	
336	The Parents' Manual—Anna W. M. Wolfe	3.00	9.00	15.00	NF
337	Ace in the Hole—Jackson Gregory	1.20	3.60	6.00	W
338	Starlight Pass—Tom Gill	1.20	3.60	6.00	W
339	The Lion and the Lamb—E. Phillips Oppenheim; c-Belarski	1.20	3.60	6.00	
340	Smart Guy—William MacHaug; aka The Affairs of O'Malley	1.20	3.60	6.00	M
341	Season for Passion—Lee Manning; c-Belarski	1.20	3.60	6.00	C
342	End of Track—Ward Weaver (Van Wyck Mason)	1.20	3.60	6.00	W
343	While Murder Waits—John Esteven; c-Belarski	1.60	4.80	8.00	M
344	The Applegreen Cat—Frances Crane; c-Belarski	4.00	12.00	20.00	M
345	Bullets at Clearwater—Edison Marshall; aka The Snowshoe Trail	1.20	3.60	6.00	W
346	Ramrod—Luke Short	1.20	3.60	6.00	W
347	Hoodlum—Charley Robertson; aka Shadow of a Cloud	1.00	3.00	5.00	E
348	Adios, O'Shaughnessy—Robert Tallman	1.20	3.60	6.00	E
349	Poison in Jest—John Dickson Carr	2.00	6.00	10.00	M
350	The Dogs Do Bark—Jonathan Stagge; 1951	2.00	6.00	10.00	M
351	Tonight Is Forever—Charles Mergendahl; aka Don't Wait Up for Spring, c-Bergey	1.20	3.60	6.00	
352	Cotton Moon—Catherine Tracy	1.20	3.60	6.00	E
353	The Big Corral—Al Cody	1.20	3.60	6.00	W
354	Gun Feud—W. C. Tuttle; aka Wandering Dogies	1.20	3.60	6.00	E
355	I'll Be Right Home, Ma—Henry Denker	1.20	3.60	6.00	E
356	This Woman Is Mine—P. J. Wolfson; aka All Women Die	1.00	3.00	5.00	E
357	How I Became a Girl Reporter—Hyman Goldberg	1.00	3.00	5.00	E
358	Mrs. Candy and Saturday Night—Robert Tallant; c-Bergey	1.00	3.00	5.00	E
359	Beyond the Rio Grande—William MacLeod Raine	1.20	3.60	6.00	W
360	The Silver Desert—Ernest Haycox	1.20	3.60	6.00	W
361	Winter Kill—Steve Fisher; c-Belarski	1.60	4.80	8.00	M
362	Never Walk Alone—Rufus King; aka The Case of the Dowager's Etchings, c-Belarski. Note: Same cover as the pulp magazine Phantom Detective, Summer 1950.	1.60	4.80	8.00	M
363	The Traitor—William L. Shirer	1.00	3.00	5.00	M
364	The Ringing of the Glass—Preston Schoyer; c-Belarski	1.20	3.60	6.00	
365	Copperbelt—Nigel Sligh	1.20	3.60	6.00	
366	Please Send Me Absolutely Free!—Arkady Leokum	1.00	3.00	5.00	E
367	Shotgun Guard—D. B. Newton	1.20	3.60	6.00	W

Popular Library 344, © Poplib

Popular Library 349, © Poplib

Popular Library 350, © Poplib

Popular Library 368, © Poplib

Popular Library 376, © Poplib

Popular Library 377, © Poplib

(POPULAR LIBRARY, continued)

		Good	Fine	N/Mint	
368	Apache Crossing—Will Ermine; Note: Same cover as the pulp magazine Giant Western, August 1949.	1.20	3.60	6.00	W
369	My Love Wears Black—Octavus Roy Cohen	1.60	4.80	8.00	M
370	The Crying Sisters—Mabel Seeley	1.20	3.60	6.00	M
371	The Strumpet Sea—Ben Ames Williams	1.60	4.80	8.00	A
372	Wintertime—Jan Valtin	1.00	3.00	5.00	E
373	The Weeping and the Laughter—Vera Caspary	1.20	3.60	6.00	E
374	Dark Drums—Wenzell Brown	1.20	3.60	6.00	E
375	Texas Sheriff—Eugene Cunningham; 1951	1.20	3.60	6.00	W
376	Trouble at Moon Dance—A. B. Guthrie, Jr.; aka Murders at Moon Dance	1.00	3.00	5.00	W
377	Shadow of Madness—Hugh Pentecost; c-Bergey	2.00	6.00	10.00	M
378	You're Lonely When You're Dead—James Hadley Chase	2.00	6.00	10.00	M
379	No Narrow Path—Catharine Whitcomb; aka The Hill of Glass, c-Belarski	1.60	4.80	8.00	E
380	Rear Guard—James Warner Bellah; aka The White Invader	1.00	3.00	5.00	W
381	Heads Off at Midnight—Francis Beeding	1.20	3.60	6.00	M
382	Dark Threat—Patricia Wentworth; c-Belarski. Note: Same cover as the pulp magazine Black Book Detective, Summer 1949.	1.20	3.60	6.00	M
383	The Man From Texas—Jackson Gregory	1.00	3.00	5.00	W
384	Range Boss—Gordon Young; aka Red Clark, Range Boss. Note: Same cover as the pulp magazine Hopalong Cassidy, Fall 1950 (No. 1).	1.20	3.60	6.00	W
385	Once Off Guard—J. H. Wallace	1.00	3.00	5.00	E
386	Cottage Sinister—Q. Patrick	1.20	3.60	6.00	M
387	Casualty—Robert Lowry	1.00	3.00	5.00	E
388	Hang My Wreath—Ward Weaver (Van Wyck Mason)	1.00	3.00	5.00	
389	This Way Out—James Ronald	1.00	3.00	5.00	M
390	Trails by Night—Tom J. Hopkins	1.00	3.00	5.00	W
391	Mooney—William Brown Meloney	1.00	3.00	5.00	E
392	Jailbait—William Bernard; illo in Parade of Pleasure	2.00	6.00	10.00	JD
393	The Bed She Made—Leslie Waller; 1952	1.00	3.00	5.00	E
394	Echo of Evil—Manuel Komroff	1.00	3.00	5.00	E
395	Day Into Night—David Westheimer; aka The Magic Fallacy	1.00	3.00	5.00	E
396	Love Me Sailor—Robert S. Close	1.00	3.00	5.00	
397	Border Feud—Tom Gill; aka Red Earth	1.00	3.00	5.00	W
398	Trail Smoke—Ernest Haycox	1.00	3.00	5.00	W
399	Whirlpool—James Leal Henderson	1.00	3.00	5.00	E
400	Slay Ride—Frank Kane; 1952	1.20	3.60	6.00	
401	Wine of Violence—Ralph Ingersoll	1.00	3.00	5.00	E
402	Main Line—Livingston Biddle, Jr.	1.00	3.00	5.00	E
403	The Reef—Keith Wheeler	1.00	3.00	5.00	E
404	Divorce—James Warner Bellah	1.00	3.00	5.00	

Popular Library 384, © Poplib

Popular Library 392, © Poplib

Popular Library 400, © Poplib

Popular Library 410, © Poplib   Popular Library 411, © Poplib   Popular Library 431, © Poplib

(POPULAR LIBRARY, continued)

		Good	Fine	N/Mint	
405	Troubled Spring—John Brick	1.00	3.00	5.00	
406	Montana Road—Harry Sinclair Drago	1.00	3.00	5.00	W
407	Bonanza Gulch—Matt Stuart	1.00	3.00	5.00	W
408	Waterfront—Ferguson Findley	2.00	6.00	10.00	E
409	One by One—Fan Nichols	1.00	3.00	5.00	E
410	The Marx Brothers—Kyle Crichton	6.00	18.00	30.00	B
411	Revolt of the Triffids—John Wyndham; aka Day of the Triffids, c-Bergey	4.00	12.00	20.00	SF
412	The Spell—Gustav Breuer	1.00	3.00	5.00	E
413	A Woman of Forty—Desmond Hall	1.00	3.00	5.00	
414	The Texas Kid—William MacLeod Raine; aka The Dam Yank	1.00	3.00	5.00	W
415	Pardners of the Dim Trails—Walt Coburn	1.00	3.00	5.00	W
416	The Perfect Frame—William Ard	1.00	3.00	5.00	E
417	A Yank on Piccadilly—C. L. McDermott	1.00	3.00	5.00	E
418	The Impudent Rifle—Dick Pearce	1.00	3.00	5.00	
419	Lower Than Angels—Walter Karig	1.00	3.00	5.00	E
420	Trial by Gunsmoke—Jim O'Mara	1.00	3.00	5.00	W
421	A Matter of Morals—Joseph Gies	1.00	3.00	5.00	E
422	The Vanquished—Alan Marcus; aka Straw to Make Brick, c-Belarski	1.00	3.00	5.00	C
423	Johnny Bogan—Leonora Baccante	1.00	3.00	5.00	E
424	Fright—George Hopley (William Irish)	3.00	9.00	15.00	M
425	Thunder Valley—Burt Arthur; 1952	1.00	3.00	5.00	W
426	The Black Door—Cleve F. Adams	1.20	3.60	6.00	M
427	More Beautiful Than Murder—Octavus Roy Cohen; c-Belarski	1.20	3.60	6.00	M
428	The Train From Pittsburgh—Julian Farsen	1.00	3.00	5.00	E
429	Two-gun Man—Gordon Young; aka Red Clark, Two-gun Man	1.00	3.00	5.00	W
430	Guardians of the Trail—Jackson Gregory	1.00	3.00	5.00	W
431	Strangler's Serenade—William Irish; c-Belarski	3.00	9.00	15.00	M
432	The Great Mail Robbery—Clarence Budington Kelland; c-Bergey	1.00	3.00	5.00	E
433	Bitter Fruit—Peter Packer; aka White Crocus	1.00	3.00	5.00	
434	So Deadly Fair—Gertrude Walker	1.00	3.00	5.00	E
435	The Lost Ones—Stevan Javellana; aka Without Seeing the Dawn	1.00	3.00	5.00	E
436	Arizona Guns—William MacLeod Raine	1.00	3.00	5.00	W
437	Six-gun Gamble—D. B. Newton	1.00	3.00	5.00	W
438	At Sundown the Tiger—Ethel Mannin	1.00	3.00	5.00	
439	Rip Tide—Lee Wichelns	1.00	3.00	5.00	
440	The Cruel Dawn—Alfred Viazzi	1.20	3.60	6.00	E
441	Thief River—Nelson Nye	1.00	3.00	5.00	W
442	Head of the Mountain—Ernest Haycox	1.00	3.00	5.00	W
443	Sweet and Deadly—Verne Chute	1.00	3.00	5.00	
444	Isle of the Damned—George John Seaton	1.00	3.00	5.00	

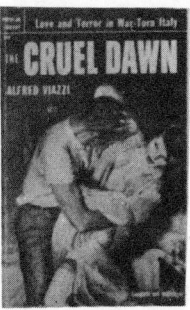

Popular Library 437, © Poplib   Popular Library 440, © Poplib   Popular Library 444, © Poplib

Popular Library 447, © Poplib

Popular Library 473, © Poplib

Popular Library 495, © Poplib

(POPULAR LIBRARY, continued)

		Good	Fine	N/Mint	
445	Timbal Gulch Trail—Max Brand	1.00	3.00	5.00	W
446	The Night and the Naked—Gordon Merrick; aka The Strumpet Wind	1.00	3.00	5.00	E
447	Dragon's Island—Jack Williamson; c-Bergey	3.00	9.00	15.00	SF
448	You Can't Catch Me—Lawrence Lariar	1.00	3.00	5.00	E
449	Gunswift—Jack Byrne	1.00	3.00	5.00	W
450	Trouble Shooter—Ernest Haycox; 1952	1.00	3.00	5.00	W
451	Maharajah—Richard Cargoe	1.20	3.60	6.00	E
452	I'll Get Mine—Thurston Scott; aka Cure It With Honey	4.00	12.00	20.00	E
453	Neither Five nor Three—Helen MacInnes	1.00	3.00	5.00	E
454	Two-edged Vengeance—W. T. Ballard	1.00	3.00	5.00	W
455	Hellgate Canyon—Fred Delano	1.00	3.00	5.00	
456	What Price Murder—Cleve F. Adams	1.20	3.60	6.00	M
457	The Boy Came Back—Charles H. Knickerbocker	1.00	3.00	5.00	E
458	Pray Love, Remember—Stephen Wendt	1.00	3.00	5.00	
459	Burmese Days—George Orwell	1.20	3.60	6.00	E
460	Rawhide Range—Ernest Haycox	1.00	3.00	5.00	W
461	Born to Trouble—Nelson Nye	1.00	3.00	5.00	W
462	A Bullet for My Love—Octavus Roy Cohen	1.20	3.60	6.00	M
463	The Big Bubble—Theodore Pratt	1.00	3.00	5.00	E
464	The Unfulfilled—W. G. Hardy	1.00	3.00	5.00	E
465	Guns of Vengeance—Jim O'Mara	1.00	3.00	5.00	W
466	The Outriders—Irving Ravetch	1.00	3.00	5.00	
467	Shakedown—Ben Kerr	1.00	3.00	5.00	
468	Dark Surrender—Peter Packer	1.00	3.00	5.00	
469	Hard to Get—Edwin Gilbert	1.00	3.00	5.00	
470	Headline Crimes of the Year—Edward D. Radin	1.20	3.60	6.00	
471	Range Beyond the Law—William MacLeod Raine	1.00	3.00	5.00	W
472	Texan on the Prod—Philip Ketchum	1.00	3.00	5.00	W
473	Bluebeard's Seventh Wife—William Irish; 1st ed., 1952	8.00	24.00	40.00	M
474	The Night Thorn—Ian Gordon; 1953	1.20	3.60	6.00	E
475	Rancher's Revenge—Max Brand	.80	2.40	4.00	W
476	Showdown—W. T. Ballard & James C. Lynch	.80	2.40	4.00	W
477	The Diary—William Ard	.80	2.40	4.00	
478	Don't Crowd Me—Evan Hunter	.80	2.40	4.00	
479	Torment—Scott Graham Williamson	.80	2.40	4.00	E
480	Superstition Range—Parker Bonner	.80	2.40	4.00	W
481	Desert of the Damned—Nelson Nye	.80	2.40	4.00	W
482	Don't Get Caught—M. E. Chaber; aka Hangman's Harvest	1.00	3.00	5.00	M
483	Ask for Linda—Fan Nichols	.80	2.40	4.00	E
484	The Girl Cage—Charles Mergendahl	.80	2.40	4.00	E
485	Glitter—A. B. Shiffrin	.80	2.40	4.00	E
486	Chaffee of Roaring Horse—Ernest Haycox	.80	2.40	4.00	W
487	Quick Trigger Law—Jim O'Mara; aka Death at War Dance	.80	2.40	4.00	W
488	Naked and Alone—Michael Lawrence	.80	2.40	4.00	
489	Duel in the Sun—Niven Busch	.80	2.40	4.00	W
490	Venables—Geoffrey Wagner	.80	2.40	4.00	E
491	Blood on the Forge—William Attaway	.80	2.40	4.00	
492	Incident at Sun Mountain—Todhunter Ballard	.80	2.40	4.00	W
493	High Mesa—Tex Grady	.80	2.40	4.00	W
494	Double Cross—Mike Moran	.80	2.40	4.00	
495	H Is for Heroin—David Hulburd	3.00	9.00	15.00	E
496	Stranger in Our Midst—Robert Carson	.80	2.40	4.00	E
497	You Can't See Around Corners—Jon Cleary	.80	2.40	4.00	
498	Texas Rawhider—Jack Barton	.80	2.40	4.00	W
499	Guns of the Barricade Bunch—Philip Ketchum	.80	2.40	4.00	W
500	Time to Kill—Terry Spain	1.20	3.60	6.00	E
501	The Closest Kin There Is—Clara Winston	.80	2.40	4.00	E
502	A Girl for Danny—William Ard	.80	2.40	4.00	

		Good	Fine	N/Mint	
503	Rickey—Charles Calitri	.80	2.40	4.00	
504	Joey Adams' Joke Book—Joey Adams	1.00	3.00	5.00	H
505	Ten Against Caesar—K. R. G. Granger	.80	2.40	4.00	
506	Fighting Cowman—Louis Trimble	.80	2.40	4.00	W
507	The Big Fear—Theo Durrant	.80	2.40	4.00	
508	The Loving and the Daring—Francoise Mallet; aka The Illusionist	.80	2.40	4.00	E
509	Rage in the Wind—Boyd Cochrell	.80	2.40	4.00	E
510	The Night Is Mine—David Davidson; aka In Another Country	.80	2.40	4.00	E
511	Renegade of Rainbow Basin—Hal G. Evarts	.80	2.40	4.00	W
512	Ramrod From Hell—Ernie Wayne	.80	2.40	4.00	
513	Beyond the Law—Edward D. Radin	.80	2.40	4.00	NF
514	Darling, I Hate You—T. S. Matthews	.80	2.40	4.00	
515	The Hard Way—Robert V. Williams	.80	2.40	4.00	
516	Island in the Sky—Ernest K. Gann	1.00	3.00	5.00	A
517	Free Grass—Ernest Haycox	.80	2.40	4.00	W
518	Rustler of the Owlhorns—Jim O'Mara	.80	2.40	4.00	W
519	Blondes Die Young—Bill Peters	.80	2.40	4.00	
520	The Tightrope—Stanley Kauffmann	.80	2.40	4.00	E
521	Six Angels at My Back—John Bell Clayton	.80	2.40	4.00	E
522	China Coaster—Don Smith	.80	2.40	4.00	E
523	Facts of Life and Love for Teenagers—Evelyn Millis Duvall	.80	2.40	4.00	NF
524	West of Quarantine—W. T. Ballard	.80	2.40	4.00	W
525	Stranger From Texas—Ray Townsend; 1953	.80	2.40	4.00	W
526	You Can't Stop Me—William Ard	.80	2.40	4.00	M
527	Bond of the Flesh—Rosamond Marshall	.80	2.40	4.00	E
528	Hooked—Will Oursler & Laurence D. Smith	2.00	6.00	10.00	E
529	Liana—Martha Gellhorn	.80	2.40	4.00	E
530	All the Way Down—M. E. Chaber	1.00	3.00	5.00	M
531	West of the Law—William MacLeod Raine	.80	2.40	4.00	W
532	The Saddle Bum—Philip Ketchum	.80	2.40	4.00	W
533	Smooth and Deadly—Quentin Reynolds; aka I, Willie Sutton	1.00	3.00	5.00	NF
534	Strange Lovers—Armando Meoni	.80	2.40	4.00	E
535	Thunder in the Dust—Alan LeMay	.80	2.40	4.00	W
536	Count Me In—Fan Nichols	.80	2.40	4.00	E
537	The Grim Canyon—Ernest Haycox	.80	2.40	4.00	W
538	Point of a Gun—Dean Owen	.80	2.40	4.00	W
539	Kiss Me Hard—Tom Brandt	.80	2.40	4.00	
540	My Enemy, the World—Guido D'Agostino	.80	2.40	4.00	E
541	This Heart, This Hunter—Hallie Burnett	.80	2.40	4.00	
542	The Ranger Way—Eugene Cunningham	.80	2.40	4.00	W
543	The Flesh and the Spirit—Charles Shaw; aka Heaven Knows, Mr. Allison	.80	2.40	4.00	E
544	The Mark of the Moon—Francis Gerard	3.00	9.00	15.00	E
545	The Silver Star—Jackson Gregory	.80	2.40	4.00	W
546	Hard Rock Rancher—William E. Vance	.80	2.40	4.00	W
547	Mother Finds a Body—Gypsy Rose Lee	.80	2.40	4.00	M
548	Stay Away, Joe—Dan Cushman; 1954	1.00	3.00	5.00	
549	Monkey on My Back—Wenzell Brown	1.20	3.60	6.00	E
550	Love for Lydia—H. E. Bates	.80	2.40	4.00	E
551	I Dive for Treasure—Lt. Harry E. Rieseberg	.80	2.40	4.00	A
552	High Iron—Todhunter Ballard	.80	2.40	4.00	W
553	Texas Breed—William MacLeod Raine	.80	2.40	4.00	W
554	Some Day I'll Kill You—Dana Chambers	.80	2.40	4.00	M
555	Martha Crane—Charles Gorham	.80	2.40	4.00	
556	Wilderness Rogue—Henry Schindall; aka Let the Spring Come	.80	2.40	4.00	A
557	Possessed—June Wetherell	.80	2.40	4.00	
558	The Tiger in Summer—Michael Keon	1.20	3.60	6.00	E
559	Be Happier, Be Healthier—Gaylord Hauser	.80	2.40	4.00	NF
560	Gunning for Trouble—L. L. Foreman	.80	2.40	4.00	W
561	Gunsight Trail—Alan LeMay	.80	2.40	4.00	W
562	I Take All—Robert Carson	.80	2.40	4.00	
563	A Secret Story—William Saroyan	.80	2.40	4.00	
564	The Sword of Satan—H. M. Mons	.80	2.40	4.00	A
565	The Innocent at Large—Noel Langley	.80	2.40	4.00	
566	Cradle of the Sun—John Claggett	1.00	3.00	5.00	A
567	Starlight Rider—Ernest Haycox	.80	2.40	4.00	W
568	Shortgrass—Hal G. Evarts	.80	2.40	4.00	W
569	A Private Party—William Ard	.80	2.40	4.00	E
570	The Violent Wedding—Robert Lowry	.80	2.40	4.00	
571	Isle of Demons—John Clarke Bowman	1.20	3.60	6.00	A
572	Country Girl—Richard McMullen	.80	2.40	4.00	
573	The Girl in the Spike-Heeled Shoes—Martin Yoseloff	.50	1.50	2.50	
574	Fighting Blood—Gordon Young	.80	2.40	4.00	W
575	The Texas Gun—Philip Ketchum; 1954	.80	2.40	4.00	W
576	The Dead Tree Gives No Shelter—Virgil Scott	.50	1.50	2.50	E
577	The Wire God—Jack Willard	.50	1.50	2.50	
578	Rainbow Road—Davenport Steward	.80	2.40	4.00	E
579	Are Your Troubles Psychosomatic?—J. A. Winter	.80	2.40	4.00	NF

Popular Library 566, © Poplib   Popular Library 590, © Poplib   Popular Library 592, © Poplib

(POPULAR LIBRARY, continued)

		Good	Fine	N/Mint	
580	We Burn Like Candles—Bernice Kevinoky; aka All the Young Summer Days	.80	2.40	4.00	
581	Dark Drums—Wenzell Brown	.80	2.40	4.00	E
582	Highgrader—Hal G. Evarts	.80	2.40	4.00	W
583	Rifle Pass—Dean Owen	.80	2.40	4.00	W
584	Run, Brother, Run!—Tom Brandt	.80	2.40	4.00	E
585	Rogue Wind—Ugo Moretti	.80	2.40	4.00	
586	Devil Take Her—Fan Nichols	.50	1.50	2.50	
587	Dark Streets of Paris—Jean-Louis Curtis	.80	2.40	4.00	
588	The Mountain—Henri Troyat	.50	1.50	2.50	
589	Guns Up—Ernest Haycox	.80	2.40	4.00	W
590	Gold Town Gunman—Ray Townsend; c-Saunders	1.00	3.00	5.00	W
591	No Angels for Me—William Ard	.80	2.40	4.00	
592	Teen-age Gangs—Madeline Darr & Dale Kramer	1.20	3.60	6.00	NF
593	The Gilded Hearse—Charles Gorham	.80	2.40	4.00	
594	The Brass God—Richard G. Hubler	.50	1.50	2.50	
595	Why We Behave As We Do—Frank S. Caprio	.80	2.40	4.00	NF
596	Frontier Feud—Will Cook	.80	2.40	4.00	W
597	Marshal of Sundown—Jackson Gregory	.80	2.40	4.00	W
598	The Innocent One—James Reach	.50	1.50	2.50	
599	The Night Is My Undoing—Delmar Jackson	.50	1.50	2.50	
600	The Feared and the Fearless—Guthrie Wilson	.50	1.50	2.50	C
601	The Naked Sword—Arthea Mitchell	.80	2.40	4.00	A
602	The Dim View—Basil Heatter	.80	2.40	4.00	E
603	Outlaw Brand—Parker Bonner	.80	2.40	4.00	W
604	Gun Law—Philip Ketchum	.80	2.40	4.00	W
605	Crimes of Passion—Edward D. Radin	.80	2.40	4.00	NF
606	The Departure—John Olden Sherry	.50	1.50	2.50	
607	Too Fast We Live—Richard Glendinning	.50	1.50	2.50	
608	The Wrath and the Wind—Alexander Key	.50	1.50	2.50	A
609	The Survivors—Ronald McKie	.50	1.50	2.50	
610	Bad Men and Good	.80	2.40	4.00	
611	Trail of the Damned—Jack Barton	.80	2.40	4.00	W
612	Hot Freeze—Martin Brett	.80	2.40	4.00	
613	The Eternal Galilean—Fulton J. Sheen	.50	1.50	2.50	NF
614	Mark of the Hunter—Gene Caesar	.50	1.50	2.50	
615	Give and Take—Thomas H. Raddall	.50	1.50	2.50	
616	Riders West—Ernest Haycox	.50	1.50	2.50	W
617	Rawhide Gunman—W. T. Ballard	.80	2.40	4.00	W
618	Ten Roads to Hell—Robert Travers	.80	2.40	4.00	
619	Naked to My Past—Frederic Wakeman; aka Mandrake Root	.50	1.50	2.50	
620	Everybody Slept Here—Elliott Arnold	.50	1.50	2.50	
621	Episode—Peter W. Denzer	.50	1.50	2.50	
622	The Last Princess—Charles O. Locke	.80	2.40	4.00	A
623	Renegade River—Ray Townsend	.50	1.50	2.50	W
624	Quick Triggers—Eugene Cunningham	.50	1.50	2.50	W
625	Flee the Night in Anger—Dan Keller; 1954	.50	1.50	2.50	
626	All Passion Spent—Chandler Brossard	.50	1.50	2.50	
627	The Naked Hunter—William Woolfolk	.50	1.50	2.50	
628	Cry the Lonely Flesh—Jesse L. Lasky, Jr.	.50	1.50	2.50	E
629	Friend or Foe?—Oreste Pinto	.50	1.50	2.50	
630	Smoke up the Valley—Monte Barrett	.50	1.50	2.50	W
631	Prairie Guns—Will Cook	.50	1.50	2.50	W
632	Now It's My Turn—M. E. Chaber	1.00	3.00	5.00	M
633	Hotel Room—Natalie Anderson Scott; 1955	.50	1.50	2.50	
634	Naked in the Night—Jon Cleary	.50	1.50	2.50	
635	The Wild Years—Donn O'Hara	.50	1.50	2.50	
636	Men and the Sea—Sterling Lord	.50	1.50	2.50	
637	Six-gun Ambush—Max Brand	.50	1.50	2.50	W

		Good	Fine	N/Mint	
638	Blizzard Range—W. T. Ballard	.50	1.50	2.50	W
639	Don't Come Crying to Me—William Ard	.50	1.50	2.50	
640	Kiss the Night Away—C. G. Lumbard; aka Senior Spring	.50	1.50	2.50	
641	The Naked I—Roy Chanslor	.50	1.50	2.50	
642	I'll Never Let You Go—Fan Nichols	.50	1.50	2.50	E
643	Boldness Be My Friend—Richard Pape	.50	1.50	2.50	
644	Vengeance Trail—Ernest Haycox	.50	1.50	2.50	W
645	Desperation Valley—Philip Ketchum	.50	1.50	2.50	
646	Up to Her Neck—John Newton Chance	.50	1.50	2.50	
647	Wide-Open Town—Robert F. Mirvish	.50	1.50	2.50	E
648	Naked Canvas—Warwick Scott	.50	1.50	2.50	E
649	Down the Dark Street—Siegel Fleisher	.50	1.50	2.50	
650	Fair Game—Karl Kramer; 1955	.50	1.50	2.50	
651	Apache Agent—Hal G. Evarts	.50	1.50	2.50	W
652	Fury at Painted Rock—Will Cook	.50	1.50	2.50	W
653	Down I Go—Ben Kerr	.50	1.50	2.50	E
654	The Nature of Love—H. E. Bates	.50	1.50	2.50	
655	Dream of Innocence—Turnley Walker	.50	1.50	2.50	
656	Passion Road—Richard Glendinning	.50	1.50	2.50	
657	You Belong to Me—Sam Ross	.50	1.50	2.50	
658	Desire in the Streets—Renato Cannavale	.50	1.50	2.50	
659	Brand of Fury—Jack Barton	.50	1.50	2.50	W
660	You Asked for It—Ian Fleming; aka Casino Royale	3.00	9.00	15.00	M
661	Live and Let Live—Chesley Wilson	.50	1.50	2.50	
662	Deep Is My Desire—Ian Gordon	.50	1.50	2.50	
663	Fast and Loose—Speed Lamkin	.50	1.50	2.50	
664	Night After Night—Leonard Nathan	.50	1.50	2.50	
665	Farewell, My Young Lover—Glenn Scott	.50	1.50	2.50	
666	Sundown Basin—Ray Townsend	.50	1.50	2.50	W
667	Blonde and Beautiful—Richard Foster (K. F. Crossen); orig., 1955	1.00	3.00	5.00	
668	Strip the Heart—Jacquin Sanders; aka Freakshow	.50	1.50	2.50	E
669	Sail the Dark Tide—Davenport Steward	.50	1.50	2.50	
670	The Bad One—Lowell Barrington	.50	1.50	2.50	
671	Drag Me Down—E. B. Stuart	.50	1.50	2.50	
672	A Time for Pleasure—Phyllis Hastings	.50	1.50	2.50	
673	Rider From Texas—Philip Ketchum	.50	1.50	2.50	W
674	Web of Passion—Edward D. Radin	.50	1.50	2.50	
675	Cry Hard, Cry Fast—John D. MacDonald; 1955	1.60	4.80	8.00	M
676	This Is My Night—Robert Lowry	.50	1.50	2.50	
677	Wicked We Love—Mordecai Richler	.50	1.50	2.50	
678	Bobby Sox—Marty Links	.50	1.50	2.50	H
679	Good-Time Girl—Conrad Maine	.50	1.50	2.50	
680	Trigger Trail—W. T. Ballard	.50	1.50	2.50	W
681	Don't Push Me Around—Elliott Gilbert	.50	1.50	2.50	
682	The Divine Romance—Fulton J. Sheen	.40	1.20	2.00	
683	The Valley of Love—H. E. Bates	.50	1.50	2.50	
684	Only the Brave—Allan R. Bosworth	.50	1.50	2.50	
685	The Big Rumble—Wenzell Brown	.80	2.40	4.00	
686	The Naked and the Damned—Robert Shafer; aka The Conquered Place	.50	1.50	2.50	
687	Bullet Range—Will Cook	.50	1.50	2.50	W
688	Surrender to Love—Charles Boswell & Lewis Thompson	.50	1.50	2.50	
689	The Lovers—Mitchell Wilson	.50	1.50	2.50	
690	The Long Watch—Robert F. Mirvish	.50	1.50	2.50	
691	All That Love Allows—Paul Darcy Boles	.50	1.50	2.50	
692	If You Are a Woman—Lee Graham	.50	1.50	2.50	
693	Desert Showdown—Max Brand; aka Trouble Trail	.50	1.50	2.50	W
694	Forbidden Valley—Thomas Thompson	.50	1.50	2.50	W
695	Blondes Are My Trouble—Martin Brett	.50	1.50	2.50	
696	I'll Cry Tomorrow—Lillian Roth	.50	1.50	2.50	
697	Contrary Pleasure—John D. MacDonald	1.00	3.00	5.00	
698	Oops! Wrong Party!—Syd Hoff	.50	1.50	2.50	H
699	The Whole Town Knew—Francis Irby Gwaltney	.50	1.50	2.50	
700	Secret River and the Trail of the Barefoot Pony—Ernest Haycox	.50	1.50	2.50	W
701	Trail Drive—Bill Gulick; aka A Thousand for the Caribou	.50	1.50	2.50	
702	Sweet and Low-down—Jack Waer	.50	1.50	2.50	
703	Lovers in Torment—Gordon Merrick	.50	1.50	2.50	
704	The Judas Kiss—Jay J. Dratler	.50	1.50	2.50	
705	A New Desire—Stanley Kauffmann	.50	1.50	2.50	
706	Angel Face—Fan Nichols	.50	1.50	2.50	
707	Rawhide Guns—Frank Bonham	.50	1.50	2.50	W
708	Ambush Range—Jack Barton	.50	1.50	2.50	W
709	Show No Mercy—Lindsay Hardy	.50	1.50	2.50	
710	The World in the Evening—Christopher Isherwood	.80	2.40	4.00	
711	Woman of Paris—Guy des Cars	.50	1.50	2.50	
712	Sigmund Freud for Everybody—Rachel Baker	.50	1.50	2.50	NF
713	The Fall of Night—Giose Rimanelli	.50	1.50	2.50	
714	Saddlebow Rancher—Ray Townsend	.50	1.50	2.50	W

	Good	Fine	N/Mint	
715 Guns Along the Chisholm—Will C. Brown	.50	1.50	2.50	W
716 After Dark, My Sweet—Jim Thompson; 1st ed., 1955	1.20	3.60	6.00	
717 Mistress of Rogues—Rosemond Marshall; 1956, aka The Dollmaster	.80	2.40	4.00	A
718 Carnival Girl—Richard Glendinning	.50	1.50	2.50	
719 These Women—Gregory d'Alessio	.50	1.50	2.50	
720 Come and Get Me—Johnny Laredo	.50	1.50	2.50	
721 Brothers on the Trail—Max Brand	.50	1.50	2.50	W
722 The Fighting Texan—Will Cook	.50	1.50	2.50	W
723 Mr. Trouble—William Ard	.50	1.50	2.50	
724 The Widow—Georges Simenon	.80	2.40	4.00	M
725 I'll Fix You—Hal Ellson; 1956	.50	1.50	2.50	
726 The Fugitive Romans—William Murray	.50	1.50	2.50	
727 Revolt of the Sinners—Ugo Zatterin	.50	1.50	2.50	
728 Gun Talk—Ernest Haycox	.50	1.50	2.50	W
729 The Vengeance Riders—Jack Barton	.50	1.50	2.50	W
730 My Love Is Violent—Thomas B. Dewey	.50	1.50	2.50	
731 The Searchers—Alan LeMay; movie tie-in	1.60	4.80	8.00	W
732 The Naked Hours—Wenzell Brown	.80	2.40	4.00	
733 The Double Life—Thomas Gallagher	.50	1.50	2.50	
734 The Violators—Israel Beckhardt & Wenzell Brown	.50	1.50	2.50	
735 Gunman From Texas—W. T. Ballard	.50	1.50	2.50	W
736 The Drifters—Allan R. Bosworth	.50	1.50	2.50	
737 You Live Once—John D. MacDonald	.80	2.40	4.00	M
738 The Persistant Image—Gladys Schmitt	.50	1.50	2.50	
739 Wilderness Virgin—John Clagett	.50	1.50	2.50	A
740 You've Got Me in Stitches—Lawrence Lariar	.50	1.50	2.50	
741 Ambush Rider—Hal G. Evarts	.50	1.50	2.50	W
742 Rawhide River—Cliff Farrell	.50	1.50	2.50	W
743 Jailbait—William Bernard	.80	2.40	4.00	JD
744 I'm No Good—Peter W. Denzer	.50	1.50	2.50	
745 The Pitfall—Jay J. Dratler	.50	1.50	2.50	
746 The Savage Streets—Floyd Miller	.50	1.50	2.50	
747 Wine of Desire—LaSelle Gilman	.50	1.50	2.50	
748 Trumpets to the West—Will Cook	.50	1.50	2.50	W
749 Death Cries in the Streets—Samuel A. Krasney	.50	1.50	2.50	
750 Border Town Girl—John D. MacDonald; 1956	.80	2.40	4.00	M
751 Hotel Fever—Arnold Gifford	.50	1.50	2.50	
752 Dark Night of Love—Calvin Clements	.50	1.50	2.50	
753 To Hate and to Love—Frieda K. Franklin	.50	1.50	2.50	
754 Let Me Alone—Donald Windham	.50	1.50	2.50	
755 The Mountain Men—Bill Gulick	.80	2.40	4.00	W
756 Hell Is a City—William Ard	.50	1.50	2.50	
757 Duke—Hal Ellson	.80	2.40	4.00	E
758 The Last Party—Robert Lowry	.50	1.50	2.50	
759 Fair in Love and War—Denton Whitson	.50	1.50	2.50	
760 I Get What I Want—Larry Heller	.50	1.50	2.50	
761 The Man From Missouri—Frank Gruber	.50	1.50	2.50	W
762 The Innocent and the Wicked—Phyllis Hastings	.50	1.50	2.50	
763 I Fear You Not—Ben Kerr	.50	1.50	2.50	
764 Why Johnny Can't Read—Rudolf Flesch	.40	1.20	2.00	
765 The Cruel Tower—William B. Hartley	.50	1.50	2.50	
766 Fraulein Lili Marlene—James Wakefield Burke	.50	1.50	2.50	
767 A Rider of the High Mesa—Ernest Haycox	.50	1.50	2.50	W
768 Gun in His Hand—Jack Barton	.50	1.50	2.50	W
769 Run...Run...Run...—Frank Taubes	.50	1.50	2.50	
770 The Actor—Niven Busch	.50	1.50	2.50	
771 A Night Out—Basil Heatter	.50	1.50	2.50	
772 Guns of the Lawless—W. T. Ballard	.50	1.50	2.50	W
773 Apache Ambush—Will Cook	.50	1.50	2.50	W
774 Walk a Wicked Mile—Robert P. Hansen	.50	1.50	2.50	
775 Behold This Woman—David Goodis; 1956	.80	2.40	4.00	
776 This Is It!—Hal Ellson	.50	1.50	2.50	
777 Love From France—Edna Bennett & Brant House	.50	1.50	2.50	
778 The Night Raiders—Hal G. Evarts	.50	1.50	2.50	W
779 Born to Gunsmoke—Thomas Thompson	.50	1.50	2.50	W
780 Murder Makes Me Mad—Ferguson Findley	.50	1.50	2.50	
781 Take All You Can Get—Steve Fisher	.80	2.40	4.00	
782 The Hustlers—Sam Ross	.50	1.50	2.50	
783 The Man From Idaho—Dan Temple	.50	1.50	2.50	W
784 The Return of the Rancher—Frank Austin	.50	1.50	2.50	W
785 Damned If He Does—Ben Kerr	.50	1.50	2.50	
786 Moods and Truths—Fulton J. Sheen	.40	1.20	2.00	NF
787 The Dream Peddlers—Floyd Miller	.50	1.50	2.50	
788 The Gunpointer—Dean Owen	.50	1.50	2.50	W
789 Powder Smoke—Jackson Gregory	.50	1.50	2.50	W
790 Run While You Can—William Woolfolk	.50	1.50	2.50	
791 He Walks by Night—Fan Nichols; 1957	.50	1.50	2.50	

		Good	Fine	N/Mint	
792	Ramrod—Luke Short	.50	1.50	2.50	W
793	Day of the .44—Jack Barton	.50	1.50	2.50	W
794	The Tramplers—Jason Manor	.50	1.50	2.50	
795	Marmaduke—Brad Anderson & Phil Leeming	.50	1.50	2.50	H
796	The Silver Desert—Ernest Haycox	.50	1.50	2.50	W
797	Six-gun Maverick—Philip Ketchum	.50	1.50	2.50	W
798	Spin the Glass Web—Max Ehrlich	.50	1.50	2.50	
799	Sabrina Kane—Will Cook	.50	1.50	2.50	W
800	Island of the Pit—Vincent James; 1957	.50	1.50	2.50	
801	The Jackson Trail—Max Brand	.50	1.50	2.50	W
802	Last-Chance Range—Dean Owen	.50	1.50	2.50	W
803	Club 17—Ben Kerr	.50	1.50	2.50	
804	On the Prod—Ernest Haycox	.50	1.50	2.50	W
805	Arizona Guns—William MacLeod Raine	.50	1.50	2.50	W
806	The Deadly Finger—Henry Kane	.80	2.40	4.00	M
807	The Girls From Goldfield—Jacquin Sanders	.50	1.50	2.50	
808	Fort Vengeance—Gordon D. Shirreffs	.50	1.50	2.50	W
809	My Brother's Wife—Harry Davis	.50	1.50	2.50	
810	Maverick Empire—Lewis Ford	.50	1.50	2.50	W
811	Flee From Terror—Martin Brett	.50	1.50	2.50	
812	Laugh Yourself Well—Eddie Davis	.50	1.50	2.50	H
813	Dead Man's Trail—Philip Ketchum	.50	1.50	2.50	
814	Silver Bullets—C. S. Park	.50	1.50	2.50	W
815	Swamp Fire—Don Kingery	.50	1.50	2.50	
816	And Where She Stops—Thomas B. Dewey	.50	1.50	2.50	
817	Calibre—Irving Shulman	.50	1.50	2.50	
818	Doctor Paradise—Jay J. Dratler	.50	1.50	2.50	
819	Let the Sky Fall—Roger Dee	.50	1.50	2.50	
820	Teen-age Gangs—Madeline Karr & Dale Kramer	.80	2.40	4.00	NF
821	The Whipping Boy—S. E. Pfoutz	.50	1.50	2.50	
822	Valley Vultures—Max Brand	.50	1.50	2.50	W
823	One Thing on My Mind—Herbert D. Kastle	.50	1.50	2.50	
824	A Girl, a Man and a River—John Hawkins & Ward Hawkins	.50	1.50	2.50	
825	Scandal in Troy—Eva Hemmer Hansen; 1957	.50	1.50	2.50	
826	The Mustangers—Jack Barton	.50	1.50	2.50	W
827	Lone Hand From Texas—Will Cook	.50	1.50	2.50	W
828	Sunset Strip—James Reach	.50	1.50	2.50	
829					
830	The Empty Trap—John D. MacDonald	.80	2.40	4.00	M
831	Dead Man Range—Ernest Haycox	.50	1.50	2.50	W
832	Massacre Creek—Gordon D. Shirreffs; 1958	.50	1.50	2.50	W
833	The Plundered Land—Coe Williams	.50	1.50	2.50	
834	Red Range—Eugene Cunningham	.50	1.50	2.50	W
835	The Avenging Gun—J. L. Bouma	.50	1.50	2.50	W

POPULAR LIBRARY EAGLE
Popular Library, Inc.

		Good	Fine	N/Mint	
EB 1	The Captain's Lady—Basil Heatter; 1953	.80	2.40	4.00	E
EB 2	Rustlers' Gap—William MacLeod Raine	.50	1.50	2.50	W
EB 3	Ward 20—James Warner Bellah	.50	1.50	2.50	E
EB 4	Whispering Range—Ernest Haycox	.50	1.50	2.50	W
EB 5	She'll Be Dead by Morning—Dana Chambers	.50	1.50	2.50	M
EB 6	The Loves of Lucrezia—Francesca Wright; 1954	.50	1.50	2.50	E
EB 7	Yellowstone Passage—Coe Williams	.50	1.50	2.50	W
EB 8	The Pale Blonde of Sands Street—William Chapman White	.50	1.50	2.50	
EB 9	Julia—Margot Bland	.50	1.50	2.50	
EB10	The Red Law—Jackson Gregory	.50	1.50	2.50	W
EB11	Macamba—Lilla van Saher	.50	1.50	2.50	E
EB12	Fight or Run—Giles A. Lutz	.50	1.50	2.50	W
EB13	Gentle Annie—MacKinlay Kantor	.50	1.50	2.50	W
EB14	Gunmen's Grass—Lewis Ford	.50	1.50	2.50	W
EB15	The G-String Murders—Gypsy Rose Lee	.50	1.50	2.50	M
EB16	Satan Was a Man—Edward Hale Bierstadt	.50	1.50	2.50	
EB17	Secret Valley—Jackson Gregory	.50	1.50	2.50	W
EB18	This Spring of Love—Charles Mergendahl	.50	1.50	2.50	
EB19	Desert Cache—Dave Barron	.50	1.50	2.50	
EB20	The Boat—Walter Gibson	.50	1.50	2.50	
EB21	The River Bend Feud—William MacLeod Raine	.50	1.50	2.50	W
EB22	Born of the Sun—Geoffrey Wagner	.50	1.50	2.50	
EB23	Troopers West—Forbes Parkhill	.50	1.50	2.50	W
EB24	Passion Is the Gale—Jane Winton	.50	1.50	2.50	
EB25	Trouble Trail—Coe Williams; 1954	.50	1.50	2.50	W
EB26	The Eagle and the Wind—Herbert E. Stover	.50	1.50	2.50	
EB27	Pistol Pardners—William MacLeod Raine; aka The Black Tolts	.50	1.50	2.50	W
EB28	The Tough Ones—Whit & Hallie Burnett	.80	2.40	4.00	

Popular Libr. Eagle EB19, © Poplib   Popular Libr. Eagle EB37, © Poplib   Popular Libr. Eagle EB71, © Poplib

(POPULAR LIBRARY EAGLE, continued)

		Good	Fine	N/Mint	
EB29	Danger Trail—J. L. Bouma	.50	1.50	2.50	W
EB30	I'll Get You Yet—James Howard	.50	1.50	2.50	
EB31	Six-gun Buckaroo—Clem Colt; aka Smoke Talk	.50	1.50	2.50	W
EB32	The Girl From Easy Street—Richard Foster (K. F. Crossen); orig., 1955	1.00	3.00	5.00	
EB33	Brush Rider—Dean Owen	.50	1.50	2.50	W
EB34	Too Hard to Handle—Derrick Nabarro	.50	1.50	2.50	
EB35	Drygulch Trail—William MacLeod Raine	.50	1.50	2.50	W
EB36	Tombolo—Nicholas Fersen	.50	1.50	2.50	
EB37	Outlaw River—Dan Temple; aka Missouri Passage	.50	1.50	2.50	W
EB38	That Girl on the River—Ted Fox	.50	1.50	2.50	E
EB39	Go for Your Gun—Coe Williams	.50	1.50	2.50	W
EB40	Tonight and Forever—Simon Kent	.50	1.50	2.50	
EB41	Texas Spurs—J. L. Bouma	.50	1.50	2.50	W
EB42	The Girl in the Red Jaguar—Jason Manor	.50	1.50	2.50	E
EB43	Reluctant Gunman—William MacLeod Raine	.50	1.50	2.50	W
EB44	Leave It to Me—George Joseph	.50	1.50	2.50	
EB45	Apache War Cry—William E. Vance	.50	1.50	2.50	W
EB46	I Like It Tough—James Howard	.50	1.50	2.50	
EB47	Fugitive's Canyon—Hal G. Evarts	.50	1.50	2.50	W
EB48	River of Eyes—Lawrence Earl	.50	1.50	2.50	
EB49	Gunfighter From Montana—Lewis Ford	.50	1.50	2.50	W
EB50	Don't Get in My Way—Frances Clippinger; 1955	.50	1.50	2.50	
EB51	Beyond the Rio Grande—William MacLeod Raine	.50	1.50	2.50	W
EB52	Time to Embrace—Joseph Foster	.50	1.50	2.50	
EB53	Fighting Indians of the West—David C. Cooke	.80	2.40	4.00	NF
EB54	Barbary Slave—Kevin Matthews	.80	2.40	4.00	A
EB55	Mesquire Maverick—Eugene Cunningham	.50	1.50	2.50	W
EB56	No Halo for Me—Jason Manor; 1956	.50	1.50	2.50	
EB57	Longhorn Stampede—Philip Ketchum	.50	1.50	2.50	W
EB58	Lament for a Lover—Patricia Highsmith	.80	2.40	4.00	
EB59	Six-gun Feud—William MacLeod Raine	.50	1.50	2.50	W
EB60	Storm Fear—Clinton Seeley	.50	1.50	2.50	
EB61	Border Vengeance—J. L. Bouman	.50	1.50	2.50	W
EB62	Strange Customs of Courtship and Marriage—William J. Fielding	.40	1.20	2.00	NF
EB63	Apache Crossing—Will Ermine	.50	1.50	2.50	W
EB64	The Battle Done—S. Leonard Rubinstein	.50	1.50	2.50	
EB65	The Elkhorn Feud—Philip Ketchum	.50	1.50	2.50	W
EB66	All or Nothing—Max Catto	.50	1.50	2.50	
EB67	Desert Feud—William MacLeod Raine	.50	1.50	2.50	W
EB68	Don't Say No—Olga Rosmanith	.50	1.50	2.50	
EB69	Hard Rock Town—Joseph Gage	.50	1.50	2.50	
EB70	Blow Out My Torch—James Howard	.50	1.50	2.50	
EB71	Montana Road—Harry Sinclair Drago	.50	1.50	2.50	W
EB72	Hard and Fast—U. S. Anderson	.50	1.50	2.50	
EB73	The Texas Kid—William MacLeod Raine	.50	1.50	2.50	W
EB74	Maracaibo—Sterling Silliphant	.50	1.50	2.50	
EB75	The Big Gun—Philip Ketchum; 1956	.50	1.50	2.50	
EB76	The Bed She Made—Leslie Waller	.50	1.50	2.50	E
EB77	Defiance Mountain—Frank Bonham	.50	1.50	2.50	W
EB78	Tory Mistress—Kevin Matthews	.80	2.40	4.00	A
EB79	Desert of the Damned—Nelson Nye	.50	1.50	2.50	W
EB80	Judas Journey—Lee Roberts; 1957	.50	1.50	2.50	
EB81	High Grass Valley—Wayne D. Overholser & William MacLeod Raine	.50	1.50	2.50	W
EB82	Free Ride—James M. Fox	.50	1.50	2.50	
EB83	Roundup—W. T. Ballard	.50	1.50	2.50	W
EB84	The Loving and the Daring—Francoise Mallet	.50	1.50	2.50	E
EB85	Man Without a Gun—Hal G. Evarts	.50	1.50	2.50	W
EB86	The Spoiled Children—Philippe Heriat	.50	1.50	2.50	

(POPULAR LIBRARY EAGLE, continued)		Good	Fine	N/Mint	
EB87	Burning Valley—J. L. Bouma	.50	1.50	2.50	W
EB88	Heaven Knows, Mr. Allison—Charles Shaw	.40	1.20	2.00	
EB89	Rawhide Rider—Thomas Thompson	.50	1.50	2.50	W
EB90	Die on Easy Street—James Howard	.50	1.50	2.50	
EB91	Trouble on the Brazos—Will C. Brown	.50	1.50	2.50	W
EB92	In Search of Love—William Fain	.50	1.50	2.50	
EB93	Trail Town Marshal—W. T. Ballard	.50	1.50	2.50	W
EB94	Duel in the Sun—Niven Busch	.50	1.50	2.50	W
EB95	I Am Fifteen...and I Don't Want to Die—Christine Arnothy	.50	1.50	2.50	
EB96	Just So Far—Floyd Miller	.50	1.50	2.50	
EB97	More Bobby Sox—Marty Links	.50	1.50	2.50	W
EB98	California Passage—Cliff Farrell	.50	1.50	2.50	W
EB99	Bullet Lease—Dan Temple	.50	1.50	2.50	W
EB100	Portrait of Rene—Harry Davis; 1957	.50	1.50	2.50	
EB101	Border Breed—William MacLeod Raine; 1958	.50	1.50	2.50	W
EB102	Stay Away, Joe—Dan Cushman	.50	1.50	2.50	
EB103	Hardcase Range—Jackson Gregory	.50	1.50	2.50	W
EB104	The Blonde and Johnny Malloy—Ben Kerr	.50	1.50	2.50	

POPULAR LIBRARY G - SERIES
Popular Library, Inc.

		Good	Fine	N/Mint	
G100	Sangaree—Frank G. Slaughter; 1952	.80	2.40	4.00	A
G101	The Nymph and the Lamp—Thomas H. Raddall	.80	2.40	4.00	
G102	From the Sea and the Jungle—Robert Carse	1.00	3.00	5.00	
G103	Mask of Glory—Dan Levin	.80	2.40	4.00	
G104	Savage Cavalier—Noel B. Gerson	1.00	3.00	5.00	A
G105	The Big Cage—Robert Lowry	.80	2.40	4.00	
G106	Courtroom—Quentin Reynolds	.80	2.40	4.00	
G107	The Golden Road—Peter Bourne	1.20	3.60	6.00	A
G108	Red Lion Inn—Robert Payne	.80	2.40	4.00	
G109	The Glorious Three—June Wetherell	.80	2.40	4.00	
G110	Congo Song—Stuart Cloete	1.00	3.00	5.00	E
G111	The Forsaken—Ferenc Kormendi	.80	2.40	4.00	
G112	Point Venus—Susanne McConnaughey	.80	2.40	4.00	E
G113	Marianne—Rhys Davies	.80	2.40	4.00	
G114	Find Me in Fire—Robert Lowry	.80	2.40	4.00	E
G115	The Naked Rich—Vivian Connell	.80	2.40	4.00	
G116	Sword of Fortune—Noel B. Gerson; 1953	1.20	3.60	6.00	A
G117	Angle of Attack—Joseph Landon	.80	2.40	4.00	
G118	The Forest Cavalier—Roy Flannagan	1.00	3.00	5.00	A
G119	Jasmine Street—Clifford Dowdey	.80	2.40	4.00	
G120	The City Beyond—Lucille Emerick	.80	2.40	4.00	
G121	Look Down in Mercy—Walter Baxter	.80	2.40	4.00	
G122	After the Big House—Fred Berson	.80	2.40	4.00	
G123	Charlie Dell—Anderson Wayne	.80	2.40	4.00	
G124	Afraid in the Dark—Mark Derby	.80	2.40	4.00	
G125	The Beach House—Stephen Longstreet	.80	2.40	4.00	
G126	The Big Rape—James Wakefield Burke	.80	2.40	4.00	
G127	The Scarlet Sword—H. E. Bates	.80	2.40	4.00	
G128	One Winter in Boston—Robert M. Smith	.80	2.40	4.00	
G129	Free and Easy—June Wetherell	.80	2.40	4.00	
G130	Tisa—Helga Moray	1.60	4.80	8.00	E
G131	The Gathering Darkness—Thomas Gallagher	.80	2.40	4.00	
G132	Watch for the Dawn—Stuart Cloete	.80	2.40	4.00	
G133	Three Comrades—Erich Maria Remarque; illo in *Parade of Pleasure*	.80	2.40	4.00	
G134	Whistle Stop—Maritta Wolff	.80	2.40	4.00	E
G135	When the Gods Are Silent—Mikhail Soloviev; B&W illo in *Parade of Pleasure*	.80	2.40	4.00	

Popular Library G102, © Poplib

Popular Library G107, © Poplib

Popular Library G130, © Poplib

		Good	Fine	N/Mint	
G136	Prince Bart—Jay Richard Kennedy	.80	2.40	4.00	
G137	Sun in Their Eyes—Monte Barrett	.80	2.40	4.00	W
G138	Blood Royal—Robert Payne	1.20	3.60	6.00	A
G139	Marie of the Isles—Robert Gaillard	.80	2.40	4.00	
G140	A House Is Not a Home—Polly Adler	.80	2.40	4.00	
G141	These Items of Desire—Louis A. Brennan	.80	2.40	4.00	
G142	The Hot and the Cool—Edwin Gilbert	.80	2.40	4.00	
G143	Rage to Love—Frank Tilsley	.80	2.40	4.00	
G144	The Strong Don't Cry—Estelle Slater; 1955	.80	2.40	4.00	
G145	The Flesh Is Real—Irving Shulman	.80	2.40	4.00	
G146	Rumble on the Docks—Frank Paley	1.20	3.60	6.00	
G147	This Is Temptation—James Ronald	.80	2.40	4.00	
G148	The Only Sin—Anne Powers	.80	2.40	4.00	
G149	Never Say Love—Pierre Sichel	.80	2.40	4.00	
G150	The Girl From Rome—Michel Durafour	.80	2.40	4.00	
G151	The Image and the Search—Walter Baxter	.80	2.40	4.00	
G152	The Golden Wildcat—Margaret Widdemer	.80	2.40	4.00	
G153	A Time to Love and a Time to Die—Erich Maria Remarque	.80	2.40	4.00	
G154	Many Loves Have I—William Brown Meloney	.80	2.40	4.00	
G155	The Luciano Story—Sid Feder, Joachim Joesten; 1956	1.20	3.60	6.00	NF
G156	Tomorrow!—Philip Wylie	1.60	4.80	8.00	SF
G157	The Iron Maiden—Edwin Lanham	.80	2.40	4.00	
G158	Between Darkness and Day—Gordon Merrick	.80	2.40	4.00	
G159	Louisiana Cavalier—Everett Webber	.80	2.40	4.00	
G160	The Tormented—Audrey Erskine Lindop	.80	2.40	4.00	
G161	Diversey—MacKinlay Kantor	.80	2.40	4.00	
G162	The Reckless Years—Virginia Oakey	.80	2.40	4.00	
G163	Sangaree—Frank G. Slaughter	.50	1.50	2.50	
G164	Red Carpet for Mamie Eisenhower—Alden Hatch	.50	1.50	2.50	
G165	Never Too Young—Joseph Weeks	.50	1.50	2.50	
G166	Headquarters—Quentin Reynolds	.80	2.40	4.00	
G167	A Room in Paris—Peggy Mann	.50	1.50	2.50	
G168	The Four Winds—David Beaty	.50	1.50	2.50	
G169	Captain Whitecap—John Clagett	.80	2.40	4.00	A
G170	Folies - Bergere—Paul Derval	.80	2.40	4.00	
G171	A Tale for Midnight—Frederic Prokosch	.80	2.40	4.00	
G172	The Other Side of Paradise—Paul Hyde Bonner	.80	2.40	4.00	
G173	The Night Is So Dark—Robert M. Coates	.50	1.50	2.50	
G174	Red Sky at Midnight—Robert F. Mirvish	.50	1.50	2.50	
G175	Children of the Dark—Irving Shulman; 1957	.80	2.40	4.00	
G176	Rogue Cavalier—Rosamond Marshall	.80	2.40	4.00	A
G177	Her French Husband—Phyllis Hastings	.50	1.50	2.50	
G178	Hot Winds of Summer—John H. Secondari	.50	1.50	2.50	
G179	The Wild Country—Louis Bromfield	.50	1.50	2.50	
G180	Hang My Wreath—Ward Weaver (Van Wyck Mason)	.80	2.40	4.00	
G181	Erika—James McGovern	.80	2.40	4.00	
G182	Girls on Parole—Katherine Sullivan	.80	2.40	4.00	
G183	Man of the World—Stanley Kauffmann	.50	1.50	2.50	
G184	The Last Voyage of the Lusitania—A. A. Hoehling, Mary Hoehling; (cover supposedly by Kelly Freas)	.50	1.50	2.50	NF
G185	Honey From a Dark Hive—Bernice Kavinoky	.50	1.50	2.50	
G186	The Sultan's Warrior—Bates Baldwin	.80	2.40	4.00	A
G187	The Quick and the Loving—Clifford Irving	.50	1.50	2.50	
G188	Episode in the Sun—Curry Holden	.50	1.50	2.50	
G189	All the Trumpets Sounded—W. G. Hardy	.50	1.50	2.50	
G190	Happy Marriage—John A. O'Brien	.50	1.50	2.50	
G191	Savage Cavalier—Noel B. Gerson	.50	1.50	2.50	
G192	The Sleepless Moon—H. E. Bates	.50	1.50	2.50	
G193	Keep the Aspidistra Flying—George Orwell	.50	1.50	2.50	
G194	A Cry of Children—John Horne Burns	.50	1.50	2.50	
G195	The Valley of God—Irene Patai	.50	1.50	2.50	
G196	Sisters of the Night—Jess Stearn	.50	1.50	2.50	
G197	On the Dodge—William MacLeod Raine	.50	1.50	2.50	W
G198	A House in Peking—Robert Payne	.50	1.50	2.50	
G199	The Miracle of Lourdes—Ruth Cranston	.50	1.50	2.50	
G200	Way of a Buccaneer—Davenport Steward	.80	2.40	4.00	A
G201	The Red Sands of Santa Maria—Bill Murphy	.50	1.50	2.50	
G202	Ten Days in August—Bernard Frizell	.50	1.50	2.50	
G203	Facts of Life and Love for Teenagers—Evelyn Millis Duvall	.50	1.50	2.50	NF
G204	Dust in the Sun—Jon Cleary	.50	1.50	2.50	
G205	Mamba—Stuart Cloete	.50	1.50	2.50	
G206	The Beach House—Stephen Longstreet	.50	1.50	2.50	
G207	Tempered Blade—Monte Barrett	.50	1.50	2.50	A
G208	Lady Sings the Blues—William Dufty & Billy Holiday; 1958	1.20	3.60	6.00	B
G209	Life Is Worth Living—Fulton J. Sheen	.40	1.20	2.00	
G210	Jubliee—John Brick	.50	1.50	2.50	
G211	Pitchman—Robin Moore	.50	1.50	2.50	

		Good	Fine	N/Mint	
G212	Work of Darkness—Jack Karney	.50	1.50	2.50	
G213	So Far From Spring—Peggy Simpson Curry	.50	1.50	2.50	
G214	Burmese Days—George Orwell	.50	1.50	2.50	E
G215	The Red Room—Francoise Mallet	.50	1.50	2.50	
G216	Joey Adams' Joke Book—Joey Adams	.50	1.50	2.50	H
G217	The Silver Lion—Noel B. Gerson	.50	1.50	2.50	
G218	Trouble Shooter—Ernest Haycox	.50	1.50	2.50	W
G219	Bond of the Flesh—Rosamond Marshall	.50	1.50	2.50	
G220	What's Left of April—Robert Lowry	.40	1.20	2.00	
G221	A House on the Rhine—Frances Faviell	.50	1.50	2.50	
G222	Walk Through the Valley—Borden Deal	.50	1.50	2.50	
G223	The Sheriff's Son—William MacLeod Raine	.50	1.50	2.50	W
G224	Sex Attitudes in the Home—Ralph G. Eckert	.40	1.20	2.00	NF
G225	The Hell Bent Kid—Charles O. Locke	.50	1.50	2.50	
G226	God Is Late—Christine Arnothy	.50	1.50	2.50	
G227	Pride of Innocence—David Buckley	.50	1.50	2.50	
G228	They Died in the Chair—Wenzell Brown	.50	1.50	2.50	
G229	Awake to Darkness—Richard McMullen	.50	1.50	2.50	E
G230	The Happy Valley—Max Brand	.50	1.50	2.50	W
G231	I Know My Love—Fan Nichols	.50	1.50	2.50	
G232	The Man From Yuma—Hal G. Evarts	.50	1.50	2.50	W
G233	Give Us This Day—Sidney Stewart	.50	1.50	2.50	
G234	The Priest—Joseph Caruso	.50	1.50	2.50	
G235	Six Angels at My Back—John Bell Clayton	.50	1.50	2.50	E
G236	Cry Scandal—William Ard	.50	1.50	2.50	
G237	Chaffee of Roaring Horse—Ernest Haycox	.50	1.50	2.50	W
G238	Texas Triggers—Eugene Cunningham	.50	1.50	2.50	W
G239	I Take the Rap—Gordon Shelly	.50	1.50	2.50	
G240	Gun Hand—Cliff Farrell	.50	1.50	2.50	W
G241	Don't Touch Me—MacKinlay Kantor	.50	1.50	2.50	
G242	Dream of a Woman—Jay J. Dratler	.50	1.50	2.50	
G243	Queen of the East—Alexander Baron	.80	2.40	4.00	
G244	From the Sea and the Jungle—Robert Carse	.50	1.50	2.50	
G245	Manhunt—Donald MacKenzie	.50	1.50	2.50	
G246	Man-Size—William MacLeod Raine	.50	1.50	2.50	W
G247	Showdown in the Sun—Bill Gulick	.50	1.50	2.50	W
G248	The Deadly Reasons—Edward D. Radin	.50	1.50	2.50	
G249	Saddle Tramp—W. T. Ballard	.50	1.50	2.50	W
G250	The Squirrel Cage—Edwin Gilbert	.50	1.50	2.50	
G251	Best Seller—William Murray	.50	1.50	2.50	
G252	The Kind of Guy I Am—Robert McAllister & Floyd Miller	.50	1.50	2.50	
G253	Liana—Martha Gellhorn	.50	1.50	2.50	E
G254	Trial by Fire—Charles Elliott	.50	1.50	2.50	
G255	Rawhide Gunman—W. T. Ballard	.50	1.50	2.50	W
G256	Caribbean Cavalier—Davenport Steward	.50	1.50	2.50	A
G257	The Silver Star—Jackson Gregory	.50	1.50	2.50	W
G258	The Rib of the Hawk—Rosamond Marshall	.50	1.50	2.50	
G259	The Violent Wedding—Robert Lowry	.50	1.50	2.50	
G260	Calendar Model—Gloria Gale	.50	1.50	2.50	
G261	Free Grass—Ernest Haycox	.50	1.50	2.50	W
G262	Take a Number—Armando T. Perretta	.50	1.50	2.50	
G263	Apache Agent—Hal G. Evarts	.50	1.50	2.50	W
G264	Square Shooter—William MacLeod Raine	.50	1.50	2.50	W
G265	This Is for Keeps—George Joseph	.50	1.50	2.50	
G266	Life Without Father—Muriel Resnik	.50	1.50	2.50	
G267	Painted Ponies—Alan LeMay	.50	1.50	2.50	W
G268	The Big Bubble—Theodore Pratt; c-Maguire	.50	1.50	2.50	E
G269	All for a Woman—Jay J. Dratler	.50	1.50	2.50	
G270	Dead or Alive—Max Brand	.50	1.50	2.50	W
G271	Cry Hard, Cry Fast—John D. MacDonald	.50	1.50	2.50	M
G272	Spiderweb Trail—Eugene Cunningham	.50	1.50	2.50	W
G273	The Life of All Living—Fulton J. Sheen	.50	1.50	2.50	
G274	Trouble at Moon Dance—A. B. Guthrie, Jr.	.50	1.50	2.50	W
G275	Tiger by the Tail—Charles Mergendahl	.50	1.50	2.50	
G276	Fury at Painted Rock—Will Cook	.50	1.50	2.50	W
G277	Don't Crowd Me—Evan Hunter	.50	1.50	2.50	
G278	Bullet Ambush—William MacLeod Raine	.50	1.50	2.50	W
G279	The Cut of the Ax—Delmar Jackson	.50	1.50	2.50	
G280	The Naked Rich—Vivian Connell	.50	1.50	2.50	
G281	A Strange Affair—Felix Jackson	.50	1.50	2.50	
G282	The Man Inside—M. E. Chaber	1.00	3.00	5.00	M
G283	Trail Smoke—Ernest Haycox	.50	1.50	2.50	W
G284	The Wicked Blade—Robert Carse	.50	1.50	2.50	
G285	Rage on the Bar—Geoffrey Wagner	.50	1.50	2.50	
G286	Showdown at Pistol Flat—C. S. Park	.50	1.50	2.50	W
G287	I'll Get Mine—Thurston Scott	.50	1.50	2.50	
G288	Shadow Valley—Gordon D. Shirreffs	.50	1.50	2.50	W

		Good	Fine	N/Mint	
G289	Seize the Day—Saul Bellow	.50	1.50	2.50	
G290	Naked to My Pride—Howard Rigsby	.50	1.50	2.50	
G291	The Devil Must—Tom Wicker	.50	1.50	2.50	
G292	Ramrod From Hell—Leslie Ernenwein	.50	1.50	2.50	W
G293	Woman of Egypt—Kevin Matthews	.80	2.40	4.00	A
G294	Buckaroo—Eugene Cunningham	.50	1.50	2.50	W
G295	The Tough Tenderfoot—William MacLeod Raine	.50	1.50	2.50	W
G296	The Closest Kin There Is—Clara Winston	.50	1.50	2.50	
G297	We Burn Like Candles—Bernice Kavinoky; 1959	.50	1.50	2.50	E
G298	Love Is a Four-letter Word—Anita Rowe Block	.40	1.20	2.00	E
G299	Gold in the Sky—Max Catto	.50	1.50	2.50	
G300	Lone Rider—Ernest Haycox	.50	1.50	2.50	W
G301	Boy With a Gun—James Dean Sanderson	.50	1.50	2.50	
G302	Go to Sleep, Jeannie—Thomas B. Dewey	.50	1.50	2.50	
G303	End of Track—Ward Weaver (Van Wyck Mason)	.50	1.50	2.50	W
G304	Cry, Brother, Cry—Jack Karney	.50	1.50	2.50	
G305	The River Bend Feud—William MacLeod Raine	.50	1.50	2.50	W
G306	The Staked Plain—Frank X. Tolbert	.50	1.50	2.50	W
G307	The Boy Came Back—Charles H. Knickerbocker	.50	1.50	2.50	E
G308	The Last Hero—Peter W. Denzer	.50	1.50	2.50	
G309	Trouble on the Massacre—W. T. Ballard	.50	1.50	2.50	W
G310	Time to Remember—Anderson Wayne	.50	1.50	2.50	
G311	The Losers—Clifford Irving	.50	1.50	2.50	
G312	The Last Princess—Charles O. Locke	.50	1.50	2.50	A
G313	Double Agent—Gene Stackelberg	.50	1.50	2.50	
G314	Guns of Abilene—James B. Chaffin	.50	1.50	2.50	W
G315	The Time of the Panther—Wesley Ford Davis	.50	1.50	2.50	
G316	Face of a Hero—Louis Falstein	.50	1.50	2.50	
G317	Dark Drums—Wenzell Brown	.50	1.50	2.50	E
G318	Riders West—Ernest Haycox	.50	1.50	2.50	W
G319	The Savage Affair—Virgil Scott	.50	1.50	2.50	
G320	Two-edged Vengeance—W. T. Ballard	.50	1.50	2.50	W
G321	Jailbait—William Bernard	.80	2.40	4.00	JD
G322	The Untamed Breed—Jack Barton	.50	1.50	2.50	W
G323	Beyond My Worth—Lillian Roth	.50	1.50	2.50	
G324	Breaking Point—Jacob Presser	.50	1.50	2.50	
G325	Ask for Linda—Fan Nichols	.50	1.50	2.50	E
G326	Starlight Rider—Ernest Haycox	.50	1.50	2.50	W
G327	Timbal Gulch Trail—Max Brand	.50	1.50	2.50	W
G328	A Private Party—William Ard	.50	1.50	2.50	E
G329	New York Call Girl—Robert Lowry	.50	1.50	2.50	E
G330	After Long Silence—Robert Gutwillig	.50	1.50	2.50	
G331	Bitter Fruit—Peter Packer	.50	1.50	2.50	
G332	Texas Sheriff—Eugene Cunningham	.50	1.50	2.50	W
G333	That Randall Girl—Samuel Edwards	.50	1.50	2.50	E
G334	A Secret Story—William Saroyan	.50	1.50	2.50	
G335	Showdown—W. T. Ballard & James C. Lynch	.50	1.50	2.50	W
G336	Johnny Bogan—Leonora Baccante	.50	1.50	2.50	E
G337	Decision at Piute Wells—Philip Ketchum	.50	1.50	2.50	W
G338	Blondes Die Young—Bill Peters	.50	1.50	2.50	
G339	The Young Life—Leo Townsend	.50	1.50	2.50	
G340	See How They Burn—Edwin Gilbert	.50	1.50	2.50	
G341	Cradle of the Sun—John Clagett	.50	1.50	2.50	A
G342	Prodigal Shepherd—Al Hirshberg & Robert Pfau	.50	1.50	2.50	
G343	The Texas Kid—William MacLeod Raine	.50	1.50	2.50	W
G344	The Night and the Naked—Gordon Merrick	.50	1.50	2.50	E
G345	Thunder in the Dust—Alan LeMay	.50	1.50	2.50	W
G346	I'll Get You Yet—James Howard	.50	1.50	2.50	
G347	Guns of the Tom Dee and The Valley of the Rogue—Ernest Haycox	.50	1.50	2.50	W
G348	Free and Easy—June Wetherell	.50	1.50	2.50	
G349	The Eagle and the Wind—Herbert E. Stover	.50	1.50	2.50	
G350	Ward 20—James Warner Bellah	.50	1.50	2.50	E
G351	Head of the Mountain—Ernest Haycox	.50	1.50	2.50	W
G352	The Tough Ones—Whit and Hallie Burnett	.50	1.50	2.50	
G353	Gold Town Gunman—Ray Townsend	.50	1.50	2.50	W
G354	Naked and Alone—Michael Lawrence	.50	1.50	2.50	
G355	Gun Law—Philip Ketchum	.50	1.50	2.50	W
G356	The Groves of Desire—Nathaniel Norsen Weinreb	.50	1.50	2.50	
G357	Drums of Empire—Robert Carse	.50	1.50	2.50	
G358	Duke—Hal Ellson	.80	2.40	4.00	
G359	Violent Valley—Wade Ashburn	.50	1.50	2.50	
G360	Love Is a Man's Affair—Fred Kerner	.50	1.50	2.50	
G361	Texas Breed—William MacLeod Raine	.50	1.50	2.50	W
G362	The Girl in the Red Jaguar—Jason Manor	.50	1.50	2.50	E
G363	Gunsight Trail—Alan LeMay	.50	1.50	2.50	W
G364	Good Housekeeping's the Better Way	.30	.90	1.50	NF
G365	Spring in Fialta—Vladimir Nabokov	.50	1.50	2.50	

(POPULAR LIBRARY G-SERIES, continued)

		Good	Fine	N/Mint	
G366	Danny and the Boys—Robert Travor	.50	1.50	2.50	
G367	Rawhide Range—Ernest Haycox	.50	1.50	2.50	W
G368	Julia—Margot Bland	.50	1.50	2.50	
G369	Rancher's Revenge—Max Brand	.50	1.50	2.50	W
G370	Rifle Pass—Dean Owen	.50	1.50	2.50	W
G371	Cindy and I—Joey Adams	.50	1.50	2.50	
G372	This Spring of Love—Charles Mergendahl	.50	1.50	2.50	
G373	The Sins of Maria—Bruce Cameron	.50	1.50	2.50	
G374	Pistol Pardners—William MacLeod Raine	.50	1.50	2.50	W
G375	So Strong a Flame—Bernice Kavinoky	.50	1.50	2.50	
G376	Lily and the Sergeant—Martin Yoseloff	.50	1.50	2.50	
G377	The Girls on the 10th Floor—Steve Allen	.40	1.20	2.00	
G378	Outlaw River—Dan Temple	.50	1.50	2.50	W
G379	Gentle Annie—MacKinlay Kantor	.50	1.50	2.50	W
G380	Marshal of Sundown—Jackson Gregory	.50	1.50	2.50	W
G381	Seek Out and Destroy—James D. Horan	.50	1.50	2.50	
G382	Aimee—M. L. Law	.50	1.50	2.50	E
G383	The Dr. Lewis Affair—Lane Johnstone	.50	1.50	2.50	
G384	Guadalcanal Diary—Richard Tregaskis	.40	1.20	2.00	C
G385	Country Girl—Richard McMullen	.50	1.50	2.50	E
G386	A Matter of Morals—Joseph Gies	.50	1.50	2.50	E
G387	Texas Spurs—J. L. Bouma	.50	1.50	2.50	W
G388	Brush Rider—Dean Owen	.50	1.50	2.50	W
G389	Gunfire Man—Philip Ketchum	.50	1.50	2.50	W
G390	Desert Feud—William MacLeod Raine	.50	1.50	2.50	W
G391	The Scarlet Guidon—Ray Toepfer	.50	1.50	2.50	
G392	The Living Wood—Louis de Wohl	.50	1.50	2.50	
G393	The Loves of Lucrezia—Francesca Wright	.50	1.50	2.50	
G394	Beyond the Rio Grande—William MacLeod Raine	.50	1.50	2.50	W
G395	Find Me in Fire—Robert Lowry	.50	1.50	2.50	E
G396	The Man From Texas—Jackson Gregory	.50	1.50	2.50	W
G397	Trouble Trail—Coe Williams	.50	1.50	2.50	W
G398	Six-gun Ambush—Max Brand	.50	1.50	2.50	W

POPULAR LIBRARY PC-SERIES
Popular Library, Inc.

		Good	Fine	N/Mint	
PC300	Adventures of Captain David Grief—Jack London	.50	1.50	2.50	A
PC400	Be My Guest—Conrad Hilton	.50	1.50	2.50	NF

POPULAR LIBRARY SP-SERIES
Popular Library, Inc.

		Good	Fine	N/Mint	
SP 2	The Adventures of Augie March—Saul Bellow; 1955	.50	1.50	2.50	
SP 3	Crossword Puzzles; 1956	1.20	3.60	6.00	NF
SP 4	The Doctors—Andre Soubiran	.50	1.50	2.50	
SP 5	Between Heaven and Hell—Francis Irby Gwaltney	.50	1.50	2.50	
SP 6	Auntie Mame—Patrick Dennis	.50	1.50	2.50	
SP 7	A Tree Grows in Brooklyn—Betty Smith	.50	1.50	2.50	
SP 8	Courtroom—Quentin Reynolds; 1957	.50	1.50	2.50	
SP 9	Roll Back the Sky—Ward Taylor	.50	1.50	2.50	
SP10	The Spear—Louis de Wohl	.50	1.50	2.50	
SP11	The Butchers—Leonard Bishop	.50	1.50	2.50	
SP12	Big Fella—Henry W. Clune; 1958	.50	1.50	2.50	
SP13	Onionhead—Weldon Hill	.50	1.50	2.50	H
SP14	Three Comrades—Erich Maria Remarque	.50	1.50	2.50	C
SP15	Webster's New World Dictionary of the American Language—David B. Guralnik	.40	1.20	2.00	NF
SP16	Guestward Ho!—Patrick Dennis & Barbara Hooton	.50	1.50	2.50	
SP17	The Nymph and the Lamp—Thomas H. Raddall	.50	1.50	2.50	E
SP18	Shadow of the Moon—M. M. Kaye	.50	1.50	2.50	
SP19	The Wind in His Fists—John Jennings	.50	1.50	2.50	A
SP20	The Forest Cavalier—Roy Flannagan	.50	1.50	2.50	A
SP21	A Time to Love and a Time to Die—Erich Maria Remarque	.50	1.50	2.50	C
SP22	If I Forget Thee—Robert S. de Ropp	.50	1.50	2.50	
SP23	Dream of Innocence—Turnley Walker	.50	1.50	2.50	
SP24	Lower the Angels—Walter Karig	.50	1.50	2.50	E
SP25	Tisa—Helga Moray; 1958	.50	1.50	2.50	A
SP26	Woman Surgeon—Else K. LaRoe	.50	1.50	2.50	
SP27	A Moment of Warmth—Francis Irby Gwaltney	.50	1.50	2.50	
SP28	Drums of Destiny—Peter Bourne	.50	1.50	2.50	A
SP29	Good Deeds Must Be Punished—Irving Shulman	.50	1.50	2.50	
SP30	The Philanderer—Stanley Kauffmann	.50	1.50	2.50	
SP31	The City of Libertines—W. G. Hardy	.50	1.50	2.50	
SP32	My Father - My Son—William Duffy & Edward G. Robinson, Jr.	1.20	3.60	6.00	
SP33	Marie of the Isles—Robert Gaillard	.50	1.50	2.50	

		Good	Fine	N/Mint	
SP34	Red Lion Inn—Robert Payne	.50	1.50	2.50	A
SP35	The Late Liz—Elizabeth Burns	.50	1.50	2.50	
SP36	A House Is not a Home—Polly Adler	.50	1.50	2.50	
SP37	Love for Lydia—H. E. Bates	.40	1.20	2.00	E
SP38	A Tale for Midnight—Frederic Prokosch	.50	1.50	2.50	
SP39	Whistle Stop—Maritta Wolff	.40	1.20	2.00	E
SP40	Blood Royal—Robert Payne	.50	1.50	2.50	A
SP41	Look Down in Mercy—Walter Baxter	.50	1.50	2.50	
SP42	The Good Housekeeping Book of Baby and Child Care—L. Emmett Holt, Jr.	.30	.90	1.50	NF
SP43	Rage to Love—Frank Tilsley	.40	1.20	2.00	
SP44	Dark Fury—Helga Moray	.50	1.50	2.50	
SP45	These Items of Desire—Louis A. Brennan	.50	1.50	2.50	
SP46	The Big Cage—Robert Lowry	.40	1.20	2.00	
SP47	The Strong Don't Cry—Estelle Slater	.50	1.50	2.50	
SP48	The Insider—James Kelly	.50	1.50	2.50	
SP49	Love Affair—Robert Carson	.50	1.50	2.50	E
SP50	Kingsblood Royal—Sinclair Lewis; 1959	.50	1.50	2.50	
SP51	The Greater Glory—Lester Gorn	.50	1.50	2.50	
SP52	The Golden Touch—Al Dewlen	.50	1.50	2.50	
SP53	The Great Days—John Dos Passos	.50	1.50	2.50	
SP100	Man Into Woman—Niels Hoyer	1.60	4.80	8.00	NF

POPULAR LIBRARY W-SERIES
Popular Library, Inc.

W400	I, James Dean—T. T. Thomas	1.60	4.80	8.00	
W500	Fire Down Below—Simon Kent	.50	1.50	2.50	
W600	The Treasury of Ribaldry - Volume 1—Louis Untermeyer	.50	1.50	2.50	

PREMIER BOOKS
Fawcett Publications, Inc.

S12	The Power of Positive Living—Douglas Lurton; 1955	.30	.90	1.50	NF
S13	How to Write and Speak Effective English—Edward Frank Allen	.30	.90	1.50	NF
S14	The Enjoyment of Love in Marriage—LeMon Clark	.30	.90	1.50	NF
S15	Best Quotations for All Occasions—Lewis C. Henry	.40	1.20	2.00	NF
S16	The Art of Thinking—Ernest Dimnet	.40	1.20	2.00	NF
S17	Mademoiselle de Maupin—Theophile Gautier	.40	1.20	2.00	
S18	Look Younger, Live Longer—Gaylord Hauser; 1956	.30	.90	1.50	NF
S19	The Way of Woman—Johnson E. Fairchild	.30	.90	1.50	NF
S20	Philosophy for Pleasure—Hector Hawton	.30	.90	1.50	NF
S21	The Fascinating Insect World of J. Henri Fabre—Edwin Way Teale	.40	1.20	2.00	NF
S22	Your Key to Happiness—Harold Sherman	.40	1.20	2.00	NF
d23	The Sex Life of Wild Animals—Eugene Burns	.40	1.20	2.00	NF
S24	The Strange Story of Our Earth—A. Hyatt Verrill	.40	1.20	2.00	NF
S25	My Life As an Indian—J. W. Schultz	.50	1.50	2.50	NF
S26	The Living Tide—N. S. Berrill	.30	.90	1.50	NF
S27	A Key to the Heavens—Leo Mattersdorf	.30	.90	1.50	NF
S28	The Wisdom and Ideas of Plato—David Appel & Eugene Freeman	.40	1.20	2.00	NF
S29	A Book About American History—George Stimpson	.40	1.20	2.00	NF
S30	The World's Ten Greatest Novels—W. Somerset Maugham	.40	1.20	2.00	
S31	The Benjamin Franklin Sampler	.40	1.20	2.00	
S32	American Ballads—David Jordan & Charles O'Brien Kennedy	.40	1.20	2.00	
S33	The Origin of Things—Julius E. Lips	.40	1.20	2.00	NF
d34	Abraham Lincoln—Emil Ludwig	.40	1.20	2.00	B
S35	Understanding Other People—Stuart Palmer	.40	1.20	2.00	NF
S36	Party Fun and Games—Alexander Van Rensselaer; 1956	.30	.90	1.50	NF
S37	According to Hoyle—Richard Frey	.30	.90	1.50	NF
S38	Unfaithful—Frank S. Caprio	.40	1.20	2.00	
S39	The Great Religions by Which Men Live—Tynette Hills & Floyd H. Ross	.40	1.20	2.00	NF
d40	George Washington—W. E. Woodward	.40	1.20	2.00	B
S41	The Home Book of Italian Cooking—Angela Catanzaro; 1957	.30	.90	1.50	NF
S42	How You Can Forecast the Weather—Eric Sloane	.30	.90	1.50	NF
S43	Discover Your Self!—Stephen Lackner	.30	.90	1.50	NF
S44	Animal Wonder World—Frank Lane	.40	1.20	2.00	NF
d45	Meet General Grant—W. E. Woodward	.40	1.20	2.00	B
S46	What Your Dreams Mean—Emil A. Gutheil	.40	1.20	2.00	NF
S47	Boswell's Johnson Sampler—James Boswell	.40	1.20	2.00	
S48	How to Make Psychology Work for You—Abraham P. Sperling	.30	.90	1.50	NF
S49	Crucibles: the Story of Chemistry—Bernard Jaffe	.40	1.20	2.00	NF
d50	Man's Emerging Mind—N. J. Berrill	.30	.90	1.50	NF
d51	The Miracle of Language—Charlton Laird	.30	.90	1.50	NF
d52	Understanding Human Nature—Alfred Adler	.30	.90	1.50	NF
d53	The Kipling Sampler—Rudyard Kipling	.40	1.20	2.00	

(PREMIER BOOKS, continued)

		Good	Fine	N/Mint	
d54	Shakespeare Without Tears—Margaret Webster	.30	.90	1.50	
d55	The Son of Man—Emil Ludwig	.30	.90	1.50	NF
d56	Fun With Mathematics—Jerome S. Meyer	.30	.90	1.50	NF
d57	Cure Your Nerves Yourself—Louis E. Bisch	.30	.90	1.50	NF
d58	Mirror for Man—Clyde Kluckhohn	.30	.90	1.50	NF
d59	The Practical Way to a Better Memory—Bruno Furst	.30	.90	1.50	NF
d60	They Walked With God—Michael Williams	.30	.90	1.50	NF
d61	The Living Thoughts of Thomas Jefferson	.40	1.20	2.00	
d62	Freedom From Money Worries—Martha & Price A. Patton; 1958	.30	.90	1.50	NF
d63	The Living Thoughts of Henry David Thoreau	.40	1.20	2.00	
d64	How to Understand Music—Oscar Thompson	.30	.90	1.50	NF
d65	Riddles of Science—J. Arthur Thomson	.30	.90	1.50	NF
d66	Becoming a Mother—Marvin H. Albert & T. R. Seidman	.30	.90	1.50	NF
d67	The Living Thoughts of Ralph Waldo Emerson	.40	1.20	2.00	
d68	See Without Glasses—Ralph MacFadyen	.30	.90	1.50	NF
d69	Magic, Myth and Medicine—D. T. Atkinson	.40	1.20	2.00	NF
d70	The Growth of Physical Science—James Jeans	.30	.90	1.50	NF
d71	How to Live With Yourself and Like It—Henry Clay Lindgren	.30	.90	1.50	NF
d72	The Living Thoughts of Machiavelli—Niccolo Machiavelli	.40	1.20	2.00	
d73	How to Use the Power of Prayer—Harold Sherman	.40	1.20	2.00	NF
d74	The Living Thoughts of Confucius—Confucius; 1959	.40	1.20	2.00	
d75	Philosophy for Pleasure—Hector Hawton	.30	.90	1.50	NF
d76	The Living Thoughts of Spinoza—Benedictus de Spinoza	.40	1.20	2.00	
d77	Your Key to Happiness—Harold Sherman	.30	.90	1.50	NF
d78	Understanding Other People—Stuart Palmer	.30	.90	1.50	NF
d79	The Story of America—Hendrik Willem Van Loon	.30	.90	1.50	NF
d80	You and the Universe—N. J. Berrill	.30	.90	1.50	NF
d81	Much Loved Books, Volume 1—James O'Donnell Bennett	.30	.90	1.50	
d82	The Living Thoughts of Darwin—Charles Darwin	.40	1.20	2.00	
d83	The Inhabited Universe—Derek D. Dempster & Kenneth W. Gatland	.30	.90	1.50	NF
d84	The Wisdom and Ideas of Plato—David Appel & Eugene Freeman	.40	1.20	2.00	
d85	Readings From World Religions—Selwyn Gurney Champion & Dorothy Short	.40	1.20	2.00	NF
d86	Discover Yourself—Stephen Lackner	.30	.90	1.50	NF

PRIZE
Century Publications

55	Love Business—William Arthur	1.00	3.00	5.00	E
63	The Common Passion—John Saxon	1.00	3.00	5.00	E
64	Too Loose—Carlotta Baker	1.00	3.00	5.00	E
88	Hell's Horseman—William Hopson	1.20	3.60	6.00	W

PRIZE LOVE NOVELS
Crestwood Publishing Co., Inc.

Digest Size

22	Old Man's Darling—John Saxon	1.00	3.00	5.00	R
23	Night Club Angel—Ralph Carter	1.00	3.00	5.00	E
24	Time for Love—Lee Jacquin	1.00	3.00	5.00	E
25	Passion's Prophecy—Thomas Stone	1.00	3.00	5.00	E
26	Sisters in Sin—Eliot Brewster	1.00	3.00	5.00	E
27	Skin Deep—Eliot Brewster	1.00	3.00	5.00	E
28	Love Racket	1.00	3.00	5.00	E

Prize 88, © Cen

Prize Love Novels 23, © Crest

Prize Love Novels 26, © Crest

Prize Mystery Novels 1, © Crest

Prize Mystery Novels 14, © Crest

Prize Mystery Novels 21, © Crest

PRIZE MYSTERY NOVELS
Crestwood Publishing Co., Inc.

Digest Size

		Good	Fine	N/Mint	
1	The Rose Petal Murders—Charles G. Givens; 1943	1.20	3.60	6.00	M
2	Murder on the Mike—Charles Saxby	1.20	3.60	6.00	M
4	Hot Ice—R. J. Casey	1.20	3.60	6.00	M
5	And Sudden Death—Cleve F. Adams	1.20	3.60	6.00	M
6	Fall Guy for Murder—Lawrence Goldman	1.20	3.60	6.00	M
7	The Great Insurance Murders—Milton Propper	1.20	3.60	6.00	M
8	The Station Wagon Murder—Milton Propper; 1944	1.20	3.60	6.00	M
9	The Third Owl—Robert J. Casey	1.00	3.00	5.00	M
10	Murder on Safari—Elspeth Huxley	1.20	3.60	6.00	M
11	The Frightened Girl—Michael Crombie	1.20	3.60	6.00	M
12	The Third Degree—Joe Barry	1.00	3.00	5.00	M
13	Sinner's Castle—S. Andrew Wood	1.20	3.60	6.00	M
14	The Purple Pony Murders—Sidney E. Porcelain; 1945	1.20	3.60	6.00	M
15	The Camp-Meeting Murders—Vance Randolph & Nancy Clemens	1.20	3.60	6.00	M
16	Murder Without Motive—R. L. Goldman	1.20	3.60	6.00	M
17	Invitation to Kill—Gardner Low	1.20	3.60	6.00	M
18	Out on Bail—R. L. Goldman	1.20	3.60	6.00	M
19	Murder for Breakfast—Peter Hunt	1.20	3.60	6.00	M
20	Murder Is Forgetful—William G. Bogart	1.20	3.60	6.00	M
21	The Wolf Howls Murder—Manning Lee Stokes; 1946	1.20	3.60	6.00	M
22	Message From a Corpse—Sam Merwin, Jr.	1.20	3.60	6.00	M
23	Never Say Die—M. Malmar	1.20	3.60	6.00	M
24	The Walls Came Tumbling Down—Jo Eisinger	1.20	3.60	6.00	M
25	The Thorne Theater Mystery—J. Willard	1.20	3.60	6.00	M
26	Death Dines Out—Theodora DuBois	1.00	3.00	5.00	M
27	It's My Own Funeral—Dana Lyon; 1947	1.20	3.60	6.00	M
28	Two Names for Death—E. P. Fenwick	1.20	3.60	6.00	M
29	The Straw Donkey Case—A. S. Fleischman	1.20	3.60	6.00	M
30	Major Crime—Oliver Keystone	1.20	3.60	6.00	M

PRIZE SCIENCE FICTION NOVELS
Crestwood Publishing Co., Inc.

Digest Size

Prize Mystery Novels 22, © Crest

Prize Mystery Novels 27, © Crest

Prize S/F Novels 10, © Crest

Prize S/F Novels 11, © Crest   Prize Western Novels 27, © Crest   Prize Western Novels 35, © Crest

		Good	Fine	N/Mint	
(PRIZE SCIENCE FICTION NOVELS, continued)					
10	Fight for Life—Murray Leinster	2.00	6.00	10.00	SF
11	Sojarr of Titan—Manly Wade Wellman; 1st ed., nd	2.00	6.00	10.00	SF

PRIZE WESTERN NOVELS
Crestwood Publishing Co., Inc.

Digest Size

20	Gunsmoke Over Utah	1.00	3.00	5.00	W
21	Lawless Range	1.00	3.00	5.00	W
22	Trail of Lost Men—Tex Holt	1.00	3.00	5.00	W
23	Wolf's Candle—Dane Coolidge	1.00	3.00	5.00	W
24	Thunder of Hoofs—Tex Holt	1.00	3.00	5.00	W
26	Trouble From Texas—Stuart Hardy	1.00	3.00	5.00	W
27	Silver City Rangers—Herbert Shappiro; 1948	1.00	3.00	5.00	W
29	Gunmaster of Saddleback—D. B. Newton	1.00	3.00	5.00	W
30	Smoke of the .45—Harry S. Drago	1.00	3.00	5.00	
32	Powder Smoke Blood—Clav Star	1.00	3.00	5.00	
34	Ramrod Vengeance—John Sims	1.00	3.00	5.00	W
35	Wyoming Trail—Walter A. Tompkins	1.00	3.00	5.00	W
36	Bravo Trail—Leigh Carder	1.00	3.00	5.00	W
37	Valley of Death—Burt Arthur	1.00	3.00	5.00	W
38	Yellow Dust—V. J. Hanson	1.00	3.00	5.00	W
39	Trouble Buster—Earl Sumner	1.00	3.00	5.00	W
40	Guns of Powder River—Lee Floren	1.00	3.00	5.00	W

PUTNAM
G. P. Putnams Sons

nn	This Is Nixon: The Man and His Work—James Keogh; 1956	1.20	3.60	6.00	NF

PYRAMID BOOKS
Almat Publishing Corp./Pyramid Books

NOTE: 1-10 do not exist.

11	Passionate Virgin—Perry Lindsay; 1949, aka Brief Pleasure	3.00	9.00	15.00	E
12	Reckless Passion—Gordon Sample	2.00	6.00	10.00	E
14	Blonde Mistress—Hall Bennett	2.00	6.00	10.00	E

Putnam nn, © Put   Pyramid Books 11, © Pyb   Pyramid Books 14, © Pyb

Pyramid Books 22, © Pyb   Pyramid Books 28, © Pyb   Pyramid Books 31, © Pyb

(PYRAMID BOOKS, continued)

		Good	Fine	N/Mint	
15	Palm Beach Apartment—Gail Jordan (Peggy Gaddis)	2.00	6.00	10.00	E
16	Set-up for Murder—Peter Cheyney; 1950	3.00	9.00	15.00	M
17	Tavern Girl—Glen Watkins	2.00	6.00	10.00	E
18	Shameless Honeymoon—Thomas Stone	2.00	6.00	10.00	E
19	The Moonstone—Wilkie Collins	2.00	6.00	10.00	M
20	Terror in Times Square—Alan Handley	3.00	9.00	15.00	M
21	Sin Street—Dorine Manners	2.00	6.00	10.00	E
22	The Dead Men Grin—Bruno Fischer	3.00	9.00	15.00	M
23	Cry Shame!—Katherine Everard	2.00	6.00	10.00	E
24	The Manatee—Nancy Bruff	1.60	4.80	8.00	E
25	The Orphan Outlaw—Clarence E. Mulford	2.00	6.00	10.00	W
26	Arizona Ranger—A. Scott Leslie	2.00	6.00	10.00	W
27	Sinful Cities of the Western World—Hendrik de Leeuw	2.00	6.00	10.00	E
28	The Shame of Mary Quinn—Clifton Cuthbert	2.00	6.00	10.00	E
29	Stairway to Death—Bruno Fischer	3.00	9.00	15.00	M
30	Madeleine—anonymous	1.60	4.80	8.00	E
31	Tough Town—Jack Karney; 1951, aka The Ragged Edge	1.60	4.80	8.00	E
32	The Divided Path—Nial Kent	1.60	4.80	8.00	E
33	Roadside Night—Erwin N. Nistler & Gerry P. Broderick	1.60	4.80	8.00	E
34	Rustlers' Range—Bradford Scott	1.60	4.80	8.00	W
35	French Doctor—Louis-Charles Royer	1.60	4.80	8.00	E
36	Tombstone Trail—A. Scott Leslie	1.60	4.80	8.00	W
37	Farm Girl—William Brown Meloney; aka Rusty to the Sun	2.00	6.00	10.00	E
38	The Raft—Robert Trumbull	1.60	4.80	8.00	A
39	Swamp Girl—Evans Wall	8.00	24.00	40.00	E
40	Texas Fury—Jackson Cole	1.60	4.80	8.00	W
41	The House of Madame Tellier—Guy de Maupassant; 1952	1.60	4.80	8.00	E
G42	The King's Mistress—Jean Plaidy; aka The Goldsmith's Wife	1.60	4.80	8.00	E
G43	Teen-Age Vice!—Courtney Ryley Cooper	2.00	6.00	10.00	JD
44	The Stranger in Boots—A. Scott Leslie	1.20	3.60	6.00	W
45	I Am a Fugitive From a Chain Gang—Robert E. Burns; movie tie-in	4.00	12.00	20.00	
46	23 Women—anonymous	3.00	9.00	15.00	
47	Thunder Range—Jackson Cole	1.20	3.60	6.00	W
G48	Cage of Lust—Allan Seager; aka Equinox	1.20	3.60	6.00	E
49	A Diary of Love—Maude Hutchins	1.20	3.60	6.00	E
G50	Yama, the Hell-Hole—Alexandre Kuprin; 1952	1.60	4.80	8.00	E
51	Border Hell—Jackson Cole	1.20	3.60	6.00	W
G52	Tillie—David Westheimer; 1952, aka Summer on the Water	1.20	3.60	6.00	E
53	The Bruiser—Jim Tully	1.20	3.60	6.00	
G54	Yankee Trader—Stanley Morton	1.60	4.80	8.00	E

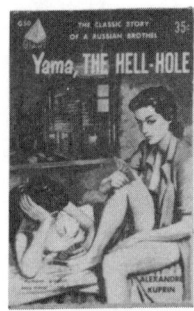

Pyramid Books 39, © Pyb   Pyramid Books G50, © Pyb   Pyramid Books G54, © Pyb

Pyramid Books 58, © Pyb

Pyramid Books G75, © Pyb

Pyramid Books 76, © Pyb

(PYRAMID BOOKS, continued)		Good	Fine	N/Mint	
55	Downfall—Bentz Plagemann	1.20	3.60	6.00	E
56	The Death Riders—Jackson Cole	1.20	3.60	6.00	W
G57	The Wild Ones—Vardis Fisher	1.20	3.60	6.00	E
58	Female Convict—as told to Vincent E. Burns	2.00	6.00	10.00	NF
G59	Sweet Man—Gilmore Millen	1.60	4.80	8.00	E
G60	Bitter Love—Dyson Taylor	1.20	3.60	6.00	E
61	The Texan—A. Scott Leslie	1.20	3.60	6.00	W
62	Let's Go Naked—ed. Don Wollheim	3.00	9.00	15.00	E
63	Apache Devil—Edwin Corle	1.60	4.80	8.00	W
G64	The Heavenly Sinner—Everett Harre	1.20	3.60	6.00	E
65	One Way Street—Nick Morino	1.20	3.60	6.00	
66	Trigger Law—Jackson Cole	1.20	3.60	6.00	W
G67	Hospital Doctor—Edward Young	1.20	3.60	6.00	E
68	Georgia Hotel—Scott Laurence	1.20	3.60	6.00	E
G69	The Brute—Guy des Cars	1.20	3.60	6.00	E
70	Massacre Canyon—Jackson Cole; 1953	1.20	3.60	6.00	W
71	A Woman of Paris—Andre Tellier	1.20	3.60	6.00	E
G72	The Dark Urge—Robert W. Taylor	1.20	3.60	6.00	E
73	Killer Country—Jackson Cole	1.20	3.60	6.00	E
74	The Come-On—Whitman Chambers	1.20	3.60	6.00	E
G75	Pirate Wench—Frank Shay; 1953	1.60	4.80	8.00	A
76	Two Years Before the Mast—Richard Henry Dana	1.60	4.80	8.00	A
G77	Stella and Joe—Lester Cohen; 1953, aka Coming Home	1.20	3.60	6.00	E
78	Blood Feud—Dave Ricks	1.20	3.60	6.00	W
79	The Heel—William L. Rohde	1.20	3.60	6.00	E
80	Beware the Lady—Cornell Woolrich; 1953, aka The Bride Wore Black	2.00	6.00	10.00	E
81	Texas Fists—Jackson Cole	1.20	3.60	6.00	W
82	Loves of Groya—Marion Chapman	1.20	3.60	6.00	E
83	The Bohemian—Jules Koslow	1.20	3.60	6.00	E
84	Love Camp—Louis-Charles Royer	3.00	9.00	15.00	E
85	Chinese Lover—Charles Pettit	2.00	6.00	10.00	E
G86	The Spitfires—Beril Becker; 1953, aka Whirlwind in Petticoats	1.20	3.60	6.00	E
87	Gun-Runners—Jackson Cole	1.20	3.60	6.00	W
G88	The Moonstone—Wilkie Collins	1.00	3.00	5.00	M
89	She-Devil—Harry Hervey	1.20	3.60	6.00	E
90	Chicago Woman—Robert O. Saber; aka The Dove	1.20	3.60	6.00	E
91	Land Grab—Jackson Cole	1.20	3.60	6.00	W
92	Road Show—Jim Tully	1.20	3.60	6.00	E
93	Houseboy—Walton Fairbanks	1.20	3.60	6.00	E
94	Sailor's Leave—Brian Moore	1.20	3.60	6.00	E

Pyramid Books 80, © Pyb

Pyramid Books 84, © Pyb

Pyramid Books G88, © Pyb

Pyramid Books 98, © Pyb   Pyramid Books 139, © Pyb   Pyramid Books 144, © Pyb

(PYRAMID BOOKS, continued)

		Good	Fine	N/Mint	
95	Showdown Trail—William Colt MacDonald; aka The Red Rider of Smoky Range	1.20	3.60	6.00	W
96	Mimi—Robert W. Taylor; 1953	1.20	3.60	6.00	E
97	The Big Fake—Murray Forbes; 1953, aka Hollow Triumph	1.00	3.00	5.00	E
98	The Sea Tyrant—Peter Freuchen	1.20	3.60	6.00	E
99	There Goes Shorty Higgins—Jack Karney	1.00	3.00	5.00	E
100	Cellini—Benvenuto Cellini; 1953	1.20	3.60	6.00	A
101	Cow Thief—William Colt MacDonald	1.20	3.60	6.00	W
102	African Mistress—Louis-Charles Royer	1.20	3.60	6.00	E
103	Backstairs—L. K. Scott	1.20	3.60	6.00	E
104	Big Mike—Charles Givens; 1953, aka Anchor Money	1.00	3.00	5.00	M
105	Lesson in Love—Emile Zola; aka Pot-Bouille	1.00	3.00	5.00	E
106	The Ordeal of Pvt. Heath—Jeb Stuart	1.00	3.00	5.00	
107	Scandal—Robert W. Taylor; orig., 1954	1.20	3.60	6.00	E
108	Texas Tornado—Jackson Cole	1.20	3.60	6.00	W
109	After Dark—Max White	1.20	3.60	6.00	E
110	The Redhead From Chicago—Louis-Charles Royer	1.20	3.60	6.00	E
111	Gun Town—Jackson Cole	1.20	3.60	6.00	W
112	Hill Man—John Garth	1.20	3.60	6.00	E
113	Sporting Lady—Gene Gauntier	1.20	3.60	6.00	E
114	The Harem—Louis-Charles Royer	1.60	4.80	8.00	E
115	Two-Gun Deputy—William Colt MacDonald	1.20	3.60	6.00	W
116	His Kind of Woman—Michael Morgan	1.20	3.60	6.00	E
117	Outlawed—Jackson Cole	1.20	3.60	6.00	W
118	Woman on the Wall—Marshall McClintock	1.20	3.60	6.00	E
119	The Great Balsamo—Maurice Zolotow	1.20	3.60	6.00	E
G120	The Counsul at Sunset—Gerald Hanley	1.00	3.00	5.00	E
121	With Sirens Screaming—Ernest Booth	1.00	3.00	5.00	E
122	I Was a Drug Addict—Leroy Street & David Loth	2.00	6.00	10.00	
123	Blind Alley—Bant Singer	1.00	3.00	5.00	E
124	Bullets High—Jackson Cole	1.00	3.00	5.00	W
125	Bold Moment—Victor H. Johnson; 1954; aka The Horncasters	1.20	3.60	6.00	E
126	The Junk Pusher—Robert W. Taylor	1.60	4.80	8.00	E
G127	Teen-Age Vice!—Courtney Ryley Cooper	1.20	3.60	6.00	NF
128	One for the Road—Robert Dietrich	1.00	3.00	5.00	E
G129	Dark Brother—Gerald Gordon	1.20	3.60	6.00	E
130	A Diary of Love—Maude Hutchins	1.00	3.00	5.00	E
131	Ex-Con—Stuart Friedman	1.00	3.00	5.00	
132	Jungle Heat—Dale Wilmer; orig., 1954	1.20	3.60	6.00	
133	Pierre's Woman—Jacques de Bout	1.00	3.00	5.00	E
134	Savage Triangle—Louis-Charles Royer	1.00	3.00	5.00	E
135	The Cheat—Robert Dietrich	1.00	3.00	5.00	E
136	Night in Manila—John Langdon	1.00	3.00	5.00	E
G137	The King's Mistress—Jean Plaidy	1.00	3.00	5.00	E
138	His Father's Wife—Day Keene; orig., 1954	1.20	3.60	6.00	E
139	I Was a House Detective—Dev Collans & Stewart Sterling; 1955	1.20	3.60	6.00	E
G140	Yankee Trader—Stanley Morton	1.00	3.00	5.00	E
G141	The Wild Ones—Vardis Fisher	1.00	3.00	5.00	E
G142	Sweet Man—Gilmore Millen	1.00	3.00	5.00	E
143	Lovers in the Sun—Robert Payne; orig., 1955	1.20	3.60	6.00	E
144	Texas Manhunt—Jackson Cole	1.00	3.00	5.00	W
G145	Cage of Lust—Allan Seager	1.00	3.00	5.00	E
G146	The Heavenly Sinner—Everett Harre	1.00	3.00	5.00	E
147	For I Have Sinned	1.00	3.00	5.00	E
148	Roadside Night—Gerry P. Broderick & Erwin N. Nistler	1.00	3.00	5.00	E
149	The Texan—A. Scott Leslie	1.00	3.00	5.00	W
G150	Devil's Cargo—Si Podolin; 1955	1.00	3.00	5.00	E
151	The Proposition—Hunt Collins	1.00	3.00	5.00	E
152	Just Married	1.00	3.00	5.00	H

		Good	Fine	N/Mint	
153	Gunsmoke Trail—Jackson Cole	1.00	3.00	5.00	W
G154	Farm Girl—William Brown Meloney	1.00	3.00	5.00	E
155	Trouble Shooter—Jackson Cole	1.00	3.00	5.00	W
156	Dangerous Game—anthology; Note: Same cover as the magazine Man's Adventure, June 1955.	1.00	3.00	5.00	A
G157	Shriek With Pleasure—Toni Howard	1.00	3.00	5.00	E
158	Diary of a Nun—Oscar de Mejo	1.00	3.00	5.00	
159	One Way Street—Nick Marino	1.00	3.00	5.00	
G160	Tell Me, Doctor—Dr. Henry B. Safford	1.00	3.00	5.00	NF
G161	Mademoiselle De Maupin—Theophile Gautier	1.00	3.00	5.00	E
162	Gun-Blaze—Jackson Cole	1.00	3.00	5.00	W
163	Bed of Hate—Si Podolin	1.00	3.00	5.00	E
164	Of a Strange Woman—James Wakefield Burke	1.00	3.00	5.00	E
165	Town Quarry—Martin Manners	1.00	3.00	5.00	E
166	French Doctor—Louis-Charles Royer	1.00	3.00	5.00	E
167	Texas Fury—Jackson Cole	1.00	3.00	5.00	W
168	Swamp Girl—Evans Wall	1.60	4.80	8.00	E
169	Shadow at Noon—Harry White (Harry Whittington)	1.20	3.60	6.00	W
G170	Strange Friends—Agnete Holk	.80	2.40	4.00	E
171	Two-Gun Devil—Jackson Cole	1.00	3.00	5.00	W
172	The Range Kid—William Colt MacDonald	1.00	3.00	5.00	W
173	Brand of Cain—Wade B. Cantrell	1.00	3.00	5.00	W
174	The Wanton Hour—Lewis Clay	.80	2.40	4.00	E
175	Madeleine—anonymous	.80	2.40	4.00	E
176	Love Off-Limits—Arthur Curtin; 1956	.80	2.40	4.00	E
G177	Pere Goriot—Honore de Balzac	.80	2.40	4.00	
178	The Texas Terror—Bradford Scott	.80	2.40	4.00	W
179	The Shame of Mary Quinn—Clifton Cuthbert	.80	2.40	4.00	E
G180	The Seed of McCoy—Jack London	1.00	3.00	5.00	A
G181	My Sister, My Bride—Merriam Modell	.80	2.40	4.00	E
182	The Owlhoot Trail—Buck Billings	.80	2.40	4.00	W
183	The World's Worst Women—Bernard O'Donnell	1.20	3.60	6.00	E
G184	A Way Home—Theodore Sturgeon (ed. by Groff Conklin)	1.20	3.60	6.00	SF
G185	The Sin Underneath—Bentz Plagemann; aka Into the Labyrinth, aka Downfall	.80	2.40	4.00	E
186	Trigger Talk—Bradford Scott	.80	2.40	4.00	
187	Gunman's Gold—Johnston McCulley	.80	2.40	4.00	W
R188	It's Never Too Late to Leave—Anna K. Daniels	.80	2.40	4.00	
G189	Shadows & Shame—John Taylor	.80	2.40	4.00	E
190	Badland's Boss—Bradford Scott	.80	2.40	4.00	W
191	Female Convict—as told to Vincent G. Burns	1.00	3.00	5.00	NF
192	Range Rebel—Gordon D. Shirreffs	.80	2.40	4.00	W
193	Taking a Turn for the Nurse—Kaz	.80	2.40	4.00	H
194	The Gunhand—Paul Evan Lehman	.80	2.40	4.00	W
195	The Six-Gun Syndicate—Norman A. Fox	.80	2.40	4.00	W
196	Let's Go Naked—ed. Donald A. Wollheim	1.20	3.60	6.00	H
G197	The Future Mr. Dolan—Charles Gorhom	.80	2.40	4.00	E
198	Hell and High Water—ed. Michael Dewell	.80	2.40	4.00	A
199	Canyon Killers—Bradford Scott	.80	2.40	4.00	W
200	The Girl on the Couch—Georgiana Hunter; 1956	.50	1.50	2.50	E
G201	Celeste—Rosamond Marshall	.50	1.50	2.50	E
R202	The House of Madame Tellier—Guy de Maupassant	.50	1.50	2.50	E
203	Lynch Law—Paul Evan	.80	2.40	4.00	W
204	The Stranger in Boots—A. Scott Leslie	.80	2.40	4.00	W
205	Playgirls, U. S. A.—Eddie Davis	.80	2.40	4.00	
G206	Creep Into Thy Narrow Bed—Leonard Bishop	.80	2.40	4.00	E
R207	Yama, the Hell-Hole—Alexandre Kuprin	.80	2.40	4.00	E
208	The Big Gun—James Cavanaugh	.80	2.40	4.00	W
209	Gunsmoke Over Texas—Bradford Scott	.80	2.40	4.00	W

Pyramid Books 156, © Pyb

Pyramid Books 183, © Pyb

Pyramid Books 209, © Pyb

(PYRAMID BOOKS, continued)		Good	Fine	N/Mint	
R210	Women and Vodka—ed. Mark Merrill	.80	2.40	4.00	E
R211	Drinkers of Darkness—Gerald Hanley	.80	2.40	4.00	E
G212	The Other Side of the Street—Shirley Jackson	1.00	3.00	5.00	
G213	The Miracle of Growth—Arnold Sundgaard	.50	1.50	2.50	NF
G214	Tomorrow and Tomorrow—Hunt Collins	1.00	3.00	5.00	SF
215	Houseboy—Walton Fairbanks	.80	2.40	4.00	E
216	Outlaw Brand—Tom West	.50	1.50	2.50	W
G217	The Man From Paris—Louis-Charles Royer	.50	1.50	2.50	E
G218	Wild Country—Noel M. Loomis	.50	1.50	2.50	E
219	The Avenger—Bradford Scott	.50	1.50	2.50	W
220	Border Blood—Bradford Scott	.50	1.50	2.50	W
221	Pyramid Crossword Book—Jack Luzzatto	1.20	3.60	6.00	NF
G222	The Jealous Mistress—Paul Elbogen	.50	1.50	2.50	E
R223	The Intimate Problems of Women—Henry B. Safford	.80	2.40	4.00	NF
G224	The Damned One—Guy des Cars	.50	1.50	2.50	E
225	A Gunman Rode North—William Hopson; 1956	.50	1.50	2.50	W
G226	Give Me a Little Something—William L. Rohde	.50	1.50	2.50	E
G227	The Love Makers—Mark Merrill	.50	1.50	2.50	E
G228	Handwriting Analysis—Dorothy Sara	.50	1.50	2.50	NF
229	Bold Moment—Victor H. Johnson; aka The Horncasters	.50	1.50	2.50	E
230	Reach for Your Guns—Curtis Bishop	.50	1.50	2.50	W
231	Flaming Lead—William Colt MacDonald	.50	1.50	2.50	W
R232	Woman Without Love—Andre Maurois	.80	2.40	4.00	E
G233	Tillie—David Westheimer	.50	1.50	2.50	E
G234	Men Against the Stars—Martin Greenberg; 1957	.80	2.40	4.00	SF
235	One for the Road—Robert Dietrich	.50	1.50	2.50	E
R236	The Hearth and the Strangeness—N. Martin Kramer	.50	1.50	2.50	E
R237	How to Help Your Husband Get Ahead—Mrs. Dale Carnegie	.40	1.20	2.00	
238	Dead Man's Trail—Bradford Scott	.50	1.50	2.50	W
G239	Feud at Five Rivers—Jack April	.50	1.50	2.50	W
G240	Sex Is Better in College—ed. Henry Boltinoff	.80	2.40	4.00	H
G241	The Night It Happened—Martin Manners	.50	1.50	2.50	E
G242	Come See Them Die—Harold Hadley	.50	1.50	2.50	
R243	Death Be Not Proud—John Gunther	.50	1.50	2.50	
G244	Gone to Texas—ed. Leo Margulies	.50	1.50	2.50	W
245	Blood Brand—Larry Lawson	.50	1.50	2.50	W
R246	Sex and Marriage—Havelock Ellis	.50	1.50	2.50	NF
G247	The Synthetic Man—Theodore Sturgeon	1.00	3.00	5.00	SF
G248	Tonight It's Me—Robert Schlick	.50	1.50	2.50	
G249	Sin Street—Dorine Manners	.50	1.50	2.50	E
250	The Gun Crasher—William L. Rohde; 1957	.50	1.50	2.50	W
251	Rimrock Raiders—Leslie Scott	.50	1.50	2.50	W
G252	Teenage Vice!—Courtney Ryley Cooper	.80	2.40	4.00	JD
G253	Unrepentant Sinners—Louis-Charles Royer	.50	1.50	2.50	
G254	The Lusty Men—William R. Cox	.50	1.50	2.50	
255	Double-Cross Ranch—Stuart Brock	.50	1.50	2.50	W
R256	Why Can't We Have a Baby?—James Henry Ferguson	.40	1.20	2.00	
R257	Crescent City—William E. Wilson	.50	1.50	2.50	
258	Powder Burn—Bradford Scott	.50	1.50	2.50	W
259	Gunhand's Play—Archie Joscelyn	.50	1.50	2.50	W
G260	The First Time—Chandler Brossard	.50	1.50	2.50	
G261	I Was a House Detective—Dev Collans & Stewart Sterling	.50	1.50	2.50	E
G262	Twilight Men—Andre Tellier	.50	1.50	2.50	
G263	Taboo—James Wakefield Burke	.80	2.40	4.00	E
264	Curse of Texas Gold—Bradford Scott	.50	1.50	2.50	W
265	Bravo Trail—Eugene Cunningham	.50	1.50	2.50	W
G266	His Father's Wife—Day Keene	.80	2.40	4.00	E
G267	The Fourth World—Daphne Athas	.50	1.50	2.50	
G268	Impossible Greeting Cards—Len Levinson	.50	1.50	2.50	
269	Gunsmoke Mesa—Dan James	.50	1.50	2.50	W
G270	Stairway to Death—Bruno Fischer	.50	1.50	2.50	M
G271	The Young Punks—ed. Leo Margulies	.80	2.40	4.00	
G272	Georgia Hotel—Scott Lawrence	.50	1.50	2.50	E
R273	Take Off Your Mask—Ludwig Eidelberg	.50	1.50	2.50	
G274	This Girl for Hire—G. G. Fickling	.80	2.40	4.00	
G275	The Fuzzy Pink Nightgown—Sylvia Tate; 1957	.50	1.50	2.50	
G276	Thunderbird Trail—William Colt MacDonald	.50	1.50	2.50	W
G277	The Law Bringers—Bliss Lomax (H. S. Drago)	.50	1.50	2.50	W
G278	Bitter Love—Dyson Taylor	.50	1.50	2.50	E
R279	Inherit the Night—Robert Christie	.50	1.50	2.50	
G280	Yellow Kid Weil—William T. Brannon	.80	2.40	4.00	B
R281	Gestapo—Edward Crankshaw	.80	2.40	4.00	
282	The Texas Hawk—Bradford Scott	.50	1.50	2.50	W
G283	V. I. P.—William L. Rohde	.50	1.50	2.50	
G284	The Name Is Chambers—Henry Kane	.80	2.40	4.00	M
G285	All His Women—Daniel Taylor	.50	1.50	2.50	
286	Two-gun Deputy—William Colt MacDonald	.50	1.50	2.50	W

(PYRAMID BOOKS, continued)		Good	Fine	N/Mint	
287	The Sheriff—Forrest Covington	.50	1.50	2.50	W
G288	Smoke Among the Plains—Vingie Roe	.50	1.50	2.50	W
R289	I Am Adam—Maxine Kaufman	.50	1.50	2.50	
R290	Frankenstein—Mary Wollstonecraft Shelley	.80	2.40	4.00	SF
G291	Isle of the Damned—George John Seaton	.80	2.40	4.00	
G292	You're Wrong, Delaney—Charles Shaw	.50	1.50	2.50	
293	Death Canyon—Bradford Scott	.50	1.50	2.50	W
294	The Range Kid—William Colt MacDonald	.50	1.50	2.50	W
G295	The Daughter—Arthur Markowitz	.50	1.50	2.50	
G296	Here's the Answer—Albert Mitchell	.50	1.50	2.50	
G297	Hospital Doctor—Edward Young	.50	1.50	2.50	E
G298	Hellflower—George O. Smith	1.00	3.00	5.00	SF
G299	Perfect 36—Ed Spingarn	.50	1.50	2.50	
R300	Michael Strogoff—Jules Verne; 1957	.50	1.50	2.50	A
G301	She-Devil—Harry Hervey	.50	1.50	2.50	E
302	Tombstone Showdown—Leslie Scott	.50	1.50	2.50	W
303	Blood-moon Range—Bob Obets	.50	1.50	2.50	W
G304	The Case of the Attic Lover—Alan Hynd	.50	1.50	2.50	
R305	Mrs. Parkington—Louis Bromfield; c-Maguire	.50	1.50	2.50	
G306	Dead Wrong—Larry Holden	.50	1.50	2.50	
307	The Hard Men—Roe Richmond; 1958, aka Riders of Red Butte	.50	1.50	2.50	W
308	Shootin' Man—Bradford Scott	.50	1.50	2.50	W
G309	Yaller Gal—Carolina Lee	.80	2.40	4.00	E
G310	The Wild Ones—Vardis Fisher	.50	1.50	2.50	E
G311	Fury With Legs—Gil Lawrence	.50	1.50	2.50	
G312	Bedlam—Andre Soubiran; c-Maguire	.50	1.50	2.50	
G313	Flame of the Osage—Fred Grove	.50	1.50	2.50	W
314	High Trail—R. D. Whitinger	.50	1.50	2.50	W
G315	City Limits—Nick Marino	.50	1.50	2.50	
R316	The Affairs of Casanova—Giacomo Casanova	.50	1.50	2.50	E
G317	French Doctor—Louis-Charles Royer	.50	1.50	2.50	E
R318	The Death of Hitler's Germany—Georges Blond	1.00	3.00	5.00	NF
319	The Blaze of Guns—Bradford Scott	.50	1.50	2.50	W
G320	Love Camp—Louis-Charles Royer	1.00	3.00	5.00	
G321	The Hills Beyond—Thomas Wolfe	.50	1.50	2.50	
G322	Twenty-one—Jack Barry	.50	1.50	2.50	
G323	Seven Days to Death—J. J. Marric	.50	1.50	2.50	M
G324	Baseball Stars of 1958—Ray Robinson	.80	2.40	4.00	S
325	Naked Spurs—Larry Lawson; 1958	.50	1.50	2.50	W
G326	House of Dolls—Ka-Tzetnik	.80	2.40	4.00	NF
G327	Take My Face—Peter Held (Jack Vance)	8.00	24.00	40.00	M
G328	The Mustard Seed—Vicki Baum	.50	1.50	2.50	
G329	Hangtree Country—Eric Allen	.50	1.50	2.50	W
R330	Hitler's Secret Service—Walter Schellenberg	1.00	3.00	5.00	NF
G331	Curve Ball Laughs—Herman L. Masin	.50	1.50	2.50	H
G332	The Skylark of Space—E. E. ''Doc'' Smith	.80	2.40	4.00	SF
333	Railtown Sheriff—Stuart Brock	.50	1.50	2.50	W
G334	The Girl on the Couch—Georgiana Hunter	.50	1.50	2.50	E
G335	Gideon's Night—J. J. Marric	.50	1.50	2.50	M
G336	Cropper's Cabin—Jim Thompson	.80	2.40	4.00	
G337	Operation Cicero—L. C. Moyzisch	.50	1.50	2.50	NF
G338	The Sleeper—Holly Roth	.50	1.50	2.50	
G339	Who?—Algis Budrys	.80	2.40	4.00	SF
R340	Brainwashing—Edward Hunter	.80	2.40	4.00	
G341	Strange Fulfillment—Denys Val Baker	.50	1.50	2.50	
G342	Never the Same Again—Gerald Tesch	.50	1.50	2.50	
G343	Bed and Broad—ed. Henry Boltinoff	.50	1.50	2.50	H
G344	A Gun for Honey—G. G. Fickling	.80	2.40	4.00	

Pyramid Books G291, © Pyb

Pyramid Books G298, © Pyb

Pyramid Books G324, © Pyb

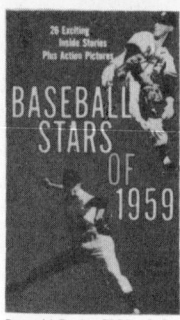

Pyramid Books G352, © Pyb   Pyramid Books G392, © Pyb   Pyramid Books G410, © Pyb

(PYRAMID BOOKS, continued)

		Good	Fine	N/Mint	
G345	Prison Girl—Wenzell Brown; c-Maguire	1.00	3.00	5.00	E
G346	Cartoons for Men Only—Sandy Nelkin	.80	2.40	4.00	H
347	The Young Texan—Paul Evan Lehman	.50	1.50	2.50	W
G348	House of Hate—W. Craig Thomas	.50	1.50	2.50	
G349	The Lost Combat—Ralph Leveridge	.50	1.50	2.50	
G350	The Name Is Malone—Craig Rice; 1958	.50	1.50	2.50	M
G351	70,000 to 1—Quentin Reynolds	.40	1.20	2.00	
G352	Rumble—Harlan Ellison; orig., 1958	10.00	30.00	50.00	JD
G353	Room to Swing—Ed Lacy; c-Maguire	.80	2.40	4.00	M
G354	Night Man—Lucille Fletcher & Allan Ullman	.50	1.50	2.50	
G355	The Case of the Nameless Corpse—Clarence Budington Kelland	.50	1.50	2.50	
G356	Lincoln's Commando—Ralph J. Roske & Charles Van Doren	.50	1.50	2.50	NF
G357	Mr. Arkadin—Orson Welles; c-Maguire	.50	1.50	2.50	
G358	Killer Colt—James Woodruff Smith	.50	1.50	2.50	W
G359	Sidewalk Caesar—Donald Honig	.50	1.50	2.50	
G360	The Megstone Plot—Andrew Garve	.50	1.50	2.50	
G361	The Scarlet Treasury of Great Confessions—Whit Burnett	.50	1.50	2.50	
G362	Good Luck to the Corpse—Max Murray	.50	1.50	2.50	M
G363	The Mad Marshal—William Colt MacDonald	.50	1.50	2.50	W
G364	The Bad Girls—Bud Clifton	.50	1.50	2.50	
G365	All Thy Conquests—Alfred Hayes	.50	1.50	2.50	
G366	Girl on the Loose—G. G. Fickling	.80	2.40	4.00	
R367	My Brother's Bride—William March	.50	1.50	2.50	
G368	The Man of Cold Rages—Jordan Park (C. M. Kornbluth)	6.00	18.00	30.00	
G369	Summer Boy—Walter Lowrey	.50	1.50	2.50	
370	Thunderbird Range—W. C. Tuttle	.50	1.50	2.50	W
G371	I Cried in the Dark—Ann Scott	.50	1.50	2.50	
G372	The Crimson in the Purple—Holly Roth; c-Maguire	.50	1.50	2.50	
G373	The Fastest Man Alive—Frank K. Everest, Jr. & John Guenther	.50	1.50	2.50	NF
G374	Death Is My Dancing Partner—Cornell Woolrich; orig., 1958	4.00	12.00	20.00	M
G375	Platoon—Adam Singer; 1958	.50	1.50	2.50	
G376	West of the Pecos—Paul Evan	.50	1.50	2.50	W
G377	Female Convict—as told to Vincent G. Burns	.80	2.40	4.00	NF
G378	An Outcast of the Islands—Joseph Conrad; orig., 1959	2.00	6.00	10.00	
G379	The Spy—Vincent Brome	.50	1.50	2.50	
G380	These Lonely, These Dead—Robert Colby	.50	1.50	2.50	
G381	The New Italian Cook Book—Rose L. Sorce	.40	1.20	2.00	NF
G382	So Soon to Die—Jeremy York	.50	1.50	2.50	
G383	The Silver Dark—Herbert Clyde Lewis	.50	1.50	2.50	
G384	Whisper of Love—Fletcher Flora	.80	2.40	4.00	
G385	The Survivor—John Ehle	.50	1.50	2.50	
G386	The Young Punks—ed. Leo Margulies	.80	2.40	4.00	
G387	The Dream and the Flesh—Vivian Connell; c-Maguire	.50	1.50	2.50	
G388	Never Smile at Children—E. T. French	.50	1.50	2.50	
389	Gallows Trail—Garth Davis	.50	1.50	2.50	W
G390	Vera—Robert Scott Taylor	.50	1.50	2.50	
G391	The Black Orchid—Edward Ronns	.50	1.50	2.50	
G392	Baseball Stars of 1959—Ray Robinson	.80	2.40	4.00	S
G393	The Lost One—Dana Lyon	.50	1.50	2.50	
394	How Sharp the Point—P. J. Wolfson; orig., 1959	.50	1.50	2.50	W
G395	So Dead, My Lovely—Day Keene; orig., 1959, c-Maguire	.80	2.40	4.00	M
396	The Longhorn Brand—Wade Hamilton	.50	1.50	2.50	W
G397	Off the Beaten Orbit—Judith Merril	.80	2.40	4.00	SF
G398	Sins of Their Fathers—Marjorie Rittwagen	.50	1.50	2.50	
G399	The Beauty Makers—Nedda Lamont	.50	1.50	2.50	
G400	The Husband—Vera Caspary; 1959	.50	1.50	2.50	
G401	Five Who Vanished—Robert Levin	.50	1.50	2.50	
G402	City of Chains—William E. Pettit	.80	2.40	4.00	

		Good	Fine	N/Mint	
403	Rimrock Renegade—Wade Hamilton	.50	1.50	2.50	W
G404	Take Off Your Mask—Ludwig Eidelberg	.50	1.50	2.50	
G405	Al Capone—John Roeburt	.80	2.40	4.00	
G406	War Fish—George Grider & Lydel Sims	.50	1.50	2.50	C
G407	The Affair—Hans Koningsberger	.50	1.50	2.50	
G408	Hilda, Take Heed—Jeremy York	.50	1.50	2.50	
409	Dead in Texas—Bradford Scott	.50	1.50	2.50	W
G410	The Power Gods—Bud Clifton	.80	2.40	4.00	JD
G411	Honey in the Flesh—G. G. Fickling	.80	2.40	4.00	
G412	The Oracle—Edwin O'Connor; c-Maguire	.50	1.50	2.50	
G413	The Shame of Mary Quinn—Clifton Cuthbert	.50	1.50	2.50	E
G414	Born Innocent—Creighton Brown-Burnham	.50	1.50	2.50	
G415	The Bride Is Much Too Beautiful—Odette Joyeux	.50	1.50	2.50	
G416	The Falling Torch—Algis Budrys	1.00	3.00	5.00	SF
G417	The Red Lily—Anatole France	.50	1.50	2.50	
R418	Five Soldiers—Paul Vialar	.50	1.50	2.50	
R419	The Divine Passion—Vardis Fisher; c-Maguire	2.00	6.00	10.00	E
420	Texas Badman—Bradford Scott	.50	1.50	2.50	W
G421	The Passionate Season—Victor Wolfson	.50	1.50	2.50	
G422	Mamma's Boarding House—John D. Fitzgerald	.50	1.50	2.50	
G423	Make Mine Love—Faber Birren	.50	1.50	2.50	
G424	The Banker's Daughter—Vladimir B. Grinioff	.50	1.50	2.50	
G425	Acts of Violence—William Kozlenko; 1959	.50	1.50	2.50	
426	The Range Terror—Bradford Scott; orig., Walt Slade western	.50	1.50	2.50	W
G427	A Really Sincere Guy—Robert Van Riper	.50	1.50	2.50	
G428	Celeste—Rosamond Marshall	.50	1.50	2.50	E
G429	Crime Cop—Larry Holden	.50	1.50	2.50	
G430	That Kind of Woman—Robert Lowry	.50	1.50	2.50	
G431	One to Grow On—Nathaniel Benchley	.50	1.50	2.50	
G432	Private Eyeful—Henry Kane; c-Maguire	.80	2.40	4.00	M
R433	10,000 Eyes—Richard Collier	.50	1.50	2.50	
G434	Four for the Future—ed. Groff Conklin	.80	2.40	4.00	SF
435	Texas Vengeance—Bradford Scott	.50	1.50	2.50	W
G436	A Diary of Love—Maude Hutchins	.50	1.50	2.50	E
G437	Slaughter Street—Louis Falstein	.50	1.50	2.50	
G438	So Love Returns—Robert Nathan	.50	1.50	2.50	
G439	The Hoods Ride In—Wenzell Brown	.80	2.40	4.00	JD
G440	No Nice Girl—Gale Wilhelm	.80	2.40	4.00	
G441	Seeds of Murder—Jeremy York	.50	1.50	2.50	
442	Gun Law—Bradford Scott	.50	1.50	2.50	W
G443	Dark Violence—Lee Bergman	.50	1.50	2.50	
G444	Cut Me In—Jack Karney	.50	1.50	2.50	
G445	But Not for Me—Edward Ronns	.50	1.50	2.50	
G446	The Magnificent Female—Cecil Saint-Laurent	.50	1.50	2.50	
R447	Leave Her to Heaven—Ben Ames Williams	.50	1.50	2.50	
G448	Dead in Bead—Day Keene; orig., 1959	1.20	3.60	6.00	M
G449	The Future Mr. Dolan—Charles Gorham	.50	1.50	2.50	
G450	Enemy in Sight—J. E. MacDonnell; 1959	.50	1.50	2.50	
G451	Guns Between Suns—William Colt MacDonald	.50	1.50	2.50	W
G452	The Divided Path—Nial Kent	.50	1.50	2.50	E
G453	Girl on the Prowl—G. G. Fickling	.80	2.40	4.00	E
454	Possessed—Anne Chamberlain	.50	1.50	2.50	
455	Holster Law—Bradford Scott; orig., 1959	.50	1.50	2.50	
G456	Hungry Men—Edward Anderson	.50	1.50	2.50	
G457	The Big Bedroom—Edward Ronns	.50	1.50	2.50	
G458	Man of Many Minds—E. Everett Evans	1.00	3.00	5.00	SF
R459	Cookbook of Fabulous Foods for People You Love—Carolyn Coggins	.40	1.20	2.00	NF
G460	Farm Girl—William Brown Meloney	.50	1.50	2.50	E

Pyramid Books R419, © Pyb

Pyramid Books G439, © Pyb

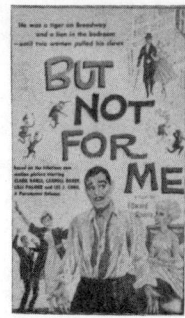

Pyramid Books G445, © Pyb

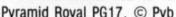

Pyramid Royal PG17, © Pyb

Quarter Books 19, © Astro

Quarter Books 39, © Astro

		Good	Fine	N/Mint	
(PYRAMID BOOKS, continued)					
G461	The Long Night—Julian Mayfield	.50	1.50	2.50	
G462	Fire in My Blood—Lady Newborough; c-Maguire	1.20	3.60	6.00	E
G463	Court Martial—Jack Ehrlich	.50	1.50	2.50	
G464	Tough Cop—John Roeburt	.50	1.50	2.50	
G465	The Loner—James Woodruff Smith	.50	1.50	2.50	
G466	Rooming House—Berton Roueche	.50	1.50	2.50	
G467	Gestapo—Edward Crankshaw	.80	2.40	4.00	
G468	The Woman Racket—Gil Lawrence	.50	1.50	2.50	
G469	Once More With Feeling	.50	1.50	2.50	

PYRAMID ROYAL
Pyramid Books

(Some Pyramid Royal editions are part of the regular Pyramid series.)

		Good	Fine	N/Mint	
PR10	The Compact Bible; 1956	.50	1.50	2.50	
PR11	The Moonstone—Wilkie Collins; 1958	.50	1.50	2.50	M
PR12	Two Years Before the Mast—Richard Henry Dana	.50	1.50	2.50	A
PG13	The Sky Block—Steve Frazee	.80	2.40	4.00	SF
PR14	I Married a Hunter—Marjorie Michael	.50	1.50	2.50	
PR15	The Lost World—Arthur Conan Doyle	.80	2.40	4.00	SF
PR16	The Scarlet Pimpernel—Baroness Orczy	.80	2.40	4.00	A
PG17	Go, Man, Go—Edgar Williams & Dave Zinkoff	.50	1.50	2.50	
PG18	Sports Laughs—Herman L. Masin	.50	1.50	2.50	H
PR19	It's Never Too Late to Love—Anna K. Daniels; 1959	.50	1.50	2.50	
PR20	The Dog Who Wouldn't Be—Farley Mowat	.50	1.50	2.50	
PR21	Pere Goriot—Honore de Balzac	.50	1.50	2.50	
PR22	The Miracle of Growth—Arnold Sundgaard	.40	1.20	2.00	NF
PR23	Handwriting Analysis—Dorothy Sara	.40	1.20	2.00	NF
PG24	Daughter of the Gold Rush—Corey Ford & Klondy Nelson	.50	1.50	2.50	
PR25	Lady Chatterley's Lover—D. H. Lawrence	.50	1.50	2.50	
PG26	At Home in India—Cynthia Bowles	.50	1.50	2.50	

PYRAMID BOOKS—R-SERIES
Pyramid Publications, Inc.

		Good	Fine	N/Mint	
R-1200	A Cellarful of Noise—Brian Epstein; 1965	3.00	9.00	15.00	NF

QUARTER BOOKS
Magazine Village, Inc./Astro Distributing Corp.

Digest Size
(See Astro)

		Good	Fine	N/Mint	
19	Bed Time Girl—James Clayford	.80	2.40	4.00	E
20	Fighting Horse Valley—Murray Leinster	2.00	6.00	10.00	W
21	Shamed—Luther Gordon; aka Made for Love, c-Rodewald	.80	2.40	4.00	E
22	Unfaithful—Luther Gordon	.80	2.40	4.00	E
23	Passion's Mistress	.80	2.40	4.00	E
24	Passion's Mistress—Luther Gordon	.80	2.40	4.00	E
25	Wanted Dead or Alive—Murray Leinster	2.00	6.00	10.00	W
26	Respectable Harlot—James Clayford; aka Unfaithful, c-Rodewald	.80	2.40	4.00	E
27	Sinful!—James Clayford; aka Love Runs Away	.80	2.40	4.00	E
28	Lure for Love—James Clayford; aka Nine O'Clock Parade, c-Gross	.80	2.40	4.00	E
29	Immoral!—Luther Gordon; aka The Naked Escape, c-Gross	.80	2.40	4.00	E
30	Marriage Can Wait	.80	2.40	4.00	E

		Good	Fine	N/Mint	
32	Careless—James Clayford	.80	2.40	4.00	E
33	Naughty Virgin—Luther Gordon; aka Women Are Freight	.80	2.40	4.00	E
34	Pleasure Girl—Luther Gordon	.80	2.40	4.00	E
35	Ecstasy—Luther Gordon	.80	2.40	4.00	E
36	Tempted—Luther Gordon; aka Pleasure Girl, c-Rodewald	.80	2.40	4.00	E
37	Love Cheat—Luther Gordon; aka Love Is No Sin, c-Gross	.80	2.40	4.00	E
38	Wolf Trap Blonde—Luther Gordon; 1949, aka Marriage Agency, c-Gross	.80	2.40	4.00	E
39	Frenchy—Harmon Bellamy	.80	2.40	4.00	E
40	Night of Passion—John Caldwell; aka Bedmates	.80	2.40	4.00	E
41	Pick-Up—Harmon Bellamy; aka Sacrifice, c-Gross	1.00	3.00	5.00	E
42	Midnight Sinner—John Caldwell	.80	2.40	4.00	E
43	Vera Is a Tramp—Gerald Foster	.80	2.40	4.00	E
44	Bad Woman—Russell Higgins; 1949	.80	2.40	4.00	E
45	Hot Number—Ross Sloane, aka Beach Brat	.80	2.40	4.00	E
46	Call Girl—Gail Jordan (Peggy Gaddis); aka Passion for Profit	.80	2.40	4.00	E
47	Sin Child—Norman Bligh; 1949	.80	2.40	4.00	E
48	As Good As Married—Perry Lindsay (Peggy Gaddis); c-Gross	.80	2.40	4.00	E
49	The Intimate Affairs of a Burlesque Queen—R. Higgins; aka Burlesque Queen	.80	2.40	4.00	E
50	Overnight Blonde—Charles E. Colohan; aka Big Blonde	.80	2.40	4.00	E
51	Wild Passion—Watkins E. Wright	.80	2.40	4.00	E
53	Virgin No More—Charles E. Colohan	.80	2.40	4.00	E
54	Illicit Desires—H. M. Appel; aka The Farmer's Daughter, c-Gross	.80	2.40	4.00	E
60	Room and Dame—Gerald Foster	.80	2.40	4.00	E
62	Everyone Loves Irene—Wright Williams; c-Gross	.80	2.40	4.00	E
63	One Night With Diane—H. Jones	.80	2.40	4.00	E
64	Bed Time Girl—James Clayford	.80	2.40	4.00	E
65	Passionate Pick-Up—Doug Duperault; c-Gross	.80	2.40	4.00	E
66	Flesh and Females—Harmon Bellamy; aka The Transgressors	.80	2.40	4.00	E
67	Shamed—Luther Gordon; aka Made for Love, c-Rodewald	.80	2.40	4.00	E
68	Marriage Can Wait—James Clayford; aka Eve in the Garden	.80	2.40	4.00	E
69	Illicit Wife—James Clayford; aka Respectable? Note: Same cover as Astro No. 15	.80	2.40	4.00	E
71	Passion's Mistress	.80	2.40	4.00	E
73	Love Life of a Hollywood Mistress—Florence Stonebraker; orig., 1950	.80	2.40	4.00	E
74	"Leg Art" Virgin—Gene Harrey; orig., 1950	.80	2.40	4.00	E
75	Sins of Allie May—Albert L. Quandt	.80	2.40	4.00	E
76	Waterfront Hotel	.80	2.40	4.00	E
77	Red-Light Babe—Doug Duperault; orig., 1950	.80	2.40	4.00	E
78	Waterfront Hotel—Norman Bligh	.80	2.40	4.00	E
79	Bad Sue—Norman Bligh	.80	2.40	4.00	E
80	Frisco Dame—Florence Stonebraker	.80	2.40	4.00	E
81	Fast, Loose, and Lovely—Norman Bligh	.80	2.40	4.00	E
82	Illicit Pleasure—Peggy Gaddis	.80	2.40	4.00	E
83	Four Men and a Dame—Florence Stonebraker	.80	2.40	4.00	E
84	Born to Be Bad	.80	2.40	4.00	E
85	The Flesh Is Weak—Florence Stonebraker	.80	2.40	4.00	E
86	Girl on the Make!—Joan Sherman (Peggy Gaddis)	.80	2.40	4.00	E
87	Ticket to Passion—Albert L. Quandt	.80	2.40	4.00	E
88	Untamed Woman—Amos Hatter	.80	2.40	4.00	E
89	The Lady Is Taboo—Norman Bligh; orig., 1951, c-Gross	.80	2.40	4.00	E
90	Flirting Eyes—Florence Stonebraker; orig., 1951	.80	2.40	4.00	E
91	Street Girl—Albert L. Quandt	.80	2.40	4.00	E
92	Three Men and a Mistress—Florence Stonebraker; c-Gross	.80	2.40	4.00	E
93	Thrill Me Suzy—Joan Sherman (Peggy Gaddis)	.80	2.40	4.00	E
94	Confessions of an Artist's Model—Norman Bligh	.80	2.40	4.00	E
95	Diary of a Pleasure Cruise—Anthony Scott; aka Stolen Sins	.80	2.40	4.00	E

QUICK READER
Royce Publishers

(3''x4¾'' small size)

		Good	Fine	N/Mint	
101	Stories of Guy de Maupassant; 1943	2.00	6.00	10.00	
102	The Killer—Stewart Edward White	2.00	6.00	10.00	
103	Nana—Emile Zola	2.00	6.00	10.00	E
104	The Chillers	3.00	9.00	15.00	
105	You'll Laugh Your Head Off	2.00	6.00	10.00	H
106	Great Short Stories—anthology	2.00	6.00	10.00	
107	The Florentine Dagger—Ben Hecht	1.60	4.80	8.00	A
108	Webster's Dictionary	1.60	4.80	8.00	NF
109	Bushido—Alexandre Pernikoff	5.00	15.00	25.00	C
110	Jane Eyre—Charlotte Bronte	2.00	6.00	10.00	
111	Here's Reading You'll Enjoy	2.00	6.00	10.00	
112	More Fun Than Looking Through a Keyhole	2.00	6.00	10.00	H
113	Murder on Shark Island—Jack DeWitt	3.00	9.00	15.00	M
114	Crime and Punishment—Fyodor Dostoyevsky	1.60	4.80	8.00	
115	How to Safeguard Your Income, Children	2.00	6.00	10.00	NF

Quick Reader 104, © Royce

Quick Reader 112, © Royce

Quick Reader 113, © Royce

(QUICK READER, continued)

		Good	Fine	N/Mint	
116	Try This for Size—anthology	2.00	6.00	10.00	
117	Count Bruga—Ben Hecht	2.00	6.00	10.00	
118	How to Tell Your Friends From the Apes—Will Cuppy	2.00	6.00	10.00	H
119	A Tale of Two Cities—Charles Dickens	2.00	6.00	10.00	
120	Time Out for Murder—Ellery Queen & others	3.00	9.00	15.00	M
121	The Curve of the Catenary—Mary Roberts Rinehart	2.00	6.00	10.00	M
122	Wuthering Heights—Emily Bronte; 1944	2.00	6.00	10.00	
123	True Murders Not Quite Solved—Alvin F. Harlow	2.00	6.00	10.00	NF
124	15 Short Short Surprise Stories—anthology	2.00	6.00	10.00	
125	Strictly on the Funny Side; 1944	2.00	6.00	10.00	H
126	Love Is a Funny Business—anthology	2.00	6.00	10.00	H
127	Celebrated Stories Made Into Movies	2.00	6.00	10.00	
128	Cat and Mouse—Hugh Pentecost	2.00	6.00	10.00	M
129	The Way of All Flesh—Samuel Butler	2.00	6.00	10.00	
130	Treasure Island—Robert Louis Stevenson	3.00	9.00	15.00	A
131	Seven Keys to Baldpate—Earl Derr Biggers; 1945	3.00	9.00	15.00	M
132	I'll Be Glad When You're Dead—Dana Lyon	2.00	6.00	10.00	M
133	Gentlemen Prefer Blondes—Anita Loos	2.00	6.00	10.00	
134	Mr. Pinkerton - Passage for One—David Frome	2.00	6.00	10.00	M
135	Humorous Ghost Stories	2.00	6.00	10.00	H
136	Gulliver's Travels—Jonathan Swift	3.00	9.00	15.00	A
137	Bedside Bedlam—anthology	2.00	6.00	10.00	H
138	Mademoiselle de Maupin—Theophile Gautier	2.00	6.00	10.00	
139	One Side Please—anthology	2.00	6.00	10.00	H
140	The Best of Edgar Allan Poe	2.00	6.00	10.00	
141	Quick Reader Bible	2.00	6.00	10.00	
142	Dr. Jekyll and Mr. Hyde—Robert Louis Stevenson	3.00	9.00	15.00	SF
143	Great Comedies Made Into Movies	2.00	6.00	10.00	
144	Unforgettable French Love Stories	2.00	6.00	10.00	
145	The Dead Man's Tale—Hugh Pentecost	2.00	6.00	10.00	M
146					
147					
148	Blind Trail at Sunrise—W. C. Tuttle	2.00	6.00	10.00	W
149	Camille—Alexandre Dumas	2.00	6.00	10.00	

QUINN
Quinn Publishing Company

Digest Size

Quick Reader 114, © Royce

Quick Reader 135, © Royce

Quinn nn, © Quinn

		Good	Fine	N/Mint	
(QUINN, continued)					
nn	The 1st World of IF—anthology	1.00	3.00	5.00	SF
nn	The 2nd World of IF—anthology	1.00	3.00	5.00	SF

RAINBOW
Magazine Productions, Inc.

Digest Size

		Good	Fine	N/Mint	
101	Thrill Girl—Gene Harvey; 1950	.80	2.40	4.00	E
102	Reno Tramp—Florence Stonebraker	.80	2.40	4.00	E
103	Wild Is the Woman—Laura Hale; orig., 1951	.80	2.40	4.00	E
104	Moment of Rapture—Jon Balmer; c-Gross	.80	2.40	4.00	E
105	Four Dames Named Sin—Mark Reed (Norman Daniels)	1.00	3.00	5.00	E
107	Street of Dark Desires—Mark Reed (Norman Daniels)	1.00	3.00	5.00	E
108	Passion Has Red Lips	.80	2.40	4.00	E
109	Her Candle Burns Hot!—Hodge Evens; 1951	.80	2.40	4.00	E
111	Walk the Evil Street—David Wade; orig., 1952	.80	2.40	4.00	E
114	Tease the Wild Flame—Mark Reed (Norman Daniels)	1.00	3.00	5.00	E
115	Carnival of Passion	.80	2.40	4.00	E
116	She Walks By Night—David Wade (Norman Daniels)	1.00	3.00	5.00	E
117	Bedroom in Hell—Norman A. Daniels	1.00	3.00	5.00	E
118	Kiss of Fire	.80	2.40	4.00	E
119	Joy Ride!—Roger Treat; c-Gross	1.00	3.00	5.00	E
120	The Nude Stranger—Mark Reed (Norman Daniels); orig., 1952	1.00	3.00	5.00	E
121	Seven Hungry Men—Lionel White; c-Gross	1.20	3.60	6.00	E
123	Vice Cop—Mark Reed (Norman Daniels)	1.00	3.00	5.00	E
124	Bedroom With a View—David Wade (Norman Daniels); orig., 1952, c-Gross	1.00	3.00	5.00	E
125	Tender Hearted Harlot—Val Munroe	.80	2.40	4.00	E
126	She Devil—Robert Turner	.80	2.40	4.00	E
127	The Big Woman—Mel Colton; orig., 1953	.80	2.40	4.00	E
128	The Twist!—Norma Dann (Norman Daniels); orig., 1953	*1.00	3.00	5.00	E
129	Only Human—David Wade (Norman Daniels); orig., 1953	1.00	3.00	5.00	E
130	Off Limits—George Bottari	.80	2.40	4.00	E

RAINBOW BOOKS
The Colonial Press, Inc.

Digest Size

		Good	Fine	N/Mint	
103	Ten Perfect Crimes—Hank Sterling; 1954	.80	2.40	4.00	NF
2	The Complete Bedside Joke Book—Howard Stackman; 1955	.80	2.40	4.00	H

READERS CHOICE LIBRARY
St. John Publishing Company

Some Digest Size

		Good	Fine	N/Mint	
nn	The Hussy—Boine Grainger	1.00	3.00	5.00	E
1	Six-Gun Law in Wrango—Frank C. Robertson; digest size	1.20	3.60	6.00	W
2	Smoky Road—Frank Gruber; digest size	1.00	3.00	5.00	W
3	Gina—George Albert Glay	1.00	3.00	5.00	M
4	The Powder Burner—Frank C. Robertson; c-Saunders	1.20	3.60	6.00	W
5	The Stranger From Texas—Allan K. Echols; digest size	1.00	3.00	5.00	W
6	Texas Lightning	1.00	3.00	5.00	W
7	Shoe the Wild Mare—Gene Fowler	1.00	3.00	5.00	W
8	Green Light for Death—Frank Kane	3.00	9.00	15.00	M
9	Smoky Joe	1.00	3.00	5.00	W

Rainbow 119, © MP

Rainbow Books 2, © CP

Readers Choice Library 1, © Stj

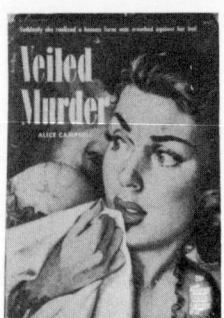

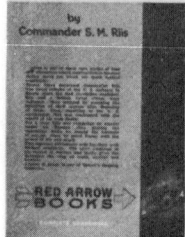

Readers Choice Library 23, © Stj   Reader's League nn, © Readers League   Red Arrow Books 7, © Red

(READERS CHOICE LIBRARY, continued)

		Good	Fine	N/Mint	
11	Stranger Than Truth—Vera Caspary	1.00	3.00	5.00	E
12	Nightmare—William Irish; aka I Wouldn't Be in Your Shoes	1.20	3.60	6.00	M
13	Western Outlaw—Frank Gruber; digest size	1.00	3.00	5.00	W
14	Trouble Shootin' Man—Frank C. Robertson; digest size	1.00	3.00	5.00	W
15	The Lock and the Key—Frank Gruber; digest size	1.00	3.00	5.00	M
16	Murder '97—Frank Gruber; digest size	1.00	3.00	5.00	M
17	Gun Crazy—Wayne D. Overholser; digest size	1.00	3.00	5.00	W
18	Bloody Saddlers—L. P. Holmes; digest size	1.00	3.00	5.00	W
19	Broken Lance—Frank Gruber; digest size	1.00	3.00	5.00	W
20	Trumpet in the Dust—Gene Fowler	1.00	3.00	5.00	E
23	Veiled Murder—Alice Campbell; digest size	1.00	3.00	5.00	M
24	Red Rustlers—Frank C. Robertson	1.00	3.00	5.00	W
25	Bonanza Queen—Zola Ross	1.00	3.00	5.00	E
27	Sinful Bargain—Michael Valbeck; aka Headlong for Heaven	1.00	3.00	5.00	E
33	Prairie Guns—E. E. Halleran; digest size	1.00	3.00	5.00	W
37	They Call It Sin—Alberta Stedman Eagan	1.00	3.00	5.00	E
38	Death Is My Lover—Stuart Brock	1.00	3.00	5.00	E
39	Lover Boy—Eric Rhodes Hayden	1.00	3.00	5.00	E

READER'S LEAGUE
Readers League of America

		Good	Fine	N/Mint	
nn	Red Harvest—Dashiell Hammett	1.60	4.80	8.00	M
nn	The Case of the Dangerous Dowager—Erle Stanley Gardner	.80	2.40	4.00	M
nn	The Four of Hearts—Ellery Queen	1.00	3.00	5.00	M
nn	Jeeves—P. G. Wodehouse	1.00	3.00	5.00	H
nn	Enter the Saint—Leslie Charteris	1.00	3.00	5.00	M
nn	The Case of the Substitute Face—Erle Stanley Gardner	.80	2.40	4.00	M
nn	The Four of Hearts—Ellery Queen	1.00	3.00	5.00	M
nn	The Pocket Entertainer; 1942	.80	2.40	4.00	NF
nn	Phantom Lady—William Irish	1.20	3.60	6.00	M
nn	The Egyptian Cross Mystery—Ellery Queen	1.00	3.00	5.00	M
nn	The Case of the Stuttering Bishop—Erle Stanley Gardner	.80	2.40	4.00	M
nn	Halfway House—Ellery Queen	1.00	3.00	5.00	M
nn	Jeeves—P. G. Wodehouse	1.00	3.00	5.00	H
nn	Topper Takes a Trip—Thorne Smith	1.00	3.00	5.00	
nn	The Chinese Parrot—Earl Derr Biggers	1.20	3.60	6.00	M
nn	The Circular Staircase—Mary Roberts Rinehart	1.00	3.00	5.00	M
nn	Abraham Lincoln—G. R. Benson	1.00	3.00	5.00	
nn	And Then There Were None—Agatha Christie	1.00	3.00	5.00	M
nn	Lost Horizon—James Hilton	1.00	3.00	5.00	
nn	Here Is Your War—Ernie Pyle	.80	2.40	4.00	
nn	Trial By Fury—Craig Rice	1.00	3.00	5.00	M

NOTE: These were special re-issues of Pocket Book titles, using the same covers and format slightly modified.

RED ARROW BOOKS
Red Arrow Books

		Good	Fine	N/Mint	
1	Thirteen at Dinner—Agatha Christie; 1939	5.00	15.00	25.00	M
2	Murder-on-Hudson—Jennifer Jones	4.00	12.00	20.00	M
3	Murders in Praed Street—John Rhode	5.00	15.00	25.00	M
4	Death in the Library—Philip Ketchum	4.00	12.00	20.00	M
5	Death Wears a White Gardenia—Zelda Popkin	4.00	12.00	20.00	M
6	My South Sea Island—Eric Musprat	4.00	12.00	20.00	
7	Yankee Komisar—Commander S. M. Riis	4.00	12.00	20.00	
8	Girl Hunt—Laurence D. Smith	4.00	12.00	20.00	
9	The Seven Sleepers—Francis Beeding	4.00	12.00	20.00	A

Red Circle 5, © Select Publs.

Red Circle 6, © Select Publs.

Red Circle 13, © Select Publs.

		Good	Fine	N/Mint	
(RED ARROW BOOKS, continued)					
10	Captain Nemesis—F. Van Wyck Mason	4.00	12.00	20.00	A
11	Windswept—Olga Moore	4.00	12.00	20.00	
12	Pirate's Purchase—Ben Ames Williams	4.00	12.00	20.00	A

RED CIRCLE
Select Publications, Inc.

(Also see Lion)

		Good	Fine	N/Mint	
1	Sex Life and You—Jules Archer & Maxine Sawyer; 1949	5.00	15.00	25.00	NF
2	Passionate Fool—John Moroso; aka Poor Passionate Fool	4.00	12.00	20.00	E
3	Leg Artist—Gene Harvey	4.00	12.00	20.00	E
4	Blonde Menace—Don Martin; aka Shed No Tears	4.00	12.00	20.00	E
5	Body or Soul—Royal Peters	4.00	12.00	20.00	E
6	Passion in the Dust—Paul Evan Lehman	3.00	9.00	15.00	W
7	Hot Date—Elliot Storm; aka Shame Girl	3.00	9.00	15.00	E
12	Why Get Married?—Token West	4.00	12.00	20.00	E
13	Carnival of Love—Anthony Scott; 1949, aka Mardi Gras Madness	4.00	12.00	20.00	E

RED DAGGER MYSTERY
Dagger House, Inc.

Digest Size

		Good	Fine	N/Mint	
21	Death for a Hussy—Allison Holt; 1946, aka Bier for a Hussy	1.20	3.60	6.00	M
23	Kill at Dusk—Philip Ketchum; 1946	1.20	3.60	6.00	M
25	Murder From the Mind—Patrick Laing; 1947	1.20	3.60	6.00	M
27	There Are Dead Men in Manhattan—John Roeburt; 1947	1.20	3.60	6.00	M
29	Blood on the Beach—H. Holley; 1947	1.20	3.60	6.00	M

RED SEAL BOOKS
Fawcett Publications, Inc.

		Good	Fine	N/Mint	
7	The Sky Tramps—Dennison O'Hara; orig., 1952	.80	2.40	4.00	E
8	Each Life to Live—Richard Gehman; orig., 1952	.80	2.40	4.00	E
9	This Woman—Albert Idell; orig., 1952	.80	2.40	4.00	E
10	Naken in the Streets—Ryerson Johnson	.80	2.40	4.00	E
11	Out of the Sea—Don Smith; orig., 1952	.80	2.40	4.00	A

Red Daggar Mystery 21, © Daggar

Red Daggar Mystery 23, © Daggar

Red Seal Books 7, © Faw

Red Seal Books 24, © Faw

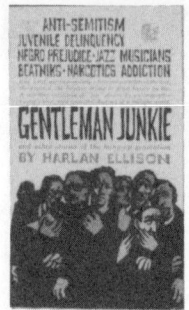

Regency RB102, © Regency Books

Regency RB118, © Regency Books

(RED SEAL BOOKS, continued)

			Good	Fine	N/Mint	
12	City of Women—Nancy Morgan; orig., 1952		1.00	3.00	5.00	E
13	The Sea Waifs—John Vail; orig., 1952		1.00	3.00	5.00	E
14	Halo for a Heel—Mike Skelly; orig., 1952		.80	2.40	4.00	E
15	Bride of the Sword—Homer Hatten		1.00	3.00	5.00	A
16	The Golden Sorrow—Theodore Pratt		.80	2.40	4.00	E
17	The Quest—O. O. Osborne; orig., 1952		.80	2.40	4.00	E
18	The Marriage Bed—H. Vernor Dixon		.80	2.40	4.00	E
19	Lili of Paris—Fay Adams; orig., 1952		.80	2.40	4.00	E
20	Girl From Town—Jack Sheridan; orig., 1952		.80	2.40	4.00	E
21	Be Still My Heart—Steve Fisher		1.00	3.00	5.00	
22	American Ballads; orig., 1952		.80	2.40	4.00	NF
23	The Magnificent Moll—John Gonzales		.80	2.40	4.00	E
24	One for Hell—Jada M. Davis		.80	2.40	4.00	E
25	Thy Name Is Woman—Hilda Van Siller; orig., 1952		1.00	3.00	5.00	E
26	This, Too, Is Love—Sam Ross		.80	2.40	4.00	E
27	Love Isn't for Now—John Vail; orig., 1953		.80	2.40	4.00	E
28	Mississippi Flame—Ryerson Johnson		.80	2.40	4.00	E
29	Fare Thee Well—Robert Spafford; orig., 1953		.80	2.40	4.00	E

REGENCY

Regency Books

		Good	Fine	N/Mint	
RB101	Firebug—Robert Bloch; orig., 1961	2.00	6.00	10.00	
RB102	Gentleman Junkie—Harlan Ellison; 1st ed., 1961	12.50	37.50	60.00	JD
RB103	Mr. Ballerina—Ronn Martin; orig., 1961	1.20	3.60	6.00	
RB104	The Brain Buyers—James Sagebiel; orig., 1961	1.20	3.60	6.00	
RB105	Divide the Night—Donald Honig; orig., 1961	1.20	3.60	6.00	
RB106	Memos From Purgatory—Harlan Ellison; 1st ed., 1961	15.00	45.00	75.00	JD
RB107	Stories by the Man Nobody Knows—B. Traven; 1st ed., 1961	2.00	6.00	10.00	
RB108	The Torment of the Kids—Hal Ellson; orig., 1961	1.60	4.80	8.00	
RB109	Weed—Clarence L. Cooper, Jr.; orig., 1961	1.60	4.80	8.00	
RB110	Some Will Not Die—Algis Budrys; orig., 1961	4.00	12.00	20.00	
RB111	What Mad Oracle?—Thomas N. Scortia; orig., 1961	3.00	9.00	15.00	
RB112	The Man in the Water—Robert Sheckley; orig., 1961	3.00	9.00	15.00	
RB113	The Eleventh Commandment—Lester Del Rey; orig., 1962	3.00	9.00	15.00	SF
RB114	Panic!—David Alexander; orig., 1962	1.20	3.60	6.00	NF
RB115	The Crooked Cops—W. T. Brannon	1.20	3.60	6.00	NF
RB116	The Dark Messenger—Clarence L. Cooper, Jr.; orig., 1962	1.20	3.60	6.00	
RB117	Muscle on Broadway—Paul B. Weston; orig., 1962	1.20	3.60	6.00	NF
RB118	Fire and the Night—Philip Jose Farmer; orig., 1962	2.00	6.00	10.00	
RB301	Philosopher of Evil/The Life and Times of the Marquis de Sade—Walter Drummond (Robert Silverberg); orig., 1962	1.60	4.80	8.00	
RB302	The Pangs of Love—ed. Chandler Brossard; 1st ed., 1962	1.60	4.80	8.00	
RB303	The Hills of Creation—Neil Elliot Blum; orig., 1962	.80	2.40	4.00	
RB304	The Hammer in the City—Paul B. Weston; orig., 1962	1.60	4.80	8.00	
RB305	Bloody Grass—Hobe Gilmore; orig., 1962	1.60	4.80	8.00	
RB306	White Man Go!—Roskolenko; orig., 1962	1.20	3.60	6.00	
RB307	In the Line of Fire—Jackson M. Bowling; orig., 1962	1.20	3.60	6.00	NF
RB308	Crimes and Chaos—Avram Davidson	3.00	9.00	15.00	
RB309	You Will Never Be the Same—Cordwainer Smith	4.00	12.00	20.00	
RB310	Damn It!—William E. Miles; orig., 1963	1.20	3.60	6.00	NF
RB311	Gilded Witch—Jack Webb; orig., 1963	1.60	4.80	8.00	
RB312	The Men of the Swastika—Hal Vetter; orig., 1963	1.20	3.60	6.00	NF
RB313	Black!—Clarence L. Cooper, Jr.; orig., 1963	1.20	3.60	6.00	
RB314	Truman and the Pendergasts—Frank Mason; orig., 1963	1.20	3.60	6.00	NF
RB315	Queen Street—Matthew Gant; orig., 1963	1.20	3.60	6.00	
RB316	Hack #777—Ed Bunin; orig., 1963	1.20	3.60	6.00	
RB317	The Rabble Rousers—Eric Frank Russell; orig., 1963	2.00	6.00	10.00	

(REGENCY, continued)	Good	Fine	N/Mint	
RB318 How to Spend Money—Walter Drummond (Robert Silverberg); orig., 1963	1.60	4.80	8.00	
RB319 KKK—Ben Haas; orig., 1963	1.20	3.60	6.00	
RB320 Hollywood, R. I. P.—I. G. Edmonds; orig., 1963	1.60	4.80	8.00	NF
RB321 The Expatriates—Mack Reynolds; orig., 1963	1.60	4.80	8.00	
RB322 The Grifters—Jim Thompson; orig., 1963	2.00	6.00	10.00	NF
RB323 Fighting Men, U. S. A.—James Warner Bellah; orig., 1963	1.20	3.60	6.00	NF
RB324 No Law But Their Own—Joe Millard; orig., 1963	1.20	3.60	6.00	NF

REGENCY SUSPENSE (See CORINTH SUSPENSE)

RETAIL DISTRIBUTORS
Retail Distributors, Inc.

		Good	Fine	N/Mint	
nn	World's Champs—Lester Bromberg; 1958	1.00	3.00	5.00	S
101	Hoodlums Los Angeles—Ted Prager & Larry Craft; 1959	1.00	3.00	5.00	NF
102	Hoodlums New York—Ted Prager & Leeds Moberley; 1959	1.00	3.00	5.00	NF

REX STOUT MYSTERY
Avon Book Company/Avon Detective-Mysteries, Inc.

Digest Size

		Good	Fine	N/Mint	
1	Includes Hammett, Stout, Christie, Steinbeck, others; 1945	4.00	12.00	20.00	M
2	Includes Hammett, Chandler, Dickson, Cain, others	3.00	9.00	15.00	M
3	Includes Hammett, Lovecraft, Irish, Carr, others; 1946	3.00	9.00	15.00	M
4	Includes Dickson, Starrett, Freeman, Blackwood, others	3.00	9.00	15.00	M
5	Includes Stout, Woolrich, Dickson, Sayers, others	3.00	9.00	15.00	M
6	Includes Bradbury, Charteris, Sayers, Ambler, others	3.00	9.00	15.00	M
7	Includes Irish, Cain, Fitzgerald, Collier, others; 1947	3.00	9.00	15.00	M
8	Includes Woolrich, Crofts, Collier, Starrett, others	3.00	9.00	15.00	M
9	Includes Boucher, Crofts, Collier, Forester, others	3.00	9.00	15.00	M

ROMANTIC NOVELS
Romantic Reprints

Digest Size

		Good	Fine	N/Mint	
nn	Dance Hall Girl—Ann Lawrence; c-Rodewald	.80	2.40	4.00	E
nn	Reckless Girl—John Saxon	.80	2.40	4.00	E
nn	Affairs of a Mistress	.80	2.40	4.00	E

ROYAL GIANT EDITION
Royal Books/Universal Publishing and Distributing Corp.

Digest Size

(Also see Universal Giant Edition)

		Good	Fine	N/Mint	
12	Jimgrim Sahib—Talbot Mundy; aka Jimgrim	3.00	9.00	15.00	A
13	Note: May not exist.				
14	Matador—Marguerite Steen	2.00	6.00	10.00	A
15	Highlights From Yank	2.00	6.00	10.00	
16	Stalingrad—Theodor Plievier	2.00	6.00	10.00	C
17	The Other Stranger—Daoma Winston; orig., 1953				E
	Adam and Two Eves—anonymous	2.00	6.00	10.00	E

Retail Distributors nn, © Retail

Rex Stout Mystery 2, © Avon

Romantic Novels nn, © Romantic Rprts.

Royal Giant Edition 19, © Univ   Royal Giant Edition 22, © Univ   Royal Giant Edition 26, © Univ

		Good	Fine	N/Mint	
(ROYAL GIANT EDITION, continued)					
18	Allan Quatermain—H. Rider Haggard				A
	King Solomon's Mines—H. Rider Haggard	3.00	9.00	15.00	A
19	Trek East—Talbot Mundy; aka The Ivory Trail	3.00	9.00	15.00	A
20	Full Moon—Talbot Mundy				A
	High Priest of California—Charles Willeford; orig., 1953	3.00	9.00	15.00	E
21	Highway Episode—George Weller; aka Clutch and Differential	2.00	6.00	10.00	E
22	Gonzaga's Woman—John Jakes; orig., 1953				E
	Affair in Araby—Talbot Mundy; aka The King in Check	3.00	9.00	15.00	A
23	The Case of Sergeant Grischa—Arnold Zweig	2.00	6.00	10.00	C
24	Roxana—Daniel Defoe	2.00	6.00	10.00	E
25	Mademoiselle De Maupin—Theophile Gautier				E
	Candide—Voltaire	2.00	6.00	10.00	E
26	The Harem of Hsi Men—anthology	5.00	15.00	25.00	E
27	Confessions of a Psychiatrist—Henry Lewis Nixon; orig., 1954				E
	The Woman He Wanted—Daoma Winston; orig., 1954	3.00	9.00	15.00	E
28	The Unnatural Son—Mark Twain; aka Puddnhead Wilson				A
	A Connecticut Yankee in King Arthur's Court—Mark Twain	2.00	6.00	10.00	F
29	The Way of All Flesh—Samuel Butler	2.00	6.00	10.00	E

RUTLEDGE BOOKS
Scholastic Book Services

Digest Size

		Good	Fine	N/Mint	
RP10	The Buccaneer—Iris Vinton; 1959, movie tie-in	.80	2.40	4.00	A

R. W.
The R. W. Company

Digest Size

		Good	Fine	N/Mint	
nn	The Vice Czar Murders—Franklin Charles	.80	2.40	4.00	M

SAINT MYSTERY LIBRARY
Great American Publications, Inc.

		Good	Fine	N/Mint	
118	Stairway to Murder—Leslie Charteris; 1959	1.20	3.60	6.00	M
119	Witness to Death—Leslie Charteris	1.20	3.60	6.00	M
120	Murder Set to Music—Leslie Charteris; title story by Fredric Brown	2.00	6.00	10.00	M

Rutledge Books RP10, © SB   R. W. nn, © R. W. Co.   Saint Mystery Library 120, © Great

		Good	Fine	N/Mint	
121	The Frightened Millionaire—Leslie Charteris	1.20	3.60	6.00	M
122	Murder Made in Moscow—Leslie Charteris; title story by Baynard Kendrick	1.20	3.60	6.00	M
123	Murder in the Family—Leslie Charteris	1.20	3.60	6.00	M
124	Death Stops at a Tourist Camp—Leslie Charteris	1.20	3.60	6.00	M
125	Red Snow in Darjeeling—Leslie Charteris; title story by Lawrence G. Blochman	1.20	3.60	6.00	M
126	Executioner's Signature—Leslie Charteris; 1960	1.20	3.60	6.00	M
127	Murder Seeks an Agent—Leslie Charteris; title story by Wenzell Brown	1.20	3.60	6.00	M
128	Let Her Kill Herself—Leslie Charteris	1.20	3.60	6.00	M
129	Innocent Bystander—Craig Rice	1.20	3.60	6.00	M
130	Death Walks in Marble Halls—Leslie Charteris; title story by Lawrence G. Blochman	1.20	3.60	6.00	M
131	Rum and Cocoa Murders—Leslie Charteris; title story by Wenzell Brown	1.00	3.00	5.00	M

SCIENCE SERVICE
Science Service

		Good	Fine	N/Mint	
nn	Science From Shipboard; 1943	.80	2.40	4.00	NF

SHOOTING SCRIPT
Catholic Digest/Catechetical Guild

		Good	Fine	N/Mint	
nn	Guilty of Treason—Emmet Lavery; 1950, movie tie-in	1.60	4.80	8.00	

SIGNET
New American Library of World Literature, Inc.

(Also see Penguin; some issued as Penguin Signet)

		Good	Fine	N/Mint	
660	100 American Poems—Selden Rodman; 1948	.80	2.40	4.00	
661	Tragic Ground—Erskine Caldwell	.80	2.40	4.00	
662	Invitation to the Waltz—Rosamond Lehman	.80	2.40	4.00	
663	As Good As Dead—Thomas B. Dewey	1.00	3.00	5.00	
664	Portrait of the Artist As a Young Man—James Joyce	.80	2.40	4.00	
665	Strange Fruit—Lillian Smith	.80	2.40	4.00	
666	The Valley of Hunted Men—Paul Evan Lehman	.80	2.40	4.00	W
667	The Pinkerton Case Book—Alan Hynd	1.00	3.00	5.00	
668	The Dim View—Basil Heatter	.80	2.40	4.00	
669	The Caballero—Johnston McCulley	.80	2.40	4.00	W
670	They Shoot Horses, Don't They?—Horace McCoy	1.20	3.60	6.00	
671	Darkness at Noon—Arthur Koestler	.80	2.40	4.00	
672	Cattle Kingdom—Alan LeMay	.80	2.40	4.00	W
673	Sons of the Saddle—William MacLeod Raine	.80	2.40	4.00	W
674	Mine Own Executioner—Nigel Balchin	.80	2.40	4.00	
675	About the Kinsey Report—Enid Curie & Donald Porter Geddes	.50	1.50	2.50	NF
676	Ariane—Claude Anet	.80	2.40	4.00	E
677	Guilty Bystander—Wade Miller	1.20	3.60	6.00	
678	The Signet Crossword Puzzle Book—Albert Morehead & Geoffrey Mott-Smith	.80	2.40	4.00	NF
679	Laramie Rides Again—Will Ermine	.80	2.40	4.00	W
680	Past All Dishonor—James M. Cain	.80	2.40	4.00	
681	Contract Bridge for Everyone—Ely Culbertson	.50	1.50	2.50	NF
682	Blood of the West—Paul Evan Lehman	.80	2.40	4.00	W
683	The Lost Weekend—Charles Jackson	1.00	3.00	5.00	
684	Slay the Murderer—Hugh Holman	1.00	3.00	5.00	M
685	Lobo Law—Will Ermine	.80	2.40	4.00	W
686	A House in the Uplands—Erskine Caldwell	.80	2.40	4.00	
687	Shore Leave—Frederic Wakeman	.80	2.40	4.00	
688	High Pockets—Herbert Shappiro	.80	2.40	4.00	

Science Service nn, © Science Svc.

Shooting Script nn, © Catechetical Guild

Signet 660, © NA

Signet 690, © NA

Signet 697, © NA

Signet 699, © NA

(SIGNET, continued)

		Good	Fine	N/Mint	
689	The Silver Tombstone—Frank Gruber	1.00	3.00	5.00	
690	No Pockets in a Shroud—Horace McCoy	1.20	3.60	6.00	
691	All the Girls We Loved—Prudencio De Pereda	.80	2.40	4.00	
692	The Old Man—William Faulkner	.80	2.40	4.00	
693	I Love You, I Love You, I Love You—Ludwig Bemelmans	.80	2.40	4.00	
694	Lawless Range—Charles N. Heckelmann	.80	2.40	4.00	W
695	Fatal Step—Wade Miller	1.20	3.60	6.00	
696	The Snake Pit—Mary Jane Ward; movie tie-in	.80	2.40	4.00	
697	Look Homeward, Angel, Part II—Thomas Wolfe	.80	2.40	4.00	
698	Black Sombrero—William Colt MacDonald	.80	2.40	4.00	W
699	I, the Jury—Mickey Spillane; used in *Parade of Pleasure*, pg. 172	3.00	9.00	15.00	M
700	Other Voices, Other Rooms—Truman Capote; 1949	1.60	4.80	8.00	
701	Finnley Wren—Philip Wylie	.80	2.40	4.00	
702	The Vehement Flame—Ludwig Lewisohn	.80	2.40	4.00	
703	Find My Killer—Manly Wade Wellman	1.20	3.60	6.00	M
704	Gold of Smoky Mesa—Johnston McCulley	.80	2.40	4.00	W
705	A Woman in the House—Erskine Caldwell	.80	2.40	4.00	
706	Last of the Conquerors—William Gardner Smith	.80	2.40	4.00	
707	The Honest Dealer—Frank Gruber	.80	2.40	4.00	
708	The Texan—Herbert Shapiro	.80	2.40	4.00	W
709	Deadlier Than the Male—James E. Gunn	1.00	3.00	5.00	
710	The Street—Ann Petry	.80	2.40	4.00	
711	Love in Dishevelment—David Greenhood	.80	2.40	4.00	
712	The Fighting Tenderfoot—William MacLeod Raine	.80	2.40	4.00	W
713	Murder As a Fine Art—Francis Bonnamy	.80	2.40	4.00	M
714	The Gilded Hearse—Charles Gorham	.80	2.40	4.00	
715	The Fall of Valor—Charles Jackson	.80	2.40	4.00	
716	We Were Strange—Robert Sylvester	.80	2.40	4.00	
717	A Son of Arizona—Charles Alden Seltzer	.80	2.40	4.00	W
718	Another Man's Poison—Hugh Holman	.80	2.40	4.00	
719	Baseball for Everyone—Joe Di Maggio	1.00	3.00	5.00	S
720	The Butterfly—James M. Cain	.80	2.40	4.00	
721	Night of Flame—Warren Desmond	.80	2.40	4.00	
722	Uneasy Street—Wade Miller	1.20	3.60	6.00	
723	The Crimson Quirt—William Colt MacDonald	.80	2.40	4.00	W
724	The Golden Sleep—Vivian Connell	.80	2.40	4.00	
725	At Heaven's Gate—Robert Penn Warren; 1949	.80	2.40	4.00	
726	The Whispering Master—Frank Gruber	.80	2.40	4.00	
727	Trigger Justice—Leslie Ernenwein	.80	2.40	4.00	W
728	Lona Hanson—Thomas Savage	.80	2.40	4.00	
729	Stranger in Town—Howard Hunt	1.00	3.00	5.00	
730	The Body in the Bed—Bill S. Ballinger	1.00	3.00	5.00	M
731	Montana Man—Paul Evan Lehman	.80	2.40	4.00	W
732	The Sure Hand of God—Erskine Caldwell	.80	2.40	4.00	E
733	Crime and Punishment—Fyodor Dostoyevsky	1.00	3.00	5.00	
734	Meet the Girls—James T. Farrell	.80	2.40	4.00	
735	Everybody Slept Here—Elliott Arnold	.80	2.40	4.00	
736	Draw the Curtain Close—Thomas B. Dewey	1.00	3.00	5.00	M
737	Brave in the Saddle—Will Ermine	.80	2.40	4.00	W
738	Nightmare Alley—William Lindsay Gresham	1.00	3.00	5.00	E
739	Beyond the Forest—Stuart Engstrand	.80	2.40	4.00	E
740	Whistling Lead—Eugene Cunningham	.80	2.40	4.00	W
741	Life in a Putty Knife Factory—H. Allen Smith	.50	1.50	2.50	H
742	Kill or Cure—William Francis	1.00	3.00	5.00	
743	Intruder in the Dust—William Faulkner	.80	2.40	4.00	
744	The Christian Demand for Social Justice—William Scarlett	.50	1.50	2.50	NF
745	The Ox-Bow Incident—Walter Van Tilburg Clark	1.20	3.60	6.00	W
746	Human Destiny—Pierre Lecomte du Nouy	.80	2.40	4.00	NF

		Good	Fine	N/Mint	
747	Walden—Henry David Thoreau	.80	2.40	4.00	
748	Mistress Glory—Susan Morley	.80	2.40	4.00	E
749	For Ever Wilt Thou Love—Ludwig Lewisohn	.80	2.40	4.00	E
750	Devil in the Flesh—Raymond Radiguet; 1949	.80	2.40	4.00	
751	Love Without Fear—Eustace Chesser	.50	1.50	2.50	NF
752	The Future Mr. Dolan—Charles Gorham	.80	2.40	4.00	JD
753	The Gamecock Murders—Frank Gruber	1.20	3.60	6.00	M
754	Kiss Tomorrow Good-bye—Horace McCoy	1.20	3.60	6.00	E
755	An American Tragedy—Theodore Dreiser	.80	2.40	4.00	
756	If He Hollers Let Him Go—Chester Himes	1.00	3.00	5.00	
757	Brother of the Cheyennes—Max Brand	.80	2.40	4.00	W
758	Clattering Hoofs—William MacLeod Raine	.80	2.40	4.00	W
759	Everybody Does It and the Embezzler—James M. Cain; aka Career in C Major	.80	2.40	4.00	
760	Georgia Boy—Erskine Caldwell; 1950	.80	2.40	4.00	
761	Country Place—Ann Petry	.80	2.40	4.00	
762	You Can Change the World—James Keller	.80	2.40	4.00	NF
763	The Weeper and the Blackmailer—Richard H. Rovere	.80	2.40	4.00	
764	Six-Shooter Showdown—William Colt MacDonald	.80	2.40	4.00	W
765	Murder All Over—Cleve F. Adams; aka Up Jumped the Devil	1.20	3.60	6.00	M
766	Appointment in Samarra—John O'Hara	.80	2.40	4.00	
767	Alien Land—Willard Savoy	.80	2.40	4.00	E
768	Dark Encounter—Howard Hunt; aka Maelstrom	1.00	3.00	5.00	
769	Margaret—Caroline Slade	.80	2.40	4.00	E
770	Two Loves—Elliott Arnold	.80	2.40	4.00	
771	Killer's Choice—Wade Miller; aka Devil on Two Sticks	1.20	3.60	6.00	M
772	Three Musketeers and a Lady—Tiffany Thayer	.80	2.40	4.00	A
773	The City and the Pillar—Gore Vidal	.80	2.40	4.00	
774	The Body Beautiful—Bill S. Ballinger	1.00	3.00	5.00	M
775	Vengeance Trail—Charles N. Heckelmann; 1950	.80	2.40	4.00	W
776	Now I Lay Me Down to Sleep—Ludwig Bemelmans	.80	2.40	4.00	
777	Laughter in the Dark—Vladimir Nabokov	.80	2.40	4.00	
778	I Am Thinking of My Darling—Vincent McHugh	.80	2.40	4.00	
779	Ellen Rogers—James T. Farrell	.80	2.40	4.00	E
780	The Restless Hands—Bruno Fischer	1.20	3.60	6.00	M
781	The Outer Edges—Charles Jackson	.80	2.40	4.00	E
782	The Buckaroo—Burt Arthur	.80	2.40	4.00	E
783	The Saxon Charm—Frederic Wakeman	.80	2.40	4.00	E
784	Double Indemnity—James M. Cain	1.00	3.00	5.00	M
785	Horseback Hellion—George Owen Baxter	.80	2.40	4.00	W
786	The Sling and the Arrow—Stuart Engstrand	.80	2.40	4.00	E
787	The Hanging Heiress—Richard Wormser	1.00	3.00	5.00	M
788	Having a Baby—Alan F. Guttmacher	.80	2.40	4.00	NF
789	The Love-Making of Max-Robert—Robert Shaplen; aka Corner of the World	.80	2.40	4.00	
790	Lily Henry—Mae Cooper	.80	2.40	4.00	
791	My Gun Is Quick—Mickey Spillane	1.20	3.60	6.00	M
792	The Shadow Rider—William Colt MacDonald	.80	2.40	4.00	W
793	Kitty Foyle—Christopher Morley	.80	2.40	4.00	
S794	Native Son—Richard Wright	1.00	3.00	5.00	
795	Healthy Babies Are Happy Babies—Josephine H. Kenyon & Ruth K. Russell	.50	1.50	2.50	NF
S796	Arch of Triumph—Erich Maria Remarque	.80	2.40	4.00	
797	A Tale of Poor Lovers—Vasco Pratolini	.80	2.40	4.00	
798	1984—George Orwell	2.00	6.00	10.00	SF
799	The Fourth Letter—Frank Gruber	1.20	3.60	6.00	
800	Fannie Farmer's Handy Cook Book; 1950	.80	2.40	4.00	NF
801	The Track of the Cat—Walter Van Tilburg Clark	.80	2.40	4.00	W
802AB	Knock on Any Door—Willard Motley	1.00	3.00	5.00	JD
803	World Full of Strangers—David Alman	.80	2.40	4.00	E
804	Night Rider—Robert Penn Warren	.80	2.40	4.00	E

Signet 754, © NA

Signet 772, © NA

Signet 784, © NA

Signet 834, © NA

Signet 884, © NA

Signet 888, © NA

(SIGNET, continued)

		Good	Fine	N/Mint	
805	The Runaways—Carl Bottume; aka The Hills Around Havana	.80	2.40	4.00	E
806	Powdersmoke Feud—William MacLeod Raine	.80	2.40	4.00	W
807	The Bandaged Nude—Robert Finnegan	1.20	3.60	6.00	
808	The New American Webster Dictionary	.80	2.40	4.00	NF
809AB	Forever Amber—Kathleen Winsor	1.00	3.00	5.00	
810	The Young Manhood of Studs Lonigan—James T. Farrell	.80	2.40	4.00	
811	The Moth—James M. Cain	.80	2.40	4.00	
812	Beyond the Moon—Edmond Hamilton	1.20	3.60	6.00	SF
813	The World Next Door—Fritz Peters	.80	2.40	4.00	
814	Room for Murder—Thomas B. Dewey	1.00	3.00	5.00	
815	Wanted - Dead or Alive—Gordon Young	.80	2.40	4.00	W
816	Tortilla Flat—John Steinbeck	1.20	3.60	6.00	
817AB	The Young Lions—Irwin Shaw	.80	2.40	4.00	
818	A Swell-Looking Girl—Erskine Caldwell; aka American Earth	.80	2.40	4.00	E
819	The Lonely—Paul Gallico	.80	2.40	4.00	
820	Shriek With Pleasure—Toni Howard	.80	2.40	4.00	E
821	Sleep No More—Sam S. Taylor	.80	2.40	4.00	
822	Trigger Man—Burt Arthur	.80	2.40	4.00	W
823	The Wastrel—Frederic Wakeman	.80	2.40	4.00	
824	State Fair—Phil Stong	1.00	3.00	5.00	
825	Knight's Gambit—William Faulkner; 1950	.80	2.40	4.00	
826	Son of the Giant—Stuart Engstrand	.80	2.40	4.00	
827	A Job of Murder—Frank Gruber	1.20	3.60	6.00	
828	Gunsmoke—Leslie Ernenwein	.80	2.40	4.00	W
829	Lilly Crackell—Caroline Slade	.80	2.40	4.00	
830	Night Unto Night—Philip Wylie	.80	2.40	4.00	E
831	Saturday Night—James T. Farrell	.80	2.40	4.00	E
832	Love Knows No Barriers—Will Thomas; aka God Is for White Folks	1.00	3.00	5.00	E
833	The Flesh Was Cold—Bruno Fischer	1.20	3.60	6.00	M
834	Heart of Darkness and the Secret Sharer—Joseph Conrad	1.20	3.60	6.00	
835	Dead Man's Gold—William Colt MacDonald	.80	2.40	4.00	W
836	Montana Riders!—Evan Evans (Max Brand); 1951	.80	2.40	4.00	
837AB	The Naked and the Dead—Norman Mailer	1.00	3.00	5.00	
838	This Very Earth—Erskine Caldwell	.80	2.40	4.00	
839	Limbo Tower—William Lindsay Gresham	.80	2.40	4.00	
840	The Sheltering Sky—Paul Bowles	.80	2.40	4.00	E
841	Black Boy—Richard Wright	1.00	3.00	5.00	
842	Two-Bit Rancher—Charles N. Heckelmann	.80	2.40	4.00	W
843	Calamity Fair—Wade Miller	1.20	3.60	6.00	E
S844	The Woman of Rome—Alberto Moravia	.80	2.40	4.00	E
845	Tiger in the Garden—Speed Lamkin	.80	2.40	4.00	E
846	The Short Cut—Ennio Flaiano	.80	2.40	4.00	E
847	The Man Who Sold the Moon—Robert A. Heinlein	1.20	3.60	6.00	SF
848	The Conquest of Happiness—Bertrand Russell	.80	2.40	4.00	
849	Brother of the Kid—Paul Evan Lehman	.80	2.40	4.00	W
850	The Private Eye—Cleve F. Adams; 1951	1.20	3.60	6.00	M
S851	The Strange Land—Ned Calmer	.80	2.40	4.00	
852	Vengeance Is Mine—Mickey Spillane; used in Parade of Pleasure, pg. 180-182	1.60	4.80	8.00	M
853	Black Gold—Jewel Gibson	1.00	3.00	5.00	E
854	Memory and Desire—Leonora Hornblow	.80	2.40	4.00	
855	The Snow Was Black—Georges Simenon	1.00	3.00	5.00	M
856	Mean As Hell—Dee Harkey	.80	2.40	4.00	
857	Meg—Theodora Keogh	1.00	3.00	5.00	
858	Dirty Eddie—Ludwig Bemelmans	.80	2.40	4.00	
859	The Consumer's Guide to Better Buying—Sidney Margolius	.50	1.50	2.50	NF
860	Follow Me Down—Shelby Foote	1.00	3.00	5.00	E
861	Prettiest Girl in Town—Thomas Fall	.80	2.40	4.00	E
862	Courage and Confidence From the Bible—Walter L. Moore	.80	2.40	4.00	NF

(SIGNET, continued)		Good	Fine	N/Mint	
863	Pylon—William Faulkner	.80	2.40	4.00	
864	Strangers and Lovers—Edwin Gran Gerry	.80	2.40	4.00	E
865	I. O. U. - Murder—William Francis; aka Rough on Rats	1.00	3.00	5.00	M
866	Trouble Town—Burt Arthur	.80	2.40	4.00	W
867	They Sought for Paradise—Stuart Engstrand	.80	2.40	4.00	
868AB	Star Money—Kathleen Winsor	.50	1.50	2.50	
869	Kneel to the Rising Sun—Erskine Caldwell	.80	2.40	4.00	
870	Time for Love—Margaret Lee Runbeck	.80	2.40	4.00	E
871	The Dog Star—Donald Windham	.80	2.40	4.00	E
872	There's No Home—Alexander Baron; aka The Wine of Etna	.50	1.50	2.50	E
873	Appointment With Fear—Donald Stokes	.80	2.40	4.00	
874	Hell for Leather—Leslie Ernenwein	.80	2.40	4.00	W
S875	Judgment Day—James T. Farrell; 1951	.80	2.40	4.00	
876	A Stretch on the River—Richard Bissell	.80	2.40	4.00	
877	Cry of Violence—Joseph Kessel; aka Sirrocco	.80	2.40	4.00	
878	A Tree of Night—Truman Capote	1.00	3.00	5.00	
879	No Luck for a Lady—Floyd Mahannah; aka The Yellow Hearse	1.20	3.60	6.00	
880	Gunsight Range—William Colt MacDonald	.80	2.40	4.00	W
881	Fertility in Marriage—Louis Portnoy & Jules Saltman	.80	2.40	4.00	NF
882	The Day After Tomorrow—Robert A. Heinlein	1.20	3.60	6.00	SF
883	Stone Cold Blonde—Adam Knight	1.20	3.60	6.00	M
884	I Should Have Stayed Home—Horace McCoy	1.20	3.60	6.00	
885	Buckskin Marshal—Will Ermine	.80	2.40	4.00	W
886	The Daughter—Arthur Markowitz	.80	2.40	4.00	
887	Soldier's Pay—William Faulkner	.80	2.40	4.00	
888	One Lonely Night—Mickey Spillane; used in Parade of Pleasure, pg. 175	2.00	6.00	10.00	M
889	Your Way to Popularity & Personal Power—James Bender & Lee Graham	.50	1.50	2.50	NF
890	The Invaders—Stuart Engstrand	.80	2.40	4.00	
891	Gunplay Valley—Joseph Wayne	.80	2.40	4.00	W
892	The Silent Dust—Bruno Fischer	1.20	3.60	6.00	M
S893	Bernard Carr—James T. Farrell	.80	2.40	4.00	E
894	Cornbread Aristocrat—Claud Garner	.80	2.40	4.00	E
895	The Triumph of Willie Pond—Caroline Slade	.80	2.40	4.00	E
896	Jubel's Children—Lenard Kaufman	.80	2.40	4.00	E
897	Portrait in Smoke—Bill S. Ballinger	1.00	3.00	5.00	M
898	A Texas Cowboy—Charles A. Siringo	.80	2.40	4.00	W
899	The Humorous Side of Erskine Caldwell	.80	2.40	4.00	
900	A Wind Is Rising—William Russell; 1951	.80	2.40	4.00	
901	Good Is for Angels—Christopher Clark	.80	2.40	4.00	E
902	Contraband—Cleve Adams; illo in Parade of Pleasure	1.20	3.60	6.00	M
903	High, Wide and Handsome—Curt Brandon	.80	2.40	4.00	
904AB	The Rains Came—Louis Bromfield	.80	2.40	4.00	
905	Thunder Mountain—Theodore Pratt	.80	2.40	4.00	
906	Love Is the One With Wings—Philip van Doren Stern	.80	2.40	4.00	
907	Anger at Innocence—William Gardner Smith	.80	2.40	4.00	
908	Murder Charge—Wade Miller	1.20	3.60	6.00	M
909	Butcher's Dozen—John Bartlow Martin	.80	2.40	4.00	
910	Let the Guns Roar!—Charles N. Heckelmann	.80	2.40	4.00	W
911	The Young Lovers—Meyor Levin	.80	2.40	4.00	
912	A Family Romance—Elizabeth Pollet	.80	2.40	4.00	
913	They Don't Dance Much—James Ross	.80	2.40	4.00	E
914	Mission: Interplanetary—A. E. Van Vogt	1.20	3.60	6.00	SF
915	The Big Kill—Mickey Spillane; used in Parade of Pleasure, pg. 178	1.20	3.60	6.00	M
916	Bugles in the Night—Arthur Herbert; 1952	.80	2.40	4.00	
917	A Streetcar Named Desire—Tennessee Williams	1.20	3.60	6.00	
918	A Place Called Estherville—Erskine Caldwell	.80	2.40	4.00	E
919	The Delicate Prey—Paul Bowles	.80	2.40	4.00	
920	Murder for Madame—Adam Knight	1.20	3.60	6.00	M

Signet 894, © NA

Signet 898, © NA

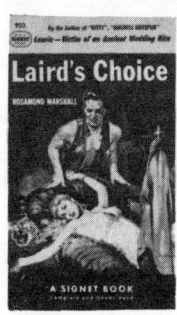

Signet 923, © NA

Signet 953, © NA Signet 959, © NA Signet 1034, © NA

(SIGNET, continued)

		Good	Fine	N/Mint	
921AB	Moulin Rouge—Pierre LaMure	.80	2.40	4.00	
922	Conjugal Love—Alberto Moravia	.80	2.40	4.00	
923	Laird's Choice—Rosamond Marshall	.80	2.40	4.00	
S924	The Promising Young Men—George Sklar	.50	1.50	2.50	
925	The Killer Brand—William Colt MacDonald; 1952	.80	2.40	4.00	W
D926	A World I Never Made—James T. Farrell	.80	2.40	4.00	E
927	Renee—H. R. Lenormand	.80	2.40	4.00	
928	Deadly Weapon—Wade Miller	1.20	3.60	6.00	M
D929	The Seven Storey Mountain—Thomas Merton	.80	2.40	4.00	
930	Finistere—Fritz Peters	.80	2.40	4.00	E
S931	The Troubled Air—Irwin Shaw	.80	2.40	4.00	
932	The Long Wait—Mickey Spillane; used in *Parade of Pleasure*, pg. 179	1.20	3.60	6.00	M
933	Southways—Erskine Caldwell	.80	2.40	4.00	
T934	The Fountainhead—Ayn Rand	1.20	3.60	6.00	
935	Montana Rides Again—Evan Evans (Max Brand)	.80	2.40	4.00	W
936	Sabotage—Cleve F. Adams	1.20	3.60	6.00	
937	Goodbye to Berlin—Christopher Isherwood	1.00	3.00	5.00	
938	Where Town Begins—Richard R. Werry	1.00	3.00	5.00	M
939	China Station—Donald R. Morris	.80	2.40	4.00	
940	Walk on the Water—Ralph Leveridge	.80	2.40	4.00	
941	There's One in Every Town—James Aswell	.80	2.40	4.00	
942	Pressure—Charles Francis Coe	.80	2.40	4.00	
943	The Green Hills of Earth—Robert A. Heinlein	1.20	3.60	6.00	SF
944	The Loved and the Lost—Morley Callaghan	.80	2.40	4.00	
945	Rock Wagram—William Saroyan	.80	2.40	4.00	
D946	No Star Is Lost—James T. Farrell	.80	2.40	4.00	
947	See How They Run—Don M. Mankiewicz	.80	2.40	4.00	
948	The Girl in His Past—Georges Simenon	1.00	3.00	5.00	M
949	The Kiss-Off—Douglas Heyes	1.00	3.00	5.00	
950	Only the Dead Know Brooklyn—Thomas Wolfe; 1952	1.00	3.00	5.00	
951	Elinda—Frances Clippinger	.80	2.40	4.00	
952	Stirrups in the Dust—Burt Arthur	.80	2.40	4.00	W
953	A Grove of Fever Trees—Daphne Rooke	.80	2.40	4.00	
S954	Mister Smith—Louis Bromfield	.80	2.40	4.00	
955	The Roman Spring of Mrs. Stone—Tennessee Williams	.80	2.40	4.00	
S956	The Stubborn Heart—Frank G. Slaughter	.80	2.40	4.00	
957	The Broken Body—Floyd Mahannah	1.20	3.60	6.00	E
958	The Double Door—Theodora Keogh	1.00	3.00	5.00	
959	The Revolt of Mamie Stover—William Bradford Huie	.80	2.40	4.00	E
960	Two Adolescents—Alberto Moravia	.80	2.40	4.00	
S961	Back Street—Fannie Hurst	.80	2.40	4.00	
962	The Face of Innocence—William Sansom	.80	2.40	4.00	
963	The Caravan Passes—George Tabori	.80	2.40	4.00	E
964	The Heart of a Man—Georges Simenon	1.00	3.00	5.00	
965	Fighting Ramrod—Charles N. Heckelmann	.80	2.40	4.00	W
966	Death Is a Round Black Ball—Mike Roscoe	1.00	3.00	5.00	M
D967	Lie Down in Darkness—William Styron	.80	2.40	4.00	
968	The Long November—James Benson Nablo	.80	2.40	4.00	
969	A Hero of Our Time—Vasco Pratolini	.80	2.40	4.00	
970	Love in a Dry Season—Shelby Foote	1.20	3.60	6.00	
S971	The Sky Is Red—Giuseppe Berto	.80	2.40	4.00	
972	Those Devils in Baggy Pants—Ross Carter	.80	2.40	4.00	C
973	The Six-Gun Kid—William MacLeod Raine	.80	2.40	4.00	W
974	Who Walk in Darkness—Chandler Brossard	.80	2.40	4.00	
D975	World Enough and Time—Robert Penn Warren; 1952	.80	2.40	4.00	
976	The Temptress—Rosamond Marshall	.80	2.40	4.00	
977	The Unvanquished—William Faulkner	.80	2.40	4.00	
978	Tobacco Road—Jack Kirkland	.80	2.40	4.00	

		Good	Fine	N/Mint	
S979	Possession—Louis Bromfield	.80	2.40	4.00	
980	The Puppet Masters—Robert A. Heinlein	1.20	3.60	6.00	SF
981	The Lonely Hearts Murders—Wenzell Brown	1.00	3.00	5.00	M
982	Gunhawk Harvest—Leslie Ernenwein	.80	2.40	4.00	W
983	Episode in Palmetto—Erskine Caldwell; 1953	.80	2.40	4.00	E
984	The Unwanted—Dante Arfelli	.80	2.40	4.00	
S985	The Age of Longing—Arthur Koestler	.80	2.40	4.00	
986	Your Body and Your Mind—Frank G. Slaughter	.80	2.40	4.00	
987	Reach to the Stars—Calder Willingham	.80	2.40	4.00	
988	Stripped for Murder—Bruno Fischer; illo in *Parade of Pleasure*	1.20	3.60	6.00	M
989	Trouble in Tombstone—Tom J. Hopkins	.80	2.40	4.00	W
990	Sailor's Choice—Carl Bottume	.80	2.40	4.00	
991	Moulded in Earth—Richard Vaughan	.80	2.40	4.00	
D992	We Fished All Night—Willard Motley	.80	2.40	4.00	
993	Act of Passion—Georges Simenon	1.00	3.00	5.00	
994	When Boyhood Dreams Came True—James T. Farrell	.80	2.40	4.00	
995	Night at the Vulcan—Ngaio Marsh	1.00	3.00	5.00	M
996	Doubtful Valley—George Garland	.80	2.40	4.00	
997	Leopard in the Grass—Desmond Stewart	.80	2.40	4.00	
998	Moira—Julian Green	.80	2.40	4.00	
S999	The Hoods—Harry Gray	1.00	3.00	5.00	
1000	Kiss Me, Deadly—Mickey Spillane; illo in *Parade of Pleasure*	1.20	3.60	6.00	M
1001	The Catcher in the Rye—J. D. Salinger	1.20	3.60	6.00	
1002	Let It Come Down—Paul Bowles	.80	2.40	4.00	
1003	Dangerous Voyage—Gore Vidal	.80	2.40	4.00	
1004	Sybil—Louis Auchincloss	.80	2.40	4.00	
1005	Blind Cartridges—William Colt MacDonald	.80	2.40	4.00	W
1006	Captive in the Night—Donald Stokes	.80	2.40	4.00	
1007	Destination: Universe!—A. E. Van Vogt	1.20	3.60	6.00	SF
1008	You and Your Heart—H. M. Marvin	.40	1.20	2.00	NF
D1009	Down All Your Streets—Leonard Bishop	.80	2.40	4.00	
S1010	Back of Town—Maritta Wolff	.80	2.40	4.00	
1011	Dream of Eden—Winston Brebner; aka The Second Circle	.80	2.40	4.00	
1012	The Blessing—Nancy Mitford	.80	2.40	4.00	
1013	Shoot to Kill—Wade Miller	1.20	3.60	6.00	M
1014	They Lived By Their Guns	1.00	3.00	5.00	
1015	Song of the Whip—Evan Evans (Max Brand)	.80	2.40	4.00	W
1016	The Courting of Susie Brown—Erskine Caldwell	.80	2.40	4.00	
S1017	Scalpel—Horace McCoy	1.20	3.60	6.00	
S1018	Dream of Innocence—Turnley Walker	.80	2.40	4.00	
1019	Barbary Shore—Norman Mailer	.80	2.40	4.00	E
1020	The Glass Harp—Truman Capote	.80	2.40	4.00	
1021	Mittee—Daphne Rooke	.80	2.40	4.00	
1022	Knife at My Back—Adam Knight	1.00	3.00	5.00	M
S1023	Spark of Life—Erich Maria Remarque	.80	2.40	4.00	E
1024	A Husband in the House—Stuart Engstrand	.50	1.50	2.50	
S1025	The Green Bay Tree—Louis Bromfield; 1953	.80	2.40	4.00	
1026	Frail Barrier—Philip Gillon	.80	2.40	4.00	
1027	The Devil's Passkey—Jimmy Shannon	.80	2.40	4.00	
1028	The Snake Stomper—Joseph Wayne	.80	2.40	4.00	W
1029	Wise Blood—Flannery O'Connor	.80	2.40	4.00	
D1030	Invisible Man—Ralph Ellison	.80	2.40	4.00	
1031	An American Dream Girl—James T. Farrell	.80	2.40	4.00	
S1032	Sartoris—William Faulkner	.80	2.40	4.00	
1033	My Life in Crime—John Bartlow Martin	.80	2.40	4.00	NF
1034	I Take This Woman—George Simenon	1.00	3.00	5.00	M
1035	To End the Night—Alex Gaby	.80	2.40	4.00	
1036	Death in the Fifth Position—Edgar Box	1.00	3.00	5.00	M
1037	Bugle's Wake—Curt Brandon	.80	2.40	4.00	W
S1038	Rage of the Soul—Vincent Sheean	.80	2.40	4.00	
S1039	Sons and Lovers—D. H. Lawrence	.80	2.40	4.00	
1040	The Darkening Door—Bill S. Ballinger	1.00	3.00	5.00	M
S1041	This Dear Encounter—Catherine Hutter	.80	2.40	4.00	
1042	The Red Carnation—Elio Vittorini	.80	2.40	4.00	
S1043	Submarine!—Edward L. Beach	.80	2.40	4.00	C
1044	Tomorrow, the Stars—Robert A. Heinlein	1.20	3.60	6.00	SF
1045	Trigger Vengeance—B. M. Bower	.80	2.40	4.00	W
1046	Brother of the Cheyennes—Max Brand	.80	2.40	4.00	W
1047	Wives and Husbands—David Duncan; c-Maguire	1.00	3.00	5.00	E
1048	By Anyother Name—Roy Michaels	.80	2.40	4.00	
1049	Street Music—Theodora Keogh	1.00	3.00	5.00	
1050	Pistol Pete—Frank Eaton; 1953	.80	2.40	4.00	W
S1051	Scollay Square—Pearl Schiff	.50	1.50	2.50	
S1052	Heaven Pays No Dividends—Richard Kaufmann; c-Maguire	.80	2.40	4.00	
1053	The Brigand—Giuseppe Berto	.50	1.50	2.50	
1054	Naked to Mine Enemies—Susan Yorke	.50	1.50	2.50	

Signet 1047, © NA

Signet 1082, © NA

Signet S1094, © NA

(SIGNET, continued)

		Good	Fine	N/Mint	
S1055	The Consumer's Guide to Better Buying—Sidney Margolius	.40	1.20	2.00	NF
1056	The Mistress—H. C. Branner	.50	1.50	2.50	
1057	No Head for Her Pillow—Sam S. Taylor	.50	1.50	2.50	
1058	Ashes—Charles Francis Coe	.50	1.50	2.50	
1059	Ranger Man—William Colt MacDonald	.80	2.40	4.00	W
1060	Riddle Me This—Mike Roscoe	1.20	3.60	6.00	
1061	The Naked Streets—Vasco Pratolini	.50	1.50	2.50	
S1062	Natural Child—Calder Willingham	.50	1.50	2.50	
1063	Home Is Upriver—Brian Horwin	.50	1.50	2.50	
1064	The Descent—Fritz Peters	.50	1.50	2.50	
1065	A Funeral for Sabella—Robert Travers	.80	2.40	4.00	
D1066	Father and Son—James T. Farrell	.80	2.40	4.00	
1067	Crime Without Punishment—Guenther Reinhardt	.80	2.40	4.00	
D1068	Confessors of the Name—Gladys Schmitt; c-Maguire	1.00	3.00	5.00	
1069	Justice Comes to Tomahawk—William MacLeod Raine	.80	2.40	4.00	W
S1070	The Best Thing That Ever Happened—Warren Leslie	.50	1.50	2.50	
S1071	The Conformist—Alberto Moravia	.50	1.50	2.50	
1072	A Cow Is Too Much Trouble in Los Angeles—Joseph Foster	.50	1.50	2.50	
1073	Four Days in a Lifetime—Georges Simenon	1.00	3.00	5.00	M
S1074	Strange Fruit—Lillian Smith	.80	2.40	4.00	
T1075	From Here to Eternity—James Jones; 1953	1.20	3.60	6.00	C
1076	The Big Sin—Jack Webb	1.00	3.00	5.00	
1077	By Gun and Spur—Joseph Wayne	.80	2.40	4.00	W
S1078	The Curve and the Tusk—Stuart Cloete	.80	2.40	4.00	
S1079	Sanctuary and Requiem for a Nun—William Faulkner	.50	1.50	2.50	
S1080	Caesar's Angel—Mary Anne Amsbary	.50	1.50	2.50	
1081	The Disguises of Love—Robie Macauley	.50	1.50	2.50	
1082	The Currents of Space—Isaac Asimov	1.20	3.60	6.00	SF
1083	The Day I Died—Lawrence Lariar	1.00	3.00	5.00	
1084	Deadlier Than the Male—James E. Gunn	1.00	3.00	5.00	
1085	The Saga of Billy the Kid—Walter Noble Burns	.80	2.40	4.00	B
S1086	Lady Chatterley's Lover—D. H. Lawrence	.80	2.40	4.00	
1087	Appointment in Samarra—John O'Hara	.80	2.40	4.00	
1088	Young Man With a Horn—Dorothy Baker	.80	2.40	4.00	
1089	Guilty Bystander—Wade Miller; 1954	1.00	3.00	5.00	M
S1090	The Mountain and the Valley—Ernest Buckler	.50	1.50	2.50	
1091	A Lamp for Nightfall—Erskine Caldwell	.50	1.50	2.50	
1092	Depends What You Mean By Love—Nicholas Monsarrat	.50	1.50	2.50	
1093	Death Before Bedtime—Edgar Box	1.00	3.00	5.00	M
S1094	Amazon Head-Hunters—Lewis Cotlow	1.20	3.60	6.00	
1095	Uncle Tom's Children—Richard Wright	1.00	3.00	5.00	
1096	Gigi and Julie de Carneilhan—Sidonie Colette	.80	2.40	4.00	
1097	The Waitress—William Fisher	.50	1.50	2.50	
S1098	The Skin—Curzio Malaparte	.50	1.50	2.50	
1099	The Center of the Stage—Gerald Sykes	.50	1.50	2.50	
1100	The Tatooed Heart—Theodora Keogh; 1954	.80	2.40	4.00	
1101	The Big Dry—George Garland	.50	1.50	2.50	
D1102	Night Shift—Maritta Wolff	.50	1.50	2.50	
1103	The Sunburned Corpse—Adam Knight	1.00	3.00	5.00	M
1104	Shiloh—Shelby Foote	1.00	3.00	5.00	
1105	The Demolished Man—Alfred Bester	1.20	3.60	6.00	SF
1106	A Breed Apart—Fleming MacLiesh	.50	1.50	2.50	
D1107	Days of My Love—Leonard Bishop	.50	1.50	2.50	
1108	Hell in His Holsters—Charles N. Heckelmann	.80	2.40	4.00	W
1109	The Brother Rico—Georges Simenon	1.00	3.00	5.00	M
1110	Portrait of the Damned—Richard McKaye; c-Maguire	1.00	3.00	5.00	
1111	Nine Stories—J. D. Salinger	.80	2.40	4.00	
1112	The Double Shuffle—James Hadley Chase	1.00	3.00	5.00	M

		Good	Fine	N/Mint	
1113	The Execution of Private Slovik—William Bradford Huie	.80	2.40	4.00	C
S1114	The Outsider—Richard Wright	1.00	3.00	5.00	
1115	The Lost Year—Robert Hazel	.50	1.50	2.50	
1116	Morning, Winter and Night—John Nairne Michaelson	.50	1.50	2.50	
1117	The Moon and the Bonfires—Cesare Pavese	.50	1.50	2.50	
S1118	My Days of Anger—James T. Farrell	.80	2.40	4.00	
1119	Murder, Madness and the Law—Louis H. Cohen; c-Maguire	.80	2.40	4.00	M
1120	Smoke Bellew—Jack London	.80	2.40	4.00	
1121	The Birds and the Bees—James Aswell	.50	1.50	2.50	
1122	The Fancy Dress Party—Alberto Moravia	.50	1.50	2.50	
S1123	The Street—Ann Petry	.80	2.40	4.00	E
1124	Belle—Georges Simenon	1.00	3.00	5.00	M
1125					
1126	The Naked Heart—John Lee Weldon; 1954	.50	1.50	2.50	
1127	The Time Masters—Wilson Tucker	1.00	3.00	5.00	SF
1128	The Long Wind—Joseph Wayne	.50	1.50	2.50	W
1129	Pajama—Richard Bissell	.50	1.50	2.50	
D1130	Trial By Darkness—Charles Gorham	.50	1.50	2.50	
S1131	Cancel All Our Vows—John D. MacDonald	1.00	3.00	5.00	M
1132	The Face of the Deep—Jacob Twersky	.50	1.50	2.50	
S1133	The Time of Man—Elizabeth Madox Roberts	.50	1.50	2.50	
1134	The Beautiful Trap—Bill S. Ballinger	1.00	3.00	5.00	M
1135	The Texan—Burt Arthur	.80	2.40	4.00	W
1136	We Are the Living—Erskine Caldwell	.50	1.50	2.50	
S1137	A House of Her Own—Robert F. Mirvish	.50	1.50	2.50	
1138	Go Tell It on the Mountain—James Baldwin	.80	2.40	4.00	
1139	Kiss and Kill—Adam Knight	1.00	3.00	5.00	M
1140	Guns of the Frontier—William MacLeod Raine	.80	2.40	4.00	W
1141					
1142	Branded—A. C. Abbott	.80	2.40	4.00	
S1143	A Law for the Lion—Louis Auchincloss	.50	1.50	2.50	
1144	The Bottom of the Bottle—Georges Simenon	1.00	3.00	5.00	M
1145	The Money Song—Arnold Shaw	.50	1.50	2.50	
1146	The Wayward Ones—Sara Harris	.80	2.40	4.00	
1147	A Kiss Before Dying—Ira Levin	.50	1.50	2.50	
S1148	The Wild Palms and the Old Man—William Faulkner	.80	2.40	4.00	
1149	The Naked Angel—Jack Webb; c-Maguire	1.00	3.00	5.00	M
S1150	Portrait of the Artist As a Young Man—James Joyce; 1955	.80	2.40	4.00	
1151	Mafia—Ed Reid	.80	2.40	4.00	
1152	Galatea—James M. Cain	.80	2.40	4.00	
1153	Serenade—James M. Cain	.80	2.40	4.00	
1154	Requiem for a Redhead—Lindsay Hardy	1.00	3.00	5.00	
1155	Awakening—Jean-Baptiste Rossi	.50	1.50	2.50	
D1156	The Chain in the Heart—Hubert Creekmore	.50	1.50	2.50	
S1157	The Hive—Camilo Jose Cela	.50	1.50	2.50	
1158	This Man and This Woman—James T. Farrell	.50	1.50	2.50	
1159	The Scattered Seed—Stuart Engstrand	.50	1.50	2.50	
1160	The Ox-Bow Incident—Walter Van Tilburg Clark	.80	2.40	4.00	W
1161	Assignment in Eternity—Robert A. Heinlein	1.20	3.60	6.00	SF
S1162	Mud on the Stars—William Bradford Huie	.50	1.50	2.50	
1163	The General's Wench—Rosamond Marshall	.80	2.40	4.00	
1164	The Black City—M. F. Caulfield	.80	2.40	4.00	
1165	The Color of His Blood—Marris Murray	.80	2.40	4.00	
1166	The Young and Hungry-Hearted—James Aswell	.50	1.50	2.50	
1167	Let the Night Cry—Charles Wells; c-Maguire	1.00	3.00	5.00	
1168	Law and Order, Unlimited—William Colt MacDonald	.80	2.40	4.00	W
D1169	Forever Amber—Kathleen Winsor	.50	1.50	2.50	
1170	Time for Love—Margaret Lee Runbeck	.50	1.50	2.50	

Signet 1134, © NA

Signet 1144, © NA

Signet 1149, © NA

Signet 1173, © NA

Signet 1188, © NA

Signet 1221, © NA

(SIGNET, continued)

		Good	Fine	N/Mint	
S1171	Search for the Sun—Charles Furcolowe	.50	1.50	2.50	
1172	A Private Stair—David Loughlin; 1955	.50	1.50	2.50	
1173	The Spider in the Cup—Norman Hales	.50	1.50	2.50	
1174	Texas Hellion—J. H. Plenn	.80	2.40	4.00	W
1175	Devil in the Flesh—Raymond Radiguet	.80	2.40	4.00	
1176	The Sling and the Arrow—Stuart Engstrand	.80	2.40	4.00	
1177	Proud Youth—Alexander Eliot	.50	1.50	2.50	
S1178	The Housewarming—George Sklar	.50	1.50	2.50	
1179	The Lie—Peggy Goodin	.50	1.50	2.50	
1180	Fatal Step—Wade Miller	1.00	3.00	5.00	M
1181	Six-Shooter Showdown—William Colt MacDonald	.80	2.40	4.00	W
1182	The Snake Pit—Mary Jane Ward	.50	1.50	2.50	
D1183	A Many-Splendored Thing—Suyin Han	.50	1.50	2.50	
1184	Thunder in the Heart—John Lee Weldon	.50	1.50	2.50	
1185	Room Clerk—Herbert Gold	.50	1.50	2.50	
1186	All the Way Home—Walter Freeman	.50	1.50	2.50	
1187	I'll Bury My Dead—James Hadley Chase	1.00	3.00	5.00	M
1188	Inspector Maigret and the Strangled Stripper—Georges Simenon; c-Maguire	1.00	3.00	5.00	M
S1189	Cheri and the Last of Cheri—Sidonie Colette	.80	2.40	4.00	
1190	Kitty—Rosamond Marshall	.50	1.50	2.50	
1191	The Final Hours—Jose Suarez Carreno	.80	2.40	4.00	
1192	A Texas Cowboy—Charles A. Siringo	.80	2.40	4.00	W
1193	River in My Blood—Richard Bissell	.80	2.40	4.00	
1194	Revolt in 2100—Robert A. Heinlein	1.20	3.60	6.00	SF
1195	The Butterfly—James M. Cain	.80	2.40	4.00	
1196	Mean As Hell—Dee Harkey	.80	2.40	4.00	
S1197	Street of the Barefoot Lovers—Joseph Foster	.50	1.50	2.50	
D1198	Love Is a Bridge—Charles Bracelen Flood	.50	1.50	2.50	
D1199	The Complete Stories of Erskine Caldwell	.50	1.50	2.50	
S1200	The Jungle Seas—Arthur A. Ageton; 1955	.50	1.50	2.50	
1201	Bamboo—Robert O. Bowen	.50	1.50	2.50	
1202	Out of the Red Brush—Kermit Daugherty	.50	1.50	2.50	
1203	Win, Place and Die!—Lawrence Lariar	.80	2.40	4.00	M
1204	Love Trap—Lionel White; orig., 1955	1.20	3.60	6.00	
S1205	Tombstone—Walter Noble Burns	.50	1.50	2.50	NF
D1206	The Cry and the Covenant—Morton Thompson	.50	1.50	2.50	
1207	Three Sinners in Paris—Toni Howard	.50	1.50	2.50	
1208	Live for Today—Vincent Sheean; c-Maguire	.80	2.40	4.00	
1209	The Fascinator—Theodora Keogh	.80	2.40	4.00	
1210	My Husband Keeps Telling Me to Go to Hell—Ella Bentley Arthur	.50	1.50	2.50	
D1211	The Hoods—Harry Grey	.80	2.40	4.00	
T1212	A Child of the Century—Ben Hecht	.50	1.50	2.50	
S1213	The Time of Indifference—Alberto Moravia	.50	1.50	2.50	
S1214	Life of Davy Crockett—Davy Crockett	.80	2.40	4.00	B
S1215	Lost Island—Graham McInnes	.50	1.50	2.50	
1216	Slice of Hell—Mike Roscoe; c-Maguire	1.20	3.60	6.00	
1217	Death Likes It Hot—Edgar Box	1.00	3.00	5.00	M
1218	The City and the Pillar—Gore Vidal	.80	2.40	4.00	
1219	Cattle Kingdom—Alan LeMay	.80	2.40	4.00	W
S1220	Darkness at Noon—Arthur Koestler	.50	1.50	2.50	
1221	The Black Donnellys—Thomas P. Kelley	.80	2.40	4.00	NF
S1222	The Eternal Voyagers—Robert F. Mirvish	.50	1.50	2.50	
1223	First Affair—Raffaele LaCapria	.50	1.50	2.50	
1224	The Space Frontiers—Roger Lee Vernon	1.00	3.00	5.00	SF
1225	The Last Kill—Charles Wells; 1955, c-Maguire	1.00	3.00	5.00	
1226	Violent Streets—Dale Kramer	1.00	3.00	5.00	
D1227	The Lovers—Kathleen Winsor	.50	1.50	2.50	
1228	Sons of the Saddle—William MacLeod Raine	.50	1.50	2.50	W

		Good	Fine	N/Mint	
D1229	Moby Dick—Herman Melville	1.00	3.00	5.00	A
1230	High Water—Richard Bissell	.80	2.40	4.00	
1231	The Farmer's Bride—Robert Hazel	.50	1.50	2.50	
1232	Hard Man With a Gun—Charles N. Heckelmann	.50	1.50	2.50	W
1233	The Damned Lovely—Jack Webb; c-Maguire	1.00	3.00	5.00	M
1234	This Thing Called Love—Harve Breit & Marc Slonim	.50	1.50	2.50	
1235	Killer's Choice—Wade Miller	1.00	3.00	5.00	M
1236	The Rose Tattoo—Tennessee Williams	.50	1.50	2.50	
D1237	The Lying Days—Nadine Gordimer	.50	1.50	2.50	
S1238	Everything Happens at Night—Bernard Wolfe	.50	1.50	2.50	
1239	Warrior's Return—Ted Pittenger	.50	1.50	2.50	
S1240	The Caves of Steel—Isaac Asimov	1.20	3.60	6.00	SF
1241	To Find a Killer—Lionel White; c-Maguire	1.20	3.60	6.00	M
1242	Web of Gunsmoke—Will Hickok	.50	1.50	2.50	W
1243	The Body in the Bed—Bill S. Ballinger	1.00	3.00	5.00	M
D1244	The Gold of Their Bodies—Charles Gorham	.50	1.50	2.50	
S1245	Satchmo—Louis Armstrong	.80	2.40	4.00	B
1246	Nights of Love and Laughter—Henry Miller	1.20	3.60	6.00	
1247	So Cold, My Bed—Sam S. Taylor; c-Maguire	1.20	3.60	6.00	
1248	Inspector Maigret and the Killers—Georges Simenon	1.00	3.00	5.00	M
S1249	The Sheltering Sky—Paul Bowles	.50	1.50	2.50	
1250	The Golden Sleep—Vivian Connell; 1955	.50	1.50	2.50	
1251	Laramie Rides Alone—Will Ermine	.50	1.50	2.50	W
S1252	Goodbye to Berlin—Christopher Isherwood	1.00	3.00	5.00	
S1253	Intruder in the Dust—William Faulkner	.50	1.50	2.50	
S1254	Heart of Darkness and the Secret Sharer—Joseph Conrad	.80	2.40	4.00	
1255	The Unholy Three and Other Stories—Louis Auchincloss	.50	1.50	2.50	
1256	The Bleeding Scissors—Bruno Fischer; c-Maguire	1.20	3.60	6.00	M
1257	Uneasy Street—Wade Miller	1.00	3.00	5.00	
1258	Montana Man—Paul Evan Lehman	.50	1.50	2.50	W
T1259	The Narrows—Ann Petry	.50	1.50	2.50	
D1260	The Farm—Louis Bromfield	.50	1.50	2.50	E
1261	How Green Was My Sex Life—Lawrence Lariar	1.00	3.00	5.00	
S1262	A Streetcar Named Desire—Tennessee Williams	.80	2.40	4.00	
D1263	The Rains Came—Louis Bromfield; 1956	.50	1.50	2.50	
1264	The Primitive—Chester Himes	.50	1.50	2.50	
T1265	Not As a Stranger—Morton Thompson	.50	1.50	2.50	
S1266	The Soft Voice of the Serpent—Nadine Gordimer	.50	1.50	2.50	
1267	Margaret—Caroline Slade	.50	1.50	2.50	
1268	Stopover for Murder—Floyd Mahannah; c-Maguire	1.20	3.60	6.00	M
1269	Whistling Lead—Eugene Cunningham	.50	1.50	2.50	
1270	Calamity Fair—Wade Miller; c-Maguire	1.20	3.60	6.00	M
S1271	Fifty Roads to Town—Earl Hammer, Jr.	.80	2.40	4.00	
1272	Love and Money—Erskine Caldwell	.50	1.50	2.50	
S1273	The Blue Hussar—Roger Nimier	.50	1.50	2.50	
1274	The Body Beautiful—Bill S. Ballinger	1.00	3.00	5.00	M
1275	The Face of Time—James T. Farrell; 1956, c-Maguire	1.00	3.00	5.00	
1276	I'll Kill You Next!—Adam Knight; c-Maguire	1.00	3.00	5.00	M
1277	Bunch Grass—Joseph Wayne	.50	1.50	2.50	W
1278	Dirty Eddie—Ludwig Bemelmans	.50	1.50	2.50	
S1279	Making of a Mistress—Susan Morley	.50	1.50	2.50	
S1280	General Billy Mitchell—Roger Burlingame	.80	2.40	4.00	B
S1281	Adventures in the Skin Trade—Dylan Thomas	.80	2.40	4.00	
S1282	I, Robot—Isaac Asimov	1.60	4.80	8.00	SF
1283	The Nightshade Ring—Lindsay Hardy	.50	1.50	2.50	
1284	Meg—Theodora Keogh	.50	1.50	2.50	
S1285	No Time for Sergeants—Mac Hyman	.50	1.50	2.50	
1286	The Big Steal—Earle Basinsky	.80	2.40	4.00	M

Signet 1233, © NA

Signet 1246, © NA

Signet 1276, © NA

Signet 1289, © NA

Signet 1311, © NA

Signet S1334, © NA

(SIGNET, continued)

		Good	Fine	N/Mint	
1287	Lobo Law—Will Ermine	.50	1.50	2.50	W
1288	Conjugal Love—Alberto Moravia	.50	1.50	2.50	
1289	Animal Farm—George Orwell	2.00	6.00	10.00	
S1290	Too Late the Phalarope—Alan Paton	.50	1.50	2.50	
D1291	The Royal Box—Frances Parkinson Keyes	.50	1.50	2.50	
S1292	The Enemy—Wirt Williams	.50	1.50	2.50	
1293	I Stole $16,000,000—Thomas P. Kelley & Herbert Emerson Wilson	.80	2.40	4.00	NF
1294	Violence in Velvet—Michael Avallone; c-Maguire	1.20	3.60	6.00	M
1295	The Lonely—Paul Gallico	.50	1.50	2.50	
1296	The Delicate Prey—Paul Bowles	.50	1.50	2.50	
1297	The Valley of Hunted Men—Paul Evan Lehman	.50	1.50	2.50	W
1298	Contraband—Cleve F. Adams	1.00	3.00	5.00	
D1299	The Third Generation—Chester Himes	.50	1.50	2.50	
1300	Washington Lowdown—Larston Farrar; 1956	.50	1.50	2.50	
1301	The Secret of Mary Magdalene—Paul Ilton	.50	1.50	2.50	
1302	Gunplay Valley—Joseph Wayne	.50	1.50	2.50	W
1303	The Six-Gun Kid—William MacLeod Raine	.50	1.50	2.50	W
1304	Winesburg, Ohio—Sherwood Anderson	.50	1.50	2.50	
D1305	Boswell's London Journal—James Boswell	.50	1.50	2.50	
S1306	A Ghost at Noon—Alberto Moravia	.50	1.50	2.50	
S1307	Murder in Paradise—Richard Gehman	.50	1.50	2.50	M
S1308	The Girl in the Dogwood Cabin—Calder Willingham	.50	1.50	2.50	
S1309	The Whispers of Love—Marguerite Duras	.50	1.50	2.50	
1310	The Killing—Lionel White; c-Maguire, movie tie-in	1.20	3.60	6.00	
1311	The Broken Doll—Jack Webb; c-Maguire	1.00	3.00	5.00	
1312	The Fastest Gun in Texas—C. J. LaRoche & J. H. Plenn	.80	2.40	4.00	
1313	The Tent of the Wicked—Robert Switzer	.50	1.50	2.50	
1314	There's One in Every Town—James Aswell	.50	1.50	2.50	
1315	Knight's Gambit—William Faulkner	.50	1.50	2.50	
1316	The Glass Playpen—Edwin Fadiman, Jr.; c-Maguire	.80	2.40	4.00	
1317	A Devil in Paradise—Henry Miller	.80	2.40	4.00	
S1318	The Black Prince and Other Stories—Shirley Ann Grau	.80	2.40	4.00	
1319	The Tooth and the Nail—Bill S. Ballinger; c-Maguire	1.00	3.00	5.00	M
1320	Shore Leave—Frederic Wakeman	.50	1.50	2.50	
1321	Portrait in Smoke—Bill S. Ballinger	.80	2.40	4.00	M
1322	Stone Cold Blonde—Adam Knight; c-Maguire	1.00	3.00	5.00	M
1323	Buckskin Marshal—Will Ermine	.50	1.50	2.50	W
1324	Delay en Route—Jerry Weil; c-Maguire	.80	2.40	4.00	
1325	The Navigator—Jules Roy; 1956	.50	1.50	2.50	
1326	Nightmare Alley—William Lindsay Gresham	.50	1.50	2.50	
1327	The Snow Was Black—Georges Simenon	.80	2.40	4.00	M
D1328	The New American Handy College Dictionary—Albert H. Morehead & Loy Morehead	.40	1.20	2.00	NF
1329	The Kiss-off—Douglas Heyes	.50	1.50	2.50	
D1330	Band of Angels—Robert Penn Warren	.50	1.50	2.50	
1331	Black Sombrero—William Colt MacDonald	.50	1.50	2.50	W
1332	Julie—Andrew L. Stone; c-Maguire	.80	2.40	4.00	
S1333	The Glass Harp and A Tree of Night—Truman Capote	.50	1.50	2.50	
1334	Baby Doll—Tennessee Williams	1.60	4.80	8.00	
1335	The Living Idol—Robert Switzer; c-Maguire	2.00	6.00	10.00	E
S1336	Nectar in a Sieve—Kamala Markandaya	.50	1.50	2.50	
S1337	The Alien Heart—Catherine Hutter	.50	1.50	2.50	
1338	Inspector Maigret in New York's Underworld—Georges Simenon; c-Maguire	1.00	3.00	5.00	M
1339	Return of the Texan—Burt Arthur	.50	1.50	2.50	W
1340	Trigger Justice—Leslie Ernenwein	.50	1.50	2.50	W
1341	The Wayward Ones—Sara Harris	1.00	3.00	5.00	
1342	Gretta—Erskine Caldwell	.50	1.50	2.50	
1343	Tea and Sympathy—Robert Anderson	.50	1.50	2.50	
1344	Good Night, Sailor—J. Inchardi	.50	1.50	2.50	

		Good	Fine	N/Mint	
S1345	A Good Man Is Hard to Find—Flannery O'Connor	.50	1.50	2.50	
S1346	Operation: Outer Space—Murray Leinster	1.20	3.60	6.00	SF
1347	Girl Running—Adam Knight	1.00	3.00	5.00	M
S1348	The Teahouse of the August Moon—Vern Sneider; movie tie-in	.50	1.50	2.50	
1349	French Girls Are Vicious—James T. Farrell	.50	1.50	2.50	
1350	Office Wife—Jerry Weil; 1957	.50	1.50	2.50	
1351	Death Is a Cold, Keen Edge—Earle Basinsky; c-Maguire	1.20	3.60	6.00	M
1352	Blood of the West—Paul Evan Lehman	.50	1.50	2.50	W
1353	The Slander of Witches—Richard Gehman	.50	1.50	2.50	
1354	Night Flight—Antoine de Saint Exupery	.50	1.50	2.50	
D1355	The Strangeland—Ned Calmer	.50	1.50	2.50	
S1356	Anastasia—Marcelle Maurette	.50	1.50	2.50	
1357	A Stranger in Eden—Desmond Stewart	.50	1.50	2.50	
1358	One Tear for My Grave—Mike Roscoe; c-Maguire	1.00	3.00	5.00	M
1359	Desire Me—Leonhard Frank	.50	1.50	2.50	
1360	Brave in the Saddle—Will Ermine	.50	1.50	2.50	W
1361	Ever Since Adam and Eve—Alfred Andriola & Mel Casson	.50	1.50	2.50	
S1362	Quicksand—William Brinkley	.50	1.50	2.50	
S1363	The Tyranny of Sex—Ludwig Lewisohn	.50	1.50	2.50	
S1364	The Girl He Left Behind—Marion Hargrove	.40	1.20	2.00	
S1365	The Angry Hills—Leon Uris	.50	1.50	2.50	C
1366	Death Rider—J. O. Barnwell; 1957	.50	1.50	2.50	
S1367	Gift From the Sea—Anne Morrow Lindbergh	.50	1.50	2.50	
D1368	1,000,000 Delinquents—Benjamin Fine	.80	2.40	4.00	
1369	Shoot to Kill—Wade Miller	1.00	3.00	5.00	M
S1370	The Short Cut—Ennio Flaiano	.50	1.50	2.50	
S1371	I Leap Over the Wall—Monica Baldwin	.50	1.50	2.50	
1372	Two Adolescents—Alberto Moravia	.50	1.50	2.50	
1373	Bullet Law—Charles N. Heckelmann	.50	1.50	2.50	W
1374	An Act of Violence—Edwin Fadiman, Jr.	.50	1.50	2.50	
D1375	The Deer Park—Norman Mailer; 1957	.50	1.50	2.50	
1376	Strangers in the House—Georges Simenon	1.00	3.00	5.00	M
1377	The Life, the Loves, the Adventures of Omar Khayyam—Manuel Komroff; movie tie-in	.50	1.50	2.50	
1378	Flight Into Terror—Lionel White; c-Maguire	1.00	3.00	5.00	
1379	The Bandaged Nude—Robert Finnegan	.50	1.50	2.50	
1380	Tortilla Flat—John Steinbeck	.80	2.40	4.00	
1381	The Story of Sandy—Susan Stanhope Wexler	.50	1.50	2.50	
1382	What Am I Doing Here?—Abner Dean	.50	1.50	2.50	
1383	Killer in the House—Borden Deal	.80	2.40	4.00	
1384	The Return of the Kid—Joseph Wayne	.50	1.50	2.50	W
S1385	The Bachelor Party—Paddy Chayefsky; movie tie-in	.50	1.50	2.50	
D1386	End As a Man—Calder Willingham	.50	1.50	2.50	
S1387	Look Not Upon Me—Denys Jones	.50	1.50	2.50	
T1388	Andersonville—MacKinlay Kantor	.80	2.40	4.00	NF
S1389	The Stars, My Destination—Alfred Bester	1.00	3.00	5.00	SF
1390	The Wastrel—Frederic Wakeman	.50	1.50	2.50	
D1391	The Long Ships—Frans G. Bengtsson	.80	2.40	4.00	W
S1392	The Girl He Left Behind—Marion Hargrove	.50	1.50	2.50	
1393	Paint on Their Faces—Jerry Weil; c-Maguire	1.00	3.00	5.00	
1394					
1395	Murder for Madame—Adam Knight	1.00	3.00	5.00	M
1396	Clattering Hoofs—William MacLeod Raine	.50	1.50	2.50	W
1397	In a Summer Season—Ludwig Lewisohn	.50	1.50	2.50	
1398	Montana Rides!—Evan Evans (Max Brand)	.50	1.50	2.50	W
1399	The Last Days of Sodom and Gomorrah—Paul Ilton; c-Maguire	1.60	4.80	8.00	E
S1400	Lizzie—Shirley Jackson; 1957	.50	1.50	2.50	
1401	Trigger Man—Burt Arthur	.50	1.50	2.50	W
1402	Ripening Seed—Sidonie Colette	.80	2.40	4.00	

Signet 1361, © NA

Signet S1387, © NA

Signet 1399, © NA

		Good	Fine	N/Mint	
1403	Quick-Trigger Country—Clem Colt	.50	1.50	2.50	W
1404	Love in the Afternoon—Claude Anet	.50	1.50	2.50	
1405	The Private Eye—Cleve F. Adams; c-Maguire	1.00	3.00	5.00	M
1406					
D1407	Beyond Desire—Pierre LaMure	.50	1.50	2.50	
S1408	More Deaths Than One—Stuart Engstrand	.50	1.50	2.50	
S1409	The Prince and the Showgirl—Terence Rattigan; movie tie-in	.50	1.50	2.50	
D1410	Heart of Darkness and the Secret Sharer—Joseph Conrad	.50	1.50	2.50	
D1411	Confessions of Felix Krull, Confidence Man—Thomas Mann	1.00	3.00	5.00	NF
S1412	A Hatful of Rain—Michael Vincente Gazzo	.50	1.50	2.50	
S1413	Sweet Smell of Success—Ernest Lehman	.50	1.50	2.50	
1414	Flint—Gil Dodge	.50	1.50	2.50	
S1415	The Night Before Chancellorsville—Shelby Foote	1.00	3.00	5.00	
1416	The Killer Brand—William Colt MacDonald	.50	1.50	2.50	W
1417	This Very Earth—Erskine Caldwell	.50	1.50	2.50	
1418	Doubtful Valley—George Garland	.50	1.50	2.50	
1419	Sabotage—Cleve F. Adams	.80	2.40	4.00	
S1420	The Deliverance of Sister Cecilia—William Brinkley & Sister Cecilia	.50	1.50	2.50	
1421	The Hitchhiker—Georges Simenon	.80	2.40	4.00	M
1422	The Bad Blonde—Jack Webb; c-Maguire	.80	2.40	4.00	
1423	The Manhunter—Matthew Gant	.50	1.50	2.50	
S1424	This Is the West—Robert West Howard	.50	1.50	2.50	NF
S1425	Pajama—Richard Bissell; 1957	.50	1.50	2.50	
S1426	Country Place—Ann Petry	.50	1.50	2.50	
1427	Double Indemnity—James M. Cain; c-Maguire	.80	2.40	4.00	
D1428	Lady Chatterley's Lover—D. H. Lawrence	.50	1.50	2.50	
1429	The Unfaithful Wife—Jules Roy	.50	1.50	2.50	
S1430	Gulf Coast Stories—Erskine Caldwell	.50	1.50	2.50	
D1431	New American Roget's College Thesaurus in Dictionary Form	.40	1.20	2.00	NF
1432	The Hard Guys—John B. Sanford	.50	1.50	2.50	
S1433	The Martian Way and Other Stories—Isaac Asimov	1.00	3.00	5.00	SF
1434	The Tight Corner—Sam Ross	.50	1.50	2.50	
1435	The Man From Yesterday—John S. Daniels	.50	1.50	2.50	
1436	Montana Rides Again—Evan Evans (Max Brand)	.50	1.50	2.50	W
S1437	Appointment in Samarra—John O'Hara	.50	1.50	2.50	
D1438	Lucy Crown—Irwin Shaw	.50	1.50	2.50	
S1439	Ruby McCollum—William Bradford Huie	.50	1.50	2.50	
1440	Coral Comes High—George P. Hunt	.50	1.50	2.50	
1441	The Mountain Boys—Paul Webb	.50	1.50	2.50	
1442	The House Next Door—Lionel White; c-Maguire	1.00	3.00	5.00	
1443	Gunsmoke in Nevada—Burt Arthur	.50	1.50	2.50	W
S1444	Double Star—Robert A. Heinlein	1.20	3.60	6.00	SF
1445	Love's Lovely Counterfeit—James M. Cain	.50	1.50	2.50	
1446	The Comedian and Other Stories—Ernest Lehman	.50	1.50	2.50	
1447	Secret of Hidden Valley—Loring Hutchinson	.50	1.50	2.50	
1448	Find My Killer—Manly Wade Wellman; c-Maguire	.80	2.40	4.00	
1449	Nobody Dies in Paris—Jerry Weil	.50	1.50	2.50	
1450	Shore Leave—Frederic Wakeman; 1957	.50	1.50	2.50	
S1451	Comfort Me With Apples—Peter De Vries	.50	1.50	2.50	
S1452	I'm Owen Harrison Harding—James Whitfield Ellison	.50	1.50	2.50	
S1453	Tip on a Dead Jockey—Irwin Shaw; movie tie-in	.50	1.50	2.50	
T1454	Marjorie Morningstar—Herman Wouk	.50	1.50	2.50	
D1455	The Field of Vision—Wright Morris	.50	1.50	2.50	
1456	A House in the Uplands—Erskine Caldwell	.50	1.50	2.50	
S1457	A Dangerous Woman—James T. Farrell	.50	1.50	2.50	
D1458	Don't Go Near the Water—William Brinkley	.40	1.20	2.00	
S1459	Submarine!—Edward L. Beach	.50	1.50	2.50	C
S1460	This Is Goggle—Bentz Plagemann	.50	1.50	2.50	
1461	Wild Town—Jim Thompson; orig., 1957, c-Maguire	1.20	3.60	6.00	
S1462	Bitter Victory—Rene Hardy	.50	1.50	2.50	
S1463	Modern Sex Life—Edwin Hirsch	.40	1.20	2.00	
S1464	The City and the Stars—Arthur C. Clarke	1.00	3.00	5.00	SF
1465	The Fugitive—Georges Simenon	.80	2.40	4.00	M
S1466	Those Devils in Baggy Pants—Ross Carter	.40	1.20	2.00	C
S1467	A Walk in the Sun—Harry Brown	.50	1.50	2.50	
T1468	The Fountainhead—Ayn Rand	1.20	3.60	6.00	
D1469	The Amazing Crime and Trial of Leopold and Loeb—Maureen McKernan	.50	1.50	2.50	NF
S1470	The Ox-Bow Incident—Walter Van Tilburg Clark	.50	1.50	2.50	W
1471	Old Soldiers Never Die—Wolf Mankowitz	.50	1.50	2.50	
1472	Kill Once, Kill Twice—Kyle Hunt; c-Maguire	.80	2.40	4.00	
1473	Bandido—Nelson Nye	.50	1.50	2.50	W
1474	The Flesh Was Cold—Bruno Fischer; c-Maguire	1.00	3.00	5.00	M
1475	Death in the Fifth Position—Edgar Box; 1957	.80	2.40	4.00	M
S1476	The FBI in Action—Ken Jones	.50	1.50	2.50	
D1477	Raquel—Lion Feuchtwanger	.50	1.50	2.50	
S1478	War!—Alex Austin	.50	1.50	2.50	C

		Good	Fine	N/Mint	
1479	A Place Called Estherville—Erskine Caldwell	.50	1.50	2.50	
1480	The Sins of Sandra Shaw—Larston Farrar; 1958	.50	1.50	2.50	
1481	Thirty Notches—Brad Ward	.50	1.50	2.50	W
1482	Guilty Bystander—Wade Miller	.50	1.50	2.50	
1483	Powdersmoke Feud—William MacLeod Raine	.50	1.50	2.50	W
1484	Death Likes It Hot—Edgar Box	.80	2.40	4.00	M
S1485	Pylon—William Faulkner; movie tie-in	.50	1.50	2.50	
D1486	Sanctuary and Requiem for a Nun	.40	1.20	2.00	
D1487	The Last Parallel—Martin Russ	.50	1.50	2.50	
T1488	The Brothers Karamazov—Fyodor Dostoyevsky	.50	1.50	2.50	
1489	Sing, Boy, Sing—Richard Vincent; movie tie-in	.50	1.50	2.50	
D1490	Too Much, Too Soon—Diana Barrymore & Gerold Frank	.50	1.50	2.50	
S1491	Kitty Foyle—Christopher Morley	.50	1.50	2.50	
1492	Violent Hours—Robert Walsh	.50	1.50	2.50	
S1493	The End of Eternity—Isaac Asimov	.80	2.40	4.00	SF
1494	The Wife of the Red-haired Man—Bill S. Ballinger	.50	1.50	2.50	M
S1495	Last of the Great Outlaws—Homer Croy	.80	2.40	4.00	NF
T1496	The Young Lions—Irwin Shaw	.50	1.50	2.50	
S1497	The Sacrilege of Alan Kent—Erskine Caldwell	.50	1.50	2.50	
D1498	Nine Stories—J. D. Salinger	.50	1.50	2.50	
S1499	Cat Man—Edward Hoagland	.50	1.50	2.50	E
S1500	Mafia—Ed Reid; 1958	.50	1.50	2.50	
S1501	The Long Hot Summer—William Faulkner; movie tie-in	.80	2.40	4.00	
S1502	Desire Under the Elms—Eugene O'Neill	.50	1.50	2.50	
D1503	Grandfather Stories—Samuel Hopkins Adams	.50	1.50	2.50	
1504	West Side Jungle—Jason Ridgway	.50	1.50	2.50	
1505	Smoke of the Gun—John S. Daniels	.50	1.50	2.50	W
D1506	Able Company—D. J. Hollands	.50	1.50	2.50	
S1507	The Tunnel of Love—Peter De Vries	.50	1.50	2.50	
1508	Cry Terror—Andrew L. Stone; c-Maguire	.80	2.40	4.00	
D1509	Sons and Lovers—D. H. Lawrence	.50	1.50	2.50	
D1510	The Conformist—Alberto Moravia	.50	1.50	2.50	
S1511	Intruder in the Dust—William Faulkner	.50	1.50	2.50	
S1512	The Invisible Flag—Peter Bamm	.50	1.50	2.50	
S1513	The Barbarian and the Geisha—Robert Payne; movie tie-in	1.00	3.00	5.00	
S1514	The Assistant—Bernard Malamud	.50	1.50	2.50	
1515	Hang By Your Neck—Henry Kane	.80	2.40	4.00	M
1516	Maverick Marshal—Nelson Nye	.50	1.50	2.50	W
S1517	Duchess Hotspur—Rosamond Marshall	.40	1.20	2.00	
T1518	Studs Lonigan—James T. Farrell	.50	1.50	2.50	
D1519	Gallery of Women—Bernard Glemser	.50	1.50	2.50	
S1520	Bitter Honeymoon—Alberto Moravia	.50	1.50	2.50	
S1521	Soldier's Three—Humphrey Slater	.40	1.20	2.00	
S1522	Company K—William March	.40	1.20	2.00	
1523	Edge of Panic—Henry Kane	.80	2.40	4.00	M
S1524	Starburst—Alfred Bester	1.00	3.00	5.00	SF
S1525	Gigi and Julie de Carneilhan—Sidonie Colette; 1958	.50	1.50	2.50	
1526	Death Before Bedtime—Edgar Box; c-Maguire	.80	2.40	4.00	M
1527	The Body—Carter Brown	.50	1.50	2.50	M
1528	The Nightwalkers—Beverley Cross	.50	1.50	2.50	
D1529	A Streetcar Named Desire—Tennessee Williams	.80	2.40	4.00	
D1530	No Time for Sergeants—Mac Hyman	.40	1.20	2.00	
S1531	Love Among the Cannibals—Wright Morris	.40	1.20	2.00	
S1532	Some Inner Fury—Kamala Markandaya	.50	1.50	2.50	
S1533	Branded West—Don Ward	.50	1.50	2.50	W
S1534	43,000 Years Later—Horace Coon	1.00	3.00	5.00	SF
S1535	A Thirsty Evil—Gore Vidal	.50	1.50	2.50	
1536	A Texan Came Riding—Frank O'Rourke	.50	1.50	2.50	W

Signet 1500, © NA

Signet 1541, © NA

Signet 1555, © NA

		Good	Fine	N/Mint	
S1537	The Green Hills of Earth—Robert A. Heinlein	1.00	3.00	5.00	SF
1538	Dame in Danger—Thomas B. Dewey; c-Maguire	1.00	3.00	5.00	
1539	The Case of the Dead Divorcee—William Holder	.80	2.40	4.00	M
1540	No Luck for a Lady—Floyd Mahannah; c-Maguire	1.00	3.00	5.00	
1541	The Restless Gun—Will Hickok	.50	1.50	2.50	W
D1542	Whispers of the Flesh—Fletcher Flora	.50	1.50	2.50	
S1543	Silent Grow the Guns—MacKinlay Kantor	.50	1.50	2.50	
S1544	The Puppet Masters—Robert A. Heinlein	.80	2.40	4.00	SF
D1545	Bread and Wine—Ignazio Silone	.40	1.20	2.00	
D1546	Bon Voyage!—Joseph & Marrijane Hayes	.40	1.20	2.00	
T1547	A Dictionary of American-English Usage—Margaret Nicholson	.40	1.20	2.00	NF
D1548	The Love-Seekers—Leonora Hornblow	.50	1.50	2.50	
T1549	The Naked and the Dead—Norman Mailer	.50	1.50	2.50	
D1550	Birdman of Alcatraz—Thomas E. Gaddis; 1958	.80	2.40	4.00	
S1551	My Fair Lady—Alan Jay Lerner; movie tie-in	1.00	3.00	5.00	
D1552	The World of Suzie Wong—Raymond Mason; movie tie-in	.80	2.40	4.00	
S1553	Selected Stories—Liam O'Flaherty	.50	1.50	2.50	
1554	Escapade—Jerry Weil	.80	2.40	4.00	
1555	Hell to Pay—William R. Cox	1.00	3.00	5.00	JD
1556	The Brass Halo—Jack Webb; c-Maguire	1.00	3.00	5.00	
S1557	The Wild Bunch—James D. Horan	.50	1.50	2.50	NF
S1558	Destination: Universe—A. E. Van Vogt	1.00	3.00	5.00	SF
S1559	Giovanni's Room—James Baldwin	.50	1.50	2.50	
S1560	My Name Is Rose—Theodora Keogh	.50	1.50	2.50	
D1561	The Girl With the Swansdown Seat—Cyril Pearl	.50	1.50	2.50	
D1562	On the Beach—Nevil Shute	.80	2.40	4.00	
S1563	From Russia, With Love—Ian Fleming	1.20	3.60	6.00	
S1564	This Very Earth—Erskine Caldwell	.50	1.50	2.50	
1565	The Blonde—Carter Brown	.50	1.50	2.50	M
1566	Damaron's Gun—Wesley Ray	.50	1.50	2.50	
T1567	Forever Amber—Kathleen Winsor	.50	1.50	2.50	
S1568	Certain Women—Erskine Caldwell	.50	1.50	2.50	
S1569	Room at the Top—John Braine	.40	1.20	2.00	
S1570	Nine Miles to Reno—Jill Stern	.50	1.50	2.50	
S1571	Henry the Last—Giuseppe Puzza	.50	1.50	2.50	
S1572	Portrait of a Mobster—Harry Grey	.80	2.40	4.00	
1573	Kill a Wicked Man—Kyle Hunt	.80	2.40	4.00	
D1574	Moulin Rouge—Pierre LaMure	.50	1.50	2.50	
D1575	The Hoods—Harry Grey; 1959	.50	1.50	2.50	
D1576	Knock on Any Door—Willard Motley	.50	1.50	2.50	
S1577	The Day After Tomorrow—Robert A. Heinlein	.80	2.40	4.00	SF
T1578	Remember Me to God—Myron S. Kaufmann	.50	1.50	2.50	
S1579	Not Yet . . .—Tereska Torres	.80	2.40	4.00	
S1580	Subways Are for Sleeping—Edmund Love	.50	1.50	2.50	
1581	The Heart of a Stranger—Lionel Olay	.50	1.50	2.50	
1582	The Doll's Smile—Eva Boros	.50	1.50	2.50	
S1583	The Deep Range—Arthur C. Clarke	1.00	3.00	5.00	SF
1584	The Getaway—Jim Thompson; orig., 1959	1.20	3.60	6.00	
1585	Formula for Murder—Bill S. Ballinger	.80	2.40	4.00	M
1586	The Case of the Strangled Starlet—James Hadley Chase	.80	2.40	4.00	M
S1587	I Want to Live!—Tabor Rawson; movie tie-in	.50	1.50	2.50	
1588	The Crimson Quirt—William Colt MacDonald	.50	1.50	2.50	W
S1589	The Sure Hand of God—Erskine Caldwell	.50	1.50	2.50	
S1590	Cat on a Hot Tin Roof—Tennessee Williams; movie tie-in	1.00	3.00	5.00	
D1591	The American Woman—Eric J. Dingwall	.50	1.50	2.50	
S1592	Journeyman—Erskine Caldwell	.50	1.50	2.50	
S1593	The Demolished Man—Alfred Bester	.80	2.40	4.00	SF
1594	The Mistress—Carter Brown	.50	1.50	2.50	M
1595	The Decks Ran Red—Andrew L. Stone	.50	1.50	2.50	
D1596	The Woman of Rome—Alberto Moravia	.50	1.50	2.50	
S1597	Sigrid and the Sergeant—Robert Buckner	.50	1.50	2.50	
S1598	Episode in Palmetto—Erskine Caldwell	.50	1.50	2.50	
S1599	The Knife—Theon Wright	.50	1.50	2.50	
D1600	America, With Love—Kathleen Winsor; 1958	.50	1.50	2.50	
D1601	The Called and the Chosen—Monica Baldwin	.50	1.50	2.50	
S1602	Summer in Salander—H. E. Bates	.50	1.50	2.50	
S1603	A Restless Breed—J. William Terry	.50	1.50	2.50	
S1604	Fortune Is a Woman—Hermes Nye	.50	1.50	2.50	
1605	Ute Country—John S. Daniels	.50	1.50	2.50	W
1606	The Corpse—Carter Brown	.50	1.50	2.50	M
1607	Gunsmoke Men—L. L. Foreman	.50	1.50	2.50	W
S1608	Trouble in July—Erskine Caldwell	.50	1.50	2.50	
S1609	Separate Tables—Terence Rattigan; 1959	.50	1.50	2.50	
S1610	Expense Account—Joe Morgan	.50	1.50	2.50	
S1611	Tragic Ground—Erskine Caldwell	.50	1.50	2.50	
S1612	Roman Tales—Alberto Moravia	.50	1.50	2.50	
S1613	Nobody Cares for Me—Sara Harris	.50	1.50	2.50	

		Good	Fine	N/Mint	
D1614	Sartoris—William Faulkner	.50	1.50	2.50	
S1615	Animal Farm—George Orwell	.80	2.40	4.00	
S1616	The Unvanquished—William Faulkner	.50	1.50	2.50	
D1617	Man of Montmartre—Ethel & Stephen Longstreet	.50	1.50	2.50	
1618	Texas Hellion—J. H. Plenn	.50	1.50	2.50	W
D1619	On the Road—Jack Kerouac	1.00	3.00	5.00	
1620	The Lover—Carter Brown	.50	1.50	2.50	M
S1621	The Courting of Susie Brown—Erskine Caldwell	.50	1.50	2.50	
S1622	The Seedling Star—James Blish	.50	1.50	2.50	SF
S1623	A Place Called Estherville—Erskine Caldwell	.50	1.50	2.50	
S1624	Saturday Night—James T. Farrell	.50	1.50	2.50	
S1625	The Blessing—Nancy Mitford; 1959	.50	1.50	2.50	
S1626	Last Train From Gun Hill—Gordon D. Shirreffs; movie tie-in	.80	2.40	4.00	W
D1627	Grandfather Stories—Samuel Hopkins Adams	.50	1.50	2.50	
D1628	The Sound and the Fury—William Faulkner; movie tie-in	.50	1.50	2.50	
D1629	Soldier's Pay—William Faulkner	.50	1.50	2.50	
D1630	Arch of Triumph—Erich Maria Remarque	.50	1.50	2.50	
1631	The Overlanders—Nelson Nye	.50	1.50	2.50	W
1632	The Caballero—Johnston McCulley	.50	1.50	2.50	W
1633	The Victim—Carter Brown	.50	1.50	2.50	M
1634	The Last Blitzkrieg—Walter Freeman	.50	1.50	2.50	
1635	The Fastest Gun in Texas—C. J. LaRoche & J. H. Plenn	.50	1.50	2.50	
1636	The Whispering Master—Frank Gruber	.50	1.50	2.50	
T1637	Some Came Running—James Jones	.50	1.50	2.50	
D1638	Darkness at Noon—Arthur Koestler	.50	1.50	2.50	
S1639	The Door Into Summer—Robert A. Heinlein	1.00	3.00	5.00	SF
D1640	1984—George Orwell	.50	1.50	2.50	SF
D1641	The Shadow and the Peak—Raymond Mason	.50	1.50	2.50	
1642	An Eye for an Eye—John B. West	.50	1.50	2.50	
D1643	The Wild Palms and the Old Man—William Faulkner	.50	1.50	2.50	
S1644	The Man Who Sold the Moon—Robert A. Heinlein	.50	1.50	2.50	SF
T1645	Never So Few—Tom T. Chamales	.50	1.50	2.50	
1646	Dormitory Women—R. V. Cassill; c-Maguire	1.00	3.00	5.00	
S1647	The Bedside Mad—William M. Gaines	1.00	3.00	5.00	H
S1648	The Mackerel Plaza—Peter De Vries	.50	1.50	2.50	
S1649	The Darling Buds of May—H. E. Bates	.50	1.50	2.50	
S1650	Miri—Peter Sourian; 1959	.50	1.50	2.50	
S1651	Wolf Whistle and Other Stories—William Bradford Huie	.50	1.50	2.50	
S1652	Beat, Beat, Beat—William F. Brown	.50	1.50	2.50	
D1653	The Intimate Henry Miller	1.00	3.00	5.00	
1654	The Loving and the Dead—Carter Brown	.50	1.50	2.50	M
1655	Slattery's Range—Richard Wormser	.50	1.50	2.50	
S1656	Some Like It Hot!—I. A. L. Diamond & Billy Wilder; movie tie-in	1.00	3.00	5.00	
D1657	Two Women—Alberto Moravia	.50	1.50	2.50	
S1658	The Silent Service—William C. Chambliss	.50	1.50	2.50	
S1659	Something About a Soldier—Mark Harris	.50	1.50	2.50	
1660	Night Ward—Noah Gordon	.50	1.50	2.50	
T1661	And Quiet Flows the Don—Mikhail Sholokhov	.50	1.50	2.50	
1662	Kiss Her Goodbye—Wade Miller	.50	1.50	2.50	
1663	Walk Softly, Witch—Carter Brown	.50	1.50	2.50	M
S1664	The Roman Spring of Mrs. Stone—Tennessee Williams	.50	1.50	2.50	
S1665	Cancel All Our Vows—John D. MacDonald	.50	1.50	2.50	M
S1666	Georgia Boy—Erskine Caldwell	.40	1.20	2.00	
D1667	The Catcher in the Rye—J. D. Salinger	.50	1.50	2.50	
T1668	The Time of the Dragons—Alice Ekert-Rotholz	.50	1.50	2.50	
D1669	Safe Conduct—Boris Pasternak	.50	1.50	2.50	
S1670	Doctor No—Ian Fleming	1.20	3.60	6.00	
S1671	The Dangerous American—A. E. Hotchner	.50	1.50	2.50	

Signet S1626, © NA

Signet 1653, © NA

Signet 1670, © NA

		Good	Fine	N/Mint	
S1672	A Lamp for Nightfall—Erskine Caldwell	.50	1.50	2.50	
S1673	The Black Cloud—Fred Hoyle	1.00	3.00	5.00	SF
1674	The Passionate—Carter Brown	.50	1.50	2.50	M
1675	Trail of the Restless Gun—Will Hickok; 1959	.50	1.50	2.50	W
1676					
1677	The Silver Tombstone Mystery—Frank Gruber	.50	1.50	2.50	M
D1678	Lola—Dario Fernandez-Florez	.50	1.50	2.50	
D1679	They Came to Cordura—Glendon Swarthout; movie tie-in	.50	1.50	2.50	
D1680	Chiara—Gene d'Olive	.50	1.50	2.50	
D1681	Ben-Hur—Lew Wallace	.50	1.50	2.50	
S1682	The Slot—John Clagett	.50	1.50	2.50	
S1683	No Time Like Tomorrow—Brian W. Aldiss	.50	1.50	2.50	SF
S1684	The Wounds of Hunger—Luis Spota	.50	1.50	2.50	
S1685	Follow Me Down—Shelby Foote	.80	2.40	4.00	
1686	Gun Code—Philip Ketchum	.50	1.50	2.50	W
1687	Violent Streets—Dale Kramer	.50	1.50	2.50	
1688	Wake Up With a Stranger—Fletcher Flora	.50	1.50	2.50	
S1689	The Loved and the Lost—Morley Callaghan	.50	1.50	2.50	
S1690	The Roman and the Slave Girl—John Medford Morgan	.50	1.50	2.50	
S1691	Crow Killer—Robert Bunker & Raymond Thorp	.50	1.50	2.50	W
D1692	Nautilus 90 North—William R. Anderson & Clay Blair, Jr.	.50	1.50	2.50	
D1693	Let No Man Write My Epitaph—Willard Motley	.50	1.50	2.50	
1694	None But the Lethal Heart—Carter Brown	.50	1.50	2.50	M
1695	Brand of a Man—Thomas Thompson	.50	1.50	2.50	W
1696	Shock Treatment—James Hadley Chase	.80	2.40	4.00	
1697	Stirrups in the Dust—Burt Arthur	.50	1.50	2.50	W
S1698	No But I Saw the Movie—Peter DeVries	.50	1.50	2.50	
S1699	Revolt in 2100—Robert A. Heinlein	.50	1.50	2.50	SF
S1700	The Big Kill—Mickey Spillane; 1959	.50	1.50	2.50	M
S1701	Son of Mad—William M. Gaines	1.00	3.00	5.00	H
Q1702	Atlas Shrugged—Ayn Rand	1.20	3.60	6.00	
S1703	Frontier—MacKinlay Kantor	.50	1.50	2.50	
1704	Manuela—William Woods	.50	1.50	2.50	
S1705	The Long Wait—Mickey Spillane	.50	1.50	2.50	M
S1706	The Eighth Day of the Week—Marek Hasko	.50	1.50	2.50	
1707	Invitation to Violence—Lionel White	1.00	3.00	5.00	
S1708	You Tell My Son—Rex Pratt	.50	1.50	2.50	
D1709	Around the World With Auntie Mame—Patrick Dennis	.50	1.50	2.50	
S1710	Vengeance Is Mine—Mickey Spillane	.50	1.50	2.50	M
S1711	Summer of the Seventeenth Doll—Ray Lawler	.50	1.50	2.50	
S1712	Entry E—Richard Frede	.50	1.50	2.50	
1713	The Wanton—Carter Brown	.50	1.50	2.50	M
1714	Apache Warpath—George Garland	.50	1.50	2.50	W
1715	Ambuscade—Frank O'Rourke	.50	1.50	2.50	
1716	The 21'' Scream—Edwin Fadiman, Jr.	.50	1.50	2.50	
T1717	The Mountain Is Young—Suyin Han	.50	1.50	2.50	
D1718	The Dharma Bums—Jack Kerouac	.80	2.40	4.00	
S1719	Galactic Cluster—James Blish	.80	2.40	4.00	SF
S1720	The Blue Angel—Heinrich Mann	.50	1.50	2.50	
S1721	Devil in the Flesh—Raymond Radiguet	.50	1.50	2.50	
1722	Suddenly by Violence—Carter Brown	.50	1.50	2.50	M
S1723	Live and Let Die—Ian Fleming	1.20	3.60	6.00	
1724	Triple Slay—Adam Knight	.80	2.40	4.00	M
D1725	Star Money—Kathleen Winsor; 1959	.40	1.20	2.00	
T1726	The Hard Blue Sky—Shirley Ann Grau	.50	1.50	2.50	
D1727	Breakfast at Tiffany's—Truman Capote	.50	1.50	2.50	
S1728	One Lonely Night—Mickey Spillane	.50	1.50	2.50	M
S1729	The Other Side of the Sky—Arthur C. Clarke	.80	2.40	4.00	SF
1730	The Longest Second—Bill S. Ballinger	.50	1.50	2.50	M
S1731	A Stretch on the River—Richard Bissell	.50	1.50	2.50	
S1732	The Incident—Marc Rivette	.50	1.50	2.50	
S1733	Kneel to the Rising Sun—Erskine Caldwell	.50	1.50	2.50	
S1734	Southways—Erskine Caldwell	.50	1.50	2.50	
S1735	We Are the Living—Erskine Caldwell	.50	1.50	2.50	
D1736	Lady Chatterley's Lover—D. H. Lawrence	.50	1.50	2.50	
S1737	Tortilla Flat—John Steinbeck	.50	1.50	2.50	
1738	The Dame—Carter Brown	.50	1.50	2.50	M
S1739	A Swell-Looking Girl—Erskine Caldwell	.50	1.50	2.50	
D1740	The Rainbow and the Rose—Nevil Shute	.50	1.50	2.50	
1741					
Q1742	A Child of the Century—Ben Hecht	.50	1.50	2.50	
S1743	The Girl in the Freudian Slip—William F. Brown	.50	1.50	2.50	
1744	The Dead-Shot Kid—Philip Ketchum	.50	1.50	2.50	W
S1745	The Fugitive Kind—Tennessee Williams; 1960, movie tie-in	.50	1.50	2.50	
D1746	Strike Heaven on the Face—Charles Calitri	.50	1.50	2.50	
S1747	The Lovely Lady—D. H. Lawrence	.50	1.50	2.50	
1748	Desperate Rider—Frank O'Rourke	.50	1.50	2.50	W

(SIGNET, continued)

		Good	Fine	N/Mint	
1749	The Guilty Are Afraid—James Hadley Chase	.80	2.40	4.00	M
1750	Terror Comes Creeping—Carter Brown	.50	1.50	2.50	M
D2939	Batman—Bob Kane; 1966. Note: Contains DC comic reprints	1.00	3.00	5.00	A

SIGNET CLASSICS
New American Library of World Literature, Inc.

		Good	Fine	N/Mint	
CD 1	Adolphe and the Red Notebook—Benjamin Constant; 1959	.40	1.20	2.00	
CD 2	The Adventures of Tom Sawyer—Mark Twain	.40	1.20	2.00	
CD 3	Animal Farm—George Orwell	.40	1.20	2.00	
CD 4	Heart of Darkness and the Secret Sharer—Joseph Conrad	.40	1.20	2.00	
CD 5	The Adventures of Huckleberry Finn—Mark Twain	.40	1.20	2.00	
CD 6	Kidnapped—Robert Louis Stevenson	.40	1.20	2.00	A
CD 7	The Return of the Native—Thomas Hardy	.40	1.20	2.00	
CD 8	The Scarlet Letter—Nathaniel Hawthorne	.40	1.20	2.00	
CD 9	The Unvanquished—William Faulkner	.40	1.20	2.00	
CD10	Wuthering Heights—Emily Bronte	.40	1.20	2.00	

SIGNET KEY
New American Library of World Literature, Inc.

		Good	Fine	N/Mint	
K300	Gandhi: His Life and Message for the World—Louis Fischer; 1954	.40	1.20	2.00	B
K301	How to Make a Success of Your Marriage—Dr. Eustace Chesser	.30	.90	1.50	NF
K302	Speak Better - Write Better - English—Horace Coon	.30	.90	1.50	NF
K303	The United States Political System and How It Works—David Cushman Coyle	.30	.90	1.50	NF
K304	A Brief History of the United States—Franklin Escher, Jr.	.30	.90	1.50	NF
K305	Flower Arrangements Anyone Can Do Anywhere—Matilda Rogers	.40	1.20	2.00	NF
K306	Lives of Destiny as Told for the Reader's Digest—Donald Culross Peattie	.40	1.20	2.00	B
Ks307	Hoyle's Rules of Games—Albert H. Morehead & Geoffrey Mott-Smith	.30	.90	1.50	NF
K308	How the Great Religions Began—Joseph Gaer	.40	1.20	2.00	NF
K309	Diet to Suit Yourself—Walter Ross	.30	.90	1.50	NF
Ks310	A Treasury of Wisdom and Inspiration—David St. Leger	.40	1.20	2.00	
Ks311	Andy's Everyday Encyclopedia—Ellen Wales	.30	.90	1.50	NF
K312	The Householder's Manual—Richard Kent	.30	.90	1.50	NF
K313	Your Way to Popularity and Personal Power—James Bender & Lee Graham	.30	.90	1.50	
Ks314	How to Help Your Child in School—Lawrence K. & Mary Frank	.30	.90	1.50	NF
KD315	God's Wonderful World—Agnes Lockie Mason & Phyllis Brown Ohanian	.40	1.20	2.00	NF
Ks316	How to Land the Job You Want—Jules Z. Willing	.30	.90	1.50	NF
Ks317	Flight Into Space—Jonathan N. Leonard	.40	1.20	2.00	NF
Ks318	Hobbies for Pleasure and Profit—Horace Coon; 1955	.30	.90	1.50	NF
KD319	The Life of Abraham Lincoln—Stefan Lorant Lorant	.40	1.20	2.00	B
Ks320	Science in Our Lives—Ritchie Calder	.30	.90	1.50	NF
K321	Benjamin Franklin—Roger Burlingame	.40	1.20	2.00	B
Ks322	The Conquest of Happiness—Bertrand Russell	.30	.90	1.50	
Ks323	The Handy Book of Gardening—Victor A. Tiedjens & Albert E. Wilkinson	.40	1.20	2.00	NF
Ks324	The United Nations and How It Works—David Cushman Coyle	.30	.90	1.50	NF
Ks325	Your Guide to Financial Security—Sidney Margolius	.30	.90	1.50	NF
Ks326	The Nature of Living Things—C. Brooke Worth & Robert K. Enders	.40	1.20	2.00	NF
Ks327	Machines That Built America—Roger Burlingame	.30	.90	1.50	NF
KD328	How to Know American Antiques—Alice Winchester	.40	1.20	2.00	NF
Ks329	Fifty Years a Surgeon—Robert T. Morris	.30	.90	1.50	NF
Ks330	The Crust of the Earth—Samuel Rapport & Helen Wright	.30	.90	1.50	NF
KD331	Stories of Famous Operas—Harold Vincent Milligan	.40	1.20	2.00	NF
Ks332	Having a Baby—Alan F. Guttmacher	.30	.90	1.50	NF
Ks333	The Web of Life—John H. Storer; 1956	.30	.90	1.50	
Ks334	The American Presidency—Clinton Rossiter	.30	.90	1.50	NF
K335	How to Live Without Liquor—Ralph A. Habas	.30	.90	1.50	

Signet D2939, © NA

Signet Key KD347, © NA

Signet Key KS360, © NA

Stallion Books 206, © Univ

Stanley Library SL-68, © Stanley Libr.

Star Books 29, © SG

		Good	Fine	N/Mint	
K336	The Unknown - Is It Nearer?—Eric J. Dingwall & John Langdon-Davies; c-Powers ..	.40	1.20	2.00	
K337	Henry Ford—Roger Burlingame	.30	.90	1.50	B
Ks338	Live Without Fear—T. V. Smith	.30	.90	1.50	
Ks339	The Meaning of the Dead Sea Scrolls—A. Powell Davies	.40	1.20	2.00	NF
KD340	American Folk Tales and Songs—Richard Chase	.40	1.20	2.00	NF
Ks341	How to Be a Better Member—Horace Coon	.30	.90	1.50	NF
Ks342	Sight Without Glasses—Harold M. Peppard	.30	.90	1.50	NF
Ks343	The Ten Commandments—A. Powell Davies	.40	1.20	2.00	NF
Ks344	Call It Experience—Erskine Caldwell	.30	.90	1.50	
Ks345	Seeds of Life—John Langdon-Davies; 1957	.30	.90	1.50	NF
KD346	How to Know the Minerals and Rocks—Richard M. Pearl	.40	1.20	2.00	NF
KD347	How to Know the Birds—Roger Tory Peterson	.40	1.20	2.00	NF
Ks348	The Eloquence of Winston Churchill—Winston Churchill	.40	1.20	2.00	NF
KD349	How to Know the American Mammals—Ivan T. Sanderson	.40	1.20	2.00	NF
Ks350	Here's How! A Round-the-World Bar Guide—Lawrence G. Blochman	.40	1.20	2.00	NF
KD351	Electronics for Everyone—Monroe Upton	.30	.90	1.50	NF
Ks352	The Shape of Tomorrow—George Soule	.30	.90	1.50	NF
KD353	How to Know and Predict the Weather—Robert Moore Fisher	.30	.90	1.50	NF
K354	Speak Better - Write Better - English—Horace Coon	.30	.90	1.50	NF
KD355	The Human Body and How It Works—Elbert Tokay	.30	.90	1.50	NF
KD356	You and Your Heart—H. M. Marvin	.30	.90	1.50	NF
KD357	Gods, Heroes and Men of Ancient Greece—W. H. D. Rouse	.40	1.20	2.00	
KD358	Pregnancy and Birth—Alan F. Guttmacher; 1958	.30	.90	1.50	NF
KD359	How the Great Religions Began—Joseph Gaer	.40	1.20	2.00	NF
Ks360	Satellites, Rockets and Outer Space—Willy Ley	.40	1.20	2.00	NF
K361	Magic House of Numbers—Irving Adler	.30	.90	1.50	NF
KD362	Buffalo Bill and the Wild West—Henry Blackman Sell & Victor Weybright	.50	1.50	2.50	B
KD363	Hoyle's Rules of Games—Albert H. Morehead & Geoffrey Mott-Smith	.30	.90	1.50	NF
Ks364	The Stars—Irving Adler	.30	.90	1.50	NF
KD365	Your Body and Your Mind—Frank G. Slaughter	.30	.90	1.50	NF
KD366					
Ks367	A Brief History of the United States—Franklin Escher, Jr.; 1959	.30	.90	1.50	NF
KD368	The Complete Italian System of Winning Bridge—Edgar Kaplan	.30	.90	1.50	NF
K369	How Life Began—Irving Adler	.30	.90	1.50	NF
Ks370	How to Spell and Increase Your Word Power—Horace Coon	.30	.90	1.50	NF
KD371	The Bible Was Right—Hugh J. Schonfield	.40	1.20	2.00	
KD372	Your Adolescent at Home and in School—Lawrence K. & Mary Frank	.30	.90	1.50	NF
KD373	The New American Guide to Colleges—Gene R. Hawes	.30	.90	1.50	NF

STALLION BOOKS
Stallion Books/Universal Publishing and Distributing Corporation

Digest Size

205	Tramp Girl	1.00	3.00	5.00	E
206	The Queer Sisters—Steve Harragan	1.20	3.60	6.00	M
207	Miami Widow—Gene Harvey	1.00	3.00	5.00	E
210	Gutter Star—D. B. Clark; orig., 1951	1.00	3.00	5.00	E
213	Reefer Club—Luke Roberts; Note: Same cover as Intimate No. 32 and virtually identical to Beacon No. B260	2.00	6.00	10.00	E

STANLEY LIBRARY
Stanley Library, Inc.

SL-67	The Oldest Profession—Jean Campbell; orig., 1958	1.20	3.60	6.00	E
SL-68	So Nice, So Wild—Max Day; orig., 1959	1.20	3.60	6.00	E
SL-69	Quarry Road—A. R. Dispaldo; orig., 1959	1.20	3.60	6.00	E

(STANLEY LIBRARY, continued)

		Good	Fine	N/Mint	
SL-70	Love Doctor—Florence Stonebraker	1.20	3.60	6.00	E
SL-72	Strictly for the Boys—Harry Whittington; orig., 1959	1.20	3.60	6.00	E
SL-73	Strange Sinner—Florence Stonebraker	1.20	3.60	6.00	E
SL-74	Bed of Fear—Doug Duperault; orig., 1959	1.20	3.60	6.00	E

STAR BOOKS
Star Guidance, Inc./Publication House, Inc.

Digest Size

1	Texas Gun Slinger—Murray Leinster	2.00	6.00	10.00	W
2	Bachelor Bait—Peggy Gaddis	.80	2.40	4.00	E
3	Outlaw Guns—Murray Leinster	2.00	6.00	10.00	W
4	Hell Cat!—Martin Gregor; aka Bodies Are Different	.80	2.40	4.00	E
5	Outlaw Deputy—Murray Leinster; 1950	2.00	6.00	10.00	W
6	The Flaming Guns—Burt Arthur	.80	2.40	4.00	W
7	Bad Hombre—Archie Joscelyn; orig., 1950, c-Gross	.80	2.40	4.00	W
8	Range Justice—Paul Evan Lehman; orig., 1950, c-Gross	.80	2.40	4.00	W
9	Border Wolves—Archie Joscelyn; c-Gross	.80	2.40	4.00	W
10	Law of the .45—Paul Evan Lehman	.80	2.40	4.00	W
11	Killer's Moon—Burt Arthur; orig., 1950, c-Gross	.80	2.40	4.00	W
12	The Black Rider—Burt Arthur; orig., 1950, c-Gross	.80	2.40	4.00	W
13	Gun-Thunder Valley—Archie Joscelyn; c-Gross	.80	2.40	4.00	W
14	The Vengeance Trail—Archie Joscelyn	.80	2.40	4.00	W
15	The Long Trail North—Lee Floren; orig., 1951. Note: Same cover as Star No. 27	.80	2.40	4.00	W
16	The Sheep Killers—Paul Evan Lehman; orig., 1951	.80	2.40	4.00	W
17	Two-Gun Trail—Lee Floren; orig., 1951, c-Gross	.80	2.40	4.00	W
18	Wyoming Outlaw—Archie Joscelyn	.80	2.40	4.00	W
19	Duel on the Range—Burt Arthur	.80	2.40	4.00	W
20	Rustler's Trail—Lee Floren; orig., 1951	.80	2.40	4.00	W
21	Black Gunsmoke—Lee Floren; orig., 1951, c-Gross	.80	2.40	4.00	W
22	Texas Vengeance—Paul Evan Lehman; c-Gross	.80	2.40	4.00	W
24	Gun-Thunder Valley—Archie Joscelyn	.80	2.40	4.00	W
26	Killers Moon—Burth Arthur	.80	2.40	4.00	W
27	Deputy's Revenge—Lee Floren; 1952, aka The Long Trail North. Note: Same cover as Star No. 15.	.80	2.40	4.00	W
28	Texas Guns—Paul Evan Lehman; aka Range Justice, c-Gross	.80	2.40	4.00	W
29	Duel at Killman Creek—Archie Joscelyn; aka Border Wolves, c-Gross	.80	2.40	4.00	W
30	Texas Outlaw—Archie Joscelyn; 1952, aka Bad Hombre, c-Gross	.80	2.40	4.00	W
42	Two-Gun Vengeance—Archie Joscelyn	.80	2.40	4.00	W
46	Two-Gun Trail—Lee Floren	.80	2.40	4.00	W
48	Texas Revenge—Archie Joscelyn	.80	2.40	4.00	W
750	Boy-Crazy—Albert L. Quandt; 1955. Note: Same cover as Original No. 721.	1.20	3.60	6.00	JD
754	Cellar Club—Albert L. Quandt	1.60	4.80	8.00	JD
758	Sinners Club—Harry Whittington; 1956	1.20	3.60	6.00	E
760	Waterfront Girl—Amos Hatter	.80	2.40	4.00	E
763	Motel Mistress—Norman Bligh	.80	2.40	4.00	E
765	River Boat Girl—Norman Bligh	.80	2.40	4.00	E
768	Ward Nurse—M. Coleman	.80	2.40	4.00	E

STORK ORIGINAL NOVEL
Star Guidance, Inc.

Digest Size

nn	Lust for Love—Wright Williams; c-Cole	2.00	6.00	10.00	E
nn	Life of Passion—Gordon Semple; orig., 1949, c-Rodewald	1.60	4.80	8.00	E
6	The Sins of Donna Kenyon—Ralph Carter	1.60	4.80	8.00	E

Star Books 30, © SG

Stork Original Novel nn, © SG

Stork Original Novel 7, © SG

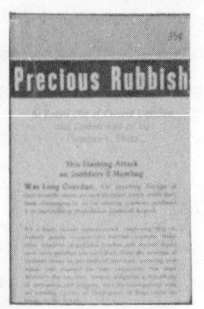

Stuart nn, © Stuart Art Gallery, Inc.　　　　Superior nn, © Duch　　　　Superior Reprints M642, © Mil

		Good	Fine	N/Mint	
(STORK ORIGINAL NOVEL, continued)					
7	Raging Passions—Thomas Stone; orig., 1950, c-Cole	2.00	6.00	10.00	E
8	Two Sinners—Lee Jackquin; c-Cole	2.00	6.00	10.00	E

STOVEL-ADVOCATE
Stovel-Advocate Press Ltd.

(Canadian)

nn	Grey Cup or Bust—Tony Allan; 1954	1.20	3.60	6.00	S
nn	Curling to Win—Ken Watson; 1955	1.20	3.60	6.00	

STUART
Stuart Art Gallery, Inc.

nn	Precious Rubbish—Theodore L. Shaw; orig., 1956	1.00	3.00	5.00	NF
nn	Critical Quackery—Theodore L. Shaw	1.00	3.00	5.00	NF

SUPERIOR
Duchess Publishing Company

Digest Size

(Canadian)

nn	True Mysteries and Murders—Robert Henry Todd & Lloyd C. Steele; 1945	1.00	3.00	5.00	NF

SUPERIOR REPRINTS
The Military Service Publishing Company

M637	White Magic—Faith Baldwin; 1944	.50	1.50	2.50	R
M638	Ol' Man Adam an' His Chillun—Roark Bradford	.50	1.50	2.50	
M639	Unexpected Night—Elizabeth Daly	.80	2.40	4.00	M
M640	An April Afternoon—Philip Wylie	.80	2.40	4.00	
M641	Family Affair—Ione Sundberg Shriber	.50	1.50	2.50	
M642	The Rynox Murder Mystery—Philip MacDonald	1.00	3.00	5.00	M
M643	Cartoons by George Price—George Price; 1945	1.20	3.60	6.00	H
M644	Embarrassment of Riches—Marjorie Fischer	.80	2.40	4.00	
M645	Murder in Mink—Robert George Dean	.80	2.40	4.00	M
M646	The Love Nest, and Other Stories—Ring Lardner	.80	2.40	4.00	H
M647	Inquest—Percival Wilde	.80	2.40	4.00	
M648	One Foot in Heaven—Hartzell Spence	.80	2.40	4.00	
M649	The Navy Colt—Frank Gruber	.80	2.40	4.00	
M650	The Informer—Liam O'Flaherty	.80	2.40	4.00	
M651	Mr. Angel Comes Aboard—Charles G. Booth	.80	2.40	4.00	
M652	This Gun for Hire—Graham Greene	.80	2.40	4.00	
M653	The House Without the Door—Elizabeth Daly	.80	2.40	4.00	M
M654	On Ice—Robert George Dean	.80	2.40	4.00	M
M655	The Mighty Blockhead—Frank Gruber	.80	2.40	4.00	
M656	Saki Sampler—H. H. Munro	1.00	3.00	5.00	F
M657	Good Night, Sheriff—Harrison R. Steeves	.80	2.40	4.00	

SUSPENSE NOVELS
Farrell Publishing Corporation

Digest Size

		Good	Fine	N/Mint	
1	Strange Pursuit—N. R. De Mexico	.80	2.40	4.00	M
2	The Case of the Lonely Lovers—Will Daemer; 1951	.80	2.40	4.00	M
3	Naked Villainy—Carl G. Hodges	.80	2.40	4.00	M

TECH MYSTERY
Tech Mysteries, Inc.

Digest Size

1	The Candle—Linton C. Hopkins	.80	2.40	4.00	M
2	Murder Is My Racket—Robert H. Leitfred	.80	2.40	4.00	M
nn	Murder Man—William Bogart	.80	2.40	4.00	M

TECH WESTERN
Tech Books, Inc.

Digest Size

1	The Black Rider—Herbert Shapiro	.80	2.40	4.00	W
2	Rainbow Trail—Herbert Shapiro	.80	2.40	4.00	W

TEMPO BOOKS
Grosset and Dunlap, Inc.

5320	Grove of Doom—Walter B. Gibson; 1966	1.00	3.00	5.00	M
5368	The Best of Creepy—1971, c-Frazetta. Note: Comic story reprints include art by Williamson, Wood & Adkins, Torres, Crandall, Frazetta, Toth, and Ditko	1.60	4.80	8.00	

THRILLER BOOK, A
Lev Gleason Publications, Inc.

3½'' x 5¾'' Size

nn	Big Shot Gangsters, Their Crimes, Careers and Deaths—Stanford Quayle; 1947, c-Cole	3.00	9.00	15.00	NF
nn	The Greatest Prison Breaks of All Time—Michael Finn; c-Cole	3.00	9.00	15.00	NF
nn	How Detectives Catch Crooks—Stanford Quayle; c-Cole	3.00	9.00	15.00	NF
nn	10 Most Terrible Crimes of All Time—Stanford Quayle; c-Cole	3.00	9.00	15.00	NF
nn	Mysteries of Magic, Mind Reading and Hypnotism Explained—Hamilton Holt; c-Cole	3.00	9.00	15.00	NF

THRILLER NOVEL CLASSIC
Novel Selections, Inc.

Digest Size

1	Secret Agent No. 1—Frederick Frost	1.00	3.00	5.00	M
2	Bulldog Drummond on Dartmoor—Gerald Fairlie	.80	2.40	4.00	
3	The Yellow Strangler—Colin Robertson	1.20	3.60	6.00	M
4	The Insidious Dr. Fu-Manchu—Sax Rohmer	1.20	3.60	6.00	M
5	Lord of Terror—Sidney Horler	1.00	3.00	5.00	M
7	Spy Meets Spy—Frederick Frost	.80	2.40	4.00	
8	Jimmy Dale and the Phantom Clue—Frank L. Packard	.80	2.40	4.00	
9	The Golden Scorpion—Sax Rohmer	1.00	3.00	5.00	M

Suspense Novels 1, © Farrell Publ.   Tempo Books 5368, © Grosset & Dunlap   Thriller Novel Classic 4, © NS

Thriller Novel Classic 30, © NS

Thrilling Novels 12, © Poplib

Thrilling Novels 22, © Poplib

(THRILLER NOVEL CLASSIC, continued)

		Good	Fine	N/Mint	
10	The White Wolf—Franklin Gregory	1.20	3.60	6.00	SF
11	Death in Four Letters—Francis Beeding	.80	2.40	4.00	M
12	The Bamboo Whistle—Frederick Frost	.80	2.40	4.00	
13	Invasion—Whitman Chambers	1.20	3.60	6.00	SF
14	Bulldog Drummond Meets a Murderess—H. C. McNeile	.80	2.40	4.00	M
15	Terror by Night—Lee Crosby	.80	2.40	4.00	M
16	The Saint in Miami—Leslie Charteris	.80	2.40	4.00	M
17	Trial by Murder—Elisabeth Sanxay Holding	.80	2.40	4.00	M
18	Murder Greets Jean Holton—Kathleen Moore Knight	.80	2.40	4.00	M
19	Eleven Were Brave—Francis Beeding	.80	2.40	4.00	
20	Night Attack—Lee Crosby	.80	2.40	4.00	
21	Design in Evil—Rufus King	.80	2.40	4.00	M
22	Cradled in Fear—Anita Boutell	.80	2.40	4.00	
23	Poison in Jest—John Dickson Carr	1.00	3.00	5.00	M
24	Deadline for Destruction—Charles L. Leonard	.80	2.40	4.00	
25	Doors to Death—Lee Crosby; aka Too Many Doors	.80	2.40	4.00	M
26	Deep Lay the Dead—Frederick C. Davis	.80	2.40	4.00	
27	Assignment to Death—Charles L. Leonard	.80	2.40	4.00	
29	The Black Path of Fear—Cornell Woolrich	1.00	3.00	5.00	M
30	The Secret of the Spa—Charles A. Leonard	1.20	3.60	6.00	
33	Murder for Empire—Kim Knight	.80	2.40	4.00	S
34	Action at World's End—Whitman Chambers	1.00	3.00	5.00	
35	Death at Abu Mina—Peter William; aka The Affair at Abu Mina	.80	2.40	4.00	
36	Death and Bitters—Kit Christian	.80	2.40	4.00	
37	Murder in Silence—George Selmark	.80	2.40	4.00	M
38	Under a Cloud—Van Siller	.80	2.40	4.00	
39	A Shroud for Shylock—Stephen Ransome	.80	2.40	4.00	M

THRILLING BOOKS/NOVELS
Popular Library, Inc.

Digest Size

		Good	Fine	N/Mint	
11	Trail Dust—Clarence E. Mulford	.80	2.40	4.00	W
12	Texas Man—William MacLeod Raine	.80	2.40	4.00	W
13	Holster Law—Gordon Young	.80	2.40	4.00	W
14	Square Deal Sanderson—Charles Alden Seltzer	.80	2.40	4.00	W
15	The Quirt—B. M. Bower	.80	2.40	4.00	W
16	Cow Country Law—Frank C. Robertson	.80	2.40	4.00	W
17	Man to Man—Jackson Gregory	.80	2.40	4.00	W
18	Guns of Paradise Bend—William White	.80	2.40	4.00	W
19	Two Rangers From Texas—Caddo Cameron	.80	2.40	4.00	W
20	Rustler's Valley—Clarence E. Mulford	.80	2.40	4.00	W
21	Trigger Gospel—Harry Sinclair Drago	.80	2.40	4.00	W
22	Hot Lead Trail—Charles Alden Seltzer; aka The Red Brand	.80	2.40	4.00	W
23	Gunman From Abilene—Gordon Young; aka Red Clark to the Rescue	.80	2.40	4.00	W
24	Heart of a Ranger—William Patterson White	.80	2.40	4.00	W
25	Longhorns of Hate—Frank C. Robertson	.80	2.40	4.00	W
27	It's Hell to Be a Ranger—Caddo Cameron	.80	2.40	4.00	W
28	Riders of the Rocker K—S. Payne	.80	2.40	4.00	W
29	Bring Me His Ears—Clarence E. Mulford	.80	2.40	4.00	W
30	Thorson of Thunder Gulch—Norman A. Fox	.80	2.40	4.00	W

TOBY
Toby Press, Inc.

Digest Size

Toby nn, © Toby

Toby nn, © Toby

Today's Crosswords nn, © Today's Cr.

(TOBY, continued)		Good	Fine	N/Mint	
nn	Dangerous People; orig., 1952	.80	2.40	4.00	NF
nn	Space Pirate—Jack Vance; orig., 1953	4.00	12.00	20.00	SF
nn	Escape; orig., 1953	.80	2.40	4.00	A
nn	Sunset Showdown—Steve Frazee; orig., 1953	1.00	3.00	5.00	W
nn	Private Lives—E. Whitfield	.80	2.40	4.00	NF
nn	The Lil Abner Square Dance Book—F. Leifer	1.20	3.60	6.00	NF
nn	You'll Die Now—Raymond Drennen	1.00	3.00	5.00	M

TODAY'S CROSSWORDS
Today's Crosswords, Inc.

nn	Today's Crossword Dictionary—ed. David Shulman; 1955	.50	1.50	2.50	NF

TOWER
Tower Publications, Inc.

42-660	Dynamo; 1966, c-Wood	1.00	3.00	5.00	
42-672	Noman; 1966, c-Wood	1.00	3.00	5.00	
42-674	Menthor; 1966, c-Wood	1.00	3.00	5.00	
42-687	The Terrific Trio; 1966, c-Wood	1.00	3.00	5.00	

NOTE: These contain comic book reprints from T.H.U.N.D.E.R. Agents, art by Wally Wood, Reed Crandall, Steve Ditko, others.

TRAVELLERS POCKET LIBRARY BEST-SELLER
Ward-Hill Books

100	Passion Is a Gentle Whip—Milton H. Gropper; 1949	1.60	4.80	8.00	E
103	Venus in Furs—Leopold Sacher-Masoch; 1949	2.00	6.00	10.00	E
104	Pagan in Silk—Irving Sinclair	1.60	4.80	8.00	E

TRIPLE NICKEL LIBRARY
Solomon & Gelman, Inc.

Digest Size

1	The Adventures of Davy Crockett	1.20	3.60	6.00	A
2	Davy Crockett and Danger From the Mountain—Nat Wilson	1.20	3.60	6.00	A
3	The Life of Wild Bill Hickok	1.20	3.60	6.00	W

Tower 42-660, © Tower Publs.

Travellers Pocket Libr. 103, © Ward-Hill

Triple Nickel Library 5, © Sol

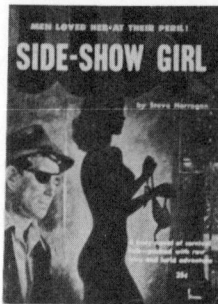

Trophy Books 402, © Royce   Uni-Books 30, © Univ   Uni-Books 42, © Univ

		Good	Fine	N/Mint	
(TRIPLE NICKEL LIBRARY, continued)					
4	1955				
5	Barbie Lane and Mystery of the Egyptian Museum—Lucy Carlton; 1955	1.20	3.60	6.00	M
6	The Power Boys and the Riddle of the Sunken Ship—Arthur Benwood; 1956	1.20	3.60	6.00	M
7	The Power Boys in the Castle of Curious Creatures—Arthur Benwood; 1956	1.20	3.60	6.00	M
8	The Power Boys and the Mystery of the Marble Face—Arthur Benwood	1.20	3.60	6.00	M

TROPHY BOOKS
Royce Publishers

401	Smile, Brother, Smile—anthology	6.00	18.00	30.00	H
402	The Pilditch Puzzle—W. B. M. Ferguson; 1946	6.00	18.00	30.00	M

20TH CENTURY THRILLER (See WHITMAN)

UNI-BOOKS
Universal Publishing and Distributing Corp.

Digest Size

3	Unfaithful Wives—Peggy Gaddis; aka Wives in Scarlet	.80	2.40	4.00	E
4	Wicked—Eleanor Gates	.80	2.40	4.00	E
6	Man Bait—Richard Grant; aka Man Hater	.80	2.40	4.00	E
7	Male for Sale—Florenz Branch	.80	2.40	4.00	E
9	Warped Women—Janet Pritchard	1.20	3.60	6.00	E
10	Without Consent—M. Pili Grilli	.80	2.40	4.00	E
13	Tormented—Richard Meeker	.80	2.40	4.00	E
14	Stripper—Wright Williams	.80	2.40	4.00	E
15	The Thing That Made Love—David V. Reed	3.00	9.00	15.00	SF
16	Raw Passion—Charles Martin	.80	2.40	4.00	W
17	Scandalous Affair	.80	2.40	4.00	E
18	Love Cheat—William Arthur	.80	2.40	4.00	E
19	Marijuana Girl—N. R. de Mexico	4.00	12.00	20.00	E
20	Side Street—Wright Williams	.80	2.40	4.00	E
21	Hideaway—Peggy Gaddis	.80	2.40	4.00	E
22	Tainted Passions—H. M. Appel	.80	2.40	4.00	E
23	Sin Ship—Janet Pritchard	.80	2.40	4.00	E
24	Badge of Shame—A. Abram	.80	2.40	4.00	E
26	The Fiend—Gerald Foster; aka Lust	1.00	3.00	5.00	E
28	Unleashed Woman—Gail Jordan (Peggy Gaddis); aka Dark Passion	.80	2.40	4.00	E
29	Brutal Kisses—H. M. Appel; aka The Farmer's Daughter	.80	2.40	4.00	E
30	Eurasian Girl—Richard Grant	1.20	3.60	6.00	E
31	Dr. Prescott's Secret—Peggy Gaddis	.80	2.40	4.00	E
32	Loves of a Girl Wrestler—Ben West; Note: Cover is almost identical to Beacon B112	1.20	3.60	6.00	E
33	White Trash—Beulan Poynter; orig., 1952	.80	2.40	4.00	E
35	Slave Ship—H. B. Drake	1.00	3.00	5.00	E
36	Hoyden of the Hills—Ann Lawrence; aka She Wanted More	.80	2.40	4.00	E
37	Student Nurse—Gail Jordan (Peggy Gaddis)	.80	2.40	4.00	E
38	Secrets of a Co-ed—Ben West	.80	2.40	4.00	E
39	Pleasure Resort Women—Gordon Semple	.80	2.40	4.00	E
41	She Devil—John Saxon	.80	2.40	4.00	E
42	Side-Show Girl—Steve Harragan	1.20	3.60	6.00	M
44	Sin Is a Redhead—Steve Harragan	1.20	3.60	6.00	M
45	Bad Sister—Evans Wall	.80	2.40	4.00	E
46	Smuggled Sin—Steve Harragan	1.20	3.60	6.00	M
47	Kiss of the Damned—Steve Harragan	1.20	3.60	6.00	M
48	Women of Paris—L. H. Brenning	.80	2.40	4.00	E

		Good	Fine	N/Mint	
49	Reefer Club—Luke Roberts	2.00	6.00	10.00	E
50	River Woman—Evans Wall	.80	2.40	4.00	E
51	Dirt Farm—Mitchell	.80	2.40	4.00	E
52	The Shayne Dame—Steve Harragan	1.20	3.60	6.00	M
53	Wild Body—Manning Clay	.80	2.40	4.00	E
54	Carney's Burlesque—Steve Harragan	1.20	3.60	6.00	M
55	Mountain Woman	.80	2.40	4.00	E
56	Her Last Lover—Kelsey Freeman; aka Last Lover	.80	2.40	4.00	E
57	Three Bad Girls—Bart Frame	.80	2.40	4.00	M
58	Cracker Girl—Harry Whittington; orig., 1953	1.20	3.60	6.00	E
59	Another Man's Wife—Margaret Carruthers	.80	2.40	4.00	E
60	Savage Eve—Jack Woodford	.80	2.40	4.00	E
62	Hungry for Love—George Willis; aka Wild Faun	.80	2.40	4.00	E
63	Passion in the Pines—Jack Woodford	.80	2.40	4.00	E
64	Cuban Heel—Steve Harragan; orig., nd	1.20	3.60	6.00	M
65	Hillbilly in High Heels—Jeff Bogar	.80	2.40	4.00	E
66	Witch on Wheels—Bill Bolton	.80	2.40	4.00	E
67	Male Virgin—Jack Woodford	.80	2.40	4.00	E
69	Confessions of a Chinatown Moll—Jeff Bogar	2.00	6.00	10.00	M
70	Wild Oats—Harry Whittington; orig., 1954	1.20	3.60	6.00	E
71	Swamp Hoyden—Jack Woodford & John B. Thompson	.80	2.40	4.00	E
72	Honey—Jack Woodford & John Thompson	.80	2.40	4.00	E
73	Cabin Fever—Orrie Hitt; orig., 1954	.80	2.40	4.00	E
75	Harlem Doctor—Luke Roberts; orig., 1953	2.00	6.00	10.00	E
76	Below the Belt—R. Lucas	.80	2.40	4.00	E
77	Bayou Girl—John B. Thompson	1.20	3.60	6.00	E
78	Out of Bounds—Ernest L. Matthews, Jr.	.80	2.40	4.00	E

UNICORN
Unicorn Press

Digest Size

nn	Everything's a Puzzle; 1953	1.00	3.00	5.00	NF

UNITED STATES PLAYING CARD COMPANY
United States Playing Card Co./Whitman Publishing Company

3768	50 Card Games for Children—Vernon Quinn; 1946	.40	1.20	2.00	NF

UNITED STATES SALES COMPANY
United States Sales Company

nn	Judge Priest Turns Detective—Irvin S. Cobb; nd	1.00	3.00	5.00	M

UNIVERSAL GIANT EDITION
Universal Publishing and Distributing Corporation

Digest Size (See Royal Giant Edition)

		Good	Fine	N/Mint	
1	Prime Sucker—Harry Whittington; orig., 1952				E
	The Hussy—Idabel Williams	4.00	12.00	20.00	E
2	Paprika—Erich von Stroheim	6.00	18.00	30.00	E
3	His Majesty O'Keefe—Klingman and Green	3.00	9.00	15.00	A
4	Dope Doll—Steve Harragan				E
	The Bigamy Kiss—Steve Harragan	6.00	18.00	30.00	E

Uni-Books 64, © Univ

Universal Giant Edition 1, © Univ

Universal Giant Edition 3, © Univ

Universal Giant Edition 8, © Univ

Vanitas V4402, © Harvard Lampoon

Venus Books 110, © SG

		Good	Fine	N/Mint	
(UNIVERSAL GIANT EDITION, continued)					
5	Bulls, Blood and Passion—David Williams; orig.				E
	The Sinful Ones—Fritz Leiber; 1st ed., 1953	5.00	15.00	25.00	SF
6	The Private Life of Julius Caesar—William Marston	3.00	9.00	15.00	E
7	Savage Mistress—Jon Hartt				E
	Concubine—Elsie Dean	3.00	9.00	15.00	
8	The Lusty Land—Valerie Taylor				E
	Forbidden Fruit—Curtis Lucas	3.00	9.00	15.00	E
9	Aphrodite's Lover—Arthur MacArthur	4.00	12.00	20.00	E
10	The Memoirs of Casanova—Jacques Casanova	3.00	9.00	15.00	E
11	The Queen's Warrant—Talbot Mundy; 1st ed., 1953				A
	Paths of Glory—Humphrey Cobb	4.00	12.00	20.00	C

UNIVERSAL ROMANCE
Universal Publishing and Distributing Corporation

Digest Size

nn	Any Man's Woman—Cecil Barr; aka It's Hard to Sin	.80	2.40	4.00	E

VALUE BOOKS
Value Books, Inc.

101	The Young Adventurer—Horatio Alger	1.20	3.60	6.00	A
102	Strive and Succeed—Horatio Alger	1.20	3.60	6.00	A
103	Do and Dare—Horatio Alger	1.20	3.60	6.00	A
104	Brave and Bold—Horatio Alger	1.20	3.60	6.00	A
105	Making His Way—Horatio Alger	1.20	3.60	6.00	A

VANITAS
The Harvard Lampoon, Inc.

V4402	Alligator—I*n Fl*m*ng (Ian Fleming); orig., 1962	3.00	9.00	15.00	H

VENUS BOOKS
Star Guidance, Inc.

Digest Size

101	Girl With My Past—Peggy Gaddis	1.00	3.00	5.00	E
102	She Wanted Love—Joan Sherman (Peggy Gaddis)	1.00	3.00	5.00	E
103	Mazie - Any Man's Girl	1.00	3.00	5.00	E
104	Beach Party—Peggy Gaddis; aka Lovers No More	1.00	3.00	5.00	E
105	Take My Love!—Peggy Gaddis; aka Shameless	1.00	3.00	5.00	E
106	Overnight—Norman Bligh; aka Harlot in Her Heart	1.00	3.00	5.00	E
107	Play Girl	1.00	3.00	5.00	E
108	Cutie—Gene Harvey; aka Passion's Slave	1.00	3.00	5.00	E
109	Lover Boy—Harmon Bellamy; aka Sacrifice, c-Gross	1.00	3.00	5.00	E
110	Hard-Boiled—Harmon Bellamy; 1950, aka Struggle	1.00	3.00	5.00	E
111	Pick-Up Alley—Albert L. Quandt	1.00	3.00	5.00	E
112	Temptation—Peggy Gaddis	1.00	3.00	5.00	E
113	Reckless—James Clayford	1.00	3.00	5.00	E
114	Confessions of a Carnival Dancer—Gene Harvey	1.00	3.00	5.00	E
115	Journey Into Ecstacy—Albert L. Quandt	1.00	3.00	5.00	E
116	One Wild Night—Peggy Gaddis	1.00	3.00	5.00	E
118	Honey - Broadway Playgirl—Peggy Gaddis	1.00	3.00	5.00	E
119	No Time for Marriage—David Charlson	1.00	3.00	5.00	E

		Good	Fine	N/Mint	
120	The Naked Night—Norman Bligh; orig., 1951	1.00	3.00	5.00	E
121	Girl of the Slum—Albert L. Quandt	1.20	3.60	6.00	E
122	Pleasure at Midnight—Peggy Gaddis	1.00	3.00	5.00	E
123	Emotions of Fire—Peggy Gaddis	1.00	3.00	5.00	E
124	She Couldn't Be Good—Gene Harvey	1.00	3.00	5.00	E
127	Painted Lips—Peggy Gaddis; orig., 1951	1.00	3.00	5.00	E
128	She Had What It Takes—Kermit Welles	1.00	3.00	5.00	E
129	Big-Time Girl—Albert L. Quandt	1.00	3.00	5.00	E
130	The Men She Knew—Norman Bligh	1.00	3.00	5.00	E
131	Tough Doll—Peggy Gaddis	1.00	3.00	5.00	E
132	Lady With a Past—Amos Hatter	1.00	3.00	5.00	E
133	She Tried to Be Good—Florence Stonebraker; orig., 1951	1.00	3.00	5.00	E
134	The Doctor's Wife—Arthur Marin	1.00	3.00	5.00	E
135	Night Nurse—David Charlson; orig., 1951	1.00	3.00	5.00	E
136	Torch Singer—William Arnold	1.00	3.00	5.00	E
137	Lost to Desire—Peggy Gaddis; orig., 1952	1.00	3.00	5.00	E
138	Reckless—Joan Sherman (Peggy Gaddis); orig., 1952	1.00	3.00	5.00	E
139	The Naked Canvas—William Arnold; orig., 1952, c-Gross	1.00	3.00	5.00	E
140	Oriental Nights—Florence Stonebraker; orig., 1952	1.60	4.80	8.00	E
141	Strip Street—Gene Harvey; orig., 1952	1.00	3.00	5.00	E
142	Unfaithful—Peggy Gaddis	1.00	3.00	5.00	E
143	Lovers in the Sun—Joan Sherman (Peggy Gaddis); orig., 1952	1.00	3.00	5.00	E
144	The Innocent Wanton—Kermit Welles; orig., 1952	1.00	3.00	5.00	E
145	Frenchie—David Charlson; orig., 1952	1.00	3.00	5.00	E
146	Call It Marriage—Gail Jordan (Peggy Gaddis); orig., 1952	1.00	3.00	5.00	E
147	Weekend of Madness—Joan Tucker	1.00	3.00	5.00	E
148	Remembered Moment—Norman Bligh; orig., 1952	1.00	3.00	5.00	E
149	Runaway Lovers—Peggy Gaddis; orig., 1952	1.00	3.00	5.00	E
150	The Affairs of a Leading Lady—Jane Manning; orig., 1952	1.00	3.00	5.00	E
151	Young Wife—Norman Bligh	1.00	3.00	5.00	E
152	Passion Is a Woman—Kale Nickerson	1.00	3.00	5.00	E
153	Sailor's Weekend—Whit Harrison (Harry Whittington); orig., 1952	1.20	3.60	6.00	E
154	Hired Girl—Amos Hatter; orig., 1953	1.00	3.00	5.00	E
156	The Doctor's Wife—A. Marin	1.00	3.00	5.00	E
158	Girl on Parole—Harry Whittington; orig., 1953, aka Man Crazy	1.20	3.60	6.00	E
159	Shanty Girl—Joan Tucker	1.00	3.00	5.00	E
160	Farmer's Wife	1.00	3.00	5.00	E
162	Wayward Nurse—Norman Bligh; c-Belarski	1.20	3.60	6.00	E
163	Private Nurse—David Charlson	1.00	3.00	5.00	E
165	Passion Is a Woman—Kate Nickerson; c-Belarski	1.20	3.60	6.00	E
166	Sailor's Weekend—Whit Harrison (Harry Whittington)	1.20	3.60	6.00	E
167	Young Secretary—Joan Tucker; orig., 1954	1.00	3.00	5.00	E
168	Backwoods Girl—Peggy Gaddis	1.00	3.00	5.00	E
169	Strip Street—Gene Harvey	1.00	3.00	5.00	E
170	Male Ward—M. Coleman; c-Belarski	1.20	3.60	6.00	E
171	Beach Girl—Joan Sherman (Peggy Gaddis); aka Lovers in the Sun	1.00	3.00	5.00	E
172	Farmer's Woman—Peggy Gaddis; orig., 1954	1.00	3.00	5.00	E
173	Young Doctor—Frank Haskell; orig., 1954, c-Belarski	1.20	3.60	6.00	E
174	Night Nurse—David Charlson	1.00	3.00	5.00	E
178	Wild Sister—K. Welles	1.00	3.00	5.00	E
180	Beach Girl—Joan Sherman (Peggy Gaddis); aka Lovers in the Sun	1.00	3.00	5.00	E
188	Young Wife—Norman Bligh	1.00	3.00	5.00	E
190	Farmer's Woman—Peggy Gaddis	1.00	3.00	5.00	E
193	Waterfront Club—Joan Tucker	1.00	3.00	5.00	E
194	Army Girl—Whit Harrison (Harry Whittington); orig., 1953, c-Belarski	1.20	3.60	6.00	E
196	Cabin Hostess—Peggy Gaddis	1.00	3.00	5.00	E

Venus Books 133, © SG

Venus Books 154, © SG

Venus Books 162, © SG

Vital Book 2, © Vital Publs.

Vital Book 3, © Vital Publs.

Vulcan Mystery 5, © Vulcan

VITAL BOOK
Vital Publications, Inc.

Digest Size

		Good	Fine	N/Mint	
1	Empire of Crime—Nicholas Carter (Richard Wormser); aka Crook's Empire	3.00	9.00	15.00	M
2	Murder Unlimited—Nicholas Carter (Richard Wormser); aka Bid for a Railroad	2.00	6.00	10.00	M
3	Death Has Green Eyes—Nicholas Carter (Richard Wormser)	2.00	6.00	10.00	M
4	Park Avenue Murder—Nicholas Carter (Richard Wormser); aka Death on Park Avenue	2.00	6.00	10.00	M

VULCAN MYSTERY
Vulcan Publishing, Inc.

Digest Size

		Good	Fine	N/Mint	
nn	The Maori Murder Case—Andrew I. Albert	1.20	3.60	6.00	M
nn	Death Meets the Deadline—David Robinson George; 1944	1.20	3.60	6.00	M
3	The Laughing Buddha Murder—Richard Foster; orig., 1944	2.00	6.00	10.00	M
4	Murder for a Hollow Shell—Andrew I. Albert; orig., 1945	1.60	4.80	8.00	M
5	The Case of the Phantom Fingerprints—Kendall Foster Crossen; orig., 1945	2.00	6.00	10.00	M
6	Curtain Call for Murder—Peter Yates	1.20	3.60	6.00	M

WASHINGTON SQUARE PRESS
Washington Square Press, Inc./Pocket Books, Inc.

W 1	English Through Pictures - Book 1—Christine Gibson & I. A. Richards; 1959	.40	1.20	2.00	NF
W 2	First Steps in Reading English—Christine Gibson & I. A. Richards	.40	1.20	2.00	NF
W 4	English Through Pictures - Book 2—Christine Gibson & I. A. Richards	.40	1.20	2.00	NF
W 8	French Through Pictures - Book 1—I. A. Richards & others	.40	1.20	2.00	NF
W18	A First Workbook of French—Christine Gibson & I. A. Richards	.40	1.20	2.00	NF
W15	German Through Pictures - Book 1—I. A. Richards & others	.40	1.20	2.00	NF
W22	Italian Through Pictures - Book 1—I. A. Richards & others	.40	1.20	2.00	NF
W30	Spanish Through Pictures - Book 1—I. A. Richards & others	.40	1.20	2.00	NF
W38	Hebrew Through Pictures - Book 1—I. A. Richards & others	.40	1.20	2.00	NF
W39	Hebrew Reader—I. A. Richards & others	.40	1.20	2.00	NF
W99	Oedipus the King—Sophocles	.40	1.20	2.00	
W100	Doctor Faustus—Christopher Marlowe	.40	1.20	2.00	
W101	The Duchess of Malfi—John Webster	.40	1.20	2.00	
W115	Macbeth—William Shakespeare	.40	1.20	2.00	
W121	Romeo and Juliet—William Shakespeare	.40	1.20	2.00	
W550	Collected Lyrics—Edna St. Vincent Millay	.40	1.20	2.00	
W551	Collected Sonnets—Edna St. Vincent Millay	.40	1.20	2.00	
W561	The Way of All Flesh—Samuel Butler	.40	1.20	2.00	
W571	The Return of the Native—Thomas Hardy; 1959	.40	1.20	2.00	

WESTERN ACTION NOVEL
Hillman Periodicals, Inc./Novel Selections

Digest Size

1	Round-up in the River—Frank C. Robertson	1.00	3.00	5.00	W
2	The Riddle of Ramrod Ridge—William Colt MacDonald	.80	2.40	4.00	W
3	Powder Smoke Fence—Bennett Foster	.80	2.40	4.00	W
4	Donovan Rides—Arthur Henry Gooden	.80	2.40	4.00	W

WESTERN NOVEL CLASSIC
Hillman Periodicals, Inc./Novel Selections

Digest Size

		Good	Fine	N/Mint	
22	The Sheriff's Son—William MacLeod Raine	.80	2.40	4.00	W
23	Brothers on the Trail—Max Brand	.80	2.40	4.00	W
24	Thunder on the Range—Frank C. Robertson	.80	2.40	4.00	W
28	Ironheart—William MacLeod Raine	.80	2.40	4.00	W
32	Thunder Ranch—Clarence E. Mulford; aka Me an' Shorty	.80	2.40	4.00	W
33	Tumbling River Range—W. C. Tuttle	.80	2.40	4.00	W
36	Hopalong Cassidy and the Eagles Brood—Clarence E. Mulford	1.00	3.00	5.00	W
37	Black Sombrero—William Colt MacDonald	.80	2.40	4.00	W
38	Red Range—Eugene Cunningham	.80	2.40	4.00	W
39	Trail's End—William MacLeod Raine	.80	2.40	4.00	W
40	War on the Cimarron—Luke Short	.80	2.40	4.00	W
43	Whistling Lead—Eugene Cunningham	.80	2.40	4.00	W
44	Roaring River Range—Arthur Henry Gooden	.80	2.40	4.00	W
45	The Feud at Single Shot—Luke Short	.80	2.40	4.00	W
46	The Tin God of Twisted River—W. C. Tuttle	.80	2.40	4.00	W
49	Murder at Two Rivers—Frederick R. Bechdolt	.80	2.40	4.00	W
50	The Dead-Line—W. C. Tuttle	.80	2.40	4.00	W
54	Cartridge Carnival—William Colt MacDonald	.80	2.40	4.00	W
55	Hash Knife of the Double Bar 8—W. C. Tuttle	.80	2.40	4.00	W
58	Hell in Paradise Valley—Dane Coolidge	.80	2.40	4.00	W
60	Trouble Trail—Tom West	.80	2.40	4.00	W
66	Saddle Hawks—Bliss Lomax	.80	2.40	4.00	W
67	Sudden Takes Charge—O. Strange	.80	2.40	4.00	W
68	Rough Mesa—J. Trace	.80	2.40	4.00	W
69	South to Sonora—Ryerson Johnson	.80	2.40	4.00	W
71	Range of Golden Hoofs—John Trace	.80	2.40	4.00	W
72	Gunsmoke in the Hills—Ray Palmer Tracy	.80	2.40	4.00	W
73	Gunsight Range—Frank R. Adams	.80	2.40	4.00	W
74	Renegade Range—Tom West	.80	2.40	4.00	W
75	Horsethief Trail—Frederick Bechdolt	.80	2.40	4.00	W
77	Guns of Ghost Valley—Claude Rister	.80	2.40	4.00	W
79	The Prodigal Bandit—Randolph Hale	.80	2.40	4.00	W
81	Black Gold Stampede—Ed Moore	.80	2.40	4.00	W
83	The Firebrand From Burnt Creek—Frank C. Robertson	.80	2.40	4.00	W
84	Blood on the Sage—Louis E. Legner	.80	2.40	4.00	W
85	Black River Ranch—Lynn Westland	.80	2.40	4.00	W
86	The Brand Stealer—Charles H. Snow	.80	2.40	4.00	W
89	Marked Man—Harold Channing Wire; Note: Same cover as Hillman No. 28	.80	2.40	4.00	W
90	Gunsmoke Galoot—Leslie Ernenwein	.80	2.40	4.00	W
91	Meddling Maverick—Tom West	.80	2.40	4.00	W
93	Lead Law—Amos Moore	.80	2.40	4.00	W
94	The Deuce of Diamonds—Charles M. Martin	.80	2.40	4.00	W
95	Badland Bill—Ranger Lee	.80	2.40	4.00	W
96	Closed Range—Bliss Lomax (H. S. Drago)	.80	2.40	4.00	W
97	The Lightning Kid—J. E. Grinstead	.80	2.40	4.00	W
99	Horsethief Pass—Charles H. Snow	.80	2.40	4.00	W
100	Barbed Wire Empire—Will Ermine	.80	2.40	4.00	W
104	The Hard Riders—Tom J. Hopkins	.80	2.40	4.00	W
105	Dakota Marshal—Lynn Westland	.80	2.40	4.00	W
106	Lawless Legion—Will Ermine	.80	2.40	4.00	W
107	Poison Springs—Eli Colter	.80	2.40	4.00	W
108	The Vultures of Vacaville—W. C. Tuttle	.80	2.40	4.00	W
109	Blow, Desert Winds—William Corcoran	.80	2.40	4.00	W

Western Novel Classic 55, © NS

Western Novel Classic 99, © NS

Western Novel Classic 108, © NS

Western Novel of the Month 4, © NS   Western Thriller 4, © Vital Publs.   West in Action 1, © Astro

WESTERN NOVEL OF THE MONTH
Hillman Periodicals, Inc./Novel Selections

Digest Size

		Good	Fine	N/Mint	
nn	Rancho Bonita—Dan James	.80	2.40	4.00	W
4	Hell on the Pecos—Ed Earl Repp	.80	2.40	4.00	W
5	The Gun Tamer—Max Brand	.80	2.40	4.00	W
6	Quick Triggers	.80	2.40	4.00	W
10	Roaring River	.80	2.40	4.00	W
11	Brand of the Outlaw	.80	2.40	4.00	W
12	Ranger Two-Rifles	.80	2.40	4.00	W
13	The Outlaw Trail—Max Brand	.80	2.40	4.00	W
16	Badman of Elk Head	.80	2.40	4.00	W
19	Suicide Ranch—Ed Earl Repp	.80	2.40	4.00	W
21	Pistol Passport—Eugene Cunningham	.80	2.40	4.00	W

WESTERN THRILLER
Vital Publications, Inc.

Digest Size

		Good	Fine	N/Mint	
4	Open Land Renegades—Tom J. Hopkins; 1948	.80	2.40	4.00	W

THE WEST IN ACTION
Astro Distributing Corporation

Digest Size

		Good	Fine	N/Mint	
1	Outlaw Sheriff—Murray Leinster; 1948	2.00	6.00	10.00	W
2	Guns Along the Western Trail—Murray Leinster	2.00	6.00	10.00	W
3	Kid Deputy—Murray Leinster; 1948	2.00	6.00	10.00	W
4	Two-Gun Showdown—Murray Leinster	2.00	6.00	10.00	W

WHITMAN
Whitman Publishing Company

		Good	Fine	N/Mint	
347	100 Games of Solitaire—Helen L. Coops	.80	2.40	4.00	NF
556	Pinocchio; 1939, movie tie-in (Disney)	8.00	24.00	40.00	
630	Universal Dream Book; 1940	1.20	3.60	6.00	NF

West in Action 3, © Astro   Whitman 556, © Whitman Publ.   Whitman 630, © Whitman Publ.

			Good	Fine	N/Mint	
(WHITMAN, continued)						
790	Murder C.O.D.—Fred MacIsaac		2.00	6.00	10.00	M
	with dust jacket		10.00	30.00	50.00	

WIDE WORLD
Peters Publishing Company

		Good	Fine	N/Mint	
1	A World in Crisis?—Allan Forester; 1952	.80	2.40	4.00	NF
2	Republicans Today—Philip Arthur; 1952	.80	2.40	4.00	NF
3	Democrats Today—Philip Arthur; 1952	.80	2.40	4.00	NF
4					
5	Cold War Politics—John Breamer; 1953	.80	2.40	4.00	NF

YOGI MYSTERIES
Wiegers Publishing Company

Digest Size

		Good	Fine	N/Mint	
nn	Death From Nowhere—Stuart Towne (Clayton Rawson)	15.00	45.00	75.00	M
nn	Man About Broadway—Herbert Crooker	2.00	6.00	10.00	M

ZENITH
Zenith Books, Inc.

		Good	Fine	N/Mint	
ZB 1	The Sisters—Charles Jackson; 1958	.80	2.40	4.00	E
ZB 2	All Over Town—George Milburn	.80	2.40	4.00	
ZB 3	Johnny Purple—John Wyllie	.80	2.40	4.00	M
ZB 4	Die Screaming—Jo Pagano; aka The Condemned	.80	2.40	4.00	M
ZB 5	The Best Cartoons From Argosy	.80	2.40	4.00	H
ZB 6	The Oral Roberts Reader—Oral Roberts	.50	1.50	2.50	
ZB 7	The Girl From Hateville—Gil Brewer	.80	2.40	4.00	E
ZB 8	Adventure in Paradise—Emile C. Schurmacher	.80	2.40	4.00	A
ZB 9	The Man Without a Face—John Eugene Hasry	.80	2.40	4.00	
ZB10	Rawhiders—Tom Roan	.80	2.40	4.00	W
ZB11	The Long Desire—Max Weatherly; 1959	.80	2.40	4.00	E
ZB12	The Rascal's Guide—Bruce Jay Friedman	.80	2.40	4.00	
ZB13	The Three Legions—Gregory Solon	.80	2.40	4.00	
ZB14	The People Maker—Damon Knight	1.00	3.00	5.00	SF
ZB15	Etched in Murder—Ken Jones	.80	2.40	4.00	M
ZB16	Lysistrata—Fletcher Flora	.80	2.40	4.00	
ZB17	Death of the Party—Ruth Fenisong	.80	2.40	4.00	M
ZB18	Blonde Bait—Ed Lacy	.80	2.40	4.00	M
ZB19	The Deadly Doll—Henry Kane	1.00	3.00	5.00	M
ZB20	Fall Girl—Richard Deming	.80	2.40	4.00	M
ZB21	Young Sinner—Elisabeth Gill	.80	2.40	4.00	E
ZB22	Georgia Girl—Bart Frame	.80	2.40	4.00	E
ZB23	A Fine and Private Place—Ann Hebson	.80	2.40	4.00	E
ZB24	Moran's Woman—Day Keene; orig., 1959	1.00	3.00	5.00	E
ZB25	The Sweet Blonde Trap—William Campbell Gault; 1959	.80	2.40	4.00	M
ZB26					
ZB27	Wayward Nymph—Elisabeth Gill	.80	2.40	4.00	E
ZB28	Your Body and Its Care—Richard E. Winter	.50	1.50	2.50	NF
ZB29	Sweet and Deadly—A. Boyd Correll & Philip MacDonald	.80	2.40	4.00	M
ZB30	Strangers on Friday—Harry Whittington	1.00	3.00	5.00	M
ZB31					
ZB32					
ZB33	The Gray Flannel Shroud—Henry Slesar	.80	2.40	4.00	M
ZB34	Frenchie—David Charlson	.80	2.40	4.00	E

Yogi Mysteries nn, © Wiegers Publ.

Zenith ZB8, © Zenith Books

Zenith ZB29, © Zenith Books

Zenith ZB30, © Zenith Books

Zenith ZB39, © Zenith Books

Zenith ZB40, © Zenith Books

(ZENITH, continued)	Good	Fine	N/Mint	
ZB35				
ZB36				
ZB37				
ZB38				
ZB39 The Blonde on Borrowed Time—B. X. Sanborn; 1960, aka The Doom-Maker	.80	2.40	4.00	M
ZB40 Corpus Earthling—Louis Charbonneau; orig., 1960	1.20	3.60	6.00	SF
ZB41				
ZB42				
ZB43 The Hot Sand of Hell—Christopher Landon; 1960, aka Ice Cold in Alex, movie tie-in .	.80	2.40	4.00	C
ZB44 Black Satin Jungle—Bart Frame; aka Indiscretions of a French Model	.80	2.40	4.00	E

Ace (Ace)
Adventure Novel Classics (ANC)
All-Picture Mystery (APM)
Amazing Stories SF Novel (AmSF)
American Folklore & Humor (AmFH)
American Library (AL)
Archer (Ar)
Argyle (Arg)
Armed Services Editions (ASE)
Arrow Mystery (ArM)
Astro (Ast)
Atlas Mystery (AtM)
Atomic Books (At)
Avon (Av)
Avon Annual (AvAn)
Avon Bedside Novel (AvBN)
Avon Book Dividend (AvBD)
Avon Detective Myst. (AvDM)
Avon Fantasy Novel (AvFN)
Avon Fantasy Reader (AvFR)
Avon Love Book Monthly (AvLBM)
Avon Monthly Novel (AvMN)
Avon Romance Novel Monthly (AvRNM)
Avon SF & Fantasy Reader (AvSF/FR)
Avon Science Fiction Reader (AvSFR)
Avon Special (AvS)
Avon Western Novel Monthly (AvWNM)
Avon Western Reader (AvWR)
Ballantine (Bal)
Banner (Bann)
Bantam (Bant)
Bantam of L.A. (BLA)
Bard (Bard)
Bart House (BH)
Beacon (Bea)
Belmont (Bel)
Berkley (Berk)
Best Detective Novel/Selection
   of the Month (BDM)
Bestseller Library/Myst. (BM)
Big Green Det. Nov. (BGDN)
Big Green Pub. (BGP)
Black Cat Det. (BCD)
Black Cat West. (BCW)
Black Knight (BK)
Bleak House (BlH)
Boblin Book (Bob)
Bonded/Chartered (B/C)
Bonded Mystery (BoM)
Bowker (Bow)
Broadway Novel Monthly (BNM)
Bronze Book (Bro)
Brussel (Bru)
Bull's Eye Det. Nov. (BEDN)
Cameo (Cam)
Candid Love Novel (CLN)
Cardinal (Card)
Carnival (Carn)
Cavalcade (Cav)
Century (Cent)
Checkerbooks (Chec)
Columbia Broadcasting Syst. (CBS)
Comet (Com)
Crest (Cre)
Crime Novel Selection (CNS)
Crossword Pleasure (CP)
Croydon (Croy)
Dagger House Myst. (DHM)
Death House (DH)
Dell (Dell)
Dell First Edition (DeFE)
Dell Ten-Cent (DeT)
Dell Told in Pictures (DeTIP)
Detective Novel Classic (DNC)
Diversey Popular Nov. (DivPoN)
Diversey Prize Nov. (DivPrN)
Diversey Romance Nov. (DivRN)

Docket Series (Doc)
Domino Mystery (Dom)
Double Action Det. (DAD)
Double Action Pocketbook (DAP)
Doubleday Doran (DD)
Duchess (Duc)
Eagle NAL (Eag)
Ecstasy Novel (Ecs)
Edell (Ed)
Eerie Series (Ee)
Eton (Et)
Exotic (Ex)
Falcon Books (Fal)
Famous Myst. Series (FMS)
Federal (Fed)
Feiner (Fei)
Femack (Fem)
Fiesta Books (Fie)
Fighting Forces Series (FFS)
Fighting Western Nov. (FWN)
Fingerprint Myst. (FiM)
Five-Star Myst. (FSM)
Galaxy SF Novels (Gal)
Gem Books (Gem)
Golden Willow (GW)
Gold Medal (GM)
Gold Star (GS)
Graphic (Gra)
Great American Pub. (GA)
Green (Gre)
Green Dragon (GD)
Griffin Books (Grif)
Gunfire Western Nov. (GWN)
Handi-books (Han)
Handi-books Western (HanW)
Hangman House (HH)
Hanro (Hanro)
Harlequin (Har)
Hart Books (Hart)
Hercules (Her)
Hillman (Hil)
Hillman Det. Nov. (HilDN)
Hip Books (Hip)
Howard (How)
Infantry Journal (IJ)
Intimate Novels (Int)
Jacket Lib. (Jac)
James (Jam)
Jonathan Myst. (JM)
Keep-Worthy Books (KW)
Knickerbocker (Kni)
Larch (Lar)
Leisure Library (Lei)
Lev Gleason Lib. (LG)
Lion (Lio)
Love Romance Series (LR)
Lucom (Luc)
Magabooks (GalM)
Magazine Village (MV)
Manhattan (Man)
Mentor (Ment)
Mercury Myst. (MM)
Merit Books (Mer)
Metro (Met)
Midwood (Mid)
Modern Short Story Monthly (AvMSSM)
Monarch (Mon)
Murder Myst. Monthly/Murder of
   Month (AvMMM)
Mystery Novel Classic (MNC)
Mystery Novel of the Month (MNM)
Newsstand Lib. (News)
Novel Library (NL)
Novel Selections (NS)
Novels, Inc. (NI)
Omnibus (Omn)
Original Novels (Orig)

Padell (Pad)
Parent's Institute (PI)
Pelican (Pel)
Penguin (Peng)
Pennant (Penn)
Pennant Myst. (PenM)
Pennant Student Ed. (PennS)
Perma Books (Perm)
Phantom Books (Phan)
Phantom Myst. (PhM)
Phoenix (Pho)
Pitman Editions (Pit)
Pocketbooks (Pk)
Pony Books (Pony)
Popular Library (Pop)
Premier (Pre)
Prize Century (Prz)
Prize Love Novel (PLN)
Quarter Books (Qua)
Quick Readers (QR)
Rainbow (Rain)
Rainbow Books (RB)
Reader's Choice Libr. (RCL)
Reader's League (RL)
Red Arrow Books (RA)
Red Circle (RC)
Red Dagger Myst. (RDM)
Red Seal Books (RS)
Regency (Reg)
Retail Dist. (Ret)
Rex Stout Myst. (RSM)
Romantic Novel (Rom)
Royal Giant (RG)
Rutledge (Rut)
R. W. Co. (RW)
Saint Myst. Libr. (SML)
Shooting Script (ShS)
Signet (Sig)
Stallion Books (Stal)
Stanley Library (Stan)
Star Books (Star)
Stork Original Novel (SON)
Stovel-Advocate (SA)
Stuart (Stu)
Superior Reprints (SuR)
Suspense Novels (Susp)
Tech Myst. (TM)
Tech Western (TW)
Thriller Book (Thr)
Thriller Novel Classic (TNC)
Thrilling Books/Novels (TN)
Toby (Toby)
Travellers Pocket Libr. (Trav)
Triple Nickel Libr. (TNL)
Trophy Books (Trop)
Uni Books (Uni)
Universal Giant (UG)
Universal Romance (UR)
Value Books (Val)
Venus (Ven)
Vital Book (Vit)
Vulcan Myst. (VulM)
Washington Square Press (WSP)
Western Action Novel (WAN)
Western Novel Classic (WNC)
Western Novel of the Month (WNM)
Western Thriller (WT)
West in Action (WIA)
Whitman (Whit)
Yogi Myst. (YM)
Zenith (Zen)
Prize Myst. Novel (PMN)
Prize SF Novel (PSFN)
Prize Western Novel (PWN)
Putnam (Put)
Pyramid (Pyr)

AUTHOR CROSS-INDEX

Aarons, Edward S.—GM 258, 280, 362, 424, 491, 568, 621, 666, 707, 749, 799, 834, 863, 895, 906, S911, 923; MM 143

Abbot, Anthony—AvMMM 25; Dell 88; GD 7; Pop 159, 286

Adams, Cleve F.—Ace D115; Dell 104; Han 2, 7, 33, 112; Har 256; MNC 43; MNM 31, 36; Peng 522; Pop 426, 456, Sig 765, 850, 902, 936, 1298, 1405, 1419

Albert, Marvin H.—GM 519, 553, 696, 756, 760, 808, 826, 846, 856, 902, 918; Pre d66

Alcott, Louisa May—Dell 296; Pk 75

Aldiss, Brian W.—Ace D369, D443, F382; Bal F555; Bea 305; Sig S1683

Aldrich, Ann—GM 509, S727, S774

Algren, Nelson—Av 185, 222, 419, 424, T108, T125, T185, T223, T324; Card C31; Cre d157; Pk 757

Allingham, Margery—Av 29; AvMMM 17, 35; BM 33, 51; BoM 12; Dell 777, D234; JM 32; MM 49, 112, 132; Peng 276, 503; Pk 329, 665; Pony 56

Ambler, Eric—Bant 1327, A1671, A1772; Dell D201, D238; Peng 511; Penn P3; Pk 193, 232, 286, 887

Amis, Kingsley—Bal 479

Anderson, Poul—Ace D110, D199, D255, D303, D335, D407, D479, D550, D568, F104, F139, F209, F425; Bal 80, 422, 483, 579, 02107; Bea 270; Berk G289

Angelo, Tony—Ar 6, 12; Lei 17

Appel, Benjamin—Av T101, T162; Bal 345K; Berk G152; Dell F81; GM 266, 385, S642, S809; Lio 39, 95, 166, LB116, LL151

Ard, William—Dell B145, 991; Mon 124; Pop 416, 477, 502, 526, 569, 591, 639, 723, 756, G236, G328

Armstrong, Charlotte—Cre 191, 247; MM 85; Pk 427, 444, 575, 805, 880, 1034, 1058, 1095

Arno, Peter—ASE 933; Pk 417, 1087

Asbury, Herbert—ASE K26; Av 263; Card C195, C251; Pk 474, 565

Asimov, Isaac—Ace D84, D110, D110 (Spec.), D125, D538, F216; Av T232, T287; Bant A1646, A1731, A1978; Gal 14; Sig 1082, S1240, S1282, S1433, S1493

Aswell, James—Av 247; Sig 941, 1121, 1166, 1314

Auchincloss, Louis—Bant F1722; Cre S320; Sig 1004, S1143, 1255

Austen, Jane—Bant FC10; Card C37; Dell LC122, LC128; Pk 63, PL9

Autry, Gene—Dell 153, 217

Avallone, Michael—Ace D259; GM 703, 718; Mid 60; Perm 244, 289, M3012; Sig 1294

Bagby, George—Bant 1197, 1226, 1308; Berk G84; BDM 4; BM 87, 113, 200; Cent 13; Dell 848, 904, 949, 997; JM 67, 71, 73, 87; MM 156; Pk 736

Bailey, H. C.—BoM 8, 16; Pk 190; Pony 52, 60, 64

Baldwin, Faith—Bant 411, 455, 471; Dell 12, 73, 116, 138, 163, 196, 236, 255, 288, 318, 368, 445, 475, 532, 574, D317; DeT 5, 30; Pk 150, 311, 380, 445, 456, 513, 603, 613, 658; Pony 51; SuR M637

Ballard, W. T.—Bant A1600; BDM 9; Card C277; Gm 259; Gra 18, 26, 65, 72; Moñ 134; Peng 566; Pop 454, 476, 492, 524, 552, 617, 638, 680, 735, 772, G249, G255, G309, G320, G335, EB83, EB93

Ballinger, Bill S.—Sig 730, 774, 897, 1040, 1134, 1243, 1274, 1319, 1321, 1494, 1585, 1730

Balzac, Honore de—Av 697, T102, T140; Bant AC17; Cre S220; Hil 12; Jac 7; Pyr G177, PR215

Bannon, Ann—GM S653, S833, S919

Barry, Joe—Ace D47; FMS 2; Han 42, 52, 63, 106; Har 43, 83, 84, 101; Phan 500; PMN 12

Baum, Vicki—Av 64, 265; BH 28; Dell 524, D239, F83; Perm P109, P208; Pyr G328

Beauchamp, Loren—Mid 7, 18, 29, 30, 65, 70

Beaumont, Charles—Bal F641; Bant A1759, A1917; Dell F94

Beeding, Francis—Av 37; Peng 544; Pop 42, 57, 71, 268, 381; RA 9; TNC 11, 19

Bellah, James Warner—Bal 44, 352K; GM 155; Lio 43; Pop 195, 380, 404, G350, EB3; Reg 323

Benchley, Robert—ASE B39, G192, M4, R5, T13, 865; Pk 449

Benet, Stephen Vincent—ASE C77, H215, L1, N3, 855, 1114; AvMSSM 31; Peng 546; Pk 360

Benson, Ben—Bant 1014, 1070, 1271, 1323, 1359, 1421, 1468, 1552, A1698, 1909, 1910, 1974, 2001; GM S583; Penn P4, P16

Bierce, Ambrose—Av 628

Biggers, Earl Derr—ASE E130; Av 17, 337, 344, 350; Dell 47; Pk 50, 133, 168, 191, 207; Pop 132; QR 131; RL nn

Binder, Otto—Bal U2271; Ban 3569

Blackburn, Thomas W.—Bant 207, 958, 1164, A1798; DeFE A171; Det 20; Penn P1

Blake, Nicholas—ASE 1031; BM 193; BCD 7; Dell D227; MM 147; Peng 543, 592; Pk 548, 742; Pop 30, 41, 60, 123

Blassingame, Wyatt—BH 5

Blish, James—Av T193, T225, T238, T268, T279; Bal 197, 256, 465K, F647; Gal 16, 19; Sig S1622, S1719

Bloch, Robert—Ace D59, S67, D265, Av 211, 494; AvMN 9; AvS nn; Bel 233; Lio 185; Reg 101

Blochman, Lawrence G.—BM 140; Dell 7, 43, 134, 156, 311, 488, 638, 740, 833; Det 19; Han 128; Pk 793; Sig Ks350

Bode, Vaughn—Ban 5869

Bodenheim, Maxwell—Av 152, 168, 191, 352, 427; AvBD 3; Bel 231; Chec 6; DivPoN 2; NL 38, 46

Bok, Hannes—Bal 01795, 02093

Bonnamy, Francis—ASE 1026; BM 147; DH 5; Peng 584, 606, 629; Sig 713

Boswell, Charles—GM 180, 334, 384, 480; Han 94; Pop 688

Bosworth, Allan R.—ASE 1299; Bant 86, 119, 929; CNS 3; DH nn, 6; Dell 858; GW 54; Pop 684, 736

Boucher, Anthony—Ace D422, D455, F105, F131, F162, F217; Bal 109; Dell 334, 591; MM 179; MNM nn; Pk 213; Pop 59, 154

Bower, B. M.—Av 374, 505; Dell 466; Pk 310; Pop 118, 157, 306; Sig 1045; TN 15

Box, Edgar—Sig 1036, 1093, 1217, 1475, 1484, 1526

Brackett, Leigh—Ace D36, D99, D103, F123, F135, F187, F422; Bant 1893; Han 32

Bradbury, Ray—Bal 41, F139, U2139, U2141, U2142; Bant 886, A944, 991, A1241, 1261, 1282, A1519, A1885, A1922

Bradley, Marion Zimmer—Ace F117, F127, F153, F273, F303, F350

Brand, Max—ASE J286, K5, L13, M14, N15, P8, Q24, R24, S23, T21, 715, 877, 908, 982, 1133, 1216, 1263, 1311; Card C368; Dell 329; Mon 126; Pk 144, 250, 316, 369, 390, 423, 491, 509, 523, 547, 584, 609, 634, 668, 687, 705, 717, 744, 781, 797, 848, 877, 895, 910, 930, 950, 979, 991, 1018, 1033, 1056, 1065, 1084, 1097, 1122,

(AUTHOR CROSS-INDEX, continued)

    1133, 1149, 1168, 1180, 1190, 1203, 1221, 1228, 1244; Pop 78, 152, 445, 475, 637, 693, 757, 801, 822, G230,
    G270, G327, G369, G398; Sig 757, 1046; WNC 23, 31; WNM 5, 13

Brandel, Marc—Av 387, 393; Bant A1332

Brennan, Dan—Ace D488, Lio 197, LB147

Brewer, Gil—Ace D123; Av 830, T335; Cre 147, 173, 229, 238, 310; GM 169, 196, 211, 277, 345, 380, 409, 418, 448,
    708, 858; Mon 107; Zen ZB7

Brock, Stuart—Ace D23, D166, D573; Dell 337; Gra 136; Pyr 255, 333; RCL 38

Bromfield, Louis—ASE I265, L7, Q34, S31, T32, 811, 845; Av 52; AvMSSM 13, 24, 34; Bant 28, 462, A869, A910, 957;
    Berk G36; BM 6; Card C138; Peng 512; Pk 56; Pop G179; Pyr R305; Sig 904AB, S954, S979, S1025, D1260, D1263

Brown, Carter—Sig 1527, 1565, 1594, 1606, 1620, 1633, 1654, 1663, 1674, 1694, 1713, 1722, 1738, 1750

Brown, Fredric—Bant 302, 361, 735, 783, 831, 835, 876, 943, 990, 1040, 1077, 1133, 1134, 1176, 1215, 1216, 1253,
    1285, 1312, 1423, 1436, A1546, 1565, 1566, 1567, A1615, A1701, 1712, 1757, A1812, 1990; DeFE 2E; Det 33;
    Penn P59

Brown, Wenzell—Av 560, 722, T235; FSM 38; GM 292, S522, 640, S734, S897, S917; Perm P186; Pop 374, 549, 581,
    685, 732, 734, G228, G317; Pyr G345, G439; Sig 981

Brown, Will C.—Dell 878, 986; DeFE A183; Pop 715, EB91

Brunner, John—Ace D335, D362, D385, D391, D421, D457, D465, D471, D507, D547, F133, F161, F215, F227, F242,
    F277, F299, F361

Brush, Katharine—Av 22, 154, 192, 239; AvMN 12; AvMSSM 48; Det 18

Buchan, John—ANC 1, 4; Bant 31, 71, 1143; Pk 69, 94

Buck, Pearl S.—AvMSSM 23; BH 21; Card C46, C105, C108, C111, C114, C308, C334, C372, GC 35, GC35, GC41, GC46; DeT
    8; MM 19; Peng 505; Pk nn(0), 11, 359, 642, 679, 951, 993

Budrys, Algis—Ball 243; Lio 230; Pyr G339, G416; Reg 110

Bulmer, Kenneth—Ace D255, D331, D369, D453, D507, F104, F209, F285, F289, F396

Burnett, W. R.—ASE G191, 017, 848(?), 1161; Av 66, 212, 329; AvMMM 33, 40; Bant 826, 888, 942, 998, 1124,
    A1331, 1547, A1819, A1871, 1973; GM 106; Hil 20; Penn P7; Pk 714

Burns, Walter Noble—Peng 514, 520; Sig 1085, S1205

Burroughs, Edgar Rice—Ace F156-F159, F168-F171, F179-F182, F189, F190, F193, F194, F203-F206, F212, F213,
    F220, F221, F232-F235, F245, F247, F256, F258, F268, F270, F280, F282; ASE M16, 022; Bal F701, F702, F711,
    F728, F739, F745-F754, F762, F770, F772, F776, F777, U2001-U2024, U2031-U2034, U2036-U2041, U2045,
    U2046, U2048, U6039; BLA 23; Dell 320, 536

Cain, James M.—ASE Q2, 766, 1058; Av 60, 99, 137, 141, 161, 174, 348, 421, 455, 479, 581, 599, 768, T285;
    AvMN 1, 17; AvMMM 6, 16, 20, 44; AvMSSM 22; MM 1; Peng 591, 621; Pk 443; Sig 680, 720, 759, 784, 811,
    1152, 1153, 1195, 1427, 1445

Cain, Paul—Av 178, 268, 496; B/C 10, 21

Caldwell, Erskine—ASE P19, 866, 945; Av 134, 151, 177, 309, 340; AvMSSM 14,30; Card C270; NS 50, 51; Peng 567,
    581, 627, 646; Pk 392; Sig 661, 686, 705, 732, 760, 818, 838, 869, 899, 918, 933, 983, 1016, 1091, 1136,
    D1199, 1272, 1342, 1417, S1430, 1456, 1479, S1497, S1564, S1568, S1589, S1592, S1598, S1608, S1611,
    S1621, S1623, S1666, S1672, S1733, S1734, S1735, S1739, Ks344

Caldwell, Taylor—Bant A760, A956, A1139, F1702, S1879; Card C202, C245, C252, C274, C311; GM 288, 525

Canning, Victor—Bant 313, 734, 834, 948, 1177; Berk 377; Har 41, 393; Perm M4121, M4139

Capote, Truman—Sig 700, 878, 1020, S1333, D1727

Capp, Al—Bal 8, 172, 350K; Pk 621

Carco, Francis—Av 302, 401, 555; Berk 337, 369, G33, G81, G140, G155, G174

Carnegie, Dale—BLA 2; Card C112, C237, C303; Perm 135; Pk 68, 891; Pop 182

Carr, John Dickson—Ace D181; ASE 1280; Av 33, 476, 621; Bant 101, 304, 365, 793, 896, 996, A1009, 1119, 1207,
    1325, 1447, A1472, 1503-1505, 1682-1684, A1847, A1849; Berk G42, G48, G60, G72, G80, G91, G101, G117,
    G129, G143, G157, G281, G287; BM 47, 78; Dell 91, 537, 564, 635, 706, 775, 859, D323; DNC 32, 40; HiIDN 1;
    MM 110; Peng 528, 532,; Pk 101, 350, 372, 436, 448; Pop 10, 19, 28, 61, 174, 282, 349; TNC 23

Carroll, Lewis—Jac 8; Pk 835

Carse, Robert—ASE A5; Bant A1820; Berk G257; DeFE 95, B109; Mon 129; Pop G102, G244, G284, G357

Carter, Nick—AtM 1, 3

Carter, Ralph—Bea B307; Cent 91, 98, 112, 122; Croy 14; Gem 101; Int 20; Kni nn; SON 6

Caspary, Ver—ASE 666, 943, 1209; BM 74; Dell D188; Pop 111, 284, 373; Pyr G400; RCL 11

Cassill, R. V.—Ace S104, S136; Av 686, 710, T173, T281, T293; GM d852, 921; Lio 216; Sig 1646

Chaber, M. E.—Ace D225; Bant 202; Perm M3080; Pk 1240, 1259; Pop 482, 530, 632, G282

Chandler, Raymond—ASE 751, 838; Av 38, 63, 88, 219; AvMMM 7, 19, 28, 43; Card C213, C344, C375; Pk 212, 320,
    389, 696, 750, 823, 846, 916, 1044

Charteris, Leslie—Av 34, 44, 71, 118, 130, 147, 321, 341, 347, 420, 432, 440, 463, 473, 477, 489, 518, 526, 533,
    544, 588, 610, 611, 619, 629, 635, 653, 663, 680, 694, 708, 718, 744, 756, 771, 803, 818, 827, 834, 848,
    T199, T234, T250, T317; AvMMM 22, 32; B/C 1-9, 11, 14, 17, 26, 27, nn; MM 141; Perm P124, M3103; Pk 257,
    272, 1233; Pop 1; RL nn; SML (edited series); TNC 16

Chase, James Hadley—Ace D135; Av 355, A436, 485; AvMN 4, 7; Et E112, E116; Han 3; Har 95, 108, 111, 124, 130,
    135, 160, 197, 199, 206, 245, 267, 316, 323, 385, 413; NL 11, 37; Pop 378; Sig 1112, 1187, 1586, 1696, 1749

Cheever, John—Bant F1833; Berk G119

Chekhov, Anton—Av T120; Bant FC5; Dell LC126

Chesterton, G. K.—ASE 984; Dell 819, D230; Pk 60, 236; Pop 153

Cheyney, Peter—Av 49, 80, 93, 114, 123, 349, 699, 712, 734, 764, 776, 797, T212, T314, T365; AvMMM 15, 21, 30,
    36; Bant 730; Et E115; Han 18; Har 354; Pyr 16

Chidsey, Donald Barr—Ace D278, D318, D364, D394, D410, D512; Av T81, T96, T134, T305, T318; BLA 25; DeFE 107;
    Gra G214; MM 6; Perm P174, P248, M4129

Christian, Paula—Cre s267

Christie, Agatha—Av 3, 46, 61, 70, 75, 85, 89, 100, 124, 164, 245, 312, 316, 317, 353, 371, 379, 410, 443, 616, 636,
    648, 658, 690, 716, 793, T149, T167, T176, T192, T204, T210, T220, T243, T245; AvMMM 26; BLA 26; BM 9, 18,
    21, 25, 32, 36, 39, 43, 48, 52, 54, 58, 61, 79, 86; Card C312, C318, C335, C349, C360-C362; Dell 8, 46, 60, 105,
    145, 172, 187, 199, 226, 257, 293, 319, 391, 454, 491, 529, 550, 570, 633, 664, 683, 753, 770, 805, 830, 855,

871, 888, 912, 937, 961, D217, D218, D235, D236, D249, D262, D288, D305, D326; Har 242, 337, 359, 377, 441; JM 7, 10, 13, 16; MM 41, 43, 46, 50, 53, 59, 66, 69, 84, 100; Pk 5, 38, 79, 88, 167, 249, 261, 285, 319, 341, 398, 451, 465, 485, 617, 753, 820, 897, 956, 1003, 1021, 1036, 1085, 1114, 1151, 1174; RL nn
Christopher, John—Av T371; Cre S273; Pk 1183
Clark, Walter van Tilburg—ASE S24, 974, 1134; Peng 521; Sig 745, 801, 1160, S1470
Clarke, Arthur C.—Bal 33, 52, 68, 97, 135, 186, 249; Card C135; Gal 3; Perm 310, M4149; Pk 989; Sig S1464, S1583, S1729
Clarke, Donald Henderson—ASE 990; Av 105, 116, 120, 149, 193, 213, 232, 237, 253, 270, 336, 351, 365, 384, 394, 397, 408, 431, 438, 456, 472, 480, 483, 503, 530, 543, 575, 593, 615, 631, 650, 656, 671, 747, T233, T300; AvMN 3, 16, 18; AvS nn; Berk 331, G34, G76, G124; NL 8, 19
Cloete, Stuart—ASE N29, 973; Card C371; Mon K50; Peng 573; Perm P147, M4102; Pop 110, G110, G132, G205; Sig S1078
Cobb, Irvin S.—U.S. Sales nn
Coburn, Walt—Ace D180, D196, D294; ASE 803; Av 749, 821, 852, 858; Berk D2013; Har 350; Pop 135, 166, 191, 250, 290, 415
Cohen, Octavus Roy—Cre S124; GM 138, 172, 650; Gra 125; Gre 14; Pop 46, 74, 88, 144, 162, 196, 264, 332, 369, 427, 462
Cole, Jackson—Cent 132; Har 100; Pop 298; Pyr 40, 47, 51, 56, 66, 70, 73, 81, 87, 91, 108, 111, 117, 124, 144, 153, 155, 162, 167, 171
Coles, Manning—Ace D389; ASE 1038, 1279; Bant 76, 118; JM 39, 57, 62, 68, 74, 90, 93; MM 63, 126, 144
Collier, John—ASE 871; Bant A1106, F1703
Collins, Wilkie—ASE M29; Pyr 19, G88, PR11
Conklin, Groff—Av T289; Bal 257; Bant 1352; Berk G3, G31, G53, G63; DeFE D9; Perm P67, P117, P254, M4022; Pk 1045, 1074; Pyr G434
Conrad, Joseph—ASE A26, G194, I264, J273, 1099; Bant F1597, FC7; Peng 619; Pyr G378; Sig 834, S1254, D1410, CD4
Cook, Will—Cre 242; GM 748, 798, 837; Mon 130; Pop 596, 631, 652, 687, 722, 748, 773, 799, 827, G276
Cooper, Jefferson—Card C262; Perm M3064, M4113, M4117; Pk 1071, 1237
Costain, Thomas B.—ASE R36, 814, 1082, 1320; Bant A818, A951, A984, A1027, F1186, F1444; Perm P2845, M5000, M5003
Coward, Noel—Av 28, 78; AvMSSM 3; DeFE D80
Coxe, George Harmon—ASE 1136; Av 143; AvMMM 39; Dell 5, 27, 58, 81, 101, 147, 169, 182, 202, 225, 240, 276, 321, 377, 423, 441, 453, 502, 522, 549, 586, 644, 678, 734, 745, 757, 799, 838, 902, 931, 970, 984, D271; DeTIP 2; JM 30; Perm M3010
Creasey, John—Av 563, 590, 641, 720, T366; Bant 1883, 1884; Dell 985; Har 116
Crofts, Freeman Wills—Av 9, 126; Peng 533, 575; Pk 105; Pop 18, 121
Cronin, A. J.—ASE D113, Q27, T33, 891, 1009, 1054; Bant 782, A930, F1042, A1050, A1060, F1321, F1429, F1474, F1536, F1537, F1624, A1719, F1947
Crossen, Kendell Foster—DeFE 32; Ee 1; FSM 15, 22; Perm M4099; VulM 5
Cummings, Ray—Ace D173, D324, D331, D497, D535, F248, F313, F343, F363, F406; AvFN 1; Duc nn
Cunningham, A. B.—Dell 313, 365, 410, 465; DNC 15, 20, 25, 30, 37, 42, 46, 52; MM 166, 199; MNC 90; MNM 32, 35
Cunningham, Eugene—ASE H222, T20, 753, 1036; Bant 77, 113; Cent 20; Dell 776, 935, 956; Pk 345, 554, 791; Pop 77, 148, 176, 234, 289, 375, 542, 624, 834, G238, G272, G294, G332, EB55; Pyr 265; Sig 740, 1269; WNC 38, 43; WNM 21, 48
Curwood, James Oliver—ASE P12, 1065; Har 162, 176, 380, 383, 406, 429; Pk 362
Cushman, Dan—Ace D49; Bal 281K; Cre d264; Dell 575, 656, 720; DeFE 67, A140; GM 142, 158, 241, 290, 332, 332, 535, 785, S828, S840; Pop 548, EB102
Daly, Elizabeth—Bant 4, 53, 78, 353, 713, 811; BM 70, 92, 112, 191, 199; JM 21; MM 151, 165; Peng 549; Sur M639, M653
Dana, Richard Henry—Bant FC20; Pyr 76, PR12
Daniels, John S.—Bant 1189, 1769; Penn P69; Sig 1435, 1505, 1605
Daniels, Norman A.—Av 864, T370; Fal 29, 38; GD 2; Rain 117
Davenport, Basil—Bal 326K; Card C118
Davis, Frederick C.—Ace D63, D499; BM 192; MNC 78; Pk 804
Davis, Norbert—Han 40, 54
Defoe, Daniel—Card C44; Peng 554; Pk PL510; RG 24
Dekobra, Maurice—Ace 585; AvBN 4; BNM 2; Dell 256; Div. Love Book Monthly 1
Delany, Samuel R.—Ace F173, F199, F261, F322, F388, F427
Delmar, Vina—Av 81, 92, 107, 121, 145, 187, 209, 286, AT51; Dell F69; DeT 9; Pk 838, 915
Dent, Lester—Ace D21, D357; BM 96, 101, 115; GM 247
Derby, Mark—Ace D458; Bant A1824; Cre S306; Dell D320; Perm 265, M3017, M3028; Pop G124
Derleth, August—ASE R33; Berk G77, G104, G116, G131, G163, G189, G249
Dick, Philip K.—Ace D103, D150, D193, D211, D249, D261, D340, D421, D457, F251, F301, F309, F337, F377, F429
Dickens, Charles—ASE A8, N31, 691; Card C35; Dell F70; Pk 14, 29, 519, PL22, PL50, PL68, PL514, PL522, PL751; QR 119
Dickson, Carter—ASE 991, 1069, 1246; Av 7; Bant A2000; Berk G214, G267; BM 34, 45; Dell 16, 65, 108, 175, 370, 481, 543, 650, 690; JM 4, 11, 14, 19, 25; MM 52; Pk 46, 86, 156, 180, 219, 231, 303, 335, 386, 478, 507, 568, 633; Pop 87
Dickson, Gordon R.—Ace D139, D164, D449, F119, F426
Dikty, T. E.—Bant 1328; Berk G233; Cre S197, S258
Disney, Doris Miles—Av T319; BM 65, 111; Dell 885, 929; MM 114
Disney, Dorothy Cameron—ASE 675; Bant 91, 761, 863; BM 53; Dell 15, 62, 76, 137; MM 34, 54, 71; Pk 152
Dobie, J. Frank—Bant 940, A1089, A1212, F1778; Penn P51
Dodge, David—ASE 1289; Dell 270, 350, 405, 478, 565, 658, D304; JM 95; Pop 168, 202, 252
Dos Passos, John—Bant FC28; Bel L510; Card C72, C131, GC26; Lio LL1, LL42; Peng 577; Pop SP53
Dostoyevsky, Fyodor—Av G1024; Bant F1735, SC4, FC30; Dell F55, LX106, LC131; QR 114; Sig 733, T1488

Douglas, Lloyd C.—ASE D118, K27, R37; Card C176, C240, C257, C269, C336, GC53, GC59; Dell 304, 380; Pk 175, 215, 352, 387, 405, 1096

Doyle, Arthur Conan—Bant 366, 704, 733; Dell D302; Har 238; Jac 10; Perm 279; Pk 95, 670; Pyr PR15

Drago, Harry Sinclair—Ace D112; ANC 33; ASE I251; Bel 235, 241; Cent 57; Cre 116; Dell 660, 789, 919; NL 16, 21; Perm M3038, M3068, M3085, M3115; Pk 1257, 1264; Pop 305, 406, EB71; PWN 30; TN 21

DuBois, Theodora—Dell 860; MM 146; MNC 96; PMN 26

Dumas, Alexandre—Ace G414; Bant F1520; Pk 36, 37; QR 149

Du Maurier, Daphne—ASE E137, T36, 1176; Card C6, C53, C68, C99, C153, C168, C216, C276, C326; DD nn; MM 18, 28; Pk 205, 403, 415, 483

Eberhart, Mignon G.—ASE 711; Bant 46, 137, 739, 849, 885; BLA 28; BM 49, 55, 60; Cent 19, 35; Dell 25, 83, 136, 161, 213, 546, 628, 669, 767, 811, 877, 955, D259; DeT 7; MM 51, 88; MNC 47, 56; Peng 501; Pk 64; Pop 2, 17, 27, 35, 73, 167, 293

Edmonds, Walter D.—ASE B52, E149, H240, J298, 677, 768, 875; Bant 708, A804, A1099, A1254, F1648; Card C121; DeT 6; Perm P132

Eisner, Simon—Lio 109, LL125

Ellison, Harlan—Ace D312, D413, D513; Pyr G352; Reg 102, 106

Ellson, Hal—Ace D522; Bal 2, 27, 103, 129, 319K; Bant 945, 1561; Hil 119; Mid 5; Mon 137; Pop 219, 725, 757, 776, G358; Reg 108

Endore, Guy—Av 323, 354; Card GC42; Dell D183; Pk 97

Epstein, Brian—Pyr R-1200

Ermine, Will—ASE 1183, 1290; Cre 120; Dell 284, 378, 592, 653, 684, 916, 932; FWN 21, 25; Penn P37; Perm M3024; Pk 719, 761, 911, 986, 1031, 1040, 1091, 1124, 1134, 1169; Pop 368, EB63; Sig 679, 685, 737, 885, 1251, 1287, 1323, 1360; WNC 100, 106

Ernenwein, Leslie—Av 659; Bant 740; Berk 368; GM 140, 156, 220, 293, 329, 361, 464, 620, 916; FWN 15; Gra 44, 62, 112, 120; Han 69, 75, 83, 93, 111; HanW 2; Har 88, 89, 143, 145, 171, 204, 355, 371, 386; Lio LB155; Pop G292; Sig 727, 828, 874, 982, 1340; WNC 90

Evans, Evan—ANC 26, 32; ASE L8, 1257; Bant 211, 254, 784, 882, 966, 1102, 1709, 1837; Peng 600, 620, 645; Penn P38; Sig 836, 935, 1015, 1398, 1436

Fair, A. A.—ASE Q10; Dell 59, 84, 109, 160, 211, 243, 254, 315, 389, 460, 472, 542, 603, 619, 620, 691, 718, 772, 778, 809, 836, 899, 939, D210-D213, D253, D309; Pk 228

Farley, Ralph Milne—Ace F304, F312; Av 285

Farmer, Philip Jose—Ace F165, F367, F412; Bal 210; Bea 277, 291; Reg 118

Farrell, James T.—Av 157, 252, 260, 290, 466, 468, 475; AvMSSM 10, 21, 41; Cre S200; Peng 603, 643; Sig 734, 779, 810, 831, S875, S893, S926, D946, 994, 1031, D1066, S1118, 1158, 1275, 1349, S1475, T1518, S1624

Fast, Howard—ASE A19, T26, 787; Av 205; Bant 30, FC44; Peng 569, 588; Pk 322, 382

Faulkner, John—Bant 972, 1023; GM 178, 238, 410, 439, 455, 633, 729, 730, 927

Faulkner, William—ASE 825; Av 12; Dell 708, D168; Peng 632, 659; Sig 692, 743, 825, 863, 887, 977, S1032, S1079, S1148, S1253, 1315, S1485, D1486, S1501, S1511, D1614, S1616, D1628, D1629, D1643, CD9

Fearing, Kenneth—ASE 1215; Av 823; Bant 93, 738; BM 67; MM 173

Fenisong, Ruth—BM 168, 185; BoM 9; Dell 808; MM 167; MNC 97; Pop 173, 245; Zen 17

Ferber, Edna—ASE E140, F165, 959, 1111; Av 51; AvMSSM 19; Bant A1754, S1843, F1912; Card C120; DeT 10; Peng 605, 617, 633, 639, 650, 653; Pk 13

Ferrars, E. X.—DNC 54; Pk 735

Fickling, G. G.—Pyr G274, G344, G366, G411, G453

Field, Peter—ASE B36, 1154, 1181, 1264, 1300; Bant 68, 104, 201, 210, 731, 775; Pk 348, 567, 683, 711, 759, 847, 882, 902, 934, 937, 962, 982, 990, 1027, 1035, 1054, 1068, 1081, 1088, 1123, 1161, 1173, 1187, 1205, 1213, 1241, 1260

Finney, Jack—Dell D274; DeFE 42, A139; Pk 1078

Fischer, Bruno—Ace D27; BM 82, 106, 130; Dell 79, 752, 817, 910; FSM 46; GW 52; GM 123, 148, 209, 270, 343, 437, 537, 591, 600, 694, 753, 755, S783, 886, 901, 928; JM 45; MM 127; PenM 3; Pk 521; Pyr 22, 29, G270; Sig 780, 833, 892, 988, 1256, 1474

Fisher, Clay—Bal 11, 40, 59; Card C373; Penn P26; Pk 927, 1108, 1137, 1159, 1186, 1209

Fisher, Steve—Bant 1376; BM 204; GM 219; Han 27; MNM nn; Pop 129, 229, 317, 361, 781; RS 21

Fisher, Vardis—ASE C3, C73, C119, C177, C253; GC 81; Pyr G57, G141, G310, R419

Fitzgerald, F. Scott—ASE 862, 1043; Bant 8, A867, A1228; Dell D140; Perm P123

Flaubert, Gustave—Bant AC35; Berk G5, BG73; Card 659; Dell LC118; Pk 240; PkL 69

Fleischman, A. S.—Ace D57,; GM 181, 223, 295, 368, 499, 514, 572; PMN 29

Fleming, Ian—Perm M3048, M3070, M3084; Pop 660; Sig S1563, S1670, S1723

Fletcher, Inglis—ASE 1238; Perm P137, P151, P171, P189, P207, P216, P268

Fletcher, J. S.—DNC 2; MNC 45; Peng 518

Flynn, Errol—Dell 195, 351

Foote, Shelby—Sig 860, 970, 1104, S1415, S1685

Ford, Leslie—Bant 16, 42, 80, 114, 303, 359; Dell 6, 61, 354, 395, 447, 505, 547, 689, 788, 908; Pk 33, 122; Pop 6, 24, 158

Foreman, L. L.—Ace D570, F360, F411; Bal 259; Cent 55; Dell 825; DeFE 11, 57, A127; Pk 627, 702, 824; Pop 560; Sig 1607

Forester, C. S.—ASE A14, E133, F157, H213, O12, Q18, 679, 709, 804, 829, 996, 1187; Bant 40, 712, 772, 816, A912, 917, 993, 1011, 1080, 1170, A1196, A1305, A1314, A1587, 1610, A1611, A1619, A1811, A1815, A1816, A2060; DeFE 30; FFS nn, nn; MM 10, 111; Pk 174

Foster, Bennett—Bant 88, 252, 255, 260, 725, 762, 808, 841, 873, 1112, 1116; Lio 17, 35, LL43; Pk 807, 1166; WAN 3

Foster, Richard—FSM 5, 13, 36; GM s853, 899; Pop 667, EB32; VulM 3

Fox, Gardner F.—Ace F299, F307, F354, F399; Av T341; Bel 227; Cre 166, 304; GM 300, 328, 360, 394, 438, 484, s549, 609, 648, 942

Fox, Norman A.—Ace D72; Bal 70; Cre 128, 137; Dell 362, 406, 480, 539, 569, 642, 694, 737, 783, 831, 864, 907, 927, 950, 969, 980, 1002; DeT 12; Han 105; Har 96; Pyr 195; TN 30

(AUTHOR CROSS-INDEX, continued)

Frazee, Steve—Cre 211, 261, 315; DeFE A135; GM 457, 613, 637, s836, 935; Lio 90, 96, 130, 150, 217, LL3, LB69, LB78, LB108, LB173; Perm M3003, M3049; Pk 1101; Pyr PG13; Toby nn

Freeman, R. Austin—Av 10, 122; Pk 184; Pop 11, 70, 122

Friend, Oscar J.—Av 299; B/C 10B; Cre S245; Han 71, 79, 101, 113; HanW 3; Har 94; Pk 1007

Fuller, Timothy—ASE T6, 744; Dell 54, 594; Pop 81, 117, 207

Gaddis, Peggy—Ace D536; Ast 14; Bea B302; Bel 244; Cam 317, 325, 337, 362; Carn 905, 915, 916; Crow 25; Croy 43, 45, 69, 82, 90; Har 368, 394, 405, 471; Orig 700; Qua 14, 82; Star 2; Uni 3, 21, 31; Ven 101, 104, 105, 112, 116, 118, 122, 123, 127, 131, 137, 142, 149, 168, 172, 190, 196

Gaines, William M.—Bal 178, 266K, 267K; Sig S1647, S1701

Gallico, Paul—ASE J290, 728, 754; Av 760; Dell 717; DeT 27; Pk 318; Sig 819, 1295

Gann, Ernest K.—ASE 015, 1200; Perm P134, P301, M4002, M4034, M4091; Pop 516

Gardner, Erle Stanley—ASE S21, 915, 1039, 1131, 1218, 1302; BM 10, 19, 22, 29, 35; Card C275, C281-C285, C291-C295, C297, C299, C302, C307, C309, C312, C320, C323, C324, C325, C329, C332, C337, C341, C345-C348, C355, C376; MM 40, 56, 58, 62; Pk 73, 90, 106, 116, 138, 157, 177, 201, 223, 242, 252, 263, 277, 287, 312, 334, 368, 378, 407, 414, 438, 464, 468, 512, 544, 561, 590, 595, 619, 643, 667, 678, 689, 724, 758, 792, 832, 855, 856, 869, 886, 909, 922, 949, 965, 976, 1009, 1010, 1029, 1041, 1052, 1063, 1089, 1092, 1107, 1121, 1127, 1138, 1155, 1170; RL nn, nn, nn

Garth, David—ASE R13; Pop 49, 84, 136

Gibson, Walter B.—AtM 2, 5; Bel 90-298; Perm P54; Tempo 5320

Gilbert, Anthony—ArM 7; Bant 51, 85, 138, 317, 768, 851, 1758; Han 29; MM 67, 91, 108, 168, 193

Gipson, Fred—Bant F1749; Perm M4168; Pk 713, 1177

Golightly, Bonnie—Av T194, T237, T310; Bel L521; Berk G92

Goodis, David—Bant 407; BM 121; Dell 221; GM 189, 226, 256, 348, 428, 530, 544, 623, 626, 652, 691; Har 311; Lio 124, 133, 186, 224, LB131; News 39; Pk 833; Pop 775

Gould, Chester—Dell nn

Grant, Maxwell—BLA 21; Bel 92-602, 92-615, 92-624, B50-647, B50-683, B50-709, B50-725, B50-737

Greene, Graham—ASE A22, 873; Bant 315, 355, 797, 971, A1217, A1306, 1316, 1333, A1424, A1480, A1669, A1773, F2004; Berk G146; Lio LL31; Peng 515, 530; SuR M652

Greene, Ward—Av 190, 266, 664; Lio 89, 115, LL55; MM 14

Gregory, Jackson—Av 13; Pop 95, 140, 160, 184, 226, 255, 313, 337, 383, 430, 545, 597, 789, G257, G380, G396, EB10, EB17, EB103; TN 17

Grey, Zane—ASE Q19, 678, 722, 797, 842, 883, 997, 1107, 1294; Bant 3, 73, 1067, 1298, A1717, A1718; Card C231, C239, C264, C333, C351; Penn P2; Pk 161, 371

Grove, Fred—Bal 251, 324K; Pyr G313

Grove, Walt—DeFE 1E, D81, B136; GM 120, 134, 545, s649, s801

Gruber, Frank—Ace D39, D196; ASE A12, S6; Av 91; AvMMM 4, 12, 23; Bant 2, 50, 114, 151, 212, 1198, 1287, 1347, 1488, 1527, A1598, 1666, 1726, 1741-1743, 1934, A1627, 1618, F1872; Card C97, C204, C370; Cent 60, 64, 72; Cre 115; Gra 119; JM 66, 72, 76, 85, 89; Lio 157, 163, LB93, LB117; MM 191; Peng 538, 545, 562, 623, 651; Penn P43; Pop 188, 761; RCL 2, 13, 15, 16, 19; SuR M649, M655

Guthrie, A. B., Jr.—ASE 1297; Card C30, C52, C267; Pk 600, 780, PL17, PL513; Pop 376, G274

Haggard, H. Rider—ASE 795, 881; Dell 339, 433; RG 18

Hall, James Norman—ASE F179, P5, T10, 725, 905; Card C34; Mon 141; Perm M4001; Pk 188, 216, 358, 457

Halleran, E. E.—ASE Q11, 951, 1206; Av 367, 507, 522; Bal 142, 153, 170, 205, 219; Bant 1004, 1385; Dell 616, 755; GWN 28; Har 58, 61; Lio 134, Pk 703, 783, 876; RCL 33

Halliday, Brett—ASE 663; ArM 8; Dell 23, 64, 78, 112, 128, 168, 184, 222, 268, 280, 323-326, 385-388, 426-429, 458, 459, 503, 533, 578, 590, 617, 668, 723, 743, 768, 803, 829, 842, 865-867, 891, 905, 914, 934, 946, 957, 958, 960, 965, 978, 981, 987-989, D248, D269, D283, D291-D293, D314, D327, D331; DeT 15; DNC 21, 26, 31; Han 15; Pop 98, 192

Hamilton, Donald—Dell 375, 473, 577; DeFE 18, 27, 46, 91, A123, B115

Hamilton, Edmond—Ace D351, F271, F319; Cre S184, S329; Gal 18; Sig 812

Hammett, Dashiell—Bel 230, 239; BM 40, 50, 62, 81; Dell 53, 90, 129, 154, 223, 308, 379, 411, 421, 452, 486, 538; JM 17, 29, 36, 40, 48, 59; MM 120, 131, 233; Perm M3043, M3074; Pk 196, 211, 241, 268, 295; RL nn

Harragan, Steve—Stal 206; Uni 42, 44, 46, 47, 52, 54, 64; UG 4

Hastings, March—Bea B190, B198, B207; Mid 53

Hatlo, Jimmy—Av 366, 524, 612, 639, 652, 707, 789, 826, 857, DeFE 78; Pk 298

Hawthorne, Nathaniel—ASE 863; Card C65, Pk 52, 551, PL15, PL26, PL59; Sig CD8

Haycox, Ernest—ASE E129, F164, I254, K14, M13, N9, P16, Q16, 683, 706, 748, 791, 837, 867, 916, 1094, 1164, 1267; Bant 25, 261, 788, A980, 1115, A1627, 1628, F1872; Card C97, C204, C370; Dell 120, 227, 317, 347, 450, 598, 618, 748, 945, 952, 975, D290; Mon 108; Pk 301, 466, 531, 573, 594, 608, 640, 790, 864, 983, 1011, 1028, 1069, 1148; Pop 85, 143, 171, 199, 235, 271, 360, 398, 442, 450, 460, 486, 517, 537, 567, 589, 616, 644, 700, 728, 767, 796, 804, 831, G218, G237, G261, G283, G300, G318, G326, G347, G351, G367, EB4

Heard, H. F.—Av 108, 625, 808; Bant 1079; Dell 44; MM 70

Heinlein, Robert A.—Ace F375; Av T261; DeT 36; Sig 847, 882, 943, 980, 1044, 1161, 1194, S1444, S1537, S1544, S1577, S1639, S1644, S1699

Hemingway, Ernest—ASE K9, 667; Av G1006; Bant 467, 717, A883, A1240, A1249; Bel L506; Berk S127; Dell D117; Perm 253, P296, M3041, M3056

Hendryx, James B.—ANC 10, 17, 41; ASE 1073, 1230; Dell 587, 876; Har 156; Pony 66; Pop 314

Henry, O.—ASE K16, 944; BM 94; Peng 595; Pk 65, 510, PL38

Henry, Will—Bant 946, 1168, A1411, A1481, A1482, A1483, 1855, A1935

Hersey, John—Bant 45, 404, 1219, 1529, AC26; Card GC12; Dell D263; DeT 25; Pk 225, 279

Heuman, William—Ace D380, F254; Av 569, 855; GM 131, 146, 187, 216, 267, 287, 310, 322, 330, 414, 429, 631, 681, 705, 842, 944; Hil 104; Pk 1112

Highsmith, Patricia—Bant 905; Dell D282; Pop EB58

Hilton, James—ASE D91, E138, 966; Av 4, 39, 42, 79, 223, 301, 325, 381; AvMSSM 5; Bant 29, A1636; Bob nn; Card C70; Pk 1, 89, 93, 118, 136, 275, 630, 1046; RL nn

Hitchcock, Alfred—Dell 92, 143, 206, 262, 264, 367, D231, D281

Hitt, Orrie—Bea B101, B104, B126, B132, B137, B139, B146, B151, B153, B158, B159, B164, B168, B169, B174, B176, B180, B186, B194, B195, B203, B209, B211, B212, B222, B227, B232, B238, B239, B250, B254, B261, B267, B274, B288, B294, B304, B325; Mid 12, 16, 23, 34, 38; Uni 73
Hodgson, William Hope—Ace D553
Holding, Elisabeth Sanxay—Bant 26; BM 167; BCD 14; BoM 14; Dell 103, 194; Har 54, 60; MM 175; MNC 58; Pk 662; Pop 189, 302
Holmes, Clellon—Ace D238; Cre S307
Holmes, H. H.—Peng 553; PhM 1
Holmes, L. P.—Ace D597, F142, F208; Bant 823, 898, 988, 1048, 1103, 1384, 1514, 1822, 1873, 2031; Gra 77, 144; Penn P13, P25; Pk 514, 675; RCL 18
Hopley, George—Pop 424
Horan, James D.—Av 330; Bant A1402; Perm M4118; Pop G381; Sig S1557
Household, Geoffrey—ASE 1165, 1248; Bant 9, 1019; BM 207; Com 12; DeT 29; Penn P11
Howard, James—Ace F130; Pk 1255; Pop G346, EB30, EB46, EB70, EB90
Howard, Robert E.—Ace D36, F305
Hubbard, L. Ron—Ace S66; Gal 29
Hudson, W. H.—ASE C71, G196, 05, 721; Bant 63, F1878; Jac 3; Pk 16
Huffaker, Clair—Cre 158, 167, 193, 222; GM 733, 736
Huggins, Roy—ASE 1088; Av 282; DeFE A176; Pk 524, 602
Hughes, Dorothy B.—ASE N11, 785, 828, 869; BoM 11; Dell 31, 48, 100, 149, 210, 853, D225; Har 44; Pk 394, 422, 454, 587, 845; SM 70
Hugo, Victor—Av T190; Bant F1526, F1678; Pk 31, 32
Hunt, Howard—Av 457; Berk 345, D2001; GM 113, 167, 268, 297, 738, S869; Har 3; Sig 729, 768
Huxley, Aldous—ASE 36; Av AT435, T75, T160, G1020, G1027, G1031, G2001, V2031; Bant A1071, 1142, F1233, A1260, A1369, A1490, A1560, F1622, A1793, AC1, AC22; Bel L516; Berk BG66
Innes, Hammond—Bant 364, 741, 890, 1024, 1058, 1125, 1516; JM 60; Perm M4079
Innes, Michael—Av 752, T351; Pk 741
Irish, William—Ace D40; ASE S20, 878, 1173; Av 104, 220; AvMMM 31, 42; BM 90; Dell 679, D207; DeT 11, 26; Gra 16, 20, 31, 81, 108; JM 31; MM 82, 135; Pk 253; Pop 137, 258, 309, 431, 473; RCL 12; RL nn
Isherwood, Christopher—ASE 1115; Av 448; Berk G153; Dell LC102; Pop 710; Sig 937, S1252
Jackson, Charles—ASE 019, 1041; Bal 36; Bel L505; Berk G1; Dell 504; Lio LL35, LL143; Sig 683, 715, 781; Zen ZB1
Jackson, Shirley—Bal 337K, 342K; Lio 14, 36; Perm M3004; Pyr G212; Sig S1400
Jakes, John—Ace D209, D220; Bea B115; Bel 204; RG 22
Jenkins, Will F.—GM 126, 161, 346; Han 62; HH 4; News 141
Jennings, John—ASE Q36, 1226, 1306; Card C22, C137; Dell D267; Perm P125, P133, P141, P157, P256, P293, M3071; Pk 1047; Pop SP19
Jordan, Gail—Cam 311, 328, 341; Cent 119; Croy 19, 23; Har 26; Kni 15, 16, nn, nn, nn, nn; News 22; NI nn; Qua 46; Uni 28, 37; Ven 146
Joyce, James—Sig 664, S1150
Judd, Cyril—Ace D227; Bea 312; Dell 760
Kane, Frank—Ace D33; Bea B111; Dell 665, 749, 785, 822, 886, 901, 918, 973, D226, D264, D280, D333; DeFE A117, A126, A142, B123, B125, B137; Fed 3, 4; Han 72; Har 126; JM 56, 64; Pop 400; RCL 8
Kane, Henry—Av 572, 602, 618, 646, 672, 703, 733, 745, 751, 761, 790, 796, T264, T276, T291; Dell 231, 316, 330, 348, 455, 535, 580, 735; DeFE A144; Pop 806; Pyr G284, G432; Sig 1515, 1523; Zen ZB19
Kantor, MacKinlay—ASE B38, G202, K6, T14, 813, 1233; Bant 753, 809, 900, A965, A1008, 1038, 1175, 1237, 1238, 1351, A1625; GM 122, 675; Peng 636; Pk 135; Pop 183, G161, G241, G379, EB13; Sig T1388, S1543, S1703
Keene, Day—Ace D11, D41, D129, D170; Av 159, 660, 684, 705, 814; Berk G258, D2003, D2020; Cre 286; GM 206, 225, 254, 372, 405, 494, 603, 617, 622, 823, 874, 931; Gra 43, 51, 58, 75, 87; Har 167, 168, 180, 185, 229, 253; Lio 68, 204, 210; Orig 712; Phan 504, 509, 513; Pyr 138, G266, G395, G448; Zen ZB24
Kelland, Clarence Budington—ANC 30; ASE D100, I255, 707, 1025; Bant 203, 257, 726, 1061; BM 197; Dell 335; Hil 16; Penn P47; Pop 432; Pyr G355
Kelton, Elmer—Bal 128, 187, 247, 304K
Kendrick, Baynard—ASE 786, 1097; Bant A902, 937; Dell 50, 95, 113, 162, 230, 273, 376; DeT 32; MM 205; Peng 616, 635
Keogh, Theodora—Av T358; Sig 857, 958, 1049, 1100, 1209, 1284, S1560
Kerouac, Jack—Av T302, T340, G1035; Sig D1619, D1718
Kersh, Gerald—Av T111; Bal 28, 268; Dell 374; Har 45; Lio 98
Ketcham, Hank—Av 519, 600, 665; Cre 298; Pk 1080, 1125, 1153, 1179, 1217
Ketchum, Philip—Ace F254; Av T322; Bal 158; Dell 1; GM 772; Pop 472, 499, 532, 575, 604, 645, 673, 797, 813, G337, G355, G389, EB57, EB65, EB75; RA 4; RDM 23; Sig 1686, 1744
Keyes, Frances Parkinson—Cre d232, d293, d314, d333; Dell 443, 561, 692; Pk 349; Sig D1291
King, Rufus—ASE 937; Bant 120; Cent 14; Dell 22, 39; DNC 33, 38; MNC 69; Pop 3, 13, 22, 31, 43, 55, 67, 97, 124, 193, 246, 276, 318, 362; TNC 21
Kipling, Rudyard—ASE G198; Bant 58, A1509, S1609; Dell LB128; MM 25; Pk 45, 616; Pre d53
Kline, Otis Adelbert—Ace D516, D531, F211, F259, F294, F321, F400; B/C 22
Knight, Adam—Bel 217; Sig 883, 920, 1022, 1103, 1139, 1276, 1322, 1347, 1395, 1724
Knight, Damon—Ace D375, F108; Lio LL13; Zen ZB14
Kornbluth, C. M.—Bal 21, 61, 86, 107, 123, 144, 303K, 335K; Bant 1317, A1492; Penn P15
Kurtzman, Harvey—Bal 93, 106, 124, 242, 263, 264, 295K, 296K, 297K, 338K; MacFadden 50-159 (w/Elder)
Kuttner, Henry—Ace F297, F306, F327, F344, F356; Av T275; Bal 30, 122; Bant 1154; Perm M3046, M3058, M4082, M4096
Lacy, Ed—Av 342, 561, 566, T253, T288; Bel 220; Et E111, E123; Perm M3036, M3106; Pk 1152; Pyr G353; Zen ZB18
Lamb, Harold—Bant 1127, A1234, A1291, A1353, A1382, A1545, FB412, FB416; Peng 516
L'Amour, Louis—Ace D52, S82, D574; Bant 1390, 1486, 1681, A1713, 1853, 1905, 1977; GM 347, 478, 516, 686, 700, 728, 893, 905
Lancaster, Bruce—Perm P149, P176, P196, P219, P234, P266, M3016

(AUTHOR CROSS-INDEX, continued)

Lardner, Ring—ASE F172, J278, 782; Bant 145, 466; SuR M646

Lariar, Lawrence—ASE 1085; Av 289, 746; CNS nn; Fem nn; Han 38, 92; Hil 125; Pop 448, 740; Sig 1083, 1203, 1261

Latimer, Jonathan—Cent 34, 100, 136; Dell D196; JM 65, 69, 77, 84; MM 38, 55, 182; Perm P194; Pk 246, 1136; Pop 4, 16, 301

Lawrence, D. H.—Av 98, 238, 248, 296, 423, 449, 587, T2, T114, T163, T218, G1021, G1025, G1028, G1038, G1039; AvMSSM 46, 49; Bel L512; Berk G17, G43, G52, G59, BG150, G290; Card C363; Peng 576, 610; Pyr PR25; Sig S1039, S1086, D1428, D1509, D1736, S1747

Lawrence, Hilda—ASE P17, 1270; BM 117, 122; Pk 336, 439, 492, 540

Lee, William—Ace D15

Lehman, Paul Evan—Ace D14, D64, D502; Av 540, 642, 715, 741, 759, 805, 806, 816, 825, 831, 843, 845, 850; Berk 332, 356, 364, 370, 372; Et E128; FWN 22, 27; Gra 34, 39, 47, 56, 66, 100; Han 73, 77, 87, 99, 107, 119; HanW 1, 4; Har 81, 82, 105, 118, 128, 172, 270, 353, 358, 404; Pyr 194, 347; RC 6; Sig 666, 682, 731, 849, 1258, 1297, 1352; Star 8, 10, 16, 22, 28

Leiber, Fritz—Ace 491, F285; Gal 28; Lio 179, LL7; UG 5

Leighton, Lee—Bal 51, 148, 255, 282K

Leinster, Murray—Ace D53, D79, D94, D146, D277, D403, D525, D528, F275; Av T202, T345; Gal 20, 25; GM s751, s832, s937; Har 281; Pk 920, 1037; PSFN 10; Qua 20, 25; Sig S1346; Star 1, 3, 5; WiA 1-4

LeMay, Alan—ASE B42, N10, R18, 868; Bant 134, 253; Cre S244; Mon 102; Pop 141, 161, 209, 261, 535, 561, 731, G267, G345, G363; Sig 672, 1219; WNC 35

Leroux, Gaston—Bru nn; Dell 24

Lewis, C. S.—Av 195, 277, T127, T157, T211

Lewis, Sinclair—ASE K24, 911, 969; Av 1, 74; AvMSSM 6; Bant 22, 705, A893, F1572; Dell F63, LC119; Lio LL113; MM 11, 17; Pk 115, 162; Pop SP50

Lockridge, Frances & Richard—ASE 747, 789, 950, 1093, 1162, 1231, 1293; Av 131, 142, 242, 363, 369, 434, 471, 484, 502, 515, 535, 583, 608, 666, 766, 800; Bant 305; Dell 229, 322; Gra 82; MM 44, 77, 129, 133, 137, 145, 154, 192, 208; Pk 166, 346, 376, 411, 501

Lomax, Bliss—Ace D22, D38, D56; ASE 780, 1022, 1288; Av 156, 462, 849; Berk 313; Cent 58, 59, 62; Dell 271, 418, 517, 581, 666, 724, 801, 942, 967, 1005; DeFE 87; GWN 21; Hil 33; Perm M3009; Pk 768, 809; Pyr D277; WNC 66, 96

London, Jack—ASE F180, G182, H221, K3, N28, 672, 1011; Card GC64; Dell LC114; Lio 92; Peng 587; Perm P41; Pk 325, 593; Pop PC300; Pyr G180; Sig 1120

Lord, Walter—Bant 1539, F1715, 1945

Louys, Pierre—Av 113, 135, 166, 257, 358, 668, G1003, G1018; Berk G46, G283

Lovecraft, H. P.—ASE 730; Av 136, T284; BH 4, 12

Macardle, Dorothy—ASE B51, 1185; Bant 90, 915

MacDonald, John D.—Cre S295; DeFE 12, 62, 85, A113, A130, A152, B112, B117, B121, B127, B134, B141; GM 124, 164, 186, 200, 240, 298, 323, 420, 481, 482, 724, 737, 767, s777, 782, s790, 792, 884, 894, s907; Pk 943; Pop 675, 697, 737, 750, 830, G271

MacDonald, Ross—Bant 1295, 1360, 1613, 1839, A2024; Pk 680, 821, 907, 971, 1020

MacDonald, Philip—Bant 146; BM 195; BoM 13; Dell D194, D247; MM 181; Peng 79, 586; Pk 70, 328; SuR M642; Zen ZB29

MacDonald, William Colt—Ace D2, D52, D216, F389, F428; ASE 712, 956, 1208, 1304; Av 343, 491, 514, 535, 536, 579, 586, 592, 678, 689, 765, 769, T353, T369; Cent 16, 56, 61, 69, 76; Cre 134, 149; Et E127; Gra 25, 50; GWN 11, 14, 17, 19, 22; Hil 19, 25, 31, 34, 102; Perm P96; Pyr 95, 101, 115, 172, 231, G276, 286, 294, G363, G451; Sig 698, 723, 764, 792, 835, 880, 925, 1005, 1059, 1168, 1181, 1331, 1416, 1588; WAN 2; WNC 37, 54

MacInnes, Helen—ASE M32; Cre d300; Pk 186, 235; Pop 453

MacLean, Alistair—Perm M4067, M4089, M4116

Maine, Charles Eric—Ace D274; Bal 218, 290K; Bant A1470

Mann, E. B.—ASE 947; Dell 333; Lio 27; Pk 694, 987, 1022, 1194

Mannix, Daniel P.—Ace G402; Bal 275K, 302K, 354K, 355K; Bant 1006

Marlowe, Stephen—Ace D77, D89, D189; Av T330; Cre 296; GM 523, 575, 627, 658, 693, 769, 813, 880, 914, d926; Gra 94

Marquand, John P.—ASE D120, E146, G208, L26, 852, 1084, 1225; Bant A805, 881, A919, A987, F1087, F1200, F1453, F1454, F1675, A1690, A1691, A1781, 1810, S2013; BM 12, 124; DeT 13; JM 49, 52, 54; MM 139; Pk 59, 258

Marric, J. J.—Berk G122, G278; Pyr G323, G335

Marsh, Ngaio—ASE 727, 760, 882, 1269; Av T254; BM 23, 64, 68; JM 3; MM 79, 203; Pk 113, 137, 221, 297, 351, 437, 475, 527, 626, 762; Sig 995

Marshall, Edison—ASE C87, 689, 841; Card C194, C233; Dell 144, 188, 233, 341, 353, 364, 422, 431, 468, 487, 530, D102, D103, D119, D122, D139, D157, D173, F67, F72, F87; Har 200, 239; Pop 128, 208, 242, 272, 345

Martin, Pete—Bant 721; Card C248; Dell D266; Peng S230

Mason, F. van Wyck—ASE D119, M31, 1234; Bant 311, F1744; BM 27, 57, 63; Card C4, C23, C57, C165, C211, C242, C365, GC2, GC6, GC9, GC17; Cent 21, 32, 70; DNC 9; Han 98; Har 74; Pk 129, 799, 929, 977, 1024, 1076, 1115, 1143, 1176, 1201, 1219, 1223; RA 10

Masur, Harold Q.—Dell 874, 944, D232, D250, D298, D329; Lio LB152; Pk 558, 704, 860, 998

Matheson, Richard—Bal 301K; Bant 1294, A1571; Cre S308; GM 417, s577, 643; Lio 137, 180

Maugham, Robin—Av 233, 333, 428, 464, 695

Maugham, W. Somerset—ASE E128, I260, L30, N14, Q31, 971; AvMSSM 8, 18, 35, 38, 43; Bant 136, 423, 810, 852, 909, 949, A1339, A1399, 1489, A1930, A1931, AC25; Bard 4; Bel L511; Berk BG213, G268; Card C19, C63, C161, C273; Cre d276; Dell D106, D176; DeT 2, 16; Har 266; Ment M60, MD203; Peng 597; Perm P74, M4056; Pk 262, 418, 581, 700, 1158; Pre s30

Maupassant, Guy de—ASE 669; Av 87, 175, 198, 459; Dell LC135; Lio LL2; Pad nn; Pk 12, PL29; Pyr 41, R202

Mayo, Jim—Ace D38, D48

McBain, Ed—Dell D306; Perm M3037, M3055, M3061, M3062, M3108, M3113, M3119, M4150

McCoy, Horace—Berk 108, 328, G134; DeFE A188; Sig 670, 690, 754, 884, S1017

McCullers, Carson—Bant 821, 822, A1091, A1156, A1235, F1761-F1764; Peng 596

McCulley, Johnston—Av 748, 779, 795, 856; Cent 131; Dell 553, D204; FWN 8; Har 260; Pyr 187; Sig 669, 704, 1632

(AUTHOR CROSS-INDEX, continued)

McGivern, William P.—Card C316; Dell 599; Pk 693, 786, 870, 961, 981, 1030, 1062, 1105, 1156, 1193

Melville, Herman—ASE A24, G209, L15; Av T117; Bant F1803, FC16; Dell LX105; Pk 612, PL28; Sig D1229

Merril, Judith—Bant 751; DeFE B103, B110, B119, B129; Lio 205, LL25; Penn P56; Pyr G397

Merritt, A.—Av 26, 43, 117, 214, 235, 315, 324, 370, 392, 413, T115, T135, T152, T161, T172, T208; AvMMM 1, 5, 11, 18, 24, 29, 34, 41

Merwin, Sam, Jr.—Ace D121; Bea 284; BCD 19; Cent 63; Gal 12, 22; GM 227; GD 30; Han 12, 44; Har 62, 70, 87, 112; PMN 22

Meyers, Harold—Av 133, 230, 359, 627, 633, 637, 643, 649, 662, 681, 698, 860, T92, T95, T227, T282

Michener, James A.—ASE 1248; Bant A884, A999, A1000, 1269, A1318, F1350, A1641, A1650, F1674, F1705, F1844; Card C226; Pk 516

Millard, Joseph—GM 129, 404, s590; Reg 324

Miller, Henry—Sig 1246, 1317, D1653

Miller, Wade (Bill Miller & Bob Wade)—Ace D518; GM 108, 139, 152, 173, 257, 279, 331, 469, 513, 521, 682, 758, s791, 810, s845, s936, 945; Gra 11, 54; Han 65; Har 99; Lio LL96; Peng 648; Sig 677, 695, 722, 771, 843, 908, 928, 1013, 1089, 1180, 1235, 1257, 1270, 1369, 1482, 1662

Milne, A. A.—Dell D321; Pk 81

Mitchell, Margaret—Perm P294, M7500

Morelli, Spike—Ar 3, 8; Lei 2, 7

Mulford, Clarence E.—ASE C72, F163, H227, I257, 759, 834, 918, 1072, 1141; Dell nn, 246; Gra 15, 23, 28, 53, 91; GWN 7; Har 107, 131; Pk 337; Pop 104, 146, 198; Pyr 25; TN 11, 20, 29; WNC 26, 32, 36

Mundy, Talbot—Bea B105; RG 12, 19, 20, 22; UG 11

Murphy, Audie—Perm P119, P214, M4029

Murray, Max—Bant 358; Dell 485, 560, 639; MM 138; Pyr G362

Nash, Ogden—ASE A3, 981, 1151; Card C158; Pk 251

Nin, Anais—Av 755

Nordhoff, Charles—ASE H238, T10, 725, 861; Card C34; Mon 141; Perm M4001; Pk 188, 216, 358, 457

Norris, Kathleen—BH 20; Pk 44, 440, 453, 480, 488, 525, 549, 599, 605, 625, 688, 710; Pony 55

North, Andrew—Ace D249, D345

Norton, Andre—Ace D69, D96, D121, D164, D199, D299, D381, D437, D461, D498, D509, D527, D534, D542, D546, F109, F147, F167, F183, F192, F197, F207, F226, F231, F236, F243, F263, F279, F287, F291, F308, F310, F315, F323, F325, F329, F332, F357, F365, F366, F386, F391, F408; Com 28

Nye, Nelson C.—Ace D6, D78, D98, D134, D180, D592, F150, F184, F224, F298, F348, F395, F418; ASE C66, O10, 1251; Av 267, 478, 758; AvWNM 1; Berk 321, 330, 343, 350, 363, G79, G99, G118, G138, G154, G234, D2006, D2018; Cre 123, 235; Dell 804; FWN 38, 41; Har 29; Hil 109; Pk 754, 1060, 1135, 1142; Pony 58; Pop 441, 461, 481, EB79; Sig 1473, 1516, 1631

O'Farrell, William—Bant 1128; Berk 373; BM 149, 179; Dell 306, 555; DeFE A120; Penn P35, P55

O'Flaherty, Liam—Bant 150, A1357; Sig S1553; SuR M650

O'Hara, John—ASE 741, 799, 817, 979, 1147; Av 31, 94, 144, 231, 258, 293, 368, 422, 661, 679, T107, T183, G2002; AvMSSM 1, 2, 29, 39, 45, 50; Bant F935, 1046, 1422, A1484, F1554, F1583, 1594, 1640, 1679; DeT 24; Peng 563, 580; Pk 27; Sig 766, 1087, S1437

O'Neill, Eugene—ASE Q35; Sig S1502

O'Rourke, Frank—Bal 10, 35, 49, 69, 82, 98, 111, 149, 211-214; Bant 720, 799, 916, 1005, 1149, 1344, 1549; Dell 966; DeFE 41, 59, 89, 104, 108, A131, A157; Har 402, 424; Penn P17; Perm M3069; Sig 1536, 1715, 1748

Orwell, George—Av T121, T144; Berk G262; Perm P267; Pop 459, G193, G214; Sig 798, 1289, S1615, D1640, CD3

Overholser, Wayne D.—ASE 1254; Dell 372, 499, 556, 624, 699, 729, 796, 815, 846, 875, 903, 924, 948, 972, 993, 1008; Pop EB81; RCL 17

Padgett, Lewis—Ace D69; Bant 107, 306, 1251; Gal 17, 26

Palmer, Stuart—BM 128, 189; Dell 18, 601, 715; DNC 18; JM 26; Perm M3079

Park, Jordan—Lio 135, 176, LL97, LB153; Pyr G368

Patrick, Quentin—Bann 2; GM 397; Pop 8, 23, 36, 47, 206, 263, 386

Patten, Lewis B.—Ace D4, F376, F423; Av T331, T339; Cre 174, 274; GM 526, 573, 602, 706, 723, 778, 815, 866, 920; Gra 151; Perm M3088

Pease, Howard—Bant 1110; Com 10, 33; Pk J71, J73, J76

Pentecost, Hugh—Cent 30; DeT 31; Pop 44, 53, 82, 109, 377; QR 128, 145

Perelman, S. J.—ASE N2, 872, 1019; Pop 240

Poe, Edgar Allan—ASE J297, 767; Card C45; Dell LB120; Pk 39, PL46; QR 140

Pohl, Frederick—Bal 16, 21, 55, 61, 89, 96, 107, 123, 130, 137, 144, 173, 192, 199, 206, 272K, 308K, 325K, 335K, 353K; Perm P145, P236

Prather, Richard S.—Berk 316, 362, G98, G241; Cre 132, 142, 255, 277; GM 127, 147, 165, 203, 233, 265, 341, 413, 425, 489, 496, 497, 504, 505, 508, 551, 592, 598, 665, 677, 712, 745, 770, s817, 818-821, 830, 838, 848-851, 860, s887, 896, d926; Lio 85

Pratt, Fletcher—Ace F257; Bal 25; Card C7; Diamond Libr. nn; FFS nn, nn; Gal 30; Peng S224

Priestley, J. B.—ASE C75, 665; Peng 535, 548

Queen, Ellery—Ace D493; ASE 680; Av 425, 450, 465, 488, 509, 523, 726, T141, T184, T242, T292, T337; BLA 1; BM 1, 3, 8, 11, 14, 17, 28, 59; Card C343, C357; Dell 4; DeT 23; JM 1, 5, 12; MM 27, 32, 36, 39, 42, 47, 57, 68, 164; Perm M3015, M3076; Pk 17, 71, 77, 99, 109, 125, 134, 146, 179, 202, 227, 245, 259, 270, 283, 313, 326, 355, 459, 471, 517, 669, 740, 822, 874, 926, 960, 1005, 1049, 1082, 1118, 1167; QR 120; RL nn, nn, nn, nn

Queen, Ellery, Jr.—Com 13

Quentin, Patrick—ASE T17, 1291; Dell 710, 759, 851, 890, D192, D261, D322; Han 53; Pk 83, 164, 420, 460, 614, 676

Rabe, Peter—Ace D297; GM 506, 520, 528, 547, 594, 612, 657, 670, 678, 710, 763, s773, s825, 864, 915, 939

Raine, William MacLeod—ASE F160, G184, L9, S18, 674, 989, 1129, 1196; Av 500; Dell 179, 238, 282, 359, 383, 424, 613, 629, 711, 793, 821, 889, 954; Hil 4, 6, 11, 24, 29, 36, 42, 101; Lio LL32; Penn P67; Perm P18; Pk 78, 473, 487, 611, 656, 691, 721, 743, 787, 815, 842; Pop 86, 145, 172, 213, 243, 256, 280, 322, 359, 414, 436, 471, 531, 553, 805, G197, G223, G246, G264, G278, G295, G305, G343, G361, G374, G390, G394, EB2, EB21, EB27, EB35, EB43, EB51, EB59, EB67, EB73, EB81, EB101; Sig 673, 712, 758, 806, 973, 1069, 1140, 1228, 1303, 1396, 1483; TN 12; WNC 22, 28, 34, 39, 47

Rand, Ayn—Sig T934, T1468, Q1702

Rawson, Clayton—Dell 69, 121, 176, 258; MM 155

Reilly, Helen—ASE 1241; Bant 1858; BM 201; Cent 29; Dell 17, 63, 114, 148, 200, 228, 287, 397, 498, 576, 621, 709, 732, 917; DNC 23; Peng 504; Pop 7, 20, 33, 48, 56, 211, 259

Remarque, Erich Maria—ASE 1177; Cre S215, d249, S337; Lio 49, LL81; Pop G133, G153, SP14, SP21; Sig S796, S1023, D1630

Reynolds, Quentin—Av T226; Bant A1785; Pop 533, G106, G166, SP8; Pyr G351

Rhodes, Eugene Manlove—ASE G190, H212, J271, K8, M6; Dell 688, D152

Rice, Craig—ASE 914, 1074, 1106, 1313; Bann 1; B/C 12, 13; Dell 461, D187, D306; Gra G203; MNM 21; Pk 237, 289, 361, 391, 434, 461, 476, 528, 651, 1189, 1215; Pop 45, 89, 253; Pyr G350; RL nn

Richter, Conrad—ASE C62, D98, 859; Bant 759, 962, 1208, 1264, 1737, A1792, A1850-A1852; Pk 413

Rinehart, Mary Roberts—Av 83; Bant 314; BM 95; Dell 40, 57, 124, 131, 166, 203, 241, 297, 361, 403, 404, 494, 506, 541, 585, 652, 782, 814, D126, D154, D165, D179, D197, D220, D242, D251, D276, D316, D330; DeT 4, 22; Pk 98, 121, 140; Pop 5, 21; QR 121; RL nn

Roberts, Kenneth—ASE H228, Q29, S38, 1014; AvMSSM 25; Perm P1655

Robertson, Frank C.—Bal 208, 232; BCW 29; FWN 39; GWN 9, 12, 15, 20, 46; RCL 1, 4, 14, 24; TN 16, 25; WAN 1; WNC 24, 83

Rohmer, Sax—Ace F283; Av 189; GM 105, 199, 283, 321, 408, 555, s684, s757, 868, s929; Gra 32, 78; Pop 217; TNC 4, 9

Roscoe, Mike—Ace D273; Sig 966, 1060, 1216, 1358

Royer, Louis-Charles—Dell 567; Pyr 35, 84, 102, 110, 114, 134, 166, G217, G253, G317, G320

Runyon, Damon—ASE 018; Av 102; AvMSSM 27; Gra 30, 69; Perm P113; Pk 53, 158, 292, 406, 1098

Russell, Eric Frank—Ace D44, D215, D315, D468, F398; Bant 1362; Berk G148; Gal 1; Perm M4120; Reg 317

Sabatini, Rafael—ANC 2, 5, 12; ASE I266, R32, 812, 1006; Av 84; AvMSSM 36; Bant 5, A1022; BH 30; Chec 7; Har 217; Pk 82; Pop 91, 241

Saki (H. H. Munro)—ASE M3; Bant 143; Peng 634; SuR M656

Sale, Richard—Ace D23; ASE S7, 1205; Dell 252; Han 13, 19; Har 59, 79; JM 20, 24; Pop 163, 205, 247, 275

Sandburg, Carl—ASE A27, N6, 1122; Dell F77, LX113-LX115

Saroyan, William—ASE A15, J272, S2; Av 19; AvMSSM 4, 12; Lio LL56; Peng 540; Pk 282; Pop 563, G334; Sig 945

Sayers, Dorothy L.—ASE 890; Av 23, 40, 176, 328, 335; AvMMM 14; BM 13, 20, 38; Pk 21, 74, 85, 130, 163, 185, 324

Schaefer, Jack—Bal 13, 22, 45, 136; Bant 833, 1297

Seltzer, Charles Alden—ANC 13; ASE T16, 833, 917, 949, 987, 1030, 1071, 1101; DNC 13; FWN 6; Pop 151, 204; Sig 717; TN 14, 22

Shakespeare, William—Card C1, C14, C15, C55; Dell LB112-LB115, LB118, LB119, LB124, LB125, LB129, LB130, LB133, LB134; Jac 5; Pk 3, 114, 532, 533, PL30, PL31, PL57, PL60, PL61, PL64, PL66, PL67, PL70; WSP W115, W121

Sheckley, Robert—Bal 73, 126; Bant A1672, A1991, A2003; Reg 112

Shelley, Mary Wollstonecraft—ASE 909; Lio 146; Pyr R290

Short, Luke—ANC 23; ASE G195, R11, 670, 874, 1184; Bal 4, 43; Bant 82, 112, 139, 140, 204, 209, 258, 702, 703, 747, 748, 791, 792, 853, 854, 911, 1063, 1075, 1104, 1105, 1293, 1346, 1356, 1373, A1401, F1417, 1446, 1466, 1485, 1531-1533, 1564, 1588, 1652, 1668, 1680, 1710, 1755, 1821, 1865, 1866, 1916, A1959, A1989, A2006, A2036; Dell 562, 606, 647, 702, 769, 826, 869, 895, 962, 963, D289; DeFE 7, 31, 68, 70, A122, A134, A151, A154, B130; DeT 1; GM 159, 720; Pop 114, 346, 792; WNC 40, 45

Silverberg, Robert—Ace D223, D237, D286, D311, D407, F123, F145, F195

Simak, Clifford D.—Ace D61, D283, D339, D517, F239; Berk G71; Dell 680; Gal 7; Perm 264

Simenon, Georges—Ace F166, F198; ASE 021; Av 757; AvMMM 8; Bant 1875, A2063; Berk 322, 340, 351, 379, G133, G145; BM 24, 41, 69; Dell 964, D279; Hil 100, 105; JM 8, 18; MM 31, 89; Peng 564, 579; Pk 141; Pop 724; Sig 855, 948, 964, 993, 1034, 1073, 1109, 1124, 1144, 1188, 1248, 1327, 1338, 1376, 1421, 1465

Siodmak, Curt—ASE 09; Bal 58; Bant 819; Dell 756; MM 87

Smith, Thorne—ASE G181, H230, J284, K15, L17, Q13, 528, 671, 922, 953; Av 69; Pk 4, 209, 314, 401, 409, 428, 447, 479, 490, 518, 546; RL nn

Sohl, Jerry—Ace D162, D381; Av T186; Bant 1278, A1952, A1971; Lio 118; Penn P75

Spain, John—Bant 968; BCD 3; DNC 35, 44; Pop 178, 239

Spillane, Mickey—Sig 699, 791, 852, 888, 915, 932, 1000, S1700, S1705, S1710, S1728

Stagge, Jonathan—ASE 1194; BM 164; MM 160; Pop 40, 52, 62, 90, 267, 350

Steinbeck, John—ASE A9, C90, T5, 690, 703, 750, 794, 1232; Av 77, 132; AvMSSM 9; Bant 7, 75, 131, 402, 752, A868, 899, 953, 1065, 1066, 1184, 1266, F1267, F1301, A1324, A1329, 1406, A1412, A1478, 1544, A1555, A1753, F1895, AC12, AC18; Dell 358, 407; MM 20; Peng 509, 599, S219; Pk 243; Pop 216; Sig 816, 1380, S1737

Stevenson, Robert Louis—ASE N13, 885; Bant 142; Card C48; Dell LC140; Jac 1; Pk 25, 123, PL14, PL34, PL49, J57; QR 130, 142; Sig CD6

Stilwell, Hart—Bant 765; Pop 331

Stoker, Bram—ASE L25, 851; Perm M4088; Pk 452

Stone, Irving—ASE L29, 693; Bant FB418; Card C10, GC32; Perm P228; Pk 344

Stout, Rex—ASE P6, 906, 1222; Av 20, 62, 82, 95, 103, 256, 714, 738, T216, T296, T374; AvMMM 9; Bant 308, 722, 824, 925, 1032, 1173, 1252, 1326, 1386, 1387, 1388, 1394, 1395, A1631-A1633, A1795-A1797, A1961, A2016; BM 31, 44; Cent 28; Dell 9, 28, 45, 70, 115, 146, 177, 235, 267, 299, 495, 540, 626, 674, D223, D252; DeT 21; JM 2, 6, 9, 15, 27, 33; Lio LL23; MM 37, 48, 72; Pk 112, 208

Sturgeon, Theodore—Av T304; Bal 46, 119, 179; Berk G280; DeFE A128, B120; Pyr G184, G247

Swados, Felice—Av 298, 430; Berk G240; DivRN 1

Tarkington, Booth—ASE C70, 844; Av 55; Bant 17, A1586, AC48

Taylor, Phoebe Atwood—Av 439; Dell 98, 171, 251; Peng 618; PenM 2; Pk 171, 204; Pop 14, 25, 126

Taylor, Valerie—Bea B116; Cre 187, S290; UG 8

Tenn, William—Bal 99, 159; Bant A1786; Perm P291

Tey, Josephine—Berk G265; Dell D255; MM 200; Pk 671, 784

Thayer, Tiffany—Av 14, 234, 291, 327, 418; Pk 673; Pop 227; Sig 772

Thomas, Dylan—Sig S1281

(AUTHOR CROSS-INDEX, continued)

Thompson, Jim—Dell 738; DeFE 22; Hil 38; Lio 99, 108, 120, 127, 149, 155, 184, 192, 201, 212, 218, LB124, LB138, LL142; Pop 716; Pyr G336; Reg 322; Sig 1461, 1584

Thoreau, Henry David—ASE 880; Ment M87, MD176; Peng 508; Pre d63; Sig 747

Thurber, James—ASE A11, I253, L2, M2, M23, N7, S5, 705, 755, 856, 970, 1016; Bant 21, 92; Dell 820

Tolstoy, Leo—ASE 1080; Av T133; Bant S1497; Dell F53; Pk 515

Torres, Tereska—Cre S243; GM 132, 379, s673; Sig S1579

Towne, Stuart—PenM 1; YM nn

Traven, R.—Pk 455; Reg 107

Treat, Lawrence—Ace D51, D189; ASE 1098; AtM nn; Av 274; Bant 1026; BDM 6; BM 157, 178, 190; BoM 10; Dell 218, 301; Her nn; MM 178; MNC 64, 68

Treece, Henry—Av T325, T363; Cre S265

Tucker, Wilson—Ace D241, D479; Av T168; Bant 1343, 1400; Dell 343, 791; Gal 11; Lio 21, LL84; MM 150; Sig 1127

Tuttle, W. C.—ASE D94, E123, I245, 1021; Av 53; Cent 15; GWN 6; Hil 2, 5, 26, 28, 37, 40; Pop 96, 149, 165, 203, 249, 297, 330, 354; Pyr 370; QR 148; WNC 27, 33, 41, 46, 50, 55, 108

Twain, Mark—ASE C76, D110, E139, F174, N1, S9; Bant 1, F1445, SC3, FC39, AC50; Bob nn; Card C107, C139; Dell LC111; Jac 9; Penn nn; Pk 497, PL39, PL42, J37, J42; RG 28; Sig CD2, CD5

Upfield, Arthur W.—Peng 658

Uris, Leon—Bant F1279, S1995, F1996; Sig S1365

Vance, Jack—Ace D295, F185, F265, F390; Bal 167; Hil 41; Toby nn

Van Dine, S. S.—Bant 60, 96, 300, 362, 756; Gra 89; Pk 248, 256, 305, 333

Van Loon, Hendrik Willem—Bant FB413; BLA 12, 20; Card GC5; Dell D142; Perm P2015, M5005; Pk 15, PL12, PL501; Pre d79

Van Vogt, A. E.—Ace D31, D53, D94, D187, D242, D391, D431, D482, F154, F253, F295; Av 548, T252; Bea 298; Berk 344, G215; Dell 696; Har 177; Sig 914, 1007, S1558

Verne, Jules—Ace D155, D245, D397, D434, D564, F191; Av T148; Cre S216; Lio LL90; Perm M4161; Pyr R300

Vestal, Stanley—ASE 1199; Bant F1662, F1687; Penn P34

Vidal, Gore—ASE 1182; Bal 94, 160; Sig 773, 1003, 1218, S1535

Viereck, George Sylvester—Ace D43; Bea B228; Cre S148; GM 260, 552

Voltaire—ASE C64; Bant AC51; Dell LC134; Lio 107, LB107; RG 25

Vonnegut, Kurt, Jr.—Bant A1262; DeFE B138

Wallace, Edgar—Av 112, 125, 173; AvMMM 3, 45; Bant 3093; BM 71; Dell 49; Har 334, 349, 352, 361, 378, 387, 395, 418, 420, 428, 444, 447, 456, 466, 475, 484, 493

Walling, R. A. J.—ASE Q15; Av 8, 16; Pk 24; Pony 49; Pop 106, 139

Warren, Robert Penn—ASE 1201; Bant A939, F1338, F1556, FC34; Berk BG35; Dell F82, LX102, LC109, LX110; DeFE F16, FE69; Sig 725, 804, D975, D1330

Webb, Jack—Cre S341; Reg 311; Sig 1076, 1149, 1233, 1311, 1422, 1556

Welles, Orson—Dell 305; Pyr G357

Wellman, Manly Wade—Ace D443; Cent 68; DeFE 52; Gal 34; PSFN 11; Sig 703, 1448

Wellman, Paul I.—ASE 1262; Bant F1915; Card C96, C141, C278, GC20, Perm P115, P129, P142, P240, 263; Pk 794

Wells, H. G.—Ace D309, D388, D537, F240; ASE T2, 698, 745, 958, 1091; Berk 380; Dell 201, 269; Pk 119, 947, 1140

Wentworth, Patricia—ASE 1166; BM 75; Dell 2; DNC 4; Pop 29, 39, 66, 79, 105, 131, 197, 232, 283, 333, 382

Wertham, Fredric—Et E106

White, Ethel Lina—BM 77; Peng 565, 598; Pop 15, 32, 54, 75, 120

White, Lionel—Ace F155; Av T361; GM 304, 470, 606, 663, 687, 775, 786; Rain 121; Sig 1204, 1241, 1310, 1378, 1442, 1707

Whitman, Walt—Card GC 25; Dell LB121; Ment MS117; Peng 523

Whittington, Harry—Ace D5, D7, D63, S95, D115, S143, D185, D201, D241, D347, F472, D510, F103, F148, F196; Av T187, T196, T241, T299, T347; Berk G250, D2004, D2019; Cre 151; Croy 35, 62; GM 190, 366, 401, 595, 611, 740, 831, 862, 889; Gra 36, 41, 46; Han 120, 131, 138; Har 120, 140, 366; Orig 702; Phan 503, 505; Stanley SL72; Star 758; Uni 58, 70; UG 1; Ven 158; Zen ZB30

Wilder, Thornton—Av 59; Bant F1789; Pk 9, 55, PL36

Wilhelm, Gale—Berk 327, 367, G111, G173; Lio 52, 70, 121, LB115; Pyr G440

Williams, Robert Moore—Ace S90, D99, D215, D322, D427, D530, F141, F149, F177, F223, F261, F335

Williams, Tennessee—Sig 917, 955, 1236, S1262, 1334, D1529, S1590, S1664, S1745

Williamson, Jack—Ace D118, D169, D555, F241; AvFN 2; Gal 2, 21; Pop 447

Winsor, Kathleen—ASE T39; Sig 809AB, 868AB, D1169, D1227, T1567, D1600, D1725

Wodehouse, P. G.—Ace D25; Dell 357, 393, 469; Hil 39; Pk 28, 495, 628; RL nn, nn

Wolfe, Thomas—ASE O31, 1013; Av 57; AvMSSM 17; Lio LL19; Peng 644; Pyr R321; Sig 697, 950

Wollheim, Donald A.—Ace D44, D73, S133, S183, D205, D277, D353, D354, D490, D508, F178, F311; Pk 214; Pyr 62, 196

Woodford, Jack—Av 138, 146, 280, 297, 402, 403; AvBN 1, 2, 5, 6; AvBD 1, 4, 6; AvMN 20; AvS nn, nn, nn; Bea B123-B125, B127, B138, B140, B213, B292; BNM 9, 10; NL 1-4, 6, 7, 36, 44; Uni 60, 63, 67, 71, 72

Woollcott, Alexander—ASE G186; Bant 39; Pk 131

Woolrich, Cornell—Av 96, 106, T354; AvMMM 27; BM 198, 206; Dell 208, D186; GM 135, 719; Han 114; JM 23, 51, 61; MM 64; Pk 271, 570; Pyr 80, G374; TNC 29

Wouk, Herman—ASE 1265; DD nn; Perm M4050; Sig T1454

Wren, Percival C.—Har 223; Perm P191, P232, M4011; Pk 35

Wylie, Philip—ASE L19, M11, Q21, S8, 774, 801; Av 216, 360, 375, 390, 571, 711, 727, T155; BLA 27; Berk BG100; Card C40, C280, GC62; Cent 18, 33; Cre S240; Dell 85, 140, 627; Pk 722; Pop G156; Sig 701, 830; SuR M640

Yates, Peter—FSM 1, 4, 16, 21, 28, 35, 37; VulM 6

Young, Chic—Dell nn

Zola, Emile—Ace S76, D182; Av 150, 167, 236, 271, T129, G1013; Bant 1020, A1244, A1290; Card C134; Dell 608; Pk 104, PL63; Pyr 105; QR 103

The Paperback Advertiser ™

<u>The</u> newspaper of the paperback community. Published every three weeks, it's the favorite place to buy and sell paperbacks. Also in each issue are featured articles and columns to keep you abreast of what's happening in the paperback world.

$6 for eight issues (six months sub)

$12 for seventeen issues (one year)

2.5 MIL PAPERBACK PLASTIC BAGS!!

Just the right size for paperbacks and digests.   2" flap allows for maximum protection.   Add $2 for postage with your order.

	4 7/8" x 8" REGULAR	5 1/4" x 8" LARGE	6" x 8" DIGEST
100	$3.00	3.00	4.00
500	12.00	13.00	14.00
1000	21.00	22.00	25.00

THE PAPERBACK BOX ™

30" x 8 x 4½

With its' own separare lid, The Paperback Box is the perfect size for storing or displaying paperbacks.   Now, for the first time there is a box for displaying books at conventions or stores, or safely storing your collection (without damaging a book!).

$2 each, or $1.50 each for 100 or more boxes.

Minimum order is ten boxes.   Add 20¢ for each box for shipping.

When you write, ask for information about the fantastic PAPERBACK CONVENTION to be held in August.

Send all orders and inquiries to: THE PAPERBACK ADVERTISER, PO Box 196, Lake Hiawatha, New Jersey) 07034

HANCERS BOOKHOUSE

Hancer's Bookhouse is not a mass merchandising book 'supermarket', and I don't 'just' sell books. I sell knowledge. I sell thrills and adventure. I sell voyages to exotic isles where the palm trees sway and cannibals lurk in the undergrowth. I sell free-fall flights in fantasy and hair-raising rides in the American West. I love books, for they are the key to all the knowledge and entertainment of mankind's lush imagination. I intend that this love is reflected in Hancer's Bookhouse.

"Without doubt, your paperback lists are the premium catalogues." - Larry Abbott

"Your last catalogue was the best paperback list I've ever seen." - Paul Rollinson

"The condition of everything I've bought from you was as nice or better as you said." - Hal Johnson

"I certainly appreciate your prompt service and your professionalism." - Talbot Smith

FOR SALE

Ace D-274 World Without Men, NM $25.00
Avon 277 Perelandra, NM, $40.00
Avon 327 One Man Show, NM $15.00
Avon 354 Werewolf of Paris, NM $35.00
Avon 389 Saturday Evening Post Book of Fantasy Stories, NM $15.00
Avon 396 His 1st Million Women, NM $15.00
Belmont L504 The Brigitte Bardot Story, NM $12.50

Dell 536 Tarzan and the Lost Empire, NM $15.00
Diversey 1, Reform School Girl, F $350.00
Pocket Book 452 Dracula, NM $20.00
Popular Library 273 The Big Eye, NM $10.00
Popular Library 326 Behind the Flying Saucers, NM $10.00
Toby nn, Space Pirate, VF $20.00

Add $2.00 per order for insured shipping.

Much more is available in my regular paperback catalogues:

References for sale: Schreuder's PAPERBACKS, USA, 1939 - 1959, $10.95 and Wells' SCIENCE FICTION AND HEROIC FANTASY INDEX, $9.95.

Send $2.00 for your copy of my latest list. Other catalogues issued periodically throughout the year are: Edgar Rice Burroughs material, Popular Fiction and Motion Picture/Television/Comic Character/Paper Miscellany. Each list is $1.00.

WANTED TO BUY

1. Vintage Paperbacks

Specific wants:

Allen & Livingston - Without Reservations
Ann Bannon - All Titles
Earl Derr Biggers - All Avon Charlie Chan Titles
Robert Bloch - All Ace and Lion Titles
Max Boddenheim - Naked on Roller Skates
Leigh Brackett - Rio Bravo
Doug Brown - Anne Bonney, Pirate Queen
Fred Brown - All Mystery Titles
E. R. Burroughs - All Armed Services and Bantam Titles
Paul Cain - All Titles
Al Capp - Lil Abner, Life of the Shmoo
Raymond Chandler - Any Avon, Armed Services Titles
J. H. Chase - 12 Chinks and a Woman
G. K. Chesterton - Man Who was Thursday
Paula Christian - All Titles
Stanton Coblentz - Into Plutonian Depths
Simon Eisner - The Naked Storm
Harlan Ellison - Rumble, Any Ace or Regency Titles
Cy Endfield - Zulu
F. R. Ewing - I, Libertine
Philip Farmer - All Beacon, Brandon, Essex House, Ballantine, Ace Titles
Ian Fleming - All Perma or Popular Library Titles
Walter Gibson, - Magic Explained
Chester Gould - Dick Tracy and The Woo-Woo Sisters
Maxwell Grant - The Shadow and the Voice of Murder
Hammett - All Dell, Jonathan, Bestseller or Mercury Titles
Peter Held - Take my Face
Richard Holden - Snow Fury
L. Ron Hubbard - Fear
William Irish - Marijuana, Six Nights of Mystery, Bluebeards Bluebeards 7th Wife, You'll Never See Me Again
Jack Kerouac - Maggie Cassidy, Tristessa

Henry Kuttner - All Mystery Titles
Otis Adelbert Kline - The Man Who Limped
Louis L'amour - All Early Ace, Bantam, Gold Medal Titles
William Lee - Junkie
H. P. Lovecraft - All Bart House and Avon Titles
George Lowther - Adventures of Superman
John D. MacDonald - Border Town Girl, Weep for Me, I Could Go On Singing
Richard Matheson - Fury on Sunday, I am Legend, Someone is Bleeding
Jim Mayo - All Titles
Paul Merchant - Sex Gang
Joe Millard - Mansion of Evil
Jordan Park - All Lion or Pyramid Titles
Helen Reilly - The Doll's Trunk Murder
Henry Slesar - 20 Million Miles to Earth
Hart Stilwell - Campus Town
Fran Striker - A Lone Ranger on Thunder Mountain
W. J. Stuart - Forbidden Planet
Felice Swados - Reform School Girl
Jim Thompson - Most Lion, Signet Titles
Stuart Towne - Death from Nowhere
Jack Vance - The Dying Earth and Most Other Titles
Kurt Vonnegut - Mother Night, Cannery in a Cat House
Barton Werper - All Tarzan Titles
Lionel White - Many Titles
Harry Whittington - Many Mystery Titles
Roy Williams - Secret World of Roy Williams
Jack Williamson - The Green Girl
George Worts - Overboard

I am also interested in books involving lesbians, drug books, dust jacketed books and John Wayne movie tie-ins. My condition requirements are generally that books are in fine or better condition.

HANCER'S BOOKHOUSE

I am interested in buying all digest - sized novels, whether mystery, western, science fiction, romance, humor. I am also interested in all titles published by Archer, Bantam of Los Angeles, Black Knight, Bleak House, Bonded, Bowker, Century, Checker, Columbia, Dell - 10c, Dell un-numbered, Green Dragon, Handi-Books, Hangman's House, Harlequin, Hillman, Hip Books, Padell, Pony, Red Arrow, Red Circle, Saint Mystery Library, Shooting Script, Trophy, Value, Whitman and Zenith.

I also have general wants for these publishers:

Ace - Many early volumes, all Ellison, L'amour, Mayo, Tolkien, Vance and cartoon titles

Armed Services Editions - Most literature, mystery, science fiction, horror titles

Avon - Many early volumes, all Chandler, Woolrich, Cain, Irish, Biggers, Hatlo titles and all cartoon, puzzle, cooking books

Bantam - Any in dust jacket, all L'amour, Padgett, Kuttner, Fred Brown titles

Beacon - Many, especially Science Fiction titles

Dell - Many, all Hammett, cartoon and crossword titles

Gold Medal - All L'amour, MacDonald, Woolrich, Millard, Rohmer, Keene, Goodis, Fisher, White, Cushman, Bannon, Aldrich, Christian, Taylor, Vonnegut titles

Lion - Most, especially Jackson, Tucker, Shelley, Willhelm Keene, Thompson, Kersh, London, Eisner, Goodis, Park, Leiber, Matheson, Bloch, Fessier, titles

Midwood - All Loren Beauchamp titles and all double books with illustrations

Monarch - All movie tie-ins

Murder Mystery Monthly - All titles

Newsstand - All Warwick, Jenkins, Fischer, Phillips titles

Novel Library - Most, especially 45 and 46

Penguin - Many mystery and literature titles, especially 534, 553, and 562

Phantom - All titles

Phoenix - All titles

Pocket Books - 1st printings of 1 - 10, Werewolf of Paris, and any in dust jacket

Pocket Books (British) - Most, especially Quo Vadis

Popular Library - Most, especially cartoon, crossword titles

Pyramid - Many, all Held, Woolrich, Royer, Wollheim, Wall, Ellison titles

Readers Choice - Most, especially Irish and Kane titles

Regency - Most, especially Ellison titles

Signet - Many, especially literature, science fiction and mystery

2. Edgar Rice Burroughs/Tarzan items of any kind, esp. books in dust wrappers, scrapbooks, magazines, pulps, comics, toys, fanzines, paper items of any kind, also any books with imitation Tarzan characters.

TARZAN
MIGHTY FIGHTER OF THE JUNGLE

3. Any books by Louis L'amour, Jim Mayo, Charles Thurley Stoneham, Johnston McCulley.

4. Any pulp magazine with a story by Jim Mayo, Louis L'amour, or Tex Burns, whether mystery, western, sports, adventure.

5. All issues of Hopalong Cassidy magazine and all Hopalong Cassidy books by Tex Burns.

6. Lone Ranger novels, especially Lone Ranger Rides and Lone Ranger on Red Butte Trail.

7. Original art or books illustrated by J. Allen St. John or Gustaf Tenggren.

8. King Kong by Edgar Wallace and many other photoplay editions like Frankenstein, Creature from Black Lagoon, especially dust jacketed volumes.

9. Professional wrestling magazines, programs, premiums, etc. from 1950 - 1970.

HANCER'S BOOKHOUSE

5813 York Avenue South
Edina, Minnesota   55410
612-922-9144

The WSA DIRECTORY Committee, under the auspices of the WSA PROGRAM, in consideration of the success of the WSA Directory, announces the forthcoming publication of a SECOND directory broader in scope than the WSA Directory. This second directory will be known as the...

FANDOM DIRECTORY

... and will list FREE OF CHARGE, ANY MEMBER OF FANDOM!!!

IF YOU ARE A COLLECTOR, DEALER, COLLECTOR-DEALER, FAN, or just an interested party, whose interests include COMICS, PULPS, PAPERBACKS, HARDBACKS, ART WORK, SCIENCE FICTION, STAR TREK, STAR WARS, or related memorabilia, and allied materials, including FANZINES, ART-ZINES, etc., YOU are entitled to be listed in the FANDOM DIRECTORY FREE OF CHARGE.

IN ADDITION... you will be entered into a newly forming INTERNATIONAL FAN LOCATION SERVICE to consist of a COMPUTERIZED data bank for instant retrieval and cross reference. The WSA FAN LOCATION SERVICE will also be open to ALL OF FANDOM and once active (on or about December 1, 1982) will provide you with the opportunity to subscribe to the service at a very nominal charge. Through the Service you will receive a computerized printout containing the NAMES, ADDRESSES, TELEPHONE NUMBERS AND OTHER INTERESTS OF ALL PERSONS WHO MEET THE QUALIFICATION CRITERIA WHICH YOU PRESCRIBE.

If you are interested in having your name listed FREE OF CHARGE in BOTH the FANDOM DIRECTORY and the WSA's newly forming FAN LOCATION SERVICE, simply fill out the data form below and send (with SASE)

TO →

MICHAEL C. WAHL, DIRECTOR
WSA PROGRAM & AFFILIATES
5250 CLEAR LAKE ROAD
GRASS LAKE, MI 49240

(NOTE: Instead of clipping the form
below, you may list your choices
on a blank sheet of paper, along
with your name, address, phone,
and a heading of "FD Status Form".)

STATUS:
[*Limit — 7]

[ ] FAN
[ ] COLLECTOR
[ ] DEALER
[ ] EDITOR
[ ] WRITER
[ ] ARTIST
[ ] PUBLISHER
[ ] STORE
[ ] ZINE
[ ] CLUB
[ ] CON CH/MAN
[ ] CONVENTION
[ ] MANUFACT/ER
[ ] SUB SERVICE
[ ] SERV. ORGAN.

INTERESTS:
[*Limit — 10]

:[ ] Comics
:[ ] Pulps
:[ ] BLB's
:[ ] Books
:[ ] Paperbacks
:[ ] Original Art
:[ ] Posters
:[ ] Portfolios
:[ ] Fanzines
:[ ] Artzines
:[ ] Prozines
:[ ] Films
:[ ] Movie Matter
:[ ] Radio
:[ ] S F

[ ] Star Trek
[ ] Star Wars
[ ] E R B
[ ] Lovecraft
[ ] Gum Cards
[ ] Beer Cans
[ ] War Games
[ ] Television
[ ] Video Tapes
[ ] Comic Strips
[ ] A P A's
[ ] Good Girl Art
[ ] Horror
[ ] Plastic Bags
[ ] Records

Check One: New [ ] Change of Address [ ]

[ ] Undergrounds
[ ] Marvel
[ ] Atlas
[ ] Timely
[ ] D C
[ ] E C
[ ] Dell
[ ] Disney
[ ] Warren
[ ] Archie
[ ] Classic Comics
[ ] Fawcett
[ ] Fiction House
[ ] Fox
[ ] Gold Key

[ ] Harvey
[ ] Quality
[ ] War Comics
[ ] Westerns
[ ] Carl Barks
[ ] Funny Animal
[ ] Golden Age
[ ] Silver Age
[ ] Super Hero
[ ] Sword &
    Sorcery
[ ] Other
    (Specify)
_____
_____
_____
_____

NAME: _____

ADDRESS: _____

CITY: _____ STATE: _____ ZIP: _____ AREA CODE: _____

TELEPHONE: _____

The WSA PROGRAM & AFFILIATES - FANDOM'S PROTECTIVE ORGANIZATION - was established in 1970 for the benefit and protection of those doing business by mail order, and is now entering its 13TH YEAR of service to Fandom.

WSA Program Division....consists of the PLEDGE to the CODE of ETHICS, available to ALL eligible fans, for the purpose of standardizing the methods used in doing business by mail order.

WRB Fraud Division......the FRAUD BUREAU dedicated to the tabulation and prosecution of ALL known mail-fraud in Fandom.

As of this writing, over 1650 people have applied for, and been granted membership in the WSA Program & Affiliates. By display of their logo (at left) or line logo ("WSA 0000"), these members exhibit their character and commitment to the continuing struggle against fraud and "sharp practices" in mail transactions. Won't YOU join them TODAY?

WSA
NO. 0000

For more information, please see our advertisement in THE COMIC BOOK PRICE GUIDE #12, or send SASE and 20¢ to the Office of the Director (address above) for membership forms.